Complexity in Computer Science

Computational complexity theory is about the fundamental capabilities and limitations of efficient computation. Framing the subject in the broader context of computer science, this guidebook is both a self-contained tutorial for beginning graduate students in all areas of computer science and a thorough reference for specialists. Using only elementary discrete math, the book rigorously covers the central concepts of time, space, and randomness in computing, as well as connections to other areas of computer science such as cryptography and machine learning. Intuitions and general techniques are emphasized. The book features full proofs, numerous concrete examples and illustrations, and hundreds of exercises.

Thomas Watson is Associate Professor of Computer Science at the University of Memphis. He received his PhD from the University of California, Berkeley. His research spans many areas of computational complexity and has been supported by an NSF CAREER award.

"Watson's *Complexity in Computer Science* is a comprehensive introduction to computational complexity. It is especially well suited for students new to the area who want to learn both the foundations of the field and its connections to other areas of computer science such as cryptography and learning theory. Its breadth and level of detail make it an invaluable resource for students."

– Shachar Lovett, University of California, San Diego

Complexity in Computer Science

THOMAS WATSON
University of Memphis

CAMBRIDGE
UNIVERSITY PRESS

CAMBRIDGE
UNIVERSITY PRESS

Shaftesbury Road, Cambridge CB2 8EA, United Kingdom

One Liberty Plaza, 20th Floor, New York, NY 10006, USA

477 Williamstown Road, Port Melbourne, VIC 3207, Australia

314–321, 3rd Floor, Plot 3, Splendor Forum, Jasola District Centre, New Delhi – 110025, India

Cambridge University Press is part of Cambridge University Press & Assessment, a department of the University of Cambridge.

We share the University's mission to contribute to society through the pursuit of education, learning and research at the highest international levels of excellence.

www.cambridge.org
Information on this title: www.cambridge.org/9781009752336
DOI: 10.1017/9781009752329

When citing this work, please include a reference to the DOI 10.1017/9781009752329

First published 2027

Cover image: Jorg Greuel/Photodisc via Getty Images

A catalogue record for this publication is available from the British Library

A Cataloging-in-Publication data record for this book is available from the Library of Congress

ISBN 978-1-009-75233-6 Hardback

Dedicated to the memory of my father, Andrew Watson

Contents

Preface *page* **xiii**

Prologue **1**
Part I: Time and Space 1
Part II: Randomness 3
Part III: Scope of Complexity 4
Part IV: Concrete Models 5

I TIME AND SPACE **7**

1 Efficient Computation **9**
1.1 Problems and Algorithms 9
1.2 Efficiency 13
1.3 Input/Output Encodings 19
1.4 The Model of Computation 23
1.5 Robustness of the Model 30
1.6 Complexity Classes 40
1.7 Time Versus Space 44
1.8 Time-Efficient Reductions 49
1.9 Space-Efficient Reductions 61
Exercises 67
Notes 71

2 Time Complexity **73**
2.1 Tractable and Seemingly Intractable Problems 73
2.2 P Versus NP 81
2.3 NP-Completeness 87
2.4 Independent Sets 98
2.5 Long Paths 102
2.6 Graph Colorings 106
2.7 Subset Sums 110
2.8 Satisfying Assignments 112
2.9 Variants of P Versus NP 126
Exercises 128
Notes 135

3 Space Complexity **137**
3.1 Logic, Games, and Recursion 137
3.2 PSPACE-Completeness 143
3.3 NL and NL-Completeness 147
3.4 Turning Verifiers into Solvers 151
3.5 NL Is Closed Under Complement 154
Exercises 156
Notes 161

4 A Time-Space Lower Bound **162**
4.1 Padding 162
4.2 Time and Space Hierarchies 166
4.3 The Polynomial Hierarchy 175
4.4 Trading Space for Time 181
4.5 Time-Space-Efficient Reductions 183
4.6 Putting It All Together 190
Exercises 191
Notes 194

5 Nonuniformity **195**
5.1 Algorithms That Take Advice 195
5.2 Logic Circuits 200
5.3 Time Versus Circuit Size 209
5.4 P-Completeness 215
5.5 Branching Programs 219
5.6 Space Versus Branching Program Size 225
Exercises 228
Notes 231

6 Parallelism **232**
6.1 Parallel Time 232
6.2 Arithmetic 238
6.3 Space Versus Parallel Time 241
6.4 L-Completeness 244
6.5 Parallelization 248
6.6 Narrow Branching Programs 252
Exercises 262
Notes 263

II	**RANDOMNESS**	**265**
7	**Randomized Computation**	**267**
7.1	Time-Efficient Randomized Algorithms	267
7.2	The Model and Complexity Classes	273
7.3	Amplification	277
7.4	Derandomizing BPP	280
7.5	Implications of Randomized Algorithms for NP	282
7.6	Concentration Bounds	284
7.7	Space-Efficient Randomized Algorithms	290
7.8	Derandomizing BPL	294
7.9	Promise Problems	300
7.10	Map of Complexity Classes	303
	Exercises	305
	Notes	308
8	**Hashing**	**310**
8.1	Randomized Hashing	310
8.2	Constructing Pairwise Uniformity	313
8.3	Isolating Witnesses	316
8.4	Approximately Counting and Sampling Witnesses	318
8.5	Hash Mixing and Applications	324
	Exercises	328
	Notes	331
9	**Error Correcting Codes**	**332**
9.1	Binary Codes	332
9.2	Bounds for Binary Codes	337
9.3	Polynomial Codes	342
9.4	Bit String Fields	346
9.5	Codes Using Bit String Fields	350
	Exercises	356
	Notes	358
10	**Heuristics**	**360**
10.1	Distributional Problems	360
10.2	Average-Case Analogue of P Versus NP	363
10.3	Worst-Case Versus Average-Case	367
10.4	Hardness Amplification	375
	Exercises	381
	Notes	383

11 Pseudorandomness **385**
11.1 Statistical Distance and Pseudorandom Generators 385
11.2 Fooling Parities, Clauses, and Terms 391
11.3 Fooling Space-Efficient Computations 394
11.4 Fooling Time-Efficient Computations 402
11.5 Extracting Randomness 409
11.6 Seeded Extractors 412
Exercises 419
Notes 423

III SCOPE OF COMPLEXITY **425**

12 Cryptography **427**
12.1 Perfectly Secure Encryption 428
12.2 Computationally Secure Encryption 431
12.3 Pseudorandom Generators from One-Way Functions 435
12.4 Pseudorandom Functions 442
12.5 Applications of Pseudorandom Functions 448
Exercises 454
Notes 456

13 Learning **458**
13.1 Probably Approximately Correct Learners 458
13.2 Consistent Learners 464
13.3 Time Complexity 469
13.4 Sample Complexity 474
13.5 Amplification and Boosting 483
13.6 Exact Learners 487
13.7 Learning Circuits 495
Exercises 500
Notes 505

14 Optimization **507**
14.1 Approximation Algorithms 508
14.2 Hardness of Approximation 514
14.3 Label Cover 522
14.4 Probabilistically Checkable Proofs 526
Exercises 538
Notes 542

15 Verification **544**
15.1 Arthur and Merlin 544
15.2 Interactive Proofs 552
15.3 Delegation and Program Checking 564
15.4 Zero-Knowledge Proofs 570
Exercises 573
Notes 576

IV CONCRETE MODELS **577**

16 Decision Trees and Branching Programs **579**
16.1 Deterministic Query Complexity 579
16.2 Randomized Query Complexity 585
16.3 Certificate Complexity 593
16.4 Sensitivity 598
16.5 Deterministic Versus Randomized 602
16.6 Decision Tree Size 606
16.7 Branching Program Size 608
Exercises 612
Notes 616

17 Communication Protocols **618**
17.1 Deterministic Communication Complexity 618
17.2 Randomized Communication Complexity 626
17.3 Asymmetry 631
17.4 Applications 634
17.5 Search Problems 638
Exercises 642
Notes 645

18 Circuits and Formulas **647**
18.1 Gate Elimination 647
18.2 Circuits and Polynomials 649
18.3 Circuits and Random Restrictions 652
18.4 Formulas and Random Restrictions 659
18.5 Formulas and Communication Protocols 663
18.6 Monotone Circuits 667
18.7 Natural Proofs Barrier 670
Exercises 673
Notes 675

Epilogue **677**
Fine-Grained Complexity 677
Parameterized Complexity 677
Proof Complexity 678
Expander Graphs 679
Harmonic Analysis 679
Program Size Complexity 680
Complexity of Counting 680
Arithmetic Complexity 680
Property Testing 681
Quantum Computing 681
Complexity Beyond Computer Science 682
Notes 682

Appendix: Discrete Math Background **685**
A.1 Combinatorics 685
A.2 Graphs 688
A.3 Probability 692
A.4 Algebra 697

References **707**

Index **737**

Preface

Why This Book?

Computational complexity theory is part of the foundation of computer science (CS). It provides fundamental insights about many areas of CS, including security, artificial intelligence, big data processing, verification, optimization, parallel computing, and distributed computing. Because computational complexity is sometimes abstract and technical, it might appear too isolated to have practical relevance. To convey how computational complexity is germane to CS as a whole, this book highlights connections to other areas of CS and emphasizes broadly useful intuitions and techniques for reasoning about computing.

Some students are reluctant to study computational complexity because it's math-heavy. This book aims to make the subject accessible to readers with limited math background. A music teacher once lamented, "They don't write easy music in hard keys." Students struggle to adapt to key signatures with lots of sharps or flats because most music written in those keys is technically demanding. For many people, mathematical rigor is a "hard key." This book provides some "easy music" to help readers acclimate and see that computational complexity is not so formidable. The Appendix reviews relevant discrete math background.

Intended Audience

This book is aimed at general CS graduate students, but it's also suitable for advanced undergraduates, students in related fields, working professionals, and armchair computer scientists.

The reader is assumed to have a typical undergraduate education in CS, though an intrepid reader can appreciate much of the book without such a background. The reader should have experience writing programs and a little familiarity with data structures (including stacks, queues, and dictionaries), algorithms (such as binary search and merge sort), discrete math, assembly language, and digital logic. The text sometimes alludes to basic concepts of operating systems, compilers, computer architecture, security, and artificial intelligence.

An important prerequisite is mathematical maturity: the ability to mentally connect notations to the abstract concepts they represent, to recognize valid logical reasoning, and to distinguish key ideas from technical details.

Goals of This Book

The foremost reason to study computational complexity is to gain insight about the essence of computing. This book offers intuition with "proof idea" sections and clarifies definitions with plenty of concrete examples. The book sometimes only presents interesting special cases—rather than general results—when they're easier to absorb. To help the reader solidify the material, each chapter ends with exercises ranging from calisthenics to guided advanced material.

This book is "batteries included": Everything is explained from first principles, without requiring the reader to fill in details. The book is both a self-contained tutorial and a thorough reference with full proofs. The reader is advised when certain proofs are ancillary and safe to skip. A few advanced "museum exhibit" theorems are stated without proof. (Full disclosure:

An auxiliary "battery" that's unfortunately not included is the existence of prime numbers and irreducible polynomials of suitable sizes. These standard theorems are a bit too deep to prove here, but we need them for constructing finite fields, so we accept them as gifts from pure math.)

This book tries to appeal to a broad CS audience by mentioning pragmatic motivations and by connecting complexity theoretic ideas to analogues elsewhere in CS. Most areas of CS benefit from computational complexity's rigorous perspective on the power and limitations of computing. The book covers subareas of complexity that form theoretical foundations of other areas of CS, such as cryptography and machine learning.

For general CS students, the book can be an accessible survey of complexity theory and provide inspiration about the benefits of rigorously formulating questions about computing. For students specializing in theoretical computer science, the book covers standard material and some advanced topics. The reader will emerge ready to study research papers in complexity.

Another goal is to rein in the necessary math background. The basic background includes logic, combinatorics, graph theory, discrete probability, and algebra limited to prime fields, polynomials, vectors, and matrices—nothing more abstract is needed. The Appendix reviews notation, terminology, proof techniques, and basic lemmas. Slightly more advanced tools—including concentration bounds and power-of-2 fields—are developed in the main text. The book entirely avoids calculus, information theory, linear programming, continuous probability, and complex numbers. Inductive proofs are phrased as iterative or recursive algorithms that maintain invariants (rather than "raw induction"), befitting the CS context.

Perhaps controversially, the main text doesn't mention researchers' names that got attached to results and definitions in the literature. For example, some people may decry this book's avoidance of the name "Markov's inequality." The goals are to avoid perpetuating any misallocation of credit (since the history of CS and math is littered with attributions of questionable veracity) and to emphasize that the results and ideas are fundamental parts of reality, independent of the circumstances of their discovery. Bibliographic references and historical context (including traditional names) are relegated to the "Notes" section in each chapter. A few exceptions are when someone's name has become a common adjective with a suffix, such as "boolean" and "cartesian."

The overarching goal is to tell a story, with plotlines woven together like a satisfying novel. This book presents computational complexity as a cohesive subject whose many threads are ultimately interconnected, rather than a collection of disparate topics. Each of the book's four parts ends with a "plot twist."

Manifesto on the Model of Computation

Turing machines are the most traditional model of computation for teaching complexity theory. This book uses the Word RAM model instead. Advantages of Word RAM include:

- It resembles how actual computers work. Turing machines' back-and-forth sequential-access tapes may give students reservations about the relevance to real-world computing. But students generally don't need convincing that Word RAM—which is an idealized assembly language—appropriately distills the essence of computation. It's possible to define random-access Turing machines with special tapes for constructing addresses to teleport tape heads, but this is awkward and doesn't fully purge sequential access from the model.
- Implementing algorithms in the Word RAM model is reasonably straightforward (and only slightly tedious). For example, the breadth-first search algorithm naturally corresponds to a modest amount of Word RAM code. Implementing algorithms as Turing machines can

be nightmarish. The author shudders to envision the state diagram of a random-access Turing machine for breadth-first search. Turing machines must fuss about determining the input size, delineating boundaries between pieces of data, doing simple operations such as addition at the bit level, and constructing memory addresses bit-by-bit. These boring details distract from the ideas and get swept under the rug ("clearly it can be done"). Word RAM helps students feel anchored because a high-level algorithm is never far from a low-level implementation.

- With Word RAM, the input size and running time conform to our intuition about algorithms. For example, consider summing N integers that fit in $O(\log N)$-bit words. With Word RAM, the input size is N words, and the running time is $O(N)$, as expected. With Turing machines, the input size is $O(N \log N)$ bits, and the running time must account for doing each addition at the bit level. Analyses of Turing machines have omnipresent polylogarithmic factors to soak up these low-level nuisances. Analyses of Word RAM implementations are consistent with our expectations about algorithms.

Disadvantages of Word RAM include:

- It's not a "theoretically minimal" model. The instruction set is chosen more for convenience than for mathematical purity. Some people find the austerity of Turing machines appealing.
- A Word RAM program must specify how the word size depends on the input size. This is extra baggage attached to a program's code. It sometimes throws a small wrench in the works, such as in the proofs of the time and space hierarchy theorems. Also, defining the set of permissible word sizes is subtle. (Some versions of Word RAM let the word size change during a computation, but the author considers that too unrealistic.)
- Combining programs that have different word sizes—or modifying programs in a way that changes the word size—requires attention to preserve the programs' intended behavior. This minor annoyance doesn't crop up with Turing machines because their "word size" is constant.

Content and Organization

This book has more than enough material for two semesters. A typical one-semester graduate complexity course would cover much of the first seven chapters and selections from other chapters. The most fundamental material is in the first seven chapters. The next two chapters cover widely useful tools (pairwise uniform hashing and error correcting codes) and are independent of each other. The rest of the chapters often use concepts from the first nine chapters but are largely independent of each other (and can be read in any order), except minor dependencies such as:

- Locally decodable codes (§ 10.3) are relevant to probabilistically checkable proofs (§ 14.4).
- Pseudorandom generators (§ 11.1) are relevant to encryption schemes (§ 12.2).
- Pseudorandom functions (§ 12.4) are relevant to hardness of learning circuits (§ 13.7) and to the natural proofs barrier (§ 18.7).
- Commitment schemes (§ 12.3) are relevant to zero-knowledge proofs (§ 15.4).
- Communication complexity of search problems (§ 17.5) is relevant to formula size complexity (§ 18.5).

Here are some of the author's editorial decisions about the selection and organization of material:

- The time-space lower bound for SATISFIABILITY (Chapter 4) serves as a unified excuse to introduce several fundamental concepts such as diagonalization and the polynomial hierarchy. Since the polynomial hierarchy is treated as more of a "means" than an "end," material about it is distributed across relevant chapters rather than in a dedicated chapter.
- The book avoids esoteric complexity classes and antiquated topics in structural complexity such as relativization, exact counting of witnesses, the isomorphism conjecture, and sparse decision problems.
- The chapters on concrete nonuniform models of computation are the last part of the book because the uniform model (Word RAM programs) is discarded at this point, and because the circuit complexity approach to P versus NP in the final chapter brings the book "full circle."
- When carving a sculpture, some perfectly good stone will be lost: The Epilogue is a teaser for important topics that didn't make it into the text for various reasons, such as being math-heavier or harder to motivate in the broader context of CS.

Acknowledgments

My perspective on computational complexity was profoundly influenced by my advisors throughout my education—Dieter van Melkebeek, Luca Trevisan, and Toniann Pitassi—and by all my collaborators, especially Mika Göös. I thank Alice Foffa, Mika Göös, Dieter van Melkebeek, Kilian Risse, Anastasia Sofronova, Polina Stankevich, Bowen Xie, and anonymous reviewers for helpful feedback. I thank Lauren Cowles, Arman Chowdhury, and Clare Dennison at Cambridge University Press for help during the publication process. The dblp website was very useful for curating references. I thank the US National Science Foundation for financial support. Finally, I thank my family for essential nontechnical support.

Prologue

Computer science is teeming with beautiful ideas. Designing and harnessing computer systems involves a marriage of logic and creativity. The freedom to express computations as arbitrary sequences of unambiguous instructions makes computer science a playground of clever shortcuts, elegant paradigms, and surprising insights. How far can we hope to go?

Computational complexity theory is about the fundamental capabilities and limitations of efficient computation. Let's explain this definition from back to front.

- *Computation* means going from an input to an output using steps that are simple enough for a machine to perform.
- An *efficient* computation uses only small amounts of resources such as time and memory space. A computation that takes eons or needs an inordinate amount of memory would be practically useless.
- Some things are beyond the reach of efficient computation. It's good to know these *limitations* so we can adjust our expectations and avoid futile attempts to compute such things.
- It's not all doom and gloom. The *capabilities* of efficient computation sometimes defy expectations.
- Complexity theory addresses *fundamental* questions. The goal isn't to have immediate practical applications, but to establish general principles about what computers can feasibly accomplish and what they can't. It helps put the "science" in "computer science."

Many subfields of complexity theory are motivated by other areas of computer science, such as security, artificial intelligence, optimization, verification, big data processing, parallel computing, and distributed computing. Complexity theory answers foundational questions about rigorously defining and provably achieving goals in these areas. If computer science were an apple tree, complexity theory would be at the roots: We don't pick apples from the roots, but the roots sustain the whole tree.

Studying computational complexity is like exploring a huge mansion with grand architecture, secret passages, and surprises behind many doors. Let's have a sneak peek.

Part I: Time and Space

An *algorithm* is a way to compute something by a sequence of elementary steps.

Time is the number of steps an algorithm takes. Here's a toy example. Given a number x, we want to compute x^4. We could evaluate $x \cdot x \cdot x \cdot x$ using three multiplications. A more insightful way is to group the product as $(x \cdot x) \cdot (x \cdot x) = (x^2)^2$: Multiply x by itself, and then multiply the resulting number by itself, to get x^4 with just two multiplications. In general, deeper understanding of a problem's structure may lead to faster algorithms.

Space is the amount of memory an algorithm uses. Here's a toy example. Given two variables x and y, we want to swap their values. Assigning $x \leftarrow y$ and then $y \leftarrow x$ wouldn't work, because the second assignment would copy the new value of x (after the first assignment) instead of the original value. Instead, we could create a new variable z (which takes extra space) and assign

$z \leftarrow x$, then $x \leftarrow y$, then $y \leftarrow z$. Here's a different algorithm, which doesn't use an extra variable. The comments explain why it works, if the original values of the variables (x, y) are (a, b):

$$\begin{aligned} &y \leftarrow x + y && \text{// now } (x, y) \text{ holds } (a, a + b) \\ &x \leftarrow y - x && \text{// now } (x, y) \text{ holds } (b, a + b) \\ &y \leftarrow y - x && \text{// now } (x, y) \text{ holds } (b, a) \end{aligned}$$

Sometimes space is a bigger issue than time: A program that gobbles up RAM like it's going out of style may run out of memory within seconds on a typical computer.

To put the notion of efficiency on a firm mathematical footing, we consider how the amount of time or space depends on the input size. Our toy examples just involved one or two variables, but a problem's input might be an array of N numbers, for example. If $N = 100$, then $N^2 = 10{,}000$ is a fairly small amount of time or space on a computer, whereas 2^N is an utterly impractical, mind-boggling amount. If we double the input size N, then N^2 gets quadrupled but 2^N gets squared, which is far worse. Thus N^2 is a reasonable amount of resources because it stays "tame" even as N gets larger, whereas 2^N gets wildly out of hand.

For many problems, people have discovered efficient algorithms that cut down on resources by cleverly exploiting the problem's structure. But many other problems have stubbornly resisted all attempts at designing efficient algorithms. Such problems are either just tough nuts to crack, or hopeless because an efficient algorithm is mathematically impossible. The latter would mean there's essentially no room for cleverness, no exploitable structure to unearth. Confirming this would require proving a *lower bound* showing that the problem is *intractable*: Every possible efficient algorithm (of which there are infinitely many) fails to solve the problem. The quest for lower bound proofs is a grand intellectual challenge. The goal is not just to dash the hopes of algorithm designers, but also to clarify *why* computing is subject to certain limitations.

One formulation of the challenge of proving lower bounds is the notorious "P versus NP" question, which asks whether the ability to efficiently recognize a solution (to a puzzle, say) always entails the ability to efficiently find a solution. This is among the most significant and difficult open questions in computer science. Its resolution would fetch a \$1,000,000 bounty from the Clay Mathematics Institute. We prove a modest lower bound, which is some of the only progress to date on P versus NP.

Many problems of practical importance are suspected to be intractable (unsolvable by efficient algorithms) even though nobody knows how to prove so. We'll see evidence that a wide variety of problems are indeed intractable: They're effectively "the same problem in disguise," so either none of them are intractable (which seems too good to be true) or all of them are (which seems more plausible). The tools for relating different problems to each other are *reductions*, which are like computer programs that make calls to a method stub whose body hasn't been implemented.

Let's not put the cart before the horse. To even conceive of proving a lower bound, we must carefully define the word "algorithm." We define a simple assembly language representing idealized computer hardware. Algorithms correspond to programs in this low-level language. We need such a definition for anchoring complexity theory in formal mathematics, but the details don't matter much. Our definition conveniently distills the essence of computing, but any programming language with certain core ingredients would suffice. Conceptual takeaway: The notion of computation transcends the arbitrary details of any particular computer or language.

To formalize the idea that time and space are valuable resources, we prove that more time—or more space—lets algorithms solve more problems.

We also prove that space is closely related to time in parallel computing, in which many processors work on different parts of a computation simultaneously, thus collectively performing a lot of computation in each time step.

Along the way, we'll see that ideas from various areas of computer science—such as interpreters (for programming languages), memory management (in operating systems), game playing (in artificial intelligence), and digital logic (in computer architecture)—actually have fundamental roles in computational complexity theory.

Part II: Randomness

Random means inherently unpredictable, like a coin toss. Unpredictability is often undesirable, but sometimes it's actually useful. Polling is an example: Suppose 1,000,000 people will choose between two candidates in an election. We're eager to predict who will win. We go down a list of people and ask them who they'll vote for, assuming for simplicity that they answer honestly. If the list orders people by age or by geographic area (for instance), then the order might be correlated with people's preferences, so the top of the list wouldn't be a representative sample. (In an extreme case, the first 499,999 people vote for candidate A, and the other 500,001 vote for B.) If we randomly reorder the list, then polling works regardless of "who will vote for whom": The top of the shuffled list is probably a representative sample that won't mislead us.

In general, random choices may thwart adverse situations that deterministic choices are susceptible to. For some problems, a randomized algorithm uses less time or space than any known deterministic algorithm. The price is that the output may be wrong, with small probability. But the efficiency improvement is often worth it, if the error probability is small enough.

The next topic is *hashing*. A hash table data structure stores a smallish subset of items (such as all English words) out of a huge set of possible items (such as all strings of 20 or fewer letters). An appropriate hash function, applied to an item, specifies where to store the item in the table. Different items might get hashed to the same place, and such collisions are a nuisance. We want collisions to be "unlikely," but we also want the hash function to be "general purpose" (not tailored to the set being stored). Randomness reconciles these opposing goals. Many hash functions used in practice aren't randomized, but a theoretical explanation for their efficacy is that their randomness was already sampled and hardcoded (once and for all). Randomized hashing is a powerful tool for solving entire categories of problems.

The next topic is *error correcting codes*. Data transmitted over an unreliable communication channel may get randomly corrupted. This happens regularly with satellite communications and with data stored on disk ("transmissions" to the future). To defend against this, the sender encodes the data so the receiver can recover the original data despite the corruption (unless there's too much corruption). Error correcting codes are indispensable in computer hardware and communication systems, and they play an important role in computational complexity.

The next topic is *heuristics*. Traditionally, complexity theory is about algorithms that produce correct output on all conceivable inputs ("worst case"). But in practice, we only care about inputs that actually arise. Heuristics are algorithms that work on "typical" inputs. To make this rigorous: A heuristic should work with high probability on a random input sampled from some realistic distribution ("average case"). Randomized algorithms give a random output, whereas heuristics get a random input.

We normally assume randomized algorithms can access an unlimited source of pure random bits. But randomness is a resource, not to be taken for granted. Physical sources might only yield a few "crude" random bits. To make such randomness suitable for randomized algorithms, we can improve the quality using a *randomness extractor*, and then improve the quantity using a *pseudorandom generator*, which "stretches" a few random bits into many bits that "look random" to all efficient algorithms. In practice, such tools often have weak theoretical guarantees. We construct extractors and pseudorandom generators with strong theoretical guarantees.

These topics may seem eclectic, but they're tightly interwoven in the tapestry of randomized complexity theory. Hash functions and error correcting codes are part of complexity theory's infrastructure since they have many applications. We'll see deep connections between heuristics, pseudorandom generators, and extractors.

Part III: Scope of Complexity

Traditionally, computational complexity is about solving problems of the form: "Given an input, find a correct output." Computation is also useful for other goals. We consider four areas of computer science featuring diverse goals: cryptography, machine learning, optimization, and verification. These topics have been annexed into complexity theory to address their foundational questions, but they're also integral parts of complexity theory because they're intertwined with traditional topics and with each other.

In *cryptography*, the goals involve protecting information from adversaries. In the classic setting, the adversary is an eavesdropper who observes communication over a channel. To ensure the eavesdropper learns nothing about the message, the sender encrypts the transmission so it appears unintelligible but can be decrypted by the intended receiver. The sender and receiver use a secret "key" that's unknown to the eavesdropper. "Secret" means "random," so cryptography is immediately related to Part II. How does cryptography fit in the framework of computational complexity? We need mathematical rigor to answer: "What exactly does it mean for an encryption scheme to be secure?" "How can we prove that an encryption scheme is secure?" (This is important because the consequences of insecurity can be disastrous.) Encryption and decryption should be efficient algorithms. Furthermore, we view eavesdroppers as somewhat efficient algorithms, because defending against computationally unlimited eavesdroppers would be impractical and overkill. Breaching the security (learning something about the message from the encrypted transmission) just needs to be intractable (impossible for somewhat efficient algorithms) because who cares if the security is breached thousands of years from now anyway? Intractability is often a curse, but it's a blessing for cryptography.

In *machine learning*, a major type of goal is to learn an unknown function such as, "Given an image, does it depict a human face?" A learning algorithm is given labeled training examples—a bunch of images, each already labeled "face" or "non-face." It then generates a hypothesis—an algorithm for predicting whether other images are faces or non-faces. Machine learning is very successful in practice, but why? Like the foundations of cryptography, a branch of computational complexity addresses foundational questions about machine learning: "What exactly does it mean for an algorithm to learn?" "How can we prove that an algorithm learns?" We'll see techniques for designing efficient learning algorithms and for showing that some learning problems are intractable.

In *optimization*, the goal is to find an "optimal" solution among all solutions that obey certain constraints. For example, an airline wants a route schedule that maximizes their profit, subject to constraints about the availability of personnel and equipment. An *approximation algorithm* finds an "almost optimal" solution, which is often good enough. Some optimization problems have efficient algorithms with very good approximation guarantees, despite the apparent intractability of finding a truly optimal solution. For other optimization problems, achieving even a modest approximation is apparently intractable. There's a whole spectrum of approximability: We classify optimization problems by how good of an approximation is achievable by efficient algorithms.

In *software verification*, a major type of goal is to ascertain that a program actually solves the problem it purports to solve. Such verification is impossible in full generality, but computational complexity provides a framework for a type of efficient verification. One application area is delegation: A party with insufficient computational resources lets a powerful but untrusted party run a computation on their behalf and help them verify that the output is correct. In another application area, an unvetted program can be modified to abort rather than produce wrong output, so that it's safe to use even if it's incorrect. A third application area is related to cryptography: Counterintuitively, B can verify that A knows a secret (like a password) without A leaking any information about what the secret is. From another perspective, A can convince B that a puzzle (such as a sudoku) is solvable, without revealing anything about how to solve it.

We'll see surprising and mutually beneficial relationships among the topics in Part III.

Part IV: Concrete Models

A major goal of computational complexity is to prove lower bounds on the amount of time or space necessary to solve important problems. Researchers have only had modest success in this endeavor. To chip away at this grand challenge, we scale back our ambitions and prove lower bounds for restricted kinds of algorithms. Compared to arbitrary algorithms, these *concrete models* of computation are relatively simple and more amenable to proving lower bounds, and they focus the spotlight on specific aspects of computation.

One such model is *decision trees*, which are like nested "if ... else"s. For example, given a three-bit input (x, y, z):

if $y = 0$:
    if $x = 0$: output 1
    else: output 0
else:
    if $z = 0$: output 0
    else: output 1

This decision tree only ever reads two of the three input bits (though which two depends on the input). Decision trees are appropriate when we focus on the amount of input we need to read. This represents practical scenarios where the input is large, and retrieving individual parts of the input is costly. Decision trees are also popular in machine learning and operations research.

Another concrete model is *communication protocols*, which specify how separate parties collaborate to solve a problem when the input is split among them. In each step, a protocol indicates which party sends the next message and what that message is, as a function of everything that party knows (their piece of the input, and the prior messages from other parties). The resource of interest is the amount of communication across the network. This represents distributed computing scenarios where local computation is considered cheap and the network is reliable. Lower bounds show that certain problems require lots of back-and-forth communication—the parties must reveal to each other lots of information about their parts of the input. Furthermore, communication complexity has surprising applications to diverse topics that don't explicitly involve communication, such as data structures and integrated circuits.

Another concrete model is *logic circuits*, which distill the inner workings of computer hardware. Since a processor can run any program, arbitrary circuits are as powerful as arbitrary algorithms. But certain restricted types of circuits—such as ones representing parallel computations—are weak enough for us to prove interesting lower bounds.

Fields of science often have branches focusing on "big things" and "small things." Biology concerns big organisms and small cellular components. Physics concerns big outer space and small subatomic particles. Computational complexity concerns "big" arbitrary algorithms and "small" concrete models of algorithms—the nuts and bolts of computation.

Part I

TIME AND SPACE

Chapter 1

Efficient Computation

1.1 Problems and Algorithms

A *computation* receives an input, executes a sequence of elementary steps, and produces an output. To unpack this concept, let's separate two questions:

(i) What is the computation supposed to accomplish?
(ii) How does the computation accomplish it?

An answer to *(i)* is a *computational problem*, or *problem* for short: a relationship between inputs and outputs, specifying what the output should be for each possible input. An answer to *(ii)* is an *algorithm*: instructions for going from input to output by elementary steps that could be performed by a computer program or patient human. A problem is a goal, and an algorithm is a way to achieve that goal. This is like "interface versus implementation" in programming. A problem may have multiple algorithms that are *correct*, meaning they *solve* the problem: For every possible input, the algorithm produces output as specified by the problem.

This book adheres to some stylistic conventions: Names of computational problems are written in SMALL CAPITALS. Problems are in rectangles. Algorithms are in rounded rectangles.

Problems and algorithms are the central characters in the story of computational complexity. Let's introduce some running examples.

1.1.1 Multiplying Numbers

MULTIPLICATION	(1.1)
Input: Nonnegative integers x and y	
Output: The product $x \cdot y$	

A "brute force" algorithm solves this problem, assuming we know how to add numbers:

Brute force algorithm for MULTIPLICATION (1.2)

```
initialize z ← 0
repeat y times:
    update z ← z + x
output z
```

Pseudocode in this book uses "←" for variable assignments, "=" for definitions and comparisons, and Python-style indentation for bodies of loops, conditionals, and subroutines.

In primary school, we learned a "better" algorithm for when x and y are large. Let's review this using base two (binary) instead of the traditional base ten. Let $y = \cdots y_2 y_1 y_0$ in binary, so

$y = \sum_j (y_j \cdot 2^j)$, where $y_j \in \{0, 1\}$ for each index j. The primary-school algorithm exploits the distributive law:

$$x \cdot y \;=\; x \cdot \textstyle\sum_j (y_j \cdot 2^j) \;=\; \sum_j (x \cdot y_j \cdot 2^j)$$

The algorithm sums the rows of a table where the jth row (the top row being the 0th) is $x \cdot y_j \cdot 2^j$ in binary, which is obtained by shifting x left by j many bit positions to get $x \cdot 2^j$ and multiplying it by the individual bit y_j of y. Denote the output $x \cdot y$ as $z = \sum_i (z_i \cdot 2^i)$.

Example. Suppose x is twenty-seven and y is twenty-two. In base ten, $x = 27$ and $y = 22$, while in base two:

$$\begin{array}{lllll} x = 11011 & \text{since} & 27 = 16+8 \quad +2+1 & = & 1\cdot 2^4 + 1\cdot 2^3 + 0\cdot 2^2 + 1\cdot 2^1 + 1\cdot 2^0 \\ y = 10110 & \text{since} & 22 = 16 \quad +4+2 & = & 1\cdot 2^4 + 0\cdot 2^3 + 1\cdot 2^2 + 1\cdot 2^1 + 0\cdot 2^0 \end{array}$$

Figure 1.1's left side computes $27 \cdot 22 = 594$ using the primary-school algorithm. The 0th and 3rd rows are "zeroed out" since $y_0 = y_3 = 0$. The 1st, 2nd, and 4th rows are shifted copies of $x = 11011$ since $y_1 = y_2 = y_4 = 1$. Blanks are equivalent to 0s. The usual addition algorithm sums the rows by processing the columns from right to left. Each individual column's bits are summed to produce a bit of the output and a "carry" value that feeds into the next column. Figure 1.1's right side shows how the output and carries are computed. The output is:

$$z = 1001010010 \quad \text{since} \quad 594 = 512+64+16+2 = 2^9 + 2^6 + 2^4 + 2^1 \qquad \blacklozenge$$

We now describe this algorithm in general. Assume x and y are both n bits long (possibly with leading 0s), so $x < 2^n$ and $y < 2^n$, which implies $x \cdot y < 2^{2n}$, so $x \cdot y$ is $2n$ bits long. The pseudocode uses three variables: i is the current column's index, j is the current row's index (as we go down the entire current column, treating blanks as 0s), and c is the carry that gets updated from one column to the next.

Primary-school algorithm for MULTIPLICATION (1.3)

view the input as binary numbers $x = x_{n-1} \cdots x_1 x_0$ and $y = y_{n-1} \cdots y_1 y_0$
initialize $c \leftarrow 0$
for $i \leftarrow 0, 1, \ldots, 2n-1$:
  for $j \leftarrow 0, 1, \ldots, n-1$:
    update $c \leftarrow c + (x_{i-j} \cdot y_j)$ (where $x_{i-j} = 0$ if $i - j < 0$ or $i - j \geq n$)
  let $z_i \leftarrow c \bmod 2$
  update $c \leftarrow \lfloor c/2 \rfloor$
output the binary number $z = z_{2n-1} \cdots z_1 z_0$

How is this better than the brute force algorithm? Though the primary-school algorithm is more complicated to describe, it's more *efficient* to run, as we discuss in §1.2.

A *decision problem*'s output is always a single bit. Such a problem asks a yes/no or true/false question, where 1 means yes/true and 0 means no/false. MULTIPLICATION isn't a decision problem, because the output has multiple bits. Here's a decision problem version of MULTIPLICATION:

MULTIPLICATION DECISION (1.4)

Input: Nonnegative integers x, y, and i
Output: The ith bit of $x \cdot y$ in binary

						1	1	0	1	1
·						1	0	1	1	0
=						0	0	0	0	0
+					1	1	0	1	1	
+				1	1	0	1	1		
+			0	0	0	0	0			
+		1	1	0	1	1				
=	1	0	0	1	0	1	0	0	1	0

column index i	carry in + bits of column =	carry out z_i
0	$(0) =$	0 0
1	$0 + (0+1) =$	0 1
2	$0 + (0+1+1) =$	1 0
3	$1 + (0+0+1+0) =$	1 0
4	$1 + (0+1+0+0+1) =$	1 1
5	$1 + (1+1+0+1) =$	1 0 0
6	$10 + (1+0+0) =$	1 1
7	$1 + (0+1) =$	1 0
8	$1 + (1) =$	1 0
9	$1 =$	1

Figure 1.1: Example of running the primary-school algorithm for MULTIPLICATION

To phrase the output as a yes/no question, we could write "Does the ith bit of $x \cdot y$ equal 1?" (The 0th bit is the least significant.) It's tempting to think, "This asks for less than MULTIPLICATION does, so the primary-school algorithm already solves this." Strictly speaking, it doesn't solve this because it doesn't even output the right number of bits. We can modify the algorithm to solve MULTIPLICATION DECISION by outputting just z_i rather than all of z (or outputting 0 if $i \geq 2n$). Technically, that small modification yields a different algorithm. This may seem pedantic, but such distinctions matter in computational complexity theory. We should be careful and precise when discussing problems and algorithms.

We'll revisit the primary-school algorithm for MULTIPLICATION, but next let's introduce our other running example.

1.1.2 Reachability in Graphs

Many problems involve paths in graphs. Navigation systems suggest how to get from one location to another. Computer networks route packets from one host to another. Let's pare these goals down to a decision problem that asks whether it's even possible to go from here to there.

In a directed graph, node t is *reachable* from node s when there exists a walk from s to t. There exists a walk from s to t (which may repeat nodes and edges) iff there exists a path from s to t (which doesn't repeat nodes or edges), by Lemma A.5.

DIRECTED REACHABILITY	(1.5)
Input: Directed graph G, nodes s and t	
Output: Is t reachable from s in G?	

Assume G has no multi-edges or self-loops, which would be irrelevant.

Every path has length (number of edges) at most $n-1$, where n is the number of nodes in G. A "brute force" algorithm tries all potential paths of length up to $n-1$ and checks whether any is actually a path from s to t:

Brute force algorithm for DIRECTED REACHABILITY (1.6)

for $\ell \leftarrow 0, 1, \ldots, n-1$:
    for every tuple of distinct nodes $(v_1, v_2, \ldots, v_{\ell+1})$ with $v_1 = s$ and $v_{\ell+1} = t$:
        if G has an edge from v_i to v_{i+1} for every $i \in \{1, 2, \ldots, \ell\}$: halt and output "yes"
output "no"

We design a better algorithm with this insight: If we've deduced that a node u is reachable from s, and u has an edge to node v, then we deduce that v is also reachable from s, via a path from s to u followed by the edge (u, v). Upon deducing that u is reachable from s, we mark u as "discovered," and then eventually we "process" u by considering each outgoing edge (u, v) and marking v as discovered (if it wasn't already), and later we process v, and so on. This kind of algorithm explores outward from s, discovering all reachable nodes. If t is reachable from s via a path $s \to v_2 \to v_3 \to \cdots \to t$, then t eventually gets discovered: v_2 gets discovered when we process s, and v_3 gets discovered when we process v_2 (if not sooner), and so on. Conversely, if t gets discovered, t must be reachable from s.

To fully specify the algorithm, we must choose which node to process in each iteration. We use a data structure to remember which nodes have been discovered but not yet processed. The *breadth-first search (BFS)* algorithm uses a *queue* data structure, which supports *enqueueing* (inserting a node) and *dequeueing* (removing the oldest remaining node). In short, enqueue = discover, and dequeue = process. After v is discovered, v waits its turn while we process nodes that have been waiting longer.

Breadth-first search algorithm for DIRECTED REACHABILITY (1.7)

if $s = t$: halt and output "yes"
mark s as discovered and initialize the queue with s
while the queue is not empty:
    dequeue a node u
    for each edge (u, v):
        if v is undiscovered:
            if $v = t$: halt and output "yes"
            mark v as discovered and enqueue v
output "no"

Example. We demonstrate BFS on the input in Figure 1.2. In the first iteration, we dequeue and process node 4, whose outgoing edges lead to the undiscovered nodes 1 and 2. We mark 1 and 2 as discovered and enqueue them for later processing. It doesn't matter which order they're enqueued in, but say we enqueue 1 first, so we dequeue and process 1 in the next iteration. Since 1's only outgoing edge leads to the already-discovered node 2, nothing needs to be done. (We don't enqueue 2 again, since it should only get processed once.) Now the queue only contains 2, so we dequeue and process 2, whose outgoing edges lead to 4 (which was already discovered) and to 5. After marking and enqueueing 5, we promptly dequeue and process 5. The outgoing edges lead to 1 (already discovered) and 3 (which is t) and 4 (already discovered). We encountered t, so we celebrate without bothering to mark and enqueue it. ♦

DIRECTED REACHABILITY may seem inadequate because the output doesn't say how to get from s to t (if t is indeed reachable from s). The following variant is more practical:

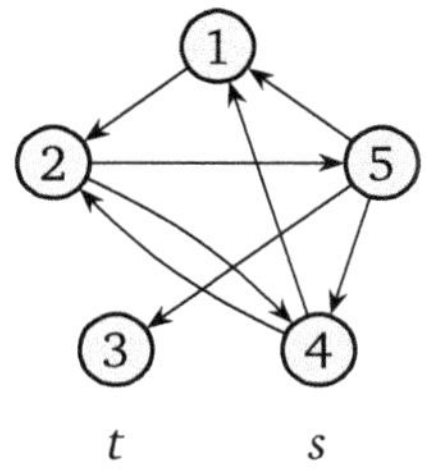

Figure 1.2: Example input for Directed Reachability

Directed Reachability Search	(1.8)
Input: Directed graph G, nodes s and t	
Output: A path from s to t in G, or report that no such path exists	

This is a *search problem*: Each input has an associated set of acceptable "solutions," and the goal is to output any acceptable solution (it doesn't matter which one) or report that the set is empty.

We can solve Directed Reachability Search with a trivial modification of brute force or with an augmented version of BFS called *extended BFS*: When a node v (other than s) gets discovered, we record which node u "caused" the discovery of v, and we deem u the "predecessor" of v. When t is encountered, we record its predecessor and begin a second phase to reconstruct a path from s to t in reverse: If v_2 is t's predecessor, and v_3 is v_2's predecessor, and so on, and s is v_ℓ's predecessor, then we output the path $s \to v_\ell \to \cdots \to v_2 \to t$.

Example. On our earlier example, extended BFS outputs the path $4 \to 2 \to 5 \to 3$. Another acceptable solution is $4 \to 1 \to 2 \to 5 \to 3$, but any algorithm only needs to find one of them. ♦

Extended BFS also solves a more stringent version of Directed Reachability Search where the output must be a shortest path (with as few edges as possible), rather than any old path, from s to t. We call this problem Directed Shortest Path. This is an *optimization problem*, which is a type of search problem where the goal is to output a "best" solution.

Extended BFS finds a shortest path because the set of discovered nodes is like a wave emanating steadily from s: Define any node v's *distance* (from s) as the length of a shortest path from s to v (or ∞ if v is unreachable from s). In the first iteration, all nodes at distance 1 are discovered, with s as their predecessor. While processing nodes at distance 1, the algorithm discovers exactly the nodes at distance 2: Every node discovered by a node at distance 1 has distance 2 (no more, and no less since otherwise it would've been discovered earlier), and conversely, every node at distance 2 is discovered by a node at distance 1 (since it has an edge from a node at distance 1 but no edge from s). In general, while dequeueing and processing nodes at distance $d-1$, the algorithm discovers and enqueues exactly the nodes at distance d. The queue's "first in, first out" property ensures that all nodes at distance $d-1$ get processed before any node at distance d does. If t has distance d, then t's predecessor has distance $d-1$, and that node's predecessor has distance $d-2$, and so on, so the path constructed by extended BFS indeed has length d.

1.2 Efficiency

How should we compare different algorithms for the same problem? We may prefer an algorithm that's easy to understand, implement, analyze, modify, or generalize. Computational complexity theory is about *efficiency*: An algorithm is more efficient than another if it uses less of some computational *resource*. The most fundamental resources are *time* and *space*.

1.2.1 Time

An algorithm's *running time* on a particular input is the number of elementary steps the algorithm executes before it halts. We discuss the precise meaning of "elementary step" in § 1.4, but an informal intuition suffices for now. In practice, we care about "wall clock time" (seconds, minutes, hours), which depends on various factors extrinsic to the algorithm, such as processor speed. The number of elementary steps is a good measure of running time because it's approximately proportional to wall clock time but is intrinsic to the algorithm.

Let's examine the running times of algorithms for MULTIPLICATION. Our first instinct might be, "In a programming language such as Java, we can multiply integers `x` and `y` with a single instruction `x * y`, so the running time is 1." That's fine if `x` and `y` are `int` or `long` values, which fit in single machine words and can be multiplied with a hardware instruction. In computational complexity, we study how running time depends on the input's "size." We discuss the general meaning of "size" in § 1.3, but for MULTIPLICATION it's the number of bits in x and y. Suppose x and y are both n bits. We impose no limit on n, so x and y could be arbitrarily large (a hundred or a million bits, or more). This is what Java's `BigInteger` class is for.

The brute force MULTIPLICATION algorithm adds x to a running sum, y times. A loop's running time is at most "number of iterations" times "steps per iteration." We won't even worry about how many steps the addition takes inside the loop, because that's "a drop in the bucket" compared to the number of iterations. Since y's value is as large as 2^n, the loop could have 2^n iterations—an exponential dependence on n. What if $n = 300$? Though 300 bits is a pitifully small amount of data, 2^{300} is a staggeringly huge number—greater than the number of atoms in the known universe. With a billion steps per second, the wall clock time would be far greater than the universe's age since the Big Bang. In practice, cryptography uses huge number arithmetic: Multiplying thousand-bit numbers (as large as 2^{1000} in value) is common, so there better be a faster algorithm!

In the primary-school MULTIPLICATION algorithm, the outer loop has $2n$ iterations, and the inner loop has n iterations. The maximum number of steps inside the inner loop doesn't depend on n: subtraction $i-j$, comparisons $i-j<0$ and $i-j \geq n$, lookups x_{i-j} and y_j, multiplication $x_{i-j} \cdot y_j$, addition $c + (x_{i-j} \cdot y_j)$, assignment to c, increment to j, and comparison $j \geq n$ to see whether the inner loop is done. This is perhaps 10 steps. The outer loop has perhaps 5 steps that aren't part of the inner loop. So the running time is at most $2n \cdot (n \cdot 10 + 5) = 20n^2 + 10n$ steps—a polynomial dependence on n. With $n = 300$ and a billion steps per second, the wall clock time would be a fraction of a second. Running the primary-school algorithm by hand, with a few steps per minute, we'd drastically outperform a computer running brute force.

The preceding paragraph was too much detail. Using big-O notation, we summarize the running time $20n^2 + 10n = O(n^2)$. At a glance, the algorithm has $O(n)$ outer iterations, $O(n)$ inner iterations, and $O(1)$ steps per iteration; multiplying these gives $O(n^2)$. Can we improve the running time? Skipping the table's blank entries decreases the running time by perhaps a factor of 2, but there would still be n^2 nonblanks, so big-O wouldn't be affected. A factor 2 speedup can be a big deal in practice, but it can also be eclipsed by the effect of larger inputs: Doubling the input size could increase a $O(n^2)$ running time by a factor of 4. Big-O captures how running time scales with the input size. The relative importance of hidden constant factors and lower-order terms diminishes as the input grows. Even with a constant factor in the billions, a $O(n^2)$-time

MULTIPLICATION algorithm would vastly outperform brute force on 300-bit numbers.

In summary: On large inputs, an algorithm's big-O running time matters much more than the execution speed or hidden constant factor.

For DIRECTED REACHABILITY, suppose the graph has n nodes and m edges, so two parameters describe the input's size. Brute force tries all tuples of distinct nodes to see if any is a path from s to t. There are more than $n!$ (n factorial) possibilities to try, which is even worse than 2^n. Brute force is totally impractical for graphs with hundreds of nodes.

Breadth-first search's running time depends on how the graph is represented and how the data structures are implemented. One common graph representation is the *adjacency matrix*, which lets algorithms look up whether (u, v) is an edge (for any nodes u and v) in $O(1)$ steps. Here and in most of this book, the *adjacency list* representation is more convenient: Each node u has a list of all nodes to which u has an edge. This enables a simple implementation of "for each edge (u, v)" when processing u, since finding the next outgoing edge only takes $O(1)$ steps. What about the queue and the set of all discovered nodes? Using simple arrays, we can implement these data structures so the following operations only take $O(1)$ steps: enqueueing, dequeueing, checking whether a node is undiscovered, and marking a node as discovered.

Let's analyze BFS's running time. For the outer loop, "number of iterations" times "steps per iteration" doesn't give the most detailed bound: There are up to n iterations (each node is processed at most once), and the number of steps in an iteration is proportional to the outdegree of the node u being processed. Since $\text{outdeg}(u) < n$, the total running time is $O(n) \cdot O(n) \cdot O(1) = O(n^2)$. We do a more careful analysis: Different outer iterations contribute different amounts to the running time. The outer iteration for processing u contributes at most $c \cdot (\text{outdeg}(u) + 1)$ steps, for a constant c. Why the $+1$? Because if $\text{outdeg}(u) = 0$, then processing u still takes a few steps (dequeueing u and seeing that u has no outgoing edges). Summing over outer iterations, the running time is $\leq \sum_u c \cdot (\text{outdeg}(u) + 1) = c \cdot \left(\sum_u \text{outdeg}(u) + \sum_u 1\right) \leq c \cdot (m + m + 1) = O(m)$ since the sum of the outdegrees counts each of the m edges once, and since the number of processed nodes is at most $m + 1$.

In computational complexity theory, we generally bound the running time in terms of a single parameter N, which is the input's "total size." For MULTIPLICATION, the input has $N = 2n$ bits, so the primary-school algorithm has running time $O(n^2) = O(N^2)$. For DIRECTED REACHABILITY, the input's adjacency list representation has size $N = n + m$, so BFS has running time $O(m) = O(N)$. For some graph algorithms, the running time depends on both size parameters, such as $O(mn)$, but we should be mindful that there are multiple ways to define big-O for functions of several variables.

1.2.2 Space

An algorithm's *memory space* on a particular input is the number of bits it uses to store intermediate results ("scratch work") during the computation. This corresponds to the amount of RAM (random-access memory) a program uses. An algorithm can store whatever data it wants in memory and retrieve that data later. It can overwrite old intermediate results (that are no longer needed) with new ones. A fundamental distinction between space and time is that space can be reused, but time cannot (alas).

The brute force MULTIPLICATION algorithm only needs $O(n)$ memory space (assuming x and y are n bits) if implemented prudently: The running sum z never exceeds $x \cdot y$, so it fits in $2n$ bits of memory. As we add another copy of x to z, we construct z's new value in another $2n$ bits of memory. After the addition, we safely forget z's old value (since we won't use it again) and overwrite it with z's new value. We also reuse the memory where we constructed z's new value for the same purpose in the next iteration, so we need not allocate any more memory for successive iterations. Remembering which iteration we're on (so we can stop after y iterations) takes n bits. We also need $O(\log n)$-bit pointers (indices) for running the addition algorithm, moving z after the addition, and incrementing the iteration counter. So we only need $O(n + \log n) = O(n)$ bits of memory at a time. We don't count the space to store the program, since that space doesn't depend on the input.

A straightforward implementation of the primary-school MULTIPLICATION algorithm uses $O(n^2)$ bits of memory for the n-by-$2n$ table. Why should we care about space? Suppose x and y each have $n =$ one million bits, and our computer executes one billion instructions per second and has 32 gigabytes of RAM. With $O(n^2)$ running time (with a reasonable hidden constant), if we start the computation before lunch, it might finish before we get back. However, n^2 bits of memory is over 100 gigabytes, so we might see an "out of RAM" error instead. Time is more often in the limelight, but sometimes space is the bottleneck.

The primary-school algorithm need not store the whole table all at once. One way to get the memory space down to $O(n)$ is to sum the rows one by one (like the brute force algorithm). It seems impossible to do better than $O(n)$ space, because the input and output are already more than n bits. But we'll show that the primary-school algorithm can get by with much less than n bits of memory if we disregard the space to store the input and output.

In computational complexity theory, the input is in a separate read-only memory segment, and the output goes in a separate write-only memory segment, and these special segments don't count toward the space. Intermediate data is stored in the read-write *work memory*. The space is the number of bits of work memory. If an algorithm's work memory is larger than its input and output, then the input, output, and intermediate data might as well be in one common memory. The segments idea is useful when the work memory is smaller than the input or output. This is motivated by practical situations where the input or output is on an external storage device, or available over a network, or not explicitly stored anywhere. If the input's individual parts can be retrieved on demand, and the output's individual parts can be sent to their destination, we don't include them in "what the algorithm is doing with its memory."

How much work memory does the primary-school MULTIPLICATION algorithm need? It stores i (index into z), j (index into y), $i-j$ (index into x), n (length of x and y), and c (carry). The inner loop reads the bits x_{i-j} and y_j from the input segment. The outer loop writes the bit z_i to the output segment. The indices and n take $O(\log n)$ bits, but the carry is more subtle to analyze. The space to store c is the log of the maximum value c could attain throughout the computation. We analyze this using a loop invariant:

Claim 1.1. *The value of c never exceeds $2n$ in the primary-school* MULTIPLICATION *algorithm.*

Proof. First, we prove that at the boundaries between outer iterations, c doesn't exceed n. This invariant holds at the beginning since $c = 0$. To see that the invariant is maintained, suppose it holds at the beginning of outer iteration i. In each inner iteration, c goes up by $x_{i-j} \cdot y_j \leq 1$. There are $\leq n$ inner iterations, so c goes up by $\leq n$ throughout the inner loop. Since $c \leq n$ before the inner loop (by assumption), we have $c \leq n + n$ after the inner loop. Outer iteration i concludes with $c \leftarrow \lfloor c/2 \rfloor \leq \lfloor 2n/2 \rfloor = n$, so the invariant indeed holds again.

The largest c could ever be is $2n$, right after some execution of the inner loop. ∎

Hence, c only needs $\lceil \log(2n+1) \rceil = O(\log n)$ bits. (In this book, logs are base 2 by default.) Summing the memory requirements for all the variables, the primary-school algorithm uses only $O(\log n)$ work space—a logarithmic dependence on n.

Now, we analyze the memory space of BFS for DIRECTED REACHABILITY. Suppose the graph has n nodes and m edges. The computation remembers the queue's contents and which nodes have been discovered. Each node needs one bit to record whether it's been discovered, which is n bits for all n nodes. The queue's space is the maximum number of items ever in the queue simultaneously, times the number of bits per item. Each node gets enqueued at most once, so the queue never holds more than n items. A node's label is $\lceil \log n \rceil$ bits. In total, the two data structures take $n + n \cdot \lceil \log n \rceil = O(n \log n)$ bits of memory. The computation also remembers other node labels and pointers, which only contribute $+O(\log n)$ bits and don't affect the overall space usage of $O(n \log n)$.

As with running time, we generally bound the memory space in terms of the total input size N. For MULTIPLICATION with $N = 2n$, the primary-school algorithm uses memory space $O(\log n) = O(\log N)$. For DIRECTED REACHABILITY with $N = n + m$, BFS uses memory space $O(n \log n) = O(N \log N)$. For *dense* graphs with $m \approx n^2$, we have $n \log n \approx \sqrt{N}$, so the actual memory space is much less than $O(N \log N)$. But the final analysis should hold for all inputs.

Outside this book, some analyses count "words" rather than bits of memory. Some references say the primary-school algorithm uses space $O(1)$ and BFS uses space $O(n) = O(N)$ because in practice, counters/indices/pointers fit in single machine words. In computational complexity theory, such variables take space $O(\log N)$ because bits (not words) are the unit of space, and the input size N is theoretically unlimited. We examine this issue in §1.3 and §1.4.

1.2.3 Complexity

With respect to a resource such as time or space:

- An algorithm's *efficiency* is the function that maps N to the maximum, over all inputs of size exactly N, of the resource usage on that input. Perhaps confusingly, a larger efficiency function means "less efficient."
- A problem's *complexity* is the efficiency of the "most efficient" algorithm that solves it. This is only an informal definition, because different algorithms could be more efficient on different input sizes, but this generally isn't a significant issue (see Exercise 1.20).

This isn't just about known algorithms, or about algorithms that could be devised using known techniques. A problem's complexity is determined by the "best" algorithm that exists mathematically, regardless of whether the algorithm has been found. "What is problem A's time complexity?" isn't a well-defined question, but it represents a collection of well-defined questions such as "Does A have an algorithm with time efficiency $O(N^2)$ or not?"

To show a problem has low complexity, we prove an *upper bound*—some algorithm is both correct and efficient. To show a problem has high complexity, we prove a *lower bound*—every algorithm is either incorrect or inefficient. *Correct* means for every input, the output is as it should be. *Efficient* means for every input, the resource usage is at most some target. Because of these $\forall$ quantifiers over inputs, correctness and efficiency are *worst-case* notions: An algorithm should perform well for every input, no matter how "bad" the input may be.

To summarize our upper bounds so far: MULTIPLICATION has time complexity $O(N^2)$ and space complexity $O(\log N)$ where $N = 2n$. DIRECTED REACHABILITY has time complexity $O(N)$ and space complexity $O(N \log N)$ where $N = n + m$. Since big-O is like "less than or equal to" for functions, these upper bounds leave open the possibility of more efficient algorithms—the problems might have even lower complexities.

In general, what does a lower bound look like? Suppose for some function T, we have a correct algorithm with time efficiency $O(T(N))$ for a problem A, and we suspect it's impossible to design a faster algorithm for A. That is, we know an upper bound of $O(T(N))$ on A's time complexity, and we conjecture a matching lower bound.

- One formulation uses little-o: No algorithm for A has time efficiency $o(T(N))$. This means for every correct algorithm, there exists $c > 0$ such that for infinitely many inputs, the running time is $\geq c \cdot T(N)$.
- A stronger formulation uses big-Omega: Every algorithm for A has time efficiency $\Omega(T(N))$. This means for every correct algorithm, there exists $c > 0$ such that for all but finitely many N, the running time is $\geq c \cdot T(N)$ for at least one input of size N.

The distinction between "not little-o" and "big-Ω" is that for big-Ω, the infinitely many inputs on which an algorithm is inefficient must be "regularly occurring"—at least one per input size. This matters in some abstract corners of computational complexity theory. When studying specific, natural problems, the distinction is usually insignificant because nothing about particular sizes of inputs makes them more difficult than other sizes. Caveat: Some problems only have inputs of certain sizes. For example, suppose we insist that in Multiplication, both x and y are exactly n bits, so the input size $N = 2n$ must be even. Then it's unreasonable to want a big-Ω lower bound, which requires algorithms to be slow for both odd and even N despite there being nothing to do for odd N. Three ways to iron out this wrinkle are:

- Change the definition of big-Ω to quantify only over valid input sizes for the problem at hand.
- Change the definition of the problem so it has valid inputs of every size N. For example, Multiplication could say x has $\lceil N/2 \rceil$ bits and y has $\lfloor N/2 \rfloor$ bits.
- Change the definition of time efficiency at N to be the maximum running time over all valid inputs of size $\leq N$ rather than size exactly N.

Ideally, we want matching upper and lower bounds for a problem. For example, if we prove that some algorithm has space efficiency $O(S(N))$ and every algorithm has space efficiency $\Omega(S(N))$, we've pinned down the problem's space complexity (within a constant factor) at $\Theta(S(N))$. Typically, lower bounds are tougher to prove than upper bounds, because an upper bound just involves exhibiting a single algorithm, whereas a lower bound involves ruling out all possible algorithms. For many problems, a $\Omega(N)$ time lower bound and $\Omega(\log N)$ space lower bound hold because with less time or space, an algorithm can't even access the entire input. Superlinear time lower bounds and superlogarithmic space lower bounds tend to be drastically harder to prove, and open questions abound. The time and space complexities of countless problems remain unresolved by a wide margin.

What is Multiplication's time complexity? It's tempting to conjecture that no algorithm beats the primary-school algorithm's $O(N^2)$ time efficiency. If we expand

$$x \cdot y \;=\; \left(\textstyle\sum_k x_k \cdot 2^k\right) \cdot \left(\textstyle\sum_j y_j \cdot 2^j\right) \;=\; \textstyle\sum_{k,j} (x_k \cdot y_j) \cdot 2^{k+j}$$

then it feels necessary to multiply each pair of bits $x_k \cdot y_j$, and there are $\Omega(N^2)$ such pairs. However, there are Multiplication algorithms with time efficiency pretty close to $O(N)$, using sophisticated mathematical tricks to bypass the explicit enumeration of all pairs of input bits.

What is Directed Reachability's space complexity? We showed a $O(N \log N)$ upper bound. The log factor can be shaved off because it arose from remembering the order of nodes in the queue, which is unnecessary (when we don't care about a path's length). We may be pessimistic about the prospect of going below $O(N)$, because it feels necessary to record at least one bit per node, to avoid endless loops of rediscovering nodes. However, we prove a $O(\log^2 N) = O((\log N)^2)$ upper bound in Chapter 3. For UNDIRECTED REACHABILITY (in which the input graph is *un*directed), the space complexity is $O(\log N)$ by a sophisticated algorithm that's beyond the scope of this book. The latter algorithm's discovery was predated by reasons to suspect it was possible, as we discuss in Chapter 7 and Chapter 11. For DIRECTED REACHABILITY, no such reasons are known, and most complexity theorists conjecture the space complexity is $\Omega(\log^2 N)$. A proof that DIRECTED REACHABILITY's space complexity is not $O(\log N)$ would already be an astounding breakthrough.

These examples show that intuition is unreliable when speculating about computational complexity. When we find an algorithm, there's usually a lingering question: Is a more efficient algorithm waiting to be discovered?

Lower bound proofs tend to be elusive because we can't make any assumptions whatsoever about the inner workings of algorithms. We must view any potential algorithm as a completely arbitrary tuple of instructions, which might have no apparent "rhyme or reason." To even conceive of rigorously proving lower bounds, we must first formalize the meanings of *problem* (§ 1.3) and *algorithm* (§ 1.4).

In the research community, the prevailing sentiment is that our goal is to understand *why* a theorem is true, not just ascertain *whether* it's true. We prefer proofs that yield insight. If DIRECTED REACHABILITY has no $O(\log N)$-space algorithm, we really want to learn *why not?* Or perhaps it has such an algorithm—who knows? The theory of computational complexity harbors many surprises, some of which we explore in this book.

1.3 Input/Output Encodings

Computers represent all information with bits. When we define a computational problem, we should specify how to represent the input and output with bits. For MULTIPLICATION this is simple—binary numbers already consist of bits. For DIRECTED REACHABILITY it's less immediate: A node's label from $\{1, 2, \ldots, n\}$ is approximately $\log n$ many bits. For the adjacency list representation, each node u has a list of the labels of nodes to which u has an edge, along with a way of locating the beginning and end of u's list. We'll see more details later, but a key takeaway of this section is that details don't matter much.

An *encoding* is an unambiguous way of representing each possible input and output value as a string of bits. *Unambiguous* means different values have different representations, so we can determine the value that any bit string represents. There isn't just one encoding for any problem—there can be many encodings that differ in how they handle various details.

- Technically, a problem's specification should include an encoding. Changing the encoding changes the problem.
- Practically, the encoding details are often left unspecified because they don't affect the problem's complexity very much. An algorithm for one reasonable encoding can be adapted to handle another reasonable encoding, without much overhead in time or space.

For example, one encoding for MULTIPLICATION has bits in most-to-least-significant order, while another encoding uses the opposite order. Formally, these are two distinct computational problems. But if an algorithm works with one order, we can tweak the algorithm to work with the other order, by changing where it looks for x's least significant bit in the input, and so on. There's not much point distinguishing between these encodings—intuitively, both are incarnations of a single problem called MULTIPLICATION.

input =	000110	000100	000111	000101	000011	000110	000010	output = 100001
	0	1	2	3	4	5	6	

Figure 1.3: Example of SMALL ITERATED ADDITION encoding

1.3.1 Word Size

In a computer, bits of data are organized into *words* of a common size. How many bits per word? This question exposes a dissonance between theory and practice. In real architectures, the word size is a constant such as 64 bits. But to express problems and algorithms naturally, individual words should fit simple data such as counters, indices, and pointers, which depend on the (arbitrarily large) input size. So the word size should depend on the input size. Let's see an example to demonstrate this clash.

SMALL ITERATED ADDITION	(1.9)
Input: Nonnegative integers $x_1, x_2, \ldots, x_N$ such that $x_i \leq N$ for each i	
Output: $x_1 + x_2 + \cdots + x_N$	

In this problem's name, SMALL means restricting each value x_i to a modest range $\{0, 1, \ldots, N\}$ (unlike MULTIPLICATION's big numbers), and ITERATED means allowing many summands.

If we encounter this problem "in the field," we might whip up a Java method `public int sum(int[] x)`. The x_i values and return value (output) should be like "`int`"s in Java, which fit in single words. But x_i in binary is $\approx \log N$ bits, and the output $x_1 + x_2 + \cdots + x_N$ could be as large as N^2, so it's $\approx \log N^2 = 2 \log N$ bits. If these must fit in 64-bit words, the input size N would be limited to $\approx 2^{32}$. That's fairly generous, which is why the word size issue isn't typically a concern in practice. But for big-O analysis, N must go to infinity, necessitating a word size with at least a logarithmic dependence on N.

Example. Suppose the input to SMALL ITERATED ADDITION is $(6, 4, 7, 5, 3, 6, 2)$ and the output is 33 (in base ten). The input size is $N = 7$, and the word size is $\lceil \log(N^2 + 1) \rceil = 6$. Figure 1.3 shows our encoding as a tuple of words, where each word is a bit string viewed as a nonnegative binary number with most-to-least-significant order. The little numbers underneath are addresses that algorithms will use to access the input's words: x_i is at address $i - 1$. ◆

From a practical standpoint, letting the word size depend on N seems preposterous, since hardware won't adjust its word size on the fly. For SMALL ITERATED ADDITION, we could modify the encoding to use a constant word size by splitting each number's binary representation across multiple words, but this wouldn't match the spirit of the problem. Letting the word size grow with N is a standard compromise to reconcile the finiteness of real computers with the infinity of big-O analysis. We just have to get used to it.

We don't want the word size to grow too fast with N, since then N wouldn't be a reasonable measure of the amount of data in the input. We only allow $O(\log N)$ word size, which is generous enough for sensible encodings.

If the word size is W, a word of data is an element of $\{0, 1\}^W$ (the set of all bit strings of length W). If the input size is N, an (encoded) input is an element of $(\{0, 1\}^W)^N$ (the set of all N-tuples of words). We should write W_N to make it explicit that different values of N can have different associated word sizes, but we often tidy up the notation by just writing W with the implicit understanding that it depends on N.

1.3.2 Computational Problems

For some problem encodings, not every element of $(\{0,1\}^W)^N$ represents a valid input. For example, in SMALL ITERATED ADDITION, if some word is greater than N, then the whole input is invalid according to the problem's definition. Two ways to deal with this are:

- Restrict our attention to encodings where every element of $(\{0,1\}^W)^N$ represents a valid input. For example, in SMALL ITERATED ADDITION, we could treat any input number greater than N as zero. An input may have multiple different representations, which is fine, but an algorithm would need to be correct and efficient on all of them. Multiple representations of an input are technically distinct inputs that "mean" the same thing.
- Allow elements of $(\{0,1\}^W)^N$ that don't represent valid inputs, but disallow giving them to algorithms. An algorithm has no burden to check whether its input is valid, and on an invalid input there's no correctness or efficiency requirement (even running forever is allowed). This is computational complexity's version of "garbage in, garbage out." We *promise* that the input will be valid (and don't care about "what if it's not"). The problem is called a *promise problem*. We specify the input-output relationship using a *partial function*, which may be undefined for some elements of the domain $(\{0,1\}^W)^N$. A *total function* is a partial function that's defined on the whole domain, so every element is a valid input.

The choice between these conventions is often immaterial but sometimes important. We allow promise problems since they simplify specifying encodings and implementing algorithms.

We're ready for our official definition of *problem*. For search problems, the definition involves *power sets*: If S is a set then $\text{pow}(S) = \{T : T \subseteq S\}$ is the set of all subsets of S.

Definition. A *computational problem* associates to each positive integer *input size* N a pair (W_N, F_N), abbreviated (W, F), such that:

- W is a positive integer *word size*, which must be $O(\log N)$.
- F is a partial function with domain $(\{0,1\}^W)^N$. The inputs on which F is defined are *valid*.
    - *Decision problem*: F has codomain $\{0,1\}$. On input x, the goal is to output $F(x)$. If $F(x) = 1$ then x is a 1-*input* or *yes-input*. If $F(x) = 0$ then x is a 0-*input* or *no-input*.
    - *Function problem*: F has codomain $(\{0,1\}^W)^M$ for some M depending on N. On input x, the goal is to output $F(x)$.
    - *Search problem*: F has codomain $\text{pow}\big((\{0,1\}^W)^M\big)$ for some M depending on N. On input x, the goal is to output an element of the set $F(x)$ or report that $F(x) = \emptyset$.

If A is a problem and x is a valid input of size N, then $A(x)$ means $F_N(x)$. ◄

For search problems, $F(x)$ is the set of acceptable solutions. Function problems (such as MULTIPLICATION) are equivalent to search problems where each valid input has exactly one acceptable solution. For function and search problems, M is the output size, and the output is encoded using the same word size as the input.

Every problem has an encoding with word size 1 (though perhaps not the most natural encoding). We could define a decision problem as a single partial function $F\colon \{0,1\}^+ \to \{0,1\}$ encompassing all input sizes, since $\{0,1\}^+$ is the set of all nonempty bit strings. This is handy when discussing general concepts, without a particular problem in mind. The point of bigger word sizes is that the two-level structure (break input into words, break words into bits) lets us express specific problems naturally, without fussing about delineating pieces of data.

$(x,y) = (10110, 01100)$

0	1	1	0	1	0	0	1	1	0
0	1	2	3	4	5	6	7	8	9

Figure 1.4: Example of MULTIPLICATION encoding

1.3.3 Example Encodings

We describe particular input/output encodings for MULTIPLICATION and DIRECTED REACHABILITY. We use these encodings when implementing the primary-school algorithm and breadth-first search after seeing our official definition of *algorithm* in § 1.4.

For MULTIPLICATION, we use word size $W_N = 1$ and have each number's bits in least-to-most-significant order (from lower to higher addresses). We promise that the input size N is even, and we view the first $N/2$ bits as x and the last $N/2$ bits as y. The output is a bit string of length $M = N$. When N is even, $F_N : \{0,1\}^N \to \{0,1\}^N$ is a total function. When N is odd, F_N is a partial function that's undefined on all inputs. Figure 1.4 shows an example, with addresses represented by little numbers underneath.

MULTIPLICATION's complexity is robust with respect to the encoding details. Other reasonable encodings differ in the bit order, the case when N is odd, and so on. We chose our encoding to make the algorithm implementation as simple as we can.

We could consider an encoding with word size > 1 and cram more input/output bits into each word. This technique is handy in practice for improving efficiency, but it doesn't capture the cleanest way to view the problem. We intended the input size N to be the number of bits in the binary representation.

For DIRECTED REACHABILITY, we use a larger word size and view each word as a binary number (with most-to-least-significant bit order) representing either a node label from $[n] = \{1,2,\ldots,n\}$, a count of some number of nodes or edges, or a pointer (address of another input word). Every node u gets a contiguous list of words holding the labels of u's outneighbors (nodes to which u has an edge) in increasing order (though the order won't matter). The encoding also needs some structure to help algorithms find the beginning and end of each node's list: Address 0 gets n (the number of nodes). For each $u \in [n]$, address u gets a pointer to the beginning of node u's list. Then starting from address $n+1$, we concatenate the lists for nodes $1,2,\ldots,n$. Node u's list consists of a word holding outdeg(u), followed by outdeg(u) many words holding u's outneighbors' labels. After node n's list, two more words hold the labels of s and t (the start and destination nodes).

Example. Figure 1.5 shows the encoding of an example input, with annotations to make the structure apparent. Words are shown in base ten for readability. The first bracket on top illustrates that the initial word 5 counts how many pointers follow. For each of those 5 words, the arrow underneath shows which address it points to. Address 6 is the start of node 1's list, address 8 is the start of node 2's list, and so on. For each node's list, the bracket on top illustrates that the first word counts how many node labels follow. For example, address 15 contains 3 because node 5 has edges to three nodes (namely nodes $1,3,4$, which are the words under the bracket). Node 3's bracket has no words since outdeg$(3) = 0$. ♦

We view DIRECTED REACHABILITY as a promise problem: Any tuple of words that doesn't conform to our encoding (with node labels not in $[n]$, or inconsistent pointers, for example) is invalid. An algorithm can assume its input legitimately represents some (G,s,t), without checking for formatting mistakes.

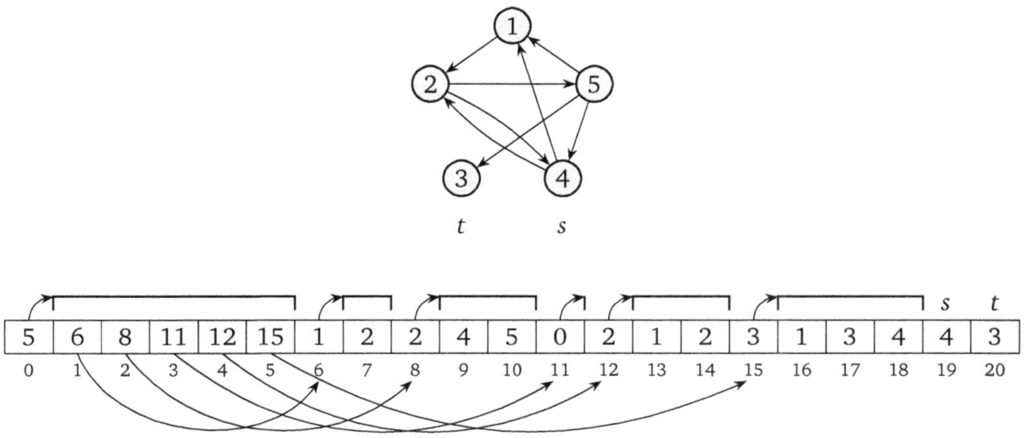

Figure 1.5: Example of DIRECTED REACHABILITY encoding

If G has n nodes and m edges, then the number of words is $N = 2n + m + 3$ because each node has two words (the pointer and outdegree), each edge (u, v) is accounted for once (in u's list), and n, s, t are the other three words. Technically, we should express algorithm efficiency and problem complexity in terms of this N, which isn't exactly the $N = n + m$ from earlier. This doesn't affect our big-O analysis, since these values of N are within a constant factor.

What word size is appropriate? Each node label and each count only needs $\lceil \log(n+1) \rceil$ bits since the possible values are $\{0, 1, \ldots, n\}$. A pointer could contain an address near the end of the input ($N - 1$ is the last address), so we can use $\lceil \log N \rceil$ bits per pointer. Since $n + 1 \le N$, word size $W_N = \lceil \log N \rceil$ is enough.

As usual, there's flexibility in designing the encoding. The outdegree words are redundant since an algorithm could calculate an outdegree by subtracting adjacent pointers. We could modify the encoding by eliminating the outdegree words, at the cost of an extra implementation step and a special case for node n, but this wouldn't affect our big-O analysis. We adopt our chosen encoding for convenience, but the details don't matter much.

Throughout this book, when a problem's input contains a graph, we assume the encoding is as above, unless specified otherwise. The same encoding works for undirected graphs, by viewing an undirected edge $\{u, v\}$ as a pair of directed edges (u, v) and (v, u).

1.4 The Model of Computation

Informally, an algorithm is a tuple of instructions specifying elementary steps of a computation. What's an "elementary step"? Many ways to flesh out the definition are essentially equivalent as long as they have certain core features. A *model of computation* is a formal definition of what constitutes algorithms. The details don't matter much because they have little impact on the complexities of problems—an algorithm in one model can be translated to another reasonable model without much loss in efficiency.

Though various models of computation would be fine, we must designate an "official" one for this book. This is a balancing act: For upper bounds, we'd prefer a feature-rich model like a high-level programming language, to facilitate specifying algorithms. For lower bounds, we'd prefer a bare-bones model, to minimize the variety of possible algorithms to rule out. The model we elaborate in this section is an idealized assembly language. It imitates how real computers work but is tidier. Algorithms are like software, and the model of computation is like hardware.

There's no formal distinction between *algorithm* and *program*. "There exists an algorithm such that ..." has literally the same meaning as "There exists a program such that ..." But by convention, *algorithm* means high-level pseudocode as in § 1.1, and *program* means actual code in our official model, and *implementation* means turning an algorithm into a program.

1.4.1 Model Definition

Memory. The memory is organized into five parts:

- The read-only *input segment*.
- The write-only *output segment*.
- The read-write *work segment*.
- The general-purpose *registers*.
- The *program counter*.

The input, output, and work segments each have an unlimited number of words, with addresses starting from 0. (Many real architectures split words into bytes, and addresses refer to bytes. In our model, addresses refer to words.) Registers and the program counter are single words.

The number of registers depends on the program but not on the input. A program can use any number of registers. This may seem unrealistic since real architectures have a fixed number of registers, but we'll see in § 1.5 that we can adapt every program to use just two registers.

The input segment's first N words are initialized with the input. The 0th register is initialized with the input size N. All other words of memory are initialized to all-0s.

Code. A program has a tuple of instructions. There are four types of instructions:

- **Data processing.** An instruction can get the contents of one or two registers, perform an arithmetic or bitwise logical operation on them, and put the result in a register. The instruction specifies which registers and which operation. It can also use a hardcoded constant ("immediate value") in place of either operand register. In a real processor, the ALU (arithmetic-logic unit) does these operations.
- **Control flow.** An instruction can make the computation *branch* (jump) to another instruction, possibly conditional on a comparison between two register (or constant) values. The program counter holds the current instruction's *line number* (an address in the *code segment* containing the instructions). The program counter is incremented after every instruction except when a branch is taken.
- **Memory access.** An instruction can *load* a word from the work segment into a register, or *store* a word from a register into the work segment. The instruction specifies two registers (or constants): the word of data being copied, and the address within the work segment. (Real architectures have fancier addressing modes. Our model only has "direct" and "register indirect" modes.) To get a word from the input segment or put a word in the output segment, we use instructions called *read* and *write* (to distinguish them from the analogous *load* and *store*). Output segment addresses must be written to consecutively.
- **Termination.** Three instructions make a computation halt: *accept* and *reject* mean "output 1" and "output 0" respectively (for solving decision problems), and *halt* means "output the output segment's contents up through the largest address that was written to" (for solving

function and search problems). For search problems, *reject* means "no acceptable solution." If none of these instructions is executed, the computation runs forever. A program's last instruction (in the tuple of instructions) must be a termination or unconditional branch.

We flesh out the instruction set in §1.4.2, but the details aren't very important.

Many instructions can use hardcoded constants in lieu of register values. A program can use arbitrarily large constants. This may seem unrealistic since real architectures have a fixed number of bits for immediate values, but we'll see in §1.5 that we can adapt every program to use just single-bit constants.

Word size. The program counter has its own special word size $\lceil \log L \rceil$ where L is the number of instructions (lines of code). Each other word of memory has size W_N (depending on the input size N), which must be large enough to hold N itself and any hardcoded constant (not including register indices and line numbers). A program Π (capital Greek pi) is a pair (I, W) where I is the tuple of instructions (code) and $W : \mathbb{N}_+ \to \mathbb{N}_+$ is the word size function, where $W(N)$ means W_N (and $\mathbb{N}_+$ is the set of positive integers).

Correctness. A program *solves* a problem iff for every valid input, it terminates with a correct output. The program and problem might not have the same word size. If the program has smaller word size than the problem, then it can't solve the problem since the input words don't fit. If the program has larger word size than the problem, then the input segment's words are the problem's input words left-padded with 0s, and the output segment's words (for function/search problems) should be the problem's output words left-padded with 0s.

Efficiency. A program's *running time* on a particular input is the number of instruction executions up through termination, which could be ∞. (A pitfall of modeling computation with a high-level programming language would be that instructions may conceal mini-algorithms, so counting instructions wouldn't accurately reflect the running time.)

A program's *memory space* on a particular input is the total number of bits in all registers and the work segment from address 0 up through the largest address accessed by a load or store (including any in-between addresses that aren't accessed). The program counter's size doesn't depend on the input, so it's not included in the memory space. If a program has R registers, accesses at most the first M words of the work segment, and has word size W, then the memory space is $\le (R+M)W$. Since R is a constant, the memory space is $O(MW)$ if the work segment is accessed, and is $O(W)$ if not. It would be reasonable to define memory space as the number of bits in the words that are actually accessed (regardless of the largest address accessed), but this wouldn't make a big difference (§1.7.3). Our definition is like allocating a contiguous block of M words of work memory for a program to manage on its own. Space can't be ∞ even if time is ∞: Addresses must fit in registers, so they can't exceed $2^W - 1$.

It might seem unfair that, for example, adding two single-word numbers is only 1 time step but $O(W)$ bits of space. This is an artifact of the "W depends on N" discord between theory and practice. Bits have always been the unit of space in computational complexity, but it's still sensible to count time steps that resemble real machine instructions.

With respect to a problem, a program's *time efficiency* and *space efficiency* are the functions $T : \mathbb{N}_+ \to \mathbb{N}$ and $S : \mathbb{N}_+ \to \mathbb{N}$ where $T(N)$ and $S(N)$ are the maximum running time and maximum memory space over all inputs of size N that are valid for the problem (and $T(N) = S(N) = 0$ if there are no valid inputs of size N). We don't care about time or space on invalid inputs.

1.4.2 Instruction Set

On the spectrum of RISC (reduced instruction set computer) versus CISC (complex instruction set computer), our model is at the RISC end. The word in register i is Reg$[i]$. The words at address i in the work/input/output segments are Mem$[i]$ / In$[i]$ / Out$[i]$. (A program can't access its "code segment.") Hardcoded constants—which may be operands in data processing or control flow instructions, or addresses or data in memory access instructions—are nonnegative binary integers, treated as whole words (left-padded with 0s).

Data processing. These instructions begin with "let". The simplest is copying one register to another:

$$\text{let Reg}[i] \leftarrow \text{Reg}[j]$$

This overwrites Reg$[i]$ with the contents of Reg$[j]$, so the old contents of Reg$[i]$ are lost and Reg$[j]$ is unchanged. In lieu of Reg$[j]$, the instruction could assign a hardcoded constant to Reg$[i]$. Other instructions are "let Reg$[i] \leftarrow \ldots$" with arithmetic or bitwise logical operations on Reg$[j]$ and Reg$[k]$:

$\text{Reg}[j] + \text{Reg}[k]$	(sum)	$\neg\text{Reg}[j]$	(not)
$\text{Reg}[j] - \text{Reg}[k]$	(difference)	$\text{Reg}[j] \wedge \text{Reg}[k]$	(and)
$\text{Reg}[j] \cdot \text{Reg}[k]$	(product)	$\text{Reg}[j] \vee \text{Reg}[k]$	(or)
$\lfloor \text{Reg}[j] / \text{Reg}[k] \rfloor$	(quotient)	$\text{Reg}[j] \oplus \text{Reg}[k]$	(xor)
$\text{Reg}[j] \bmod \text{Reg}[k]$	(remainder)	$\text{Reg}[j] \gg \text{Reg}[k]$	(shift right)
$\lfloor \log_2(\text{Reg}[k]) \rfloor$	(logarithm)	$\text{Reg}[j] \ll \text{Reg}[k]$	(shift left)

The register indices i, j, k need not be distinct. These instructions can have hardcoded constants in lieu of Reg$[j]$ and/or Reg$[k]$.

For arithmetic instructions, a word in $\{0,1\}^W$ is a nonnegative integer in $\{0, 1, \ldots, 2^W - 1\}$. Sum/difference/product are done "mod 2^W" so there's no overflow or negative numbers. (Bits that would be "too significant" to fit in a word are dropped.) Quotient/remainder/logarithm yield Reg$[i] \leftarrow 0$ if Reg$[k] = 0$. (A program is responsible for anticipating divide-by-0 and log-of-0, since our model has no runtime errors.)

To do signed arithmetic using two's complement to represent negative numbers (as real computers do), a program can treat the positive integers $2^{W-1}, \ldots, 2^W - 1$ as the negative integers $-2^{W-1}, \ldots, -1$ respectively. The "mod 2^W" arithmetic automatically handles signs correctly for sum/difference/product (but division would require consideration), so signed arithmetic is available even though the model officially only has unsigned numbers.

A bitwise shift instruction obtains the new contents of Reg$[i]$ from Reg$[j]$ by dropping Reg$[k]$ many bits off one end and filling in the other end with 0s. For example, $1 \ll \text{Reg}[k]$ is $2^{\text{Reg}[k]}$ in binary if Reg$[k] < W$. The logarithm instruction might feel out of place, but it's tasteful to include because it's the inverse of the exponentiation provided by shift left: $\lfloor \log_2(\text{Reg}[k]) \rfloor$ is the position of the leftmost 1 in Reg$[k]$ (where position 0 is the rightmost bit).

Control flow. An unconditional branch updates the program counter to point to another instruction, and execution continues from there:

$$\text{goto line } \ell$$

The value of ℓ is hardcoded in the instruction. We number lines from 0, so $0 \le \ell < L$ where L is the number of lines of code. A conditional branch compares the contents of two registers (or a constant in lieu of either register). If the condition is true, it updates the program counter to ℓ. If the condition is false, it increments the program counter as usual.

$$\text{if Reg}[i] = \text{Reg}[j] \text{ then goto line } \ell$$

We can also use $\neq$, $<$, $\leq$, $>$, $\geq$ for the comparison. These treat words as unsigned integers, so a program must compensate if it uses two's complement.

Memory access. Addresses are nonnegative binary integers.

Get word from work segment address Reg$[j]$ into Reg$[i]$:	load Reg$[i] \leftarrow$ Mem[Reg$[j]$]
Put word from Reg$[i]$ into work segment address Reg$[j]$:	store Mem[Reg$[j]$] $\leftarrow$ Reg$[i]$
Get word from input segment address Reg$[j]$ into Reg$[i]$:	read Reg$[i] \leftarrow$ In[Reg$[j]$]
Put word from Reg$[i]$ into next output segment address:	write Reg$[i]$

We allow $i = j$. There can be a constant in lieu of Reg$[i]$ (the data) and/or Reg$[j]$ (the address), except that load and read can't have a constant in lieu of Reg$[i]$.

A read instruction with address $\geq N$ gets an all-0 word. The first write instruction executed writes to Out[0], the second write instruction executed writes to Out[1], and so on. We disallow "write Out[Reg$[j]$] $\leftarrow$ Reg$[i]$" because it's susceptible to abuse: Writing to a high address while leaving gaps of "unwritten-to" addresses would let a program produce a large output without being charged for the time to write each word—it could get all-0 words in the output for free. Also, writing to the same output address more than once would let a program use it as a kind of work memory without being charged for the space—it could put a word there, then later decide whether to leave that word or overwrite it. Our write instruction forces programs to write each output word exactly once.

Termination. As explained in §1.4.1, three instructions make the computation stop and announce the output:

accept reject halt

1.4.3 Example Programs

For "hello world," we write a program solving Small Iterated Addition from §1.3.1. A loop adds each input number (one by one) to a running sum. We don't use the work segment; the registers are enough space.

- Reg[0] is initialized to N, and we won't change it.
- Reg[1] is the loop counter and an address (pointer) into the input.
- Reg[2] is the current number from the input.
- Reg[3] is the running sum.

Reg[1], Reg[2], Reg[3] are initialized to 0, though for Reg[2] it doesn't matter.

Program for Small Iterated Addition (1.10)

```
0. read Reg[2] ← In[Reg[1]]
1. let Reg[3] ← Reg[3] + Reg[2]
2. let Reg[1] ← Reg[1] + 1
3. if Reg[1] < Reg[0] then goto line 0
4. write Reg[3]
5. halt
```

The loop is line 0 through line 3. Line 0 reads the next input number. Line 1 adds it to the running sum. Line 2 increments the loop counter. Line 3 branches to the top for another iteration if more input remains. Line 4 puts the running sum at address 0 in the output segment. Since this is the only output word accessed, it's the entire output when the program halts on line 5.

The program works with word size $\lceil \log(N^2+1) \rceil$ since Reg[0], Reg[1], Reg[2] never exceed N and Reg[3] never exceeds N^2, assuming the input is valid. (The problem promises $x_i \leq N$ for each i.) This illustrates that a program's word size should depend on N, so words can hold simple data that would be `int` variables in Java, say. The program has time efficiency $O(N)$ and space efficiency $O(\log N)$ since each register holds $O(\log N)$ bits. Since the program has no load or store instructions, only registers contribute to the space.

Next, we implement the primary-school algorithm for MULTIPLICATION and the breadth-first search algorithm for DIRECTED REACHABILITY with the input/output encodings from §1.3.3. To improve readability of these programs, we use human-friendly aliases for registers, and indentation to show the correspondence with the pseudocode's nested loops.

The top of Figure 1.6 shows our program for MULTIPLICATION. The input segment has x's bits followed by y's bits (with each bit in a separate word) in least-to-most-significant order, so $\text{In}[k] = x_k$ and $\text{In}[n+k] = y_k$ for each $k \in \{0,\ldots,n-1\}$. We use aliases for Reg[0],...,Reg[9]:

$$\begin{aligned}
N &= \text{input size}\\
n &= N/2\\
c &= \text{carry value, and running sum for each column}\\
i &= \text{outer loop counter}\\
j &= \text{inner loop counter}\\
ptr &= \text{pointer for input addresses } i-j \text{ (to read } x_{i-j}\text{) and } n+j \text{ (to read } y_j\text{)}\\
xbit &= x_{i-j}\\
ybit &= y_j\\
zbit &= z_i\\
prod &= \text{temporary holder for } x_{i-j}\cdot y_j
\end{aligned}$$

All registers except N are initialized to 0, but we only rely on this for c and i. We must reinitialize j each time the inner loop starts (line 2). The heart is $c \leftarrow c + (x_{i-j} \cdot y_j)$ (line 7 through line 11), but before that we check if $i - j < 0$ (line 4) or $i - j \geq n$ (line 6) and skip updating c if either holds. For line 4, why not compare $ptr < 0$ after computing $ptr \leftarrow i - j$, similar to line 6? Since our model only has unsigned arithmetic, that comparison would always be false—negative numbers wrap around to large positive numbers. (This is a common bug in real-world programs that use unsigned integers.) Comparing $i < j$ sidesteps the issue. The bits of z are written to separate words of the output segment, so $\text{Out}[i] = z_i$. The first $N = 2n$ output segment words are the output upon termination.

The program works with word size $\lceil \log(N+1) \rceil$ (which is greater than the problem's word size of 1) since each register never exceeds N (see Claim 1.1 regarding c). The program has time efficiency $O(N^2)$ and space efficiency $O(\log N)$, as we claimed earlier.

The bottom of Figure 1.6 shows our program for DIRECTED REACHABILITY. The work segment layout is:

- Address 0 goes to waste since this slightly simplifies the implementation.
- Addresses $1,\ldots,n$ record which nodes have been discovered: $\text{Mem}[u]$ is 1 or 0 to indicate whether node u is discovered or undiscovered, respectively. The initialization automatically makes all nodes undiscovered at the beginning.

Implementation of the primary-school algorithm for Multiplication (1.11)

```
0.  let n ← ⌊N/2⌋
1.  if i ≥ N then goto line 19
2.      let j ← 0
3.      if j ≥ n then goto line 14
4.          if i < j then goto line 12
5.          let ptr ← i − j
6.          if ptr ≥ n then goto line 12
7.          read xbit ← In[ptr]
8.          let ptr ← n + j
9.          read ybit ← In[ptr]
10.         let prod ← xbit · ybit
11.         let c ← c + prod
12.         let j ← j + 1
13.         goto line 3
14.     let zbit ← c mod 2
15.     write zbit
16.     let c ← ⌊c/2⌋
17.     let i ← i + 1
18.     goto line 1
19. halt
```

Implementation of the breadth-first search algorithm for Directed Reachability (1.12)

```
0.  let ptr ← N − 2
1.  read s ← In[ptr]
2.  let ptr ← N − 1
3.  read t ← In[ptr]
4.  if s ≠ t then goto line 6
5.      accept
6.  store Mem[s] ← 1
7.  read head ← In[0]
8.  let head ← head + 1
9.  store Mem[head] ← s
10. let tail ← head + 1
11. if head = tail then goto line 28
12.     load u ← Mem[head]
13.     let head ← head + 1
14.     read ptr ← In[u]
15.     read outdeg ← In[ptr]
16.     let end ← ptr + outdeg
17.     if ptr = end then goto line 11
18.         let ptr ← ptr + 1
19.         read v ← In[ptr]
20.         load disc ← Mem[v]
21.         if disc = 1 then goto line 17
22.         if v ≠ t then goto line 24
23.             accept
24.         store Mem[v] ← 1
25.         store Mem[tail] ← v
26.         let tail ← tail + 1
27.         goto line 17
28. reject
```

Figure 1.6: Implementations of algorithms

- Addresses $n+1,\ldots,2n$ are the queue: The label of the first node to be enqueued goes at address $n+1$, the second to be enqueued goes at address $n+2$, and so on. The queue's current contents are at addresses *head*, $head+1$, ..., $tail-1$. The next place to dequeue is *head*. The next place to enqueue is *tail*. The queue is empty iff $head = tail$. Since each node is enqueued at most once, the queue need not "wrap around" the allocated space.

We use aliases for Reg[0], ..., Reg[10]:

$$
\begin{aligned}
N &= \text{input size}\\
ptr &= \text{pointer for accessing various input words}\\
s &= \text{start node}\\
t &= \text{destination node}\\
head &= \text{queue's head pointer}\\
tail &= \text{queue's tail pointer}\\
u &= \text{node being processed}\\
outdeg &= \text{node } u\text{'s outdegree}\\
end &= \text{pointer to the last entry in } u\text{'s list}\\
v &= \text{other endpoint of an edge out of } u\\
disc &= \text{indicator of whether } v \text{ is discovered}
\end{aligned}
$$

Line 0 through line 5 gets s and t and accepts if $s = t$. Line 6 marks s as discovered, and line 7 through line 10 sets up the queue to contain s (with $head = n+1$ and $tail = n+2$). The outer loop (line 11 through line 27) iterates until the queue is empty. Line 12 and line 13 dequeue u. Line 14 through line 16 finds the beginning and end of u's list. The inner loop (line 17 through line 27) iterates through the list's entries (pointed to by *ptr*). Line 19 through line 21 gets v and continues to the next inner iteration if v was already discovered. Then, the program accepts if $v = t$, and otherwise marks v as discovered (line 24) and enqueues v (line 25 and line 26).

The program works with word size $\lceil \log(N+1) \rceil$ since each register never exceeds N: For *ptr* and *end* this is clear since they point into the input; $s, t, u, v, outdeg$ never exceed the number of nodes $n \le N$; *head* and *tail* never exceed $2n+1 \le N$; *disc* is always 0 or 1. The program has time efficiency $O(N)$ and space efficiency $O(N \log N)$, as we claimed earlier.

Computational complexity theory is mostly *not* about dealing with such code. There are much bigger fish to fry, which transcend the low-level details. But the formalism of the model of computation is always behind the scenes, supporting the theory.

1.5 Robustness of the Model

There's a lot of leeway in defining a model of computation. As long as the model has sufficient representation of the four essential ingredients—data processing, control flow, memory access, and termination—we can add (and sometimes remove) various instructions without significantly changing the complexities of problems. This is because any program that uses the extra instructions can be adapted to accomplish the same thing, almost as efficiently, without those instructions. We illustrate this in §1.5.1.

Programs can use as many registers as they want, and hardcoded constants as large as they want. We prove in §1.5.2 that essentially nothing is lost if programs can only use two registers and one-bit constants.

§1.5.3 has some observations about memory access, which will simplify some things later.

Another issue has to do with word sizes. A program's word size should just provide appropriate space to store basic units of data in individual words. A computation might be sensitive to the exact word size, but in § 1.5.4 we show that increasing the word size doesn't mess things up if we impose restrictions to preclude abuse of the word size.

Upshot: Don't fret about the model. An intuitive understanding of computation is good enough, because the formal underpinning is very resilient.

1.5.1 Adding and Removing Instructions

Base+offset addressing. Instead of specifying a memory address with just a register ("indirect mode") or constant ("direct mode"), we could specify it as a sum of two values, each of which is a register or constant. This is handy for accessing a data structure in a contiguous block of memory: The *base* points to the start of the data structure, and *offsets* refer to components of the data structure. This feature is merely a convenience because we can split a "base+offset" memory access into two official instructions: calculate the absolute address, then do the access with register indirect mode.

For "load", since we're about to overwrite Reg$[i]$, we might as well use it for the address:

$$\text{load Reg}[i] \leftarrow \text{Mem}[\text{Reg}[j] + \text{Reg}[k]] \quad \rightsquigarrow \quad \begin{array}{l} \text{let Reg}[i] \leftarrow \text{Reg}[j] + \text{Reg}[k] \\ \text{load Reg}[i] \leftarrow \text{Mem}[\text{Reg}[i]] \end{array}$$

This also works with constants in lieu of Reg$[j]$ or Reg$[k]$.

For "store", it's more subtle. We must handle all possible combinations of i, j, k being equal and constants in lieu of any registers. A worrisome example is "store Mem[Reg$[i] + c$] $\leftarrow$ Reg$[i]$" for a constant c: Which register should we put the address Reg$[i]+c$ into? Using Reg$[i]$ would mess up the data being stored, and commandeering another register might derail the computation. Fortunately, our model lets the modified program use more registers than the original program. Pulling a new "register h" out of thin air to hold the address:

$$\text{store Mem}[\text{Reg}[j] + \text{Reg}[k]] \leftarrow \text{Reg}[i] \quad \rightsquigarrow \quad \begin{array}{l} \text{let Reg}[h] \leftarrow \text{Reg}[j] + \text{Reg}[k] \\ \text{store Mem}[\text{Reg}[h]] \leftarrow \text{Reg}[i] \end{array}$$

We need not feel guilty about introducing a new register, because we can always go down to two registers (§ 1.5.2). This also works with constants in lieu of Reg$[i]$, Reg$[j]$, or Reg$[k]$.

After applying these substitutions, target line numbers of branches may be messed up. Let $\lambda(\ell)$ be the new line number of the instruction from line ℓ of the original program. (λ is lower-case Greek lambda.) We update the target of each conditional and unconditional branch:

$$\text{goto line } \ell \quad \rightsquigarrow \quad \text{goto line } \lambda(\ell)$$

Time and space only go up by constant factors.

Indirect branching. This means the target line number is in a register (and if the register points to a nonexistent line, then the indirect branch instruction is ignored). To simulate this:

$$\text{goto line Reg}[i] \quad \rightsquigarrow \quad \begin{array}{l} \text{if Reg}[i] = 0 \text{ then goto line } \lambda(0) \\ \text{if Reg}[i] = 1 \text{ then goto line } \lambda(1) \\ \text{if Reg}[i] = 2 \text{ then goto line } \lambda(2) \\ \vdots \end{array}$$

To simulate a conditional indirect branch, we precede the block of "if"s with a conditional branch that jumps over the block if the condition is false. $\lambda(\ell)$ is the new line number (after doing all the substitutions) of the instruction from line ℓ of the original program. We also update the target line numbers of preexisting "direct" branches.

The original line numbers become hardcoded constants as comparison operands. We need not feel guilty about introducing large new constants, because we can always go down to one-bit constants (§ 1.5.2).

A technical nuisance: Operand constants—including the ones we just introduced—must fit in the word size for every N. Our modified program might be illegal for the silly reason that these "line number constants" take more than W_N bits when N is small. To bypass this, we apply a different substitution using a fresh "register h":

$$\text{goto line Reg}[i] \quad \rightsquigarrow \quad \begin{array}{l} \text{let Reg}[h] \leftarrow \text{Reg}[i] \\ \text{if Reg}[h] = 0 \text{ then goto line } \lambda(0) \\ \text{let Reg}[h] \leftarrow \text{Reg}[h] - 1 \\ \text{if Reg}[h] = 0 \text{ then goto line } \lambda(1) \\ \text{let Reg}[h] \leftarrow \text{Reg}[h] - 1 \\ \text{if Reg}[h] = 0 \text{ then goto line } \lambda(2) \\ \vdots \end{array}$$

The modified program is legal and equivalent to the original. (For small N, if some original line numbers don't fit in a word, then the original program couldn't indirectly branch to those lines.)

Time and space only go up by constant factors depending on the original program's size.

Subroutine calls. We use base+offset addressing and indirect branching to create a subroutine call mechanism. ("Subroutine" has fewer connotations than similar terms like "method" and "procedure.") Part of the work memory is designated as a *call stack*. (Real architectures sometimes deem the call stack a separate segment.) Each item on the call stack is a *stack frame*, which is a contiguous block of memory holding data associated with a subroutine invocation: local variables and arguments, return address (line number where execution resumes when the subroutine returns), and previous values of registers the subroutine uses. One register is designated as the *frame pointer*, which points to the start of the currently executing invocation's stack frame.

- A subroutine call *pushes* a frame associated with the new invocation. This involves initializing local variables, saving the return address, saving the contents of registers (including the frame pointer), updating the frame pointer, and branching to the subroutine.
- During execution of the subroutine, the program uses the frame pointer as the base, and uses different offsets to access local variables and arguments within the frame.
- A return statement *pops* the frame. This involves putting the return value at a designated place, restoring saved register contents, and doing an indirect branch to the saved return address, so the caller picks up where it left off.

There are various details to iron out, but we can do it all with official instructions and features we already added to the model.

Adding other instructions. Whipping up new registers is helpful for augmenting the instruction set. For example, we simulate a hypothetical instruction "let $\text{Reg}[i] \leftarrow \lfloor\sqrt{\text{Reg}[j]}\rfloor$" by inserting a mini-algorithm to compute $\lfloor\sqrt{\text{Reg}[j]}\rfloor$ using auxiliary registers. The time overhead for "square root" wouldn't be a constant factor—it would depend on the word size—but would be a small price to pay.

For floating point arithmetic, "just do it in software." Treating two registers as the mantissa and exponent, we simulate arithmetic operations with mini-algorithms using auxiliary registers, incurring a low time overhead depending on the word size.

When writing high-level pseudocode, we assume all these features are available. In programming language parlance, these are syntactic sugar—features that sweeten the programming process but can be "de-sugared" down to core instructions.

Removing instructions. We can remove some instructions without crippling the model. For example, we express "xor" with "and", "or", and "not" by replacing "let $\mathrm{Reg}[i] \leftarrow \mathrm{Reg}[j] \oplus \mathrm{Reg}[k]$" with instructions evaluating $(\mathrm{Reg}[j] \wedge (\neg \mathrm{Reg}[k])) \vee ((\neg \mathrm{Reg}[j]) \wedge \mathrm{Reg}[k])$ using auxiliary registers to hold intermediate results. The same goes for the logarithm instruction—we can compute $\lfloor \log_2(\mathrm{Reg}[k]) \rfloor$ efficiently using auxiliary registers.

To completely purge "xor" and "log" from the model, these instructions shouldn't be reintroduced if we modify a program to use two registers and one-bit constants. The proof in § 1.5.2 creates no "xor" or "log" instruction that wasn't already there, so "xor" and "log" are indeed superfluous and can be safely removed from our instruction set.

We won't identify a "theoretically minimal" instruction set—that's off topic. The point is that we can push and pull the model definition in reasonable directions without significantly altering its capabilities. The concept of efficient computation is a sturdy facet of reality.

1.5.2 Number of Registers and Size of Constants

A *tight* program has only two registers and one-bit hardcoded constants (except target line numbers of branches).

Theorem 1.2. *For every program, there exists a tight program such that for every input with the original program's word size:*

- *Correctness: The programs produce the same output as each other (or both run forever).*
- *Efficiency: The new program's time and space are only constant factors larger than the original's, and the new word size is only an additive constant larger (where these constants depend on the original program).*

Proof idea. To get by with just two registers, we designate some words of work memory to hold the contents of the original program's registers, and just load or store a couple at a time, whenever the program needs to access them.

To get by with just one-bit constants, we use a bundle of instructions to construct any large constant in a register, one bit at a time, and then use the register in lieu of the constant.

These two issues seem independent but are interrelated: Decreasing the number of registers introduces large constants. Building a constant bit-by-bit requires an available register.

The modified program might need to access work segment addresses beyond the reach of the original word size. So we increase the word size. But that might change the program's behavior: If some instructions make 1s spill over into a word's new most significant bits, then the original program might have relied on those bits disappearing under the original word size. To preserve the program's behavior and output, we use extra instructions to "zero out" the new most significant bits whenever this complication might arise. Thus every word of memory (except the program counter) effectively has the original word size. ■

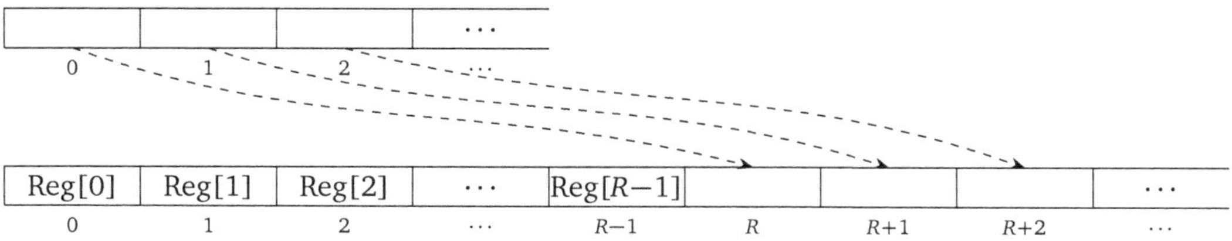

Figure 1.7: Scooting the work segment over to make room for registers

The formal proof is slightly laborious and skippable by anyone comfortable with the idea.

Proof (ancillary). First, we deal with the number of registers. Suppose the original program uses $R > 2$ many registers. The new program keeps those registers' contents in its work segment's first R words, and scoots the original program's work segment over to occupy the rest of the new program's work segment (Figure 1.7). The original Reg[i] resides at the new Mem[i] for each $i \in \{0, 1, \ldots, R-1\}$, and the original Mem[$i$] resides at the new Mem[$i+R$].

Since Reg[0] is initialized with the input size N, the new program's first instruction is "store Mem[0] ← Reg[0]". Then, each original instruction gets replaced as follows. (We only illustrate one data processing instruction and one control flow instruction; the rest are similar.)

let Reg[i] ← Reg[j] + Reg[k]	⇝	load Reg[0] ← Mem[j] load Reg[1] ← Mem[k] let Reg[0] ← Reg[0] + Reg[1] store Mem[i] ← Reg[0]
if Reg[i] = Reg[j] then goto line ℓ	⇝	load Reg[0] ← Mem[i] load Reg[1] ← Mem[j] if Reg[0] = Reg[1] then goto line $\lambda(\ell)$
load Reg[i] ← Mem[Reg[j]]	⇝	load Reg[0] ← Mem[j] let Reg[0] ← Reg[0] + R load Reg[0] ← Mem[Reg[0]] store Mem[i] ← Reg[0]
store Mem[Reg[j]] ← Reg[i]	⇝	load Reg[0] ← Mem[j] let Reg[0] ← Reg[0] + R load Reg[1] ← Mem[i] store Mem[Reg[0]] ← Reg[1]
read Reg[i] ← In[Reg[j]]	⇝	load Reg[0] ← Mem[j] read Reg[0] ← In[Reg[0]] store Mem[i] ← Reg[0]
write Reg[i]	⇝	load Reg[0] ← Mem[i] write Reg[0]

$\lambda(\ell)$ is the new line number (after all substitutions and the new first instruction) of the instruction from line ℓ of the original program. It's straightforward to handle hardcoded constants in lieu of registers. For example, in "let Reg[i] ← Reg[j] + Reg[k]" if there's a constant c instead of

Substitution	Constant	Construct in which register?
let	j, or in lieu of Reg[j]	Reg[0]
	k, or in lieu of Reg[k]	Reg[1]
	i	Reg[1]
if	i, or in lieu of Reg[i]	Reg[0]
	j, or in lieu of Reg[j]	Reg[1]
load	j, or in lieu of Reg[j]	Reg[0]
	R	Reg[1]
	i	Reg[1]
store	j, or in lieu of Reg[j]	Reg[0]
	R	Reg[1]
	i, or in lieu of Reg[i]	Reg[1]
read	j, or in lieu of Reg[j]	Reg[0]
	i	Reg[1]
write	i, or in lieu of Reg[i]	Reg[0]

Figure 1.8: Where to construct constants

Reg[j], then the substitution's third line becomes "let Reg[0] $\leftarrow c +$ Reg[1]" and we remove the first line "load Reg[0] $\leftarrow$ Mem[j]". The new program only uses two registers.

Now, we deal with the size of constants. We can construct any hardcoded constant c in a register using bitwise-or and shift left. First, we place c's most significant 1 in the register's least significant position. Then, we shift the register left until we're ready to insert c's next most significant 1 in the register's least significant position, by bitwise-or-ing with 1, and so on. Thus c "slides in" from the right. Since new constants can only be one bit, shifting left by more than one position is accomplished by repeatedly shifting left by one. Here's the example of constructing the binary number 11010 (26 in base ten):

let Reg[0] $\leftarrow$ 26 $\rightsquigarrow$ let Reg[0] $\leftarrow$ 1
let Reg[0] $\leftarrow$ Reg[0] $\ll$ 1
let Reg[0] $\leftarrow$ Reg[0] $\vee$ 1
let Reg[0] $\leftarrow$ Reg[0] $\ll$ 1
let Reg[0] $\leftarrow$ Reg[0] $\ll$ 1
let Reg[0] $\leftarrow$ Reg[0] $\vee$ 1
let Reg[0] $\leftarrow$ Reg[0] $\ll$ 1

We do this for each hardcoded constant (except target line numbers) right before where it's used—including the constants i, j, k, R in our earlier substitutions such as "load Reg[0] $\leftarrow$ Mem[i]" and "let Reg[0] $\leftarrow$ Reg[0] $+R$". We must be careful about which register to construct the constant in, since we only have two registers to work with (Figure 1.8). Now, each hardcoded constant is only one bit. We update the target line numbers in the branch substitutions after including all these instructions.

The original program's hardcoded constants fit in single words (by assumption), but the constants i, j, k, R might not fit when N is small. Also, even if R fits, the address $\text{Reg}[0] + R$ (in the load and store substitutions) might not fit, if the original program accesses addresses near the top of its range. So we increase the word size from W_N to $W_N + r$ where $r = \lceil \log(R+1) \rceil$.

To faithfully simulate the original program, the new program zeroes out the r most significant bits of each word in its work segment, leaving only the W_N least significant bits (as the original program expects for its registers and work segment). In the "let" substitution, after "let $\text{Reg}[0] \leftarrow \text{Reg}[0] + \text{Reg}[1]$" but before constructing i in Reg[1], we create a mask in Reg[1] that has 0s in the most significant r bits and 1s in the least significant W_N bits, and we bitwise-and the mask with the data word that's being assigned:

$$
\begin{aligned}
&\text{let Reg}[1] \leftarrow \neg 0 \\
&\left.\begin{aligned}
&\text{let Reg}[1] \leftarrow \text{Reg}[1] \gg 1 \\
&\vdots \\
&\text{let Reg}[1] \leftarrow \text{Reg}[1] \gg 1
\end{aligned}\right\} r \text{ times} \\
&\text{let Reg}[0] \leftarrow \text{Reg}[0] \wedge \text{Reg}[1]
\end{aligned}
$$

Masking is unnecessary in the memory access substitutions—the word being stored/written was already masked since it came from the new program's work segment or input segment. (Each input word fits in W_N bits.)

This replicates the original program's register contents and work segment, since operations that might overflow are done "mod 2^W" anyway. (If the original program did two's complement for negative numbers, the new program does "two's complement in the least significant W_N bits.") The new computation proceeds as the original would have with word size W_N: Each comparison (in conditional branches) has the same outcome as in the original, and the output is the same, except each output word is left-padded with 0s.

Time only goes up by a constant factor since each instruction is replaced with a constant-size bundle of instructions. Space only goes up by a constant factor since the word size and number of words of work memory both go up by additive constants. ■

1.5.3 Memory Access

We observe three simple lemmas that will be handy later:

- A program might as well never read past the end of the input, because it would just get an all-0 word.
- If a program uses only a constant number of words of the work segment, then it might as well use none, since it could use extra registers instead.
- If a program uses multiple work segments, then it might as well use just one, which combines all the work segments.

Lemma 1.3. *For every program, there exists a program that never reads past the input, and such that for every input:*

- *Correctness: The programs produce the same output as each other (or both run forever).*
- *Efficiency: The new program's time and space are only constant factors larger than the original's, and the word size is unchanged.*

Proof. We introduce an auxiliary register nicknamed N and insert "let $N \leftarrow \text{Reg}[0]$" before the first instruction, to remember the input size in case the program overwrites Reg[0]. We do the following substitution (and update the target line numbers of all branches):

read $\text{Reg}[i] \leftarrow \text{In}[\text{Reg}[j]]$	$\rightsquigarrow$	if $\text{Reg}[j] < N$ then goto 3 lines below let $\text{Reg}[i] \leftarrow 0$ goto 2 lines below read $\text{Reg}[i] \leftarrow \text{In}[\text{Reg}[j]]$

Time and space only go up by constant factors. ∎

A *register-only* program has no load/store instructions and no work segment.

Lemma 1.4. *For every program and every constant M, there exists a register-only program such that for every input on which the original program doesn't access any work segment address $\geq M$:*

- *Correctness: The programs produce the same output as each other (or both run forever).*
- *Efficiency: The new program's time and space are only constant factors larger than the original's (where these constants depend on M), and the word size is unchanged.*

Proof. Suppose the original program has R registers. To modify it to a register-only program, we relocate the contents of $\text{Mem}[0], \ldots, \text{Mem}[M-1]$ to new registers $\text{Reg}[R], \ldots, \text{Reg}[R+M-1]$. (This is the inverse of the idea behind Theorem 1.2, where we eliminated registers by relocating their contents to the work segment.) For $m \in \{0, 1, \ldots, M-1\}$, loading/storing $\text{Mem}[m]$ corresponds to copying data from/to $\text{Reg}[R+m]$. Since the address m may be indirect (held in a register), we need "indirect indexing for registers," which we de-sugar like indirect branching:

load $\text{Reg}[i] \leftarrow \text{Mem}[\text{Reg}[j]]$	$\rightsquigarrow$	let $\text{Reg}[i] \leftarrow \text{Reg}[R + \text{Reg}[j]]$
	$\rightsquigarrow$	if $\text{Reg}[j] \neq m$ then goto 3 lines below let $\text{Reg}[i] \leftarrow \text{Reg}[R+m]$ goto line after this whole substitution (all three lines: $\forall m$)
store $\text{Mem}[\text{Reg}[j]] \leftarrow \text{Reg}[i]$	$\rightsquigarrow$	let $\text{Reg}[R + \text{Reg}[j]] \leftarrow \text{Reg}[i]$
	$\rightsquigarrow$	if $\text{Reg}[j] \neq m$ then goto 3 lines below let $\text{Reg}[R+m] \leftarrow \text{Reg}[i]$ goto line after this whole substitution (all three lines: $\forall m$)

Then, we update the target line numbers of preexisting branch instructions.

The addresses $m \in \{0, 1, \ldots, M-1\}$ become hardcoded constants as comparison operands. If $M-1$ doesn't fit in the word size when N is small, we get around this—without increasing the word size—using the same trick as for indirect branching (§1.5.1). Time and space only go up by constant factors depending on M. The new program faithfully simulates the original program if the latter doesn't access any work segment address $\geq M$. ∎

Sometimes it's convenient to have multiple work segments $\text{Mem}_1, \text{Mem}_2, \ldots, \text{Mem}_K$, which are accessed using instructions like "load $\text{Reg}[i] \leftarrow \text{Mem}_k[\text{Reg}[j]]$". This feature helps us organize data, but it doesn't increase the model's power:

Lemma 1.5. *For every program with multiple work segments, there exists a program with one work segment, such that for every input with the original program's word size:*

$\mathrm{Mem}_1[0]$	$\mathrm{Mem}_2[0]$	$\cdots$	$\mathrm{Mem}_K[0]$	$\mathrm{Mem}_1[1]$	$\mathrm{Mem}_2[1]$	$\cdots$	$\mathrm{Mem}_K[1]$	$\mathrm{Mem}_1[2]$	$\cdots$
0	1	$\cdots$	$K-1$	K	$K+1$	$\cdots$	$2K-1$	$2K$	$\cdots$

Figure 1.9: Interleaving K work segments into one

- *Correctness: The programs produce the same output as each other (or both run forever).*
- *Efficiency: The new program's time and space are only constant factors larger than the original's, and the new word size is only an additive constant larger (where these constants depend on the original number of work segments).*

Proof. A simple way to combine K work segments into one is to interleave them (Figure 1.9). For any $k \in \{1,\ldots,K\}$, an original load or store to $\mathrm{Mem}_k[m]$ instead goes to $\mathrm{Mem}[K \cdot m + k - 1]$, using an auxiliary register to calculate the new address. The catch is that although the original word size can hold m, it might not hold $K \cdot m + k - 1$. Adding $\lceil \log(K+1) \rceil$ to the word size fixes this. To preserve the program's behavior, we vigilantly zero out the new most significant bits after every "let" instruction (except those for calculating the address) as in the proof of Theorem 1.2. Time and space only go up by constant factors: The number of words of the new work segment is at most K times the maximum number of words of any original work segment. ∎

1.5.4 Specifying and Changing the Word Size

A program's word size should provide appropriate "breathing room"—enough space per word to store basic data such as counters and pointers. If a program needs M words of work memory, then it needs word size $\geq \log M$ to fit load/store addresses in registers. Allowing a constant factor leeway in the word size is reasonable. For example, if a program uses $2^{\sqrt{N}}$ words of work memory, then word size $O(\sqrt{N})$ is appropriate.

Exactly which word size functions $W : \mathbb{N}_+ \to \mathbb{N}_+$ should we allow? An arbitrary function W contains infinite information since there are infinitely many input sizes N. But a program should have a finite specification, including the word size function. We restrict programs to use "simple" word sizes, so they can't smuggle hard-to-compute information via W. For example, $O(\log N)$ includes bizarre functions with no finite description, but we may require a program to use a very simple word size $c \log N$ for a positive integer constant c. Technically, $c \log N$ is shorthand for $c \cdot \max(\lceil \log_2(N) \rceil, 1)$. We allow arbitrarily large c so programs aren't constrained to use smaller words than would be natural.

In general, what is simple enough? Our definition will permit reasonable word sizes and prohibit exotic word sizes that let contraband information seep into a computation. The idea is that $W(N)$ should be efficiently computable from N. Informally, W is (T,S)*-constructible* iff some *constructor* program computes W in time T and space S. There's a "chicken and egg" conundrum: What word size do we use when computing the word size? We require a constructor to be oblivious to its own word size, so if we run it with a bigger word size, it does the same thing and still produces $W(N)$. We imagine each register has unlimited size, but only bits that are "used" count toward the space. This precludes computations that find a register's left end by exploiting modular arithmetic or bitwise-not.

Definition. W is (T,S)*-constructible* iff there exists a program such that:

- There are no load/store/read/write/accept/reject instructions.
- Each register can hold any nonnegative integer.

- With Reg[0] initialized to N and all other registers initialized to 0:
  - It halts with $W(N)$ in Reg[1].
  - The running time is at most $T(N)$.
  - At every step, each register's value fits in the least significant $S(N)$ bits (and so does any hardcoded constant). ◀

If we run such a program using registers of any finite size $\geq S(N)$, it "won't notice" and will still construct $W(N)$.

Example. $W = \max(2\lceil\log(N+1)\rceil, 7)$ is $(O(1), O(\log N))$-constructible by the following constructor program. Since our model has $\lfloor\log_2\rfloor$ but not $\lceil\log_2\rceil$, line 3 checks whether $N+1$ is a power of 2, and if not, then line 4 adds 1 to the floor to get the ceiling. Line 6 does the max.

Example constructor (1.13)

```
0. let Reg[2] ← Reg[0] + 1
1. let Reg[1] ← ⌊log₂(Reg[2])⌋
2. let Reg[3] ← 1 ≪ Reg[1]
3. if Reg[3] = Reg[2] then goto line 5
4. let Reg[1] ← Reg[1] + 1
5. let Reg[1] ← 2 · Reg[1]
6. if Reg[1] ≥ 7 then goto line 8
7. let Reg[1] ← 7
8. halt
```

The time is $O(1)$. The space is $O(\log N)$ since no register exceeds $N+1$, and hardcoded constants are 3 bits. ◆

Example.

- N^d is $(O(1), O(\log N))$-constructible for every integer d.
- $\lceil\sqrt{N}\rceil$ is $(O(\log N), O(\log N))$-constructible by binary search (comparing squared candidate values to N).
- $\lceil N^d\rceil$ is $(O(\log N), O(\log N))$-constructible for every rational d, similarly.
- 2^N is $(O(1), O(N))$-constructible.
- 3^N is $(O(\log N), O(N))$-constructible by the well-known "repeated squaring" algorithm. ◆

The definition of constructibility is somewhat complicated but is fortunately "self-obviating": Any program's constructible word size can be rounded up to a very simple word size with little impact on the program's efficiency. Increasing the word size is even relevant in practice: A 64-bit machine can't "just run" a 32-bit program—it needs a "compatibility mode," which incurs some overhead. Here is "compatibility mode for theory," showing that our model is robust with respect to increasing the word size.

Lemma 1.6. *For every program with (T, S)-constructible word size W, and every $U \geq \max(W, S)$, there exists a program with word size U such that for every input with word size W:*

- *Correctness: The programs produce the same output as each other (or both run forever).*
- *Efficiency: If the original program's time and space are T^* and S^*, then the new program's time and space are only constant factors larger than $T^* + T$ and $S^* \cdot U/W$.*

Proof idea. Constructibility of W lets the new program create a mask to "zero out" all but the least significant W bits of each word as it runs the original program. So although the word size is $U \geq W$, the program gets executed as if the word size were W. ■

Proof. Abbreviate $W(N)$ as W, and so on. The new program first runs W's constructor program using separate registers, after copying N from Reg[0] to the register corresponding to the constructor's Reg[0]. The constructor works since $U \geq S$. After constructing W, the new program evaluates $(1 \ll W) - 1$ to create a mask in an auxiliary Reg[h], with 1s in the least significant W bits and 0s in the most significant $U - W$ bits. Then, the new program runs the original program but after every "let Reg[i] $\leftarrow \ldots$", it inserts "let Reg[i] $\leftarrow$ Reg[i] $\wedge$ Reg[h]" to zero out the bits that wouldn't exist under the original word size W. This makes the word size effectively W, so the original program's behavior and output are preserved.

The new time is $\leq T + 3 + 2T^*$. The original program contributes $S^* \cdot U/W$ to the new space because the new program uses the same number of words of memory as the original, but now each word has U bits instead of W bits. The constructor's registers and Reg[h] take $O(U)$ space, which doesn't dominate the overall space, since $U \leq S^* \cdot U/W$ follows from $S^* \geq W$. ■

Takeaway: A program's exact word size doesn't matter, as long as it's not a covert source of information. The cumbersome definition of constructibility renders itself unnecessary.

1.6 Complexity Classes

Complexity classes "classify" computational problems according to how efficiently they can be solved. A complexity class is the set of all problems solvable within a certain efficiency constraint. If a particular problem is an element of a particular complexity class, then the problem has low complexity in a sense. If the problem isn't in the class, it has high complexity. Most complexity classes only contain decision problems, to capture the essence of efficient computation while avoiding minor hassles associated with function/search problems.

We use SANS SERIF CAPITALS for complexity class names. TIME[T] contains every decision problem with a $O(T(N))$-time program, and SPACE[S] contains every decision problem with a $O(S(N))$-space program. We'll see the formal definitions soon.

A program's word size should be small and constructible, so the program can't hide too much computation in individual instructions and in the word size specification. We combine these requirements into a streamlined definition: W is *U-bounded* iff $W \leq U$ and W is (U, U)-constructible (meaning $W(N)$ is computable from N in time U and space U).

A program's U-bounded word size can be rounded up to U with little overhead in time and space (Lemma 1.6). A common case is that a program's *log-bounded* (which means $O(\log N)$-bounded) word size can be rounded up to $c \log N$ for an integer c: Time only goes up by a constant factor plus $O(\log N)$. Space only goes up by a constant factor since the word size was already $\geq \log N$ (since N fits in a register).

All logarithms are base 2 unless specified otherwise, and we usually omit ceilings and floors when they're unimportant, such as pretending $\log N$ is always an integer.

1.6.1 Time Classes

For time T, we allow word size $\geq \log T$ so words can hold values up to T, such as counters and pointers. A constant factor leeway in the word size is reasonable, so we allow $O(\log T)$-bounded word size. If $T < N$, we allow $O(\log N)$-bounded word size so words can hold pointers to the input, and Reg[0] can hold N. For example, binary search (Exercise 1.2) takes $O(\log N)$ time but needs word size $O(\log N)$, not $O(\log(\log N))$. A problem's word size need not be constructible but must be $O(\log N)$ and at most the program's word size.

Definition. For every function $T(N)$, $\mathsf{TIME}[T]$ is the set of all decision problems for which there exists a correct program with $O(T)$ time efficiency and $O(\log\max(T,N))$-bounded word size. ◄

We showed Multiplication Decision $\in \mathsf{TIME}[N^2]$ and Directed Reachability $\in \mathsf{TIME}[N]$. Sometimes people get sloppy and write Multiplication $\in \mathsf{TIME}[N^2]$, but technically that's wrong since Multiplication isn't a decision problem.

TIME[a set of functions] is the union of $\mathsf{TIME}[T]$ over all T in the set. Let

$$\operatorname{poly} N \;=\; \{T : \text{there exists a constant } d \text{ such that } T = O(N^d)\}$$

be the set of functions that only grow polynomially fast. This includes functions that aren't polynomials per se but are at most a polynomial, such as $N\log N \le N^2$.

$$\mathsf{TIME}[\operatorname{poly} N] \;=\; \bigcup_{T\in \operatorname{poly} N} \mathsf{TIME}[T] \;=\; \bigcup_d \mathsf{TIME}[N^d]$$
$$\mathsf{TIME}[2^{\operatorname{poly} N}] \;=\; \bigcup_{T\in \operatorname{poly} N} \mathsf{TIME}[2^T] \;=\; \bigcup_d \mathsf{TIME}[2^{O(N^d)}]$$

These two classes have special names:

Definition.

- $\mathsf{P} = \mathsf{TIME}[\operatorname{poly} N]$ (Polynomial time)
- $\mathsf{EXP} = \mathsf{TIME}[2^{\operatorname{poly} N}]$ (Exponential time) ◄

We often shorten "polynomial" to "poly": $A \in \mathsf{P}$ iff A is a decision problem with a poly-time program—which has $O(N^d)$ time efficiency (for a constant d) and log-bounded word size (which we may assume is $c\log N$ for an integer c). Likewise, $A \in \mathsf{EXP}$ iff A is a decision problem with an exponential-time program—which has $2^{O(N^d)}$ time efficiency (for a constant d) and poly-bounded word size (which we may assume is cN^e for integers c and e). Not all decision problems are in EXP: Some problems require superexponential time, and some can't be solved by any program at all, regardless of efficiency.

If A is a function/search problem, we can't say $A \in \mathsf{P}$ or $A \in \mathsf{EXP}$, but we can say A has a poly-time program (with log-bounded word size) or exponential-time program (with poly-bounded word size).

An *inclusion* is a complexity class being a subset of another. A *separation* is a complexity class being *not* a subset of another. The inclusion $\mathsf{P} \subseteq \mathsf{EXP}$ holds because any program showing $A \in \mathsf{P}$ also shows $A \in \mathsf{EXP}$, since polynomials grow slower than exponentials. (We'll see many inclusions in this book, but proving them usually involves modifying the program.) We prove the separation $\mathsf{EXP} \not\subseteq \mathsf{P}$ in §4.2 by proving a superpolynomial time lower bound for a problem in EXP. Thus the *strict inclusion* $\mathsf{P} \subsetneq \mathsf{EXP}$ holds.

Another named complexity class is $\mathsf{E} = \mathsf{TIME}[2^{O(N)}]$ (*linear exponential* time). Though $\mathsf{TIME}[T]$ has an implicit big-O, we make the big-O explicit in the exponent because $2^{O(N)}$ is not $O(2^N)$. We won't study E often in this book. Let

$$\operatorname{polylog} N \;=\; \{T : \text{there exists a constant } d \text{ such that } T = O(\log^d N)\}$$

be the set of functions that only grow polylogarithmically fast. These are subpolynomial since $\log^d N = o(N^e)$ for all constants d (however large) and $e > 0$ (however small). We generally deem polylog time factors insignificant, so we dub $\mathsf{TIME}[N \operatorname{polylog} N]$ *quasi-linear* time.

1.6.2 Why P?

P is the most important class—the central hub of complexity theory. A *tractable* problem has an "efficient" algorithm, and the most common definition of tractability is having a poly-time algorithm. MULTIPLICATION DECISION and DIRECTED REACHABILITY are tractable. One reason to focus on P is because it's more robust than the TIME[T] classes. TIME[T] is sensitive to:

- The input/output encoding: For example, a graph problem might be in TIME[N] with adjacency matrix encoding but not with adjacency list encoding.
- The model of computation: For example, a problem might be in TIME[N] when the model has a log instruction but not otherwise.

P is far less finicky: Expelling a problem from P would require drastic changes to the encoding or the model. For example, only polynomial slowdown is incurred by converting adjacency list to adjacency matrix, or by computing logs using other instructions. EXP is similarly robust.

Like any celebrity, P has detractors. Criticisms leveled at P include:

"Allowing arbitrarily high-degree polynomials is too generous." A $O(N^{100})$-time algorithm is hopelessly impractical even on tiny inputs, but the problem it solves is in P. A counterpoint is that such algorithms are rarely the fastest in practice: Almost every useful problem known to be in P is also known to be in TIME[N^6] or better. There's a big theoretical chasm between polynomial and superpolynomial time. If a $O(N^{100})$-time algorithm is discovered for a problem previously only known to be in EXP, then a deep insight about the problem's structure must have been revealed. Once that cat is out of the bag, researchers typically capitalize on the new understanding to significantly improve the time efficiency. A similar criticism is that even with $O(N)$ time, big-O could conceal a terrible constant like 2^{100}. But it's rarely so bad in practice.

"Requiring worst-case performance is too restrictive." A poly-time algorithm must be correct and fast on every single valid input. But an algorithm that's wrong or slow on some contrived inputs might work great on real-world inputs. By declaring bad inputs invalid, we'd have a promise problem in P, but that's not very satisfactory because a problem shouldn't be a moving target. Instead, *average-case complexity* (Chapter 10) is about algorithms that work on "typical" inputs, without specifying which inputs those are.

"It doesn't account for randomness or other physical resources." Randomized algorithms (Chapter 7) produce correct output with high probability, which may be good enough in practice. But it's conjectured that every randomized poly-time algorithm can be converted to a deterministic (non-randomized) poly-time algorithm (Chapter 11). A bigger threat to P's status as the definition of tractability comes from bizarre properties of quantum physics. Counterintuitive behavior of subatomic particles could be harnessed to solve some problems much faster than any deterministic or randomized algorithm. Practical realization of quantum computing remains a major engineering challenge. Quantum complexity is beyond the scope of this book.

1.6.3 Space Classes

For space S, we allow word size $\geq \log S$ so words can hold values up to S, such as counters and pointers. A constant factor leeway in the word size is reasonable, so we allow $O(\log S)$-bounded word size. If $S < N$, we allow $O(\log N)$-bounded word size so words can hold pointers to the input, and Reg[0] can hold N.

Definition. For every function $S(N)$, SPACE[S] is the set of all decision problems for which there exists a correct program with $O(S)$ space efficiency and $O(\log \max(S, N))$-bounded word size. ◄

We showed MULTIPLICATION DECISION $\in$ SPACE[$\log N$] and DIRECTED REACHABILITY $\in$ SPACE[$N \log N$]. We prove DIRECTED REACHABILITY $\in$ SPACE[$\log^2 N$] in Chapter 3.

Definition.

- L = SPACE[$\log N$] (Logarithmic space)
- PSPACE = SPACE[$\mathrm{poly}\, N$] (Polynomial space) ◀

$A \in$ L iff A is a decision problem with a log-space program—which has $O(\log N)$ space efficiency and log-bounded word size (which we may assume is $c \log N$ for an integer c). Likewise, $A \in$ PSPACE iff A is a decision problem with a poly-space program—which has $O(N^d)$ space efficiency (for a constant d) and log-bounded word size (which we may assume is $c \log N$ for an integer c). We won't study EXPSPACE = SPACE[$2^{\mathrm{poly}\, N}$].

SPACE[S] is meaningful when $S \geq \log N$, since a program's word size is necessarily $\geq \log N$. A log-space program can only use a constant number of words of the work segment (on valid inputs) and therefore might as well be register-only (with no work segment and no load/store instructions) by Lemma 1.4. This clean characterization is worth highlighting:

Observation 1.7. *L is the set of all decision problems for which there exists a correct register-only program with log-bounded word size.* ■

(This ■ means no separate proof is needed.)

Like with P and EXP: If A is a function/search problem, we can't say $A \in$ L or $A \in$ PSPACE, but we can say A has a log-space or poly-space program (with log-bounded word size). The strict inclusion L $\subsetneq$ PSPACE holds because the inclusion L $\subseteq$ PSPACE is trivial and we prove the separation PSPACE $\not\subseteq$ L in §4.2. The classes L and PSPACE are robust with respect to the encoding and the model, though for L the reason is less clear and we postpone discussion to §1.9.

Now, we consider time and space together. TISP[T, S] contains every decision problem with a program that uses $O(T)$ time and $O(S)$ space. For example, MULTIPLICATION DECISION $\in$ TISP[N^2, $\log N$]. To contrast TISP[T, S] with TIME[T] $\cap$ SPACE[S]:

- $A \in$ TISP[T, S] means some program for A uses $O(T)$ time and $O(S)$ space.
- $A \in$ TIME[T] $\cap$ SPACE[S] means some program for A uses $O(T)$ time and some possibly different program for A uses $O(S)$ space.

Presumably TIME[T] $\cap$ SPACE[S] $\not\subseteq$ TISP[T, S]: We can't always have the best of both worlds. But TISP[T, S] $\subseteq$ TIME[T] $\cap$ SPACE[S] should hold: TISP[T, S] $\subseteq$ TIME[T] by ignoring space, and TISP[T, S] $\subseteq$ SPACE[S] by ignoring time. To ensure this, the word size should be both $O(\log \max(T, N))$-bounded and $O(\log \max(S, N))$-bounded.

Definition. For all functions $T(N)$ and $S(N)$, TISP[T, S] is the set of all decision problems for which there exists a correct program with $O(T)$ time efficiency, $O(S)$ space efficiency, and $O(\log \max(\min(T, S), N))$-bounded word size. ◀

If $T \in \mathrm{poly}\, N$ and $S \in \mathrm{poly}\, N$, we may assume the word size is $c \log N$ for an integer c. If sets of functions stand in for T and S, then the TISP class is the union of TISP[T, S] over all pairs (T, S) from the respective sets. For example,

$$\mathsf{TISP}[\mathrm{poly}\, N, \mathrm{polylog}\, N] = \bigcup_{(T,S)\in(\mathrm{poly}\, N)\times(\mathrm{polylog}\, N)} \mathsf{TISP}[T, S]$$

which equals $\bigcup_d$ TISP[N^d, $\log^d N$] by rounding both exponents up to the same constant d.

1.7 Time Versus Space

In this section, we prove inclusions that relate time and space:

- We convert space to time with an exponential blowup: $\mathsf{SPACE}[S] \subseteq \mathsf{TIME}[2^{O(S)}]$, so $\mathsf{L} \subseteq \mathsf{P}$ and $\mathsf{PSPACE} \subseteq \mathsf{EXP}$.
- We convert time to space with a log factor blowup: $\mathsf{TIME}[T] \subseteq \mathsf{SPACE}[T \log T]$ if $T \geq N$, so $\mathsf{P} \subseteq \mathsf{PSPACE}$.

The four main robust classes form complexity theory's "backbone":

$$\mathsf{L} \subseteq \mathsf{P} \subseteq \mathsf{PSPACE} \subseteq \mathsf{EXP}$$

Each of these three inclusions is widely believed to be strict, but these conjectures all remain unproven. The separation $\mathsf{P} \neq \mathsf{EXP}$ leaves a frustrating but amusing state of affairs:

- Most researchers conjecture that both $\mathsf{P} \neq \mathsf{PSPACE}$ and $\mathsf{PSPACE} \neq \mathsf{EXP}$ hold.
- We know for sure at least one of them holds, but with no indication of which one.
- Proving either one would be an earth-shattering achievement. ("Jaw-dropping" is too mild a description.) Nobody is aware of any viable approach that might work any time soon.

An analogous situation comes from $\mathsf{L} \neq \mathsf{PSPACE}$ implying that either $\mathsf{L} \neq \mathsf{P}$ or $\mathsf{P} \neq \mathsf{PSPACE}$.

In § 4.1 we prove another result about the backbone: If $\mathsf{L} = \mathsf{P}$ then $\mathsf{PSPACE} = \mathsf{EXP}$. The converse is not known to hold, though.

1.7.1 From Space to Time

Theorem 1.8. $\mathsf{SPACE}[S] \subseteq \mathsf{TIME}[2^{O(S)}]$ *for every* $S \geq \log N$.

Proof idea. For any program that uses $O(S)$ space, if it terminates at all, then it must terminate within $2^{O(S)}$ steps. We show the contrapositive. At any moment, the computation is in one of only $2^{O(S)}$ possible "configurations." If it hasn't halted within $2^{O(S)}$ steps, then by the pigeonhole principle, it must have repeated some configuration. Once the program experiences such déjà vu, it's doomed to repeat history forever: Upon reaching some configuration a second time, the computation will undergo the same sequence of steps as it did after the first time, until it reaches that configuration a third time ("déjà vu all over again"), and so on, ad infinitum. ■

The concept of configurations is useful throughout this book:

Definition. Consider a program with L lines of code, R registers, and word size W. Suppose on a particular input, the program never accesses any work segment address $\geq M$, so the memory space is $\leq (R+M)W$. A *configuration* consists of a line number and contents of all R registers and the work segment's first M words:

$$\big(\ell, \mathrm{Reg}[0], \ldots, \mathrm{Reg}[R-1], \mathrm{Mem}[0], \ldots, \mathrm{Mem}[M-1]\big) \in \{0,1\}^{\log L} \times (\{0,1\}^W)^R \times (\{0,1\}^W)^M$$

We assume L is a power of 2 (by appending dummy instructions if necessary), so $\{0,1\}^{\log L}$ is the set of all line numbers. ◄

A configuration is a snapshot of the state of a computation (including the program counter) at a moment in time. It's like "full debug info": If we pause a particular program running on a particular input, then the current configuration contains all information needed to resume the execution where we left off. The next configuration just depends on the program, input, and current configuration. (The program and input aren't part of a configuration because they don't change during the execution.)

Proof of Theorem 1.8. Suppose $A \in \mathsf{SPACE}[S]$ by a program Π with $O(S)$ space efficiency and $O(\log \max(S,N))$-bounded word size. Say Π has L lines of code, R registers, and word size W. Consider any valid input x of size N, and let $M-1$ be the largest address accessed by a load or store on input x (or $M=0$ if no load or store is executed). The memory space is $(R+M)W \leq cS$ for some constant c. Since a configuration has $\log L + (R+M)W \leq \log L + cS$ bits, there are $T = L2^{cS}$ possible configurations.

Since Π is correct on input x, it eventually halts. We claim that it halts within $T-1$ steps. Suppose for contradiction it executes at least T steps. Let $C_0, C_1, C_2, \ldots$ be the sequence of configurations the computation goes through, where C_0 is the initial configuration and C_t is the configuration after step t. Since this sequence has length $> T$ but each configuration comes from a set of size $\leq T$, we have $C_{t'} = C_t$ for some $t' > t$. Since the computation knows only the current configuration and not how it got there, it proceeds after step t' exactly as it did after step t. That is, $C_{t'+1} = C_{t+1}$ and then $C_{t'+2} = C_{t+2}$ and so on, up to $C_{t'+(t'-t)} = C_{t+(t'-t)} = C_{t'} = C_t$. Thus after step $t' + (t'-t)$ it again repeats the same cycle of configurations, returning to $C_{t'+2(t'-t)} = C_t$. Repeating this reasoning shows that $C_{t+k(t'-t)} = C_t$ for every integer $k \geq 0$ and thus Π runs forever on x, which is a contradiction.

Π has $2^{O(S)}$ time efficiency since it halts within $L2^{cS}-1$ steps for all valid inputs of size N. Since W is trivially also $O(S)$-bounded (as $S \geq \log N$), we conclude $A \in \mathsf{TIME}[2^{O(S)}]$. ■

1.7.2 From Time to Space

Since load/store addresses must fit in single words, a program with word size $O(\log T)$ can only access work segment addresses up to $2^{O(\log T)} = \operatorname{poly} T$. This implies $\mathsf{TIME}[T] \subseteq \mathsf{SPACE}[\operatorname{poly} T]$ if $T \geq N$, which already yields $\mathsf{P} \subseteq \mathsf{PSPACE}$. We prove a stronger inclusion:

Theorem 1.9. $\mathsf{TIME}[T] \subseteq \mathsf{SPACE}[T \log T]$ *for every* $T \geq N$.

Proof idea. A program can load/store only one word per step, so if it runs in time $O(T)$, then it accesses only $O(T)$ addresses. This is a total of $O(T \log T)$ bits of memory since the word size is $O(\log T)$. If it accessed only the first $O(T)$ work segment addresses, we'd be done. But it may access some higher addresses, leaving gaps of never-accessed addresses. Since our definition of memory space is based on the largest address accessed, the program's space efficiency might not be $O(T \log T)$. We modify the program so it solves the same problem but is frugal with space. We consolidate the accessed work memory so there's no unused space. This is like fragmentation issues that operating systems contend with. We "defragment" by rearranging the accessed memory words into a contiguous block. When the original program wants to load/store a word, the modified program figures out the new address where that word is kept. This is a job for a *dictionary* data structure, which maintains a set of (key, value) pairs such that each possible key is in at most one pair, and which supports these operations:

- Lookup: Given a key k, find k's associated value v, or report that k isn't present.
- Update: Given a key k and a value v, change k's associated value to v, or insert (k, v) if k wasn't already present.

For our defragmentation, a key is a work segment address, and its associated value is the word that would reside there for the original program. Load = lookup, and store = update.

Time efficiency doesn't matter for this theorem, so for the dictionary, we just use an unordered list of (key, value) pairs. Each operation iterates through the list looking for the desired key. If an update doesn't find the key, then it appends the (key, value) pair to the list. ■

Proof. Suppose $A \in \mathsf{TIME}[T]$ by a program Π with $O(T)$ time efficiency and $O(\log T)$-bounded word size (since $T \geq N$). We turn Π into a program Π' with the same code except for load/store substitutions (and updated target line numbers of branches). Π' views its work segment as a list of *items*, each of which is a pair of words: a work segment address (*key*) and what Π would have at that address (*value*). The keys are ordered according to the first time at which Π stores to that address. For example, after Π stores $\mathrm{Mem}[8] \leftarrow 1$, then $\mathrm{Mem}[6] \leftarrow 2$, then $\mathrm{Mem}[8] \leftarrow 3$, then $\mathrm{Mem}[7] \leftarrow 4$, then $\mathrm{Mem}[6] \leftarrow 5$, the work segment of Π' would contain $(8, 3, 6, 5, 7, 4, \ldots)$.

Π' uses three extra registers: the length of the list, a pointer for iterating through the list, and a key from the list (to compare against the desired key). For each "load $\mathrm{Reg}[i] \leftarrow \mathrm{Mem}[\mathrm{Reg}[j]]$" and "store $\mathrm{Mem}[\mathrm{Reg}[j]] \leftarrow \mathrm{Reg}[i]$" in Π, Π' instead iterates through all items until it finds a key that equals $\mathrm{Reg}[j]$, and then:

- "load": Π' loads the associated value into $\mathrm{Reg}[i]$, from the address after where the key is. If no key equals $\mathrm{Reg}[j]$ (Π is loading from an address it never stored to), Π' assigns 0 to $\mathrm{Reg}[i]$.
- "store": Π' stores $\mathrm{Reg}[i]$ to the associated value, at the address after where the key is. If no key equals $\mathrm{Reg}[j]$, Π' stores the words $(\mathrm{Reg}[j], \mathrm{Reg}[i])$ as a new item at the end of the list, and updates the "list length" register.

Π' solves A because it faithfully simulates Π. It has $O(T \log T)$ space efficiency because it only accesses the first $O(T)$ work segment addresses (at most two addresses per original store) and the word size is $O(\log T)$.

There's a slight catch: Since Π' accesses twice as many words of work memory as Π, the addresses might not quite fit in the word size. But if Π' notices that they don't fit, then only the first $O(T)$ words of work memory are addressable anyway, in which case Π' can run Π unmodified, knowing that it already uses $O(T \log T)$ space. So it's not necessary to change the word size.

Of course the $O(\log T)$-bounded word size is also $O(\log(T \log T))$-bounded, so we conclude $A \in \mathsf{SPACE}[T \log T]$. ■

If $T < N$, the same proof yields $\mathsf{TIME}[T] \subseteq \mathsf{SPACE}[T \log N]$ since the word size is $O(\log N)$.

1.7.3 Simultaneous Time and Space Bounds

$\mathsf{SPACE}[S] \subseteq \mathsf{TISP}[2^{O(S)}, S]$ because in the proof of Theorem 1.8, the program doesn't change. $\mathsf{TIME}[T] \subseteq \mathsf{TISP}[T^2, T \log T]$ because in the proof of Theorem 1.9, for each of the $O(T)$ original loads and stores, the modified program may look through $O(T)$ items to find the desired key, resulting in $O(T^2)$ time efficiency. This can be improved to $\mathsf{TIME}[T] \subseteq \mathsf{TISP}[T \log T, T \log T]$ using a more sophisticated dictionary (a self-balancing search tree). We prove a slightly weaker version with time $O(T \log^2 T)$ instead of $O(T \log T)$. This is good enough for our purposes (since we usually won't care about polylog time factors), and the proof is elementary and self-contained.

Theorem 1.10. $\mathsf{TIME}[T] \subseteq \mathsf{TISP}[T \log^2 T, T \log T]$ *for every* $T \geq N$.

Proof idea. Suppose in the proof of Theorem 1.9, we change the dictionary to keep the list of items sorted in increasing order of the keys. A load takes $O(\log T)$ time, using binary search to

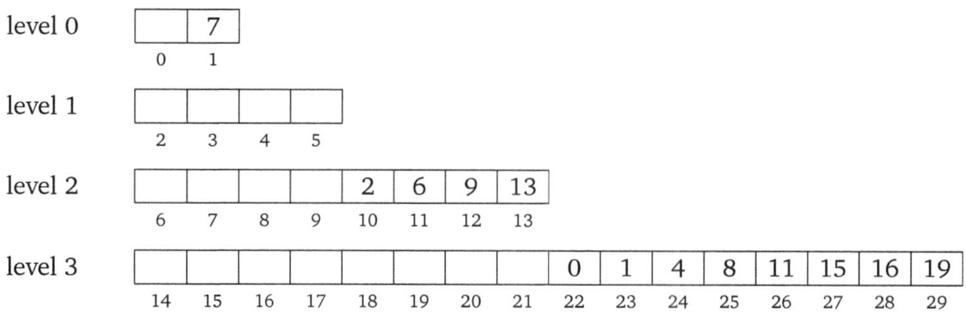

Figure 1.10: Levels of slots

locate the desired key. The time for a store depends on whether the store is *fresh*, meaning it's the original program's first store to this address. A nonfresh store takes $O(\log T)$ time. A fresh store still takes $O(T)$ time because after determining where the key should be, we must shift over all subsequent items (with larger keys) to make room to insert the new item: We need "insertion sort" to maintain the invariant that the keys are sorted.

A sorted list is good for loads and nonfresh stores, while an unsorted list has an advantage for fresh stores—appending to the list only takes $O(1)$ time. We combine and balance these approaches to make all loads and stores fast. We use a "list of lists" where each inner list is sorted but the outer list has no particular order. For example, we could have $O(\sqrt{T})$ inner lists, each of length $O(\sqrt{T})$. Then a load or nonfresh store takes $O(\sqrt{T}\log T)$ time (using binary search on each inner list), and a fresh store also takes $+\,O(\sqrt{T})$ time to insert into one of the inner lists. Thus $O(T)$ loads and stores take total time $O(T^{1.5}\log T)$ and space $O(T\log T)$.

We do even better with fewer inner lists, of varying lengths, and imitating "merge sort" (rather than insertion sort) to maintain sortedness after an insertion. This doesn't achieve $O(\log^2 T)$ time for every load/store, but it achieves $O(\log^2 T)$ time averaged over all loads/stores—this style of reasoning is called *amortized analysis*. ■

Proof (ancillary). We turn any program Π with $O(T)$ time efficiency and $O(\log T)$-bounded word size into an equivalent program Π' with $O(T\log^2 T)$ time efficiency, $O(T\log T)$ space efficiency, and the same word size. We just change the loads and stores.

We partition the work segment of Π' into *slots*, where slot $i \in \mathbb{N}$ is the pair of addresses $2i$ and $2i+1$. A slot can either be empty or hold an item, which is a (key, value) pair representing an address and the word Π would have at that address in its work segment. We worry later about how to tell whether a slot is empty.

We partition the sequence of slots into *levels*, where level $\ell \in \mathbb{N}$ contains $2\cdot 2^\ell$ many slots (specifically, slots $2^{\ell+1}-2,\dots,2^{\ell+2}-3$). Π' maintains the invariant that for each level, either all slots are empty, or the first half of the slots are empty and the second half are full and have keys in increasing order. Thus if level ℓ is nonempty, it has exactly 2^ℓ items. Figure 1.10 shows an example, where the little numbers underneath are slot numbers, and each nonempty slot shows only a key (with no value).

The invariant ensures that Π' uses only the first $O(T)$ words of its work segment. This is because if L is the greatest level that's ever nonempty, then the number of keys is $\geq 2^L$ but also $\leq O(T)$, so $2^L \leq O(T)$. The highest slot number is $2^{L+2}-3$, and the highest work segment address is $2(2^{L+2}-3)+1 \leq O(T)$. Since the word size is $O(\log T)$, the space is $O(T\log T)$.

Π' uses a register to remember how many keys are currently in the dictionary. This number's bits indicate which levels are nonempty: If the ℓth bit (0th = least significant) is 1 then level ℓ is half-full, and if the ℓth bit is 0 then level ℓ is empty. Thus we can tell whether a particular slot is empty in $O(1)$ time by examining a bit of this register. Junk can be left in empty slots.

To accomplish "load Reg[i] $\leftarrow$ Mem[Reg[j]]" or "store Mem[Reg[j]] $\leftarrow$ Reg[i]", Π' first locates the key Reg[j] by doing binary search on each nonempty level. If the key is found, its associated value is copied to or from Reg[i]. Otherwise, a load assigns 0 to Reg[i], and a fresh store inserts the item (Reg[j], Reg[i]) into the dictionary somehow. The number of nonempty levels is $\le L+1 \le O(\log T)$, and each binary search takes $O(\log T)$ time since each level has $\le O(T)$ keys. So the time per original load/store is $O(\log^2 T)$ except for a fresh store's insertion.

To insert a (k, v) pair (assuming the key k isn't already present), Π' uses *cascade insertion*. If level 0's second half is empty, we put (k, v) there. Otherwise, we put (k, v) in level 0's first half, which breaks the invariant, and then we rearrange items to restore the invariant. This pseudocode moves keys around, but their associated values are implicitly moved with the keys.

Cascade insertion algorithm (1.14)

```
if level 0 is empty: put k in slot 1 and stop
put k in slot 0
for ℓ ← 0,1,2,... until level ℓ+1 is empty:
    merge the two halves of level ℓ into the first half of level ℓ+1:
        initialize i ← 1; let a_1 < a_2 < ··· < a_{2^ℓ} denote the keys of the first half of level ℓ
        initialize j ← 1; let b_1 < b_2 < ··· < b_{2^ℓ} denote the keys of the second half of level ℓ
        for h ← 1,2,...,2^{ℓ+1}:
            if i ≤ 2^ℓ and either j > 2^ℓ or a_i < b_j:
                move a_i to the hth slot of level ℓ+1; increment i
            else:
                move b_j to the hth slot of level ℓ+1; increment j
merge the two halves of level ℓ into the second half of level ℓ+1
```

Figure 1.11 shows an example.

For intuition, when we increment the "number of keys" register, the least significant 1s all get flipped to 0s until we encounter a 0, which becomes a 1. So when rearranging items, levels $0, 1, 2, \ldots$ should become empty until we encounter an already-empty level, which becomes half-full with all the items from previous levels along with the fresh item. (Recall $2^{\ell+1} = (2^0 + 2^1 + \cdots + 2^\ell) + 1$.) Making level 0 full triggers a cascade where a full level gets moved (and sorted in the process) to the first half of the next level, thus making that level full, and so on. For each round of the cascade, both halves of the full level are already sorted, so we just have to merge them (like in merge sort): We repeatedly compare the smallest remaining first-half key with the smallest remaining second-half key, and move the smaller of the two to the next slot in the next level (and when one half is exhausted, we just move the rest of the other half).

A cascade insertion can be very time-consuming if the first empty level is far down, so a fresh store doesn't always take $O(\log^2 T)$ time. But we prove that the total time of the cascade insertions, over all fresh stores, is $O(T \log T)$: There are $O(T)$ keys and $O(\log T)$ levels. Each key progresses through the levels but never goes backward to a previous level. Thus the total amount of time spent moving any particular key is $O(\log T)$. The key might be compared to many other keys, but we "charge" a comparison to whichever key gets moved. More precisely, we partition the time steps of all cascade insertions into phases, using "key moves" as boundaries. Each phase

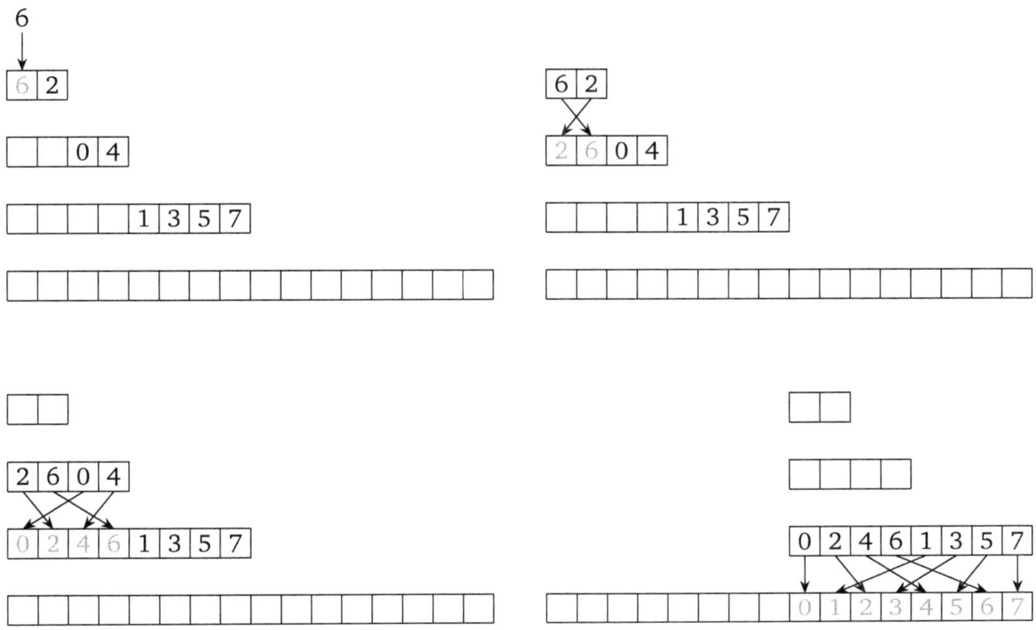

Figure 1.11: Cascade insertion example

is $O(1)$ steps, which get charged to the key that's moved at the end of the phase. So the total time for insertions is $(O(T)$ keys$) \cdot (O(\log T)$ phases per key$) \cdot (O(1)$ steps per phase$)$.

The overall time efficiency of Π' is: $O(T)$ for original non-load/non-store instructions, plus $O(T \log^2 T)$ for all load/store binary searches, plus $O(T \log T)$ for all fresh store insertions.

As in the proof of Theorem 1.9, Π' can abandon the dictionary approach if it discovers the word size is too small, and just run Π using $O(T)$ time and $O(T \log T)$ space in that case. ■

If $T < N$, the same proof yields $\mathsf{TIME}[T] \subseteq \mathsf{TISP}[T \log^2 T, T \log N]$ since the word size is $O(\log N)$.

We mentioned in §1.4.1 that it wouldn't make a big difference if we defined memory space as the number of bits in words that are actually accessed (regardless of the biggest address). This is because the proof of Theorem 1.10 shows that for every program running in time $O(T)$ and space $O(S)$ under this alternative definition of space, there exists an equivalent program running in time $O(T \log^2 S)$ and space $O(S)$ under our official definition of space.

1.8 Time-Efficient Reductions

Reductions relate the complexities of different computational problems. A reduction from problem A to problem B shows that "if B has an efficient algorithm, then so does A," and the contrapositive, "if A doesn't have an efficient algorithm, then neither does B." It turns an upper bound for B into an upper bound for A, and turns a lower bound for A into a lower bound for B.

This is "reducing A to B." We should dispel preconceptions about the word "reduce": In ordinary English it means making something smaller, but that's not a great analogy here. Computational complexity appropriated the word "reduce" and assigned it a new, technical meaning.

1.8.1 Oracle Reductions

Informally, a reduction from A to B is an algorithm that solves A by making use of any algorithm that solves B. To illustrate, consider a more general version of DIRECTED REACHABILITY:

DIRECTED SUBSET REACHABILITY	(1.15)
Input: Directed graph G, subsets S and T of G's set of nodes	
Output: Do there exist nodes $s \in S$ and $t \in T$ such that t is reachable from s?	

Instead of designing an algorithm from scratch, we can take advantage of any algorithm for DIRECTED REACHABILITY: To solve DIRECTED SUBSET REACHABILITY on input (G, S, T), we loop through all pairs $(s,t) \in S \times T$ and run any DIRECTED REACHABILITY algorithm on (G,s,t) to see whether t is reachable from s, and we accept iff at least one run of the DIRECTED REACHABILITY algorithm accepts. We just reduced A = DIRECTED SUBSET REACHABILITY to B = DIRECTED REACHABILITY. The reduction itself was simple because we didn't have to "reinvent the wheel."

Using BFS, which takes $O(N)$ time, our algorithm for DIRECTED SUBSET REACHABILITY would take $O(N^3)$ time because the loop might try $O(N^2)$ pairs (s,t). We'll soon see a more efficient reduction between these problems, but first let's elaborate on the concept of reductions.

Note that our example reduction treated the DIRECTED REACHABILITY algorithm as a black box whose inner workings were irrelevant. We could plug in any DIRECTED REACHABILITY algorithm (even the brute force one) and the reduction would still solve DIRECTED SUBSET REACHABILITY correctly (albeit less efficiently).

Reductions are common in real-world programming. Suppose a software library provides functionality that's relevant but not exactly what we need. Without modifying the library, we might be able to use it by writing wrapper code around it. Rather than "roll our own," we reduce from our desired functionality to the library's. We need not know or care how the library is implemented—we just assume it somehow accomplishes what it's supposed to.

We can reduce A to B without being aware of any algorithm for B at all. A reduction is not a complete algorithm for A—it's an algorithm with a "B-shaped hole." If an efficient algorithm for B becomes available, we could plug it into the reduction to get a complete, efficient algorithm for A. Reductions are like thought experiments: "If we had an algorithm for B, what could we do with it?" Even if we had no idea how to solve DIRECTED REACHABILITY, we could design an efficient reduction from DIRECTED SUBSET REACHABILITY, relating these problems' complexities.

We view a hypothetical algorithm for B as a subroutine we can call despite the lack of any code for the subroutine's body. (In C/C++ we would say "declared but not defined.") Running the hypothetical algorithm means we call this stub, pass it arguments that form an input to B, and pretend it instantaneously solves B and returns the correct output. In real programming, there's nothing fishy about making calls to a subroutine stub and assuming a correct body for the subroutine will be written eventually.

In complexity theory lingo, to *query the oracle* means "call the subroutine stub representing the hypothetical algorithm." Dubbing it "the oracle for B" evokes a magical entity that answers any question of the form: "Here's y, what's $B(y)$?" A reduction translates an A-question into any number of B-questions whose answers help to answer the A-question efficiently. In other words, a reduction solves A by delegating some work to the oracle for B. This explains the etymology of "reduce": A reduction does part of the work of solving A, thereby "decreasing" the amount of work remaining—all that's left is to solve B.

A *query* is any particular input to B that a reduction asks the oracle about. A reduction can make as many queries as it wants, and each query can depend on the answers received from the oracle for previous queries. This general kind of reduction is named an *oracle reduction*, to distinguish it from restricted kinds. We'll see a formal definition in §1.8.5, but for now:

Definition. An *oracle reduction* from problem A to problem B is an algorithm that solves A with access to an *oracle* that solves B: The reduction can write any valid input y to B in a designated part of its memory and do a *query* to get $B(y)$ in one time step. If B is a search problem, the reduction must solve A no matter which acceptable solution the oracle returns for each query.

The notation $A \le_p^o B$ means there exists a polynomial-time oracle reduction from A to B. In particular, on an input of size N, such a reduction makes at most $\text{poly}\, N$ many queries, and the size of each query is at most $\text{poly}\, N$. ◀

In " $\le_p^o$ " the subscript stands for "poly-time" and the superscript stands for "oracle." The "$\le$" notation is not ideal but has prevailed historically. It doesn't mean A is "less than or equal to" B, but it suggests that A's complexity can't be much higher than B's complexity.

Figure 1.12 illustrates the flow of execution of a reduction interacting with an oracle. The oracle for B is shown as a dashed box because it's a hypothetical algorithm. Given input x, the reduction computes and eventually produces a query y_1. Control is transferred to the oracle, which magically returns $B(y_1)$. Control is transferred back to the reduction, which computes and may produce another query y_2, and so on. Figure 1.12 depicts three queries, but it could be any number, including zero. After getting the answer to a query, the reduction decides whether to make another query and if so, what the next query should be, and if not, what to output.

A reduction can ignore the oracle (make no queries), so a self-contained poly-time algorithm for A is automatically an oracle reduction to literally any problem B. Reductions are useful when we don't already have an efficient algorithm for A.

Our earlier reduction was:

Oracle reduction from Directed Subset Reachability to Directed Reachability (1.16)

```
on input (G,S,T):
    for each node s ∈ S:
        for each node t ∈ T:
            query the oracle on input (G,s,t)
            if the oracle accepted: accept
    reject
```

1.8.2 Mapping Reductions

A *mapping reduction* is an oracle reduction that always makes exactly one query and outputs the same answer the oracle returns. Since the only work is to go from the input to the query, we usually just specify a mapping reduction as a function that *maps* an input x to a query y such that $A(x) = B(y)$ (Figure 1.13). We can combine a mapping reduction with any algorithm for B to obtain an algorithm for A: Run the mapping reduction on x to get y, then run the algorithm for B to get $B(y)$, then output the same thing for $A(x)$. A mapping reduction translates an A-question into one equivalent B-question.

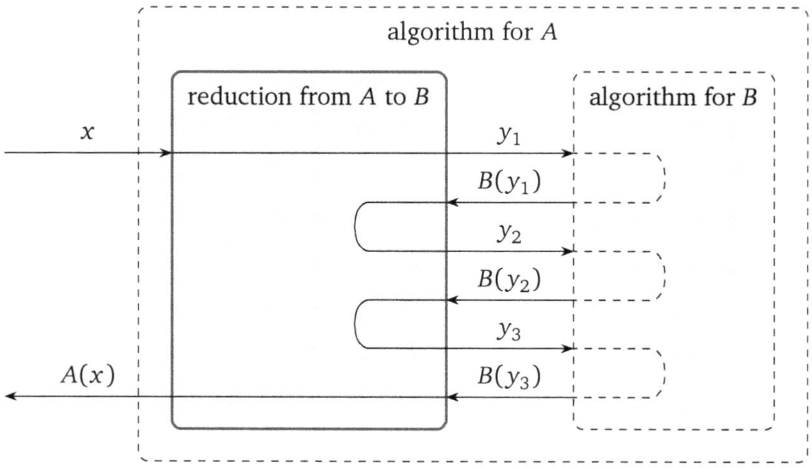

Figure 1.12: Oracle reduction

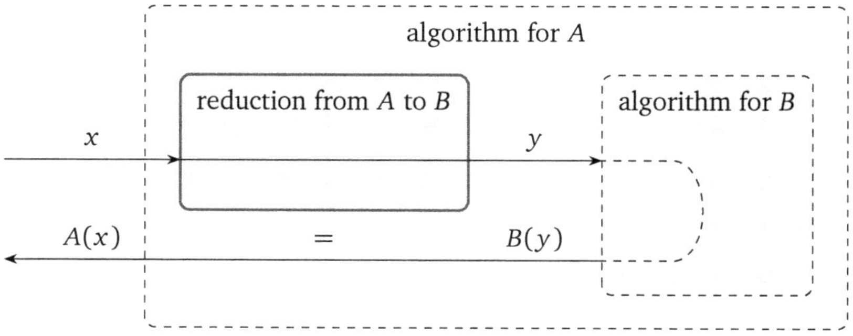

Figure 1.13: Mapping reduction

Definition. Assume A and B are both decision problems or both function problems. A *mapping reduction* from A to B is an algorithm that computes a function F: (A's valid inputs) $\rightarrow$ (B's valid inputs) such that $A(x) = B(F(x))$ for every valid input x to A.

The notation $A \leq_p^m B$ means there exists a polynomial-time mapping reduction from A to B. In particular, on an input of size N, such a reduction produces a query of size at most poly$N$. ◀

In "$\leq_p^m$" the subscript stands for "poly-time" and the superscript stands for "mapping."

We could define mapping reductions for search problems, but we won't need them.

Our oracle reduction from A = Directed Subset Reachability to B = Directed Reachability in §1.8.1 wasn't a mapping reduction, since it made many queries. We now show $A \leq_p^m B$ by efficiently mapping (transforming) an input of A to an equivalent input of B:

Mapping reduction from Directed Subset Reachability to Directed Reachability (1.17)

map (G, S, T) to (G', s', t') where:
    G' contains G along with:
        a new node s' with edges to all nodes of S
        a new node t' with edges from all nodes of T

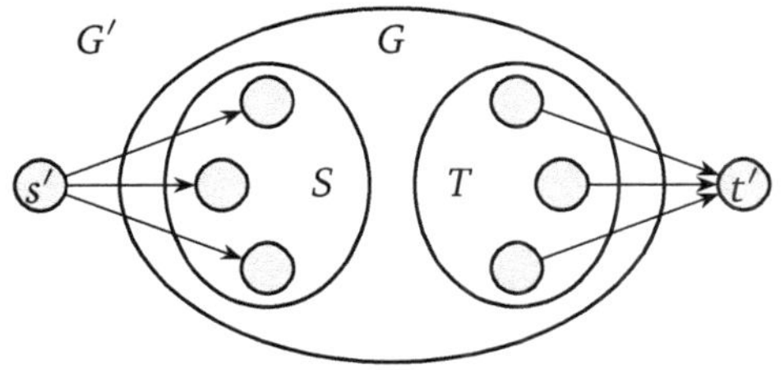

Figure 1.14: Mapping reduction from DIRECTED SUBSET REACHABILITY to DIRECTED REACHABILITY

See Figure 1.14. The oracle internally renames the arguments (G', s', t') as (G, s, t), which are like parameter names in a DIRECTED REACHABILITY subroutine. The reduction uses the "primed" names to avoid a name clash with the G, s, t that appear in the definition of DIRECTED SUBSET REACHABILITY. It's simple to see the reduction is correct, but let's formalize this to illustrate the format of such proofs.

Claim 1.11. $A(G, S, T) = B(G', s', t')$.

Proof. We show that "there exist $s \in S$ and $t \in T$ such that t is reachable from s in G" iff "t' is reachable from s' in G'."

$\Rightarrow$: Assume G has a path $s \to \cdots \to t$ for some $s \in S$ and $t \in T$. Then $s' \to s \to \cdots \to t \to t'$ is a path in G'.

$\Leftarrow$: Assume G' has a path $s' \to s \to \cdots \to t \to t'$. Then $s \to \cdots \to t$ is a path in G (it doesn't use any new nodes or new edges of G'), and $s \in S$ since $s' \to s$ is an edge, and $t \in T$ since $t \to t'$ is an edge. (If S and T overlap then we could have $s = t$, which is fine since that node would be a path of length 0 from S to T.) ■

This mapping reduction runs in time $O(N)$ and produces a query of size $O(N)$. Using BFS to answer the query in $O(N)$ time, we get a DIRECTED SUBSET REACHABILITY algorithm with time efficiency $O(N)$.

By the way, in the opposite direction, DIRECTED REACHABILITY $\leq_p^m$ DIRECTED SUBSET REACHABILITY by mapping (G, s, t) to $(G, \{s\}, \{t\})$.

For an example involving function problems, consider a more general version of SMALL ITERATED ADDITION:

ITERATED ADDITION	(1.18)
Input: Nonnegative integers $x_1, x_2, \ldots, x_n$ represented in binary with m bits each	
Output: $x_1 + x_2 + \cdots + x_n$ in binary	

Each x_i is a separate number (not an individual bit of a single number x). The input encoding has n and m (two words) and $x_1, \ldots, x_n$ (one word per bit), so the input size is $N = 2 + nm$.

We can decompose the primary-school MULTIPLICATION algorithm into a mapping reduction from MULTIPLICATION to ITERATED ADDITION, together with an ITERATED ADDITION algorithm.

Mapping reduction from MULTIPLICATION to ITERATED ADDITION	(1.19)

map (x,y) to $(q_0,q_1,\ldots,q_{n-1})$ where:
  n is the number of bits in each of $x = x_{n-1}\cdots x_0$ and $y = y_{n-1}\cdots y_0$
  $m = 2n-1$
  $q_j = x\cdot y_j\cdot 2^j$ represented with m bits, for each $j\in\{0,\ldots,n-1\}$	

To avoid a name clash, the arguments $(q_0,\ldots,q_{n-1})$ passed to the oracle have different names than the corresponding input parameters $(x_1,\ldots,x_n)$ in the definition of ITERATED ADDITION. (We used q to stand for "query.") The reduction is correct since $x\cdot y = x\cdot\sum_{j=0}^{n-1}(y_j\cdot 2^j) = \sum_j q_j$.

The primary-school MULTIPLICATION algorithm contains the standard "carry algorithm" for ITERATED ADDITION. The latter algorithm runs in linear time, but we should be careful: If we say $O(N)$ time, it's unclear whether N is the size of the input to MULTIPLICATION or the size of the query to ITERATED ADDITION. It's best to give distinct names to the input sizes of the two problems. Let's use N for MULTIPLICATION and M for ITERATED ADDITION. The reduction runs in time $O(N^2)$ and produces a query of size $M = O(N^2)$, and the carry algorithm runs in time $O(M) = O(N^2)$. Thus the primary-school MULTIPLICATION algorithm has time efficiency $O(N^2)$.

1.8.3 Decision Versus Search

As a warmup, let's consider decision versus function problems. Reducing a decision problem to a related function problem is often trivial. For example, if we can compute the product of two numbers, then of course we can compute any particular bit of the product:

Reduction from MULTIPLICATION DECISION to MULTIPLICATION	(1.20)

on input (x,y,i):
  query the oracle on input (x,y) to get $z = x\cdot y$
  output z_i, or output 0 if z has at most i bits	

In the opposite direction, we can compute the product by computing its bits one by one:

Reduction from MULTIPLICATION to MULTIPLICATION DECISION	(1.21)

on input (x,y), where x and y each have $N/2$ bits:
  for $i\leftarrow 0,1,\ldots,N-1$:
    query the oracle on input (x,y,i) to get $z_i\in\{0,1\}$
  output the binary number $z = z_{N-1}\cdots z_0$	

This isn't the most efficient way to solve MULTIPLICATION. We could ignore the oracle and solve MULTIPLICATION from scratch. If we didn't know how to solve MULTIPLICATION efficiently—or if a MULTIPLICATION DECISION implementation were conveniently available—this reduction would exploit the decision problem black box to solve the function problem without hassle.

This reduction is *nonadaptive*, which means the queries don't depend on the oracle's answers to previous queries: The reduction knows in advance which queries it will make. The answers to the queries are only used to form the output, not to form other queries.

We turn to decision versus search. Reductions from search problems to related decision problems are handy for several results in this book. Let's illustrate the idea with this search problem (introduced in §1.1.2) and a related decision problem:

DIRECTED SHORTEST PATH	(1.22)
Input: Directed graph G, nodes s and t	
Output: A shortest path from s to t in G, or report that t is not reachable from s	

DIRECTED SHORTEST PATH DECISION	(1.23)
Input: Directed graph G, nodes s and t, nonnegative integer k	
Output: Does there exist a path of length $\leq k$ from s to t in G?	

Pretend we don't know DIRECTED SHORTEST PATH can be solved in linear time by the extended BFS algorithm, but we can make calls to a hypothetical algorithm for DIRECTED SHORTEST PATH DECISION. How can we construct a shortest path from s to t with the aid of an oracle that only gives one bit of information at a time?

For starters, we determine the distance (length of a shortest path) from s to t by querying the oracle on inputs (G,s,t,k) for different values of k, to find the smallest k for which the oracle accepts. If the actual distance is d, the oracle accepts when $k \geq d$ and rejects when $k < d$. We can do binary search to find d in about $\log n$ queries (where n is the number of nodes) or just try all possibilities from 0 to $n-1$, which would still be poly time.

After finding d, we figure out which edge our path of length d should start with. For each edge (s,v), we formulate the question "Is it safe to have (s,v) be the first edge?" as the query "Does there exist a path of length $\leq d-1$ from v to t?" After identifying a safe edge (s,v) with the oracle's help, we repeat this with v's outgoing edges to pick the path's next edge, and so on. This is a *greedy* approach—the reduction commits to each edge of the path in sequence, and never changes its mind. Suppose we've built a path from s to some node u so far. To determine whether an edge (u,v) is safe to append to our path, we have the oracle "smell" whether v is in the right direction—whether the distance from v to t is less than the distance from u to t.

Reduction from DIRECTED SHORTEST PATH to DIRECTED SHORTEST PATH DECISION (1.24)

```
on input (G,s,t):
    find the smallest d ∈ {0,1,...,n−1} for which the oracle accepts input (G,s,t,d)
    if no such d exists: halt and report that t is not reachable from s
    let u_0 = s
    for ℓ = 1,2,...,d:
        for each edge (u_{ℓ−1}, v):
            query the oracle on input (G,v,t,d−ℓ)
            if the oracle accepted: let u_ℓ = v and continue to the next outer iteration
    output u_0 → u_1 → ··· → u_{d−1} → u_d
```

This first finds the distance $d = \text{dist}(s,t)$. Then, assuming t is reachable from s, the outer loop invariant is $\text{dist}(u_\ell,t) \leq d-\ell$. (This distance is exactly $d-\ell$, but we only need $\leq$ for the proof.) The invariant holds for $\ell = 0$ by the definition of d. To see that the invariant is maintained, suppose it holds for $\ell-1$: $\text{dist}(u_{\ell-1},t) \leq d-\ell+1$. The oracle accepts at least one of the queries $(G,v,t,d-\ell)$ in outer iteration ℓ, because removing the first edge $(u_{\ell-1},v)$ of a path from $u_{\ell-1}$ to t of length $\leq d-\ell+1$ yields a path from v to t of length $\leq d-\ell$. Multiple outgoing edges of $u_{\ell-1}$ might make the oracle accept, but whichever one the reduction finds first, the invariant will hold for ℓ: $\text{dist}(u_\ell,t) \leq d-\ell$. Since the invariant holds at the end when $\ell = d$, we have

$u_d = t$ since $\text{dist}(u_d, t) \le d - d = 0$. Thus the output is correct: $u_0 \to \cdots \to u_d$ is a path from s to t of length d. Though the reduction doesn't explicitly avoid repeating nodes (as required by the definition of *path*), there indeed won't be any repeats since otherwise G would have an even shorter path from s to t (by removing cycles as in Lemma A.5), contradicting the definition of d.

This reduction is *adaptive* because the answer to a query $(G, v, t, d - \ell)$ affects subsequent queries: If the oracle accepts, then the next queries correspond to outgoing edges of this v, otherwise they don't.

This illustrates the style of search-to-decision reductions in a familiar context. Compared to using extended BFS to solve the problem from scratch, this reduction has no advantage in time efficiency but has an advantage in space efficiency (§1.9.3).

1.8.4 Properties of Reductions

Lemma 1.12. *If $A \le_p^o B$ and B has a poly-time program, then so does A. In particular, for all decision problems A and B, if $A \le_p^o B$ and $B \in \mathsf{P}$ then $A \in \mathsf{P}$.*

Proof idea. We create a program for A that runs the reduction and uses the program for B to answer each oracle query. This is like what a linker does: Given compiled code that makes calls to an external subroutine whose implementation is in another file, a linker combines them into a complete, executable program.

The time efficiency of B's program is a function of B's input size, not of A's input size. If we run the reduction on an input of size N and it produces a query of size M, then B's program takes $\text{poly}\, M$ time to answer the query. Since the reduction runs in $\text{poly}\, N$ time, it makes only $\text{poly}\, N$ many queries, each of $\text{poly}\, N$ size. So A's program has time efficiency:

$$\underbrace{\text{poly}\, N}_{\substack{\text{time of}\\ \text{reduction}}} + \underbrace{\text{poly}\, N}_{\substack{\text{number}\\ \text{of queries}}} \cdot \underbrace{\text{poly}}_{\substack{\text{time of } B\text{'s}\\ \text{program}}} \Big(\underbrace{\text{poly}\, N}_{\substack{\text{query}\\ \text{size}}}\Big) = \text{poly}\, N$$

■

The next lemma is the *transitive property* of reductions.

Lemma 1.13. *If $A \le_p^o B$ and $B \le_p^o C$ then $A \le_p^o C$. If $A \le_p^m B$ and $B \le_p^m C$ then $A \le_p^m C$.*

Proof idea. If we can translate A-questions to B-questions, and we can translate B-questions to C-questions, then by chaining these together we can translate A-questions to C-questions. An A-to-C reduction can run the A-to-B reduction but use the B-to-C reduction to answer each B oracle query. This solves A by making C oracle queries, and it still runs in poly time. See Figure 1.15 and Figure 1.16. ■

We formally define reductions in §1.8.5 and then formally prove these two lemmas in §1.8.6. But an intuitive understanding of reductions is usually good enough.

1.8.5 Formal Definition

We likened oracles to subroutines, but instead of representing oracles with the subroutine call mechanism from § 1.5.1, we add dedicated features to our model of computation. We use pseudocode for high-level "reduction algorithms" and implement them as low-level "reduction programs" in our model.

First, consider reductions to a decision problem B. We have a write-only *query segment* and two new instructions:

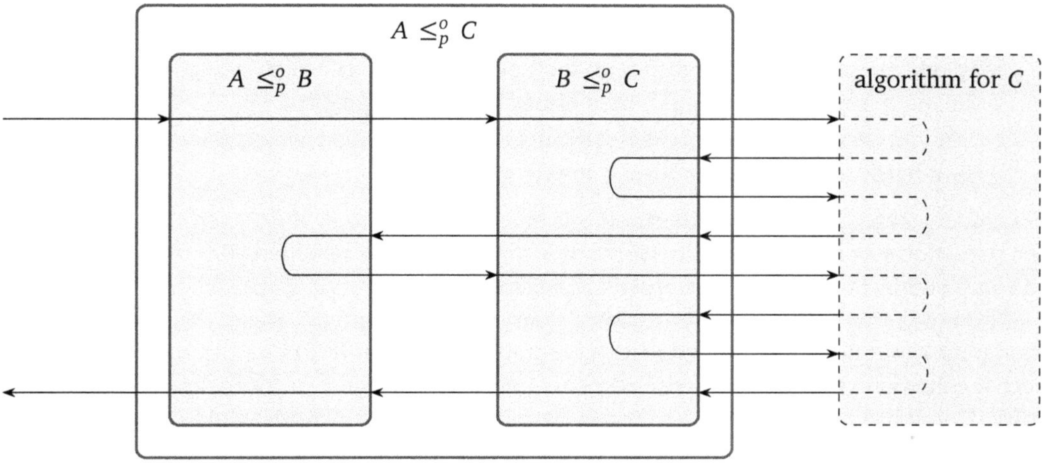

Figure 1.15: Chaining oracle reductions together

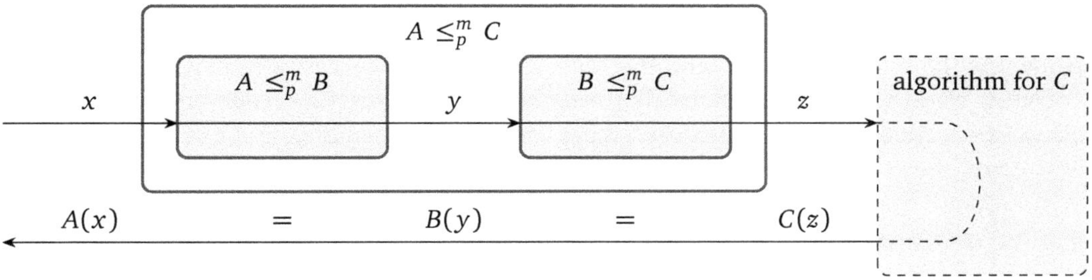

Figure 1.16: Chaining mapping reductions together

- "write-query Reg[i]" puts the word from Reg[i] (or a hardcoded constant) into the next query segment address (like the "write" instruction for the output segment).
- "query Reg[i] $\leftarrow$ Answer" treats the query segment's contents (up through the largest address written to) as an input y to B, puts $B(y)$ (which is 0 or 1) into Reg[i], and erases the query segment (resetting every word to all-0). This counts as one time step.

After a query step, subsequent write-query steps will write to addresses $0, 1, 2, \ldots$ again (in that order), and the next query step will let y be the words written by those subsequent write-query steps. There are subtleties in defining a query step's behavior:

- If y is an invalid input to B, the reduction "freezes" by keeping the program counter on the query instruction for all future steps. This represents that a hypothetical program for B might not halt on an invalid input. Thus, on a valid input to A, a reduction from A to B can't make an invalid query to B, because then the reduction wouldn't halt.
- If B's word size (depending on the size of y) is greater than the reduction's word size (depending on the size of the reduction's input), then each word of y is left-padded with 0s to form the input to B. If B's word size is less than the reduction's word size, then any y with a 1 in the "extra" most significant bits is necessarily an invalid input to B.

Now, suppose B is a function problem. We have a read-only *answer segment* for holding each oracle query's result. We still have "write-query Reg[i]", but instead of "query Reg[i] $\leftarrow$ Answer" we have two new instructions:

- "query" erases the answer segment, then puts $B(y)$ into the answer segment (where y is the query segment's contents), then erases the query segment.
- "read-answer $\text{Reg}[i] \leftarrow \text{Ans}[\text{Reg}[j]]$" puts the word from answer segment address $\text{Reg}[j]$ (or a hardcoded constant address) into $\text{Reg}[i]$.

For a query step: The reduction freezes if y is an invalid input to B. If B's word size doesn't equal the reduction's word size, then the words of $B(y)$ are either left-padded with 0s or truncated to the least significant bits to fit the answer segment.

If B is a search problem, the instruction "query $\text{Reg}[i] \leftarrow$ Found?" erases the answer segment, then puts 1 into $\text{Reg}[i]$ and an arbitrary acceptable solution of $B(y)$ into the answer segment if such a solution exists and otherwise just puts 0 into $\text{Reg}[i]$, then erases the query segment. To solve A, a reduction must generate correct output no matter which acceptable solution appears in the answer segment after each query.

$A \leq_p^o B$ means there exists a reduction to B that solves A with poly$N$ time efficiency and log-bounded word size, where N is A's input size.

$A \leq_p^m B$ means $A \leq_p^o B$ via a reduction that, for every valid input to A, performs exactly one query and outputs the same answer. For function problems, we might as well assume the answer segment is the output segment, and the "query" instruction causes termination. For decision problems, we might as well assume that instead of "query $\text{Reg}[i] \leftarrow$ Answer" we just have a "query" instruction that's equivalent to "accept" or "reject" depending on the oracle's answer. In these cases, the accept/reject/halt instructions are out of commission.

1.8.6 Formal Proofs of Properties of Reductions

Warmup for proof of Lemma 1.12. We prove the important special case of mapping reductions between decision problems: If $A \leq_p^m B$ and $B \in \mathsf{P}$ then $A \in \mathsf{P}$.

Let $\Pi_{A\leq B}$ be a poly-time mapping reduction from A to B. Let Π_B be a poly-time program for B. It suffices to design a poly-time program Π_A for A using three work segments (Lemma 1.5):

- Mem_1 corresponds to $\Pi_{A\leq B}$'s work segment.
- Mem_2 corresponds to $\Pi_{A\leq B}$'s query segment and Π_B's input segment.
- Mem_3 corresponds to Π_B's work segment.

Π_A's registers are:

- $\Pi_{A\leq B}$'s registers.
- Π_B's registers, renamed $\text{Reg}_B[\,]$ to distinguish them from $\Pi_{A\leq B}$'s registers.

Π_A contains $\Pi_{A\leq B}$'s code with $\text{Mem}_1[\,]$ instead of $\text{Mem}[\,]$ in load/store instructions, followed by Π_B's code with $\text{Reg}_B[\,]$ instead of $\text{Reg}[\,]$ and with $\text{Mem}_3[\,]$ instead of $\text{Mem}[\,]$. We do these substitutions in $\Pi_{A\leq B}$'s code:

write-query $\text{Reg}[i]$	$\rightsquigarrow$	store $\text{Mem}_2[\text{Reg}_B[0]] \leftarrow \text{Reg}[i]$ let $\text{Reg}_B[0] \leftarrow \text{Reg}_B[0] + 1$
query	$\rightsquigarrow$	goto 0th line of Π_B's code

When the execution gets to Π_B, $\text{Reg}_B[0]$ has been initialized with the query size. We do this substitution in Π_B's code:

read $\text{Reg}[i] \leftarrow \text{In}[\text{Reg}[j]]$	$\rightsquigarrow$	load $\text{Reg}_B[i] \leftarrow \text{Mem}_2[\text{Reg}_B[j]]$

We also update the target line numbers of all branches.

Π_A solves A because $\Pi_{A\leq B}$ solves A assuming the query is answered correctly, and Π_B answers the query correctly. $\Pi_{A\leq B}$ and Π_B might not agree on the word size, but we deal with this snag momentarily.

Suppose $\Pi_{A\leq B}$ has time efficiency $O(N^c)$ and Π_B has time efficiency $O(M^d)$ where M is the query size. For Π_A's time efficiency: $\Pi_{A\leq B}$'s contribution is still $O(N^c)$ since it's at most twice the unmodified $\Pi_{A\leq B}$'s time (after accounting for the write-query substitution). Since $M \leq O(N^c)$ (as each write-query is a time step of $\Pi_{A\leq B}$), the execution of Π_B contributes $O(O(N^c)^d) = O(N^{cd})$ time. Thus Π_A runs in time $O(N^c) + O(N^{cd}) = O(N^{cd})$ (assuming $d \geq 1$).

Back to the word size issue: We may assume $\Pi_{A\leq B}$ uses word size $c' \log N$ and Π_B uses word size $d' \log M$, for integers c' and d'. Since $M \leq eN^c$ for an integer e, the intended word size for Π_B is $\leq d' \log(eN^c)$. Thus, the log-bounded word size $\max\big(c' \log N,\, d' \log(eN^c)\big)$ is big enough for Π_A. As usual, Π_A zeroes out the most significant bits of each word, leaving $c' \log N$ bits for $\Pi_{A\leq B}$'s words and $d' \log M$ bits for Π_B's words. This only increases the time by a constant factor. ■

For function/search problems, we deal with the answer segment. To handle multiple queries, we reinitialize all of Π_B's memory for each query. The details are unenlightening.

Proof of Lemma 1.12 (ancillary). First, assume B is a function problem.

Let $\Pi_{A\leq B}$ be a poly-time oracle reduction from A to B. Let Π_B be a poly-time program for B. It suffices to design a poly-time program Π_A for A using four work segments (Lemma 1.5):

- Mem_1 corresponds to $\Pi_{A\leq B}$'s work segment.
- Mem_2 corresponds to $\Pi_{A\leq B}$'s query segment and Π_B's input segment.
- Mem_3 corresponds to Π_B's work segment.
- Mem_4 corresponds to Π_B's output segment and $\Pi_{A\leq B}$'s answer segment.

Π_A's registers are:

- $\Pi_{A\leq B}$'s registers.
- Π_B's registers, renamed $\text{Reg}_B[\,]$ to distinguish them from $\Pi_{A\leq B}$'s registers.
- Three more registers, nicknamed *qsize*, *bsize*, *asize*, to remember the sizes of the contents of Mem_2, Mem_3, Mem_4 respectively.

Π_A runs $\Pi_{A\leq B}$ using $\text{Mem}_1[\,]$ instead of $\text{Mem}[\,]$, and with these substitutions:

write-query $\text{Reg}[i]$	⇝	store $\text{Mem}_2[qsize] \leftarrow \text{Reg}[i]$ let $qsize \leftarrow qsize + 1$
query	⇝	erase Mem_4 erase Mem_3 let $\text{Reg}_B[0] \leftarrow qsize$ let $\text{Reg}_B[i] \leftarrow 0$ } $\forall i \neq 0$ a copy of Π_B's code erase Mem_2
read-answer $\text{Reg}[i] \leftarrow \text{Ans}[\text{Reg}[j]]$	⇝	load $\text{Reg}[i] \leftarrow \text{Mem}_4[\text{Reg}[j]]$
erase Mem_2	⇝	if $qsize = 0$ then goto 4 lines below let $qsize \leftarrow qsize - 1$ store $\text{Mem}_2[qsize] \leftarrow 0$ goto 3 lines above

Similarly, "erase Mem_3" uses *bsize*, and "erase Mem_4" uses *asize*. We update Π_B's code to use $\text{Reg}_B[\,]$ instead of Reg[ ], and $\text{Mem}_3[\,]$ instead of Mem[ ], and with these substitutions:

read $\text{Reg}[i] \leftarrow \text{In}[\text{Reg}[j]]$	$\rightsquigarrow$	load $\text{Reg}_B[i] \leftarrow \text{Mem}_2[\text{Reg}_B[j]]$
write $\text{Reg}[i]$	$\rightsquigarrow$	store $\text{Mem}_4[\mathit{asize}] \leftarrow \text{Reg}_B[i]$ let $\mathit{asize} \leftarrow \mathit{asize} + 1$
store $\text{Mem}[\text{Reg}[j]] \leftarrow \text{Reg}[i]$	$\rightsquigarrow$	if $\text{Reg}_B[j] < \mathit{bsize}$ then goto 2 lines below let $\mathit{bsize} \leftarrow \text{Reg}_B[j] + 1$ store $\text{Mem}_3[\text{Reg}_B[j]] \leftarrow \text{Reg}_B[i]$
halt	$\rightsquigarrow$	goto next "erase Mem_2"

If B is a decision problem, the "query $\text{Reg}[i] \leftarrow$ Answer" substitution is the "query" substitution but without "erase Mem_4" (there's no answer segment), and this copy of Π_B's code has:

accept	$\rightsquigarrow$	let $\text{Reg}[i] \leftarrow 1$ goto next "erase Mem_2"
reject	$\rightsquigarrow$	let $\text{Reg}[i] \leftarrow 0$ goto next "erase Mem_2"

If B is a search problem, the "query $\text{Reg}[i] \leftarrow$ Found?" substitution is the "query" substitution for function problems, but this copy of Π_B's code has:

halt	$\rightsquigarrow$	let $\text{Reg}[i] \leftarrow 1$ goto next "erase Mem_2"
reject	$\rightsquigarrow$	let $\text{Reg}[i] \leftarrow 0$ erase Mem_4 goto next "erase Mem_2"

We also update the target line numbers of all branches.

(We duplicate Π_B's code for every query instruction, which is poor programming style, but that doesn't matter here. To avoid the duplication, we could branch to a unique copy of Π_B, then indirectly branch back to the calling point when Π_B is done.)

Π_A solves A because $\Pi_{A\le B}$ solves A assuming each query is answered correctly, and Π_B answers each query correctly. We deal with the word size issue just like in the warmup proof, though now different runs of Π_B may have different query sizes and thus need different effective word sizes.

Suppose $\Pi_{A\le B}$ has time efficiency $O(N^c)$ and Π_B has time efficiency $O(M^d)$ where $M = \mathit{qsize}$ is the query size. We bound Π_A's time efficiency by partitioning the steps into five groups, and bounding each group's contribution to the time. The five groups are: $\Pi_{A\le B}$, the executions of Π_B, and the "erase Mem_2", "erase Mem_3", and "erase Mem_4" phases.

$\Pi_{A\le B}$'s contribution is still $O(N^c)$ after accounting for the substitutions. If $M_1, \ldots, M_p$ are the sizes of queries made by $\Pi_{A\le B}$ on a particular valid input of A, then $M_1 + \cdots + M_p \le O(N^c)$, so Π_B's total contribution is $O(M_1^d + \cdots + M_p^d) \le O((M_1 + \cdots + M_p)^d) \le O(N^{cd})$, since expanding $(M_1 + \cdots + M_p)^d$ yields $M_1^d + \cdots + M_p^d$ plus other nonnegative terms.

The total contribution of all "erase Mem_2" phases is $O(N^c)$ since each iteration of the erase loop corresponds to a write-query step of $\Pi_{A\le B}$. The total contribution of all "erase Mem_4" phases is $O(N^{cd})$ since each iteration of the erase loop corresponds to a write step of Π_B.

The contribution of one "erase Mem_3" phase is proportional to the highest address stored to by the previous execution of Π_B, which is poly$N$ since the word size is $O(\log N)$. We can improve the total contribution to $O(N^{cd})$ by using an extra work segment to record which addresses Π_B stores to, and just erasing those addresses.

So Π_A has time efficiency $O(N^{cd})$ with the "erase Mem_3" modification. ■

Proof of Lemma 1.13 (ancillary). We just outline the proof; it's nearly identical to Lemma 1.12. First, we show this for oracle reductions. The A-to-C reduction has work segments corresponding to the A-to-B reduction's work/query/answer segments and the B-to-C reduction's work segment. The A-to-C reduction's query/answer segments correspond to the B-to-C reduction's query/answer segments. The A-to-C reduction has registers corresponding to the registers of the A-to-B and B-to-C reductions, and extra registers to remember the sizes of work segments it needs to erase. The A-to-C reduction runs the A-to-B reduction and replaces each B query with a run of the B-to-C reduction, using the same instruction substitutions as in the proof of Lemma 1.12. This solves A assuming each C query is answered correctly. The analysis of the time efficiency and word size is as in Lemma 1.12. (The proof of Lemma 1.5 also works for reductions, provided we zero out the new most significant bits after each "read-answer".)

For mapping reductions, we observe that the proof for oracle reductions preserves the "mapping" property: Assume A, B, C are all decision problems or all function problems. On input x, the A-to-B mapping reduction makes one query y, such that $A(x) = B(y)$. This query is answered by the B-to-C mapping reduction, which makes one query z, such that $B(y) = C(z)$. So on input x, the A-to-C reduction makes one query z, such that $A(x) = C(z)$, and is thus a mapping reduction. ■

1.9 Space-Efficient Reductions

1.9.1 Log-Space Mapping Reductions

The notation $A \leq_\ell^m B$ means there exists a log-space mapping reduction from A to B (which are both decision problems or both function problems). As usual, the space includes the registers and work segment but not the input or output segments. It doesn't include the query segment. (If it did, log-space reductions could only produce queries with $O(\log N)$ bits, which is very restrictive.) The mapping reduction examples from §1.8.2 only need log space:

Example. Multiplication $\leq_\ell^m$ Iterated Addition: We map $(x, y) = (x_{n-1} \cdots x_0, y_{n-1} \cdots y_0)$ to $(q_0, \ldots, q_{n-1})$ where $q_j = x \cdot y_j \cdot 2^j$ has $m = 2n - 1$ bits. As we write the encoding of $(q_0, \ldots, q_{n-1})$, we hold $j \in \{0, \ldots, n-1\}$ and $i \in \{0, \ldots, m-1\}$ in registers and use more registers to compute $q_{j,i} = x_{i-j} \cdot y_j$ (the ith least significant bit of the query's jth number) for each pair (j, i) with $0 \leq i - j < n$, and $q_{j,i} = 0$ for other pairs (j, i). Each register has $O(\log N)$ bits, so the reduction has space efficiency $O(\log N)$ even though the query is at least $nm = \Omega(N^2)$ bits. ♦

Example. Directed Subset Reachability $\leq_\ell^m$ Directed Reachability: We map (G, S, T) (where G has n nodes) to (G', s', t') where G' contains G and nodes $s' = n + 1$ (with edges to all nodes of S) and $t' = n + 2$ (with edges from all nodes of T). As we write the encoding of (G', s', t'), we mostly just copy G, using a register to remember where we are and a register to hold each word as it's copied. For each node $u \in [n]$, we check whether $u \in T$ and if so, append t' to u's adjacency list and shift all subsequent lists over. Then, s' has adjacency list S, and t' has an empty adjacency list. At the beginning, as we go through the list of pointers to the adjacency lists, we remember how many nodes so far are in T, and update each pointer accordingly. ♦

Every log-space program is poly-time, since there are only poly many possible configurations and the computation wouldn't halt if it ever repeated a configuration (Theorem 1.8). This also holds for mapping reductions if configurations don't include the query segment:

Lemma 1.14. *Every log-space mapping reduction is poly-time, so if $A \leq_{\ell}^{m} B$ then $A \leq_{p}^{m} B$.* ∎

Poly-time mapping reductions transfer time complexity bounds from one problem to another: If $A \leq_{p}^{m} B$ and B has a poly-time program, then so does A (Lemma 1.12). There's an analogue for space:

Lemma 1.15. *If $A \leq_{\ell}^{m} B$ and B has a log-space program, then so does A. In particular, for all decision problems A and B, if $A \leq_{\ell}^{m} B$ and $B \in \mathsf{L}$ then $A \in \mathsf{L}$.*

Now we see why L is robust with respect to the problem encoding, as mentioned in § 1.6.3: Different encodings of a problem are technically different problems, but we can convert between reasonable encodings with log-space mapping reductions, so either all versions of the problem are in L or none are (Lemma 1.15). Also, L is robust with respect to the model of computation because the adaptations in § 1.5 only involve new registers and a constant number of work segment words.

Proof idea for Lemma 1.15. In the poly-time setting (Lemma 1.12), we combined a reduction and a program for B into a program for A, in which the reduction's query segment became a work segment. In the log-space setting, we can't do that, because we'd suddenly be charged for the previously "free" query segment.

For example, to get a log-space MULTIPLICATION algorithm from a log-space ITERATED ADDITION algorithm, we can't afford to store the entire query and then run the ITERATED ADDITION algorithm on it. The primary-school MULTIPLICATION algorithm instead calculates each bit of the query on the fly when it's needed—and then forgets it—rather than calculating them all up front. This blurs the boundary between the reduction and the algorithm it's interacting with.

In general, the idea is to never store the whole query at once. Whenever B's program wants to read a word of its input (the query), we pause B's program and compute the desired word by running the reduction and ignoring the query it generates, until it gets to the address being read by B's program. We reuse the same memory every time we run the reduction. If B's program reads the same word multiple times, we resist the temptation to store the word for future lookup—we just recompute it by rerunning the reduction, as many times as needed. This program for A might not be impressively fast, but it just needs the space of the reduction plus the space of B's program, both of which are $O(\log N)$. ∎

This illustrates a paradigm for designing space-efficient algorithms:

Recompute intermediate results to avoid wasting space storing them.

Here's the complementary paradigm for designing time-efficient algorithms:

Store intermediate results to avoid wasting time recomputing them.

Before we formally prove Lemma 1.15, we precisely define *log-space mapping reduction*. Recall that a mapping reduction to B can use these instructions:

- "write-query $\text{Reg}[i]$" puts the word from $\text{Reg}[i]$ (or a hardcoded constant) into the next query segment address.
- "query" treats the query segment's contents (up through the largest address written to) as an input y to B, and terminates the execution with $B(y)$ as the output. If B is a decision problem, this is equivalent to "accept" or "reject". If B is a function problem, this is equivalent to "halt" where the answer segment and output segment are one and the same.

$A \leq_\ell^m B$ means there exists a mapping reduction to B that solves A with $O(\log N)$ space efficiency and log-bounded word size (where N is A's input size), where the input, query, and answer/output segments don't count toward the space. We may assume such a reduction is register-only, as in Observation 1.7.

Proof of Lemma 1.15. Let $\Pi_{A\leq B}$ be a register-only mapping reduction from A to B, and let Π_B be a register-only program for B, both with log-bounded word size. We design a register-only program Π_A for A using these registers:

- $\Pi_{A\leq B}$'s registers.
- Π_B's registers, renamed $\text{Reg}_B[\,]$ to distinguish them from $\Pi_{A\leq B}$'s registers.
- Two more registers, nicknamed N and $qaddr$.

Π_A first has "let $N \leftarrow \text{Reg}[0]$", which puts A's input size in the N register for safekeeping, in case $\Pi_{A\leq B}$ overwrites $\text{Reg}[0]$. Then, Π_A initializes $\text{Reg}_B[0]$ to the query size using a copy of $\Pi_{A\leq B}$'s code with these substitutions:

write-query $\text{Reg}[i]$	$\rightsquigarrow$	let $\text{Reg}_B[0] \leftarrow \text{Reg}_B[0]+1$
query	$\rightsquigarrow$	goto 0th line of Π_B's code

Then, Π_A has Π_B's code with $\text{Reg}_B[\,]$ instead of $\text{Reg}[\,]$ and with this substitution:

read $\text{Reg}[i] \leftarrow \text{In}[\text{Reg}[j]]$	$\rightsquigarrow$	let $qaddr \leftarrow 0$ let $\text{Reg}[0] \leftarrow N$ let $\text{Reg}[k] \leftarrow 0$ $\quad\}\ \forall k \neq 0$ another copy of $\Pi_{A\leq B}$'s code

This new copy of $\Pi_{A\leq B}$'s code (there's one copy per "read" line in Π_B) computes the word that would be at address $\text{Reg}_B[j]$ of the query segment, and puts it in $\text{Reg}_B[i]$. To accomplish this, we modify the code to use the $qaddr$ register to remember how many words have been "written" to the (nonexistent) query segment so far, and stop when it reaches the desired word:

write-query $\text{Reg}[k]$	$\rightsquigarrow$	if $qaddr \neq \text{Reg}_B[j]$ then goto 3 lines below let $\text{Reg}_B[i] \leftarrow \text{Reg}[k]$ goto next line of Π_B's code let $qaddr \leftarrow qaddr + 1$

We assume Π_B never reads past its input (Lemma 1.3), so this copy of $\Pi_{A\leq B}$ won't reach a "query" instruction—we must have $\text{Reg}_B[j] <$ query size.

We also update the target line numbers of all branches.

Π_A solves A because it faithfully simulates Π_B on $\Pi_{A\leq B}$'s query. Though $\Pi_{A\leq B}$ and Π_B might not agree on which word size to use, we handle this as in Lemma 1.12: Since $\Pi_{A\leq B}$ runs in time $\text{poly}N$ (Lemma 1.14), the query has size $M \leq \text{poly}N$, and Π_B expects word size $O(\log M) = O(\log N)$. We choose a log-bounded word size large enough for running both $\Pi_{A\leq B}$

and Π_B, and we persistently zero out all but the intended number of bits in the registers for both computations. This only uses a few extra registers for the masks. Since Π_A is register-only and has word size $O(\log N)$, it has space efficiency $O(\log N)$. ■

The transitive property (like Lemma 1.13) holds by the same proof as Lemma 1.15, except using a B-to-C reduction in place of the program for B:

Lemma 1.16. *If $A \leq_\ell^m B$ and $B \leq_\ell^m C$ then $A \leq_\ell^m C$.* ■

1.9.2 Log-Space Oracle Reductions

The notation $A \leq_\ell^o B$ means there exists a log-space oracle reduction from A to B, where the query segment doesn't count toward the space. We only let B be a decision problem, to avoid the issue of whether the answer segment counts toward the space. (For mapping reductions, the answer segment is the output segment, which doesn't count anyway.) Such a reduction can use "write-query Reg[i]" and "query Reg[i] $\leftarrow$ Answer", which puts the bit $B(y)$ into Reg[i] and erases the query segment. Such a reduction has log-bounded word size, and is register-only without loss of generality.

Lemma 1.17. *Every log-space oracle reduction to a decision problem is poly-time, so if B is a decision problem and $A \leq_\ell^o B$ then $A \leq_p^o B$.*

Proof. This is more subtle than for $\leq_\ell^m$ (Lemma 1.14). A configuration is the contents of the program counter and registers (assuming the reduction is register-only), which is $O(\log N)$ bits, so there are only $2^{O(\log N)} = \text{poly}\,N$ possible configurations on an input of size N. But the reduction isn't necessarily doomed to run forever if it repeats a configuration, since the future execution can depend on the query segment, which isn't part of the configuration.

Consider any valid input. Partition the computation steps into phases delimited by queries. The last phase ends with a termination step, and each other phase ends with a query step.

If two phases start with the same configuration, then the reduction wouldn't halt: The query segment is empty at these steps, so the execution after a repeated configuration would be the same as after the first occurrence, leading to an endless loop (as in Theorem 1.8). Since the reduction halts, it has only poly$N$ many phases.

Within a phase (not including the configuration after the phase's query step, which is the first configuration of the next phase), if two configurations were the same, then the reduction wouldn't halt: The query segment may be different at these two steps, but it doesn't affect the execution until the query. Thus, a repeated configuration within a phase would lead to an endless loop (as in Theorem 1.8), possibly writing an infinitely long query.

In summary, the reduction runs in poly$N$ time = (poly$N$ phases) $\cdot$ (poly$N$ time/phase). ■

Lemma 1.18. *If $A \leq_\ell^o B$ and $B \in \mathsf{L}$ then A has a log-space program.*

Proof idea. Like in Lemma 1.15, whenever B's program wants to read a word of the query, we fetch the word by rerunning the reduction and discarding the other query words as we go. But with adaptive queries, we shouldn't rerun the reduction from the beginning, which would involve redoing earlier queries. We just rerun the reduction's latest phase, starting after the most recent query (or the beginning if we're working on the first query). At the start of each phase, we save the reduction's current configuration in extra registers, so we can restore this configuration to kick off each rerun during the next query. To restore the program counter, we do an indirect branch (§1.5.1). ■

Proof (ancillary). Let $\Pi_{A\le B}$ be a register-only oracle reduction from A to B, and let Π_B be a register-only program for B, both with log-bounded word size. We design a register-only program Π_A for A using these registers:

- Three copies of $\Pi_{A\le B}$'s registers, named Reg[ ], $\text{Reg}_{\text{snapshot}}[\,]$, and $\text{Reg}_{\text{replay}}[\,]$.
- Π_B's registers, renamed $\text{Reg}_B[\,]$.
- Two more registers, nicknamed *qsite* and *qaddr*.

Π_A has "let $\text{Reg}_{\text{snapshot}}[0] \leftarrow \text{Reg}[0]$" followed by $\Pi_{A\le B}$'s code with these substitutions:

write-query Reg[i]	$\rightsquigarrow$	let $\text{Reg}_B[0] \leftarrow \text{Reg}_B[0]+1$

And for the qth "query" instruction (qth in terms of lines of code, not computation steps):

query Reg[h] $\leftarrow$ Answer	$\rightsquigarrow$	a copy of Π_B's code	
		let $\text{Reg}_B[k] \leftarrow 0$	$\}\ \forall k$
		let $\text{Reg}_{\text{snapshot}}[k] \leftarrow \text{Reg}[k]$	$\}\ \forall k$
		let *qsite* $\leftarrow q$	

Here, $q \in \{1,2,\ldots\}$ is a hardcoded constant. This copy of Π_B's code uses $\text{Reg}_B[\,]$ and the following substitutions:

accept	$\rightsquigarrow$	let Reg[h] $\leftarrow 1$ goto line after this copy of Π_B's code
reject	$\rightsquigarrow$	let Reg[h] $\leftarrow 0$ goto line after this copy of Π_B's code

And for the rth "read" instruction in this copy of Π_B's code:

read Reg[i] $\leftarrow$ In[Reg[j]]	$\rightsquigarrow$	let *qaddr* $\leftarrow 0$	
		let $\text{Reg}_{\text{replay}}[k] \leftarrow \text{Reg}_{\text{snapshot}}[k]$	$\}\ \forall k$
		if *qsite* $= s$ then goto line $\ell_{q,r,s}$	$\}\ \forall s$
		another copy of $\Pi_{A\le B}$'s code	

Here, each $s \in \{1,2,\ldots\}$ is a hardcoded constant, and $\ell_{q,r,s}$ is the number of the line following the sth "query" in this copy of $\Pi_{A\le B}$'s code (which is the rth copy within the qth copy of Π_B's code). If *qsite* $= 0$ then the block of "if"s falls through to the 0th line of the copy.

This copy of $\Pi_{A\le B}$'s code computes the word that would be at address $\text{Reg}_B[j]$ of the query segment, and puts it in $\text{Reg}_B[i]$. To do this, it replays $\Pi_{A\le B}$'s computation from just after the previously performed query (which was the *qsite*th "query" instruction), or from the beginning if no query was previously performed (*qsite* $= 0$). The Reg[ ] contents from that moment were saved in $\text{Reg}_{\text{snapshot}}[\,]$, and they now get recalled into $\text{Reg}_{\text{replay}}[\,]$, which the copy of $\Pi_{A\le B}$'s code uses. It uses *qaddr* to detect when the desired word becomes available, with the same substitution as in the proof of Lemma 1.15 (assuming Π_B never reads past its input):

write-query Reg[k]	$\rightsquigarrow$	if *qaddr* $\neq \text{Reg}_B[j]$ then goto 3 lines below let $\text{Reg}_B[i] \leftarrow \text{Reg}_{\text{replay}}[k]$ goto line after this copy of $\Pi_{A\le B}$'s code let *qaddr* $\leftarrow$ *qaddr* $+1$

We remove any "write" instructions from this copy of $\Pi_{A\le B}$'s code.

We also update the target line numbers of all branches.

Π_A solves A because $\Pi_{A\le B}$ solves A assuming each query is answered correctly, and Π_B answers each query correctly since each "read" gets the desired word. We handle the word size as in Lemma 1.15, using the fact that each query has size at most poly N since $\Pi_{A\le B}$ runs in poly N time (Lemma 1.17). We also ensure the word size is big enough for the q and s constants. Since Π_A is register-only and has word size $O(\log N)$, it has space efficiency $O(\log N)$. ■

The transitive property holds by the same proof as Lemma 1.18, except using a B-to-C reduction in place of the program for B:

Lemma 1.19. *If $A \le_\ell^o B$ and $B \le_\ell^o C$ then $A \le_\ell^o C$, assuming B and C are decision problems.* ■

1.9.3 Decision Versus Search

This chapter's finale is a log-space search-to-decision reduction for Directed Reachability.

Lemma 1.20. Directed Shortest Path $\le_\ell^o$ Directed Shortest Path Decision.

Proof. The reduction in § 1.8.3 only needs log space: When finding the distance d from s to t, it only needs registers to remember the current guess for d and copy the input to the query segment. When finding a path, it only needs registers to remember the loop counter ℓ and latest node $u_{\ell-1}$, iterate through $u_{\ell-1}$'s adjacency list, and copy things to the query segment. It can output the path as it goes along. The previous nodes $u_0, \dots, u_{\ell-2}$ need not be remembered since they were already written to the output segment. ■

Lemma 1.21. Directed Shortest Path Decision $\le_\ell^m$ Directed Reachability.

Proof. Map (G, s, t, k) to (G', s', t') where G' is a "layered" version of G. There are $k+1$ layers in G', numbered $0, 1, \dots, k$. Each layer is a copy of G but with the edges going to the next layer, and layer k has no outgoing edges. Each copy of t in G', except the one in layer k, also has a "horizontal" edge to the next layer's copy of t (as if t had a self-loop in G). Node s' corresponds to s in layer 0, and node t' corresponds to t in layer k. Non-s' nodes in layer 0 and non-t' nodes in layer k (and all their edges) are optional because they can't be on a path from s' to t'.

Figure 1.17 shows an example yes-input. The bold edges show how a path from s to t of length $2 \le k = 3$ corresponds to a path from s' to t'. The gray nodes and edges are optional.

Formally, from $G = (V, E)$ define $G' = (V', E')$ where $V' = V \times \{0, 1, \dots, k\}$ and for each $j \in \{0, \dots, k-1\}$, we have $\big((u, j), (v, j+1)\big) \in E'$ for each $(u, v) \in E$, and $\big((t, j), (t, j+1)\big) \in E'$. Define $s' = (s, 0)$ and $t' = (t, k)$.

We argue that G has a path from s to t of length $\le k$ iff G' has a path from s' to t':

$\Rightarrow$: Assume G has a path from s to t of length $d \le k$. Follow the corresponding sequence of nodes from s' through the successive layers of G' to reach the copy of t in layer d, then follow $k-d$ horizontal edges to reach t'. Formally, a path $s = u_0 \to u_1 \to \cdots \to u_d = t$ becomes a path $s' = (u_0, 0) \to (u_1, 1) \to \cdots \to (u_d, d) \to (u_d, d+1) \to \cdots \to (u_d, k) = t'$.

$\Leftarrow$: Assume G' has a path from s' to t'. The corresponding sequence of nodes in G—stopping as soon as we reach t, and trimming out any cycles—is a path from s to t of length $\le k$. Formally, $s' = (v_0, 0) \to (v_1, 1) \to \cdots \to (v_k, k) = t'$ becomes a walk $s = v_0 \to v_1 \to \cdots \to v_d = t$ where $d \le k$ is the first layer with $v_d = t$.

The reduction can be implemented in log space because while writing G', it only needs to remember the current node (u, j) and some pointers for consulting u's adjacency list in G. We may assume $k \le n-1$ (where G has n nodes), so each layer index j fits in one word. ■

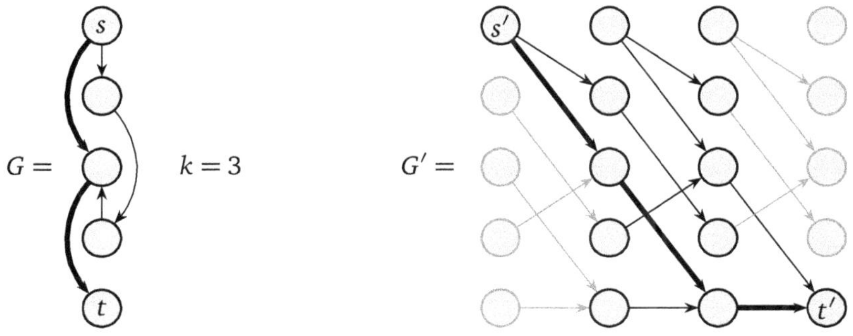

Figure 1.17: Layered version of a graph

Theorem 1.22. DIRECTED REACHABILITY SEARCH $\leq_\ell^o$ DIRECTED REACHABILITY.

Proof. DIRECTED REACHABILITY SEARCH is less stringent than DIRECTED SHORTEST PATH, and:

DIRECTED SHORTEST PATH	$\leq_\ell^o$	DIRECTED SHORTEST PATH DECISION	(Lemma 1.20)
	$\leq_\ell^m$	DIRECTED REACHABILITY	(Lemma 1.21)

■

It's unknown whether DIRECTED REACHABILITY has a log-space program. But if it does, then so does DIRECTED REACHABILITY SEARCH (Theorem 1.22 and Lemma 1.18).

Exercises

1.1 Implement an algorithm in our official model for finding the minimum and maximum of a list of numbers with $O(N)$ time efficiency and $O(\log N)$ space efficiency.

MIN AND MAX	(1.25)
Input: Nonnegative integers $x_1, x_2, \ldots, x_N$ such that $x_i \leq N$ for each i	
Output: $\min(x_1, x_2, \ldots, x_N)$ and $\max(x_1, x_2, \ldots, x_N)$	

1.2 Show CONTAINMENT IN SORTED LIST $\in$ TISP[$\log N$, $\log N$] by implementing the binary search algorithm in our official model.

CONTAINMENT IN SORTED LIST	(1.26)
Input: Nonnegative integers $x_1 \leq x_2 \leq \cdots \leq x_n$ and y such that $x_n \leq n$ and $y \leq n$	
Output: Does there exist an i such that $x_i = y$?	

The input size is $N = n + 1$, the problem's word size is $\lceil \log N \rceil$, the input encoding is $x_1, x_2, \ldots, x_n, y$ with one value per word, and it's promised that $x_1 \leq x_2 \leq \cdots \leq x_n \leq n$ and $y \leq n$.

1.3 Implement an algorithm in our official model showing GREATER THAN $\in$ TISP$[N, \log N]$, where the input encoding is the same as for MULTIPLICATION in §1.3.3.

GREATER THAN	(1.27)
Input:	Nonnegative integers x and y represented in binary
Output:	Is $x > y$?

1.4 Show ELEMENT DISTINCTNESS $\in$ TIME$[N]\cap$SPACE$[\log N]$ and implement both algorithms in our official model.

ELEMENT DISTINCTNESS	(1.28)
Input:	Nonnegative integers $x_1, x_2, \ldots, x_N$ such that $x_i \le N^2$ for each i
Output:	Are $x_1, x_2, \ldots, x_N$ all distinct (that is, no two are equal)?

1.5 Implement the extended BFS algorithm for DIRECTED REACHABILITY SEARCH (and DIRECTED SHORTEST PATH) in our official model. For convenience, assume the output encoding is the labels of nodes on a path backward from t to s (so output segment address 0 gets t). In particular, the output size may depend on the input, not just on the input size. Your program should reject if there's no path from s to t, and use the halt instruction otherwise.

1.6 This is about dags and topological orders (§A.2.3). Implement an algorithm solving the following search problem with time efficiency $O(N)$ and word size $O(\log N)$ in our official model. Assume the same input encoding as DIRECTED REACHABILITY except there's no s or t.

TOPOLOGICAL ORDER	(1.29)
Input:	Directed graph G
Output:	A topological order of G, or report that none exists

For $u \in \{1, 2, \ldots, n\}$, let Mem$[u]$ be node u's indegree. Use Mem$[n+1], \ldots,$ Mem$[2n]$ for a queue of nodes that have indegree 0. When a node u is dequeued and processed, the algorithm puts u next in the topological order and effectively deletes u by decrementing the indegree of each node v to which u has an edge, and enqueueing v if its indegree became 0. Your program should reject if G is not a dag, and use the halt instruction otherwise. It's OK if your program executes some write instructions before rejecting.

1.7 Show TRIANGLE DETECTION $\in$ TISP$[N^{1.5}, \log N]$. Write pseudocode (not actual code in our model) and analyze the time and space efficiencies. Assume the graph has no multi-edges or self-loops.

TRIANGLE DETECTION	(1.30)
Input:	Undirected graph G encoded as an adjacency matrix
Output:	Does G have a cycle of length 3?

1.8 **(a)** Show MOST SIGNIFICANT BIT OF MEDIAN $\in \mathsf{TISP}[\sqrt{N}, \log N]$ using pseudocode.

MOST SIGNIFICANT BIT OF MEDIAN	(1.31)
Input:	Nonnegative integers $x_1, \ldots, x_n$ where each x_i is represented in binary with n bits (so $x_i < 2^n$) and n is odd
Output:	The most significant bit (position $n-1$) of the median of $x_1, \ldots, x_n$

(b) Show LEAST SIGNIFICANT BIT OF MEDIAN $\in \mathsf{TIME}[N] \cap \mathsf{SPACE}[\log N]$ using pseudocode.

1.9 Design an algorithm (using pseudocode) for GENERAL ITERATED ADDITION with $O(N)$ time efficiency and $O(\log N)$ word size.

GENERAL ITERATED ADDITION	(1.32)
Input:	Nonnegative integers $x_1, x_2, \ldots, x_n$ represented in binary
Output:	$x_1 + x_2 + \cdots + x_n$ in binary

The input numbers may have different bit-lengths from each other (unlike in ITERATED ADDITION), so the input size N is essentially the sum of the bit-lengths. The specific input encoding isn't important, but assume it's n, then pointers to the beginnings of the individual x_i numbers, then the numbers themselves with one word per bit (reminiscent of our DIRECTED REACHABILITY encoding), so $N = 1 + n + \sum_{i=1}^{n}(\text{bit-length of } x_i)$.

1.10 A *forest* is an undirected graph with no cycles—that is, each connected component is a tree. Show FOREST REACHABILITY $\in \mathsf{L}$ using pseudocode. (It's considerably harder to prove the more general result that UNDIRECTED REACHABILITY $\in \mathsf{L}$.)

FOREST REACHABILITY	(1.33)
Input:	Forest G, nodes s and t
Output:	Is t reachable from s in G?

Hint: You can escape a maze by keeping your left hand on the wall, without making a map.

1.11 Show that each of the following instructions can be added to the model of computation without increasing its power. Specifically, show that every program using the instruction can be converted to a program that's equivalent (as in Theorem 1.2) but doesn't use the instruction. Do not rely on auxiliary registers for this exercise—develop substitutions that only employ the registers the original program was already using. Handle all possible combinations of register indices being equal and constants standing in for any registers.

(a) Bitwise-iff: "let $\text{Reg}[i] \leftarrow \text{Reg}[j] \Leftrightarrow \text{Reg}[k]$"

(b) Bitwise-implication: "let $\text{Reg}[i] \leftarrow \text{Reg}[j] \Rightarrow \text{Reg}[k]$"

1.12 In Java, >> denotes *signed shift right*, meaning the leftmost bits get filled in with copies of the leftmost bit of the number being shifted, while >>> denotes unsigned shift right (which always fills in with 0s). Since our model uses $\gg$ for unsigned shift right, let's do the opposite of Java by using $\ggg$ for signed shift right. Show that every program using

$\ggg$ can be converted to a program that's equivalent (as in Theorem 1.2) but doesn't use $\ggg$. You may employ an auxiliary register.

1.13 For each of the following instructions, show that it can be removed from the model of computation without decreasing the model's power. (This is not asking you to remove all three simultaneously.) Specifically, show that every program using the instruction can be converted to an equivalent tight program (as in Theorem 1.2) that doesn't use the instruction. This involves adjusting the proof of Theorem 1.2 to avoid reintroducing the instruction.

(a) Bitwise-and

(b) Bitwise-or

(c) Bitwise-not

1.14 Prove that for every log-space program that uses "write Out[Reg[j]] $\leftarrow$ Reg[i]" instructions (and doesn't use our official "write" instruction), there exists a log-space program that always produces the same output as the original program, has the same word size, and uses only our official "write" instruction.

1.15 Prove that $\mathsf{P} = \mathsf{L}$ (where the classes contain promise problems) iff $\mathsf{P} = \mathsf{L}$ with the classes redefined to contain total problems only.

1.16 For a directed graph in which each edge is labeled with a nonnegative "height" value, define a path's height as the height of a highest edge on the path. Design an algorithm (using pseudocode) for the following function problem with $O(N \log N)$ time efficiency and $O(\log N)$ word size, by giving an oracle reduction to DIRECTED REACHABILITY.

DIRECTED MIN PATH HEIGHT	(1.34)
Input:	Directed graph G in which each edge has a height label in $\{1,\ldots,m\}$ where m is the number of edges, nodes s and t
Output:	Minimum height of any path from s to t in G, or report that no such path exists

1.17 Implement the mapping reduction from MULTIPLICATION to ITERATED ADDITION from §1.8.2 in our official model.

1.18 **(a)** Explain why for all decision problems A and B, if $A \leq_p^o B$ and $B \in \mathsf{EXP}$ then $A \in \mathsf{EXP}$.

(b) Let $\mathsf{QUASIP} = \mathsf{TIME}[2^{\text{polylog} N}]$, and let $A \leq_{qp}^o B$ mean there exists an oracle reduction from A to B with $2^{\text{polylog} N}$ time efficiency and polylog-bounded word size. Explain why for all decision problems A and B, if $A \leq_{qp}^o B$ and $B \in \mathsf{QUASIP}$ then $A \in \mathsf{QUASIP}$.

1.19 **(a)** Prove that UNDIRECTED CONNECTIVITY $\leq_\ell^o$ UNDIRECTED REACHABILITY using only $n-1$ oracle queries, where n is the number of nodes in the input graph.

UNDIRECTED CONNECTIVITY	(1.35)
Input: Undirected graph G	
Output: Is G connected?	

(b) Prove that UNDIRECTED CONNECTIVITY $\leq_\ell^m$ UNDIRECTED REACHABILITY.

1.20 This exercise justifies why it's generally safe to assume a problem has well-defined time and space complexities: If different programs are more efficient on different inputs, we can combine them to get "the best of both worlds." Let Π_1 and Π_2 be programs that solve the same decision problem and have the same word size. Prove that there exist programs Π_3 and Π_4 that also solve that problem and have word sizes larger by only an additive constant, and such that the following hold for every valid input x. (Feel free to use Lemma 1.5.)

(a) The running time of $\Pi_3(x)$ is at most a constant factor higher than the minimum of the running time of $\Pi_1(x)$ and the running time of $\Pi_2(x)$. Hint: This is like how an operating system creates the illusion of parallelism (on a single-core processor) by switching back and forth between different processes.

(b) The memory space of $\Pi_4(x)$ is at most a constant factor higher than the minimum of the memory space of $\Pi_1(x)$ and the memory space of $\Pi_2(x)$.

(c) Update your programs Π_3 and Π_4 to handle function and search problems.

Notes

Now that we're "off to the races," here are references for further reading on traditional complexity theory: Texts surveying much of the field (like this book does) include [407, 149, 557, 319, 196, 28, 376, 559]. Texts developing complexity theory in the historical context of automata and computability include [252, 334, 497, 249, 117].

An input to a computational problem is also called an "instance." A decision problem is also called a "language" because it can be viewed as a set of strings—the encodings of all 1-inputs. A search problem is also called a "relation."

An algorithm's efficiency is also sometimes called the algorithm's "complexity." We prefer to reserve the word "complexity" for assessing computational problems (best efficiency of any correct algorithm), to draw a clear line between these two concepts.

Like MULTIPLICATION, the DIVISION problem can be solved in $O(\log N)$ space [124], but that's much more difficult to prove. Some sophisticated MULTIPLICATION and DIVISION algorithms have time efficiencies pretty close to $O(N)$ [472, 178, 235].

In the computational complexity literature, algorithms (or programs) are often called "machines" since the original general-purpose model of computation is called "Turing machines" [525]. Our model from §1.4 is called "Word RAM" (standing for Random-Access Machine, not Random-Access Memory). This way of expressing computations dates back to the genesis of digital computers, but credit for introducing the Word RAM model in the theory literature usually goes to [173]. This was predated by other RAM models where words can store arbitrarily large values [140].

Computability theory is about which computational problems can be solved by algorithms at all, regardless of efficiency. Our model is unsuitable for studying computability, because the word size automatically limits the space (since an address must fit in a word), which in turn limits the time (Theorem 1.8). For computability theory (with no bounds on a computation's resources) we need a model with a mechanism for accessing arbitrarily large memory addresses, such as sequential access, or pointers spanning multiple words, or letting the word size grow during the computation. Our model is suitable for complexity theory since we can select the word size large enough to accommodate whatever resource bounds we have in mind.

Sometimes "easy" and "hard" are used as synonyms for tractable and intractable, respectively. The idea that "polynomial time" corresponds to "tractable" is typically attributed to [131, 153, 421, 154]. The TIME and SPACE complexity classes are sometimes called "DTIME" and "DSPACE" where D stands for "deterministic." TISP[poly N, polylog N] is also called SC, which stands for "Steve's class" in honor of Stephen Cook.

We defined complexity classes such as P to contain promise problems, but lots of the literature uses names like prP ("promise P") for this and reserves names such as P for classes of total problems.

Oracle reductions are also called "Turing reductions" (after [526]) and "Cook reductions" (after [136]). Mapping reductions are also called "many-one reductions" and "Karp reductions" (after [292]).

Least Significant Bit of Median $\in$ L (Exercise 1.8.b) appears in [404].

Chapter 2

Time Complexity

2.1 Tractable and Seemingly Intractable Problems

This section introduces some problems that are in EXP but not known to be in P. Many people conjecture these problems aren't in P, because intensive research has not turned up any algorithms substantially faster than brute force. But researchers are thoroughly stumped about how to prove that these problems don't have polynomial-time algorithms. In this chapter, we'll see it's no coincidence that these problems have the same status: Despite their lack of resemblance, they are effectively the same problem in disguise!

2.1.1 Independent Sets

An *independent set* in an undirected graph is a subset of nodes S such that no edge has both endpoints in S.

INDEPENDENT SET	(2.1)
Input: Undirected graph G, nonnegative integer k	
Output: Does there exist an independent set of size $\geq k$ in G?	

Example. How big of an independent set can we find in the graph G in Figure 2.1? If we pick the center node, it would preclude all other nodes (since it's adjacent to all other nodes), so the size would be only 1. Does this G have an independent set of size 2? Yes—we can pick any nonadjacent pair of nodes, such as the top node and either one of the two bottom nodes. Is there an independent set of size 3? No—any set of 3 nodes on the outer cycle would contain 2 adjacent nodes. In summary, $(G,2)$ is a yes-input of INDEPENDENT SET, and $(G,3)$ is a no-input. ♦

This problem represents situations where we want to pick many things but are constrained by pairwise conflicts: For each edge, we can pick at most one endpoint. These examples hint at the practical relevance of INDEPENDENT SET:

- Nodes are projects a company could take on, and an edge means two projects can't both be taken on—perhaps they both require some personnel or resource that can't be shared between projects. Can the company pursue a large set of projects?
- Nodes are locations on a map, and an edge means two locations' labels would overlap. Can we display lots of labels without any overlap?
- Nodes are people, and an edge means two people can't serve together on a committee due to incompatible personalities. Can we select a large committee?

INDEPENDENT SET $\in$ PSPACE by brute force: Try all sets of size k, and see if any is independent. (Every subset of an independent set is also independent, so we may assume the problem

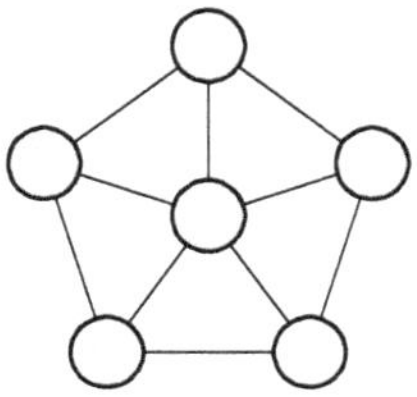

Figure 2.1: Example for INDEPENDENT SET

definition says "$= k$" rather than "$\geq k$".) We only need polynomial space to remember the current set and check whether it's independent, and we reuse the space from one set to the next.

> Brute force algorithm for INDEPENDENT SET (2.2)
>
> for every subset S consisting of k of G's nodes:
>   for each edge $\{u, v\}$ in G:
>   if $u \in S$ and $v \in S$: continue to the next subset
>   accept
> reject

In the worst case, this takes exponential time: If G has n nodes, then the number of outer iterations is $\binom{n}{k}$, which is $\geq 2^n/(n+1)$ for some k since $\sum_{k=0}^{n} \binom{n}{k} = 2^n$. Brute force can be sped up somewhat, but all known algorithms for INDEPENDENT SET still take exponential time. Nobody has discovered an insight that bypasses exhaustive search altogether. The ad hoc reasoning we applied to our earlier example graph doesn't generalize to arbitrary graphs.

Brute force runs in polynomial time on inputs where k is a constant, since $\binom{n}{k} \leq n^k$. Thus for each constant k, the following problem is in P:

k-INDEPENDENT SET	(2.3)
Input: Undirected graph G	
Output: Does there exist an independent set of size $\geq k$ in G?	

We're talking about an infinite list of decision problems: one problem for each choice of k. Rather than being an input parameter, k is now fixed by the problem definition. For example, 7-INDEPENDENT SET $\in$ P by trying all $\binom{n}{7} \leq n^7$ sets of 7 nodes of G (with $k = 7$ hardcoded in the algorithm). In fact, k-INDEPENDENT SET $\in$ L since it only takes log space to remember the current set S and iterate through all edges to check if S is independent.

2.1.2 Long Paths

Recall DIRECTED SHORTEST PATH DECISION $\in$ P (§1.8.3). Changing the desired path length from "$\leq k$" to "$\geq k$" makes a world of difference. No poly-time algorithm is known for this problem:

DIRECTED LONGEST PATH DECISION	(2.4)
Input: Directed graph G, distinct nodes s and t, nonnegative integer k	
Output: Does there exist a path of length $\geq k$ from s to t in G?	

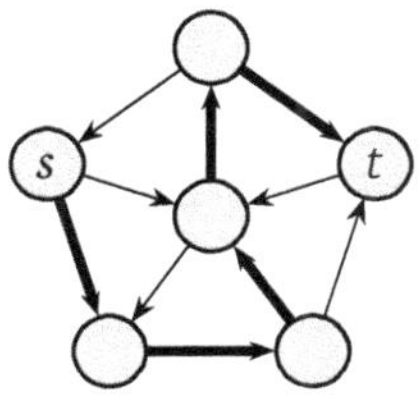

Figure 2.2: Example for DIRECTED FULL PATH

By definition, a path doesn't revisit nodes. For short paths, revisiting nodes would just create cycles that could be chopped off (Lemma A.5). For long paths, visiting certain nodes early may create blockades that frustrate an algorithm's attempts to visit more nodes later. The need for global coordination across the whole path stymies efforts to design a poly-time algorithm.

The special case $k = n-1$ (where n is the number of nodes) already exhibits the apparent intractability of DIRECTED LONGEST PATH DECISION. A *full path* has $n-1$ edges (it visits every node exactly once). We distinguish this case as a named problem, and for brevity we omit "DECISION" from the name.

DIRECTED FULL PATH	(2.5)
Input: Directed graph G, distinct nodes s and t	
Output: Does there exist a path from s to t that visits every node in G?	

DIRECTED FULL PATH SEARCH is the problem of finding such a path if one exists.

Example. In the graph G in Figure 2.2, the bold edges form a full path from s to t, so (G, s, t) is a yes-input of DIRECTED FULL PATH. There's no full path from t to s, so (G, t, s) is a no-input. ♦

Another perspective: A walk from s to t may repeat nodes and edges. Instead of taking as many steps as possible while visiting each node at most once (a path), we can take as few steps as possible while visiting each node at least once. To walk from s to t and visit all nodes along the way, at least $n-1$ steps are necessary, but do $n-1$ steps suffice? This is DIRECTED FULL PATH. Variants known as TRAVELING SALESPERSON problems are inspired by a hypothetical character who wants to peddle wares at every location and minimize the total amount of travel. These problems show up in industrial applications such as vehicle routing, robot motion planning, scheduling tasks on computers, and computational biology.

DIRECTED FULL PATH $\in$ PSPACE by brute force: Try all permutations of all nodes starting with s and ending with t, and see if any forms a path. We only need polynomial space to remember the current permutation and check whether it's a path, and we reuse the space from one permutation to the next.

Brute force algorithm for DIRECTED FULL PATH (2.6)

```
for every permutation (v_1, v_2, ..., v_n) of G's nodes with v_1 = s and v_n = t:
    for i ← 1, 2, ..., n−1:
        if G doesn't have an edge from v_i to v_{i+1}: continue to the next permutation
    accept
reject
```

This takes exponential time: The number of outer iterations (permutations of the $n-2$ nodes besides s and t) is $(n-2)! = 2^{\Theta(n \log n)}$, since $n! \leq n^n$ (round each factor up to n) and $n! \geq (n/2)^{n/2}$ (round half the factors down to $n/2$, and the other half down to 1). This can be sped up to $2^n \cdot \operatorname{poly} n$, but every known algorithm for DIRECTED FULL PATH takes exponential time. It seems exhaustive search can be tempered but not eliminated for this problem.

Here's a problem that looks similar but is tractable. A trail from s to t may repeat nodes but doesn't repeat edges. A *full trail* traverses every edge (exactly once).

DIRECTED FULL TRAIL	(2.7)
Input:	Directed graph G, distinct nodes s and t
Output:	Does there exist a trail from s to t that traverses every edge in G?

Despite their resemblance, DIRECTED FULL PATH and DIRECTED FULL TRAIL are very different. The latter is in P (indeed, in L): When a trail passes through a node, this can't block future transits if the node's indegree equals its outdegree—we can't get stuck at a node if we can pair up the incoming and outgoing edges. Formalizing this insight shows that G has a full trail from s to t iff $\operatorname{indeg}(v) = \operatorname{outdeg}(v)$ for all $v \notin \{s, t\}$ and $\operatorname{outdeg}(s) = \operatorname{indeg}(s)+1$ and $\operatorname{indeg}(t) = \operatorname{outdeg}(t)+1$ and the undirected version of G is connected except for isolated nodes. These properties are simple to check in linear time. No analogous characterization is known for full paths. Seemingly innocuous changes to a problem's definition can have huge impacts on its complexity.

2.1.3 Graph Colorings

Consider an undirected graph $G = (V, E)$ and a positive integer k. A *k-color assignment* specifies a color for each node of G using a set of k allowed colors. Viewing colors as elements of $[k] = \{1, 2, \ldots, k\}$, a k-color assignment is a function $c \colon V \to [k]$ where $c(v)$ is node v's color. If G has n nodes, there are k^n different k-color assignments.

A *proper k-coloring* is a k-color assignment c such that every edge of G is *multicolored*, meaning its endpoints have different colors: $c(u) \neq c(v)$ for every $\{u, v\} \in E$. A proper k-coloring partitions the set of nodes V into at most k many independent sets: All nodes with a particular color form an independent set since no two of them are adjacent.

GRAPH k-COLORING	(2.8)
Input:	Undirected graph G
Output:	Does there exist a proper k-coloring of G?

Except in this problem's name, we avoid the bare word "coloring" because for some people it means color assignment, while for others it means proper coloring. Like k-INDEPENDENT SET, we have an infinite list of problems: GRAPH 1-COLORING, GRAPH 2-COLORING, and so on. Yes-inputs of GRAPH 1-COLORING are graphs with no edges.

Example. The graph in Figure 2.3 is a no-input of GRAPH 3-COLORING. Suppose the colors are red, green, and blue. Since colors are interchangeable, the middle node might as well be red, and the top node might as well be green. Clockwise around the outer cycle, the next node must be blue in a proper 3-coloring, since it's adjacent to red and green nodes. Similarly, the next two nodes must be green and blue respectively. No color is available for the remaining node, since it

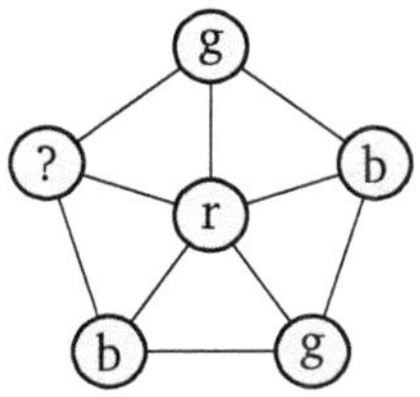

Figure 2.3: Example for GRAPH 3-COLORING

has neighbors of all three colors. This graph is a yes-input of GRAPH 4-COLORING, since we could assign the remaining node yellow to get a proper 4-coloring. ♦

A natural motivation comes from coloring a 2-dimensional map's regions so no two bordering regions share a color. This is equivalent to properly coloring the graph where nodes are regions, and two nodes are adjacent when the regions share a border. Assuming each region is contiguous and that touching at a corner doesn't count as "bordering," such a graph is *planar*, meaning it can be drawn on paper without any edges crossing each other. A deep theorem (whose only known proofs involve computer assistance) says every planar graph has a proper 4-coloring.

Register allocation in compilers is a classic application of graph coloring. Suppose we're compiling a high-level program that has more variables than there are registers available in the target architecture. In a simplified version, we'd like to assign each variable a register—to hold the value while the variable is being used—such that no register is assigned to two variables that might be used simultaneously. (If some variables are only needed at separate times, they can safely share a register.) Assuming there are only k registers—viewed as colors—this is equivalent to properly k-coloring the graph where nodes are variables, and two nodes are adjacent when the variables can't share a register.

Another application is bandwidth allocation. Radio stations and cell phone towers are assigned frequencies for broadcasting wireless signals. Transmitters that are too close to each other can't use the same frequency, since they would interfere. Assuming there are only k possible frequencies—viewed as colors—this is equivalent to properly k-coloring the graph where nodes are transmitters, and two nodes are adjacent when the transmitters are close enough to interfere.

GRAPH k-COLORING $\in$ PSPACE for every k by brute force: Try all k-color assignments, and see if any is proper. We only need polynomial space to remember the current assignment and check whether it's proper, and we reuse the space from one assignment to the next.

Brute force algorithm for GRAPH k-COLORING (2.9)

```
for every k-color assignment c to G's nodes:
    for each edge {u, v} in G:
        if c(u) = c(v): continue to the next assignment
    accept
reject
```

This takes exponential time since there are k^n outer iterations. More sophisticated algorithms achieve smaller bases in the exponential, but no subexponential-time algorithm is known even for GRAPH 3-COLORING.

Theorem 2.1. GRAPH 2-COLORING $\in$ P.

In fact, GRAPH 2-COLORING $\in$ L, but that's more difficult to prove (Exercise 3.11).

Proof idea. What's special about $k = 2$ colors is that each edge has two endpoints. After assigning node u a color, any neighbor v must get the opposite color. Looking for a proper 2-coloring, we're led around by the nose. This is a *greedy* approach—we commit to each node's color as we go, and never reconsider.

With $k = 3$ colors, after coloring u, there would be two options for coloring a neighbor v, and this choice could have "long-range repercussions" affecting the options for coloring distant parts of G. Looking for a proper 3-coloring, we'd be navigating a bewildering expanse of possibilities, seemingly requiring some form of exhaustive search. ■

Proof. We start with two observations:

- G has a proper 2-coloring iff each connected component has a proper 2-coloring, so we can color G by coloring its connected components independently of each other.
- Swapping the colors in a proper 2-coloring (for any connected component) yields another proper 2-coloring, so we can safely begin by picking any node and assigning it any color.

These are the only degrees of freedom. After assigning a color to one node, there's only one way to color the rest of its connected component (if a proper 2-coloring exists at all).

Greedy algorithm for GRAPH 2-COLORING (2.10)

```
for each connected component:
    pick an arbitrary node s in the component and assign it an arbitrary color
    run BFS starting from s, assigning colors to nodes as they're discovered:
        whenever a node u causes the discovery of a node v: give v the opposite color as u
if this 2-color assignment is proper: accept
else: reject
```

If the algorithm accepts, then G has a proper 2-coloring, since the algorithm found one. To conclude that the algorithm is correct, we show the converse: Suppose G has a proper 2-coloring. To see that the algorithm accepts, we claim it maintains the invariant that G has a proper 2-coloring that agrees with the algorithm's 2-color assignment to the nodes discovered so far. The invariant is maintained when we color the first node s in a connected component, due to the interchangeability of colors in that component. During BFS, if the invariant holds before we color v, then it continues to hold after we color v, because in every proper 2-coloring, the edge $\{u, v\}$ is multicolored. At termination, the invariant guarantees that the algorithm's final 2-color assignment is proper, so the algorithm accepts. ■

For each connected component, all nodes at even distance from s get the same color as s, and all nodes at odd distance get the other color. This helps us characterize graphs that are *bipartite* (properly 2-colorable), meaning the set of nodes can be partitioned into two parts such that every edge goes between the parts.

Theorem 2.2. *G is bipartite iff G has no odd-length cycle.*

Proof. $\Rightarrow$: Suppose for contradiction G has a proper 2-coloring and an odd-length cycle. Starting at any node on the cycle, the colors must strictly alternate around the cycle. But since the cycle has odd length, the last node (before revisiting the starting node) would have the same color as the starting node, which is a contradiction since these nodes are adjacent.

$\Leftarrow$: Suppose G is not bipartite. Since the 2-color assignment found by the algorithm from Theorem 2.1 is not proper, some edge $\{u, v\}$ is not multicolored. Thus the distances from s to u

and from s to v are either both even or both odd. These two distances must be equal because if they weren't, then one of them would be even and the other odd (since adjacent nodes must differ by at most 1 in their distances from s). Call this common distance d. As in extended BFS, consider the "predecessor paths" from u back to s and from v back to s. These two paths of length d join up at some node w and stay merged for the remaining d' edges on the way to s, where d' is the distance from s to w. Combining the path segment from u to w (length $d-d'$), the path segment from v to w (length $d-d'$), and the edge $\{u,v\}$ itself (length 1), we have a cycle of length $2(d-d')+1$, which is odd. ∎

2.1.4 Subset Sums

Our previous problems dealt with graphs, but now we'll see an apparently intractable problem with a numerical flavor. Given n numbers $x_1, x_2, \ldots, x_n$, is it possible to add up some of them to hit a target number t exactly? Like Multiplication and Iterated Addition (Chapter 1), we allow arbitrarily large binary numbers, and the input size N is essentially the total number of bits in $x_1, \ldots, x_n$ and t. (Here, x_i is an entire number, not an individual bit of a number.) "Adding up some of them" means picking a subset I of the indices $[n] = \{1, 2, \ldots, n\}$ and summing those x_i for which $i \in I$. Thus, in the summation, a value may appear as many times (and no more) as it occurs in the input list $x_1, \ldots, x_n$.

Subset Sum	(2.11)
Input:	Positive integers $x_1, x_2, \ldots, x_n$ and t, represented in binary with m bits each
Output:	Does there exist a set $I \subseteq [n]$ such that $\sum_{i \in I} x_i = t$?

Example. Using base ten for convenience, let $n = 5$ and $(x_1, \ldots, x_5) = (4, 3, 9, 4, 12)$ and $t = 17$. This is a yes-input of Subset Sum since with $I = \{1, 3, 4\}$ we have $x_1 + x_3 + x_4 = 4 + 9 + 4 = 17$. It would be a no-input if $t = 18$; we can check this by trying every $I \subseteq [5]$ and seeing that $\sum_{i \in I} x_i$ is never 18. ♦

For practical motivation, perhaps our freight vehicle has a weight limit of t, and clients want us to transport items that have weights $x_1, \ldots, x_n$. If we charge by weight, then to maximize revenue, we should choose a set of items so the shipment's weight is exactly the limit, if possible.

Subset Sum ∈ PSPACE by brute force: Try all sets I, and see if any has $\sum_{i \in I} x_i = t$. We only need polynomial space to remember the current set and compute the sum and compare it to the target, and we reuse the space from one set to the next.

Brute force algorithm for Subset Sum (2.12)

```
for every I ⊆ [n]:
    compute z ← Σ_{i∈I} x_i using a poly-time algorithm for ITERATED ADDITION
    if z = t: accept
reject
```

This takes exponential time since there are 2^n iterations. Faster algorithms are known, but they still take exponential time.

Let m be the bit-length of each input number. The case $n = O(\log m)$ (large numbers but few of them) is tractable because brute force has $2^{O(\log m)} = \operatorname{poly} m$ iterations. The case $m = O(\log n)$ (small numbers but many of them) is also tractable, but this is less straightforward: Each input number has value $\leq 2^m = 2^{O(\log n)} = \text{poly}\, n$. For concreteness, say $x_i \leq n^2$ for all i. The biggest possible sum is $\sum_{i\in[n]} x_i \leq n \cdot n^2$, so we might as well have $t \leq n^3$. For this version (which we name analogously to SMALL ITERATED ADDITION), we encode the input with one word per number, so the input size is $N = n + 1$.

SMALL SUBSET SUM	(2.13)
Input: Positive integers $x_1, x_2, \ldots, x_n$ and t, such that $x_i \leq n^2$ for all i, and $t \leq n^3$	
Output: Does there exist a set $I \subseteq [n]$ such that $\sum_{i\in I} x_i = t$?	

Brute force still takes exponential time for this problem. To design a poly-time algorithm, we use the *dynamic programming* technique.

Theorem 2.3. SMALL SUBSET SUM $\in$ P.

Proof. There are 2^n ways to do the summation, but the sums are confined to $\{0, 1, \ldots, n^3\}$, so we can afford the time to examine each possible value of the sum. Say a value s is *achievable* iff there exists $I \subseteq [n]$ such that $\sum_{i\in I} x_i = s$. We compute the set S of all achievable values, and check whether t is among them. We build up S gradually, by constructing the sequence of sets $S_0, S_1, S_2, \ldots, S_n$ where S_j is defined like S but only using the first j numbers $x_1, \ldots, x_j$. That is, $S_j = \{\sum_{i\in I} x_i : I \subseteq [j]\} \subseteq \{0, 1, \ldots, n^3\}$. Then $S_n = S$.

For the base case, $S_0 = \{0\}$ because summing nothing yields 0. (Formally, the only $I \subseteq [0] = \emptyset$ is $I = \emptyset$, and the empty sum $\sum_{i\in\emptyset} x_i$ is defined as 0.) How do we go from S_{j-1} to S_j? For starters, $S_{j-1} \subseteq S_j$ since it's not mandatory to include x_j in a summation. (Every value achievable from $x_1, \ldots, x_{j-1}$ is also achievable from $x_1, \ldots, x_j$.) To account for summations that include x_j, we take the values achievable from $x_1, \ldots, x_{j-1}$ and add x_j to them. Defining a shorthand notation $S_{j-1} + x_j = \{s + x_j : s \in S_{j-1}\}$, we have $S_j = S_{j-1} \cup (S_{j-1} + x_j)$. (The intuition for beating brute force is that for each $s \in S_{j-1}$, there might be many ways to achieve s from $x_1, \ldots, x_{j-1}$, but we need not waste time adding x_j onto all those different ways, since they would all yield $s + x_j$.)

We can represent S_j with a bit string of length $n^3 + 1$, where each bit indicates whether a particular value is achievable from $x_1, \ldots, x_j$. We compute S_j by bitwise-or-ing S_{j-1} with "S_{j-1} shifted by x_j." Let's not worry about such details in the pseudocode:

Dynamic programming algorithm for SMALL SUBSET SUM (2.14)

```
let S_0 ← {0}
for j ← 1,2,...,n:
    for each s ∈ S_{j-1}:
        insert s and s + x_j into S_j (if not already there)
if t ∈ S_n: accept
else: reject
```

With n outer iterations and at most n^3 inner iterations, the time efficiency is $O(n^4) = O(N^4)$. ■

Since SMALL SUBSET SUM $\in$ P, the apparent intractability of SUBSET SUM hinges on very large input numbers (or fractional numbers with very high precision). Admittedly, many real-world applications don't feature such extreme numbers.

2.2 P Versus NP

2.2.1 Verifying Witnesses

Independent Set, Directed Full Path, Graph 3-Coloring, and Subset Sum have something in common: Trying all possibilities to find what we seek takes exponential time, but if someone shows us what we seek, we could verify in polynomial time that it's indeed what we seek. This is like detecting a needle in a haystack: Sifting through all the hay is slow, but if a mysterious stranger plunges his hand into the haystack and withdraws a needle, we could quickly verify that it's indeed a needle. Yes-inputs are haystacks with at least one needle. No-inputs are haystacks with no needle. The stranger could convince us a needle exists by showing us one.

A *verifier* algorithm determines whether something from a haystack is a needle. A verifier V takes an input x and an auxiliary input w (separated by a semicolon in the notation) and accepts or rejects, indicating whether or not w is a needle from x's haystack. For a decision problem A:

$$\text{Solver } \Pi: \quad A(x) = 1 \iff \big(\Pi(x) \text{ accepts}\big)$$

$$\text{Verifier } V: \quad A(x) = 1 \iff \big(\exists w: \; V(x;w) \text{ accepts}\big)$$

Instead of determining whether x is a yes-input from scratch, a verifier is open to being convinced that x is a yes-input. If $V(x;w)$ accepts, then w convinced V that x is a yes-input, and we say w is a *witness* (needle). If $V(x;w)$ rejects, then w didn't convince V that x is a yes-input (but a different w might). An input is a yes-input iff it's possible to convince a verifier of this. There's no requirement to convince a verifier that an input is a no-input. (How could someone convince us a haystack is needleless?) Unlike solvers, verifiers have asymmetry between "yes" and "no."

Let's step into the verifier's shoes for our running example problems.

Independent Set: A big graph G is on a whiteboard. The mysterious stranger says G has an independent set of size k. "Oh yeah? Prove it! Which nodes?" The stranger makes some marks on the board. If he doesn't mark k nodes, or if he marks both endpoints of some edge, we say, "Nice try. We're not falling for that." Otherwise, we say, "I'll be darned. You're right!" A witness is an independent set of size k.

Verifier for Independent Set (2.15)

```
given input (G, k) and purported witness S:
    if S isn't a subset consisting of k of G's nodes: reject
    for each edge {u, v} in G:
        if u ∈ S and v ∈ S: reject
    accept
```

Directed Full Path: The stranger says G has a full path from s to t. We ask him to trace such a path with a marker. We pay close attention, so we won't be duped if he doesn't start at s, doesn't end at t, misses a node, repeats a node, or jumps between nodes without following an edge. If everything checks out, we thank him for the help and part ways convinced that we have a yes-input. A witness is a full path from s to t.

Verifier for DIRECTED FULL PATH (2.16)

given input (G, s, t) and purported witness w:
  if w isn't a permutation $(v_1, v_2, \ldots, v_n)$ of G's nodes with $v_1 = s$ and $v_n = t$: reject
  for $i \leftarrow 1, 2, \ldots, n-1$:
    if G doesn't have an edge from v_i to v_{i+1}: reject
  accept

GRAPH 3-COLORING: The stranger says G has a proper 3-coloring. We challenge him to substantiate his claim, and he accedes by taking three colors of markers to the board. If he doesn't illustrate a proper 3-coloring, then we won't be fooled, because we can quickly check whether only three colors are used and every edge is multicolored. But if he does, then we can't deny that the graph is a yes-input. A witness is a proper 3-coloring.

Verifier for GRAPH 3-COLORING (2.17)

given input G and purported witness c:
  if c isn't a 3-color assignment to G's nodes: reject
  for each edge $\{u, v\}$ in G:
    if $c(u) = c(v)$: reject
  accept

SUBSET SUM: The stranger says some of the numbers $x_1, \ldots, x_n$ can be added to achieve t. To persuade us, he says which numbers to sum. We efficiently compute the sum on our own. If this doesn't yield t, we express our disapproval of his shenanigans by rejecting. A witness is a set of indices that yields the target sum.

Verifier for SUBSET SUM (2.18)

given input $(x_1, \ldots, x_n, t)$ and purported witness I:
  if I isn't a subset of $[n]$: reject
  compute $z \leftarrow \sum_{i \in I} x_i$ using a poly-time algorithm for ITERATED ADDITION
  if $z \neq t$: reject
  accept

For each of these problems, the brute force algorithm from § 2.1 repeatedly runs a verifier V for each possible w, accepts if V accepts for at least one w, and rejects if V rejects for all w. We inspect each thing in the haystack, accept if we find a needle, and reject if we exhaust the haystack without finding a needle. (The tractable variants of these problems have "magnetic needles" we can find without sifting through all the hay.) To obtain a verifier from such a brute force algorithm, we can extract the loop body and replace "continue to the next possibility" by "reject." Actually, a verifier must be so skeptical, it can't trust that w corresponds to one of the possibilities that the brute force algorithm iterates over. The verifier should first check whether w is a legitimate possibility and reject if not.

2.2.2 The Complexity Class NP

P is the class of all decision problems with poly-time solvers. NP is the class of all decision problems with poly-time verifiers. The archaic moniker "NP" stands for "Nondeterministic Polynomial time" because the witness is "not determined"—it's a missing piece of information needed to run a

Verifier program for GRAPH 3-COLORING (2.19)

```
 0. read n ← In[0]
 1. if u = n then goto line 6
 2.     let u ← u + 1
 3.     read-witness ucol ← Wit[u]
 4.     if ucol ≤ 2 then goto line 1
 5.     reject
 6. let u ← 0
 7. if u = n then goto line 19
 8.     let u ← u + 1
 9.     read-witness ucol ← Wit[u]
10.     read ptr ← In[u]
11.     read deg ← In[ptr]
12.     let end ← ptr + deg
13.     if ptr = end then goto line 7
14.         let ptr ← ptr + 1
15.         read v ← In[ptr]
16.         read-witness vcol ← Wit[v]
17.         if ucol ≠ vcol then goto line 13
18.         reject
19. accept
```

Figure 2.4: Implementation of the verifier for GRAPH 3-COLORING

verifier. INDEPENDENT SET, DIRECTED FULL PATH, GRAPH 3-COLORING, and SUBSET SUM are in NP but not known to be in P. Unlike P, NP doesn't represent realistic computation—alas, no mysterious strangers supply us with witnesses in the real world. NP's raison d'être is to gather important problems that share a distinctive trait. Presumably not all problems in PSPACE have this trait, since poly-space algorithms can do more than search for a needle in a haystack.

We use pseudocode for high-level "verifier algorithms" and implement them as low-level "verifier programs" in an augmented version of our official model of computation. The read-only *witness segment* holds the purported witness w. The instruction "read-witness Reg[i] ← Wit[Reg[j]]" puts the word from witness segment address Reg[j] (or a hardcoded constant address) into Reg[i].

Example. In Figure 2.4, we implement our verifier for GRAPH 3-COLORING. We encode the input like DIRECTED REACHABILITY (§ 1.3.3) but with no distinguished s and t, and with u and v in each other's list of neighbors if $\{u, v\}$ is an undirected edge. For a witness, Wit[u] $\in \{0, 1, 2\}$ is the color of node $u \in [n]$ (ignoring Wit[0]). The verifier uses word size $O(\log N)$ and registers nicknamed *n, u, v, ucol, vcol, ptr, deg, end*. The left column checks that each node is assigned a color from $\{0, 1, 2\}$. (We can't assume the witness segment encodes a 3-color assignment.) The right column checks that each edge $\{u, v\}$ is multicolored. For simplicity, the implementation redundantly checks each edge twice (once from the perspective of u having neighbor v, and again with the roles of the endpoints swapped). ♦

Definition. A *verifier* for a decision problem A is a program V such that for every valid input x,

$$A(x) = 1 \iff \big(\exists w : \; V(x; w) \text{ accepts}\big)$$

and $V(x; w)$ terminates for all w. A verifier skeptically entertains the claim that "x is a yes-input":

- *Completeness* (true claims can be proven):
  For every yes-input x, some w (a *witness*) makes V accept.
- *Soundness* (false claims can't be proven):
  For every no-input x, no w makes V accept.

The running time of $V(x;w)$ is the maximum of the number of execution steps and $1+$the highest witness segment address accessed. The time efficiency $T(N)$ of V is the maximum running time of $V(x;w)$ over all valid x of size N and all w. ◄

A may be a promise problem, so x is promised to be a valid input. But there's never a promise on w. A verifier must scrutinize w with utmost distrust. If V has word size W (depending on x's size N), then each word of w can be any element of $\{0,1\}^W$. In principle, w could be an infinite sequence of words, but we may assume w is finite since a verifier can only read finitely many words.

The definition of running time also "charges" for the time the stranger takes to write down all words of w up to the highest one V looks at. If we only charged for execution steps (like for a solver), then V might judge a purported witness of size N^2 in only $O(N)$ time by picking and choosing which words to read. (This wouldn't make much difference, though—see Exercise 2.6.) If V has time efficiency $\leq T$ and word size W, we may assume $w \in (\{0,1\}^W)^T$ since V never reads beyond w's first T words.

Definition.

- NTIME$[T]$ is the set of all decision problems for which there exists a correct verifier with $O(T)$ time efficiency and $O(\log \max(T,N))$-bounded word size.
- NP $=$ NTIME$[\text{poly}N]$ ◄

For NP, we may round the verifier's word size up to $c \log N$ for an integer c, like for P but with the extra step of zeroing out the new most significant bits of each word that's read from the witness segment (or just rejecting if those new bits aren't already 0s).

Observation 2.4. P $\subseteq$ NP. *More generally,* TIME$[T] \subseteq$ NTIME$[T]$.

"Proof". A solver is a verifier that ignores the purported witness. We need not listen to a stranger if we can convince ourselves. ■

Lemma 2.5. NP $\subseteq$ PSPACE. *More generally,* NTIME$[T] \subseteq$ SPACE$[T \log T]$ *for every* $T \geq N$.

Proof idea. We can plug a verifier into the brute force algorithm template: Run the verifier for every possible w, and accept iff at least one run accepts. We only need poly space to remember the current candidate w and recycle the verifier's space from one w to the next. ■

Proof. Suppose $A \in$ NTIME$[T]$ by a verifier V with $O(T)$ time efficiency and $O(\log T)$-bounded word size. By the definition of running time, V only accesses the first $O(T)$ words of its witness segment. We may also assume V only accesses the first $O(T)$ words of its work segment, because the proof of Theorem 1.9 doesn't interfere with V's witness segment.

To show $A \in$ SPACE$[T \log T]$, we design a program Π that solves A. We have Π use V's registers and a few extra registers. It's fine for Π to have two work segments (Lemma 1.5): Mem_1 corresponds to V's witness segment, and Mem_2 corresponds to V's work segment. Π contains V's code, modified to use $\text{Mem}_2[\,]$ instead of $\text{Mem}[\,]$ in load/store instructions, and:

$$\text{read-witness Reg}[i] \leftarrow \text{Wit}[\text{Reg}[j]] \quad \rightsquigarrow \quad \text{load Reg}[i] \leftarrow \text{Mem}_1[\text{Reg}[j]]$$

Π encloses V's code in a loop and replaces each of V's reject instructions with a branch to a new section of code at the bottom of the loop body. This new section erases Mem_2, resets V's registers to their initial values, updates Mem_1 to the next possible w, and decides whether to reject or branch to the top of the loop for another iteration.

To get the next w: Π increments $\text{Mem}_1[0]$. If that rolled over to 0, then Π increments $\text{Mem}_1[1]$. If that also rolled over to 0, then Π increments $\text{Mem}_1[2]$, and so on until some word doesn't roll over.

To decide whether to reject: One of Π's extra registers keeps track of the highest Mem_1 address a that V has ever accessed, out of all the iterations so far. When updating w, if $\text{Mem}_1[0], \ldots, \text{Mem}_1[a]$ all roll over and $\text{Mem}_1[a+1]$ gets incremented from 0 to 1, then Π rejects. This is because if Π continued to iterate through all possibilities of $\text{Mem}_1[0], \ldots, \text{Mem}_1[a]$ again, V would reject them all again, never noticing that something changed at a higher Mem_1 address. Thus if Π rejects, then V rejects for all w, so $A(x) = 0$. Conversely, if Π accepts, then V accepts for some w, so $A(x) = 1$. Hence Π solves A.

Π only uses the first $O(T)$ words of Mem_1 and Mem_2. Since Π has the same $O(\log T)$ word size as V, it only uses $O(T \log T)$ bits of space. ■

The complexity class "backbone" is now:

$$\mathsf{L} \subseteq \mathsf{P} \subseteq \mathsf{NP} \subseteq \mathsf{PSPACE} \subseteq \mathsf{EXP}$$

It's widely conjectured that none of these classes are equal, though nobody even knows how to prove that $\mathsf{L} \neq \mathsf{NP}$, or that $\mathsf{P} \neq \mathsf{PSPACE}$, or that $\mathsf{NP} \neq \mathsf{EXP}$. But the lion's share of the publicity and notoriety goes to the question of whether $\mathsf{P} \neq \mathsf{NP}$.

2.2.3 The Big Question

"Does $\mathsf{P} = \mathsf{NP}$?" is among the most consequential and difficult open questions in computer science and math. Computational complexity theory is rife with similarly formidable questions, but P versus NP is the "poster child" that epitomizes these challenges. It's so significant that the Clay Mathematics Institute has offered a \$1,000,000 bounty on its resolution, as one of seven "Millennium Prize Problems." Why is P versus NP so consequential and so difficult to resolve?

Why is it consequential? $\mathsf{P} = \mathsf{NP}$ would mean every decision problem with a fast verifier also has a fast solver. If someone could convince us the correct output is "yes," we could convince ourselves almost as quickly. This seems too good to be true, so most researchers conjecture $\mathsf{P} \neq \mathsf{NP}$. The distinction between "deciding whether a solution exists" and "finding a solution if one exists" is insignificant, by search-to-decision reductions (§1.8.3 and §2.3.5). The essence of P versus NP is whether the ability to recognize what we're looking for entails the ability to find it. This is familiar to everyone: When racking our brains trying to solve a puzzle such as sudoku, if someone shows us a solution, we can check it with hardly any effort (either spoiler or salvation, depending on our level of frustration). The notion of "efficient computation" formalizes the terms "recognize" and "find."

Let's daydream about the ramifications of $\mathsf{P} = \mathsf{NP}$. Across natural sciences, social sciences, engineering, and business, many practical problems have a common trait: Checking a solution seems easier than finding a solution. Suppose the goal is to design a bridge, electronic circuit, airline schedule, or investment portfolio, obeying certain constraints. Verifying that a proposed design fulfills the requirements is often simple compared to devising the design. $\mathsf{P} = \mathsf{NP}$ would unleash a revolution in design automation: All these problems—for which a solution is easy to recognize—would suddenly be amenable to finding a solution quickly. (The financial consequences could make the million dollar prize seem measly.)

In computer science, $\mathsf{P} = \mathsf{NP}$ would enable dramatic improvements in machine learning (Chapter 13), optimization (Chapter 14), and software verification (Chapter 15). A downside is that cryptography (Chapter 12) would be severely crippled. Most nontrivial cryptography relies on the assumption that $\mathsf{P} \neq \mathsf{NP}$, because "breaching the security" can be cast as an NP problem that should be intractable for attackers. If $\mathsf{P} = \mathsf{NP}$, we'd have to adapt to diminished cybersecurity protections.

$\mathsf{P} = \mathsf{NP}$ would deeply influence automated theorem proving. The informally defined problem "Given as input a mathematical proposition, does it have a reasonably short proof?" is in NP. A proof is a witness that convinces us a theorem is true. Proofs should be elementary to verify by a human or a computer program such as a proof assistant. $\mathsf{P} = \mathsf{NP}$, together with a search-to-decision reduction, would yield the ultimate automated theorem prover: a fast algorithm to resolve any mathematical conjecture by constructing a proof of its truth or falsehood (assuming a not-too-long proof exists). So there's a good chance that by proving $\mathsf{P} = \mathsf{NP}$, we could claim not only this Millennium Prize but also all the other outstanding Millennium Prizes!

Following this reasoning to an amusingly self-referential extreme, we might expect that if $\mathsf{P} = \mathsf{NP}$, then a proof of $\mathsf{P} = \mathsf{NP}$ would be easy to find. So some people construe the apparent difficulty of proving $\mathsf{P} = \mathsf{NP}$ as (flimsy) evidence that $\mathsf{P} \neq \mathsf{NP}$. A catch is that although a proof of $\mathsf{P} = \mathsf{NP}$ would imply that poly-time algorithms exist for our favorite NP problems, the proof might be nonconstructive, giving no indication of what those algorithms are! Or, the algorithms might be woefully impractical, with $O(N^{100})$ time efficiency. So even if a proof of $\mathsf{P} = \mathsf{NP}$ is theoretically "self-revealing," we might remain blind to it. If we knew that a poly-time algorithm existed for INDEPENDENT SET (for example), we couldn't necessarily code up a practical program for INDEPENDENT SET. But we're fantasizing anyway, so let's not depress ourselves.

Wandering into philosophical territory, some people generalize the "design automation" interpretation of $\mathsf{P} = \mathsf{NP}$ to "creativity automation." Creating great works of art—say, music or literature—seems more difficult than recognizing their greatness. $\mathsf{P} = \mathsf{NP}$ is like saying that anyone who can appreciate an excellent song or novel could also be a stellar composer or author. Ingenuity could be replaced by flowcharts. It's a thought-provoking analogy, but the scope of $\mathsf{P} = \mathsf{NP}$ is limited to "appreciation" that's objective enough to be done by computers.

What would be the effect of proving $\mathsf{P} \neq \mathsf{NP}$? It would tell us there exists a decision problem with a fast verifier but no fast solver. Lots of problems in NP aren't known to be in P, so $\mathsf{P} \neq \mathsf{NP}$ is the default assumption consistent with our current understanding of computation. If we proved $\mathsf{P} \neq \mathsf{NP}$, nothing would change except we'd have the intellectual satisfaction of seeing our suspicion confirmed. But the proof would almost certainly require brilliant ideas, the likes of which no one has ever seen. History has shown that deep technical ideas tend to find new applications, sometimes far-flung from the arena in which the ideas were developed. So besides being one of the greatest intellectual achievements of all time, a proof of $\mathsf{P} \neq \mathsf{NP}$ would likely unlock a giant treasure chest of techniques and insights about computation. We can't predict what other spectacular results might ensue.

Why is it difficult? We shouldn't hold our breath. Trying to settle P versus NP is like pondering how to scale a towering obelisk with no apparent footholds. Many flawed proofs have appeared and continue to appear (including both P = NP claims and P ≠ NP claims), but no attempts have come close to succeeding. Failed attempts to show P ≠ NP often hinge on an implicit assumption that any algorithm must follow some recognizable pattern, like "trying all possibilities." It may be hard to imagine an alternative, but that doesn't mean no alternative is possible. Suppose a deranged programmer spews out ten thousand lines of inexplicable spaghetti code with no discernible logic, and claims it solves GRAPH 3-COLORING in quadratic time. Despite our incredulity, what if they are right, by some miracle? A lower bound statement contains a $\forall$ quantifier over the set of all algorithms, and "for all" means "for *all*." The range of possible behaviors of arbitrary algorithms is too unwieldy to get a grip on. A P ≠ NP proof would need to explain why, for example, brute force can only be improved somewhat—but not too much—for GRAPH 3-COLORING, yet totally circumvented for GRAPH 2-COLORING.

Why is P versus NP beyond the reach of our finest proof techniques? Complexity theorists have formulated some "barrier theorems" showing that certain types of proofs are doomed to fail. These "meta-theorems" cordon off entire avenues, preemptively condemning some proof ideas as dead ends. The barriers provide a "sniff test" for evaluating a claimed P versus NP proof: If it doesn't try to overcome the known barriers, don't take it seriously. We prove a barrier theorem at the end of the book (§18.7).

Now what? Progress on P versus NP is largely stalled, but the shadow of P versus NP looms over the whole field, serving as a constant source of inspiration and awe as we explore the surrounding landscape. This question is worth studying for its own sake, and it stands alongside other foundational scientific questions such as "What is a complete set of physical laws that govern the universe?" and "How did life arise?" The quest to unravel the P versus NP mystery continues to advance our knowledge about the capabilities of computers in many ways.

2.3 NP-Completeness

It's no coincidence that none of INDEPENDENT SET, DIRECTED FULL PATH, GRAPH 3-COLORING, SUBSET SUM are known to be in P. These problems are NP-*complete*, which intuitively means they're among the "hardest" in NP—the least likely to be in P. (NP-"completeness" is unrelated to "completeness and soundness" from §2.2.2.)

P ≠ NP only says that at least one NP problem is not in P. But in fact, P ≠ NP would automatically imply that every NP-complete problem is not in P. In other words: Proving P = NP seems to require designing poly-time algorithms for all NP problems. But in fact, it would suffice to design a poly-time algorithm for any one NP-complete problem.

So the entire P versus NP question is wrapped up inside each individual NP-complete problem. If we pick our favorite NP-complete problem and determine with certainty whether or not it's in P, we will have resolved P versus NP, and fame and fortune will be ours.

2.3.1 The Definition

Recall $A \leq_p^m B$ means there exists a poly-time mapping reduction from problem A to problem B. Such a reduction is an algorithm that "maps" any given A-input x to an equivalent B-input y: If we run a hypothetical algorithm for B on input y, the output would also solve A on input x. Here's a recap of basic properties of mapping reductions (Lemma 1.12 and Lemma 1.13):

Lemma 2.6. *For all decision problems A, B, C:*

(i) If $A \leq_p^m B$ and $B \in \mathsf{P}$ then $A \in \mathsf{P}$.

(ii) If $A \leq_p^m B$ and $B \leq_p^m C$ then $A \leq_p^m C$. ■

Definition. A decision problem B is NP-*complete* when $B \in \mathsf{NP}$ and $A \leq_p^m B$ for every $A \in \mathsf{NP}$. ◄

It's not obvious that such a beast even exists. The definition asks for a lot. NP contains infinitely many problems (such as the trivial problem "Does the input equal k?" for each integer k), so proving that B is NP-complete involves designing infinitely many reductions, one from each $A \in \mathsf{NP}$. This is doable by designing a recipe for turning verifiers into reductions. NP-complete problems not only exist, they abound. Amazingly, the whole of NP, with its immense variety of problems, can be embedded inside each individual NP-complete problem.

Why not allow oracle reductions ($\leq_p^o$), rather than just mapping reductions, in the definition of NP-completeness? We could, and some people do, but this wouldn't affect much. There are virtually no known problems for which oracle reductions buy us anything over mapping reductions for NP-completeness.

A decision problem B is NP-*hard* when $A \leq_p^m B$ for every $A \in \mathsf{NP}$ but B isn't necessarily in NP. Function and search problems can't be in NP (since NP only contains decision problems), but we say a function or search problem B is NP-hard when $A \leq_p^o B$ for every $A \in \mathsf{NP}$. We allow oracle reductions here since mapping reductions between decision and non-decision problems don't make sense (a "type mismatch").

Let's formalize the idea that NP-complete problems are the hardest in NP:

Lemma 2.7. *Suppose B is* NP*-complete. Then $B \in \mathsf{P}$ iff $\mathsf{P} = \mathsf{NP}$.*

Proof. $\Leftarrow$: Assume $\mathsf{P} = \mathsf{NP}$. Then $B \in \mathsf{P}$ because $B \in \mathsf{NP}$.

$\Rightarrow$: Assume $B \in \mathsf{P}$. Then $\mathsf{NP} \subseteq \mathsf{P}$ because for every $A \in \mathsf{NP}$, we have $A \leq_p^m B$, which implies $A \in \mathsf{P}$ (Lemma 2.6.*(i)*). Since $\mathsf{P} \subseteq \mathsf{NP}$, we conclude $\mathsf{P} = \mathsf{NP}$. ■

Corollary 2.8. *Either all* NP*-complete problems are in* P*, or none are.*

Proof. By Lemma 2.7, if $\mathsf{P} = \mathsf{NP}$ then every NP-complete problem is in P, and if $\mathsf{P} \neq \mathsf{NP}$ then every NP-complete problem is not in P. ■

Since it's widely conjectured that $\mathsf{P} \neq \mathsf{NP}$, we construe NP-completeness as evidence that a problem is not in P.

In this chapter, we prove that Independent Set, Directed Full Path, Graph 3-Coloring, and Subset Sum are NP-complete. In practice, if we need to solve one of these, or any other NP-complete problem, we shouldn't waste time trying to devise a poly-time algorithm that works on literally all inputs. But we need not give up entirely. It may be productive to scale back our ambition and exploit the structure of the particular inputs at hand. NP-completeness doesn't preclude a good enough algorithm for a specific practical situation. For example, faced with the Subset Sum problem, if our application only has fairly small input numbers, then we can use an efficient Small Subset Sum algorithm. Furthermore, we can argue to our boss that it would be pointless to fire us for failing to find a poly-time algorithm for an NP-complete problem—many smart people already tried.

To prove that a specific decision problem C is NP-complete, we can use this template:

(1) Show $C \in \mathsf{NP}$.
(2) Pick a problem B that we already know is NP-complete.
(3) Show $B \leq_p^m C$.

This works since for every $A \in \mathsf{NP}$, we have $A \leq_p^m B \leq_p^m C$ and therefore $A \leq_p^m C$ (Lemma 2.6.*(ii)*). Doing the reduction backward is a common mistake: Reducing C to B is not the same as reducing B to C.

For *(1)*, it's often clear what a witness should be. For *(2)*, it's generally wise to pick a B that resembles C, but there's no recipe for success. Step *(3)* is the bulk of the effort. Fortunately, we only have to design this one reduction, not infinitely many.

"Which came first, the chicken or the egg?" Using the template to show something is NP-complete requires already knowing that something else is NP-complete. To get the ball rolling, we must prove that some problem is NP-complete from first principles, with no shortcut. We undertake this project in §2.8. Our first NP-complete problem is called SATISFIABILITY, or SAT for short—we define it soon. Once we have this "mother of all NP-complete problems," the snowball begins rolling down the hill. Reducing SAT to other NP problems shows that those problems are also NP-complete. So we add them to our arsenal of known NP-complete problems, and they become available to pick as the B in the template. Having more options for B makes it easier to prove that more problems are NP-complete. Adding *those* problems to our arsenal makes it *even easier* to show that *even more* problems are NP-complete, and the rest is history.

How many NP-complete problems are there?

- Practical answer: Many thousands. Every week, researchers discover that some problems of interest are NP-complete.
- Mathematical answer: Infinitely many. For example, GRAPH k-COLORING is NP-complete for each $k \geq 3$.
- Philosophical answer: Just one. Since all NP-complete problems are interreducible with each other, they are "the same" problem wearing different clothes.

It's easy to get the false impression that NP is partitioned into just two types of problems: P and NP-complete (assuming $\mathsf{P} \neq \mathsf{NP}$). But it's known that if $\mathsf{P} \neq \mathsf{NP}$ then there exist NP-*intermediate* problems, which are in NP but neither in P nor NP-complete. We won't prove this theorem. There aren't many examples of candidate NP-intermediate problems. A notable candidate is a decision version of the FACTORING function problem: "Given a positive integer, find its prime factorization." Most well-studied problems in NP are known or conjectured to be either in P or NP-complete.

2.3.2 Normal Form Logic Formulas

To introduce the seminal SATISFIABILITY problem, we first discuss logic formulas. This section's concepts permeate the book.

A boolean function $f\colon \{0,1\}^n \to \{0,1\}$ has a tuple of *variables* $x = x_1 x_2 \cdots x_n$ where each x_i can be assigned either 0 or 1. An *assignment* $a = a_1 a_2 \cdots a_n \in \{0,1\}^n$ specifies which bit a_i to plug in for each variable x_i. Evaluating f on assignment a yields the bit $f(a)$. As usual, x sometimes refers to the variables and sometimes refers to the variables' values (an assignment being plugged in). The truth table of f has 2^n rows, where the left side has all assignments a, and the right side has the corresponding bits $f(a)$. (We associate true with 1 and false with 0.)

A logic formula is a parenthesized expression using the connectives $\wedge$ (and), $\vee$ (or), $\neg$ (not), with variables as building blocks. A formula expresses a boolean function $f\colon \{0,1\}^n \to \{0,1\}$:

x_1	x_2	x_3	positive literal x_1	negative literal $\overline{x_2}$	width-2 term $x_1 \wedge \overline{x_2}$	width-2 clause $\overline{x_1} \vee x_2$	3-term 2-DNF $(x_1 \wedge \overline{x_2}) \vee (\overline{x_2} \wedge \overline{x_3}) \vee (x_1 \wedge x_3)$	3-clause 2-CNF $(\overline{x_1} \vee x_2) \wedge (x_2 \vee x_3) \wedge (\overline{x_1} \vee \overline{x_3})$
0	0	0	0	1	0	1	1	0
0	0	1	0	1	0	1	0	1
0	1	0	0	0	0	1	0	1
0	1	1	0	0	0	1	0	1
1	0	0	1	1	1	0	1	0
1	0	1	1	1	1	0	1	0
1	1	0	1	0	0	1	0	1
1	1	1	1	0	0	1	1	0

Figure 2.5: Logic formula examples

Plug in an assignment a for x and evaluate the formula to get $f(a)$. A formula for f may be more succinct than f's truth table.

A very simple type of formula is a *literal*, which is a variable x_i or a negated variable $\overline{x_i}$ (compact notation for $\neg x_i$). A literal's truth table has $2^n/2$ many 0s and $2^n/2$ many 1s (on the right side).

A *term* is a conjunction (and) of literals that correspond to distinct variables (for example, $\overline{x_2} \wedge x_4 \wedge \overline{x_5}$). A *clause* is a disjunction (or) of literals that correspond to distinct variables (for example, $x_2 \vee \overline{x_4} \vee x_5$). The number of literals in a term or clause is its *width*. The negation of a width-k term is a width-k clause (and vice versa) since pulling the negation inside flips the conjunction to a disjunction and flips each literal's sign. A width-k term's truth table has 2^{n-k} many 1s and $2^n - 2^{n-k}$ many 0s. A width-k clause's truth table has 2^{n-k} many 0s and $2^n - 2^{n-k}$ many 1s. A width-1 term or clause is just a literal. Empty terms and clauses are allowed: A width-0 term always evaluates to 1 (since every literal is 1 if there are no literals). A width-0 clause always evaluates to 0 (since no literal is 1 if there are no literals).

A *disjunctive normal form formula (DNF)* is a disjunction of terms (an "or" of "and"s of literals). A *conjunctive normal form formula (CNF)* is a conjunction of clauses (an "and" of "or"s of literals). The negation of a DNF is a CNF (and vice versa). In a *k-DNF* or *k-CNF*, each term or clause has width exactly k. The negation of a k-DNF is a k-CNF (and vice versa).

Example. See Figure 2.5.

- $(x_1 \wedge \overline{x_2}) \vee (\overline{x_2} \wedge \overline{x_3}) \vee (x_1 \wedge x_3)$ is a 2-DNF with three terms. After negating: $(\overline{x_1} \vee x_2) \wedge (x_2 \vee x_3) \wedge (\overline{x_1} \vee \overline{x_3})$ is a 2-CNF with three clauses.
- $(\overline{x_1} \vee x_3 \vee x_4) \wedge (\overline{x_2} \vee x_3 \vee \overline{x_5})$ is a 3-CNF with two clauses. After negating: $(x_1 \wedge \overline{x_3} \wedge \overline{x_4}) \vee (x_2 \wedge \overline{x_3} \wedge x_5)$ is a 3-DNF with two terms. ♦

A 1-DNF is like a clause, and a 1-CNF is like a term, except repeated variables are allowed: A 1-DNF might redundantly contain $(x_1) \vee (x_1) \vee \cdots$ or might contain $(x_1) \vee (\overline{x_1}) \vee \cdots$ and thus always evaluate to 1. A 1-CNF might redundantly contain $(x_1) \wedge (x_1) \wedge \cdots$ or might contain $(x_1) \wedge (\overline{x_1}) \wedge \cdots$ and thus always evaluate to 0. An empty DNF (with no terms) always evaluates to 0. An empty CNF (with no clauses) always evaluates to 1.

DNFs and CNFs are "universal" types of formulas, capable of expressing any truth table:

x_1	x_2	x_3	$f(x)$	DNF	CNF
0	0	0	0		$(x_1 \vee x_2 \vee x_3)$
0	0	1	1	$(\overline{x_1} \wedge \overline{x_2} \wedge x_3)$	
0	1	0	1	$\vee\ (\overline{x_1} \wedge x_2 \wedge \overline{x_3})$	
0	1	1	0		$\wedge\ (x_1 \vee \overline{x_2} \vee \overline{x_3})$
1	0	0	1	$\vee\ (x_1 \wedge \overline{x_2} \wedge \overline{x_3})$	
1	0	1	0		$\wedge\ (\overline{x_1} \vee x_2 \vee \overline{x_3})$
1	1	0	0		$\wedge\ (\overline{x_1} \vee \overline{x_2} \vee x_3)$
1	1	1	1	$\vee\ (x_1 \wedge x_2 \wedge x_3)$	

Figure 2.6: Example of expressing a function as a DNF and as a CNF

Lemma 2.9. *Every $f\colon \{0,1\}^n \to \{0,1\}$ can be expressed as a DNF and as a CNF, specifically an n-DNF with at most 2^n terms and an n-CNF with at most 2^n clauses.*

Proof idea. DNF: For each row where f's truth table has a 1, we create a term with a 1 in that row and 0s in all other rows. "Or"ing these terms together replicates f's truth table.

CNF: Define the *complement* function $\overline{f}$ by $\overline{f}(a) = \overline{f(a)}$ for every assignment a. Negating a DNF for $\overline{f}$ yields a CNF for f. To describe this CNF directly, without the "double negation" detour: For each row where f's truth table has a 0, we create a clause with a 0 in that row and 1s in all other rows, and we "and" these clauses together. ∎

Proof. DNF: For each assignment $b \in \{0,1\}^n$, define a width-n term T_b that has x_i if $b_i = 1$ and has $\overline{x_i}$ if $b_i = 0$ (for each index $i \in [n]$). Thus $T_b(a) = 1$ if $a = b$, and $T_b(a) = 0$ if $a \neq b$. We have $f = \bigvee_{b\,:\,f(b)=1} T_b$ because for every assignment a, if $f(a) = 1$ then T_a is a term in the DNF and $T_a(a) = 1$, and if $f(a) = 0$ then for every term T_b in the DNF we have $a \neq b$ (since $f(b) = 1$) and thus $T_b(a) = 0$.

CNF: For each assignment $b \in \{0,1\}^n$, define a width-n clause C_b that has x_i if $b_i = 0$ and has $\overline{x_i}$ if $b_i = 1$ (for each index $i \in [n]$). Thus $C_b(a) = 0$ if $a = b$, and $C_b(a) = 1$ if $a \neq b$. We have $f = \bigwedge_{b\,:\,f(b)=0} C_b$ because for every assignment a, if $f(a) = 0$ then C_a is a clause in the CNF and $C_a(a) = 0$, and if $f(a) = 1$ then for every clause C_b in the CNF we have $a \neq b$ (since $f(b) = 0$) and thus $C_b(a) = 1$. ∎

Example. Figure 2.6 demonstrates the proof of Lemma 2.9 with the 3-bit parity function, which evaluates to 1 iff the number of 1s in x is odd: $f(x) = x_1 \oplus x_2 \oplus x_3$ where $\oplus$ is xor. ♦

2.3.3 Satisfying Assignments

An assignment *satisfies* a formula iff it makes the formula evaluate to 1. A formula is *satisfiable* iff there exists an assignment that satisfies it.

Satisfiability (or Sat for short)	(2.20)
Input: CNF formula φ	
Output: Is φ satisfiable?	

φ (lower-case phi) is the Greek version of f, standing for "formula."

To satisfy a CNF, every clause must have at least one literal that evaluates to 1 (a positive literal whose variable is assigned 1, or a negative literal whose variable is assigned 0). Each clause is a constraint, and each of its literals is an opportunity to satisfy the constraint.

Example. Consider this CNF with variables $x = x_1x_2x_3$:

$$\varphi = (x_1 \vee \overline{x_2}) \wedge (\overline{x_1} \vee \overline{x_3}) \wedge (\overline{x_1} \vee x_2 \vee x_3) \wedge (x_1 \vee x_2)$$

Let's try to find a satisfying assignment. We can satisfy the first clause $(x_1 \vee \overline{x_2})$ via its first literal by assigning $x_1 = 1$; let's see where this leads us. We don't have to worry about the first clause anymore (unless we change our mind about our assignment to x_1), but the second clause's $\overline{x_1}$ literal now evaluates to 0, so we should assign $x_3 = 0$ to satisfy this clause via its $\overline{x_3}$ literal. In the third clause $(\overline{x_1} \vee x_2 \vee x_3)$, the first and third literals now evaluate to 0, so our only chance to satisfy it is by assigning $x_2 = 1$. Now we have a full assignment $x = 110$, so let's cross our fingers that the rest of φ is satisfied. Indeed, the last clause has a literal that evaluates to 1—in fact, both its literals satisfy it, but we don't get "extra credit" for this. We found a satisfying assignment, so φ is a yes-input of SAT. Does φ have any other satisfying assignments? Not with $x_1 = 1$, because the rest of the assignment was forced in that case. How about with $x_1 = 0$? This would satisfy the middle two clauses, but then we'd need $x_2 = 0$ to satisfy the first clause and $x_2 = 1$ to satisfy the last clause, which is impossible. Thus $x = 110$ is the only satisfying assignment of φ. Adding the clause $(\overline{x_2} \vee x_3)$, for example, would make this CNF unsatisfiable and thus a no-input of SAT. ♦

This example's ad hoc reasoning doesn't generalize to arbitrary CNFs. The interplay among clauses can be very intricate, leaving us little choice but to wade through the morass of possible assignments. Nobody has found a poly-time, or even subexponential-time, algorithm for SAT.

Theorem 2.10. SAT *is* NP-*complete.*

This is among the most influential and central results in computational complexity. It's evidence that SAT $\notin$ P. We have SAT $\in$ NP because given an assignment $a \in \{0,1\}^n$ as a purported witness, a poly-time verifier can plug in $x = a$ and evaluate φ to check whether it's satisfied. We prove that SAT is NP-hard in §2.8, and we take this for granted until then.

Why focus on CNFs and not DNFs? The variant of SAT where the input is a DNF is trivial because a DNF is satisfiable iff it's nonempty (has at least one term). The problem "Given a DNF, does it have at least one unsatisfying assignment?" is equivalent to SAT since the two problems mapping reduce to each other by negating the input formula.

SAT has such infamy that extensive effort has gone into defying its NP-completeness. People have written and deployed SAT solving programs that work well on CNFs that arise in many practical applications. SAT's flexibility as a generic constraint satisfaction problem makes SAT solvers useful for computer aided design, software and hardware verification (such as model checking), artificial intelligence, and cryptanalysis, for example. There are even SAT solving competitions. But a SAT solver that's correct and efficient on every CNF is likely a pipe dream.

Consider a special case of SAT where all clauses in the input CNF have width exactly k:

k-SAT	(2.21)
Input: k-CNF formula φ	
Output: Is φ satisfiable?	

1-SAT is in P (in fact, in L) because a 1-CNF is satisfiable iff it doesn't contain any opposite literals $(x_i) \wedge (\overline{x_i})$. We can satisfy such a 1-CNF by assigning $x_i = 1$ if (x_i) is present, or $x_i = 0$ if $(\overline{x_i})$ is present, and if neither is present then x_i's value doesn't matter.

2-SAT is in P but is neither known nor widely believed to be in L. Recall the key for efficiently solving GRAPH 2-COLORING: Once we assign a color to an endpoint of an edge, the other endpoint's color is forced. 2-SAT is more subtle: For a clause $(x_i \vee x_j)$, once we assign $x_i = 0$ or $x_j = 0$, we're forced to assign the other variable 1. But if we first assign $x_i = 1$ or $x_j = 1$, then the other variable's value is not forced. Similar reasoning applies to clauses with negative literals. Thus 2-SAT is on a longer leash than GRAPH 2-COLORING, but the leash is still short enough to rein in the complexity. Exercise 2.12 is a guided proof that 2-SAT has a poly-time oracle reduction to DIRECTED REACHABILITY and is thus in P.

There's a big jump from 2 to 3:

Theorem 2.11. 3-SAT *is* NP-*complete.*

We prove this in §2.3.4 using the template from §2.3.1: Since SAT is NP-complete, we can just show SAT $\leq_p^m$ 3-SAT rather than reduce every NP problem to 3-SAT.

Theorem 2.11 supersedes Theorem 2.10. After adding 3-SAT to our arsenal of known NP-complete problems, there's no reason to reduce from the general SAT problem when proving other problems are NP-complete—we might as well reduce from 3-SAT.

SAT's encoding details aren't important, but we assume an encoding reminiscent of DIRECTED REACHABILITY (§1.3.3): The input starts with two words containing the number of variables and number of clauses, followed by pointers to the starts of the clause descriptions, followed by the clause descriptions. Each clause description has a word for the width and then two words per literal: the variable index and the sign (positive or negative). Up to constant factors, the size of a CNF with no empty clauses is the number of literal occurrences (sum of widths of clauses). For k-SAT, we may omit the pointers and omit the width word from each clause description.

2.3.4 Adjusting Clause Width

Proof idea for Theorem 2.11. Let's design a poly-time mapping reduction from SAT to 3-SAT.

How about this? "Given φ, query the SAT oracle on φ and output the same answer. Since every 3-CNF is a CNF, this solves 3-SAT." This reduces 3-SAT to SAT, which is backward! We can show a problem is NP-complete by reducing *from* an NP-complete problem, but reducing *to* an NP-complete problem shows nothing. Similarly, we can show a problem is in P by reducing *to* a problem in P, but reducing *from* a problem in P shows nothing.

Let's try again, with our head screwed on straight. Given a CNF φ, we must efficiently map (transform) it to a 3-CNF ψ (lower-case Greek psi) such that φ is satisfiable iff ψ is satisfiable. It would be great if we could just rewrite φ as a 3-CNF ψ on the same variables, having the same truth table. Since that's not always possible, we add new variables. Thus φ and ψ won't express the same function, but as long as they're both satisfiable or both unsatisfiable, our work here will be done. Any width-3 clauses of φ go unchanged into ψ.

- Any clause of width < 3 needs to get widened, but we can't just insert a variable, which might make ψ easier to satisfy than φ. We counterbalance this by adding more clauses.
- Any clause of width > 3 needs to get split into narrower clauses, but we can't just partition its literals, which might make ψ harder to satisfy than φ. We counterbalance this by inserting more literals.

The following two claims make progress on one clause at a time, by replacing it with two clauses whose widths are closer to 3 without affecting whether the CNF is satisfiable. We keep doing this until all clauses have width 3. ■

Claim 2.12. *Suppose we map a CNF φ to a CNF ψ by replacing some clause C with two clauses $(C \vee y) \wedge (C \vee \overline{y})$ where y is any variable not in C. Then φ is satisfiable iff ψ is satisfiable.*

Proof. $\Rightarrow$: If φ has a satisfying assignment, then the same assignment satisfies ψ: All clauses besides those replacing C remain satisfied, and any satisfied literal in C is also satisfied in both $(C \vee y)$ and $(C \vee \overline{y})$, so those two clauses are satisfied regardless of y's value.

$\Leftarrow$: If ψ has a satisfying assignment, then the same assignment satisfies φ: All clauses besides C remain satisfied. If $y = 0$ then C is satisfied since $(C \vee y)$ is satisfied but not by y. If $y = 1$ then C is satisfied since $(C \vee \overline{y})$ is satisfied but not by $\overline{y}$. ■

Claim 2.13. *Suppose we map a CNF φ to a CNF ψ by replacing some clause C with two clauses $(C_1 \vee y) \wedge (C_2 \vee \overline{y})$ where $C_1 \vee C_2$ is some partition of C's literals into two parts, and y is a fresh variable that's not in φ. Then φ is satisfiable iff ψ is satisfiable.*

Proof. $\Rightarrow$: If φ has a satisfying assignment, then the same assignment, together with some value of y, satisfies ψ: All clauses besides those replacing C remain satisfied. If C has a satisfied literal in C_1, then the same literal satisfies $(C_1 \vee y)$, and assigning $y = 0$ satisfies $(C_2 \vee \overline{y})$. If C has a satisfied literal in C_2, then the same literal satisfies $(C_2 \vee \overline{y})$, and assigning $y = 1$ satisfies $(C_1 \vee y)$.

$\Leftarrow$: If ψ has a satisfying assignment, then the same assignment (ignoring y) satisfies φ: All clauses besides C remain satisfied. If $y = 0$ then C_1 (and hence C) is satisfied since $(C_1 \vee y)$ is satisfied but not by y. If $y = 1$ then C_2 (and hence C) is satisfied since $(C_2 \vee \overline{y})$ is satisfied but not by $\overline{y}$. ■

Example. Let's transform $(x_1) \wedge (\overline{x_1} \vee x_2 \vee x_3 \vee \overline{x_4} \vee x_5 \vee \overline{x_6})$ to an equivalent 3-CNF.

Figure 2.7 applies Claim 2.12 to the width-1 clause (x_1) yielding two width-2 clauses, and applies Claim 2.12 again to each of those. Instead of introducing the fresh variable y_1, we could have used one of $x_2, \dots, x_6$. We also could have reused y_2 instead of introducing y_3.

There are many ways to split up a wide clause by applying Claim 2.13 repeatedly. A traditional way is to peel off two literals at a time. These two literals, together with the fresh variable, become a width-3 clause. Then, we repeat with the remaining original literals and the negated fresh variable. Suppose we always peel off the most recent negated fresh variable along with the next original literal. This produces a chain where each width-3 clause contains one of the original literals (or two, in the first and last resulting clauses), with fresh variables "linking" adjacent clauses. Figure 2.8 shows an example using fresh variables y_4, y_5, y_6 for the links. Why can't we go down to width 2? If we peel off only one literal (forming a width-2 clause with a fresh variable), the leftover clause would lose that literal but gain the negated fresh variable, so it would be as wide as the original clause—no progress. That's what's special about width 3. ♦

Proof of Theorem 2.11. 3-SAT $\in$ NP since SAT $\in$ NP. It suffices to show SAT $\leq_p^m$ 3-SAT since SAT is NP-complete (Theorem 2.10).

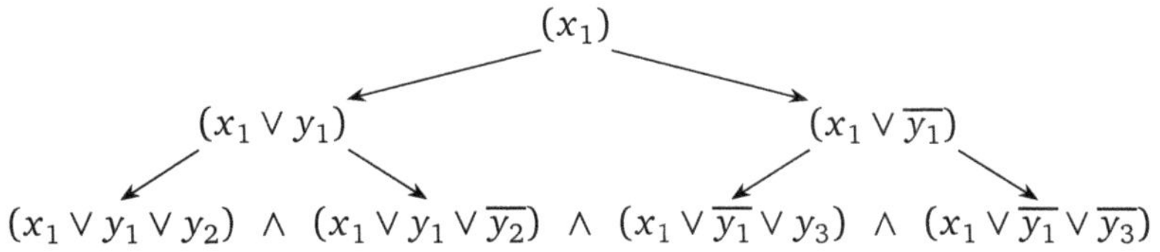

Figure 2.7: Example of widening clauses

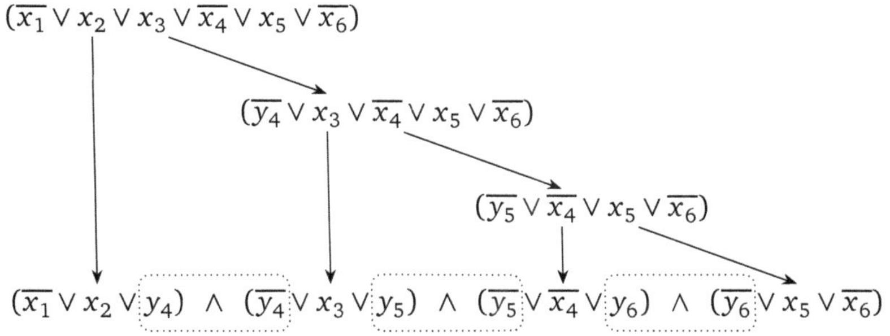

Figure 2.8: Example of narrowing clauses

Mapping reduction from SAT to 3-SAT (2.22)

map CNF φ to 3-CNF ψ using fresh variables $y_1, y_2, \dots$:
  initialize $\psi \leftarrow \varphi$
  for $i \leftarrow 1, 2, \dots$ until ψ is a 3-CNF:
    pick a clause C of width $k \neq 3$ in the current ψ
    if $k < 3$: replace C with $(C \vee y_i) \wedge (C \vee \overline{y_i})$ in ψ
    if $k > 3$: replace C with $(C_1 \vee y_i) \wedge (C_2 \vee \overline{y_i})$ in ψ,
      where C_1 is two of C's literals and C_2 is the rest of C's literals

This maintains the invariant that φ is satisfiable iff ψ is satisfiable (Claim 2.12 and Claim 2.13). The φ and ψ in the claims actually correspond to the current ψ and next ψ in a loop iteration. Each clause of width $k < 3$ in φ becomes 2^{3-k} many width-3 clauses in the final ψ. Each clause of width $k > 3$ in φ becomes $k-2$ many width-3 clauses in the final ψ. The reduction only needs linear time, by iterating over φ's clauses and directly transforming each to the corresponding set of width-3 clauses, without bothering to store intermediate CNFs. ∎

The same reasoning shows that k-SAT is NP-complete for each integer $k \geq 3$.

2.3.5 Search-to-Decision Reduction

Merely knowing whether a satisfying assignment exists is not always adequate.

SAT SEARCH (2.23)

Input: CNF formula φ

Output: A satisfying assignment for φ, or report that φ is unsatisfiable

Recall we can find a shortest path from s to t in a graph by repeatedly consulting an oracle for a related decision problem (§ 1.8.3). Similarly, we can find a satisfying assignment with the help of a SAT oracle:

Theorem 2.14. SAT SEARCH $\leq_p^o$ SAT.

SAT SEARCH can't be NP-complete (since it's not a decision problem), but it's "as good as" NP-complete:

Corollary 2.15. SAT SEARCH *has a poly-time program iff* P = NP.

Proof of Corollary 2.15. SAT SEARCH has a poly-time program iff SAT ∈ P (Theorem 2.14 and Lemma 1.12) iff P = NP (Lemma 2.7) because SAT is NP-complete (Theorem 2.10). ■

Proof idea for Theorem 2.14. The oracle can tell us whether φ is satisfiable, and we reject if it's not. Suppose φ is satisfiable and has variables $x_1x_2\cdots x_n$. Each oracle query gives one bit of information, and we need n bits for an assignment, so we make n more queries. The ith query asks which bit to assign to x_i.

The first query should be "Does φ have a satisfying assignment with $x_1 = 1$?" If it does, we commit to $x_1 = 1$ and keep going. Otherwise, since φ is satisfiable, some (in fact, every) satisfying assignment has $x_1 = 0$, so we commit to $x_1 = 0$. This question doesn't quite look like a SAT query. The oracle will turn up its nose at any question that's not exactly of the form "Is this CNF satisfiable?" We make the question into a SAT query by *contracting* φ: We create a CNF ψ by plugging in (hardcoding) $x_1 = 1$ and simplifying φ accordingly. The satisfying assignments to ψ's variables $x_2\cdots x_n$ are exactly the assignments that, together with $x_1 = 1$, would satisfy φ. This ψ is the query. (Another approach is to append the clause (x_1) to φ.)

The second query shouldn't be "Does φ have a satisfying assignment with $x_2 = 1$?" since φ might have a satisfying assignment with $x_1 = 1$ and a different satisfying assignment with $x_2 = 1$ but no satisfying assignment with $x_1x_2 = 11$. We must honor our commitment about x_1.

After assigning $x_1\cdots x_{i-1}$, we decide whether to assign $x_i = 1$ or $x_i = 0$ by asking the oracle whether φ has a satisfying assignment that agrees with our assignment to $x_1\cdots x_{i-1}$ and also has $x_i = 1$. To speak the oracle's language, we give it a contracted version of φ.

This is a *greedy* approach—we forge ahead and never reconsider earlier decisions. ■

Here's some terminology. A *partial assignment* to variables $x_1\cdots x_n$ is an element of $\{0,1,*\}^n$, for example $*10{*}{*}0{*}1$ if $n = 8$. A *star* $*$ means the variable remains unassigned. A partial assignment with no stars is an ordinary assignment. An assignment $b \in \{0,1\}^n$ is *consistent with* a partial assignment $a \in \{0,1,*\}^n$ iff $b_i = a_i$ for all i such that $a_i \neq *$. For example, 010 is consistent with $*1*$, and 10101 is consistent with $1{*}{*}0{*}$. (Stars are like wildcards in pattern matching, but here a $*$ must match exactly one bit.)

The *restriction* of a function $f\colon \{0,1\}^n \to \{0,1\}$ under a partial assignment a is the function $f|_a$ obtained from f by hardcoding a's assigned bits: $f|_a$ takes an assignment to a's star variables and evaluates f on the "filled out" assignment. If a has k stars, then $f|_a\colon \{0,1\}^k \to \{0,1\}$. For example, $f|_{*1*}(00) = f(010)$ and $f|_{1**0*}(011) = f(10101)$. We obtain $f|_a$'s truth table from f's truth table by deleting all rows inconsistent with a and deleting all columns of non-$*$ variables. We usually have $f|_a$ inherit f's variable names despite gaps between indices of unassigned variables.

Example. Figure 2.9 shows the restriction of the 3-bit parity function f under the partial assignment $a = *1*$. Here, x_3 is the "2nd" variable of $f|_a$, but we retain 3 as its index. ♦

x_1	x_2	x_3	$f(x_1x_2x_3)$
0	0	0	0
0	0	1	1
0	1	0	1
0	1	1	0
1	0	0	1
1	0	1	0
1	1	0	0
1	1	1	1

x_1	x_3	$f\vert_{*1*}(x_1x_3)$
0	0	1
0	1	0
1	0	0
1	1	1

Figure 2.9: Restriction of the 3-bit parity function under the partial assignment $*1*$

The *contraction* of a CNF φ under a partial assignment a is the CNF $\varphi|_a$ obtained from φ by deleting each clause that has at least one literal that evaluates to 1 under a (since the clause is already satisfied), and deleting from all other clauses any literals that evaluate to 0 under a (leaving only literals whose variables are $*$s in a). If φ expresses f, then $\varphi|_a$ expresses $f|_a$. Given φ and a, we can find $\varphi|_a$ in linear time.

Example. We contract a CNF φ under the partial assignment $a = *0*1$:

$$\begin{aligned}
\varphi &= (x_1 \vee \overline{x_2}) \wedge (\overline{x_1} \vee x_2 \vee x_3) \wedge (x_1 \vee \overline{x_3}) \wedge (x_2 \vee x_4) \wedge (x_2 \vee x_3 \vee \overline{x_4}) \\
&\ (x_1 \vee 1) \wedge (\overline{x_1} \vee 0 \vee x_3) \wedge (x_1 \vee \overline{x_3}) \wedge (0 \vee 1) \wedge (0 \vee x_3 \vee 0) \\
\varphi|_a &= (\overline{x_1} \vee x_3) \wedge (x_1 \vee \overline{x_3}) \wedge (x_3)
\end{aligned}$$ ♦

Our search-to-decision reduction for SAT assigns variables from left to right, so it always has a partial assignment with an assigned prefix $a_1 \cdots a_i \in \{0,1\}^i$ and unassigned suffix $a_{i+1} \cdots a_n = * \cdots *$. The general definition (any subset of variables can be stars) is useful for other things.

Proof of Theorem 2.14. This reduction solves SAT SEARCH using a SAT oracle:

Reduction from SAT SEARCH to SAT (2.24)

```
on input φ with variables x1x2···xn:
    query the oracle on input φ, and reject if the oracle rejected
    initialize a ← **···* (partial assignment to φ's variables)
    for i ← 1,2,...,n:
        let b be the same partial assignment as a except that b_i = 1
        query the oracle on input φ|_b
        if the oracle accepted: update a_i ← 1
        if the oracle rejected: update a_i ← 0
    output a
```

Assume the oracle says φ is satisfiable. The loop maintains the invariant that φ has a satisfying assignment consistent with a, in other words, $\varphi|_a$ is satisfiable. If the oracle accepts, then of course the invariant continues to hold since the new a equals the b for which the oracle just said $\varphi|_b$ is satisfiable. To see that the invariant is maintained if the oracle rejects, assume the old $\varphi|_a$ (at the beginning of the iteration) has a satisfying assignment. This assignment must have $x_i = 0$ (otherwise it would satisfy $\varphi|_b$), so it also satisfies the new $\varphi|_a$ after letting $a_i \leftarrow 0$.

When the loop terminates, $a \in \{0,1\}^n$ is an assignment. By the loop invariant, φ has a satisfying assignment that's consistent with a, which must be a itself, so the output is correct.

The reduction runs in polynomial time. (To speed things up, the reduction can remember the current $\varphi|_a$ and just plug in a bit for x_i and contract to get $\varphi|_b$ or the next $\varphi|_a$.) ■

2.4 Independent Sets

Theorem 2.16. Independent Set *is* NP-*complete.*

Before proving this, we use it to deduce that some related problems are also NP-complete.

2.4.1 Related Problems

A *node cover* (or *vertex cover*) in an undirected graph is a subset of nodes S such that every edge has at least one endpoint in S. Each node in S "covers" its incident edges, and all edges must be covered. For example, suppose nodes and edges represent computers and communication links in a network, and a computer can use certain software to monitor the traffic on its links. A node cover is a choice of computers to install the software on, so all links are monitored.

Node covers are related to independent sets. For $G=(V,E)$ and $S \subseteq V$, let $\overline{S} = V \setminus S$ be the *complement* subset containing all other nodes of G. Note that $|\overline{S}| = |V| - |S|$.

Claim 2.17. *For every undirected graph G and every subset S of nodes, S is an independent set in G iff $\overline{S}$ is a node cover in G.*

Proof. For every $G=(V,E)$ and $S \subseteq V$:

$$\begin{aligned} S \text{ is an independent set in } G &\iff \neg\big(\exists\ \{u,v\} \in E : u \in S \text{ and } v \in S\big) \\ &\iff \big(\forall\ \{u,v\} \in E : u \in \overline{S} \ \text{ or } \ v \in \overline{S}\big) \iff \overline{S} \text{ is a node cover in } G \end{aligned}$$

Figure 2.10 shows an example. ■

The full set of nodes is always a node cover. Can we detect a node cover with few nodes?

Node Cover (or Vertex Cover)	(2.25)
Input: Undirected graph G, nonnegative integer k	
Output: Does there exist a node cover of size $\leq k$ in G?	

Corollary 2.18. Node Cover *is* NP-*complete.*

Proof. Node Cover $\in$ NP by a verifier that checks that the purported witness is a node cover containing at most k of G's nodes. Since Independent Set is NP-complete, it suffices to show Independent Set $\leq_p^m$ Node Cover. Map (G,k) to $(G, n-k)$ where n is the number of nodes in G. This reduction takes poly time and is correct since G has an independent set of size $\geq k$ iff G has a node cover of size $\leq n-k$ (Claim 2.17). ■

A *clique* in an undirected graph is a subset of nodes S such that every pair of nodes in S has an edge between them. For example, if nodes and edges represent people and friendships in a social network, then a clique is a group of mutual friends.

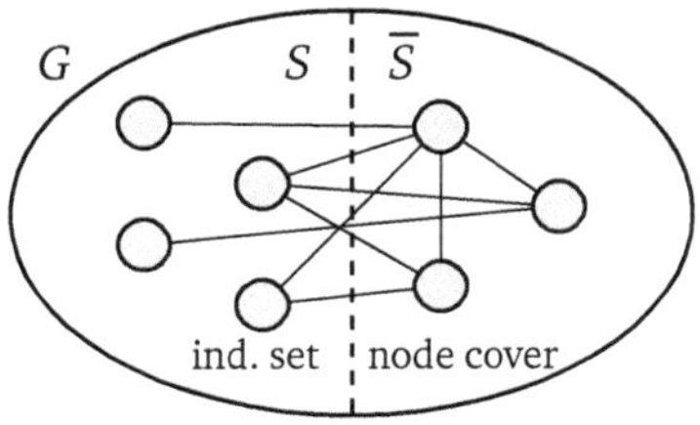

Figure 2.10: Independent set versus node cover

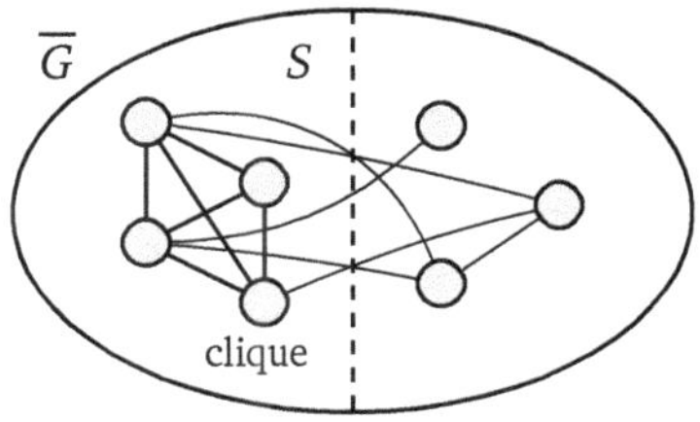

Figure 2.11: Independent set versus clique

Cliques are related to independent sets. For $G = (V, E)$, denote the set of all non-edges by $\overline{E} = \big\{\{u, v\} \subseteq V \,:\, u \neq v \text{ and } \{u, v\} \notin E\big\}$, and let $\overline{G} = (V, \overline{E})$ be the *complement* graph, whose edges are G's non-edges. We're assuming graphs have no multi-edges or self-loops.

Claim 2.19. *For every undirected graph G and every subset S of nodes, S is an independent set in G iff S is a clique in $\overline{G}$.*

Proof. For every $G = (V, E)$ and $S \subseteq V$:

$$\begin{aligned} S \text{ is an independent set in } G &\iff \neg\big(\exists \text{ distinct } u, v \in S : \{u, v\} \in E\big) \\ &\iff \big(\forall \text{ distinct } u, v \in S : \{u, v\} \in \overline{E}\big) \iff S \text{ is a clique in } \overline{G} \end{aligned}$$

Figure 2.11 continues the example from Figure 2.10. ∎

Any edge's two endpoints are always a clique. Can we detect a clique with many nodes?

CLIQUE	(2.26)
Input: Undirected graph G, nonnegative integer k	
Output: Does there exist a clique of size $\geq k$ in G?	

Corollary 2.20. CLIQUE *is* NP*-complete.*

Proof. CLIQUE $\in$ NP by a verifier that checks that the purported witness is a clique containing at least k of G's nodes. Since INDEPENDENT SET is NP-complete, it suffices to show INDEPENDENT SET $\leq_p^m$ CLIQUE. Map (G, k) to $(\overline{G}, k)$. This reduction takes poly time and is correct since G has an independent set of size $\geq k$ iff $\overline{G}$ has a clique of size $\geq k$ (Claim 2.19). ∎

2.4.2 INDEPENDENT SET Is NP-Complete

Proof idea. We reduce from 3-SAT. This is our first example of reducing between problems that seem unrelated (logic formulas versus graphs). We want to transform any 3-CNF φ into a graph G and number k, such that 3-SAT witnesses somehow correspond to INDEPENDENT SET witnesses. A natural first idea is to make satisfying assignments directly correspond to independent sets of size k, but we'd get stuck trying to use edges to enforce the same constraints as the clauses.

Consider a different verifier for 3-SAT: Instead of expecting a satisfying assignment as the witness, the new verifier expects the witness to say which literal to satisfy in each clause, and it checks that no two of these literals conflict (x_i and $\overline{x_i}$). If φ is satisfiable, then an appropriate witness makes this new verifier accept. Conversely, if a witness makes this verifier accept, then

$$\varphi = (\overline{x_1} \vee \overline{x_2} \vee \overline{x_3}) \wedge (x_1 \vee x_2 \vee \overline{x_3}) \wedge (\overline{x_2} \vee x_3 \vee x_4) \wedge (x_2 \vee \overline{x_3} \vee x_4)$$

$G =$

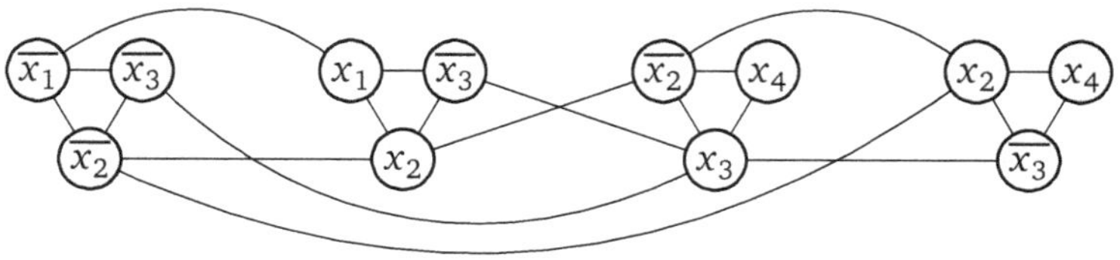

$k = 4$

Figure 2.12: Example of reducing 3-SAT to INDEPENDENT SET

some assignment agrees with the witness and satisfies φ. For example, if the witness says some clauses are satisfied by $\overline{x_i}$ literals but none are satisfied by x_i literals, then assign $x_i = 0$.

We design (G, k) so witnesses for the new verifier correspond to independent sets of size k. If nodes represent occurrences of literals, then edges are perfect for enforcing the "no two conflicting literals" constraints. We must also force an independent set S to contain one node for each clause, like the new 3-SAT witness. By making a triangle (a clique of size 3) on each clause's nodes, S must have at most one node per clause. Then by setting the size threshold k appropriately, S must have at least one node per clause. Thus S can't "compensate" for an unsatisfied clause by picking two literals to satisfy in another clause. ■

In reductions, it's common to design little structures known as *gadgets* to translate constraints from one problem to another. In this proof, a triangle is a gadget associated with a clause.

Proof of Theorem 2.16. We observed INDEPENDENT SET ∈ NP in § 2.2. Since 3-SAT is NP-complete, it suffices to show 3-SAT $\leq_p^m$ INDEPENDENT SET. Map φ to (G, k) where:

- G is the following graph: For each clause of φ, create a triangle whose three nodes represent the clause's literals. Put an "inter-clause" edge between any two nodes representing opposite literals (x_i and $\overline{x_i}$).
- k is the number of clauses in φ.

Figure 2.12 shows an example. This reduction takes poly time since the number of nodes is the number of literal occurrences in φ, and there can be at most quadratically more edges than nodes. To show that it's correct, we argue that φ is satisfiable iff G has an independent set of size $\geq k$:

⇒: Assume φ is satisfiable, and consider a satisfying assignment. For each clause, pick one of its satisfied literals (it doesn't matter which one, if the clause has multiple satisfied literals) and include the corresponding node in S. Then S has size k, and it's an independent set because:

- An edge in a clause's triangle gadget can't have both endpoints in S, since S only contains one node per clause.
- An inter-clause edge can't have both endpoints in S, since each node in S represents a satisfied literal, and x_i and $\overline{x_i}$ can't be simultaneously satisfied by an assignment.

⇐: Assume G has an independent set S of size $\geq k$.

- The triangle edges ensure S contains at most one node from any clause gadget. By the pigeonhole principle, S has exactly one node per clause gadget. (Nodes in S are $\geq k$ pigeons flying into k different holes corresponding to clauses in φ.)

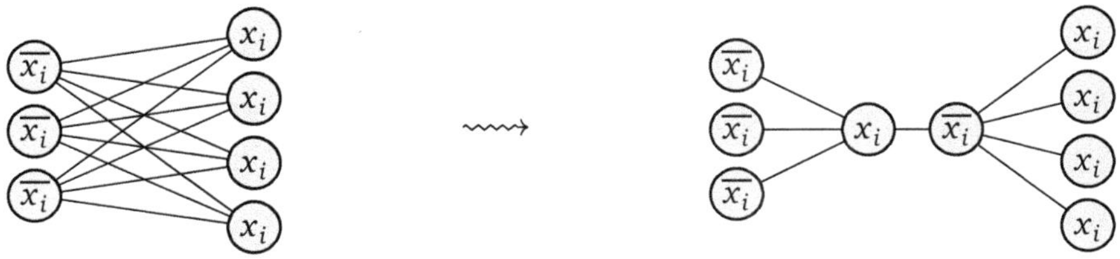

Figure 2.13: Gadget to replace a complete bipartite subgraph

- The inter-clause edges ensure for each variable x_i, S has either no x_i nodes or no $\overline{x_i}$ nodes.

For each x_i, assign $x_i = 0$ if S has no x_i nodes, and assign $x_i = 1$ if S has no $\overline{x_i}$ nodes. If S has neither x_i nor $\overline{x_i}$ nodes, then it doesn't matter how we assign x_i. This assignment satisfies φ since every clause in φ has a literal represented by a node in S, and every node in S represents a satisfied literal. Thus φ is satisfiable. ■

2.4.3 A Faster Reduction

The reduction we just designed takes quadratic time in the worst case. This is good enough for NP-completeness, but as we'll see later, faster reductions are sometimes useful.

Theorem 2.21. 3-SAT $\leq_p^m$ INDEPENDENT SET *via a linear-time reduction.*

Proof idea. In our previous reduction, G could be quadratically larger than φ due to the edges between all pairs of nodes representing opposite literals. For example, if φ had m clauses, with x_1 in half the clauses and $\overline{x_1}$ in the other half, then G had $(m/2)^2$ edges between those nodes. For each x_i, G had a *complete bipartite subgraph* between the x_i nodes and the $\overline{x_i}$ nodes. We cut down the number of edges by introducing two more nodes as in Figure 2.13. These two new nodes are a gadget associated with the variable x_i. By adjusting k, we force S to contain one of these two nodes. If S has the new x_i node, it can't have any $\overline{x_i}$ node. If S has the new $\overline{x_i}$ node, it can't have any x_i node. So instead of enforcing clause-to-clause consistency, we make S choose an assignment and we enforce consistency with this. Thus S corresponds to a 3-SAT witness that includes a satisfying assignment *and* says which literal gets satisfied in each clause. ■

Proof. Map φ to (G, k) where:

- G is the following graph: For each clause of φ, create a triangle whose three nodes represent the clause's literals. For each variable x_i of φ, create two nodes representing x_i and $\overline{x_i}$ with an edge between them. Give each clause gadget node an edge to the variable gadget node representing the opposite literal.
- k is the number of clauses plus the number of variables in φ.

Figure 2.14 shows an example. This reduction takes linear time since each variable and each clause in φ corresponds to a constant number of nodes and edges in G. To show that it's correct, we argue that φ is satisfiable iff G has an independent set of size $\geq k$:

$\Rightarrow$: Assume φ is satisfiable, and consider a satisfying assignment. For each clause gadget and each variable gadget, pick one node representing a satisfied literal (x_i if $x_i = 1$, or $\overline{x_i}$ if $x_i = 0$) and include it in S. Then S has size k, and it's an independent set because:

$$\varphi = (\overline{x_1} \vee \overline{x_2} \vee \overline{x_3}) \wedge (x_1 \vee x_2 \vee \overline{x_3}) \wedge (\overline{x_2} \vee x_3 \vee x_4) \wedge (x_2 \vee \overline{x_3} \vee x_4)$$

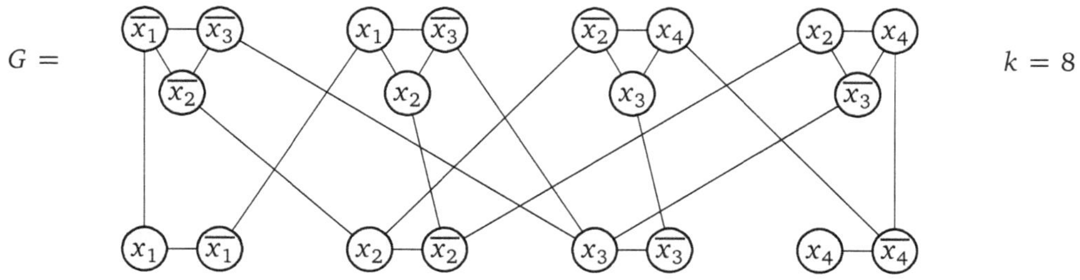

Figure 2.14: Example of reducing 3-SAT to INDEPENDENT SET in linear time

- An edge in a clause gadget or variable gadget can't have both endpoints in S, since S only contains one node per gadget.
- A clause-to-variable edge can't have both endpoints in S, since each node in S represents a satisfied literal, and x_i and $\overline{x_i}$ can't be simultaneously satisfied by an assignment.

$\Leftarrow$: Assume G has an independent set S of size $\geq k$.

- The clause gadget and variable gadget edges ensure S contains at most one node from any gadget. By the pigeonhole principle, S has exactly one node from each of the k gadgets.
- The clause-to-variable edges ensure that if S has the x_i variable gadget node then S has no $\overline{x_i}$ nodes, and if S has the $\overline{x_i}$ variable gadget node then S has no x_i nodes.

For each x_i, assign $x_i = 1$ if S has the x_i variable gadget node, and assign $x_i = 0$ if S has the $\overline{x_i}$ variable gadget node. This assignment satisfies φ since every clause in φ has a literal represented by a node in S, and every node in S represents a satisfied literal. Thus φ is satisfiable. ■

2.5 Long Paths

Theorem 2.22. DIRECTED FULL PATH *is* NP-*complete.*

Before proving this, we use it to deduce that some related problems are also NP-complete.

2.5.1 Related Problems

A *full cycle* visits every node in a graph. By definition, a cycle doesn't revisit nodes, so a full cycle visits each of the n nodes exactly once, using n edges.

DIRECTED FULL CYCLE	(2.27)
Input: Directed graph G	
Output: Does there exist a cycle that visits every node in G?	

Corollary 2.23. DIRECTED FULL CYCLE *is* NP-*complete.*

Proof idea. One idea is to reduce DIRECTED FULL PATH to DIRECTED FULL CYCLE by inserting an edge from t to s. If the original graph G has a full path from s to t, then the new graph G'

Figure 2.15: Counterexample for reducing DIRECTED FULL PATH to DIRECTED FULL CYCLE

has a full cycle, namely (t,s) plus the full path. But the converse doesn't always hold: If G' has a full cycle, then G might not have a full path from s to t (as the counterexample in Figure 2.15 shows), since G' might not have a full cycle using the new edge (t,s) as we intended. If it did, we could remove that edge to get a full path from s to t. To force every full cycle to use (t,s), we can either split this edge into two edges with a new node in the middle (which must be visited), or remove all other edges into s, or remove all other edges out of t. Let's do the first option. ∎

Proof. DIRECTED FULL CYCLE $\in$ NP by a verifier that checks that the purported witness is a full cycle in G. Since DIRECTED FULL PATH is NP-complete, it suffices to show DIRECTED FULL PATH $\le_p^m$ DIRECTED FULL CYCLE. Map (G,s,t) to a graph G' that contains G and edges (t,u), (u,s) where u is a new node. This reduction takes poly time. To show that it's correct, we argue that G has a full path from s to t iff G' has a full cycle:

$\Rightarrow$: Adding (t,u), (u,s) to a full path from s to t in G yields a full cycle in G'.

$\Leftarrow$: A full cycle in G' visits u, and the only way to do that is with the edges (t,u), (u,s). Removing those edges yields a full path from s to t in G. ∎

UNDIRECTED FULL PATH	(2.28)
Input: Undirected graph G, distinct nodes s and t	
Output: Does there exist a path from s to t that visits every node in G?	

Corollary 2.24. UNDIRECTED FULL PATH *is* NP-*complete.*

Proof idea. If we just erase the directions of edges, then a full path in the resulting undirected graph might use edges in the "wrong" directions. We create some new nodes, so that the requirement to visit these new nodes forces a full path to use edges in the "right" directions. For example, if a path enters and leaves a node along undirected edges that were both originally incoming edges, then it will miss its only chance to visit one of the new nodes. ∎

Proof. UNDIRECTED FULL PATH $\in$ NP by a verifier that checks that the purported witness is a full path from s to t in G. Since DIRECTED FULL PATH is NP-complete, it suffices to show DIRECTED FULL PATH $\le_p^m$ UNDIRECTED FULL PATH. Map (G,s,t) (where G is directed) to (G',s',t') (where G' is undirected) as follows (Figure 2.16). Each node v in G becomes a gadget in G' with three nodes v_{in}, v_{mid}, v_{out} and two edges $\{v_{\text{in}}, v_{\text{mid}}\}$, $\{v_{\text{mid}}, v_{\text{out}}\}$. Each edge (u,w) in G becomes the edge $\{u_{\text{out}}, w_{\text{in}}\}$ in G'. Let $s' = s_{\text{in}}$ and $t' = t_{\text{out}}$. This reduction takes poly time. To show that it's correct, we argue that G has a full path from s to t iff G' has a full path from s' to t':

$\Rightarrow$: When a full path from s to t in G visits a node v, we go through v_{in}, v_{mid}, v_{out}, in that order, in G'. This forms a full path from s' to t' in G'.

$\Leftarrow$: If a full path from s' to t' in G' has the intended form—for each v, the path visits v_{in}, v_{mid}, v_{out} consecutively, in that order—then it naturally corresponds to a full path from s to t in G.

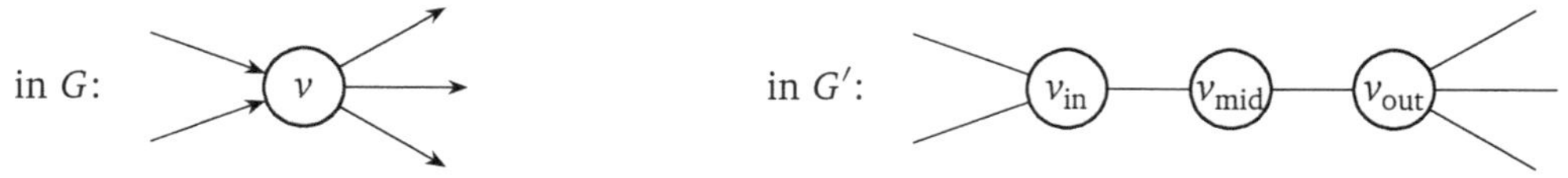

Figure 2.16: Reducing Directed Full Path to Undirected Full Path

We argue that the path must have the intended form. If the path enters v's gadget at v_{in} then it must immediately proceed to v_{mid} since otherwise when it visits v_{mid} (as it must since it's full), it would have to come from v_{out} (since it can't revisit v_{in}) and get stuck at v_{mid} (since it can't revisit v_{in} or v_{out}), so it couldn't reach t'. After v_{mid}, it must proceed to v_{out}. But what if the path enters v's gadget at v_{out}? That can't happen, because the path starts at s' and leaves s's gadget at s_{out}, from which it must enter the gadget of another node u at u_{in} and leave at u_{out}, from which it must enter some other w_{in}, and so on, all the way to t's gadget. ■

Combining these techniques shows that Undirected Full Cycle is NP-complete too.

2.5.2 Directed Full Path Is NP-Complete

Proof idea. We reduce from 3-Sat. For some nodes, the ability to visit them in different orders corresponds to the ability to assign each variable different values. For other nodes, the requirement to visit them corresponds to the requirement to satisfy each clause. For each "clause node," we create three opportunities to visit it, like the three opportunities to satisfy the clause.

Each full path from s to t corresponds to a 3-Sat witness that includes a satisfying assignment and says which literal gets satisfied in each clause, like in the proof of Theorem 2.21. ■

Proof of Theorem 2.22. We observed Directed Full Path $\in$ NP in §2.2. Since 3-Sat is NP-complete, it suffices to show 3-Sat $\leq_p^m$ Directed Full Path. Map φ to (G, s, t) as follows. Each of φ's n variables has a gadget as shown in Figure 2.17. In x_i's gadget, the vertical chain has $3k_i + 3$ nodes, where k_i is the number of clauses that contain x_i or contain $\overline{x_i}$. These gadgets are joined so x_i's gadget's left node is x_{i-1}'s gadget's right node, for $i > 1$. Each clause of φ has a gadget with one node. For each literal in the clause, this node has a pair of edges from/to a pair of consecutive nodes in the vertical chain of the corresponding variable's gadget:

- If the clause has x_i, these edges are from the upper node and to the lower node in the pair.
- If the clause has $\overline{x_i}$, these edges are from the lower node and to the upper node in the pair.

The pairs of consecutive nodes on x_i's gadget's chain (with edges to/from the clause nodes) are separated from each other and from the top and bottom nodes—there are extra chain nodes in between them. Each chain has enough nodes available for this. Finally, s is x_1's gadget's left node, and t is x_n's gadget's right node. Figure 2.20 shows an example.

This reduction takes linear time since each variable and each clause in φ corresponds to a constant number of nodes and edges in G. To show that it's correct, we argue that φ is satisfiable iff G has a full path from s to t:

$\Rightarrow$: Assume φ is satisfiable, and consider a satisfying assignment. Consider this path from s to t: For each variable x_i, if $x_i = 1$ then traverse x_i's gadget by going down the chain (Figure 2.18), and if $x_i = 0$ then traverse x_i's gadget by going up the chain (Figure 2.19). This path visits all nodes except the clause nodes. For each clause, pick one of its satisfied literals (it doesn't matter which one, if it has multiple satisfied literals) and make a detour to visit the clause node while

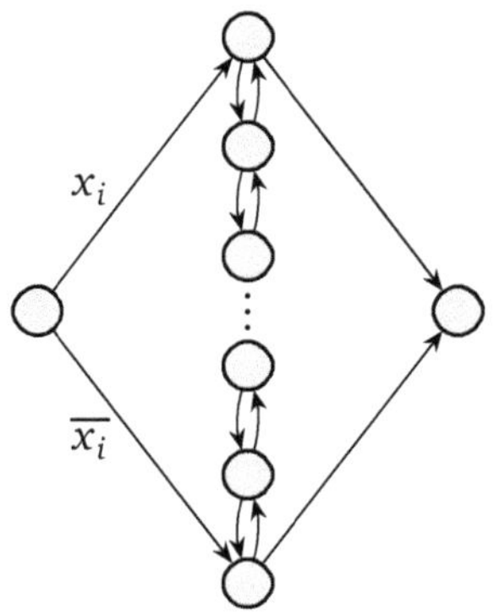

Figure 2.17: Variable gadget

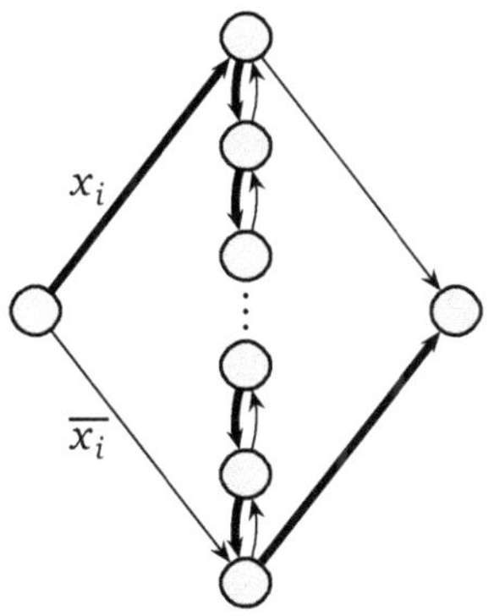

Figure 2.18: Assigning $x_i = 1$

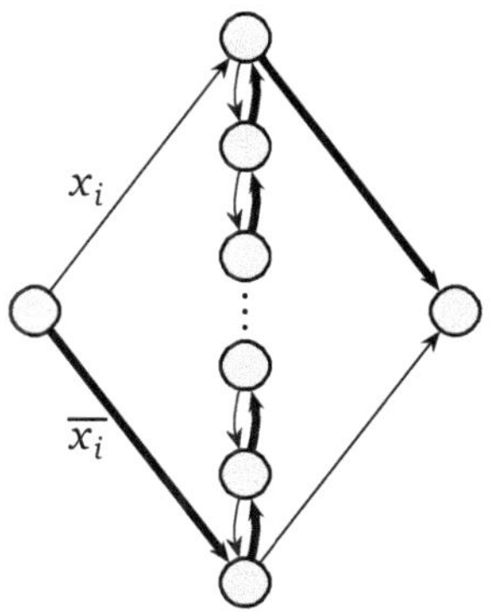

Figure 2.19: Assigning $x_i = 0$

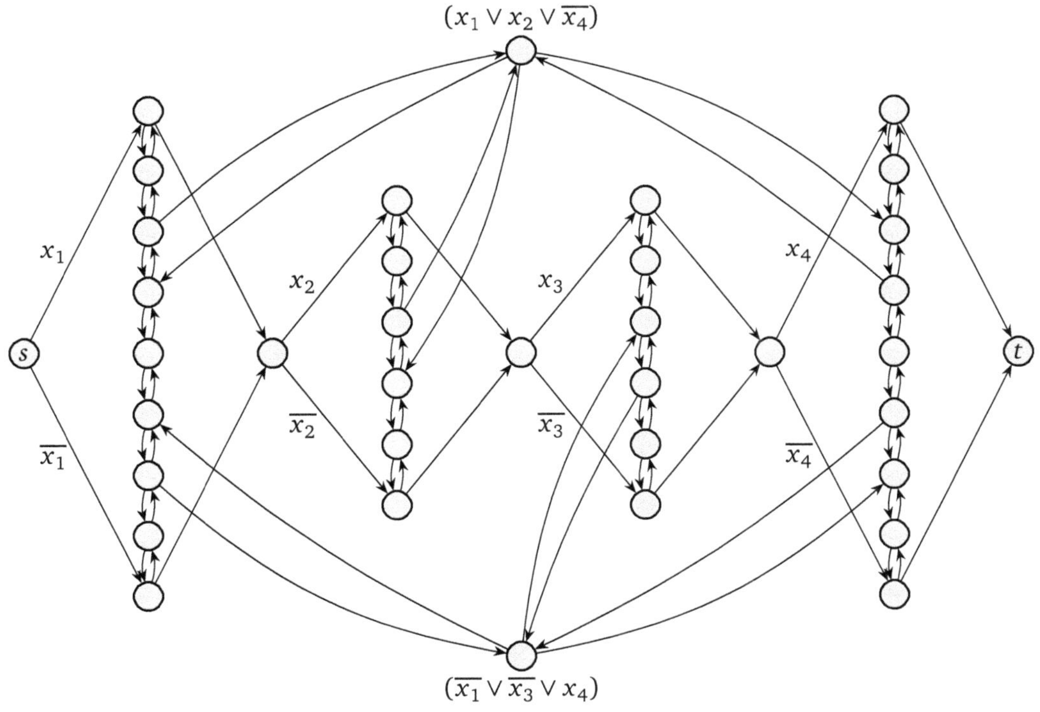

Figure 2.20: Reducing 3-SAT on input $(x_1 \vee x_2 \vee \overline{x_4}) \wedge (\overline{x_1} \vee \overline{x_3} \vee x_4)$ to DIRECTED FULL PATH

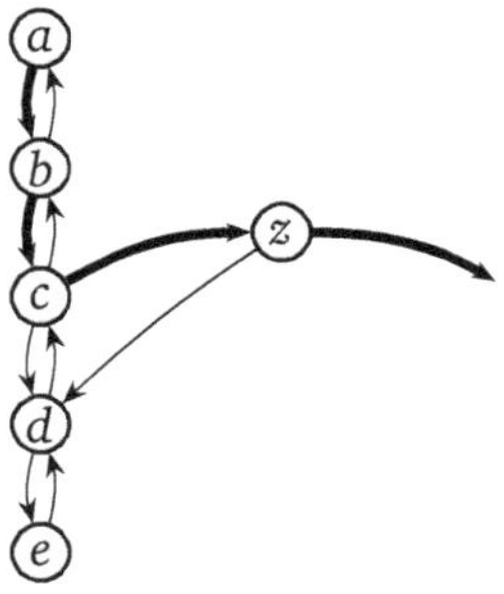

Figure 2.21: An unintended path

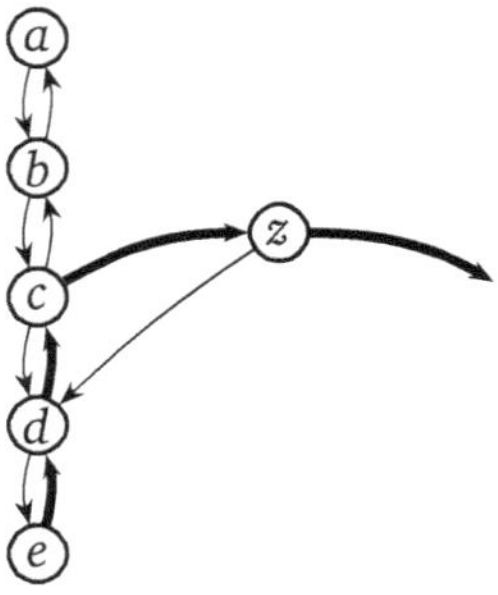

Figure 2.22: Another unintended path

traversing the chain in that variable's gadget. Since the literal is satisfied, the chain is traversed in the correct direction to do the detour and keep going in the same direction: Either $x_i = 1$ and the clause has x_i, in which case the original path and the detour both go down the chain, or $x_i = 0$ and the clause has $\overline{x_i}$, in which case the original path and the detour both go up the chain. Thus G has a full path from s to t.

$\Leftarrow$: Assume G has a full path from s to t. First, suppose this path has the intended form—at each clause node, the path goes back to the same variable gadget it just came from. Then the path corresponds to an assignment to φ's variables: x_i's gadget's chain is traversed either down all the way (assign $x_i = 1$) or up all the way (assign $x_i = 0$). This assignment satisfies φ since the detour that visits any clause node must come from a variable's chain being traversed in the direction that satisfies that literal in the clause. Thus φ is satisfiable.

We argue that the path must have the intended form. Suppose for contradiction that at some clause node, the path goes to a different variable gadget than it just came from. This could happen in two ways:

- Figure 2.21: Such a path must enter d from e, since d's only other incoming edges are from c and z but the path goes elsewhere from c and z. The path gets stuck at d since d's only outgoing edges are to c and e, which are already visited.
- Figure 2.22: Such a path must enter b from a, since b's only other incoming edge is from c but the path goes elsewhere from c. The path gets stuck at b since b's only outgoing edges are to a and c, which are already visited. (This is why b must be a separator node.)

These figures assume the path enters the clause node from a gadget corresponding to a positive literal, but the same reasoning works for negative literals. ■

2.6 Graph Colorings

Theorem 2.25. GRAPH 3-COLORING *is* NP-*complete.*

Before proving this, we use it to deduce that some related problems are also NP-complete.

2.6.1 Related Problems

Corollary 2.26. *For every* $k \geq 3$, GRAPH k-COLORING *is* NP-*complete.*

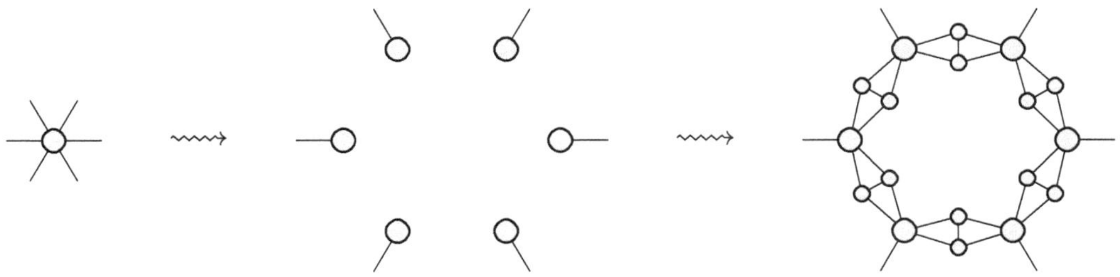

Figure 2.23: Reducing GRAPH 3-COLORING to DEGREE-5 3-COLORING

Proof. We argue that for every $k \geq 3$, GRAPH k-COLORING $\leq_p^m$ GRAPH $(k+1)$-COLORING. Since GRAPH 3-COLORING is NP-complete, this implies that GRAPH 4-COLORING is NP-complete, which implies that GRAPH 5-COLORING is NP-complete, and so on.

Map G to a graph G' that contains G and a new node u that has edges to all nodes of G. This reduction takes poly time. To show that it's correct, we argue that G has a proper k-coloring iff G' has a proper $(k+1)$-coloring:

$\Rightarrow$: Extending a proper k-coloring of G by assigning color $k+1$ to u yields a proper $(k+1)$-coloring of G': Each edge of G is still multicolored, and each edge $\{u, v\}$ is multicolored since u has color $k+1$ and v doesn't.

$\Leftarrow$: In a proper $(k+1)$-coloring of G', we may assume u has color $k+1$ since colors are interchangeable. Ignoring u, this yields a proper k-coloring of G: Each edge of G is still multicolored, and each node v of G has one of the first k colors since the edge $\{u, v\}$ is multicolored in G'. ■

A node's *degree* is the number of edges touching the node.

DEGREE-d k-COLORING	(2.29)
Input: Undirected graph G where every node has degree $\leq d$	
Output: Does there exist a proper k-coloring of G?	

DEGREE-3 3-COLORING $\in$ P and DEGREE-4 3-COLORING is NP-complete, but those theorems are somewhat difficult to prove. We just prove this:

Corollary 2.27. DEGREE-5 3-COLORING *is* NP-*complete.*

Proof. DEGREE-5 3-COLORING $\in$ NP since GRAPH 3-COLORING $\in$ NP. Since GRAPH 3-COLORING is NP-complete, it suffices to show GRAPH 3-COLORING $\leq_p^m$ DEGREE-5 3-COLORING. Map G to G' as follows. First, split each node of degree $e > 5$ into e many nodes of degree 1 (one node per incident edge). Then, join these "external" nodes into a circular gadget with $2e$ "internal" nodes as illustrated in Figure 2.23 (which shows $e = 6$ and smaller internal nodes). The resulting graph G' is a valid input to DEGREE-5 3-COLORING since each external node has degree 5, each internal node has degree 3, and each unmodified node from G still has degree ≤ 5. This reduction takes poly time since G' is only a constant factor larger than G. To show that it's correct, we argue that G has a proper 3-coloring iff G' has a proper 3-coloring:

$\Rightarrow$: We can turn a proper 3-coloring of G into a proper 3-coloring of G': Each unmodified node retains its color. For each other node v of G, assign the external nodes in v's gadget the same color as v, and use the other two colors to properly color the internal nodes in v's gadget.

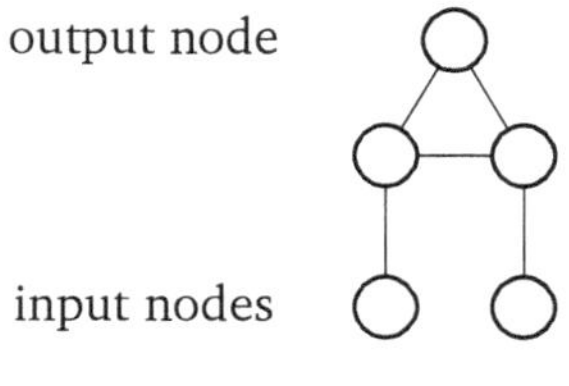

Figure 2.24: 2-bit $\vee$ gadget

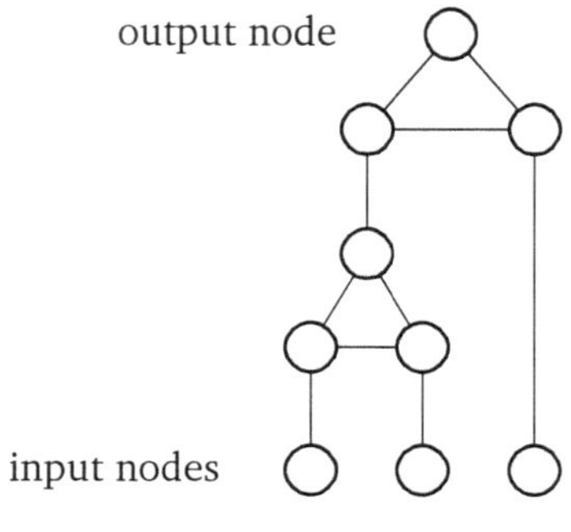

Figure 2.25: 3-bit $\vee$ gadget

$\Leftarrow$: Assume G' has a proper 3-coloring. All external nodes in a gadget must have the same color as each other: If an external node is red, then going around the circle, the next internal nodes must be green and blue (since they're adjacent to a red node and to each other), which forces the next external node to be red (since it's adjacent to both those internal nodes), and so on.

To turn this into a proper 3-coloring of G: Each unmodified node retains its color. Assign each other node v of G the same color as its gadget's external nodes. Each edge in G is multicolored since its endpoints have the same colors as the corresponding edge's endpoints in G'. ■

2.6.2 Graph 3-Coloring Is NP-Complete

Proof idea. We reduce from 3-Sat. Colors are interchangeable, but bits aren't interchangeable in assignments to a CNF's variables. To let proper 3-colorings correspond to satisfying assignments, we break the symmetry among colors: We include a designated "reference edge" in the graph and declare that this edge's endpoints have particular colors, which is OK by the interchangeability of colors. For any other node, different colors have different meanings based on the node's relationship to the reference edge. We turn a 3-CNF into a graph like in the proof of Theorem 2.21, but now our clause gadget is more complicated than just a triangle. ■

Proof of Theorem 2.25. We observed Graph 3-Coloring $\in$ NP in § 2.2. Since 3-Sat is NP-complete, it suffices to show 3-Sat $\leq_p^m$ Graph 3-Coloring.

First, we design a clause gadget. Assume the colors are $\{0, 1, 2\}$ where $0, 1$ are bits and 2 is a "neutral" color. In the 2-bit $\vee$ gadget of Figure 2.24:

(i) For every proper 3-coloring, if the input nodes are colored $0, 0$ then the output node must be colored 0 (since the middle nodes must be colored $1, 2$ or $2, 1$).

(ii) If the input nodes are colored $0, 1$ or $1, 0$ or $1, 1$ then the rest of the gadget can be properly 3-colored so the output node has color 1 (by assigning color 0 to a middle node that's adjacent to an input node colored 1, and assigning color 2 to the other middle node).

We can compute 3-bit $\vee$ by applying a 2-bit $\vee$ to two of the input bits, and applying another 2-bit $\vee$ to the third input bit and the output bit from the first 2-bit $\vee$. The gadget of Figure 2.25 thus combines two copies of the gadget from Figure 2.24 and has these properties:

(i′) For every proper 3-coloring, if the input nodes are colored $0, 0, 0$ then the output node must be colored 0.

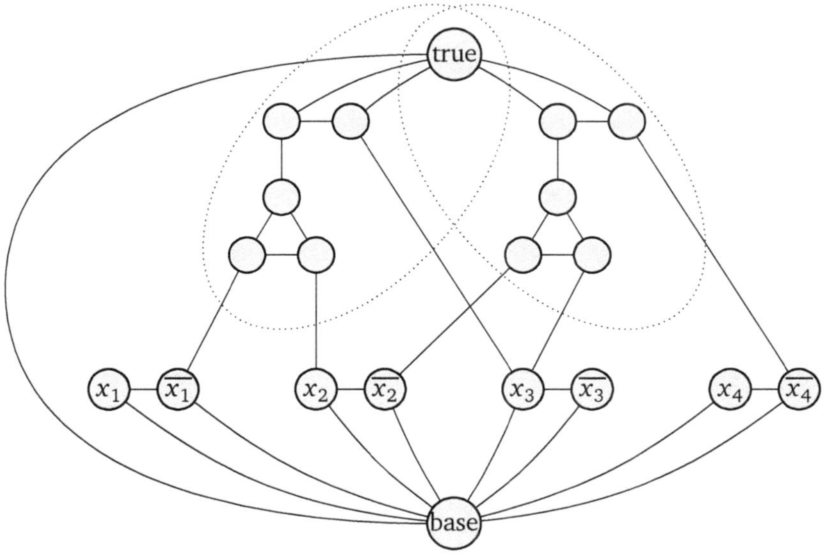

Figure 2.26: Reducing 3-SAT on input $(\overline{x_1} \vee x_2 \vee x_3) \wedge (\overline{x_2} \vee x_3 \vee \overline{x_4})$ to GRAPH 3-COLORING

(ii′) If the input nodes are colored with bits and at least one of them is 1, then the rest of the gadget can be properly 3-colored so the output node has color 1.

For the reduction, map φ to a graph G as follows. There are two distinguished nodes "base" and "true" with an edge between them (the "reference edge"). Each variable x_i of φ has a gadget with two nodes labeled x_i and $\overline{x_i}$ forming a triangle with "base". Each clause of φ has a copy of the 3-bit $\vee$ gadget from Figure 2.25, where the input nodes are the variable gadget nodes labeled by the clause's literals, and the output node is "true" (so all clause gadgets share their output node). Figure 2.26 shows an example.

This reduction takes linear time since each variable and each clause in φ corresponds to a constant number of nodes and edges in G. To show that it's correct, we argue that φ is satisfiable iff G has a proper 3-coloring:

$\Rightarrow$: Assume φ is satisfiable, and consider a satisfying assignment. Let "base" have color 2 and "true" have color 1. Color the variable gadget nodes according to the satisfying assignment: Node x_i's color is variable x_i's value, and node $\overline{x_i}$'s color is the opposite bit. Since each clause is satisfied, each clause gadget has at least one 1 among its input nodes and hence can be properly 3-colored with "true" having color 1, by *(ii′)*. Thus G has a proper 3-coloring.

$\Leftarrow$: Assume G has a proper 3-coloring. Since colors are interchangeable, we may assume "base" has color 2 and "true" has color 1. For each variable x_i, the nodes $x_i, \overline{x_i}$ must be colored $0, 1$ or $1, 0$ since they're adjacent to each other and to "base". Assign each variable x_i the same bit as node x_i's color, and note that the literal $\overline{x_i}$ is the same bit as node $\overline{x_i}$'s color. For each clause gadget, the output node is colored 1, so at least one of its input nodes must be colored 1, by the contrapositive of *(i′)*. Each clause is therefore satisfied by this assignment to φ's variables. Thus φ is satisfiable. ∎

2.7 Subset Sums

Theorem 2.28. Subset Sum *is* NP*-complete.*

Before proving this, we use it to deduce that some related problems are also NP-complete.

2.7.1 Related Problems

Subset Sum to Zero	(2.30)
Input:	Integers $x_1, x_2, \dots, x_n$ represented in binary with m bits each
Output:	Does there exist a nonempty set $I \subseteq [n]$ such that $\sum_{i \in I} x_i = 0$?

The input numbers could be negative. One of the m bits in a number is its sign. The set I must be nonempty because otherwise the answer would always be "yes" since $\sum_{i \in \emptyset} x_i = 0$.

For convenience, we introduce the shorthand notation $x_I = \sum_{i \in I} x_i$.

Corollary 2.29. Subset Sum to Zero *is* NP*-complete.*

Proof. Subset Sum to Zero $\in$ NP by a verifier that checks that the purported witness is an $I \neq \emptyset$ such that $x_I = 0$, using an Iterated Addition algorithm to check that the sum of all positive x_i with $i \in I$ equals the sum of all negative x_i with $i \in I$. Since Subset Sum is NP-complete, it suffices to show Subset Sum $\leq_p^m$ Subset Sum to Zero. Map $(x_1, \dots, x_n, t)$ to $(x_1, \dots, x_n, x_{n+1})$ where $x_{n+1} = -t$. This reduction takes poly time. To show that it's correct, we argue that there exists an $I \subseteq [n]$ such that $x_I = t$ iff there exists a nonempty $I' \subseteq [n+1]$ such that $x_{I'} = 0$:

$\Rightarrow$: Assume $x_I = t$. Letting $I' = I \cup \{n+1\}$, we have $I' \neq \emptyset$ and $x_{I'} = x_I - t = 0$.

$\Leftarrow$: Assume $I' \neq \emptyset$ and $x_{I'} = 0$. We must have $n+1 \in I'$, because $x_1, \dots, x_n$ are positive and thus no nonempty subset of them sums to 0. Letting $I = I' \setminus \{n+1\}$, we have $x_I = x_{I'} - (-t) = t$. ■

The next problem is a simple form of load balancing: Can we distribute n jobs of varying lengths between two machines so the load is perfectly balanced?

Balanced Partition	(2.31)
Input:	Positive integers $x_1, x_2, \dots, x_n$ represented in binary with m bits each
Output:	Does there exist a set $I \subseteq [n]$ such that $\sum_{i \in I} x_i = \sum_{i \notin I} x_i$?

Corollary 2.30. Balanced Partition *is* NP*-complete.*

Proof idea. Balanced Partition is the special case of Subset Sum where the sum of all x_i is exactly twice the target t. If the total sum is less than $2t$ in Subset Sum, we create a new number x_{n+1} to bring the total sum up to $2t$. If the total sum is greater than $2t$, we can't bring it down to $2t$, but we increase t and observe that hitting a small target is the same as the complement set hitting a large target. ■

Proof. Balanced Partition $\in$ NP by a verifier that checks that the purported witness is an I such that $x_I = x_{[n] \setminus I}$, using an Iterated Addition algorithm. Since Subset Sum is NP-complete, it suffices to show Subset Sum $\leq_p^m$ Balanced Partition. On input $(x_1, \dots, x_n, t)$:

- If $x_{[n]} = 2t$ then map to $(x_1, \ldots, x_n)$. This is correct because for all $I \subseteq [n]$, we have $x_I = t$ iff $x_I = x_{[n] \setminus I}$.
- If $x_{[n]} < 2t$ then map to $(x_1, \ldots, x_n, x_{n+1})$ where $x_{n+1} = 2t - x_{[n]}$. Observe that $x_{[n+1]} = x_{[n]} + x_{n+1} = 2t$ and thus for all $I' \subseteq [n+1]$, we have $x_{I'} = x_{[n+1] \setminus I'}$ iff $x_{I'} = t$. To show the reduction is correct, we argue that there exists $I \subseteq [n]$ such that $x_I = t$ iff there exists $I' \subseteq [n+1]$ such that $x_{I'} = t$:

  $\Rightarrow$: Assume $x_I = t$. Letting $I' = I$, we have $x_{I'} = t$.

  $\Leftarrow$: Assume $x_{I'} = t$. Then $x_{[n+1] \setminus I'} = t$ as well, so letting I be either I' or $[n+1] \setminus I'$ (whichever doesn't contain $n+1$), we have $I \subseteq [n]$ and $x_I = t$.
- If $x_{[n]} > 2t$ then we first change the input to $(x_1, \ldots, x_n, t')$ where $t' = x_{[n]} - t$. This doesn't change the SUBSET SUM answer, because for all $I \subseteq [n]$, we have $x_I = t$ iff $x_{[n] \setminus I} = t'$. Now since $x_{[n]} < 2t'$, we apply the mapping from the previous bullet.

In all cases, the reduction takes poly time. ■

2.7.2 SUBSET SUM Is NP-Complete

Proof idea. We reduce from 3-SAT. Selecting which numbers to sum is analogous to selecting an assignment to the 3-CNF's variables. For each bit position of the numbers, the requirement to hit the target number is analogous to the requirement to satisfy a clause. We should be mindful of carries—the sum in a bit position might affect more significant bit positions if there's a carry. Also, satisfying *at least* one literal per clause doesn't quite align with the goal of summing *exactly* to the target. To fix this, we put two extra "fake literals" in each clause, which can "mop up" so there are exactly three satisfied literals per clause. ■

Proof of Theorem 2.28. We observed SUBSET SUM $\in$ NP in §2.2. Since 3-SAT is NP-complete, it suffices to show 3-SAT $\leq_p^m$ SUBSET SUM. Let $x_1, \ldots, x_n$ denote the variables of φ, not the input numbers of SUBSET SUM, and let k be the number of clauses. Map φ to an input to SUBSET SUM as follows. Each number is $n + 2k$ bits long. Associate the n least significant bit positions with φ's variables. Group the other $2k$ bit positions into k adjacent pairs associated with φ's clauses. (We use pairs since the number of literals per clause is three, which in binary is two bits.)

For each variable x_i, create two numbers a_i, b_i. Selecting a_i corresponds to assigning $x_i = 1$, and selecting b_i corresponds to assigning $x_i = 0$. To enforce that exactly one of a_i, b_i is selected, put 1 in x_i's associated bit position for each of a_i, b_i, t.

For each clause, put 01 in its associated bit positions for each of the three numbers corresponding to the clause's literals: a_i if it contains x_i, or b_i if it contains $\overline{x_i}$. Thus, if we sum a selection of $a_1, b_1, \ldots, a_n, b_n$ corresponding to an assignment, then this pair of bits in the sum will say how many satisfied literals the clause has. To enforce that one, two, or three literals are satisfied, put 11 (representing three) for these bits of t, and create two numbers c_j, d_j (for the jth clause) both having 01 for these bits. The purpose of c_j, d_j is to "mop up" and hit the target if the clause has only one or two satisfied literals.

In summary, map φ to $(a_1, b_1, \ldots, a_n, b_n, c_1, d_1, \ldots, c_k, d_k, t)$ where:

- a_i has 1 in the x_i position and 01 in the positions of each clause containing x_i.
- b_i has 1 in the x_i position and 01 in the positions of each clause containing $\overline{x_i}$.
- c_j and d_j both have 01 in the jth clause's positions.
- t is all 1s.

$a_1 =$	0	0	0	0	0	0	0	1	x_1
$b_1 =$	0	0	0	1	0	0	0	1	$\overline{x_1}$
$a_2 =$	0	0	0	1	0	0	1	0	x_2
$b_2 =$	0	1	0	0	0	0	1	0	$\overline{x_2}$
$a_3 =$	0	1	0	1	0	1	0	0	x_3
$b_3 =$	0	0	0	0	0	1	0	0	$\overline{x_3}$
$a_4 =$	0	0	0	0	1	0	0	0	x_4
$b_4 =$	0	1	0	0	1	0	0	0	$\overline{x_4}$
$c_1 =$	0	0	0	1	0	0	0	0	$(\overline{x_1} \vee x_2 \vee x_3)$ mop up
$d_1 =$	0	0	0	1	0	0	0	0	
$c_2 =$	0	1	0	0	0	0	0	0	$(\overline{x_2} \vee x_3 \vee \overline{x_4})$ mop up
$d_2 =$	0	1	0	0	0	0	0	0	
$t =$	1	1	1	1	1	1	1	1	

Figure 2.27: Reducing 3-SAT on input $(\overline{x_1} \vee x_2 \vee x_3) \wedge (\overline{x_2} \vee x_3 \vee \overline{x_4})$ to SUBSET SUM

Figure 2.27 shows an example. This reduction takes poly time since the total number of bits is $(n+2k) \cdot (2n+2k+1)$, which is quadratic in the size of φ. To show that it's correct, we argue that φ is satisfiable iff some selection of $a_1, b_1, \ldots, a_n, b_n, c_1, d_1, \ldots, c_k, d_k$ sums to t:

$\Rightarrow$: Assume φ is satisfiable, and consider a satisfying assignment. For each variable x_i, select a_i if $x_i = 1$, or select b_i if $x_i = 0$. For the jth clause, select both, one, or neither of c_j, d_j depending on whether the clause has one, two, or three satisfied literals, respectively. The selected numbers sum to t: In the x_i position, the selected numbers have one 1 (from a_i or b_i) and the rest are 0, so they sum to 1 with no carry out. For the jth clause's positions, the selected numbers have three 01s (from one, two, or three literals and two, one, or zero of c_j, d_j) and the rest are 00, so they sum to 11 with no carry out.

$\Leftarrow$: Assume there exists a selection that sums to t. Since t has a 1 in the x_1 position, exactly one of a_1, b_1 must be selected, with no carry out. Repeating this reasoning shows that for each variable x_i, exactly one of a_i, b_i must be selected. Assign $x_i = 1$ if a_i is selected, or $x_i = 0$ if b_i is selected. This assignment satisfies φ: The 1st clause's positions have 11 in t and five 01s in all the other numbers, so exactly three of these numbers with 01 must be selected, summing to 11 with no carry out. Since at most two of these can be c_1, d_1, at least one selected number must correspond to a literal that satisfies the 1st clause. Repeating this reasoning shows that each clause is satisfied. Thus φ is satisfiable. ■

2.8 Satisfying Assignments

Figure 2.28 shows the tree of NP-completeness reductions we've designed. We now lay the foundation by proving that SAT is NP-complete (Theorem 2.10).

2.8.1 Expressiveness of CNFs

First, we describe primitives for designing CNFs to represent computations.

Let $p = p_{W-1} \cdots p_0$ be a word of W many variables. We index variables this way (as opposed to $p_1 \cdots p_W$) to view them as bit positions of a binary number when we want to. Let $a =$

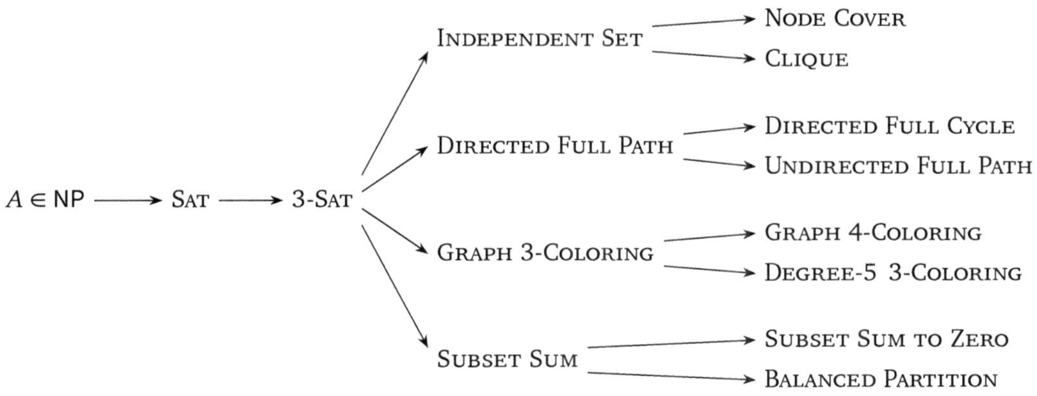

Figure 2.28: Tree of reductions, where $\longrightarrow$ represents $\leq_p^m$

$a_{W-1} \cdots a_0 \in \{0,1\}^W$ be an assignment. We write "$p_i = a_i$" to mean the literal p_i if $a_i = 1$, or the literal $\overline{p_i}$ if $a_i = 0$. We write "$p_i \neq a_i$" for the opposite literal.

- "$p = a$" denotes $(p_{W-1} = a_{W-1}) \wedge \cdots \wedge (p_0 = a_0)$, which evaluates to 1 iff p is assigned a. This is a 1-CNF with W clauses.
- "$p \neq a$" denotes $(p_{W-1} \neq a_{W-1} \vee \cdots \vee p_0 \neq a_0)$, which evaluates to 1 iff p is not assigned a. This is a W-CNF with 1 clause.

Example. "$p = 101$" means $(p_2) \wedge (\overline{p_1}) \wedge (p_0)$, and "$p \neq 101$" means $(\overline{p_2} \vee p_1 \vee \overline{p_0})$. ♦

Let $q = q_{W-1} \cdots q_0$ be another word of variables. We write "$p_i = q_i$" to mean the pair of clauses $(p_i \vee \overline{q_i}) \wedge (\overline{p_i} \vee q_i)$, which is equivalent to $p_i \Leftrightarrow q_i$.

- "$p = q$" denotes $(p_{W-1} = q_{W-1}) \wedge \cdots \wedge (p_0 = q_0)$, which evaluates to 1 iff the assignment to p equals the assignment to q. This is a 2-CNF with $2W$ clauses.

Expressing "$p \neq q$" with a CNF requires 2^W clauses (Exercise 2.33).

We can also represent conditionals with CNFs. Suppose a is an assignment to p, and φ and ψ are CNFs that don't involve the p variables.

- "if $p = a$ then φ" is equivalent to "$p \neq a$ or φ". To express this, we insert the literals $p_{W-1} \neq a_{W-1} \vee \cdots \vee p_0 \neq a_0$ into each clause of φ. This new CNF has the same number of clauses as φ, and each clause's width is increased by W.
- "if $p \neq a$ then ψ" is equivalent to "$p = a$ or ψ". To express this, we take W copies of ψ and insert the literal $p_i = a_i$ into each clause of the ith copy. This new CNF has W times as many clauses as ψ, and each clause's width is increased by 1 in each copy.
- "if $p = a$ then φ else ψ" is equivalent to "(if $p = a$ then φ) and (if $p \neq a$ then ψ)".

A handy case is "if $u = a$ then $p = q$ else $p = r$" with four words of variables p, q, r, u. Our recipe expresses this as a CNF with $2W$ clauses of width $W + 2$ and $2W^2$ clauses of width 3.

Example. To express "if $u = 01$ then $p = q$ else $p = r$" (where $W = 2$ and $a_1 a_0 = 01$):

$$\overbrace{(u_1 \vee \overline{u_0} \vee p_1 \vee \overline{q_1}) \wedge (u_1 \vee \overline{u_0} \vee \overline{p_1} \vee q_1) \wedge (u_1 \vee \overline{u_0} \vee p_0 \vee \overline{q_0}) \wedge (u_1 \vee \overline{u_0} \vee \overline{p_0} \vee q_0)}^{\text{“if } u = 01 \text{ then } p = q\text{”}}$$
$$\left.\begin{aligned} &\wedge (\overline{u_1} \vee p_1 \vee \overline{r_1}) \wedge (\overline{u_1} \vee \overline{p_1} \vee r_1) \wedge (\overline{u_1} \vee p_0 \vee \overline{r_0}) \wedge (\overline{u_1} \vee \overline{p_0} \vee r_0) \\ &\wedge (u_0 \vee p_1 \vee \overline{r_1}) \wedge (u_0 \vee \overline{p_1} \vee r_1) \wedge (u_0 \vee p_0 \vee \overline{r_0}) \wedge (u_0 \vee \overline{p_0} \vee r_0) \end{aligned}\right\} \text{“if } u \neq 01 \text{ then } p = r\text{”}$$ ♦

We can also express nested conditionals. Suppose b is an assignment to another word of variables v. To express "if $v = b$ then: if $u = a$ then $p = q$ else $p = r$" (where the dangling "else" goes with the inner "if"), we just insert the literals for "$v \neq b$" into each clause of "if $u = a$ then $p = q$ else $p = r$". This is the mechanism for representing "store" instructions.

To express "$p \leq a$" for a binary number $a \in \{0,1\}^W$: For every index i such that $a_i = 0$, include the clause "$(p_{W-1} \cdots p_i) \neq (a_{W-1} \cdots a_{i+1} 1)$".

Example. With $W = 6$, "$p \leq 010010$" means:

$$(p_5 \neq 1) \wedge (p_5 p_4 p_3 \neq 011) \wedge (p_5 p_4 p_3 p_2 \neq 0101) \wedge (p_5 p_4 p_3 p_2 p_1 p_0 \neq 010011)$$ ♦

To express other things, we can use Lemma 2.9, which says every function on n variables has a CNF with $\leq 2^n$ clauses: "$p \leq q$", "$p = q + r$", and so forth denote CNFs that evaluate to 1 iff the predicate inside the quotes is true (where $+, -, \cdot$ are done mod 2^W). Some of these only need poly W many clauses, while others need $2^{O(W)}$ clauses, which is still good enough for NP-completeness of SAT.

2.8.2 SAT Is NP-Complete

Proof idea. For every $A \in$ NP, we turn a poly-time verifier V into a poly-time mapping reduction to SAT, which maps x to a CNF ψ:

- Verifier: $A(x) = 1$ iff some witness makes V accept.
- Reduction: $A(x) = 1$ iff some assignment satisfies ψ.

For wishful thinking, suppose V itself is a CNF φ (depending on x's size), so $V(x; w)$ accepts iff $\varphi(x, w) = 1$. We could plug any input into the x variables and contract φ (§2.3.5) to get a CNF ψ such that $\psi(w) = \varphi(x, w)$. This would be a correct reduction to SAT:

$$A(x) = 1 \iff \big(\exists w : V(x; w) \text{ accepts}\big) \iff \big(\exists w : \varphi(x, w) = 1\big) \iff \psi \text{ is satisfiable}$$

Lemma 2.9 expresses V as an exponentially large CNF. Not every poly-time computation can be expressed as a poly-size CNF. To salvage this proof, we turn any poly-time verifier into a poly-size CNF verifier for the same problem A but with different witnesses.

Let's step into the verifier's shoes. The mysterious stranger is eager to convince us $A(x) = 1$. We have a plan for how to check whatever witness he shows us, but we're too lazy to run this poly-time verification algorithm ourselves. How can the stranger make our job even easier? By doing our job for us! For the new witness, we want to see the original witness and full details of how the original verification computation would transpire: For every time step and every memory location, what word would be there? We assess this *transcript* using "local consistency checks." For example, if a step executes "let Reg[i] ← Reg[j]", we make sure the stranger doesn't sneak some other value into Reg[i]. Each check is a small CNF.

Upshot: Checking that a computation was done correctly (given the transcript) is simpler than doing the computation. If the latter is fast, then the former only needs a small CNF. ■

Space

Time	PC	Reg[0]	Reg[1]	$\cdots$	Reg[$R-1$]	Mem[0]	Mem[1]	$\cdots$	Mem[$M-1$]
0	$0\cdot\cdot0$	N	$0\cdots0$	$\cdots$	$0\cdots0$	$0\cdots0$	$0\cdots0$	$\cdots$	$0\cdots0$
1				$\cdots$				$\cdots$	
2				$\cdots$				$\cdots$	
$\vdots$	$\vdots$	$\vdots$	$\vdots$		$\vdots$	$\vdots$	$\vdots$		$\vdots$
$T-1$				$\cdots$				$\cdots$	
T				$\cdots$				$\cdots$	

Figure 2.29: Computation transcript

A *configuration* (§ 1.7.1) of a verifier is the contents of the program counter (PC), registers, and work segment. The witness segment, like the input segment, isn't in a configuration since it doesn't change during the computation.

Definition. Consider any verifier V, input x of size N, and purported witness w. Suppose $V(x;w)$ has running time $\leq T$ and never accesses any work segment address $\geq M$. The *transcript* of $V(x;w)$ (with respect to T and M) is the table with rows indexed $0,1,\ldots,T$ where row t is the configuration after step t of $V(x;w)$. If V has L lines of code, R registers, and word size W, then each row represents:

$$\big(\text{PC, Reg}[0], \ldots, \text{Reg}[R-1], \text{Mem}[0], \ldots, \text{Mem}[M-1]\big) \in \{0,1\}^{\log L} \times (\{0,1\}^W)^R \times (\{0,1\}^W)^M$$

Row 0 is the initial configuration, with N in Reg[0] and all-0 words everywhere else. Once the computation reaches an accept or reject configuration, it freezes: All subsequent rows (down through row T) have that same configuration. See Figure 2.29. ◀

Proof of Theorem 2.10. We observed SAT $\in$ NP in § 2.3.3. Suppose $A \in$ NP by a poly-time verifier V. We show $A \leq_p^m$ SAT. The reduction first ignores the input and builds a CNF φ with groups of variables for the input x, purported witness w, and transcript y, such that:

$$\varphi(x,w,y) = 1 \iff \big(y \text{ is the transcript of } V(x;w), \text{ and } y\text{'s last row is an accept configuration}\big)$$

By the "freezing" property, y's last row shows V's output even if V terminates earlier. Therefore:

$$V(x;w) \text{ accepts} \iff \big(\exists y : \varphi(x,w,y) = 1\big)$$

Then, the reduction reads the input, contracts $\varphi(x,w,y)$ with the input plugged in for x, and outputs the resulting CNF $\psi(w,y)$:

$$A(x) = 1 \iff \big(\exists w : V(x;w) \text{ accepts}\big) \iff \big(\exists w,y : \varphi(x,w,y) = 1\big) \iff \psi \text{ is satisfiable}$$

Suppose V has L lines, R registers, word size W, and time efficiency $\leq T = cN^d$ (for integers c,d), and doesn't access any work segment address $\geq M = 2^W$. Then φ has these variables:

- $x = x_0 \cdots x_{N-1}$ for the input, where each x_i is a word of W variables.
- $w = w_0 \cdots w_{T-1}$ for the purported witness, where each w_i is a word of W variables. (By the definition of time efficiency, V doesn't access any witness segment address $\geq T$.)

- $y = y_0 \cdots y_T$ for the transcript of $V(x; w)$, where each row y_t consists of $y_{t,s}$ for all $s \in \{\text{PC}, \text{Reg}[0], \ldots, \text{Reg}[R-1], \text{Mem}[0], \ldots, \text{Mem}[M-1]\}$, where $y_{t,\text{PC}}$ is $\log L$ variables and each $y_{t,\text{Reg}[i]}$ and each $y_{t,\text{Mem}[m]}$ is a word of W variables. Actually, y_0 is hardcoded with the initial configuration, with $y_{0,\text{Reg}[0]} = N$ and with 0s elsewhere.

Let $\varphi = \varphi_{\text{transcript}} \wedge \varphi_{\text{accept}}$ where $\varphi_{\text{transcript}}$ checks that y is the transcript of $V(x; w)$, and φ_{accept} checks that y's last row is an accept configuration. We may assume V has only one accept instruction, say at line ℓ_{accept} (by replacing other accept instructions with "goto line ℓ_{accept}"), so $\varphi_{\text{accept}} =$ "$y_{T,\text{PC}} = \ell_{\text{accept}}$". Let $\varphi_{\text{transcript}} = \bigwedge_{t \in \{1,\ldots,T\}} \varphi_t$ where φ_t checks that y_t is the configuration after one step from y_{t-1}. Let $\varphi_t = \bigwedge_s \varphi_{t,s}$ where $\varphi_{t,s}$ checks that $y_{t,s}$ is the word at location s after one step from y_{t-1}. Let $\varphi_{t,s} = \bigwedge_{\ell \in \{0,\ldots,L-1\}} \varphi_{t,s,\ell}$ where $\varphi_{t,s,\ell}$ checks that if $y_{t-1,\text{PC}} = \ell$ then $y_{t,s}$ is the word at location s after one step from y_{t-1} (executing line ℓ). In summary, φ is the conjunction of φ_{accept} and $\varphi_{t,s,\ell}$ over all possibilities of:

When: $t \in \{1, \ldots, T\}$
Where: $s \in \{\text{PC}, \text{Reg}[0], \ldots, \text{Reg}[R-1], \text{Mem}[0], \ldots, \text{Mem}[M-1]\}$
How: $\ell \in \{0, \ldots, L-1\}$

Most $\varphi_{t,s,\ell} =$ "if $y_{t-1,\text{PC}} = \ell$ then $y_{t,s} = y_{t-1,s}$" check that the word at location s is unchanged. If line ℓ isn't a control flow instruction, then $\varphi_{t,\text{PC},\ell} =$ "if $y_{t-1,\text{PC}} = \ell$ then $y_{t,\text{PC}} = \ell + 1$" checks that the PC is incremented. Here are the other cases, depending on the instruction at line ℓ:

- "let $\text{Reg}[i] \leftarrow \text{Reg}[j] + \text{Reg}[k]$" (or another data processing instruction):

$$\varphi_{t,\text{Reg}[i],\ell} = \text{"if } y_{t-1,\text{PC}} = \ell \text{ then } y_{t,\text{Reg}[i]} = y_{t-1,\text{Reg}[j]} + y_{t-1,\text{Reg}[k]}\text{"}$$

- "goto line h":

$$\varphi_{t,\text{PC},\ell} = \text{"if } y_{t-1,\text{PC}} = \ell \text{ then } y_{t,\text{PC}} = h\text{"}$$

- "if $\text{Reg}[i] = \text{Reg}[j]$ then goto line h" (or another comparison):

$$\begin{aligned} \varphi_{t,\text{PC},\ell} = \text{"if } y_{t-1,\text{PC}} = \ell \text{ then: if } y_{t-1,\text{Reg}[i]} = y_{t-1,\text{Reg}[j]} &\text{ then } y_{t,\text{PC}} = h \\ &\text{ else } y_{t,\text{PC}} = \ell + 1\text{"} \end{aligned}$$

- "store $\text{Mem}[\text{Reg}[j]] \leftarrow \text{Reg}[i]$": Any work segment address m might be stored to, so $\varphi_{t,\text{Mem}[m],\ell}$ checks that $\text{Mem}[m]$ gets the value of $\text{Reg}[i]$ if m is the destination address $\text{Reg}[j]$, and is otherwise unchanged:

$$\begin{aligned} \varphi_{t,\text{Mem}[m],\ell} = \text{"if } y_{t-1,\text{PC}} = \ell \text{ then: if } y_{t-1,\text{Reg}[j]} = m &\text{ then } y_{t,\text{Mem}[m]} = y_{t-1,\text{Reg}[i]} \\ &\text{ else } y_{t,\text{Mem}[m]} = y_{t-1,\text{Mem}[m]}\text{"} \end{aligned}$$

- "load $\text{Reg}[i] \leftarrow \text{Mem}[\text{Reg}[j]]$": Any work segment address m might be loaded from, so $\varphi_{t,\text{Reg}[i],\ell}$ checks, for every possible m separately, that $\text{Reg}[i]$ gets the value of $\text{Mem}[m]$ if m is the source address $\text{Reg}[j]$:

$$\begin{aligned} \varphi_{t,\text{Reg}[i],\ell} &= \textstyle\bigwedge_{m \in \{0,\ldots,M-1\}} \varphi_{t,\text{Reg}[i],\ell,m} \text{ where} \\ \varphi_{t,\text{Reg}[i],\ell,m} &= \text{"if } y_{t-1,\text{PC}} = \ell \text{ then: if } y_{t-1,\text{Reg}[j]} = m \text{ then } y_{t,\text{Reg}[i]} = y_{t-1,\text{Mem}[m]}\text{"} \end{aligned}$$

- "read" is like "load" but with $m \in \{0, \ldots, N-1\}$ and with x_m instead of $y_{t-1,\text{Mem}[m]}$. We assume V never reads past the input, since Lemma 1.3 also holds for verifiers.
- "read-witness" is like "load" but with $m \in \{0, \ldots, T-1\}$ and with w_m instead of $y_{t-1,\text{Mem}[m]}$.

If a hardcoded constant is in lieu of, say, Reg[j], then define $\varphi_{t,s,\ell}$ with fresh variables instead of $y_{t-1,\mathrm{Reg}[j]}$, and contract it with the constant plugged in.

Each $\varphi_{t,s,\ell}$ is a *component*, unless (s,ℓ) is a *retrieval*—meaning line ℓ is a load/read/read-witness and s is the destination register—in which case each $\varphi_{t,s,\ell,m}$ is a component. Each component involves $O(1)$ words, and $\varphi_{\mathrm{transcript}}$ is the conjunction of all components.

How big is φ? Each component has $O(W)$ variables and $\leq 2^{O(W)} \leq 2^{O(\log N)} = \mathrm{poly}\,N$ clauses (Lemma 2.9). The number of nonretrieval components $\varphi_{t,s,\ell}$ is $\leq T \cdot (1+R+M) \cdot L = O(T \cdot M)$ since R and L are constants. The number of retrieval components $\varphi_{t,s,\ell,m}$ is $\leq T \cdot 1 \cdot L \cdot M = O(T \cdot M)$ since they only arise for one s, namely line ℓ's destination register (and since we may assume $N \leq M$ for "read" and $T \leq M$ for "read-witness"). The total number of components is $O(T \cdot M) \leq (\mathrm{poly}\,N) \cdot 2^{O(\log N)} = \mathrm{poly}\,N$. Thus φ has $\mathrm{poly}\,N$ size, and φ's description is explicit enough for the reduction to write φ and the contraction ψ in $\mathrm{poly}\,N$ time. ■

2.8.3 Quasi-Quadratic-Time Reductions

Something is unsettling about our proof that SAT is NP-complete: The CNF's size (and the reduction's time efficiency) has an exponential dependence on the verifier's word size. For example, if the verifier runs in $O(N)$ time but uses word size $100 \log N$, the reduction produces a CNF with over $2^{100 \log N} = N^{100}$ clauses. Ideally, the reduction's time efficiency should be comparable to the verifier's, regardless of the hidden constant in $W = O(\log N)$. For concreteness, we focus on linear-time verifiers. *Quasi-linear* means $N \,\mathrm{polylog}\, N$. *Quasi-quadratic* means $N^2 \,\mathrm{polylog}\, N$.

Theorem 2.31. *For every $A \in \mathrm{NTIME}[N]$, $A \leq_p^m$ SAT via a quasi-quadratic-time reduction.*

We strengthen this from quasi-quadratic to quasi-linear in §2.8.4.

Proof idea for Theorem 2.31. In the proof that SAT is NP-complete, φ's size depended exponentially on W for two reasons:

(i) There were $O(T \cdot M)$ components, where $M = 2^W$ was the trivial bound on the number of words of the work segment.

(ii) Each component involved $O(W)$ variables but sometimes as many as 2^W clauses.

To deal with *(i)*: Theorem 1.10 brings M down to $O(T)$ with only a polylog T factor slowdown. (Theorem 1.10 is for solvers but also holds for verifiers since the witness segment is irrelevant.) With $T = O(N)$, φ now has $N^2 \,\mathrm{polylog}\, N$ components. If each component had size $\mathrm{poly}\,W = \mathrm{polylog}\, N$ instead of $2^{O(W)} = \mathrm{poly}\,N$, we'd be done.

To deal with *(ii)*: Recall that we decreased the verification complexity from "poly time" to "poly size CNF" by soliciting more help from the stranger. We further apply this idea to the components. To perform a check with only $\mathrm{poly}\,W$ size, we crawl back to the stranger for even more help. For example, checking $p \neq q$ requires size $\geq 2^W$ unaided but only $O(W)$ if the stranger shows us the bitwise-xor $p \oplus q$ as part of the witness: We check that this word indeed equals $p \oplus q$ (by checking each bit position separately) and has at least one 1. ■

With the SAT encoding from the end of §2.3.3, a CNF's size is O(sum of widths of clauses) assuming no clause is empty.

Proof of Theorem 2.31. We extend the proof of Theorem 2.10, assuming $A \in \mathrm{NTIME}[N]$. First, we modify the verifier V as in Theorem 1.10, so V uses only the first $M = O(N)$ words of the work segment and has time efficiency $\leq T = O(N \log^2 N)$. We modify φ to have size $N^2 \operatorname{polylog} N$ with auxiliary variables z in addition to x, w, y, such that:

$$V(x;w) \text{ accepts with transcript } y \iff \big(\exists z : \varphi(x,w,y,z) = 1\big)$$

Obtaining ψ as the contraction of φ with the actual input plugged in for x:

$$\begin{aligned} A(x) = 1 &\iff \big(\exists w : V(x;w) \text{ accepts}\big) \\ &\iff \big(\exists w, y : V(x;w) \text{ accepts with transcript } y\big) \\ &\iff \big(\exists w, y, z : \varphi(x,w,y,z) = 1\big) \\ &\iff \psi \text{ is satisfiable} \end{aligned}$$

The new φ will be explicit enough for the reduction to write φ and ψ in $N^2 \operatorname{polylog} N$ time.

φ is the conjunction of φ_{accept} and $O(T \cdot M) = O(N^2 \log^2 N)$ components. Many components, including all retrieval components $\varphi_{t,s,\ell,m}$, only need $O(W^3)$ size. We replace each other component $\varphi_{t,s,\ell}$ by an "equivalent" CNF $\varphi'_{t,s,\ell}$ of size $O(W^3)$, so the modified φ has size $O(N^2 \log^2 N) \cdot O(W^3) = O(N^2 \log^5 N)$. "Equivalent" means it involves auxiliary variables $z_{t,s,\ell}$ and for every assignment to $\varphi_{t,s,\ell}$'s variables, $\varphi_{t,s,\ell}$ is satisfied iff $\varphi'_{t,s,\ell}$ is satisfied for at least one assignment to $z_{t,s,\ell}$. Then z consists of all $z_{t,s,\ell}$ groups.

For each component, "if $y_{t-1,\text{PC}} = \ell$ then" only increases the size by a constant factor depending on L, so we ignore it. Many components are equality checks such as "$y_{t,s} = y_{t-1,s}$" or "$y_{t,\text{PC}} = \ell + 1$", which have size $O(W)$ (and no auxiliary variables). Each memory access component fits in the framework from §2.8.1 and has size $O(W^2)$. Now, we go through the other components. The details aren't important. Let p, q, r abbreviate the relevant groups of variables $y_{t,\text{Reg}[i]}$, $y_{t-1,\text{Reg}[j]}$, $y_{t-1,\text{Reg}[k]}$. Index a word's variables as $p = p_{W-1} \cdots p_0$.

Bitwise logic. Size $O(W)$ suffices for "$p = \neg q$", "$p = q \wedge r$", "$p = q \vee r$", and "$p = q \oplus r$": For each index i, "$p_i = \neg q_i$", "$p_i = q_i \wedge r_i$", "$p_i = q_i \vee r_i$", and "$p_i = q_i \oplus r_i$" are size-$O(1)$ CNFs.

Shifting and logarithm. These only need size $O(W^3)$ using the framework from §2.8.1. See Figure 2.30. For each $a \leq W - 1$, "$p = q \ll a$" is the equality check "$p_{W-1} \cdots p_a = q_{W-1-a} \cdots q_0$ and $p_{a-1} \cdots p_0 = 0 \cdots 0$". For "$p = q \ll r$": The contrapositive of the last "if" is "if $p \neq 0 \cdots 0$ then $r \leq W - 1$". Size $O(W^2)$ suffices for "$r \leq W - 1$", and "if $p \neq 0 \cdots 0$ then" increases the size by a factor $O(W)$, so the last line has size $O(W^3)$. Each of the other W lines has size $O(W^2)$, so the total size is $O(W^3)$. Similarly, "$p = q \gg r$" and "$p = \lfloor \log_2(q) \rfloor$" have size $O(W^3)$.

Addition and subtraction. "$p = q + r$" is a tricky size-$O(W^3)$ CNF (Exercise 2.35). It's easier if we use auxiliary variables: Imagine running the standard addition algorithm and assigning the carry bits to auxiliary variables $c = c_W \cdots c_1 = z_{t,s,\ell}$. Checking "$p = q + r$ with carries c" ($\varphi'_{t,s,\ell}$) is simpler than "$p = q + r$" ($\varphi_{t,s,\ell}$). Specifically, "$p = q + r$" holds iff there exists an assignment to c such that "$c_{i+1} p_i = c_i + q_i + r_i$" for each index $i \in \{0, \ldots, W-1\}$, where $c_{i+1} p_i$ is a 2-bit binary number and $c_0 = 0$. So $\varphi'_{t,s,\ell}$ is a conjunction of W size-$O(1)$ CNFs and thus has size $O(W)$. The overflow bit c_W gets dropped with "mod 2^W" arithmetic. We express "$p = q - r$" as "$q = p + r$".

Multiplication. For "$p = q \cdot r$", imagine running the primary-school algorithm but instead of summing the table by columns, we sum it by rows. Because of "mod 2^W" arithmetic, each row is truncated to the least significant W bits. Each bit of the table depends on one bit of q and one bit of r. For each $j \in \{0, \ldots, W-1\}$, we have a group of auxiliary variables v_j for the bits of the

"$p = q \ll r$":	"$p = \lfloor \log_2(q) \rfloor$":
if $r = 0$ then $p = q$	if $p = 0$ then $q_{W-1} \cdots q_1 = 0 \cdots 000$
if $r = 1$ then $p = q \ll 1$	if $p = 1$ then $q_{W-1} \cdots q_1 = 0 \cdots 001$
if $r = 2$ then $p = q \ll 2$	if $p = 2$ then $q_{W-1} \cdots q_2 = 0 \cdots 01$
$\vdots$	$\vdots$
if $r = W-1$ then $p = q \ll (W-1)$	if $p = W-1$ then $q_{W-1} = 1$
if $r \geq W$ then $p = 0 \cdots 0$	$p \leq W-1$

Figure 2.30: CNFs to check shifting and logarithm

truncated sum of the 0th through jth rows. Then $\varphi'_{t,s,\ell}$ checks that $v_{W-1} = p$ and $v_0 = $ (0th row) and $v_j = v_{j-1} +$ (jth row) for each $j \geq 1$ using the addition check described above. Thus, $z_{t,s,\ell}$ is all v_j groups and carry variables for each intermediate sum. The size of $\varphi'_{t,s,\ell}$ is $O(W^2)$.

Comparisons. For conditional branches, let p stand for $y_{t-1,\mathrm{Reg}[i]}$ instead of $y_{t,\mathrm{Reg}[i]}$. For each $? \in \{=, \neq, <, \leq, \geq, >\}$, let $\overline{?} \in \{=, \neq, <, \leq, \geq, >\}$ be the negated comparison. Recall:

$$\varphi_{t,\mathrm{PC},\ell} \;=\; \text{"(if } p \,?\, q \text{ then } y_{t,\mathrm{PC}} = h\text{) and (if } p \,\overline{?}\, q \text{ then } y_{t,\mathrm{PC}} = \ell + 1\text{)"}$$

These "if"s have the same form, so let's just consider the second one. The contrapositive is "if $y_{t,\mathrm{PC}} \neq \ell + 1$ then $p \,?\, q$". The "if $y_{t,\mathrm{PC}} \neq \ell + 1$ then" only increases the size by a constant factor, so we just show how to express "$p \,?\, q$" with $O(W)$ size. "$p = q$" doesn't need auxiliary variables. "$p \neq q$" can use the xor trick from the proof idea, but instead let's demonstrate a technique using our addition check: We introduce auxiliary variables r, and $\varphi'_{t,\mathrm{PC},\ell}$ checks "$p = q + r$ and $r \neq 0$" (with auxiliary carry variables). For "$p \geq q$", checking "$p = q + r$ and $r \geq 0$" doesn't make sense with "mod 2^W" arithmetic. Instead, check "$p = q + r$" with nonmodular arithmetic (checking overflow = 0). For "$p > q$", check "$p = q + r$ and $r \neq 0$" with nonmodular arithmetic. Finally, "$p \leq q$" is "$q \geq p$", and "$p < q$" is "$q > p$".

Quotient and remainder. Change the variable group abbreviations so q, r, u, v mean quotient, remainder, numerator, denominator. For "$q = \lfloor u/v \rfloor$", introduce auxiliary variables r and check "$r < v$ and $u = q \cdot v + r$" using our "less than" check and multiplication check (adapted to nonmodular arithmetic by not truncating the rows, and with r as an extra summand row). For "$r = u \bmod v$", introduce auxiliary variables q and check "$r < v$ and $u = q \cdot v + r$". Since division by 0 yields quotient 0 and remainder 0 (to avoid runtime errors), enclose these in "if $v \neq 0$ then … else $q = 0$" and "if $v \neq 0$ then … else $r = 0$". The size is $O(W^3)$. ■

2.8.4 Quasi-Linear-Time Reductions

The following result supersedes Theorem 2.31. *Quasi-linear* means N polylog N.

Theorem 2.32. *For every* $A \in \mathsf{NTIME}[N]$, $A \leq_p^m$ SAT *via a quasi-linear-time reduction.*

Corollary 2.33. *For all* $d \geq 1$, *if* SAT $\in \mathsf{TIME}[N^d]$ *then* $\mathsf{NTIME}[N] \subseteq \mathsf{TIME}[N^d \operatorname{polylog} N]$.

Proof of Corollary 2.33. Assume SAT $\in \mathsf{TIME}[N^d]$. Consider any $A \in \mathsf{NTIME}[N]$. To solve A in time N^d polylog N: Run the reduction of Theorem 2.32, which takes time N polylog N and yields a CNF of size N polylog N, then run the SAT algorithm on this CNF, which takes time $O((N \operatorname{polylog} N)^d) = N^d \operatorname{polylog} N$. ■

A practical consequence is that to solve an NP-complete problem, we could apply a very efficient reduction to SAT and hope the CNFs are handled well by industrial-strength SAT solvers.

Our reduction from SAT to 3-SAT (§2.3.4) takes linear time. Theorem 2.32 and Corollary 2.33 also hold for 3-SAT and for any NP problem with a linear-time (or quasi-linear-time) reduction from 3-SAT, such as INDEPENDENT SET, DIRECTED FULL PATH, and GRAPH 3-COLORING.

Proof idea for Theorem 2.32. In the proof of Theorem 2.31, y was a transcript with N polylog N rows and N polylog N columns. We can't afford that many variables now. Let's keep the $y_{t,\mathrm{PC}}$ and $y_{t,\mathrm{Reg}[i]}$ variables but axe the $y_{t,\mathrm{Mem}[m]}$ variables: The stranger shows us the verifier's program counter and register contents at each step, but not the work segment.

This isn't too far-fetched. Data processing, control flow, and termination instructions don't care about the work segment. The $y_{t,\mathrm{Mem}[m]}$ variables were only for checking consistency of memory accesses: A load from Mem$[m]$ should get the word most recently stored there. We can check this in another way: If step t is a load, find the latest step $t' < t$ that loads or stores at the same address, and check that they have the same data (by comparing the relevant registers). Thus all $y_{t,\mathrm{Mem}[m]}$ are redundant—the information can be gleaned from registers. But φ would need clauses for each pair of steps, so it would still have quadratic size.

Let's make-believe that the verifier is *oblivious*: For every step, the type of memory access (load/store/neither) and address (if it's a load/store) depend only on the time t and input size N, not on the input x or witness w. Then φ wouldn't have to "search" for the relevant store, since we could hardcode the time t'. CNFs are inherently oblivious—they can't change their clauses after looking at the assignment—so obliviousness of the verifier would enable a fairly lossless conversion from time efficiency to CNF size. Let's put this idea on the back burner.

Next idea: Suppose we had a list of all load/store steps sorted by address: all Mem[0] accesses in chronological order, followed by all Mem[1] accesses in chronological order, and so on. We could check consistency by just examining adjacent pairs in the list: Each load should have the same data as the previous entry (which could be a load or store), or have the 0 word if these two entries access different addresses.

The stranger can supply this sorted list (as an assignment to new variables in φ), but we must check that his list is accurate, which would take quadratic size without further help. What if the stranger runs a quasi-linear-time sorting algorithm (such as merge sort) and gives us the transcript to check? Sounds like we're back to square one: "How to check a transcript with a quasi-linear-size CNF" is the puzzle we're trying to solve!

We combine our ideas: Only the sorting algorithm needs to be oblivious. Merge sort is not oblivious, since which entries get compared (during a merge) depends on the results of earlier comparisons. A fancier version of merge sort is oblivious and almost as efficient.

We handle the input and witness segments similarly to the work segment. ■

We represent oblivious sorting algorithms with *sorting networks*. These have practical applications in computer hardware, particularly in graphics processing units (GPUs).

A *comparison network* operates on an array of n numbers. In each step, it compares two entries and swaps them if necessary to make the smaller come before the bigger of the two numbers. A comparison network is a sequence of *comparators*, each of which sorts two entries at a prespecified pair of positions. The sequence of comparators depends on n but not on the array contents. To visualize a comparison network: The array positions are horizontal lines, indexed $1, \ldots, n$ from top to bottom. Each comparator is a vertical line connecting the two positions being compared. Time flows from left to right: Two numbers enter a comparator from the left and get sorted, so the smaller leaves on the upper right and the bigger leaves on the lower right.

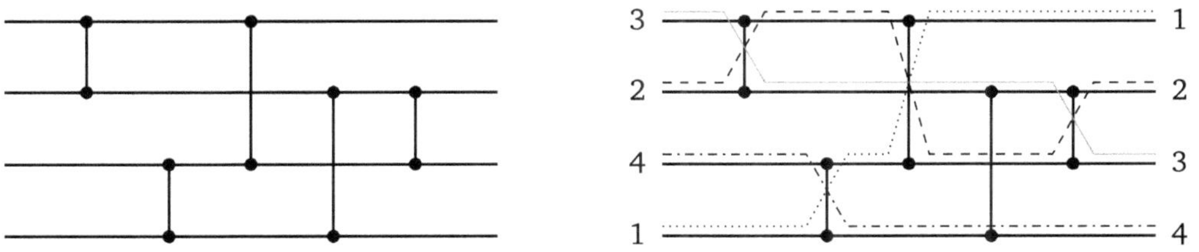

Figure 2.31: Example sorting network

A *sorting network* is a comparison network that sorts: If we plug any array of n numbers in the left, the sorted version comes out the right.

Example. In Figure 2.31, the left side shows a comparison network with $n = 4$, which first compares positions 1 and 2, then compares positions 3 and 4, then positions 1 and 3, and so on. The right side runs this comparison network on input array $(3, 2, 4, 1)$. Though it's not obvious, this is a sorting network. ♦

In a comparison network, endpoints of comparators split horizontal lines into segments called *wires*. A wire carries an array entry's value between consecutive accesses to that position, or before the first or after the last access. A comparison network with k comparators has $n + 2k$ wires because there are n input wires, and each comparator creates two new wires.

A simple sorting network construction is oblivious bubble sort: Compare positions $n-1$ and n, then $n-2$ and $n-1$, then $n-3$ and $n-2$, and so on, then 1 and 2. This bubbles the smallest number up to position 1. Then, do that again but stopping at position 2, to bubble the next-smallest up to position 2, and so on. This has $\Theta(n^2)$ comparators.

Theorem 2.34. *For all n, some sorting network has $O(n \log^2 n)$ comparators. Moreover, some algorithm finds this sorting network in time $O(n \log^2 n)$ given n.*

We prove this in § 2.8.5. Sorting networks with $O(n \log n)$ comparators exist, but they're much tougher to design. $O(n \log^2 n)$ is good enough for us.

The array entries need not be numbers. They can be anything, if we can implement a comparator to determine which of two entries should come before the other according to some desired "sorted order."

Proof of Theorem 2.32. We adapt the proof of Theorem 2.31. Now the proof won't mention M (the work segment size), so we need not make $M = O(N)$. We remove from φ all $y_{t,\mathrm{Mem}[m]}$ variables and all clauses that mention any $y_{t,\mathrm{Mem}[m]}$ or x or w. Here's what remains:

- Variables: x, w, $y = y_0 \cdots y_T$ where $y_t = y_{t,\mathrm{PC}}\, y_{t,\mathrm{Reg}[0]} \cdots y_{t,\mathrm{Reg}[R-1]}$, and the auxiliary z.
- Clauses: $\varphi_{\mathrm{accept}}$ and all $\varphi_{t,s,\ell}$ or $\varphi'_{t,s,\ell}$ components for $s \in \{\mathrm{PC}, \mathrm{Reg}[0], \ldots, \mathrm{Reg}[R-1]\}$ except when (s, ℓ) is a retrieval.

This has size N polylog N. To compensate for the missing retrievals, we append $\varphi_{\mathrm{Mem}} \wedge \varphi_{\mathrm{In}} \wedge \varphi_{\mathrm{Wit}}$:

- φ_{Mem} checks that each load gets the word most recently stored to that address (according to y's previous rows) or gets the 0 word if the address was never stored to.
- φ_{In} checks that each read gets the relevant word of x.
- φ_{Wit} checks that each read-witness gets the relevant word of w.

We design φ_{Mem} involving y and new auxiliary variables z_{Mem} so that:

$$\big(\exists z_{\text{Mem}} : \varphi_{\text{Mem}}(y, z_{\text{Mem}}) = 1\big) \iff \big(\forall t \in \{1, \dots, T\} : \text{if line } y_{t-1,\text{PC}} \text{ is "load Reg}[i] \leftarrow \dots\text{"} \text{ then } y_{t,\text{Reg}[i]} \text{ is as it should be}\big)$$

We define $\varphi_{\text{Mem}} = \varphi_{\text{Mem, distill}} \wedge \varphi_{\text{Mem, sort}} \wedge \varphi_{\text{Mem, validate}}$:

- $\varphi_{\text{Mem, distill}}$ checks that groups of variables $v_1 \cdots v_T$ (in z_{Mem}) distill the information in y relevant to the work segment: v_t says whether step t is a load or store or neither, and says the address being accessed and data being copied if it's a load or store.
- $\varphi_{\text{Mem, sort}}$ checks that groups of variables $u_1 \cdots u_T$ (in z_{Mem}) are $v_1 \cdots v_T$ sorted by address in nondescending order, preserving the relative order of steps that access the same address (a *stable* sort), with non-load/non-store steps at the end. We turn a sorting network into a CNF for this.
- $\varphi_{\text{Mem, validate}}$ checks consistency of $u_1 \cdots u_T$: Each load has the same data as the previous group if they access the same address, and otherwise has data 0 since the address wasn't accessed before. This indirectly checks consistency of $v_1 \cdots v_T$: Each load has the same data as the most recent step that accessed the same address (via a load or store), or data 0 if there's no such step.

Details follow.

- $\varphi_{\text{Mem, distill}}$ has the following check for all t and ℓ, where v_t consists of $v_{t,\text{load?}}$ (one bit), $v_{t,\text{store?}}$ (one bit), $v_{t,\text{addr}}$ (one word), $v_{t,\text{data}}$ (one word). Depending on line ℓ:

load Reg$[i] \leftarrow$ Mem[Reg$[j]$]:	"if $y_{t-1,\text{PC}} = \ell$ then $v_t = (1,\ 0,\ y_{t-1,\text{Reg}[j]},\ y_{t,\text{Reg}[i]})$"
store Mem[Reg$[j]$] $\leftarrow$ Reg$[i]$:	"if $y_{t-1,\text{PC}} = \ell$ then $v_t = (0,\ 1,\ y_{t-1,\text{Reg}[j]},\ y_{t-1,\text{Reg}[i]})$"
neither load nor store:	"if $y_{t-1,\text{PC}} = \ell$ then $v_t = (0,\ 0,\ \text{don't care},\ \text{don't care})$"

  Each such check has size poly W = polylog N, so $\varphi_{\text{Mem, distill}}$ has size N polylog N.

- $\varphi_{\text{Mem, sort}}$ checks that $u_1 \cdots u_T$ is $v_1 \cdots v_T$ sorted in this way: First are all v_t with $v_{t,\text{load?}} = 1$ or $v_{t,\text{store?}} = 1$, in nondecreasing order of $v_{t,\text{addr}}$, preserving the relative order of steps having the same value of $v_{t,\text{addr}}$. All other v_t are at the end, in any order. Figure 2.32 shows an example. Consider the sorting network from Theorem 2.34 with $n = T = O(N)$ and with $O(N \log^2 N)$ comparators and wires. Number the input wires $1, \dots, T$ from top to bottom, and number the other wires $T+1, T+2, \dots$ in some way. Wire i has a group of variables $v_i = v_{i,\text{load?}}\ v_{i,\text{store?}}\ v_{i,\text{addr}}\ v_{i,\text{data}}$. Thus $v_1 \cdots v_T$ are the input wire groups, and $u_1 \cdots u_T$ are aliases for the output wire groups, and other v_i groups are new (in z_{Mem}). For each comparator, say with wires h (upper left), i (lower left), j (upper right), and k (lower right), $\varphi_{\text{Mem, sort}}$ checks that those groups obey our comparison rules:

  "if $(v_{i,\text{load?}}$ or $v_{i,\text{store?}})$ and $\big((\overline{v_{h,\text{load?}}}$ and $\overline{v_{h,\text{store?}}})$ or $v_{h,\text{addr}} > v_{i,\text{addr}}\big)$
  then $(v_j = v_i$ and $v_k = v_h)$ (swap)
  else $(v_j = v_h$ and $v_k = v_i)$ " (no swap)

  As required for a stable sort, this checks that the comparator does not swap when $v_{h,\text{addr}} = v_{i,\text{addr}}$ and $(v_{h,\text{load?}}$ or $v_{h,\text{store?}})$ and $(v_{i,\text{load?}}$ or $v_{i,\text{store?}})$. Each comparator check can be expressed with size poly W = polylog N using auxiliary variables (we'll see a demonstration soon with $\varphi_{\text{Mem, validate}}$), so $\varphi_{\text{Mem, sort}}$ has size N polylog N.

t	v_t	u_t
1	(1, 0, 7,)	(0, 1, 5,)
2	(0, 1, 5,)	(1, 0, 5,)
3	(0, 0, ,)	(1, 0, 7,)
4	(1, 0, 5,)	(0, 1, 7,)
5	(0, 0, ,)	(0, 0, ,)
6	(0, 1, 7,)	(0, 0, ,)

Figure 2.32: Example of sorting distilled information about work segment accesses

- $\varphi_{\text{Mem, validate}}$ checks consistency of $u_1 \cdots u_T$:

$$\text{For } t = 1\text{: “if } u_{1,\text{load?}} \text{ then } u_{1,\text{data}} = 0\text{”}$$

$$\text{For each } t > 1\text{: “if } u_{t,\text{load?}} \text{ then: if } u_{t-1,\text{addr}} = u_{t,\text{addr}} \text{ then } u_{t,\text{data}} = u_{t-1,\text{data}} \text{ else } u_{t,\text{data}} = 0\text{”}$$

This indirectly checks consistency of $v_1 \cdots v_T$:

$$\text{For each } t\text{: if } v_{t,\text{load?}} \text{ then } v_{t,\text{data}} = \begin{cases} v_{t',\text{data}} & \text{for the greatest } t' < t \text{ with} \\ & (v_{t',\text{load?}} \text{ or } v_{t',\text{store?}}) \text{ and } v_{t',\text{addr}} = v_{t,\text{addr}} \\ 0 & \text{if there's no such } t' \end{cases}$$

For each t, the check can be expressed with size $\text{poly}\, W = \text{polylog}\, N$, so $\varphi_{\text{Mem, validate}}$ has size $N \,\text{polylog}\, N$. For example, to express “if $u_{t-1,\text{addr}} = u_{t,\text{addr}}$ then $u_{t,\text{data}} = u_{t-1,\text{data}}$”, which is equivalent to “$u_{t-1,\text{addr}} \neq u_{t,\text{addr}}$ or $u_{t,\text{data}} = u_{t-1,\text{data}}$”, we introduce an auxiliary variable and insert it into each clause of “$u_{t-1,\text{addr}} \neq u_{t,\text{addr}}$” (which itself involves auxiliary variables) and insert its negation into each clause of “$u_{t,\text{data}} = u_{t-1,\text{data}}$”.

φ_{In} is like φ_{Mem} but for read instead of load. To “initialize” the input segment, we prepend to the transcript phantom “store In[m] $\leftarrow x_m$” steps for $m \in \{0, \ldots, N-1\}$:

- $\varphi_{\text{In, distill}}$ checks that new groups of variables $v_0 \cdots v_{-(N-1)}$ capture these phantom stores ($v_{-m} = (0, 1, m, x_m)$ for each m) and $v_1 \cdots v_T$ distill the information in y about read steps.
- $\varphi_{\text{In, sort}}$ checks that $v_0 \cdots v_{-(N-1)}$ and $v_1 \cdots v_T$ all get sorted together into $u_1 \cdots u_{N+T}$, using a sorting network with $n = N + T$.
- $\varphi_{\text{In, validate}}$ exploits the fact that reads never precede phantom stores:

$$\text{For each } t > 1\text{: “if } u_{t,\text{read?}} \text{ then } u_{t,\text{data}} = u_{t-1,\text{data}}\text{”}$$

φ_{Wit} is like φ_{In} but for read-witness instead of read. We prepend to the transcript phantom “store Wit[m] $\leftarrow w_m$” steps for $m \in \{0, \ldots, T-1\}$.

Since $z_{\text{Mem}}, z_{\text{In}}, z_{\text{Wit}}$ are disjoint sets of variables, we technically should have used $v_{\text{Mem}}, v_{\text{In}}, v_{\text{Wit}}$ instead of just reusing the letter v, and likewise for u. ■

2.8.5 Sorting Network Construction

Proof of Theorem 2.34 (ancillary). We may assume $n \geq 2$ is a power of 2 because if it's not, then we can let $n' < 2n$ be the next power of 2, construct a sorting network for n' with

Odd-even merge sort	(2.32)
sort($x_1,\dots,x_n$):	merge($x_1,\dots,x_n$):
if $n = 2$: apply comparator to (x_1,x_2)	if $n = 2$: apply comparator to (x_1,x_2)
else:	else:
sort($x_1,\dots,x_{n/2}$)	merge($x_1,x_3,x_5,\dots,x_{n-1}$)
sort($x_{n/2+1},\dots,x_n$)	merge($x_2,x_4,x_6,\dots,x_n$)
merge($x_1,\dots,x_n$)	apply comparators to these pairs:
	(x_2,x_3), (x_4,x_5), ..., (x_{n-2},x_{n-1})

Figure 2.33: Odd-even merge sort

$O(n'\log^2 n') = O(n\log^2 n)$ comparators, and delete comparators involving any of the fake positions $n+1,\dots,n'$.

Figure 2.33 shows *odd-even merge sort*. The recursive subroutine sort($x_1,\dots,x_n$) generates a sorting network on array entries $x_1,\dots,x_n$. Figure 2.34 depicts the sorting network's recursive structure. The example sorting network in Figure 2.31 is odd-even merge sort for $n = 4$. When sort() or merge() is called, the arguments (such as $x_{n/2+1},\dots,x_n$ or $x_1,x_3,x_5,\dots,x_{n-1}$) get internally renamed as $x_1,\dots,x_n$ in the subroutine, even though they actually represent a subset of the original array positions.

We prove that the comparison network generated by sort($x_1,\dots,x_n$) is indeed a sorting network: If we plug any array of n numbers in the left, the sorted version comes out the right. We may assume the array contains distinct numbers, by imagining that equal entries are perturbed slightly to make them distinct. Analogous to ordinary merge sort, the following lemma implies that sort() maintains the invariant that it generates a sorting network on whichever array positions are specified as the arguments, assuming n is a power of 2.

Lemma 2.35. *The comparison network generated by* merge($x_1,\dots,x_n$) *is a merging network: If* $x_1 < \cdots < x_{n/2}$ *and* $x_{n/2+1} < \cdots < x_n$ *then after applying the network,* $x_1 < \cdots < x_n$.

Proof of Lemma 2.35 (ancillary). merge() maintains the invariant that it generates a merging network on whichever array positions are specified as the arguments, assuming n is a power of 2. The base case $n = 2$ is trivial. To show that merge($x_1,\dots,x_n$) maintains this invariant, assume merge($x_1,x_3,\dots,x_{n-1}$) and merge($x_2,x_4,\dots,x_n$) each generate a merging network.

- Let $a_1 < \cdots < a_{n/2}$ be the initial values of the "top half" entries $x_1,\dots,x_{n/2}$.
- Let $b_1 < \cdots < b_{n/2}$ be the initial values of the "bottom half" entries $x_{n/2+1},\dots,x_n$.
- Let $c_1,\dots,c_n$ be the values of all entries $x_1,\dots,x_n$ after the two recursive merges:
  $c_1 < c_3 < \cdots < c_{n-1}$ is the merging of $a_1 < a_3 < \cdots < a_{n/2-1}$ with $b_1 < b_3 < \cdots < b_{n/2-1}$.
  $c_2 < c_4 < \cdots < c_n$ is the merging of $a_2 < a_4 < \cdots < a_{n/2}$ with $b_2 < b_4 < \cdots < b_{n/2}$.

We claim that to sort $c_1,\dots,c_n$ (finalize the merge), each number c_i belongs at position i or $i+1$ if i is even, or at position i or $i-1$ if i is odd. Thus, $c_1,\dots,c_n$ is almost sorted except c_2,c_3 might be swapped, and c_4,c_5 might be swapped, and so on. The (x_2,x_3), (x_4,x_5), ... comparators fix this, so the values are indeed sorted at the end—the merging of $a_1 < \cdots < a_{n/2}$ with $b_1 < \cdots < b_{n/2}$.

To prove the claim, suppose c_i came from the top half, say $c_i = a_j$. (An analogous argument works if c_i came from the bottom half.) To see where c_i belongs in the sorted order, we count how many numbers from the array are $\le c_i$. Exactly j many numbers from the top half are $\le c_i$, namely $a_1 < a_2 < \cdots < a_j = c_i$. How many from the bottom half?

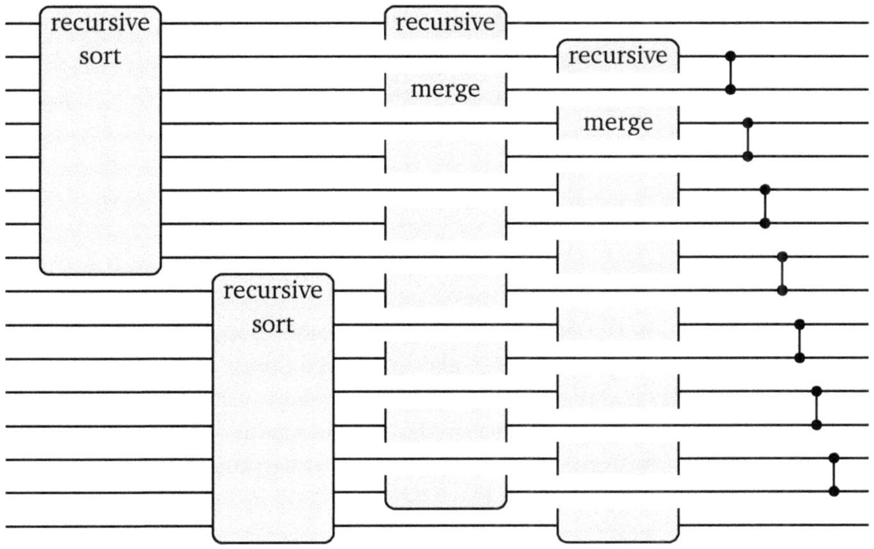

Figure 2.34: Odd-even merge sort with $n = 16$

- If i is even: Let k be such that $c_2 < c_4 < \cdots < c_i$ is the merging of $a_2 < a_4 < \cdots < a_j$ with $b_2 < b_4 < \cdots < b_k$. Then $i = j + k$ and $b_k < c_i < b_{k+2}$, but b_{k+1} could be either $> c_i$ or $< c_i$. Thus there are either k or $k+1$ many numbers from the bottom half that are $\leq c_i$, namely $b_1 < b_2 < \cdots < b_k$ and possibly b_{k+1}. In total, there are either $j + k = i$ or $j + (k+1) = i + 1$ many numbers that are $\leq c_i$, so c_i belongs in position i or $i + 1$.
- If i is odd: Let k be such that $c_1 < c_3 < \cdots < c_i$ is the merging of $a_1 < a_3 < \cdots < a_j$ with $b_1 < b_3 < \cdots < b_k$. Then $i = j + k + 1$ and $b_k < c_i < b_{k+2}$, but b_{k+1} could be either $> c_i$ or $< c_i$. Thus there are either k or $k+1$ many numbers from the bottom half that are $\leq c_i$, namely $b_1 < b_2 < \cdots < b_k$ and possibly b_{k+1}. In total, there are either $j + k = i - 1$ or $j + (k+1) = i$ many numbers that are $\leq c_i$, so c_i belongs in position $i - 1$ or i. ■

Now, we analyze the efficiency. First, consider a call to merge($x_1, \ldots, x_n$). It spawns two recursive calls, each on $n/2$ entries. Both of those calls spawn two further recursive calls, each on $n/4$ entries, and so on. Say a call to merge() is at *depth d* if its argument list has $n/2^d$ many array positions. There are 2^d calls at depth $d \in \{0, 1, \ldots, (\log n) - 1\}$. Each call at depth $d < (\log n) - 1$ directly generates $(n/2^d)/2 - 1$ comparators (not counting those generated by its descendant calls); round this up to $n/2^d$ for simplicity. Each base case call at depth $d = (\log n) - 1$ (on $n/2^d = 2$ entries) generates $1 \leq n/2^d$ comparator. Thus, a call to merge($x_1, \ldots, x_n$) results in $\leq \sum_{d=0}^{(\log n)-1} 2^d \cdot n/2^d = \sum_{d=0}^{(\log n)-1} n = n \log n$ comparators. We bound the running time similarly: For some constant e, each call at depth d takes $\leq en/2^d$ steps, including writing the argument lists of the child calls and doing other subroutine call miscellanea, but not including the time spent executing descendant calls. Thus, the total running time of merge($x_1, \ldots, x_n$) is $\leq \sum_{d=0}^{(\log n)-1} 2^d \cdot en/2^d = \sum_{d=0}^{(\log n)-1} en = en \log n$.

Now, consider a call to sort($x_1, \ldots, x_n$). There are 2^d calls to sort() at depth $d \in \{0, 1, \ldots, (\log n) - 1\}$. Each sort() call at depth $d < (\log n) - 1$ generates $\leq (n/2^d) \log(n/2^d) \leq (n/2^d) \log n$ comparators via its call to merge(), not counting the descendant calls to sort(). Each base case sort() call generates $1 \leq (n/2^d) \log n$ comparator. Thus, a call to sort($x_1, \ldots, x_n$) results in $\leq \sum_{d=0}^{(\log n)-1} 2^d \cdot (n/2^d) \log n = \sum_{d=0}^{(\log n)-1} n \log n = n \log^2 n$ comparators. We bound the running time similarly: For some constant e', each call at depth d takes $\leq e'n/2^d$ steps (not including descendant calls) plus $\leq e(n/2^d)\log(n/2^d) \leq e(n/2^d)\log n$ steps for its merge() call. Thus, the total running time of sort($x_1, \ldots, x_n$) is $\leq \sum_{d=0}^{(\log n)-1} 2^d \cdot (e'n/2^d + e(n/2^d)\log n) = \sum_{d=0}^{(\log n)-1} (e'n + en\log n) \leq (e'+e)n\log^2 n$. ■

2.9 Variants of P Versus NP

2.9.1 Complementation

If A is a decision problem, then $\overline{A}$ is the *complement* decision problem, where $\overline{A}(x) = \overline{A(x)}$ for each valid input x. ($\overline{A}$ has the same word size and same valid inputs as A.) For example, $\overline{\text{SAT}}$ asks whether φ is *not* satisfiable. If $\mathcal{C}$ is a class of decision problems, then co$\mathcal{C} = \{\overline{A} : A \in \mathcal{C}\}$ is the class of complements of problems in $\mathcal{C}$. The prefix "co" stands for "complement." For example, coP contains all decision problems for which some poly-time program accepts no-inputs and rejects yes-inputs.

Observation 2.36. coP = P.

Proof. To see that P $\subseteq$ coP, consider any $A \in$ P. Some poly-time program solves A. If we change each "accept" instruction to "reject" and vice versa, then it solves $\overline{A}$ with the same efficiency, so $\overline{A} \in$ P and thus $A \in$ coP. Symmetrically, coP $\subseteq$ P. ■

When co$\mathcal{C} = \mathcal{C}$, we say $\mathcal{C}$ is *closed under complement*. L, P, PSPACE, and EXP are closed under complement since they have symmetry between "yes" and "no." But NP doesn't have such symmetry. An efficient verifier can be convinced the answer is "yes," but can't necessarily be convinced the answer is "no." Confirming the presence of a needle in a haystack is quick if a stranger finds one, but confirming the absence of needles may require inspecting all the hay.

coNP is a "mirror image" of the asymmetric NP: It contains problems for which suitable witnesses convince a poly-time verifier that no-inputs are no-inputs. We have $A \in$ coNP iff for some poly-time verifier V and every valid input x:

$$A(x) = 0 \iff \big(\exists w : V(x;w) \text{ accepts}\big)$$

There's no apparent reason for NP to be closed under complement. After all, why would witnesses for yes-inputs entail witnesses for no-inputs? For example, SAT $\in$ NP but presumably SAT $\notin$ coNP. It seems unlikely that someone could quickly convince us a CNF has no satisfying assignment. Proving coNP $\neq$ NP would be at least as difficult as proving P $\neq$ NP, because P = NP implies coNP = coP = P = NP. It's unknown whether coNP = NP implies P = NP.

What goes wrong if we try to show coNP = NP by just flipping the verifier's output, like with coP = P? Suppose $A \in$ NP by verifier V. Let $\overline{V}$ be V but with each "accept" instruction changed to "reject" and vice versa. Is $\overline{A} \in$ NP by verifier $\overline{V}$? For each yes-input of $\overline{A}$ (no-input of A), $\overline{V}$ accepts (V rejects) for all w and hence for some w, as we want. But for each no-input of $\overline{A}$ (yes-input of A), $\overline{V}$ rejects (V accepts) for some w but not necessarily for all w.

A decision problem B is coNP-*complete* when $B \in$ coNP and $A \leq_p^m B$ for every $A \in$ coNP. Note that B is coNP-complete iff $\overline{B}$ is NP-complete, since $A \leq_p^m B$ for every $A \in$ coNP iff $\overline{A} \leq_p^m \overline{B}$ for every $\overline{A} \in$ NP.

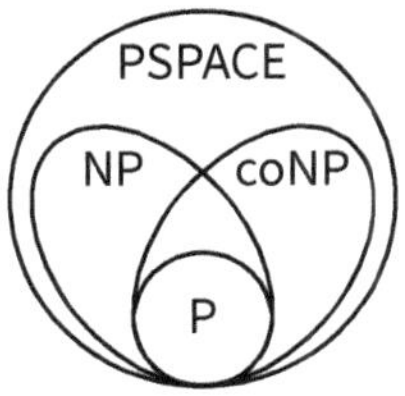

Figure 2.35: Relationship among P, NP, coNP, and PSPACE

TAUTOLOGY (or TAUT for short)	(2.33)
Input: DNF formula φ	
Output: Does every assignment satisfy φ?	

Observation 2.37. TAUT *is* coNP-*complete.*

Proof. $\overline{\text{TAUT}} \in \mathsf{NP}$ by a verifier that evaluates φ on the assignment w and accepts iff φ is not satisfied. $\overline{\text{TAUT}}$ is NP-hard because $\text{SAT} \le_p^m \overline{\text{TAUT}}$ by mapping CNF φ to DNF $\overline{\varphi}$, which works since φ has a satisfying assignment iff $\overline{\varphi}$ has an unsatisfying assignment. ■

Figure 2.35 depicts each complexity class as an oval enclosing "points" representing problems in the class. For example, $\mathsf{P} \subseteq \mathsf{NP} \cap \mathsf{coNP}$ since the P oval is in the intersection of the NP and coNP ovals. It's generally assumed that $\mathsf{P} \ne \mathsf{NP} \cap \mathsf{coNP}$, that is, some problem has efficiently-verifiable witnesses for both yes- and no-inputs, but has no poly-time program. Conviction in this conjecture is less widespread than for $\mathsf{P} \ne \mathsf{NP}$, though. Not many interesting problems are known to be in $\mathsf{NP} \cap \mathsf{coNP}$ but not known to be in P.

2.9.2 Exponential Time

NEXP is to EXP as NP is to P: $\mathsf{NEXP} = \mathsf{NTIME}[2^{\text{poly}\,N}]$ is the class of all decision problems with exponential-time verifiers. EXP versus NEXP is a scaled up analogue of P versus NP. In §4.1 we prove that $\mathsf{EXP} \ne \mathsf{NEXP}$ implies $\mathsf{P} \ne \mathsf{NP}$, so $\mathsf{EXP} \ne \mathsf{NEXP}$ would be even harder to prove than $\mathsf{P} \ne \mathsf{NP}$.

A decision problem B is EXP-*complete* when $B \in \mathsf{EXP}$ and $A \le_p^m B$ for every $A \in \mathsf{EXP}$.

Lemma 2.38. *Suppose B is* EXP-*complete. Then $B \notin \mathsf{P}$.*

Proof. Suppose for contradiction B is EXP-complete and $B \in \mathsf{P}$. For every $A \in \mathsf{EXP}$, we have $A \le_p^m B \in \mathsf{P}$ and so $A \in \mathsf{P}$. Thus $\mathsf{EXP} \subseteq \mathsf{P}$, contradicting $\mathsf{EXP} \not\subseteq \mathsf{P}$, which we prove in §4.2. ■

NP-completeness is evidence that a problem isn't in P, but EXP-completeness is definitive proof that a problem isn't in P. We won't discuss any particular EXP-complete problems, since they're less common.

2.9.3 Log-Space Reductions

We now segue into Chapter 3 on space complexity.

B is NP-*complete via log-space mapping reductions* ($\le_\ell^m$) when $B \in \mathsf{NP}$ and $A \le_\ell^m B$ for every $A \in \mathsf{NP}$. Using Lemma 1.15, we get an analogue of Lemma 2.7:

Lemma 2.39. *Suppose B is* NP*-complete via* $\le_\ell^m$. *Then $B \in$* L *iff* L $=$ NP. ■

Theorem 2.40. Sat *is* NP*-complete via* $\le_\ell^m$.

Proof. To prove $A \le_\ell^m$ Sat for any $A \in$ NP, we show that the mapping reduction from § 2.8.2 only needs log space. The reduction builds $\varphi = \varphi_{\text{accept}} \wedge \bigwedge_{t,s,\ell} \varphi_{t,s,\ell}$, then contracts $\varphi(x,w,y)$ with the actual input plugged in for x to get $\psi(w,y)$. Recall that $\varphi_{t,s,\ell}$ checks that $y_{t,s}$ is the word at location s after one step from configuration y_{t-1} if this step executes line ℓ. If (s,ℓ) is a retrieval, then $\varphi_{t,s,\ell} = \bigwedge_m \varphi_{t,s,\ell,m}$ over all possible source addresses m.

We use the Sat encoding from the end of § 2.3.3. The number of w, y variables is $TW + T \cdot (\log L + (R+M)W)$ where M is the work segment size (not the query size). To compute the number of clauses, we do a preliminary run of computing the clause descriptions, but only count how many. To compute the pointers to the clause descriptions, we do another preliminary run, but only heed the addresses. Then, we do the real run.

Writing the clauses of φ_{accept} is straightforward. For the other clauses: Four registers hold t, s, ℓ, m. In nested loops over all values of t, s, ℓ, we write $\varphi_{t,s,\ell}$. If (s,ℓ) is a retrieval, then in another inner loop over all values of m, we write $\varphi_{t,s,\ell,m}$.

Each component depends on at most five words. To write a component using the CNF recipe from Lemma 2.9, we use five registers to iterate over all possible values of the words the component depends on. For each possibility, we check whether the component evaluates to 0 and if so, write the clause "these variables $\ne$ those values" (using another register to iterate through the relevant variables). If line ℓ is a "read", we don't iterate over possible values of the relevant x variables—we hardcode the actual values, so the CNF is already contracted to the query ψ.

The reduction is register-only with log-bounded word size, and is hence log-space. ■

To prove that C is NP-complete via $\le_\ell^m$, we can use a familiar template: Show $C \in$ NP and $B \le_\ell^m C$ for some B that we already know is NP-complete via $\le_\ell^m$. This works since for every $A \in$ NP, we have $A \le_\ell^m B \le_\ell^m C$ and therefore $A \le_\ell^m C$ (Lemma 1.16). The reductions in this chapter only need log space if implemented with care, so all NP-complete problems in this chapter are NP-complete via $\le_\ell^m$.

Exercises

2.1 Consider "color" assignments $c\colon V \to \{\text{rock}, \text{scissors}, \text{paper}\}$ for a directed graph $G = (V,E)$. Rock beats scissors, and scissors beats paper, and paper beats rock. Prove that this problem is in P:

Rock Scissors Paper Coloring	(2.34)
Input: Directed graph G	
Output: Does there exist c such that for every edge (u,v), $c(u)$ beats $c(v)$?	

2.2 Run the poly-time algorithm for Small Subset Sum (from Theorem 2.3) by hand, on input $(x_1, x_2, x_3, x_4) = (7, 3, 4, 10)$ and $t = 19$. Show each of the sets S_0, S_1, S_2, S_3, S_4.

2.3 For each of the following problems, implement a linear-time verifier in our official model.

(a) 3-SAT: You may assume the input encoding consists of n (the number of variables), m (the number of clauses), and then m groups of six words. Each group represents one clause, with each literal having a pair of words—one word with the variable's index in $[n]$, and one word that's 0 if the variable is negated and 1 if it's unnegated.

(b) INDEPENDENT SET

(c) DIRECTED FULL PATH

2.4 Prove that for all decision problems A and B, if $A \leq_p^m B$ and $B \in \mathsf{NP}$ then $A \in \mathsf{NP}$.

2.5 Suppose $A \in \mathsf{NP}$ and $B \in \mathsf{NP}$ have the same word size and same valid inputs as each other. Define the decision problems $A \vee B$ and $A \wedge B$ (which share the same word size and valid inputs as A and B) by $(A \vee B)(x) = A(x) \vee B(x)$ and $(A \wedge B)(x) = A(x) \wedge B(x)$.

(a) Prove $A \vee B \in \mathsf{NP}$. (NP is *closed under or*.)

(b) Prove $A \wedge B \in \mathsf{NP}$. (NP is *closed under and*.)

2.6 Prove that if decision problem A has a verifier with $O(T)$ time efficiency only counting execution steps (not counting the highest witness segment address) and $O(\log \max(T, N))$-bounded word size, then $A \in \mathsf{NTIME}[T]$.

2.7 Define $f: \{0,1\}^n \to \{0,1\}$ by $f(x) = 1$ iff the bits of x are in sorted order (all 0s precede all 1s).

(a) Express f with an n-DNF having $n+1$ terms.

(b) Express f with a 2-CNF having $n-1$ clauses.

2.8 For $n \geq 3$, define $f: \{0,1\}^n \to \{0,1\}$ by $f(x) = 1$ iff x has at least three 1s. A *monotone* DNF or CNF has no negative literals. The *size* of a DNF or CNF is the number of literal occurrences.

(a) Express f with a monotone DNF of size $\leq n^3$.

(b) Express f with a monotone CNF of size $\leq n^3$.

2.9 Prove that every unsatisfiable k-CNF has at least 2^k many clauses.

2.10 For each of the following variants of SAT, either prove that it's in P or prove that it's NP-complete. The input is always a CNF $\varphi(x_1 x_2 \cdots x_n)$.

(a) Do there exist at least three satisfying assignments for φ?

(b) Does there exist an assignment that satisfies none of φ's clauses?

(c) Does there exist an assignment that satisfies all but one of φ's clauses?

(d) Does there exist an assignment that satisfies some but not all of φ's clauses?

(e) Does there exist a satisfying assignment for φ such that $x_i x_{i+1} \neq 11$ for all $i < n$?

(f) Does there exist a satisfying assignment for φ such that $x_i x_{i+1} \neq 10$ for all $i < n$?

2.11 Prove that SAT remains NP-complete under each of the following conditions on the input.

(a) No clause contains both a positive literal and a negative literal.
Hint: Use a 2-CNF to express that two variables are assigned opposite bits.

(b) No variable occurs (positively or negatively) in more than three clauses.
Hint: Use a 2-CNF to express that a set of variables are all assigned the same bit.

2.12 Prove that the following poly-time algorithm solves 2-SAT SEARCH. Instead of assigning bits to variables, this pseudocode assigns 1 to literals—assigning 1 to $\overline{x_i}$ means assigning 0 to x_i. For any variable x_i, use ℓ_i to denote either of the literals $x_i, \overline{x_i}$. For any 2-CNF φ, define its *implication graph*: For each variable x_i, there are two nodes representing the literals x_i and $\overline{x_i}$. For each clause $(\ell_i \vee \ell_j)$ of φ, there are two directed edges $\overline{\ell_i} \to \ell_j$ and $\overline{\ell_j} \to \ell_i$ because the clause is equivalent to $(\overline{\ell_i} \Rightarrow \ell_j)$ and to $(\overline{\ell_j} \Rightarrow \ell_i)$.

Algorithm for 2-SAT SEARCH	(2.35)

```
construct φ's implication graph
for each variable x_i:
    if x_i and ¬x_i are reachable from each other: reject
for each variable x_i:
    if x_i is not yet assigned:
        if x_i is reachable from ¬x_i: assign 1 to x_i and to all literals reachable from x_i
        else:                         assign 1 to ¬x_i and to all literals reachable from ¬x_i
```

2.13 **(a)** Contract the following CNF under the partial assignment 1∗∗0:

$$(\overline{x_2} \vee x_3 \vee x_4) \wedge (x_2 \vee \overline{x_4}) \wedge (\overline{x_1} \vee \overline{x_3} \vee x_4) \wedge (x_1 \vee x_2 \vee x_4) \wedge (x_1) \wedge (x_2 \vee \overline{x_3}) \wedge (x_4)$$

(b) Explain how to contract a DNF, and demonstrate by contracting the following DNF under the partial assignment 01∗∗:

$$(x_2 \wedge x_3) \vee (x_1 \wedge \overline{x_3}) \vee (\overline{x_1} \wedge x_4) \vee (\overline{x_1} \wedge x_2 \wedge \overline{x_3} \wedge \overline{x_4}) \vee (\overline{x_1} \wedge \overline{x_2}) \vee (x_3 \wedge \overline{x_4})$$

2.14 Design poly-time search-to-decision reductions for the following problems, without relying on their NP-completeness.

(a) INDEPENDENT SET

(b) DIRECTED FULL PATH

(c) GRAPH 3-COLORING

(d) SUBSET SUM

2.15 Prove that every NP-complete problem has a poly-time search-to-decision reduction. More precisely: If A is NP-complete and V is a poly-time verifier for A with time efficiency $\le T = cN^d$ (for integers c, d) and word size W, then $B \le_p^o A$ where B is the following search problem:

FIND WITNESS FOR V	(2.36)
Input:	Valid input x to A
Output:	$w \in (\{0,1\}^W)^T$ such that $V(x; w)$ accepts, or report that no such w exists

2.16 A decision problem A is *downward self-reducible* when $A \le_p^o A$ via a reduction that, on inputs of size N, only makes queries of size $< N$.

(a) Prove that SAT is downward self-reducible.

(b) Prove that if A has a downward self-reduction that makes at most one query on each input, then $A \in$ P.

2.17 Prove that if an undirected graph with n nodes has a proper k-coloring, then it has a node cover of size at most $n - n/k$.

2.18 Prove CLIQUE $\in$ SPACE$[\sqrt{N}\log N]$.

2.19 Prove INDEPENDENT HALF is NP-complete.

INDEPENDENT HALF	(2.37)
Input:	Undirected graph G
Output:	Does there exist an independent set containing at least half of G's nodes?

2.20 A *shy set* in an undirected graph is a subset S of nodes such that each node in S has at most one neighbor in S. Prove SHY SET is NP-complete.

SHY SET	(2.38)
Input:	Undirected graph G, nonnegative integer k
Output:	Does there exist a shy set of size $\geq k$ in G?

2.21 Prove STINGY 2-SAT is NP-complete.

STINGY 2-SAT	(2.39)
Input:	2-CNF φ, nonnegative integer k
Output:	Does φ have a satisfying assignment with $\leq k$ many variables assigned 1?

2.22 A *dominating set* in an undirected graph is a subset S of nodes such that every node in the graph is either in S or adjacent to at least one node in S. (Each node in S "dominates" itself and its neighbors.) Prove DOMINATING SET is NP-complete.

DOMINATING SET	(2.40)
Input:	Undirected graph G, nonnegative integer k
Output:	Does there exist a dominating set of size $\leq k$ in G?

2.23 An *almost clique* in an undirected graph G (with no multi-edges or self-loops) is a subset S of nodes such that G has all but one of the $\binom{|S|}{2}$ possible edges between pairs of nodes in S. Prove ALMOST CLIQUE is NP-complete.

ALMOST CLIQUE	(2.41)
Input:	Undirected graph G, nonnegative integer k
Output:	Does there exist an almost clique of size $\geq k$ in G?

2.24 Prove that the following promise problem is NP-hard.

Independent Set Gap Counting	(2.42)
Input:	Undirected graph G, positive integer k
Output:	1 if G has $\geq 2^k$ many independent sets (of any sizes) 0 if G has $\leq 2^{k-1}$ many independent sets (of any sizes) undefined otherwise

Hint: Reduce from Independent Set by replacing each of the n nodes with a group of $n+1$ nodes (for a total of $n(n+1)$ nodes) and replacing each edge with a complete bipartite graph between groups.

2.25 In this problem, the input does not specify the start and destination nodes.

Any Directed Full Path	(2.43)
Input:	Directed graph G
Output:	Do there exist nodes s and t such that G has a full path from s to t?

(a) Prove Directed Full Path $\leq_p^m$ Any Directed Full Path.

(b) Prove Any Directed Full Path $\leq_p^m$ Directed Full Path without relying on the latter problem's NP-completeness.

2.26 For an undirected graph with n nodes, an *equitable* k-color assignment has exactly n/k nodes of each color (which is only possible if n/k is an integer).

Equitable k-Coloring	(2.44)
Input:	Undirected graph G
Output:	Does there exist an equitable proper k-coloring of G?

(a) Prove Equitable 2-Coloring $\in$ P.

(b) Prove Connected Equitable 3-Coloring is NP-complete. In this problem, G is required to be connected.

2.27 Prove Barely 3-Sat is NP-complete by reducing from Graph 3-Coloring.

Barely 3-Sat	(2.45)
Input:	3-CNF φ
Output:	Does there exist an assignment satisfying exactly one literal in each clause of φ?

2.28 Prove Balanced Tripartition is NP-complete.

Balanced Tripartition	(2.46)
Input:	Positive integers $x_1, x_2, \ldots, x_n$ represented in binary with m bits each
Output:	Does there exist a partition of $[n]$ into three sets I, J, K such that $\sum_{i \in I} x_i = \sum_{j \in J} x_j = \sum_{k \in K} x_k$?

2.29 **(a)** Define FULL PATH IN A DAG like DIRECTED FULL PATH but requiring the graph to be acyclic. Prove FULL PATH IN A DAG $\in$ P.

(b) Prove EXACT PATH LENGTH IN A DAG is NP-complete.

EXACT PATH LENGTH IN A DAG	(2.47)
Input:	Directed acyclic graph G without multi-edges, nodes s and t, positive binary integer length ℓ_e for each edge e, positive binary integer T
Output:	Does there exist a path of length exactly T from s to t in G?

(c) Define SMALL EXACT PATH LENGTH IN A DAG similarly but requiring $\ell_e \le n^2$ for each edge e, and $T \le n^3$, where n is the number of nodes in G. Prove SMALL EXACT PATH LENGTH IN A DAG $\in$ P.

2.30 A *k-not-all-equal (k-NAE) clause* is a set of k literals corresponding to k distinct variables, and is satisfied by an assignment iff these literals don't all have the same value (that is, at least one literal is 1 and at least one literal is 0). For example, the 3-NAE clause $\neg(x_1 \Leftrightarrow \overline{x_2} \Leftrightarrow x_3)$ says the assignment to $x_1x_2x_3$ must be neither 010 nor 101. A *k-NAE formula* is a conjunction of k-NAE clauses. Such a formula is satisfiable iff there exists an assignment satisfying all its clauses.

k-NOT-ALL-EQUAL SATISFIABILITY (or k-NAE SAT for short)	(2.48)
Input:	k-NAE formula φ
Output:	Is φ satisfiable?

(a) Prove 2-NAE SAT $\in$ P by reducing to GRAPH 2-COLORING.

(b) Prove 4-NAE SAT is NP-complete by reducing from 3-SAT.

(c) Prove 3-NAE SAT is NP-complete by reducing from 4-NAE SAT.

(d) MAX CUT DECISION is the variant of GRAPH 2-COLORING where we only need at least k edges (rather than all edges) to be multicolored. Prove MAX CUT DECISION is NP-complete by reducing from 3-NAE SAT.

MAX CUT DECISION	(2.49)
Input:	Undirected graph G, nonnegative integer k
Output:	Does there exist a partition of G's set of nodes into two parts (a *cut*), such that the number of edges with endpoints in both parts (*crossing* the cut) is $\ge k$?

Hint: Use the same construction of G as in our linear-time reduction from 3-SAT to INDEPENDENT SET (Theorem 2.21).

(e) Prove MAX 2-SAT DECISION is NP-complete by reducing from MAX CUT DECISION.

MAX 2-SAT DECISION	(2.50)
Input:	2-CNF formula φ, nonnegative integer k
Output:	Does there exist an assignment satisfying at least k clauses of φ?

(f) Give a new proof that GRAPH 3-COLORING is NP-complete by reducing from 3-NAE SAT. Hint: Use the same construction of G as in our linear-time reduction from 3-SAT to INDEPENDENT SET (Theorem 2.21), but add a new node adjacent to all variable gadget nodes.

2.31 (a) Prove NODE DISJOINT PATHS is NP-complete by reducing from 3-SAT.

NODE DISJOINT PATHS	(2.51)
Input:	Directed graph G, pairs of nodes $(s_1, t_1), (s_2, t_2), \ldots, (s_k, t_k)$
Output:	Does there exist a path from s_i to t_i for each $i \in [k]$, such that these k paths are node disjoint (no two of them share any node)?

(b) Prove EDGE DISJOINT PATHS is NP-complete by reducing from NODE DISJOINT PATHS.

EDGE DISJOINT PATHS	(2.52)
Input:	Directed graph G, pairs of nodes $(s_1, t_1), (s_2, t_2), \ldots, (s_k, t_k)$
Output:	Does there exist a path from s_i to t_i for each $i \in [k]$, such that these k paths are edge disjoint (no two of them share any edge)?

2.32 For every $a \in \{0,1\}^W$, express "$p > a$" with a CNF of size poly W without negative literals.

2.33 Prove that every CNF expressing "$p \neq q$" (without auxiliary variables) has at least 2^W clauses, where p and q are words of W variables each. Hint: Consider assignments of the form $(p,q) = (a,a)$ where $a \in \{0,1\}^W$. Show that no two such assignments can falsify the same clause in the CNF.

2.34 In the proof of Theorem 2.31, we expressed "$p = \lfloor \log_2(q) \rfloor$" with a CNF of size $O(W^3)$.

(a) Express it with a CNF of size $O(W^2 \log W)$.

(b) We remarked that size $O(W^2)$ suffices for the "$p \leq W-1$" part. Show that actually size $O(W)$ suffices.

2.35 Prove that the following CNF expresses "$p = q + r$" (mod 2^W) with size $O(W^3)$, where p, q, r are words of W variables each. For every pair of indices $i > j$ and every $a_i b_i c_i \in \{0,1\}^3$, include this clause:

$$\text{“}p_i q_i r_i \neq a_i b_i c_i \text{ or } p_{i-1} \cdots p_{j+1} \neq 0 \cdots 0 \text{ or } q_j r_j \neq 11\text{”} \quad \text{when } a_i = b_i \oplus c_i$$
$$\text{“}p_i q_i r_i \neq a_i b_i c_i \text{ or } p_{i-1} \cdots p_{j+1} \neq 1 \cdots 1 \text{ or } q_j r_j \neq 00\text{”} \quad \text{when } a_i \neq b_i \oplus c_i$$

Also, for every index i and every $a_i b_i c_i$ with $a_i \neq b_i \oplus c_i$, include this clause:

$$\text{“}p_i q_i r_i \neq a_i b_i c_i \text{ or } p_{i-1} \cdots p_0 \neq 1 \cdots 1\text{”}$$

2.36 Prove that if $\mathsf{NTIME}[N] \subseteq \mathsf{P}$ then $\mathsf{NTIME}[N] \subseteq \mathsf{TIME}[N^d]$ for some constant d. Why isn't this automatic from the definitions?

2.37 Draw the sorting network for odd-even merge sort with $n = 8$.

2.38 Show that Not a Sorting Network ∈ NP.

Not a Sorting Network	(2.53)
Input:	A comparison network
Output:	No if it's a sorting network, yes if it's not

2.39 Suppose B is NP-complete. Prove that $B \in$ coNP iff coNP = NP.

2.40 Prove that the following decision problem is (NP ∩ coNP)-complete.

Which Is Satisfiable	(2.54)
Input:	CNFs φ_0 and φ_1 such that one of them is satisfiable and the other isn't
Output:	$i \in \{0, 1\}$ such that φ_i is satisfiable

2.41 Prove that if NP ≠ PSPACE then NP ∪ coNP ≠ PSPACE.

2.42 Prove that for all decision problems A and B, if $A \leq_p^o B$ and $B \in$ NP ∩ coNP then $A \in$ NP ∩ coNP.

Notes

The brute force algorithm format from §2.1 is also known by the Russian word "perebor."

Witnesses are also called "certificates."

The P versus NP question and NP-completeness are due to [136, 331, 292], though letters penned by John Nash and by Kurt Gödel in the 1950s anticipated P versus NP. Surveys on P versus NP and NP-completeness include [182, 496, 1]. In hindsight, we could pick more descriptive names for these complexity classes, but the cryptic acronyms P and NP have stuck—exemplifying the old quote, "There are only two hard things in computer science: cache invalidation and naming things."

An independent set in a graph is also called a "stable set." What we call a "full path" is usually called a "Hamiltonian path," "Rudrata path," or "traceable path." What we call a "full trail" is usually called an "Eulerian trail." Directed Full Trail ∈ P is based on "Euler's theorem" and "Hierholzer's algorithm." Graph 3-Coloring can be solved in $O(1.3289^n)$ time, where n is the number of nodes [55]. Degree-3 3-Coloring ∈ P follows from "Brooks' theorem" [92]. NP-completeness of Degree-4 3-Coloring is due to [183]. Small Subset Sum ∈ TIME$[N^3]$ [413], and a faster algorithm is known when t is smaller [316].

In digital logic literature, DNF and CNF are called "sum of products" and "product of sums" respectively (viewing $\vee$ and $\wedge$ as analogous to $+$ and $\times$), and the DNF and CNF from the proof of Lemma 2.9 are called "sum of minterms" and "product of maxterms."

Some people define k-Sat allowing clauses to have width $\leq k$ (not exactly k). 2-Sat ∈ P, in fact, 2-Sat ∈ TIME$[N]$ are due to [323, 158, 33]. It's known that Sat ∈ TIME$[1.0646^N \operatorname{poly} N]$ [410], and 3-Sat can be solved in $O(1.32793^n)$ time, where n is the number of variables [343].

The quasi-linear-time reduction to Sat using sorting networks (Theorem 2.32) is due to [364, 270]. The odd-even merge sorting network is due to [50]. A sorting network of size $O(n \log n)$ is due to [14]. Not a Sorting Network (Exercise 2.38) is NP-complete [275, 128].

The existence of NP-intermediate problems if $\mathsf{P} \neq \mathsf{NP}$ is known as "Ladner's theorem" [325]. A deep "dichotomy theorem" says that constraint satisfaction problems—which are like k-SAT but the constraints don't have to be clauses—are never NP-intermediate [468, 98, 577].

EDGE DISJOINT PATHS (Exercise 2.31.b) is NP-complete even when $k = 2$ [170].

If $\mathcal{C}$ is some complexity class of decision problems, then $\mathsf{P}^{\mathcal{C}}$ denotes the class of all decision problems A for which there exists $B \in \mathcal{C}$ such that $A \leq_p^o B$ (A is "oracle reducible to $\mathcal{C}$"). Exercise 2.42 says $\mathsf{P}^{\mathsf{NP} \cap \mathsf{coNP}} = \mathsf{NP} \cap \mathsf{coNP}$.

Chapter 3

Space Complexity

Chapter 2 was about the prospect of showing that certain problems aren't in P. This chapter is about the prospect of showing that certain problems aren't in L.

Along the way, we'll meet the complexity classes NL and NPSPACE, which are verifier analogues of L and PSPACE, like how NP and NEXP are verifier analogues of P and EXP. Figure 3.1 organizes these complexity classes. Spoiler alert: NL = coNL and NPSPACE = PSPACE. Space is very different from time.

3.1 Logic, Games, and Recursion

At the heart of space complexity lies a connection between superficially unrelated things: logic formulas with quantifiers, two-player games, and recursive algorithms.

3.1.1 Quantified Formulas

The input to SAT is a CNF formula $\varphi(x_1 x_2 \cdots x_n)$, and the output indicates whether

$$\exists x_1\ \exists x_2 \cdots \exists x_n : \ \varphi(x_1 x_2 \cdots x_n) = 1$$

where each quantifier's domain is $\{0,1\}$. We generalize the problem to allow nested $\exists$ and $\forall$ quantifiers. This has practical applications in model checking and in AI planning—deciding what to do ($\exists$) under uncertainty ($\forall$) about the environment and the future.

QUANTIFIED SATISFIABILITY (or QSAT for short)	(3.1)
Input: CNF formula $\varphi(x_1 x_2 \cdots x_n)$ where n is even	
Output: $\exists x_1\ \forall x_2\ \exists x_3\ \forall x_4 \cdots \exists x_{n-1}\ \forall x_n : \ \varphi(x_1 x_2 \cdots x_n) = 1$?	

We don't require all variables $x_1 \cdots x_n$ to be present in φ—some could be dummy variables that are quantified with $\exists$ or $\forall$ but aren't in any of φ's clauses. Thus it doesn't matter that quantifiers strictly alternate $\exists\,\forall\,\exists\,\forall \cdots$. We could achieve a different sequence of quantifiers such as $\forall\,\exists\,\exists\,\forall\,\forall\,\forall\,\exists$ with a valid input to QSAT by inserting quantifiers with dummy variables and updating all variable indices (Figure 3.2). We assume QSAT's input encoding has a word for each variable, including dummy variables. Thus $n < N$, and each variable index fits in a word of size $\log N$.

Example. $\varphi(x_1 x_2 x_3 x_4) = (x_1 \vee x_4) \wedge (\overline{x_1} \vee x_2 \vee \overline{x_3}) \wedge (\overline{x_2} \vee x_3)$ is a yes-input of QSAT because there exists a value of x_1 such that for both values of x_2, there exists a value of x_3 (which may depend on the value of x_2) such that for both values of x_4, all of φ's clauses are satisfied. Specifically: Let $x_1 = 1$ (satisfying the first clause). Then if $x_2 = 0$ (satisfying the third clause), let $x_3 = 0$ (satisfying the second clause) so φ is satisfied regardless of x_4's value. On the other hand, if

	Time	Space
Solvers	P, EXP	L, PSPACE
Verifiers	NP, NEXP	NL, NPSPACE

Figure 3.1: Major complexity classes

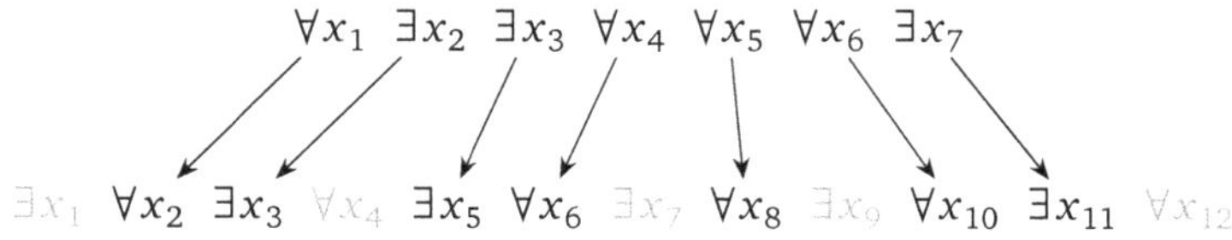

Figure 3.2: Example of inserting dummy quantifiers so that quantifiers alternate

$x_2 = 1$ (satisfying the second clause), let $x_3 = 1$ (satisfying the third clause) so φ is satisfied regardless of x_4's value.

Figure 3.3 shows φ's *evaluation tree.* Root-to-leaf paths correspond to assignments: Going to the left child means assigning the next variable 0. Going right means assigning 1. For example, left–right–left–right means $x_1x_2x_3x_4 = 0101$. Each leaf's label is φ's value under the corresponding assignment. The bold edges show why this is a yes-input: Each node at an odd-index layer ($\exists$ quantifier) has a bold edge to one child. Each node at an even-index layer ($\forall$ quantifier) has bold edges to both children. All leaves reached by totally bold paths are labeled 1. ♦

We view a QSAT input as a game where two players take turns assigning values to variables in the prescribed order: Player 1 (P1) assigns x_1, then Player 2 (P2) assigns x_2, then P1 assigns x_3, then P2 assigns x_4, and so on. If the resulting assignment satisfies φ, then P1 wins, otherwise P2 wins. That is, P1 controls the $\exists$-quantified variables and wants every clause to be satisfied, and P2 controls the $\forall$-quantified variables and wants at least one clause to be unsatisfied.

$$\begin{aligned} &\exists x_1\ \forall x_2\ \exists x_3\ \forall x_4 \cdots :\ \varphi(x_1x_2\cdots x_n) = 1 \\ \Leftrightarrow\ &(\exists \text{ move for P1})\ (\forall \text{ moves for P2})\ (\exists \text{ move for P1})\ (\forall \text{ moves for P2})\ \cdots :\ \text{P1 wins} \end{aligned}$$

For a yes-input, P1 has a *winning strategy* that specifies how to play in all possible circumstances, to guarantee that φ gets satisfied: For each odd i and each assignment to $x_2x_4\cdots x_{i-1}$ played by P2 so far, the strategy says which bit to assign x_i. For a no-input, P2 has a winning strategy that guarantees φ is unsatisfied regardless of what P1 does. For every input, one of the players has a winning strategy (possibly more than one winning strategy), and the other player has no winning strategy. Solving QSAT means determining which player has a winning strategy.

Example. In Figure 3.3, the bold edges depict P1's winning strategy: Play $x_1 = 1$, and then if P2 plays $x_2 = 0$ then P1 responds with $x_3 = 0$, and if P2 plays $x_2 = 1$ then P1 responds with $x_3 = 1$. P1 has only one winning strategy for this input. ♦

Example. $\varphi(x_1x_2x_3x_4) = (x_1 \vee \overline{x_2} \vee \overline{x_4}) \wedge (\overline{x_1} \vee \overline{x_3} \vee x_4) \wedge (x_2 \vee x_3 \vee \overline{x_4})$ is a no-input of QSAT. We exhibit a winning strategy for P2. Let's negate QSAT's output and pull the negation inside:

$$\neg\big(\exists x_1\ \forall x_2\ \exists x_3\ \forall x_4 :\ \varphi(x_1x_2x_3x_4) = 1\big) \Leftrightarrow \big(\forall x_1\ \exists x_2\ \forall x_3\ \exists x_4 :\ \varphi(x_1x_2x_3x_4) = 0\big)$$

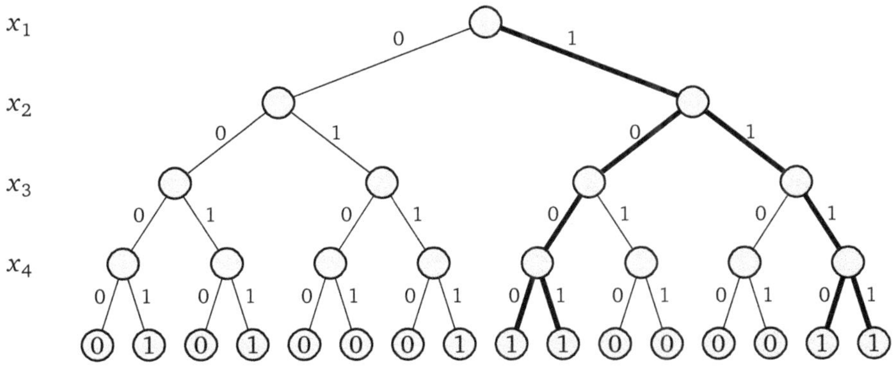

Figure 3.3: Evaluation tree for $\varphi(x_1x_2x_3x_4) = (x_1 \vee x_4) \wedge (\overline{x_1} \vee x_2 \vee \overline{x_3}) \wedge (\overline{x_2} \vee x_3)$

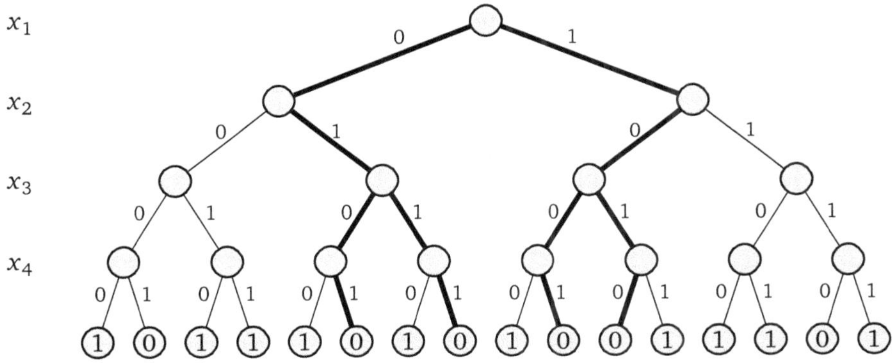

Figure 3.4: Evaluation tree for $\varphi(x_1x_2x_3x_4) = (x_1 \vee \overline{x_2} \vee \overline{x_4}) \wedge (\overline{x_1} \vee \overline{x_3} \vee x_4) \wedge (x_2 \vee x_3 \vee \overline{x_4})$

This says that for both x_1 moves P1 could make, P2 has an x_2 move such that for both x_3 moves P1 could make, P2 has an x_4 move such that φ is unsatisfied. For this φ, P2 has only one winning strategy, depicted by bold edges in the evaluation tree in Figure 3.4: If P1 plays $x_1 = 0$ then P2 responds with $x_2 = 1$, and then regardless of what P1 plays for x_3, P2 plays $x_4 = 1$ (so the first clause is unsatisfied). On the other hand, if P1 plays $x_1 = 1$ then P2 responds with $x_2 = 0$, and then whatever P1 plays for x_3, P2 responds by making $x_4 \neq x_3$ (so either the second or third clause is unsatisfied). Since this is a winning strategy for P2, all leaves reached by totally bold paths are labeled 0. ♦

Lemma 3.1. QSAT ∈ PSPACE.

Proof idea. Perhaps QSAT ∈ NP? After all, QSAT asks whether there exists a winning strategy for P1, so a stranger could convince us φ is a yes-input by showing us such a strategy as the witness, and we could verify that the strategy is indeed winning. Unfortunately, a strategy is an exponentially large thing, so we couldn't even look at it all in polynomial time. A strategy specifies one bit (to assign x_i) for each $x_2x_4 \cdots x_{i-1} \in \{0,1\}^{(i-1)/2}$ for each odd $i \in [n]$. Thus a witness would have $\sum_{i\in\{1,3,\ldots,n-1\}} 2^{(i-1)/2} = 2^0 + 2^1 + 2^2 + \cdots + 2^{n/2-1} = 2^{n/2} - 1$ many bits (Lemma A.1). It's unknown whether QSAT has a significantly faster verifier.

Our poly-space algorithm for QSAT uses recursion (implemented with the subroutine call mechanism from § 1.5.1) to traverse the evaluation tree. How can we analyze the amount of space a recursive algorithm uses? Each call has a stack frame in the work memory. When a call returns, its stack frame space becomes available for reuse by another call. For example, using letters to identify calls: If call A spawns call B, then A is paused while B runs with a separate stack frame. If B returns and A resumes and spawns call C, then C's stack frame can occupy the same space B's did. If C spawns call D, then A and C are both paused while D runs. If D returns and C resumes and spawns call E, then E's stack frame can occupy the same space D's did. This example has five stack frames (calls) but only needs space for three at a time.

Since memory space is determined by the "high water mark," it's at most the recursion depth (number of stack frame "slots") times the number of bits per stack frame. A recursive algorithm uses poly$N$ space if the depth is only poly$N$ and each stack frame is only poly$N$ bits.

In our recursive algorithm for QSAT, each call solves the "subgame" rooted at some node in the evaluation tree. Each non-leaf call spawns two calls corresponding to the children. This is a version of the basic "game tree evaluation" algorithm in AI. ■

Proof. We design a subroutine "wins" that has access to the input $\varphi(x_1 \cdots x_n)$, takes arguments $i \in [n+1]$ and $a_1 \cdots a_{i-1} \in \{0,1\}^{i-1}$, and returns the bit indicating whether the player whose turn it is (P1 if i is odd, P2 if i is even) has a winning strategy for the rest of the game, assuming $x_1 \cdots x_{i-1} = a_1 \cdots a_{i-1}$ has already been played. To solve QSAT, call wins(1, empty string), where the empty string corresponds to the evaluation tree's root.

The current player can win iff they can make a move so the other player cannot then win:

Recursive algorithm for QSAT (3.2)

wins($i, a_1 \cdots a_{i-1}$):
  if $i = n+1$: evaluate and return $\varphi(a_1 \cdots a_n)$
  return $\neg\text{wins}(i+1, a_1 \cdots a_{i-1}0) \vee \neg\text{wins}(i+1, a_1 \cdots a_{i-1}1)$

This recursive subroutine maintains the invariant that:

$$\text{wins}(i, a_1 \cdots a_{i-1}) = 1 \iff \exists x_i\ \forall x_{i+1}\ \exists x_{i+2} \cdots :\ \varphi(a_1 \cdots a_{i-1} x_i \cdots x_n) = \begin{cases} 1 & \text{if } i \text{ is odd} \\ 0 & \text{if } i \text{ is even} \end{cases}$$

This holds for the base cases since $n+1$ is odd: $\text{wins}(n+1, a_1 \cdots a_n) = 1 \iff \varphi(a_1 \cdots a_n) = 1$. To see that $\text{wins}(i, a_1 \cdots a_{i-1})$ maintains the invariant when $i \le n$, assume the invariant holds for both $\text{wins}(i+1, a_1 \cdots a_{i-1}0)$ and $\text{wins}(i+1, a_1 \cdots a_{i-1}1)$. If i is odd then the return value is:

$$\begin{aligned} \text{wins}(i, a_1 \cdots a_{i-1}) = 1 &\iff \text{wins}(i+1, a_1 \cdots a_{i-1}0) = 0 \vee \text{wins}(i+1, a_1 \cdots a_{i-1}1) = 0 \\ &\iff \neg\big(\exists x_{i+1}\ \forall x_{i+2} \cdots :\ \varphi(a_1 \cdots a_{i-1} 0 x_{i+1} \cdots x_n) = 0\big) \vee \\ &\qquad \neg\big(\exists x_{i+1}\ \forall x_{i+2} \cdots :\ \varphi(a_1 \cdots a_{i-1} 1 x_{i+1} \cdots x_n) = 0\big) \\ &\iff \big(\forall x_{i+1}\ \exists x_{i+2} \cdots :\ \varphi(a_1 \cdots a_{i-1} 0 x_{i+1} \cdots x_n) = 1\big) \vee \\ &\qquad \big(\forall x_{i+1}\ \exists x_{i+2} \cdots :\ \varphi(a_1 \cdots a_{i-1} 1 x_{i+1} \cdots x_n) = 1\big) \\ &\iff \exists x_i\ \forall x_{i+1}\ \exists x_{i+2} \cdots :\ \varphi(a_1 \cdots a_{i-1} x_i x_{i+1} \cdots x_n) = 1 \end{aligned}$$

The $\vee$ corresponds to $\exists x_i$. The same reasoning works for even i.

The argument i is the depth of a call, so the overall recursion depth is $n+1 \le N$. Each stack frame needs $O(N)$ bits to store the call's arguments and other local data, if we pack $O(\log N)$ bits of $a_1 \cdots a_{i-1}$ into a word. The space efficiency is:

$$\big(N \text{ stack frames at a time}\big) \cdot \big(O(N) \text{ bits per stack frame}\big) = O(N^2) \text{ bits}$$ ■

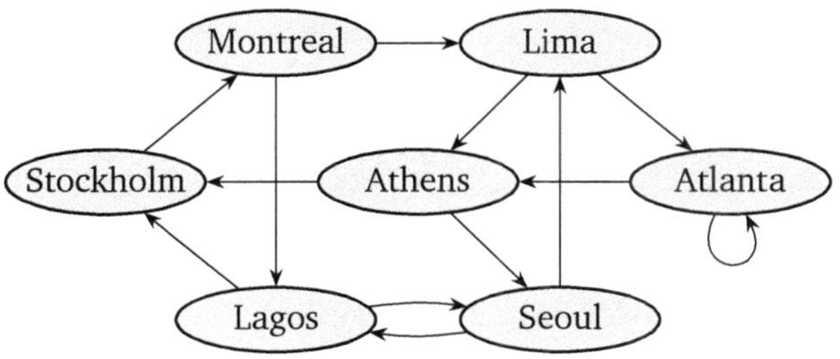

Figure 3.5: Example geography graph

A streamlined version yields QSAT $\in$ SPACE$[N]$: Instead of each stack frame having a separate copy of its $a_1 \cdots a_{i-1}$, it's enough to store one global copy of the current $a_1 \cdots a_{i-1}$.

What about improving the running time? Short-circuit $\vee$ would avoid some unnecessary calls: If the first recursive call returns 0, we could already return 1 without making the second recursive call. This is a special case of "alpha-beta pruning" in AI. We could sometimes even avoid the first recursive call: Under the partial assignment $a_1 \cdots a_{i-1} * \cdots *$, if every clause has a literal that's already 1, or if all literals in some clause are already 0, then we could return the answer straight away because the subgame's winner is already determined. These optimizations speed up the algorithm on some inputs, but it still takes exponential time in the worst case.

3.1.2 Path Forming Game

In the children's game of *geography*, two players take turns naming cities, starting with a designated city and without repeating any city. Each city must begin with the same letter the previous city ended with. For example, Seoul → Lima → Athens → Stockholm → $\cdots$. A player loses when they get stuck because they can't name an allowed city.

We represent this game with a directed graph where nodes are cities, and an edge from node u to node v means u's city's last letter equals v's city's first letter. Starting at a designated node s, the players take turns choosing edges of a path: P1 picks an edge from s to some node, then P2 picks an outgoing edge from that node, and so on. The game ends when the current node's outgoing edges all lead to nodes already on the path; the player whose turn it is loses.

Example. See Figure 3.5. (Atlanta's self-loop is useless since repeating nodes is disallowed.)

If $s =$ Lima then P1 has a winning strategy: P1 should go to Athens (not to Atlanta). If P2 goes to Seoul, then P1 goes to Lagos, and then P2 must go to Stockholm (since revisiting Seoul isn't an option), and then P1 goes to Montreal, at which point P2 loses since the outgoing edges lead to Lima and Lagos, which were both already visited. On the other hand, if P2 goes from Athens to Stockholm, then P1 goes to Montreal, and then P2 must go to Lagos (since revisiting Lima isn't an option), and then P1 goes to Seoul, at which point P2 loses since the only outgoing edges lead to Lima and Lagos, which were both already visited.

If $s =$ Montreal then P2 has a winning strategy: If P1 goes to Lagos, then P2 can go to Stockholm, and P1 loses. On the other hand, if P1 goes to Lima, then P2 should go to Atlanta, and then P1 must go to Athens, and then P2 can go to Stockholm, and P1 loses. ♦

We generalize this path forming game to all directed graphs, not just graphs arising from "last letter / first letter" relationships among city names.

GEOGRAPHY	(3.3)
Input: Directed graph G, node s	
Output: Does Player 1 have a winning strategy in the path forming game on G starting at s?	

The logic perspective is that P1 has a winning strategy iff:

$$(\exists \text{ move for P1}) \ (\forall \text{ moves for P2}) \ (\exists \text{ move for P1}) \ \cdots : \ \text{P2 has no available moves}$$

Each node in the game tree represents a path from s in G, and the children represent ways to extend the path by one edge. Each leaf in the game tree represents a path that can't be extended.

A strategy for P1 says, for each even-length path that may have been played so far, which outgoing edge P1 should take to extend the path. Like QSAT, GEOGRAPHY doesn't seem to be in NP, since a strategy is exponentially large.

Lemma 3.2. GEOGRAPHY $\in$ PSPACE.

Proof idea. A recursive algorithm explores the exponentially large game tree using only poly space, since the tree has poly depth. To see who could win given some path played so far, we try each possible next move, and recursively see who could win the rest of the game following that move. ■

Proof. We design a subroutine "wins" that has access to the input (G, s), takes as an argument a path $v_1 \to v_2 \to \cdots \to v_i$ played so far (starting at $v_1 = s$), and returns the bit indicating whether the player whose turn it is (P1 if i is odd, P2 if i is even) has a winning strategy for the rest of the game. To solve GEOGRAPHY, call wins(s) where the argument is a path with one node and no edges.

The current player can win iff they can make a move so the other player cannot then win:

Recursive algorithm for GEOGRAPHY (3.4)

```
wins(v_1, v_2, ..., v_i):
    for each edge (v_i, v) in G such that v ∉ {v_1, ..., v_i}:
        if wins(v_1, ..., v_i, v) = 0: return 1
    return 0
```

This recursive subroutine maintains the invariant that wins$(v_1, \ldots, v_i) = 1$ iff in the path forming game on G starting at v_i and with nodes $v_1, \ldots, v_{i-1}$ excluded, the player who goes first (which may be P1 or P2 from the overall game on G) has a winning strategy. This holds for the base cases, when v_i has no playable outgoing edges: wins$(v_1, \ldots, v_i) = 0$ because the current player has already lost. For non-base cases, the invariant is maintained because wins$(v_1, \ldots, v_i) = 1$ iff there exists a playable edge (v_i, v) (a move for the current player) such that wins$(v_1, \ldots, v_i, v) = 0$, which means whoever played (v_i, v) has a winning strategy (from v with $v_1, \ldots, v_i$ excluded) since their opponent (who must play from v) doesn't.

Since i is the depth of a call, and a base case must be reached when all n nodes are on the path (or sooner), the overall recursion depth is $\leq n \leq N$. Each stack frame needs poly N bits to store the call's argument and other local data. The space efficiency is:

$$\big(N \text{ stack frames at a time}\big) \cdot \big(\text{poly} N \text{ bits per stack frame}\big) \ = \ \text{poly} N \text{ bits}$$ ■

3.2 PSPACE-Completeness

3.2.1 Definition and Results

A decision problem B is PSPACE-*complete* when $B \in \mathsf{PSPACE}$ and $A \leq_p^m B$ for every $A \in \mathsf{PSPACE}$. Also, B is PSPACE-*complete via* $\leq_\ell^m$ when $B \in \mathsf{PSPACE}$ and $A \leq_\ell^m B$ for every $A \in \mathsf{PSPACE}$.

Lemma 3.3.

(i) Suppose B is PSPACE*-complete. Then $B \in \mathsf{P}$ iff $\mathsf{P} = \mathsf{PSPACE}$.*
(ii) Suppose B is PSPACE*-complete via $\leq_\ell^m$. Then $B \notin \mathsf{L}$.*

Proof. *(i)*: This is like the corresponding Lemma 2.7 for NP-completeness.

(ii): This is like the corresponding Lemma 2.38 for EXP-completeness: Suppose for contradiction B is PSPACE-complete via $\leq_\ell^m$ and $B \in \mathsf{L}$. For every $A \in \mathsf{PSPACE}$, we have $A \leq_\ell^m B \in \mathsf{L}$ and so $A \in \mathsf{L}$ (Lemma 1.15). Thus $\mathsf{PSPACE} \subseteq \mathsf{L}$, contradicting $\mathsf{PSPACE} \nsubseteq \mathsf{L}$, which we prove in §4.2. ■

Theorem 3.4. QSat *is* PSPACE*-complete via* $\leq_\ell^m$, *so* QSat $\notin \mathsf{L}$.

Theorem 3.5. Geography *is* PSPACE*-complete via* $\leq_\ell^m$, *so* Geography $\notin \mathsf{L}$.

We prove Theorem 3.4 from first principles in §3.2.2. To deduce Theorem 3.5 in §3.2.3, we use a familiar template for showing that C is PSPACE-complete via $\leq_\ell^m$: Show $C \in \mathsf{PSPACE}$ and $B \leq_\ell^m C$ for some B that we already know is PSPACE-complete via $\leq_\ell^m$. This works since for every $A \in \mathsf{PSPACE}$, we have $A \leq_\ell^m B \leq_\ell^m C$ and therefore $A \leq_\ell^m C$ (Lemma 1.16).

k-QSat is defined like QSat except φ is a k-CNF. We have 1-QSat $\in \mathsf{L}$ since a 1-CNF is a yes-input iff it's satisfiable and no $\forall$-quantified variable appears in any clause. It's known that 2-QSat $\in \mathsf{P}$, but it's neither known nor widely believed that 2-QSat $\in \mathsf{L}$.

Corollary 3.6. 3-QSat *is* PSPACE*-complete via* $\leq_\ell^m$, *so* 3-QSat $\notin \mathsf{L}$.

Proof. 3-QSat $\in \mathsf{PSPACE}$ since QSat $\in \mathsf{PSPACE}$ (Lemma 3.1). It suffices to show QSat $\leq_\ell^m$ 3-QSat since QSat is PSPACE-complete via $\leq_\ell^m$. The reduction from Sat to 3-Sat in §2.3.4 turns a CNF $\varphi(x_1 \cdots x_n)$ into a 3-CNF $\psi(x_1 \cdots x_n, y_1 \cdots y_m)$ such that for every assignment to $x_1 \cdots x_n$:

$$\varphi(x_1 \cdots x_n) = 1 \iff \exists y_1 \, \exists y_2 \cdots \exists y_m : \psi(x_1 \cdots x_n, y_1 \cdots y_m) = 1$$

To make the quantifiers strictly alternate between $\exists$ and $\forall$ as in the definition of QSat, intersperse $\forall$ quantifiers using dummy variables $z_1 \cdots z_m$:

$$\begin{aligned} &\exists x_1 \, \forall x_2 \cdots \exists x_{n-1} \, \forall x_n : \varphi(x_1 \cdots x_n) = 1 \\ \iff &\exists x_1 \, \forall x_2 \cdots \exists x_{n-1} \, \forall x_n \, \exists y_1 \, \forall z_1 \cdots \exists y_m \, \forall z_m : \psi(x_1 \cdots x_n, y_1 z_1 \cdots y_m z_m) = 1 \end{aligned}$$

Mapping φ to this ψ is a correct log-space reduction from QSat to 3-QSat. ■

What about real board games, such as Checkers, Chess, Go, Reversi, and Hex? Since they're played on constant-size boards and hence can theoretically be solved in constant time (a staggeringly huge constant), we generalize games to arbitrary-size boards. Since there would be no input besides the board size, we let the input be an arbitrary placement of pieces on the board, and ask which player can win from that point. Generalized Reversi and Hex are PSPACE-complete. Generalized Checkers, Chess, and Go are EXP-complete and thus not in P (Lemma 2.38). Those three games aren't known to be in PSPACE, because they can last for exponentially many moves, so the natural recursive algorithms have exponential depth. Even some single-player games, such as sliding block puzzles, are PSPACE-complete.

3.2.2 Quantified Formulas

Proof idea for Theorem 3.4. To reduce $A \in \mathsf{PSPACE}$ to QSAT, we turn a poly-space computation (which may take exponential time) into a poly-time computation with quantifiers: We partition the time steps into two *epochs* and use $\exists$ to "guess" the poly-size *checkpoint* configuration between the epochs, and use $\forall$ to cover both epochs, so we can just run one epoch. This achieves a factor 2 speedup with 2 quantifiers. To achieve a further factor 2 speedup with 2 more quantifiers, we repeat this by dividing epochs into sub-epochs. After poly many rounds, we achieve an exponential factor speedup using poly many quantifiers. This is like the *divide and conquer* algorithm design technique. ■

Proof of Theorem 3.4. QSAT $\in \mathsf{PSPACE}$ (Lemma 3.1). To prove that QSAT is PSPACE-hard via $\leq_\ell^m$, we consider any $A \in \mathsf{PSPACE}$ and show $A \leq_\ell^m$ QSAT.

Suppose $A \in \mathsf{PSPACE}$ by a program Π with L lines, R registers, space efficiency $\leq S = aN^b$ (for integers a, b), and word size W. Consider any valid input x of size N. Define $M = S/W - R$ (and assume M is an integer) so $\Pi(x)$ never accesses any work segment address $\geq M$. A configuration in $\{0,1\}^{\log L} \times (\{0,1\}^W)^R \times (\{0,1\}^W)^M$ represents the program counter, all R registers, and the work segment's first M words. Let $K = \log L + S$ be the number of bits in a configuration. Recall that $\Pi(x)$ takes at most 2^K steps (Theorem 1.8). When $\Pi(x)$ terminates, imagine it continues taking steps but with the configuration frozen. Assume Π has only one possible accept configuration. (Specifically, Π has only one accept instruction, and before accepting, Π assigns 0 to all registers and erases its work segment.)

We use the letters B, C, D for configurations. "$B \rightsquigarrow_t D$" means that running Π on input x for exactly t steps from configuration B results in configuration D, and that none of these t steps access any work segment address $\geq M$. (Space efficiency only concerns configurations that arise during the computation of $\Pi(x)$. Other configurations might try to access a work segment address $\geq M$, even if x is valid.) The key is that for all B and D and all even t:

$$\begin{aligned} B \rightsquigarrow_t D &\iff \exists C : (B \rightsquigarrow_{t/2} C) \text{ and } (C \rightsquigarrow_{t/2} D) \\ &\iff \exists C\ \forall e \in \{0,1\} : (B' \rightsquigarrow_{t/2} D') \text{ where } (B', D') = \begin{cases} (B, C) & \text{if } e = 0 \\ (C, D) & \text{if } e = 1 \end{cases} \end{aligned}$$

C is the "checkpoint" configuration between two epochs of the t steps from the "beginning" B to the "destination" D. The bit e indicates which epoch to focus on.

Defining B_0 as the initial configuration and D_0 as the unique accept configuration,

$$\begin{aligned} A(x) = 1 &\iff \underbrace{B_0 \rightsquigarrow_{2^K} D_0} \\ &\iff \exists C_1\ \forall e_1 : \underbrace{B_1 \rightsquigarrow_{2^{K-1}} D_1} \\ &\iff \exists C_2\ \forall e_2 : \underbrace{B_2 \rightsquigarrow_{2^{K-2}} D_2} \\ &\iff \cdots \\ &\iff \exists C_K\ \forall e_K : B_K \rightsquigarrow_1 D_K \end{aligned}$$

where for each $i \in [K]$:

$$(B_i, D_i) = \begin{cases} (B_{i-1}, C_i) & \text{if } e_i = 0 \\ (C_i, D_{i-1}) & \text{if } e_i = 1 \end{cases}$$

We condense this to:

$$A(x) = 1 \iff \exists C_1\ \forall e_1\ \exists C_2\ \forall e_2 \cdots \exists C_K\ \forall e_K : \Pi'(x, C_1, e_1, \ldots, C_K, e_K) \text{ accepts}$$

Algorithm to determine whether $B_K \rightsquigarrow_1 D_K$ (3.5)

```
Π′(x, C_1, e_1, ..., C_K, e_K):
    let B ← initial configuration, and D ← unique accept configuration
    for i ← 1, 2, ..., K:
        if e_i = 0: update D ← C_i
        if e_i = 1: update B ← C_i
    run Π for one step from configuration B with x in the input segment
    if this results in configuration D: accept
    else: reject
```

If B loads or stores at an address $\geq M$, then by definition it can't result in D. Π' runs in time linear in its input size $O(N + K^2) = O(S^2) \in \text{poly}\, N$. We apply the proof that SAT is NP-complete via $\leq_\ell^m$ (Lemma 2.39) to Π' even though Π' isn't a verifier (there's no witness w). This yields a CNF $\varphi(x, C_1, e_1, \ldots, C_K, e_K, y)$ where x is a group of variables (the input to A), each C_i is a group of variables (a configuration), each e_i is one variable, and y is a group of extra variables (the transcript of Π'), such that:

$$\Pi'(x, C_1, e_1, \ldots, C_K, e_K) \text{ accepts} \iff \exists y : \varphi(x, C_1, e_1, \ldots, C_K, e_K, y) = 1$$

The reduction computes φ in $O(\log N)$ space given N (the size of x), and it contracts φ with the actual input plugged in for x to get a CNF ψ such that:

$$A(x) = 1 \iff \exists C_1\ \forall e_1 \cdots \exists C_K\ \forall e_K\ \exists y : \psi(C_1, e_1, \ldots, C_K, e_K, y) = 1$$

Each $\exists C_i$ and $\exists y$ consists of many consecutive $\exists$ quantifiers for individual variables. After interspersing dummy variables so the quantifiers strictly alternate as in the definition of QSAT, we have $A(x) = 1$ iff ψ is a yes-input of QSAT, so the reduction is correct. ∎

3.2.3 Path Forming Game

Proof idea for Theorem 3.5. We reduce from QSAT. Given a CNF, we design a graph such that winning strategies in the QSAT game correspond to winning strategies in the GEOGRAPHY game. Choosing which bit to assign the next variable corresponds to choosing which edge to take next. But the condition for P1 winning QSAT ($\forall$ clause $\exists$ satisfied literal) is more complicated than the condition for P1 winning GEOGRAPHY (P2 gets stuck). So we extend the QSAT game by two moves: After the assignment is chosen, P2 picks a clause and then P1 picks a literal from that clause. P1 wins if the literal is satisfied, and P2 wins if it's not. These extra moves don't affect who can win the QSAT game. Now, the winning conditions of the games are in concordance: P1 being unable to pick a satisfied literal corresponds to P1 getting stuck in the graph. ∎

Proof of Theorem 3.5. GEOGRAPHY $\in$ PSPACE (Lemma 3.2). Since QSAT is PSPACE-complete via $\leq_\ell^m$ (Theorem 3.4), it suffices to show QSAT $\leq_\ell^m$ GEOGRAPHY. Map $\varphi(x_1 \cdots x_n)$ to (G, s) as follows. For each variable x_i, G has a diamond gadget as shown in Figure 3.6, which must be traversed from left to right. Going through the node labeled x_i corresponds to assigning $x_i = 0$, thus satisfying the literal $\overline{x_i}$ and leaving the $\overline{x_i}$ node available to visit later. Going through the

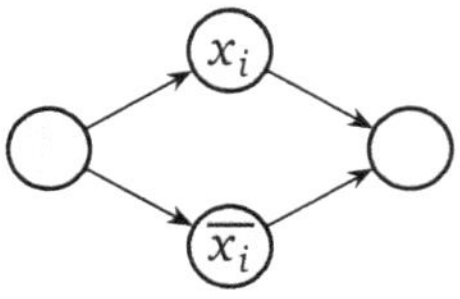

Figure 3.6: Variable gadget for reducing QSAT to GEOGRAPHY

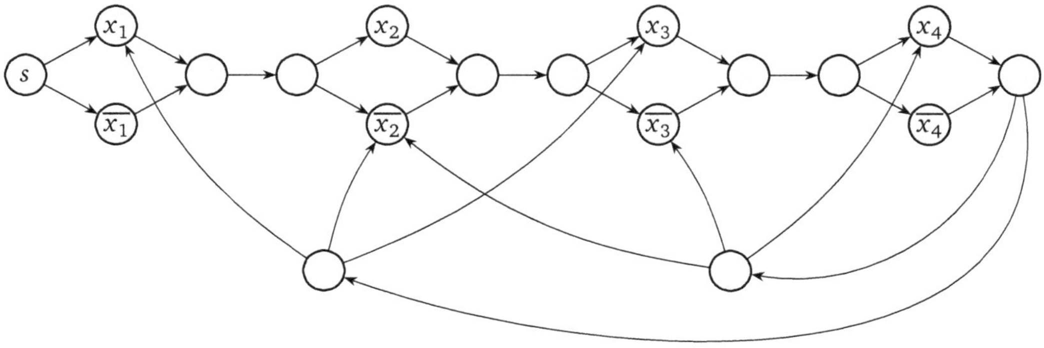

Figure 3.7: Reducing QSAT on input $\varphi(x_1x_2x_3x_4) = (x_1 \vee \overline{x_2} \vee x_3) \wedge (\overline{x_2} \vee \overline{x_3} \vee x_4)$ to GEOGRAPHY

node labeled $\overline{x_i}$ corresponds to assigning $x_i = 1$, thus satisfying the literal x_i and leaving the x_i node available to visit later. We string these variable gadgets together: The right node of x_i's gadget has an edge to the left node of x_{i+1}'s gadget, for each $i < n$. The left node of x_1's gadget is the start node s. The right node of x_n's gadget has edges to nodes that represent φ's clauses. Each clause's node has edges to the nodes labeled with the clause's literals (in the variable gadgets). Figure 3.7 shows an example.

To show this log-space mapping reduction is correct, we argue that P1 has a winning strategy on φ iff P1 has a winning strategy in the path forming game on G starting at s:

$\Rightarrow$: Assume P1 has a winning strategy on φ, and consider one such strategy. Here's a winning strategy for P1 on (G, s):

Winning strategy for Player 1 in GEOGRAPHY (3.6)

for $i \leftarrow 1, \ldots, n$:
  if i is odd:
    if P1 would assign $x_i = 0$: P1 goes to node x_i
    if P1 would assign $x_i = 1$: P1 goes to node $\overline{x_i}$
    P2 must go to x_i's right node, and then P1 goes to x_{i+1}'s left node
  if i is even:
    if P2 goes to node x_i: P1 imagines that P2 assigned $x_i = 0$
    if P2 goes to node $\overline{x_i}$: P1 imagines that P2 assigned $x_i = 1$
    P1 goes to x_i's right node, and then P2 must go to x_{i+1}'s left node if $i < n$
P2 goes from x_n's right node to some clause's node
P1 goes to the node corresponding to some satisfied literal of that clause

Each iteration of the i loop starts at the left node of x_i's gadget. Upon reaching x_n's right node, the players have simulated the QSAT gameplay of choosing an assignment to $x_1 \cdots x_n$. The unvisited nodes so far correspond to literals satisfied by this assignment. Since P1 followed the winning strategy on φ, this assignment satisfies φ. Thus no matter which clause's node P2 goes to, P1 can indeed find a satisfied literal's node to go to. At this point, P2 is stuck and loses since the only outgoing edge leads to the gadget's right node, which was already visited. Thus this strategy guarantees that P1 wins the path forming game.

$\Leftarrow$: Like the $\Rightarrow$ direction, we turn any winning strategy for P2 on φ into a winning strategy for P2 on (G,s). Upon reaching x_n's right node, the path so far corresponds to an assignment that doesn't satisfy φ. Thus P2 can go to some unsatisfied clause's node, and P1 will be stuck and lose: All outgoing edges lead to nodes that were already visited since their literals are unsatisfied. ■

3.3 NL and NL-Completeness

3.3.1 NL

For defining NL, should the witness segment count toward the verifier's space? If it counts, NL would equal L because a witness w would only be $O(\log N)$ bits, so a log-space solver could try all possible w. If it doesn't count, NL would equal NP because we could turn a poly-time verifier with witness w into a log-space verifier with witness (w, y) where y is the original verifier's transcript: If a stranger is keen to convince us, then he can also do our poly-time work for us, and we only need log space to check that he did it right.

For an interesting definition of NL, we don't count the witness segment toward the space, but instead of random access to the witness segment, we only allow one-way sequential access. A *streaming verifier* is like an ordinary verifier but instead of "read-witness Reg[i] $\leftarrow$ Wit[Reg[j]]", it uses "read-witness Reg[i]", which puts the witness segment's next unread word into Reg[i]. A streaming verifier takes one pass through the witness w, as the words of w "stream by." It can't re-read any word of w. If it wants to remember a word of w, it can keep the word in its registers or work segment and be charged for the space. The memory space of a streaming verifier V on input x is the maximum over all w of the number of bits in the registers and work segment (up through the largest address accessed) of $V(x;w)$.

As with ordinary verifiers, a streaming verifier V is correct for a decision problem A iff for every valid input x,

$$A(x) = 1 \iff \big(\exists w:\ V(x;w) \text{ accepts}\big)$$

and $V(x;w)$ terminates for all w.

Definition.

- NSPACE[S] is the set of all decision problems for which there exists a correct streaming verifier with $O(S)$ space efficiency and $O(\log \max(S,N))$-bounded word size.
- NL = NSPACE[$\log N$]
- NPSPACE = NSPACE[$\text{poly}\, N$] ◄

Observation 3.7. L ⊆ NL *and* PSPACE ⊆ NPSPACE. *More generally,* SPACE[S] ⊆ NSPACE[S]. ■

Lemma 3.8. *Every streaming verifier with space efficiency S has time efficiency $O(2^S)$.*

Proof. Suppose V is a streaming verifier (for a problem A) with L lines and space efficiency S. On a valid input x of size N, there are $T = L2^S$ possible configurations. Suppose for contradiction there exists w such that $V(x;w)$ runs for at least T steps and hence repeats a configuration C. Then $V(x;w)$ might not run forever, since it might read different words from w after repeating C. But there exists w' such that $V(x;w')$ runs forever, contradicting V's correctness: Say $V(x;w)$ reads $w_0,\ldots,w_i$ before the first occurrence of C and reads $w_{i+1},\ldots,w_j$ between the first and second occurrences of C. Define w' as $w_0,\ldots,w_i$ followed by infinitely many copies of $w_{i+1},\ldots,w_j$. Each copy of $w_{i+1},\ldots,w_j$ makes $V(x;w')$ go through the same sequence of configurations, returning to C ad infinitum. ■

Lemma 3.8 implies $\mathsf{NSPACE}[S] \subseteq \mathsf{NTIME}[2^{O(S)}]$ and thus $\mathsf{NL} \subseteq \mathsf{NP}$ and $\mathsf{NPSPACE} \subseteq \mathsf{NEXP}$. This is because we can turn a streaming verifier into a verifier with random access to the witness segment, using an extra register to remember the address of the witness segment's next unread word. We'll soon see better inclusions.

The following holds for the same reason as log-space solvers (Observation 1.7).

Observation 3.9. NL *is the set of all decision problems for which there exists a correct register-only streaming verifier with log-bounded word size.* ■

A complexity class is only as interesting as its problems. What's in NL?

Lemma 3.10. Directed Reachability ∈ NL.

Proof idea. Suppose we ask the stranger to show us a path from s to t as the witness. We follow along as he says which nodes to visit, checking that each step uses an edge of G and that the path starts at s and ends at t. To check that the witness is a path—which shouldn't repeat any node—we'd need lots of space to remember which nodes have been visited. But nobody said it must be a path. The witness can be a walk, which may repeat nodes and edges. This is enough to convince us t is reachable from s. To prevent an endless wild goose chase, we reject once we've taken n steps, since $n-1$ steps are enough to reach t. Log space suffices since we only need to remember where we are (not where we've been) and how many steps we've taken. We only need one-way sequential access to the witness, because the walk so far is irrelevant after we've checked it—we never need to recall how we got to the current node. ■

Proof. Let V be a streaming verifier such that $V(G,s,t;w)$ accepts iff w represents a walk from s to t in G of length $\leq n-1$ (where G has n nodes):

$$\begin{aligned} t \text{ is reachable from } s \text{ in } G &\iff \exists \text{ walk from } s \text{ to } t \text{ in } G \text{ of length} \leq n-1 \\ &\iff \exists w:\ V(G,s,t;w) \text{ accepts} \end{aligned}$$

V uses registers u and ℓ for the current node and the length of the walk so far. For each step, V increments ℓ and checks that $\ell \leq n-1$, then reads w's next word and checks that it represents an outgoing edge of u, then updates u to the edge's other endpoint. It accepts when t is reached. V always terminates since ℓ is incremented in each step but never exceeds n. It has $O(\log N)$ space efficiency since it only uses registers with word size $O(\log N)$.

In Figure 3.8, we implement V in our model using the input encoding from §1.3.3. At line 5, V maintains the loop invariant that it has traversed a walk from s to u of length ℓ. In the ith iteration, V gets the next node on the walk by viewing w_{i-1} as an index into u's adjacency list. This index should be ≥ 1 and $\leq u$'s outdegree, so if it's not then V rejects. ■

Directed Shortest Path Decision ∈ NL by rejecting once ℓ exceeds k from the input.

Streaming verifier program for Directed Reachability (3.7)

```
 0. read n ← In[0]
 1. let ptr ← N − 2
 2. read u ← In[ptr]
 3. let ptr ← N − 1
 4. read t ← In[ptr]
 5. if u = t then goto line 16
 6.     let ℓ ← ℓ + 1
 7.     if ℓ = n then goto line 17
 8.     read ptr ← In[u]
 9.     read outdeg ← In[ptr]
10.     read-witness index
11.     if index > outdeg then goto line 17
12.     if index = 0 then goto line 17
13.     let ptr ← ptr + index
14.     read u ← In[ptr]
15.     goto line 5
16. accept
17. reject
```

Figure 3.8: Implementation of the streaming verifier for Directed Reachability

3.3.2 NL-Completeness

L versus NL has almost the same reputation as P versus NP. It's unknown whether L = NL, but it's widely conjectured that L ≠ NL. Analogous to NP-completeness, NL-completeness is evidence that certain problems aren't in L since they're the "hardest" in NL.

A decision problem B is NL-*complete* when $B \in \mathsf{NL}$ and $A \leq_\ell^m B$ for every $A \in \mathsf{NL}$. Why $\leq_\ell^m$ instead of $\leq_p^m$? We'll soon see that NL ⊆ P. It would be silly to allow reductions that are more powerful than NL itself—a poly-time reduction could solve an NL problem without the oracle. Completeness for a complexity class should involve reductions that are weaker than the class, because translating a question should be easier than answering it.

Lemma 3.11. *Suppose B is* NL-*complete. Then $B \in \mathsf{L}$ iff* L = NL.

Proof. ⇐: Assume L = NL. Then $B \in \mathsf{L}$ because $B \in \mathsf{NL}$.

⇒: Assume $B \in \mathsf{L}$. Then NL ⊆ L because for every $A \in \mathsf{NL}$, we have $A \leq_\ell^m B$, which implies $A \in \mathsf{L}$ (Lemma 1.15). Since L ⊆ NL, we conclude L = NL. ■

Corollary 3.12. *Either all* NL-*complete problems are in* L, *or none are.*

Proof. By Lemma 3.11, if L = NL then every NL-complete problem is in L, and if L ≠ NL then every NL-complete problem is not in L. ■

Directed Reachability is the canonical NL-complete problem, like how Sat is the canonical NP-complete problem. This is evidence that Directed Reachability ∉ L.

Theorem 3.13. Directed Reachability *is* NL-*complete.*

We prove this soon. Directed Reachability Search is "as good as" NL-complete, like how Sat Search is "as good as" NP-complete (Corollary 2.15):

Corollary 3.14. Directed Reachability Search *has a log-space program iff* L = NL.

Proof. DIRECTED REACHABILITY SEARCH has a log-space program iff DIRECTED REACHABILITY $\in$ L (Theorem 1.22 and Lemma 1.18) iff L = NL (Lemma 3.11) because DIRECTED REACHABILITY is NL-complete (Theorem 3.13). ■

Corollary 3.15. NL $\subseteq$ P.

Proof. For every $A \in$ NL, we have $A \leq_\ell^m$ DIRECTED REACHABILITY $\in$ P and thus $A \in$ P. ■

To prove that C is NL-complete, we can use a familiar template: Show $C \in$ NL and $B \leq_\ell^m C$ for some B that we already know is NL-complete. This works since for every $A \in$ NL, we have $A \leq_\ell^m B \leq_\ell^m C$ and therefore $A \leq_\ell^m C$ (Lemma 1.16). For example, DIRECTED SHORTEST PATH DECISION is NL-complete: It's in NL, and DIRECTED REACHABILITY $\leq_\ell^m$ DIRECTED SHORTEST PATH DECISION by mapping (G,s,t) to $(G,s,t,n-1)$ where n is the number of nodes in G. Some other NL-complete problems are 2-SAT (Exercise 3.14) and 2-QSAT.

Proof idea for Theorem 3.13. We can't use the template, since we don't know another NL-complete problem to reduce from. To prove the theorem from first principles, we turn any log-space streaming verifier V into a reduction to DIRECTED REACHABILITY. The computation of $V(x;w)$ is like a walk in a directed graph where nodes are configurations and edges are computation steps. Possibilities of w correspond to walks. If $V(x;w)$ accepts, then w corresponds to a walk that reaches a particular target node t. One-way sequential access to w means each "read-witness" step can get potentially any word, regardless of prior steps, like how a walk can take any outgoing edge from a node, regardless of how the walk got to that node. ■

Proof of Theorem 3.13. DIRECTED REACHABILITY $\in$ NL (Lemma 3.10). To prove that DIRECTED REACHABILITY is NL-hard, we consider any $A \in$ NL and show $A \leq_\ell^m$ DIRECTED REACHABILITY. Suppose $A \in$ NL by a register-only streaming verifier V with L lines, R registers, and log-bounded word size W. Consider any valid input x of size N. A configuration in $\{0,1\}^{\log L} \times (\{0,1\}^W)^R$ represents the program counter and all R registers.

Map x to (G,s,t) as follows. G has nodes corresponding to all possible configurations, of which there are $L2^{RW} \in \operatorname{poly} N$. Node s corresponds to the initial configuration. Node t is extra (not corresponding to a configuration) and has no outgoing edges. To define the outgoing edges of the node v_C for configuration C, consider V's instruction at line C_{PC}:

- Data processing or control flow: v_C has an edge to $v_{C'}$ where C' is the configuration after one step of V from C.
- "read Reg[i] $\leftarrow$ In[Reg[j]]": v_C has an edge to $v_{C'}$ where C' is the configuration after one step of V on input x from C. That is, C' is C except $C'_{\mathrm{Reg}[i]} = \mathrm{In}[C_{\mathrm{Reg}[j]}]$ and $C'_{\mathrm{PC}} = C_{\mathrm{PC}} + 1$.
- "read-witness Reg[i]": v_C has 2^W edges (one for each possible next word of V's witness segment) to all nodes $v_{C'}$ where C' is C except $C'_{\mathrm{Reg}[i]} =$ anything and $C'_{\mathrm{PC}} = C_{\mathrm{PC}} + 1$.
- "accept": v_C has an edge to t.
- "reject": v_C has no outgoing edges.

This reduction only needs log space to loop through the nodes and create their adjacency lists. To show that it's correct, we argue that $V(x;w)$ accepts for some w iff G has a walk from s to t:

$\Leftarrow$: When a walk from s to t leaves a "read-witness" node, define w's next word according to the edge the walk takes. The walk's nodes correspond to successive configurations of the computation of $V(x;w)$. Since the only way to enter t is from an "accept" configuration, $V(x;w)$ accepts.

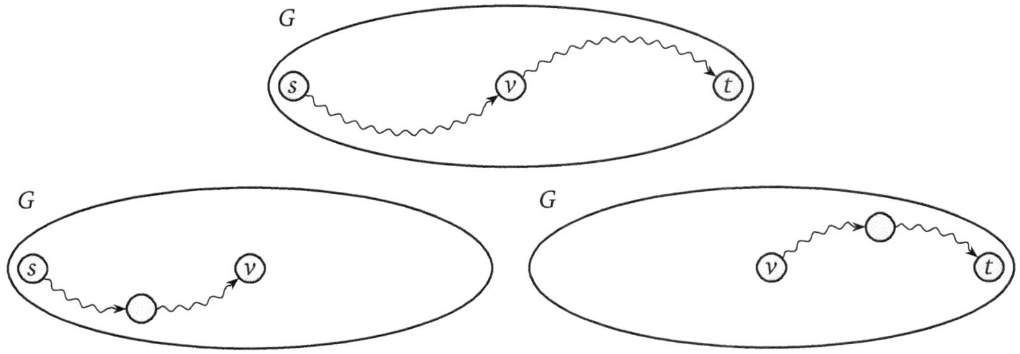

Figure 3.9: DIRECTED REACHABILITY game

⇒: If $V(x;w)$ accepts, then its sequence of configurations corresponds to a walk from s to t. When the computation reaches a "read-witness" configuration, w's next word says which edge to take. Since $V(x;w)$ accepts, this walk reaches an "accept" node, from which it steps to t.

In summary: $A(x)=1 \iff \big(\exists w:\ V(x;w) \text{ accepts}\big) \iff \big(\exists \text{ walk from } s \text{ to } t \text{ in } G\big)$ ■

3.4 Turning Verifiers into Solvers

It's conjectured that turning verifiers into solvers generally requires exponential time overhead. In contrast, we can turn streaming verifiers into solvers with only quadratic space overhead.

3.4.1 Middle-First Search

Let $\mathsf{L}^2 = \mathsf{SPACE}[\log^2 N]$.

Theorem 3.16. DIRECTED REACHABILITY $\in \mathsf{L}^2$.

Proof idea. Breadth-first search is fast but uses lots of space. We design a *middle-first search* algorithm that uses much less space but is much slower. This is a time-space tradeoff.

We use the connection between logic, games, and recursion (§ 3.1). Player 1 claims t is reachable from s, and player 2 claims it isn't, so they go toe-to-toe. P1 says which node v is the midpoint on a path from s to t. P2 picks either "s to v" or "v to t" and says, "If you're right, then this section should be a path of half the length. Show me this section's midpoint." P1 obliges, and P2 picks one of the two subsections (which should have a quarter the length of the original path), and so on. See Figure 3.9. Like binary search, they zoom in on a particular edge on the path. P1 wins if G actually has that edge, and P2 wins if it doesn't.

The game starts with $u \leftarrow s$ and $w \leftarrow t$ and has $\log n$ rounds. In each round, P1 picks v and P2 picks whether to update $w \leftarrow v$ (restrict to first half) or $u \leftarrow v$ (restrict to second half). A path from s to t provides P1 a winning strategy, since the path length is initially $< n$ and gets halved in each round. Conversely, a winning strategy for P1 yields a walk (and hence a path) from s to t. A walk's two halves are decoupled because "how we got to the midpoint" doesn't influence our options for the rest of the walk. The logic perspective is:

$$t \text{ is reachable from } s \iff \exists \text{ midpoint } \forall \text{ half } \exists \text{ midpoint } \forall \text{ half} \cdots :\ u = w \text{ or } (u,w) \text{ is an edge}$$

Though playing the game is quick, evaluating the whole game tree is not: The tree has depth $O(\log n)$ and branching factor $O(n)$, so the number of leaves is $O(n)^{O(\log n)} = 2^{O(\log^2 n)}$, which is super-polynomial. But the recursive algorithm's space efficiency benefits from the small depth. The call stack stores $O(\log n)$ nodes, each of which is $O(\log n)$ bits. ■

Proof. Say the input is (G, s, t) where $G = (V, E)$ has n nodes, and let $K = \lceil \log(n-1) \rceil$. We design a subroutine "mfs" that has access to the input (G, s, t), takes arguments $u \in V$, $w \in V$, and $k \in \{0, 1, \ldots, K\}$, and returns the bit indicating whether the distance from u to w is $\leq 2^k$ in G. (The distance is ∞ if w is unreachable from u.) To solve DIRECTED REACHABILITY, call mfs(s, t, K) since the distance from s to t is $\leq n-1 \leq 2^K$ if t is reachable from s.

Middle-first search algorithm for DIRECTED REACHABILITY (3.8)

```
mfs(u, w, k):
    if k = 0:
        if u = w or (u, w) ∈ E: return 1
        else: return 0
    else:
        for each v ∈ V:
            if mfs(u, v, k − 1) ∧ mfs(v, w, k − 1) = 1: return 1
        return 0
```

This recursive subroutine maintains the invariant that:

$$\text{mfs}(u, w, k) = 1 \iff \exists \text{ walk of length} \leq 2^k \text{ from } u \text{ to } w \text{ in } G$$

This holds for the base cases when $k = 0$. To see that mfs(u, w, k) maintains the invariant when $k > 0$, assume the invariant holds for all mfs$(u, v, k-1)$ and mfs$(v, w, k-1)$.

$\Rightarrow$: If mfs$(u, w, k) = 1$ then mfs$(u, v, k-1) \wedge$ mfs$(v, w, k-1) = 1$ for some v, so there exist walks of lengths $\leq 2^{k-1}$ from u to v and from v to w. Concatenating these walks yields a walk of length $\leq 2^{k-1} + 2^{k-1} = 2^k$ from u to w.

$\Leftarrow$: Suppose there exists a walk of length $\leq 2^k$ from u to w. If the length is $\leq 2^{k-1}$ then let $v = w$, otherwise let v be the node after the first 2^{k-1} edges on the walk and note that the walk has $\leq 2^k - 2^{k-1} = 2^{k-1}$ edges after v. Splitting the walk at v yields walks of lengths $\leq 2^{k-1}$ from u to v and from v to w, so mfs$(u, v, k-1) \wedge$ mfs$(v, w, k-1) = 1$ and thus mfs$(u, w, k) = 1$.

A call's depth is $K - k + 1$, so the overall recursion depth is $K + 1 \leq O(\log N)$. Each stack frame needs $O(\log N)$ bits for the arguments u, w, k and other local data such as v. The space efficiency is:

$$\big(O(\log N) \text{ stack frames at a time}\big) \cdot \big(O(\log N) \text{ bits per stack frame}\big) = O(\log^2 N) \text{ bits}$$ ■

Corollary 3.17. $\mathsf{NL} \subseteq \mathsf{L}^2$.

Proof. For every $A \in \mathsf{NL}$, we have $A \leq_\ell^m$ DIRECTED REACHABILITY $\in \mathsf{L}^2$ (Theorem 3.13 and Theorem 3.16), so $A \in \mathsf{L}^2$ by essentially the same proof as Lemma 1.15: On an input to A of size N, run a $O(\log^2 M)$-space program for DIRECTED REACHABILITY on the reduction's query of size $M \leq \text{poly} N$, recomputing each word of the query (as needed) with $+O(\log N)$ space. ■

Problems that are PSPACE-complete via $\le_\ell^m$, such as QSAT and GEOGRAPHY, are not in L^2 (since we prove PSPACE $\not\subseteq L^2$ in §4.2) and hence not in NL.

DIRECTED REACHABILITY has a poly-time algorithm and a polylog-space algorithm. Does it have an algorithm that's simultaneously poly-time and polylog-space? It's unknown whether NL $\subseteq$ TISP[poly$N$, polylog$N$], but it's conjectured that we can't have our cake and eat it too.

3.4.2 PSPACE = NPSPACE

Since it's widely believed that P $\ne$ NP, this may be a surprise:

Theorem 3.18. PSPACE = NPSPACE.

Proof idea. One way to prove this is by "scaling up" NL $\subseteq L^2$ using a technique we'll see in §4.1. Another way is to observe that the proof that QSAT is PSPACE-complete (§3.2.2) also shows that QSAT is NPSPACE-complete: Reduce $A \in$ NPSPACE to QSAT $\in$ PSPACE in the same way, and when configuration B is a "read-witness", Π' checks that configuration D can follow from B in one step. For both these proofs, the main idea is to recursively evaluate the game tree of middle-first search on a graph where nodes are configurations and edges are computation steps of a streaming verifier. We give a self-contained, streamlined proof. ■

Proof. Suppose $A \in$ NPSPACE by a streaming verifier V with L lines, R registers, space efficiency $\le S = aN^b$ (for integers a, b), and word size W. Consider any valid input x of size N. Define $M = S/W - R$ (and assume M is an integer) so $V(x;w)$ never accesses any work segment address $\ge M$. A configuration in $\{0,1\}^{\log L} \times (\{0,1\}^W)^R \times (\{0,1\}^W)^M$ represents the program counter, all R registers, and the work segment's first M words. Let $K = \log L + S$ be the number of bits in a configuration. For all w, $V(x;w)$ takes at most 2^K steps (Lemma 3.8). When $V(x;w)$ terminates, imagine it continues taking steps but with the configuration frozen. Assume V has only one possible accept configuration.

We use the letters B, C, D for configurations. "$B \rightsquigarrow_t D$" means there exists w such that running $V(x;w)$ for exactly t steps from configuration B results in configuration D, and that none of these t steps access any work segment address $\ge M$. We claim that for all B and D and all even t:

$$B \rightsquigarrow_t D \iff \exists C: (B \rightsquigarrow_{t/2} C) \text{ and } (C \rightsquigarrow_{t/2} D)$$

$\Leftarrow$: If $t/2$ steps of $V(x;w')$ lead B to C, and $t/2$ steps of $V(x;w'')$ lead C to D, then t steps of $V(x;w)$ lead B to D, where w is the concatenation of w' and w''. This is because of one-way sequential access to w: After consuming w' and reaching C, the computation will proceed as if it started in C and the witness segment started with w''.

$\Rightarrow$: Assume t steps of $V(x;w)$ lead B to D. Let C be the configuration after $t/2$ steps, and split w into w' read by the first $t/2$ steps, and w'' read by the last $t/2$ steps. We have $B \rightsquigarrow_{t/2} C$ since $t/2$ steps of $V(x;w')$ lead B to C by definition. We have $C \rightsquigarrow_{t/2} D$ since $t/2$ steps of $V(x;w'')$ lead C to D since they proceed the same as the last $t/2$ steps of $V(x;w)$, because of one-way sequential access to w.

We design a subroutine "mfs" that has access to the input x, takes arguments B, D, and $k \in \{0,1,\dots,K\}$, and returns the bit indicating whether $B \rightsquigarrow_{2^k} D$. To solve A, call mfs(B_0, D_0, K) where B_0 is the initial configuration and D_0 is the unique accept configuration:

$$A(x) = 1 \iff \big(\exists w: V(x;w) \text{ accepts}\big) \iff B_0 \rightsquigarrow_{2^K} D_0 \iff \text{mfs}(B_0, D_0, K) = 1$$

If B is a "read-witness", then "can follow from" means D is B but with anything in the target register and with the PC incremented. If B loads or stores at an address $\geq M$, then D can't follow from B.

Middle-first search for PSPACE = NPSPACE (3.9)

```
mfs(B, D, k):
    if k = 0:
        if D can follow from B after one step of V with x in the input segment: return 1
        else: return 0
    else:
        for each configuration C:
            if mfs(B, C, k − 1) ∧ mfs(C, D, k − 1) = 1: return 1
        return 0
```

This recursive subroutine maintains the invariant that $\mathrm{mfs}(B,D,k)=1 \iff B \rightsquigarrow_{2^k} D$. This holds for the base cases when $k=0$. By our claim, $\mathrm{mfs}(B,D,k)$ maintains the invariant when $k>0$:

$$\begin{aligned} \mathrm{mfs}(B,D,k)=1 &\iff \exists C:\ \mathrm{mfs}(B,C,k-1)\wedge \mathrm{mfs}(C,D,k-1)=1 \\ &\iff \exists C:\ (B \rightsquigarrow_{2^{k-1}} C) \text{ and } (C \rightsquigarrow_{2^{k-1}} D) \\ &\iff B \rightsquigarrow_{2^k} D \end{aligned}$$

A call's depth is $K-k+1$, so the overall recursion depth is $K+1\leq O(S)$. Each stack frame needs $O(S)$ bits for the arguments B, D, k and other local data such as C. The space efficiency is:

$$\big(O(S) \text{ stack frames at a time}\big)\cdot\big(O(S) \text{ bits per stack frame}\big) \;=\; O(S^2) \text{ bits}$$

We conclude $A \in \mathsf{SPACE}[S^2] \subseteq \mathsf{PSPACE}$. ■

3.5 NL Is Closed Under Complement

Since it's widely believed that $\mathsf{NP} \neq \mathsf{coNP}$, this may be a surprise:

Theorem 3.19. $\mathsf{NL} = \mathsf{coNL}$.

Proof idea. We prove $\overline{\text{DIRECTED REACHABILITY}} \in \mathsf{NL}$. The stranger wants to convince us there *does not* exist a path from s to t in G.

First, suppose we somehow know how many nodes are reachable from s. To convince us t is not one of those nodes, the stranger can say which nodes are reachable from s and convince us he's right by showing how to reach those nodes: For each node, he says whether it's reachable from s and if so, shows a walk of length $\leq n-1$ from s to that node. We reject if any walk doesn't pass inspection or if he demonstrates how to reach too few nodes. Otherwise, we accept after seeing that t is not among the nodes reachable from s.

Before doing that, we enlist the stranger's help to figure out how many nodes are reachable from s. For each $d \leftarrow 1,2,\ldots,n-1$, we figure out how many nodes have distance $\leq d$ from s. Distance $\leq n-1$ covers all reachable nodes. To count the nodes having distance $\leq d$, we let the stranger say which nodes have distance $\leq d$ and which don't. To convince us v has distance $\leq d$, the stranger shows a walk of length $\leq d$. To convince us v has distance $> d$, he reconvinces us which nodes have distance $\leq d-1$ similarly to the previous paragraph (since we remember how many such nodes there are), and we check that none of them has an edge to v. We only need log space because after learning how many nodes have distance $\leq d$, we can forget how many have distance $\leq d-1$. ■

Lemma 3.20. *For all decision problems A and B, if $A \leq_\ell^m B$ and $B \in \mathsf{NL}$ then $A \in \mathsf{NL}$.*

Proof of Lemma 3.20. Assume $A \leq_\ell^m B$ by reduction F, and $B \in \mathsf{NL}$ by streaming verifier V. Then $A \in \mathsf{NL}$ by a streaming verifier V' that, on input x, runs V on input $F(x)$ using the same purported witness w. This is correct because:

$$A(x)=1 \iff B(F(x))=1 \iff \big(\exists w:\ V(F(x);w) \text{ accepts}\big) \iff \big(\exists w:\ V'(x;w) \text{ accepts}\big)$$

V' terminates for all w since V does. We make V' run in log space as in the proof of Lemma 1.15: V' first runs the reduction to compute the size of $F(x)$—without writing $F(x)$—so V knows how big its input is. Then whenever V reads a word of $F(x)$, V' computes the word by rerunning the reduction and ignoring the other words of $F(x)$. We use masking so the reduction and V run with their intended word sizes. The w for V is actually the masked version of the w for V'. ■

Proof of Theorem 3.19. We prove $\mathsf{coNL} \subseteq \mathsf{NL}$. Complementing both sides yields $\mathsf{NL} \subseteq \mathsf{coNL}$, so $\mathsf{NL} = \mathsf{coNL}$. It suffices to prove $\overline{\text{DIRECTED REACHABILITY}} \in \mathsf{NL}$ since then for every $A \in \mathsf{coNL}$ we have $A \leq_\ell^m \overline{\text{DIRECTED REACHABILITY}}$ (since DIRECTED REACHABILITY is NL-complete) and thus $A \in \mathsf{NL}$ (Lemma 3.20).

Figure 3.10 shows a log-space streaming verifier V for $\overline{\text{DIRECTED REACHABILITY}}$. Let S_d be the set of all nodes with distance $\leq d$ from s, so S_{n-1} is the set of all nodes reachable from s. In iteration d, *curcount* counts how many nodes v are in S_d, while *prevcount* remembers how many nodes are in S_{d-1} (from iteration $d-1$). Before the loop, *curcount* $\leftarrow 1$ because $S_0 = \{s\}$ has one node. In each iteration of the v loop, w's next word indicates whether $v \in S_d$. If this word isn't 1, V checks that $v \notin S_d$ by using *tempcount* to recount how many nodes u are in S_{d-1}. In each iteration of the u loop, w's next word indicates whether $u \in S_{d-1}$.

By design, V always terminates. To show that V is correct, we argue that t is unreachable from s in G iff there exists w such that $V(G,s,t;w)$ accepts:

$\Rightarrow$: Assume $t \notin S_{n-1}$. We describe a w that makes V accept. Consider iteration d. For each v: If $v \in S_d$, let w have a 1 followed by a walk from s to v of length $\leq d$. If $v \notin S_d$, let w have a 0 and then for each u in the innermost loop: If $u \in S_{d-1}$, let w have a 1 followed by a walk from s to u of length $\leq d-1$. If $u \notin S_{d-1}$, let w have a 0.

We claim V maintains the invariant that it doesn't reject, and *curcount* $= |S_d|$ at the end of iteration d. Assume *prevcount* $= |S_{d-1}|$ in iteration d. Note that V doesn't reject any "walk check." If $v \notin S_d$, then for all $u \in S_{d-1}$ we have $u \neq v$ and (u,v) isn't an edge, so *tempcount* reaches $|S_{d-1}|$ and thus V doesn't reject due to *tempcount* < *prevcount*. Each $v \in S_d$ causes an increment to *curcount*. This proves the claim. In conclusion, V accepts when $d = n-1$ and $v = t$, since $t \notin S_{n-1}$.

$\Leftarrow$: Assume $V(G,s,t;w)$ accepts. Intuitively, w must have the intended form as in the $\Rightarrow$ direction, otherwise V would reject.

We claim V maintains the invariant that *curcount* $= |S_d|$ at the end of iteration d. To show iteration d maintains the invariant, we assume *prevcount* $= |S_{d-1}|$ in iteration d, and we argue that for all v, we have $v \in S_d$ iff v causes an increment to *curcount*:

Streaming verifier for $\overline{\text{DIRECTED REACHABILITY}}$ (3.10)

```
V(G,s,t;w) where G has n nodes:
    curcount ← 1
    for d ← 1,2,...,n−1:
        prevcount ← curcount and curcount ← 0
        for each node v:
            if w's next word = 1:
                if w's next words aren't a walk from s to v of length ≤ d: reject
                increment curcount
            else:
                tempcount ← 0
                for each node u ≠ v such that (u,v) isn't an edge in G:
                    if w's next word = 1:
                        if w's next words aren't a walk from s to u of length ≤ d−1: reject
                        increment tempcount
                if tempcount < prevcount: reject
                if d = n−1 and v = t: accept
    reject
```

Figure 3.10: Streaming verifier for proving $\overline{\text{DIRECTED REACHABILITY}} \in \mathsf{NL}$

⇐: Suppose v causes an increment to *curcount*. This means w's next word is 1 in the v iteration and V doesn't reject the "walk check" here, so $v \in S_d$.

⇒: Suppose for contradiction $v \in S_d$ but v doesn't cause an increment to *curcount*. We'll show that V rejects, contradicting the assumption that V accepts. If w's next word is 1 in the v iteration, then V rejects the "walk check" (otherwise *curcount* would get incremented). So assume w's next word isn't 1. If $v \in S_{d-1}$ then let $u^* = v$, otherwise let $u^* \in S_{d-1}$ be v's predecessor on some shortest path from s to v. Since either $u^* = v$ or (u^*, v) is an edge, the innermost loop has no iteration with $u = u^*$. Each $u \notin S_{d-1}$ can't cause an increment to *tempcount* since V would reject the "walk check." Thus *tempcount* only counts nodes in S_{d-1} but misses u^*, so V rejects because $\textit{tempcount} < |S_{d-1}| = \textit{prevcount}$.

This proves the claim. In conclusion, $t \in S_{n-1}$ iff t causes an increment to *curcount* when $d = n-1$. Since V accepts, t doesn't cause an increment to *curcount* when $d = n-1$. Therefore $t \notin S_{n-1}$.

Since V is register-only and no register ever exceeds N in value, word size $O(\log N)$ suffices. Thus V has $O(\log N)$ space efficiency. ■

In summary, $\mathsf{NL} \subseteq \mathsf{P} \cap \mathsf{L}^2 \cap \mathsf{coNL}$.

Exercises

3.1 For the QSAT input $\varphi(x_1x_2x_3x_4) = (x_1 \vee \overline{x_2} \vee \overline{x_3}) \wedge (\overline{x_1} \vee x_2 \vee \overline{x_4}) \wedge (x_2 \vee x_3 \vee x_4)$, draw the evaluation tree, determine which player has a winning strategy, and find a winning strategy.

3.2 **(a)** Consider the version of QSAT in which the input CNF is *monotone*, meaning it has no negative literals. Prove that this problem is in L.

(b) Consider the version of 3-QSAT in which each clause of the input CNF φ has at least one literal for which the opposite literal appears nowhere in φ. Prove that this problem $\le_\ell^m$ 2-QSAT (which is known to be in NL).

(c) Consider the version of QSAT in which the input CNF has at most $c \log n$ clauses, for some constant c. Prove that this problem is in P.

3.3 For each possible starting city in the example geography graph in Figure 3.5, determine which player has a winning strategy, and find a winning strategy.

3.4 NODE KAYLES is a two-player game version of INDEPENDENT SET. The players take turns picking different nodes of an undirected graph, such that the set of all picked nodes is always an independent set. A player loses if they cannot move because every unpicked node is adjacent to at least one picked node. "Kayles" comes from a French word for "bowling" because knocking down a node (a bowling pin) also knocks down its neighbors. Prove NODE KAYLES $\in$ PSPACE.

NODE KAYLES	(3.11)
Input:	Undirected graph G
Output:	Does Player 1 have a winning strategy in the game on G described above?

3.5 QSAT's input can have dummy variables, which are quantified but appear in no clauses. Prove that QSAT would remain PSPACE-complete via $\le_\ell^m$ even if dummy variables are disallowed—that is, every quantified variable must be in at least one clause (and we still require the quantifiers to strictly alternate $\exists x_1 \, \forall x_2 \cdots \exists x_{n-1} \, \forall x_n$).

3.6 MISÈRE GEOGRAPHY is like GEOGRAPHY except the player who gets stuck wins (whereas they would lose in GEOGRAPHY).

(a) Show that MISÈRE GEOGRAPHY is *not* the same as $\overline{\text{GEOGRAPHY}}$.

(b) Prove that MISÈRE GEOGRAPHY is PSPACE-complete via $\le_\ell^m$.

3.7 In the game of geography, each node has a string label, and an edge (u, v) means u's label's last letter equals v's label's first letter. If two nodes' labels have the same last letter, then these nodes must have the same set of outneighbors, namely all nodes whose label starts with that letter. Thus, such graphs are *string compatible*, which means every pair of nodes with an outneighbor in common have *all* their outneighbors in common. Prove that GEOGRAPHY remains PSPACE-complete via $\le_\ell^m$ even if the input graph must be string compatible.

3.8 Search-to-decision reductions wouldn't make much sense for PSPACE-complete problems, since the object we're searching for—such as a winning strategy in a game—has exponential size. Instead, we design "play-to-decision" reductions. Just knowing that Player 1 has a winning strategy in a QSAT game isn't much help for actually playing the game. This search problem asks what move P1 should make in any given situation:

PLAY QSAT	(3.12)
Input:	CNF $\varphi(x_1 \cdots x_n)$ where n is even, and $a_1 \cdots a_{i-1} \in \{0,1\}^{i-1}$ where $i < n$ is odd
Output:	A bit a_i such that $\forall x_{i+1}\ \exists x_{i+2} \cdots \forall x_n :\ \varphi(a_1 \cdots a_{i-1} a_i x_{i+1} \cdots x_n) = 1$, or report that none exists

Prove PLAY QSAT $\leq_p^o$ QSAT. Thus if QSAT $\in$ P, then P1 has a poly-time algorithm for winning a game regardless of P2's moves, assuming a winning strategy exists for P1.

3.9 Two-player game versions of NP-complete problems are not automatically PSPACE-hard or even NP-hard. Prove SUBSET SUM GAME $\in$ L.

SUBSET SUM GAME	(3.13)
Input:	Positive integers $x_1, x_2, \ldots, x_n$ (where n is even) and t, represented in binary with m bits each
Output:	Does Player 1 have a winning strategy in the following game? P1 picks whether $1 \in I$, then P2 picks whether $2 \in I$, then P1 picks whether $3 \in I$, then P2 picks whether $4 \in I$, and so on At the end, if $\sum_{i \in I} x_i = t$ then P2 wins, otherwise P1 wins.

3.10 Prove that the class NTIME$[T]$ would remain the same if we changed the definition to use streaming verifiers instead of ordinary verifiers. We're not concerned with space efficiency here—the point is that random access and one-way sequential access to the witness are equivalent in the context of time efficiency.

3.11 **(a)** In this exercise, you'll prove GRAPH 2-COLORING $\in$ L by reducing it to UNDIRECTED REACHABILITY (which is in L by a difficult proof). For any undirected graph G, define G_{bip} as the bipartite graph that has two nodes u_{left} and u_{right} for each node u of G, and has two edges $\{u_{\text{left}}, v_{\text{right}}\}$ and $\{u_{\text{right}}, v_{\text{left}}\}$ for each edge $\{u, v\}$ of G. Prove that this reduction shows GRAPH 2-COLORING $\leq_\ell^o$ UNDIRECTED REACHABILITY:

Reduction from GRAPH 2-COLORING to UNDIRECTED REACHABILITY (3.14)

```
on input G:
    for each node u of G:
        query the oracle on input (G_bip, u_left, u_right)
        if the oracle accepted: reject
    accept
```

(b) Prove GRAPH 2-COLORING $\leq_\ell^m$ $\overline{\text{UNDIRECTED REACHABILITY}}$.

(c) Prove 2-XOR SAT $\leq_\ell^m$ GRAPH 2-COLORING, and thus 2-XOR SAT $\in$ L.

2-XOR SAT	(3.15)
Input:	A conjunction of constraints of the form $(\ell_i \oplus \ell_j)$ where ℓ_i and ℓ_j are literals
Output:	Is this formula satisfiable?

3.12 A directed graph is *strongly connected* when for every ordered pair of nodes u, v, there exists a path from u to v. Prove STRONG CONNECTIVITY is NL-complete.

STRONG CONNECTIVITY	(3.16)
Input:	Directed graph G
Output:	Is G strongly connected?

3.13 Recall the layering technique from the proof of Lemma 1.21.

(a) Prove DAG DECISION is NL-complete. Hint: NL = coNL.

DAG DECISION	(3.17)
Input:	Directed graph G
Output:	Is G acyclic?

(b) Prove DIRECTED REACHABILITY ON A DAG is NL-complete. This problem is defined like DIRECTED REACHABILITY but in the input, G is acyclic. (This result doesn't immediately follow from the proof that DIRECTED REACHABILITY is NL-complete, since there could be cycles in unreachable parts of the graphs from that proof.)

(c) Prove UNDIRECTED SHORTEST PATH DECISION is NL-complete. This problem is defined like DIRECTED SHORTEST PATH DECISION but in the input, G is undirected.

3.14 Prove 2-SAT is NL-complete.

(a) Prove 2-SAT $\in$ NL using Exercise 2.12.

(b) Prove 2-SAT is NL-hard.

3.15 Prove that this problem is NL-complete using NL-completeness of 2-SAT (Exercise 3.14).

(2 OUT OF 3)-SAT	(3.18)
Input:	3-CNF formula φ
Output:	Does there exist an assignment that satisfies at least two literals in each clause?

3.16 Prove that this problem is NL-complete using NL-completeness of 2-SAT (Exercise 3.14).

GRAPH 3-COLORING WITH FORBIDDEN COLORS	(3.19)
Input:	Undirected graph G, and a "forbidden" color f_v for each node v
Output:	Does G have a proper 3-coloring c with $c(v) \neq f_v$ for each node v?

(a) Prove GRAPH 3-COLORING WITH FORBIDDEN COLORS $\in$ NL.

(b) Define BIPARTITE 2-SAT like 2-SAT but φ has variables $x_1 \cdots x_n$ and $y_1 \cdots y_n$ and each clause involves one x variable and one y variable. Prove BIPARTITE 2-SAT is NL-complete.

(c) Prove GRAPH 3-COLORING WITH FORBIDDEN COLORS is NL-hard. Hint: Reduce from

BIPARTITE 2-SAT. Have a node for each possible literal. Of the colors $\{0, 1, 2\}$, forbid color 2 for x nodes, and forbid color 1 for y nodes.

3.17 The UNORDERED QSAT game is like the QSAT game except in each turn, the current player gets to pick any remaining (unassigned) variable and pick which bit to assign it. Thus, the variables can be played in any order, not necessarily the order $x_1x_2 \cdots x_n$ prescribed in the input. Player 1 wins iff φ gets satisfied.

UNORDERED QSAT	(3.20)
Input:	CNF formula $\varphi(x_1x_2 \cdots x_n)$ where n is even
Output:	Does Player 1 have a winning strategy in the game on φ described above?

k-UNORDERED QSAT is defined like UNORDERED QSAT but φ is a k-CNF.

(a) Prove UNORDERED QSAT $\in$ PSPACE.

(b) Prove 4-UNORDERED QSAT is NL-hard using NL-hardness of 2-SAT (Exercise 3.14).

(c) Prove 2-UNORDERED QSAT $\in$ L.

3.18 The one-player *pebble game* is played on a directed acyclic graph (dag) with exactly one sink (a node with no outneighbors) using k many pebbles. Initially, each node has no pebble. In each move, the player can either:

- Pick a node v that has no pebble but each of v's inneighbors has a pebble (or v has no inneighbors) and put a pebble on v, as long as the dag has at most k pebbles at a time.
- Or, pick a node v that has a pebble, and remove the pebble from v. This pebble becomes available to use in future moves.

The player wins iff they put a pebble on the sink. Prove PEBBLE GAME $\in$ PSPACE. Hint: NPSPACE.

PEBBLE GAME	(3.21)
Input:	Dag G with exactly one sink, positive integer k
Output:	Is it possible to win the pebble game on G using only k pebbles?

3.19 Prove that for all decision problems A and B, if $A \leq_\ell^o B$ and $B \in$ NL then $A \in$ NL. (This generalizes Lemma 3.20 from mapping reductions to oracle reductions.) Hint: Exercise 2.42.

3.20 We proved that $\mathsf{NL} \subseteq \mathsf{P} \cap \mathsf{L}^2 \cap \mathsf{coNL}$. Now, prove that for every function S:

$$\mathsf{NSPACE}[S] \subseteq \mathsf{TIME}[2^{O(S)}] \cap \mathsf{SPACE}[S^2] \cap \mathsf{coNSPACE}[S]$$

You don't have the luxury of assuming $S(N)$ itself is efficiently computable.

3.21 A streaming verifier V for a decision problem A is *unambiguous* iff for every 1-input x, $V(x; w)$ accepts for only one w (considering only the words of w that $V(x; w)$ reads). UL is the set of all decision problems for which there exists an unambiguous log-space streaming verifier. (Note that $\mathsf{L} \subseteq \mathsf{UL} \subseteq \mathsf{NL}$. We study the poly-time counterpart UP in Chapter 8.)

Say a directed graph is *unambiguous* iff for all nodes u and v such that v is reachable from u, there's only one shortest path from u to v. Prove that this problem is in UL:

UNAMBIGUOUS DIRECTED REACHABILITY	(3.22)
Input: Unambiguous directed graph G, nodes s and t	
Output: Is t reachable from s in G?	

Hint: This is similar to the proof of NL = coNL (Theorem 3.19). Besides remembering the number of nodes with distance $\leq d$ from s, the streaming verifier should also remember the sum of the distances of all these nodes from s.

Notes

QSAT is also known as TRUE QUANTIFIED BOOLEAN FORMULA (TQBF). PSPACE-completeness of 3-QSAT is due to [507]. 2-QSAT $\in$ P, in fact 2-QSAT $\in$ NL $\cap$ TIME[N], is due to [33]. [112] proved that an "alternating polynomial time" complexity class AP equals PSPACE, giving another perspective on the PSPACE-completeness of QSAT.

PSPACE-completeness of GEOGRAPHY is due to [469, 337]. The variant of GEOGRAPHY with an undirected input graph is in P [172], though the undirected variant would become PSPACE-complete if we allow nodes but not edges to be repeated [172] or if we consider the misère version (like in Exercise 3.6) [442].

Under suitable generalizations, Checkers [447], Chess [171], and Go [446] are EXP-complete, and Reversi [268] and Hex [159, 441] are PSPACE-complete.

$\mathsf{NL} \subseteq \mathsf{L}^2$ and PSPACE = NPSPACE are often called "Savitch's theorem" [464]. NL = coNL is often called the "Immerman–Szelepcsényi theorem" [258, 510].

It's widely believed that L $\neq$ NL. Remarkably, though, every problem in NL can be solved in log space using a polynomial amount of extra memory that may initially contain arbitrary data and must contain that same data again at the end of the computation [95]. In other words, it's useful to "borrow" memory from other computations, even though that memory must be "returned" exactly as it was. This model is called "catalytic space" by analogy with chemical catalysts, which facilitate chemical reactions but appear as if they don't participate in the reactions, since they end up the same as they started.

NODE KAYLES from Exercise 3.4 is PSPACE-complete [469].

Exercise 3.17.b is due to [424]. Exercise 3.17.c is due to [423]. 5-UNORDERED QSAT is PSPACE-complete [423]. 6-UNORDERED QSAT is PSPACE-complete even when restricted to monotone CNFs [424].

PEBBLE GAME from Exercise 3.18 is PSPACE-complete [188]. For every constant d and every n-node dag where each node has indegree $\leq d$, the pebble game can be won with $k = O(n/\log n)$ pebbles [253].

Exercise 3.21 is due to [440], which also gave evidence that NL = UL, based on combining Exercise 3.21 with an "isolation lemma" from [381]. It's known that $\mathsf{NL} \subseteq \mathsf{UTISP}[\text{poly}N, \log^{1.5} N]$ [366].

Chapter 4

A Time-Space Lower Bound

It's conjectured that $\mathsf{P} \neq \mathsf{NP}$, in other words, SAT $\notin \mathsf{TIME}[N^d]$ for all d. We don't even know how to prove that SAT $\notin \mathsf{TIME}[N]$ or that SAT $\notin \mathsf{SPACE}[\log N]$. What can we prove?

Theorem 4.1. *For all $d < \sqrt{2}$,* SAT $\notin \mathsf{TISP}[N^d, \operatorname{polylog} N]$.

That is, we rule out any SAT algorithm with some modest time bound and a simultaneous sublinear space bound. This *time-space lower bound* is a far cry from what we hope to prove, but we'll take what we can get. Theorem 4.1 also holds for many other NP-complete problems, including 3-SAT, INDEPENDENT SET, DIRECTED FULL PATH, and GRAPH 3-COLORING.

Theorem 4.1 is one of the few known results in the direction of $\mathsf{P} \neq \mathsf{NP}$. Its proof serves as a unified excuse to introduce several fundamental ideas of computational complexity, so this chapter is essential even if the reader trusts Theorem 4.1.

4.1 Padding

4.1.1 Scaling Inclusions

Theorem 4.2. *If* $\mathsf{P} = \mathsf{NP}$ *then* $\mathsf{EXP} = \mathsf{NEXP}$.

Proof idea. For every problem A, we show these implications for a related problem A_{pad}:

$$\begin{array}{ccc} A \in \mathsf{NEXP} & & A \in \mathsf{EXP} \\ \Downarrow & & \Uparrow \\ A_{\text{pad}} \in \mathsf{NP} & \Rightarrow & A_{\text{pad}} \in \mathsf{P} \end{array}$$

$\Rightarrow$ holds by the assumption $\mathsf{P} = \mathsf{NP}$. To make $\Downarrow / \Uparrow$ hold, we let A_{pad} be effectively A but somehow more efficiently verifiable/solvable than A. Efficiency is a function of the input size. If we artificially change the input size but don't change the computation, its efficiency becomes a different function. We enlarge the input by appending irrelevant *padding* words.

- Given the padded input, a computation meant for the original input can ignore the padding. Its efficiency becomes a smaller function since the padded input is larger.
- Given the original input, a computation meant for the padded input can pretend the padding is present. Its efficiency becomes a larger function since the original input is smaller.

For example, if a computation takes $O(2^N)$ steps on an original input of size N, then on the padded input of size $M = 2^N$, it still takes $O(2^N) = O(M)$ steps, which is linear time. Conversely, if a computation takes $O(M)$ steps on a padded input of size $M = 2^N$, then on the original input of size N, it still takes $O(M) = O(2^N)$ steps. This proof hinges on a silly hack, but it's mathematically legitimate. By technically changing the problem, we can be "dishonest" about the input size without changing the output. ■

Definition. For any decision problem A and any strictly increasing function $\text{pad}: \mathbb{N}_+ \to \mathbb{N}_+$ (which means $\text{pad}(N+1) > \text{pad}(N)$ for all N, and therefore $\text{pad}(N) \geq N$ for all N), define:

A_{pad}	(4.1)
Input: Valid input x of size N to A, followed by $\text{pad}(N) - N$ many 0 words	
Output: $A(x)$	

N denotes A's input size, and M denotes A_{pad}'s input size. If $M = \text{pad}(N)$, then A_{pad}'s word size for M is A's word size for N. If $M \neq \text{pad}(N)$ for all N, then A_{pad} has no valid inputs of size M. For any valid input x of size N to A, let x_{pad} denote the corresponding valid input of size $M = \text{pad}(N)$ to A_{pad}, so $A_{\text{pad}}(x_{\text{pad}}) = A(x)$. ◄

When juggling multiple computational problems, it's wise to use different letters for their input sizes. When we discussed reductions from A to B, we used N and M for their respective input sizes. Now, we use N and M for the input sizes of A and A_{pad}. It might be confusing that $\mathsf{TIME}[N]$ and $\mathsf{TIME}[M]$ are the same class (exactly the same set of decision problems). When we ask whether a particular problem is in this class, we use whichever letter denotes the problem's input size. With our convention, we could ask whether $A \in \mathsf{TIME}[N]$ and whether $A_{\text{pad}} \in \mathsf{TIME}[M]$.

Proof of Theorem 4.2. Assuming $\mathsf{NP} \subseteq \mathsf{P}$, we prove $\mathsf{NEXP} \subseteq \mathsf{EXP}$. Suppose $A \in \mathsf{NEXP}$ by a verifier V. Then for some function pad, we have $A_{\text{pad}} \in \mathsf{NP}$ by a verifier V_{pad} where $V_{\text{pad}}(x_{\text{pad}}; w)$ runs $V(x; w)$ (using the word size V expects) and outputs the same thing:

Verifier for A_{pad}	(4.2)
$V_{\text{pad}}(x_{\text{pad}}; w)$: run V but with Reg[0] initialized to $N = \text{pad}^{-1}(M)$	

V sees x in the input segment because x_{pad}'s padding words match the 0 words that would exist beyond x if the input segment were initialized with x instead of with x_{pad}. This V_{pad} is correct:

$$A_{\text{pad}}(x_{\text{pad}}) = 1 \iff A(x) = 1 \iff \big(\exists w:\ V(x; w) \text{ accepts}\big) \iff \big(\exists w:\ V_{\text{pad}}(x_{\text{pad}}; w) \text{ accepts}\big)$$

If V has time efficiency $O(2^{N^d})$ and word size eN^d for integers $d, e \geq 1$, then for $\text{pad}(N) = 2^{N^d}$, V_{pad} has time efficiency $O(M) = O(2^{N^d})$ and word size $e \log M = eN^d$. (Computing $N = \log^{1/d} M$ takes $O(\log\log M)$ time by binary search.)

Since $A_{\text{pad}} \in \mathsf{NP}$, we have $A_{\text{pad}} \in \mathsf{P}$ by a program Π_{pad}. Then $A \in \mathsf{EXP}$ by a program Π where $\Pi(x)$ runs $\Pi_{\text{pad}}(x_{\text{pad}})$ (using the word size Π_{pad} expects) and outputs the same thing:

Program for A	(4.3)
$\Pi(x)$: run Π_{pad} but with Reg[0] initialized to $M = \text{pad}(N)$	

Π_{pad} sees x_{pad} in the input segment because it thinks $M-N$ of the 0 words beyond x are actually padding words that are part of the input. This Π is correct:

$$A(x)=1 \iff A_{\text{pad}}(x_{\text{pad}})=1 \iff \Pi_{\text{pad}}(x_{\text{pad}}) \text{ accepts} \iff \Pi(x) \text{ accepts}$$

If Π_{pad} has time efficiency $O(M^c)$ and word size $e'\log M$ for integers $c, e' \geq 1$, then Π has time efficiency $O(2^{cN^d}) = O(M^c)$ and word size $e'N^d = e'\log M$. (Computing $M = 2^{N^d}$ takes $O(1)$ time, and M fits in a single word.) ■

Padding is a general technique for proving "If a certain inclusion of complexity classes holds, then a scaled up version also holds." (It doesn't work for "scaling down" because we can't shrink inputs without destroying them.) For this chapter's time-space lower bound, we need a scaling result involving a simultaneous space bound, which doesn't affect the proof.

For convenience, we assume quantities like N^a are rounded up to integers, without bothering to write $\lceil N^a \rceil$. For any rational $a = u/v$ where $u, v \geq 1$ are integers, we can compute N^a in $O(\log N)$ time and $O(\log N)$ space by doing binary search to find the vth root of N^u.

Theorem 4.3. *For all rational $a \geq 1$ and all $b > 0$ and $c > 0$, if* $\mathsf{NTIME}[N] \subseteq \mathsf{TISP}[N^b, N^c]$ *then* $\mathsf{NTIME}[N^a] \subseteq \mathsf{TISP}[N^{ab}, N^{ac}]$.

Proof idea. With $\text{pad}(N) = N^a$:

$$\begin{array}{ccc} A \in \mathsf{NTIME}[N^a] & & A \in \mathsf{TISP}[N^{ab}, N^{ac}] \\ \Downarrow & & \Uparrow \\ A_{\text{pad}} \in \mathsf{NTIME}[M] & \Rightarrow & A_{\text{pad}} \in \mathsf{TISP}[M^b, M^c] \end{array}$$

■

Proof. This echoes the proof of Theorem 4.2, so we'll be brief.

Suppose $A \in \mathsf{NTIME}[N^a]$ by a verifier V with word size $e\log N^a$ for an integer $e \geq 1$. Let $\text{pad}(N) = N^a$. Then $A_{\text{pad}} \in \mathsf{NTIME}[M]$ by a verifier V_{pad} where $V_{\text{pad}}(x_{\text{pad}}; w)$ runs $V(x; w)$ by telling V the input size is $N = \text{pad}^{-1}(M) = M^{1/a}$, with time efficiency $O(M) = O(N^a)$ and word size $e\log M = e\log N^a$. (We assume e is large enough that intermediate values for computing N fit in individual words.)

Assuming $\mathsf{NTIME}[M] \subseteq \mathsf{TISP}[M^b, M^c]$, we have $A_{\text{pad}} \in \mathsf{TISP}[M^b, M^c]$ by a program Π_{pad} with word size $e'\log M$ for an integer $e' \geq 1$. Then $A \in \mathsf{TISP}[N^{ab}, N^{ac}]$ by a program Π where $\Pi(x)$ runs $\Pi_{\text{pad}}(x_{\text{pad}})$ by telling Π_{pad} the input size is $M = \text{pad}(N) = N^a$, with time efficiency $O(N^{ab}) = O(M^b)$ and space efficiency $O(N^{ac}) = O(M^c)$ and word size $e'\log N^a = e'\log M$. (We assume e' is large enough to accommodate computing M.) ■

4.1.2 A Word Size Issue

Theorem 4.4. *If* $\mathsf{L} = \mathsf{P}$ *then* $\mathsf{PSPACE} = \mathsf{EXP}$.

Proof idea. There's an annoying asymmetry: L, P, and PSPACE use word size $O(\log N)$, but EXP uses word size $\text{poly}N$. The padding technique shows that if $\mathsf{L} = \mathsf{P}$ then every problem in EXP has a program with space $\text{poly}N$ and word size $\text{poly}N$. To get the word size down to $O(\log N)$ as needed for PSPACE, we chop up each word of size $\text{poly}N$ into words of size $O(\log N)$ and simulate big word operations (such as arithmetic) "in software" using small words. Addresses are the only data we can't chop up—a load/store/read address must fit in one word. Since the program uses space $\text{poly}N$, each address fits in $O(\log N)$ bits anyway. ■

Proof. Assuming $\mathsf{P} \subseteq \mathsf{L}$, we prove $\mathsf{EXP} \subseteq \mathsf{PSPACE}$. Suppose $A \in \mathsf{EXP}$ by a program Π with time efficiency $O(2^{N^d})$ and word size eN^d for integers $d, e \geq 1$. Let $\mathrm{pad}(N) = 2^{N^d}$. Then $A_{\mathrm{pad}} \in \mathsf{P}$ by a program Π_{pad} where $\Pi_{\mathrm{pad}}(x_{\mathrm{pad}})$ runs $\Pi(x)$ by telling Π the input size is $N = \mathrm{pad}^{-1}(M)$, with time efficiency $O(M) = O(2^{N^d})$ and word size $e \log M = eN^d$.

Since $A_{\mathrm{pad}} \in \mathsf{P}$, we have $A_{\mathrm{pad}} \in \mathsf{L}$ by a program Π'_{pad} with space efficiency $O(\log M)$ and word size $e' \log M$ for an integer $e' \geq 1$. Then A can be solved by a program Π' where $\Pi'(x)$ runs $\Pi'_{\mathrm{pad}}(x_{\mathrm{pad}})$ by telling Π'_{pad} the input size is $M = \mathrm{pad}(N)$, with space efficiency $O(N^d) = O(\log M)$ and word size $W = e'N^d = e' \log M$. To see that $A \in \mathsf{PSPACE}$, apply Lemma 4.5 (below) to turn Π' into a program with space efficiency $O(N^d)$ and some log-bounded word size W'. This is possible since $\log(O(N^d))$, $\log(N+1)$, and A's word size are all $O(\log N)$, and W is $(O(1), W')$-constructible since e' and d are integers. ■

In § 1.5.4 we saw how to run a program using a bigger word size than intended. Using a smaller word size than intended requires an upper bound on the space. In practice, there's no simple "compatibility mode" for running a 64-bit program on a 32-bit machine. The main barrier is the address space: If the program uses most of the 2^{64} possible addresses, we're out of luck since that much memory isn't addressable with 32-bit words. But if a 32-bit address space is enough, we could rewrite the program to do other 64-bit hardware operations in software, incurring a modest slowdown. Let's see the "theory version." This lemma decreases the word size to the theoretical limit imposed by the need to fit the following data into single words: memory addresses, the input size N, and input/output words. We state this lemma in a general form, which we also need in §4.2.

Lemma 4.5. *If A is solvable in simultaneous time T and space S with word size W, then A is solvable in simultaneous time $O(TW^2)$ and space $O(S)$ with word size W', assuming $W \geq W' \geq \max(\log(10S/W'),\ \log(N+1),\ A\text{'s word size})$ and W is $(O(1), W')$-constructible.*

Proof (ancillary). Consider a program that solves A in time T and space S with word size W. We first modify it to a program Π that solves A in time $O(T)$ and space $5S$ with word size W, such that:

- It never reads past the input. This uses one extra register (Lemma 1.3).
- Each "let" instruction's destination register is different from its operands. We make each "let" put its result in an extra register and then copy it to the intended destination.
- Each quotient or remainder instruction actually computes both, puts them in extra registers, and copies the desired one to the intended destination.
- It only has 1-bit hardcoded constants. We forge any constant bit-by-bit in an extra register.

These modifications incur a constant-factor time overhead. Only 4 extra registers are needed, so the space overhead is at most a factor 5 (since in the most extreme case, the original program uses 1 register and no work memory, and Π uses 5 registers).

We design a program Π' that solves A in time $O(TW^2)$ and space $O(S)$ with word size W'. A *big word* has W bits. A *small word* has W' bits. Partition the work memory of Π' into contiguous *blocks* of $B = \lceil W/W' \rceil$ small words each. A block holds a big word since Π' will ensure a block's most significant $BW' - W$ bits are 0 ("wasted"). Suppose Π has R registers. Block i holds $\mathrm{Reg}[i]$ of Π if $0 \leq i < R$, or holds $\mathrm{Mem}[i-R]$ of Π if $i \geq R$.

First, Π' moves N from $\mathrm{Reg}[0]$ to block 0 and calculates W, W', B in $O(1)$ time. (The constructor for W works with registers of size W'.) Then, Π' runs Π but replaces each non-termination instruction with a bundle of instructions to simulate the big word operation using small words.

Each instruction of Π takes at most $O(W^2)$ time to simulate. The hardcoded constants of Π' (such as the 1-bit constants of Π) fit in the new word size W'.

Memory access. Since Π uses space $5S$ and Π' wastes at most half its bits, Π' accesses at most the first $10S$ bits of its work segment. Thus each "load"/"store" address of Π' fits in $\log(10S/W') \leq W'$ bits (one small word). For "load $\text{Reg}[i] \leftarrow \text{Mem}[\text{Reg}[j]]$", Π' loads block j's least significant small word into an *addr* register, then copies block *addr* $+R$ to block i by looping over all B small words (loading to and then storing from a *temp* register, and using other registers to calculate addresses). Each "read" address fits in $\log N \leq W'$ bits (one small word) since Π never reads past the input. Each word that's read or written fits in one small word since A's word size is $\leq W'$. For "read $\text{Reg}[i] \leftarrow \text{In}[\text{Reg}[j]]$", Π' loads block j's least significant small word into *addr*, reads In[*addr*] into *temp*, then stores *temp* to block i's least significant small word and 0 to its other words. Simulating "store" and "write" are similar.

Control flow. For "if $\text{Reg}[i] > \text{Reg}[j]$ then goto line ℓ", Π' loops over the small words of blocks i and j, from most to least significant, until it encounters small words that differ between the blocks. If Π branches to line ℓ, Π' branches to the corresponding line $\lambda(\ell)$. Other comparisons are handled similarly.

Data processing. For "let $\text{Reg}[i] \leftarrow \text{Reg}[j] \wedge \text{Reg}[k]$" and similarly $\vee$ and $\oplus$, Π' operates on the individual small words of the corresponding blocks. Handling $\neg$ is similar, but Π' zeroes out block i's wasted bits. For "let $\text{Reg}[i] \leftarrow \text{Reg}[j] \gg \text{Reg}[k]$", Π' checks whether block k's big word is $\geq W$ and if so, zeroes out block i, and otherwise keeps the shift amount in a register and copies block j's bits to the correct places in block i one at a time, with simple arithmetic and bit manipulation. Handling $\ll$ is similar, but Π' ensures block i's wasted bits stay 0. For "let $\text{Reg}[i] \leftarrow \lfloor \log_2(\text{Reg}[k]) \rfloor$", Π' finds block k's most significant 1 and stores its location to block i. For "let $\text{Reg}[i] \leftarrow \text{Reg}[j] + \text{Reg}[k]$", Π' runs the standard carry algorithm, ignoring any final carry out. Handling $-$ is like $+$ but using two's complement. For $\cdot$, Π' runs the primary-school algorithm but sums the table by rows, keeping the current running sum in the destination block. For / and mod, Π' runs the standard long division algorithm, maintaining the "current quotient" and "current remainder" in the blocks corresponding to the relevant registers of Π, and then copies the desired one to the destination block. For these data processing simulations, all pointers and counters fit in small words (registers of Π'), and the operand blocks don't get clobbered by intermediate results, since the destination register is different. ∎

4.2 Time and Space Hierarchies

We prove that more time or space lets us solve some problems that can't be solved with less time or space: $\mathsf{TIME}[N] \subsetneq \mathsf{TIME}[N^2] \subsetneq \mathsf{TIME}[N^3] \subsetneq \cdots$ and $\mathsf{SPACE}[\log N] \subsetneq \mathsf{SPACE}[\log^2 N] \subsetneq \mathsf{SPACE}[\log^3 N] \subsetneq \cdots$ are infinite hierarchies, with each class strictly larger than the previous. Computational resources are indeed valuable: More time or space gives more power.

4.2.1 Writing an Interpreter

One ingredient for proving our hierarchy theorems is an *interpreter* (or *universal program* in complexity theory jargon). This is a program that takes as input the code of a program Π, simulates Π step by step, and outputs the same thing as if Π were executed directly. Interpreters for real programming languages abound. Unsurprisingly, we can write one for our model of computation. Both the interpreter and Π (the "interpretee") are programs in our model. Like real-world interpreters, ours has some overhead compared to a direct execution of Π. We develop a time-efficient interpreter in this section and a space-efficient interpreter in §4.2.3.

Our interpreter uses more registers and bigger constants than Π, so we assume Π is already *tight*, with only two registers and one-bit constants (Theorem 1.2). We represent each of Π's L lines of code as a word of size $\log L+10$: The least significant 10 bits specify the type of instruction (opcode), destination register, and operand registers or constants. (10 bits are enough since our instruction set has only 27 types and the code is tight.) For branch instructions, the most significant $\log L$ bits are the target line number.

The interpreter's input says what program Π to simulate (instructions I and word size W), on what input x, and for how many steps T. Here, W is just a number (not a function), and $I_W(x)$ means running the code I with word size W on input x.

INTERPRETATION	(4.4)
Input: Tight code I, $W \le \log T$, $x \in (\{0,1\}^W)^M$, padding of size T	
Output: Does $I_W(x)$ accept within T steps?	

The encoding begins with three words: L (size of I), M (size of x), and T (size of padding). Also, W is one word. INTERPRETATION has input size $N = 4 + L + M + T$ and word size $\log N + 10$, which is big enough for I (since a line of code is $\log L + 10$ bits) and for x (since $W \le \log T$). In a valid input, each word of x has 0s in all but the least significant W bits, and each line of I represents a legitimate instruction, and the last line is a termination or unconditional branch.

Lemma 4.6. INTERPRETATION $\in \mathsf{TIME}[N]$.

Proof. Figure 4.1 shows the interpreter's code with syntactic sugar that's simple to de-sugar. The interpreter uses word size $\log N + 10$ and these registers:

- Reg[0] and Reg[1] hold the same values as they would in the computation being simulated.
- L, M, T, W hold the corresponding words from the input.
- *mask* is used to make the simulation have effective word size W.
- t counts the number of steps simulated so far.
- *pc* holds the current line number (program counter) of I.
- *instr* holds the instruction currently being simulated.
- Another register holds intermediate results in various calculations.

Reg[0] gets reinitialized to x's size. Reg[1] is already initialized to 0. If $W < \lceil \log(M+1) \rceil$ then the simulation isn't allowed since M wouldn't fit in Reg[0] with W bits, so the interpreter rejects.

Each loop iteration simulates one fetch-execute cycle by fetching the next instruction from I with "read *instr* $\leftarrow$ In[3 + *pc*]" and then doing whatever that instruction says to do. The code shows representative cases of instructions, and the $\vdots$ hides all other cases. The *pc* register is incremented after each cycle, so the next cycle defaults to I's next line.

Data processing. To clarify notation, consider the first case: if *instr* = "let Reg[0] $\leftarrow$ Reg[1]". The "let Reg[0] $\leftarrow$ Reg[1]" stands for the 10-bit constant representing this instruction. Most data processing cases use *mask* to zero out all but the least significant W bits of the result, so the simulation has effective word size W.

```
Interpreter                                                                    (4.5)
read L ← In[0], M ← In[1], T ← In[2], W ← In[3 + L]
if W < ⌈log(M + 1)⌉: reject
let mask ← (1 ≪ W) − 1
let Reg[0] ← M
for t ← 1, 2, ..., T:
    read instr ← In[3 + pc]
    if instr = "let Reg[0] ← Reg[1]":                 let Reg[0] ← Reg[1]
    if instr = "let Reg[0] ← Reg[0] + Reg[1]":        let Reg[0] ← (Reg[0] + Reg[1]) ∧ mask
    if instr = "goto line ...":                       let pc ← (instr ≫ 10) − 1
    if instr = "if Reg[0] = Reg[1] then ...":         if Reg[0] = Reg[1]: let pc ← (instr ≫ 10) − 1
    if instr = "load Reg[0] ← Mem[Reg[1]]":           load Reg[0] ← Mem[Reg[1]]
    if instr = "store Mem[Reg[1]] ← Reg[0]":          store Mem[Reg[1]] ← Reg[0]
    if instr = "read Reg[0] ← In[Reg[1]]":            read Reg[0] ← In[4 + L + Reg[1]]
    if instr = "accept":                              accept
    if instr = "reject":                              reject
    ⋮
    let pc ← pc + 1
reject
```

Figure 4.1: Interpreter

Control flow. Consider the unconditional branch case: if $instr =$ "goto line ...". The "goto line ..." stands for the 10-bit constant for "goto", excluding the target line number. The "if $instr =$" only checks the least significant 10 bits of $instr$, so technically it should be "if $(instr \wedge 1023) =$". The body of this "if" extracts the target line number with "$instr \gg 10$" and subtracts 1 to offset the "increment pc" that happens at the end of every iteration. Conditional branches are similar.

Memory access. The "load" and "store" cases are straightforward. For "read", address Reg[1] in x is address $4 + L + \text{Reg}[1]$ in the interpreter's input. Reading past the end of x may get a padding word, which is 0 anyway. Any "write" instructions get ignored since it only matters whether the computation accepts.

Termination. The interpreter accepts or rejects if the simulated computation does. It treats "halt" as "reject". If the computation hasn't terminated within T iterations, then it hasn't accepted, so the interpreter rejects when time is up. Since each iteration takes $O(1)$ steps, the interpreter runs in $O(T) \leq O(N)$ time. ■

4.2.2 Time Hierarchy

Theorem 4.7. *For all $a > b \geq 1$, $\mathsf{TIME}[N^a] \not\subseteq \mathsf{TIME}[N^b]$.*

Proof idea. What computation quintessentially takes $O(N^a)$ time and therefore presumably can't be sped up? How about "simulating an arbitrary computation for N^a steps"? Sweeping details under the rug, let's frame this as a decision problem A: Given a program Π and x, would $\Pi(x)$ accept within N^a steps? We can solve A in $O(N^a)$ time using an interpreter.

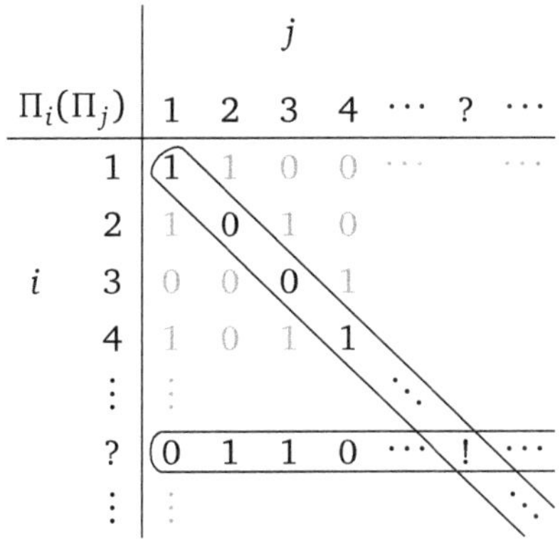

Figure 4.2: Diagonalization

We prove that A can't be solved much faster than $O(N^a)$. The philosophical upshot is that computation doesn't admit general shortcuts. Predicting an arbitrary computation's output can't be faster than just running the computation. This is no surprise, but it's less obvious than it seems. Of the infinite set of possible programs that run faster than $O(N^a)$, it's conceivable one of them miraculously solves A. Such an extraordinary program would be a crystal ball that foresees the output of any N^a-step computation before that computation finishes. This is too good to be true because it would enable a paradox in which a program peers into its own future to see what it's destined to output, and then deliberately outputs the opposite. The paradoxical program must provide its own code to the crystal ball. It can't access its "code segment" in our model, but it can get its own code via the input: The paradoxical program takes the code of an arbitrary program Π as input, asks the crystal ball what Π would output if given Π's own code as the input x, and then flips the crystal ball's answer. When Π happens to be the paradoxical program itself, $\Pi(\Pi)$ outputs the opposite of what the crystal ball says it does (a contradiction).

Another perspective: We contrive a decision problem B that can't be solved too fast (in $< N^a$ steps). For each too-fast program Π, there should exist an input x such that $\Pi(x)$ doesn't output $B(x)$. Which x? Let x be the code of Π itself (denoted $x = \Pi$) and define $B(\Pi)$ as the opposite of what $\Pi(\Pi)$ outputs. We can solve B in $O(N^a)$ time using an interpreter.

This technique is called *diagonalization*. Why? Let $\Pi_1, \Pi_2, \Pi_3, \ldots$ be an infinite list of all possible too-fast programs. Imagine the infinite table where the entry at row i and column j is what Π_i would output ($1 =$ accept, $0 =$ reject) given Π_j's code as input. We want to define B so the sequence $B(\Pi_1), B(\Pi_2), B(\Pi_3), \ldots$ is *not* a row of this table. For every row, there should exist a column where it disagrees with B's sequence. Let row i disagree with B at column i, which is along the infinite diagonal: Define B to disagree with row 1 at column 1 and disagree with row 2 at column 2 and so on, so B's sequence is the diagonal's bitwise negation. The punchline is that no Π_i solves B, since $\Pi_i(\Pi_i) \neq B(\Pi_i)$ means Π_i fails to solve B on input Π_i. See Figure 4.2, which populates the table with example bits.

Some complications arise due to big-O concealing an arbitrarily large constant factor:

- The smaller time bound $O(N^b)$ might exceed N^a for small N. We might miss our chance to ensure Π_i fails to solve B, if the relevant N is too small.
- We must decrease the hidden constant factor in Π_i's $O(\log N)$ word size so the constant doesn't depend on i. We can do this (§4.1.2) after getting Π_i's space usage under control (§1.7.3). ■

Giving a program its own code as input may seem a silly mental experiment, but it has a practical application: *self-compilation* (*bootstrapping*). We can write a C++ compiler in C++. After translating our compiler to machine code (using a preexisting compiler), we can run it to compile any C++ program—including itself! This may yield more efficient machine code than the preexisting compiler did. Despite the mental acrobatics, nothing mysterious is going on.

Proof of Theorem 4.7. Let c be a rational number with $a \geq c > b$. Recall $I_W(x)$ means running the code I with word size W on input x.

(call this problem A, with input size N)	(4.6)
Input: Tight code $I,\ W \leq c \log M,\ x \in (\{0,1\}^W)^M$	
Output: Does $I_W(x)$ accept within M^c steps?	

A has input size $N = 3 + L + M$ (the encoding begins with words L, M) and word size $c \log N + 10$.

(call this problem B, with input size M)	(4.7)
Input: Tight code $I,\ W$ such that $\log M + 10 \leq W \leq c \log M$	
Output: Does $I_W(I, W)$ reject within M^c steps?	

B has input size $M = L + 1$ and word size $\log M + 10 + \log c$. We require $\log M + 10 \leq W$ so the words of I (each $\log L + 10$ bits) fit in the word size W for running I.

There's a linear-time mapping reduction from B to A: Map (I, W) to $\big(\overline{I}, W, (I, W)\big)$ where $\overline{I}$ is I but with each "accept" instruction changed to "reject" and vice versa.

We claim that $A \in \mathsf{TIME}[N^a]$ and $B \notin \mathsf{TIME}[M^b]$. This implies $A \notin \mathsf{TIME}[N^b]$, so A shows $\mathsf{TIME}[N^a] \not\subseteq \mathsf{TIME}[N^b]$, and $B \in \mathsf{TIME}[M^a]$, so B shows $\mathsf{TIME}[M^a] \not\subseteq \mathsf{TIME}[M^b]$. We only needed one such problem, but we defined both because A embodies the upper bound and B embodies the lower bound.

$A \in \mathsf{TIME}[N^a]$: On input (I, W, x), run a linear-time program for INTERPRETATION on input $(I, W, x, \text{padding of size } M^c)$. This takes $O(N^c) \leq O(N^a)$ time since the latter input has size $O(N^c)$. Computing $T = M^c$ takes $O(\log N)$ time since c is rational; this is why we introduced c.

Suppose for contradiction $B \in \mathsf{TIME}[M^b]$. By Claim 4.8 (below), some program Π with tight code I solves B in time $O(M^b \log^4 M)$ with word size $b \log M + e$ for some constant e. Let $W = b \log M + e$ be Π's word size when M is the size of input (I, W). Then $\Pi(I, W) = I_W(I, W) \neq B(I, W)$, so Π fails to solve B on input (I, W), as long as:

- $\Pi(I, W)$ terminates within M^c steps: Assuming the big-O means "$\leq d M^b \log^4 M$ for all $M \geq M_0$" for some constants d and M_0, we need $d M^b \log^4 M \leq M^c$ and $M \geq M_0$.
- (I, W) is a valid input: We need $W \leq c \log M$. (We have $\log M + 10 \leq B$'s word size $\leq W$ anyway.)

These hold if M is large enough, since $b < c$. We make M large enough by appending dummy instructions to I without affecting its behavior.

This concludes the proof of the time hierarchy theorem, except for the following claim. ■

Claim 4.8. *If $B \in \mathsf{TIME}[M^b]$ then some tight program solves B in time $O(M^b \log^4 M)$ with word size $b \log M + e$ for some constant e.*

Proof. We decrease space to $\approx M^b$, then decrease word size to $\approx b \log M$, then make it tight.

By Theorem 1.10, $B \in \mathsf{TISP}[M^b \log^2 M,\ M^b \log M]$. We may assume such a program has word size $e_1 \log M$ for an integer e_1. Say it uses space $\le S = e_2 M^b \log M$ for a constant e_2. By Lemma 4.5, B is solvable in time $O(M^b \log^4 M)$ with word size $W' = b \log M + 10 + \log(e_1 e_2 c)$ since $W' \ge \max\big(\log(10S/W'),\ \log(M+1),\ B\text{'s word size}\big)$ and $e_1 \log M$ is $(O(1), W')$-constructible. By Theorem 1.2, B is solvable by a tight program in time $O(M^b \log^4 M)$ with word size $b \log M + e$ where $e = 10 + \log(e_1 e_2 c) +$ another constant. ∎

Theorem 4.9. $\mathsf{EXP} \not\subseteq \mathsf{P}$.

Proof idea. This is like the proof of Theorem 4.7, but instead of ruling out $O(N^b)$-time programs for a particular degree b, we rule out all poly-time programs with any degree. We redefine the problems to ask about an exponential number of steps. We discard A and just use B to streamline the proof and bypass some annoyances in this setting. ∎

Proof. We prove $\mathsf{TIME}[2^M] \not\subseteq \mathsf{TIME}[2^{M/2}]$, which implies the theorem since $\mathsf{TIME}[2^M] \subseteq \mathsf{EXP}$ and $\mathsf{P} \subseteq \mathsf{TIME}[2^{M/2}]$. Change B's definition (from the proof of Theorem 4.7) to say "2^M steps" in the output (instead of "M^c steps") and allow $W \le M$ in the input (instead of $W \le c \log M$).

$B \in \mathsf{TIME}[2^M]$: On input (I, W), run a linear-time program for Interpretation on input $\big(\bar{I}, W, (I, W), \text{padding of size } 2^M\big)$. This takes $O(2^M)$ time with $O(M)$-bounded word size.

Suppose for contradiction $B \in \mathsf{TIME}[2^{M/2}]$. Like in Claim 4.8, some program Π with tight code I solves B in time $O(2^{M/2} M^4)$ with word size $M/2 + e$ for some constant e. Let $W = M/2 + e$ be Π's word size when M is the size of input (I, W). Then $\Pi(I, W) = I_W(I, W) \ne B(I, W)$, so Π fails to solve B on input (I, W), as long as $O(2^{M/2} M^4) \le 2^M$ and $W \le M$. These hold if M is large enough, which we ensure by appending dummy instructions to I. ∎

4.2.3 Space Hierarchy

We present a version of the space hierarchy theorem focusing on polylog rather than poly space. The upper and lower bounds can be quite close to each other.

Theorem 4.10. *For all rational* $a > 1$, $\mathsf{SPACE}[\log^a N] \not\subseteq \mathsf{SPACE}[o(\log^a N)]$.

Interpretation for Space	(4.8)
Input: Tight code I, $W \le S/2$, $x \in (\{0,1\}^W)^M$, padding of size 2^S	
Output: Does $I_W(x)$ accept within S bits of memory?	

This has input size $N = 4 + L + M + 2^S$ (the encoding begins with words L, M, S) and word size $\log N + 10$. "Bits of memory" means the registers and work segment. We require $W \le S/2$ since I's two registers already contribute $2W$ to the memory space.

Lemma 4.11. Interpretation for Space $\in \mathsf{L}$.

Proof idea. The interpreter limits its space—even when the simulated computation would use too much—by checking whether each load/store address would be too big. And though we don't care about the interpreter's running time, it must terminate even if the simulated computation wouldn't. To ensure this, the interpreter sets its alarm clock so that when time is up, it rejects because the computation must have repeated a configuration and therefore wouldn't terminate. ∎

Proof. This interpreter is similar to the one in Lemma 4.6. It has "$S \leftarrow \text{In}[2]$" instead of "$T \leftarrow \text{In}[2]$". Before the "for $t \leftarrow 1, 2, \ldots, T$" loop, it has "let $T \leftarrow L \cdot (1 \ll S)$", which is the number of possible configurations with L lines of code and S bits of memory. If such a computation takes more than T steps, it would run forever (Theorem 1.8), so the interpreter rejects. Word size $2\log N > \log L + S$ is enough for T to fit in one of the interpreter's registers.

The interpreter uses a register named *mem* to hold the entire contents of the simulated computation's work segment: *mem*'s least significant W bits are Mem[0], and *mem*'s next W bits are Mem[1], and so on. For "load Reg[0] $\leftarrow$ Mem[Reg[1]]" and "store Mem[Reg[1]] $\leftarrow$ Reg[0]", the interpreter first checks if $(\text{Reg}[1] + 3) \cdot W > S$ and rejects if so. This is because accessing address Reg[1] means the simulated computation uses at least $\text{Reg}[1] + 1$ many work segment words, and 2 registers, and hence $(\text{Reg}[1] + 3) \cdot W$ bits of memory. If this is $\leq S$ then:

"load" case: let $\text{Reg}[0] \leftarrow (mem \gg (\text{Reg}[1] \cdot W)) \wedge mask$

"store" case: let $mem \leftarrow (mem \wedge \neg(mask \ll (\text{Reg}[1] \cdot W))) \vee (\text{Reg}[0] \ll (\text{Reg}[1] \cdot W))$

Since the interpreter is register-only, it has $O(\log N)$ space efficiency. ■

Proof of Theorem 4.10. This problem has word size $\max(\log M + 10, \log(\log^a M))$:

(call this problem B, with input size M)	(4.9)
Input: Tight code I, W such that $\log M + 10 \leq W \leq (\log^a M)/2$	
Output: Does $I_W(I, W)$ reject within $\log^a M$ bits of memory?	

$B \in \mathsf{SPACE}[\log^a M]$: On input (I, W), run a log-space program for Interpretation for Space on input $(\bar{I}, W, (I, W), \text{padding of size } 2^{\log^a M})$ where $\bar{I}$ is I but with each "accept" instruction changed to "reject" and vice versa. Since the latter input has size $O(2^{\log^a M})$ (and isn't stored in memory), this takes $O(\log^a M)$ space with $O(\log^a M)$-bounded word size, including computing $\log^a M$ and $2^{\log^a M}$ since a is rational. By Lemma 4.5, we can decrease the word size to $O(\log M)$ since $\log(O(\log^a M))$ and B's word size are both $O(\log M)$. The original $O(\log^a M)$ word size might not be constructible in $O(1)$ time as in Lemma 4.5, but time doesn't matter here.

Suppose for contradiction $B \in \mathsf{SPACE}[o(\log^a M)]$. By Theorem 1.2, some program Π with tight code I solves B in space $o(\log^a M)$ with word size $O(\log M)$. Let W be Π's word size when M is the size of input (I, W). Then $\Pi(I, W) = I_W(I, W) \neq B(I, W)$, so Π fails to solve B on input (I, W), as long as $\Pi(I, W)$ terminates within $\log^a M$ bits of memory and (I, W) is a valid input, with $W \leq (\log^a M)/2$. These hold if M is large enough, which we ensure by appending dummy instructions to I. ■

Corollary 4.12. $\mathsf{PSPACE} \not\subseteq \mathsf{L}$.

Proof. For example, $\mathsf{PSPACE} \supseteq \mathsf{SPACE}[\log^2 N] \not\subseteq \mathsf{SPACE}[o(\log^2 N)] \supseteq \mathsf{L}$. ■

4.2.4 Time Hierarchy for Verifiers

We use this result in the proof of this chapter's time-space lower bound:

Theorem 4.13. *For all $a > b \geq 1$, $\mathsf{NTIME}[N^a] \not\subseteq \mathsf{NTIME}[N^b]$.*

Proof idea. In the standard time hierarchy proof (§ 4.2.2), B's input is the code of a too-fast program Π, and B's output is "Does $\Pi(\Pi)$ reject?" Let's try to incorporate a witness w. Now B's input is the code of a too-fast verifier V, and what should B's output be?

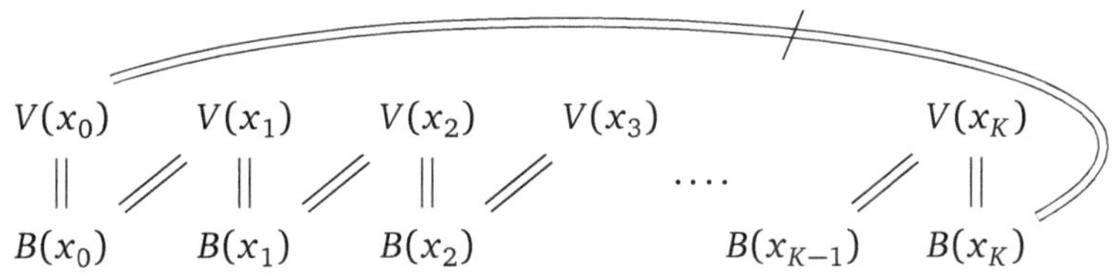

Figure 4.3: Contradiction in the proof of the time hierarchy for verifiers

- For the upper bound, we'd like "$\exists w: V(V;w)$ rejects?" so a not-too-fast verifier for B could simulate $V(V;w)$ and output the opposite.
- For the lower bound, we'd like "$\forall w: V(V;w)$ rejects?" so a too-fast verifier V for B would yield the contradiction

$$\big(\exists w: V(V;w) \text{ accepts}\big) \Leftrightarrow B(V)=1 \Leftrightarrow \big(\forall w: V(V;w) \text{ rejects}\big)$$

  where the first $\Leftrightarrow$ is by V's correctness, and the second $\Leftrightarrow$ is by B's definition.

Our desired quantifiers for w don't match. We reconcile this using *delayed diagonalization*.

Lower bound: We define B so that a too-fast verifier V for B would yield a contradiction on a sequence of inputs $x_0, x_1, \ldots, x_K$ where $x_J = (V\text{'s code, padding of size } J)$, and $V(x_J)$ denotes the bit indicating whether $\exists w: V(x_J;w)$ accepts. See Figure 4.3. The vertical "="s are by V's correctness, and the diagonal "="s are by B's definition. That is, V would have to cooperate in transferring the incorrect output between x_0 and x_K.

Upper bound: Here's a not-too-fast verifier for $B(x_J)$: If $J < K$ then simulate $V(x_{J+1})$. If $J = K$ then brute force simulate $V(x_0)$ and complement the answer, by simulating $V(x_0;w)$ for each w and accepting iff they all reject. The brute force complementation's running time is exponential in the size of x_0 and thus linear in the size of x_K if K is exponentially large.

Unlike in the standard time hierarchy, diagonalizing against V involves multiple inputs, for which V has different word sizes. So instead of including a single word size value in the inputs, we include information to enable computing V's word size for any input size. ∎

By the way, a space hierarchy for verifiers can be proven by standard (not delayed) diagonalization, using space-efficient complementation (Theorem 3.19).

VERIFIER INTERPRETATION WITH WITNESS	(4.10)
Input: Tight code I, $W \le \log T$, $x \in (\{0,1\}^W)^M$, $w \in (\{0,1\}^W)^T$	
Output: Does $I_W(x;w)$ accept within T steps?	

Lemma 4.14. VERIFIER INTERPRETATION WITH WITNESS $\in$ TIME$[N]$.

Proof. This is like INTERPRETATION $\in$ TIME$[N]$ (Lemma 4.6) but with a new case:

if *instr* = "read-witness Reg[0] $\leftarrow$ Wit[Reg[1]]": if Reg[1] $\ge T$: reject
read Reg[0] $\leftarrow$ In[$4 + L + M +$ Reg[1]]

We reject if Reg[1] $\ge T$ because reading witness segment address Reg[1] means the verifier's running time (number of "steps") is $\ge$ Reg[1] + 1 by definition (§2.2.2). Also, reading past x won't always get 0 words, so we update the "read Reg[0] $\leftarrow$ In[Reg[1]]" case to assign 0 to Reg[0] if Reg[1] $\ge M$. ∎

VERIFIER INTERPRETATION	(4.11)
Input: Tight code I, $W \le \log T$, $x \in (\{0,1\}^W)^M$, padding of size T	
Output: Does there exist $w \in (\{0,1\}^W)^T$ such that $I_W(x;w)$ accepts within T steps?	

Lemma 4.15. VERIFIER INTERPRETATION $\in$ NTIME$[N]$.

Proof. This interpreter is a verifier that views its witness segment's first T words as w. It rejects if any of these words doesn't fit in W bits. Otherwise, it's as in Lemma 4.6 but with this case:

if *instr* = "read-witness Reg[0] ← Wit[Reg[1]]": if Reg[1] $\ge T$: reject
read-witness Reg[0] ← Wit[Reg[1]] ■

Proof of Theorem 4.13. Let c and d be rational numbers with $a \ge c > d \ge b$. We show that this problem B is in NTIME$[N^c] \subseteq$ NTIME$[N^a]$ but not in NTIME$[N^d] \supseteq$ NTIME$[N^b]$.

(call this problem B, with input size N)	(4.12)
Input: Tight code I of size L, e such that $10 \le e \le (c-d)\log L$, padding of size J	
Output: Let $K = 2^{L^{c+1}}$. Let $J' = J+1$ if $J < K$, and $J' = 0$ otherwise. Let $x = (I, e, \text{padding of size } J')$ of size M. Let $T = M^c$ and $W = d\log M + e$. Does there exist $w \in (\{0,1\}^W)^T$ such that $I_W(x;w)$ accepts within T steps? Flip the answer if $J' = 0$.	

$B \in$ NTIME$[N^c]$: This verifier is correct by definition:

Verifier for B (4.13)

```
compute K, x, T, W as in B's definition
if J < K:
    run the verifier from Lemma 4.15 on input (I, W, x, padding of size T)
    output the same thing
else:
    for each w ∈ ({0,1}^W)^T:
        run the program from Lemma 4.14 on input (I, W, x, w)
        if it accepted: reject
    accept
```

Computing T and W takes time $O(\log N)$ since c and d are rational. (The need to compute W is why we introduced d instead of using b.) The $J < K$ case takes time $O(N^c)$ since the input to VERIFIER INTERPRETATION has size $4 + L + M + T = O(M^c) = O(N^c)$. For the $J \ge K$ case, there are 2^{TW} iterations, each of which takes time $O(L^c)$ since the input to VERIFIER INTERPRETATION WITH WITNESS has size $4 + L + M + T = O(M^c) = O(L^c)$, so this case takes time $2^{TW} \cdot O(L^c) = 2^{O(L^c \log L)} \cdot O(L^c) = O(K) = O(N) = O(N^c)$. In both cases, W is valid as part of the input since $e \le (c-d)\log L \le (c-d)\log M$ implies $W = d\log M + e \le c\log M = \log T$.

Suppose for contradiction $B \in$ NTIME$[N^d]$. Like in Claim 4.8, some verifier V with tight code I verifies B in time $O(N^d \log^4 N)$ with word size $d\log N + e$ for some constant $e \ge 10$. Consider the sequence of inputs $x_0, x_1, \ldots, x_K$ where $x_J = (I, e, \text{padding of size } J)$. Since $d < c$, we can ensure L is large enough (by appending dummy instructions to I) that V runs in time N^c on input x_J, and $e \le (c-d)\log L$ so x_J is a valid input. Let $V(x_J)$ denote the bit indicating whether $\exists w: V(x_J;w)$ accepts.

- $V(x_J) = B(x_J)$ for each J since V is correct and x_J is valid.
- $B(x_J) = V(x_{J+1})$ for each $J < K$ and $B(x_K) \ne V(x_0)$ by B's definition and the fact that V runs in time $T = M^c$ and has word size $W = d\log M + e$ on input $x_{J'}$ of size M.

Contradiction: $V(x_0) = B(x_0) = V(x_1) = B(x_1) = V(x_2) = \cdots = V(x_K) = B(x_K) \ne V(x_0)$. ■

Just as an exponential-time version of the time hierarchy theorem yielded EXP $\not\subseteq$ P:

Theorem 4.16. NEXP $\not\subseteq$ NP. ■

4.3 The Polynomial Hierarchy

The *polynomial hierarchy* (or "polynomial-time hierarchy," not to be confused with the unrelated "time hierarchy theorem") is a collection of complexity classes generalizing NP by allowing a constant number of quantifiers, alternating between $\exists$ and $\forall$. Although the polynomial hierarchy doesn't appear in the statement of this chapter's time-space lower bound, it serves as a "playing field" for the proof. Let's motivate the polynomial hierarchy with some example problems.

CNFs and DNFs are fundamental in digital logic hardware design. The size (number of literal occurrences) affects chip area and energy consumption. In the field of *logic synthesis*, lots of effort has gone into heuristics to find small CNFs/DNFs in practice. The following problem just asks whether a given CNF can be improved or is already the smallest possible:

Smaller CNF	(4.14)
Input:	CNF φ
Output:	Does there exist a CNF that's smaller than φ but expresses the same function as φ?

This problem doesn't seem to be in NP: Though a stranger could show us a smaller CNF, it's unclear how he could quickly convince us that it agrees with φ on all of the exponentially many assignments. This problem doesn't seem to be in coNP either: Though a stranger could quickly convince us that a particular smaller CNF disagrees with φ on some assignment, it's unclear how he could do this for all of the exponentially many smaller CNFs. We need two quantifiers.

Here's another problem involving two quantifiers.

Exact Independent Set	(4.15)
Input:	Undirected graph G, nonnegative integer k
Output:	Is k the size of a largest independent set in G?

This asks whether there's an independent set of size $\ge k$ ("$\exists$") and every independent set has size $\le k$ ("$\forall$"). This problem doesn't seem to be in NP: Though we could be convinced the maximum independent set size is $\ge k$, how could we be convinced it's $\le k$? This problem doesn't seem to be in coNP either: Though we could be convinced when the maximum independent set size is $> k$, how could we be convinced when it's $< k$?

4.3.1 Quantifiers

Definition. $\Sigma_1\mathsf{P}$ is an alias for NP, and $\Pi_1\mathsf{P}$ is the set of all decision problems A for which there exists a poly-time verifier V such that for every valid input x:

$$A(x) = 1 \iff \big(\forall w: \; V(x; w) \text{ accepts}\big)$$ ◀

$\Pi_1\mathsf{P}$ is like $\Sigma_1\mathsf{P}$ but with $\forall$ instead of $\exists$. The archaic reason for the notation Σ and Π (capital Greek sigma and pi) is that they also mean "sum" and "product," vaguely resembling how $\exists$ and $\forall$ mean "or" and "and." The subscript 1 means there's one quantifier.

Observation 4.17. $\Pi_1\mathsf{P} = \mathsf{coNP}$.

Proof. To see that $\Pi_1\mathsf{P} \subseteq \mathsf{coNP}$, suppose $A \in \Pi_1\mathsf{P}$ by a poly-time verifier V. Then $\overline{A} \in \mathsf{NP}$, and thus $A \in \mathsf{coNP}$, by the verifier $\overline{V}$ that outputs the opposite bit as V:

$$A(x) = 0 \iff \neg\big(\forall w: \; V(x; w) \text{ accepts}\big) \iff \big(\exists w: \; V(x; w) \text{ rejects}\big) \iff \big(\exists w: \; \overline{V}(x; w) \text{ accepts}\big)$$

The same reasoning shows $\mathsf{coNP} \subseteq \Pi_1\mathsf{P}$. ■

The polynomial hierarchy's classes are stratified into levels by the number of quantifiers: $\Sigma_\ell\mathsf{P}$ has ℓ quantifiers, starting with $\exists$, and $\Pi_\ell\mathsf{P}$ has ℓ quantifiers, starting with $\forall$. An *ℓ-witness verifier* V has witness segments $\text{Wit}_1, \ldots, \text{Wit}_\ell$, accessed with "read-witness $\text{Reg}[i] \leftarrow \text{Wit}_k[\text{Reg}[j]]$". Let $V(x; w_1; w_2; \cdots; w_\ell)$ denote the computation of V on input x with w_k in Wit_k for each $k \in [\ell]$. The running time of $V(x; w_1; \cdots; w_\ell)$ is the maximum of the number of execution steps and $1 +$ the highest address accessed in any of the witness segments. So if V has time efficiency $\leq T$ and word size W, we may assume $w_k \in (\{0,1\}^W)^T$ for each k.

Definition. For each integer $\ell \geq 0$:

- $\Sigma_\ell\mathsf{TIME}[T]$ is the set of all decision problems A for which there exists an ℓ-witness verifier V with $O(T)$ time efficiency and $O(\log \max(T, N))$-bounded word size, such that for every valid input x:

  $$A(x) = 1 \iff \big(\exists w_1 \; \forall w_2 \; \exists w_3 \; \cdots : \; V(x; w_1; w_2; \cdots; w_\ell) \text{ accepts}\big)$$

  The quantifiers alternate, so the last one is $\exists w_\ell$ if ℓ is odd, or $\forall w_\ell$ if ℓ is even.
- $\Sigma_\ell\mathsf{P} \; = \; \Sigma_\ell\mathsf{TIME}[\text{poly} N]$
- $\Pi_\ell\mathsf{TIME}[T]$ is the set of all decision problems A for which there exists an ℓ-witness verifier V with $O(T)$ time efficiency and $O(\log \max(T, N))$-bounded word size, such that for every valid input x:

  $$A(x) = 1 \iff \big(\forall w_1 \; \exists w_2 \; \forall w_3 \; \cdots : \; V(x; w_1; w_2; \cdots; w_\ell) \text{ accepts}\big)$$

  The quantifiers alternate, so the last one is $\forall w_\ell$ if ℓ is odd, or $\exists w_\ell$ if ℓ is even.
- $\Pi_\ell\mathsf{P} \; = \; \Pi_\ell\mathsf{TIME}[\text{poly} N]$ ◀

This subsumes the definition of $\Sigma_1\mathsf{P}$ and $\Pi_1\mathsf{P}$. The polynomial hierarchy's 0th level is $\mathsf{P} = \Sigma_0\mathsf{P} = \Pi_0\mathsf{P}$ since a 0-witness verifier is just a solver.

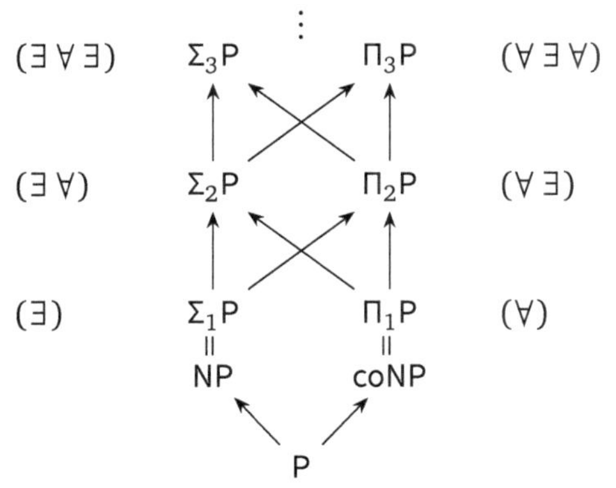

Figure 4.4: The polynomial hierarchy, where $\mathcal{C}_1 \longrightarrow \mathcal{C}_2$ means $\mathcal{C}_1 \subseteq \mathcal{C}_2$

SMALLER CNF $\in \Sigma_2$P by a 2-witness verifier V that views w_1 as a CNF ψ and w_2 as an assignment a, and $V(\varphi;\psi;a)$ checks that ψ is smaller than φ and that $\psi(a) = \varphi(a)$. Presumably SMALLER CNF $\notin \Pi_2$P, though.

EXACT INDEPENDENT SET $\in \Sigma_2$P by a 2-witness verifier V that views w_1 and w_2 as subsets of G's nodes, and $V(G,k;w_1;w_2)$ checks that w_1 is independent and has $\geq k$ nodes and that w_2 either is not independent or has $\leq k$ nodes. The order of these quantifiers doesn't matter—w_1 and w_2 are "decoupled" from each other—so swapping them shows EXACT INDEPENDENT SET $\in \Pi_2$P also. This problem is in both level 2 classes but presumably in neither level 1 class.

Π_1P $=$ coΣ_1P and Σ_1P $=$ coΠ_1P (Observation 4.17) generalizes to all levels: Pulling a negation across ℓ quantifiers flips them all to the opposite types.

Observation 4.18. Π_ℓP $=$ coΣ_ℓP *and* Σ_ℓP $=$ coΠ_ℓP *for every* ℓ. ■

P $\subseteq$ NP $\cap$ coNP generalizes to all levels: Both classes of each level are contained in both classes of the next level (Figure 4.4).

Observation 4.19. $\Sigma_\ell\mathsf{P} \cup \Pi_\ell\mathsf{P} \subseteq \Sigma_{\ell+1}\mathsf{P} \cap \Pi_{\ell+1}\mathsf{P}$ *for every* ℓ.

Proof. $\Sigma_\ell\mathsf{P} \subseteq \Sigma_{\ell+1}\mathsf{P}$ and $\Pi_\ell\mathsf{P} \subseteq \Pi_{\ell+1}\mathsf{P}$ by tacking a dummy quantifier on the back end: An ℓ-witness verifier is an $(\ell+1)$-witness verifier that ignores $\mathrm{Wit}_{\ell+1}$.

$\Sigma_\ell\mathsf{P} \subseteq \Pi_{\ell+1}\mathsf{P}$ and $\Pi_\ell\mathsf{P} \subseteq \Sigma_{\ell+1}\mathsf{P}$ by tacking a dummy quantifier on the front end: We turn any ℓ-witness verifier into an $(\ell+1)$-witness verifier that accesses $\mathrm{Wit}_2, \ldots, \mathrm{Wit}_{\ell+1}$ instead of $\mathrm{Wit}_1, \ldots, \mathrm{Wit}_\ell$ (respectively) and ignores the new Wit_1. ■

Since $\bigcup_\ell \Sigma_\ell\mathsf{P} \subseteq \bigcup_\ell \Pi_{\ell+1}\mathsf{P} = \bigcup_\ell \Pi_\ell\mathsf{P}$ and $\bigcup_\ell \Pi_\ell\mathsf{P} \subseteq \bigcup_\ell \Sigma_{\ell+1}\mathsf{P} = \bigcup_\ell \Sigma_\ell\mathsf{P}$, we can define a single complexity class for the whole polynomial hierarchy:

Definition. $\mathsf{PH} = \bigcup_\ell \Sigma_\ell\mathsf{P} = \bigcup_\ell \Pi_\ell\mathsf{P}$ ◄

Lemma 4.20. PH $\subseteq$ PSPACE.

Proof idea. We could use recursion like in the proof that QSAT $\in$ PSPACE (Lemma 3.1). But since the number of quantifiers doesn't depend on the input, we just use nested loops instead. ■

Proof. We show $\Sigma_\ell \mathsf{P} \subseteq \mathsf{PSPACE}$ for every ℓ. For convenience, let's just do $\ell = 4$. Suppose $A \in \Sigma_4\mathsf{P}$ by a 4-witness verifier V with time efficiency $\leq T = cN^d$ (for integers c, d) and log-bounded word size W. The following algorithm solves A on input x of size N. The kth loop iterates over all $w_k \in (\{0,1\}^W)^T$.

Solver using a 4-witness verifier (4.16)

```
for each w1:
    for each w2:
        for each w3:
            for each w4:
                run V(x; w1; w2; w3; w4) and let b ∈ {0,1} be its output
                if b = 0: break out of w4 loop
            if b = 1: break out of w3 loop
        if b = 0: break out of w2 loop
    if b = 1: break out of w1 loop
output b
```

Let's see why this is correct, from the inside out.

- For every w_1, w_2, w_3: After the w_4 loop, b indicates whether $\forall w_4 : V$ accepts. (Either the loop breaks with $b = 0$ upon finding a w_4 for which V rejects, or it exhausts all w_4 and finishes with $b = 1$.)
- For every w_1, w_2: After the w_3 loop, b indicates whether $\exists w_3\ \forall w_4 : V$ accepts. (Either the loop breaks with $b = 1$ upon finding a w_3 for which $\forall w_4 : V$ accepts, or it exhausts all w_3 and finishes with $b = 0$.)
- For every w_1: After the w_2 loop, b indicates whether $\forall w_2\ \exists w_3\ \forall w_4 : V$ accepts.
- After the w_1 loop, b indicates whether $\exists w_1\ \forall w_2\ \exists w_3\ \forall w_4 : V$ accepts.

An implementation can keep each w_k in a separate work segment Mem_k, and replace V's "read-witness from Wit_k" instructions with "load from Mem_k", and use Mem_5 for V's work segment. Remembering the current w_1, w_2, w_3, w_4 takes $O(TW) = O(N^d \log N)$ bits of space. Running V takes $\operatorname{poly} N$ space, which gets reused for all runs of V. Since the program has $\operatorname{poly} N$ space efficiency and log-bounded word size, $A \in \mathsf{PSPACE}$. ■

We can adapt the proof to show $\Sigma_\ell \mathsf{TIME}[T] \subseteq \mathsf{SPACE}[T \log T]$ for every ℓ and every $T \geq N$.

4.3.2 Instigating a Collapse

Smaller CNF and Exact Independent Set are in level 2 but presumably not in level 1 of the polynomial hierarchy. Nevertheless, their complexities are related to P versus NP: If $\mathsf{P} = \mathsf{NP}$ then Exact Independent Set $\in \mathsf{P}$ because Exact Independent Set $\leq_p^o$ Independent Set $\in \mathsf{NP}$: On input (G, k), query the oracle on (G, k) and on $(G, k+1)$ and accept iff the first query's answer is yes and the second query's answer is no. If $\mathsf{P} = \mathsf{NP}$ then Smaller CNF $\in \mathsf{P}$, but the reason is more subtle and doesn't use a reduction.

Suppose $\mathcal{C}_1 \subseteq \mathcal{C}_2$ is an inclusion of complexity classes. We say $\mathcal{C}_2$ *collapses* to $\mathcal{C}_1$ iff $\mathcal{C}_1 = \mathcal{C}_2$.

- Theorem 4.9 says "EXP does not collapse to P."
- Theorem 4.2 says "If NP collapses to P, then NEXP collapses to EXP."

We prove that if NP collapses to P, then PH collapses to P. (A collapse from level 1 to level 0 would make all higher levels collapse all the way down, too.)

Theorem 4.21. *If* P = NP *then* P = PH.

Proof idea. We'd like to prove that for every $A \in \mathsf{PH}$, there exists $B \in \mathsf{NP}$ such that if $B \in \mathsf{P}$ then $A \in \mathsf{P}$. This sounds like a job for reductions—how about we show $A \leq_p^o B$? Unfortunately, this is not possible unless PH unconditionally collapses to level 2 (Exercise 4.13). Since it's widely believed that PH doesn't collapse to any level, we need an idea not based on reductions.

Intuitively, the P = NP hypothesis eliminates a $\exists$ quantifier with only polynomial slowdown. The hypothesis also implies P = coNP, which eliminates a $\forall$ quantifier. We can peel off any number of quantifiers, one at a time, until none remain. To collapse level $\ell+1$ to level ℓ by peeling off the last quantifier:

$$\begin{array}{ccc} A \in \Sigma_{\ell+1}\mathsf{P} & & A \in \Sigma_\ell \mathsf{P} \\ \Downarrow & & \Uparrow \\ B \in \mathsf{NP} & \Rightarrow & B \in \mathsf{P} \end{array}$$

$\Rightarrow$ holds by the hypothesis. To make $\Downarrow$ and $\Uparrow$ hold, we define B so it asks about just the last of the $\ell+1$ witnesses for A. We relocate the other ℓ witnesses to the input for $\Downarrow$ and reinstate them as witnesses for $\Uparrow$. ■

Proof. Assume P = NP. We argue that $\Sigma_{\ell+1}\mathsf{P} \subseteq \Sigma_\ell\mathsf{P}$ for every ℓ. This yields the theorem since then $\Sigma_\ell\mathsf{P} \subseteq \Sigma_{\ell-1}\mathsf{P} \subseteq \Sigma_{\ell-2}\mathsf{P} \subseteq \cdots \subseteq \Sigma_0\mathsf{P} = \mathsf{P}$ and thus $\mathsf{PH} = \bigcup_\ell \Sigma_\ell\mathsf{P} = \mathsf{P}$.

Suppose $A \in \Sigma_{\ell+1}\mathsf{P}$ by an $(\ell+1)$-witness verifier V with time efficiency $\leq T = cN^d$ (for integers c, d) and log-bounded word size W. First, assume ℓ is even.

FINAL $\exists$ OF V (call this problem B, with input size M) (4.17)
Input: $x, w_1, \ldots, w_\ell$ where $x \in (\{0,1\}^W)^N$ is a valid input to A, and each $w_k \in (\{0,1\}^W)^T$
Output: Does there exist $w_{\ell+1} \in (\{0,1\}^W)^T$ such that $V(x; w_1; \cdots; w_\ell; w_{\ell+1})$ accepts?

The input encoding has 1 word for the value of N, then N words for x, then T words for w_1, and so on, so B's input size is $M = 1 + N + \ell T = \Theta(N^d)$.

$B \in \mathsf{NP}$ by a verifier U where $U(x, w_1, \ldots, w_\ell; w_{\ell+1})$ runs $V(x; w_1; \cdots; w_\ell; w_{\ell+1})$. Specifically: U first computes T and W from N. Then, it runs V, modified to read $x, w_1, \ldots, w_\ell$ from the input segment and $w_{\ell+1}$ from the witness segment, and with masking so the effective word size is W. Whenever V accesses $\mathrm{In}, \mathrm{Wit}_1, \ldots, \mathrm{Wit}_\ell$, instead U calculates the corresponding address in its input and reads the word from there. Whenever V accesses $\mathrm{Wit}_{\ell+1}$, instead U accesses Wit and rejects if the word doesn't fit in the least significant W bits. The time efficiency of U is $O(T(N)) = O(M)$, and U is correct by definition:

$$B(x, w_1, \ldots, w_\ell) = 1 \iff \big(\exists w_{\ell+1} : U(x, w_1, \ldots, w_\ell; w_{\ell+1}) \text{ accepts}\big)$$

From our assumption that $\mathsf{NP} \subseteq \mathsf{P}$, we have $B \in \mathsf{P}$ by a program Π. Thus $A \in \Sigma_\ell\mathsf{P}$ by an ℓ-witness verifier V' where $V'(x; w_1; \cdots; w_\ell)$ runs $\Pi(x, w_1, \ldots, w_\ell)$. Specifically: V' first computes T and W from N. Then, it runs Π, modified to read x from In and w_k from Wit_k. Whenever Π does a read, V' gives it N if the address is 0, and otherwise V' calculates where the desired word resides within $\mathrm{In}, \mathrm{Wit}_1, \ldots, \mathrm{Wit}_\ell$, reads it from that segment, and masks it to keep only the least significant W bits. Thus in Π's input, w_k is the masked first T words of Wit_k, and for convenience, w_k also denotes the unmasked contents of Wit_k. Masking doesn't affect the truth of any $\exists$ or $\forall$ quantifier. The time efficiency of V' is $\max(\operatorname{poly} M, O(N^d)) = \operatorname{poly} N^d = \operatorname{poly} N$ since Π takes $\operatorname{poly} M$ time and each w_k has $O(N^d)$ size. V' is correct because for every valid input x:

$$\begin{aligned} A(x)=1 &\iff \big(\exists w_1 \cdots \forall w_\ell\ \exists w_{\ell+1} :\ V(x;w_1;\cdots;w_\ell;w_{\ell+1}) \text{ accepts}\big) \\ &\iff \big(\exists w_1 \cdots \forall w_\ell :\ \Pi(x,w_1,\ldots,w_\ell) \text{ accepts}\big) \\ &\iff \big(\exists w_1 \cdots \forall w_\ell :\ V'(x;w_1;\cdots;w_\ell) \text{ accepts}\big) \end{aligned}$$

Now, assume ℓ is odd. Let $B = $ FINAL $\forall$ OF V, which asks whether for all $w_{\ell+1}$, $V(x;w_1;\cdots;w_\ell;w_{\ell+1})$ accepts. Then $B \in \Pi_1\mathsf{P} = \mathsf{coNP}$. Since $\mathsf{P} = \mathsf{NP}$ implies $\mathsf{P} = \mathsf{coNP}$, we have $B \in \mathsf{P}$ by a program Π. Thus $A \in \Sigma_\ell\mathsf{P}$ by an ℓ-witness verifier V' where $V'(x;w_1;\cdots;w_\ell)$ runs $\Pi(x,w_1,\ldots,w_\ell)$. ■

Here's the version we use for this chapter's time-space lower bound:

Theorem 4.22. *For all $b \geq 1$, if $\mathsf{NTIME}[N] \subseteq \mathsf{TIME}[N^b]$ then $\Sigma_2\mathsf{TIME}[N] \subseteq \mathsf{NTIME}[N^b]$.*

Proof. Assume $\mathsf{NTIME}[N] \subseteq \mathsf{TIME}[N^b]$. Suppose $A \in \Sigma_2\mathsf{TIME}[N]$ by a 2-witness verifier V with time efficiency $\leq T = cN$ (for an integer c) and log-bounded word size W. Define $B = $ FINAL $\forall$ OF V like in the previous proof. Then $B \in \Pi_1\mathsf{TIME}[M]$ by a verifier U where $U(x,w_1;w_2)$ runs $V(x;w_1;w_2)$ (or accepts if some word of w_2 doesn't fit in W bits). The time efficiency of U is $O(T(N)) = O(M)$, and U is correct by definition:

$$B(x,w_1)=1 \iff \big(\forall w_2 :\ V(x;w_1;w_2) \text{ accepts}\big) \iff \big(\forall w_2 :\ U(x,w_1;w_2) \text{ accepts}\big)$$

Since $\Sigma_1\mathsf{TIME}[M] \subseteq \mathsf{TIME}[M^b]$ implies $\Pi_1\mathsf{TIME}[M] \subseteq \mathsf{TIME}[M^b]$, we have $B \in \mathsf{TIME}[M^b]$ by a program Π. Thus $A \in \mathsf{NTIME}[N^b]$ by a verifier V' where $V'(x;w_1)$ runs $\Pi(x,w_1)$. The time efficiency of V' is $O(\max(M^b,N)) = O(N^b)$ since $b \geq 1$, and V' is correct because for every valid input x:

$$\begin{aligned} A(x)=1 &\iff \big(\exists w_1\ \forall w_2 :\ V(x;w_1;w_2) \text{ accepts}\big) \\ &\iff \big(\exists w_1 :\ \Pi(x,w_1) \text{ accepts}\big) \\ &\iff \big(\exists w_1 :\ V'(x;w_1) \text{ accepts}\big) \end{aligned}$$ ■

A similar proof shows that if any level besides P is closed under complement, then the whole polynomial hierarchy collapses to that level:

Theorem 4.23. *For every $\ell \geq 1$, if $\Sigma_\ell\mathsf{P} = \Pi_\ell\mathsf{P}$ then PH collapses to $\Sigma_\ell\mathsf{P} = \Pi_\ell\mathsf{P}$.*

Instead of full details, let's see the idea. Exercise 4.11 asks for a careful proof for $\ell = 1$.

Proof idea. We illustrate why $\Sigma_2\mathsf{P} = \Pi_2\mathsf{P}$ implies $\Sigma_4\mathsf{P} \subseteq \Sigma_2\mathsf{P}$. Representing classes with their quantifier sequences (such as $\exists\ \forall\ \exists\ \forall$ for $\Sigma_4\mathsf{P}$), the argument looks like this:

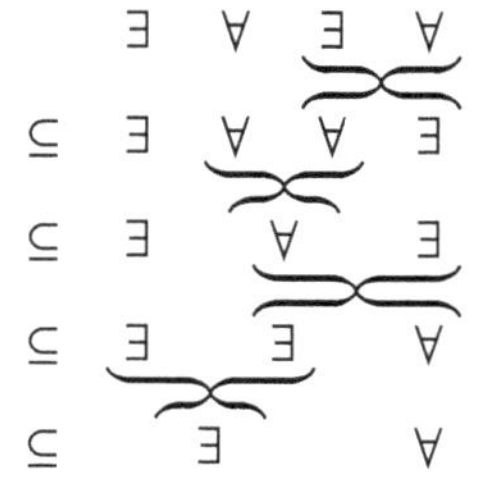

($\Sigma_2\mathsf{P} \subseteq \Pi_2\mathsf{P}$)

(merging $\forall$ quantifiers)

($\Pi_2\mathsf{P} \subseteq \Sigma_2\mathsf{P}$)

(merging $\exists$ quantifiers)

In more detail, suppose $A \in \Sigma_4\mathsf{P}$ by a 4-witness verifier V. Define $B =$ FINAL $\exists\,\forall$ OF V:

$$B(x, w_1, w_2) = 1 \iff \big(\exists w_3\ \forall w_4 : \ V(x; w_1; w_2; w_3; w_4) \text{ accepts}\big)$$

$B \in \Sigma_2\mathsf{P}$ by a 2-witness verifier U where $U(x, w_1, w_2; w_3; w_4)$ runs $V(x; w_1; w_2; w_3; w_4)$. From our assumption that $\Sigma_2\mathsf{P} \subseteq \Pi_2\mathsf{P}$, we have $B \in \Pi_2\mathsf{P}$ by a 2-witness verifier U':

$$B(x, w_1, w_2) = 1 \iff \big(\forall w_2'\ \exists w_3' : \ U'(x, w_1, w_2; w_2'; w_3') \text{ accepts}\big)$$

(The word size for w_2' and w_3' might be larger than V's word size.) Thus $A \in \Sigma_3\mathsf{P}$ by a 3-witness verifier V' where $V'(x; w_1; w_2, w_2'; w_3')$ runs $U'(x, w_1, w_2; w_2'; w_3')$. This V' is correct because:

$$\begin{aligned} A(x) = 1 &\iff \big(\exists w_1\ \forall w_2\ \exists w_3\ \forall w_4 : \ V(x; w_1; w_2; w_3; w_4) \text{ accepts}\big) \\ &\iff \big(\exists w_1\ \forall w_2\ \forall w_2'\ \exists w_3' : \ U'(x, w_1, w_2; w_2'; w_3') \text{ accepts}\big) \\ &\iff \big(\exists w_1\ \forall w_2, w_2'\ \exists w_3' : \ V'(x; w_1; w_2, w_2'; w_3') \text{ accepts}\big) \end{aligned}$$

Similar reasoning then yields $A \in \Sigma_2\mathsf{P}$ using FINAL $\forall\,\exists$ OF V'. ■

4.4 Trading Space for Time

The time hierarchy theorem says that speeding up computations is not always possible. For example, $\mathsf{TIME}[N^3] \not\subseteq \mathsf{TIME}[N^2]$. Perhaps a space bound would weaken the left side enough for a speedup such as $\mathsf{TISP}[N^3, N] \subseteq \mathsf{TIME}[N^2]$? Perhaps some quantifiers would strengthen the right side enough for a speedup such as $\mathsf{TIME}[N^3] \subseteq \Sigma_2\mathsf{TIME}[N^2]$? Neither of those inclusions is known to hold, but by making both concessions simultaneously, we prove a general speedup $\mathsf{TISP}[N^3, N] \subseteq \Sigma_2\mathsf{TIME}[N^2]$ using the divide and conquer technique (§3.2.2).

Theorem 4.24. *For all rational $b > c > 0$, $\mathsf{TISP}[N^b, N^c] \subseteq \Sigma_2\mathsf{TIME}[N^{(b+c)/2}]$.*

Proof idea. Consider a computation that runs in time T and space S. The transcript is the table whose rows are the successive configurations the computation goes through on a particular input. If $T > S$ then the transcript is taller than it is wide. We'd like to save time by stepping through a few rows rather than all of them. We partition the time steps into *epochs* and just run one epoch. To check the whole computation, we use a $\forall$ quantifier over the epochs. To run an epoch, we need to know the *checkpoint* configuration at the start of the epoch. To get that configuration without running the whole computation up to that point, we use an $\exists$ quantifier. To harmonize all the epochs, the $\exists$ witness contains all the checkpoints.

$$\begin{aligned} \text{computation accepts} \iff\ & \exists \text{ configurations } C_0, C_1, \ldots, C_E \text{ where } C_0 = \text{initial and } C_E \text{ accepts} \\ & \forall \text{ index } e \in \{1, \ldots, E\} \\ & C_{e-1} \text{ leads to } C_e \text{ in } T/E \text{ steps} \end{aligned}$$

See Figure 4.5. Running one of E equally sized epochs takes T/E time. We must also count the witness sizes toward the time. The $\forall$ witness is tiny, but we should worry about the $\exists$ witness, which has size $S \cdot E$ since each configuration has size S. Many short epochs would make it fast but with a big witness. Few long epochs would make it slow but with a small witness. To balance the tradeoff and minimize the verifier's time $\max(T/E, S \cdot E)$, we set $T/E = S \cdot E$ and solve for $E = \sqrt{T/S}$. We achieve time efficiency $\sqrt{T \cdot S}$. This is the geometric mean of T and S, which lies between T and S. We need $T > S$ since otherwise we wouldn't get a speedup. ■

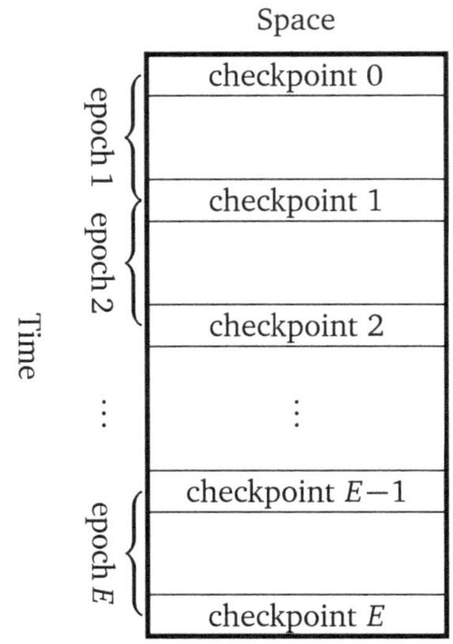

Figure 4.5: Chopping up a transcript into epochs delimited by checkpoints

Proof. Suppose $A \in \mathsf{TISP}[N^b, N^c]$ by a program Π with L lines, R registers, time efficiency $\leq T = aN^b$, space efficiency $\leq S = aN^c$ (for an integer a), and log-bounded word size W. Consider any valid input x of size N. Partition the T time steps into $E = N^{(b-c)/2}$ many *epochs*, each of duration $D = T/E$ steps. Assume E and D are integers—if not, then round E and D up to integers and redefine T as $E \cdot D$. Define $M = S/W - R$ (and assume M is an integer) so $\Pi(x)$ never accesses any work segment address $\geq M$. A configuration is $1+R+M$ words representing the program counter, all R registers, and the work segment's first M words. *Checkpoints* are configurations between consecutive epochs or before the first or after the last epoch. If $\Pi(x)$ terminates before the end of the last epoch, we "run out the clock" by freezing the terminal configuration for all remaining time steps.

$A \in \Sigma_2\mathsf{TIME}[N^{(b+c)/2}]$ by a 2-witness verifier V that views $w_1 = (C_0, C_1, \ldots, C_E)$ as a tuple of purported checkpoint configurations and views $w_2 = e$ as an epoch's index:

2-witness verifier for A (4.18)

$V(x; C_0, C_1, \ldots, C_E; e)$:
- if some C_i isn't a legitimate configuration: reject
- if C_0 isn't the initial configuration, or C_E isn't an accept configuration: reject
- if $e \notin \{1, \ldots, E\}$: accept
- run Π for D steps from configuration C_{e-1} with x in the input segment
- if the resulting configuration is C_e: accept
- else: reject

To see that V is correct, we show that $A(x) = 1 \iff \big(\exists w_1\ \forall w_2 :\ V(x; w_1; w_2) \text{ accepts}\big)$.

$\Rightarrow$: Suppose $A(x) = 1$. Let $C_0, \ldots, C_E$ be the actual checkpoints of $\Pi(x)$—that is, C_i is the configuration after epoch i. Then C_E is an accept configuration since $\Pi(x)$ accepts within T steps, and for all $e \in \{1, \ldots, E\}$, C_{e-1} leads to C_e in D steps by definition, so $V(x; C_0, \ldots, C_E; e)$ accepts.

$\Leftarrow$: Suppose there exist $C_0,\ldots,C_E$ such that for all e, $V(x;C_0,\ldots,C_E;e)$ accepts. Since C_0 is the initial configuration and V accepts with $e=1$, C_1 is the configuration of $\Pi(x)$ after epoch 1. This implies that since V accepts with $e=2$, C_2 is the configuration of $\Pi(x)$ after epoch 2, and so on. Thus $\Pi(x)$ reaches the accept configuration C_E, so $A(x)=1$ since $\Pi(x)$ accepts.

Running Π for one epoch takes $O(D)=O(N^{(b+c)/2})$ steps, and w_1 is $(1+R+M)(E+1)=O((N^c/\log N)\cdot N^{(b-c)/2})=O(N^{(b+c)/2})$ words, and w_2 is one word, so V runs in time $O(N^{(b+c)/2})$.

Here are some implementation details to crystallize the proof. V has registers $\mathrm{Reg}[0],\ldots,$ $\mathrm{Reg}[R-1]$ like Π, as well as registers nicknamed $W,E,D,M,mask,e,t,pc$, and some auxiliary registers. V's code has a "prelude," then a modified copy of Π's code, then a "postlude."

Prelude. First, V computes W,E,D,M, and $mask \leftarrow (1 \lll W)-1$ from N, which takes $O(\log N)$ time since b and c are rational. Then, V uses its auxiliary registers to iterate through the words of w_1, checking that each C_i is legitimate (the line number is in $\{0,\ldots,L-1\}$ and each other word fits in the least significant W bits), that $C_0=(0,N,0,0,\ldots)$, and that the line number in C_E is an accept instruction of Π. To "boot" Π with configuration C_{e-1}, V uses its auxiliary registers to read and copy the words of C_{e-1} into $(pc,\mathrm{Reg}[0],\ldots,\mathrm{Reg}[R-1],\mathrm{Mem}[0],\ldots,\mathrm{Mem}[M-1])$, where pc is one of V's registers (not V's program counter). Then, V does an indirect branch (§1.5.1) into the copy of Π's code, to the group of instructions corresponding to line pc of Π.

Copy of Π's code. The invariant is that $(pc,\mathrm{Reg}[0],\ldots,\mathrm{Reg}[R-1],\mathrm{Mem}[0],\ldots,\mathrm{Mem}[M-1])$ holds the configuration Π would be in after t steps from configuration C_{e-1} with x in the input segment, where t is one of V's registers. To maintain this, insert these three lines before the instruction from line ℓ of Π, for each ℓ:

let $pc \leftarrow \ell$ (where ℓ is a hardcoded constant)
if $t=D$ then goto postlude (the invariant holds here)
let $t \leftarrow t+1$

After each of Π's data processing instructions that might cause overflow in $\mathrm{Reg}[i]$, insert "let $\mathrm{Reg}[i] \leftarrow \mathrm{Reg}[i] \wedge mask$" so the effective word size for Π is W even if V's word size is bigger. In each of Π's control flow instructions, change "goto line h" to "goto line $\lambda(h)$" where $\lambda(h)$ is the number of V's "let $pc \leftarrow h$" line, which was inserted before the instruction from line h of Π. Replace each of Π's termination instructions with "goto postlude" because all subsequent configurations of Π—including the next checkpoint—are frozen to the current configuration.

Postlude. V checks that $C_e=(pc,\ \mathrm{Reg}[0],\ \ldots,\ \mathrm{Reg}[R-1],\ \mathrm{Mem}[0],\ \ldots,\ \mathrm{Mem}[M-1])$. ■

4.5 Time-Space-Efficient Reductions

We saw reductions respecting time efficiency (§1.8) and space efficiency (§1.9). We now define a special type of mapping reduction that respects time and space simultaneously.

4.5.1 Focused Reductions

When we combine a mapping reduction from A to B with a program for B to get a program for A: Storing the whole query at once saves time but wastes space. Computing any word of the query when it's needed—by rerunning the reduction and waiting for the desired word—saves space but wastes time. A win-win version computes any word of the query promptly, without waiting for the reduction to unproductively generate the preceding words:

Definition. A *focused* reduction from A to B (which are both decision problems or both function problems) is an F: (A's valid inputs) $\to$ (B's valid inputs) such that $A(x) = B(F(x))$ and the query $F(x)$ has size (number of words) at most poly$N$ (for every valid input x of size N to A), and these function problems are solvable in simultaneous polylog$N$ time and $O(\log N)$ space:

SIZE OF F	(4.19)
Input:	Valid input x to A
Output:	Size of $F(x)$

WORD OF F	(4.20)
Input:	Valid input x to A, and $i \in \{0, 1, \ldots, \text{query size} - 1\}$
Output:	Word at address i of $F(x)$

The notation $A \leq_f^m B$ means there exists a focused reduction from A to B. ◄

Let's revisit our mapping reduction examples from § 1.8.2 and § 1.9.1.

Example. MULTIPLICATION $\leq_f^m$ ITERATED ADDITION: It takes $O(1)$ time and $O(\log N)$ space to compute the query size $2 + n \cdot (2n - 1) = O(N^2)$ and to compute any word of the query: n, $m = 2n - 1$, and $q_{j,i} = x_{i-j} \cdot y_j$ or $q_{j,i} = 0$. ♦

Example. DIRECTED SUBSET REACHABILITY $\leq_f^m$ DIRECTED REACHABILITY: Assume DIRECTED SUBSET REACHABILITY's encoding is like DIRECTED REACHABILITY (§ 1.3.3) but instead of s and t at the end, each set S and T is encoded with the set's size (one word) and a *sorted* list of nodes in the set, and the input's block of pointers includes pointers to the S and T descriptions. Given (G, S, T), the query is (G', s', t'). Computing the query size $M = N + 2$ is trivial. Computing the query's ith word takes $O(\log^2 N)$ time and $O(\log N)$ space: If the ith word is the pointer to node i's adjacency list, we update the pointer by doing binary search in the T list to see how many prior nodes are in T (and thus have t' in their adjacency lists), since node i's adjacency list gets pushed over by that much. If the ith word is in a node's adjacency list, we find which node by doing binary search in the new block of pointers (where computing any pointer involves a nested binary search in T). If the node is in T, we increment the outdegree word and let t' be the last node in the list. The adjacency list of s' is just the description of S. ♦

Lemma 4.25. *If $A \leq_f^m B$ then $A \leq_\ell^m B$.*

Proof. Assuming $A \leq_f^m B$, we can realize the mapping F as follows:

Mapping reduction using a focused reduction (4.21)

on input x:
    run the program for SIZE OF F on input x to get the query size M
    for $i \leftarrow 0, 1, \ldots, M - 1$:
        run the program for WORD OF F on input (x, i) to write the next word of $F(x)$

This mapping reduction uses log space: Solving Size of F takes log space. Solving Word of F takes log space, which is recycled across all iterations. Beyond that, the reduction only needs registers for N, M, i, and masks to let each part of the computation use its intended word size. ■

We can combine a focused reduction from A to B with a time-space-efficient program for B to get a time-space-efficient program for A. We state this for decision problems to keep it tidy:

Lemma 4.26. *If $A \leq_f^m B$ with query size $\leq Q(N)$ and $B \in \mathsf{TISP}[T, S]$ then*

$$A \in \mathsf{TISP}[T(Q(N)) \cdot \operatorname{polylog} N,\ S(Q(N)) + \log N]$$

assuming $T \in \operatorname{poly} M$ and $S \in \operatorname{poly} M$ are nondecreasing.

Proof idea. To solve A on input x, we run B's program on input $F(x)$. First, we use the program for Size of F to tell B's program how big its input is. Whenever B's program reads a word, we pause it and use the program for Word of F to promptly generate the word.

On the query of size $\leq Q(N)$, B's program takes time $O(T(Q(N)))$ and space $O(S(Q(N)))$. The reduction programs cause a $\cdot \operatorname{polylog} N$ time overhead and $+O(\log N)$ space overhead. We assume T and S are nondecreasing (which is normal for resource bounds) to avoid the bizarre situation that a smaller query, of size $M < Q(N)$, takes time $T(M)$ or space $S(M)$ that overshoots the target upper bound of $T(Q(N))$ or $S(Q(N))$. ■

Proof (ancillary). Let F be the focused reduction's mapping, with register-only programs Π_{size} for Size of F and Π_{word} for Word of F. Let Π_B be the program for B. We design a program Π_A for A using registers Reg[0] (nicknamed N), and $\text{Reg}_{\text{size}}[\,]$ for Π_{size}, and $\text{Reg}_{\text{word}}[\,]$ for Π_{word}, and $\text{Reg}_B[\,]$ for Π_B. First, Π_A initializes $\text{Reg}_B[0]$ to the query size by having "let $\text{Reg}_{\text{size}}[0] \leftarrow N$" followed by Π_{size}'s code with $\text{Reg}_{\text{size}}[\,]$ instead of Reg[ ] and with this substitution:

write Reg[i]	$\rightsquigarrow$	let $\text{Reg}_B[0] \leftarrow \text{Reg}_{\text{size}}[i]$ goto 0th line of Π_B's code

We need not wait for a "halt" instruction, because the word Π_{size} writes is the query size. Then, Π_A has Π_B's code with $\text{Reg}_B[\,]$ instead of Reg[ ] and with this substitution:

read Reg[i] ← In[Reg[j]]	$\rightsquigarrow$	let $\text{Reg}_{\text{word}}[0] \leftarrow N+1$ let $\text{Reg}_{\text{word}}[k] \leftarrow 0$ a copy of Π_{word}'s code	 $\}\ \forall k \neq 0$

The input to Word of F has size $N+1$ because in addition to the N words of x, it has a word for an address into $F(x)$. We assume Π_B never reads past its input, so $\text{Reg}_B[j]$ is a valid address, which is the last word of the input to Word of F. This copy of Π_{word}'s code has $\text{Reg}_{\text{word}}[\,]$ instead of Reg[ ] and these substitutions:

read Reg[h] ← In[Reg[k]]	$\rightsquigarrow$	if $\text{Reg}_{\text{word}}[k] \neq N$ then goto 3 lines below let $\text{Reg}_{\text{word}}[h] \leftarrow \text{Reg}_B[j]$ goto 2 lines below read $\text{Reg}_{\text{word}}[h] \leftarrow \text{In}[\text{Reg}_{\text{word}}[k]]$
write Reg[k]	$\rightsquigarrow$	let $\text{Reg}_B[i] \leftarrow \text{Reg}_{\text{word}}[k]$ goto next line of Π_B's code

We need not wait for "halt", because the word Π_{word} writes is what's at address $\text{Reg}_B[j]$ of $F(x)$.

On input x, Π_A faithfully simulates Π_B on the query $F(x)$, because $\text{Reg}_B[0]$ is supplied with the query size and each "read" gets the desired word. Thus, it outputs $B(F(x)) = A(x)$ and solves A. As usual, we choose a log-bounded word size large enough for all constituent programs, and use masks so each program effectively runs with its intended word size.

Say the query has size M, which depends on x. Π_B takes $O(T(M))$ steps, which is $O(T(Q(N)))$ since $M \leq Q(N)$ and T is nondecreasing. Each "read" step takes polylog N time. Π_B uses $O(S(M))$ bits of memory, which is $O(S(Q(N)))$ since $M \leq Q(N)$ and S is nondecreasing. An additional $O(\log N)$ bits are used for doing all the "read"s.

There's a catch: Say Π_B has word size $W_M = \Theta(\log M)$ and Π_A has word size $W'_N = \Theta(\log N)$. If $W'_N > W_M$, each word's extra bits are wasted but still count toward the space. Only a constant fraction of the bits are wasted if $M \geq N$ (as is typical). Otherwise, let Π_A pack $\lfloor W'_N / W_M \rfloor$ words of size W_M into each word of size W'_N, so less than half the bits are wasted. To access a packed word in $O(1)$ time, Π_A does arithmetic to locate it and bit manipulation to extract it. ■

Here's the transitive property:

Lemma 4.27. *If $A \leq_f^m B$ with query size $\leq Q(N)$, and $B \leq_f^m C$ with query size $\leq Q'(M)$, then $A \leq_f^m C$ with query size $\leq Q'(Q(N))$, assuming Q and Q' are nondecreasing.*

Proof. Let F be the A-to-B mapping and F' be the B-to-C mapping. Then $F''(x) = F'(F(x))$ is an A-to-C mapping. If x has size N and $F(x)$ has size $M \leq Q(N)$, then $F''(x)$ has size $\leq Q'(M) \leq Q'(Q(N))$ since Q' is nondecreasing. To compute Size of F'' or Word of F'' on input x, run the corresponding program for Size of F' or Word of F' on input $F(x)$. First, tell that program its input size using the program for Size of F. Whenever the program for Size of F' or Word of F' wants to read a word of $F(x)$, use the program for Word of F. These programs for Size of F'' and Word of F'' take time

$$\underbrace{\text{polylog}\, N}_{\substack{\text{time for}\\ \text{Size of } F}} + \underbrace{\text{polylog}\, Q(N)}_{\substack{\text{time for}\\ \text{Size/Word of } F'}} \cdot \underbrace{\text{polylog}\, N}_{\substack{\text{time for}\\ \text{Word of } F}} = \text{polylog}\, N$$

since $Q \in \text{poly}\, N$. Similarly, both programs take space $O(\log N)$. ■

4.5.2 Ultimate Reduction to Sat

We come to the ultimate version of "Sat is NP-complete," superseding Theorem 2.32 (quasi-linear-time reductions) and Theorem 2.40 (log-space reductions). We state it for linear-time verifiers:

Theorem 4.28. *For every $A \in \mathsf{NTIME}[N]$, $A \leq_f^m$ Sat with quasi-linear query size.*

Here's the upshot we use for this chapter's time-space lower bound:

Theorem 4.29. *For all $b > d \geq 1$ and $c > 0$, if Sat $\in \mathsf{TISP}[N^d, \text{polylog}\, N]$ then $\mathsf{NTIME}[N] \subsetneq \mathsf{TISP}[N^b, N^c]$.*

Proof. For every $A \in \mathsf{NTIME}[N]$, $A \leq_f^m$ Sat with quasi-linear query size (Theorem 4.28) and Sat $\in \mathsf{TISP}[N^d, \text{polylog}\, N]$ (by assumption), so by Lemma 4.26:

$$\begin{aligned} A &\in \mathsf{TISP}[(N\, \text{polylog}\, N)^d \cdot \text{polylog}\, N,\ \text{polylog}(N\, \text{polylog}\, N) + \log N] \\ &= \mathsf{TISP}[N^d\, \text{polylog}\, N,\ \text{polylog}\, N] \\ &\subsetneq \mathsf{TISP}[N^b, N^c] \end{aligned}$$

■

Theorem 4.28 is the only property of SAT we need for Theorem 4.1. This property also holds for any B such that SAT $\leq_f^m B$ with quasi-linear query size, by transitivity of focused reductions (Lemma 4.27). We designed linear-time reductions from SAT to 3-SAT (§2.3.4) and from 3-SAT to INDEPENDENT SET (§2.4.3), DIRECTED FULL PATH (§2.5.2), and GRAPH 3-COLORING (§2.6.2). These reductions have linear query size and can be focused. Hence, no algorithm solves 3-SAT, INDEPENDENT SET, DIRECTED FULL PATH, or GRAPH 3-COLORING in time $O(N^d)$ and space $\operatorname{polylog} N$, for any $d < \sqrt{2}$.

The rest of this section is the proof of Theorem 4.28, which is safe to skip. It dissects the argument from §2.8 but doesn't introduce new ideas. The following lemma, which we prove at the end of this section, is a focused construction of the sorting network from §2.8.5.

Lemma 4.30. *Consider the odd-even merge sorting network for power-of-2 array size n. The following can be computed in simultaneous $O(\log^3 n)$ time and $O(\log n)$ space:*

(i) Given n, find the number of comparators.
(ii) Given n and the index of a comparator, find the indices of its four wires.

Proof of Theorem 4.28 (ancillary). We argue that the mapping reduction from §2.8.4, which produces a quasi-linear-size CNF, can be focused. A small catch is that since Lemma 4.30 is for powers of 2, the sorting networks for $\varphi_{\text{Mem, sort}}$, $\varphi_{\text{In, sort}}$, $\varphi_{\text{Wit, sort}}$ should have power-of-2 array sizes: We insert dummy time steps to bring the sizes up to powers of 2, and $\varphi_{\text{Mem, distill}}$, $\varphi_{\text{In, distill}}$, $\varphi_{\text{Wit, distill}}$ check that the v variables for dummy steps don't represent memory accesses. Plugging in the real input for x only affects $\varphi_{\text{In, distill}}$, which becomes $\psi_{\text{In, distill}}$. The reduction produces a CNF $\psi(w, y, z)$ with eleven parts:

$$\begin{aligned}\psi \;=\; \varphi_{\text{accept}} \wedge \varphi_{\text{main}} &\wedge \varphi_{\text{Mem, distill}} \wedge \varphi_{\text{Mem, sort}} \wedge \varphi_{\text{Mem, validate}}\\ &\wedge \psi_{\text{In, distill}} \wedge \varphi_{\text{In, sort}} \wedge \varphi_{\text{In, validate}}\\ &\wedge \varphi_{\text{Wit, distill}} \wedge \varphi_{\text{Wit, sort}} \wedge \varphi_{\text{Wit, validate}}\end{aligned}$$

Each part is a conjunction of at most $N \operatorname{polylog} N$ components, each of size $\operatorname{polylog} N$:

- φ_{accept} is considered a single component.
- φ_{main} is the conjunction of all $\varphi_{t,s,\ell}$ or $\varphi'_{t,s,\ell}$ components where (s, ℓ) is not a retrieval.
- $\varphi_{\text{Mem, distill}}$ has one component per (real time step, line of code) pair and per dummy step.
- $\varphi_{\text{Mem, sort}}$ has one component per comparator in the sorting network.
- $\varphi_{\text{Mem, validate}}$ has one component per time step (real and dummy).
- In and Wit are like Mem but include components for phantom stores.

We partition each part into a constant number of types of components. Components of the same type have the same number of clauses, same sequence of clause widths, and same number of z variables—they're identical except for which literals appear.

- φ_{main} has one type per (s, ℓ) that's not a retrieval.
- $\varphi_{\text{Mem, distill}}$ has one type per ℓ (for real steps) and one type for dummy steps.
- $\psi_{\text{In, distill}}$ and $\varphi_{\text{Wit, distill}}$ are like $\varphi_{\text{Mem, distill}}$ but with an additional type for phantom stores.
- $\varphi_{\text{Mem, validate}}$ has two types since the first component is different from the rest.
- Each other part has one type.

Using the definitions and Lemma 4.30.*(i)*, it's elementary to compute the following in $\operatorname{polylog} N$ time and $O(\log N)$ space (letting # mean "number of"):

- # components of each type.

- # clauses, sequence of clause widths, and # z variables per component of each type.
- # clauses $= \sum_{\text{types}}$ (# components of type) $\cdot$ (# clauses per component of type).
- # z variables $= \sum_{\text{types}}$ (# components of type) $\cdot$ (# z variables per component of type).
- # variables.

ψ's encoding has two words for # variables and # clauses, then a block of pointers to clause descriptions, then all the clause descriptions. Fix a natural order of all clauses (grouping them by type and by component within each type) and a natural order of all variables (ordering z variables in the same way as the corresponding components). A clause description has one word for the width and two words per literal (the variable index and sign). Using the definitions and Lemma 4.30.*(ii)*, it's elementary to compute any component's description (all its clauses' descriptions) in polylog$N$ time and $O(\log N)$ space given the component's type and index (such as t). Now, we explain how to realize F, which maps x to ψ. To compute SIZE OF F:

$$2 + (\text{\# clauses}) + \sum_{\text{types}} (\text{\# components of type}) \cdot (\text{description size per component of type})$$

To compute WORD OF F: If the address is 0 or 1, we saw how to compute # variables and # clauses. If the address is in the block of pointers, we determine which component (type and index) the pointed-to clause is in (by calculations like for # clauses) and then compute the clause's address:

$$\begin{aligned}&2 + (\text{\# clauses})\\&\quad + \textstyle\sum_{\text{preceding types}} (\text{\# components of that type}) \cdot (\text{description size per component of that type})\\&\quad + (\text{\# preceding components of target type}) \cdot (\text{description size per component of target type})\\&\quad + \textstyle\sum_{\text{preceding clauses of target component}} (\text{description size of clause})\end{aligned}$$

Finally, suppose the address is in a clause description. We determine which clause by doing binary search in the block of pointers (computing any pointer as explained above). Once we know which type, component, clause, and word within the clause description, we compute the whole component's description and pick out the desired word. ■

Proof of Lemma 4.30 (ancillary). The top of Figure 4.6 shows the algorithm for *(i)*. We use variables ℓ, m, n for sizes of arrays (always powers of 2) and a, b for comparator counts.

Let sort$_n$ be the sorting network generated by sort() for array size n. Let merge$_n$ be the merging network generated by merge() for array size n.

count-comp-merge(n) returns the number of comparators in merge$_n$. It maintains the loop invariant that b is the number of comparators in merge$_m$. It takes $O(\log n)$ time since the loop has $\leq \log n$ iterations, and $O(\log n)$ space since it only uses registers with values $\leq$ poly$n$.

count-comp-sort(n) returns the number of comparators in sort$_n$. It maintains the loop invariant that a is the number of comparators in sort$_\ell$. It takes $O(\log^2 n)$ time and $O(\log n)$ space.

The bottom of Figure 4.6 shows the algorithm for *(ii)*. We use variables i, j, k for (1-based) indices of comparators and p, q, r for (1-based) array positions.

We define the wire indices in sort$_n$ as follows: The input wires are $1, \ldots, n$, and the wires leaving the ith comparator are $n + 2i - 1$ (upper right) and $n + 2i$ (lower right). Given i, the tricky part is to find the indices of the wires entering the ith comparator (upper left and lower left): We must find which two comparators those two wires leave from, or determine that they're input wires. We first use find-pos-sort() to find the two array positions compared by the ith comparator, and then for both of those positions, we use find-comp-sort() to find the indices of all comparators that touch that position, so we can determine which (if any) precedes i.

Algorithm to count comparators in odd-even merge sort (4.22)

count-comp-sort(n):
- initialize $\ell \leftarrow 2$ and $a \leftarrow 1$
- while $\ell < n$:
  - $\ell \leftarrow 2\ell$
  - $a \leftarrow 2a + \text{count-comp-merge}(\ell)$
- return a

count-comp-merge(n):
- initialize $m \leftarrow 2$ and $b \leftarrow 1$
- while $m < n$:
  - $m \leftarrow 2m$
  - $b \leftarrow 2b + m/2 - 1$
- return b

Algorithm to find a comparator's wire indices in odd-even merge sort (4.23)

find-pos-sort(n, i):
- $\ell \leftarrow n$ and $j \leftarrow i$ and $o \leftarrow 0$
- while $\ell > 2$:
  - $a \leftarrow \text{count-comp-sort}(\ell/2)$
  - if $j > 2a$:
    - return $\text{find-pos-merge}(\ell, j-2a)+o$
  - if $j > a$: $j \leftarrow j - a$ and $o \leftarrow o + \ell/2$
  - $\ell \leftarrow \ell/2$
- return $(1,2) + o$

find-pos-merge(n, i):
- $m \leftarrow n$ and $k \leftarrow i$ and $s \leftarrow 1$ and $t \leftarrow 0$
- while $m > 2$:
  - $b \leftarrow \text{count-comp-merge}(m/2)$
  - if $k > 2b$:
    - return $s\cdot\big(2(k-2b), 2(k-2b)+1\big)-t$
  - if $k > b$: $k \leftarrow k - b$
  - else: $t \leftarrow t + s$
  - $s \leftarrow 2s$
  - $m \leftarrow m/2$
- return $s \cdot (1,2) - t$

find-comp-sort(n, p):
- $\ell \leftarrow n$ and $q \leftarrow p$ and $g \leftarrow 0$
- while $\ell > 2$:
  - $a \leftarrow \text{count-comp-sort}(\ell/2)$
  - $\text{find-comp-merge}(\ell, q, g + 2a)$
  - if $q > \ell/2$: $q \leftarrow q - \ell/2$ and $g \leftarrow g + a$
  - $\ell \leftarrow \ell/2$
- write $1 + g$

find-comp-merge(n, p, g):
- $m \leftarrow n$ and $r \leftarrow p$ and $h \leftarrow g$
- while $m > 2$:
  - $b \leftarrow \text{count-comp-merge}(m/2)$
  - if $1 < r < m$: write $\lfloor r/2 \rfloor + 2b + h$
  - if r is even: $r \leftarrow r/2$ and $h \leftarrow h + b$
  - else: $r \leftarrow (r+1)/2$
  - $m \leftarrow m/2$
- write $1 + h$

find-wires(n, i):
- $(p_{\text{upper}}, p_{\text{lower}}) \leftarrow \text{find-pos-sort}(n, i)$
- upper right wire $= n + 2i - 1$
- $\text{find-comp-sort}(n, p_{\text{upper}})$
- if i was the last index written:
  - upper left wire $= p_{\text{upper}}$
- else:
  - say j was written after i
  - $(q_{\text{upper}}, q_{\text{lower}}) \leftarrow \text{find-pos-sort}(n, j)$
  - upper left wire $=$
    $$\begin{cases} n+2j-1 & \text{if } q_{\text{upper}} = p_{\text{upper}} \\ n+2j & \text{if } q_{\text{lower}} = p_{\text{upper}} \end{cases}$$

(continued from previous column)
- lower right wire $= n + 2i$
- $\text{find-comp-sort}(n, p_{\text{lower}})$
- if i was the last index written:
  - lower left wire $= p_{\text{lower}}$
- else:
  - say k was written after i
  - $(r_{\text{upper}}, r_{\text{lower}}) \leftarrow \text{find-pos-sort}(n, k)$
  - lower left wire $=$
    $$\begin{cases} n+2k-1 & \text{if } r_{\text{upper}} = p_{\text{lower}} \\ n+2k & \text{if } r_{\text{lower}} = p_{\text{lower}} \end{cases}$$

Figure 4.6: Focused construction of the odd-even sorting network find-pos-merge(n, i) returns the pair of array positions compared by the ith comparator in merge_n. It maintains the loop invariant that the positions of the ith comparator in merge_n are the positions of the kth comparator in merge_m scaled by factor s and shifted by $-t$. Scaling and shifting are componentwise: $s \cdot (1,2) - t$ means $(s \cdot 1 - t, s \cdot 2 - t)$. The $k > 2b$ case handles the comparators at the end of merge_m. If $b < k \leq 2b$, the desired comparator is the $(k-b)$th in the "even" copy of $\text{merge}_{m/2}$, and we must scale the positions by an extra factor of 2. If $k \leq b$, the desired comparator is the kth in the "odd" copy of $\text{merge}_{m/2}$, and if its positions in $\text{merge}_{m/2}$ are $(p_{\text{upper}}, p_{\text{lower}})$, then its positions in merge_m are $2 \cdot (p_{\text{upper}}, p_{\text{lower}}) - 1$, so its positions in merge_n are $s \cdot \big(2 \cdot (p_{\text{upper}}, p_{\text{lower}}) - 1\big) - t = (2s) \cdot (p_{\text{upper}}, p_{\text{lower}}) - (t+s)$, which is why we update $t \leftarrow t+s$ and $s \leftarrow 2s$. This subroutine takes $O(\log^2 n)$ time and $O(\log n)$ space.

find-pos-sort(n, i) returns the pair of array positions compared by the ith comparator in sort_n. It maintains the loop invariant that the positions of the ith comparator in sort_n are the positions of the jth comparator in sort_ℓ shifted by offset $+o$. If $j > 2a$, the desired comparator is the $(j-2a)$th in the copy of merge_ℓ. If $a < j \leq 2a$, the desired comparator is the $(j-a)$th in the bottom copy of $\text{sort}_{\ell/2}$, and we must shift the positions by an extra $\ell/2$. If $j \leq a$, the desired comparator is the jth in the top copy of $\text{sort}_{\ell/2}$. This subroutine takes $O(\log^3 n)$ time and $O(\log n)$ space.

find-comp-merge(n, p, g) writes (outputs) the indices of all comparators that touch position p in merge_n, in reverse order and with g added to each of these indices. It maintains the loop invariant that the indices remaining to be written are those that touch position r in merge_m, in reverse order and shifted by h. If $1 < r < m$, some comparator from the end of merge_m touches r. If r is even, the remaining comparators that touch r are those that touch $r/2$ in the second copy of $\text{merge}_{m/2}$. If r is odd, the remaining comparators that touch r are those that touch $(r+1)/2$ in the first copy of $\text{merge}_{m/2}$. This subroutine takes $O(\log^2 n)$ time and $O(\log n)$ space.

find-comp-sort(n, p) writes the indices of all comparators that touch position p in sort_n, in reverse order. It maintains the loop invariant that the indices remaining to be written are those that touch position q in sort_ℓ, in reverse order and shifted by g. It takes $O(\log^3 n)$ time and $O(\log n)$ space.

find-wires(n, i) computes the indices of the ith comparator's four wires in sort_n because find-pos-sort() and find-comp-sort() are correct. Instead of running find-comp-sort() as a black box, find-wires() contains inline copies of find-comp-sort() modified to discard each index written until i is encountered. The whole algorithm takes $O(\log^3 n)$ time and $O(\log n)$ space.

(To avoid running find-pos-sort(n, j) and find-pos-sort(n, k), we could straightforwardly modify find-comp-sort() and find-comp-merge() so each comparator index gets tagged with whether p is its upper or lower array position.) ■

4.6 Putting It All Together

Theorem 4.1 (restated). *For all $d < \sqrt{2}$,* SAT $\notin$ TISP[N^d, polylog N].

Proof idea. We use *indirect diagonalization*: We assume the theorem is false and argue that this contradicts another theorem—specifically a time hierarchy (§4.2)—that was proved by "direct diagonalization." We want to speed up arbitrary computations under the hypothesis that SAT can be solved time-space efficiently. Because of the ultimate reduction to SAT (§4.5), we can work with NTIME[N] rather than just SAT. We speed up space-bounded computations at the price of introducing quantifiers (§4.4). To reach a contradiction, we must eliminate those quantifiers without too much slowdown. The polynomial hierarchy's collapse property (§4.3) does that using our hypothesis. Straightforward application of the space-bounded speedup would result in sublinear time, which wouldn't dovetail with the collapse, which works for linear time. We fix this by scaling things up using padding (§4.1).

Where does the time exponent $\sqrt{2}$ come from? The $\sqrt{\ }$ is because the speedup uses two quantifiers, so we must apply the hypothesis twice (once per quantifier), which squares the slowdown exponent. The 2 (inside the $\sqrt{\ }$) is because the speedup has $1/2$ in the exponent, and the total slowdown must not outweigh that (to get a contradiction). ■

The proof combines these five ingredients, restated for convenience.

Scaling Lemma (Theorem 4.3). *For all rational $a \geq 1$ and all $b > 0$ and $c > 0$:*

$$\mathsf{NTIME}[N] \subseteq \mathsf{TISP}[N^b, N^c] \Rightarrow \mathsf{NTIME}[N^a] \subseteq \mathsf{TISP}[N^{ab}, N^{ac}]$$

Hierarchy Lemma (Theorem 4.13). *For all $a > b \geq 1$:*

$$\mathsf{NTIME}[N^a] \not\subseteq \mathsf{NTIME}[N^b]$$

Collapse Lemma (Theorem 4.22). *For all $b \geq 1$:*

$$\mathsf{NTIME}[N] \subseteq \mathsf{TIME}[N^b] \Rightarrow \Sigma_2\mathsf{TIME}[N] \subseteq \mathsf{NTIME}[N^b]$$

Speedup Lemma (Theorem 4.24). *For all rational $b > c > 0$:*

$$\mathsf{TISP}[N^b, N^c] \subseteq \Sigma_2\mathsf{TIME}[N^{(b+c)/2}]$$

Completeness Lemma (Theorem 4.29). *For all $b > d \geq 1$ and $c > 0$:*

$$\textsc{Sat} \in \mathsf{TISP}[N^d, \operatorname{polylog} N] \Rightarrow \mathsf{NTIME}[N] \subseteq \mathsf{TISP}[N^b, N^c]$$

Proof of Theorem 4.1. Suppose for contradiction $\textsc{Sat} \in \mathsf{TISP}[N^d, \operatorname{polylog} N]$ for some $1 \leq d < \sqrt{2}$. Since $d^2 < 2$, there exist rational constants $b > d$ and $c > 0$ such that $(b+c)b < 2$. Defining $a = 2/(b+c)$, we have $a > b$ and $(ab+ac)/2 = 1$. Now,

$$\mathsf{NTIME}[N] \subseteq \mathsf{TISP}[N^b, N^c] \text{ and so } \mathsf{NTIME}[N^a] \subseteq \mathsf{TISP}[N^{ab}, N^{ac}] \subseteq \Sigma_2\mathsf{TIME}[N] \subseteq \mathsf{NTIME}[N^b]$$

by the Completeness Lemma, Scaling Lemma, Speedup Lemma, Collapse Lemma respectively. This contradicts the Hierarchy Lemma. ■

Exercises

4.1 **(a)** Prove that if $\mathsf{SPACE}[N] \subseteq \mathsf{TIME}[N^3]$ then $\mathsf{SPACE}[N^2] \subseteq \mathsf{TIME}[N^6]$.
(b) Prove that if $\mathsf{TIME}[N^2] \subseteq \mathsf{NTIME}[N]$ then $\mathsf{TIME}[N^6] \subseteq \mathsf{NTIME}[N^3]$.

4.2 **(a)** Prove that if $\mathsf{PSPACE} \neq \mathsf{NEXP}$ then $\mathsf{L} \neq \mathsf{NP}$.
(b) Prove that if $\mathsf{PSPACE} \neq \mathsf{NP}$ then for every $d > 0$, $\mathsf{SPACE}[N^d] \not\subseteq \mathsf{NP}$.

4.3 Prove that if $\mathsf{EXP} \neq \mathsf{NEXP}$ then for every $d > 0$, $\mathsf{NTIME}[2^{\log^d N}] \not\subseteq \mathsf{TIME}[N^{\operatorname{polylog} N}]$.

4.4 Prove that if $\mathsf{L} \subseteq \mathsf{TIME}[\operatorname{polylog} N]$ then $\mathsf{P} = \mathsf{PSPACE}$.

4.5 **(a)** Prove that $\mathsf{TIME}[N] \subseteq \mathsf{L}$ iff $\mathsf{L} = \mathsf{P}$.

(b) Prove that $\mathsf{TIME}[N] \neq \mathsf{L}$.

(c) Prove that $\mathsf{NTIME}[N] \subseteq \mathsf{P}$ iff $\mathsf{P} = \mathsf{NP}$.

(d) Prove that $\mathsf{NTIME}[N] \neq \mathsf{P}$.

4.6 Disprove this: For all decision problems A and B, if $A \leq_p^m B$ and $B \in \mathsf{E}$ then $A \in \mathsf{E}$.

4.7 The time hierarchy theorem says that for some problem in $\mathsf{TIME}[N^a]$, every correct program (with log-bounded word size) does not have $O(N^b)$ time efficiency (where $b < a$). Explain why something stronger is true: Every such program has $\omega(N^b)$ time efficiency. Does this also work for the time hierarchy for verifiers?

4.8 **(a)** Prove that for all $a > b \geq 1$, $\mathsf{NTIME}[N^a] \not\subseteq \mathsf{coNTIME}[N^b]$ using standard (not delayed) diagonalization.

(b) Adjust the proof of Theorem 4.1 (§4.6) to use $\mathsf{NTIME}[N^a] \not\subseteq \mathsf{coNTIME}[N^b]$ instead of $\mathsf{NTIME}[N^a] \not\subseteq \mathsf{NTIME}[N^b]$.

4.9 Prove Critical Graph 3-Coloring $\in \Sigma_2\mathsf{P} \cap \Pi_2\mathsf{P}$.

Critical Graph 3-Coloring	(4.24)
Input:	Undirected graph G
Output:	Is it true that G is not properly 3-colorable, but for every node v, deleting v would make it properly 3-colorable?

4.10 Prove that if Independent Set $\in \mathsf{P}$ then Robust Independent Set $\in \mathsf{P}$.

Robust Independent Set	(4.25)
Input:	Undirected graph G, nonnegative integer k
Output:	Does every set of at least half of G's nodes contain an independent set of size k?

4.11 Prove that if $\mathsf{NP} = \mathsf{coNP}$ then $\mathsf{NP} = \mathsf{PH}$ (the polynomial hierarchy collapses to level 1).

4.12 Prove for all rational $b \geq 1$, if $\mathsf{NTIME}[N] \subseteq \mathsf{TIME}[N^b]$ then $\Pi_3\mathsf{TIME}[N] \subseteq \mathsf{coNTIME}[N^{b^2}]$.

4.13 Prove that for all decision problems A and B, if $A \leq_p^o B$ and $B \in \mathsf{NP} \cup \mathsf{coNP}$ then $A \in \Sigma_2\mathsf{P} \cap \Pi_2\mathsf{P}$.

4.14 **(a)** Prove Π_2Sat is $\Pi_2\mathsf{P}$-complete.

Π_2Sat	(4.26)
Input:	CNF φ with two groups of variables x and y
Output:	Is it true that for every assignment to x, there exists an assignment to y such that φ is satisfied?

(b) Prove Σ_2SAT is NP-complete. Modify the definition to make it Σ_2P-complete.

Σ_2SAT	(4.27)
Input:	CNF φ with two groups of variables x and y
Output:	Does there exist an assignment to x such that for every assignment to y, φ is satisfied?

(c) Prove that if there exists a PH-complete problem, then PH collapses.

4.15 **(a)** Prove UNIQUE SAT $\in \Sigma_2\mathsf{P} \cap \Pi_2\mathsf{P}$.

UNIQUE SAT	(4.28)
Input:	CNF φ
Output:	Does φ have exactly one satisfying assignment (no more, no less)?

(b) Prove that $\overline{\text{SAT}} \leq_f^m$ UNIQUE SAT with linear query size.

(c) Prove that for all $d < \sqrt{2}$, UNIQUE SAT $\notin \mathsf{TISP}[N^d, \operatorname{polylog} N]$.

4.16 **(a)** Prove that for focused reductions (§4.5.1), if we drop the polylog N time requirement but keep the $O(\log N)$ space requirement (for both SIZE OF F and WORD OF F), then $\leq_f^m$ would become equivalent to $\leq_\ell^m$.

(b) Prove that $\mathsf{P} \neq \mathsf{L}$ iff there exist decision problems A and B such that $A \leq_p^m B$ but not $A \leq_\ell^m B$.

4.17 **(a)** Generalize Theorem 4.1 to SAT $\notin \mathsf{TISP}[N^d, N^e]$ for all d and e such that $(d+e)d < 2$.

(b) Theorem 4.1 focused on maximizing the time bound: SAT $\notin \mathsf{TISP}[N^d, \operatorname{polylog} N]$ if $d < \sqrt{2}$. Now, maximize the space bound: SAT $\notin \mathsf{TISP}[N \operatorname{polylog} N, N^e]$ if $e < 1$.

4.18 **(a)** Prove that for all rational $b > c > 0$, $\mathsf{TISP}[N^b, N^c] \subseteq \Sigma_3\mathsf{TIME}[N^{(b+2c)/3}]$. (The exponent $\frac{1}{3}b + \frac{2}{3}c$ is a weighted average of b and c that's skewed more toward c than $\frac{1}{2}b + \frac{1}{2}c$ is. Hence we get more speedup with 3 quantifiers than with 2.)

(b) Prove that for all $d < \sqrt[3]{3}$, SAT $\notin \mathsf{TISP}[N^d, \operatorname{polylog} N]$. (Note that $\sqrt[3]{3} > \sqrt{2}$.)

4.19 **(a)** Prove $\mathsf{L} \subseteq \bigcup_\ell \Sigma_\ell\mathsf{TIME}[N]$.

(b) Prove SAT $\notin \mathsf{TIME}[N] \cap \mathsf{L}$.

4.20 Define $\mathsf{NTISP}[T, S]$ as the set of all decision problems for which there exists a correct streaming verifier with $O(T)$ time efficiency, $O(S)$ space efficiency, and $O(\log \max(\min(T, S), N))$-bounded word size.

(a) Prove that for all rational $b > c > 0$, $\mathsf{NTISP}[N^b, N^c] \subseteq \Sigma_3\mathsf{TIME}[N^{(b+c)/2}]$.

(b) Prove that for all $d < \sqrt[3]{2}$, SAT $\notin \mathsf{coNTISP}[N^d, \operatorname{polylog} N]$. Hint: See Exercise 4.8, Exercise 4.11, and Exercise 4.12.

4.21 This extends Exercise 4.19 and Exercise 4.20.

(a) Prove $\mathsf{NL} \subseteq \bigcup_\ell \Sigma_\ell\mathsf{TIME}[N]$.

(b) Prove SAT $\notin \mathsf{coNTIME}[N] \cap \mathsf{NL}$.

Notes

Time-space lower bounds for SAT and related problems are surveyed in [364]. Theorem 4.1 is due to [167], which also improved the bound on the time exponent from $\sqrt{2} \approx 1.414$ to $(1+\sqrt{5})/2 \approx 1.618$. The state of the art is SAT $\notin \mathsf{TISP}[N^d, \text{polylog}\, N]$ for all $d < 2\cos(\pi/7) \approx 1.801$, due to [560]. The latter result's proof combines the same ingredients from this chapter in a more sophisticated way, and [102] showed that it's impossible to get a bigger time exponent if we only consider proofs that use these ingredients.

A time hierarchy theorem was first shown (for a different model) in [234], which is widely regarded as the genesis of computational complexity theory. A space hierarchy theorem was first shown in [504]. A time hierarchy for verifiers was first shown in [137] and was later sharpened and simplified in [476, 576]. These hierarchy theorems require the time and space bounds to be efficiently constructible given N, as is the case for ordinary polynomials and exponentials. The hierarchies are false for some contrived, hard-to-compute time and space bounds [521, 83].

Besides proving time and space hierarchies, diagonalization is useful for various other theorems, including the existence of NP-intermediate problems assuming $\mathsf{P} \neq \mathsf{NP}$ [325]. In an ironic twist, diagonalization can be used to prove that diagonalization *cannot* be used to resolve P versus NP. In more detail, a proof "relativizes" if it works even when all computations are replaced with oracle reductions to some arbitrary decision problem. Proofs based on diagonalization relativize. A barrier theorem from [45] says that no relativizing proof can show $\mathsf{P} = \mathsf{NP}$ or show $\mathsf{P} \neq \mathsf{NP}$. An even stronger type of barrier was developed in [3].

The polynomial hierarchy was defined in [368], though its collapse property (Theorem 4.21) was mentioned earlier in [292]. The notation for $\Sigma_\ell \mathsf{P}$ and $\Pi_\ell \mathsf{P}$ sometimes has P as a superscript: Σ_ℓ^{P} and Π_ℓ^{P}. Various complete problems for levels of the polynomial hierarchy (such as in Exercise 4.14) are cataloged in [466, 467]. Though it's unknown whether SMALLER CNF is $\Sigma_2\mathsf{P}$-complete, a more general problem is $\Sigma_2\mathsf{P}$-complete [527]—on input (φ, k), it asks whether there exists a CNF that's equivalent to φ and has size $\leq k$. EXACT INDEPENDENT SET is in, and complete for, a complexity class called DP.

Exercise 4.19.a is due to [387, 288]. Exercise 4.19.b is due to [166].

Chapter 5

Nonuniformity

Nonuniformity means using different algorithms for different input sizes. The model we studied so far is *uniform* because a single algorithm handles inputs of all sizes. How helpful could it be to design an algorithm tailored to a particular input size? One way to model this is with algorithms that take *advice* about how to handle inputs of any particular size. Another way is with new, inherently nonuniform models known as *logic circuits* (related to time) and *branching programs* (related to space). Throughout this book, it's sometimes more convenient to work with nonuniform models anyway, when uniformity is not the focus. Logic circuits and branching programs also facilitate the study of parallel algorithms and streaming algorithms.

5.1 Algorithms That Take Advice

5.1.1 Precomputation

Suppose we know which problem A we'll need to solve and what the input size N will be, but we don't yet know the input. In the meantime, how can we prepare to solve A efficiently once the input arrives? One idea is to solve A on all valid inputs of size N in advance and store the answers in a lookup table. Then, when we get the input, we look up the answer straight away. This can be practical if N is fairly small. If N is large, this may require a colossal amount of precomputation, since there may be exponentially many valid inputs.

In this chapter, we don't care how much computational effort is expended before the input arrives—we just consider the space for storing the resulting information that will help us solve A once we get the input. A straightforward lookup table has exponential size. What if we limit ourselves to polynomial size? Might it speed things up to have a small lookup table of common subproblems or other data?

Let's incorporate this into our model. We give a program *advice*—information that depends on the input size but not on the input—in a read-only *advice segment*. The instruction "read-advice $\text{Reg}[i] \leftarrow \text{Adv}[\text{Reg}[j]]$" puts the word from advice segment address $\text{Reg}[j]$ (or a hardcoded constant address) into $\text{Reg}[i]$. We posit the existence of an infinite *advice sequence* $a_1, a_2, \ldots$ where a_N is the tuple of words in the advice segment when the input has size N. We don't care where a_N comes from—it needn't be the result of a computation—we simply assume it somehow exists. The running time of $\Pi(x; a_N)$ is the maximum of the number of execution steps and $1 +$ the highest advice segment address accessed, like with verifiers (§2.2.2). If Π runs in poly time, then the advice has poly size, meaning a_N has poly$N$ bits. Like memory space, we measure advice size in bits, not words.

Definition. P/poly is the set of all decision problems A for which there exist a poly-time advice-taking program Π and a sequence of poly-size advice $a_1, a_2, \ldots$ such that for every valid input x of size N:

$$A(x) = 1 \iff \Pi(x; a_N) \text{ accepts}$$ ◄

P/poly stands for "P with poly much advice." The / notation does not mean division.

Unlike a verifier's witness, the advice is trustworthy. Π must be correct when given the "right" advice (a_N), but all bets are off if Π is given "wrong" advice ($\neq a_N$). We may assume Π runs in poly time even when given wrong advice, because Π can count its steps and terminate after poly many steps no matter what.

This model of "algorithms that take advice" is *nonuniform* because $a_1, a_2, \ldots$ may be totally unrelated to each other. The advice for different input sizes may alter Π's behavior so thoroughly that $\Pi(\ ; a_1)$, $\Pi(\ ; a_2)$, ... are essentially infinitely many different algorithms (one per input size). A uniform program has a finite description, but a nonuniform program doesn't—its description includes the infinite sequence $a_1, a_2, \ldots$.

For P/poly, Π has word size $O(\log N)$, but it doesn't matter whether the word size is efficiently constructible (§ 1.5.4): If it's not, we could round it up to $c \log N$ for an integer c, and include the exact original word size as part of the advice, and use masking to effectively run Π with this intended word size. In retrospect, the whole point of constructibility was to prevent nonuniformity from seeping in via the word size.

NP $\not\subseteq$ P/poly would be at least as difficult to prove as NP $\not\subseteq$ P, since P $\subseteq$ P/poly. We know EXP $\not\subseteq$ P (Theorem 4.9), but EXP $\not\subseteq$ P/poly is not known. Even NEXP $\not\subseteq$ P/poly is not known. Diagonalization doesn't yield nonuniform lower bounds.

Poly-size advice doesn't seem very useful for most natural problems, because changing the input size doesn't fundamentally change the problem. Though it's conceivable we could solve SAT efficiently on CNFs of size 1,000 in one way, and on CNFs of size 1,001 in a totally different way, this flexibility seems unlikely to help. But next we'll see that for a contrived problem, a little advice goes a long way. Most problems in P/poly that people care about are known or conjectured to be in P, but P/poly $\not\subseteq$ P does hold. In fact, something much stronger holds:

Theorem 5.1. *Some decision problem is solvable in constant time with one bit of advice but not solvable by any uniform program with any constructible word size, regardless of efficiency.*

Proof. We use diagonalization to define a decision problem A with word size 1 and with one valid input of each size N, say the all-0s input, denoted 0^N. For each pair (I, J) where I is code and J is code of a word size constructor, we pick a distinct value of N and define $A(0^N) \in \{0, 1\}$ as the opposite of the output of I on input 0^N with word size determined by J on input N (and if either of those computations runs forever, then $A(0^N)$ doesn't matter). By definition, every uniform program (with a constructible word size) fails to solve A on some input 0^N. But A can be solved in constant time by reading one bit of advice $a_N = A(0^N)$ and outputting it. ∎

P $\neq$ P/poly isn't about efficiency. Nonuniform programs just have an unfair advantage since they can stash infinite information in their advice.

L/poly is the log-space analogue of P/poly and the nonuniform analogue of L. The advice segment doesn't count toward the space. (If it counted, then a poly amount of advice wouldn't make sense for log-space programs.) We allow random access to the advice, unlike NL's one-way sequential access to the witness. We have L $\subsetneq$ L/poly, like P $\subsetneq$ P/poly. Also, L/poly $\subseteq$ P/poly by the same proof that L $\subseteq$ P (Theorem 1.8). It's a major open question whether L/poly = P/poly. We know PSPACE $\not\subseteq$ L (Corollary 4.12), but PSPACE $\not\subseteq$ L/poly is not known. Even NEXP $\not\subseteq$ L/poly is not known. Though nonuniformity doesn't seem especially useful for upper bounds, it throws a big wrench in the works for proving lower bounds.

It's straightforward to define EXP/poly and PSPACE/poly. The classes NP/poly, NEXP/poly, and NL/poly are also defined like their uniform counterparts: A nonuniform verifier V for A has a witness segment and an advice segment, and there exists a sequence of poly-size advice $a_1, a_2, \ldots$ such that for every valid input x of size N,

$$A(x) = 1 \iff \big(\exists w: \ V(x; w; a_N) \text{ accepts}\big)$$

and $V(x; w; a_N)$ terminates for all w. We won't have much to say about nonuniform verifiers, except some interesting exercises at the end of this chapter.

5.1.2 Reductions

Here's the nonuniform analogue of Lemma 1.12.

Lemma 5.2. *For all decision problems A and B, if $A \leq_p^o B$ and $B \in$ P/poly then $A \in$ P/poly.*

Proof idea. We solve A by running the reduction and answering each query using B's nonuniform program, which requires advice that depends on the query size. Since the query size doesn't just depend on A's input size, we collect all the relevant advice for B into the advice for A. ■

Proof. Let $\Pi_{A \leq B}$ be a poly-time oracle reduction from A to B. Let Π_B be a poly-time program with advice $b_1, b_2, \ldots$ for B. We design a poly-time program Π_A with advice $a_1, a_2, \ldots$ for A.

Assume $\Pi_{A \leq B}$ has time efficiency $\leq T = cN^d$ (for integers c, d). On a valid input, every query has size $\leq T$. For all N, define $a_N = (b_1, b_2, \ldots, b_T)$. On input x of size N, $\Pi_A(x; a_N)$ runs $\Pi_{A \leq B}(x)$ and answers each oracle query y of size $M \leq T$ by running $\Pi_B(y; b_M)$. We modify each of Π_B's "read-advice" instructions to find the desired word of b_M within a_N.

Π_A solves A because $\Pi_{A \leq B}$ solves A assuming each query is answered correctly, and Π_B answers each query correctly. Since b_M has size $O(M^e)$ for an integer e, a_N has size $O\big(\sum_{M=1}^{T} M^e\big) \leq O(T \cdot T^e) \leq O(N^{(1+e)d}) \in \operatorname{poly} N$. Thus Π_A is poly-time, with poly-size advice. ■

Similarly, we have a nonuniform analogue of Lemma 1.18:

Lemma 5.3. *For all decision problems A and B, if $A \leq_\ell^o B$ and $B \in$ L/poly then $A \in$ L/poly.* ■

A complexity class's complete problems are the least likely to be efficiently solvable:

- Suppose A is NP-complete. Then $A \in$ P/poly iff NP $\subseteq$ P/poly.
- Suppose A is NP-complete via $\leq_\ell^m$. Then $A \in$ L/poly iff NP $\subseteq$ L/poly.
- Suppose A is PSPACE-complete. Then $A \in$ P/poly iff PSPACE $\subseteq$ P/poly.
- Suppose A is PSPACE-complete via $\leq_\ell^m$. Then $A \in$ L/poly iff PSPACE $\subseteq$ L/poly.
- Suppose A is NL-complete. Then $A \in$ L/poly iff NL $\subseteq$ L/poly.

Lemma 5.2 also works for function and search problems:

Lemma 5.4. *If $A \leq_p^o B$ and B has a poly-time nonuniform program, then so does A.* ■

5.1.3 A Limitation of Nonuniformity

If someone believes the polynomial hierarchy doesn't collapse, then the following should convince them that poly-size advice isn't helpful for solving NP-complete problems.

Theorem 5.5. *If* NP $\subseteq$ P/poly *then* PH $= \Sigma_2$P $= \Pi_2$P.

Proof idea. Assuming NP $\subseteq$ P/poly, it suffices to prove Π_2P $\subseteq$ Σ_2P. Suppose $A \in \Pi_2$P by a 2-witness verifier V:

$$A(x)=1 \iff \big(\forall w_1\ \exists w_2 : V(x;w_1;w_2) \text{ accepts}\big)$$

Here, w_2 depends on w_1. We want to modify V so w_2 doesn't depend on w_1, since then we could swap the quantifiers so $\exists$ precedes $\forall$, thus showing $A \in \Sigma_2$P. First attempt: The assumption NP $\subseteq$ P/poly turns $\exists w_2$ into advice that doesn't depend on w_1 and can thus be specified with a $\exists$ quantifier preceding $\forall w_1$. In more detail: Consider FINAL $\exists$ OF $V \in$ NP (§4.3.2): On input (x, w_1), the output is whether $\exists w_2 : V(x;w_1;w_2)$ accepts. By assumption, FINAL $\exists$ OF $V \in$ P/poly by a poly-time program Π with advice $a_1, a_2, \ldots$. For every input (x, w_1) of size M:

$$\big(\exists w_2 : V(x;w_1;w_2) \text{ accepts}\big) \iff \Pi(x,w_1;a_M) \text{ accepts}$$

Our new 2-witness verifier V' (for showing $A \in \Sigma_2$P) must be uniform and thus can't have a_M for advice. Instead, V' has $\exists b$ for a purported value of a_M. Since a_M doesn't depend on w_1, the new $\exists b$ can precede $\forall w_1$. Letting $V'(x;b;w_1)$ run $\Pi(x,w_1;b)$, we envision the correctness of V' as:

$$\begin{aligned} A(x)=1 &\iff \big(\quad \forall w_1\ \exists w_2 : V(x;w_1;w_2) \text{ accepts}\big)\\ &\iff \big(\quad \forall w_1 : \Pi(x,w_1;a_M) \text{ accepts}\big)\\ &\iff \big(\exists b\ \forall w_1 : \Pi(x,w_1;b) \text{ accepts}\big)\\ &\iff \big(\exists b\ \forall w_1 : V'(x;b;w_1) \text{ accepts}\big) \end{aligned}$$

$\Rightarrow$ holds with $b = a_M$, but there's an issue with $\Leftarrow$:

$$\big(\exists b\ \forall w_1 : \Pi(x,w_1;b) \text{ accepts}\big) \not\Rightarrow \big(\forall w_1 : \Pi(x,w_1;a_M) \text{ accepts}\big)$$

because Π might incorrectly accept when given wrong advice $b \neq a_M$. To prevent V' from accepting unless $\exists w_2 : V(x;w_1;w_2)$ accepts, we use a search-to-decision reduction to find a w_2 and verify that $V(x;w_1;w_2)$ accepts. If no such w_2 exists, then V' will reject even if b is wrong advice—blood can't be squeezed from a stone. We substitute SAT for FINAL $\exists$ OF V since SAT is NP-complete and has a convenient search-to-decision reduction (§2.3.5). ■

Proof. Assume NP $\subseteq$ P/poly. Since SAT $\in$ NP $\subseteq$ P/poly and SAT SEARCH $\leq_p^o$ SAT (Theorem 2.14), SAT SEARCH has a poly-time program Π with advice $a_1, a_2, \ldots$ (Lemma 5.4). For every satisfiable CNF φ of size M, $\Pi(\varphi; a_M)$ outputs an assignment that satisfies φ. Assume Π clocks itself so it runs in poly time even with wrong advice ($\neq a_M$).

To prove PH $= \Sigma_2$P $= \Pi_2$P, it suffices to prove Π_2P $\subseteq \Sigma_2$P (Theorem 4.23). Suppose $A \in \Pi_2$P by a 2-witness verifier V with time efficiency $\leq T = cN^d$ (for integers c, d) and log-bounded word size W.

FINAL $\exists$ OF V	(5.1)
Input: x, w_1 where $x \in (\{0,1\}^W)^N$ is a valid input to A, and $w_1 \in (\{0,1\}^W)^T$	
Output: Does there exist $w_2 \in (\{0,1\}^W)^T$ such that $V(x;w_1;w_2)$ accepts?	

FINAL $\exists$ OF $V \in$ NP by a verifier U where $U(x,w_1;w_2)$ runs $V(x;w_1;w_2)$. Since SAT is NP-complete (Theorem 2.10), FINAL $\exists$ OF $V \leq_p^m$ SAT by a reduction that maps (x, w_1) to a CNF φ_{x,w_1} such that:

$$\big(\exists w_2 : V(x;w_1;w_2) \text{ accepts}\big) \iff \varphi_{x,w_1} \text{ is satisfiable}$$

Using a SAT encoding that allows any amount of padding, we may assume φ_{x,w_1} is padded up to some size M that depends on N but not on x or w_1.

We prove $A \in \Sigma_2\mathsf{P}$:

2-witness verifier for A (5.2)

$V'(x;b;w_1)$:
  run the mapping reduction to get φ_{x,w_1}
  run $\Pi(\varphi_{x,w_1};b)$ to get an assignment y
  if y satisfies φ_{x,w_1}: accept
  else: reject

(Technicality: If b's words don't all fit in Π's word size, V' rejects. If w_1's words don't all fit in V's word size, V' accepts.)

$$\begin{aligned} A(x)=1 &\iff \big(\quad \forall w_1\ \exists w_2 : V(x;w_1;w_2) \text{ accepts}\big) \\ &\iff \big(\quad \forall w_1 : \varphi_{x,w_1} \text{ is satisfiable}\big) \\ &\iff \big(\exists b\ \forall w_1 : \Pi(\varphi_{x,w_1};b) \text{ satisfies } \varphi_{x,w_1}\big) \\ &\iff \big(\exists b\ \forall w_1 : V'(x;b;w_1) \text{ accepts}\big) \end{aligned}$$

$\Rightarrow$ holds with $b = a_M$, and $\Leftarrow$ holds trivially. V' is poly-time since b and w_1 have poly$N$ size, and the mapping reduction runs in poly$(N+T) =$ poly$N$ time, and $\Pi(\varphi_{x,w_1};b)$ runs in poly$M =$ poly$N$ time even when $b \neq a_M$, and evaluating $\varphi_{x,w_1}(y)$ takes poly$N$ time. ■

5.1.4 Another Limitation of Nonuniformity

Theorem 5.6. *If* $\mathsf{PSPACE} \subseteq \mathsf{P/poly}$ *then* $\mathsf{PSPACE} = \Sigma_2\mathsf{P} = \Pi_2\mathsf{P}$.

Proof idea. Consider turning a poly-space program into a poly-time 2-witness verifier:

$$\exists \text{ accepting transcript } \forall \text{ time step } t\text{: row } t \text{ follows from row } t-1$$

The transcript is exponentially long, so it can't be the $\exists$ witness. The assumption $\mathsf{PSPACE} \subseteq \mathsf{P/poly}$ lets us retrieve any row of the transcript "on demand" in poly time, given the right advice as the $\exists$ witness. And wrong advice can't convince us an accepting transcript exists if it doesn't exist.

Exercise 5.6 asks for an alternative proof using PSPACE-completeness of QSAT. ■

Proof. Assume $\mathsf{PSPACE} \subseteq \mathsf{P/poly}$. To prove $\mathsf{PSPACE} = \Sigma_2\mathsf{P} = \Pi_2\mathsf{P}$, it suffices to prove $\mathsf{PSPACE} \subseteq \Sigma_2\mathsf{P}$ since $\Sigma_2\mathsf{P} \subseteq \mathsf{PSPACE}$ (Lemma 4.20) and PSPACE is closed under complement.

Suppose $A \in \mathsf{PSPACE}$ by a program Π with L lines and space efficiency $\leq S = cN^d$ (for integers c, d). On a valid input x of size N, each configuration is $K = \log L + S$ bits, and $\Pi(x)$ takes at most $T = 2^K$ steps (Theorem 1.8). When $\Pi(x)$ terminates, imagine it continues taking steps but with the configuration frozen.

CONFIGURATION OF Π	(5.3)
Input:	Valid input x of size N to A, and $t \in \{0,1,\dots,T\}$ represented in binary
Output:	The configuration after t steps of $\Pi(x)$

Bit of Configuration of Π	(5.4)
Input: Valid input x of size N to A, $t \in \{0,1,\ldots,T\}$ represented in binary, and $k \in [K]$	
Output: The kth bit of the configuration after t steps of $\Pi(x)$	

Bit of Configuration of $\Pi \in$ PSPACE by a program that runs $\Pi(x)$ for t steps (using extra work memory for the clock) and then extracts the configuration's kth bit. By assumption, Bit of Configuration of $\Pi \in$ P/poly. We have Configuration of $\Pi \leq_p^o$ Bit of Configuration of Π by a reduction that queries the oracle for each $k \in [K]$. Thus Configuration of Π has a poly-time program Π' with advice $a_1, a_2, \ldots$ (Lemma 5.4). Assume Π' clocks itself so it runs in poly time even with wrong advice ($\neq a_M$).

We prove $A \in \Sigma_2$P:

2-witness verifier for A (5.5)

```
V(x; b; t):
    run Π′(x, t; b) to get a configuration C
    if t = 0 and C isn't the initial configuration: reject
    if t = T and C isn't an accept configuration: reject
    if t > 0:
        run Π′(x, t − 1; b) to get a configuration B
        if C doesn't follow from B after one step of Π with x in the input segment: reject
    accept
```

(Technicality: If b's words don't all fit in Π''s word size, V rejects. If $t > T$, V accepts.) We argue:

$$A(x) = 1 \iff \big(\exists b\ \forall t:\ V(x;b;t) \text{ accepts}\big)$$

$\Rightarrow$: Suppose $A(x) = 1$ and thus $\Pi(x)$ accepts. Let $b = a_M$ where M is the common size of all (x,t). The configurations output by $\Pi'(x,0;b), \Pi'(x,1;b), \ldots, \Pi'(x,T;b)$ are the transcript of $\Pi(x)$, which starts with the initial configuration and ends with an accept configuration, and each configuration (except the 0th) follows from the previous. Thus for all t, $V(x;b;t)$ accepts.

$\Leftarrow$: Suppose b is such that for all t, $V(x;b;t)$ accepts. The configurations output by $\Pi'(x,0;b)$, $\Pi'(x,1;b), \ldots, \Pi'(x,T;b)$ start with the initial configuration and end with an accept configuration, and each configuration (except the 0th) follows from the previous. Thus this is an accepting transcript of $\Pi(x)$, so $A(x) = 1$.

V is poly-time since b, t have poly$N$ size, and $\Pi'(x,t;b)$, $\Pi'(x,t-1;b)$ run in poly$M$ = poly$N$ time even when $b \neq a_M$, and checking that C follows from B takes poly$N$ time. ■

5.2 Logic Circuits

We introduce a model of computation that corresponds to the combinational digital logic in a processor's hardware. This model captures nonuniform time complexity, and its simplicity makes it convenient for other things.

5.2.1 Model Definition

In a directed graph, *source* nodes have indegree 0, and *sink* nodes have outdegree 0.

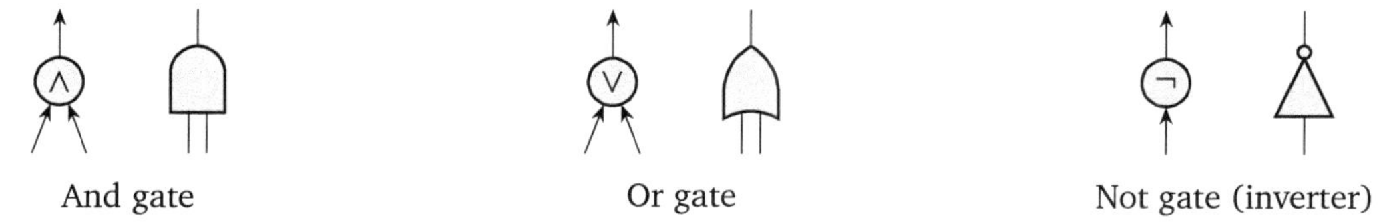

Figure 5.1: Notation for gates in logic circuits

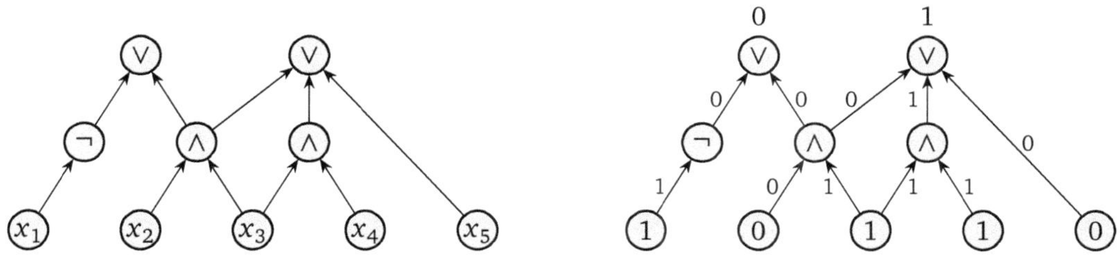

Figure 5.2: Example of evaluating a circuit

Definition. A *logic circuit*—or *circuit* for short—is a dag (directed acyclic graph) where sources are input variables, nonsource nodes are *gates* labeled $\wedge$ (and), $\vee$ (or), or $\neg$ (not), edges are *wires*, and some nodes (input nodes or gates) are designated as output nodes. *Fan-in* and *fan-out* mean indegree and outdegree. Each $\neg$ gate has fan-in 1. In a *bounded-fan-in* circuit, $\wedge$ and $\vee$ gates have fan-in 2. In an *unbounded-fan-in* circuit, $\wedge$ and $\vee$ gates may have any fan-ins ≥ 2.

A circuit with n input nodes and m output nodes is a kind of algorithm to compute a function $f\colon \{0,1\}^n \to \{0,1\}^m$. Each wire carries a bit. Each gate applies its operator to the bits on its incoming wires and sends the resulting bit on its outgoing wires. *Evaluating* a circuit means plugging in an assignment of bits for the input nodes and getting the output bits from the output nodes. ◀

Figure 5.1 shows how gates are drawn in computational complexity literature, compared to the equivalent notation in digital logic literature.

Example. The left side of Figure 5.2 shows a circuit that computes some $f\colon \{0,1\}^5 \to \{0,1\}^2$, and the right side evaluates the circuit to compute $f(10110) = 01$. ◆

If $m = 1$, the output node might as well be a sink. If $m > 1$, an output node need not be a sink, since it might be useful for computing other output bits. A node that's both a source and a sink is an input variable that's unused, except perhaps as an output bit. We may remove any node from which no output node is reachable. In particular, we may remove unused input nodes, so a circuit for f may have fewer than n input nodes if f doesn't depend on all its variables.

Sometimes C denotes both a circuit and the function $C\colon \{0,1\}^n \to \{0,1\}^m$ it computes. Also, we sometimes draw input nodes without circles.

A circuit's *size* is the number of nodes plus the number of wires. A bounded-fan-in circuit has at most twice as many wires as nodes (since each node has at most two incoming wires), so we consider its size to be the number of nodes when we don't care about constant factors.

A *formula* is a circuit where every non-output gate has fan-out 1 and there's only one output node, which has fan-out 0. Input nodes may have any fan-out. Another perspective: We duplicate input nodes so they have fan-out 1, in which case the formula is a rooted tree (an *in-tree*, since

Figure 5.3: Example of a formula and its tree version

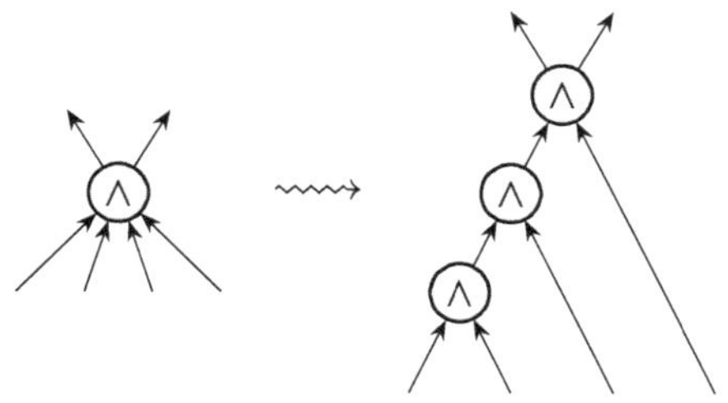

Figure 5.4: Unbounded to bounded fan-in

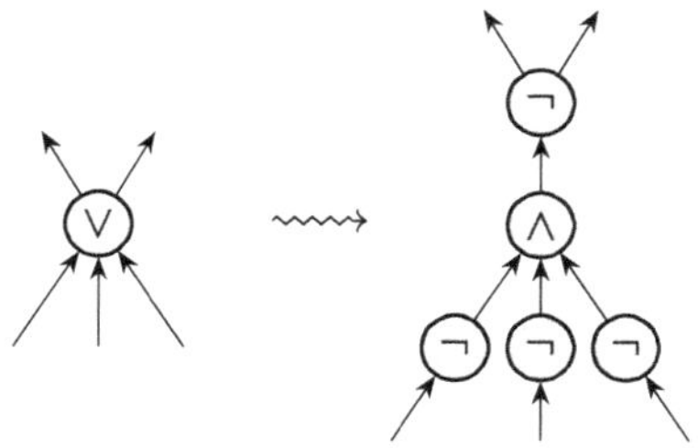

Figure 5.5: Eliminating ∨ gates

edges point toward the root). Figure 5.3 shows the example formula $(x_1 \vee \overline{x_2} \vee x_3) \wedge (x_2 \vee x_3 \vee \overline{x_4})$. CNFs and DNFs are types of formulas.

The circuit model is inherently nonuniform because a circuit only handles inputs with a particular number of bits n. Solving a computational problem with inputs of varying sizes requires an infinite *family* of circuits—one for each input size. To solve a decision problem A that has word size W_N, we need a family of circuits $C_1, C_2, \ldots$ (which may be unrelated to each other) where C_N has $n = NW_N$ input nodes and one output node, such that $C_N(x) = A(x)$ for every valid input x of size N. Ditto for function problems, where C_N has the appropriate number of output nodes. When we describe a circuit's size with big-O notation, we have a family of circuits in mind.

Technicality: Recall that if a uniform program's word size is bigger than A's word size, then the extra bits in each word of the input segment are automatically 0s. Similarly, we can let each input word in a circuit have extra input nodes, assigned 0 (pretending A has a bigger word size). This circumvents one minor nuisance later.

5.2.2 Robustness of the Model

Two circuits are *equivalent* when they compute the same function as each other.

Fan-in. We can change any unbounded-fan-in circuit into an equivalent bounded-fan-in circuit, by replacing each $\wedge$ gate of fan-in > 2 with a group of $\wedge$ gates of fan-in 2, and similarly for $\vee$ gates (Figure 5.4). The size at most triples. Thus we may assume circuits have bounded fan-in when we don't care about constant factors.

Gate types. We can change any circuit into an equivalent circuit with no $\vee$ gates—only $\wedge$ and $\neg$ gates—by replacing each $\vee$ gate with an $\wedge$ gate with $\neg$ gates on its incoming and outgoing wires (Figure 5.5). The size at most triples. Similarly, we can change any circuit into an equivalent

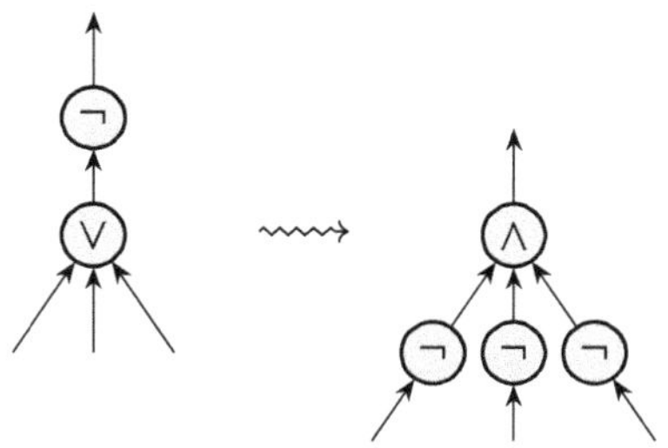

Figure 5.6: Pushing ¬ gates down

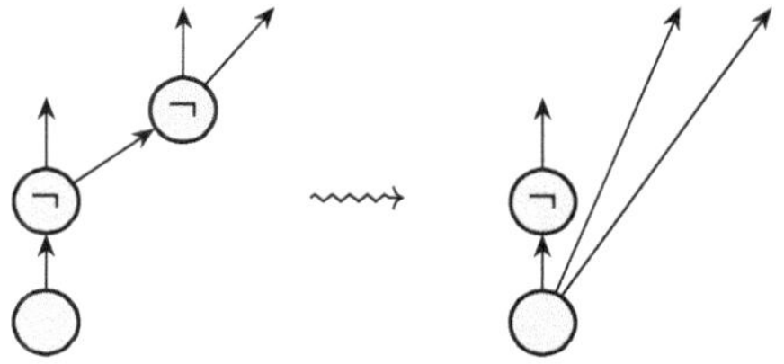

Figure 5.7: Bypassing double ¬

Figure 5.8: Partner of an input node

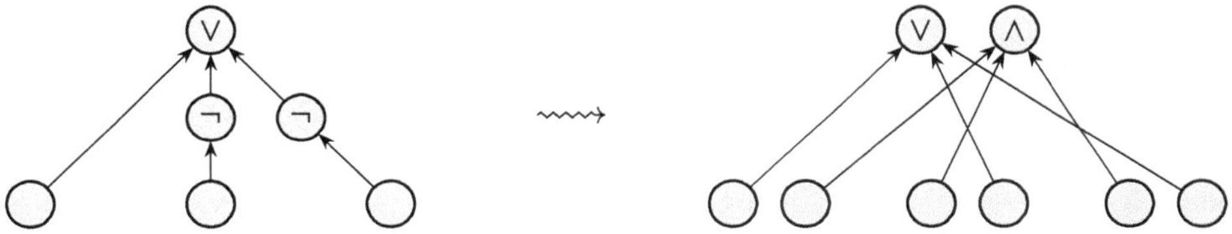

Figure 5.9: Partners of ∧ and ∨ gates

circuit with no ∧ gates—only ∨ and ¬ gates. But we can't always eliminate ¬ gates, because no combination of ∧ and ∨ simulates ¬. A *monotone* circuit has no ¬ gates. ("Mono" means "only one": When we flip input bits from 0 to 1, a monotone circuit's output bits can change in only one direction—from 0 to 1.)

Negations only at the inputs. We can change any circuit into an equivalent circuit where each ¬ gate's incoming wire is from an input node—that is, the circuit is monotone but with literals (input variables and their negations) feeding into it. First, consider formulas. We can push a ¬ gate through an ∧ or ∨ gate, flipping the latter gate to the other type (Figure 5.6). We repeat this until all ¬ gates reach the formula's input nodes or cancel out with other ¬ gates. It's trickier for general circuits because among a gate's outgoing wires, some may go to ¬ gates while others don't. First, there's no reason to have a wire from a ¬ gate to another ¬ gate, since then the latter gate's outgoing wires could instead bypass both gates (Figure 5.7). Now, we modify the circuit by removing the existing ¬ gates and giving each non-¬ node v (input, ∧, or ∨) a "partner" node named $\overline{v}$ that computes the opposite bit. We visualize $\overline{v}$ as sitting to v's right. An input node's partner is a ¬ gate (Figure 5.8). Consider an original ∧ or ∨ gate v (Figure 5.9): The gate $\overline{v}$ has the other type (∨ or ∧). If v had a wire from a non-¬ node u, then v still has a wire from u, and $\overline{v}$ gets a wire from $\overline{u}$. If v had a wire from a ¬ gate that had a wire from a non-¬ node w, then v gets a wire from $\overline{w}$, and $\overline{v}$ gets a wire from w. Each original non-¬ output node remains an output node. For each original ¬ output node with an edge from a non-¬ node v, the new circuit uses $\overline{v}$ as the output node instead. The whole transformation at most triples the circuit's size.

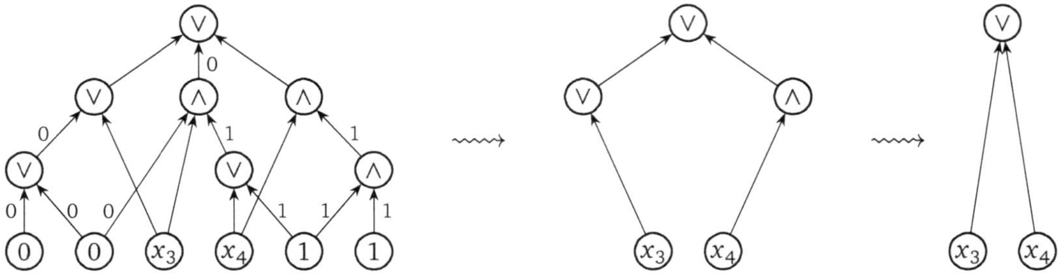

Figure 5.10: Contracting a circuit with $a = 00{*}{*}11$

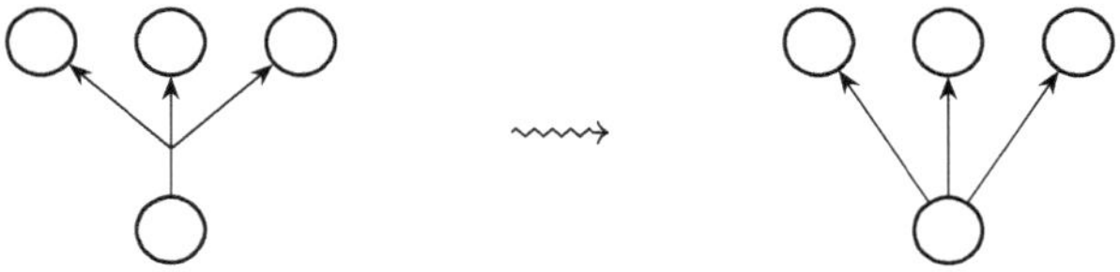

Figure 5.11: Splitting wires

Constant bits. How about allowing "constant nodes" that are like input nodes but hardwired to 0 or to 1? We could pick any input node x_i and use $x_i \wedge \neg x_i$ for constant 0 and use $x_i \vee \neg x_i$ for constant 1. Another perspective: Suppose we have a partial assignment $a \in \{0, 1, *\}^n$ and a circuit C that computes $f\colon \{0,1\}^n \to \{0,1\}^m$. If $a_i \in \{0,1\}$ then we replace the input node x_i with a constant node a_i. We *contract* C by *partially evaluating* it with a plugged in, like how we contract a CNF by plugging in a partial assignment and simplifying accordingly (§2.3.5). This yields a circuit $C|_a$ that computes the restriction $f|_a$, with input nodes corresponding to $*$s in a. Contracting a formula yields a formula. To partially evaluate $C(a)$:

- An $\vee$ gate emits 0 if all incoming wires have 0s.
- An $\vee$ gate emits 1 if at least one incoming wire has a 1.
- An $\wedge$ gate emits 0 if at least one incoming wire has a 0.
- An $\wedge$ gate emits 1 if all incoming wires have 1s.
- A $\neg$ gate emits the opposite bit if the incoming wire has a bit.

To get the contracted circuit $C|_a$, delete each node that emits a constant bit and each node that no longer has any path to an output node. If this leaves any $\wedge$ gates or $\vee$ gates with fan-in 1, delete each such gate and make its outgoing wires come from its predecessor instead. Figure 5.10 shows an example. The size doesn't increase. There's a catch: If an output node is deleted because it had fan-in 1, then follow the predecessor chain backward to a non-deleted node, and designate that as the output node instead. If an output node is deleted because it became a constant, then replace it with gates that compute the constant. The upshot is that we may use constant 0 and constant 1 nodes in circuits and formulas when convenient.

Splitting wires. We can allow "splitting" a wire into multiple wires all carrying the same bit. This is the same as having multiple wires emanate from a node (Figure 5.11). It's convenient for organizing a circuit into subcircuits.

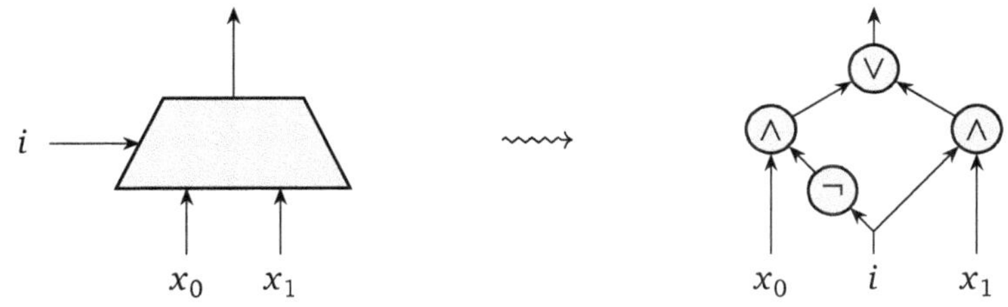

Figure 5.12: Multiplexer notation

5.2.3 Multiplexers

A *multiplexer* circuit—or *mux* for short—does "if then else". It computes $\mathrm{Mux}\colon \{0,1\}^3 \to \{0,1\}$ defined by $\mathrm{Mux}(x_0, x_1, i) = x_i$. That is, i is the *selector* or *index* input bit specifying which other input bit to forward to the output. If $i = 0$ then the output is x_0, and if $i = 1$ then the output is x_1. The DNF $(x_0 \wedge \bar{i}) \vee (x_1 \wedge i)$ computes this. Figure 5.12 shows the special notation for muxes in circuit diagrams. If we contract this circuit with $x_0 x_1 i = {*}{*}0$, then x_0 becomes the output node. If we contract it with $x_0 x_1 i = {*}{*}1$, then x_1 becomes the output node. We often use muxes as components in bigger circuits, in which case $x_0 x_1 i$ may be other gates rather than input nodes. The selector is a single incoming wire, which gets split inside the mux.

We generalize this "2-to-1 mux" to a "2^k-to-1 mux" with k many selector bits forming a binary number i specifying which one of 2^k many x input bits to output. Define $\mathrm{Mux}_k\colon \{0,1\}^{2^k+k} \to \{0,1\}$ by $\mathrm{Mux}_k(x,i) = x_i$ where $x = x_0 \cdots x_{2^k-1}$ and $i = i_{k-1} \cdots i_0$. One way to compute this generalizes the 2-to-1 mux DNF: For each $j \in \{0,1\}^k$, include the term $(x_j \wedge \text{“}i = j\text{”})$. With $k = 2$:

$$\mathrm{Mux}_2(x_0x_1x_2x_3,\, i_1i_0) \;=\; (x_0 \wedge \overline{i_1} \wedge \overline{i_0}) \;\vee\; (x_1 \wedge \overline{i_1} \wedge i_0) \;\vee\; (x_2 \wedge i_1 \wedge \overline{i_0}) \;\vee\; (x_3 \wedge i_1 \wedge i_0)$$

On any assignment (x,i), the term with $i = j$ evaluates to x_i, and all other terms evaluate to 0. This 2^k-term $(k+1)$-DNF for Mux_k has size $O(2^k \cdot k)$. We modify this into a somewhat smaller equivalent formula—of size $O(2^k)$ but no longer a DNF—by "factoring out" each bit of i as much as possible. We factor out "$\wedge\, i_{k-1}$" from half the terms and "$\wedge\, \overline{i_{k-1}}$" from the other half. Within both halves, we factor out "$\wedge\, i_{k-2}$" and "$\wedge\, \overline{i_{k-2}}$", and so on. With $k = 2$:

$$\mathrm{Mux}_2(x_0x_1x_2x_3,\, i_1i_0) \;=\; \big(\big((x_0 \wedge \overline{i_0}) \;\vee\; (x_1 \wedge i_0)\big) \wedge \overline{i_1}\big) \;\vee\; \big(\big((x_2 \wedge \overline{i_0}) \;\vee\; (x_3 \wedge i_0)\big) \wedge i_1\big)$$

This yields a tree of 2-to-1 muxes. Figure 5.13 shows this with $k = 3$. The bottom row uses i_0 to select one bit from each pair of x bits whose indices differ only in their least significant bit. This is repeated up the tree using i's other bits. This resembles a single-elimination tournament among $x_0 \cdots x_{2^k-1}$ where each 2-to-1 mux is a match-up, and x_i is the overall winner. The number of 2-to-1 muxes is $2^{k-1} + 2^{k-2} + \cdots + 2^0 = 2^k - 1$ (Lemma A.1), and each 2-to-1 mux contributes $O(1)$ to the size. Thus the size is $O(2^k)$, which is linear in the input size. This circuit is a formula since each 2-to-1 mux's x inputs (which may be gates in the 2^k-to-1 mux) have fan-out 1, and its selector is an input node.

To bundle wires together (perhaps representing a word), we draw them as a single arrow with a slash through it. A "2-bundles-to-1-bundle mux" consists of a 2-to-1 mux applied to each bundle's first bit, and another applied to each bundle's second bit, and so on, all sharing the same selector. Figure 5.14 shows this with three wires per bundle. The same thing works for a 2^k-bundles-to-1-bundle mux.

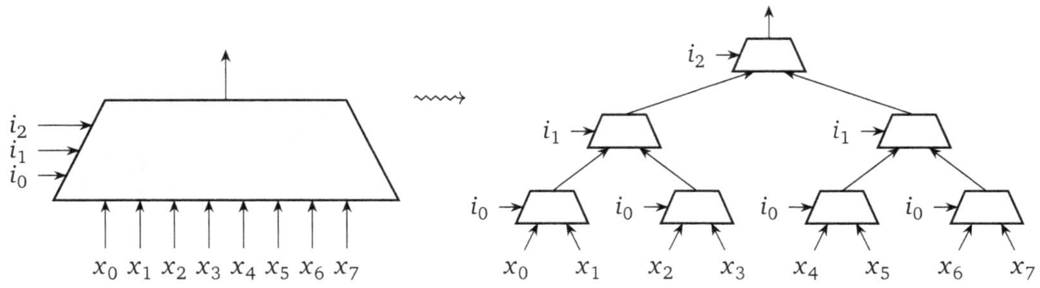

Figure 5.13: 2^3-to-1 mux

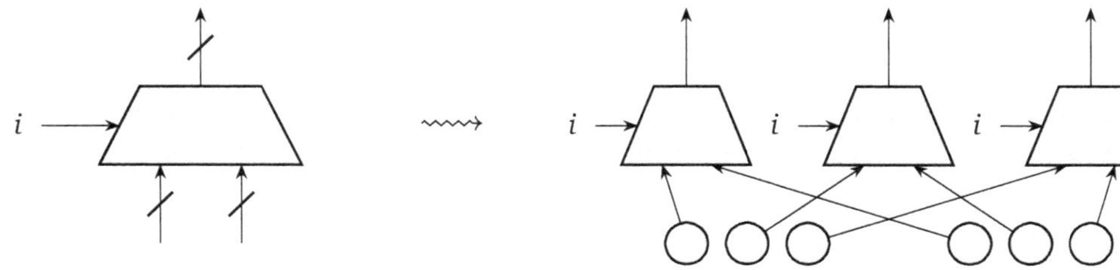

Figure 5.14: Mux with three wires per bundle

5.2.4 Circuit Complexity

In this section, we consider decision problems that have word size 1 and are total (every possible input is valid). Such a problem is a function $F\colon \{0,1\}^+ \to \{0,1\}$, viewed as an infinite family of functions $F_1, F_2, \ldots$ where $F_N\colon \{0,1\}^N \to \{0,1\}$ handles inputs of size N: $F_N(x) = F(x)$ for all $x \in \{0,1\}^N$. The *circuit size complexity* of F is the function that maps N to the size of a smallest circuit that computes F_N. The *formula size complexity* of F is defined analogously. (Circuit/formula size complexities are well-defined, unlike uniform time/space complexities, which are only vaguely defined since there might be no single program that's best for all N.)

Theorem 5.7. *Every* $F\colon \{0,1\}^+ \to \{0,1\}$ *has formula size complexity* $O(2^N)$.

Proof. We compute F_N using a 2^N-to-1 multiplexer formula of size $O(2^N)$ (§5.2.3) with the input x as the selector (which we called i before) and with constants for the bits being selected: x selects $F_N(x)$ to output. Figure 5.15 shows an example. ∎

Theorem 5.8. *Some* $F\colon \{0,1\}^+ \to \{0,1\}$ *has circuit size complexity* $\Omega(2^N/N)$.

Proof idea. For each input size, there are more functions than "small" circuits to compute them. There are 2^{2^N} functions $F_N\colon \{0,1\}^N \to \{0,1\}$. The number of size-$s$ circuits is $\approx s^{2s}$, and when $s = \frac{1}{2} \cdot 2^N/N$, this is $< (2^N)^{2s} = (2^N)^{2^N/N} = 2^{2^N}$. ∎

Proof. Since we don't care about constant factors in the circuit size, we just consider the number of nodes in bounded-fan-in circuits. We show that for all large enough N, there exists $F_N\colon \{0,1\}^N \to \{0,1\}$ that's not computed by any circuit with $s = \lfloor 2^N/2N \rfloor$ nodes. There are 2^{2^N} functions $F_N\colon \{0,1\}^N \to \{0,1\}$ since each of the 2^N many $x \in \{0,1\}^N$ has 2 options for $F_N(x)$. Since each circuit computes only one function, it suffices to show there are fewer than 2^{2^N} circuits

x_2	x_1	x_0	$F_3(x)$
0	0	0	1
0	0	1	0
0	1	0	1
0	1	1	1
1	0	0	0
1	0	1	0
1	1	0	1
1	1	1	0

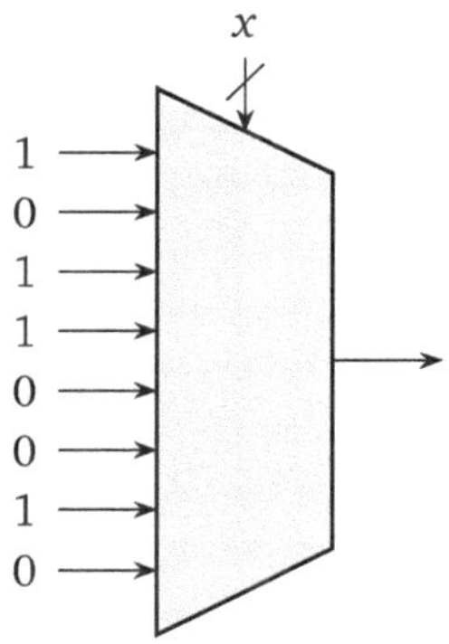

Figure 5.15: Example of computing an arbitrary function with a multiplexer

with s nodes. Say nodes are numbered $1,\ldots,s$ with the first N being the input nodes and the last being the output. A $\neg$ gate has $\leq s$ options for its inneighbor, and an $\wedge$ or $\vee$ gate has $\leq s^2$ options for its two inneighbors, so each gate has $\leq s+2s^2 < 3s^2$ possibilities. The number of circuits with s nodes is thus $< (3s^2)^s < (2^{2N})^s \leq 2^{2N\cdot 2^N/2N} = 2^{2^N}$. We overcounted: Some options lead to illegal "circuits" with cycles, and each legal circuit is counted multiple times with different orderings of the nodes, but that's OK. ■

For every N, there are *far* fewer small circuits than functions, so almost all functions require large circuits. This proof is *nonconstructive*—it doesn't pinpoint any particular function requiring large circuits, despite the abundance of such functions.

We showed the highest possible circuit size complexity is $O(2^N)$ and $\Omega(2^N/N)$. It's actually $\Theta(2^N/N)$ (Exercise 5.11.a). The highest possible formula size complexity is $\Theta(2^N/\log N)$.

Next, we have a circuit size hierarchy theorem, analogous to the time and space hierarchies (§4.2) but simpler to prove.

Theorem 5.9. *For all $a > b \geq 1$, some $F\colon \{0,1\}^+ \to \{0,1\}$ has circuit size complexity $O(N^a)$ but not $O(N^b)$.*

Proof idea. Here's an idea that doesn't work: There are more circuits of size $O(N^a)$ than of size $O(N^b)$. That's true, but different circuits of size $O(N^a)$ might compute the same function as each other, so circuits of size $O(N^a)$ might all compute the same functions as circuits of size $O(N^b)$.

Instead, we already know some F has circuit size complexity $O(2^N)$ but not $O((2^N)^{0.99})$, for example. To scale these bounds from exponential to polynomial, we use padding (§4.1), which scales inclusions up and separations down. Previously, padding bits were promised to be 0s. Since we're dealing with total functions, we let padding bits be anything. The padding amount is hardwired (not computed) since the circuit model is nonuniform. ■

Proof. We know some $G\colon \{0,1\}^+ \to \{0,1\}$ with input size M has circuit size complexity $O(2^M)$ (Theorem 5.7) and $\Omega(2^M/M)$ (Theorem 5.8). Let $\text{pad}(M) = \lceil 2^{M/a} \rceil$. Define $F\colon \{0,1\}^+ \to \{0,1\}$ by $F(x_1\cdots x_N) = G(x_1\cdots x_M)$ (ignoring $x_{M+1}\cdots x_N$) if $N = \text{pad}(M)$ for some $M \leq N$, and otherwise $F(x_1\cdots x_N)$ is a constant (say, 1).

F has circuit size complexity $O(N^a)$: To compute F_N when $N = \text{pad}(M)$ for some $M \leq N$, apply a circuit for G_M of size $O(2^M) = O(N^a)$ to the first M of the N input nodes.

F doesn't have circuit size complexity $O(N^b)$: Suppose for contradiction it does. To compute G_M, let $N = \text{pad}(M)$ and assume $N \geq M$ (otherwise compute G_M with a constant-size circuit since M is at most a constant depending on a), and take a circuit for F_N of size $O(N^b) = O(2^{bM/a})$ and plug in arbitrary constants (say, 0s) for all but the first M input nodes. Since $b/a < 1$, we have $2^{bM/a} \le o(2^M/M)$, so this contradicts G having circuit size complexity $\Omega(2^M/M)$. ■

5.2.5 Arithmetic

We design families of poly-size circuits for the arithmetic operations from our uniform model's instruction set (§ 1.4.2). The input is two words $x = x_{W-1} \cdots x_0$ and $y = y_{W-1} \cdots y_0$ viewed as binary numbers in $\{0, \ldots, 2^W - 1\}$. The input size is $2W$ bits.

Comparisons. To compute whether $x = y$, use a CNF of size $O(W)$ (§ 2.8.1). To compute whether $x < y$, note that $x < y$ iff there exists an index i such that $x_i = 0$ and $y_i = 1$ and $x_j = y_j$ for all $j > i$: The output $\vee$ gate corresponds to $\exists i$, and the ith incoming wire is from the CNF $\overline{x_i} \wedge y_i \wedge$"$x_{W-1} \cdots x_{i+1} = y_{W-1} \cdots y_{i+1}$" (and when $i = W-1$, this is just $\overline{x_{W-1}} \wedge y_{W-1}$). This circuit has size $O(W^2)$, which can be improved to $O(W)$ (Exercise 5.13.a). To compute whether $x \le y$, feed an $x < y$ circuit and an $x = y$ circuit into an $\vee$ gate. Other comparisons ($\ne$, $>$, $\ge$) are analogous.

Addition. To compute $z = (x + y) \bmod 2^W$, use a *ripple carry adder* composed of W *full adder* components that compute Add: $\{0,1\}^3 \to \{0,1\}^2$ where $\text{Add}(x_i, y_i, c_{\text{in}}) = c_{\text{out}} z_i$ is the binary representation of $x_i + y_i + c_{\text{in}}$. The ith full adder's c_{in} (carry in) is the $(i-1)$st full adder's c_{out} (carry out), or $c_{\text{in}} = 0$ if $i = 0$. To do "mod 2^W", discard the last c_{out}, which would have been z_W. Each full adder has size $O(1)$, so the total size is $O(W)$.

Subtraction. We reduce from subtraction to addition using two's complement. To compute $(x - y) \bmod 2^W$, first bitwise-negate y to get $y' = (2^W - 1) - y$, then add 1 to get $y'' = (2^W - y) \bmod 2^W$, and then compute $(x + y'') \bmod 2^W = (x + 2^W - y) \bmod 2^W = (x - y) \bmod 2^W$ using an "addition mod 2^W" circuit. The total size is $O(W)$.

Multiplication. Recall the reduction from MULTIPLICATION to ITERATED ADDITION (§ 1.8.2). Compute $(x \cdot y) \bmod 2^W = (a_0 + \cdots + a_{W-1}) \bmod 2^W$ where $a_j = (x \cdot y_j \cdot 2^j) \bmod 2^W$. Each bit of each a_j is either 0 or (a bit of x) $\wedge$ (a bit of y). To compute the iterated sum row by row, feed a_0 and a_1 into an "addition mod 2^W" circuit, then feed $(a_0 + a_1) \bmod 2^W$ and a_2 into another copy of that circuit, and so on. The total size is $O(W^2)$.

Division. To compute the quotient and remainder of x/y, first do binary search to find the quotient, which is the greatest $q = q_{W-1} \cdots q_0$ such that $y \cdot q \le x$. After computing $q_{W-1} \cdots q_{i+1}$, let $q_i = 1$ if $y \cdot (q_{W-1} \cdots q_{i+1} 10 \cdots 0) \le x$ and let $q_i = 0$ if not. That is, for each $i \leftarrow W-1, \ldots, 0$, feed y and $q_{W-1} \cdots q_{i+1} 10 \cdots 0$ into a multiplication circuit (not mod 2^W), feed the result and x into a $\le$ circuit, and let q_i be the comparison's result. At the end, compute the remainder $x - y \cdot q$. To handle divide-by-0, bitwise-$\wedge$ the output with the result of a $y \ne 0 \cdots 0$ comparison. The total size is $O(W^3)$.

Logarithm. $\lfloor \log x \rfloor$ is the index of the most significant 1 in x. For each $i \in \{0, \ldots, W-1\}$, $z_i = \overline{x_{W-1}} \wedge \cdots \wedge \overline{x_{i+1}} \wedge x_i$ indicates whether $i = \lfloor \log x \rfloor$. If $x \ne 0 \cdots 0$ then $z_{\lfloor \log x \rfloor} = 1$ and all other z_i are 0s. If $x = 0 \cdots 0$ then all z_i are 0s. For each $j \in \{0, \ldots, \lceil \log W \rceil\}$, the jth bit of $\lfloor \log x \rfloor$ is the $\vee$ of all z_i for which the jth bit of i is 1. This circuit has size $O(W^2)$, which can be improved to $O(W \log W)$ (Exercise 5.13.b). In digital logic parlance, we built a *priority encoder*.

Shifting. We lump this in with arithmetic because shifting left or right by y means multiplying or dividing by 2^y. We may assume W is a power of 2 because we can round W up to a power of 2 and use 0s for a word's new most significant bits. To compute $x \gg y$ (computing $x \ll y$ is similar), first use a W-bundles-to-1-bundle mux whose selector is y's least significant $\log W$ bits, to choose one of the bundles $0 \cdots 0 x_{W-1} \cdots x_i$ (with i many 0s on the left) for $i \in \{0, \ldots, W-1\}$. Then, use a 2-bundles-to-1-bundle mux to choose either that result if $y < W$, or $0 \cdots 0$ if $y \geq W$. The total size is $O(W^2)$.

5.3 Time Versus Circuit Size

5.3.1 From Size to Time

The time it takes to evaluate a circuit is essentially the circuit's size.

CIRCUIT EVALUATION	(5.6)
Input: Circuit C with n input nodes and one output node, assignment $a \in \{0,1\}^n$	
Output: $C(a)$	

We encode C like any directed graph, but with each node labeled by a gate type or variable index and with an adjacency list of inneighbors (rather than outneighbors).

Lemma 5.10. CIRCUIT EVALUATION $\in$ $\mathsf{TIME}[N]$.

Proof idea. Suppose a gate v has wires from u and w. To determine which bit v emits, we need to know what u and w emit. We process nodes in a topological order (§ A.2.3), so each wire goes from an earlier node to a later node. Thus, we've already determined u's and w's bits by the time they're needed for v. This is an example of dynamic programming: We only care about the output node, but we evaluate every node (a subproblem) and store its value for future reference. Every time the bit that v emits is needed for another gate (having a wire from v), we look up the bit rather than recompute it. ■

Proof. Say C has m nodes, with input nodes $x_1, \ldots, x_n$. This algorithm uses an array *value* where *value*$[i]$ gets the bit that node v_i emits when assignment a is plugged into C.

Algorithm for CIRCUIT EVALUATION (5.7)

topologically order C's nodes $v_1, v_2, \ldots, v_m$
for $i \leftarrow 1, 2, \ldots, k$ where v_k is the output node:
    if v_i is an input node x_j: $value[i] \leftarrow a_j$
    if v_i is a $\neg$ gate with a wire from v_j: $value[i] \leftarrow \neg value[j]$
    if v_i is an $\wedge$ gate with wires from $v_{j_1}, \ldots, v_{j_d}$: $value[i] \leftarrow value[j_1] \wedge \cdots \wedge value[j_d]$
    similarly if v_i is an $\vee$ gate
output *value*$[k]$

C has a topological order since it's a dag (Theorem A.9), so $j < i$ for a $\neg$ gate and $j_1, \ldots, j_d < i$ for an $\wedge$ or $\vee$ gate. By definition, the algorithm correctly fills out the *value* array and outputs $C(a) = value[k]$. A topological order can be found in linear time by the proof of Theorem A.9. The rest of the algorithm also takes linear time since it spends constant time per wire and per input node. ■

Surprisingly, Circuit Evaluation $\in$ SPACE[$\sqrt{N}$ polylog N]. This is difficult to prove.

5.3.2 From Time to Size

Theorem 5.11. *Every problem in* TIME[T] *has circuit size complexity at most* T^2 polylog T*, assuming* $T \geq N$.

Thus every problem in P has a poly-size circuit family. This opens an angle of attack for proving P $\neq$ NP: Try to prove a superpolynomial circuit size lower bound for an NP-complete problem. This seems approachable since the circuit model is simple—just wires and a few types of gates. But despite some intriguing progress (Chapter 18), this approach has not panned out.

Proof idea for Theorem 5.11. We turn any program into a circuit. Real processors use digital logic to run arbitrary programs. Ignoring optimizations like pipelining and caching, a processor has a big blob of combinational logic implementing the fetch-execute cycle. We hardwire the instructions instead of fetching them from a "code segment," since we can tailor our circuit to a particular program. Unlike a real processor, we can't reevaluate the same blob of combinational logic for different time steps, because our model has no sequential logic (no flip-flops or clock). Instead, we "unroll the loop" by copying the fetch-execute logic for as many steps as needed. Each copy takes a configuration (contents of the PC, registers, and work segment) on incoming wires, executes one step of the program, and sends the updated configuration to the next copy.

The T^2 is essentially "time multiplied by space." (A time-T computation only needs $\approx T$ space.) Our circuit must keep tabs on everything at all times, because the gates and wires are fixed in advance but the program's memory accesses aren't. It's unknown whether it's possible to do better than T^2. ■

Proof of Theorem 5.11. Suppose $A \in$ TIME[T]. We design a family of size-T^2 polylog T circuits solving A. We have $A \in$ TISP[$T \log^2 T$, $T \log T$] (Theorem 1.10) by a program Π with L lines, R registers, time efficiency $T' \leq O(T \log^2 T)$, space efficiency $S \leq O(T \log T)$, and word size $W \leq O(\log T)$. Consider any valid input x of size N. Define $M = S/W - R$ so $\Pi(x)$ never accesses any work segment address $\geq M$. Assume L and M are powers of 2. Assume Π has a unique accept instruction at line ℓ_{accept} and doesn't read past the input (Lemma 1.3).

We describe a circuit for A on inputs of size N. There are $n = NW$ nodes for the bits of the input x. If A's word size is $< W$, then some of these nodes are constant 0s (left-padding), and the rest are actual input nodes. Π's transcript is like scaffolding for the circuit. For each $t \in \{0, 1, \ldots, T'\}$, a bundle of wires y_t carries the configuration after step t of $\Pi(x)$. This y_t consists of bundles $y_{t,s}$ for all $s \in \{\text{PC}, \text{Reg}[0], \ldots, \text{Reg}[R-1], \text{Mem}[0], \ldots, \text{Mem}[M-1]\}$. We hardwire y_0 with the initial configuration. For each $t \in \{1, \ldots, T'\}$, an identical subcircuit computes y_t from y_{t-1} and x. Finally, $y_{T'}$ feeds into a subcircuit that outputs whether $y_{T',\text{PC}} = \ell_{\text{accept}}$. The circuit solves A since it outputs 1 iff $\Pi(x)$ accepts. See Figure 5.16, which has wires pointing downward like how time flows from top to bottom in a transcript. The input x feeds into the subcircuits, but the figure omits x for simplicity.

Computing y_t from y_{t-1} and x: For each s, a subcircuit separately computes $y_{t,s}$. See Figure 5.17.

Computing $y_{t,s}$ from y_{t-1} and x: Let $y_{t-1,-\text{PC}}$ denote y_{t-1} without $y_{t-1,\text{PC}}$. For each line $\ell \in \{0, \ldots, L-1\}$ of Π's code, a subcircuit separately computes the word $y_{t,s,\ell}$ that would be at location s after executing line ℓ with $y_{t-1,-\text{PC}}$ in the registers and work segment. Then, $y_{t,s}$ is chosen from $y_{t,s,0}, \ldots, y_{t,s,L-1}$ by an L-bundles-to-1-bundle mux whose selector is $y_{t-1,\text{PC}}$. See Figure 5.18.

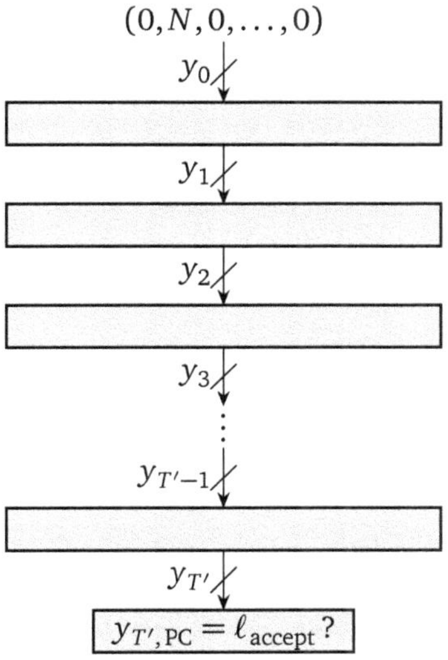

Figure 5.16: Circuit simulating a program

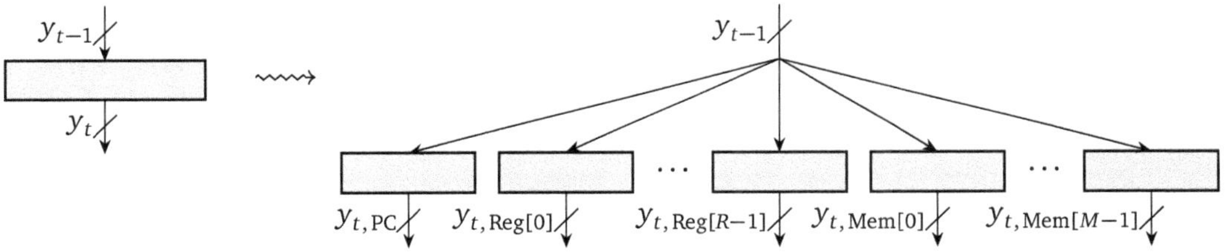

Figure 5.17: Breaking down a time step according to memory location

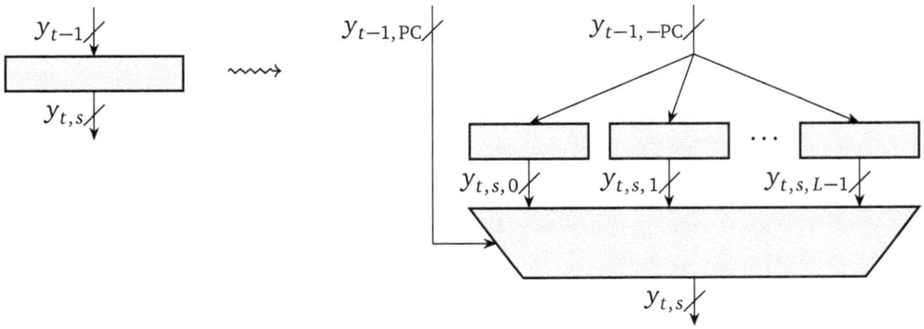

Figure 5.18: Breaking down according to instruction being executed

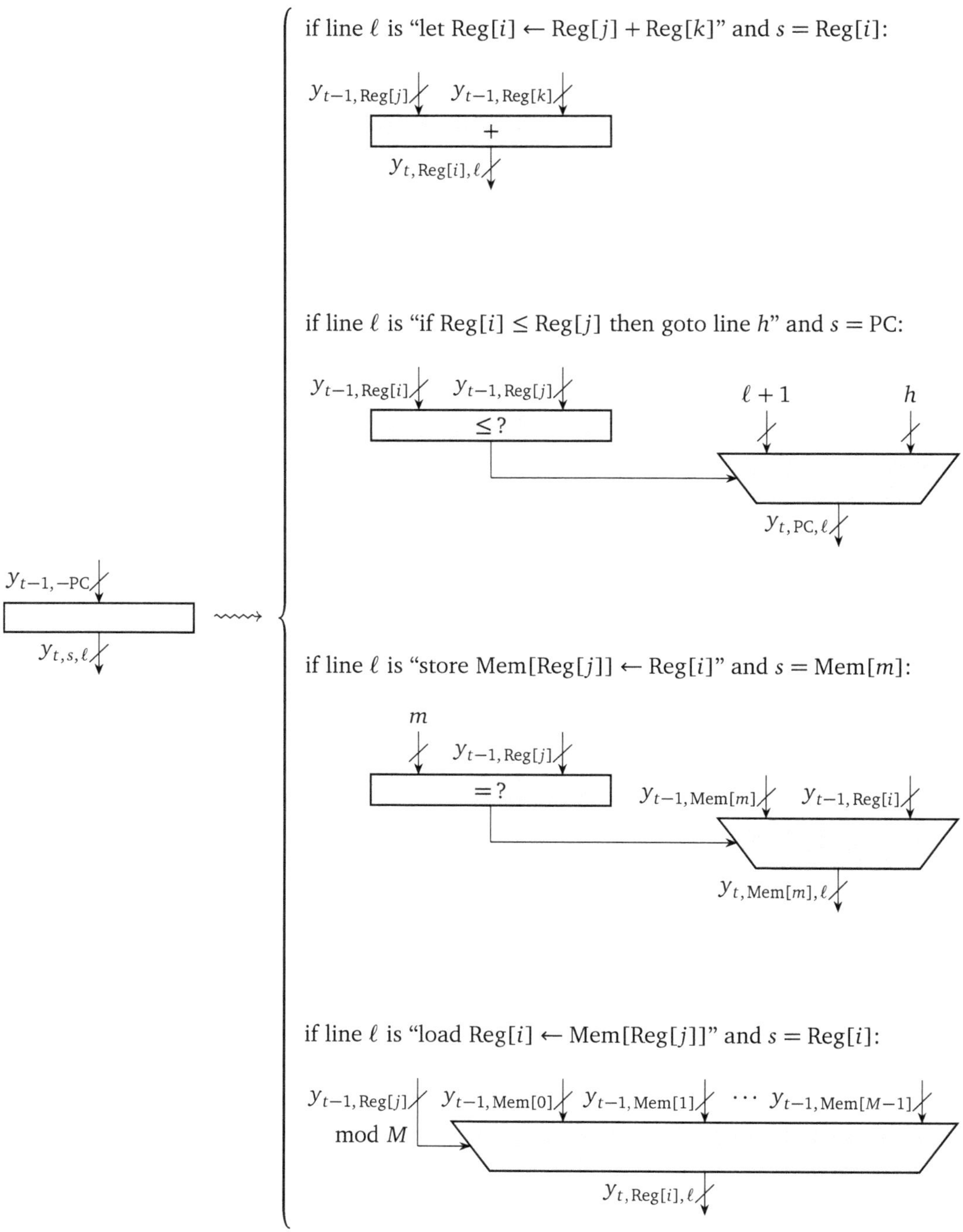

Figure 5.19: Computing a memory location's contents after executing a particular instruction

Computing $y_{t,s,\ell}$ from $y_{t-1,-\mathrm{PC}}$ and x: Figure 5.19 shows representative cases depending on s and the instruction at line ℓ.

- **Data processing.** Suppose s is the destination register. A circuit from §5.2.5 computes $y_{t,s,\ell}$ from the relevant registers of y_{t-1}. If an operand is a constant, we use constant bits instead of wires from y_{t-1}. If $s = \mathrm{PC}$ then $y_{t,s,\ell} = \ell + 1$ (a constant).
- **Control flow.** Suppose $s = \mathrm{PC}$. If line ℓ is an unconditional branch, then $y_{t,s,\ell}$ is the target line number (a constant). Otherwise, $y_{t,s,\ell}$ is either the target line number or $\ell + 1$, chosen by a 2-bundles-to-1-bundle mux whose selector is the result of comparing the relevant registers of y_{t-1} (or constants) using a circuit from §5.2.5.
- **Memory access.** Suppose line ℓ is a store and $s = \mathrm{Mem}[m]$ for some m. Then $y_{t,s,\ell}$ is either the word being stored (which is a register of y_{t-1} or a constant) or the old word $y_{t-1,s}$, chosen by a 2-bundles-to-1-bundle mux whose selector is the result of comparing whether m equals the destination address (which is a register of y_{t-1} or a constant). Now, suppose line ℓ is a load and s is the destination register. Then, $y_{t,s,\ell}$ is chosen from $y_{t-1,\mathrm{Mem}[0]}, \ldots, y_{t-1,\mathrm{Mem}[M-1]}$ by an M-bundles-to-1-bundle mux whose selector is the least significant $\log M$ bits of the source address (which is a register of y_{t-1} or a constant). If the source address is $\geq M$, then $y_{t,s,\ell}$ doesn't matter since Π wouldn't execute such a step on a valid input anyway. Read is like load, but one of the N words of x is chosen by a mux whose selector is the source address's least significant $\lceil \log N \rceil$ bits, which is enough since Π never reads past x. If $s = \mathrm{PC}$ then $y_{t,s,\ell} = \ell + 1$.
- **Termination.** We freeze the configuration: Each $y_{t,s,\ell}$ is the same wires as $y_{t-1,s}$.

In all other cases, $y_{t,s,\ell}$ is just $y_{t-1,s}$.

How big is this circuit? The subcircuit for $y_{t,s,\ell}$ has size $\mathrm{poly}\, W \leq \mathrm{polylog}\, T$ unless line ℓ is a load or read and s is the destination register—a *retrieval* as in §2.8.2—in which case it has size $O(MW)$ or $O(NW)$, which are $\leq T\, \mathrm{polylog}\, T$. Though we said all of $y_{t-1,-\mathrm{PC}}$ feeds into these subcircuits, each nonretrieval subcircuit only needs a constant number of words from $y_{t-1,-\mathrm{PC}}$. The number of nonretrieval subcircuits is $\leq T' \cdot (1 + R + M) \cdot L \leq O(T' \cdot M) \leq T^2\, \mathrm{polylog}\, T$. The number of retrieval subcircuits is $\leq T' \cdot 1 \cdot L \leq T\, \mathrm{polylog}\, T$ since they only arise for one s, namely line ℓ's destination register. Thus the total size of these subcircuits is:

$$\begin{aligned} &\leq (T^2\, \mathrm{polylog}\, T \text{ nonretrievals}) \cdot (\mathrm{polylog}\, T \text{ size per nonretrieval}) + \\ &\quad (T\, \mathrm{polylog}\, T \text{ retrievals}) \cdot (T\, \mathrm{polylog}\, T \text{ size per retrieval}) \\ &= T^2\, \mathrm{polylog}\, T \end{aligned}$$

These collectively dwarf the final $y_{T',\mathrm{PC}} = \ell_{\mathrm{accept}}$ and the muxes for all $y_{t,s}$. Thus the circuit has size $T^2\, \mathrm{polylog}\, T$. ■

5.3.3 Size Characterizes Time

Theorem 5.12. *For every decision problem A, we have $A \in \mathsf{P/poly}$ iff A has a poly-size circuit family.*

Because of this, some people define P/poly using poly-size circuit families instead of poly-time programs with advice.

Proof idea. To turn a circuit into a nonuniform program: The advice describes the circuit, and the program evaluates the circuit. To turn a nonuniform program into a circuit: Treat the advice as part of the input, turn the resulting uniform program into a circuit, and hardwire the advice in the circuit. ■

Proof. $\Leftarrow$: Suppose a poly-size circuit family $C_1, C_2, \ldots$ solves A. For each N, let the advice a_N be the encoding of C_N. Define a program Π such that on input x of size N, $\Pi(x; a_N)$ runs a linear-time program for CIRCUIT EVALUATION (Lemma 5.10) on input (C_N, x), and outputs the same bit. This solves A since the circuit does: $\Pi(x; a_N) = C_N(x) = A(x)$. The time efficiency of Π is linear in the size of (C_N, x), which is poly N. Thus $A \in \mathsf{P/poly}$.

$\Rightarrow$: Suppose $A \in \mathsf{P/poly}$ by a poly-time program Π with advice $a_1, a_2, \ldots$. Consider this promise problem:

A WITH Π'S ADVICE (call this problem B, with input size M)	(5.8)
Input: Valid input x of size N to A, and a_N	
Output: $A(x)$	

In the input, we promise a_N is Π's intended advice: If $b_N \neq a_N$, then (x, b_N) is an invalid input to B. The input encoding starts with the word N.

$B \in \mathsf{P}$ by a program Π' where $\Pi'(x, a_N)$ runs $\Pi(x; a_N)$. This solves B since $\Pi'(x, a_N) = \Pi(x; a_N) = A(x) = B(x, a_N)$. The time efficiency of Π' is poly N = poly M. (Details: We modify each "read" and "read-advice" to calculate the desired word's address within the input (x, a_N) and read it from there, and we may assume Π has log-bounded word size.)

By Theorem 5.11, a poly-size circuit family $D_1, D_2, \ldots$ solves B. We turn this into a poly-size circuit family $C_1, C_2, \ldots$ that solves A. For each N, let M be the size of inputs to B of the form (x, a_N), and obtain C_N from D_M by hardwiring the bits of N and a_N and contracting (§5.2.2), leaving only x for the input nodes. This solves A since $C_N(x) = D_M(x, a_N) = B(x, a_N) = A(x)$. The size of D_M, and thus the size of C_N, is poly M = poly N.

(Instead of detouring through B, we could adjust Theorem 5.11 to create circuits with input nodes for the advice segment's bits, by treating "read-advice" like "read".) ■

Circuits can also characterize the uniform complexity class P. To make the circuit model uniform, we require a family's circuits to be generated by a uniform program given N. Thus a program does the precomputation that only depends on the input size, and then a circuit does the computation that depends on the input.

Definition. A *generator* for a circuit family $C_1, C_2, \ldots$ is a uniform program that has no input segment, starts with N in Reg[0], and writes the encoding of C_N to the output segment. A *poly-time-uniform* circuit family has a generator running in poly N time with log-bounded word size. A *log-space-uniform* circuit family has a generator running in $O(\log N)$ space with log-bounded word size. ◄

A poly-time-uniform circuit family is poly-size since the generator only has time to write the encoding of a poly-size circuit. A log-space-uniform circuit family is poly-time-uniform (and poly-size) since the generator can't repeat any of its poly N many configurations without running forever (Theorem 1.8). A log-space generator might as well be register-only.

Theorem 5.13. *For every decision problem A, the following are equivalent:*

(i) $A \in \mathsf{P}$.
(ii) A has a poly-time-uniform circuit family.
(iii) A has a log-space-uniform circuit family.

Proof. *(iii)* $\Rightarrow$ *(ii)*: This holds since every log-space-uniform circuit family is poly-time-uniform.

(ii) $\Rightarrow$ *(i)*: Suppose a poly-time-uniform circuit family $C_1, C_2, \ldots$ solves A. Define a program Π such that on input x of size N, $\Pi(x)$ runs the generator to get C_N, then runs a linear-time program for CIRCUIT EVALUATION (Lemma 5.10) on input (C_N, x), and outputs the same bit. This solves A since the circuit does: $\Pi(x) = C_N(x) = A(x)$. The time efficiency of Π is poly N for running the generator, plus poly N for evaluating C_N. Thus $A \in \mathsf{P}$.

(i) $\Rightarrow$ *(iii)*: In the proof of Theorem 5.11, the circuit family for A is log-space-uniform if we let $T = cN^d$ (for integers c, d) and increase A's word size to W. (This is why at the end of §5.2.1, we allowed extra input nodes in circuits: The generator need not construct A's actual word size to determine the number of input nodes.) In more detail, we use registers to iterate through the possibilities of t, s, ℓ, and write the encoding of the subcircuit for computing $y_{t,s,\ell}$ and the mux that chooses one of these for $y_{t,s}$. Each subcircuit is a mux or comparison/arithmetic/bitwise logic circuit or combination thereof, all of which we can generate in log space by the definitions in §5.2.3 and §5.2.5. ∎

(ii) $\Rightarrow$ *(iii)* doesn't say every poly-time-uniform circuit family is log-space-uniform. It says every poly-time-uniform circuit family can be converted to a different circuit family that solves the same problem but is log-space-uniform. Most of the work of generating a circuit can be offloaded onto the circuit itself.

5.4 P-Completeness

A decision problem B is P-*complete* when $B \in \mathsf{P}$ and $A \leq_\ell^m B$ for every $A \in \mathsf{P}$. It wouldn't make sense to allow $\leq_p^m$ since then the reduction could solve A without the oracle. As usual:

Lemma 5.14. *Suppose B is* P*-complete. Then* $B \in \mathsf{L}$ *iff* $\mathsf{L} = \mathsf{P}$, *and* $B \in \mathsf{NL}$ *iff* $\mathsf{NL} = \mathsf{P}$. ∎

P-completeness is evidence that certain problems aren't in NL (much less in L) since they're the "hardest" in P.

5.4.1 Evaluating Circuits

Theorem 5.15. CIRCUIT EVALUATION *is* P*-complete.*

Proof. CIRCUIT EVALUATION $\in \mathsf{P}$ (Lemma 5.10). Every $A \in \mathsf{P}$ has a log-space-uniform circuit family $C_1, C_2, \ldots$ (Theorem 5.13), so $A \leq_\ell^m$ CIRCUIT EVALUATION by mapping x of size N to (C_N, x). This is correct since $A(x) = 1 \iff C_N(x) = 1 \iff (C_N, x)$ is a 1-input of CIRCUIT EVALUATION. It uses log space to run the generator to get C_N. ∎

Here's the template for proving that a problem C is P-complete: Show $C \in \mathsf{P}$ and $B \leq_\ell^m C$ for some B that we already know is P-complete. Let's use this template now.

MONOTONE CIRCUIT EVALUATION is like CIRCUIT EVALUATION but the circuit has no $\neg$ gates.

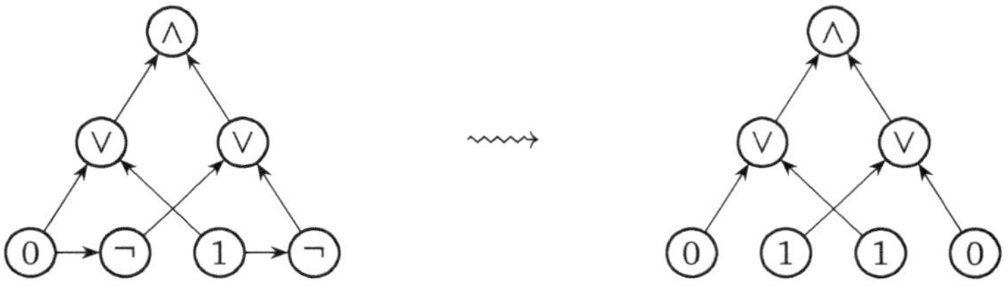

Figure 5.20: Example of reducing CIRCUIT EVALUATION to MONOTONE CIRCUIT EVALUATION

Theorem 5.16. MONOTONE CIRCUIT EVALUATION *is* P-*complete.*

Proof. MONOTONE CIRCUIT EVALUATION $\in$ P since CIRCUIT EVALUATION $\in$ P. It suffices to show CIRCUIT EVALUATION $\leq_\ell^m$ MONOTONE CIRCUIT EVALUATION since CIRCUIT EVALUATION is P-complete. Map (C,a) to (C',a') as follows. First, change C into an equivalent circuit where every $\neg$ gate's incoming wire is from an input node (§5.2.2). Then, obtain C' by replacing each $\neg$ gate with a new input node, and have a' assign this node the opposite of what a assigns to whichever input node fed into the $\neg$ gate. Figure 5.20 shows an example. This log-space mapping reduction is correct since $C(a) = C'(a')$. ■

5.4.2 Path Forming Game on a Dag

Recall the path forming game from § 3.1.2. The associated problem GEOGRAPHY is PSPACE-complete (Theorem 3.5), but the situation changes when the input graph is acyclic:

Theorem 5.17. GEOGRAPHY ON A DAG *is* P-*complete.*

Proof idea. To design a poly-time algorithm for GEOGRAPHY ON A DAG, we use dynamic programming rather than recursion. It never matters how the players got to the current node. Since there are no cycles, previously visited nodes never block subsequent moves, and the game only ends upon reaching a sink.

To reduce MONOTONE CIRCUIT EVALUATION to GEOGRAPHY ON A DAG, note that $\vee$ gates are like $\exists$ quantifiers, and $\wedge$ gates are like $\forall$ quantifiers, and use the connection between games and quantifiers (§3.1). Starting at the output gate—which is like the first quantifier—the players form a path backward toward the input. At an $\vee$ gate, P1 picks an incoming wire. At an $\wedge$ gate, P2 picks an incoming wire. P1 claims the circuit evaluates to 1, and P2 claims it evaluates to 0, and whoever is right can ensure that every wire they traverse carries that same bit. ■

In Chapter 3 we saw that poly-space computations are games in disguise. Now, we know that poly-time computations are also games in disguise! CIRCUIT EVALUATION embodies the familiar perspective of computing from input to output. GEOGRAPHY ON A DAG offers the alternative perspective of playing a game from the output backward to the input.

Proof of Theorem 5.17. The following algorithm shows GEOGRAPHY ON A DAG $\in$ TIME$[N]$. It uses an array *wins* where *wins*$[i]$ gets the bit indicating whether the current player has a winning strategy for the rest of the game, assuming they're at node v_i. The current player can win iff they can make a move so the other player cannot then win:

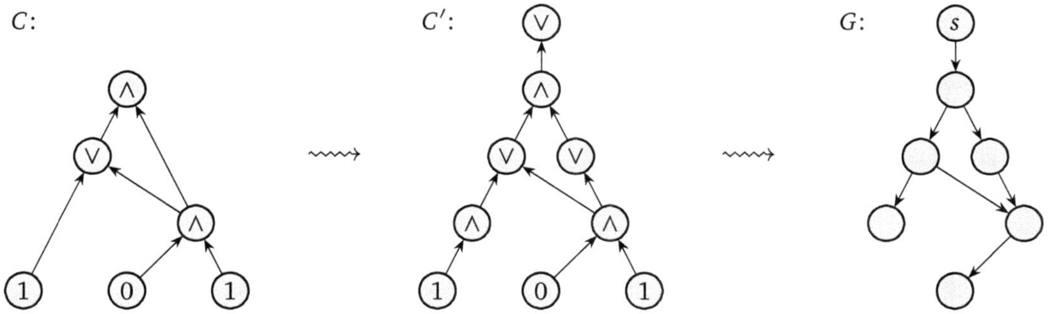

Figure 5.21: Example of reducing MONOTONE CIRCUIT EVALUATION to GEOGRAPHY ON A DAG

Algorithm for GEOGRAPHY ON A DAG	(5.9)

topologically order G's nodes $v_1, v_2, \ldots, v_n$
for $i \leftarrow n, n-1, \ldots, k$ where $v_k = s$:
  if v_i has outdegree 0: $wins[i] \leftarrow 0$
  else if v_i has edges to $v_{j_1}, \ldots, v_{j_d}$: $wins[i] \leftarrow \neg wins[j_1] \vee \cdots \vee \neg wins[j_d]$
output $wins[k]$

G has a topological order since it's a dag (Theorem A.9). If v_i has outdegree 0, then $wins[i] = 0$ because the current player just lost. Otherwise $j_1, \ldots, j_d > i$, so $wins[j_1], \ldots, wins[j_d]$ were already computed. The algorithm correctly computes $wins[i]$ because $wins[i] = 1$ iff $wins[j_h] = 0$ for some edge (v_i, v_{j_h}) (which is necessarily a legal move since if v_{j_h} were on the path so far, it would create a cycle), which means whoever played (v_i, v_{j_h}) has a winning strategy (from v_i) since their opponent (who must play from v_{j_h}) doesn't. Thus the output $wins[k]$ indicates whether P1 can win starting from s.

A topological order can be found in linear time, by the proof of Theorem A.9. The rest of the algorithm also takes linear time since it spends constant time per edge and per node.

Next, it suffices to show MONOTONE CIRCUIT EVALUATION $\leq_\ell^m$ GEOGRAPHY ON A DAG since MONOTONE CIRCUIT EVALUATION is P-complete. Map (C, a) to (G, s) as follows.

Recall we can ensure a QSAT input's quantifiers alternate $\exists \forall \exists \forall \cdots \exists \forall$ by inserting dummy quantifiers if necessary. We do a similar thing with a circuit by inserting dummy $\vee$ and $\wedge$ gates, which have fan-in 1 and just propagate their incoming bit. We change C into an equivalent circuit C' where every path from the output node backward to an input node has the form $\vee \leftarrow \wedge \leftarrow \vee \leftarrow \wedge \leftarrow \cdots \vee \leftarrow \wedge \leftarrow$:

- If the output isn't an $\vee$ gate, give it a wire to a dummy $\vee$ gate, which becomes the output.
- If a wire connects an input node to an $\vee$ gate, cut the wire in two with a dummy $\wedge$ gate.
- If a wire connects an $\wedge$ gate to an $\wedge$ gate, cut the wire in two with a dummy $\vee$ gate.
- If a wire connects an $\vee$ gate to an $\vee$ gate, cut the wire in two with a dummy $\wedge$ gate.

Obtain G from C' by reversing all edge directions and deleting all input nodes that a assigns 1. Let s be the output node. Figure 5.21 shows an example.

G is a dag since C' is a dag and reversing all edge directions can't create a cycle. Every s-to-sink path in G has the form $\vee \rightarrow \wedge \rightarrow \vee \rightarrow \wedge \rightarrow \cdots \vee \rightarrow \wedge$ and then if the last $\wedge$ node has any outneighbors, they must be sinks corresponding to input nodes assigned 0. That last $\wedge$ node is a sink in G iff it evaluates to 1 in C'. In the path forming game on G starting at s, P1 plays at

$\vee$ nodes, and P2 plays at $\wedge$ nodes.

To show this log-space mapping reduction is correct, we argue that $C(a) = 1$ iff P1 has a winning strategy on (G,s). (In Figure 5.21, the circuit evaluates to 0, and P2 has a winning strategy.)

$\Rightarrow$: Assume $C(a) = 1$ and thus s evaluates to 1 in C'. A winning strategy for P1 on (G,s) can maintain the invariant that every node on the path evaluates to 1 in C'. This holds for s by assumption. P1 can maintain the invariant since if an $\vee$ gate evaluates to 1, then at least one incoming wire in C' (outgoing edge in G) carries 1. P2 must maintain the invariant since if an $\wedge$ gate evaluates to 1, then all incoming wires in C' carry 1. The game ends at an $\wedge$ that evaluates to 1 and is thus a sink in G, so P1 wins since it's P2's turn.

$\Leftarrow$: Assume $C(a) = 0$ and thus s evaluates to 0 in C'. A winning strategy for P2 on (G,s) can maintain the invariant that every node on the path evaluates to 0 in C'. This holds for s by assumption. P2 can maintain the invariant since if an $\wedge$ gate evaluates to 0, then at least one incoming wire in C' (outgoing edge in G) carries 0. P1 must maintain the invariant since if an $\vee$ gate evaluates to 0, then all incoming wires in C' carry 0. The last $\wedge$ on the path evaluates to 0 and is thus not a sink in G, so P2 can go from there to a sink corresponding to an input node assigned 0. Then, P2 wins since it's P1's turn. ■

5.4.3 NP-Completeness Redux

An assignment *satisfies* a circuit with one output node iff it makes the circuit evaluate to 1. A circuit with one output node is *satisfiable* iff there exists an assignment that satisfies it.

CIRCUIT SATISFIABILITY (or CIRCUIT SAT for short)	(5.10)
Input: Circuit C with one output node	
Output: Is C satisfiable?	

Theorem 5.18. CIRCUIT SAT *is* NP-*complete via* $\leq_{\ell}^{m}$.

We prove NP-hardness of CIRCUIT SAT from first principles, even though it follows immediately from NP-hardness of SAT (Theorem 2.10 and Theorem 2.40) since CNFs are circuits.

Proof idea. To reduce $A \in \mathsf{NP}$ to CIRCUIT SAT, we turn A's verifier into a circuit with input nodes for both the input x and the purported witness w, and we hardwire the actual input for x. The verifier accepts w iff w satisfies the circuit. ■

Proof. CIRCUIT SAT $\in \mathsf{NP}$ by a verifier that, given input C and an assignment a as a purported witness, runs a linear-time program for CIRCUIT EVALUATION (Lemma 5.10) on input (C,a) to check whether a satisfies C. Now, suppose $A \in \mathsf{NP}$ by a verifier V with time efficiency $\leq T = cN^d$ (for integers c,d) and log-bounded word size W.

OUTPUT OF V WITH WITNESS (call this problem B, with input size M)	(5.11)
Input: Valid input x of size N to A, and purported witness $w \in (\{0,1\}^W)^T$	
Output: $V(x;w)$	

The input encoding starts with the word N, so B's input size is $M = 1 + N + T$.

$B \in \mathsf{P}$ by a program Π where $\Pi(x,w)$ runs $V(x;w)$. The time efficiency of Π is poly $N =$ poly M. (Details: We modify each "read" and "read-witness" to calculate the desired word's address within the input (x,w), and read it from there.)

By Theorem 5.13, a log-space-uniform circuit family $D_1, D_2, \ldots$ solves B. Thus $A \leq_\ell^m$ CIRCUIT SAT by mapping input x of size N to a circuit C_x as follows: Calculate the size M of inputs to B of the form (x,w), run the generator to get D_M, and obtain C_x from D_M by hardwiring the bits of N and x, leaving only w for the input nodes. For every assignment to w, we have $V(x;w) = B(x,w) = D_M(x,w) = C_x(w)$. This log-space mapping reduction is correct since $A(x) = 1 \iff (\exists w : V(x;w) \text{ accepts}) \iff C_x$ is satisfiable.

(Instead of detouring through B, we could adjust Theorem 5.13 to create circuits with input nodes for the witness segment's bits, by treating "read-witness" like "read".) ■

To reprove the NP-completeness of SAT, we can show CIRCUIT SAT $\leq_\ell^m$ SAT by mapping C to φ as follows: φ has variables $x = x_1 \cdots x_n$ and $y = y_1 \cdots y_m$ associated with C's input nodes and gates respectively. For each gate, φ has clauses checking that the gate's variable has the same bit the gate would emit, depending on the variables for the incoming bits. For example, these clauses check that $y_i \wedge y_j = y_k$:

$$((y_i \wedge y_j) \Rightarrow y_k) \wedge (\overline{y_i} \Rightarrow \overline{y_k}) \wedge (\overline{y_j} \Rightarrow \overline{y_k}) \equiv (\overline{y_i} \vee \overline{y_j} \vee y_k) \wedge (y_i \vee \overline{y_k}) \wedge (y_j \vee \overline{y_k})$$

Also, φ has a width-1 clause checking that the output node's variable is assigned 1. For every assignment to x, we have $C(x) = 1$ iff there exists an assignment to y such that $\varphi(x,y) = 1$. That is, y must be the values of all gates, like a "transcript" of evaluating C. This log-space mapping reduction is correct since $(\exists x : C(x) = 1) \iff (\exists x, y : \varphi(x,y) = 1)$. (We can show CIRCUIT SAT $\leq_\ell^m$ 3-SAT by first making C have bounded fan-in.)

Thus CIRCUIT SAT can be the "mother of all NP-complete problems," providing an alternative to the proof in § 2.8.2 that SAT is NP-complete. This also yields quasi-quadratic-time reductions for NTIME$[N]$ as in § 2.8.3, since "time to circuit size" has only quasi-quadratic overhead (Theorem 5.11). But this doesn't bypass the proof in § 2.8.4 for quasi-linear-time reductions—it's unknown if time can be converted to circuit size with subquadratic overhead.

5.5 Branching Programs

We introduce a model of computation that captures nonuniform space complexity, like how circuits capture nonuniform time complexity. *Branching programs* (also known as *binary decision diagrams*) have practical applications in computer aided design software and in model checking.

5.5.1 Model Definition

Despite the name, branching programs aren't "programs" as in our uniform model (§ 1.4).

Definition. A *branching program* is a dag with a designated start node, and where each nonsink node is labeled by an input variable and has two outgoing edges labeled 0 and 1, and with two sinks labeled 0 (reject) and 1 (accept).

A branching program is a kind of algorithm to compute a function $f : \{0,1\}^n \to \{0,1\}$. On input $a \in \{0,1\}^n$, it traverses a path from the start node: At a node labeled x_i, it *queries* (reads) this input bit and follows the edge labeled a_i. It outputs the label of the sink reached. ◄

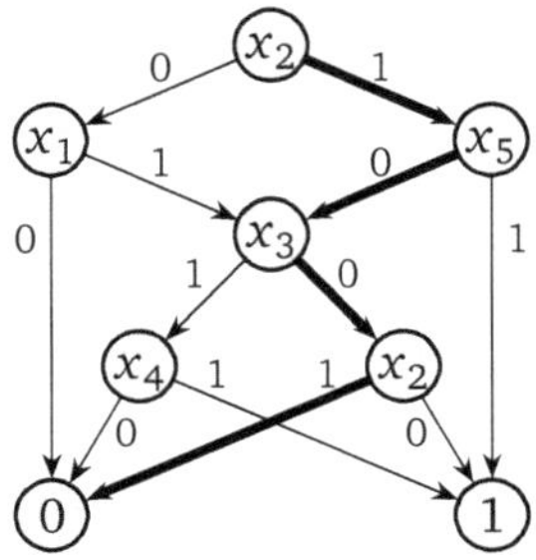

Figure 5.22: Example branching program

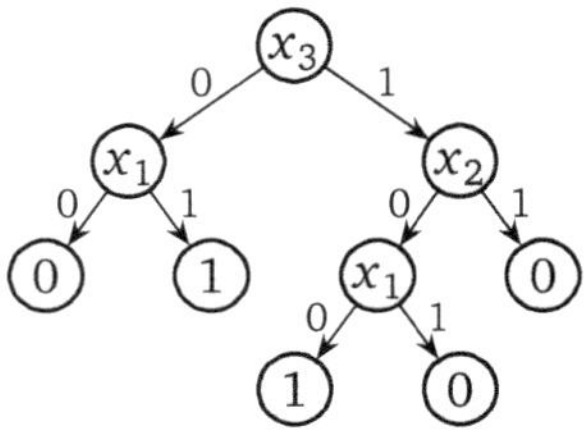

Figure 5.23: Example decision tree

Example. Figure 5.22 shows a branching program. The start node is at the top. The output nodes are at the bottom. The bold edges show the path for computing $f(01010) = 0$. It reads $x_2 = 1$ and follows the 1-edge, then reads $x_5 = 0$ and follows the 0-edge, then reads $x_3 = 0$ and follows the 0-edge, then reads $x_2 = 1$ again and follows the 1-edge to the 0 output node. Rereading x_2 is not redundant: This branching program "forgets" x_2's value upon reaching the x_3 node since it could have gotten there by either $x_2x_1 = 01$ or $x_2x_5 = 10$. The latter two cases share the part after the x_3 node, and the computation may or may not need to recall x_2 (depending on x_3's value). ♦

The start node may be an output node, in which case the branching program immediately outputs that bit. We may remove any node that's unreachable from the start node.

Sometimes B denotes both a branching program and the function $B\colon \{0,1\}^n \to \{0,1\}$ it computes.

A branching program's *size* is the number of nodes. There are at most twice as many edges as nodes, so we don't count the edges when we don't care about constant factors.

Recall that a tree-like circuit is a formula, and we duplicate input nodes so it's really a tree. A tree-like branching program is a *decision tree*, and we duplicate output nodes so it's really a tree (an *out-tree*, since edges point away from the root). Figure 5.23 shows an example. At each internal node in a decision tree, the 0-edge goes to the left child, and the 1-edge goes to the right child. There's no reason to reread an input variable along any root-to-leaf path—a decision tree never forgets. In the name, "decision" refers not to solving decision problems, but to nodes deciding whether to step left or right.

The branching program model is inherently nonuniform because a branching program only handles inputs with a particular number of bits n. To solve a decision problem A that has word size W_N, we need an infinite family of branching programs $B_1, B_2, \ldots$ where B_N has $n = NW_N$ input variables, such that $B_N(x) = A(x)$ for every valid input x of size N. As with circuits, we can let extra input variables represent left-padding the input words with 0s. When we describe a branching program's size with big-O notation, we have a family of branching programs in mind.

5.5.2 Robustness of the Model

Unconditional branches. A branching program's non-output nodes are conditional branches. Sometimes it's convenient to allow "unconditional branches," which are unlabeled nodes with outdegree 1. At such a node, the computation steps to the outneighbor without reading any input bit. To simulate an unconditional branch, we make all incoming edges bypass this and

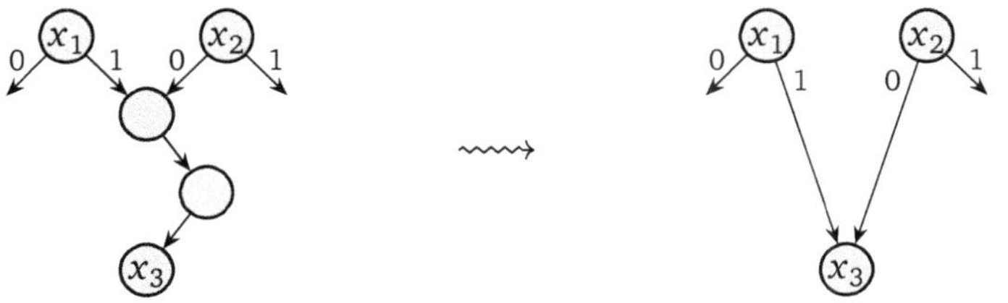

Figure 5.24: Bypassing unconditional branch nodes

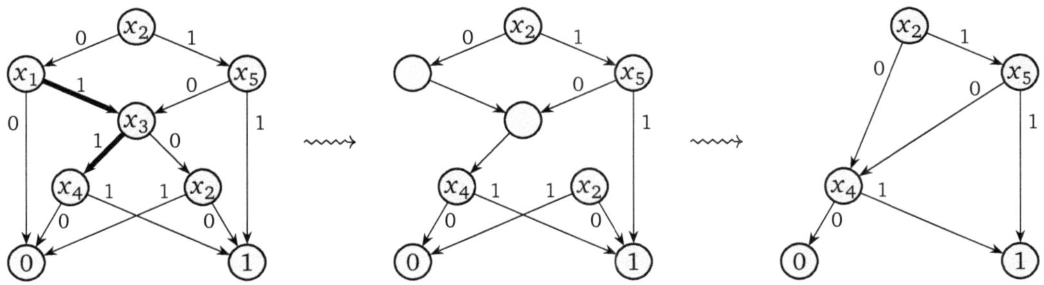

Figure 5.25: Contracting a branching program with $a = 1{*}1{*}{*}$

any subsequent unconditional branch nodes (Figure 5.24). If the start node is an unconditional branch, we follow the path to a node that's not an unconditional branch, and make that the start.

Constant bits. To replace an input variable x_i with a constant bit a_i, we make all nodes labeled x_i unconditional branches with just their outgoing edges labeled a_i. If we have a partial assignment $a \in \{0,1,*\}^n$ and a branching program B that computes $f\colon \{0,1\}^n \to \{0,1\}$, we *contract* B by plugging in a (bypassing the unconditional branches and deleting unreachable nodes) to get a branching program $B|_a$ that computes the restriction $f|_a$, with variables corresponding to $*$s in a. Contracting a decision tree yields a decision tree. Figure 5.25 contracts the branching program from Figure 5.22 with $a = 1{*}1{*}{*}$.

Reading multiple bits at once. To simulate a node that reads $k > 1$ variables and has 2^k outgoing edges (corresponding to the values in $\{0,1\}^k$ of those variables), we replace it with a decision tree that reads the variables one at a time, remembering the values read so far (Figure 5.26). There's one node for the first variable being read, two nodes for the second variable, four nodes for the third, and so on, and 2^{k-1} nodes for the kth variable. This increases the size by a factor $\le \sum_{i=0}^{k-1} 2^i = 2^k - 1$.

5.5.3 Branching Program Complexity

The *branching program size complexity* of $F\colon \{0,1\}^+ \to \{0,1\}$ is the function that maps N to the size of a smallest branching program that computes $F_N\colon \{0,1\}^N \to \{0,1\}$, where $F_N(x) = F(x)$ for all $x \in \{0,1\}^N$. The *decision tree size complexity* of F is defined analogously. Recall that the highest possible size complexities are $\Theta(2^N/N)$ for circuits and $\Theta(2^N/\log N)$ for formulas (§5.2.4). The highest possible size complexities are $\Theta(2^N/N)$ for branching programs and $\Theta(2^N)$ for decision trees.

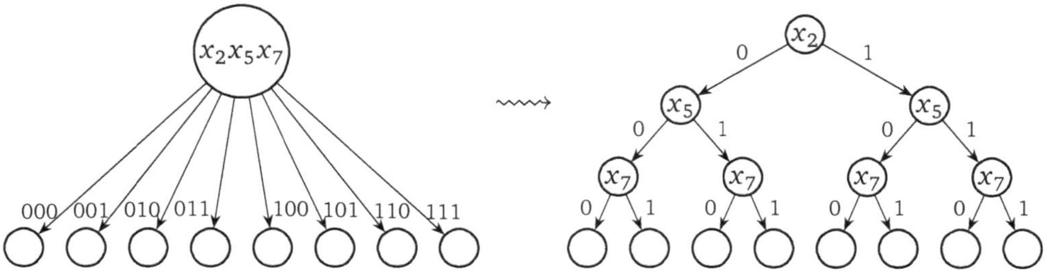

Figure 5.26: Reading multiple bits at once

x_1	0	0	0	0	1	1	1	1
x_2	0	0	1	1	0	0	1	1
x_3	0	1	0	1	0	1	0	1
$F_3(x)$	0	1	1	0	1	0	0	1

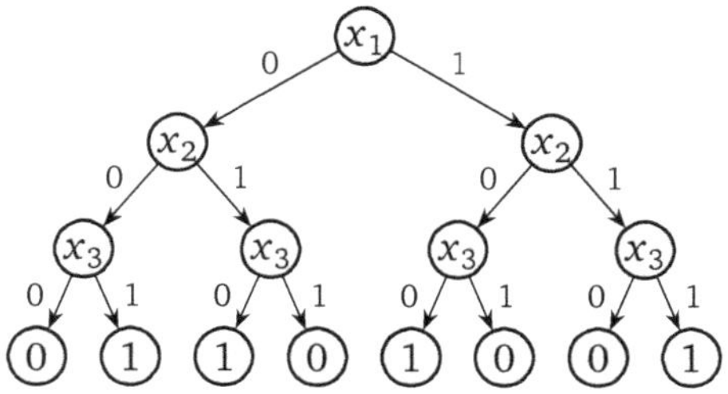

Figure 5.27: Example of computing an arbitrary function with a decision tree

Theorem 5.19. *Every $F: \{0,1\}^+ \to \{0,1\}$ has decision tree size complexity $O(2^N)$.*

Proof. We compute F_N using a node that reads all N bits at once, and for each $a \in \{0,1\}^N$ it has an edge labeled a to an output node labeled $F_N(a)$. As explained in § 5.5.2, we turn this into a decision tree of size $O(2^N)$ that reads the input bits one at a time, with one leaf per input. Intuitively, if we turn F_N's truth table on its side, it resembles a decision tree. Figure 5.27 shows an example. ■

Theorem 5.20. *Some $F: \{0,1\}^+ \to \{0,1\}$ has branching program size complexity $\Omega(2^N/N)$.*

Proof. We use a counting argument like the analogous result for circuits: There are 2^{2^N} functions F_N but at most $s(Ns^2)^{s-2} < 2^{2^N}$ branching programs with $s = \lfloor 2^N/2N \rfloor$ nodes, since there are s options for the start node, and each non-output node has N options for which input variable it reads and $\le s^2$ options for its two outneighbors. ■

Theorem 5.21. *Some $F: \{0,1\}^+ \to \{0,1\}$ has decision tree size complexity $\Omega(2^N)$.*

Proof idea. We have nonconstructive lower bound proofs for circuits (Theorem 5.8), formulas (Exercise 5.12), and branching programs (Theorem 5.20). For decision trees, we pinpoint a particular F, namely Parity: $\{0,1\}^+ \to \{0,1\}$ defined by Parity$(x) = 1$ iff x has an odd number of 1s. (Figure 5.27 shows Parity$_3$.) Decision trees for Parity can never afford to miss reading any input bit, because every bit always affects the output. ■

Proof. We claim that in every decision tree computing Parity$_N$, every root-to-leaf path reads all N variables, and hence the tree has 2^N leaves corresponding to all 2^N inputs. Suppose for contradiction some root-to-leaf path doesn't read some variable x_i. Let $a \in \{0,1\}^N$ be an input leading to this leaf. Let b be a except $b_i = \overline{a_i}$. Then b leads to the same leaf as a since they

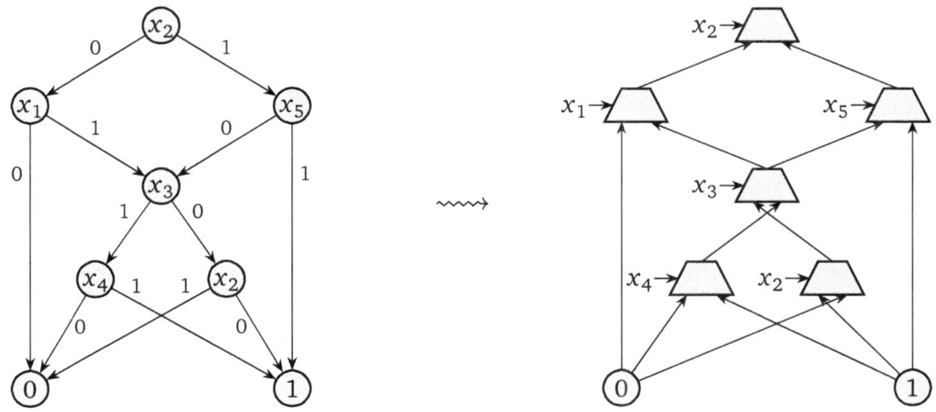

Figure 5.28: Example of turning a branching program into a circuit

only differ in a bit the path doesn't read, so the decision tree outputs the same bit on inputs a and b. But $\text{PARITY}_N(a) \neq \text{PARITY}_N(b)$ since a has exactly one more or one fewer 1 than b, so the decision tree errs on either a or b. ∎

Every F has branching program size complexity $O(2^N/N)$ (Exercise 5.11.b). A branching program size hierarchy holds by the same reasoning as the circuit size hierarchy (Theorem 5.9).

5.5.4 Branching Programs Versus Circuits

We introduced four nonuniform models: circuits, formulas (tree circuits), branching programs, and decision trees (tree branching programs). Every decision problem's size complexities are interleaved as follows, ignoring constant factors:

$$\text{circuit} \leq \text{branching program} \leq \text{formula} \leq \text{decision tree}$$

Theorem 5.22.

(i) Every size-s branching program is equivalent to some size-$O(s)$ circuit.
(ii) Every size-s formula is equivalent to some size-$O(s)$ branching program.
(iii) Every size-s decision tree is equivalent to some size-$O(s)$ formula.

Proof. *(i)*: We turn any branching program B into a circuit C:

- B's output nodes become constant nodes in C.
- B's non-output nodes become muxes in C with the input variables as selectors.
- B's edges become wires in C but with the directions reversed.
- B's edge labels become the indices of wires entering the muxes in C.
- B's start node becomes C's output.

For every node v in B, the associated mux (or constant) in C computes what B would output if v were the start node. Every node in B corresponds to $O(1)$ gates and wires in C, so C's size is $O(B\text{'s size})$. Figure 5.28 applies this to the branching program from Figure 5.22.

(iii): When applied to a decision tree, the transformation from *(i)* yields a formula.

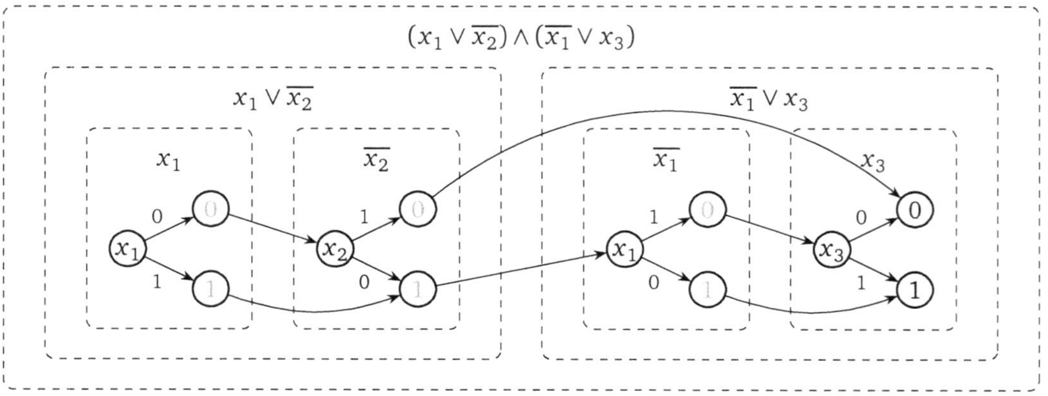

Figure 5.29: Example of turning a formula into a branching program

(ii): Assume the formula has bounded fan-in and has negations only on the input variables, which increases the size by only a constant factor (§ 5.2.2). We give a recursive algorithm that turns any such formula φ into a branching program B. For the base cases when φ is a literal x_i or $\overline{x_i}$, B's start node reads x_i and has edges to the output nodes:

- If $\varphi = x_i$: The 0-edge goes to the reject node. The 1-edge goes to the accept node.
- If $\varphi = \overline{x_i}$: The 1-edge goes to the reject node. The 0-edge goes to the accept node.

For non-base cases, the algorithm makes two recursive calls to find branching programs B_1 and B_2 equivalent to the left and right subformulas φ_1 and φ_2, and combines them as follows: B's start node is B_1's start node. B's output nodes are B_2's output nodes.

- If $\varphi = \varphi_1 \vee \varphi_2$: B_1's reject node unconditionally branches to B_2's start node.
  B_1's accept node unconditionally branches to B_2's accept node.
- If $\varphi = \varphi_1 \wedge \varphi_2$: B_1's accept node unconditionally branches to B_2's start node.
  B_1's reject node unconditionally branches to B_2's reject node.

"Short-circuit" $\vee$ and $\wedge$ avoids duplicating B_2 (which would blow up the size). Every literal occurrence in φ corresponds to three nodes in B (before bypassing unconditional branches), so B's size is $O(\varphi\text{'s size})$. Figure 5.29 applies this to the formula $(x_1 \vee \overline{x_2}) \wedge (\overline{x_1} \vee x_3)$, showing the branching program from left to right and with the intermediate output bits grayed out. ■

By Theorem 5.22:

- Every F has decision tree size complexity $O(2^N)$ (Theorem 5.19) implies every F has formula size complexity $O(2^N)$ (Theorem 5.7).
- Some F has circuit size complexity $\Omega(2^N/N)$ (Theorem 5.8) implies some F has branching program size complexity $\Omega(2^N/N)$ (Theorem 5.20).
- Every F has branching program size complexity $O(2^N/N)$ (Exercise 5.11.b) implies every F has circuit size complexity $O(2^N/N)$ (Exercise 5.11.a).

Combining the proof of the circuit size hierarchy (Theorem 5.9) with Theorem 5.19 shows that for all $a > b \geq 1$, some F has $O(N^a)$ decision tree size complexity but not $O(N^b)$ circuit size complexity. This simultaneously implies hierarchies for all four size complexity measures, by Theorem 5.22.

5.6 Space Versus Branching Program Size

5.6.1 From Size to Space

The space it takes to evaluate a branching program is essentially the log of the branching program's size.

BRANCHING PROGRAM EVALUATION	(5.12)
Input: Branching program B with n input variables, assignment $a \in \{0,1\}^n$	
Output: $B(a)$	

Lemma 5.23. BRANCHING PROGRAM EVALUATION $\in$ L.

Proof. This algorithm simulates B on input a:

Algorithm for BRANCHING PROGRAM EVALUATION (5.13)

```
initialize v ← B's start node
while v isn't an output node:
    read a_i, where x_i is v's label
    update v ← other endpoint of v's edge labeled a_i
output v's label
```

Each iteration reads v's label and v's adjacency list from B. This algorithm outputs $B(a)$ and takes log space since it only remembers $O(1)$ words at a time: v, i, a_i, and pointers into the input. ■

5.6.2 From Space to Size

Theorem 5.24. *Every problem in* SPACE$[S]$ *has branching program size complexity at most* $2^{O(S)}$.

Thus every problem in L has a poly-size branching program family. This opens an angle of attack for proving L $\neq$ NL: Try to prove a superpolynomial branching program size lower bound for an NL-complete problem. This approach is stalled, like the circuit complexity approach to P $\neq$ NP. In §16.7 we prove an almost quadratic lower bound on branching program size for a problem in L. But even for problems in NEXP, no superquadratic lower bound is known.

Proof idea for Theorem 5.24. We represent a program with a directed graph where nodes are configurations and edges are computation steps. This resembles the proof that DIRECTED REACHABILITY is NL-complete (Theorem 3.13). In that proof, the input was fixed and the witness could be anything, but now the input can be anything (of a particular size) and there's no witness.

A snag is that a branching program must be a dag, but the configuration graph might have cycles. No valid input uses all edges of a cycle (since otherwise it wouldn't halt), but different inputs could use different edges of a cycle. Figure 5.30's left side shows a "branching program" with a cycle (the self-loop) that's reachable from the start node but is never used. Figure 5.30's right side shows a more serious example that's like a roundabout (traffic circle) with the start node in the middle. No matter where we enter the roundabout, we'll exit before getting all the way around. Though the cycle is never fully traversed on any input, all its edges play roles for different inputs.

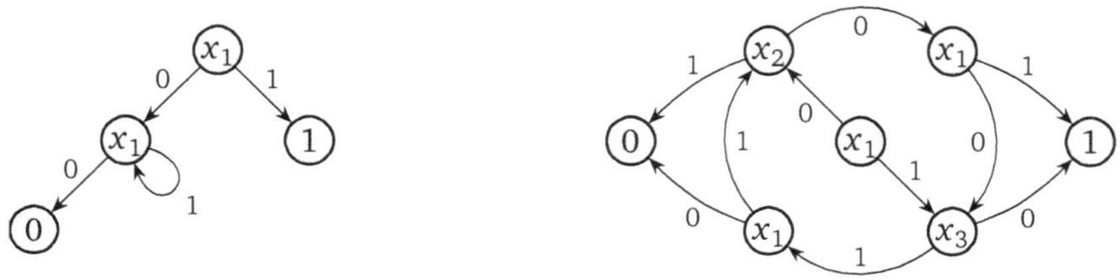

Figure 5.30: Configuration graphs could have cycles, but branching programs must not

We can't just delete cycles, since every edge might serve a purpose. Instead, we use the layering technique from Lemma 1.21. We create layers of nodes corresponding to time steps. This prevents cycles since edges only go forward in time. ■

Proof of Theorem 5.24. Suppose $A \in \mathsf{SPACE}[S]$. We design a family of size-$2^{O(S)}$ branching programs solving A. Let Π be a program for A with L lines, R registers, space efficiency $S' \le O(S)$, and word size $W \le O(\log \max(S,N))$. Consider any valid input x of size N. Define $M = S'/W - R$ so $\Pi(x)$ never accesses any work segment address $\ge M$. A configuration in $\{0,1\}^{\log L} \times (\{0,1\}^W)^R \times (\{0,1\}^W)^M$ represents the program counter, all R registers, and the work segment's first M words. Let $T = L2^{S'} \le 2^{O(S)}$ be the number of configurations. Recall that $\Pi(x)$ takes fewer than T steps (Theorem 1.8).

We describe a branching program for A on inputs of size N. Letting W' be A's word size, there are $n = NW'$ variables for the bits of the input x. There are T^2 non-output nodes, corresponding to pairs (C,t) where C is a configuration and $t \in \{0,1,\ldots,T-1\}$ is a time step. The computation path corresponds to Π's transcript: The branching program visits (C,t) iff Π is in configuration C after step t. The start node is (initial configuration, 0), and all other nodes with $t = 0$ are unnecessary. To define the outgoing edges of node (C,t) when $t < T-1$, consider Π's instruction at line C_{PC}:

- Data processing, control flow, or "load"/"store": (C,t) unconditionally branches to $(C',t+1)$ where C' is the configuration after one step of Π from C. Caveat: C might load or store at an address $\ge M$, in which case (C,t) won't be visited on any valid input, but for simplicity we keep the node and have it branch to an output node.
- "read Reg[i] $\leftarrow$ In[Reg[j]]": Let $m = C_{\text{Reg}[j]}$ and first assume $m < N$. The node (C,t) reads all W' bits of x_m, and the outgoing edge labeled $a_m \in \{0,1\}^{W'}$ goes to $(C',t+1)$ where C' is C except $C'_{\text{Reg}[i]} = a_m$ (left padded with 0s if $W' < W$) and $C'_{\text{PC}} = C_{\text{PC}} + 1$. If $m \ge N$ (reading past the input) then (C,t) unconditionally branches to $(C',t+1)$ where C' is C except $C'_{\text{Reg}[i]} = 0$ and $C'_{\text{PC}} = C_{\text{PC}} + 1$.
- "accept" or "reject": (C,t) unconditionally branches to the 1 or 0 output node, respectively. This also applies when $t = T-1$.

Nontermination nodes with $t = T-1$ won't be visited on any valid input, but for simplicity we keep them and have them branch to an output node. The graph is a dag since each edge goes from a layer t to layer $t+1$ or to an output node—the layers provide a topological order.

For every valid input of size N, this branching program outputs 1 iff Π accepts. As shown in §5.5.2, we can bypass unconditional branch nodes and expand "read a whole word" nodes into trees that read one bit at a time, which increases the size by a factor $\le 2^{W'}$. Since $W' \le O(\log N) \le O(S)$, the total number of non-output nodes is $\le 2^{W'} \cdot T^2 \le 2^{O(S)} \cdot (2^{O(S)})^2 \le 2^{O(S)}$. ■

5.6.3 Size Characterizes Space

We showed that poly-size circuits capture P/poly (Theorem 5.12), and uniform poly-size circuits capture P (Theorem 5.13). We now show that poly-size branching programs capture L/poly, and uniform poly-size branching programs capture L.

Theorem 5.25. *For every decision problem A, we have $A \in$ L/poly iff A has a poly-size branching program family.*

Because of this, some people define L/poly using poly-size branching program families instead of log-space programs with advice.

Proof. $\Leftarrow$: Suppose a poly-size branching program family $B_1, B_2, \ldots$ solves A. For each N, let the advice a_N be the encoding of B_N. Define a program Π such that on input x of size N, $\Pi(x; a_N)$ runs a log-space program for BRANCHING PROGRAM EVALUATION (Lemma 5.23) on input (B_N, x), and outputs the same bit. This solves A since the branching program does: $\Pi(x; a_N) = B_N(x) = A(x)$. The space efficiency of Π is logarithmic in the size of (B_N, x), which is poly N. Thus $A \in$ L/poly. (Details: Instead of storing (B_N, x) in the work segment, we modify each "read" to calculate the desired word's address within x or within a_N, and read it from there.)

$\Rightarrow$: Suppose $A \in$ L/poly by a log-space program Π with advice $a_1, a_2, \ldots$. Let A' (with input size M) be the promise problem A WITH Π'S ADVICE defined in the proof of Theorem 5.12: The input is (x, a_N) and the output is $A(x)$. (We called this problem B before, but we're using B for branching programs now.)

$A' \in$ L by a program Π' where $\Pi'(x, a_N)$ runs $\Pi(x; a_N)$. This solves A' since $\Pi'(x, a_N) = \Pi(x; a_N) = A(x) = A'(x, a_N)$. The space efficiency of Π' is $O(\log N) = O(\log M)$.

By Theorem 5.24, a poly-size branching program family $D_1, D_2, \ldots$ solves A'. We turn this into a poly-size branching program family $B_1, B_2, \ldots$ that solves A. For each N, let M be the size of inputs to A' of the form (x, a_N), and obtain B_N from D_M by plugging in the bits of N and a_N and contracting (§ 5.5.2), leaving only x for the input variables. This solves A since $B_N(x) = D_M(x, a_N) = A'(x, a_N) = A(x)$. The size of D_M, and thus the size of B_N, is poly M = poly N. ■

Definition. A *generator* for a branching program family $B_1, B_2, \ldots$ is a uniform program that has no input segment, starts with N in Reg[0], and writes the encoding of B_N to the output segment. A *log-space-uniform* branching program family has a generator running in $O(\log N)$ space with log-bounded word size. ◀

A log-space-uniform branching program family is automatically poly-size.

Theorem 5.26. *For every decision problem A, we have $A \in$ L iff A has a log-space-uniform branching program family.*

Proof. $\Leftarrow$: Suppose a log-space-uniform branching program family $B_1, B_2, \ldots$ solves A. Define a program Π such that on input x of size N, $\Pi(x)$ runs a log-space program for BRANCHING PROGRAM EVALUATION (Lemma 5.23) on input (B_N, x) (obtaining the words of B_N by rerunning the generator as often as needed, to avoid storing B_N), and outputs the same bit. This solves A since the branching program does: $\Pi(x) = B_N(x) = A(x)$. The space efficiency of Π is $O(\log N)$ for running the generator (repeatedly), plus $O(\log N)$ for evaluating B_N. Thus $A \in$ L.

$\Rightarrow$: In the proof of Theorem 5.24, the branching program family for A is log-space-uniform if we let $S' = cW$ (for an integer c) and increase A's word size to W. In more detail, we use registers to iterate through the possibilities of C and t, and simulate steps of Π to find the outneighbors $(C', t+1)$. We also only need log space for bypassing unconditional branches and expanding "read a whole word" nodes. ■

Exercises

5.1 Prove that $\mathsf{P} \subseteq \mathsf{L/poly}$ iff $\mathsf{P/poly} = \mathsf{L/poly}$.

5.2 A *sparse* decision problem has only $\operatorname{poly} N$ many 1-inputs of each size N. Prove that for every decision problem A, we have $A \in \mathsf{P/poly}$ iff there exists a sparse decision problem B such that $A \leq_p^o B$.

5.3 Prove $\mathsf{NEXP/poly}$ is closed under complement.

5.4 Define $\mathsf{P/log}$ like $\mathsf{P/poly}$ but with $O(\log N)$ bits of advice rather than $\operatorname{poly} N$ bits. Prove that if $\mathsf{NP} \subseteq \mathsf{P/log}$ then $\mathsf{P} = \mathsf{NP}$.

5.5 Prove that if $\mathsf{NP} \subseteq \mathsf{coNP/poly}$ then $\mathsf{PH} = \Sigma_3\mathsf{P} = \Pi_3\mathsf{P}$. Hint: Instead of using a search-to-decision reduction to prevent mistakes due to wrong advice, use a quantifier.

5.6 Give another proof that if $\mathsf{PSPACE} \subseteq \mathsf{P/poly}$ then $\mathsf{PSPACE} = \Sigma_2\mathsf{P} = \Pi_2\mathsf{P}$ (Theorem 5.6), using PSPACE-completeness of QSAT (Theorem 3.4) and a play-to-decision reduction for QSAT (Exercise 3.8).

5.7 Prove that if $\mathsf{EXP} \subseteq \mathsf{P/poly}$ then $\mathsf{EXP} = \Sigma_2\mathsf{P} = \Pi_2\mathsf{P}$.

5.8 (a) A *round-robin tournament* is a directed graph such that for every pair of distinct nodes u and v, exactly one of (u, v) or (v, u) is an edge. Prove that in every round-robin tournament with n nodes, some node has outdegree $\geq (n-1)/2$.

(b) Prove that in every round-robin tournament with $n \geq 2$ nodes, there exists a set S of $\lfloor \log n \rfloor$ many nodes such that each node not in S has an edge from at least one node in S.

(c) For any decision problem A, define this related search problem:

A SELECT	(5.14)
Input: Valid inputs x and y to A such that either $A(x) = 1$ or $A(y) = 1$	
Output: Any $z \in \{x, y\}$ such that $A(z) = 1$	

Prove that if A SELECT has a poly-time program Π, then $A \in \mathsf{P/poly}$. Hint: For every input size N, define a round-robin tournament whose nodes are A's 1-inputs of size N, and for every pair of nodes $x < y$ (using lexicographic comparison), if $\Pi(x, y) = y$ then (x, y) is an edge, and if $\Pi(x, y) = x$ then (y, x) is an edge.

5.9 Define $f\colon \{0,1\}^3 \to \{0,1\}$ by $f(x) = 1$ iff x has exactly one or two 1s. Design an unbounded-fan-in circuit for f with only four gates.

5.10 We saw in § 5.2.2 that every circuit can be turned into an equivalent bounded-fan-in circuit. Show that every circuit can be turned into an equivalent *bounded-fan-out* circuit (meaning every gate has fan-out ≤ 2) with only a constant factor increase in size.

5.11 **(a)** Prove that every $F\colon \{0,1\}^+ \to \{0,1\}$ has circuit size complexity $O(2^N/N)$. Hint: In the proof of Theorem 5.7, the tree's bottom few levels must have many redundant 2-to-1 muxes, which always evaluate to the same bit as each other, no matter what the input is.

(b) Give a similar proof showing a qualitatively stronger result: Every $F\colon \{0,1\}^+ \to \{0,1\}$ has branching program size complexity $O(2^N/N)$.

5.12 Prove that some $F\colon \{0,1\}^+ \to \{0,1\}$ has formula size complexity $\Omega(2^N/\log N)$.

5.13 **(a)** Design a family of $O(W)$-size circuits that compute whether $x < y$, given W-bit binary numbers x and y as input.

(b) Design a family of $O(W \log W)$-size circuits that compute $\lfloor \log x \rfloor$, given a W-bit binary number x as input.

5.14 This exercise is like a time hierarchy where the lower bound is nonuniform and the upper bound is uniform but uses quantifiers.

(a) Prove that for every integer $d \ge 1$, $\Sigma_4\mathsf{P}$ contains a problem whose circuit size complexity is $> N^d$ for all large enough N. Hint: Consider the set S_N of all circuits of size $\le N^{d+1}$ (with N input nodes and one output node) for which there's no equivalent circuit of size $\le N^d$. For all large enough N, S_N is nonempty by the circuit size hierarchy (Theorem 5.9). Let C_N be the lexicographically first (in terms of encoding) circuit in S_N. Let A be the total decision problem (with word size 1) solved by this circuit family. Thus, A has circuit size complexity $> N^d$ for all large enough N. Prove $A \in \Sigma_4\mathsf{P}$.

(b) Prove that for every integer $d \ge 1$, $\Sigma_2\mathsf{P}$ contains a problem whose circuit size complexity is not $\le N^d$. (It's open whether "not $\le N^d$" can be improved to $> N^d$. This is like how "not big-O" doesn't imply little-ω.) Hint: If $\mathsf{NP} \subseteq \mathsf{P/poly}$ then $\mathsf{PH} = \Sigma_2\mathsf{P}$ (Theorem 5.5).

5.15 Prove that if $\mathsf{P} = \mathsf{NP}$ then E contains a total decision problem (with word size 1) with the maximum possible circuit size complexity for all N. Hint: If $\mathsf{P} = \mathsf{NP}$ then $\mathsf{P} = \Sigma_2\mathsf{P} = \Pi_2\mathsf{P}$ (Theorem 4.21). On an input x of size N, first find the maximum over all $f\colon \{0,1\}^N \to \{0,1\}$ of the size of a smallest circuit for f. Then, find an $f\colon \{0,1\}^N \to \{0,1\}$ such that a smallest circuit for f has that maximum possible size. Output $f(x)$.

5.16 Design a family of poly-size (in fact, quasi-linear-size) monotone circuits solving the problem MAJORITY: $\{0,1\}^+ \to \{0,1\}$ defined by MAJORITY$(x) = 1$ iff x has more 1s than 0s. Hint: Use a sorting network (Theorem 2.34).

5.17 **(a)** Prove that the variant of CIRCUIT EVALUATION where the circuit has only one input node is P-complete.

(b) Prove that the variant of CIRCUIT EVALUATION where every gate is $\wedge$ is NL-complete. Hint: DIRECTED REACHABILITY ON A DAG is NL-complete (Exercise 3.13.b).

5.18 Consider the variant of the path forming game on a dag where the loser is determined not by whose turn it is when they reach a sink, but by which sink they reach: G has exactly

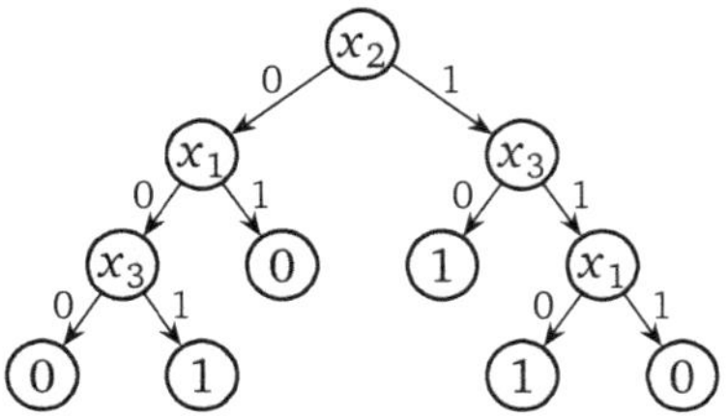

Figure 5.31: Decision tree for Exercise 5.20.a

two sinks, labeled "P1 loses" and "P2 loses." The players start at s and take turns picking which edge to follow next, until they reach a sink. Prove GEOGRAPHY ON A DAG WITH TARGETS is P-complete.

GEOGRAPHY ON A DAG WITH TARGETS	(5.15)
Input: Dag G with two sinks, node s	
Output: Does Player 1 have a winning strategy in the game described above?	

5.19 Prove ALL GATES CIRCUIT SAT $\in$ L.

ALL GATES CIRCUIT SAT	(5.16)
Input: Circuit C	
Output: Does there exist an assignment that makes every gate of C evaluate to 1?	

5.20 **(a)** Turn the decision tree in Figure 5.31 into an equivalent formula using the proof of Theorem 5.22.*(iii)*, and contract the formula to eliminate the constant bits.

(b) Turn the formula $(\overline{x_2} \wedge x_3) \vee (x_1 \wedge \overline{x_4})$ into an equivalent branching program using the proof of Theorem 5.22.*(ii)*, and bypass the unconditional branch nodes.

5.21 Uniform circuits capture P. CIRCUIT SAT is NP-complete. Uniform branching programs capture L. Do you think BRANCHING PROGRAM SAT is NL-complete? Why or why not?

5.22 **(a)** A *directed switching network* is a triple (G, s, t) where G is a dag with multi-edges allowed and where each edge is either unlabeled or labeled with a literal, and s and t are nodes in G. It computes a function $f: \{0,1\}^n \to \{0,1\}$ where for all $x \in \{0,1\}^n$, $f(x) = 1$ iff there exists a path from s to t in G only using edges that are unlabeled or labeled by literals that evaluate to 1. (This is inspired by how some electrical communication networks identify a communication path between s and t.) Prove that for every decision problem A, we have $A \in$ NL/poly iff A has a poly-size directed switching network family.

(b) A *skew circuit* is a circuit in which $\neg$ gates are only on the input variables, and every $\wedge$ gate has at most one inneighbor that isn't a literal. Prove that for every decision problem A, we have $A \in$ NL/poly iff A has a poly-size skew circuit family.

Notes

The definition of P/poly, along with Theorem 5.5 (if NP ⊆ P/poly then PH collapses, known as the "Karp–Lipton theorem"), Theorem 5.6, and Exercise 5.7, are due to [293].

"Concrete" models such as circuits, formulas, branching programs, and decision trees are the topic of Part IV. Texts focusing on this aspect of complexity theory include [555, 463, 552, 278].

Formulas that only have $\wedge$, $\vee$, and $\neg$ gates are known as "De Morgan formulas" to distinguish them from formulas with other kinds of gates such as $\oplus$.

The highest possible circuit size and branching program size complexities are $\Omega(2^N/N)$ (Theorem 5.8) [484] and $O(2^N/N)$ (Exercise 5.11) [380, 353]. The highest possible formula size complexity is $\Omega(2^N/\log N)$ (Exercise 5.12) [443] and $O(2^N/\log N)$ [354].

Circuit Evaluation $\in$ SPACE[$\sqrt{N}$ polylog N] is due to [563]. See [482] for a streamlined proof.

For a compendium of P-complete problems, see [219].

Theorem 5.11 (small circuits can simulate time-efficient programs) originated in [462]. Theorem 5.24 (small branching programs can simulate space-efficient programs) originated in [132, 419].

L/poly can also be characterized with poly-size "log-width" circuits [412].

Regarding sparse decision problems (defined in Exercise 5.2), "Mahaney's theorem" says that if P $\neq$ NP then no NP-hard decision problem is sparse [360]; a slick proof appears in [223]. Similar results are known for other classes: If P $\neq$ NP then no coNP-hard decision problem is sparse [169]. If L $\neq$ P then no P-hard decision problem is sparse [105]. If L $\neq$ NL then no NL-hard decision problem is sparse [106].

Exercise 5.5 is due to [572]. Exercise 5.8 is due to [477]. Exercise 5.14 is due to [287]. Exercise 5.22.b is due to [543].

Chapter 6

Parallelism

So far, we studied *sequential* computation, in which instructions are executed one after another. In *parallel* computation, multiple instructions are executed simultaneously by separate processors (or cores on the same processor). This speeds things up by performing more work per time step. The practical benefit cannot be overstated.

Some problems are amenable to parallelism—we can decompose them into subproblems that can be solved independently of each other—while other problems aren't. Parallel time complexity is closely related to space complexity.

Circuits are well suited for modeling parallel computation. Incorporating parallelism into our uniform model from § 1.4 would be more cumbersome.

6.1 Parallel Time

6.1.1 Depth

A circuit's *depth* (or *height*) is the largest number of $\wedge$ and $\vee$ gates on any path from an input node to an output node. In other words, it's the length of a longest input-to-output path, not counting $\neg$ gates. We don't charge for $\neg$ gates because we can push them to the inputs (§5.2.2) and imagine sources labeled by literals (x_i or $\overline{x_i}$) rather than having separate input nodes and $\neg$ gates. Depth-2 unbounded-fan-in circuits with one output node are equivalent to CNFs and DNFs, although such circuits may have "clauses" or "terms" with repeated variables and have wires between $\wedge$ gates or between $\vee$ gates. For example, the depth-2 circuit $(\overline{x_1} \vee x_2) \wedge (x_3 \wedge \overline{x_4}) \wedge (x_5 \vee \overline{x_5})$ is equivalent to the CNF $(\overline{x_1} \vee x_2) \wedge (x_3) \wedge (\overline{x_4})$.

Likewise, a branching program's *depth* (or *height*) is the length of a longest path from the start node to an output node. We study this complexity measure in Chapter 16.

We prove that if we only care about depth (not about size), then dags are equivalent to trees: A circuit might as well be a formula, and a branching program might as well be a decision tree. We can still bound the tree's size in terms of the depth and—for circuits—in terms of the *fan-in*, which is the maximum fan-in of any $\wedge$ or $\vee$ gate. (Bounded fan-in means fan-in 2.)

Theorem 6.1.

(i) Every depth-d fan-in-k circuit with one output node is equivalent to some depth-d fan-in-k size-$O(k^d)$ formula. If the circuit is monotone, so is the formula.
(ii) Every depth-d branching program is equivalent to some depth-d size-$O(2^d)$ decision tree.

Proof idea. *(i)*: If a gate v has fan-out > 1, then v's value is shared among its outneighbors. We "unshare" by duplicating v, so each outneighbor gets a separate, redundant copy. We repeat this for all gates down the circuit. Exhaustively unsharing everything yields a formula with spectacular redundancy but with unchanged depth and fan-in. The formula's input-to-output paths correspond to the circuit's input-to-output paths.

(ii): This uses the same idea as *(i)*, which is why we prove *(ii)* here even though we won't need it in this chapter. ■

Proof. The size bounds will follow because if a tree has depth d and each node has $\leq k$ children (where $k \geq 2$), then the number of nodes is $\leq 1 + k + k^2 + \cdots + k^d = (k \cdot k^d - 1)/(k-1) < 2k^d$ (a geometric sum) since each level has at most k times as many nodes as the previous level.

(i): Consider any depth-d fan-in-k circuit C with one output node. Assume C is monotone but with "literal nodes" (labeled x_i or $\overline{x_i}$) as the sources, since this doesn't affect the depth or fan-in (§5.2.2). A node v's *subcircuit* consists of all nodes from which v is reachable, and v is considered the output node of its subcircuit.

We design a recursive subroutine "make-formula" that has access to C and takes a node v as an argument. It maintains the invariant that each call make-formula(v) returns the root of a fresh copy of a formula equivalent to, and with the same depth and fan-in as, v's subcircuit.

Algorithm to turn a circuit into a formula (6.1)

make-formula(v):
  if v is a literal node: return a copy of v
  if v is an $\wedge$ or $\vee$ gate with inneighbors $v_1, \ldots, v_j$:
    let $u_1 \leftarrow$ make-formula(v_1), $\ldots$, $u_j \leftarrow$ make-formula(v_j)
    return a new gate u with the same type as v and with inneighbors $u_1, \ldots, u_j$

Thus make-formula(C's output node) creates a depth-d fan-in-k formula equivalent to C. Since make-formula doesn't introduce $\neg$ gates, the formula is monotone if C is monotone.

(ii): Consider any depth-d branching program B. A node v's *sub-branching program* consists of all nodes reachable from v, and v is considered the start node of its sub-branching program.

We design a recursive subroutine "make-decision-tree" that has access to B and takes a node v as an argument. It maintains the invariant that each call make-decision-tree(v) returns the root of a fresh copy of a decision tree equivalent to, and with the same depth as, v's sub-branching program.

Algorithm to turn a branching program into a decision tree (6.2)

make-decision-tree(v):
  if v is an output node: return a copy of v
  if v has a 0-edge to node v_0 and a 1-edge to node v_1:
    let $u_0 \leftarrow$ make-decision-tree(v_0) and $u_1 \leftarrow$ make-decision-tree(v_1)
    return a new node u with the same label as v and with 0-edge to u_0 and 1-edge to u_1

Thus make-decision-tree(B's start node) creates a depth-d decision tree equivalent to B. ■

Example. Figure 6.1 demonstrates make-formula. Each node in the formula corresponds to a subroutine call. The formula has three copies of the circuit's bottom left $\vee$ gate because the circuit has three paths from that gate to the output node.

Figure 6.2 demonstrates make-decision-tree. Each node in the decision tree corresponds to a subroutine call. The decision tree has three copies of the branching program's bottom left x_3 node because the branching program has three paths to that node from the start node. In the decision tree, 0-edges go left and 1-edges go right, even though sometimes it looks the other way in the branching program. ♦

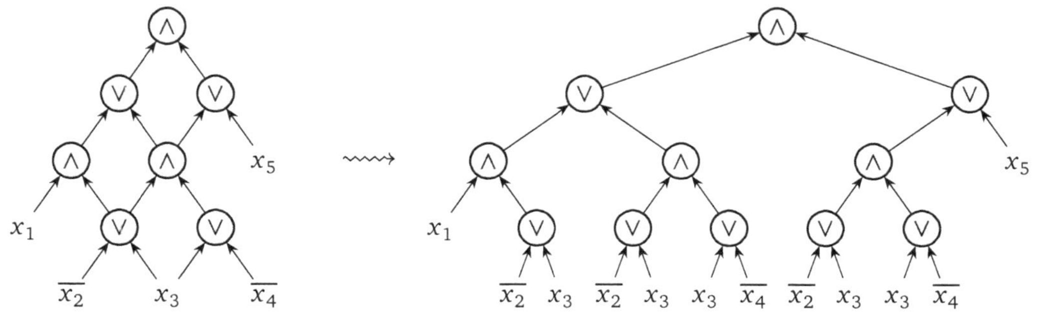

Figure 6.1: Example of turning a circuit into a formula

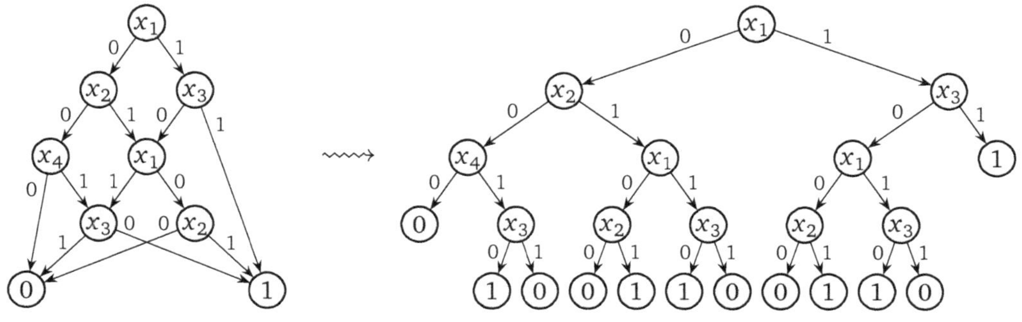

Figure 6.2: Example of turning a branching program into a decision tree

6.1.2 Parallel Computation with Bounded Fan-In

To model parallel computation using circuits, each gate is a baby processor that performs one simple operation. If two gates are unreachable from each other (neither depends on the other's value), they can be evaluated at the same time. If we partition a circuit's nodes into layers so all wires go from lower layers to higher layers—a *topological layering*—then all gates in the same layer can compute their values simultaneously in a single time step. The number of layers is the "running time," and the circuit's size is the "total amount of work."

In more detail: Push $\neg$ gates to the inputs and define a node v's *depth* as the length of a longest path from any literal to v. If (v, w) is a wire, then w has larger depth than v because appending (v, w) to a longest literal-to-v path yields an even longer literal-to-w path. To get a topological layering, let layer $d \in \{0, 1, 2, \ldots\}$ contain all nodes with depth d. The circuit's depth is the number of layers, not counting layer 0 (which just contains the literals). Depth corresponds to parallel time.

Consider AND: $\{0,1\}^+ \to \{0,1\}$. Computing AND_N takes one $\wedge$ gate with fan-in N. What about with bounded fan-in? We can keep a "running $\wedge$" by iteratively $\wedge$ing each input bit with the $\wedge$ of the previous bits (Figure 5.4). This is very sequential—later gates must wait for all earlier gates. The depth is $N-1$. We can achieve a much smaller depth $\lceil \log N \rceil$: Associativity of $\wedge$ means we can group the bits however we want, so let's divide and conquer: Recursively compute $\wedge$ on the first half of the bits and—in parallel—recursively compute $\wedge$ on the second half, and then combine the resulting two bits with an $\wedge$ gate. If N is a power of 2, this yields a perfect binary tree of $\wedge$ gates, with depth $\log N$. Layer 1 computes $\wedge$ on pairs of adjacent bits,

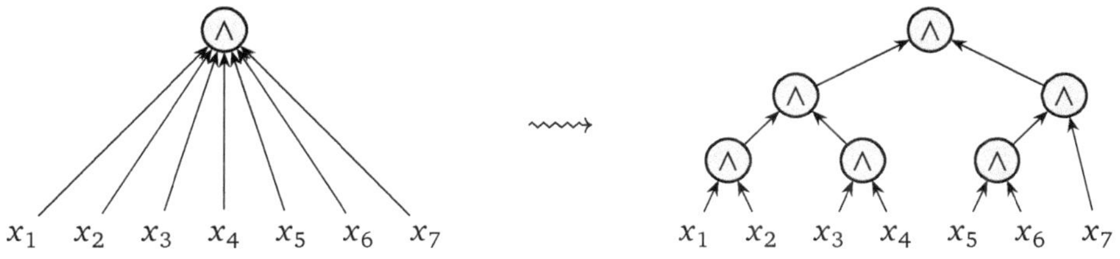

Figure 6.3: Shallow circuit for $\textsc{And}_7$

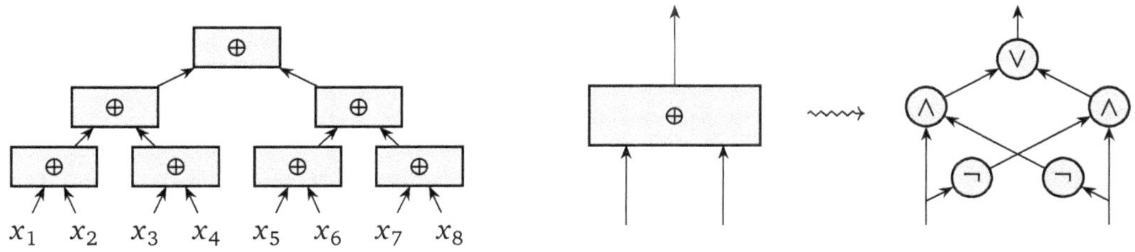

Figure 6.4: Shallow circuit for $\textsc{Parity}_8$

effectively reducing $\textsc{And}_N$ to $\textsc{And}_{N/2}$, and so on for each level. If N isn't a power of 2, round it up to $2^{\lceil \log N \rceil}$ and plug in 1s for the extra bits (Figure 6.3).

Consider $\textsc{Parity}\colon \{0,1\}^+ \to \{0,1\}$ defined by $\textsc{Parity}(x) = 1$ iff x has an odd number of 1s. In other words, $\textsc{Parity}_N(x) = (x_1 + x_2 + \cdots + x_N) \bmod 2$. Like $\textsc{And}$, we can compute $\textsc{Parity}$ sequentially with a "running sum mod 2" of the input bits, or we can do it faster in parallel since "sum mod 2" is associative. Xor is "sum mod 2" of two bits: $a \oplus b = (a \wedge \overline{b}) \vee (\overline{a} \wedge b)$. A tree of xors computes $\textsc{Parity}_N$ (Figure 6.4). The size is $O(N)$. The depth is $2\lceil \log N \rceil$ since each of the $\lceil \log N \rceil$ many levels of xors has a layer of $\vee$ gates and a layer of $\wedge$ gates. This circuit isn't a formula, because each xor splits its incoming wires. By Theorem 6.1.*(i)*, we can turn this bounded-fan-in circuit into a formula of size:

$$O(2^{\text{depth}}) = O\big(2^{2\lceil \log N \rceil}\big) = O\big((2^{\log N + 1})^2\big) = O(N^2)$$

This is optimal: We prove in §18.5 that every formula family for $\textsc{Parity}$ has size $\Omega(N^2)$, regardless of depth. So although augmenting the model with "xor gates" would only affect circuit size complexity by a constant factor, it would significantly affect formula size complexity.

6.1.3 Parallel Computation with Unbounded Fan-In

What about computing $\textsc{Parity}$ with unbounded-fan-in circuits? Like every decision problem, $\textsc{Parity}$ has a family of depth-2 circuits (CNFs or DNFs) of size $O(N2^N)$ (Lemma 2.9). We interpolate between the extremes of "log depth, linear size" and "depth 2, exponential size":

Theorem 6.2. *For every integer $d \geq 2$,* $\textsc{Parity}$ *has a family of unbounded-fan-in depth-d circuits of size $O\big(N2^{N^{1/(d-1)}}\big)$.*

Proof idea. Use divide and conquer. Since there's a limited depth budget, divide the input bits into $m > 2$ groups, to get to the base cases sooner. For the conquer step, compute the parity of m

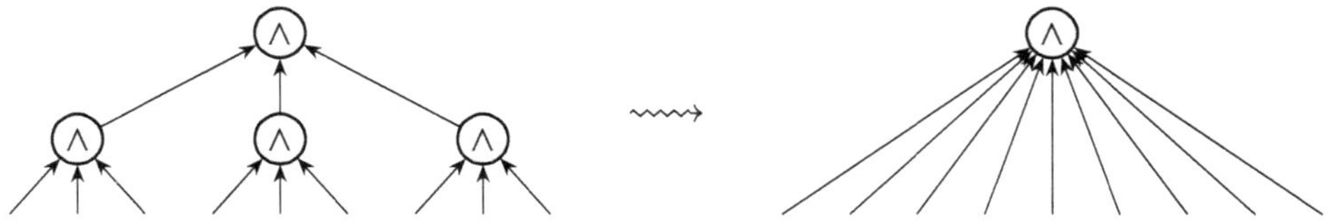

Figure 6.5: Merging adjacent layers of gates

bits (which are the parities of the m groups) with a "brute force" CNF or DNF, which contributes two layers of gates. With $d/2$ levels of recursion, this yields a depth-d circuit on $N = m^{d/2}$ input bits, with size $O(m^{d/2}2^m) = O\big(N2^{N^{1/(d/2)}}\big)$. To improve $d/2$ to $d-1$, merge adjacent layers of the same type of gates (Figure 6.5). Choose CNFs or DNFs at each level to merge as many pairs of layers as possible. ■

Proof. Abbreviate $\textsc{Parity}_N$ as $\oplus_N$. For all integers $d \geq 2$ and $m \geq 2$, we design an unbounded-fan-in depth-d size-$O(m^{d-1}2^m)$ circuit $C_{d,m}$ with two output nodes that compute $\oplus_{m^{d-1}}$ and $\overline{\oplus_{m^{d-1}}}$ on the same input. To compute $\oplus_N$ where $N = m^{d-1}$, use $C_{d,m}$, which has size $O\big(N2^{N^{1/(d-1)}}\big)$, and discard the node computing $\overline{\oplus_N}$. If N doesn't have the form m^{d-1}, define $m = \lceil N^{1/(d-1)} \rceil$ and plug in 0s for the extra input bits in $C_{d,m}$, which still has size $O\big(N2^{N^{1/(d-1)}}\big)$.

The $\neg$ gates of $C_{d,m}$ are at the inputs. Layer 0 contains the literals. Other layers alternate between $\wedge$ and $\vee$: Layer i has $\wedge$ gates if i is odd, and has $\vee$ gates if i is even.

$C_{2,m}$ is DNFs of size $O(m2^m)$ computing $\oplus_m$ and $\overline{\oplus_m}$ (Lemma 2.9). To build $C_{d,m}$ for $d > 2$, partition the m^{d-1} input bits into m groups of m^{d-2} bits, apply m copies of $C_{d-1,m}$ to the m groups, and combine the results to compute

$$\oplus_{m^{d-1}}(x_1 \cdots x_{m^{d-1}}) = \oplus_m\big(\oplus_{m^{d-2}}(x_1 \cdots x_{m^{d-2}}) \cdots \oplus_{m^{d-2}}(x_{(m-1)m^{d-2}+1} \cdots x_{m^{d-1}})\big)$$

and its complement: First, assume d is odd. To compute $\oplus_{m^{d-1}}$, use a CNF of size $O(m2^m)$ for $\oplus_m$ in which each positive or negative literal is the node computing $\oplus_{m^{d-2}}$ or $\overline{\oplus_{m^{d-2}}}$ (respectively) in the corresponding copy of $C_{d-1,m}$. To compute $\overline{\oplus_{m^{d-1}}}$, use a CNF for $\overline{\oplus_m}$ similarly. Merge the CNFs' $\vee$ gates with the output $\vee$ gates of the copies of $C_{d-1,m}$, yielding a single layer of $\vee$ gates. If d is even, use DNFs for $\oplus_m$ and $\overline{\oplus_m}$, and merge their $\wedge$ gates with the output $\wedge$ gates of the copies of $C_{d-1,m}$.

$C_{d,m}$ has d layers because $C_{d-1,m}$ has $d-1$ layers and the CNFs or DNFs for $\oplus_m$ and $\overline{\oplus_m}$ add one more layer (after the merging). $C_{d,m}$ has size $O(m^{d-1}2^m)$ because it combines $1 + m + m^2 + \cdots + m^{d-2} = (m^{d-1}-1)/(m-1)$ many CNFs and DNFs, each of size $O(m2^m)$. ■

This is nearly optimal: We prove in § 18.3 that every depth-d circuit family for $\textsc{Parity}$ has size $2^{\Omega(N^{1/(d-1)})}$.

6.1.4 Complexity Classes

We define classes of problems solvable by efficient parallel algorithms, meaning polylog N parallel time and poly N total work.

Definition. For every integer $i \geq 0$:

- NC^i is the set of all decision problems for which there exists a correct log-space-uniform family of bounded-fan-in circuits with depth $O(\log^i N)$.
- AC^i is defined like NC^i but allowing unbounded fan-in. ◄

Log-space-uniform circuit families are automatically poly-size. The generator need not be a parallel algorithm: Precomputation (based on the input size) can be sequential, and parallelism kicks in when the input arrives. These classes are contained in P (Theorem 5.13).

The acronyms NC and AC are uninformative but entrenched. NC stands for "Nick's class" in honor of one of its original proponents. (The N in NC is not the same N as in NP and NL.) AC stands for "alternating circuits" because gates alternate between $\wedge$ and $\vee$ along a literal-to-output path—even though that has nothing to do with depth or with bounded versus unbounded fan-in. (The C in AC is not the same C as in NC.)

In these class names, i is a superscript (as opposed to a subscript as in $\Sigma_i\mathsf{P}$) because i is the exponent of $\log N$ for the depth. NC^0 and AC^0 are defined with circuits of depth $O(\log^0 N) = O(1)$. A bounded-fan-in depth-d circuit depends on at most 2^d input bits, so NC^0 isn't very interesting—it only contains decision problems whose output depends on a constant number of input bits.

For NC^1 and AC^0, we may assume the circuits are actually formulas by Theorem 6.1.*(i)*: For NC^1, we can turn bounded-fan-in circuits of depth $O(\log N)$ into bounded-fan-in formulas of depth $O(\log N)$ and size $2^{O(\log N)} = \text{poly} N$. For AC^0, we can turn unbounded-fan-in circuits of depth $O(1)$ and size poly$N$ (and thus fan-in poly$N$) into formulas of depth $O(1)$ and size $(\text{poly} N)^{O(1)} = \text{poly} N$. This preserves log-space uniformity.

$\mathsf{NC}^i \subseteq \mathsf{AC}^i$ since bounded fan-in is a special case of unbounded fan-in. AC^i and NC^{i+1} might seem incomparable since AC^i allows bigger fan-in and NC^{i+1} allows bigger depth, but actually:

Lemma 6.3. $\mathsf{AC}^i \subseteq \mathsf{NC}^{i+1}$ *for all* $i \geq 0$.

Proof. Replace any fan-in-k $\wedge$ gate by a tree of fan-in-2 $\wedge$ gates, with depth $\lceil \log k \rceil$ and size $O(k)$ (§ 6.1.2), and similarly for $\vee$ gates. Since poly-size circuits have poly fan-in, doing this to all $\wedge$ and $\vee$ gates increases the depth by a factor $\log(\text{poly} N) = O(\log N)$ and the size by a factor poly$N$. Thus we turn unbounded-fan-in poly-size circuits of depth $O(\log^i N)$ into bounded-fan-in poly-size circuits of depth $O(\log N) \cdot O(\log^i N) = O(\log^{i+1} N)$. This preserves log-space uniformity. ■

We have an interleaved hierarchy of parallel complexity classes:

$$\mathsf{NC}^0 \subseteq \mathsf{AC}^0 \subseteq \mathsf{NC}^1 \subseteq \mathsf{AC}^1 \subseteq \mathsf{NC}^2 \subseteq \mathsf{AC}^2 \subseteq \cdots \subseteq \mathsf{P}$$

$\mathsf{NC}^0 \neq \mathsf{AC}^0$ because AND $\in \mathsf{AC}^0$ but AND $\notin \mathsf{NC}^0$ since AND depends on all its input bits. $\mathsf{AC}^0 \neq \mathsf{NC}^1$ because PARITY $\in \mathsf{NC}^1$ (§6.1.2) but PARITY $\notin \mathsf{AC}^0$. It's conjectured that all other inclusions in this hierarchy are strict too. But for all we know, $\mathsf{PH} = \mathsf{NC}^1$ might hold.

Like $\mathsf{PH} = \bigcup_\ell \Sigma_\ell \mathsf{P} = \bigcup_\ell \Pi_\ell \mathsf{P}$, define $\mathsf{NC} = \bigcup_i \mathsf{NC}^i$ and $\mathsf{AC} = \bigcup_i \mathsf{AC}^i$ and note that $\mathsf{NC} = \mathsf{AC}$ by Lemma 6.3.

Let's define nonuniform versions of these classes. Since the poly-size requirement is no longer implied by a generator, we add it to the definition explicitly.

Definition. For every integer $i \geq 0$:

- $\mathsf{NC}^i/\mathsf{poly}$ is the set of all decision problems for which there exists a correct family of bounded-fan-in poly-size circuits with depth $O(\log^i N)$.
- $\mathsf{AC}^i/\mathsf{poly}$ is defined like $\mathsf{NC}^i/\mathsf{poly}$ but allowing unbounded fan-in. ◄

These classes are contained in P/poly (Theorem 5.12). The notation $\mathsf{NC}^i/\mathsf{poly}$ and $\mathsf{AC}^i/\mathsf{poly}$ is analogous to P/poly but is somewhat nonstandard—some people let NC^i denote the nonuniform class and just write "log-space-uniform NC^i" for what we call NC^i, and similarly for AC^i. We have $\mathsf{NC}^i \subseteq \mathsf{NC}^i/\mathsf{poly}$ and $\mathsf{AC}^i \subseteq \mathsf{AC}^i/\mathsf{poly}$ since log-space-uniform is a special case of nonuniform. Like in the uniform setting,

$$\mathsf{NC}^0/\mathsf{poly} \subseteq \mathsf{AC}^0/\mathsf{poly} \subseteq \mathsf{NC}^1/\mathsf{poly} \subseteq \mathsf{AC}^1/\mathsf{poly} \subseteq \mathsf{NC}^2/\mathsf{poly} \subseteq \mathsf{AC}^2/\mathsf{poly} \subseteq \cdots \subseteq \mathsf{P}/\mathsf{poly}$$

and $\mathsf{NC}/\mathsf{poly} = \bigcup_i \mathsf{NC}^i/\mathsf{poly} = \bigcup_i \mathsf{AC}^i/\mathsf{poly} = \mathsf{AC}/\mathsf{poly}$. It's conjectured that all inclusions in this hierarchy are strict, but only the first two are known: $\mathsf{NC}^0/\mathsf{poly} \neq \mathsf{AC}^0/\mathsf{poly}$ because of AND, and $\mathsf{AC}^0/\mathsf{poly} \neq \mathsf{NC}^1/\mathsf{poly}$ because of PARITY:

Theorem 6.4. PARITY $\notin \mathsf{AC}^0/\mathsf{poly}$.

This theorem is a landmark in computational complexity. We give two proofs of it in Chapter 18. Can we generalize these nonuniform lower bound techniques to prove $\mathsf{NP} \nsubseteq \mathsf{P}/\mathsf{poly}$ by handling circuits with larger depth? Unfortunately, all known techniques break down at $\mathsf{NC}^1/\mathsf{poly}$. For all we know, $\mathsf{NEXP} \subseteq \mathsf{NC}^1/\mathsf{poly}$ might hold.

6.2 Arithmetic

If A isn't a decision problem, we can't say $A \in \mathsf{AC}^0$ or $A \in \mathsf{NC}^1$ (for example), since those classes only contain decision problems. Instead, we say A has an "AC^0-type" (log-space-uniform unbounded-fan-in constant-depth) or "NC^1-type" (log-space-uniform bounded-fan-in log-depth) circuit family, allowing multiple output nodes.

In §5.2.5 we designed AC^0-type circuits for comparisons, log, and shifting. But our circuits for $+, -, \cdot, /$ were highly sequential. Let's rectify this.

6.2.1 ADDITION and SUBTRACTION

Theorem 6.5. ADDITION *and* SUBTRACTION *have* AC^0*-type circuit families.*

Proof idea. In a ripple carry adder, each coordinate waits for its carry-in, which waits for the previous carry-in, which waits for the carry-in before that, and so on. Instead, we compute each carry-in directly, independently of the others. A carry-in is 1 iff some prior coordinate *generates* a carry-out of 1 and all intervening coordinates *propagate* that carry. We check this by examining all prior coordinates in parallel. This *carry look-ahead adder* is used in real processors. ■

Proof. For ADDITION on input $x = x_{n-1} \cdots x_0$ and $y = y_{n-1} \cdots y_0$, classify each coordinate $i \in \{0, \ldots, n-1\}$ according to three cases:

- Propagate carry: If $x_i \oplus y_i = 1$ then the carry-out equals the carry-in.
- Generate carry: If $x_i = y_i = 1$ then the carry-out is 1 regardless of the carry-in.
- Absorb carry: If $x_i = y_i = 0$ then the carry-out is 0 regardless of the carry-in.

Two layers of gates compute which case each coordinate is. Coordinate i's carry-in is 1 iff there exists a coordinate $j < i$ that generates a carry and all coordinates k with $j < k < i$ propagate the carry. Compute i's carry-in with an $\vee$ gate corresponding to $\exists j$, having wires from $\wedge$ gates checking the cases of j and $\forall k$. This contributes two layers. Finally, the ith bit of $x + y$ is $x_i \oplus y_i \oplus (i\text{'s carry-in})$, computed with two layers. This log-space-uniform circuit family has depth $O(1)$ and size $O(n^3)$ due to the "nested loops" over i, j, k.

In §5.2.5 we designed a reduction from SUBTRACTION to ADDITION. Combining this with our AC^0-type circuits for ADDITION yields AC^0-type circuits for SUBTRACTION. ■

ADDITION DECISION $\in \mathsf{AC}^0$: Given input (x, y, i), compute $x + y$ with an AC^0-type circuit, then use a poly-size DNF mux (§5.2.3) with i selecting which bit of $x + y$ to output.

6.2.2 MULTIPLICATION and ITERATED ADDITION

Theorem 6.6. MULTIPLICATION *and* ITERATED ADDITION *have* NC^1*-type circuit families.*

Proof idea. The usual reduction from MULTIPLICATION to ITERATED ADDITION (§1.8.2) is NC^0-type (each query bit depends on $O(1)$ input bits), so it suffices to prove this for ITERATED ADDITION. The goal is to compute $x_1 + \cdots + x_n$ where each x_i is a binary number. Since $+$ is associative, we could compute $x_1 + x_2$ and $x_3 + x_4$ and $x_5 + x_6$ and so on in parallel, and then sum pairs of those results, and so on, repeatedly halving the number of numbers to sum. Using AC^0-type circuits for ADDITION, we get an AC^1-type circuit—a "tree" of $\log n$ levels of AC^0-type circuits. To achieve a similar depth but with bounded fan-in, we can't just plug in NC^0-type circuits for ADDITION, since those don't exist. We design an NC^0-type circuit for something almost as good: Instead of turning two numbers into one number (their sum), the NC^0-type circuit turns three numbers into two numbers that have the same sum as the original three numbers. Each level decreases the number of numbers by a factor 2/3 instead of 1/2. ■

Proof. ITERATED ADDITION's input is $(x_1, \ldots, x_n)$ where each x_i is an m-bit binary number. Different pairs (n, m) might lead to the same input size N. We design a circuit $C_{n,m}$ tailored to any particular (n, m), with $n \cdot m$ many input nodes. A circuit for ITERATED ADDITION on input size N combines all relevant $C_{n,m}$ circuits and selects the right one using an NC^1-type mux.

First, we design an NC^0-type circuit D_m that takes three binary numbers $a, b, c \in \{0,1\}^m$ and outputs two binary numbers $d, e \in \{0,1\}^{m+1}$ such that $a+b+c = d+e$. For each $i \in \{0, \ldots, m-1\}$, the two-bit binary representation of $a_i + b_i + c_i$ is $e_{i+1}d_i$, and we let $d_m = e_0 = 0$. That is, for each coordinate, we sum the three bits and put the sum's two bits into different numbers, so the coordinates don't interfere with each other. Figure 6.6 shows an example. This works since:

$$\begin{aligned} a+b+c &= \textstyle\sum_{i=0}^{m-1} (a_i + b_i + c_i) \cdot 2^i = \sum_{i=0}^{m-1} (e_{i+1} \cdot 2 + d_i) \cdot 2^i \\ &= \textstyle\sum_{i=0}^{m-1} d_i \cdot 2^i + \sum_{i=0}^{m-1} e_{i+1} \cdot 2^{i+1} = d + e \end{aligned}$$

Each bit of (d, e) depends on only three bits of (a, b, c), so D_m is an NC^0-type circuit of size $O(m)$.

For $C_{2,m}$, we turn AC^0-type circuits for ADDITION (Theorem 6.5) into NC^1-type circuits. Now, we design $C_{n,m}$ for $n \geq 3$. Assuming n is divisible by 3, $C_{n,m}(x_1, \ldots, x_n)$ first computes

$$D_m(x_1, x_2, x_3),\ D_m(x_4, x_5, x_6),\ \ldots,\ D_m(x_{n-2}, x_{n-1}, x_n)$$

and then feeds the resulting $2n/3$ many $(m+1)$-bit numbers into $C_{2n/3, m+1}$. If n isn't divisible by 3, then the one or two leftover input numbers get fed into the next level directly (appending a leading

$$\begin{array}{rccccc} & & 1 & 0 & 0 & 1 \\ + & & 1 & 0 & 1 & 1 \\ + & & 1 & 0 & 0 & 0 \\ \hline = & 0 & 1 & 0 & 1 & 0 \\ + & 1 & 0 & 0 & 1 & 0 \end{array}$$

Figure 6.6: $9+11+8=10+18$

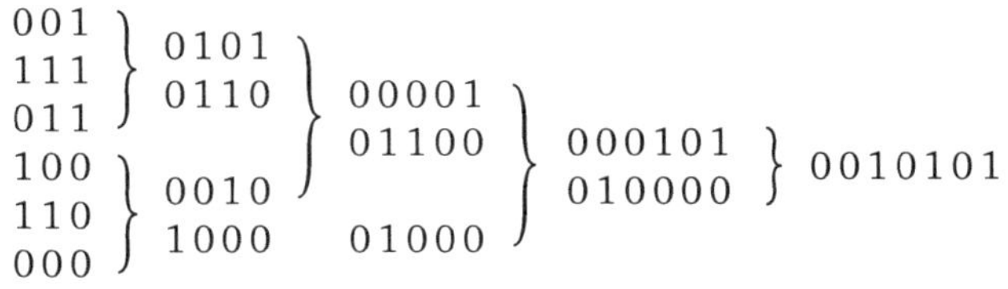

Figure 6.7: Running $C_{6,3}$: $1+7+3+4+6+0=21$

0, and without going through a copy of D_m). Thus after the first level, $n' = 2\lfloor n/3 \rfloor + (n \bmod 3)$ many numbers go into $C_{n',m+1}$. Figure 6.7 shows an example.

$C_{n,m}$ is correct since the levels maintain the invariant that the sum of the current numbers equals $x_1 + \cdots + x_n$. How many levels does $C_{n,m}$ have? If we pretend every n is divisible by 3, then level i would have $(2/3)^i n$ many outgoing numbers, so we reach $(2/3)^i n = 2$ after level $i = \log_{3/2}(n/2) = O(\log n)$. To incorporate leftover numbers into the analysis, note that $n' \leq (2/3)n + 2$ so level i has at most

$$\tfrac{2}{3}(\cdots \tfrac{2}{3}(\tfrac{2}{3}(\tfrac{2}{3}n+2)+2)+2\cdots)+2 = (2/3)^i n + (2/3)^{i-1}2 + (2/3)^{i-2}2 + \cdots + 2 = (2/3)^i n + O(1)$$

outgoing numbers, since the geometric series converges. Thus $C_{n,m}$ has $\log_{3/2}(n/2) + O(1) = O(\log n)$ levels. Also, m goes up by 1 at each level, so each copy of $D_{m'}$ has $m' \leq m + O(\log n)$ and depth $O(1)$ and size $O(m') \leq \operatorname{poly} N$. The final $C_{2,m'}$ at the output has $m' \leq m + O(\log n)$ and depth $O(\log m') \leq O(\log N)$ and size $\operatorname{poly} m' \leq \operatorname{poly} N$. Thus $C_{n,m}$ has total depth $O(\log n) \cdot O(1) + O(\log N) = O(\log N)$ and total size $(\operatorname{poly} N) \cdot (\operatorname{poly} N) + \operatorname{poly} N = \operatorname{poly} N$. The circuit family we designed is log-space-uniform.

To solve Multiplication, apply the primary-school reduction to Iterated Addition: On n-bit numbers x and y, use $C_{n,2n-1}$ where each input bit of $C_{n,2n-1}$ is either 0 or some $x_i \wedge y_j$. The depth is $O(\log n^2) + 1 = O(\log N)$, and it's still log-space-uniform. ■

Division (given binary numbers x and y, find the quotient and remainder of x/y) also has an NC^1-type circuit family. This is challenging to prove and is beyond the scope of this book. Parallel algorithms for Division are quite different from standard algorithms.

6.2.3 Lower Bounds

Iterated Addition doesn't have an $\mathsf{AC}^0/\mathsf{poly}$-type circuit family, because if it did, then Parity $\in \mathsf{AC}^0/\mathsf{poly}$ (contradicting Theorem 6.4) by summing the input bits and outputting the least significant bit of the sum. Reducing Parity to Multiplication is trickier:

Theorem 6.7. Multiplication *doesn't have an* $\mathsf{AC}^0/\mathsf{poly}$*-type circuit family.*

Proof idea. On input w to Parity, we create binary numbers x and y such that w's bits form a column in the table of the primary-school Multiplication algorithm. The corresponding bit of $x \cdot y$ (sum of the table's rows) should be $\left(\sum_i w_i\right) \bmod 2 = \text{Parity}(w)$, except that carries might interfere with this since it's not the least significant column. We insert enough 0s to absorb any carries, effectively isolating the columns from each other: x is the "expanded" version of w, and y is like x but with 1s instead of w's bits. Figure 6.8 illustrates this with $N = 5$ and inserting two 0s between adjacent bits of w (and omitting the table's jth row when $y_j = 0$). ■

$$
\begin{array}{c*{25}{c}}
 &&&&&&&&&&&&& w_4 & 0 & 0 & w_3 & 0 & 0 & w_2 & 0 & 0 & w_1 & 0 & 0 & w_0 \\
\cdot &&&&&&&&&&&&& 1 & 0 & 0 & 1 & 0 & 0 & 1 & 0 & 0 & 1 & 0 & 0 & 1 \\
\hline
= &&&&&&&&&&&&& w_4 & 0 & 0 & w_3 & 0 & 0 & w_2 & 0 & 0 & w_1 & 0 & 0 & w_0 \\
+ &&&&&&&&&& w_4 & 0 & 0 & w_3 & 0 & 0 & w_2 & 0 & 0 & w_1 & 0 & 0 & w_0 \\
+ &&&&&&& w_4 & 0 & 0 & w_3 & 0 & 0 & w_2 & 0 & 0 & w_1 & 0 & 0 & w_0 \\
+ &&&& w_4 & 0 & 0 & w_3 & 0 & 0 & w_2 & 0 & 0 & w_1 & 0 & 0 & w_0 \\
+ & w_4 & 0 & 0 & w_3 & 0 & 0 & w_2 & 0 & 0 & w_1 & 0 & 0 & w_0 \\
\hline
= &&&&&&&&&&&&& \oplus
\end{array}
$$

Figure 6.8: Reducing PARITY to MULTIPLICATION

Proof (ancillary). Assume MULTIPLICATION has an $\mathsf{AC}^0/\mathsf{poly}$-type circuit family. We show that this implies PARITY $\in \mathsf{AC}^0/\mathsf{poly}$, contradicting Theorem 6.4. For every input $w \in \{0,1\}^N$ to PARITY, we define a query $(x,y) \in (\{0,1\}^m)^2$ to MULTIPLICATION such that PARITY(w) equals a particular bit of the product $z = x \cdot y$, and each bit of (x,y) depends on at most one bit of w. Then on input w, a circuit for PARITY$_N$ can apply a circuit for MULTIPLICATION$_{2m}$ on input (x,y), and output the relevant bit of z. This circuit still has depth $O(1)$ and size $\operatorname{poly} 2m = \operatorname{poly} N$.

Given $w = w_{N-1} \cdots w_0$, let $\ell = \lceil \log N \rceil$ and $m = (N-1)\ell + 1$ and define $x = x_{m-1} \cdots x_0$ and $y = y_{m-1} \cdots y_0$ by $x_{i\ell} = w_i$ and $y_{i\ell} = 1$ for all $i \in \{0, \ldots, N-1\}$, and all other bits of x and y are 0s. We claim that PARITY$(w) = z_{(N-1)\ell}$. We have

$$
\begin{aligned}
z = x \cdot y = \left(\textstyle\sum_{i=0}^{N-1} w_i \cdot 2^{i\ell}\right) \cdot \left(\textstyle\sum_{j=0}^{N-1} 1 \cdot 2^{j\ell}\right) &= \textstyle\sum_{i=0}^{N-1} w_i \cdot \sum_{j=0}^{N-1} 2^{(i+j)\ell} \\
&= \textstyle\sum_{i=0}^{N-1} w_i \cdot \sum_{k=i}^{i+(N-1)} 2^{k\ell} = \sum_{k=0}^{2(N-1)} s_k \cdot 2^{k\ell}
\end{aligned}
$$

where $s_k = \sum_{i=\max(k-(N-1),0)}^{\min(k,N-1)} w_i$. For all $k < N-1$, we have $s_k = \sum_{i=0}^{k} w_i \le k+1 \le N-1 \le 2^\ell - 1$. Hence:

$$
\textstyle\sum_{k=0}^{N-2} s_k \cdot 2^{k\ell} \le \sum_{k=0}^{N-2} (2^\ell - 1) \cdot 2^{k\ell} \le \sum_{k=0}^{N-2} \left(2^{(k+1)\ell} - 2^{k\ell}\right) = 2^{(N-1)\ell} - 1 < 2^{(N-1)\ell}
$$

For all $k > N-1$, we have $2^{k\ell} > 2^{(N-1)\ell}$. Thus for all $k \neq N-1$, $s_k \cdot 2^{k\ell}$ doesn't contribute to the coefficient of $2^{(N-1)\ell}$ in z's binary expansion. Denoting $s = s_{N-1}$, we have $s = \lfloor s/2 \rfloor \cdot 2 + (s \bmod 2)$, so:

$$
s \cdot 2^{(N-1)\ell} = \lfloor s/2 \rfloor \cdot 2^{(N-1)\ell+1} + (s \bmod 2) \cdot 2^{(N-1)\ell}
$$

It follows that $z_{(N-1)\ell} = s \bmod 2 = \left(\sum_{i=0}^{N-1} w_i\right) \bmod 2 = $ PARITY(w). ■

6.3 Space Versus Parallel Time

Recall these inclusions:

- Space: $\mathsf{L} \subseteq \mathsf{NL} \subseteq \mathsf{L}^2$
- Parallel time: $\mathsf{NC}^1 \subseteq \mathsf{AC}^1 \subseteq \mathsf{NC}^2$

We prove that these classes are interleaved and hence space is closely related to parallel time:

$$
\mathsf{NC}^1 \subseteq \mathsf{L} \subseteq \mathsf{NL} \subseteq \mathsf{AC}^1 \subseteq \mathsf{NC}^2 \subseteq \mathsf{L}^2
$$

6.3.1 From Parallel Time to Space

Theorem 6.8. $\mathsf{NC}^1 \subseteq \mathsf{L}$ *and* $\mathsf{NC}^1/\mathsf{poly} \subseteq \mathsf{L}/\mathsf{poly}$.

Proof. $\mathsf{NC}^1/\mathsf{poly} \subseteq \mathsf{L}/\mathsf{poly}$ because if $A \in \mathsf{NC}^1/\mathsf{poly}$ then A has a poly-size formula family (Theorem 6.1.*(i)*), so A has a poly-size branching program family (Theorem 5.22.*(ii)*), so $A \in \mathsf{L}/\mathsf{poly}$ (Theorem 5.25). $\mathsf{NC}^1 \subseteq \mathsf{L}$ also holds because these transformations are log-space-uniform.

Another perspective: By Lemma 5.10, we can evaluate a circuit in time proportional to its size, using "bottom-up" dynamic programming. Now, we evaluate a circuit in space proportional to its depth, using "top-down" recursion. Assuming A has bounded-fan-in log-depth circuits $C_1, C_2, \ldots$, we design a recursive subroutine "eval" that has access to the input x of size N and to C_N (as advice, or by rerunning the generator whenever a word of C_N's encoding is needed), takes a node v of C_N as an argument, and returns v's value when x is plugged into C_N. To solve A, call eval(output node). Assuming $\neg$ gates are only at the inputs:

Recursive algorithm to evaluate a circuit (6.3)

```
eval(v):
    if v is a literal: return v's value on input x
    if v = v0 ∨ v1: return eval(v0) ∨ eval(v1)
    if v = v0 ∧ v1: return eval(v0) ∧ eval(v1)
```

The recursion depth is C_N's depth plus 1, so it's $O(\log N)$. Each stack frame uses $O(\log N)$ bits for v and $O(1)$ bits for the return address. The space efficiency is:

$$\big(O(\log N) \text{ stack frames at a time}\big) \cdot \big(O(\log N) \text{ bits per stack frame}\big) = O(\log^2 N) \text{ bits}$$

To bring the space down to $O(\log N)$: Instead of storing v, the stack frame uses one bit to remember whether v is u_0 or u_1, where u is the parent call's node. This information is enough to identify v, by looking at all ancestor stack frames and tracing the path from the output node backward to v. (In practice, keeping one shared copy of this path information in the heap may be preferable to poking around in other calls' stack frames.) Now, the space efficiency is

$$\big(O(\log N) \text{ stack frames at a time}\big) \cdot \big(O(1) \text{ bits per stack frame}\big) + \big(O(\log N) \text{ bits for path tracing}\big)$$

which is $O(\log N)$ bits. We pack all the stack frames into one word and extract individual stack frames using bit manipulation. ∎

The same reasoning shows $\mathsf{NC}^2 \subseteq \mathsf{L}^2$ and $\mathsf{NC}^2/\mathsf{poly} \subseteq \mathsf{L}^2/\mathsf{poly}$.

6.3.2 From Space to Parallel Time

Theorem 6.9. $\mathsf{NL} \subseteq \mathsf{AC}^1$ *and* $\mathsf{NL}/\mathsf{poly} \subseteq \mathsf{AC}^1/\mathsf{poly}$.

Proof idea. This is like middle-first search from $\mathsf{NL} \subseteq \mathsf{L}^2$ and $\mathsf{PSPACE} = \mathsf{NPSPACE}$ (§3.4): Try all possible midpoint configurations (for an accepting transcript) in parallel, and recursively check the two halves in parallel. Each level of recursion corresponds to $O(1)$ layers of gates. The proof of $\mathsf{NL} \subseteq \mathsf{L}^2$ yielded a superpolynomial-time algorithm because many recursive calls recomputed the same intermediate results. But our circuit has poly size because it computes each intermediate result only once. ∎

Proof. Suppose $A \in \mathsf{NL}$ by a register-only streaming verifier V with L lines, R registers, and log-bounded word size W. Consider any valid input x of size N. A configuration in $\{0,1\}^{\log L} \times (\{0,1\}^W)^R$ represents the program counter and all R registers. Let $K = \log L + RW$ be the number of bits in a configuration. For all w, $V(x;w)$ takes at most 2^K steps (Lemma 3.8). When $V(x;w)$ terminates, imagine it continues taking steps but with the configuration frozen. Assume V has only one possible accept configuration.

We use the letters B, C, D for configurations. (For now, C doesn't stand for "circuit.") "$B \rightsquigarrow_t D$" means there exists w such that running $V(x;w)$ for exactly t steps from configuration B results in configuration D. As in the proof of $\mathsf{PSPACE} = \mathsf{NPSPACE}$ (Theorem 3.18), for all B, D, and $k > 0$:

$$B \rightsquigarrow_{2^k} D \iff \exists C : (B \rightsquigarrow_{2^{k-1}} C) \text{ and } (C \rightsquigarrow_{2^{k-1}} D)$$

We design an unbounded-fan-in circuit that solves A on inputs of size N. For all B, D, and $k \in \{0,1,\ldots,K\}$, the circuit has a node $v_{B,D,k}$ that evaluates to 1 iff $B \rightsquigarrow_{2^k} D$. The output node is $v_{B_0,D_0,K}$ where B_0 is the initial configuration and D_0 is the unique accept configuration:

$$A(x) = 1 \iff \big(\exists w : V(x;w) \text{ accepts}\big) \iff B_0 \rightsquigarrow_{2^K} D_0 \iff v_{B_0,D_0,K} \text{ evaluates to 1 on input } x$$

- When $k > 0$: $v_{B,D,k} = \bigvee_C \big(v_{B,C,k-1} \wedge v_{C,D,k-1}\big)$. Each $k > 0$ contributes a layer of $\vee$ gates and a layer of $\wedge$ gates.
- When $k = 0$: If line B_{PC} of V is "read $\mathrm{Reg}[i] \leftarrow \mathrm{In}[\mathrm{Reg}[j]]$" and $B_{\mathrm{Reg}[j]} < N$ and $D_{\mathrm{PC}} = B_{\mathrm{PC}} + 1$ and $D_{\mathrm{Reg}[k]} = B_{\mathrm{Reg}[k]}$ for all $k \neq i$, then $v_{B,D,0}$ is the width-W term "$x_{B_{\mathrm{Reg}[j]}} = D_{\mathrm{Reg}[i]}$". For all other B and D, $v_{B,D,0}$ is a constant bit. Thus $k = 0$ contributes one layer.

The circuit has depth $2K + 1 \le O(\log N)$ and has size $\mathrm{poly}\,N$ since each $v_{B,D,k}$ contributes at most $O(2^K) \le \mathrm{poly}\,N$ to the size, and there are $2^K \cdot 2^K \cdot (K+1) \le \mathrm{poly}\,N$ many $v_{B,D,k}$. The circuit has a simple enough definition to be log-space-uniform. Thus $A \in \mathsf{AC}^1$.

Similarly, if $A \in \mathsf{NL/poly}$ then $A \in \mathsf{AC}^1\mathsf{/poly}$ by hardwiring the advice in the circuit. ∎

Lemma 6.10. *For all decision problems A and B, if $A \le_\ell^m B$ and $B \in \mathsf{AC}^1$ then $A \in \mathsf{AC}^1$.*

Proof idea. We get log-depth circuits for A by turning the log-space reduction into log-depth circuits and combining these with log-depth circuits for B. To turn the reduction into circuits, we generalize $\mathsf{L} \subseteq \mathsf{AC}^1$ from decision problems to functions with multi-bit outputs. We could adapt the proof of $\mathsf{L} \subseteq \mathsf{AC}^1$, but instead let's use $\mathsf{L} \subseteq \mathsf{AC}^1$ as a black box. ∎

Proof. Let F: (A's valid inputs) $\to$ (B's valid inputs) be a log-space mapping reduction from A to B. Let $D_1, D_2, \ldots$ be a log-space-uniform family of unbounded-fan-in log-depth circuits for B. We design a log-space-uniform family of unbounded-fan-in log-depth circuits $C_1, C_2, \ldots$ for A.

Recall Size of F and Word of F (§4.5.1). Let $M \in \mathrm{poly}\,N$ be an upper bound on F's query size on valid inputs to A of size N. The actual query size could be any $m \le M$, so C_N contains parallel copies of $D_1, D_2, \ldots, D_M$. The outputs of these copies go into a mux whose selector will be the output of Size of F on input x, picking the output of D_m where m is x's actual query size. For each k, the input to D_k will be the output of Word of F for all inputs (x,i) with $i \in \{0,\ldots,k-1\}$. If $i \ge m$ then (x,i) is an invalid input to Word of F, so garbage gets fed into $D_{m+1}, \ldots, D_M$, but that doesn't matter since the mux selects D_m's output anyway.

Define decision problems Bit of Size of F and Bit of Word of F where the input also includes an index j, and the output is the jth bit of the output of Size of F or Word of F. Then Bit of Size of $F \in \mathsf{L}$ and Bit of Word of $F \in \mathsf{L}$ by programs that run the log-space program for

F but instead of writing the query, they keep track of how many query words would have been written so far, and use bit manipulation to extract the desired bit from the desired word. Since $\mathsf{L} \subseteq \mathsf{NL} \subseteq \mathsf{AC}^1$ (Theorem 6.9), Bit of Size of F and Bit of Word of F have log-space-uniform families of unbounded-fan-in log-depth circuits.

In C_N, the bits of the mux's selector come from parallel copies of the circuit for Bit of Size of F—one copy for each possible index j. The bits of the inputs to $D_1, \ldots, D_M$ come from parallel copies of the circuit for Bit of Word of F—one copy for each pair (i, j) where $i \in \{0, \ldots, M-1\}$.

C_N has depth $O(\log N)$ (for the circuits for Bit of Size of F and Bit of Word of F) plus $O(\log M) = O(\log N)$ (for $D_1, \ldots, D_M$) plus 2 (for the mux). Also, C_N combines poly$N$ many circuits of size poly$N$, and C_N has a simple enough definition to be log-space-uniform. ∎

P-completeness is evidence that a problem can't be solved in small space. Using Lemma 6.10, P-completeness is evidence that a problem can't even be solved in small parallel time:

Lemma 6.11. *Suppose B is* P*-complete. Then $B \in \mathsf{AC}^1$ iff $\mathsf{AC}^1 = \mathsf{P}$.* ∎

Besides AC^1, analogues of Lemma 6.10 and Lemma 6.11 hold for NC^2, AC^2, NC^3, and so on, and for the nonuniform counterparts of these classes.

6.4 L-Completeness

Among problems in P, the P-complete ones are least likely to be in $\mathsf{NC} = \mathsf{AC}$. Among problems in L, the L-complete ones are least likely to be in NC^1. It wouldn't make sense to define "B is L-complete" by requiring $A \leq_\ell^m B$ for every $A \in \mathsf{L}$, since a log-space reduction could solve A without the oracle. The complexity of reducing A to B shouldn't exceed the smaller target complexity class, which is NC^1 in this case.

6.4.1 Parallel Reductions

The notation $A \leq_{nc^1}^m B$ means there exists a mapping reduction from A to B (which are both decision problems or both function problems) computed by an NC^1-type circuit family. Unlike with $\leq_p^m$ and $\leq_\ell^m$, the query size with $\leq_{nc^1}^m$ can only depend on the input size, not on the input. To sidestep this minor nuisance, we assume B's encoding allows any amount of padding.

Lemma 6.12. *If $A \leq_{nc^1}^m B$ then $A \leq_\ell^m B$.*

Proof. Suppose F: (A's valid inputs) $\to$ (B's valid inputs) is a mapping reduction from A to B, computed by a log-space-uniform family of bounded-fan-in log-depth circuits $C_1, C_2, \ldots$. On input x of size N, a log-space program can compute $F(x) = C_N(x)$ by evaluating C_N's output nodes like in $\mathsf{NC}^1 \subseteq \mathsf{L}$ (Theorem 6.8), rerunning the generator to get each word of C_N's encoding whenever needed. ∎

Lemma 6.13. *For all decision problems A, B, and C:*

(i) If $A \leq_{nc^1}^m B$ and $B \in \mathsf{NC}^1$ then $A \in \mathsf{NC}^1$.
(ii) If $A \leq_{nc^1}^m B$ and $B \leq_{nc^1}^m C$ then $A \leq_{nc^1}^m C$.

Proof. *(i)*: Let $D_1, D_2, \ldots$ be an NC^1-type circuit family computing a mapping reduction from A to B. Let $E_1, E_2, \ldots$ be an NC^1-type circuit family solving B. We design an NC^1-type circuit family solving A: On inputs of size N, feed D_N's output into E_M, where $M \in \text{poly}N$ is the query size. This is correct since $A(x) = B(D_N(x)) = E_M(D_N(x))$. This bounded-fan-in circuit family for A has depth $O(\log N) + O(\log M) = O(\log N)$ and size $\text{poly}N + \text{poly}M = \text{poly}N$ and is log-space-uniform.

We prove *(ii)* in the same way, but where $E_1, E_2, \ldots$ is an NC^1-type circuit family computing a mapping reduction from B to C. The combination of D_N and E_M computes a mapping reduction from A to C since $A(x) = B(D_N(x)) = C(E_M(D_N(x)))$. ■

A decision problem B is L-*complete* when $B \in \mathsf{L}$ and $A \leq^m_{nc^1} B$ for every $A \in \mathsf{L}$.

Lemma 6.14. *Suppose B is* L*-complete. Then $B \in \mathsf{NC}^1$ iff $\mathsf{NC}^1 = \mathsf{L}$.*

Proof. $\Leftarrow$: Assume $\mathsf{NC}^1 = \mathsf{L}$. Then $B \in \mathsf{NC}^1$ because $B \in \mathsf{L}$.

$\Rightarrow$: Assume $B \in \mathsf{NC}^1$. Then $\mathsf{L} \subseteq \mathsf{NC}^1$ because for every $A \in \mathsf{L}$, we have $A \leq^m_{nc^1} B$, which implies $A \in \mathsf{NC}^1$ (Lemma 6.13.*(i)*). Since $\mathsf{NC}^1 \subseteq \mathsf{L}$ (Theorem 6.8), we conclude $\mathsf{NC}^1 = \mathsf{L}$. ■

6.4.2 Following a Path

In Branching Program Evaluation (§5.6.1), the input is an n-variable branching program B and an assignment $a \in \{0,1\}^n$, and the output is $B(a)$.

Theorem 6.15. Branching Program Evaluation *is* L*-complete.*

Proof. Branching Program Evaluation $\in \mathsf{L}$ (Lemma 5.23). Every $A \in \mathsf{L}$ has a log-space-uniform branching program family $B_1, B_2, \ldots$ (Theorem 5.26), so $A \leq^m_{nc^1}$ Branching Program Evaluation by mapping x of size N to (B_N, x). This is correct since $A(x) = 1 \iff B_N(x) = 1 \iff (B_N, x)$ is a 1-input of Branching Program Evaluation. It is NC^1-type (indeed, NC^0-type) because each query bit is either hardwired (depending only on N) or a bit of x, and a log-space generator for the reduction circuit can determine the hardwired bits by running the log-space generator to get B_N. ■

Here's the template for proving that a problem C is L-complete: Show $C \in \mathsf{L}$ and $B \leq^m_{nc^1} C$ for some B that we already know is L-complete. This works since for every $A \in \mathsf{L}$, we have $A \leq^m_{nc^1} B \leq^m_{nc^1} C$ and therefore $A \leq^m_{nc^1} C$ (Lemma 6.13.*(ii)*). Let's use this template now.

An *in-tree* is like an undirected rooted tree but with each edge directed from child to parent, that is, a dag where one node has outdegree 0 (the root) and each other node has outdegree 1.

In-Tree Reachability	(6.4)
Input: In-tree G, nodes s and t	
Output: Is t reachable from s in G?	

Theorem 6.16. In-Tree Reachability *is* L*-complete.*

Proof. In-Tree Reachability $\in \mathsf{L}$ by an algorithm that follows the unique path from s to the root and accepts iff it encounters t. This needs log space for the current node and pointers into the input.

It suffices to show Branching Program Evaluation $\leq^m_{nc^1}$ In-Tree Reachability since Branching Program Evaluation is L-complete. Map (B, a) to (G, s, t) as follows. First, define

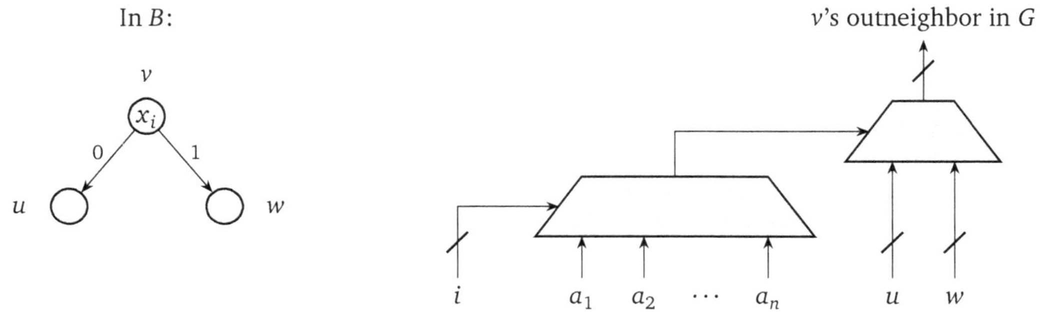

Figure 6.9: Computing a node's outneighbor for L-completeness of IN-TREE REACHABILITY

a dag B_a by keeping only B's edges that are consistent with a: For each node labeled x_i, keep its outgoing edge labeled a_i and discard the edge labeled $\overline{a_i}$. Note that B_a consists of two disjoint in-trees rooted at the accept and reject nodes, and $B(a) = 1$ iff the start node is in the accept node's in-tree. Let G be B_a but with a new edge from the accept node to the reject node—so G is an in-tree rooted at the reject node—and let s be the start node and t be the accept node. This is correct since $B(a) = 1$ iff G's unique path from s reaches t.

We show how to compute this reduction with an NC^1-type (indeed, AC^0-type) circuit family. In the encoding of (B, a), each non-output node v has three words: the index i of the variable being read, the 0-edge's other endpoint u, and the 1-edge's other endpoint w. In the encoding of (G, s, t) (§1.3.3), each non-output node's adjacency list has two words: the outdegree which is 1, and the outneighbor's index. Figure 6.9 shows how to compute the outneighbor's index. (We should also have dummy bits for "a_0", "a_{n+1}", "a_{n+2}" and so on, so the first mux has a power-of-2 many a input bits.) The encoding of (G, s, t) also has words for the output nodes' adjacency lists, the number of nodes, and pointers to all the adjacency lists, which are trivial to compute from the size of B and the size of a. The circuit is simple enough to be log-space-uniform.

This circuit depends on the sizes of B and a. To get a circuit that depends only on the size N of (B, a), combine all the relevant circuits and use a mux to select the appropriate one. ■

An *out-tree* is like an undirected rooted tree but with each edge directed from parent to child, that is, a dag where one node has indegree 0 (the root) and each other node has indegree 1.

OUT-TREE REACHABILITY	(6.5)
Input: Out-tree G, nodes s and t	
Output: Is t reachable from s in G?	

Theorem 6.17. OUT-TREE REACHABILITY *is* L*-complete.*

Proof. OUT-TREE REACHABILITY $\in$ L by an algorithm that follows the unique path backward from t to the root and accepts iff it encounters s. For each step, the algorithm loops through all nodes to either find the one with an edge to the current node or determine that the current node is the root. This needs log space for the current node and candidate parent node (in the inner loop) and pointers into the input.

It suffices to show IN-TREE REACHABILITY $\leq^m_{\mathsf{NC}^1}$ OUT-TREE REACHABILITY since IN-TREE REACHABILITY is L-complete. Map (G, s, t) to (H, t, s) where the out-tree H is the in-tree G but with all edge directions reversed. This is correct since G has a path from s to t iff H has a path from t to s.

Computing this reduction with NC^1-type circuits is not straightforward, since in the encoding of (H,t,s) (§ 1.3.3), different nodes may have different numbers of outneighbors. We prove in § 6.4.3 that NC^1-type circuits can convert any directed graph's adjacency list encoding to its adjacency matrix encoding (Lemma 6.18) and vice versa (Lemma 6.19). To reverse the edge directions in any graph (not just a tree), we convert to adjacency matrix, transpose the matrix trivially, and then convert back to adjacency list. ■

Undirected Reachability is also L-complete: Proving that it's in L is difficult, but Exercise 6.6 shows that it's L-hard even when every connected component is a tree.

Upshot: AC^1 can handle graph reachability problems, but NC^1 seemingly can't, even for trees.

6.4.3 Robustness of the Parallel Model

L is robust with respect to the input encoding, because log-space mapping reductions can translate between different reasonable encodings (§ 1.9.1). NC^1 is also fairly robust, but we can't take this for granted, since loops with many iterations aren't allowed. We prove that when the input is a graph, it doesn't matter whether we use the adjacency list encoding or adjacency matrix encoding, because NC^1-type mapping reductions can translate between these encodings.

We consider directed graphs with self-loops allowed but multi-edges not allowed. The adjacency list encoding (§ 1.3.3) is the number of nodes (one word), and then pointers to the nodes' lists, and then each node's list, which consists of its outdegree (one word) and outneighbors (in any order). The adjacency matrix encoding is the number of nodes (one word) followed by the matrix in row-major order with one entry per word, where the entry in row u and column v is 1 iff (u,v) is an edge.

Lemma 6.18. *Some AC^0-type circuit family converts any directed graph's adjacency list encoding to its adjacency matrix encoding.*

Proof (ancillary). Say the input graph is $G=(V,E)$ where $V=[n]$, with adjacency list encoding $x_0x_1\cdots x_{N-1}$ where each x_i is a word. Since the input size N doesn't uniquely determine the number of nodes n, we design circuits tailored to each possibility of n, and then choose the right one using a mux whose selector is x_0 (the actual value of n). So consider any particular n.

For each pair of nodes $(u,v)\in V\times V$, our circuit computes the bit in row u and column v of G's adjacency matrix, indicating whether $(u,v)\in E$:

- For all $i\in\{n+1,\dots,N-1\}$ and $d\in\{0,\dots,n\}$, compute whether $(u,v)\in E$ assuming u's list starts at address i and $\text{outdeg}(u)=d$: $g_{u,v,i,d}$ is the DNF "$x_{i+1}=v \vee x_{i+2}=v \vee\cdots\vee x_{i+d}=v$". (Here, $x_Nx_{N+1}\cdots$ are all-0 words.)
- For all $i\in\{n+1,\dots,N-1\}$, compute whether $(u,v)\in E$ assuming u's list starts at address i: $g_{u,v,i}$ gets the value of one of $g_{u,v,i,0},\dots,g_{u,v,i,n}$, chosen using a mux whose selector is x_i (the assumed value of $\text{outdeg}(u)$).
- Finally, compute whether $(u,v)\in E$: $g_{u,v}$ gets the value of one of $g_{u,v,n+1},\dots,g_{u,v,N-1}$, chosen using a mux whose selector is x_u (the actual pointer to the start of u's list).

We designed a log-space-uniform unbounded-fan-in constant-depth poly-size circuit family. ■

Lemma 6.19. *Some NC^1-type circuit family converts any directed graph's adjacency matrix encoding to its adjacency list encoding.*

Proof (ancillary). Say the input graph is $G = (V, E)$ where $V = [n]$, and $x_{u,v}$ is the bit in row u and column v of the adjacency matrix.

For each node u, our circuit first computes u's list (outdegree and outneighbors in increasing order) without worrying about where it will go in G's adjacency list encoding:

- Compute $\text{outdeg}(u) = \sum_v x_{u,v}$ by summing row u's bits using an NC^1-type circuit for Iterated Addition (Theorem 6.6).
- For all $i \in \{1, \ldots, n\}$ and $v \in V$, compute whether v is u's ith outneighbor (in increasing order of u's outneighbors): $g_{u,i,v}$ is the bit $x_{u,v} \wedge \left(i = \sum_{w \leq v} x_{u,w}\right)$, computed using an NC^1-type circuit for Iterated Addition.
- For all $i \in \{1, \ldots, n\}$, compute the index of u's ith outneighbor, or the all-0 word if $i >$ $\text{outdeg}(u)$: First, the binary number $g_{u,i,n} \cdots g_{u,i,1}\, 0$ equals 2^v where v is u's ith outneighbor, or zero if $i > \text{outdeg}(u)$. To compute v from this, use an NC^1-type (or even AC^0-type) circuit for logarithm (§5.2.5).

Next, for each node u, our circuit computes the address where u's list goes in G's adjacency list encoding: $p_u = 1 + n + \sum_{w<u}(1 + \text{outdeg}(w))$ since the encoding has one word for n, then n words for the pointers $p_1, \ldots, p_n$, and then the lists of the nodes $1, \ldots, n$. Having already computed each $\text{outdeg}(w)$, compute p_u using an NC^1-type circuit for Iterated Addition.

Finally, to obtain G's adjacency list encoding: Shift each node u's list (including the all-0 padding words) to the right by p_u words, using an NC^1-type (or even AC^0-type) circuit for shifting (§5.2.5). Then, bitwise-$\vee$ these all together, along with $n, p_1, \ldots, p_n$ for the words at addresses $0, 1, \ldots, n$.

We designed a log-space-uniform bounded-fan-in log-depth circuit family. ■

6.5 Parallelization

Can we always turn an efficient algorithm in one of our nonuniform models (circuit, branching program, formula, or decision tree) into a fast parallel algorithm? The circuit model is presumably not amenable to parallelization, but the other three models are. This provides a technique to obtain fast parallel algorithms: Design an algorithm in one of those models, and turn it into a fast parallel algorithm using a recipe from this section.

6.5.1 Branching Programs and Decision Trees

Theorem 6.20. *Every poly-size branching program family is equivalent to some unbounded-fan-in log-depth poly-size circuit family.*

Proof idea. Theorem 5.22.*(i)* turns any branching program into an equivalent circuit that's unfortunately as deep as the branching program. Instead, we use $\mathsf{L/poly} \subseteq \mathsf{AC}^1\mathsf{/poly}$ (Theorem 5.25 and Theorem 6.9). Let's do a streamlined proof. ■

Proof. For any branching program B with N input variables and $n \leq \text{poly}\, N$ nodes, we design an equivalent circuit C. Let $K = \lceil \log(n-1) \rceil$, so B always takes at most $n - 1 \leq 2^K$ steps. When B reaches an output node, imagine it continues taking steps but stays at that node.

For all nodes u and w of B, and all $k \in \{0, 1, \ldots, K\}$, C has a node $g_{u,w,k}$ that evaluates to 1 on input x iff running B on input x starting at u for 2^k steps leads to w. The output node of C is $g_{s,t,K}$ where s is B's start node and t is B's accept node.

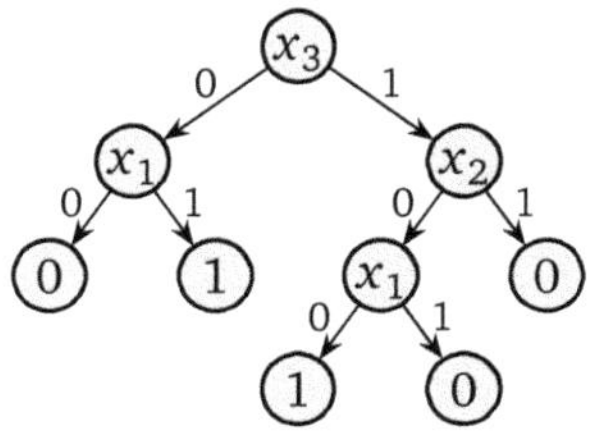

DNF: $(\overline{x_3} \wedge x_1) \vee (x_3 \wedge \overline{x_2} \wedge \overline{x_1})$

CNF: $(x_3 \vee x_1) \wedge (\overline{x_3} \vee x_2 \vee \overline{x_1}) \wedge (\overline{x_3} \vee \overline{x_2})$

Figure 6.10: Example of turning a decision tree into a depth-2 formula

- When $k > 0$: $g_{u,w,k} = \bigvee_v \left(g_{u,v,k-1} \wedge g_{v,w,k-1}\right)$. Each $k > 0$ contributes a layer of $\vee$ gates and a layer of $\wedge$ gates.
- When $k = 0$: If u is labeled x_i with 1-edge to w, then $g_{u,w,0}$ is the input node x_i. If u is labeled x_i with 0-edge to w, then $g_{u,w,0}$ is $\overline{x_i}$. If both of those are true, or if u and w are the same output node, then $g_{u,w,0}$ is constant 1. Otherwise, $g_{u,w,0}$ is constant 0. Thus $k = 0$ contributes no layers.

C has depth $2K \le O(\log n) \le O(\log N)$ and has size poly$N$ since each $g_{u,w,k}$ contributes $O(n) \le$ poly$N$ to the size, and there are $n \cdot n \cdot (K+1) \le$ poly$N$ many $g_{u,w,k}$. ■

Theorem 6.20 also holds for formulas and decision trees in place of branching programs. But we can do even better for these tree-like models: For formulas we improve the circuit's fan-in to 2 (§6.5.2), and for decision trees we improve the circuit's depth to 2:

Theorem 6.21. *Every poly-size decision tree family is equivalent to some poly-size DNF and CNF families.*

Proof idea. Theorem 5.22.*(iii)* turns any decision tree into an equivalent formula that's unfortunately as deep as the decision tree. Instead, a fast parallel algorithm can evaluate a decision tree by trying all possible root-to-leaf paths in parallel, and for each root-to-leaf path, checking the values of all variables along the path in parallel. ■

Proof. For any decision tree T with N input variables and $\ell \le$ poly$N$ leaves, we design an equivalent DNF φ. For each leaf labeled 1 in T, φ has a term that accepts exactly the inputs that lead to that leaf: For each node labeled x_i on the root-to-leaf path, the term contains the literal $\overline{x_i}$ if the path takes the 0-edge, or the literal x_i if the path takes the 1-edge. Then φ is equivalent to T since $\varphi(x) = 1$ iff x leads to some leaf labeled 1 iff $T(x) = 1$. Since T has $\ell \le$ poly$N$ leaves and each term has size $\le N$, φ has size poly$N$.

To design a CNF equivalent to T: Negate each leaf's label in T, turn the resulting decision tree into a DNF, and negate this DNF. That is, for each leaf labeled 0 in T, the CNF has a clause that accepts exactly the inputs that don't lead to that leaf. ■

Figure 6.10 shows an example.

6.5.2 Formulas

Theorem 6.22. *Every poly-size formula family is equivalent to some bounded-fan-in log-depth formula family.*

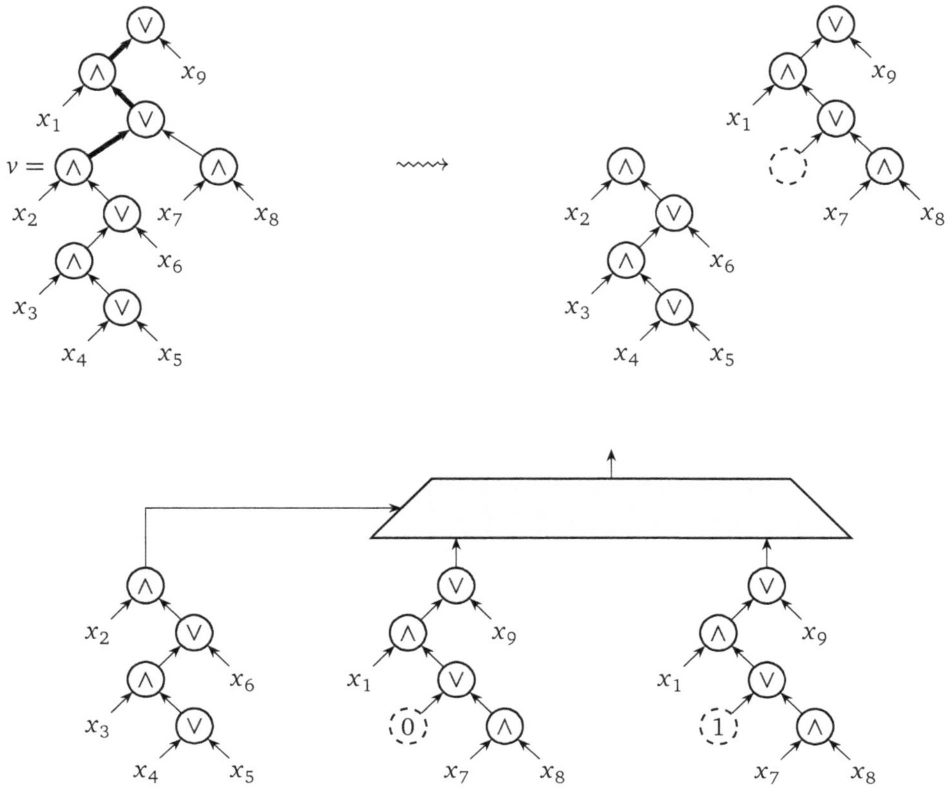

Figure 6.11: Balancing $(x_1 \wedge ((x_2 \wedge ((x_3 \wedge (x_4 \vee x_5)) \vee x_6)) \vee (x_7 \wedge x_8))) \vee x_9$

Proof idea. A small-but-deep formula φ must be fairly "unbalanced," with some subformulas much bigger than their sibling subformulas. To reorganize φ and make it more balanced, we first find a node v whose subformula is approximately half the size of the whole formula φ. We sever the wire to v's parent, so the "rest of φ" is also about half of φ but has a hole where v's subformula was. We'd like to put v's subformula in parallel with the rest of φ, as if they're siblings. But the rest of φ depends on v's value, so how can we evaluate it without waiting for v? By trying both possible bits (to plug into the hole) and then using a mux to select the right one retrospectively, after v's subformula is evaluated. This yields a circuit, not a formula (since the selector wire gets split inside the mux), but we fix this by duplicating v's subformula. We recurse to balance v's subformula and balance the rest of φ. ■

Example. Figure 6.11 demonstrates one balancing step (without recursing). To find v, start at the root and repeatedly descend to whichever child has more leaves in its subformula, until reaching a node whose subformula has at most two-thirds of all the leaves. The formula in Figure 6.11 has 9 leaves.

- The root's left subtree has 8 leaves and its right subtree has 1, so go to the left child.
- This node's left subtree has 1 leaf and its right subtree has 7, so go to the right child.
- This node's left subtree has 5 leaves and its right subtree has 2, so go to the left child.
- Stop here since 5 is at most two-thirds of the 9 leaves. ♦

Lemma 6.23. *In every rooted tree with $\ell \geq 2$ leaves and where each node has at most two children, some node's subtree has at most $2\ell/3$ but more than $\ell/3$ leaves.*

Proof of Lemma 6.23. For any such tree, the following algorithm finds such a node v. A node's "number of leaves" is its subtree's number of leaves.

> Algorithm to find a subtree with approximately half of the leaves (6.6)
>
> initialize $v \leftarrow$ the root
> while v has $> 2\ell/3$ leaves:
>   if v has only one child: update $v \leftarrow v$'s child
>   else: update $v \leftarrow$ whichever child of v has more leaves (breaking a tie arbitrarily)

Inside the loop, v is not a leaf since v has $> 2\ell/3 \geq 4/3 > 1$ leaves. The algorithm stops at some v with $\leq 2\ell/3$ leaves. We claim that this v has $> \ell/3$ leaves. Since the root has $\ell > 2\ell/3$ leaves, v is not the root. Thus v has a parent u, and u has $> 2\ell/3$ leaves since the algorithm didn't stop at u. Also, u has two children, since otherwise v would have as many leaves as u and the algorithm wouldn't stop at v either. Since v has at least as many leaves as u's other child, v has at least half as many leaves as u. Thus v has $> (2\ell/3)/2 = \ell/3$ leaves. ■

Proof of Theorem 6.22. It suffices to prove that every bounded-fan-in poly-size formula family is equivalent to some bounded-fan-in log-depth circuit family (Theorem 6.1.*(i)*).

For any node v in a formula φ, let φ_v denote v's subformula, and for both $b \in \{0,1\}$, define $\varphi_{v=b}$ from φ by replacing φ_v with the constant b and contracting.

We design a subroutine "balance" that takes a bounded-fan-in formula φ as an argument and returns an equivalent (but shallower) bounded-fan-in circuit C.

> Algorithm to balance a formula (6.7)
>
> balance(φ):
>   if φ has only one leaf: return φ
>   if φ has $\ell \geq 2$ leaves:
>   find a node v with $\leq 2\ell/3$ but $> \ell/3$ leaves in φ using Lemma 6.23
>   let $C_v \leftarrow$ balance(φ_v) and $C_{v=0} \leftarrow$ balance($\varphi_{v=0}$) and $C_{v=1} \leftarrow$ balance($\varphi_{v=1}$)
>   return a circuit C with a mux whose selector is the output of C_v
>   and whose other two inputs are the outputs of $C_{v=0}$ and $C_{v=1}$

This recursive subroutine maintains the invariant that balance(φ) is equivalent to φ. This holds by definition for the base cases when φ has only one leaf. For non-base cases, the invariant is maintained because if C_v, $C_{v=0}$, $C_{v=1}$ are equivalent to φ_v, $\varphi_{v=0}$, $\varphi_{v=1}$ then for every input x, letting $b = C_v(x) = \varphi_v(x)$ we have $C(x) = C_{v=b}(x) = \varphi_{v=b}(x) = \varphi(x)$, so C is equivalent to φ.

Base cases correspond to literals, which contribute nothing to the depth. Each level of recursion corresponds to a level of muxes, contributing two layers of $\wedge$ and $\vee$ gates. If φ has $\ell \geq 2$ leaves, then φ_v has $\leq 2\ell/3$ leaves and $\varphi_{v=0}$, $\varphi_{v=1}$ each have $< \ell - \ell/3 = 2\ell/3$ leaves since φ_v has $> \ell/3$ leaves. Since ℓ gets multiplied by $\leq 2/3$ at each level, each formula passed to a call at level i has $\leq (2/3)^{i-1}\ell$ leaves. Thus the recursion always reaches a base case after $\leq \log_{3/2}(\ell)$ levels, so C has depth $\leq 2\log_{3/2}(\ell)$.

Applying this to a bounded-fan-in poly-size formula family yields an equivalent family of bounded-fan-in circuits of depth $\leq 2\log_{3/2}(\mathrm{poly}\, N) = O(\log N)$. ■

Hence, these nonuniform models are equally powerful, and they all capture NC^1/poly:

- Bounded-fan-in log-depth circuits.
- Bounded-fan-in log-depth formulas.
- Poly-size formulas.

We add a surprise entry to this list in §6.6.

The proof of Theorem 6.22 yields an algorithm to balance a formula in poly time but more than log space. A log-space-uniform analogue of Theorem 6.22 does hold—where the new formula family is log-space-uniform if the original is—so a problem is in NC^1 iff it has a log-space-uniform poly-size formula family. But it takes a different approach to prove this: Using the difficult theorem that Formula Evaluation $\in$ NC^1 (which we won't prove), a log-space generator can generate a poly-size formula φ and a bounded-fan-in log-depth formula ψ for Formula Evaluation, and hardwire φ's encoding as part of ψ's input, to get a bounded-fan-in log-depth formula equivalent to φ.

In summary: Circuits correspond to P. Branching programs correspond to L. Formulas correspond to NC^1.

A monotone analogue of Theorem 6.22 also holds:

Theorem 6.24. *Every poly-size monotone formula family is equivalent to some bounded-fan-in log-depth monotone formula family.*

Proof idea. The proof of Theorem 6.22 doesn't immediately work for this, because even if the original formula is monotone, the muxes introduce $\neg$ gates. Fortunately, we can just remove the negations from the muxes, and the proof still works: The cases where the mutilated muxes would make mistakes actually won't arise if the formula is monotone. ■

Proof. Like the ordinary mux $(y_0 \wedge \overline{b}) \vee (y_1 \wedge b)$, which evaluates to y_b, define the *monotone mux* $y_0 \vee (y_1 \wedge b)$, which evaluates to y_b unless $y_0 = 1$ and $y_1 = 0$ and $b = 1$. Apply the proof of Theorem 6.22 to a monotone formula φ but using monotone muxes instead of ordinary muxes. The resulting circuit C is already a monotone formula, and it's equivalent to φ: For every input x, we have $\varphi_{v=0}(x) \leq \varphi_{v=1}(x)$ because when the constant flips from 0 to 1, no $\wedge$ or $\vee$ gate on the v-to-root path flips from 1 to 0. Since it cannot be that $\varphi_{v=0}(x) = 1$ and $\varphi_{v=1}(x) = 0$, the monotone mux outputs the correct bit, like an ordinary mux would. ■

Nonmonotone balancing (Theorem 6.22) follows from monotone balancing (Theorem 6.24) by pushing $\neg$ gates to the inputs, replacing negative literals with fresh variables (like reducing Circuit Evaluation to Monotone Circuit Evaluation in §5.4), balancing the resulting monotone formula, and then changing the fresh variables back to the original negative literals. This yields a formula directly, avoiding the size increase from the circuit-to-formula conversion.

6.6 Narrow Branching Programs

Formula depth is closely related to branching program *width*. We can convert shallow formulas to narrow branching programs and vice versa. Thus, width approximately measures how time-efficient of a parallel algorithm we can obtain from a space-efficient algorithm.

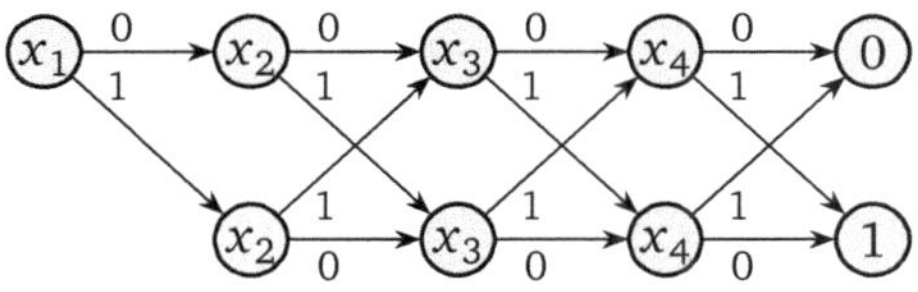

Figure 6.12: Example layered branching program

6.6.1 Layered Branching Programs

In a *layered* branching program, nodes are partitioned into a sequence of layers with the start node in the first layer and the accept and reject nodes in the last layer, and with each edge going from some layer to the next layer. We typically visualize layers as columns. A layered branching program's depth (number of non-output layers) is often called its *length*. A layered branching program's *width* is the maximum number of nodes in any non-output layer. (The output layer has 2 nodes, but as a technicality, we allow the width to be 1 without counting the output layer.) The number of non-output nodes is $\leq$ length $\cdot$ width. A branching program uses log(size) bits to remember which node it's at, and a layered branching program uses log(length) bits to remember which layer, plus log(width) bits to remember which node in that layer. Informally, length = time and log(width) = "space other than the clock."

Example. Figure 6.12 shows a layered branching program computing PARITY_4. The top row means the parity of the input so far is 0, and the bottom row means it's 1. This has length 4 and width 2. It uses $\log(4) = 2$ bits to remember how much of the input it has read, and $\log(2) = 1$ bit to remember the parity of the input so far. ♦

To simulate an unconditional branch node in a layered branching program, we can't just bypass the node, which would violate the layering. Instead, we let the node read any input bit and have its edges go to the same node as each other.

Layered branching programs are as powerful as non-layered ones:

Theorem 6.25. *Every size-s branching program is equivalent to some width-s length-s layered branching program.*

Proof. We use the layering technique from §1.9.3. For any branching program B with s nodes, define a layered branching program B' with $s-1$ layers, each of which is a copy of B but with edges going to the next layer. Formally: Let V be the set of nodes in B. Then $V' = V \times \{1, 2, \ldots, s-1\}$ is the set of nodes in B'. For all $v \in V$ and $j \in \{1, \ldots, s-2\}$:

- If v is labeled x_i with 0-edge to u and 1-edge to w in B, then (v, j) is labeled x_i with 0-edge to $(u, j+1)$ and 1-edge to $(w, j+1)$ in B'.
- If v is an output node in B, then (v, j) unconditionally branches to $(v, j+1)$ in B'.

The nodes $(v, s-1)$ have no outgoing edges. Assuming v_{start}, v_{accept}, and v_{reject} are the start, accept, and reject nodes of B, let $(v_{\text{start}}, 1)$, $(v_{\text{accept}}, s-1)$, and $(v_{\text{reject}}, s-1)$ be the start, accept, and reject nodes of B'. Delete from B' all nodes that are unreachable from the start node. This ensures that layer $s-1$ only contains the output nodes, because any path from the start node to a non-output node in layer $s-1$ would correspond to a path of $s-1$ many non-output nodes in B, which is impossible.

B' is layered, with layer j consisting of the (v, j) nodes. B' has width $\leq s$ and length $s-2 \leq s$. Finally, B and B' are equivalent because for every input a, $B(a)$ accepts iff $B'(a)$ accepts:

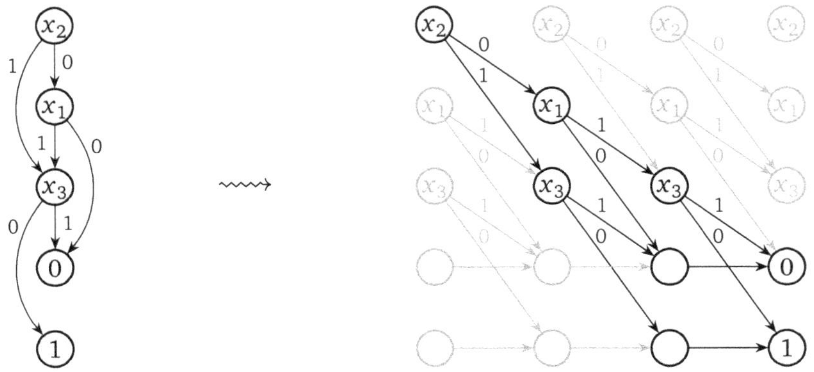

Figure 6.13: Example of turning a branching program into a layered branching program

⇒: If the computation path of $B(a)$ is $v_{\text{start}} = v_1 \to v_2 \to \cdots \to v_k = v_{\text{accept}}$ then $k \leq s-1$ since the path never repeats nodes and never visits v_{reject}, and so the computation path of $B'(a)$ is:

$$(v_{\text{start}}, 1) = (v_1, 1) \to (v_2, 2) \to \cdots \to (v_k, k) \to (v_k, k+1) \to \cdots \to (v_k, s-1) = (v_{\text{accept}}, s-1)$$

⇐: If the computation path of $B'(a)$ is

$$(v_{\text{start}}, 1) = (v_1, 1) \to (v_2, 2) \to \cdots \to (v_k, k) \to (v_k, k+1) \to \cdots \to (v_k, s-1) = (v_{\text{accept}}, s-1)$$

which first reaches v_{accept} in some layer $k \leq s-1$, then the computation path of $B(a)$ is $v_{\text{start}} = v_1 \to v_2 \to \cdots \to v_k = v_{\text{accept}}$. ■

Figure 6.13 shows an example, with gray nodes and edges deleted since they're unreachable from the start node.

6.6.2 Branching Program Width Versus Formula Depth

Width-2 layered branching programs can't compute all boolean functions, though this isn't obvious and we won't prove it. The following theorem implies that width-3 layered branching programs can compute all boolean functions since depth-2 formulas can (Lemma 2.9).

Theorem 6.26. *Every unbounded-fan-in depth-d size-s formula is equivalent to some width-$(d+1)$ length-s layered branching program.*

Proof idea. The conversion of formulas to non-layered branching programs (Theorem 5.22.*(ii)*) uses short-circuit evaluation: If an ∨'s left side evaluates to 1, the branching program skips to the accept node. If an ∧'s left side evaluates to 0, the branching program skips to the reject node. To make the branching program layered, we create dedicated "lanes" of nodes for these short-circuit evaluations to have "stopovers" in all layers en route to the output layer. Each layer of gates in the formula gives rise to a lane of nodes in the branching program, contributing 1 to the width. ■

Proof. Assume the formula has negations only on the input variables, which doesn't increase the depth or the number of leaves. We give a recursive algorithm that turns any such formula φ into a layered branching program B whose width is φ's depth plus 1, and whose length is φ's number of leaves.

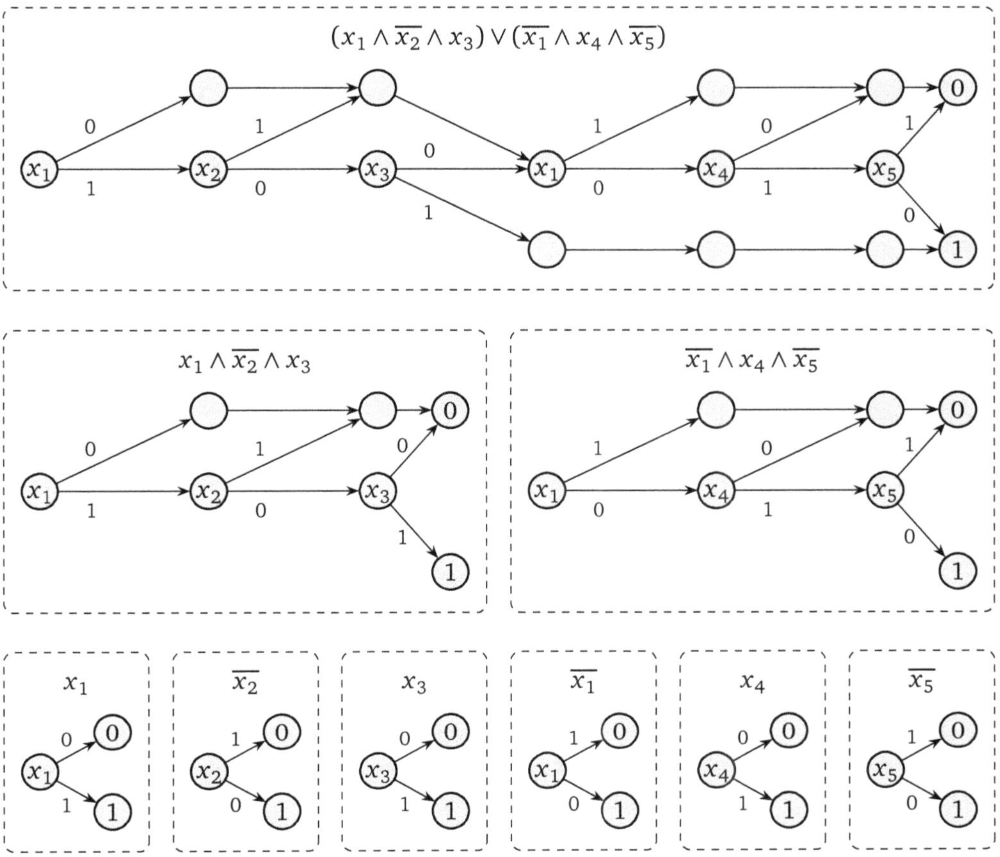

Figure 6.14: Example of turning a depth-2 formula into a width-3 layered branching program

The base cases are when φ is just a literal x_i or $\overline{x_i}$, which has depth 0 and 1 leaf. Then B's start node reads x_i and has edges to the output nodes:

- If φ is x_i: The 0-edge goes to the reject node. The 1-edge goes to the accept node.
- If φ is $\overline{x_i}$: The 1-edge goes to the reject node. The 0-edge goes to the accept node.

B has width 1 (since we don't count the output layer toward the width) and length 1.

For non-base cases, the algorithm recursively finds layered branching programs $B_1, \ldots, B_k$ equivalent to the subformulas $\varphi_1, \ldots, \varphi_k$ (of the output gate's children) and combines them: B's start node is B_1's start node. B's output nodes are B_k's output nodes. The output nodes of $B_1, \ldots, B_{k-1}$ are removed, so B's layers are B_1's non-output layers, followed by B_2's non-output layers, and so on, followed by all layers of B_k. Also, B has a new lane of nodes—one node in every non-output layer—which each unconditionally branch to the next node in this lane.

- If $\varphi = \varphi_1 \vee \cdots \vee \varphi_k$:
  The new lane's last node unconditionally branches to the accept node.
  For each $i \in \{1, \ldots, k-1\}$: Edges to B_i's reject node instead go to B_{i+1}'s start node.
  Edges to B_i's accept node instead go into the new lane.

- If $\varphi = \varphi_1 \wedge \cdots \wedge \varphi_k$:
  The new lane's last node unconditionally branches to the reject node.
  For each $i \in \{1, \ldots, k-1\}$: Edges to B_i's accept node instead go to B_{i+1}'s start node.
  Edges to B_i's reject node instead go into the new lane.

B's width is the maximum width of $B_1, \ldots, B_k$ plus 1, and B's length is the sum of the lengths of $B_1, \ldots, B_k$. Thus, this algorithm maintains the invariant that B is equivalent to φ, and B's width is φ's depth plus 1, and B's length is φ's number of leaves. ■

Figure 6.14 shows an example.

We went from depth to width. Now, we go from width to depth.

Theorem 6.27. *Every width-w length-ℓ layered branching program is equivalent to some bounded-fan-in depth-$((\lceil \log w \rceil + 1)\lceil \log \ell \rceil)$ formula.*

Proof idea. In the conversion of poly-size branching programs to unbounded-fan-in log-depth poly-size circuits (Theorem 6.20), each $\vee$ gate has unbounded fan-in because it tries every potential midpoint node for a path between two particular nodes in the branching program. In a width-w layered branching program, the midpoint node must be in a particular layer, so there are only w possibilities. Thus each $\vee$ gate only needs fan-in w and can be replaced by a depth-$\lceil \log w \rceil$ tree of bounded-fan-in $\vee$ gates, like in the proof that $\mathsf{AC}^i \subseteq \mathsf{NC}^{i+1}$ (Lemma 6.3). ■

Proof. For any width-w length-ℓ layered branching program B, we design an equivalent bounded-fan-in depth-$((\lceil \log w \rceil + 1)\lceil \log \ell \rceil)$ circuit C, which can be converted to a bounded-fan-in formula of the same depth (Theorem 6.1.*(i)*). Let $K = \lceil \log \ell \rceil$. Adding dummy layers if necessary, we may assume B has length exactly 2^K, with layers numbered $0, 1, \ldots, 2^K$. For every $k \in \{0, 1, \ldots, K\}$, every $j \in \{1, 2, 3, \ldots, 2^{K-k}\}$, every node u in layer $(j-1)2^k$, and every node w in layer $j2^k$, C has a node $g_{u,w}$ that evaluates to 1 on input a iff running B on input a starting at u for 2^k steps leads to w. C's output node is $g_{s,t}$ where s is B's start node and t is B's accept node.

- When $k > 0$: $g_{u,w} = \bigvee_v (g_{u,v} \wedge g_{v,w})$ where the $\bigvee$ is over nodes v in layer $j2^k - 2^{k-1}$, halfway between layers $(j-1)2^k$ and $j2^k$. The layers of u, v, w are consecutive multiples of 2^{k-1}. Each $k > 0$ contributes to C a layer of fan-in-2 $\wedge$ gates and a layer of fan-in-w $\vee$ gates, which we replace with depth-$\lceil \log w \rceil$ trees of fan-in-2 $\vee$ gates.
- When $k = 0$: If u is labeled x_i with 1-edge to w, then $g_{u,w}$ is the input node x_i. If u is labeled x_i with 0-edge to w, then $g_{u,w}$ is $\overline{x_i}$. If both of those are true, then $g_{u,w}$ is constant 1. Otherwise, $g_{u,w}$ is constant 0. Thus $k = 0$ contributes no layers to C.

C has depth $(\lceil \log w \rceil + 1)\lceil \log \ell \rceil$ since there are $K = \lceil \log \ell \rceil$ possibilities of $k > 0$. ■

6.6.3 A Surprise

The complexity class of all decision problems solvable by poly-width poly-length layered branching program families is $\mathsf{L/poly}$ (Theorem 6.25 and Theorem 5.25). What about the complexity class of all decision problems solvable by *constant*-width poly-length layered branching program families? Let's call this class $\mathcal{C}$ in lieu of a real name. $\mathsf{AC}^0/\mathsf{poly} \subseteq \mathcal{C} \subseteq \mathsf{NC}^1/\mathsf{poly}$ (Theorem 6.26 and Theorem 6.27) and $\mathcal{C} \neq \mathsf{AC}^0/\mathsf{poly}$ since PARITY $\in \mathcal{C}$ but PARITY $\notin \mathsf{AC}^0/\mathsf{poly}$ (Theorem 6.4). For a while, $\mathcal{C} \neq \mathsf{NC}^1/\mathsf{poly}$ was conjectured since there was no indication that such branching programs could do much more than simulate constant-depth formulas and modular counting. That conjecture was amazingly refuted: $\mathcal{C} = \mathsf{NC}^1/\mathsf{poly}$. Despite the lack of syntactic resemblance,

i	$p(i)$
1	3
2	1
3	5
4	2
5	4

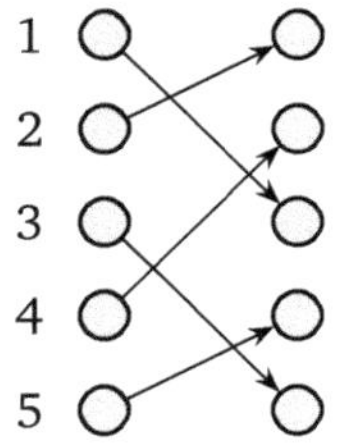

i	$p^{-1}(i)$
1	2
2	4
3	1
4	5
5	3

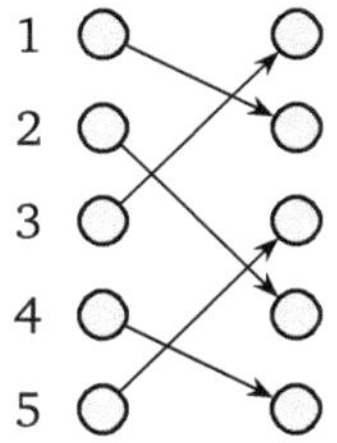

Figure 6.15: Example permutation and its inverse

constant-width poly-length layered branching programs are equal in power to bounded-fan-in log-depth formulas, and thus also to poly-size formulas. This striking perspective on parallel computation adds to the list of characterizations of $\mathsf{NC}^1/\mathsf{poly}$ in §6.5.2.

Theorem 6.28. *For every decision problem A, we have $A \in \mathsf{NC}^1/\mathsf{poly}$ iff A has a constant-width poly-length layered branching program family.*

This is a corollary of the following result:

Theorem 6.29. *Every bounded-fan-in depth-d formula is equivalent to some width-5 length-4^d layered branching program.*

Proof of Theorem 6.28. $\Rightarrow$: Suppose a bounded-fan-in log-depth formula family $\varphi_1, \varphi_2, \ldots$ solves A. Turn each φ_N into B_N using Theorem 6.29. The width-5 length-$4^{O(\log N)} = \text{poly} N$ layered branching program family $B_1, B_2, \ldots$ solves A.

$\Leftarrow$: Suppose a width-w poly-length layered branching program family $B_1, B_2, \ldots$ solves A, where w is a constant. Turn each B_N into φ_N using Theorem 6.27. The bounded-fan-in depth-$(\lceil \log w \rceil + 1)\lceil \log(\text{poly} N) \rceil = O(\log N)$ formula family $\varphi_1, \varphi_2, \ldots$ solves A. ■

Theorem 6.26 turns log-depth formulas into log-width layered branching programs. To get the width down to a constant (while retaining poly length), we need a totally different idea. The proof of Theorem 6.29 is elegant but lacks a simple intuition. Let's sit back and enjoy the proof in the next two sections.

We're ending Part I on a high note. This theorem is regarded as a great plot twist in the story of computational complexity theory.

6.6.4 Permutations

A *permutation* on $[w] = \{1, 2, \ldots, w\}$ is a function $p\colon [w] \to [w]$ such that each element of $[w]$ appears exactly once among $p(1), p(2), \ldots, p(w)$ (that is, p is a bijection). We represent p as a directed graph where node $i \in [w]$ on the left side of the graph has an edge to node $p(i)$ on the right side. The *inverse* of a permutation p is the permutation p^{-1} on $[w]$ such that $p^{-1}(p(i)) = i$ for all $i \in [w]$. We obtain the graph of p^{-1} from the graph of p by swapping the left and right sides and reversing the edge directions. Figure 6.15 shows an example permutation on $[5]$ and its inverse.

The *composition* of permutations p and q on $[w]$ is the permutation pq on $[w]$ defined by $(pq)(i) = q(p(i))$ for all i (first apply p, then apply q). This is sometimes denoted $q \circ p$, but here we denote it pq to reflect how the graphs are combined from left to right: We form pq's graph

i	$p(i)$	$q(i)$	$(pq)(i)$
1	3	4	2
2	1	1	4
3	5	2	5
4	2	3	1
5	4	5	3

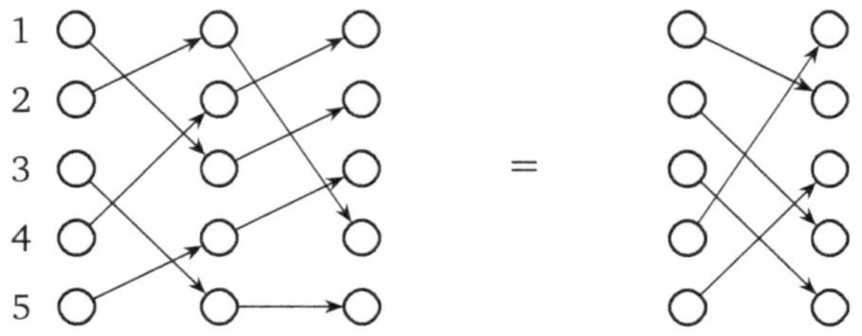

Figure 6.16: Example of composition of permutations

by treating the right side of p's graph as the left side of q's graph and turning each path of two edges into a single edge. Figure 6.16 shows an example.

Composition is associative: $(pq)r = p(qr) = pqr$ is defined by $(pqr)(i) = r(q(p(i)))$. Composition is not commutative: pq may or may not equal qp.

The *identity* permutation $e\colon [w] \to [w]$ is defined by $e(i) = i$ for all i. All edges are horizontal in e's graph. We have $e^{-1} = e$ and $p^{-1}p = e = pp^{-1}$ for all permutations $p\colon [w] \to [w]$.

In a *cyclic* permutation p, the sequence $1, p(1), p(p(1)), p(p(p(1))), \ldots$ visits every element of $[w]$ exactly once before returning to 1. (The choice of 1 as the starting point is arbitrary.) In Figure 6.16, p is cyclic $(1,3,5,4,2,1,\ldots)$ but q and pq aren't. A cyclic permutation's inverse is also cyclic. A composition of cyclic permutations is not necessarily cyclic.

Claim 6.30. *For all cyclic permutations p and q on $[w]$, there exists a (not necessarily cyclic) permutation r on $[w]$ such that $p = rqr^{-1}$.*

Proof idea. First r "relabels" the elements of $[w]$, then q does the cycle, then r^{-1} relabels the elements back. ■

Proof. Let $p^0 = e$, $p^1 = p$, $p^2 = pp$, $p^3 = ppp$, and so on. (Since we use "multiplication notation" for composition, it's fitting to use "exponentiation notation" too.) Since p and q are cyclic, each element of $[w]$ occurs exactly once among $p^0(1), p^1(1), p^2(1), \ldots, p^{w-1}(1)$ and exactly once among $q^0(1), q^1(1), q^2(1), \ldots, q^{w-1}(1)$. Thus $r\colon [w] \to [w]$ defined by $r(p^j(1)) = q^j(1)$ for all $j \in \{0,1,\ldots,w-1\}$ is a permutation. For $j \geq w$, we have $r(p^j(1)) = r(p^{j \bmod w}(1)) = q^{j \bmod w}(1) = q^j(1)$. Then $p = rqr^{-1}$ because for all $i \in [w]$, assuming $i = p^j(1)$, we have:

$$(rqr^{-1})(i) = r^{-1}(q(r(i))) = r^{-1}(q(q^j(1))) = r^{-1}(q^{j+1}(1)) = p^{j+1}(1) = p(p^j(1)) = p(i)$$

■

The next claim comes "out of the blue," but it's the crucial gadget in the proof of Theorem 6.29.

Claim 6.31. *For some cyclic permutations s and t on $[5]$, $sts^{-1}t^{-1}$ is a cyclic permutation.*

Proof. Figure 6.17 shows such permutations. ■

What's special about width 5 in Theorem 6.29 is that permutations as in Claim 6.31 exist for $w = 5$ but not for $w < 5$. A proper explanation of this phenomenon involves group theory in abstract algebra, but that detour would be unnecessary for our purpose.

i	$s(i)$	$t(i)$	$(sts^{-1}t^{-1})(i)$
1	2	3	3
2	3	1	5
3	4	5	2
4	5	2	1
5	1	4	4

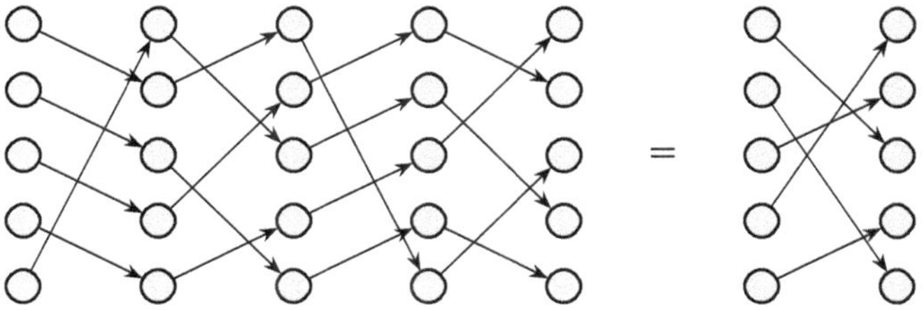

Figure 6.17: Cyclic permutation gadget

6.6.5 Permutation Branching Programs

Definition. A *w-permutation branching program* is like a layered branching program except:

- There's no designated start node or output nodes.
- Each layer has exactly w nodes.
- In each layer except the last, all nodes are labeled with the same variable.
- For each layer except the last, the 0-edges to the next layer form a permutation, and the 1-edges to the next layer form a permutation.
- The last layer's nodes are unlabeled and have no outgoing edges.

Each layer except the last specifies an input variable x_i, a permutation on $[w]$ for if $x_i = 0$, and a permutation on $[w]$ for if $x_i = 1$.

If B is a w-permutation branching program and a is an input, then the "output" $B(a)$ is the following permutation on $[w]$: For each layer except the last, select the a_i-edges where x_i is the variable being read, and compose these permutations over all layers. ◀

If we run B on input a starting at node i in the first layer, then the computation ends at node $B(a)(i)$ in the last layer. Figure 6.18 shows an example 3-permutation branching program B and the permutation $B(01)$ obtained by plugging in $a = 01$.

We allow "unconditional branch" layers, which read no variable and just have a permutation of unlabeled edges to the next layer. Unconditional branch layers don't count toward the length, because we can bypass them in either of the two ways shown in Figure 6.19. An unconditional branch in the next-to-last layer must use the first way. An unconditional branch in the first layer must use the second way. The "question mark" nodes could be either unlabeled or labeled with a variable.

We can compose w-permutation branching programs B_1 and B_2 to obtain a w-permutation branching program B_1B_2 in which B_1's last layer is B_2's first layer. For all a, we have $(B_1B_2)(a) = B_1(a)B_2(a)$. To compose a w-permutation branching program B with a permutation p on $[w]$, we create an unconditional branch layer whose edges are p. For all a, we have $(Bp)(a) = B(a)p$ and $(pB)(a) = pB(a)$.

Definition. Recall e is the identity permutation on $[w]$. If $p \neq e$ is a permutation on $[w]$, then a *p-permutation branching program* is a w-permutation branching program B such that for every input $a \in \{0,1\}^n$, $B(a)$ is either p ("accept") or e ("reject"). A p-permutation branching program computes a function $f\colon \{0,1\}^n \to \{0,1\}$ where $f(a) = 1$ iff $B(a)$ accepts. ◀

Lemma 6.32. *For every cyclic permutation p on $[5]$, every bounded-fan-in depth-d formula is equivalent to some length-4^d p-permutation branching program.*

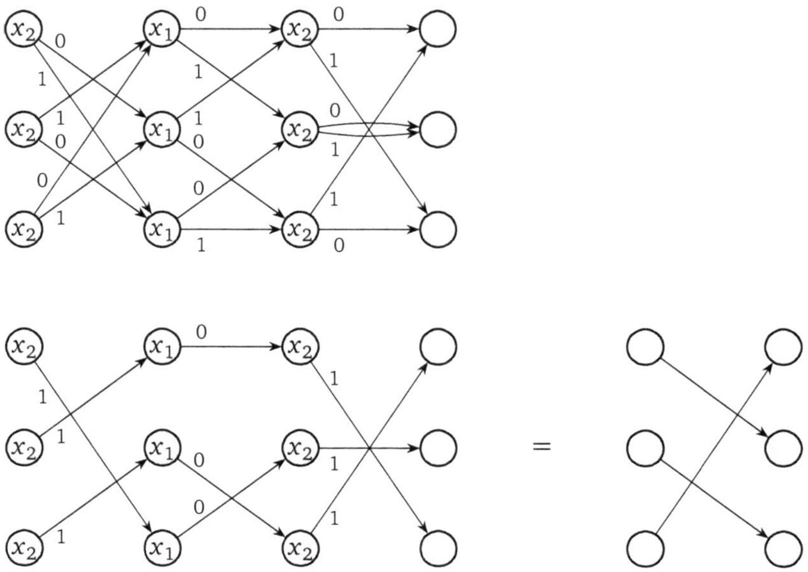

Figure 6.18: Example 3-permutation branching program B and the permutation $B(01)$

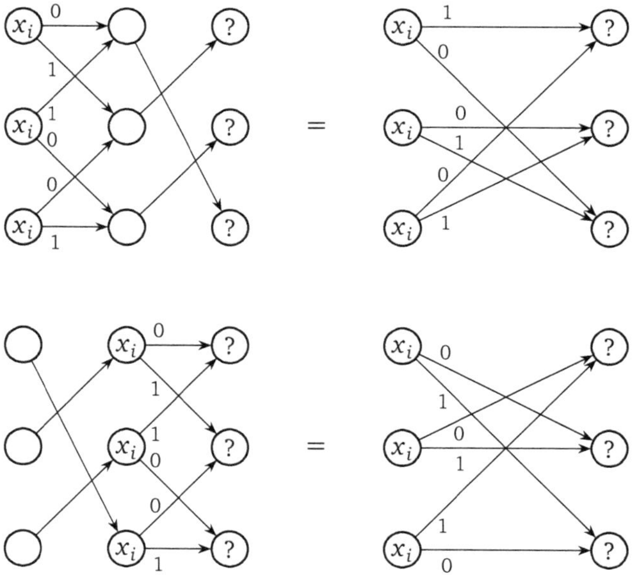

Figure 6.19: Two ways to bypass an unconditional branch layer

Proof of Theorem 6.29. Let p be any cyclic permutation on $[5]$, say with $p(1) = 2$. Every bounded-fan-in depth-d formula φ is equivalent to some length-4^d p-permutation branching program B (Lemma 6.32). Convert B to a layered branching program B':

- Node 1 in the first layer is the start node.
- Node 1 in the last layer is the reject node.
- Node 2 in the last layer is the accept node.

B' is equivalent to B and to φ because for every input a:

- $\varphi(a) = 1 \Rightarrow B(a) = p \Rightarrow B(a)(1) = p(1) = 2 \Rightarrow B'(a)$ accepts
- $\varphi(a) = 0 \Rightarrow B(a) = e \Rightarrow B(a)(1) = e(1) = 1 \Rightarrow B'(a)$ rejects

B' has the same width and length as B.

Technicality: The last layer of B' should only have the two output nodes, so delete the other three nodes and redirect their incoming edges to either output node. It doesn't matter which output node, since these edges aren't used on any input. ■

Proof of Lemma 6.32. We may assume a formula has no $\vee$ gates—only $\wedge$ and $\neg$ gates—without affecting the depth (Figure 5.5). We design a recursive subroutine "to-pbp" that takes as arguments a cyclic permutation p on $[5]$ and a bounded-fan-in formula φ without $\vee$ gates, and returns a p-permutation branching program B equivalent to φ. Here, s and t are cyclic permutations on $[5]$ such that $q = sts^{-1}t^{-1}$ is cyclic (Claim 6.31).

Algorithm to turn a shallow formula into a narrow permutation branching program (6.8)

```
to-pbp(p, φ):
    if φ = x_i:
        B ← length-1 5-permutation branching program that:
            reads x_i, uses p for the 1-edges, and uses e for the 0-edges
    if φ = ¬φ_1:
        B_1 ← to-pbp(p^{-1}, φ_1)
        B ← B_1 p
    if φ = φ_1 ∧ φ_2:
        B_1 ← to-pbp(s, φ_1), B_2 ← to-pbp(t, φ_2), B_3 ← to-pbp(s^{-1}, φ_1), B_4 ← to-pbp(t^{-1}, φ_2)
        r ← permutation such that p = rqr^{-1} (Claim 6.30)
        B ← rB_1B_2B_3B_4r^{-1}
    return B
```

This subroutine maintains the invariant that B is equivalent to φ. This holds by definition for the base cases when φ is a variable x_i:

- $\varphi(a) = 1 \Rightarrow B(a) = p$
- $\varphi(a) = 0 \Rightarrow B(a) = e$

To see that the invariant is maintained when $\varphi = \neg\varphi_1$, assume B_1 is equivalent to φ_1. For every input a, since $B(a) = B_1(a)p$:

- $\varphi(a) = 1 \Rightarrow \varphi_1(a) = 0 \Rightarrow B_1(a) = e \Rightarrow B(a) = ep = p$
- $\varphi(a) = 0 \Rightarrow \varphi_1(a) = 1 \Rightarrow B_1(a) = p^{-1} \Rightarrow B(a) = p^{-1}p = e$

To see that the invariant is maintained when $\varphi = \varphi_1 \wedge \varphi_2$, assume B_1, B_2, B_3, B_4 are equivalent to $\varphi_1, \varphi_2, \varphi_1, \varphi_2$ respectively. For every input a, since $B(a) = rB_1(a)B_2(a)B_3(a)B_4(a)r^{-1}$:

- $\varphi(a)=1 \Rightarrow$
  $\varphi_1(a)=1$ and $\varphi_2(a)=1 \Rightarrow$
  $B_1(a)=s$ and $B_2(a)=t$ and $B_3(a)=s^{-1}$ and $B_4(a)=t^{-1} \Rightarrow$
  $B(a)=rsts^{-1}t^{-1}r^{-1}=rqr^{-1}=p$

- $\varphi(a)=0 \Rightarrow \begin{cases} \varphi_1(a)=1 \text{ and } \varphi_2(a)=0 \Rightarrow B(a)=rses^{-1}er^{-1}=rss^{-1}r^{-1}=rer^{-1}=e \\ \varphi_1(a)=0 \text{ and } \varphi_2(a)=1 \Rightarrow B(a)=retet^{-1}r^{-1}=rtt^{-1}r^{-1}=rer^{-1}=e \\ \varphi_1(a)=0 \text{ and } \varphi_2(a)=0 \Rightarrow B(a)=reeeer^{-1}=rer^{-1}=e \end{cases}$

This subroutine also maintains the invariant that the length of B (not counting unconditional branch layers, which can be bypassed) is $\leq 4^{\text{depth of } \varphi}$. This holds by definition for the base cases when φ is a variable x_i, since φ has depth 0 and B has length $1=4^0$. The invariant is maintained when $\varphi=\neg\varphi_1$ because B and B_1 have the same length, and φ and φ_1 have the same depth. The invariant is maintained when $\varphi=\varphi_1 \wedge \varphi_2$ because if φ has depth d then φ_1 and φ_2 each have depth $\leq d-1$ and so:

$$\begin{aligned} \text{length of } B &= \text{length of } B_1 + \text{length of } B_2 + \text{length of } B_3 + \text{length of } B_4 \\ &\leq 4^{\text{depth of } \varphi_1} + 4^{\text{depth of } \varphi_2} + 4^{\text{depth of } \varphi_1} + 4^{\text{depth of } \varphi_2} \\ &\leq 4^{d-1}+4^{d-1}+4^{d-1}+4^{d-1} \ = \ 4^d \end{aligned}$$ ■

Exercises

6.1 Turn the circuit in Figure 6.20 into a formula using the proof of Theorem 6.1.*(i)*.

6.2 Prove that for all $i \geq 1$, if $\mathsf{NC}^{i+1}=\mathsf{NC}^i$ then $\mathsf{NC}=\mathsf{NC}^i$, and similarly if $\mathsf{AC}^{i+1}=\mathsf{AC}^i$ then $\mathsf{AC}=\mathsf{AC}^i$. This is like the polynomial hierarchy's collapse property (Theorem 4.23).

6.3 Prove that SQUARING doesn't have an AC^0/poly-type circuit family.

SQUARING	(6.9)
Input: Nonnegative binary integer x	
Output: x^2	

6.4 In a *semi-unbounded-fan-in* circuit, $\wedge$ gates have bounded fan-in, $\vee$ gates have unbounded fan-in, and $\neg$ gates are only on the input variables. Define SAC^i as the set of all decision problems for which there exists a correct log-space-uniform family of semi-unbounded-fan-in circuits with depth $O(\log^i N)$. The S stands for "semi."

(a) Why does it matter that $\neg$ gates are only allowed on the input variables?

(b) Prove $\mathsf{NL} \subseteq \mathsf{SAC}^1 \subseteq \mathsf{AC}^1$.

6.5 In § 6.4.1 we said an NC^1-type mapping reduction's query size can only depend on its input size. Now, let's allow the query size to depend on the input: A circuit computing the reduction outputs a separate word containing the query size M, and among the other output words, the first M are the query and the rest are garbage. Prove that with this more general definition, if $A \leq^m_{nc^1} B$ and $B \in \mathsf{NC}^1$ then $A \in \mathsf{NC}^1$ (like Lemma 6.13).

6.6 Prove FOREST REACHABILITY is L-complete. Exercise 1.10 already asked you to prove FOREST REACHABILITY $\in$ L.

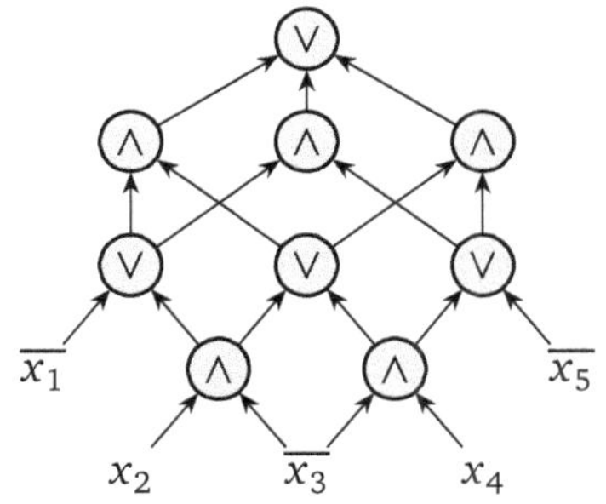

Figure 6.20: Circuit for Exercise 6.1

6.7 Prove that CIRCUIT EVALUATION $\in \mathsf{NC}^1$ iff $\mathsf{NC}^1 = \mathsf{P}$.

6.8 In Theorem 6.22 we proved that every formula with ℓ leaves is equivalent to some bounded-fan-in formula with depth $\leq 2\log_{3/2}(\ell) < 3.42\log_2(\ell)$. Improve the depth to $\leq 3\log_2(\ell)$. Hint: First, prove that in every rooted tree with $\ell \geq 2$ leaves and where each node has at most two children, some node has $> \ell/2$ leaves but both of its children have $\leq \ell/2$ leaves.

6.9 For odd $N \geq 3$, define $F_N\colon \{0,1\}^N \to \{0,1\}$ by:

$$F_N(x) = x_1 \vee \big(x_2 \wedge \big(x_3 \vee \big(x_4 \wedge \big(\cdots x_{N-2} \vee \big(x_{N-1} \wedge x_N\big)\cdots\big)\big)\big)\big)$$

This decision problem F is known as AND-OR PATH.

(a) Prove F has a bounded-fan-in monotone formula family of depth $2\log N + O(1)$.

(b) Prove F has a bounded-fan-in monotone formula family of depth $d\log N + O(1)$ for some $d < 1.5$.

(c) Prove that Exercise 6.9.b implies that ADDITION has a bounded-fan-in circuit family of depth $d\log N + O(1)$ for some $d < 1.5$.

6.10 A layered branching program is *oblivious* iff in each layer except the output layer, all nodes are labeled with the same variable. (The proofs of Theorem 6.26 and Theorem 6.29 yielded oblivious layered branching programs.)

(a) Prove that every width-w length-ℓ layered branching program is equivalent to some width-$2w$ length-ℓw oblivious layered branching program.

(b) Improve the width from $2w$ to $\lfloor 1.5w \rfloor$ (still with length ℓw).

6.11 Define MAJORITY: $\{0,1\}^+ \to \{0,1\}$ by MAJORITY$(x) = 1$ iff x has more 1s than 0s.

(a) Prove MAJORITY has a linear-width linear-length layered branching program family.

(b) Prove MAJORITY $\in \mathsf{NC}^1$ and thus MAJORITY has a constant-width poly-length layered branching program family.

Notes

The size blow-up in the circuit-to-formula conversion of Theorem 6.1.*(i)* can't be improved in general [449].

NC is named in honor of Nick Pippenger.

Division has an NC^1-type circuit family [124]. This improves the earlier result that Division has an NC^1/poly-type circuit family [52].

$\mathsf{NC}^1 \subseteq \mathsf{L}$ (Theorem 6.8) is due to [84].

A survey of L-complete problems such as Forest Reachability (Exercise 6.6) appears in [138] (not relying on the more recent result that Undirected Reachability $\in$ L).

It's conjectured that P/poly $\not\subseteq$ NC/poly $=$ AC/poly, so arbitrary circuits can't be parallelized without significantly increasing their size. Here are two results showing that circuits can be parallelized to a small extent: Every size-s circuit is equivalent to some bounded-fan-in depth-$O(s/\log s)$ circuit [408, 152]. Every bounded-fan-in log-depth linear-size circuit family is equivalent to some unbounded-fan-in depth-3 subexponential-size circuit family [531, 534, 546].

Formula balancing (Theorem 6.22) was first shown in [503]. The original proof (§ 6.5.2) showed that every formula with ℓ leaves is equivalent to some bounded-fan-in formula with depth $\leq 3.42\log_2(\ell)$. After a series of improvements on the depth, the state-of-the-art is $1.73\log_2(\ell)$ [309]. For the monotone case (Theorem 6.24), the depth can't be improved to $1.06\log_2(\ell)$ [479], but no such lower bound is known for the nonmonotone case. If we don't care about the constant factor in the depth, then the size blow-up can be improved to almost linear: For every constant $c > 1$ (no matter how close to 1), there exists a constant $d \geq 1$ such that every formula with ℓ leaves is equivalent to some bounded-fan-in formula with depth $\leq d\log_2(\ell)$ and with $\leq \ell^c$ leaves [93, 81].

Formula Evaluation $\in \mathsf{NC}^1$ is due to [100, 101].

The fact that width-2 layered branching programs can't compute all boolean functions is due to [87].

The characterization of NC^1/poly by constant-width poly-length layered branching program families (Theorem 6.28) is known as "Barrington's theorem" [48]. The length 4^d in Theorem 6.29 can be improved to 3.51^d [104]. If we don't care about the width (as long as it's a constant), then the length can be improved to almost 2^d: For every constant $b > 2$ (no matter how close to 2), there exists a constant $w \geq 5$ such that every bounded-fan-in depth-d formula is equivalent to some width-w length-b^d layered branching program [130].

SAC^1 (Exercise 6.4) is closed under complement [85] (by adapting the proof that NL is closed under complement) and equals another class known as LOGCFL [542].

Regarding Exercise 6.9: And-Or Path actually has a bounded-fan-in monotone formula family of depth $\log N + \log(\log N) + O(1)$ [222], which is optimal up to the additive constant [134]. For bounded-fan-in nonmonotone formulas for And-Or Path, a depth lower bound of $\log N + (1 - o(1))\log(\log(\log N))$ is known [135].

Majority has a poly-size formula family by Exercise 6.11.b, and the state-of-the-art size upper bound is $O(N^{3.91})$ [478]. Majority also has a $O(N^{5.3})$-size monotone formula family [535, 251].

Part II

RANDOMNESS

Chapter 7

Randomized Computation

Randomness may seem like the antithesis of computation, but sometimes randomness can speed things up. For example, to predict an election's outcome, we may poll a small random subset of voters. A *randomized algorithm* can access a source of randomness, such as a sequence of random numbers. If we run a randomized algorithm again on the same input, it may sample different random numbers and produce different output. To solve a computational problem, a randomized algorithm must produce correct output with "high" probability. Depending on our tolerance for error, a success probability of 90% or 99.999% may be good enough. There's a tradeoff: A *deterministic* (non-randomized) algorithm is guaranteed to give correct output, while a randomized algorithm might be more efficient but have a small chance of erroneous output.

7.1 Time-Efficient Randomized Algorithms

7.1.1 Testing Univariate Polynomial Identities

Our first example of a randomized algorithm involves polynomials. Given two expressions that use addition, subtraction, and multiplication, how can we check whether they express the same polynomial as each other? This is a basic primitive in computer algebra systems such as Maple and Mathematica. We could, with some effort, expand the expressions to their canonical forms and compare all the coefficients. A simpler but less reliable way to check if the polynomials are identical is to plug a value into the original expressions.

Example. On the left are two expressions P and Q. On the right are their canonical forms.

$$\begin{aligned} P(x) &= (x+1)(x-2)(3x-4) \qquad & P(x) &= 3x^3-7x^2-2x+8 \\ Q(x) &= 5x+(-x^2+4)(-3x+2) \qquad & Q(x) &= 3x^3-2x^2-7x+8 \end{aligned}$$

They're distinct polynomials because the coefficients don't all match. But let's pretend we were too lazy to expand P and Q. Let's plug some value a into the original expressions:

$$\begin{aligned} P(0) &= (0+1)(0-2)(3\cdot 0-4) &&= 8 \\ Q(0) &= 5\cdot 0+(-0^2+4)(-3\cdot 0+2) &&= 8 \end{aligned}$$

This shows the method is error-prone because $P(a)=Q(a)$ might hold even when the polynomials are distinct. Retrying with different values of a, we find $P(1)=2$ and $Q(1)=2$ which is inconclusive again, but then $P(2)=0$ and $Q(2)=10$ tells us the polynomials are definitely distinct. We got unlucky plugging in 0 and 1. ♦

In general, we probably won't get unlucky if we plug in a *random* value a. If the polynomials are identical, then $P(a)=Q(a)$ with probability 1. If the polynomials are distinct and both have degree $\leq d$, then they agree on at most d points: $P(a) = Q(a)$ for at most d many values a (Corollary A.21). So if we pick a uniformly random a from any set of $3d$ numbers, say $\{1, 2, \ldots, 3d\}$, then $P(a) \neq Q(a)$ with probability $\geq 2/3$. If we pick a uniformly random a from $\{1, 2, \ldots, 100d\}$, then $P(a) \neq Q(a)$ with probability ≥ 0.99.

A drawback of integers and real numbers is that calculations may yield "runaway" numbers, necessitating "big number arithmetic" such as the primary-school MULTIPLICATION algorithm (§1.1.1). To avoid this minor nuisance, we consider polynomials over finite fields. If p is a prime number, then $\mathbb{Z}_p = \{0, 1, \ldots, p-1\}$ is a field with these arithmetic operators (§A.4.1):

- $a + b$ means $(a + b) \bmod p$
- $a - b$ means $(a - b) \bmod p$
- $a \cdot b$ means $(a \cdot b) \bmod p$
- $a \,/\, b$ means $(a \cdot b^{-1}) \bmod p$
  where $b^{-1} \in \mathbb{Z}_p$ is the unique element such that $(b \cdot b^{-1}) \bmod p = 1$, assuming $b \neq 0$

The commutative, associative, distributive, and other familiar arithmetic properties hold for $\mathbb{Z}_p$. Prime fields are convenient because they're finite: Numbers stay confined to $\{0, 1, \ldots, p-1\}$ no matter what calculations we do, and $+$, $-$, and $\cdot$ operations take $O(1)$ steps.

An *arithmetic formula* over $\mathbb{Z}_p$ is a rooted tree where each internal node is a $+$, $-$, or $\cdot$ gate with two children (bounded fan-in) and each leaf is labeled by either the variable x or a constant in $\mathbb{Z}_p$. Unbounded fan-in would be fine for $+$ and $\cdot$ gates but not for $-$ gates. An arithmetic formula expresses a polynomial. Figure 7.1 shows an example. We call a tree's root its *top node* to avoid confusion with a polynomial's roots (field elements on which it evaluates to 0).

Arithmetic formulas (over the same field) are considered *identical* iff they express the same canonical-form polynomial as each other. Over a finite field, non-identical arithmetic formulas may compute the same function as each other (such as x^2 and x over $\mathbb{Z}_2$), though that can't happen if both have degree less than the field size.

UNIVARIATE POLYNOMIAL IDENTITY TESTING (or UPIT for short)	(7.1)
Input: Prime $p \leq N$, arithmetic formulas φ and ψ with degree $\leq p/3$ over $\mathbb{Z}_p$	
Output: Are φ and ψ identical?	

The requirement $p \leq N$ is unimportant but ensures that a number fits in a word with $\log N$ bits.

Here's the special case where ψ is the *zero polynomial*, in which all coefficients are 0 in the canonical form. If φ is identical to the zero polynomial, we say φ is *identically zero*.

UNIVARIATE POLYNOMIAL ZERO TESTING (or UPZT for short)	(7.2)
Input: Prime $p \leq N$, arithmetic formula φ with degree $\leq p/3$ over $\mathbb{Z}_p$	
Output: Is φ identically zero?	

UPZT $\leq_p^m$ UPIT by mapping φ to (φ, a constant 0 node), and UPIT $\leq_p^m$ UPZT by mapping (φ, ψ) to $\varphi - \psi$, since φ and ψ are identical iff $\varphi - \psi$ is identically zero. (We're omitting p from the input for clarity.) So we just consider UPZT.

We'll describe a linear-time randomized algorithm for UPZT, but first, we observe UPZT $\in$ P. We design a deterministic recursive subroutine "expand" that has access to the input (p, φ) of size N, takes a node v of φ as an argument, and returns the tuple of coefficients $(c_d, \ldots, c_1, c_0) \in \mathbb{Z}_p^{d+1}$ of v's subformula's canonical-form polynomial $c_d x^d + \cdots + c_1 x + c_0$. For each $i > d$, c_i is implicitly

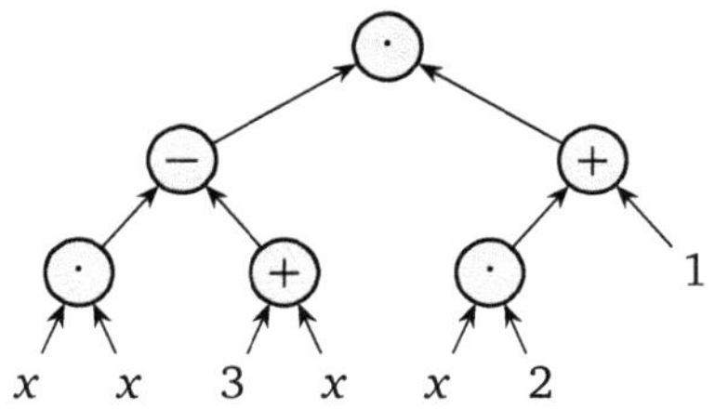

$((x \cdot x) - (3 + x)) \cdot ((x \cdot 2) + 1)$

Canonical form: $2x^3 + 4x^2 + 3x + 2$

Figure 7.1: Example arithmetic formula over $\mathbb{Z}_5$

0. To solve UPZT, check that expand(top node) returns the empty tuple (all coefficients are 0).

Algorithm to expand a univariate arithmetic formula (7.3)

expand(v):
- if v is a leaf labeled x: return $(1, 0)$
- if v is a leaf labeled $c_0 \in \mathbb{Z}_p$: return (c_0)
- if v has left child v_1 and right child v_2:
  - let $(\ldots, a_1, a_0) \leftarrow$ expand(v_1) and $(\ldots, b_1, b_0) \leftarrow$ expand(v_2)
  - return $(\ldots, c_1, c_0)$ with leading 0s removed, where for each index i:
    - if v is a + gate: $c_i = a_i + b_i$
    - if v is a − gate: $c_i = a_i - b_i$
    - if v is a · gate: $c_i = a_i b_0 + a_{i-1} b_1 + a_{i-2} b_2 + \cdots + a_0 b_i$

This has poly$N$ time efficiency because each subformula has degree $< N$. (Though φ has degree $\leq p/3 \leq N/3$, some subformulas may have monomials of degree $> p/3$ that eventually cancel out.) There are at most N calls, and each call takes $O(N^2)$ time, not counting its descendant calls. Faster polynomial multiplication algorithms exist (for handling · gates), but we're not too picky about time efficiency here.

Another deterministic poly-time algorithm for UPZT simply evaluates φ on each field element. We design a recursive subroutine "eval" that has access to (p, φ) and to $a \in \mathbb{Z}_p$, takes a node v of φ as an argument, and returns v's value when $x = a$ is plugged in. To solve UPZT, call eval(top node) with each $a \in \mathbb{Z}_p$, and accept iff each of these calls returns 0.

Algorithm to evaluate a univariate arithmetic formula (7.4)

eval(v):
- if v is a leaf labeled x: return a
- if v is a leaf labeled $c \in \mathbb{Z}_p$: return c
- if v has left child v_1 and right child v_2:
  - if v is a + gate: return eval(v_1) + eval(v_2)
  - if v is a − gate: return eval(v_1) − eval(v_2)
  - if v is a · gate: return eval(v_1) · eval(v_2)

This works since over $\mathbb{Z}_p$, the zero polynomial is the only polynomial of degree $< p$ that always evaluates to 0. Each call to eval(top node) takes $O(N)$ time, so this algorithm for UPZT has time efficiency $O(pN) = O(N^2)$.

At last, we state the $O(N)$-time randomized algorithm for UPZT: Instead of iterating over all $a \in \mathbb{Z}_p$, pick one a uniformly at random and accept iff eval(top node) returns 0. If φ is identically zero, then $\varphi(a) = 0$ for all a, so the algorithm accepts with probability 1. Otherwise, φ has at most $p/3$ roots (Theorem A.20), so the algorithm accepts (errs) with probability $\leq (p/3)/p = 1/3$.

Since the mapping reduction from UPIT to UPZT takes $O(N)$ time, we also get a $O(N)$-time randomized algorithm for UPIT.

7.1.2 Testing Multivariate Polynomial Identities

An *n-variate* polynomial P has variables $x_1, x_2, \ldots, x_n$. A *root* of P is an assignment of field elements $(a_1, a_2, \ldots, a_n)$ on which P evaluates to 0. The canonical form of P is a sum of monomials (each of which is a coefficient times a product of variables raised to natural number exponents) after combining monomials that have the same exponents. For example, $(2x_1 - x_2)(x_1x_2 + 2x_1^2)$ has canonical form $4x_1^3 - x_1x_2^2$. Variable x_i's *individual degree* $\deg_{x_i}(P)$ is the highest exponent of x_i in any monomial with nonzero coefficient in P's canonical form. The *total degree* $\deg(P)$ is the largest sum of exponents of any monomial with nonzero coefficient in P's canonical form.

The crux of our randomized univariate polynomial identity testing algorithm was that a nonzero polynomial of degree d has at most d roots. An analogous but subtler property holds for multivariate polynomials. A multivariate polynomial of total degree d may have more than d roots. For example, $x_1 + x_2$ has p roots over $\mathbb{Z}_p$, namely $(a, -a)$ for all $a \in \mathbb{Z}_p$. The following lemma says $\leq d/p$ fraction of the p^n many assignments are roots.

Lemma 7.1. *Over the prime field $\mathbb{Z}_p$, every nonzero n-variate polynomial of total degree d has at most dp^{n-1} many roots.*

Proof. Assume $d < p$ since otherwise the lemma trivially holds. We do a "proof by algorithm." We design a recursive subroutine "find-non-roots" that, given a nonzero polynomial $P(x_1, \ldots, x_n)$ of total degree d over $\mathbb{Z}_p$, finds at least $p^n - dp^{n-1}$ non-roots of P (assignments on which P doesn't evaluate to 0). The idea is to factor out the powers of a single variable—thus rearranging P into a univariate polynomial whose "coefficients" are multivariate polynomials in the other variables—and recurse.

Algorithm to find many non-roots of a low total degree polynomial (7.5)

find-non-roots(P):
  if $n = 1$: return the set of all non-roots of P
  arrange P as $\sum_{i=0}^{e} P_i(x_1, \ldots, x_{n-1}) \cdot x_n^i$ where $e = \deg_{x_n}(P)$ and each P_i is a polynomial
  initialize $R \leftarrow \emptyset$
  for each $(a_1, \ldots, a_{n-1}) \in$ find-non-roots(P_e):
    for each non-root a_n of the univariate polynomial $P(a_1, \ldots, a_{n-1}, x_n)$:
      insert $(a_1, \ldots, a_{n-1}, a_n)$ into R
  return R

This maintains the invariant that if P has total degree $d \geq 0$, then find-non-roots(P) returns a set of at least $p^n - dp^{n-1}$ (but not necessarily all) non-roots of P. This holds for the base cases when $n = 1$ because P has at least $p - d$ non-roots (Theorem A.20). To see that find-non-roots(P) maintains the invariant when $n \geq 2$, assume the invariant holds for find-non-roots(P_e). Since P is nonzero and e is x_n's individual degree, P_e is nonzero. Also, P_e has total degree $\leq d - e$ since if it had a monomial of total degree $> d - e$, then multiplying this monomial by x_n^e would yield a monomial of total degree $> d$ in P. Thus by the invariant, find-non-roots(P_e) returns a set of at least $p^{n-1}-(d-e)p^{n-2}$ non-roots of P_e. Consider any such non-root $(a_1,\ldots,a_{n-1})$. The univariate polynomial $P(a_1,\ldots,a_{n-1},x_n)$ has degree $e \geq 0$ since the coefficient of x_n^e is $P_e(a_1,\ldots,a_{n-1}) \neq 0$. Thus at least $p-e$ many a_n are such that $P(a_1,\ldots,a_{n-1},a_n) \neq 0$ (Theorem A.20). In total, R contains at least

$$\left(p^{n-1}-(d-e)p^{n-2}\right)\cdot(p-e) \;=\; p^n-(d-e)p^{n-1}-ep^{n-1}+e(d-e)p^{n-2} \;\geq\; p^n-dp^{n-1}$$

non-roots of P (by dropping $e(d-e)p^{n-2}$ and canceling $+ep^{n-1}-ep^{n-1}$). ■

Multivariate arithmetic formulas are like univariate arithmetic formulas, except each leaf is labeled by any variable x_i or by a constant.

> **Polynomial Identity Testing** (or PIT for short) (7.6)
>
> Input: Prime $p \leq N$, n-variate arithmetic formulas φ and ψ with total degree $\leq p/3$ over $\mathbb{Z}_p$
>
> Output: Are φ and ψ identical?

> **Polynomial Zero Testing** (or PZT for short) (7.7)
>
> Input: Prime $p \leq N$, n-variate arithmetic formula φ with total degree $\leq p/3$ over $\mathbb{Z}_p$
>
> Output: Is φ identically zero?

As in the univariate setting, PZT $\leq_p^m$ PIT by mapping φ to (φ, a constant 0 node), and PIT $\leq_p^m$ PZT by mapping (φ,ψ) to $\varphi-\psi$, so we just consider PZT.

Computing an arithmetic formula's total degree is at least as hard as solving PZT, since PZT asks whether the total degree is $-\infty$. PIT and PZT are promise problems because algorithms need to work when the input formulas have total degree $\leq p/3$, but need not check whether the latter holds.

PIT and PZT are not known to be in P. A multivariate arithmetic formula's canonical-form polynomial may be exponentially large—for example, $(x_1+1)(x_2+1)\cdots(x_n+1)$ has 2^n monomials—so expanding a formula takes exponential time and space. Evaluating a formula on all p^n assignments takes poly space but still exponential time.

Evaluating φ on a single assignment $(a_1,\ldots,a_n)$ takes $O(N)$ time like in the univariate setting. Thus we have a $O(N)$-time randomized algorithm for PZT: Pick a uniformly random assignment, evaluate φ on it, and accept iff φ evaluates to 0. If φ is identically zero, then the algorithm accepts with probability 1. Otherwise, φ has at most $(p/3)p^{n-1}$ roots (Lemma 7.1), so the algorithm accepts (errs) with probability $\leq (p/3)p^{n-1}/p^n = 1/3$. Since the mapping reduction from PIT to PZT takes $O(N)$ time, we also get a $O(N)$-time randomized algorithm for PIT.

7.1.3 The Random Subsum Principle

In this section, we prove a lemma that we use to analyze a randomized algorithm in the next section. We also use it many more times throughout this book—the random subsum principle is a gift that keeps on giving.

In the field $\mathbb{Z}_2 = \{0,1\}$, addition and subtraction are both "xor," and multiplication is "and." We view bit strings $v \in \{0,1\}^n$ and $w \in \{0,1\}^n$ as vectors over $\mathbb{Z}_2$, so all arithmetic is mod 2 here:

- $v \oplus w \in \{0,1\}^n$ is the componentwise sum (bitwise xor): $(v \oplus w)_i = v_i \oplus w_i$ for all i.
- $v \ominus w \in \{0,1\}^n$ is the componentwise difference, which equals $v \oplus w$ over $\mathbb{Z}_2$.
- $v \odot w \in \{0,1\}$ is the dot product: $v \odot w = v_1 w_1 \oplus v_2 w_2 \oplus \cdots \oplus v_n w_n$.
  We have $v \odot w = 1$ iff $v_i = w_i = 1$ for an odd number of indices i. The word "subsum" comes from $v \odot w = \sum_{i\,:\,w_i=1} v_i$ (the 1s of w indicate which bits of v to sum).

We could use $+, -, \cdot$, but we prefer the circled notation $\oplus, \ominus, \odot$ when the field is $\mathbb{Z}_2$.

Linearity means $(v \oplus w) \odot x = (v \odot x) \oplus (w \odot x)$ for all $v, w, x \in \{0,1\}^n$:

$$\textstyle\sum_i (v_i \oplus w_i) x_i \;=\; \sum_i (v_i x_i \oplus w_i x_i) \;=\; \left(\sum_i v_i x_i\right) \oplus \left(\sum_i w_i x_i\right)$$

$0^n = 00 \cdots 0$ denotes the vector of n many 0s. (This is not exponentiation.)

Lemma 7.2. *Assuming $x \in \{0,1\}^n$ is sampled uniformly at random:*

(i) $\mathbf{Pr}[v \odot x = 0] = 1/2$ *for all $v \in \{0,1\}^n$ such that $v \neq 0^n$.*

(ii) $\mathbf{Pr}[v \odot x = w \odot x] = 1/2$ *for all $v, w \in \{0,1\}^n$ such that $v \neq w$.*

Proof. *(i)*: Let i be an index such that $v_i = 1$ (it doesn't matter which one). Consider any *partners* $y, z \in \{0,1\}^n$, meaning $y_i \neq z_i$ and $y_j = z_j$ for all $j \neq i$. Then $y \ominus z$ has a 1 at index i and 0s everywhere else. By linearity, $(v \odot y) \ominus (v \odot z) = v \odot (y \ominus z) = v_i = 1$. This means $v \odot y \neq v \odot z$, so exactly one of them is 0. Partitioning $\{0,1\}^n$ into partner pairs, we see that $v \odot x = 0$ for exactly half of all $x \in \{0,1\}^n$.

Another perspective: Instead of thinking of x as randomly selecting which bits of v to sum, think of v as deterministically selecting which bits of x to sum. The xor of some uniformly random, fully independent bits is uniformly random, so it's 0 with probability $1/2$.

(ii): If $v \neq w$ then $v \ominus w \neq 0^n$, so by linearity and *(i)*:

$$\mathbf{Pr}[v \odot x = w \odot x] \;=\; \mathbf{Pr}\big[(v \odot x) \ominus (w \odot x) = 0\big] \;=\; \mathbf{Pr}\big[(v \ominus w) \odot x = 0\big] \;=\; 1/2 \qquad \blacksquare$$

7.1.4 Verifying Matrix Multiplication

Matrix Multiplication is a function problem of great practical importance: Given $n \times n$ matrices A and B, the goal is to compute AB, which is the $n \times n$ matrix whose entry in row i and column j is $(AB)_{i,j} = \sum_{k=1}^{n} A_{i,k} B_{k,j}$ (the dot product of row i of A and column j of B). A straightforward algorithm computes AB by looping over all n^2 possibilities of (i,j) and evaluating the dot product by looping over all n possibilities of k. This takes time $O(n^3) = O(N^{1.5})$ where $N = 2n^2$ is the input size, assuming each number fits in a word. Much more sophisticated algorithms run in time $O(n^{2.38}) = O(N^{1.19})$. It's unknown whether matrices can be multiplied in nearly-linear time.

Consider the decision problem of verifying matrix multiplication: The input also includes a matrix C, and the goal is to check whether C is the product AB. We just consider the field $\mathbb{Z}_2$, though what we're about to do works over any field (Exercise 7.3).

Matrix Multiplication Verification	(7.8)
Input: $n \times n$ matrices A, B, C over $\mathbb{Z}_2$	
Output: Does $AB = C$?	

A straightforward deterministic algorithm computes AB using a Matrix Multiplication algorithm and then compares AB to C. We solve Matrix Multiplication Verification faster using randomization. Think of AB and C as functions that map a column vector x to the column vectors $(AB)x$ and Cx. Like POLYNOMIAL IDENTITY TESTING, we test whether these functions are identical by plugging in a random x and checking that $(AB)x = Cx$. We compute Cx straightforwardly by the definition of matrix-vector product. What about computing $(AB)x$? Trying to compute AB (and then multiply it by x) would bring us back to where we started. Instead, we exploit associativity: $(AB)x = A(Bx)$. We compute Bx and then $A(Bx)$, using two matrix-vector products.

Algorithm for MATRIX MULTIPLICATION VERIFICATION (7.9)

pick a column vector $x \in \{0,1\}^n$ uniformly at random
compute $u \leftarrow Bx$ and $v \leftarrow Au$ and $w \leftarrow Cx$
if $v = w$: accept
else: reject

To compute a matrix-vector product such as $u = Bx$: An outer loop over i computes each $u_i = B_i \odot x = \sum_{j=1}^{n} B_{i,j} x_j$ (the dot product of row i of B and x) using an inner loop over j. This takes $O(n^2) = O(N)$ time for each matrix-vector product. Comparing v and w takes $O(n)$ time. Thus this algorithm has time efficiency $O(N)$.

Why is this algorithm correct? If $AB = C$ then:

$$\mathbf{Pr}[\text{algorithm accepts}] = \mathbf{Pr}[v = w] = \mathbf{Pr}\big[(AB)x = Cx\big] = 1$$

If $AB \neq C$ then some row i of AB is different from row i of C, so by the random subsum principle (Lemma 7.2.*(ii)*) applied to the vectors $(AB)_i \neq C_i$:

$$\mathbf{Pr}[\text{algorithm accepts}] = \mathbf{Pr}[v = w] \leq \mathbf{Pr}[v_i = w_i] = \mathbf{Pr}\big[(AB)_i \odot x = C_i \odot x\big] = 1/2$$

Error probability $1/2$ sounds unimpressive since we could achieve that by just outputting a uniformly random bit. But the error probability is $1/2$ only when $AB \neq C$, and is 0 when $AB = C$. We can decrease the error probability by *amplification*: Run the algorithm twice—where the second run's x is independent of the first run's x—and accept iff both runs accept. If $AB = C$ then the acceptance probability is $1 \cdot 1 = 1$, and if $AB \neq C$ then the acceptance (error) probability is $\leq (1/2) \cdot (1/2) = 1/4$.

7.2 The Model and Complexity Classes

7.2.1 The Model of Randomized Computation

A randomized program can "toss a coin" repeatedly to generate random bits. Each toss yields 1 (heads) with probability 1/2, and 0 (tails) with probability 1/2. The tosses are fully independent.

We augment our model of computation with a *randomness segment* filled with the outcomes of all coin tosses. The instruction "read-rand Reg[i]" puts the randomness segment's next unread word into Reg[i], like "read-witness Reg[i]" for a streaming verifier (§3.3.1). Thus a program with word size W can get W coin tosses per time step. We could allow "read-rand Reg[i] $\leftarrow$ Rand[Reg[j]]" but there's no reason to read the randomness segment's words out of order. Unless Reg[j] contains an address that was previously read from, "read-rand" would get a fresh random word, which might as well be from the next unread address.

A word of the randomness segment is a uniformly random binary number in $\{0,1,\ldots,2^W-1\}$. What if we want a uniformly random number in another range such as $\{0,1,\ldots,m-1\}$ (where

$m \le 2^W$) as in our POLYNOMIAL IDENTITY TESTING algorithm? If m is a power of 2 and $a \in \{0, \ldots, 2^W - 1\}$ is uniformly distributed, then $(a \bmod m) \in \{0, \ldots, m-1\}$ is uniformly distributed (a's least significant $\log m$ bits). Assuming m isn't a power of 2, we divide 2^W by m to decompose $2^W = qm + r$ where $q \ge 1$ is the quotient and $r = (2^W \bmod m) \in \{1, \ldots, m-1\}$ is the remainder. If we condition on the event $a < qm$, then $(a \bmod m) \in \{0, \ldots, m-1\}$ is uniformly distributed because for each $i \in \{0, \ldots, m-1\}$, we have $(a \bmod m) = i$ for q many values of $a < qm$, namely $i, m+i, 2m+i, \ldots, (q-1)m+i$, so $\mathbf{Pr}\big[(a \bmod m) = i \,\big|\, a < qm\big] = q/qm = 1/m$. We have $\mathbf{Pr}[a \ge qm] = r/2^W < m/2^W$, which is small if we use a large enough word size W, and in this event a program can just abort (give up and terminate). This small contribution to the error probability generally won't matter, as we'll see in §7.3. In summary, a program can get perfectly uniform samples from $\{0, \ldots, m-1\}$, with a small probability of aborting.

Randomness is a computational resource. When designing randomized algorithms, we assume an unlimited number of uniformly random bits are available. But in practice, we can't take this for granted. Physical sources of randomness, such as keystroke timing or noise in microscopic phenomena, yield a limited number of bits, which might not be uniformly distributed—individual bits might be biased, or the bits might not be independent. To run randomized algorithms, we need to turn such a source into many bits that are "as good as uniform" (Chapter 11). Our idealized model decouples "obtaining good randomness" and "using it in algorithms."

7.2.2 Randomized Complexity Classes

$\Pi(x; r)$ denotes a randomized program Π running on input x with r in the randomness segment. We say Π solves a decision problem A with error probability ε (or that Π is an ε-error randomized program for A) iff for every valid input x, $\mathbf{Pr}_r\big[\Pi(x; r) \ne A(x)\big] \le \varepsilon$ and $\Pi(x; r)$ terminates for all r. The time efficiency $T(N)$ of Π is the maximum running time of $\Pi(x; r)$ over all valid x of size N and all r. If Π has time efficiency $\le T$ and word size W, we may assume $r \in (\{0,1\}^W)^T$.

Definition.

- $\mathsf{BPTIME}[T]$ is the set of all decision problems for which there exists a $1/3$-error randomized program with $O(T)$ time efficiency and $O(\log \max(T, N))$-bounded word size.
- $\mathsf{BPP} = \mathsf{BPTIME}[\text{poly}\, N]$ (Bounded-error Probabilistic Polynomial time) ◂

A decision problem is in BPP iff some poly-time randomized program accepts 1-inputs with probability $\ge 2/3$ and 0-inputs with probability $\le 1/3$. We have $\mathsf{P} \subseteq \mathsf{BPP}$, and BPP is closed under complement. Bounded-error means $\varepsilon < 1/2$ is a constant (bounded away from $1/2$). We'll see in §7.3 that $\mathsf{BPTIME}[T]$ and BPP don't depend on the constant ε as long as $0 < \varepsilon < 1/2$. The choice of $\varepsilon = 1/3$ is convenient but not special. If we allowed $\varepsilon = 1/2$, BPP would contain literally every decision problem by outputting a coin toss, which has error probability $1/2$ on every input (a "shot in the dark"). The complexity class PP (unbounded-error Probabilistic Polynomial time) is defined like BPP but only requiring $\mathbf{Pr}_r\big[\Pi(x; r) \ne A(x)\big] < 1/2$. Since an error probability like $1/2 - 1/2^N$ has miniscule advantage over outputting a coin toss, PP doesn't correspond to practical computations.

BPP allows *two-sided error*: A program may err (output the wrong bit) with probability $\le \varepsilon$ on both 1-inputs and 0-inputs. *One-sided error* means a program may err with probability $\le \varepsilon$ on 1-inputs but never errs on 0-inputs.

Definition.

- RTIME$[T]$ is the set of all decision problems for which there exists a 1/3-one-sided-error randomized program with $O(T)$ time efficiency and $O(\log \max(T, N))$-bounded word size.
- RP = RTIME$[\text{poly} N]$ (Randomized Polynomial time) ◀

Though "probabilistic" and "randomized" are synonyms, the latter word is used for one-sided error in complexity class names—an arbitrary convention.

A decision problem is in RP iff some poly-time randomized program accepts 1-inputs with probability $\geq 2/3$ and 0-inputs with probability 0. (So if the program outputs 1, then the correct output is definitely 1.) We have P $\subseteq$ RP $\subseteq$ BPP. We'll see in § 7.3 that RTIME$[T]$ and RP don't depend on the constant ε as long as $0 < \varepsilon < 1$.

RP $\subseteq$ NP by treating the randomness segment as the witness segment: A one-sided-error randomized program is a (streaming) verifier because on a 1-input, it accepts for at least one r (in fact, for most r), and on a 0-input, it accepts for no r. The haystack is either mostly needles or devoid of needles.

RP is not known to be closed under complement. A decision problem is in coRP iff some poly-time randomized program accepts 0-inputs with probability $\geq 2/3$ and 1-inputs with probability 0. Like coNP = Π_1P (Observation 4.17), we can swap acceptance and rejection: A decision problem is in coRP iff some poly-time randomized program accepts 1-inputs with probability 1 and 0-inputs with probability $\leq 1/3$. Thus coRP corresponds to erring on "the other side" (0-inputs rather than 1-inputs). We showed in § 7.1 that Polynomial Identity Testing and Matrix Multiplication Verification are in coRTIME$[N]$.

Zero-sided error sounds like an oxymoron, but it means a program never outputs the wrong bit but may *abort* with probability $\leq \varepsilon$ on both 1-inputs and 0-inputs. We augment the model with an "abort" instruction, which outputs a special symbol $\perp$ (pronounced *bottom*) meaning "I don't know." This is a lesser kind of error because a program admits that its output isn't correct.

Definition.

- ZPTIME$[T]$ is the set of all decision problems for which there exists a 1/3-zero-sided-error randomized program with $O(T)$ time efficiency and $O(\log \max(T, N))$-bounded word size.
- ZPP = ZPTIME$[\text{poly} N]$ (Zero-sided-error Probabilistic Polynomial time) ◀

A decision problem is in ZPP iff some poly-time randomized program accepts 1-inputs with probability $\geq 2/3$ and aborts with the remaining probability, and rejects 0-inputs with probability $\geq 2/3$ and aborts with the remaining probability. We have P $\subseteq$ ZPP, and ZPP is closed under complement.

Lemma 7.3. ZPP = RP $\cap$ coRP.

Proof. ZPP $\subseteq$ RP $\cap$ coRP: Suppose $A \in$ ZPP by a randomized program Π. Then $A \in$ RP by a randomized program that's Π but with "abort" replaced by "reject". Since ZPP is closed under complement, we also have $\overline{A} \in$ ZPP $\subseteq$ RP and thus $A \in$ coRP.

RP $\cap$ coRP $\subseteq$ ZPP: Suppose $A \in$ RP by a randomized program Π_1 and $\overline{A} \in$ RP by a randomized program Π_0. Then $A \in$ ZPP by this randomized program Π:

Zero-sided-error program for A using one-sided-error programs for A and $\overline{A}$	(7.10)
run Π_1 and Π_0 on the same input if Π_1 accepted: accept if Π_0 accepted: reject if neither accepted: abort	

(It doesn't matter whether Π uses the same or independent randomness for running Π_1 and Π_0.) It's impossible for both Π_1 and Π_0 to accept the same valid input. Π is correct because:

$$\begin{aligned} A(x)=1 &\Rightarrow \mathbf{Pr}\big[\Pi_1(x)\text{ accepts}\big] \geq 2/3 \text{ and } \mathbf{Pr}\big[\Pi_0(x)\text{ accepts}\big]=0 \\ &\Rightarrow \mathbf{Pr}\big[\Pi(x)\text{ accepts}\big] \geq 2/3 \text{ and } \mathbf{Pr}\big[\Pi(x)\text{ rejects}\big]=0 \\ A(x)=0 &\Rightarrow \mathbf{Pr}\big[\Pi_0(x)\text{ accepts}\big] \geq 2/3 \text{ and } \mathbf{Pr}\big[\Pi_1(x)\text{ accepts}\big]=0 \\ &\Rightarrow \mathbf{Pr}\big[\Pi(x)\text{ rejects}\big] \geq 2/3 \text{ and } \mathbf{Pr}\big[\Pi(x)\text{ accepts}\big]=0 \end{aligned}$$ ■

The same proof shows $\mathsf{ZPTIME}[T]=\mathsf{RTIME}[T]\cap\mathsf{coRTIME}[T]$ for all T. Thus $\mathsf{ZPTIME}[T]$ and ZPP (like $\mathsf{RTIME}[T]$ and RP) don't depend on the constant ε as long as $0<\varepsilon<1$.

In summary, $\mathsf{P} \subseteq \mathsf{ZPP} \subseteq \mathsf{RP} \subseteq \mathsf{BPP}$.

7.2.3 Derandomization

Most pairs of complexity classes are assumed to be unequal by default. Remarkably, for P and BPP, the prevailing belief is the opposite:

Conjecture 7.4. $\mathsf{P}=\mathsf{BPP}$.

We'll see evidence for this in Chapter 11. $\mathsf{P}=\mathsf{BPP}$ would mean randomness can only enable polynomial speedups—we could turn any randomized poly-time algorithm into a deterministic poly-time algorithm. It would imply that "sidedness" doesn't matter ($\mathsf{P}=\mathsf{ZPP}=\mathsf{RP}=\mathsf{BPP}$) and that RP is closed under complement (since P is).

$\mathsf{BPP} \subseteq \mathsf{PSPACE}$ holds by brute force, like $\mathsf{NP} \subseteq \mathsf{PSPACE}$ (Lemma 2.5): Suppose $A \in \mathsf{BPP}$ by a 1/3-error randomized program Π with time efficiency $\leq T = cN^d$ (for integers c,d) and word size W. A deterministic poly-space program can compute $A(x)$ by running $\Pi(x;r)$ for each $r \in (\{0,1\}^W)^T$ and accepting iff a majority of the runs accept, reusing the space from one run to the next.

Despite the widespread belief that $\mathsf{BPP}=\mathsf{P}$, nobody even knows how to prove $\mathsf{BPP} \neq \mathsf{NEXP}$.

Not many interesting problems are known to be in BPP but not known to be in P. Polynomial Identity Testing is the most famous such problem—it's in coRP but not known to be in ZPP. Historically, important randomized algorithms have often been *derandomized* by carefully replacing the random choices with deterministic choices that work just as well. It's unsurprising that this is possible if one believes $\mathsf{P}=\mathsf{BPP}$. A notable success story involves this problem:

Primality Testing	(7.11)
Input: Binary integer $x \geq 2$ Output: Is x prime?	

Primality Testing was first shown to be in coRP, and then in RP and therefore ZPP (Lemma 7.3), but those algorithms resisted attempts at poly-time derandomization. Years later,

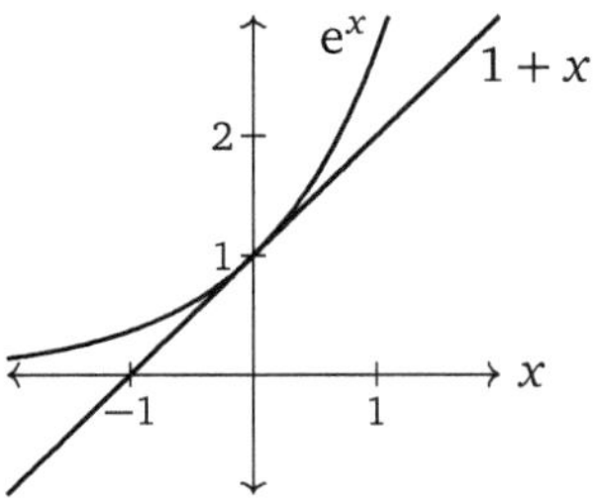

Figure 7.2: $1+x \leq e^x$

researchers discovered a new randomized algorithm, which soon succumbed to derandomization. Now, the theorem PRIMALITY TESTING $\in$ P is a landmark in computer science and mathematics. In practice, though, PRIMALITY TESTING is still usually solved with randomized algorithms, which are faster than the known deterministic algorithms. A tiny error probability is a small price to pay for the speedup.

7.3 Amplification

Amplification means modifying a randomized algorithm to increase its success probability. This tool is ubiquitous in randomized complexity theory.

7.3.1 One-Sided Error

Lemma 7.5. *If a coin with tails probability $\leq 1-\delta$ is tossed $n \geq \frac{1}{\delta}\ln\frac{1}{\varepsilon}$ times, then the probability that all tosses are tails is $\leq \varepsilon$.*

The natural logarithm (ln) arises from the handy observation that the plot of $1+x$ is entirely under the plot of e^x (Figure 7.2) where $e \approx 2.72$ (non-italic) is the base of the natural log:

Fact 7.6. $1+x \leq e^x$ *for every real number x.* ∎

Proof of Lemma 7.5. Since the tosses are fully independent and each toss is tails with probability $\leq 1-\delta$, the probability that all n tosses are tails is

$$\leq (1-\delta)^n \leq (e^{-\delta})^n \leq e^{-\delta\cdot\frac{1}{\delta}\ln\frac{1}{\varepsilon}} = e^{\ln\varepsilon} = \varepsilon$$

using Fact 7.6 with $x=-\delta$. ∎

For any decision problem A, we can turn any $(1-\delta)$-one-sided-error program Π into an ε-one-sided-error program Π' that runs Π at least $\frac{1}{\delta}\ln\frac{1}{\varepsilon}$ times—with fresh randomness for each run—and accepts iff at least one run accepts. This works because:

- If $A(x)=0$ then $\mathbf{Pr}\big[\Pi(x) \text{ accepts}\big]=0$, so $\mathbf{Pr}\big[\Pi'(x) \text{ accepts}\big]=0$.
- If $A(x)=1$ then $\mathbf{Pr}\big[\Pi(x) \text{ rejects}\big] \leq 1-\delta$, so each run of $\Pi(x)$ is like a coin toss with tails probability $\leq 1-\delta$ where tails $=$ reject and heads $=$ accept, so $\mathbf{Pr}\big[\Pi'(x) \text{ rejects}\big] = \mathbf{Pr}\big[\text{all tosses are tails}\big] \leq \varepsilon$.

If $\delta > 0$ and $\varepsilon > 0$ are constants (not functions of N), then $\frac{1}{\delta}\ln\frac{1}{\varepsilon}$ is a constant. We can decrease error probability from any constant < 1 to any constant > 0 with only a constant factor overhead in time. Thus $\mathsf{RTIME}[T]$ doesn't depend on the error probability as long as it's a constant strictly between 1 and 0, because this only affects the hidden constant in $O(T)$.

What if δ and ε depend on N? If $\delta \geq 1/\operatorname{poly} N$ and $\varepsilon \geq 1/2^{\operatorname{poly} N}$, then $\frac{1}{\delta}\ln\frac{1}{\varepsilon} \leq \operatorname{poly} N$. We can decrease error probability from $1 - 1/N^b$ to $1/2^{N^c}$ with only $O(N^{b+c})$ factor overhead in time. Thus RP doesn't depend on the error probability as long as it's between $1 - 1/\operatorname{poly} N$ and $1/2^{\operatorname{poly} N}$.

Errors are extraordinarily unlikely if the error probability is $\leq 1/2^{100}$, say. For practical purposes, such a randomized program may be deemed as reliable as a deterministic program.

7.3.2 Two-Sided Error

Lemma 7.7. *If a coin with tails probability $\leq \frac{1}{2} - \delta$ is tossed $n \geq \frac{1}{2\delta^2}\ln\frac{1}{\varepsilon}$ times where n is odd, then the probability that a majority of the tosses are tails is $\leq \varepsilon$.*

We assume n is odd so we never have to break a tie for determining the majority.

Proof. Assume the tails probability is exactly $\frac{1}{2} - \gamma$ where $\gamma \geq \delta$. Consider any particular outcome in which a majority, say $k > n/2$, of the tosses are tails. This outcome has probability $(\frac{1}{2}-\gamma)^k(\frac{1}{2}+\gamma)^{n-k}$ since there's a $\frac{1}{2}-\gamma$ factor for each tails and a $\frac{1}{2}+\gamma$ factor for each heads. To get a clean upper bound on this probability, first change some $\frac{1}{2}-\gamma$ factors to $\frac{1}{2}+\gamma$ factors until there are $\lceil\frac{n}{2}\rceil$ of the former and $\lfloor\frac{n}{2}\rfloor$ of the latter. To get a perfect balance, increase one $\frac{1}{2}-\gamma$ factor to $(\frac{1}{2}-\gamma)^{1/2}(\frac{1}{2}+\gamma)^{1/2}$. Thus each majority-tails outcome has probability:

$$\leq \left(\tfrac{1}{2}-\gamma\right)^{n/2}\left(\tfrac{1}{2}+\gamma\right)^{n/2} = \left(\tfrac{1}{4}-\gamma^2\right)^{n/2} \leq \left(\tfrac{1}{4}-\delta^2\right)^{n/2}$$

Summing over all majority-tails outcomes, of which there are $\leq 2^n = 4^{n/2}$ (the number of *all* possible outcomes), the probability that a majority of the tosses are tails is

$$\leq 4^{n/2}\left(\tfrac{1}{4}-\delta^2\right)^{n/2} = \left(1-4\delta^2\right)^{n/2} \leq \left(e^{-4\delta^2}\right)^{n/2} \leq e^{-4\delta^2\cdot\frac{1}{4\delta^2}\ln\frac{1}{\varepsilon}} = e^{\ln\varepsilon} = \varepsilon$$

using Fact 7.6 with $x = -4\delta^2$. ■

For any decision problem A, we can turn any $(\frac{1}{2}-\delta)$-error program Π into an ε-error program Π' that runs Π an odd number $\geq \frac{1}{2\delta^2}\ln\frac{1}{\varepsilon}$ of times—with fresh randomness for each run—and accepts iff a majority of the runs accept. This works because for every valid input x, each run of $\Pi(x)$ is like a coin toss with tails probability $\leq \frac{1}{2} - \delta$ where heads means the run outputs $A(x)$ and tails means the run errs, so $\mathbf{Pr}\big[\Pi'(x) \neq A(x)\big] = \mathbf{Pr}[\text{a majority of the tosses are tails}] \leq \varepsilon$.

If $\delta > 0$ and $\varepsilon > 0$ are constants, then $\frac{1}{2\delta^2}\ln\frac{1}{\varepsilon}$ is a constant. We can decrease error probability from any constant $< \frac{1}{2}$ to any constant > 0 with only a constant factor overhead in time. Thus $\mathsf{BPTIME}[T]$ doesn't depend on the error probability as long as it's a constant strictly between $\frac{1}{2}$ and 0, because this only affects the hidden constant in $O(T)$.

If $\delta \geq 1/\operatorname{poly} N$ and $\varepsilon \geq 1/2^{\operatorname{poly} N}$, then $\frac{1}{2\delta^2}\ln\frac{1}{\varepsilon} \leq \operatorname{poly} N$. We can decrease error probability from $\frac{1}{2} - 1/N^b$ to $1/2^{N^c}$ with only $O(N^{2b+c})$ factor overhead in time. Thus BPP doesn't depend on the error probability as long as it's between $\frac{1}{2} - 1/\operatorname{poly} N$ and $1/2^{\operatorname{poly} N}$.

Randomized programs for search problems generally aren't amenable to amplification. If $\mathbf{Pr}\big[\Pi(x) \text{ outputs an acceptable solution}\big] \geq 2/3$, there might not exist an acceptable solution z

such that $\mathbf{Pr}\big[\Pi(x) \text{ outputs } z\big] \geq 2/3$. Independent runs of $\Pi(x)$ might output different solutions, in which case how would we know which solution to output? If a deterministic poly-time program can check whether a solution is acceptable (say, if the goal is to find a witness for a verifier), then amplification is possible like in the one-sided-error setting: Π' runs Π multiple times independently and checks whether each run outputs an acceptable solution. Π' outputs an acceptable solution if it finds one, and rejects otherwise.

7.3.3 Reductions and Randomized Algorithms

For all decision problems A and B, if $A \leq_p^m B$ and $B \in \mathsf{BPP}$ then $A \in \mathsf{BPP}$ by a randomized program that runs the reduction to map input x to query y, then runs B's randomized program to output $B(y) = A(x)$ with probability $\geq 2/3$. This also works for one-sided error: If $A \leq_p^m B$ and $B \in \mathsf{RP}$ then $A \in \mathsf{RP}$. Handling oracle reductions is more involved for two-sided error and is not known to be possible for one-sided error.

Lemma 7.8. *For all decision problems A and B, if $A \leq_p^o B$ and $B \in \mathsf{BPP}$ then $A \in \mathsf{BPP}$.*

Proof idea. We want to solve A by running the reduction and using B's randomized program to answer each query. But B's program might answer a query incorrectly, which would derail the rest of the reduction:

- The reduction might make different queries and produce a different output than if all queries were answered correctly.
- It might not halt in poly time (or halt at all).
- It might make an invalid query, in which case B's program might not halt in poly time.

To make our program for A correct, we ensure that with high probability, all queries are answered correctly. By default, each query has $\leq 1/3$ error probability, which accumulates over multiple queries. To ensure the error probability is $\leq 1/3$ even after the accumulation, we amplify each query to have a very low error probability. The amount of amplification depends on A's input size, not on the query size.

To make our program for A efficient, we have an alarm clock abort the computation if it takes too long (which only happens if some query was answered incorrectly). ■

Proof. Let $\Pi_{A \leq B}$ be an oracle reduction from A to B that, on an input of size N, clocks itself so it halts within $T = aN^b$ steps (for integers a, b) regardless of whether the queries are answered correctly. Let Π_B be a $1/3$-error randomized program for B that, on an input of size M, clocks itself so it halts within $T'(M) = cM^d$ steps (for integers c, d) regardless of whether the input is valid. For valid inputs y, we can decrease $\Pi_B(y)$'s error probability from $1/3 = 1/2 - \delta$ to $\varepsilon = 1/3T$ by running it $13\log_2(3T) \geq 18\ln(3T) = \frac{1}{2\delta^2}\ln\frac{1}{\varepsilon}$ times and accepting iff a majority of the runs accept. We design a randomized program Π_A for A, which takes an input x of size N:

Randomized program for A using a randomized oracle for B	(7.12)
run $\Pi_{A \leq B}(x)$:	
answer each query y by running $\Pi_B(y)$, amplified to have error probability $\leq 1/3T$	
output the same bit as $\Pi_{A \leq B}(x)$ does	

$\Pi_{A \leq B}(x)$, and thus $\Pi_A(x)$, outputs $A(x)$ if each query is answered correctly. Say $\Pi_{A \leq B}(x)$ makes

$Q \le T$ many queries $y_1, y_2, \ldots, y_Q$ if they are answered correctly.

$$\begin{aligned}
&\mathbf{Pr}\big[\Pi_A(x) \neq A(x)\big] \\
\le\ &\mathbf{Pr}\big[\text{some query of } \Pi_{A\le B}(x) \text{ is answered incorrectly}\big] \\
=\ &\textstyle\sum_{i=1}^{Q} \mathbf{Pr}\big[y_1, \ldots, y_{i-1} \text{ are answered correctly but } y_i \text{ isn't}\big] \\
\le\ &\textstyle\sum_{i=1}^{Q} \mathbf{Pr}\big[y_i \text{ is answered incorrectly} \,\big|\, y_1, \ldots, y_{i-1} \text{ were answered correctly}\big] \\
=\ &\textstyle\sum_{i=1}^{Q} \mathbf{Pr}\big[\text{the amplified } \Pi_B(y_i) \text{ errs}\big] \\
\le\ &\textstyle\sum_{i=1}^{Q} 1/3T \;=\; Q/3T \;\le\; 1/3
\end{aligned}$$

The third line follows from the second by partitioning the event (that some query is answered incorrectly) according to which query is the first to be answered incorrectly. The fifth line follows from the fourth since the amplified $\Pi_B(y_i)$ uses fresh randomness, independent of the randomness for answering prior queries (though a similar argument would work even if we reused the randomness for answering each query).

Since $\Pi_{A\le B}$ takes $\le T$ steps, it makes $\le T$ queries, each of size $\le T$. On a query of size $M \le T$, the unamplified Π_B takes $\le T'(M) \le T'(T)$ steps, and the amplification incurs a factor $O(\log T)$ overhead in time. Thus Π_A has time efficiency $O\big(T + T \cdot T'(T) \cdot \log T\big) = O(N^{b+bd} \log N) \in$ poly$N$. ■

7.4 Derandomizing BPP

Let's make progress toward confirming the conjecture BPP = P. We saw BPP ⊆ PSPACE (§7.2.3), which also works for unbounded error: PP ⊆ PSPACE. Now, we'll see derandomization techniques that exploit bounded error.

7.4.1 Nonuniform Derandomization

Theorem 7.9. BPP ⊆ P/poly.

Proof idea. Consider a $1/3$-error randomized program. For every input of size N, most outcomes of the randomness are "good" (yield correct output). We want to "swap the quantifiers" to show that some outcome is good for every input of size N simultaneously, so this outcome can be advice. We just use amplification to make the error probability $< 1/(\text{number of inputs of size } N)$. This is the probabilistic method (§A.3.3): We prove a suitable outcome exists nonconstructively, without an efficient way to find such an outcome. ■

Proof. Suppose $A \in$ BPP and A has word size $W = O(\log N)$, so inputs of size N are in $(\{0,1\}^W)^N$. By amplification, A has a poly-time randomized program Π with error probability $< 2^{-NW}$. Say Π has time efficiency T and word size W'. For any input size N, the randomness r is uniformly distributed over $(\{0,1\}^{W'})^T$. For each valid input x of size N, let $B_x = \{r : \Pi(x;r) \neq A(x)\}$ be the "bad" event that Π errs on input x. There are at most 2^{NW} valid inputs x of size N, and $\mathbf{Pr}[B_x] < 2^{-NW}$ for each such x, so by a union bound:

$$\mathbf{Pr}\Big[\textstyle\bigcup_{\text{valid } x \text{ of size } N} B_x\Big] \le \textstyle\sum_{\text{valid } x \text{ of size } N} \mathbf{Pr}[B_x] < 2^{NW} \cdot 2^{-NW} = 1$$

Hence there exists an outcome $r \notin \bigcup_{\text{valid } x \text{ of size } N} B_x$, so $\Pi(x;r) = A(x)$ for every valid x of size N. Treating this r as advice for input size N (and adjusting Π to read r from the advice segment), we obtain a poly-time nonuniform program for A, so $A \in$ P/poly. ■

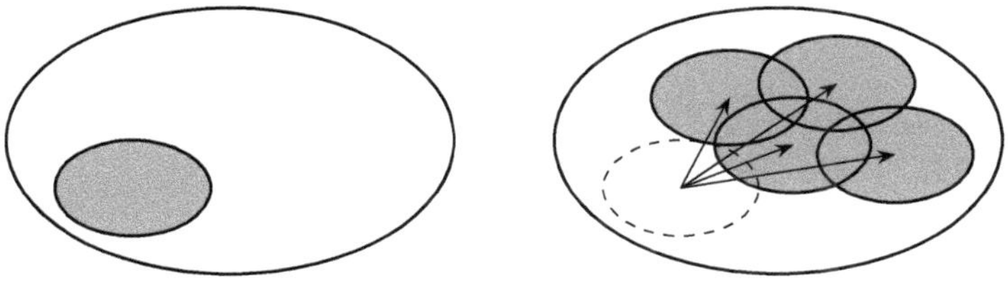

Figure 7.3: Union of shifts of a set of strings

7.4.2 Derandomization with Quantifiers

Theorem 7.10. $\mathsf{BPP} \subseteq \Sigma_2\mathsf{P}$.

Proof idea. *Shifting* a set $R \subseteq \{0,1\}^n$ by a string $s \in \{0,1\}^n$ means bitwise xoring each string in R with s, yielding the set $R \oplus s = \{r \oplus s : r \in R\} \subseteq \{0,1\}^n$ of the same size. For example:

$$\{011, 100, 111\} \oplus 101 = \{011 \oplus 101,\ 100 \oplus 101,\ 111 \oplus 101\} = \{110, 001, 010\}$$

Suppose $A \in \mathsf{BPP}$ by a randomized program Π. For an input x, let R_x be the event that $\Pi(x)$ accepts. Consider whether the union of a few shifts of R_x can cover the whole sample space:

If $A(x) = 0$ then R_x is quite small (after amplification), so the union of a few shifts of R_x can't be big enough to cover the whole space. Figure 7.3 illustrates this: The big ovals are the sample space. On the left, the shaded oval is R_x. On the right, the shaded ovals are shifts of R_x.

If $A(x) = 1$ then R_x is large, and we use the probabilistic method to prove the existence of a few shifts of R_x whose union covers the whole space: If we pick the shifts randomly, then each outcome of the sample space has very high probability of being in at least one of the shifts.

In summary, $A \in \Sigma_2\mathsf{P}$ because:

$$A(x) = 1 \iff (\exists \text{ a few shifts of } R_x)\ (\forall \text{ outcome } r)\ (r \text{ is in the union of the shifts}) \qquad \blacksquare$$

Proof. Suppose $A \in \mathsf{BPP}$, say $A \in \mathsf{BPTIME}[N^d]$ for an integer d. By amplification, A has a $1/N^{d+1}$-error randomized program Π with time efficiency $\le T = cN^d \log N$ (for an integer c) and log-bounded word size W. Define a 2-witness verifier $V(x; s; r)$:

- $s = (s_1, \ldots, s_k)$ where each $s_i \in (\{0,1\}^W)^T$ for $k = TW = O(N^d \log^2 N)$.
- $r \in (\{0,1\}^W)^T$.
- $V(x; s; r)$ runs $\Pi(x; r \oplus s_i)$ for each i and accepts iff at least one of these runs accepts.

To see that V is correct, we show that $A(x) = 1 \iff \big(\exists s\ \forall r : V(x; s; r) \text{ accepts}\big)$:

$\Leftarrow$: Assume $A(x) = 0$, so $\mathbf{Pr}_r\big[\Pi(x; r) \text{ accepts}\big] \le 1/N^{d+1}$. For every s:

$$\begin{aligned}
\mathbf{Pr}_r\big[V(x; s; r) \text{ accepts}\big] &= \mathbf{Pr}_r\big[\exists i : \Pi(x; r \oplus s_i) \text{ accepts}\big] && \text{(definition of } V\text{)} \\
&\le \textstyle\sum_i \mathbf{Pr}_r\big[\Pi(x; r \oplus s_i) \text{ accepts}\big] && \text{(union bound)} \\
&\le \textstyle\sum_i 1/N^{d+1} && (r \oplus s_i \text{ is uniformly distributed}) \\
&= k/N^{d+1} \le 1/3 < 1 && \text{(assuming } N \text{ is large enough)}
\end{aligned}$$

Thus $\forall s\ \exists r : V(x; s; r)$ rejects.

$\Rightarrow$: Assume $A(x) = 1$, so $\mathbf{Pr}_r\big[\Pi(x;r) \text{ rejects}\big] \le 1/N^{d+1} \le 1/3$. For uniformly random s:

$$\begin{aligned}
\mathbf{Pr}_s\big[\exists r : V(x;s;r) \text{ rejects}\big] &\le \textstyle\sum_r \mathbf{Pr}_s\big[V(x;s;r) \text{ rejects}\big] && \text{(union bound)}\\
&= \textstyle\sum_r \mathbf{Pr}_s\big[\forall i : \Pi(x;r\oplus s_i) \text{ rejects}\big] && \text{(definition of } V)\\
&= \textstyle\sum_r \prod_i \mathbf{Pr}_{s_i}\big[\Pi(x;r\oplus s_i) \text{ rejects}\big] && (s_1,\dots,s_k \text{ are independent})\\
&\le \textstyle\sum_r \prod_i 1/3 && (r\oplus s_i \text{ is uniformly distributed})\\
&= 2^{TW}/3^k \le 1/3 < 1 && \text{(assuming } N \text{ is large enough)}
\end{aligned}$$

Thus $\exists s\ \forall r : V(x;s;r)$ accepts.

Since V has time efficiency $O(kT)$, we have $A \in \Sigma_2\mathsf{TIME}[N^{2d}\log^3 N] \subseteq \Sigma_2\mathsf{P}$. ∎

Since BPP is closed under complement, we also have $\mathsf{BPP} \subseteq \Pi_2\mathsf{P}$.

7.5 Implications of Randomized Algorithms for NP

Can randomness help us solve NP-complete problems efficiently? Not if we believe $\mathsf{NP} \ne \mathsf{P} = \mathsf{BPP}$. Also not if we believe the polynomial hierarchy doesn't collapse: $\mathsf{NP} \subseteq \mathsf{BPP}$ implies $\mathsf{NP} \subseteq \mathsf{P/poly}$ (Theorem 7.9) implies $\mathsf{PH} = \Sigma_2\mathsf{P}$ (Theorem 5.5).

In this section, we prove that the assumption $\mathsf{NP} \subseteq \mathsf{BPP}$ is "self-strengthening" in two ways: We can improve the right side from BPP to RP, or we can improve the left side from NP to PH. This yields an elegant equivalence: NP collapses to RP iff PH collapses to BPP.

7.5.1 NP Collapses to RP

Theorem 7.11. $\mathsf{NP} \subseteq \mathsf{BPP}$ *iff* $\mathsf{NP} = \mathsf{RP}$.

Proof idea. Two-sided-error randomized algorithms for NP-complete problems might as well have one-sided error, because a search-to-decision reduction can prevent mistakes on 0-inputs. We reject if the reduction doesn't find a witness, so we always reject if no witness exists. ∎

Proof. $\Leftarrow$: If $\mathsf{NP} = \mathsf{RP}$ then $\mathsf{NP} \subseteq \mathsf{RP} \subseteq \mathsf{BPP}$.

$\Rightarrow$: Assume $\mathsf{NP} \subseteq \mathsf{BPP}$. To show $\mathsf{NP} = \mathsf{RP}$, it suffices to show SAT $\in$ RP since SAT is NP-complete. We have SAT SEARCH $\le_p^o$ SAT (Theorem 2.14) and SAT $\in$ BPP, so SAT SEARCH has a poly-time randomized algorithm that outputs a satisfying assignment with probability $\ge 2/3$ if one exists (by the same proof as Lemma 7.8).

One-sided-error randomized algorithm for SAT assuming $\mathsf{NP} \subseteq \mathsf{BPP}$ (7.13)

on input φ:
    run the randomized algorithm for SAT SEARCH on input φ
    if it output an assignment that satisfies φ: accept
    if it rejected or output an assignment that doesn't satisfy φ: reject

This poly-time algorithm accepts with probability $\ge 2/3$ if φ is satisfiable and with probability 0 if φ is unsatisfiable, so SAT $\in$ RP. ∎

7.5.2 PH Collapses to BPP

Efficient algorithms for NP collapse the polynomial hierarchy:

- If $\mathsf{NP} \subseteq \mathsf{P}$ then $\mathsf{PH} \subseteq \mathsf{P}$ (Theorem 4.21).
- If $\mathsf{NP} \subseteq \mathsf{BPP}$ then $\mathsf{PH} \subseteq \mathsf{BPP}$ (we prove this now).
- If $\mathsf{NP} \subseteq \mathsf{P/poly}$ then $\mathsf{PH} \subseteq \Sigma_2\mathsf{P}$ (Theorem 5.5).

The BPP result is intermediate between the other two since $\mathsf{P} \subseteq \mathsf{BPP} \subseteq \mathsf{P/poly}$ (Theorem 7.9) and $\mathsf{P} \subseteq \mathsf{BPP} \subseteq \Sigma_2\mathsf{P}$ (Theorem 7.10).

Theorem 7.12. $\mathsf{NP} \subseteq \mathsf{BPP}$ *iff* $\mathsf{PH} = \mathsf{BPP}$.

Proof idea. Like in the proof that if $\mathsf{NP} \subseteq \mathsf{P}$ then $\mathsf{PH} \subseteq \mathsf{P}$, we use the hypothesis $\mathsf{NP} \subseteq \mathsf{BPP}$ to peel off quantifiers one at a time. We treat the last quantifier as a verifier and turn it into a randomized algorithm. Unfortunately, this turns the second-to-last quantifier into a randomized verifier, rather than a deterministic verifier, so we can't immediately apply the hypothesis $\mathsf{NP} \subseteq \mathsf{BPP}$ to it. Fortunately, a heaping helping of amplification gets the randomness "out of the way," exposing the second-to-last quantifier so we can apply the hypothesis to it. We repeat this process for all the quantifiers: amplify, then swap randomness and quantifier, then use hypothesis to turn quantifier into even more randomness. ■

Proof. $\Leftarrow$: If $\mathsf{PH} = \mathsf{BPP}$ then $\mathsf{NP} \subseteq \mathsf{PH} \subseteq \mathsf{BPP}$.

$\Rightarrow$: Assume $\mathsf{NP} \subseteq \mathsf{BPP}$ and thus also $\mathsf{coNP} \subseteq \mathsf{BPP}$, since BPP is closed under complement. Since $\mathsf{BPP} \subseteq \mathsf{PH}$ (Theorem 7.10), it suffices to prove $\mathsf{PH} \subseteq \mathsf{BPP}$. We first prove $\Sigma_2\mathsf{P} \subseteq \mathsf{BPP}$, and we later explain how the proof generalizes to all levels of PH. Suppose $A \in \Sigma_2\mathsf{P}$ by a 2-witness verifier V with time efficiency $\leq T = cN^d$ (for integers c, d) and log-bounded word size W:

$$A(x) = 1 \iff \big(\exists w_1\ \forall w_2 :\ V(x; w_1; w_2) \text{ accepts}\big)$$

FINAL ∀ OF V (call this problem B, with input size M)	(7.14)
Input: x, w_1 where $x \in (\{0,1\}^W)^N$ is a valid input to A, and $w_1 \in (\{0,1\}^W)^T$	
Output: Is it true that for all $w_2 \in (\{0,1\}^W)^T$, $V(x; w_1; w_2)$ accepts?	

$B \in \Pi_1\mathsf{P} = \mathsf{coNP}$ by a verifier U where $U(x, w_1; w_2)$ runs $V(x; w_1; w_2)$. So by assumption, $B \in \mathsf{BPP}$. By amplification, B has a randomized program Π with error probability $\varepsilon = 2^{-TW}/6$, time efficiency $\leq T' = c'M^{d'}$ (for integers c', d'), and log-bounded word size W'.

$$\begin{aligned}
A(x) = 1 &\Rightarrow \exists w_1 :\ B(x, w_1) = 1 \\
&\Rightarrow \exists w_1 :\ \mathbf{Pr}_r\big[\Pi(x, w_1; r) \text{ accepts}\big] \geq 1 - \varepsilon \geq 5/6 \\
&\Rightarrow \mathbf{Pr}_r\big[\exists w_1 :\ \Pi(x, w_1; r) \text{ accepts}\big] \geq 5/6 \\
&\Rightarrow \mathbf{Pr}_r\big[C(x, r) = 1\big] \geq 5/6 \qquad \text{(where } C \text{ is defined below)}
\end{aligned}$$

$$\begin{aligned}
A(x) = 0 &\Rightarrow \forall w_1 :\ B(x, w_1) = 0 \\
&\Rightarrow \forall w_1 :\ \mathbf{Pr}_r\big[\Pi(x, w_1; r) \text{ accepts}\big] \leq \varepsilon \\
&\Rightarrow \mathbf{Pr}_r\big[\exists w_1 :\ \Pi(x, w_1; r) \text{ accepts}\big] \leq 2^{TW} \cdot \varepsilon = 1/6 \qquad \text{(union bound)} \\
&\Rightarrow \mathbf{Pr}_r\big[C(x, r) = 1\big] \leq 1/6 \qquad \text{(where } C \text{ is defined below)}
\end{aligned}$$

In summary, $\mathbf{Pr}_r\big[C(x,r) \neq A(x)\big] \leq 1/6$ for every valid input x.

(call this problem C, with input size L)	(7.15)
Input: x, r where $x \in (\{0,1\}^W)^N$ is a valid input to A, and $r \in (\{0,1\}^{W'})^{T'}$	
Output: Does there exist $w_1 \in (\{0,1\}^W)^T$ such that $\Pi(x, w_1; r)$ accepts?	

$C \in \mathsf{NP}$ by a verifier U' where $U'(x,r;w_1)$ runs $\Pi(x,w_1;r)$. So by assumption, $C \in \mathsf{BPP}$. By amplification, C has a 1/6-error poly-time randomized program Π'.

Define a randomized program $\Pi''(x;r,q)$ that samples r and q independently and runs $\Pi'(x,r;q)$. This Π'' solves A with error probability 1/3 because for every valid input x:

$$\begin{aligned}
\mathbf{Pr}_{r,q}\big[\Pi''(x;r,q) \neq A(x)\big] &= \mathbf{Pr}_{r,q}\big[\Pi'(x,r;q) \neq A(x)\big] \\
&\leq \mathbf{Pr}_{r,q}\big[\Pi'(x,r;q) \neq C(x,r) \text{ or } C(x,r) \neq A(x)\big] \\
&\leq \max_r\big(\mathbf{Pr}_q\big[\Pi'(x,r;q) \neq C(x,r)\big]\big) + \mathbf{Pr}_r\big[C(x,r) \neq A(x)\big] \\
&\leq \max_r(1/6) + 1/6 \\
&= 1/3
\end{aligned}$$

Also, Π'' has time efficiency $\operatorname{poly} L = \operatorname{poly} N$. Hence $A \in \mathsf{BPP}$.

The same argument works for all higher levels of PH as well: $\Sigma_2\mathsf{P} \subseteq \mathsf{BPP}$ implies $\Sigma_3\mathsf{P} \subseteq \mathsf{BPP}$ implies $\Sigma_4\mathsf{P} \subseteq \mathsf{BPP}$ and so on. To see this, assume $\Sigma_\ell\mathsf{P} \subseteq \mathsf{BPP}$ and thus also $\Pi_\ell\mathsf{P} \subseteq \mathsf{BPP}$. Suppose $A \in \Sigma_{\ell+1}\mathsf{P}$ by an $(\ell+1)$-witness verifier V. Letting $B = $ FINAL $\forall\exists\cdots$ OF V, we have $B \in \Pi_\ell\mathsf{P} \subseteq \mathsf{BPP}$, so we can show $A \in \mathsf{BPP}$ in the same way as before—by amplifying a randomized program for B enough that the randomness can be swapped with $\exists w_1$, and using $\mathsf{NP} \subseteq \mathsf{BPP}$ to turn $\exists w_1$ into more randomness. ∎

7.6 Concentration Bounds

A random variable associates a number to each outcome in a probability space. For example, if a randomized program Π always halts on input y, then the running time of $\Pi(y)$ is a random variable X, where $X(r)$ is the running time of $\Pi(y;r)$.

Suppose a probability space has distribution D over sample space S. A random variable is a function $X : S \to \mathbb{R}$. For each $x \in \mathbb{R}$, the event "$X = x$" is $X^{-1}(x) = \{s \in S : X(s) = x\}$. The expectation of X is $\mathbf{E}[X] = \sum_x \mathbf{Pr}[X = x] \cdot x$, which is intuitively the "center" of the distribution $X(D)$ over $\mathbb{R}$. But we can't always "expect" a sample from X to be near the expectation: If $\mathbf{Pr}[X = 100] = 1/2 = \mathbf{Pr}[X = -100]$, then X's value is never close to $\mathbf{E}[X] = 0$.

Concentration bounds state that some kinds of random variables are "concentrated" around their expectation, meaning the random variable's value is probably close to the expectation. We now prove three concentration bounds, which are useful for analyzing randomized algorithms.

7.6.1 Nonnegative Random Variables

A random variable $X : S \to \mathbb{R}$ is *nonnegative* iff $X(s) \geq 0$ for all $s \in S$.

Lemma 7.13. $\mathbf{Pr}[X \geq t] \leq \mathbf{E}[X]/t$ *for every nonnegative random variable X and every $t > 0$.*

Proof. Round each value $x < t$ down to 0, and round each value $x \geq t$ down to t:

$$\mathbf{E}[X] = \textstyle\sum_x \mathbf{Pr}[X = x] \cdot x \geq \sum_{x<t} \mathbf{Pr}[X = x] \cdot 0 + \sum_{x \geq t} \mathbf{Pr}[X = x] \cdot t = \mathbf{Pr}[X \geq t] \cdot t \qquad ∎$$

Lemma 7.13 implies that a nonnegative random variable's value is unlikely to be far above the expectation: If $\mathbf{E}[X] > 0$ and $k > 1$ then $\mathbf{Pr}\big[X \geq k \cdot \mathbf{E}[X]\big] \leq \mathbf{E}[X]/(k \cdot \mathbf{E}[X]) = 1/k$.

Application: "poly running time in expectation" might as well be "poly running time always":

Theorem 7.14. *$A \in$ BPP if A has a bounded-error randomized program that has* poly$N$ *running time in expectation (for every valid input) and log-bounded word size.*

Proof. Suppose Π is such a $1/3$-error randomized program for A, with $\mathbf{E}[\text{running time}] \leq T = cN^d$ (for integers c, d) for every valid input of size N. An alarm clock can prematurely stop Π in the unlikely event that it runs too long:

Always-efficient randomized program for A	(7.16)
$\Pi'(x; r)$:	
run $\Pi(x; r)$ for $10T$ steps	
if it halted within $10T$ steps: output the same bit as $\Pi(x; r)$	
else: output an arbitrary bit	

Π' always halts in $O(T)$ time, and it could err if Π either errs or runs too long:

$$\begin{aligned}
\mathbf{Pr}\big[\Pi'(x) \neq A(x)\big] &\leq \mathbf{Pr}\big[\Pi(x) \neq A(x) \text{ or } \Pi(x)\text{'s running time} > 10T\big] \\
&\leq \mathbf{Pr}\big[\Pi(x) \neq A(x)\big] + \mathbf{Pr}\big[\Pi(x)\text{'s running time} > 10T\big] && \text{(union bound)} \\
&\leq 1/3 + \mathbf{E}\big[\Pi(x)\text{'s running time}\big]/10T && \text{(Lemma 7.13)} \\
&\leq 1/3 + 1/10 \ < \ 0.44
\end{aligned}$$

Thus $A \in$ BPP by amplification. ■

Similarly, we characterize ZPP with programs that never abort but sometimes take more than polynomial time:

Theorem 7.15. *$A \in$ ZPP iff A has a randomized program that always outputs the correct bit and has* poly$N$ *running time in expectation (for every valid input) and log-bounded word size.*

Proof. $\Leftarrow$: Suppose Π is such a randomized program for A, with $\mathbf{E}[\text{running time}] \leq T = cN^d$ (for integers c, d) for every valid input of size N. Then $A \in$ ZPP by a randomized program that runs Π for $3T$ steps, outputs the same bit as Π if it halted within $3T$ steps, and otherwise aborts. This program always halts in $O(T)$ time, never outputs the wrong bit since Π never does, and aborts with probability $\mathbf{Pr}[\Pi\text{'s running time} > 3T] \leq \mathbf{E}[\Pi\text{'s running time}]/3T \leq 1/3$ for every valid input of size N (Lemma 7.13).

$\Rightarrow$: Suppose $A \in$ ZPP by a $1/3$-zero-sided-error randomized program Π. Consider a randomized program Π' that runs Π repeatedly (with fresh randomness for each run) until Π doesn't abort, and then outputs the same bit as Π. Each run of Π is like a coin toss with heads probability $p \geq 2/3$ where tails = abort. The number of runs of Π until it doesn't abort (number of coin tosses until getting a heads) is a geometric random variable with parameter p, which has expectation $1/p \leq 3/2$ (Lemma A.11). Since each run of Π takes poly$N$ time, $\mathbf{E}[\text{running time of } \Pi'] \leq (3/2) \cdot \text{poly}N \leq \text{poly}N$. The output of Π' is correct with probability 1 since the output of Π is correct whenever it doesn't abort. This doesn't quite mean the output of Π' is always correct, since Π' may (albeit with probability 0) run forever and produce no output, if every run of Π aborts. Let's fix this: In the extremely unlikely event that Π' runs way too long, we shut it down and resort to brute force. Suppose Π has time efficiency $\leq T = cN^d$ (for integers c, d) and word size W.

Always-correct randomized program for A (7.17)
$\Pi''(x)$:
repeat TW times:
run $\Pi(x)$ with fresh randomness
if it didn't abort: output the same bit
for each $r \in (\{0,1\}^W)^T$:
run $\Pi(x; r)$
if it didn't abort: output the same bit

$\Pi''(x)$ always outputs $A(x)$ since $\Pi(x)$ outputs $A(x)$ when it doesn't abort, and $\Pi(x)$ doesn't always abort. Let X be the running time of $\Pi''(x)$. Let B be the event that $\Pi''(x)$ halts in the first loop, so $\mathbf{Pr}[\overline{B}] \leq 3^{-TW}$ since $\Pi(x)$ aborts with probability $\leq 1/3$. By the law of total expectation:

$$\begin{aligned} \mathbf{E}[X] &= \mathbf{Pr}[B] \cdot \mathbf{E}[X \mid B] + \mathbf{Pr}[\overline{B}] \cdot \mathbf{E}[X \mid \overline{B}] \\ &\leq 1 \cdot \big((3/2) \cdot O(T)\big) + 3^{-TW} \cdot \big((TW + 2^{TW}) \cdot O(T)\big) \;\leq\; O(T) \end{aligned}$$ ■

7.6.2 Variance

Variance quantifies how concentrated a random variable is. A low-variance random variable is concentrated around its expectation. A high-variance one is spread out—its value "varies" a lot.

The *variance* of X is $\mathbf{Var}[X] = \mathbf{E}\big[(X - \mathbf{E}[X])^2\big]$. The square "penalizes" values of X that are far from $\mathbf{E}[X]$ much more than it penalizes values close to $\mathbf{E}[X]$. Figure 7.4 shows an example.

The following concentration bound will be useful in Chapter 8. It concerns $\big|X - \mathbf{E}[X]\big|$, which is the distance between X's value and its expectation.

Lemma 7.16. $\mathbf{Pr}\big[\big|X - \mathbf{E}[X]\big| \geq d\big] \leq \mathbf{Var}[X]/d^2$ *for every random variable X and every $d > 0$.*

Proof. A square is always nonnegative, so by Lemma 7.13:

$$\mathbf{Pr}\big[\big|X - \mathbf{E}[X]\big| \geq d\big] \;=\; \mathbf{Pr}\big[(X - \mathbf{E}[X])^2 \geq d^2\big] \;\leq\; \mathbf{E}\big[(X - \mathbf{E}[X])^2\big]/d^2 \;=\; \mathbf{Var}[X]/d^2$$ ■

Let's develop tools for calculating variance. Here, $\mathbf{E}[X]^2$ means $(\mathbf{E}[X])^2$.

Lemma 7.17. $\mathbf{Var}[X] = \mathbf{E}[X^2] - \mathbf{E}[X]^2$ *for every random variable X.*

Proof. First, we clarify some potential sources of confusion. We can view a number as a constant random variable, so $\mathbf{E}[7] = 7$, for example. Since $\mathbf{E}[X]^2$ is just a number, we have $\mathbf{E}\big[\mathbf{E}[X]^2\big] = \mathbf{E}[X]^2$. Also, linearity of expectation tells us $\mathbf{E}[7X] = 7\mathbf{E}[X]$, for example. Since $\mathbf{E}[X]$ is just a number, we have $\mathbf{E}\big[\mathbf{E}[X]X\big] = \mathbf{E}[X]\mathbf{E}[X]$.

Expanding the square and using linearity of expectation:

$$\begin{aligned} \mathbf{Var}[X] &= \mathbf{E}\big[(X - \mathbf{E}[X])^2\big] = \mathbf{E}\big[X^2 - 2\mathbf{E}[X]X + \mathbf{E}[X]^2\big] \\ &= \mathbf{E}[X^2] - 2\mathbf{E}[X]\mathbf{E}[X] + \mathbf{E}[X]^2 \;=\; \mathbf{E}[X^2] - \mathbf{E}[X]^2 \end{aligned}$$ ■

An indicator random variable X always has value 0 or 1, so $\mathbf{E}[X] = \mathbf{Pr}[X = 1]$.

s	$\mathbf{Pr}[s]$	$X(s)$
a	0.1	3
b	0.2	5
c	0.3	5
d	0.4	8

$$\mathbf{E}[X] \;=\; 0.1\cdot 3 + 0.5\cdot 5 + 0.4\cdot 8 \;=\; 6$$

$$\mathbf{Var}[X] \;=\; 0.1\cdot(3-6)^2 + 0.5\cdot(5-6)^2 + 0.4\cdot(8-6)^2 \;=\; 3$$

Figure 7.4: Example of variance calculation

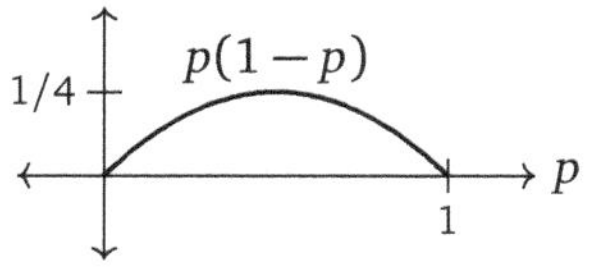

Figure 7.5: $p(1-p) \le 1/4$

Lemma 7.18. *If X is an indicator random variable with* $\mathbf{E}[X] = p$*, then* $\mathbf{Var}[X] = p(1-p) \le 1/4$.

Proof. Since $0^2 = 0$ and $1^2 = 1$, we have $X^2 = X$ and $\mathbf{E}[X^2] = \mathbf{E}[X] = p$. By Lemma 7.17, $\mathbf{Var}[X] = \mathbf{E}[X^2] - \mathbf{E}[X]^2 = p - p^2 = p(1-p)$, which is $\le 1/4$ since $1/4 - p(1-p) = (p-1/2)^2 \ge 0$ (Figure 7.5). ■

Lemma 7.19. *If X and Y are independent random variables, then* $\mathbf{Var}[X+Y] = \mathbf{Var}[X] + \mathbf{Var}[Y]$.

Proof. Since X and Y are independent, $\mathbf{E}[XY] = \mathbf{E}[X]\mathbf{E}[Y]$ (Lemma A.12). Thus by Lemma 7.17 and linearity of expectation:

$$\begin{aligned}
\mathbf{Var}[X+Y] &= \mathbf{E}\big[(X+Y)^2\big] - \mathbf{E}[X+Y]^2 \\
&= \mathbf{E}\big[X^2 + 2XY + Y^2\big] - \big(\mathbf{E}[X] + \mathbf{E}[Y]\big)^2 \\
&= \mathbf{E}[X^2] + 2\mathbf{E}[XY] + \mathbf{E}[Y^2] - \mathbf{E}[X]^2 - 2\mathbf{E}[X]\mathbf{E}[Y] - \mathbf{E}[Y]^2 \\
&= \big(\mathbf{E}[X^2] - \mathbf{E}[X]^2\big) + 2\big(\mathbf{E}[XY] - \mathbf{E}[X]\mathbf{E}[Y]\big) + \big(\mathbf{E}[Y^2] - \mathbf{E}[Y]^2\big) \\
&= \mathbf{Var}[X] + 0 + \mathbf{Var}[Y]
\end{aligned}$$
■

The binomial random variable X with parameters n and p is the number of heads in n tosses of a coin with heads probability p. Let X_i be the indicator for the ith toss being heads, so $X = X_1 + \cdots + X_n$ and $\mathbf{E}[X_i] = p$ and $\mathbf{Var}[X_i] = p(1-p) \le 1/4$ (Lemma 7.18). By linearity of expectation:

$$\mathbf{E}[X] \;=\; \mathbf{E}[X_1 + \cdots + X_n] \;=\; \mathbf{E}[X_1] + \cdots + \mathbf{E}[X_n] \;=\; p + \cdots + p \;=\; pn$$

Since $X_1, \ldots, X_n$ are fully independent, Lemma 7.19 implies:

$$\mathbf{Var}[X] \;=\; \mathbf{Var}[X_1 + \cdots + X_n] \;=\; \mathbf{Var}[X_1] + \cdots + \mathbf{Var}[X_n] \;\le\; 1/4 + \cdots + 1/4 \;=\; n/4$$

Thus Lemma 7.16 implies that for all $\gamma > 0$:

$$\mathbf{Pr}\big[|X - pn| \ge \gamma n\big] \;\le\; \mathbf{Var}[X]/(\gamma n)^2 \;\le\; 1/4\gamma^2 n$$

That is, the fraction of tosses that are heads is probably within $\pm\gamma$ of p. Next, we prove the much stronger bound $\mathbf{Pr}\big[|X - pn| \ge \gamma n\big] \le 2\mathrm{e}^{-\gamma^2 n}$.

7.6.3 Sums of Independent Random Variables

Lemma 7.20. *If X is the number of heads in n tosses of a coin with heads probability p, and $0 < \gamma \leq 1/2$, then $\mathbf{Pr}\big[X \geq (p+\gamma)n\big]$ and $\mathbf{Pr}\big[X \leq (p-\gamma)n\big]$ are both $\leq e^{-\gamma^2 n}$.*

This implies that if a coin with heads probability $p \geq \frac{1}{2} + \delta$ is tossed $n \geq \frac{1}{\delta^2} \ln \frac{1}{\varepsilon}$ times where n is odd, then the probability that a majority of the tosses are tails is:

$$\mathbf{Pr}[X \leq n/2] \;\leq\; \mathbf{Pr}\big[X \leq (p-\delta)n\big] \;\leq\; e^{-\delta^2 n} \;\leq\; \varepsilon$$

This matches Lemma 7.7 except for a factor of $\frac{1}{2}$ in n. Actually, Lemma 7.20 is true with $e^{-2\gamma^2 n}$ (which exactly captures Lemma 7.7), but that's trickier to prove.

Corollary 7.21. *Given a coin with unknown heads probability p, we can estimate p within $\pm\gamma$ with probability $\geq 1-\varepsilon$ by tossing the coin $n \geq \frac{1}{\gamma^2} \ln \frac{2}{\varepsilon}$ times and using the fraction of heads as the estimate.*

Proof. Letting X be the number of heads, Lemma 7.20 implies:

$$\mathbf{Pr}\big[|X/n - p| \geq \gamma\big] \;=\; \mathbf{Pr}\big[X \geq (p+\gamma)n\big] + \mathbf{Pr}\big[X \leq (p-\gamma)n\big] \;\leq\; 2e^{-\gamma^2 n} \;\leq\; \varepsilon \qquad \blacksquare$$

Let's apply this to polling: Each person will vote for candidate A or candidate B. Let p be the fraction of people who will vote for A. Polling a uniformly random person (and assuming they respond honestly) is like tossing a coin with heads probability p. If we poll $n \geq \frac{1}{\gamma^2} \ln \frac{2}{\varepsilon}$ people selected independently and uniformly at random (so someone might get polled more than once, but that's OK), then with probability $\geq 1-\varepsilon$, the fraction of "A" responses is within $\pm\gamma$ of p. For example, polling 10,000 people yields an estimate within 2% of p with probability $\geq$ 95%. The population size doesn't matter.

Another application: The definition of BPP says a randomized program should accept 1-inputs with probability $\geq d$ and 0-inputs with probability $\leq c$, for some constants $0 < c < 1/2 < d < 1$. Actually, nothing is special about $1/2$:

Corollary 7.22. *$A \in$ BPP if A has a poly-time randomized program that accepts 1-inputs with probability $\geq d$ and 0-inputs with probability $\leq c$, for some constants $0 < c < d < 1$.*

Proof. For any valid input x, running this program Π is like tossing a coin where heads = accept. By Corollary 7.21, we can estimate the heads probability p within $\gamma = (d-c)/3$ with probability $\geq 1-\varepsilon = 2/3$ by running $\Pi(x)$ at least $\frac{1}{\gamma^2} \ln \frac{2}{\varepsilon} = O(1)$ times independently. We define a poly-time randomized program Π' that accepts iff this estimate of p is $> (c+d)/2$.

- If $A(x) = 1$ then $p \geq d$, so with probability $\geq 2/3$, the estimate of p is $\geq d - \gamma > (c+d)/2$ and $\Pi'(x)$ accepts.
- If $A(x) = 0$ then $p \leq c$, so with probability $\geq 2/3$, the estimate of p is $\leq c + \gamma < (c+d)/2$ and $\Pi'(x)$ rejects. $\blacksquare$

Proof idea for Lemma 7.20. The key for exploiting independence of the tosses is that the expectation of a product of fully independent random variables equals the product of their expectations (Lemma A.12). Since X is a sum of fully independent random variables, we convert it to a product by using it as an exponent. $\blacksquare$

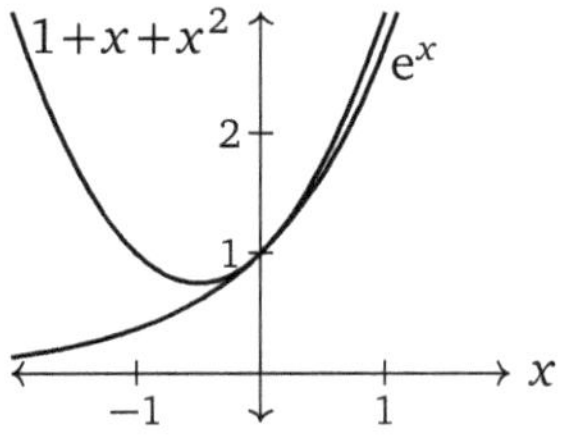

Figure 7.6: $e^x \le 1 + x + x^2$ for all $x \le 1$

$1 + x$ is a very good approximation of e^x when x is close to 0. It's off by at most x^2 since the plot of e^x is under the plot of $1 + x + x^2$ for $x \le 1$ (Figure 7.6):

Fact 7.23. $e^x \le 1 + x + x^2$ *for all* $x \le 1$. ■

Proof of Lemma 7.20. Let X_i be the indicator for the ith toss being heads, so $X = X_1 + \cdots + X_n$ is the number of heads and $\mathbf{E}[X_i] = p$. For some $0 \le a \le 1$ to be specified later,

$$\mathbf{Pr}\big[X \ge (p+\gamma)n\big] = \mathbf{Pr}\big[X - pn \ge \gamma n\big] = \mathbf{Pr}\big[e^{a(X-pn)} \ge e^{a\gamma n}\big] \le \mathbf{E}\big[e^{a(X-pn)}\big] / e^{a\gamma n}$$

by Lemma 7.13, since the random variable $e^{a(X-pn)}$ is nonnegative. We have

$$\mathbf{E}\big[e^{a(X-pn)}\big] = \mathbf{E}\big[e^{a((X_1-p)+\cdots+(X_n-p))}\big] = \mathbf{E}\big[e^{a(X_1-p)} \cdots e^{a(X_n-p)}\big] = \mathbf{E}\big[e^{a(X_1-p)}\big] \cdots \mathbf{E}\big[e^{a(X_n-p)}\big]$$

since $X_1, \ldots, X_n$ are fully independent and thus $e^{a(X_1-p)}, \ldots, e^{a(X_n-p)}$ are fully independent. For each i:

$$\begin{aligned}
\mathbf{E}\big[e^{a(X_i-p)}\big] &\le \mathbf{E}\big[1 + a(X_i-p) + a^2(X_i-p)^2\big] && \text{(Fact 7.23 with } x = a(X_i-p) \le 1\text{)}\\
&= 1 + a\big(\mathbf{E}[X_i] - p\big) + a^2\mathbf{E}\big[(X_i-p)^2\big] && \text{(linearity of expectation)}\\
&= 1 + a^2\mathbf{Var}[X_i] && \text{(definition of variance)}\\
&\le 1 + a^2/4 && \text{(Lemma 7.18)}\\
&\le e^{a^2/4} && \text{(Fact 7.6 with } x = a^2/4\text{)}
\end{aligned}$$

Combining everything:

$$\mathbf{Pr}\big[X \ge (p+\gamma)n\big] \le e^{a^2/4} \cdots e^{a^2/4} / e^{a\gamma n} = e^{(a^2/4)n} / e^{a\gamma n} = e^{-(a\gamma - a^2/4)n}$$

Choosing $a = 2\gamma \le 1$, we have $a\gamma - a^2/4 = \gamma^2$ in the exponent.

Let $Y_i = 1 - X_i$ be the indicator for the ith toss being tails, so $\mathbf{E}[Y_i] = 1 - p$. Let $Y = Y_1 + \cdots + Y_n = n - X$ be the number of tails. Swapping the roles of heads and tails in the above argument:

$$\mathbf{Pr}\big[X \le (p-\gamma)n\big] = \mathbf{Pr}\big[n - X \ge n - (p-\gamma)n\big] = \mathbf{Pr}\big[Y \ge ((1-p)+\gamma)n\big] \le e^{-\gamma^2 n}$$ ■

Essentially the same proof works even when $X_1, \ldots, X_n$ aren't identically distributed and aren't indicators. Exercise 7.12 asks for the details.

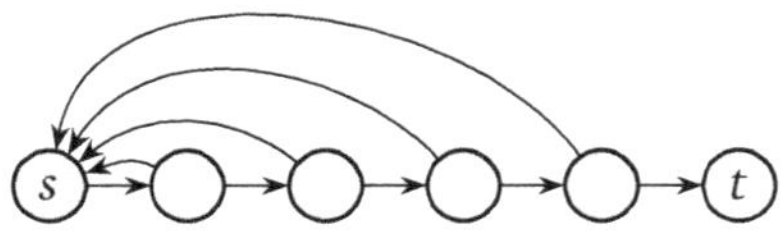

Figure 7.7: Directed graph that foils the random walk algorithm

7.7 Space-Efficient Randomized Algorithms

7.7.1 Randomized Logarithmic Space

The randomness segment doesn't count toward a program's space—only the registers and work segment count. To remember the outcomes of coin tosses for future reference, a program can keep them in its registers or work segment and "pay" for the space. (Not much is known about space complexity in the more powerful model with "read-rand Reg[i] ← Rand[Reg[j]]" instead of "read-rand Reg[i]".)

Every randomized program Π with space efficiency S has time efficiency $O(2^S)$ for the same reason as streaming verifiers (Lemma 3.8): If Π runs long enough to repeat a configuration, we could make Π repeat the cycle of configurations forever by replicating the section of r that caused the cycle. Running forever isn't allowed when solving a problem.

The definitions of two-sided, one-sided, and zero-sided error carry over from the time-efficient setting. The complexity classes $\mathsf{BPL} = \mathsf{BPSPACE}[\log N]$, $\mathsf{RL} = \mathsf{RSPACE}[\log N]$, and $\mathsf{ZPL} = \mathsf{ZPSPACE}[\log N]$ are defined analogously to their time-efficient counterparts. The amplification properties and $\mathsf{ZPL} = \mathsf{RL} \cap \mathsf{coRL}$ hold as in the time-efficient setting.

Here's the most famous demonstration of randomness in space-efficient computation:

UNDIRECTED REACHABILITY	(7.18)
Input: Undirected graph G, nodes s and t	
Output: Is t reachable from s in G?	

Theorem 7.24. UNDIRECTED REACHABILITY $\in \mathsf{RL}$.

Proof idea. We take a *random walk* from s, wandering aimlessly around s's connected component. If we stumble upon t, then we know t is reachable from s. Otherwise, we give up after a while. We only need log space to remember which node we're at and how many steps we've taken (to know when to give up). We prove that after only poly many steps, the random walk has essentially forgotten where it started: It's equally likely to be anywhere in s's connected component, so it has $\geq 1/n$ probability of being at t (if t is reachable). Extending the random walk's length by a factor $O(n)$ increases the probability of reaching t from $1/n$ to $2/3$.

For DIRECTED REACHABILITY, a random walk is generally too slow. Suppose the directed graph is just a path from s to t on which every node has an edge back to s (Figure 7.7). Each step has probability $1/2$ of "resetting" to s, so the probability of getting to t without resetting is $\approx 1/2^n$ (an incredibly lucky streak). A random walk probably takes $\approx 2^n$ trials to find t, so the timer needs $\geq n$ bits of memory. In an undirected graph, traveling back along an edge is always an option, so it's impossible to fall into a trap that requires extraordinary luck to escape. ■

Proof. Assume G has no multi-edges or self-loops (which would be irrelevant). We use the notation i and j for nodes—instead of the more traditional u and v—because in the analysis we use u and v for vectors.

Random walk algorithm for UNDIRECTED REACHABILITY (7.19)

```
if s = t: accept
i ← s
repeat 6n^4 log n times, where n is the number of nodes in G:
    i ← a uniformly random neighbor of i
    if i = t: accept
reject
```

This takes log space because it only needs $O(\log N)$-bit registers to remember n, s, t, i, the loop counter, and pointers into the input.

The algorithm traverses a walk from s. If t is unreachable from s, the algorithm rejects with probability 1 because it can't reach t. Assuming t is reachable from s, we need to prove that a $(6n^4 \log n)$-step random walk from s visits t with probability $\geq 2/3$. We defer this proof to §7.7.2 and §7.7.3. ∎

A different analysis shows that $O(n^3)$ steps suffice (Exercise 7.13). Some graphs require $\Omega(n^3)$ steps. Our weaker analysis, yielding $O(n^4 \log n)$, is good enough since it still only needs log space.

A "crown jewel" of complexity theory is a full derandomization of the random walk algorithm:

Theorem 7.25. UNDIRECTED REACHABILITY $\in$ L.

This theorem's sophisticated proof is beyond the scope of this book. It's a culmination of much effort on derandomization. For example, UNDIRECTED REACHABILITY was previously known to be in SPACE$[\log^{4/3} N]$, as well as in ZPL by ideas similar to the proof of NL $=$ coNL (Theorem 3.19).

Like the P $=$ BPP conjecture, it's widely believed that all randomized algorithms can be derandomized with only a constant factor increase in space:

Conjecture 7.26. L $=$ BPL.

This would be quite challenging to prove, but it's plausibly within reach! We'll see progress toward proving L $=$ BPL in §7.8 and §11.3.

7.7.2 Analysis of the Random Walk

Lemma 7.27. *For every connected undirected n-node graph (with no multi-edges or self-loops), and for all nodes $s \neq t$, a $(6n^4 \log n)$-step random walk from s visits t with probability $\geq 2/3$.*

To prove the correctness of the random walk algorithm for UNDIRECTED REACHABILITY when t is reachable from s, we apply Lemma 7.27 to s's connected component. In the proof of Theorem 7.24, n was the number of nodes in the whole graph, but when we apply Lemma 7.27, n is the number of nodes in s's connected component. That doesn't matter, since a longer random walk has an even higher probability of visiting t.

Proof of Lemma 7.27. Consider any connected undirected n-node graph G and any nodes $s \neq t$. Every node has degree $< n$ since G has no multi-edges or self-loops. Assume the set of nodes is $[n] = \{1, 2, \ldots, n\}$. To facilitate the analysis, we define a directed graph G' on the same nodes $[n]$: Each undirected edge $\{i, j\}$ of G becomes a pair of directed edges (i, j) and (j, i) in G', and we add enough directed self-loops so each node in G' has outdegree n and indegree n. In particular, each node has at least one self-loop in G'.

A random walk in G' is equivalent to a random walk in G except it's *lazy* because it may dawdle by taking self-loops. We prove that in G', a $(6n^4 \log n)$-step random walk from s visits t with probability $\geq 2/3$. This implies the same for the non-lazy random walk in G.

Lemma 7.28. *Let $\ell = 2n^3 \log n$. For every node q in G', an ℓ-step random walk from q ends at t with probability $\geq 1/2n$.*

Before proving Lemma 7.28, we use it to finish the proof of Lemma 7.27. Partition the $3n\ell$-step random walk from s into $3n$ phases of ℓ steps each. Intuitively, Lemma 7.28 says each phase contributes a factor $\leq 1 - 1/2n$ to the probability of never visiting t. Let's formalize this.

For each $k \in \{0, 1, \ldots, 3n\}$, let A_k be the event that at the end of phase k, the walk is not at t. The "end of phase 0" is the very beginning of the walk, so A_0 is the whole sample space since $s \neq t$. Partition A_k into events $A_{k,q}$ according to the current node $q \neq t$ at the end of phase k. Lemma 7.28 says $\mathbf{Pr}\big[A_k \,\big|\, A_{k-1,q}\big] \leq 1 - 1/2n$ for all $k \in \{1, \ldots, 3n\}$ and $q \neq t$. Let $B_k = A_0 \cap A_1 \cap \cdots \cap A_k$. Partitioning B_{k-1} into the events $A_{k-1,q} \cap B_{k-1}$ for $q \neq t$, we have:

$$\begin{aligned}
\mathbf{Pr}\big[A_k \,\big|\, B_{k-1}\big] &= \textstyle\sum_{q\neq t} \mathbf{Pr}\big[A_{k-1,q} \,\big|\, B_{k-1}\big] \cdot \mathbf{Pr}\big[A_k \,\big|\, A_{k-1,q} \cap B_{k-1}\big] && \text{(law of total probability)} \\
&= \textstyle\sum_{q\neq t} \mathbf{Pr}\big[A_{k-1,q} \,\big|\, B_{k-1}\big] \cdot \mathbf{Pr}\big[A_k \,\big|\, A_{k-1,q}\big] && \text{(conditional independence)} \\
&\leq \textstyle\sum_{q\neq t} \mathbf{Pr}\big[A_{k-1,q} \,\big|\, B_{k-1}\big] \cdot (1 - 1/2n) && \text{(Lemma 7.28)} \\
&= (1 - 1/2n)
\end{aligned}$$

The conditional independence means the walk's behavior in phase k depends only on which node the phase starts at, not on how the walk got to that node.

If the walk never visits t, then it doesn't visit t at the boundaries between phases, so

$$\mathbf{Pr}[\text{never visit } t] \;\leq\; \mathbf{Pr}[B_{3n}] \;=\; \textstyle\prod_{k=1}^{3n} \mathbf{Pr}\big[A_k \,\big|\, B_{k-1}\big] \;\leq\; (1 - 1/2n)^{3n} \;\leq\; \mathrm{e}^{-3n/2n} \;\leq\; 1/3$$

by the chain rule and Fact 7.6 with $x = -1/2n$. ∎

Proof of Lemma 7.28. Let T be the $n \times n$ transition matrix of G': $T_{i,j}$ is the probability that a step from node i goes to node j. Suppose v is any $1 \times n$ row vector representing a distribution over nodes: v_i is the probability of being at node i. If we start at a random node sampled from v and take one step of a random walk, then the row vector vT represents the resulting distribution over nodes. One step gets us a little closer to the uniform distribution $u = \begin{bmatrix} 1/n & \cdots & 1/n \end{bmatrix}$, where "closeness" is measured by $\Delta(v) = \sum_{i=1}^{n} (v_i - u_i)^2$ (and Δ is capital Greek delta):

Lemma 7.29. $\Delta(vT) \leq \mathrm{e}^{-1/n^3} \Delta(v)$ *for every distribution vector v.*

Before proving Lemma 7.29, we use it to finish the proof of Lemma 7.28. Let w be the row vector representing the initial distribution: $w_q = 1$ and $w_i = 0$ for all $i \neq q$.

$$\Delta(w) \;=\; (1 - 1/n)^2 + (n-1) \cdot (0 - 1/n)^2 \;\leq\; (1 - 1/n) + n \cdot (1/n)^2 \;=\; 1$$

Then wT is the distribution after one step, and $(wT)T = wT^2$ is the distribution after two steps, and so on, and wT^ℓ is the distribution after ℓ steps. The sequence $w, wT, wT^2, wT^3, \ldots$ gets closer and closer to u, by repeated application of Lemma 7.29:

$$\Delta(wT^\ell) \le e^{-1/n^3}\Delta(wT^{\ell-1}) \le e^{-1/n^3}e^{-1/n^3}\Delta(wT^{\ell-2}) \le \cdots \le e^{-\ell/n^3}\Delta(w) \le e^{-\ell/n^3} \le 1/4n^2$$

Letting $v = wT^\ell$, we have $(v_t - u_t)^2 \le \Delta(v) \le 1/4n^2$, so $|v_t - u_t| \le \sqrt{1/4n^2} = 1/2n$ and thus $v_t \ge u_t - 1/2n = 1/2n$. ■

Claim 7.30. $uT = u$.

Proof of Claim 7.30. Each node in G' has outdegree n and indegree n (with the added self-loops), so $T_{i,j} =$ (number of (i,j) edges)/ outdeg(i) = (number of (i,j) edges)/n and $\sum_i T_{i,j} =$ indeg$(j)/n = n/n = 1$ and thus $(uT)_j = \sum_i u_i T_{i,j} = \frac{1}{n}\sum_i T_{i,j} = 1/n = u_j$ for each j. ■

We use the standard notation $\|x\| = \sqrt{x \cdot x}$ for any vector x. For every scalar c, we have $\|cx\| = \sqrt{c^2(x \cdot x)} = |c|\,\|x\|$. Note that $\Delta(v) = (v-u)\cdot(v-u) = \|v-u\|^2$. The following key lemma, which we prove in §7.7.3, is at the tip of an iceberg called *spectral graph theory*.

Lemma 7.31. $\|xT\|^2 \le e^{-1/n^3}\|x\|^2$ *for every* $x \in \mathbb{R}^n$ *with* $\sum_i x_i = 0$.

Proof of Lemma 7.29. For $x = v - u$, we have $\sum_i x_i = \sum_i v_i - \sum_i u_i = 1 - 1 = 0$. By Claim 7.30 and Lemma 7.31:

$$\Delta(vT) = \|vT-u\|^2 = \|vT-uT\|^2 = \|(v-u)T\|^2 \le e^{-1/n^3}\|v-u\|^2 = e^{-1/n^3}\Delta(v) \quad ■$$

7.7.3 Spectral Lemma

Proof of Lemma 7.31 (ancillary). Consider any x with $\sum_i x_i = 0$. Let $y = xT$. To prove $\|y\|^2 \le (1 - 1/n^3)\|x\|^2 \le e^{-1/n^3}\|x\|^2$, we show $\|x\|^2 - \|y\|^2 \ge \|x\|^2/n^3$.

Since $\sum_j T_{i,j} = 1$ for each i, and $\sum_i T_{i,j} = 1$ for each j, and $y_j = \sum_i x_i T_{i,j}$ for each j:

$$\begin{aligned}
\|x\|^2 &= x\cdot x = \textstyle\sum_i 1x_i^2 = \sum_i(\sum_j T_{i,j})x_i^2 &&= \textstyle\sum_{i,j} T_{i,j}x_i^2\\
\|y\|^2 &= y\cdot y = \textstyle\sum_j 1y_j^2 = \sum_j(\sum_i T_{i,j})y_j^2 &&= \textstyle\sum_{i,j} T_{i,j}y_j^2\\
\|y\|^2 &= y\cdot y = \textstyle\sum_j y_jy_j = \sum_j(\sum_i x_i T_{i,j})y_j &&= \textstyle\sum_{i,j} T_{i,j}x_iy_j
\end{aligned}$$

We combine the expressions in the rightmost column using $x_i^2 + y_j^2 - 2x_iy_j = (x_i - y_j)^2$:

$$\begin{aligned}
\|x\|^2 - \|y\|^2 &= \|x\|^2 + \|y\|^2 - 2\|y\|^2\\
&= \left(\textstyle\sum_{i,j} T_{i,j}x_i^2\right) + \left(\sum_{i,j} T_{i,j}y_j^2\right) - 2\left(\sum_{i,j} T_{i,j}x_iy_j\right)\\
&= \textstyle\sum_{i,j} T_{i,j}(x_i^2 + y_j^2 - 2x_iy_j)\\
&= \textstyle\sum_{i,j} T_{i,j}(x_i - y_j)^2\\
&= \tfrac{1}{n}\textstyle\sum_{\text{edges }(i,j)}(x_i - y_j)^2
\end{aligned}$$

The last line follows because $T_{i,j} =$ (number of (i,j) edges)/n. If node i has multiple self-loops, then (i,i) occurs multiple times in the sum over all edges.

Thus to prove $\|x\|^2 - \|y\|^2 \ge \|x\|^2/n^3$, we need to show $\sum_{\text{edges }(i,j)}(x_i - y_j)^2 \ge \|x\|^2/n^2$. Let h be a node with maximum value of x_h, and let k be a node with minimum value of x_k.

Claim 7.32. $x_h - x_k \geq \|x\|/\sqrt{n}$.

Proof. Since $\sum_i x_i = 0$, we have $x_h \geq 0$ and $x_k \leq 0$. We claim that either $x_h \geq \|x\|/\sqrt{n}$, in which case $x_h - x_k \geq \|x\|/\sqrt{n} - 0$, or $x_k \leq -\|x\|/\sqrt{n}$, in which case $x_h - x_k \geq 0 - (-\|x\|/\sqrt{n})$. Suppose for contradiction that $x_h < \|x\|/\sqrt{n}$ and $x_k > -\|x\|/\sqrt{n}$. This means $-\|x\|/\sqrt{n} < x_i < \|x\|/\sqrt{n}$ for every i, so $x_i^2 < \|x\|^2/n$ and thus $\|x\|^2 = \sum_i x_i^2 < \sum_i \|x\|^2/n = \|x\|^2$, a contradiction. ■

Since G is connected, there exists a path from h to k. Renumbering the nodes, we assume $h = 1$ and the undirected path is:

$$1 - 2 - 3 - 4 - 5 - \cdots - k$$

(The path might have fewer than five nodes, but we wrote plenty of nodes to help illustrate something in a moment.) In the corresponding directed path from 1 to k in G', edge $(1,2)$ contributes $(x_1 - y_2)^2$, edge $(2,3)$ contributes $(x_2 - y_3)^2$, and so on. Since one edge involves y_2 while the other involves x_2, things don't "align" at node 2 (or at the other nodes). To smooth this out, we instead alternate the edge directions along the path. Assuming for now that k is odd:

$$1 \rightarrow 2 \leftarrow 3 \rightarrow 4 \leftarrow 5 \rightarrow \cdots \leftarrow k$$

We show that these edges already contribute at least $\|x\|^2/n^2$. (We need not consider the nonnegative contributions of other edges in G'.) The calculation looks nicest if we rewrite $(x_{i+1} - y_i)^2$ as $(y_i - x_{i+1})^2$ when i is even.

$$\begin{aligned}
&\textstyle\sum_{\text{edges }(i,j)}(x_i - y_j)^2 \\
&\geq (x_1 - y_2)^2 + (y_2 - x_3)^2 + \cdots + (x_{k-2} - y_{k-1})^2 + (y_{k-1} - x_k)^2 \\
&\geq \tfrac{1}{k-1}\left(|x_1 - y_2| + |y_2 - x_3| + \cdots + |x_{k-2} - y_{k-1}| + |y_{k-1} - x_k|\right)^2 && \text{(Corollary A.27)} \\
&\geq \tfrac{1}{k-1}\left|(x_1 - y_2) + (y_2 - x_3) + \cdots + (x_{k-2} - y_{k-1}) + (y_{k-1} - x_k)\right|^2 && \text{(Lemma A.28)} \\
&= \tfrac{1}{k-1}(x_1 - x_k)^2 \\
&\geq \tfrac{1}{k-1}(\|x\|/\sqrt{n})^2 && \text{(Claim 7.32)} \\
&= \|x\|^2/(k-1)n
\end{aligned}$$

Corollary A.27 and Lemma A.28 used the vector $(x_1 - y_2,\ y_2 - x_3,\ \ldots,\ x_{k-2} - y_{k-1},\ y_{k-1} - x_k)$.

If k is even, the last edge on the "alternating path" points into k, so we get $\frac{1}{k-1}(x_1 - y_k)^2$ near the end of the calculation. To patch this up, we tack a self-loop at k onto the path:

$$1 \rightarrow 2 \leftarrow 3 \rightarrow 4 \leftarrow 5 \rightarrow \cdots \rightarrow k \circlearrowleft$$

Now the last two terms at the beginning of the calculation are $(x_{k-1} - y_k)^2 + (y_k - x_k)^2$. Carrying this through the calculation, we get a $-y_k + y_k$ cancellation and end up with $\frac{1}{k}(x_1 - x_k)^2 \geq \frac{1}{k}(\|x\|/\sqrt{n})^2 = \|x\|^2/kn$. (The fraction out front is $\frac{1}{k}$ since the vector for Corollary A.27 now has k components.) This is why we needed a self-loop at every node.

Whether k is odd or even, we have $\sum_{\text{edges }(i,j)}(x_i - y_j)^2 \geq \|x\|^2/kn \geq \|x\|^2/n^2$ since $k \leq n$. ■

7.8 Derandomizing BPL

Let's make progress toward confirming the conjecture BPL = L. For starters, by essentially the same proof as BPP ⊆ P/poly (Theorem 7.9):

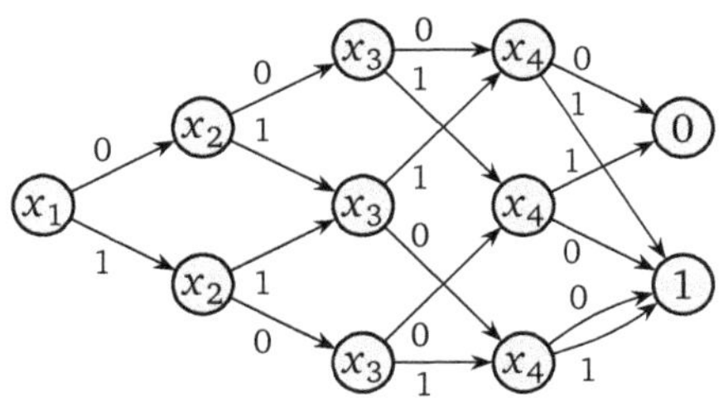

Figure 7.8: Example length-4 width-3 streaming branching program

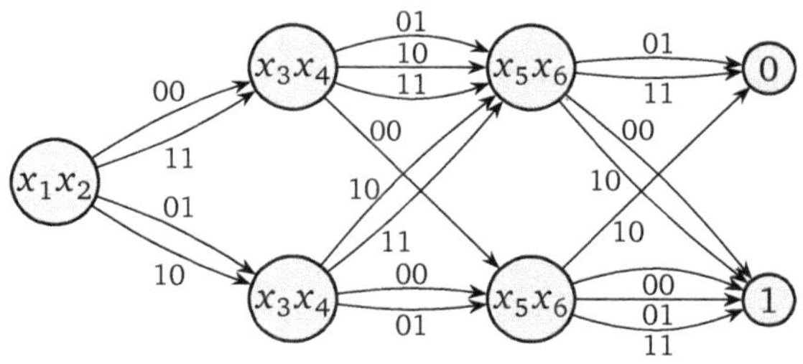

Figure 7.9: Example length-3 width-2 block-size-2 streaming branching program

Theorem 7.33. $\mathsf{BPL} \subseteq \mathsf{L/poly}$. ∎

Next, we prove $\mathsf{BPL} \subseteq \mathsf{P}$ (§ 7.8.2) and $\mathsf{BPL} \subseteq \mathsf{L}^2$ (§ 7.8.3) and $\mathsf{BPL} \subseteq \mathsf{NC}^2$ (§ 7.8.4), which subsumes the former two inclusions since $\mathsf{NC}^2 \subseteq \mathsf{P} \cap \mathsf{L}^2$. In § 11.3 we use a more advanced technique to prove $\mathsf{BPL} \subseteq \mathsf{TISP}[\text{poly} N, \log^2 N]$, which also subsumes $\mathsf{BPL} \subseteq \mathsf{P} \cap \mathsf{L}^2$. It's known that $\mathsf{BPL} \subseteq \mathsf{L}^{1.5}$ and $\mathsf{BPL} \subseteq \mathsf{AC}^1$, but the proofs are beyond the scope of this book. This section's results also hold for unbounded error: $\mathsf{PL} \subseteq \mathsf{NC}^2$. But $\mathsf{BPL} \subseteq \mathsf{TISP}[\text{poly} N, \log^2 N]$ and $\mathsf{BPL} \subseteq \mathsf{L}^{1.5}$ and $\mathsf{BPL} \subseteq \mathsf{AC}^1$ rely on bounded error, so the analogous inclusions for PL might not hold.

7.8.1 Streaming Branching Programs

When derandomizing BPL, it helps to view a computation as a certain kind of branching program.

In a *layered* branching program (§6.6.1), nodes are partitioned into a sequence of layers with the start node in the first layer and the accept and reject nodes in the last layer, and with each edge going from some layer to the next layer. The *length* is the number of non-output layers. The *width* is the maximum number of nodes in any non-output layer.

A *streaming* branching program is a layered branching program where the ith layer's nodes read the ith input bit. A streaming branching program always reads all input bits in order, from left to right, and the length is the number of input bits. Figure 7.8 shows an example.

In a streaming branching program with *block size* k, each non-output node reads a contiguous block of k input bits and has 2^k outgoing edges. The first layer reads the first k bits, and the second layer reads the next k bits, and so on. Figure 7.9 shows an example.

As observed in §5.5.2, we can turn any streaming branching program with block size k into an equivalent streaming branching program (with block size 1) by replacing each non-output node with a decision tree that reads the block's bits one at a time. This increases the length by a factor k and the width by a factor 2^{k-1}.

Lemma 7.34. *Suppose Π is a randomized program with L lines and word size W, and with running time $\leq T$ and memory space $\leq S$ on some input x. There exists a length-T width-$L2^S$ block-size-W streaming branching program B_x such that $\mathbf{Pr}_r[B_x(r) \text{ accepts}] = \mathbf{Pr}_r[\Pi(x;r) \text{ accepts}]$ for uniformly random $r \in (\{0,1\}^W)^T$.*

Proof idea. Theorem 5.24 turned space-efficient programs into small branching programs. The input was x in that proof, but now x is fixed and B_x's input is the randomness r. Since $\Pi(x)$ takes one pass through r from left to right, B_x will also read r from left to right. The subtlety is that B_x must relentlessly read r's next word in every single step, whereas $\Pi(x)$ can read r's next word "when it gets around to it." Since r's coordinates are interchangeable, it never matters which fresh random word $\Pi(x)$ reads. We imagine that $\Pi(x)$ "reads but ignores" r's next word in each step that doesn't access the randomness segment. ■

Proof. Π has at most $L2^S$ possible configurations on input x. In B_x, the nodes in layer $t \in \{0, \ldots, T-1\}$ (which read the word r_t) correspond to pairs (C, t) where C is any configuration (except configurations that load or store at too high an address and thus wouldn't be reached). The start node is (initial configuration, 0), and all other nodes with $t = 0$ are unnecessary. To define the outgoing edges of node (C, t) when $t < T - 1$, consider Π's instruction at line C_{PC}:

- Not a "read-rand" instruction: All 2^W edges go to $(C', t+1)$ where C' is the configuration after one step of $\Pi(x)$ from C. If the instruction is "accept" or "reject", then $C' = C$.
- "read-rand Reg[i]": The edge labeled $r_t \in \{0,1\}^W$ goes to $(C', t+1)$ where C' is C except $C'_{\mathrm{Reg}[i]} = r_t$ and $C'_{\mathrm{PC}} = C_{\mathrm{PC}} + 1$.

For each node $(C, T-1)$: If C executes "accept" then all 2^W edges go to the accept node. If C executes "reject" then all 2^W edges go to the reject node. Otherwise, $(C, T-1)$ can't be reached (since $\Pi(x)$ always halts within T steps), so it doesn't matter which output node its edges go to.

$B_x(r) = \Pi'(x; r)$ where Π' is like Π except that a "read-rand" in step t gets r_{t-1} rather than r's next unread word. That is, $\Pi'(x)$ reads $r_0, r_1, r_2, \ldots$ in order, one word in every step, but disregards r_{t-1} if step t isn't a "read-rand". With Π, all unread words of r are at the end, but with Π', these irrelevant words may occur throughout r. Rearranging r's words doesn't affect the acceptance probability:

$$\mathbf{Pr}_r\big[\Pi(x;r) \text{ accepts}\big] \;=\; \mathbf{Pr}_r\big[\Pi'(x;r) \text{ accepts}\big] \;=\; \mathbf{Pr}_r\big[B_x(r) \text{ accepts}\big]$$

Formally, this is because there exists a bijection $f\colon (\{0,1\}^W)^T \to (\{0,1\}^W)^T$ such that $\Pi(x;r) = \Pi'(x; f(r))$: If $\Pi(x;r)$ reads r_i in step t, then $f(r)_{t-1} = r_i$, and r's unread words are moved to $f(r)$'s remaining coordinates. This is an injection, and hence a bijection, because if $r \neq r'$ then $f(r) \neq f(r')$: If i is the least index such that $r_i \neq r'_i$, then $f(r)_j = r_i \neq r'_i = f(r')_j$ for some j. ■

Corollary 7.35. *For every $A \in \mathsf{BPL}$, there exists a deterministic log-space program that, given a valid input x, produces a poly-size streaming branching program B_x such that $\mathbf{Pr}_r\big[B_x(r) \neq A(x)\big] \leq 1/3$. In fact, the mapping from x to B_x can be computed by an NC^0-type circuit family.*

Proof. Suppose Π is a log-space 1/3-error randomized program for A. For every valid x of size N, Π runs in time $\operatorname{poly} N$ and space $O(\log N)$, so the streaming branching program from Lemma 7.34 has length $\operatorname{poly} N$ and width $2^{O(\log N)} = \operatorname{poly} N$ and thus size $\operatorname{poly} N$. We convert this to a block-size-1 streaming branching program—which we also call B_x for convenience—that's a factor $2^{O(\log N)} = \operatorname{poly} N$ larger since Π has word size $O(\log N)$. We have $\mathbf{Pr}_r\big[B_x(r) \neq A(x)\big] = \mathbf{Pr}_r\big[\Pi(x;r) \neq A(x)\big] \leq 1/3$. It's routine to see that B_x's encoding can be computed in log space, given x. Furthermore, the size of B_x's encoding depends only on N, and each bit of B_x's encoding is either a constant (depending on N but not on x) or a bit of x (for configurations that execute a "read"). Thus the mapping from x to B_x is NC^0-type. ■

7.8.2 Time-Efficient Derandomization

Theorem 7.36. $\mathsf{BPL} \subseteq \mathsf{P}$.

Proof idea. By Corollary 7.35, it suffices to compute the probability that a streaming branching program accepts a uniformly random input. Paths from the start node to the output nodes exactly correspond to inputs, so it suffices to compute the number of paths from the start node to the accept node. (Edge labels are now irrelevant.) We use dynamic programming: Once we compute the number of paths from a node v to the accept node, we store this number and use it when processing each of v's inneighbors. These numbers get too large for individual words, so we need big number arithmetic.

Another approach is to compute the number of paths from the start node to each node v, and use this number when processing each of v's outneighbors. This is reminiscent of, but simpler than, the "forward algorithm" for Hidden Markov Models in AI. ■

Proof. Suppose $A \in \mathsf{BPL}$. For any valid input x, consider the length-n streaming branching program B_x from Corollary 7.35: $A(x) = 1$ iff $\mathbf{Pr}_r[B_x(r) = 1] \geq 1/2$ for uniformly random $r \in \{0,1\}^n$. Since the inputs $r \in \{0,1\}^n$ correspond to the 2^n many paths from the start node to the output nodes, $A(x) = 1$ iff B_x has $\geq 2^n/2$ paths from the start node to the accept node. The following algorithm for A fills an array *numpaths* indexed by the nodes of B_x, where *numpaths*$[v]$ gets the number of paths from v to the accept node.

Time-efficient derandomization of BPL (7.20)

```
obtain B_x
numpaths[accept node] ← 1
numpaths[reject node] ← 0
for ℓ ← n, n−1, ..., 1:
    for each node v in layer ℓ:
        say v's outneighbors are u and w
        numpaths[v] ← numpaths[u] + numpaths[w]
if numpaths[start node] ≥ 2^n/2: accept
else: reject
```

Each node v in layer ℓ has $\leq 2^{n-\ell+1}$ paths to the accept node, so *numpaths*$[v]$ has $\leq n-\ell+2 \leq n+1$ bits and takes $O(n)$ time to compute with an ADDITION algorithm. This algorithm for A takes poly time to obtain B_x, plus poly time for each of the poly many nodes of B_x. Hence $A \in \mathsf{P}$. ■

7.8.3 Space-Efficient Derandomization

Theorem 7.37. $\mathsf{BPL} \subseteq \mathsf{L}^2$.

Proof idea. As before, it suffices to compute the number of paths from the start node to the accept node in the streaming branching program B_x. We generalize middle-first search (§3.4.1) to "middle-first counting." Denote the number of paths from node u to node w by $p_{u,w}$. If layer ℓ is halfway between u and w, then $p_{u,w} = \sum_{\text{node } v \text{ in layer } \ell} p_{u,v} \cdot p_{v,w}$ by basic counting principles: We partition the set of paths from u to w according to the midpoint v. The set of paths from u to v to w is like a cartesian product (set of paths from u to v) × (set of paths from v to w).

We turn this idea into a recursive subroutine "mfc" that has access to B_x, takes arguments u and w (where w is in a later layer than u), and returns $p_{u,w}$.

Middle-first counting algorithm (7.21)

mfc(u, w):
  say u is in layer k, and w is in layer m
  if $m = k+1$: return the number of (u, w) edges
  $\ell \leftarrow \lfloor (k+m)/2 \rfloor$
  return $\sum_{\text{node } v \text{ in layer } \ell} \text{mfc}(u, v) \cdot \text{mfc}(v, w)$

For each v in layer ℓ, this makes recursive calls mfc(u, v) and mfc(v, w) and then computes the product with a MULTIPLICATION algorithm. Then, it uses an ITERATED ADDITION algorithm to sum these products over all v in layer ℓ. This has logarithmic recursion depth. A straightforward implementation would store the big numbers in their entirety, using poly space per stack frame. We get by with log space per stack frame by using log-space programs for MULTIPLICATION and ITERATED ADDITION, recomputing individual bits of numbers whenever needed. The subroutine needs an extra argument for the desired bit's index. ∎

Proof. Suppose $A \in \mathsf{BPL}$. For any valid input x, consider the length-n streaming branching program B_x from Corollary 7.35: $A(x) = 1$ iff B_x has $\geq 2^n/2 = 2^{n-1}$ paths from the start node to the accept node. Denote the number of paths from node u to node w by $p_{u,w}$, which has $\leq n+1$ bits since $p_{u,w} \leq 2^n$.

We design a recursive subroutine "mfc" that has access to B_x (which can be computed from x using log space), takes arguments u and w (where w is in a later layer than u) and $i \in \{0, 1, \ldots, n\}$, and returns the ith bit of $p_{u,w}$. (The 0th bit is the least significant.) To solve A, call mfc(start node, accept node, $n-1$) and mfc(start node, accept node, n) and output the $\vee$ of these bits.

Space-efficient derandomization of BPL (7.22)

mfc(u, w, i):
  say u is in layer k, and w is in layer m
  if $m = k+1$: return the ith bit of the number of (u, w) edges
  $\ell \leftarrow \lfloor (k+m)/2 \rfloor$
  run a log-space program for ITERATED ADDITION DECISION:
    ask it for the ith bit of the sum of $(n+1)$-bit numbers indexed by nodes v in layer ℓ
    when it wants to read the vth number's jth bit:
      run a log-space program for MULTIPLICATION DECISION:
        ask it for the jth bit of the product of two $(n+1)$-bit numbers
        when it wants to read the 1st number's hth bit: call mfc(u, v, h)
        when it wants to read the 2nd number's hth bit: call mfc(v, w, h)
  return the bit output by the ITERATED ADDITION DECISION program

This maintains the invariant that mfc(u, w, i) returns the ith bit of $p_{u,w}$. This holds by definition for the base cases when $m = k+1$. To see that mfc(u, w, i) maintains the invariant when $m > k+1$, assume the invariant holds for all mfc(u, v, h) and mfc(v, w, h) calls. The MULTIPLICATION DECISION program is run with $p_{u,v}$ as the 1st number and $p_{v,w}$ as the 2nd number. The ITERATED ADDITION DECISION program is run with $p_{u,v} \cdot p_{v,w}$ as the vth number. Thus mfc(u, w, i) returns the ith bit of $\sum_{v \text{ in layer } \ell} p_{u,v} \cdot p_{v,w} = p_{u,w}$.

If n is a power of 2, the recursion depth is $\log n + 1$ because $m-k$ starts at n and gets halved in every recursive call (since ℓ is halfway between k and m). If n isn't a power of 2, the recursion depth is no more than it would be for the next power of 2, which is $\le 2n$. Thus the recursion depth is $\le \log(2n)+1 \le O(\log N)$. Each stack frame only needs $O(\log N)$ bits to store the call's arguments and other local data, including the memory used by the ITERATED ADDITION DECISION and MULTIPLICATION DECISION programs. The space efficiency is:

$$\big(O(\log N) \text{ stack frames at a time}\big) \cdot \big(O(\log N) \text{ bits per stack frame}\big) \;=\; O(\log^2 N) \text{ bits}$$

Thus $A \in \mathsf{L}^2$. ■

7.8.4 Parallel Derandomization

Theorem 7.38. $\mathsf{BPL} \subseteq \mathsf{NC}^2$.

Proof idea. For $\mathsf{NL} \subseteq \mathsf{AC}^1$ (Theorem 6.9), we implemented middle-first search with an AC^1-type circuit. We similarly implement middle-first counting with an NC^2-type circuit, using NC^1-type circuits for MULTIPLICATION and ITERATED ADDITION (Theorem 6.6). ■

Proof. Suppose $A \in \mathsf{BPL}$. For any valid input x of size N, consider the length-n streaming branching program B_x from Corollary 7.35: $A(x) = 1$ iff B_x has $\ge 2^n/2 = 2^{n-1}$ paths from the start node to the accept node. Adding dummy layers if necessary, we may assume n is a power of 2. We index the layers from 0 (start node) to n (output nodes). Note that n and the set of nodes in each layer depend only on N. Only the edges depend on x. Denote the number of paths from node u to node w by $p_{u,w}$, which has $\le n+1$ bits since $p_{u,w} \le 2^n$.

We design a circuit C_N. At the bottom is the NC^0-type mapping from x to B_x's encoding. For every $d \in \{0, 1, \ldots, \log n\}$ and every node u whose layer index is a multiple of 2^d (note that 0 is a multiple of 2^d) and every node w whose layer index is the next multiple of 2^d, a bundle of $n+1$ wires in C_N will carry $p_{u,w}$ in binary. Then C_N's output is the $\vee$ of the $(n-1)$st and nth bits of $p_{\text{start node, accept node}}$.

For $d = 0$: C_N computes $p_{u,w}$ (the number of (u,w) edges) by consulting B_x's encoding for the identities of u's two outneighbors (which are in fixed locations in the encoding), comparing both to w, and letting $p_{u,w}$ be 0, 1, or 2 depending on whether neither, one, or both outneighbors are w.

For $d > 0$: Let ℓ be the layer index halfway between u and w. Then C_N computes $p_{u,w} = \sum_{v \text{ in layer } \ell} p_{u,v} \cdot p_{v,w}$: For each v in layer ℓ, it uses an NC^1-type circuit for MULTIPLICATION to compute $p_{u,v} \cdot p_{v,w}$. (The latter wire bundles are lower in C_N since the layer indices of u, v, w are consecutive multiples of 2^{d-1}.) Then, it uses an NC^1-type circuit for ITERATED ADDITION to sum these products over all v in layer ℓ. It keeps only the least significant $n+1$ bits of the sum, since the more significant bits are always 0.

The circuits for MULTIPLICATION and ITERATED ADDITION have size polynomial in their input size, and depth logarithmic in their input size. Since their input size is $\operatorname{poly} N$, they have size $\operatorname{poly}(\operatorname{poly} N) = \operatorname{poly} N$ and depth $O(\log(\operatorname{poly} N)) = O(\log N)$. There are only $\operatorname{poly} N$ triples (u, v, w), so C_N has size $\operatorname{poly} N$. Each d contributes $O(\log N)$ to C_N's depth because C_N performs the associated $p_{u,w}$ computations in parallel. There are only $\log n + 1 = O(\log N)$ possibilities of d, so C_N has depth $O(\log^2 N)$.

This log-space-uniform bounded-fan-in circuit family solves A, so $A \in \mathsf{NC}^2$. ■

7.9 Promise Problems

In a *promise problem* (§1.3.1), some inputs may be *invalid*, with undefined output. We "promise" that a program will never get an invalid input. We don't care what a program would output on an invalid input. In a *total problem*, every possible input is valid. A possible input is an element of $(\{0,1\}^W)^N$ where W is the problem's word size.

We defined all complexity classes to allow promise problems. In Part I, this was just a technicality. For many promise problems, we can efficiently check whether an input is valid. (For example, we can check in linear time whether an input to DIRECTED REACHABILITY conforms to our encoding.) Such problems might as well be total, with invalid inputs redefined as no-inputs, since an efficient algorithm can detect an invalid input and reject. But suppose we can't efficiently check whether an input is valid. A deterministic algorithm that solves a promise problem (and terminates on invalid inputs) also solves some total problem, since we could declare whatever it outputs on invalid inputs to be correct. But a randomized algorithm that solves a promise problem might not solve any total problem, since it may accept with "illegal probability" (between 1/3 and 2/3 for two-sided error) on invalid inputs. With randomized complexity classes, "promise versus total" matters.

- §7.9.1: BPP and BPL have complete promise problems but aren't known to have complete total problems.
- §7.9.2: "If P = RP then P = BPP" holds for promise problems but isn't known for total problems. ("If L = RL then L = BPL" isn't even known for promise problems.)
- §7.9.3: Tight randomized time and space hierarchies are known for promise problems but not for total problems. A modest randomized space hierarchy is known for total problems.

7.9.1 Complete Problems

When defining BPP-completeness, should we use $\le_p^m$ or $\le_\ell^m$? On one hand, $\le_p^m$ is natural for studying P versus BPP. On the other hand, $\le_\ell^m$ is natural because if we conjecture P = BPP, we'd expect BPP-completeness to coincide with P-completeness (§5.4). So we say a decision problem B is BPP-*complete* when $B \in$ BPP and $A \le_\ell^m B$ for every $A \in$ BPP.

CIRCUIT GAP MAJORITY	(7.23)
Input: Circuit C such that $C(r) = 1$ for either $\ge 2/3$ or $\le 1/3$ of all inputs $r \in \{0,1\}^n$	
Output: Does $C(r) = 1$ for $\ge 2/3$ of all inputs r?	

CIRCUIT SAT (§5.4.3) is similar but asks whether $C(r) = 1$ for > 0 or 0 of all inputs r. Whether we view CIRCUIT SAT as a total or promise problem is a minor detail. But CIRCUIT GAP MAJORITY is inherently a promise problem, because it's not just about checking whether the input conforms to some encoding: If $C(r) = 1$ for $< 2/3$ and $> 1/3$ of all r, then C is an invalid input, and it's not simple to check whether this holds, since there are exponentially many r.

Lemma 7.39. CIRCUIT GAP MAJORITY *is* BPP-*complete.*

Proof. CIRCUIT GAP MAJORITY $\in$ BPP: Given input C and a uniformly random $r \in \{0,1\}^n$, run a poly-time program for CIRCUIT EVALUATION (Lemma 5.10) on input (C, r) to check whether $C(r) = 1$. The acceptance probability is $\ge 2/3$ on 1-inputs and $\le 1/3$ on 0-inputs. (On invalid inputs, the acceptance probability may be $< 2/3$ and $> 1/3$, but that doesn't matter.)

Suppose $A \in \mathsf{BPP}$ by a randomized program Π with time efficiency $\leq T = cN^d$ (for integers c, d) and log-bounded word size W.

OUTPUT OF Π WITH RANDOMNESS (call this problem B, with input size M)	(7.24)
Input: Valid input x of size N to A, and $r \in (\{0,1\}^W)^T$	
Output: $\Pi(x; r)$	

$B \in \mathsf{P}$ by a program Π' where $\Pi'(x, r)$ runs $\Pi(x; r)$. By Theorem 5.13, a log-space-uniform circuit family $D_1, D_2, \ldots$ solves B. Thus $A \leq_\ell^m$ CIRCUIT GAP MAJORITY by mapping input x of size N to a circuit C_x as follows: Calculate the size M of inputs to B of the form (x, r), run the generator to get D_M, and obtain C_x from D_M by hardwiring the bits of N and x, leaving only r for the input nodes. For every assignment to r, we have $\Pi(x; r) = B(x, r) = D_M(x, r) = C_x(r)$. This log-space mapping reduction is correct since:

$$A(x) = 1 \Rightarrow \mathbf{Pr}_r\big[\Pi(x;r) \text{ accepts}\big] \geq 2/3 \Rightarrow \big(C_x(r) = 1 \text{ for} \geq 2/3 \text{ of all } r\big)$$
$$A(x) = 0 \Rightarrow \mathbf{Pr}_r\big[\Pi(x;r) \text{ accepts}\big] \leq 1/3 \Rightarrow \big(C_x(r) = 1 \text{ for} \leq 1/3 \text{ of all } r\big)$$ ∎

No BPP-complete total problems are known, though of course they exist if $\mathsf{P} = \mathsf{BPP}$.

When defining BPL-completeness, should we use $\leq_\ell^m$ or $\leq_{nc^1}^m$? On one hand, $\leq_\ell^m$ is natural for studying L versus BPL. On the other hand, $\leq_{nc^1}^m$ is natural because if we conjecture $\mathsf{L} = \mathsf{BPL}$, we'd expect BPL-completeness to coincide with L-completeness (§ 6.4). So we say a decision problem B is BPL-*complete* when $B \in \mathsf{BPL}$ and $A \leq_{nc^1}^m B$ for every $A \in \mathsf{BPL}$.

STREAMING BRANCHING PROGRAM GAP MAJORITY	(7.25)
Input: Streaming branching program B such that $B(r) = 1$ for either $\geq 2/3$ or $\leq 1/3$ of all inputs $r \in \{0,1\}^n$	
Output: Does $B(r) = 1$ for $\geq 2/3$ of all inputs r?	

Lemma 7.40. STREAMING BRANCHING PROGRAM GAP MAJORITY *is* BPL-*complete.*

Proof. STREAMING BRANCHING PROGRAM GAP MAJORITY $\in \mathsf{BPL}$: Given input B and a uniformly random $r \in \{0,1\}^n$, evaluate $B(r)$ by following a path from the start node and reading the successive bits of r to determine which edges to take. This only uses log space to remember the current node and pointers into the input. Corollary 7.35 says $A \leq_{nc^1}^m$ STREAMING BRANCHING PROGRAM GAP MAJORITY (in fact, $\leq_{nc^0}^m$) for every $A \in \mathsf{BPL}$. ∎

No BPL-complete total problems are known, though of course they exist if $\mathsf{L} = \mathsf{BPL}$.

7.9.2 Instigating a Collapse

Theorem 7.41. *If* $\mathsf{P} = \mathsf{RP}$ *then* $\mathsf{P} = \mathsf{BPP}$.

Proof idea. Recall the proof that if $\mathsf{P} = \mathsf{NP}$ then $\mathsf{P} = \Sigma_2\mathsf{P}$ (Theorem 4.21): We use the assumption $\mathsf{P} = \mathsf{NP} = \mathsf{coNP}$ to remove one quantifier, and then again to remove another quantifier.

Imagine an analogue of the polynomial hierarchy that, instead of NP-type ($\exists$) and coNP-type ($\forall$) quantifiers, has RP-type and coRP-type "quantifiers": Wherever the polynomial hierarchy requires "at least one" witness to have some property, we instead require "most" witnesses to have the property. This new hierarchy's second level actually equals BPP: The proof that $\mathsf{BPP} \subseteq \Sigma_2\mathsf{P}$ (Theorem 7.10) shows "at least one" using the probabilistic method, which yields "most" as a bonus. To collapse this new hierarchy, we use the assumption $\mathsf{P} = \mathsf{RP} = \mathsf{coRP}$ to remove one "quantifier," and then again to remove another "quantifier."

This proof needs RP to contain promise problems, because invalid inputs fill the void between "none" and "most." The proof of "if $\mathsf{P} = \mathsf{NP}$ then $\mathsf{P} = \Sigma_2\mathsf{P}$" works for total problems because there's no void between "none" and "at least one." ■

Proof. Assume $\mathsf{P} = \mathsf{RP}$ and thus $\mathsf{P} = \mathsf{coRP}$ since P is closed under complement. Suppose $A \in \mathsf{BPP}$. In the proof of Theorem 7.10, we designed a poly-time 2-witness verifier $V(x;s;r)$ such that the following hold, where $\widehat{\exists}$ means "for at least 2/3 fraction of":

$$A(x) = 1 \Rightarrow \big(\widehat{\exists} s\ \forall r : V(x;s;r) \text{ accepts}\big)$$
$$A(x) = 0 \Rightarrow \big(\forall s\ \widehat{\exists} r : V(x;s;r) \text{ rejects}\big)$$

(call this problem B)	(7.26)
Input: Valid input x to A, and s such that either: $\big(\forall r : V(x;s;r) \text{ accepts}\big)$ or $\big(\widehat{\exists} r : V(x;s;r) \text{ rejects}\big)$	
Output: Is it true that $\forall r : V(x;s;r)$ accepts?	

B is inherently a promise problem because (x,s) is an invalid input if $V(x;s;r)$ accepts for $> 1/3$ but < 1 fraction of all r.

$B \in \mathsf{coRP}$ by a randomized program Π where $\Pi(x,s;r)$ runs $V(x;s;r)$. Thus $B \in \mathsf{P}$ by a deterministic program Π'. Assume Π' clocks itself so it terminates in poly time even on invalid inputs. (It can't always tell whether the input is invalid, but if it runs too long then the input is invalid.) Then $A \in \mathsf{RP}$ by a randomized program Π'' where $\Pi''(x;s)$ runs $\Pi'(x,s)$:

$$A(x) = 1 \Rightarrow \big(\widehat{\exists} s : B(x,s) = 1\big) \Rightarrow \mathbf{Pr}_s\big[\Pi''(x;s) \text{ accepts}\big] \geq 2/3$$
$$A(x) = 0 \Rightarrow \big(\forall s : B(x,s) = 0\big) \Rightarrow \mathbf{Pr}_s\big[\Pi''(x;s) \text{ rejects}\big] = 1$$

If $A(x) = 1$ then (x,s) may be an invalid input to B for some s, but that doesn't matter: Π'' still accepts with probability $\geq 2/3$ and always runs in poly time. Thus $A \in \mathsf{P}$. ■

7.9.3 Time and Space Hierarchies

The deterministic hierarchy theorems for time (Theorem 4.7) and space (Theorem 4.10) hold even for total problems: A program can check whether the input is valid in linear time and log space, so we can redefine invalid inputs as no-inputs. Soon, we'll see what goes wrong in the randomized setting. First, let's see how a modest randomized space hierarchy for total problems follows from the deterministic space hierarchy and space-efficient derandomization. For any $a \geq 1$, let $\mathsf{L}^a = \mathsf{SPACE}[\log^a N]$ and $\mathsf{BPL}^a = \mathsf{BPSPACE}[\log^a N]$.

Theorem 7.42. *For all $a > 1$, $\mathsf{BPL}^a \not\subseteq \mathsf{BPL}$ even when the classes are defined to contain only total problems.*

Proof idea. First, let's prove this for $a > 2$: If $\mathsf{BPL}^a \subseteq \mathsf{BPL}$ then $\mathsf{L}^a \subseteq \mathsf{BPL}^a \subseteq \mathsf{BPL} \subseteq \mathsf{L}^2$ (Theorem 7.37), contradicting the deterministic space hierarchy for total problems. To get a tighter randomized space hierarchy (though not as tight as the deterministic one, which handles a mere constant factor gap between the upper and lower bounds), we use padding to show that a small collapse would imply a bigger collapse. ■

Proof. Suppose for contradiction $\mathsf{BPL}^a \subseteq \mathsf{BPL}$ for some $a > 1$. We may assume a is rational. By a padding argument (§4.1), $\mathsf{BPL}^{a^{d+1}} \subseteq \mathsf{BPL}^{a^d}$ for every integer $d \geq 0$:

$$A \in \mathsf{BPL}^{a^{d+1}} \Rightarrow A_{\text{pad}} \in \mathsf{BPL}^a \Rightarrow A_{\text{pad}} \in \mathsf{BPL} \Rightarrow A \in \mathsf{BPL}^{a^d} \quad \text{where } \mathrm{pad}(N) = \lceil 2^{\log^{a^d}(N)} \rceil$$

In §4.1, A_{pad} is defined as a promise problem, with the padding promised to be 0s. We instead define A_{pad} as a total problem where the padding can be any bits: If a program reads from the padding, it should pretend it reads a 0 word.

Let k be an integer such that $a^k > 2$. Then

$$\mathsf{L}^{a^k} \subseteq \mathsf{BPL}^{a^k} \subseteq \mathsf{BPL}^{a^{k-1}} \subseteq \mathsf{BPL}^{a^{k-2}} \subseteq \cdots \subseteq \mathsf{BPL}^{a^2} \subseteq \mathsf{BPL}^a \subseteq \mathsf{BPL} \subseteq \mathsf{L}^2$$

by Theorem 7.37. This contradicts Theorem 4.10, which holds for total problems. ■

Theorem 7.43. *For all $a > b \geq 1$, $\mathsf{BPTIME}[N^a] \not\subseteq \mathsf{BPTIME}[N^b]$.*

Proof idea. Recall the proof of the deterministic time hierarchy (Theorem 4.7): We define a problem B whose input is the code of a too-fast program Π, and let $B(\Pi) = \overline{\Pi(\Pi)}$. That is, B's output is the opposite of what Π would output if given its own code as input. A not-too-fast program solves B using an interpreter to simulate $\Pi(\Pi)$. Every too-fast program Π fails to solve B on input Π by definition.

To adapt this to the randomized setting, a natural attempt is to define a problem B whose input is the code of a too-fast randomized program Π, and let:

$$B(\Pi) = \begin{cases} 0 & \text{if } \mathbf{Pr}\big[\Pi(\Pi) \text{ accepts}\big] \geq 2/3 \\ 1 & \text{if } \mathbf{Pr}\big[\Pi(\Pi) \text{ accepts}\big] \leq 1/3 \\ \text{undefined} & \text{otherwise} \end{cases}$$

Upper bound: A not-too-fast randomized program solves B using a randomized interpreter to simulate $\Pi(\Pi)$, and flipping the output. It's essential that B is a promise problem, because otherwise the program for B would need to accept with probability $\geq 2/3$ or $\leq 1/3$ even when $1/3 < \mathbf{Pr}\big[\Pi(\Pi) \text{ accepts}\big] < 2/3$, and it's unknown whether that can be done efficiently.

Lower bound: We'd like to say every too-fast randomized program Π fails to solve B on input Π. But that only holds if Π is a valid input to B, since otherwise failure on input Π is impossible, and Π might solve B on all valid inputs. We fix this using delayed diagonalization (§4.2.4). The proof of the time hierarchy for verifiers (Theorem 4.13) needs delayed diagonalization because complementing a verifier takes exponential time. But complementing a randomized program is trivial. We now need delayed diagonalization because forcing an input to be valid involves iterating over all possible outcomes of the randomness, which takes exponential time.

Exercise 7.21 asks for the details, which are just like in the time hierarchy for verifiers. ■

7.10 Map of Complexity Classes

It's a good time to reflect on how far we've come. Figure 7.10 shows the known inclusions among our core complexity classes. Arrows $C_1 \longrightarrow C_2 \longrightarrow C_3$ mean $C_1 \subseteq C_2 \subseteq C_3$ and thus $C_1 \subseteq C_3$ holds even though the map doesn't show the arrow $C_1 \longrightarrow C_3$.

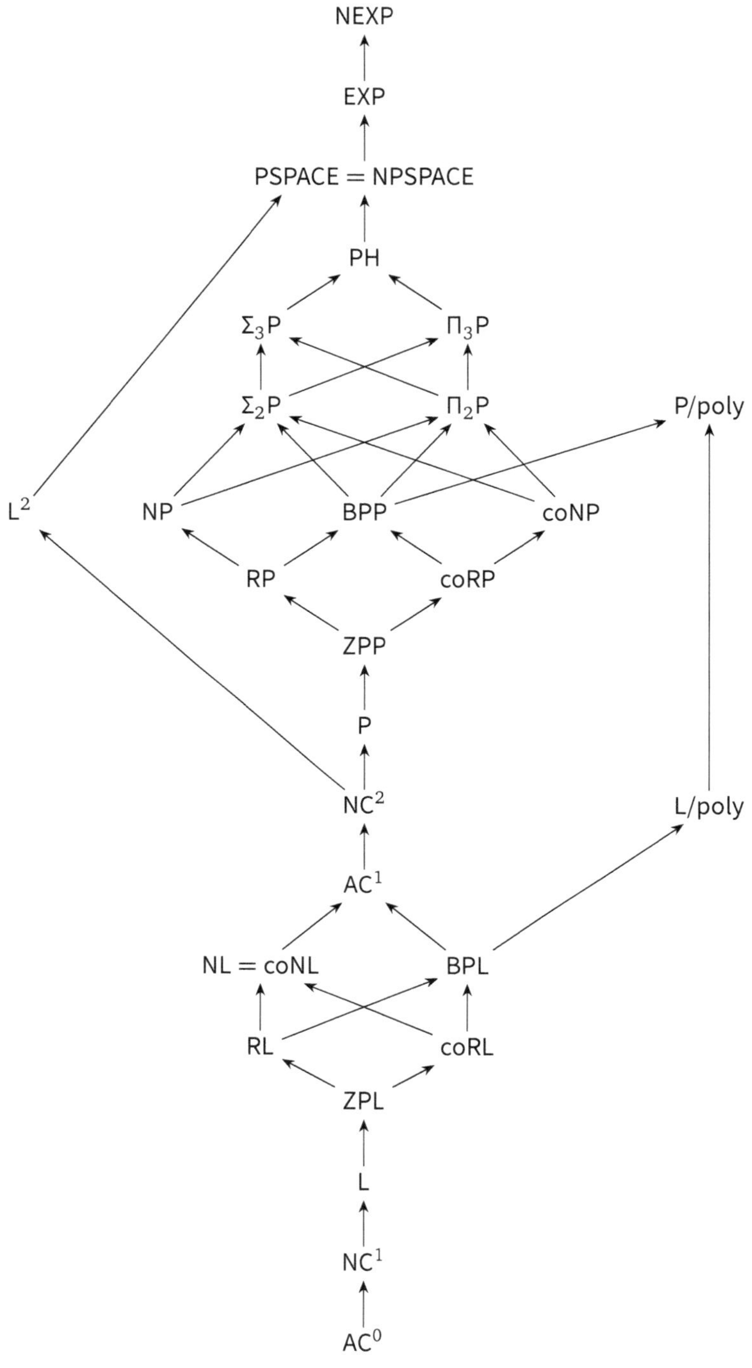

Figure 7.10: Map of major complexity classes, where $\mathcal{C}_1 \longrightarrow \mathcal{C}_2$ means $\mathcal{C}_1 \subseteq \mathcal{C}_2$

Exercises

7.1 Prove Evaluate to Zero Everywhere is coNP-complete.

Evaluate to Zero Everywhere (or EZE for short)	(7.27)
Input: n-variate arithmetic formula φ over $\mathbb{Z}_2$	
Output: Does $\varphi(a) = 0$ hold for all $a \in \mathbb{Z}_2^n$?	

7.2 **(a)** An *arithmetic circuit* is a dag (with multi-edges allowed) where each source is labeled by a variable or a constant, and each nonsource node is a bounded-fan-in $+$, $-$, or $\cdot$ gate, and there's a designated output node. Circuit Polynomial Identity Testing (CPIT) is like Polynomial Identity Testing but the input has arithmetic circuits instead of arithmetic formulas. Prove Circuit Polynomial Identity Testing $\in$ coRP.

(b) A multivariate polynomial is *multilinear* iff each variable has individual degree ≤ 1. Prove that for every $f: \{0,1\}^n \to \{0,1\}$ and every field, at most one multilinear canonical-form polynomial P is such that $P(a) = f(a)$ for all $a \in \{0,1\}^n$.

(c) A branching program (§5.5.1) is *read-once* iff every path from the start node reads each variable at most once (that is, no path from the start node contains multiple nodes labeled by the same variable). Two branching programs (with the same variables) are *equivalent* iff they compute the same function as each other. Prove Read-Once Branching Program Equivalence $\in$ coRP.

Read-Once Branching Program Equivalence (or ROBP Eq for short) (7.28)
Input: Read-once branching programs A and B with n variables
Output: Are A and B equivalent?

You may use (without proof) the existence of a prime between $3n$ and $6n$. Hint: Show ROBP Eq $\leq_p^m$ CPIT and use Exercise 7.2.a and Exercise 7.2.b.

7.3 Prove that the linear-time randomized algorithm for Matrix Multiplication Verification (§7.1.4) also works over the integers (instead of $\mathbb{Z}_2$). You may assume each matrix entry is an integer from $\{0, 1, \ldots, n\}$.

7.4 Prove NP $\subseteq$ PP.

7.5 A permutation is an element of $[n]^n = [n] \times \cdots \times [n]$ in which each element of $[n]$ appears exactly once, such as $(4, 2, 5, 1, 3) \in [5]^5$. Prove that the probability that a uniformly random element of $[n]^n$ is a permutation is $\leq ne^{-n+1}$.

7.6 By definition, $A \in$ BPP iff $\exists$ a poly-time randomized program Π such that $\forall N$:

$$\forall \text{ valid } x \text{ of size } N : \ \mathbf{Pr}_r\big[\Pi(x;r) = A(x)\big] \geq 2/3$$

Prove that $A \in$ BPP iff $\exists$ a poly-time randomized program Π such that $\forall N$:

$$\mathbf{Pr}_r\big[\forall \text{ valid } x \text{ of size } N : \ \Pi(x;r) = A(x)\big] \geq 2/3$$

7.7 $\mathsf{S_2P}$ (the S stands for "symmetric") is the set of all decision problems A for which there exists a poly-time 2-witness verifier V such that:

$$A(x)=1 \Rightarrow \big(\exists w_1\ \forall w_2 : V(x;w_1;w_2) \text{ accepts}\big)$$
$$A(x)=0 \Rightarrow \big(\exists w_2\ \forall w_1 : V(x;w_1;w_2) \text{ rejects }\big)$$

Intuitively, a lawyer claiming that $A(x)=1$ produces w_1, and simultaneously, a lawyer claiming that $A(x)=0$ produces w_2, and V is the judge. Whichever lawyer is right should be able to convince the judge regardless of what the other lawyer says.

(a) Prove $\mathsf{S_2P} \subseteq \Sigma_2\mathsf{P} \cap \Pi_2\mathsf{P}$.

(b) Prove $\mathsf{BPP} \subseteq \mathsf{S_2P}$. Hint: Adapt the proof that $\mathsf{BPP} \subseteq \Sigma_2\mathsf{P}$ (Theorem 7.10) so that $r=(r_1,\ldots,r_\ell)$ where each $r_j \in (\{0,1\}^W)^T$, for a suitably large ℓ. Let $V(x;s;r)$ run $\Pi(x;r_j \oplus s_i)$ for each i and j, and accept iff $\forall j\ \exists i : \Pi(x;r_j \oplus s_i)$ accepts.

7.8 Prove that the following promise problem has an unbounded-fan-in depth-3 size-$N^{O(\log N)}$ monotone formula family.

GAP MAJORITY	(7.29)
Input: $x \in \{0,1\}^N$ with either $< N/k$ many 0s or $< N/k$ many 1s, where $k=\lceil \log N \rceil$	
Output: Does x have more 1s than 0s?	

Hint: Follow the proof that $\mathsf{BPP} \subseteq \Sigma_2\mathsf{P}$ (Theorem 7.10). The output is an $\vee$ gate of fan-in N^k, analogous to $\exists$ in $\Sigma_2\mathsf{P}$. The middle layer is $\wedge$ gates of fan-in N, analogous to $\forall$ in $\Sigma_2\mathsf{P}$. The bottom layer is $\vee$ gates of fan-in k. The input variable indices are analogous to the outcomes r in BPP. Instead of shifting using bitwise-xor, you can shift using "addition mod N" where the input variable indices are $\{0,1,\ldots,N-1\}$.

7.9 Prove that $\mathsf{NP} \subseteq \mathsf{coRP}$ iff $\mathsf{PH} = \mathsf{ZPP}$.

7.10 A *catalytic* program's work segment is initialized with arbitrary words, and can be modified during the computation, but must be restored to its initial contents before the program terminates. That is, it must appear as if the work segment was unused. This represents "lending" a program memory that's filled with extraneous data, under the condition that the program leaves the data intact. The work segment is like a catalyst in chemistry—a substance that facilitates a chemical reaction by participating in the reaction and returning to its original state by the end (appearing as if it didn't participate).

The class CL (catalytic log space) is the set of all decision problems solvable by catalytic programs with log-bounded word size. Only the registers count toward the space. For every valid input and every possible initial contents of the work segment, the program must terminate with the correct output and with the work segment containing its initial contents again. It's not obvious how to exploit the work segment under this constraint, but surprisingly, it's known that $\mathsf{AC}^1 \subseteq \mathsf{CL}$ and in particular, $\mathsf{NL} \subseteq \mathsf{CL}$ and $\mathsf{BPL} \subseteq \mathsf{CL}$.

Prove $\mathsf{CL} \subseteq \mathsf{ZPP}$. Hint: Initialize the work segment randomly and use Theorem 7.15.

7.11 Prove that if you toss n coins, which may have different heads probabilities, then:

$$\mathbf{Pr}[\text{get all tails}] \le e^{-\mathrm{E}[\text{number of heads}]}$$

7.12 Adapt the proof of Lemma 7.20 to show that if $X = X_1 + \cdots + X_n$ is a sum of fully independent random variables with $0 \le X_i \le 1$ for each i, and $0 < \gamma \le 1/2$, then $\mathbf{Pr}\big[X \ge \mathbf{E}[X] + \gamma n\big]$ and $\mathbf{Pr}\big[X \le \mathbf{E}[X] - \gamma n\big]$ are both $\le e^{-\gamma^2 n}$.

7.13 We proved that a $O(n^4 \log n)$-step random walk solves UNDIRECTED REACHABILITY. Now, you'll show that $O(n^3)$ steps suffice, using a different analysis. You may use the following theorem without proof: For every connected undirected graph $G = (V, E)$ (with no multi-edges or self-loops) and every node v, if we take an infinite random walk from v, then $\mathbf{E}[\text{number of steps to return to } v] = 2|E|/\deg(v)$. (Rough intuition: An infinite random walk spends equal fractions of time traversing each edge in each direction, and thus spends $\deg(v)/2|E|$ fraction of time at v. Since the time between consecutive visits to v is $2|E|/\deg(v)$ on average, that must be the expectation. Formalizing this is subtle.)

- **(a)** Prove that for every connected undirected graph $G = (V, E)$ and every edge $\{u, v\}$, if we take an infinite random walk from u, then $\mathbf{E}[\text{number of steps to visit } v] \le 2|E| - 1$.
- **(b)** Prove that for every connected undirected graph $G = (V, E)$ and all nodes $s \ne t$, an infinite random walk from s visits t within $6n|E| \le O(n^3)$ steps with probability $\ge 2/3$.

7.14 A directed graph is *balanced* iff $\text{indeg}(i) = \text{outdeg}(i)$ for every node i. Now, you'll prove that the following generalization of UNDIRECTED REACHABILITY is in RL.

BALANCED DIRECTED REACHABILITY	(7.30)
Input: Balanced directed graph G (with no multi-edges or self-loops), nodes s and t	
Output: Is t reachable from s in G?	

- **(a)** Prove that for every directed graph $G = (V, E)$ and every partition of V into nonempty sets U and W, we have $\sum_{i \in U} \text{indeg}(i) - \sum_{i \in U} \text{outdeg}(i) = |E \cap (W \times U)| - |E \cap (U \times W)|$ (that is, number of edges from W to U, minus number of edges from U to W).
- **(b)** Prove that for every balanced directed graph, if it's weakly connected (ignoring the arrow directions yields a connected undirected graph) then it's strongly connected.
- **(c)** Prove BALANCED DIRECTED REACHABILITY $\le_\ell^m$ UNDIRECTED REACHABILITY and thus BALANCED DIRECTED REACHABILITY $\in$ RL.
- **(d)** Prove an analogue of Lemma 7.31 for balanced directed graphs: Suppose G' is a strongly connected directed n-node graph in which each node has outdegree n, indegree n, and at least one self-loop. Let T be the transition matrix of G'. Prove that $\|xT\|^2 \le e^{-1/2n^3} \|x\|^2$ for every $x \in \mathbb{R}^n$ with $\sum_i x_i = 0$.
- **(e)** The algorithm for BALANCED DIRECTED REACHABILITY from Exercise 7.14.c doesn't find a walk from s to t, because it may traverse edges backward. Use Exercise 7.14.d to prove that the "forward-only" random walk algorithm finds a walk from s to t within $O(n^4 \log n)$ steps with high probability (if t is reachable from s).

7.15 Define BP*L like BPL but allowing "read-rand Reg[i] $\leftarrow$ Rand[Reg[j]]" instead of "read-rand Reg[i]" (and still not counting the randomness segment toward the space). Prove BPL $\subseteq$ BP*L $\subseteq$ L/poly.

7.16 Prove that $\mathsf{NL} \subseteq \mathsf{BPL}$ iff $\mathsf{NL} = \mathsf{RL}$.

7.17 Prove that if $\mathsf{P} = \mathsf{NP}$ then $\mathsf{P} = \mathsf{BPP}$, even when the classes are defined to contain only total problems.

7.18 In §7.9.2 we claimed that BPP equals the second level of the "RP analogue of the polynomial hierarchy," and we proved that BPP is contained in the second level.

(a) Prove that the second level is contained in BPP: If A has a poly-time 2-witness verifier V such that

$$A(x)=1 \Rightarrow \left(\widehat{\exists} w_1\ \forall w_2 :\ V(x;w_1;w_2) \text{ accepts}\right)$$
$$A(x)=0 \Rightarrow \left(\forall w_1\ \widehat{\exists} w_2 :\ V(x;w_1;w_2) \text{ rejects }\right)$$

then $A \in \mathsf{BPP}$.

(b) Prove that this entire hierarchy collapses to the second level: If A has a poly-time ℓ-witness verifier V such that

$$A(x)=1 \Rightarrow \left(\widehat{\exists} w_1\ \forall w_2\ \widehat{\exists} w_3\ \forall w_4 \cdots :\ V(x;w_1;w_2;\cdots;w_\ell) \text{ accepts}\right)$$
$$A(x)=0 \Rightarrow \left(\forall w_1\ \widehat{\exists} w_2\ \forall w_3\ \widehat{\exists} w_4 \cdots :\ V(x;w_1;w_2;\cdots;w_\ell) \text{ rejects }\right)$$

then $A \in \mathsf{BPP}$.

7.19 Prove that $\mathsf{RP} = \mathsf{coRP}$ iff $\mathsf{BPP} = \mathsf{ZPP}$ (when the classes contain promise problems).

7.20 Prove that if $\mathsf{P} = \mathsf{BPP}$ (for promise problems) then:

(a) $\mathsf{BPTIME}[N] \subseteq \mathsf{TIME}[N^d]$ for some constant d. Hint: Use BPP-completeness.

(b) BPP has a time hierarchy for total problems: $\mathsf{BPTIME}[N^a] \not\subseteq \mathsf{BPTIME}[N]$ for all $a > 1$.

7.21 Use delayed diagonalization to prove Theorem 7.43: For all $a > b \geq 1$, $\mathsf{BPTIME}[N^a] \not\subseteq \mathsf{BPTIME}[N^b]$ (when the classes contain promise problems).

Notes

Some standard references on randomized algorithms and other applications of probability in computing are [378, 375, 19].

Lemma 7.1 is a version of the "Schwartz–Zippel lemma" [474, 578] and was known even earlier [405, 143]. The algorithm for Matrix Multiplication Verification (§7.1.4) is known as "Freivalds' algorithm" [174].

Two-sided-error randomized algorithms are known as "Monte Carlo" algorithms. Zero-sided-error randomized algorithms (particularly with the characterization from Theorem 7.15) are known as "Las Vegas" algorithms.

Primality Testing $\in$ coRP is due to [370, 422, 501]. Primality Testing $\in$ ZPP is due to [7]. Primality Testing $\in \mathsf{TIME}[N^{O(\log\log N)}]$ is due to [8]. Primality Testing $\in$ P is due to [10], based on derandomizing a randomized algorithm from [9].

Other success stories of randomized computation include beating brute force for k-Sat [473], parallel algorithms for finding matchings in graphs [347, 295, 381], and Element Distinctness $\in \mathsf{BPTISP}[N^{1.5} \operatorname{polylog} N, \operatorname{polylog} N]$ [118, 356].

BPP $\subseteq$ P/poly (Theorem 7.9) is due to [5, 62]. BPP $\subseteq \Sigma_2$P (Theorem 7.10) is due to [495, 327]. Quadratic time overhead is necessary for "black-box" proofs of BPP $\subseteq \Sigma_2$P [545], but quasi-linear time overhead suffices if we use three quantifiers: BPTIME[N] $\subseteq \Sigma_3$TIME[N polylog N] [144, 545].

NP $\subseteq$ BPP iff NP $=$ RP (Theorem 7.11) is due to [189, 315]. NP $\subseteq$ BPP iff PH $=$ BPP (Theorem 7.12) is due to [574].

Coin tosses are also called "Bernoulli trials." Lemma 7.13 is known as "Markov's inequality." Theorem 7.15 is due to [189]. Lemma 7.16 is known as "Chebyshev's inequality." The variance of a random variable X is also denoted $\sigma^2(X)$, with $\sigma(X) = \sqrt{\mathbf{Var}[X]}$ known as the "standard deviation" of X. Lemma 7.20 is known as a "Chernoff–Hoeffding bound" [123, 247]. A standard reference on concentration bounds and their applications to randomized algorithms is [150].

Undirected Reachability $\in$ RL (Theorem 7.24, specifically the proof from Exercise 7.13) is due to [15]. Undirected Reachability $\in$ ZPL is due to [85]. Undirected Reachability $\in$ L is due to [437], with a simplified proof due to [453]. Furthermore, the proof yields a log-space algorithm for Undirected Reachability Search. The proof of the spectral lemma (§7.7.3) is based on [20].

BPL $\subseteq$ NC^2 $\subseteq$ P $\cap$ L^2 (Theorem 7.38) is due to [86]. BPL $\subseteq$ L$^{1.5}$ is due to [459], and a slight improvement is due to [254]. BPL $\subseteq$ AC^1 is due to [122].

Our proof that if P $=$ RP then P $=$ BPP (Theorem 7.41) is due to [575, 96].

Though a randomized time hierarchy for total problems is not known, such a hierarchy holds when one bit of nonuniform advice is allowed (and if given wrong advice, programs may accept with probability between $1/3$ and $2/3$). The simplest proof of this is due to [365].

In Chapter 4, we proved Sat $\notin$ TISP[N^d, polylog N] for all $d < \sqrt{2}$. No lower bound of the form Sat $\notin$ BPTISP[N^d, polylog N] is known for any $d > 1$. But randomized time-space lower bounds are known for problems higher in the polynomial hierarchy: Π_2Sat $\notin$ BPTISP[N^d, polylog N] for all $d < 2$ [144]. (Π_2Sat was defined in Exercise 4.14.a.)

If P $=$ BPP (when the classes contain promise problems) then NEXP $\subseteq$ P/poly [261]. This explains why derandomizing BPP seems so difficult—it would require proving a super-polynomial nonuniform circuit size lower bound for NEXP. Derandomizing Circuit Polynomial Identity Testing (Exercise 7.2.a) would imply a super-polynomial nonuniform arithmetic circuit size lower bound for NEXP [282]. This explains why derandomizing Circuit Polynomial Identity Testing (or coRP more generally) seems so difficult.

Exercise 7.2.c is due to [68].

Exercise 7.5 says the probability that a uniformly random element of $[n]^n$ is a permutation is $O(ne^{-n})$. It's actually $\Theta(\sqrt{n}e^{-n})$ by "Stirling's formula."

Exercise 7.7 is due to [107, 455]. Every problem in S$_2$P has a poly-time zero-sided-error randomized oracle reduction to a problem in NP [103].

Exercise 7.10 and AC^1 $\subseteq$ CL are due to [95]. BPL $\subseteq$ CL can be strengthened to use only $O(\log^2 N)$ rather than poly N catalytic work space [420].

Balanced Directed Reachability (from Exercise 7.14) was considered in [15]. Balanced Directed Reachability Search has a log-space algorithm [439].

Chapter 8

Hashing

Hashing is a technique for implementing set (or dictionary) data structures. It's also a powerful tool in computational complexity. In this chapter, we develop a rigorous theory of hashing and use it to prove some theorems about complexity. More applications follow in later chapters.

8.1 Randomized Hashing

8.1.1 Set Data Structures

A *set* data structure maintains a subset S of elements from a *universe* set U of possible elements. For example, perhaps S is all English words, and U is all strings of at most 20 characters. (A *dictionary* data structure is similar but each element is called a *key* and has an associated *value*, such as the definition of an English word.) A set data structure supports these operations:

- Lookup: Given $u \in U$, determine whether $u \in S$.
- Insert: Given $u \in U$, update $S \leftarrow S \cup \{u\}$ (so S is unchanged if u was already in S).
- Delete: Given $u \in U$, update $S \leftarrow S \setminus \{u\}$ (so S is unchanged if u wasn't in S).

A simple implementation is a boolean array indexed by U's elements: The uth entry is true iff $u \in S$. All three operations are straightforward and time-efficient. But if U is much larger than S, then this implementation is very space-inefficient.

Another simple implementation is an array containing S's elements. This is space-efficient, but operations sometimes require traversing the whole array, which is time-inefficient.

Hash tables are a popular time- and space-efficient way to implement sets. The table is an array where each entry is either "empty" or an element of S. The element $u \in S$ is stored at index $h(u)$, where $h\colon U \to T$ is an efficiently computable *hash function* from the universe U to the table's indices T.

- Lookup: Compute $h(u)$ and see whether the table entry at this index is u.
- Insert: Compute $h(u)$ and store u at this index if it wasn't already there.
- Delete: Compute $h(u)$ and remove u from this index if it was there.

This works great if there are no collisions among elements of S. A *collision* is when $h(u) = h(u')$ for two elements $u \neq u'$, so u and u' want to share the same entry in the table. There are several ways to cope with collisions, but it's preferable not to have collisions. Major programming languages offer hash table implementations of sets, either built into the syntax (such as `{...}` in Python) or in the standard library (such as Java's `HashSet` class).

The pigeonhole principle says that if $|T| < |U|$ then for every h, there exist distinct elements of U that collide (h can't be an injection). But hash tables work well in practice because if the hash function h is "well chosen" and the table T is "somewhat larger" than the set S, then collisions among elements of S are "unlikely." We will formalize these vague terms in quotes. First, "unlikely" means "with low probability," so the hash function should be randomized.

8.1.2 Randomized Hash Functions

A *randomized hash function* is a function $h\colon R \times U \to T$ where R is the sample space, U is the universe of possible elements, and T is the table indices. Upon sampling a uniformly random $r \in R$, we get a deterministic hash function $h_r\colon U \to T$ defined by $h_r(u) = h(r, u)$. In practice, hash functions are deterministic, but they're like randomized hash functions where $r \in R$ was already sampled and hardcoded, once and for all.

For example, consider sampling a uniformly random function from U to T. The outcomes in R correspond to all $|T|^{|U|}$ functions from U to T. This means we sample $h_r(u) \in T$ uniformly at random for every $u \in U$, fully independently of each other. If T is large then collisions are unlikely because for every pair $u \neq u'$:

$$\begin{aligned} \mathbf{Pr}_r\big[h_r(u) = h_r(u')\big] &= \textstyle\sum_{t\in T} \mathbf{Pr}_r\big[h_r(u) = t \text{ and } h_r(u') = t\big] \\ &= \textstyle\sum_{t\in T} \mathbf{Pr}_r\big[h_r(u) = t\big] \cdot \mathbf{Pr}_r\big[h_r(u') = t\big] \\ &= \textstyle\sum_{t\in T} (1/|T|) \cdot (1/|T|) \\ &= 1/|T| \end{aligned}$$

But if U is huge, then storing r takes a lot of space—no better than the simple boolean array implementation of sets. We'll see constructions with much smaller r, where collisions are still unlikely:

Definition. A randomized hash function $h\colon R \times U \to T$ is *pairwise avoiding* iff for every pair of distinct elements $u \neq u'$ of U, we have $\mathbf{Pr}_r\big[h_r(u) = h_r(u')\big] \leq 1/|T|$. ◀

That is, two elements are no more likely to collide than they would be for a uniformly random hash function. Sometimes we need a slightly stronger property:

Definition. A randomized hash function $h\colon R \times U \to T$ is *pairwise uniform* iff for every pair of distinct elements $u \neq u'$ of U, the pair $\big(h_r(u), h_r(u')\big)$ is uniformly distributed over T^2. ◀

That is, for all $t \in T$ and $t' \in T$, we have $\mathbf{Pr}_r\big[h_r(u) = t \text{ and } h_r(u') = t'\big] = 1/|T|^2$. Stated another way: $h_r(u)$ is uniformly distributed over T for each u, and h is *pairwise independent*: $h_r(u)$ and $h_r(u')$ are independent of each other for all $u \neq u'$, which means that for all t and t', the events "$h_r(u) = t$" and "$h_r(u') = t'$" are independent.

Claim 8.1. *If h is pairwise uniform, then h is pairwise avoiding.*

Proof. If h is pairwise uniform, then for all $u \neq u'$:

$$\mathbf{Pr}_r\big[h_r(u) = h_r(u')\big] = \textstyle\sum_{t\in T} \mathbf{Pr}_r\big[h_r(u) = t = h_r(u')\big] = \textstyle\sum_{t\in T} 1/|T|^2 = 1/|T| \qquad \blacksquare$$

Some theorems need pairwise uniformity. But even when we only need a pairwise avoiding hash function, we'll use a pairwise uniform one anyway.

$h\colon \{0,1\}^2 \times \{1,2,3\} \to \{0,1\}$

h	1	2	3
00	0	0	0
01	0	1	1
10	1	0	1
11	1	1	0

$h\colon \{0,1\}^3 \times \{0,1\}^2 \to \{0,1\}$

h	00	01	10	11
000	0	0	0	0
001	1	1	1	1
010	0	1	0	1
011	1	0	1	0
100	0	0	1	1
101	1	1	0	0
110	0	1	1	0
111	1	0	0	1

Figure 8.1: Examples of pairwise uniform hash functions

Example. Figure 8.1 shows two pairwise uniform hash functions.

In the example on the left, the row corresponding to an outcome $r = r_1 r_2 \in \{0,1\}^2$ is $\big(h_r(1),\ h_r(2),\ h_r(3)\big) = (r_1,\ r_2,\ r_1 \oplus r_2)$. This h is pairwise uniform because in columns 1 and 2, the pairs $(0,0)$, $(0,1)$, $(1,0)$, $(1,1)$ appear equally often (once each) over all rows, and similarly for columns 1 and 3, and similarly for columns 2 and 3. This demonstrates that pairwise independence doesn't imply full independence: $(r_1,\ r_2,\ r_1 \oplus r_2)$ aren't fully independent (since two of them determine the third) but they're pairwise independent. This h's first row ($r = 00$) seems counterproductive because everything collides: $h_r(1) = h_r(2) = h_r(3)$. We could remove this row (so r becomes uniform over $\{01, 10, 11\}$) and the hash function would remain pairwise avoiding (each pair would collide with probability $1/3 \le 1/2$) but wouldn't be pairwise uniform.

The example on the right is pairwise uniform because in each pair of columns, the pairs $(0,0)$, $(0,1)$, $(1,0)$, $(1,1)$ appear equally often (twice each) over all rows. The first two rows ($r = 000$ and $r = 001$) seem counterproductive since everything collides. After removing these two rows, each pair of elements would collide with probability $1/3$, but the hash function wouldn't be pairwise uniform. ♦

8.1.3 Table Size

If we store a set $S \subseteq U$ using a pairwise avoiding hash function $h\colon R \times U \to T$, how big should the table T be? Practical implementations of hash tables resize themselves—and switch the hash function accordingly—as S grows. Let's just assume we know how big S may be.

We should have $|T| \ge |S|$ since otherwise two elements of S would certainly collide. If $|T| = |S|$ then having no collisions is possible but unlikely since there's no leeway. We don't want too much leeway, since the table would be mostly wasted space. How much leeway is enough?

If we want no collisions at all, T should be quadratically larger than S:

Lemma 8.2. *Consider a set $S \subseteq U$ and a pairwise avoiding hash function $h\colon R \times U \to T$. If $|T| \ge 2|S|^2$ then with probability $\ge 3/4$, no two elements of S collide.*

Proof. Assume $|T| \ge 2|S|^2$.

$$\begin{aligned}
\mathbf{Pr}_r\big[\exists s \ne s' \text{ in } S:\ h_r(s) = h_r(s')\big] &\le \textstyle\sum_{s \ne s' \text{ in } S} \mathbf{Pr}_r\big[h_r(s) = h_r(s')\big] && \text{(union bound)}\\
&\le \textstyle\sum_{s \ne s' \text{ in } S} 1/|T| && \text{(pairwise avoiding)}\\
&= \tbinom{|S|}{2}/|T| \le |S|^2/2|T| \le 1/4
\end{aligned}$$

■

If we're OK with a small fraction of S colliding, T can be just a constant factor larger than S:

Lemma 8.3. *Consider a set $S \subseteq U$ and a pairwise avoiding hash function $h: R \times U \to T$. If $|T| \geq 16|S|$ then with probability $\geq 3/4$, at least $3/4$ of the elements of S do not collide with any element of S.*

Proof. Assume $|T| \geq 16|S|$. For each unordered pair $s \neq s'$ in S, let $X_{s,s'}$ be the indicator random variable for the event that $h_r(s) = h_r(s')$ (over uniformly random $r \in R$). Then $\mathbf{E}[X_{s,s'}] \leq 1/|T|$ since h is pairwise avoiding. Let $X = \sum_{s \neq s' \text{ in } S} X_{s,s'}$ be the number of pairs that collide. By linearity of expectation:

$$\mathbf{E}[X] = \textstyle\sum_{s \neq s' \text{ in } S} \mathbf{E}[X_{s,s'}] \leq \sum_{s \neq s' \text{ in } S} 1/|T| = \binom{|S|}{2}/|T| \leq |S|^2/2|T| \leq |S|/32$$

By Lemma 7.13, $\mathbf{Pr}\big[X \geq |S|/8\big] \leq \mathbf{E}[X]/(|S|/8) \leq 1/4$. Each collision involves only two elements of S, so at most $2X$ elements of S are involved in collisions. So with probability $\geq 3/4$ we have $X \leq |S|/8$, in which case at most $|S|/4$ elements of S are involved in collisions. ■

8.2 Constructing Pairwise Uniformity

8.2.1 Using Finite Fields

Lemma 8.4. *For every prime p, this randomized hash function is pairwise uniform:*

$$h: \mathbb{Z}_p^2 \times \mathbb{Z}_p \to \mathbb{Z}_p \qquad \textit{defined by} \qquad h_{a,b}(u) = au + b$$

The table is as large as the universe (both have size p), which is not helpful for implementing set data structures. But such hash functions still have other applications in computational complexity.

Proof. Consider any $u \neq u'$. For every t and every t', the system of equations

$$\begin{aligned} au + b &= t \\ au' + b &= t' \end{aligned}$$

has a unique solution for the two unknowns a and b: Rearranging the first equation to $b = t - au$ and substituting this in the second equation yields $au' + (t - au) = t'$ which rearranges to $a(u' - u) = t' - t$ and thus $a = (t' - t)/(u' - u)$ since $u' - u \neq 0$. Substituting this back into the first equation yields $b = t - ((t' - t)/(u' - u))u$. Thus $\mathbf{Pr}_{a,b}\big[h_{a,b}(u) = t \text{ and } h_{a,b}(u') = t'\big] = 1/p^2$. ■

8.2.2 Using Matrices

We use the following lemma to analyze this section's hash functions.

Lemma 8.5. *For any distribution over pairs of bits $yz \in \{0,1\}^2$, if each of y, z, and $y \oplus z$ is uniform over $\{0,1\}$, then yz is uniform over $\{0,1\}^2$.*

Proof. Let $a = \mathbf{Pr}[yz = 00]$, $b = \mathbf{Pr}[yz = 01]$, $c = \mathbf{Pr}[yz = 10]$, $d = \mathbf{Pr}[yz = 11]$. By assumption, $a + b = \mathbf{Pr}[y = 0] = 1/2$ and $a + c = \mathbf{Pr}[z = 0] = 1/2$ and $a + d = \mathbf{Pr}[y \oplus z = 0] = 1/2$. These equations imply $b = c = d = 1/2 - a$. Combining this with $a + b + c + d = 1$ yields $a + 3(1/2 - a) = 1$ and thus $a = b = c = d = 1/4$. ■

If the universe is bit strings except for the all-0 string, then to achieve pairwise uniformity, we can multiply by a random matrix over $\mathbb{Z}_2$:

Lemma 8.6. *For all positive integers m and n, this randomized hash function is pairwise uniform:*

$$h\colon \{0,1\}^{mn} \times \big(\{0,1\}^n \setminus \{0^n\}\big) \to \{0,1\}^m \qquad \textit{defined by} \qquad h_A(u) = Au$$

where A is an $m \times n$ matrix, u is a nonzero $n \times 1$ vector, and the field is $\mathbb{Z}_2$.

Proof. Consider any two nonzero vectors $u \neq u'$. Let $y = Au$ and $z = Au'$. We need to show that (y, z) is uniform over $(\{0,1\}^m)^2$. For each $i \in [m]$, we have $y_i = A_i \odot u$ and $z_i = A_i \odot u'$ where A_i is A's ith row and $\odot$ is the dot product over $\mathbb{Z}_2$. Since A's rows are fully independent, it suffices to show that $y_i z_i$ is uniform over $\{0,1\}^2$ for each i. This follows from Lemma 8.5 by the random subsum principle (Lemma 7.2): y_i is uniform since $u \neq 0^n$, and z_i is uniform since $u' \neq 0^n$, and $y_i \oplus z_i$ is uniform since $u \neq u'$. ∎

If the universe is bit strings (including the all-0 string), then to achieve pairwise uniformity, we can multiply by a random matrix and add a random vector over $\mathbb{Z}_2$:

Lemma 8.7. *For all positive integers m and n, this randomized hash function is pairwise uniform:*

$$h\colon \{0,1\}^{mn+m} \times \{0,1\}^n \to \{0,1\}^m \qquad \textit{defined by} \qquad h_{A,b}(u) = Au + b$$

where A is an $m \times n$ matrix, b is an $m \times 1$ vector, u is an $n \times 1$ vector, and the field is $\mathbb{Z}_2$.

Proof. $Au + b$ is the same as:

$$\begin{bmatrix} A & b \end{bmatrix} \begin{bmatrix} u \\ 1 \end{bmatrix}$$

We append column b to A to obtain a uniformly random $m \times (n+1)$ matrix. We append a 1 to u to obtain a nonzero $(n+1) \times 1$ vector. Then, we do matrix-vector multiplication.

For all $u \neq u'$, Lemma 8.6 says $(Au + b,\ Au' + b)$ is uniform over $(\{0,1\}^m)^2$. ∎

In §8.1.2, the second example of a pairwise uniform hash function is Lemma 8.7 with $m = 1$ and $n = 2$.

8.2.3 Saving Random Bits

The pairwise uniform hash functions from §8.2.2 use $O(mn)$ random bits. Now, we design a pairwise uniform hash function using just $O(m + n)$ random bits.

In a *diagonal-constant* matrix A, the entries along each "upper-left to lower-right diagonal" are the same: $A_{i,j}$ only depends on $i - j$. Such a matrix is determined by its *principal* entries in the leftmost column and the top row—the rest of the entries are just copied along the diagonals. Figure 8.2 shows an example.

To sample a uniformly random $m \times n$ diagonal-constant matrix over $\mathbb{Z}_2$, we just need to sample the $m + n - 1$ many principal bits uniformly at random.

Lemma 8.8. *Over the field $\mathbb{Z}_2$, if A is a uniformly random $m \times n$ diagonal-constant matrix and u is any nonzero $n \times 1$ vector, then Au is a uniformly random $m \times 1$ vector.*

$$\begin{bmatrix} 0 & 1 & 0 & 1 & 1 & 0 \\ 0 & 0 & 1 & 0 & 1 & 1 \\ 1 & 0 & 0 & 1 & 0 & 1 \\ 0 & 1 & 0 & 0 & 1 & 0 \end{bmatrix} \qquad \begin{bmatrix} 0 & 1 & 0 & 1 & 1 & 0 \\ 0 & 0 & 1 & 0 & 1 & 1 \\ 1 & 0 & 0 & 1 & 0 & 1 \\ 0 & 1 & 0 & 0 & 1 & 0 \end{bmatrix}$$

Figure 8.2: Example diagonal-constant matrix

Proof idea. Each bit of Au is the xor of some principal bits of A. Thus $(Au)_1$ is uniform. And $(Au)_2$ may depend on some of the same principal bits that $(Au)_1$ did, but it depends on at least one principal bit that $(Au)_1$ didn't, which makes $(Au)_2$ uniform and independent of $(Au)_1$. This reasoning shows that each bit of Au is uniform and independent of the previous bits of Au. ■

Proof. Index A's rows from 0 to $m-1$ and A's columns from 0 to $n-1$. Index A's principal entries as:

$$\begin{bmatrix} a_0 & a_1 & a_2 & \cdots & a_{n-1} \\ a_{-1} & a_0 & a_1 & \cdots & a_{n-2} \\ a_{-2} & a_{-1} & a_0 & \cdots & a_{n-3} \\ \vdots & \vdots & \vdots & \ddots & \vdots \\ a_{1-m} & a_{2-m} & a_{3-m} & \cdots & a_{n-m} \end{bmatrix}$$

Let $J = \{j \in \{0,\ldots,n-1\} : u_j = 1\}$, which is nonempty since $u \neq 0^n$. For each $i \in \{0,\ldots,m-1\}$, let $J-i = \{j-i : j \in J\}$, and let a_{J-i} be the principal bits indexed by $J-i$. Then $(Au)_i = \oplus(a_{J-i})$ is the xor of the bits a_{J-i}.

For any $m \times 1$ vector c, we prove that $\mathbf{Pr}[Au = c] = 2^{-m}$. Let k be the smallest index in J. We ignore $a_{1-m}, \ldots, a_{k-m}$ since Au doesn't depend on them. We claim that for every outcome of $a_{k+1}, \ldots, a_{n-1}$, there's exactly one outcome of $a_{k-m+1}, \ldots, a_k$ such that $Au = c$. Let $K = J \setminus \{k\}$, so $(Au)_i = \oplus(a_{J-i}) = a_{k-i} \oplus \oplus(a_{K-i})$. ($K$ might be empty, in which case $\oplus(a_{K-i}) = 0$.)

Algorithm to find the unique $a_{k-m+1}, \ldots, a_k$ such that $(Au)_i = c_i$ for all i (8.1)

for $i \leftarrow 0, 1, \ldots, m-1$:
  let $a_{k-i} \leftarrow c_i \oplus \oplus(a_{K-i})$

In the ith iteration, the bits a_{K-i} have already been determined since they're among $a_{k-i+1}, \ldots, a_k$ (calculated in previous iterations) and $a_{k+1}, \ldots, a_{n-1}$ (which we're conditioning on). ■

The pairwise uniform construction from Lemma 8.7 works even when the matrix A is diagonal-constant, in which case the hash function only needs $m+n-1$ random bits for A's principal entries, and m random bits for b:

Lemma 8.9. *For all positive integers m and n, this randomized hash function is pairwise uniform:*

$$h\colon \{0,1\}^{2m+n-1} \times \{0,1\}^n \to \{0,1\}^m \qquad \textit{defined by} \qquad h_{A,b}(u) = Au + b$$

where A is an $m \times n$ diagonal-constant matrix, b is an $m \times 1$ vector, u is an $n \times 1$ vector, and the field is $\mathbb{Z}_2$.

Proof. Consider any $u \neq u'$. Let $y = Au + b$ and $z = Au' + b$. We need to show that (y, z) is uniform over $(\{0,1\}^m)^2$. Since $y - z = (Au + b) - (Au' + b) = A(u - u')$ and $u - u' \neq 0^n$, Lemma 8.8 says $y - z$ is uniform over $\{0,1\}^m$. For any $t \in \{0,1\}^m$ and $t' \in \{0,1\}^m$,

$$\begin{aligned}
\mathbf{Pr}\big[y = t \text{ and } z = t'\big] &= \mathbf{Pr}\big[y = t \text{ and } y - z = t - t'\big] \\
&= \mathbf{Pr}\big[y = t \,\big|\, y - z = t - t'\big] \cdot \mathbf{Pr}\big[y - z = t - t'\big] && \text{(chain rule)} \\
&= \mathbf{Pr}\big[b = t - Au \,\big|\, y - z = t - t'\big] \cdot \mathbf{Pr}\big[y - z = t - t'\big] \\
&= 2^{-m} \cdot 2^{-m}
\end{aligned}$$

since b is uniform and independent of A, and since $y - z$ only depends on A (not on b). ■

It's known that if $h \colon \{0,1\}^\ell \times \{0,1\}^n \to \{0,1\}^m$ is any pairwise uniform hash function, then $\ell \geq 2m$ and $\ell \geq m + n$. Thus the construction from Lemma 8.9 is within a constant factor of the optimal number of random bits.

8.3 Isolating Witnesses

If an NP problem has *at most one* witness for each input, does this help us solve the problem? Not in general: For every NP problem, we can use a pairwise uniform hash function to randomly *isolate* a unique witness (when a witness exists), so if an efficient randomized algorithm can detect the existence of a unique witness, then the original NP problem also has an efficient randomized algorithm.

8.3.1 Unambiguous Polynomial Time

For problems in NP, every 1-input has *at least one* witness. We define the complexity class UP ("Unambiguous Polynomial time") containing problems where every 1-input has *exactly one* witness and every 0-input has no witness. ("Ambiguous" means having more than one witness.) The definition has a wrinkle. Recall that if V is a verifier for A, then for every input x:

$$\begin{aligned}
A(x) = 1 &\Rightarrow V(x; w) \text{ accepts for at least one } w \\
A(x) = 0 &\Rightarrow V(x; w) \text{ accepts for no } w
\end{aligned}$$

If $V(x; w)$ accepts, then it would still accept if we sneakily modify a word of w that $V(x; w)$ doesn't read. Thus, 1-inputs technically have infinitely many witnesses. For "exactly one" to make sense, we only consider *plain* witnesses w, meaning w has all-0 words at all addresses that $V(x; w)$ doesn't read. We say V is an *unambiguous* verifier for A when for every input x:

$$\begin{aligned}
A(x) = 1 &\Rightarrow V(x; w) \text{ accepts for exactly one plain } w \\
A(x) = 0 &\Rightarrow V(x; w) \text{ accepts for no } w
\end{aligned}$$

Definition. UP is the set of all decision problems for which there exists a poly-time unambiguous verifier. ◀

P ⊆ UP ⊆ NP because a solver is an unambiguous verifier, and an unambiguous verifier is a verifier. It's generally conjectured that P ≠ UP ≠ NP. Here's an example problem in UP:

UNAMBIGUOUS SATISFIABILITY (or UNAMBIGUOUS SAT for short)	(8.2)
Input: CNF formula φ with at most one satisfying assignment	
Output: Is φ satisfiable?	

UNAMBIGUOUS SAT $\in$ UP by an unambiguous verifier that checks whether the purported witness satisfies φ: It reads w's first n words (assuming φ has n variables), rejects if any word is > 1, and otherwise evaluates φ with this assignment $a \in \{0,1\}^n$ plugged in, and accepts iff $\varphi(a) = 1$. UNAMBIGUOUS SAT is inherently a promise problem (§ 7.9) because it's not simple to check whether φ has at most one satisfying assignment.

8.3.2 Isolation via Hashing

Theorem 8.10. *If* UP $\subseteq$ RP *then* NP $\subseteq$ RP.

Proof idea. We follow the pattern $A \in \mathsf{NP} \Rightarrow B \in \mathsf{UP} \Rightarrow B \in \mathsf{RP} \Rightarrow A \in \mathsf{RP}$: Every $A \in \mathsf{NP}$ has a one-sided-error randomized mapping reduction to some $B \in \mathsf{UP}$. A 1-input may have many witnesses, and we want to "isolate" one of them ("eliminate" all the rest). Let $h\colon R \times U \to T$ be a pairwise uniform hash function where U is the set of all potential witnesses. We eliminate every witness that doesn't hash to some specific target $t \in T$. (It doesn't matter what t is, so we arbitrarily pick the all-0 string.) For some 1-input, let $S \subseteq U$ be the set of actual witnesses. If T is much larger than S, probably no witness will hash to t. If T is much smaller than S, probably multiple witnesses will hash to t. If $|T| \approx |S|$, there's a decent probability that exactly one witness will hash to t and survive. To specify the table size, we need an estimate of $|S|$. By guessing $\log|S|$ randomly, we get a good enough estimate with small-but-not-too-small probability. ■

Lemma 8.11. *For all pairwise uniform $h\colon R \times U \to T$ and $S \subseteq U$ and $t \in T$:*

$$\mathbf{Pr}_r\big[h_r(s) = t \text{ for exactly one } s \in S\big] \geq \tfrac{|S|}{|T|}\big(1 - \tfrac{|S|}{|T|}\big)$$

Proof of Lemma 8.11. Here, s and s' are always elements of S:

$$\begin{aligned}
&\mathbf{Pr}_r\big[h_r(s) = t \text{ for exactly one } s\big] \\
&= \textstyle\sum_s \mathbf{Pr}_r\big[h_r(s) = t \text{ and } h_r(s') \neq t \text{ for all } s' \neq s\big] \\
&= \textstyle\sum_s \big(\mathbf{Pr}_r\big[h_r(s) = t\big] - \mathbf{Pr}_r\big[h_r(s) = t = h_r(s') \text{ for some } s' \neq s\big]\big) \\
&\geq \textstyle\sum_s \big(\mathbf{Pr}_r\big[h_r(s) = t\big] - \sum_{s' \neq s} \mathbf{Pr}_r\big[h_r(s) = t = h_r(s')\big]\big) && \text{(union bound)} \\
&= \textstyle\sum_s \big(\frac{1}{|T|} - \sum_{s' \neq s} \frac{1}{|T|^2}\big) && \text{(pairwise uniformity)} \\
&= \tfrac{|S|}{|T|}\big(1 - \tfrac{|S|-1}{|T|}\big) \geq \tfrac{|S|}{|T|}\big(1 - \tfrac{|S|}{|T|}\big)
\end{aligned}$$

■

Proof of Theorem 8.10. Assume UP $\subseteq$ RP. Suppose $A \in \mathsf{NP}$ by a verifier V with time efficiency $\leq T = cN^d$ (for integers c, d) and log-bounded word size W. On a valid input x of size N, the potential witnesses are elements of $(\{0,1\}^W)^T = \{0,1\}^n$ where $n = TW$. For each m, let $h^m\colon \{0,1\}^{2m+n-1} \times \{0,1\}^n \to \{0,1\}^m$ be the pairwise uniform hash function from Lemma 8.9. (Or, we could use Lemma 8.7.)

(call this problem B)	(8.3)
Input:	x,m,r where x is a valid input of size N to A, $m \in [n+1]$, and $r \in \{0,1\}^{2m+n-1}$
Output:	1 if there's exactly one $w \in \{0,1\}^n$ such that $\big(V(x;w)$ accepts and $h_r^m(w) = 0^m\big)$ 0 if there's no such w undefined otherwise

$B \in \mathsf{UP}$ by an unambiguous verifier V' where $V'(x,m,r;w)$ reads w's first n bits and accepts iff $V(x;w)$ accepts and $h_r^m(w) = 0^m$. Thus $B \in \mathsf{RP}$ by a randomized program Π. Assume Π clocks itself so it terminates in poly time even on invalid inputs.

Consider a poly-time randomized program Π' where $\Pi'(x)$ samples a uniformly random $m \in [n+1]$ and a uniformly random $r \in \{0,1\}^{2m+n-1}$ and runs $\Pi(x,m,r)$. This Π' runs in poly time even when it runs Π on an invalid input to B.

Suppose $A(x) = 0$, so $V(x;w)$ accepts for no w. For all m and r, we have $B(x,m,r) = 0$ and so $\mathbf{Pr}\big[\Pi(x,m,r) \text{ accepts}\big] = 0$. Thus $\mathbf{Pr}\big[\Pi'(x) \text{ accepts}\big] = 0$.

Suppose $A(x) = 1$, so $V(x;w)$ accepts for some w. Let $S = \big\{w \in \{0,1\}^n : V(x;w) \text{ accepts}\big\}$. Since $1 \le |S| \le 2^n$, we have $2^\ell/3 \le |S| < 2^{\ell+1}/3$ for some $\ell \in [n+1]$, and thus $1/3 \le |S|/2^\ell < 2/3$. By Lemma 8.11:

$$\mathbf{Pr}_r\big[B(x,\ell,r) = 1\big] \;=\; \mathbf{Pr}_r\big[h_r^\ell(w) = 0^\ell \text{ for exactly one } w \in S\big] \;\ge\; \tfrac{|S|}{2^\ell}\big(1 - \tfrac{|S|}{2^\ell}\big) \;\ge\; 2/9$$

Combining everything using the chain rule:

$$\begin{aligned}
&\mathbf{Pr}\big[\Pi'(x) \text{ accepts}\big]\\
&= \mathbf{Pr}_{m,r,q}\big[\Pi(x,m,r;q) \text{ accepts}\big]\\
&\ge \mathbf{Pr}_{m,r,q}\big[m = \ell \text{ and } B(x,m,r) = 1 \text{ and } \Pi(x,m,r;q) \text{ accepts}\big]\\
&= \mathbf{Pr}_m[m = \ell] \cdot \mathbf{Pr}_r\big[B(x,\ell,r) = 1\big] \cdot \mathbf{Pr}_{r,q}\big[\Pi(x,\ell,r;q) \text{ accepts} \,\big|\, B(x,\ell,r) = 1\big]\\
&\ge \tfrac{1}{n+1} \cdot \tfrac{2}{9} \cdot \tfrac{2}{3}\\
&= \Omega(1/n)
\end{aligned}$$

By amplification (§7.3.1), $A \in \mathsf{RP}$. ■

In this proof, B is inherently a promise problem. It's unknown whether $\mathsf{UP} \subseteq \mathsf{RP}$ implies $\mathsf{NP} \subseteq \mathsf{RP}$ when the classes only contain total problems.

8.4 Approximately Counting and Sampling Witnesses

Given an input to an NP problem, computing the number of witnesses is at least as hard as deciding whether the number of witnesses is ≥ 1 (solving the NP problem). But in the opposite direction, deciding whether a witness exists doesn't seem helpful for counting the witnesses.

What if we'd be happy with an approximation of the number of witnesses, instead of the exact number? For starters, *additive* approximate counting is straightforward: Suppose $\{0,1\}^n$ is the set of all potential witnesses, and $S \subseteq \{0,1\}^n$ is the set of actual witnesses for some input. To approximate the fraction of witnesses $p = |S|/2^n$ within $\pm\gamma$, we can run the verifier several times on randomly sampled elements of $\{0,1\}^n$ and output the fraction of runs that accept. Each run is like a coin toss with heads probability p. By Corollary 7.21, $\frac{1}{\gamma^2}\ln\frac{2}{\varepsilon}$ tosses suffice to estimate p within $\pm\gamma$ with probability $\ge 1-\varepsilon$.

If $|S| = 2^{n/2}$, for example, then the number of witnesses is exponentially large but is an exponentially small fraction of $\{0,1\}^n$, so just outputting 0 is an excellent additive approximation of $|S|/2^n = 2^{-n/2}$. But suppose we want a *multiplicative* approximation, within a factor (times or divided by) $1+\gamma$. Then outputting 0 won't cut it, and if we sample uniformly random elements of $\{0,1\}^n$, we probably won't encounter any witness.

Multiplicative approximate counting is at least as hard as deciding whether the number of witnesses is ≥ 1 (since an approximation of 0 must be 0, and an approximation of > 0 must be > 0). But surprisingly, it's no harder than that. We use pairwise uniform hashing to design a poly-time randomized algorithm that approximates the number of witnesses within a factor $1 + 1/\operatorname{poly} N$ using an oracle for an NP problem (§ 8.4.1). For example, this implies that if SAT $\in$ BPP, then a poly-time randomized algorithm can multiplicatively approximate the number of satisfying assignments of a given CNF. This also leads to a poly-time algorithm that samples a uniformly random witness using an NP oracle (§8.4.2), which has an application to computational learning theory in Chapter 13.

Circuits play the role of verifiers in this section: Suppose $A \in$ NP by a verifier V. For any input x with n-bit witnesses, turn V into a poly-size circuit $C\colon \{0,1\}^n \to \{0,1\}$ (with x hardwired) such that $C(w) = V(x;w)$ for all w (§ 5.3.2). Then $S = \{w : C(w) = 1\} \subseteq \{0,1\}^n$ is x's set of witnesses. We design algorithms for approximating $|S|$ and for sampling a uniformly random element of S, using an NP oracle.

Nonnegative numbers x and y are *within a factor* $b \geq 1$ iff $x \leq by$ and $y \leq bx$.

8.4.1 Approximate Counting

CIRCUIT SAT COUNTING	(8.4)
Input:	Circuit C with one output node
Output:	The number of satisfying assignments of C

Let $S = \{w : C(w) = 1\} \subseteq \{0,1\}^n$ be the set of witnesses (satisfying assignments of C). For CIRCUIT SAT COUNTING (or any function problem whose output is a nonnegative integer), a *randomized approximation scheme* is a randomized program that takes as input C and parameters $0 < \gamma \leq 1$ and $0 < \varepsilon < 1$, and outputs an integer $z \geq 0$ such that:

$$\mathbf{Pr}\big[z \text{ and } |S| \text{ are within a factor } 1+\gamma\big] \;\geq\; 1-\varepsilon$$

A *fully poly-time* randomized approximation scheme (FPRAS) has $\operatorname{poly}\big(\frac{N}{\gamma}\log\frac{1}{\varepsilon}\big)$ time efficiency and $O\big(\log\big(\frac{N}{\gamma}\log\frac{1}{\varepsilon}\big)\big)$-bounded word size. When $\gamma \geq 1/\operatorname{poly} N$ and $\varepsilon \geq 1/2^{\operatorname{poly} N}$, the program has $\operatorname{poly} N$ time efficiency and $O(\log N)$-bounded word size.

Usually, time efficiency and word size are functions of N alone, but here they depend on γ and ε. "Non-fully poly-time" would mean the degree of the "poly" depends on γ and ε.

Theorem 8.12. *If* NP $\subseteq$ BPP *then* CIRCUIT SAT COUNTING *has a fully poly-time randomized approximation scheme.*

Proof idea. By a search-to-decision reduction, we can consider the promise problem of deciding whether $|S|$ is above some threshold or below some lower threshold. We hash the witnesses (elements of S) into a table whose size is approximately the upper threshold. If $|S|$ is above the upper threshold, then probably at least one witness hashes to a specific target t (which we arbitrarily pick to be the all-0 string). If $|S|$ is below the lower threshold, then probably no witness hashes to t. This yields a randomized reduction to the NP problem of deciding whether there exists a witness that hashes to t. ■

Lemma 8.13. *For all pairwise uniform $h: R \times U \to T$ and $S \subseteq U$ and $t \in T$ and $K \leq |S|$:*

$$\tfrac{|S|}{|T|} \geq \mathbf{Pr}_r\big[h_r(s) = t \text{ for some } s \in S\big] \geq \tfrac{K}{|T|}\big(1 - \tfrac{K}{|T|}\big)$$

Proof of Lemma 8.13. By a union bound:

$$\mathbf{Pr}_r\big[h_r(s) = t \text{ for some } s \in S\big] \leq \textstyle\sum_{s \in S} \mathbf{Pr}_r\big[h_r(s) = t\big] = \sum_{s \in S} \tfrac{1}{|T|} = \tfrac{|S|}{|T|}$$

Consider any $K \leq |S|$ and any subset $S' \subseteq S$ of size exactly K. By Lemma 8.11:

$$\mathbf{Pr}_r\big[h_r(s) = t \text{ for some } s \in S\big] \geq \mathbf{Pr}_r\big[h_r(s) = t \text{ for exactly one } s \in S'\big] \geq \tfrac{K}{|T|}\big(1 - \tfrac{K}{|T|}\big)$$ ■

Proof of Theorem 8.12. The proof has three steps.

Step 1. We prove that it suffices to consider $\gamma = 1$ (a factor 2 approximation). For $\gamma < 1$, let ℓ be the least integer such that $2^{1/\ell} \leq 1 + \gamma$. For a circuit $C: \{0,1\}^n \to \{0,1\}$, define a circuit $C': (\{0,1\}^n)^\ell \to \{0,1\}$ where $C'(w_1, \ldots, w_\ell) = C(w_1) \wedge \cdots \wedge C(w_\ell)$. Then $S' = \{w' : C'(w') = 1\} \subseteq \{0,1\}^{n\ell}$ is the cartesian product $S^\ell = S \times \cdots \times S$. If z' and $|S'|$ are within a factor 2, then $z = (z')^{1/\ell}$ and $|S| = |S'|^{1/\ell}$ are within a factor $2^{1/\ell} \leq 1 + \gamma$. Assuming some program takes input C' and outputs z' such that $\mathbf{Pr}\big[z' \text{ and } |S'| \text{ are within a factor } 2\big] \geq 1 - \varepsilon$, we modify it to a program that takes input C and outputs $z = (z')^{1/\ell}$ such that $\mathbf{Pr}\big[z \text{ and } |S| \text{ are within a factor } 1 + \gamma\big] \geq 1 - \varepsilon$. (Rounding z to an integer is a slight nuisance, but let's not be pedantic about it.) We have $\ell = O(1/\gamma)$ since $2^{\gamma/2} \leq e^{\gamma/2} \leq 1 + \gamma/2 + (\gamma/2)^2 \leq 1 + \gamma$ (Fact 7.23). Thus $\text{poly}\big(N' \log \tfrac{1}{\varepsilon}\big)$ time on input C' becomes $\text{poly}\big(\tfrac{N}{\gamma} \log \tfrac{1}{\varepsilon}\big)$ time on input C.

Step 2. Assume $\gamma = 1$, and use the original notation C, w, S, z instead of step 1's C', w', S', z'.

(call this problem A)		(8.5)
Input:	Circuit C with n variables, and $k \in \{0, 1, \ldots, n\}$	
Output:	1 if $\|S\| \geq 2^k$	
	0 if $\|S\| < 2^{k-1}$	
	undefined otherwise	

In step 3, we prove $A \in$ BPP by a randomized program Π, if NP $\subseteq$ BPP. Assume Π clocks itself so that even on an invalid input, it terminates in poly time (and may accept with any probability).

```
Randomized approximation scheme for CIRCUIT SAT COUNTING assuming NP ⊆ BPP    (8.6)
on input (C, 1, ε):
    for every k ∈ {0, 1, ..., n}: run Π(C, k), amplified to have error ε/(n + 1)
    if at least one run accepted: output 2^k for the greatest k such that Π(C, k) accepted
    else: output 0
```

This runs in $\text{poly}\big(N \log \tfrac{1}{\varepsilon}\big)$ time. We could speed it up with binary search, but we're not picky.

Say that k is *valid* iff (C, k) is a valid input to A. We claim that if $\Pi(C, k) = A(C, k)$ for all valid k (that is, no run of Π errs), then the algorithm outputs some z within a factor 2 of $|S|$:

- If $|S| = 0$ then $A(C,k) = 0$ for all k, so $z = 0$.
- If $|S| = 2^n$ then $A(C,n) = 1$, so $z = 2^n$.
- If $0 < |S| < 2^n$ so $2^{\ell-1} \le |S| < 2^\ell$ for some $\ell \in \{1,\dots,n\}$, then $A(C,\ell)$ is undefined and $A(C,\ell-1) = 1$ and $A(C,k) = 0$ for all $k > \ell$, so either $z = 2^\ell$ or $z = 2^{\ell-1}$ (depending on whether $\Pi(C,\ell)$ accepts), both of which are within a factor 2 of $|S|$.

$$\begin{aligned}
\mathbf{Pr}\big[z \text{ and } |S| \text{ aren't within a factor } 2\big] &\le \mathbf{Pr}\big[\Pi(C,k) \ne A(C,k) \text{ for some valid } k\big] \\
&\le \textstyle\sum_{\text{valid } k} \mathbf{Pr}\big[\Pi(C,k) \ne A(C,k)\big] && \text{(union bound)} \\
&\le \textstyle\sum_{\text{valid } k} \varepsilon/(n+1) && \text{(correctness of } \Pi) \\
&\le \varepsilon
\end{aligned}$$

Step 3. We prove $A \in \mathsf{BPP}$ assuming $\mathsf{NP} \subseteq \mathsf{BPP}$. For each m, let $h^m\colon \{0,1\}^{2m+n-1} \times \{0,1\}^n \to \{0,1\}^m$ be the pairwise uniform hash function from Lemma 8.9. (Or, we could use Lemma 8.7.)

(call this problem B)	(8.7)
Input: Circuit C with n variables, $k \in \{0,1,\dots,n\}$, and $r \in \{0,1\}^{2m+n-1}$ where $m = k+2$	
Output: Does there exist $w \in S$ such that $h^m_r(w) = 0^m$?	

By Lemma 8.13, we have a randomized mapping reduction from A to B:

$$\begin{aligned}
A(C,k) = 0 &\Rightarrow \mathbf{Pr}_r\big[B(C,k,r) = 1\big] < 2^{k-1}/2^m = 1/8 \\
A(C,k) = 1 &\Rightarrow \mathbf{Pr}_r\big[B(C,k,r) = 1\big] \ge \tfrac{2^k}{2^m}\big(1 - \tfrac{2^k}{2^m}\big) = \tfrac{1}{4}\big(1 - \tfrac{1}{4}\big) = 3/16
\end{aligned}$$

$B \in \mathsf{NP}$ by a verifier V where $V(C,k,r;w)$ accepts iff $C(w) = 1$ and $h^m_r(w) = 0^m$. Thus $B \in \mathsf{BPP}$ by a poly-time 0.01-error randomized program Π. Define a poly-time randomized program Π' for A where $\Pi'(C,k)$ samples a uniformly random $r \in \{0,1\}^{2m+n-1}$ and runs $\Pi(C,k,r)$, which uses its own randomness q. By the law of total probability:

$$\begin{aligned}
\mathbf{Pr}_{r,q}\big[\Pi'(C,k;r,q) \text{ accepts}\big] = {} & \mathbf{Pr}_{r,q}\big[\Pi(C,k,r;q) \text{ accepts} \,\big|\, B(C,k,r) = 1\big] \cdot \mathbf{Pr}_r\big[B(C,k,r) = 1\big] + \\
& \mathbf{Pr}_{r,q}\big[\Pi(C,k,r;q) \text{ accepts} \,\big|\, B(C,k,r) = 0\big] \cdot \mathbf{Pr}_r\big[B(C,k,r) = 0\big]
\end{aligned}$$

Combining everything:

$$\begin{aligned}
A(C,k) = 0 &\Rightarrow \mathbf{Pr}\big[\Pi'(C,k) \text{ accepts}\big] \le 1 \cdot (1/8) + 0.01 \cdot 1 \le 0.14 \\
A(C,k) = 1 &\Rightarrow \mathbf{Pr}\big[\Pi'(C,k) \text{ accepts}\big] \ge 0.99 \cdot (3/16) + 0 \cdot 0 \ge 0.18
\end{aligned}$$

By Corollary 7.22, $A \in \mathsf{BPP}$. ■

8.4.2 Approximate Sampling

In a *sampling problem* (as opposed to a decision, function, or search problem), the goal is to output a sample from a probability distribution that depends on the input. When the distribution is uniform over all witnesses of a 1-input of an NP problem, we can approximately sample using an approximate counting algorithm.

CIRCUIT SAT APPROXIMATE SAMPLING	(8.8)
Input:	Circuit C such that $S = \{w : C(w) = 1\}$ is nonempty, $0 < \gamma \leq 1$, and $0 < \varepsilon < 1$
Output:	An element of S or abort, such that for each $w \in S$, $\mathbf{Pr}[\text{output is } w]$ is within a factor $1 + \gamma$ of $1/\lvert S\rvert$, and $\mathbf{Pr}[\text{abort}] \leq \varepsilon$

Theorem 8.14. *If* NP $\subseteq$ BPP *then* CIRCUIT SAT APPROXIMATE SAMPLING *has a fully poly-time randomized program.*

Proof idea. Let's turn an exact counter into an exact sampler. The same approach turns an approximate counter into an approximate sampler. This sampling-to-counting reduction resembles a search-to-decision reduction.

Witnesses are satisfying assignments of C. Define the *witness tree*: Start with the perfect binary tree of depth n where left edges are labeled 0 and right edges are labeled 1. Identify each node u with the bit string labeling the root-to-u path: The root is the empty string, and each internal node u has left child $u0$ and right child $u1$, and the leaves are the elements of $\{0,1\}^n$. Now, delete each node that's not a prefix of any witness. The remaining leaves are the witnesses, and each remaining node is a prefix of at least one witness.

To sample a uniformly random leaf, take a random walk from the root, but in each step, go to the left child or right child with probabilities proportional to the numbers of leaves in those subtrees. Let ℓ_u be the number of leaves in u's subtree. If u was deleted then $\ell_u = 0$. If $|u| < n$ then $\ell_u = \ell_{u0} + \ell_{u1}$.

Algorithm for exact sampling using exact counting (8.9)

initialize $u \leftarrow$ empty string
while $|u| < n$:
  with probability $\ell_{u0}/(\ell_{u0} + \ell_{u1})$: update $u \leftarrow u0$
  otherwise: update $u \leftarrow u1$
output u

Note that the probability of updating $u \leftarrow u1$ is $\ell_{u1}/(\ell_{u0} + \ell_{u1})$. To compute ℓ_u for any node u, we need to count the witnesses with u as a prefix—and these are just the witnesses for a related circuit. So counting witnesses enables sampling witnesses. ■

Example. Figure 8.3 shows a witness tree.

- At the root: $\mathbf{Pr}[\text{go left}] = 3/8$ and $\mathbf{Pr}[\text{go right}] = 5/8$. Suppose we go right.
- At node 1: $\mathbf{Pr}[\text{go left}] = 3/5$ and $\mathbf{Pr}[\text{go right}] = 2/5$. Suppose we go left.
- At node 10: $\mathbf{Pr}[\text{go left}] = 1/3$ and $\mathbf{Pr}[\text{go right}] = 2/3$. Suppose we go right.
- At node 101: $\mathbf{Pr}[\text{go left}] = 1/2$ and $\mathbf{Pr}[\text{go right}] = 1/2$. Suppose we go left.

We reach node 1010 with probability $\frac{5}{8} \cdot \frac{3}{5} \cdot \frac{2}{3} \cdot \frac{1}{2} = \frac{1}{8} = \frac{1}{|S|}$. Each factor's numerator cancels the next factor's denominator. ♦

Proof of Theorem 8.14 (ancillary). Assuming NP $\subseteq$ BPP, CIRCUIT SAT COUNTING has a fully poly-time randomized approximation scheme Π (Theorem 8.12).

Consider any valid input (C, γ, ε) to CIRCUIT SAT APPROXIMATE SAMPLING. For each $u \in \{0,1\}^{\leq n}$, define the circuit C_u as the contraction of C with u plugged in for the first $|u|$ bits, and:

$$S_u = \{v : C_u(v) = 1\} = \{v : uv \in S\} \subseteq \{0,1\}^{n-|u|}$$

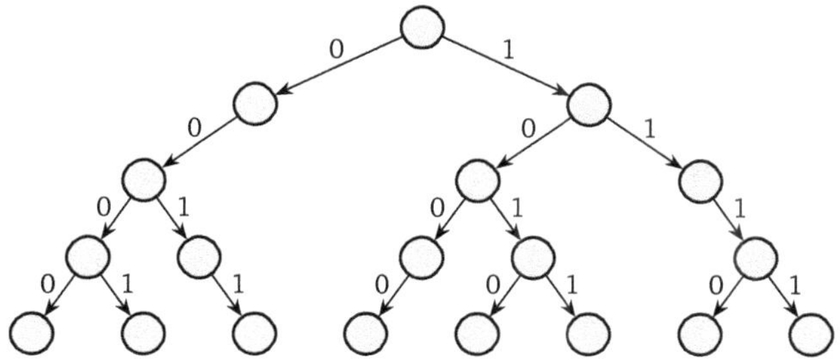

Figure 8.3: Witness tree for $S = \{0000, 0001, 0011, 1000, 1010, 1011, 1110, 1111\}$

Define $\gamma' = \gamma/16n$ and $\varepsilon' = \min(\gamma'/2^n, \varepsilon/2n)$. We have:

$$\mathbf{Pr}\big[\Pi(C_u, \gamma', \varepsilon') \text{ and } |S_u| \text{ are within a factor } 1+\gamma'\big] \geq 1-\varepsilon'$$

The following algorithm for CIRCUIT SAT APPROXIMATE SAMPLING samples a string in S bit by bit, using Π to estimate the next bit's distribution conditioned on the bits sampled so far. Here, z_u is the algorithm's estimate of $|S_u|$. (In the proof idea, ℓ_u was the actual value of $|S_u|$.)

Algorithm for approximate sampling using approximate counting (8.10)

initialize $u \leftarrow$ empty string
while $|u| < n$:
  $z_{u0} \leftarrow \Pi(C_{u0}, \gamma', \varepsilon')$ and $z_{u1} \leftarrow \Pi(C_{u1}, \gamma', \varepsilon')$
  if $z_{u0} = 0 = z_{u1}$: abort
  with probability $z_{u0}/(z_{u0}+z_{u1})$: update $u \leftarrow u0$
  otherwise: update $u \leftarrow u1$
if $C(u) = 1$: output u
else: abort

For any iteration in which neither run of Π errs:

- z_{u0} and $|S_{u0}|$ are within a factor $1+\gamma'$. In particular, $z_{u0} = 0$ iff $|S_{u0}| = 0$.
- z_{u1} and $|S_{u1}|$ are within a factor $1+\gamma'$. In particular, $z_{u1} = 0$ iff $|S_{u1}| = 0$.

If the algorithm doesn't abort, then its output is in S by definition. We prove that if the algorithm aborts, then some run of Π errs, so by a union bound:

$$\mathbf{Pr}[\text{abort}] \leq \mathbf{Pr}[\text{some run of } \Pi \text{ errs}] \leq 2n\varepsilon' \leq \varepsilon$$

First, we claim the algorithm maintains the invariant that if no run of Π errs, then $S_u \neq \emptyset$ (it stays inside the witness tree) and it doesn't abort inside the loop. This holds at the beginning by the assumption $S \neq \emptyset$. Each iteration maintains the invariant because if $S_u \neq \emptyset$ then $S_{u0} \neq \emptyset$ or $S_{u1} \neq \emptyset$, so $z_{u0} > 0$ or $z_{u1} > 0$, so this iteration doesn't abort, and if it updates $u \leftarrow ub$ (for some $b \in \{0,1\}$) with positive probability, then $z_{ub} > 0$ and so $S_{ub} \neq \emptyset$. This proves the claim. It follows that if no run of Π errs, then $S_u \neq \emptyset$ after the loop (S_u contains the empty string), so $u \in S$ and the algorithm doesn't abort.

Now, we prove that for each $w \in S$, $\mathbf{Pr}[\text{output is } w]$ is within a factor $1+\gamma$ of $1/|S|$. Consider

$$A_0 \supseteq B_1 \supseteq A_1 \supseteq B_2 \supseteq A_2 \supseteq \cdots \supseteq B_n \supseteq A_n$$

where A_i is the event that $u_1 \cdots u_i = w_1 \cdots w_i$ and no run of Π errs in the first i iterations (so A_0 is the whole sample space), and B_i is the event that $u_1 \cdots u_{i-1} = w_1 \cdots w_{i-1}$ and no run of Π errs in the first i iterations. If B_i holds, then in the ith iteration (with $u = u_1 \cdots u_{i-1} = w_1 \cdots w_{i-1}$), the algorithm picks $u_i = w_i$ with approximately the right probability:

$$\frac{z_{uw_i}}{z_{u0}+z_{u1}} \quad \text{and} \quad \frac{|S_{uw_i}|}{|S_{u0}|+|S_{u1}|} = \frac{|S_{uw_i}|}{|S_u|} \quad \text{are within a factor } (1+\gamma')^2$$

- $\mathbf{Pr}[A_i \mid B_i]$ and $|S_{w_1\cdots w_i}| / |S_{w_1 \cdots w_{i-1}}|$ are within a factor $(1+\gamma')^2 \le e^{2\gamma'}$ (Fact 7.6).
- $\mathbf{Pr}[B_i \mid A_{i-1}] \ge 1-2\varepsilon' \ge 1/e^{4\varepsilon'} \ge 1/e^{2\gamma'}$ (Fact 7.23).

By the chain rule,

$$\mathbf{Pr}[A_n] = \textstyle\prod_{i=1}^n \mathbf{Pr}[B_i \mid A_{i-1}] \cdot \mathbf{Pr}[A_i \mid B_i] \quad \text{and} \quad 1/|S| = \textstyle\prod_{i=1}^n 1 \cdot |S_{w_1\cdots w_i}| / |S_{w_1\cdots w_{i-1}}|$$

are within a factor:

$$\textstyle\prod_{i=1}^n e^{2\gamma'} \cdot e^{2\gamma'} = e^{4\gamma' n} = e^{\gamma/4} \le 1+\gamma/4+(\gamma/4)^2 \le 1+\gamma/2 \qquad \text{(Fact 7.23)}$$

Therefore,

$$\mathbf{Pr}[\text{output is } w] \ge \mathbf{Pr}[A_n] \ge 1/(1+\gamma/2)|S| \ge 1/(1+\gamma)|S|$$
$$\mathbf{Pr}[\text{output is } w] \le \mathbf{Pr}[A_n] + \mathbf{Pr}[\text{some run of } \Pi \text{ errs}] \le (1+\gamma/2)/|S| + \gamma/2|S| = (1+\gamma)/|S|$$

because $\mathbf{Pr}[\text{some run of } \Pi \text{ errs}] \le 2n\varepsilon' \le (\gamma/8)/2^n \le \gamma/2|S|$ since $|S| \le 2^n$.

Since Π runs in time $\text{poly}(\frac{N'}{\gamma'} \log \frac{1}{\varepsilon'}) = \text{poly}(\frac{N'n}{\gamma} \log \frac{1}{\varepsilon})$ on inputs of size N', the sampling algorithm runs in time $\text{poly}(\frac{N}{\gamma} \log \frac{1}{\varepsilon})$. ■

Define Circuit Sat Exact Sampling like Circuit Sat Approximate Sampling, except there's no γ, and the output distribution is exactly uniform over S, conditioned on not aborting. We proved that Circuit Sat Approximate Sampling has a fully poly-time randomized program with an NP oracle. Even Circuit Sat Exact Sampling has such a program—the proof uses hashing directly (without detouring through counting) and is beyond the scope of this book.

8.5 Hash Mixing and Applications

Now, we'll see a handy property of pairwise uniform hash functions: For all $S \subseteq U$ and $Q \subseteq T$, the fraction of S that hashes into Q is probably close to the fraction of T that's in Q. We'll see two applications in this section and several more later in the book.

8.5.1 The Lemma

Lemma 8.15. *For all pairwise uniform $h: R \times U \to T$ and nonempty $S \subseteq U$ and $Q \subseteq T$ and $\varepsilon > 0$, letting the random variable X be the number of $s \in S$ such that $h_r(s) \in Q$:*

$$\mathbf{Pr}_r\big[\big|X/|S| - |Q|/|T|\big| \ge \varepsilon\big] \le |Q|/|S|\,|T|\,\varepsilon^2$$

Example. We visualize this in Figure 8.4. An arrow from u to t means $h_r(u) = t$. A 2/6 fraction of S's elements hash into Q. A 3/8 fraction of T's elements are in Q. ♦

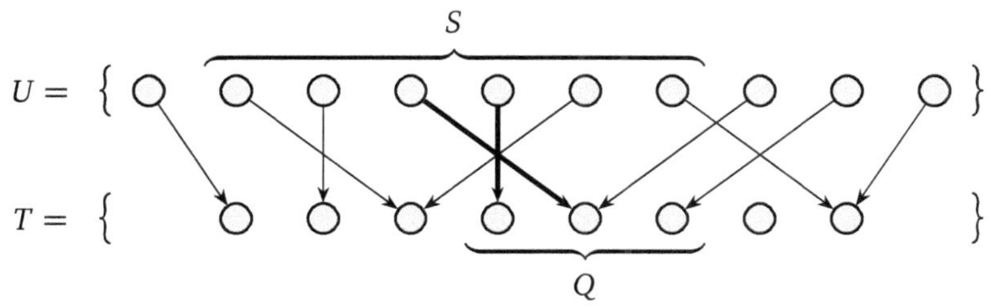

Figure 8.4: Visualization of hash mixing

The proof uses the concentration bound based on variance (§7.6.2). Recall that if X and Y are independent random variables, then $\mathbf{Var}[X+Y] = \mathbf{Var}[X] + \mathbf{Var}[Y]$ (Lemma 7.19). This implies that if $X = X_1 + \cdots + X_n$ is a sum of fully independent random variables, then $\mathbf{Var}[X] = \mathbf{Var}[X_1] + \cdots + \mathbf{Var}[X_n]$. In fact, additivity of variance holds under a weaker assumption:

Lemma 8.16. *If $X = X_1 + \cdots + X_n$ is a sum of pairwise independent random variables, then $\mathbf{Var}[X] = \mathbf{Var}[X_1] + \cdots + \mathbf{Var}[X_n]$.*

Proof of Lemma 8.16. For $i \neq j$, we have $\mathbf{E}[X_i X_j] = \mathbf{E}[X_i]\mathbf{E}[X_j]$ since X_i and X_j are independent (Lemma A.12). By Lemma 7.17 and linearity of expectation:

$$\begin{aligned}
\mathbf{Var}[X] &= \mathbf{E}\big[\big(\textstyle\sum_i X_i\big)^2\big] - \mathbf{E}\big[\textstyle\sum_i X_i\big]^2 \\
&= \mathbf{E}\big[\textstyle\sum_{i,j} X_i X_j\big] - \big(\textstyle\sum_i \mathbf{E}[X_i]\big)^2 \\
&= \textstyle\sum_{i,j} \mathbf{E}[X_i X_j] - \sum_{i,j} \mathbf{E}[X_i]\mathbf{E}[X_j] \\
&= \big(\textstyle\sum_i \mathbf{E}[X_i^2] + \sum_{i\neq j} \mathbf{E}[X_i X_j]\big) - \big(\sum_i \mathbf{E}[X_i]^2 + \sum_{i\neq j} \mathbf{E}[X_i]\mathbf{E}[X_j]\big) \\
&= \textstyle\sum_i \big(\mathbf{E}[X_i^2] - \mathbf{E}[X_i]^2\big) + \sum_{i\neq j}\big(\mathbf{E}[X_i X_j] - \mathbf{E}[X_i]\mathbf{E}[X_j]\big) \\
&= \textstyle\sum_i \mathbf{Var}[X_i] + \sum_{i\neq j} 0
\end{aligned} \quad \blacksquare$$

Proof of Lemma 8.15. For each $s \in S$, let the random variable X_s indicate whether $h_r(s) \in Q$. Since $h_r(s)$ is uniformly distributed over T, we have $\mathbf{E}[X_s] = \mathbf{Pr}_r\big[h_r(s) \in Q\big] = |Q|/|T|$ and $\mathbf{Var}[X_s] = \mathbf{E}[X_s]\big(1 - \mathbf{E}[X_s]\big) \leq |Q|/|T|$ (Lemma 7.18). Let $X = \sum_{s\in S} X_s$ be the number of $s \in S$ such that $h_r(s) \in Q$. By linearity of expectation, $\mathbf{E}[X] = \sum_{s\in S} \mathbf{E}[X_s] = |S|\,|Q|/|T|$. Since $h_r(s)$ (over all s) are pairwise independent, the X_s random variables are pairwise independent, so $\mathbf{Var}[X] = \sum_{s\in S} \mathbf{Var}[X_s] \leq |S|\,|Q|/|T|$ (Lemma 8.16). By Lemma 7.16:

$$\mathbf{Pr}_r\big[\big|X/|S| - |Q|/|T|\big| \geq \varepsilon\big] = \mathbf{Pr}_r\big[\big|X - \mathbf{E}[X]\big| \geq \varepsilon|S|\big] \leq \mathbf{Var}[X]/(\varepsilon|S|)^2 \leq |Q|/|S|\,|T|\,\varepsilon^2 \quad \blacksquare$$

Corollary 8.17. *For all pairwise uniform $h\colon R \times U \to T$ and nonempty $S \subseteq U$ and $Q \subseteq T$:*

$$\mathbf{Pr}_r\big[h_r(s) \notin Q \textit{ for all } s \in S\big] \leq |T|/|S|\,|Q|$$

Proof. By Lemma 8.15 with $\varepsilon = |Q|/|T|$:

$$\begin{aligned}
\mathbf{Pr}_r\big[h_r(s) \notin Q \text{ for all } s \in S\big] = \mathbf{Pr}_r[X = 0] &\leq \mathbf{Pr}_r\big[\big|X/|S| - |Q|/|T|\big| \geq \varepsilon\big] \\
&\leq |Q|/|S|\,|T|\,\varepsilon^2 = |T|/|S|\,|Q|
\end{aligned} \quad \blacksquare$$

8.5.2 Randomness-Efficient Amplification

The default way to amplify a two-sided-error randomized algorithm (§7.3.2) is to run it multiple times—with fresh randomness for each run—and output the majority vote of the runs. Getting error probability $1/\operatorname{poly} N$ in this way requires $O(\log N)$ runs and a $O(\log N)$ factor overhead in the number of random bits. Randomness shouldn't be taken for granted, though. If we only allow a constant factor overhead in the number of random bits, the default amplification only yields a constant error probability. With hashing, we get the best of both worlds: $1/\operatorname{poly} N$ error probability with a constant factor overhead in randomness (and $\operatorname{poly} N$ factor overhead in time):

Theorem 8.18. *Suppose decision problem A has a $1/3$-error poly-time randomized program using $\leq m = aN^b$ random bits (for integers a, b). Then for every integer $c \geq 1$, A has a $1/N^c$-error poly-time randomized program using $\leq 2m + O(\log N)$ random bits.*

Proof idea. We still run the original program multiple times and output the majority vote of the runs, but the runs need not be fully independent. They only need this property: The fraction of runs that err is probably close to the original error probability (and is thus unlikely to be $\geq 1/2$ if the original error probability is $\leq 1/3$). Pairwise independence is almost as good as full independence for this (by the hash mixing lemma) but needs less randomness. ∎

Proof. Let Π be the original randomized program. For every valid input x of size N, we have $\mathbf{Pr}_q\big[\Pi(x;q) \neq A(x)\big] \leq 1/3$ over uniformly random $q \in \{0,1\}^m$. Define $n = c\lceil \log N \rceil + 4$ and let $h\colon \{0,1\}^{2m+n-1} \times \{0,1\}^n \to \{0,1\}^m$ be the pairwise uniform hash function from Lemma 8.9. Define a randomized program Π' that takes uniformly random $r \in \{0,1\}^{2m+n-1}$:

Randomness-efficient amplification using a pairwise uniform hash function (8.11)

```
Π′(x; r):
    for each s ∈ {0,1}^n: run Π(x; h_r(s))
    if more than half the runs accepted: accept
    else: reject
```

By Lemma 8.15 with $S = U = \{0,1\}^n$, $T = \{0,1\}^m$, $Q = \big\{q \in T : \Pi(x;q) \neq A(x)\big\}$ (so $|Q|/|T| \leq 1/3$), $\varepsilon = 1/6$, and $X = \big|\{s \in S : h_r(s) \in Q\}\big|$ (the number of runs of Π that err):

$$\begin{aligned}\mathbf{Pr}_r\big[\Pi'(x;r) \neq A(x)\big] \;\leq\; \mathbf{Pr}_r\big[X/|S| \geq 1/2\big] \;&\leq\; \mathbf{Pr}_r\big[\big|X/|S| - |Q|/|T|\big| \geq \varepsilon\big] \\ &\leq\; |Q|/|S|\,|T|\,\varepsilon^2 \;\leq\; 12/2^n \;\leq\; 1/N^c\end{aligned}$$

Π' is poly-time because there are only $2^n = O(N^c)$ possibilities of s. ∎

Even better randomness-efficient amplification is possible using so-called *expander graphs*. Such graphs have many other applications in computational complexity, including the proof that UNDIRECTED REACHABILITY $\in$ L.

8.5.3 Streaming Algorithms

Streaming algorithms only have space to remember a limited summary of the input as it streams past. For example, a network router may keep statistics about packets flowing through. Streaming algorithms take one pass through the input from left to right, like how streaming verifiers (§3.3.1) and randomized algorithms (§7.7.1) take one pass through the witness and the randomness.

Instead of "read Reg[i] ← In[Reg[j]]", a streaming program uses "read Reg[i]", which puts the input segment's next unread word (or an "end of input" signifier) into Reg[i]. With linear space, a streaming algorithm could just copy the input to the work segment, to which it has unfettered access. With sublinear space, things get interesting.

Example. Suppose the input is $n-1$ many distinct numbers from $[n] = \{1,2,\ldots,n\}$ (in any order) and the output should be the number that's missing from the input. This is straightforward in linear time by recording, for each $i \in [n]$, whether i has appeared in the input. It's straightforward in log space by checking whether 1 is in the input, then taking another pass to check whether 2 is in the input, and so on. A log-space streaming algorithm can't do either of those things but can do something more insightful: Subtracting the sum of the input numbers from $n(n+1)/2 = 1+2+\cdots+n$ yields the missing number. This only uses log space for the running sum and the final subtraction. ♦

A common set-up is that the input (data stream) is a length-m sequence of elements from $[n]$, and the output depends only on how many times each element occurs in the input (not on where they occur). We may want to compute the number of distinct elements that occur at least once in the input. For example, with $n = 5$ and $m = 6$, the input $(2,5,2,4,4,2)$ has three distinct elements: 2, 4, and 5. Practical applications include determining the number of unique visitors to a particular website recently, or the number of different search queries submitted to a search engine. Algorithms for this problem are important components of big data processing systems. Even when we're not limited to a single pass through the input, a streaming algorithm may nevertheless be the most practical.

Space-efficiently counting distinct elements is possible if we use randomness and settle for an approximation. (We prove in §17.4.1 that both concessions are necessary.) A hashing-based algorithm yields a multiplicative approximation, reminiscent of approximately counting NP witnesses (§8.4.1).

Theorem 8.19. *There exists a $O(\log n)$-space randomized streaming algorithm that, given an input from $[n]^m$, approximates the number of distinct elements within a factor 7 with error probability 1/3.*

The space bound doesn't depend on m because the algorithm doesn't need to know how long the input will be or how much of the input has gone by already.

Proof idea. Suppose we "hash" each element of $[n]$ to a uniformly random real number between 0 and 1. If the input stream has k distinct elements, then their hash values are probably almost evenly spread out, like $\frac{1}{k+1}, \frac{2}{k+1}, \ldots, \frac{k}{k+1}$ if we sorted them. Thus 1/(min of these values) probably approximates $k+1$. We won't worry about the insignificant $+1$. For each element in the stream, we compute its hash value (which is the same every time we encounter this element), and we keep track of the min, and finally output $1/\min$. A pairwise uniform hash function with discretized hash values is good enough. We just need space to remember the hash function's randomness and the "running min" and to evaluate the hash function. ■

Proof. Let $h\colon R \times [n] \to \{\frac{1}{n}, \frac{2}{n}, \ldots, \frac{n}{n}\}$ be a pairwise uniform hash function.

Streaming algorithm to approximate the number of distinct elements (8.12)

on input $(x_1,\ldots,x_m) \in [n]^m$:
  pick a uniformly random $r \in R$
  output $1/\min\big(h_r(x_1),\ldots,h_r(x_m)\big)$

To implement this in $O(\log n)$ space: Assume n has been rounded up to a power of 2, so $[n]$ and $\{\frac{1}{n}, \frac{2}{n}, \ldots, \frac{n}{n}\}$ are represented as $\{0,1\}^{\log n}$. Using h from Lemma 8.9, r is a $O(\log n)$-bit string, and $h_r(x_i)$ is computable in $O(\log n)$ space. For each x_i, the algorithm compares $h_r(x_i)$ to a "running min" variable.

Let $S = \{x_1, \ldots, x_m\} \subseteq [n]$ be the set of distinct elements in the input. Let $k = |S|$ be the number of distinct elements. Let "min" stand for $\min\big(h_r(x_1), \ldots, h_r(x_m)\big) = \min_{s \in S}\big(h_r(s)\big)$. We argue that $\mathbf{Pr}\big[7k \geq 1/\min \geq k/7\big] \geq 2/3$, in other words, $\mathbf{Pr}\big[1/7k \leq \min \leq 7/k\big] \geq 2/3$. By a union bound:

$$\begin{aligned}\mathbf{Pr}\big[\min < 1/7k\big] &= \mathbf{Pr}\big[h_r(s) < 1/7k \text{ for some } s \in S\big] \\ &\leq \textstyle\sum_{s \in S} \mathbf{Pr}\big[h_r(s) < 1/7k\big] \;\leq\; \sum_{s \in S} 1/7k \;=\; 1/7\end{aligned}$$

By hash mixing (Corollary 8.17) with $Q = \{\frac{1}{n}, \frac{2}{n}, \ldots, \frac{7}{k}\}$ assuming $7n/k$ is an integer:

$$\mathbf{Pr}\big[\min > 7/k\big] \;=\; \mathbf{Pr}\big[h_r(s) > 7/k \text{ for all } s \in S\big] \;\leq\; n/(k \cdot 7n/k) \;=\; 1/7$$

If $7n/k$ isn't an integer, then using $\lfloor 7n/k \rfloor$, the bound becomes $\leq n/\big(k \cdot (7n/k - 1)\big) = n/(7n-k) \leq n/6n = 1/6$. (This is why h's codomain needs size $\geq n \geq k$.) Thus:

$$\mathbf{Pr}\big[\min < 1/7k \text{ or } \min > 7/k\big] \;\leq\; 1/7 + 1/6 \;\leq\; 1/3$$ ■

There are more sophisticated variants of this algorithm. The theoretically best one achieves approximation factor $1 + \gamma$ with error probability ε in space $O\big(\log n + \frac{1}{\gamma^2} \log \frac{1}{\varepsilon}\big)$. In practice, the "HyperLogLog" variant is widely used.

Exercises

8.1 Suppose we store a set $S \subseteq U$ using a pairwise avoiding hash function $h \colon R \times U \to T$. *Chaining* is a standard way to handle collisions: The table entry at index t points to the head of a linked list (chain) of all $s \in S$ such that $h_r(s) = t$. Given $u \in U$, to determine whether $u \in S$, we compute $h_r(u)$ and traverse the linked list at this table entry, comparing u to each element in the list. A lookup's running time depends on the chain's length.

(a) Prove that with probability $\geq 3/4$ over r, every chain has length $< 3|S|/\sqrt{|T|}$, assuming $3|S|/\sqrt{|T|} \geq 2$.

(b) Consider this problem (which appeared in Exercise 1.4):

ELEMENT DISTINCTNESS	(8.13)
Input: Nonnegative integers $x_1, x_2, \ldots, x_N$ such that $x_i \leq N^2$ for each i	
Output: Are $x_1, x_2, \ldots, x_N$ all distinct (that is, no two are equal)?	

Here's a popular algorithm in practice. Now, you'll analyze the algorithm rigorously.

Hashing algorithm for ELEMENT DISTINCTNESS (8.14)

```
for i ← 1,...,N:
    insert x_i into a hash table
    if the value x_i was already in the hash table: reject
accept
```

Assume the hash table is implemented with chaining using a pairwise avoiding hash function $h: R \times U \to T$ where $\{0,\ldots,N^2\} \subseteq U$ and $|T| \geq N$. We append x_i to the chain at index $h_r(x_i)$ if it wasn't already there. The worst possible number of comparisons is $\binom{N}{2} = \Theta(N^2)$, because if $x_1,\ldots,x_N$ are all distinct and hash to the same index, then each x_i gets compared to all previous x_j. Prove that the expectation (over uniformly random $r \in R$) of the number of comparisons is $O(N)$.

8.2 Suppose $k \geq 2$ is an integer and $|U| \geq k$. A randomized hash function $h: R \times U \to T$ is *k-wise uniform* iff for every tuple of k distinct elements $(u_1,\ldots,u_k) \in U^k$, the tuple $\big(h_r(u_1),\ldots,h_r(u_k)\big)$ is uniformly distributed over T^k.

Prove that for every prime $p \geq k$, this randomized hash function is k-wise uniform:

$$h: \mathbb{Z}_p^k \times \mathbb{Z}_p \to \mathbb{Z}_p \qquad \text{defined by} \qquad h_{r_{k-1},\ldots,r_0}(u) = r_{k-1}u^{k-1} + r_{k-2}u^{k-2} + \cdots + r_1 u + r_0$$

That is, view $r = (r_{k-1},\ldots,r_0)$ as coefficients of a polynomial of degree $\leq k-1$, and evaluate this polynomial with u plugged in. (Lemma 8.4 is the special case $k = 2$.)

8.3 Recall the randomized hash functions from §8.2.2 and §8.2.3, where A is a random $m \times n$ matrix, b is a random $m \times 1$ vector, u is an $n \times 1$ vector, and the field is $\mathbb{Z}_2$:

- Au is pairwise uniform for $u \neq 0^n$.
- $Au + b$ is pairwise uniform for all u.
- $Au + b$ is pairwise uniform for all u when A is diagonal-constant.

For each of the following, prove or disprove it.

(a) Au is pairwise avoiding for all u.

(b) Au is pairwise avoiding for all u when A is diagonal-constant.

(c) Au is pairwise uniform for $u \neq 0^n$ when A is diagonal-constant and $n, m \geq 2$.

8.4 **(a)** Prove that $A \in \mathsf{UP}$ iff there exist integers c, d and a poly-time verifier V such that for every valid input x of size N, V never reads beyond w's first cN^d words, and:

$$A(x) = 1 \Rightarrow V(x; w) \text{ accepts for exactly one } w \text{ of size } cN^d$$
$$A(x) = 0 \Rightarrow V(x; w) \text{ accepts for no } w \text{ of size } cN^d$$

"Size cN^d" means all words of w beyond the first cN^d words are 0s.

(b) Prove UNAMBIGUOUS SAT is UP-complete.

8.5 Our proof that if $\mathsf{UP} \subseteq \mathsf{RP}$ then $\mathsf{NP} \subseteq \mathsf{RP}$ (Theorem 8.10) used pairwise uniform hash functions. Adapt the proof to use pairwise avoiding hash functions. Hint: Instead of using 0^m as the target, pick a uniformly random target. Use Lemma 8.3 for the analysis.

8.6 Prove that if $\mathsf{UP} \subseteq \mathsf{BPP}$ then $\mathsf{NP} \subseteq \mathsf{RP}$.

8.7 **(a)** Use Theorem A.26 (which says $(v \cdot w)^2 \leq (v \cdot v)(w \cdot w)$ for all vectors v and w) to prove that $\mathbf{Pr}[X > 0] \geq \mathbf{E}[X]^2/\mathbf{E}[X^2]$ for every nonnegative random variable X that's not constant 0.

(b) Use Exercise 8.7.a to prove that for all pairwise uniform $h: R \times U \to T$ and $S \subseteq U$ and $t \in T$:

$$\mathbf{Pr}_r\big[h_r(s) = t \text{ for some } s \in S\big] \geq \tfrac{|S|}{|S|+|T|}$$

(This is always better than the corresponding bound from Lemma 8.13.) Hint: Let X be the number of $s \in S$ such that $h_r(s) = t$.

8.8 Prove that for a randomized approximation scheme for CIRCUIT SAT COUNTING, error probability 1/3 could be amplified to ε by running it $O(\log \frac{1}{\varepsilon})$ times (with fresh randomness for each run) and outputting the median of the values output by these runs. Why doesn't outputting the mean work?

8.9 We proved that if $\mathsf{NP} \subseteq \mathsf{BPP}$ then CIRCUIT SAT COUNTING has a fully poly-time randomized approximation scheme (Theorem 8.12). Adapt this to have one-sided error: If $S = \emptyset$ then the approximation scheme always outputs 0.

8.10 Prove that if $\mathsf{P} = \mathsf{NP}$ then CIRCUIT SAT COUNTING has a fully poly-time deterministic approximation scheme.

8.11 In this exercise, you'll see how to approximately count and sample satisfying assignments for DNFs in poly time (without an NP oracle).

Let $S \subseteq \{0,1\}^n$ be the set of assignments that satisfy a DNF $\varphi = T_1 \vee \cdots \vee T_m$. Let S_i be the set of assignments that satisfy the term T_i, so $S = S_1 \cup \cdots \cup S_m$ and $|S_i| = 2^{n-(\text{width of } T_i)}$. We can sample a uniformly random element of S_i in poly time. For example, if $T_i = (x_2 \wedge \overline{x_4} \wedge x_7)$ then we assign $x_2 = 1$, $x_4 = 0$, $x_7 = 1$ and assign the other $n-3$ variables uniformly at random. Let S_i' be the set of assignments that satisfy T_i but not $T_1 \vee \cdots \vee T_{i-1}$, so $S_1', \ldots, S_m'$ partitions S according to the first satisfied term. Given $a \in S_i$, we can determine whether $a \in S_i'$ in poly time by evaluating $\neg\big(T_1(a) \vee \cdots \vee T_{i-1}(a)\big)$. To estimate $|S_i'|/|S_i|$ within $\pm\gamma$ with probability $\geq 1-\varepsilon$, we sample $O\big(\frac{1}{\gamma^2} \log \frac{1}{\varepsilon}\big)$ elements of S_i independently and uniformly at random, view each sample as a coin toss where heads means "$\in S_i'$", and use the fraction of heads as the estimate (Corollary 7.21).

(a) Prove that this algorithm is correct and fully poly-time:

Randomized approximation scheme for DNF SAT COUNTING (8.15)

on input $(\varphi, \gamma, \varepsilon)$:
    for each $i \in [m]$:
        compute some q_i within $\pm\gamma/2m$ of $\lvert S_i'\rvert/\lvert S_i\rvert$ with probability $\geq 1-\varepsilon/m$
    output $\sum_{i=1}^{m} q_i \lvert S_i\rvert$

(b) To approximately sample a uniformly random satisfying assignment, we can reduce to approximate counting as in §8.4.2. But we can do even better from first principles.

DNF SAT EXACT SAMPLING (8.16)	
Input:	DNF φ with at least one term, and $0 < \varepsilon < 1$
Output:	A satisfying assignment of φ or abort, such that $\mathbf{Pr}[\text{abort}] \leq \varepsilon$ and conditioned on not aborting, the output is uniformly distributed over all satisfying assignments of φ

Prove that this algorithm is correct except $\mathbf{Pr}[\text{abort}] \leq 1 - 1/m$. Explain how to amplify this to $\mathbf{Pr}[\text{abort}] \leq \varepsilon$.

Algorithm for DNF SAT EXACT SAMPLING (8.17)

sample $i \in [m]$ uniformly at random
with probability $1 - |S_i| / \max(|S_1|, \ldots, |S_m|)$: abort
sample $a \in S_i$ uniformly at random
if $a \notin S'_i$: abort
output a

8.12 Prove that for all pairwise uniform $h \colon R \times U \to T$ and nonempty $S \subseteq U$ and $f \colon S \to T$:

$$\mathbf{Pr}_r\big[h_r(s) \neq f(s) \text{ for all } s \in S\big] \;\leq\; |T|/|S|$$

Notes

The definitions of pairwise avoiding and pairwise uniform hash functions are due to [109]. In [109] and much of the literature, pairwise avoiding is called “2-universal” and pairwise uniform is called “strongly 2-universal” or sometimes just “pairwise independent.” The pairwise uniform hash functions in §8.2.1 and §8.2.2 are due to [109], and the one in §8.2.3 is due to [540, 202]. If $h \colon R \times U \to T$ is pairwise uniform, then $|R| \geq |U|(|T|-1)+1$ [505], so if $h \colon \{0,1\}^\ell \times \{0,1\}^n \to \{0,1\}^m$ is pairwise uniform, then $\ell \geq m+n$.

See [351] for a survey on applications of pairwise uniform hashing in complexity theory.

UNAMBIGUOUS SAT is sometimes called “UNIQUE SAT”. Unfortunately, “UNIQUE SAT” may also refer to the problem of deciding whether φ has exactly one satisfying assignment, without the promise that it has at most one satisfying assignment (Exercise 4.15).

“If UP $\subseteq$ RP then NP $\subseteq$ RP” (Theorem 8.10) is known as the “Valiant–Vazirani theorem” [537]. There’s evidence that the isolation probability of $\Omega(1/n)$ can’t be improved [142].

Approximate counting of witnesses in poly time with an NP oracle (Theorem 8.12) is due to [506, 537, 209]. Reducing approximate sampling to approximate counting (Theorem 8.14) is due to [273, 492]. Exact sampling of witnesses in poly time with an NP oracle is due to [57].

Randomness-efficient amplification using pairwise uniformity (Theorem 8.18) is due to [126]. Randomness-efficient amplification using expander graphs is due to [133, 267].

For overviews of streaming algorithms, see [383, 330]. The hashing-based streaming algorithm for approximating the number of distinct elements (Theorem 8.19) is due to [163, 18]. The optimally-efficient algorithm (in terms of n, γ, ε) is due to [66]. The HyperLogLog algorithm is due to [162]. A simple, non-hashing-based algorithm is due to [111].

Exercise 8.5 is due to [351]. Exercise 8.11 is due to [294].

Chapter 9

Error Correcting Codes

Sometimes we need to transmit a message over an unreliable or noisy communication channel, which may accidentally corrupt parts of the transmission (Figure 9.1). For example:

- Packets sent through a computer network may be lost.
- Radio transmissions—such as between cellular network devices or between a spacecraft and earth—are susceptible to electromagnetic interference.
- Persistent storage devices—such as flash memory and hard drives—occasionally flip some stored bits. The "channel" is time: Writing data is a transmission to the future, and what's read might not match what was written.

Sometimes, errors can be handled by retransmitting the message, but that's often impractical. *Error correcting codes* handle errors by encoding the message using carefully designed redundancy, so when the resulting *codeword* is partially corrupted by the channel, it can be decoded to the original message despite the errors and with no retransmission (Figure 9.2). Error correcting codes have great practical importance. They're also useful tools for understanding randomness in computational complexity, as we'll see in subsequent chapters. This chapter covers basic theory and constructions of error correcting codes.

9.1 Binary Codes

9.1.1 Definitions

Previously, "code" meant a program's instructions. Now, a *code* is a function $E\colon \{0,1\}^k \to \{0,1\}^n$. If $m \in \{0,1\}^k$ is the message, then $E(m) \in \{0,1\}^n$ is the codeword sent over the channel. Here, k is the message length, n is the codeword length, and "E" stands for "encoder."

- An *erasure* is a mild error where a transmitted bit is replaced with a special symbol $\perp$ (pronounced *bottom*) meaning "the bit is unknown; there's an error here." Sometimes we consider channels where errors can only be erasures. The decoder is a function $D\colon \{0,1,\perp\}^n \to \{0,1\}^k$. If $r \in \{0,1,\perp\}^n$ is the received word, which matches $E(m)$ except for the $\perp$s, then $D(r) \in \{0,1\}^k$ should be the message m.
- A *bit flip* is a more severe error where a transmitted bit is replaced with the opposite bit. The receiver can't see which bits got flipped. In this setting, the decoder is a function $D\colon \{0,1\}^n \to \{0,1\}^k$. If $r \in \{0,1\}^n$ is the received word, which may differ from $E(m)$ on some bits, then $D(r) \in \{0,1\}^k$ should be the message m.

The goal is to design codes such that decoding is possible if there aren't too many errors. The number of errors we can handle depends on the code's *distance*, which we define below.

Recall that the distance between two bit strings $a, b \in \{0,1\}^n$ is the number of coordinates on which they differ: $\operatorname{dist}(a,b) = \big|\{i : a_i \neq b_i\}\big|$. We have $\operatorname{dist}(a,c) \leq \operatorname{dist}(a,b) + \operatorname{dist}(b,c)$ for

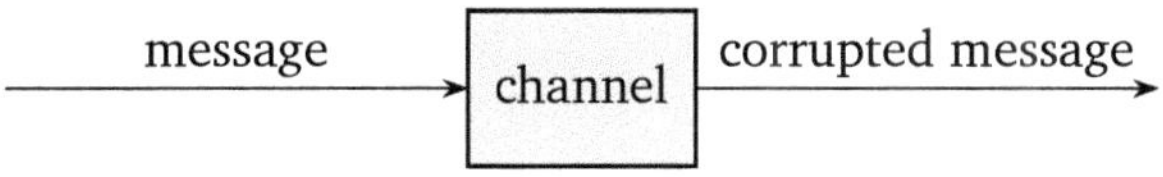

Figure 9.1: Unreliable communication channel

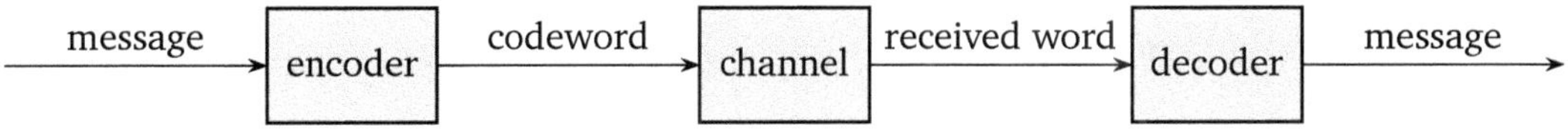

Figure 9.2: Encoding and decoding

all a, b, c because if $a_i \neq c_i$ then either $a_i \neq b_i$ or $b_i \neq c_i$. This is called the *triangle inequality* by analogy with the fact that in a triangle, one side's length (the geometric distance between two vertices) is at most the sum of the other two sides' lengths.

Definition. The *distance* of a code E is the minimum distance between the codewords of any two distinct messages: $\text{dist}(E) = \min_{m_1 \neq m_2} \text{dist}\big(E(m_1), E(m_2)\big)$. ◀

(Here, m_1 and m_2 are entire messages, not bits of some message m.)

$\text{dist}(E) = d$ means every pair of codewords has distance $\geq d$, and at least one pair has distance exactly d. If $\text{dist}(E)$ is large, then all codewords are distant from each other. Figure 9.3 depicts distances between codewords as geometric distances between points.

How many errors can we correct if $\text{dist}(E) = d$?

- Erasure channel: Decoding is possible if $< d$ many erasures occur. Only one codeword agrees with the received word r (on the non-erased coordinates) because otherwise, two codewords would have distance $< d$ from each other (differing only on r's erased coordinates).

Erasure decoder (9.1)

$D(r)$:
    if r has $< d$ erasures and agrees with some codeword $E(m)$: output m
    else: the output doesn't matter

- Bit flip channel: Decoding is possible if $< d/2$ many bit flips occur. Only one codeword is within distance $< d/2$ of the received word r because otherwise, two codewords would both have distance $< d/2$ from r and thus have distance $< d/2 + d/2 = d$ from each other, by the triangle inequality.

Bit flip decoder (9.2)

$D(r)$:
    if r is within distance $< d/2$ of some codeword $E(m)$: output m
    else: the output doesn't matter

The set of all received words r that decode to a particular message m is a *ball* of radius $< d/2$ centered at the codeword $E(m)$. These balls are disjoint, as Figure 9.4 depicts.

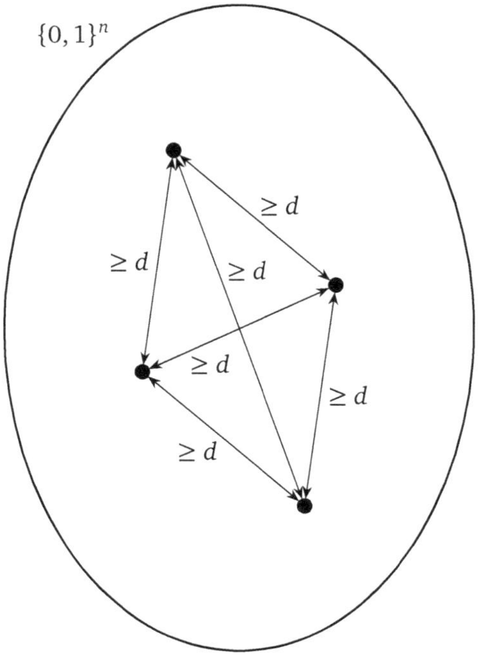

Figure 9.3: Distant codewords

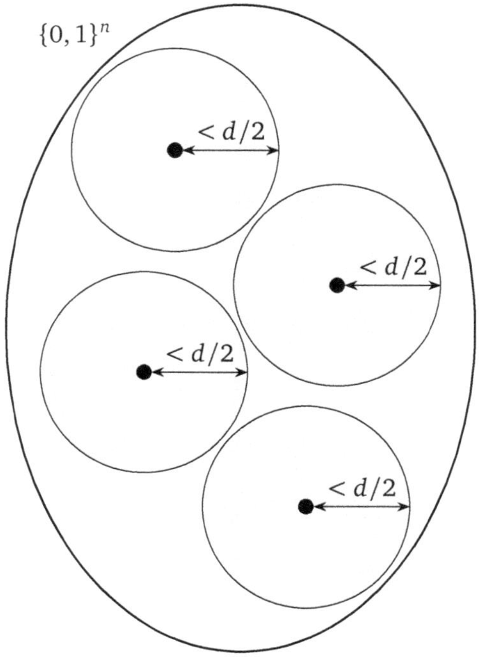

Figure 9.4: Disjoint balls

If errors occur randomly and independently with somewhat small probability in each coordinate, then by a concentration bound (Lemma 7.20), the number of errors is probably not too high, in which case a code with large enough distance can handle the errors.

Designing a code with codeword length n involves tension between competing requirements:

- We want a large distance d, to handle many errors. The *relative distance* d/n determines the fraction of coordinates that can be errors.
- We want a large message length k, to transmit a lot of information per codeword. The *rate* k/n measures the density of information.
- We want efficient encoding and decoding. Brute force decoders try all possible messages and are thus inefficient.

Achieving any two of these is not difficult. Achieving all three simultaneously takes some work.

"Code" usually means an infinite *family* of codes that are defined in the same way but with different codeword lengths. To discuss an arbitrary code from the family, we leave n unspecified.

9.1.2 Simple Constructions

Let's warm up with three simple error correcting codes.

Repetition code. The message length is $k = 1$. The codeword is n copies of the message bit: $E(0) = 0^n$ and $E(1) = 1^n$. These two codewords are at distance n, so the code has distance n.

- $< n$ erasures: $D(r)$ outputs any non-erased bit of r. For example, $D(\bot\bot\bot 1\bot) = 1$.
- $< n/2$ bit flips: $D(r)$ outputs the majority value of r's bits. For example, $D(01010) = 0$.

The repetition code has a supreme relative distance of 1 but an abysmal rate of $1/n$.

Parity code. The codeword length is $n = k+1$. The codeword $E(m)$ is the message m followed by the bit $\oplus(m)$, which is the parity (xor) of m's bits. For example, $E(11010) = 110101$ because $\oplus(11010) = 1$. The codewords are all of the strings with parity 0, that is, even weight (where a bit string's weight is the number of 1s in it). For example, $\oplus(110101) = 0$ and $\text{weight}(110101) = 4$, which is even. The code has distance 2: Changing an even-weight string to another even-weight string requires flipping at least two bits (since flipping only one bit would make the weight go up or down by one and thus yield an odd-weight string), so $\text{dist}(E) \geq 2$ (as in Theorem A.3). Also, $\text{dist}(E) \leq 2$ since the codewords 0^n and 110^{n-2} have distance 2.

- < 2 erasures: $D(r)$ first recovers the codeword by replacing the $\bot$ with the parity of all the non-erased bits (to make the whole string have parity 0), and then outputs the codeword's first $k = n-1$ bits. For example, $D(1\bot0101) = 11010$ because the $\bot$ was $\oplus(10101) = 1$.
- < 1 bit flips: Sorry, the parity code can't handle any bit flips. If one bit flip occurs, then it's possible to detect that there's an error (since the received word has odd weight) but not to correct it (since the flipped bit might be at any coordinate). Real-world barcode numbers often end with a "check digit" for a similar purpose.

The parity code has a terrible relative distance of $2/n$ but an excellent rate of $(n-1)/n$.

Dot product code. The codeword length is $n = 2^k$. The n bits of the codeword $E(m)$ are indexed by all strings $x \in \{0,1\}^k$, and the bit at index x is $m \odot x$, where $\odot$ is the dot product over $\mathbb{Z}_2$. For example, with $k = 3$:

$$\begin{aligned} E(m) &= \big(m \odot 000,\ m \odot 001,\ m \odot 010,\ m \odot 011,\ m \odot 100,\ m \odot 101,\ m \odot 110,\ m \odot 111\big) \\ E(101) &= 01011010 \end{aligned}$$

Every pair of codewords has distance $n/2$, because if $m_1 \neq m_2$ then $m_1 \odot x \neq m_2 \odot x$ for exactly half of all x, by the random subsum principle (Lemma 7.2.*(ii)*). Thus the code has distance $n/2$. (We could omit the $x = 0^k$ coordinate since all codewords have 0 there, but it's tidier to retain this coordinate.)

For starters, how can we decode if no errors occur? For each $i \in [k]$, let $e^i \in \{0,1\}^k$ have a 1 at index i and 0s everywhere else. If the received word r equals the codeword $E(m)$, then $r_{e^i} = m \odot e^i = m_i$ (the ith bit of the message m), so we can retrieve all bits of m directly from r.

To salvage this approach when r_{e^i} might be an error, we exploit linearity to recover m_i from elsewhere in r. Say $x \in \{0,1\}^k$ is *good for i* if r_x and $r_{x \oplus e^i}$ are not errors, and say x is *bad for i* otherwise. (Note that $x \oplus e^i$ is x with the ith bit flipped.) If x is good for i then:

$$r_x \oplus r_{x \oplus e^i} = (m \odot x) \oplus \big(m \odot (x \oplus e^i)\big) = m \odot \big(x \oplus (x \oplus e^i)\big) = m \odot e^i = m_i$$

- $< n/2$ erasures: To recover m_i, the decoder finds an x that's good for i. Such an x exists by the probabilistic method. For a uniformly random x:

$$\mathbf{Pr}[x \text{ is bad for } i] \leq \mathbf{Pr}[r_x = \bot] + \mathbf{Pr}[r_{x \oplus e^i} = \bot] < 1/2 + 1/2 = 1$$

by a union bound and the fact that $x \oplus e^i$ is also uniformly distributed.

Erasure decoder for the dot product code (9.3)

$D(r)$:
 for each $i \in [k]$:
  for each $x \in \{0,1\}^k$:
   if $r_x \neq \bot$ and $r_{x \oplus e^i} \neq \bot$: let $m_i \leftarrow r_x \oplus r_{x \oplus e^i}$ and break out of the x loop
 output $m_1 \cdots m_k$

- $< n/4$ bit flips: Now, the decoder can't tell whether any particular x is good for i, but we know that most x are good for i:

$$\mathbf{Pr}[x \text{ is bad for } i] \leq \mathbf{Pr}\big[r_x \neq m \odot x\big] + \mathbf{Pr}\big[r_{x \oplus e^i} \neq m \odot (x \oplus e^i)\big] < 1/4 + 1/4 = 1/2$$

Bit flip decoder for the dot product code (9.4)

$D(r)$:
 for each $i \in [k]$:
  for each $x \in \{0,1\}^k$: let $vote_x \leftarrow r_x \oplus r_{x \oplus e^i}$
  let $m_i \leftarrow$ majority bit among $vote_x$ over all x
 output $m_1 \cdots m_k$

The dot product code has a good relative distance of $1/2$ but a pretty bad rate of $(\log n)/n$.

9.1.3 Linear Codes

$E\colon \{0,1\}^k \to \{0,1\}^n$ is *linear* iff $E(m_1 + m_2) = E(m_1) + E(m_2)$ for all $m_1 \in \{0,1\}^k$ and $m_2 \in \{0,1\}^k$, viewing bit strings as vectors over $\mathbb{Z}_2$ (so $+$ and $-$ are bitwise xor). That is, the encoding of a sum equals the sum of the encodings. This automatically extends to more than two summands: $E(m_1 + m_2 + m_3 + \cdots) = E(m_1) + E(m_2) + E(m_3) + \cdots$.

To determine a linear code's distance, the following lemma conveniently lets us consider individual codewords instead of pairs of codewords.

Lemma 9.1. *The distance of a linear code* $E\colon \{0,1\}^k \to \{0,1\}^n$ *equals the minimum weight of any nonzero message's codeword:* $\operatorname{dist}(E) = \min_{m \neq 0^k} \operatorname{weight}\big(E(m)\big)$.

Proof.

$$\begin{aligned}
\operatorname{dist}(E) &= \min_{m_1 \neq m_2} \operatorname{dist}\big(E(m_1), E(m_2)\big) && \text{(definition of dist}(E)) \\
&= \min_{m_1 \neq m_2} \operatorname{weight}\big(E(m_1) + E(m_2)\big) && \text{(definition of bitwise xor)} \\
&= \min_{m_1 \neq m_2} \operatorname{weight}\big(E(m_1 + m_2)\big) && (E \text{ is linear}) \\
&= \min_{m \neq 0^k} \operatorname{weight}\big(E(m)\big) && (m_1 \neq m_2 \text{ iff } m_1 + m_2 \neq 0^k)
\end{aligned}$$

■

Encoding a linear code is equivalent to vector-matrix multiplication:

Lemma 9.2. $E\colon \{0,1\}^k \to \{0,1\}^n$ *is linear iff there exists a* $k \times n$ *matrix* G *such that* $E(m) = mG$ *over* $\mathbb{Z}_2$*, viewing* m *as a* $1 \times k$ *vector and* $E(m)$ *as a* $1 \times n$ *vector.*

Such a G is called a *generator* matrix.

Proof. $\Leftarrow$: Suppose there exists a generator matrix G for E. For all m_1 and m_2,

$$E(m_1+m_2) = (m_1+m_2)G = m_1G+m_2G = E(m_1)+E(m_2)$$

by the distributive property of matrix multiplication. Thus E is linear.

$\Rightarrow$: Suppose E is linear. For each $i \in [k]$, consider the message $e^i \in \{0,1\}^k$ with a 1 at index i and 0s everywhere else. Define G's ith row G_i to be $E(e^i)$. For any message $m \neq 0^k$:

$$E(m) = E\left(\sum_{i:m_i=1} e^i\right) = \sum_{i:m_i=1} E(e^i) = \sum_i m_i G_i = mG$$

Also, $E(0^k)+E(0^k) = E(0^k+0^k) = E(0^k)$, and subtracting $E(0^k)$ from both sides yields $E(0^k) = 0^n = 0^kG$. Thus G is a generator matrix for E. ■

We viewed a vector-matrix product as a linear combination of rows: $mG = \sum_i m_i G_i$. We can also view it as dot products with columns: The jth bit of the codeword mG is the dot product of the message m and G's jth column. Thus each codeword bit is the parity of some message bits.

The three example codes from §9.1.2 are linear:

Repetition code. The $1 \times n$ generator matrix is all 1s. For example, with $n=4$:

$$E(0) = \begin{bmatrix}0\end{bmatrix}\begin{bmatrix}1 & 1 & 1 & 1\end{bmatrix} = \begin{bmatrix}0 & 0 & 0 & 0\end{bmatrix}$$

The code has distance n: The only nonzero message's codeword has weight n.

Parity code. The $k \times (k+1)$ generator matrix is the $k \times k$ identity matrix followed by an all-1s column. For example, with $k=4$:

$$E(0110) = \begin{bmatrix}0 & 1 & 1 & 0\end{bmatrix}\begin{bmatrix}1 & 0 & 0 & 0 & 1\\ 0 & 1 & 0 & 0 & 1\\ 0 & 0 & 1 & 0 & 1\\ 0 & 0 & 0 & 1 & 1\end{bmatrix} = \begin{bmatrix}0 & 1 & 1 & 0 & 0\end{bmatrix}$$

The code has distance 2: For every nonzero message, the codeword is nonzero and even-weight, so it has weight ≥ 2. Also, the codeword of the nonzero message 10^{k-1} has weight only 2.

Dot product code. The $k \times 2^k$ generator matrix has all possible columns. For example, with $k=3$:

$$E(101) = \begin{bmatrix}1 & 0 & 1\end{bmatrix}\begin{bmatrix}0 & 0 & 0 & 0 & 1 & 1 & 1 & 1\\ 0 & 0 & 1 & 1 & 0 & 0 & 1 & 1\\ 0 & 1 & 0 & 1 & 0 & 1 & 0 & 1\end{bmatrix} = \begin{bmatrix}0 & 1 & 0 & 1 & 1 & 0 & 1 & 0\end{bmatrix}$$

The code has distance $n/2$: For every nonzero message m, the codeword has weight $n/2$ because $m \odot x = 1$ for exactly half of all x, by the random subsum principle (Lemma 7.2.*(i)*).

9.2 Bounds for Binary Codes

An *asymptotically good* family of codes has relative distance $\Omega(1)$ and rate $\Omega(1)$ (but isn't necessarily efficiently encodable and decodable): For some constants $a > 0$ and $b > 0$, every code in

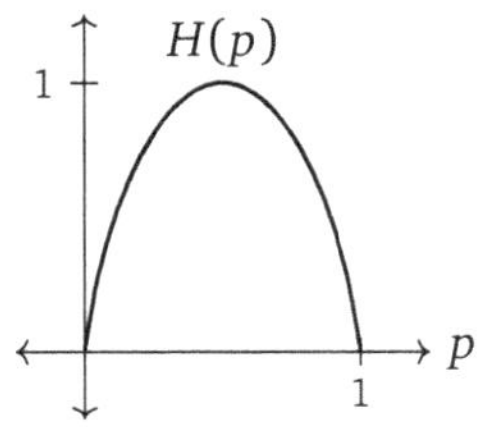

Figure 9.5: Binary entropy function

the family has relative distance $\geq a$ and rate $\geq b$. Such codes achieve the first two of the three requirements from the end of §9.1.1.

None of the examples from §9.1.2 were asymptotically good. We design an asymptotically good family with an efficient encoder in §9.5.3. For now, we prove that asymptotically good families exist. Furthermore, there's a tradeoff between relative distance and rate—we can improve either by sacrificing the other. We'll see limitations on the relationship between relative distance and rate—they can't both be too good simultaneously. Determining the precise tradeoff is a significant open question.

9.2.1 Codes Can Be Good

There exist asymptotically good families of codes where the tradeoff between relative distance and rate is captured by the *binary entropy function* H:

$$H(p) = \begin{cases} p\log_2(1/p)+(1-p)\log_2(1/(1-p)) & \text{if } 0<p<1 \\ 0 & \text{if } p=0 \text{ or } p=1 \end{cases}$$

This has maximum $H(1/2)=1$. See Figure 9.5.

Theorem 9.3. *For all n and all $p < 1/2$, there exists a code with codeword length n, relative distance $> p$, and rate $> 1-H(p)-1/n$.*

For example, this yields a family of codes with relative distance > 0.2 and rate $> 1-H(0.2)-1/n \geq 0.25$ for large enough n. So if the channel may flip up to 10% of the bits, then the codeword only needs to be 4 times as long as the message.

Proof idea for Theorem 9.3. We construct a set of codewords using a greedy algorithm that repeatedly picks any codeword that's far enough from all previously selected codewords. (It doesn't matter which message gets which codeword.) By definition, this yields the desired relative distance. To bound the rate, we need to know how many codewords we can pick before getting stuck (with no option for the next codeword). Each selected codeword "rules out" all prospective codewords that are nearby. As long as the set of ruled out codewords isn't too big, the algorithm can continue for many iterations before exhausting all options. ∎

The *ball* of radius d centered at $c \in \{0,1\}^n$ is the set of all $b \in \{0,1\}^n$ such that $\text{dist}(b,c) \leq d$. A ball's size depends only on d and n, and the dependence is captured by the binary entropy function.

Lemma 9.4. *A ball of radius $d \leq n/2$ in $\{0,1\}^n$ has size $\leq (2^n)^{H(d/n)}$.*

Proof of Lemma 9.4. If $d = 0$ then the ball has size $1 = (2^n)^0$, so assume $d > 0$. The ball's exact size is $\sum_{i=0}^{d}\binom{n}{i}$ since choosing a string at distance exactly i from the center means choosing a set of i bit positions to flip, and there are $\binom{n}{i}$ many such sets. Letting $p = d/n$:

$$(2^n)^{H(p)} \;=\; 2^{np\log(1/p)} \cdot 2^{n(1-p)\log(1/(1-p))} \;=\; (1/p)^{np} \cdot (1/(1-p))^{n-np} \;=\; 1/p^d(1-p)^{n-d}$$

Relating these two quantities using the binomial formula (§A.1.2),

$$\text{size of ball}\,\big/\,(2^n)^{H(p)} \;=\; \textstyle\sum_{i=0}^{d}\binom{n}{i}p^d(1-p)^{n-d} \;\le\; \sum_{i=0}^{n}\binom{n}{i}p^i(1-p)^{n-i} \;=\; \big(p+(1-p)\big)^n \;=\; 1$$

because $p \le 1-p$ and thus $p^d(1-p)^{n-d} \le p^i(1-p)^{n-i}$ for $i \le d \le n/2$. ∎

(We could use Lemma 7.20 to bound the probability of getting $\le d$ heads in n fair coin tosses. This implies that a ball has size $\le (2^n)^{1-(1/2-d/n)^2}$. But Lemma 9.4 is tighter than that.)

Proof of Theorem 9.3. Let $d = \lfloor pn \rfloor < n/2$ and $k = \big\lfloor n(1-H(d/n)) \big\rfloor > n(1-H(p))-1$.

Greedy construction of a code $E\colon \{0,1\}^k \to \{0,1\}^n$	(9.5)
for each $m \in \{0,1\}^k$: let $E(m) \in \{0,1\}^n$ be any string such that $\text{dist}\big(E(m), E(m')\big) > d$ for all previous m'	

In each iteration, there indeed exists such an $E(m)$ because the number of strings that are within distance d of $E(m')$ for at least one previous m' is:

$$\begin{aligned}
&\le (\text{number of previous } m') \cdot (\text{size of ball of radius } d) \\
&\le (2^k - 1) \cdot (2^n)^{H(d/n)} && \text{(Lemma 9.4)} \\
&< 2^{n(1-H(d/n))} \cdot 2^{nH(d/n)} && \text{(definition of } k\text{)} \\
&= 2^n
\end{aligned}$$

E has relative distance $\ge (d+1)/n > p$ and rate $k/n > 1-H(p)-1/n$. ∎

The following supersedes Theorem 9.3 because the statement is identical except now the code is linear.

Theorem 9.5. *For all n and all $p < 1/2$, there exists a linear code with codeword length n, relative distance $> p$, and rate $> 1-H(p)-1/n$.*

Proof. We use the probabilistic method. Let $d = \lfloor pn \rfloor < n/2$ and $k = \big\lfloor n(1-H(d/n)) \big\rfloor > n(1-H(p))-1$. For a uniformly random $k \times n$ generator matrix G, define the code $E\colon \{0,1\}^k \to \{0,1\}^n$ by $E(m) = mG$. We claim that $\mathbf{Pr}\big[\text{dist}(E) > d\big] > 0$, so there exists E with relative distance $\ge (d+1)/n > p$ and rate $k/n > 1-H(p)-1/n$.

If $m \ne 0^k$ then mG is uniformly distributed because it's the sum (bitwise xor) of some rows of G, which are uniformly distributed and fully independent. Also, weight$(mG) \le d$ iff mG is in the ball of radius d centered at 0^n.

$$\begin{aligned}
\mathbf{Pr}\big[\text{dist}(E) \le d\big] &= \mathbf{Pr}\big[\exists m \ne 0^k : \text{weight}(mG) \le d\big] && \text{(Lemma 9.1)} \\
&\le \textstyle\sum_{m \ne 0^k} \mathbf{Pr}\big[\text{weight}(mG) \le d\big] && \text{(union bound)} \\
&= (\text{number of } m \ne 0^k) \cdot (\text{size of ball of radius } d)/2^n \\
&\le (2^k - 1) \cdot (2^n)^{H(d/n)}/2^n && \text{(Lemma 9.4)} \\
&< 2^{n(1-H(d/n))} \cdot 2^{nH(d/n)}/2^n && \text{(definition of } k\text{)} \\
&= 1
\end{aligned}$$

∎

9.2.2 Codes Can't Be Too Good

Theorem 9.6. *If* $E: \{0,1\}^k \to \{0,1\}^n$ *has distance* d*, then* $k \leq n-d+1$.

Proof. By the pigeonhole principle, at least two of the 2^k codewords agree on their first $k-1$ bits (since there are $2^{k-1} < 2^k$ possibilities for this prefix) and thus have distance $\leq n-(k-1)$. Hence $d \leq n-k+1$. ■

Theorem 9.6 says that a code with relative distance p must have rate $\leq 1-p+1/n$. For example, if the relative distance is > 0.2 then the rate is $< 1-0.2+1/n$ and is thus ≤ 0.8 for large enough n. So if the channel may flip up to 10% of the bits, then the codeword must be at least $1/0.8 = 1.25$ times as long as the message.

The asymptotically good codes from § 9.2.1 have relative distance $< 1/2$, with the rate approaching 0 as the relative distance approaches $1/2$. Theorem 9.6 says that relative distance $> 1/2$ would require rate $< 1/2$. But the actual situation is worse—asymptotically good codes simply can't have relative distance $> 1/2$:

Theorem 9.7. *If* $E: \{0,1\}^k \to \{0,1\}^n$ *has distance* $d > n/2$*, then* $2^k \leq 1/(1-n/2d)$.

Thus, if the relative distance is a constant $> 1/2$, then the message length is at most a constant. For example, if the channel may flip up to 30% of the bits, so a code needs relative distance > 0.6, then the number of possible messages must be $\leq 1/(1-1/(2\cdot 0.6)) = 6$, so the message length is $\leq \lfloor \log 6 \rfloor = 2$ bits.

The repetition code has relative distance $1 > 1/2$ but a constant message length of 1. The dot product code has relative distance exactly $1/2$ and a nonconstant but still fairly small message length of $\log n$, straddling the boundary between the desolation of relative distance $> 1/2$ and the fertility of relative distance $< 1/2$.

Proof idea for Theorem 9.7. We "count something in two different ways." On one hand, if a code has large distance, then pairs of codewords have "lots of disagreement." On the other hand, there can't be too much disagreement overall, because for any individual coordinate, all codewords with 1 there agree on that bit, and all codewords with 0 there agree on that bit. ■

Proof of Theorem 9.7. Let $K = 2^k$ be the number of messages. Let D be the number of pairs $(\{m_1, m_2\}, i)$ where $\{m_1, m_2\}$ is an unordered pair of distinct messages whose codewords differ at coordinate i, that is, $E(m_1)_i \neq E(m_2)_i$. On one hand:

$$D = \sum_{\{m_1,m_2\}} \operatorname{dist}\big(E(m_1), E(m_2)\big) \geq \sum_{\{m_1,m_2\}} d = \binom{K}{2} d$$

On the other hand, letting K_i be the number of messages whose codewords have 1 at coordinate i,

$$D = \sum_i K_i(K-K_i) \leq \sum_i K^2/4 = nK^2/4$$

because $K_i(K-K_i)$ is the number of unordered pairs of distinct messages whose codewords differ at coordinate i (since K_i codewords have 1 at i, and $K-K_i$ codewords have 0 at i), and because $K^2/4 - K_i(K-K_i) = (K/2-K_i)^2 \geq 0$. Combining these two inequalities:

$$\begin{aligned} \binom{K}{2} d &\leq nK^2/4 \\ K-1 &\leq K(n/2d) && \text{(dividing both sides by } Kd/2) \\ K(1-n/2d) &\leq 1 && \text{(rearranging)} \\ K &\leq 1/(1-n/2d) && \text{(dividing both sides by } 1-n/2d) \end{aligned}$$

The inequality's direction didn't flip, because $1-n/2d > 0$ by the assumption $d > n/2$. ■

See Exercise 9.8 for stronger limitations on the tradeoff between relative distance and rate.

9.2.3 List Decoding

This topic has applications in several areas of computational complexity. We'll just see the tip of the iceberg. This section's theorem isn't needed for the rest of this chapter, but we use it in §11.6 and in Exercise 9.8.

What if a code has distance d, but the channel might flip $e \geq d/2$ many bits? Multiple codewords may be within distance e of the received word. We could at least hope to find the list of all such codewords and their associated messages. A list decoder tells the receiver, "The original message was one of these, but I'm not sure which one." That's better than nothing. Of course, we want the list to be small. The following theorem says the list is indeed small if e is somewhat less than d, and d is somewhat less than $n/2$. This means list decoding is possible in principle, and it launches the quest for efficient list decoding algorithms.

Theorem 9.8. *If $E\colon \{0,1\}^k \to \{0,1\}^n$ has relative distance $1/2-\varepsilon$ where $\varepsilon > 0$, then each ball in $\{0,1\}^n$ of relative radius $\leq 1/2-\sqrt{\varepsilon}$ contains $\leq 1/\varepsilon$ many codewords.*

This is a corollary of the following technical variant of Theorem 9.7. Instead of restricting d to be $> n/2$, this lemma restricts d in terms of the average weight of all codewords. Here, we consider codes with an arbitrary set of messages S rather than $\{0,1\}^k$.

Lemma 9.9. *Suppose $E\colon S \to \{0,1\}^n$ has distance d and average codeword weight w. Define $\delta = 1/2-d/n$ and $\gamma = 1/2-w/n$. If $\delta < 2\gamma^2$ then $|S| \leq 1/(2\gamma^2-\delta)$.*

Proof of Theorem 9.8. Consider any ball B of relative radius $\leq 1/2-\sqrt{\varepsilon}$ centered at some $r \in \{0,1\}^n$. Define $S = \{m \in \{0,1\}^k : E(m) \in B\}$ as the set of all messages whose codeword is in the ball. Define $E'\colon S \to \{0,1\}^n$ by $E'(m) = E(m) \oplus r$. (Intuitively, this shifts the ball to have center 0^n.) Then $\text{dist}(E') \geq \text{dist}(E)$ because $\text{dist}(E'(m_1), E'(m_2)) = \text{dist}(E(m_1), E(m_2))$ for all distinct $m_1, m_2 \in S$. Thus E' has relative distance $1/2-\delta$ for some $\delta \leq \varepsilon$. Also, for every $m \in S$ we have $\text{weight}(E'(m)) = \text{dist}(r, E(m)) \leq (1/2-\sqrt{\varepsilon})n$ since $E(m) \in B$. Thus E' has average codeword weight $(1/2-\gamma)n$ for some $\gamma \geq \sqrt{\varepsilon}$. We have $\delta \leq \varepsilon < 2\varepsilon \leq 2\gamma^2$ (since $\varepsilon > 0$), so Lemma 9.9 says $|S| \leq 1/(2\gamma^2-\delta) \leq 1/(2\varepsilon-\varepsilon) = 1/\varepsilon$. ■

Proof of Lemma 9.9 (ancillary). Let $K = |S|$ be the number of messages. Let K_i be the number of messages whose codewords have 1 at coordinate i.

$$\begin{aligned}
\tbinom{K}{2}d &\leq \textstyle\sum_i K_i(K-K_i) && \text{(as in the proof of Theorem 9.7)}\\
&= K\textstyle\sum_i K_i - \sum_i K_i^2 \\
&\leq K\textstyle\sum_i K_i - \left(\sum_i K_i\right)^2/n && \text{(Corollary A.27)}\\
&= K(Kw) - (Kw)^2/n && \left(\textstyle\sum_i K_i = \sum_m \text{weight}(E(m)) = Kw\right)\\
&= K^2(w - w^2/n)
\end{aligned}$$

$$(K-1)2dn \leq K(4wn - 4w^2) \qquad \text{(multiplying both sides by } 4n/K\text{)}$$

$$\begin{aligned}
2dn &\geq K(-4wn + 4w^2 + 2dn) && \text{(rearranging)}\\
&= K\big((n^2-4wn+4w^2)-(n^2-2dn)\big) && \text{(inserting } +n^2-n^2 \text{ with foresight)}\\
&= K\big((n-2w)^2 - n(n-2d)\big)\\
&= K\big((2n\gamma)^2 - n(2n\delta)\big) && \text{(definition of } \delta \text{ and } \gamma\text{)}
\end{aligned}$$

$$K(2\gamma^2-\delta) \leq d/n \qquad \text{(dividing both sides by } 2n^2\text{)}$$
$$\leq 1 \qquad (d \leq n)$$

Dividing both sides by $2\gamma^2-\delta > 0$ doesn't flip the inequality's direction. ■

Theorem 9.7 corresponds to $S = \{0,1\}^k$ and $d > n/2$. In this case, $\delta < 0 \leq 2\gamma^2$ automatically, so Lemma 9.9 says $2^k \leq 1/{-\delta}$. If we don't sloppily bound $d/n \leq 1$ at the end of the proof of Lemma 9.9, then we exactly recover Theorem 9.7: $2^k \leq (d/n)/{-\delta} = 1/(1-n/2d)$.

9.3 Polynomial Codes

9.3.1 Nonbinary Codes

Besides the alphabet $\{0,1\}$, sometimes we consider codes over an alphabet with $q \geq 2$ symbols, say $\mathbb{Z}_q = \{0,1,\ldots,q-1\}$. Such a code is called *q-ary*. "Binary" means 2-ary. The basic definitions and theorems straightforwardly generalize from binary to q-ary. Here's a brief summary.

A q-ary code is a function $E\colon \mathbb{Z}_q^k \to \mathbb{Z}_q^n$. The analogue of a bit flip error is a *symbol change* error: The channel changes a codeword symbol to any one of the other $q-1$ symbols.

The distance between two tuples $a, b \in \mathbb{Z}_q^n$ is the number of coordinates on which they differ: $\text{dist}(a,b) = \big|\{i : a_i \neq b_i\}\big|$. Each coordinate is "all or nothing": Either $a_i = b_i$ or not. (There's no notion of a_i being "close" to b_i.) This q-ary distance obeys the triangle inequality.

The distance of a q-ary code E is $\text{dist}(E) = \min_{m_1 \neq m_2} \text{dist}\big(E(m_1), E(m_2)\big)$ as usual. If $\text{dist}(E) = d$, we can decode from $< d$ many erasures or from $< d/2$ many symbol changes, like in the binary setting. The relative distance and rate are still defined as d/n and k/n.

Theorem 9.6 doesn't depend on the alphabet size:

Theorem 9.10. *If $E\colon \mathbb{Z}_q^k \to \mathbb{Z}_q^n$ has distance d, then $k \leq n-d+1$.*

Proof. By the pigeonhole principle, at least two of the q^k codewords agree on their first $k-1$ symbols (since there are $q^{k-1} < q^k$ possibilities for this prefix) and thus have distance $\leq n-(k-1)$. Hence $d \leq n-k+1$. ■

If q is prime then $\mathbb{Z}_q$ forms a field, so we can do arithmetic with symbols. In this case, we say E is linear iff $E(m_1+m_2) = E(m_1)+E(m_2)$ for all messages m_1 and m_2, and $E(cm) = cE(m)$ for every symbol (scalar) c and every message (vector) m. (The condition $E(cm) = cE(m)$ held automatically in the binary setting, so we excluded it from the definition of linear binary codes.)

The weight of a vector in $\mathbb{Z}_q^n$ is the number of coordinates with nonzero values (the distance from 0^n). Lemma 9.1 and Lemma 9.2 generalize to the q-ary setting straightforwardly:

Lemma 9.11. *For every prime q:*

(i) If $E\colon \mathbb{Z}_q^k \to \mathbb{Z}_q^n$ is linear then $\text{dist}(E) = \min_{m \neq 0^k} \text{weight}\big(E(m)\big)$.
(ii) $E\colon \mathbb{Z}_q^k \to \mathbb{Z}_q^n$ is linear iff there exists a $k \times n$ matrix G such that $E(m) = mG$ over $\mathbb{Z}_q$. ■

9.3.2 Definition of Polynomial Codes

Polynomial codes have wide-ranging practical applications in CDs, DVDs, QR codes, DSL, satellite communications, and more. They're useful building blocks for constructing binary codes, as we'll see in §9.5.

Intuitively, the message is a low-degree polynomial's coefficients, and the codeword is the polynomial's values (with different field elements plugged in).

Definition. For any prime q and $k \in [q-1]$, the *polynomial code* $E_{q,k}\colon \mathbb{Z}_q^k \to \mathbb{Z}_q^q$ has alphabet size q, message length k, and codeword length $n = q$. The message is treated as coefficients of a univariate polynomial of degree $< k$ over the field $\mathbb{Z}_q$. The codeword coordinate at index $a \in \mathbb{Z}_q$ is the evaluation of the message polynomial with a plugged in.

$$\begin{aligned} \text{message:} \qquad M &= (M_{k-1}, M_{k-2}, \dots, M_0) = M_{k-1}x^{k-1} + M_{k-2}x^{k-2} + \dots + M_0 \\ \text{codeword:} \qquad E_{q,k}(M) &= \big(M(0), M(1), \dots, M(q-1)\big) \end{aligned}$$

◀

We use M instead of m for the message because by convention, we denote polynomials with capital letters. $E_{q,1}$ is a q-ary repetition code, with distance q.

Claim 9.12. $\operatorname{dist}(E_{q,k}) = q - k + 1$.

Proof. $\operatorname{dist}(E_{q,k}) \le q-k+1$ by Theorem 9.10, and $\operatorname{dist}(E_{q,k}) \ge q-k+1$ because distinct polynomials of degree $\le k-1$ agree on $\le k-1$ points (Corollary A.21) and thus disagree on $\ge q-(k-1)$ points. ■

Polynomial codes are linear. $E_{q,k}$'s generator matrix is

$$G_{q,k} = \begin{bmatrix} 0^{k-1} & 1^{k-1} & 2^{k-1} & \cdots & (q-1)^{k-1} \\ 0^{k-2} & 1^{k-2} & 2^{k-2} & \cdots & (q-1)^{k-2} \\ \vdots & \vdots & \vdots & & \vdots \\ 0^1 & 1^1 & 2^1 & \cdots & (q-1)^1 \\ 0^0 & 1^0 & 2^0 & \cdots & (q-1)^0 \end{bmatrix}$$

where $0^0 = 1$. Let's use linearity to reiterate why $\operatorname{dist}(E_{q,k}) \ge q-k+1$: Any nonzero polynomial of degree $\le k-1$ has $\le k-1$ roots (Theorem A.20), so the codeword has weight $\ge q-(k-1)$.

Example. For $q = 5$ and $k = 3$, the polynomial code $E_{5,3}\colon \mathbb{Z}_5^3 \to \mathbb{Z}_5^5$ is defined by:

$$\begin{aligned} \text{message:} \qquad M &= (M_2, M_1, M_0) = M_2x^2 + M_1x + M_0 \\ \text{codeword:} \qquad E_{5,3}(M) &= \big(M(0), M(1), M(2), M(3), M(4)\big) \end{aligned}$$

For example:

$$\begin{aligned} \text{message:} \qquad M &= (3, 4, 2) = 3x^2 + 4x + 2 \\ \text{codeword:} \qquad E_{5,3}(M) &= (2, 4, 2, 1, 1) \end{aligned}$$

For instance, we calculated $M(1) = 3 \cdot 1^2 + 4 \cdot 1 + 2 = 3 + 4 + 2 = 4$ and $M(3) = 3 \cdot 3^2 + 4 \cdot 3 + 2 = 2 + 2 + 2 = 1$.

$E_{5,3}$ has distance $5 - 3 + 1 = 3$, so it's possible to correct two erasures or one symbol change. The generator matrix is:

$$G_{5,3} = \begin{bmatrix} 0^2 & 1^2 & 2^2 & 3^2 & 4^2 \\ 0^1 & 1^1 & 2^1 & 3^1 & 4^1 \\ 0^0 & 1^0 & 2^0 & 3^0 & 4^0 \end{bmatrix} = \begin{bmatrix} 0 & 1 & 4 & 4 & 1 \\ 0 & 1 & 2 & 3 & 4 \\ 1 & 1 & 1 & 1 & 1 \end{bmatrix}$$

◆

9.3.3 Decoding from Erasures

Decoding Polynomial Codes from Erasures	(9.6)
Input: Prime q and $k \in [q-1]$ and received word $r \in (\mathbb{Z}_q \cup \{\perp\})^q$ such that: r has $< q-k+1$ many $\perp$s and agrees with $E_{q,k}(M)$ for some M	
Output: M	

Theorem 9.13. Decoding Polynomial Codes from Erasures *has a poly-time algorithm.*

Proof. If r has more than k non-erasures, we can ignore some of them and pretend r has exactly k non-erasures, because our decoder works in that case anyway.

Let $a_1, a_2, \ldots, a_k$ be the indices of non-erasures in r, and let $b_j = r_{a_j}$ for each $j \in [k]$ (so $a_j, b_j \in \mathbb{Z}_q$). Given M's values at k distinct points, namely $M(a_j) = b_j$ for each j, we recover M by interpolating a polynomial of degree $\leq k-1$ through these points.

For each $i \in [k]$, define the *indicator* polynomial I_i of degree $k-1$ such that $I_i(a_i) = 1$ and $I_i(a_j) = 0$ for all $j \in [k]$ with $j \neq i$:

$$I_i(x) = \frac{\prod_{h \neq i}(x - a_h)}{\prod_{h \neq i}(a_i - a_h)}$$

The denominator is a nonzero constant since $a_i - a_h \neq 0$ for all $h \neq i$. The numerator has degree $k-1$ since it has $k-1$ factors, each of degree 1. We indeed have

$$I_i(a_i) = \frac{\prod_{h \neq i}(a_i - a_h)}{\prod_{h \neq i}(a_i - a_h)} = 1 \qquad \text{and} \qquad I_i(a_j) = \frac{\prod_{h \neq i}(a_j - a_h)}{\prod_{h \neq i}(a_i - a_h)} = 0$$

for each $j \neq i$, since the numerator contains a factor $a_j - a_j = 0$. The decoder outputs the polynomial $P = \sum_{i=1}^{k} b_i \cdot I_i$, which has degree $< k$ since each I_i does, and which interpolates through the given points:

$$P(a_j) = \sum_{i=1}^{k} b_i \cdot I_i(a_j) = b_j \cdot 1 + \sum_{i \neq j} b_i \cdot 0 = b_j$$

$P = M$ because P and M have degree $< k$ and agree on k points (Corollary A.21).

For each i, expanding I_i's numerator $\prod_{h \neq i}(x - a_h)$ to its canonical form takes poly time (§7.1.1). Thus the decoder runs in poly time. ∎

Example. Suppose $q = 7$, $k = 3$, and $r = (2, \perp, \perp, 1, \perp, 6, \perp)$. The goal is to find the unique polynomial M of degree ≤ 2 over $\mathbb{Z}_7$ such that $M(0) = 2$ and $M(3) = 1$ and $M(5) = 6$. We have $(a_1, a_2, a_3) = (0, 3, 5)$ and $(b_1, b_2, b_3) = (2, 1, 6)$.

$$I_1 = \frac{(x-3)(x-5)}{(0-3)(0-5)} = \frac{x^2+6x+1}{1} = 1x^2+6x+1$$

$$I_2 = \frac{(x-0)(x-5)}{(3-0)(3-5)} = \frac{x^2+2x+0}{1} = 1x^2+2x+0$$

$$I_3 = \frac{(x-0)(x-3)}{(5-0)(5-3)} = \frac{x^2+4x+0}{3} = 5x^2+6x+0$$

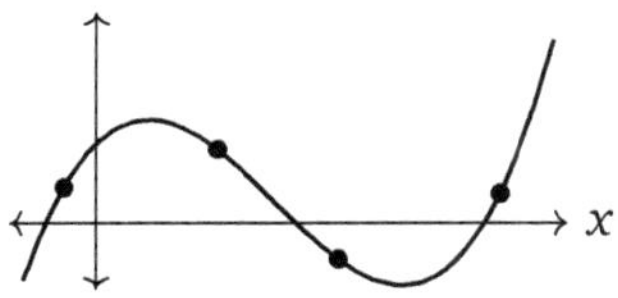

Figure 9.6: Real polynomial interpolation

$$\begin{aligned} M &= 2I_1 + 1I_2 + 6I_3 \\ &= (2x^2+5x+2)+(1x^2+2x+0)+(2x^2+1x+0) \\ &= 5x^2+1x+2 \end{aligned}$$

Let's double-check that this polynomial indeed interpolates through the given points:

$$M(0) = 5\cdot 0^2 + 1\cdot 0 + 2 = 2 \qquad M(3) = 5\cdot 3^2 + 1\cdot 3 + 2 = 1 \qquad M(5) = 5\cdot 5^2 + 1\cdot 5 + 2 = 6$$

The message was $M = (5,1,2)$. The uncorrupted codeword was $E_{7,3}(M) = (2,1,3,1,2,6,6)$. ♦

This algorithm also works with the field of real numbers in place of $\mathbb{Z}_q$. Given some points in the plane with distinct x coordinates, the algorithm finds the lowest-degree polynomial that passes through those points (Figure 9.6). This has applications in numerical analysis.

9.3.4 Decoding from Symbol Changes

DECODING POLYNOMIAL CODES FROM SYMBOL CHANGES	(9.7)
Input: Prime q and $k \in [q-1]$ and received word $r \in \mathbb{Z}_q^q$ such that: $\operatorname{dist}\big(r, E_{q,k}(M)\big) < (q-k+1)/2$ for some M	
Output: M	

Theorem 9.14. DECODING POLYNOMIAL CODES FROM SYMBOL CHANGES *has a poly-time algorithm.*

This result is fundamental but we won't need it, so we'll be brief with the proof.

Proof (ancillary). Let $e = \lfloor (q-k)/2 \rfloor$. By assumption, some polynomial M of degree $\le k-1$ is such that $r_a \ne M(a)$ for $\le e$ many $a \in \mathbb{Z}_q$. Define the polynomial $Q(x) = \prod_{a : r_a \ne M(a)} (x-a)$ of degree $\le e$, whose roots are the "error coordinates." Define the polynomial $P = Q \cdot M$ of degree $\le e+k-1$. We have $P(a) = Q(a)\cdot r_a$ for every $a \in \mathbb{Z}_q$ because if $Q(a)=0$ then both sides are 0, and if $Q(a) \ne 0$ then $r_a = M(a)$ and thus both sides are $Q(a)\cdot M(a)$.

If the decoder knew P and Q, it could do polynomial division (Lemma A.22) to recover $M = P/Q$. But it doesn't know P or Q, so it attempts to find them. Note that "$P(a) = Q(a)\cdot r_a$ for every $a \in \mathbb{Z}_q$" is a system of linear equations over $\mathbb{Z}_p$ (one equation per a) where the unknowns are the $e+k$ many coefficients of P and the $e+1$ many coefficients of Q. (This is potentially confusing since it swaps the roles of "coefficient" and "variable.") The coefficients of the actual P and Q are a solution to this system. It's well known that there exists a poly-time algorithm which, given a system of linear equations, finds a solution if one exists (virtually the same algorithm as in Theorem A.29). Thus the decoder can find polynomials P' and Q' whose coefficients are a solution to the system. It's OK if P' and Q' aren't the desired P and Q, because $P' = Q'\cdot M$ anyway:

P' and $Q' \cdot M$ have degree $\le e+k-1 < q-e$ and agree on $\ge q-e$ points since $P'(a) = Q'(a) \cdot M(a)$ for every a such that $r_a = M(a)$, so they're the same polynomial (Corollary A.21).

There's a catch: If Q' is the zero polynomial, the decoder can't recover $M = P'/Q'$. Indeed, P' and Q' might be the zero polynomials since those are always a solution to the system. We fix this by hardcoding the coefficient of x^e to 1 in Q' (so this coefficient is no longer an unknown in the system), to ensure Q' has degree exactly e and is thus nonzero. The system is still solvable since the coefficients of $x^{e-\deg(Q)}P$ and $x^{e-\deg(Q)}Q$ are a solution.

In summary, the poly-time decoder solves the system to find P' and nonzero Q', and then does polynomial division to find $M = P'/Q'$. ■

9.4 Bit String Fields

$\mathbb{Z}_q$ is a field (with modular arithmetic) iff q is prime. Sometimes, we need $\{0,1\}^\ell$ to be a field. Addition and subtraction are both bitwise xor, which obeys the commutative, associative, and inverse axioms, with 0^ℓ as the additive identity. But how should we define multiplication and division? If $\ell > 1$ then we can't view bit strings as binary numbers and do arithmetic mod 2^ℓ, since we wouldn't have multiplicative inverses (and addition and subtraction wouldn't be bitwise xor). Instead, we interpret bit strings as polynomials over $\mathbb{Z}_2$ and do arithmetic modulo a certain polynomial of degree ℓ. To prove that this is a field, we must establish the existence of multiplicative inverses.

In this section, we only consider univariate polynomials over the field $\mathbb{Z}_2$, but everything generalizes straightforwardly to univariate polynomials over the field $\mathbb{Z}_q$ for any prime q.

9.4.1 Multiplicative Inverses

Dividing a polynomial A by a nonzero polynomial M yields unique polynomials Q (the quotient) and R (the remainder) such that $A = Q \cdot M + R$ and $\deg(R) < \deg(M)$ (Lemma A.22). We define $A \bmod M$ as the remainder R. The mod operator has the following properties (like the analogous properties for integers):

$$\begin{aligned}(A+B) \bmod M &= \big((A \bmod M) + (B \bmod M)\big) \bmod M\\(A-B) \bmod M &= \big((A \bmod M) - (B \bmod M)\big) \bmod M\\(A \cdot B) \bmod M &= \big((A \bmod M) \cdot (B \bmod M)\big) \bmod M\end{aligned}$$

A "mod M" *multiplicative inverse* of A is a polynomial B such that $(A \cdot B) \bmod M = 1$ (where 1 is the constant polynomial, of degree 0) and $\deg(B) < \deg(M)$.

Example. Let $M = x^3 + x + 1$ and $A = x^2 + x$. Then $B = x + 1$ is a "mod M" multiplicative inverse of A because $(A \cdot B) \bmod M = 1$:

$$A \cdot B = x^3 + x^2 + x^2 + x = x^3 + x = 1 \cdot M + 1$$ ♦

A nonconstant polynomial P is *irreducible* (analogous to an integer being prime) when it can't be factored nontrivially: There do not exist nonconstant polynomials A and B such that $P = A \cdot B$.

Example. Let's see why $P = x^3 + x + 1$ is irreducible. If it were reducible, it would equal some degree-1 polynomial times some degree-2 polynomial. The degree-1 polynomials are x and $x+1$.

The degree-2 polynomials are x^2 and x^2+1 and x^2+x and x^2+x+1. None of these pairs multiplies to P. For example:

$$(x+1)\cdot(x^2+x+1) \;=\; (x^3+x^2+x)+(x^2+x+1) \;=\; x^3+1 \neq P \qquad \blacklozenge$$

Recall that for every prime p, every nonzero $a \in \mathbb{Z}_p$ has a unique "mod p" multiplicative inverse (Theorem A.16). Here's the analogue for polynomials:

Theorem 9.15. *For every irreducible polynomial P, every nonzero polynomial A with* $\deg(A) < \deg(P)$ *has a unique* "mod P" *multiplicative inverse.*

The proof echoes Theorem A.16 but with upper-case letters (polynomials) instead of lower-case letters (integers). A reader with faith in Theorem 9.15 may skip the proof.

Two nonzero polynomials (A, B) are *coirreducible* to each other (analogous to integers being coprime) when they have no common divisor besides 1—that is, there's no nonconstant polynomial D such that $A = Q_1D$ and $B = Q_2D$ for some polynomials Q_1 and Q_2. Recall that the zero polynomial has degree $-\infty$. Since an irreducible P is coirreducible to every nonzero A with $\deg(A) < \deg(P)$, Theorem 9.15 is a corollary of the following:

Theorem 9.16. *If* $0 \le \deg(A) < \deg(B)$ *and (A, B) are coirreducible, then A has a unique* "mod B" *multiplicative inverse.*

Proof idea. We design a recursive subroutine to find such an inverse. Two lemmas tell us what arguments to pass to the recursive call, and what to do with the call's return value. We say A is "mod B" invertible when A has a "mod B" multiplicative inverse.

	(A, B) are coirreducible		A is "mod B" invertible	
Lemma 9.17	$\Downarrow$		$\Uparrow$	Lemma 9.18
	$(B \bmod A, A)$ are coirreducible	$\Rightarrow$	$(B \bmod A)$ is "mod A" invertible	
		recursion		$\blacksquare$

Lemma 9.17. *If* $0 < \deg(A) < \deg(B)$ *and (A, B) are coirreducible, then* $0 \le \deg(B \bmod A) < \deg(A)$ *and $(B \bmod A, A)$ are coirreducible.*

Proof of Lemma 9.17 (ancillary). Assuming $0 < \deg(A) < \deg(B)$, we show that if either $(B \bmod A)$ is the zero polynomial or $(B \bmod A, A)$ aren't coirreducible, then (A, B) aren't coirreducible. If $(B \bmod A)$ is the zero polynomial, then the nonconstant polynomial A itself is a common divisor of A and B. Now, suppose $(B \bmod A, A)$ aren't coirreducible, so $(B \bmod A) = Q_1D$ and $A = Q_2D$ for some nonconstant polynomial D and polynomials Q_1 and Q_2. Since $B = Q_3A + (B \bmod A)$ for some polynomial Q_3, we have $B = Q_3Q_2D + Q_1D = (Q_3Q_2 + Q_1)D$. Thus D is also a divisor of both A and B, so (A, B) aren't coirreducible. $\blacksquare$

Lemma 9.18. *If* $0 < \deg(A) < \deg(B)$ *and* $(B \bmod A)$ *is* "mod A" *invertible, then A is* "mod B" *invertible.*

Proof of Lemma 9.18 (ancillary). Assume $0 < \deg(A) < \deg(B)$ and $(B \bmod A)$ has a "mod A" multiplicative inverse S, which means $(B \bmod A)S \bmod A = 1$, in other words $(B \bmod A)S = Q_1A + 1$ for some polynomial Q_1. Combining this with $B = Q_2A + (B \bmod A)$ for some polynomial Q_2, we get $(B - Q_2A)S = Q_1A + 1$. Rearranging this yields $A(-Q_1 - Q_2S) = (-S)B + 1$, which says $AT = Q_3B + 1$ where $T = -Q_1 - Q_2S$ and $Q_3 = -S$. This means $AT \bmod B = 1$, so A has a "mod B" multiplicative inverse $(T \bmod B)$ since $A(T \bmod B) \bmod B = AT \bmod B = 1$. $\blacksquare$

Proof of Theorem 9.16 (ancillary). The following recursive subroutine maintains the invariant that if $0 \le \deg(A) < \deg(B)$ and (A,B) are coirreducible, then find-inverse(A,B) returns a "mod B" multiplicative inverse of A.

Algorithm to find a multiplicative inverse of a polynomial	(9.8)

```
find-inverse(A, B):
    if A = 1: return 1
    S ← find-inverse(B mod A, A)
    return (−Q1 − Q2 S) mod B where:
        Q1 is the quotient of (B mod A)S divided by A
        Q2 is the quotient of B divided by A
```

The base cases are when $A = 1$ and the subroutine returns 1, which is correct since $(1 \cdot 1) \bmod B = 1$. To prove that find-inverse(A,B) maintains the invariant when $\deg(A) > 0$, we assume the invariant holds for find-inverse$(B \bmod A, A)$ and show that it also holds for find-inverse(A,B). Suppose $0 < \deg(A) < \deg(B)$ and (A,B) are coirreducible. Then $0 \le \deg(B \bmod A) < \deg(A)$ and $(B \bmod A, A)$ are coirreducible by Lemma 9.17. Thus S is a "mod A" multiplicative inverse of $(B \bmod A)$ by the invariant. The return value $(-Q_1 - Q_2 S) \bmod B$ is a "mod B" multiplicative inverse of A by the proof of Lemma 9.18. The recursion terminates since the first argument's degree decreases (but stays nonnegative) in each successive call, so it eventually reaches a base case.

Now that we know A has at least one "mod B" multiplicative inverse (since find-inverse(A,B) returns one), we show that A has only one such inverse. Assuming T and U are "mod B" multiplicative inverses of A, we show that $T = U$. Doing all calculations "mod B": We have $A(T - U) = AT - AU = 1 - 1 = 0$. Multiplying both sides by T, the left side becomes $T(A(T-U)) = (TA)(T-U) = 1 \cdot (T-U) = T - U$, while the right side becomes $T \cdot 0 = 0$. In summary, $(T - U) \bmod B = 0$, which implies $T = U$ since $\deg(T), \deg(U) < \deg(B)$. ■

9.4.2 Fields via Polynomials

If p is a prime number, then $\mathbb{Z}_p$ is a field where arithmetic is modulo p. Analogously, if P is an irreducible polynomial of degree ℓ over $\mathbb{Z}_2$, then $\{0,1\}^\ell$ is a field where each element is the coefficients of a polynomial of degree $< \ell$ over $\mathbb{Z}_2$, and arithmetic is modulo P. For example, $011001 \in \{0,1\}^6$ corresponds to $0x^5 + 1x^4 + 1x^3 + 0x^2 + 0x + 1 = x^4 + x^3 + 1$. We denote the field $\{0,1\}^\ell$ as $\mathbb{F}_{2^\ell}$, omitting the dependence on P from the notation.

- $A + B = A - B = A \oplus B$. Both operators are bitwise xor. Addition and subtraction in the field $\mathbb{F}_{2^\ell}$ are equivalent to addition and subtraction of vectors in $\mathbb{Z}_2^\ell$. The "mod P" doesn't affect $+$ and $-$ since the degree stays $< \ell$ anyway.
- $A \cdot B = (A \cdot B) \bmod P$ where $\cdot$ on the left is multiplication in the field $\mathbb{F}_{2^\ell}$, and $\cdot$ on the right is ordinary multiplication of polynomials.
- $A/B = A \cdot B^{-1}$ where $\cdot$ is field multiplication and B^{-1} is B's unique "mod P" multiplicative inverse guaranteed by Theorem 9.15 (assuming B is nonzero).

These operators $+, -, \cdot, /$, along with the additive and multiplicative identities $0\cdots00$ and $0\cdots01$ (corresponding to the constant polynomials), obey the field axioms from §A.4.1.

+	00	01	10	11
00	00	01	10	11
01	01	00	11	10
10	10	11	00	01
11	11	10	01	00

·	00	01	10	11
00	00	00	00	00
01	00	01	10	11
10	00	10	11	01
11	00	11	01	10

/	00	01	10	11
00		00	00	00
01		01	11	10
10		10	01	11
11		11	10	01

Figure 9.7: Addition/subtraction and multiplication and division tables for the field $\mathbb{F}_4$

Example. Let's use the irreducible polynomial $P = x^2 + x + 1$ to view $\mathbb{F}_4 = \{0,1\}^2$ as a field.

$$\begin{aligned} 00 &= 0x + 0 = 0 \\ 01 &= 0x + 1 = 1 \\ 10 &= 1x + 0 = x \\ 11 &= 1x + 1 = x + 1 \end{aligned}$$

00 is the additive identity, and 01 is the multiplicative identity, so $01^{-1} = 01$. We have $10 \cdot 11 = 01$ because $\big(x \cdot (x+1)\big) \bmod P = (x^2 + x) \bmod P = 1$, so $10^{-1} = 11$ and $11^{-1} = 10$. Figure 9.7 shows the addition/subtraction and multiplication and division tables: $A + B$ and $A \cdot B$ and A/B are at row A, column B. ♦

Example. In §9.4.1 we saw that $P = x^3 + x + 1$ is irreducible, so we can use P to view $\mathbb{F}_8 = \{0,1\}^3$ as a field. We also saw that $110 = x^2 + x$ and $011 = x + 1$ are each other's multiplicative inverses modulo P. Here are two example calculations:

$$101/110 = 101 \cdot 011 = \big((x^2+1)\cdot(x+1)\big) \bmod P = (x^3 + x^2 + x + 1) \bmod P = x^2 = 100$$
$$111/011 = 111 \cdot 110 = \big((x^2+x+1)\cdot(x^2+x)\big) \bmod P = (x^4 + x) \bmod P = x^2 = 100$$

The second example uses the polynomial division $x^4 + x = x \cdot P + x^2$. ♦

Assuming we know an irreducible polynomial P of degree ℓ, we can compute arithmetic operations in the field $\mathbb{F}_{2^\ell} = \{0,1\}^\ell$ in poly ℓ time. (Don't confuse "polynomial" time efficiency and the "polynomials" corresponding to field elements.) Ordinary addition/subtraction/multiplication of polynomials take poly ℓ time, and "mod P" takes poly ℓ time by the proof of Lemma A.22, and finding the multiplicative inverse (for division in $\mathbb{F}_{2^\ell}$) takes poly ℓ time by the proof of Theorem 9.15.

It doesn't matter which irreducible polynomial we use to define the field, but how do we find such a polynomial, or even know that it exists? In practice, people consult tables of all irreducible polynomials of specific degrees. For computational complexity, we need irreducible polynomials of arbitrarily large degrees.

Theorem 9.19.

(i) For every integer $\ell \geq 1$, there exists an irreducible polynomial of degree ℓ.
(ii) For every integer $e \geq 0$, the polynomial $x^{2\cdot 3^e} + x^{3^e} + 1$ is irreducible.

The polynomials from *(ii)* are $x^2 + x + 1$, and $x^6 + x^3 + 1$, and $x^{18} + x^9 + 1$, and so on. These are convenient because they provide a known irreducible polynomial having degree within a factor 3 of any target degree, which is sufficient for our purposes.

Proving Theorem 9.19 would take us too far afield (no pun intended), so we just accept it as a gift from pure math.

9.5 Codes Using Bit String Fields

9.5.1 Bit Strings as Symbols

A code over the alphabet $\mathbb{Z}_q$ is a function $E\colon \mathbb{Z}_q^k \to \mathbb{Z}_q^n$. Similarly, a code over the alphabet $\{0,1\}^\ell$ is a function $E\colon (\{0,1\}^\ell)^k \to (\{0,1\}^\ell)^n$. Such 2^ℓ-ary codes are useful intermediate tools for constructing binary codes.

Each element of $\{0,1\}^\ell$ is considered a single symbol, and 0^ℓ is the "zero symbol."

Example. $\text{dist}\big((110, 010, 011), (111, 010, 101)\big) = 2$ because $110 \neq 111$ and $010 = 010$ and $011 \neq 101$. It doesn't matter that 110 and 111 differ in one bit position while 011 and 101 differ in two bit positions—each symbol's "internal structure" is irrelevant.

$\text{weight}\big((101, 010, 000, 111)\big) = 3$ because $101 \neq 000$ and $010 \neq 000$ and $000 = 000$ and $111 \neq 000$. It doesn't matter how many 1s a symbol has internally, only whether it has at least one 1. ♦

Flattening a vector $v \in (\{0,1\}^\ell)^n$ means concatenating its components into one big bit string $v' \in \{0,1\}^{\ell n}$ (erasing the boundaries between components). For example, $(110, 010, 111)' = 110010111$. (Elsewhere in this book, we sometimes equate a vector with its flattened version, but here we must distinguish them.) Note that $\text{dist}(v', w') = \sum_{i=1}^n \text{dist}(v_i, w_i) \geq \text{dist}(v, w)$ for all $v, w \in (\{0,1\}^\ell)^n$, because if $v_i \neq w_i$, contributing 1 to $\text{dist}(v,w)$, then v_i and w_i differ in at least one of their ℓ bit positions, so $\text{dist}(v_i, w_i) \geq 1$, contributing at least 1 to $\text{dist}(v', w')$. Similarly, $\text{weight}(v') = \sum_{i=1}^n \text{weight}(v_i) \geq \text{weight}(v)$.

We can turn a 2^ℓ-ary code $E\colon (\{0,1\}^\ell)^k \to (\{0,1\}^\ell)^n$ into a binary code $E'\colon \{0,1\}^{\ell k} \to \{0,1\}^{\ell n}$ by flattening both the message and the codeword: $E'(m') = E(m)'$. For example, if $E\big((01, 10)\big) = (11, 01, 00)$ then $E'(0110) = 110100$. Note that E' has the same rate $\ell k/\ell n = k/n$ as E does, and $\text{dist}(E') \geq \text{dist}(E)$ because for all distinct $m_1, m_2 \in (\{0,1\}^\ell)^k$:

$$\text{dist}\big(E'(m_1'), E'(m_2')\big) = \text{dist}\big(E(m_1)', E(m_2)'\big) \geq \text{dist}\big(E(m_1), E(m_2)\big)$$

But E' has relative distance $\text{dist}(E')/\ell n$, which may be a factor ℓ lower than $\text{dist}(E)/n$, the relative distance of E.

In §9.4.2, we endowed $\{0,1\}^\ell$ with arithmetic operations to make it into a field $\mathbb{F}_{2^\ell}$. (And $\mathbb{F}_2$ coincides with $\mathbb{Z}_2$.) We typically assume these operations are defined using the convenient irreducible polynomial from Theorem 9.19.*(ii)*, but the specific polynomial isn't important now.

As with $\mathbb{Z}_q$ (for prime q), we say $E\colon \mathbb{F}_{2^\ell}^k \to \mathbb{F}_{2^\ell}^n$ is linear iff $E(m_1 + m_2) = E(m_1) + E(m_2)$ for all $m_1, m_2 \in \mathbb{F}_{2^\ell}^k$, and $E(cm) = cE(m)$ for all $c \in \mathbb{F}_{2^\ell}$ and $m \in \mathbb{F}_{2^\ell}^k$. The usual properties of linear codes still hold since they only rely on the field axioms, not on the details of any specific field:

Lemma 9.20. *For every ℓ:*

(i) If $E\colon \mathbb{F}_{2^\ell}^k \to \mathbb{F}_{2^\ell}^n$ is linear then $\text{dist}(E) = \min_{m \neq (0^\ell)^k} \text{weight}\big(E(m)\big)$.

(ii) $E\colon \mathbb{F}_{2^\ell}^k \to \mathbb{F}_{2^\ell}^n$ is linear iff there exists a $k \times n$ matrix G such that $E(m) = mG$ over $\mathbb{F}_{2^\ell}$. ■

Linearity and flattening get along well with each other:

Observation 9.21. $v' + w' = (v + w)'$ *for all* $v, w \in \mathbb{F}_{2^\ell}^k$.

Proof. $v' + w'$ uses bitwise xor (vector addition in $\mathbb{Z}_2^{\ell k}$), and $v + w$ uses bitwise xor on each of the k components (vector addition in $\mathbb{F}_{2^\ell}^k$). It doesn't matter whether we flatten before or after bitwise xoring everything. ■

Lemma 9.22. *If* $E\colon \mathbb{F}_{2^\ell}^k \to \mathbb{F}_{2^\ell}^n$ *is linear then* $E'\colon \mathbb{Z}_2^{\ell k} \to \mathbb{Z}_2^{\ell n}$ *is linear.*

Proof. Assume E is linear (over $\mathbb{F}_{2^\ell}$). For all $m_1, m_2 \in \mathbb{F}_{2^\ell}^k$:

$$\begin{aligned}
E'(m_1' + m_2') &= E'((m_1+m_2)') && \text{(Observation 9.21)}\\
&= E(m_1+m_2)' && \text{(definition of } E')\\
&= (E(m_1)+E(m_2))' && (E \text{ is linear})\\
&= E(m_1)' + E(m_2)' && \text{(Observation 9.21)}\\
&= E'(m_1') + E'(m_2') && \text{(definition of } E')
\end{aligned}$$

Thus E' is linear (over $\mathbb{Z}_2$). ■

9.5.2 Polynomial Codes

The elements of $\mathbb{F}_{2^\ell}$ play the role of numbers, so we can use them as coefficients of polynomials, and plug them into polynomials. It's best to forget that we defined arithmetic operations by treating elements of $\mathbb{F}_{2^\ell}$ as polynomials over $\mathbb{Z}_2$ (because "plugging a polynomial into a polynomial whose coefficients are polynomials" sounds confusing). We just view elements of $\mathbb{F}_{2^\ell}$ as symbols with "black box" arithmetic operations available. Now, a superscript on a bit means repetition, such as $0^3 = 000$, while a superscript on a bit string means exponentiation using field multiplication, such as $101^3 = 101 \cdot 101 \cdot 101$.

For $q = 2^\ell$, define the polynomial code $E_{q,k}$ as in §9.3.2 but with $\mathbb{F}_q$ instead of $\mathbb{Z}_q$.

Example. Let $\ell = 2$ and $k = 3$. Recall the field $\mathbb{F}_4 = \{0,1\}^2$ defined with the irreducible polynomial x^2+x+1 (§9.4.2). In the polynomial code $E_{4,3}\colon \mathbb{F}_4^3 \to \mathbb{F}_4^4$, the message is the three coefficients of a polynomial of degree < 3 over $\mathbb{F}_4$, and the codeword is the evaluations of the message polynomial on all four elements of $\mathbb{F}_4$:

$$\begin{aligned}
\text{message:}\quad & M = (M_2, M_1, M_0) = M_2x^2 + M_1x + M_0\\
\text{codeword:}\quad & E_{4,3}(M) = \big(M(00),\ M(01),\ M(10),\ M(11)\big)
\end{aligned}$$

For example:

$$\begin{aligned}
\text{message:}\quad & M = (10,\ 00,\ 01) = 10x^2 + 00x + 01 = 10x^2 + 01\\
\text{codeword:}\quad & E_{4,3}(M) = (01,\ 11,\ 00,\ 10)
\end{aligned}$$

This codeword's coordinates are:

$$\begin{aligned}
M(00) &= 10 \cdot 00^2 + 01 = 00 + 01 = 01\\
M(01) &= 10 \cdot 01^2 + 01 = 10 + 01 = 11\\
M(10) &= 10 \cdot 10^2 + 01 = 01 + 01 = 00\\
M(11) &= 10 \cdot 11^2 + 01 = 11 + 01 = 10
\end{aligned}$$

$E_{4,3}$ has distance $4-3+1 = 2$, so it's possible to correct one erasure. An erasure would obscure an entire symbol, so the received word might be $(01,\ 11,\ \perp,\ 10)$.

The generator matrix is:

$$G_{4,3} = \begin{bmatrix} 00^2 & 01^2 & 10^2 & 11^2\\ 00^1 & 01^1 & 10^1 & 11^1\\ 00^0 & 01^0 & 10^0 & 11^0 \end{bmatrix} = \begin{bmatrix} 00 & 01 & 11 & 10\\ 00 & 01 & 10 & 11\\ 01 & 01 & 01 & 01 \end{bmatrix}$$ ♦

9.5.3 Asymptotically Good Binary Codes

The asymptotically good family of binary codes in §9.2.1 wasn't efficiently encodable. Now, we finally design an asymptotically good, poly-time encodable family of binary codes. (We won't worry about decoding.)

A first attempt is to flatten polynomial codes. For $n = q = 2^\ell$ and $k = q/2$, the polynomial code $E_{q,k}$ has rate $k/n = 1/2$ and relative distance $(n-k+1)/n > 1/2$ but a large alphabet. Unfortunately, after flattening, the relative distance is no longer $\Omega(1)$, because although the distance doesn't go down, the codeword length goes up by a factor ℓ. Here's the idea to fix this. A flattened polynomial code is linear, so its distance is the minimum weight of any nonzero message's codeword. For any nonzero message polynomial M, we'd like the flattened codeword to have weight $\Omega(\ell q)$. We know $\Omega(q)$ many $a \in \mathbb{F}_q$ have $M(a) \neq 0$ and thus each contribute weight ≥ 1 to the flattened codeword, but we'd like them each to contribute $\Omega(\ell)$. If these values $M(a) \neq 0$ were all distinct, then $\Omega(1)$ fraction of them would each contribute $\Omega(\ell)$, because few strings in $\mathbb{F}_q$ don't have weight $\Omega(\ell)$. We ensure this distinctness property with a simple modification of the polynomial code, which only doubles the codeword length: For each a, the coordinate with $M(a)$ gets a companion coordinate with $M(a)\cdot a$. If $a \neq b$ have the same value $M(a) = M(b) \neq 0$, then at least their companions have different values $M(a)\cdot a \neq M(b)\cdot b$.

Definition. For any $q = 2^\ell$ and $k \in [q-1]$, the *augmented polynomial code* $E^*_{q,k} : \mathbb{F}_q^k \to \mathbb{F}_q^{2q}$ has alphabet size q, message length k, and codeword length $n = 2q$. The message M is treated as coefficients of a univariate polynomial of degree $< k$ over $\mathbb{F}_q$. For each $a \in \mathbb{F}_q$, the codeword $E^*_{q,k}(M)$ contains the pair of symbols $M(a)$ and $M(a)\cdot a$. ◀

Example. Let's revisit the example from §9.5.2. The augmented polynomial code $E^*_{4,3}$ is:

$$\text{message:} \quad M = (M_2, M_1, M_0) = M_2x^2 + M_1x + M_0$$

$$\text{codeword:} \quad E^*_{4,3}(M) = \begin{pmatrix} M(00), & M(00)\cdot 00, \\ M(01), & M(01)\cdot 01, \\ M(10), & M(10)\cdot 10, \\ M(11), & M(11)\cdot 11 \end{pmatrix}$$

For example, recall that with the ordinary polynomial code:

$$\text{message:} \quad M = (10, 00, 01)$$

$$\text{codeword:} \quad E_{4,3}(M) = \big(M(00), M(01), M(10), M(11)\big) = (01, 11, 00, 10)$$

With the augmented polynomial code:

$$\text{message:} \quad M = (10, 00, 01)$$

$$\text{codeword:} \quad E^*_{4,3}(M) = \begin{pmatrix} 01, & 01\cdot 00, \\ 11, & 11\cdot 01, \\ 00, & 00\cdot 10, \\ 10, & 10\cdot 11 \end{pmatrix} = \begin{pmatrix} 01, & 00, \\ 11, & 11, \\ 00, & 00, \\ 10, & 01 \end{pmatrix}$$

With the flattened augmented polynomial code:

$$\text{message:} \quad M' = 100001$$

$$\text{codeword:} \quad E^{*\prime}_{4,3}(M') = 0100111100001001$$

♦

Theorem 9.23. *For large enough $q = 2^\ell$ and $k = q/2$, the flattened augmented polynomial code $E^{*\prime}_{q,k}$ has rate $1/4$ and relative distance $> 1/30$.*

Proof (ancillary). Let's declutter by omitting the q, k subscript from the codes. $E^{*\prime}$ has message length ℓk and codeword length $2\ell q$ and thus rate $\ell k/2\ell q = 1/4$. Now, we analyze the distance. E^* is linear over $\mathbb{F}_q$, so $E^{*\prime}$ is linear over $\mathbb{Z}_2$ (Lemma 9.22), so by Lemma 9.1:

$$\text{dist}(E^{*\prime}) \;=\; \min_{M' \neq 0^{\ell k}} \text{weight}\big(E^{*\prime}(M')\big) \;=\; \min_{M \neq (0^\ell)^k} \text{weight}\big(E^*(M)'\big)$$

Consider any $M \neq (0^\ell)^k$, corresponding to a nonzero polynomial of degree $< k$ over $\mathbb{F}_q$. There do not exist $a, b \in \mathbb{F}_q$ such that $a \neq b$ and $M(a) = M(b) \neq 0^\ell$ and $M(a) \cdot a = M(b) \cdot b$ (because dividing both sides of $M(a) \cdot a = M(b) \cdot b$ by $M(a) = M(b) \neq 0^\ell$ would yield $a = b$). This means that over all $a \in \mathbb{F}_q$ with $M(a) \neq 0^\ell$, the pairs $(M(a),\, M(a) \cdot a)$ are distinct. Thus the number of such a with $\text{weight}\big((M(a),\, M(a) \cdot a)'\big) \leq \ell/5$ is at most the number of strings in $\{0,1\}^{2\ell}$ with weight $\leq \ell/5$. The ball in $\{0,1\}^{2\ell}$ of radius $\ell/5 = (2\ell)/10$ centered at $0^{2\ell}$ has size

$$\leq\; (2^{2\ell})^{H(1/10)} \;<\; (2^{2\ell})^{0.47} \;=\; q^{0.94} \;<\; q/6$$

for large enough q (Lemma 9.4). At least $q - k + 1 > q/2$ many $a \in \mathbb{F}_q$ have $M(a) \neq 0^\ell$ (since M has $\leq k - 1$ roots), and $> q/2 - q/6 = q/3$ of them have $\text{weight}\big((M(a),\, M(a) \cdot a)'\big) > \ell/5$, so:

$$\text{weight}\big(E^*(M)'\big) \;=\; \textstyle\sum_{a \in \mathbb{F}_q} \text{weight}\big((M(a),\, M(a) \cdot a)'\big) \;>\; (q/3) \cdot (\ell/5) \;=\; (2\ell q)/30$$

Thus $E^{*\prime}$ has relative distance $> 1/30$. ∎

Encoding a flattened augmented polynomial code only involves poly q many additions and multiplications in $\mathbb{F}_q$, and each arithmetic operation takes poly ℓ = polylog q time (assuming $\mathbb{F}_q$ is defined with the simple irreducible polynomial from Theorem 9.19.*(ii)*). Thus the codes with $k = q/2$ from Theorem 9.23 are encodable in poly k time.

Even though $E^{*\prime}_{q,k}$ is binary, we needed the arithmetic properties of $\mathbb{F}_q$ to define and analyze it. This illustrates why bit string fields are important even if one only cares about binary codes.

9.5.4 Concatenated Codes

Concatenation is a way of combining two codes, referred to as the *outer* and *inner* codes. The message is first encoded with the outer code, and then each symbol of the outer codeword is treated as a message and encoded with the inner code. The final codeword consists of all these inner codewords. (Perhaps "composition" would be a better name than "concatenation.")

Definition. *Concatenating* $E_{\text{out}} \colon (\{0,1\}^\ell)^k \to (\{0,1\}^\ell)^n$ and $E_{\text{in}} \colon \{0,1\}^\ell \to \{0,1\}^h$ yields a binary code $E = E_{\text{in}} \circ E_{\text{out}} \colon \{0,1\}^{\ell k} \to \{0,1\}^{hn}$ where for every $m \in (\{0,1\}^\ell)^k$:

$$E(m') \;=\; \big(E_{\text{in}}(E_{\text{out}}(m)_1),\; E_{\text{in}}(E_{\text{out}}(m)_2),\; \ldots,\; E_{\text{in}}(E_{\text{out}}(m)_n)\big)'$$

See Figure 9.8. ◀

Example. If $E_{\text{out}}(01,10) = (11,01,00)$ and $E_{\text{in}}(11) = 101$ and $E_{\text{in}}(01) = 100$ and $E_{\text{in}}(00) = 011$ then:

$$E(0110) \;=\; E\big((01,10)'\big) \;=\; (101,\, 100,\, 011)' \;=\; 101100011$$ ◆

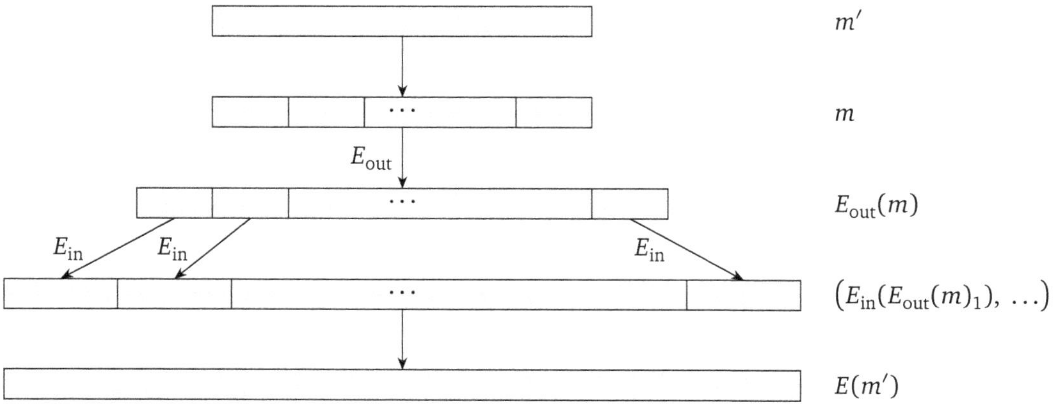

Figure 9.8: Code concatenation

The concatenated code E has rate $\ell k/hn = (k/n) \cdot (\ell/h)$, which is E_{out}'s rate times E_{in}'s rate. Letting $d = \text{dist}(E)$ and $d_{\text{out}} = \text{dist}(E_{\text{out}})$ and $d_{\text{in}} = \text{dist}(E_{\text{in}})$, we have $d \geq d_{\text{out}} \cdot d_{\text{in}}$ because for all distinct $m_1, m_2 \in (\{0,1\}^\ell)^k$, we have $E_{\text{out}}(m_1)_i \neq E_{\text{out}}(m_2)_i$ for at least d_{out} many coordinates $i \in [n]$, and for each such i, we have $E_{\text{in}}(E_{\text{out}}(m_1)_i)_j \neq E_{\text{in}}(E_{\text{out}}(m_2)_i)_j$ for at least d_{in} many coordinates $j \in [h]$, so $E(m_1')_{i,j} \neq E(m_2')_{i,j}$ for at least $d_{\text{out}} \cdot d_{\text{in}}$ many coordinates $(i,j) \in [n] \times [h]$.

Example. Let's revisit the example from §9.5.2. Concatenating the polynomial code $E_{\text{out}} = E_{4,3}$: $(\{0,1\}^2)^3 \to (\{0,1\}^2)^4$ with the dot product code $E_{\text{in}}: \{0,1\}^2 \to \{0,1\}^4$ yields the following code $E = E_{\text{in}} \circ E_{\text{out}}$:

$$\begin{aligned}
&\text{message:} & M' &= (M_2, M_1, M_0)' \qquad \text{where } M = M_2x^2 + M_1x + M_0 \\
&\text{codeword:} & E(M') &= \big(M(00)\odot 00 \;\; M(00)\odot 01 \;\; M(00)\odot 10 \;\; M(00)\odot 11, \\
&&& \quad\; M(01)\odot 00 \;\; M(01)\odot 01 \;\; M(01)\odot 10 \;\; M(01)\odot 11, \\
&&& \quad\; M(10)\odot 00 \;\; M(10)\odot 01 \;\; M(10)\odot 10 \;\; M(10)\odot 11, \\
&&& \quad\; M(11)\odot 00 \;\; M(11)\odot 01 \;\; M(11)\odot 10 \;\; M(11)\odot 11 \big)'
\end{aligned}$$

For example, recall that with the polynomial code:

$$\begin{aligned}
&\text{message:} & M &= (10,\, 00,\, 01) \\
&\text{codeword:} & E_{\text{out}}(M) &= \big(M(00),\, M(01),\, M(10),\, M(11)\big) \\
&&&= (01,\, 11,\, 00,\, 10)
\end{aligned}$$

With the "polynomial concatenated with dot product" code:

$$\begin{aligned}
&\text{message:} & M' &= 100001 \\
&\text{codeword:} & E(M') &= \big(01\odot 00 \;\; 01\odot 01 \;\; 01\odot 10 \;\; 01\odot 11, \quad = \big(0101, \\
&&& \quad\; 11\odot 00 \;\; 11\odot 01 \;\; 11\odot 10 \;\; 11\odot 11, \qquad\quad 0110, \\
&&& \quad\; 00\odot 00 \;\; 00\odot 01 \;\; 00\odot 10 \;\; 00\odot 11, \qquad\quad 0000, \\
&&& \quad\; 10\odot 00 \;\; 10\odot 01 \;\; 10\odot 10 \;\; 10\odot 11 \big)' \qquad\quad 0011 \big)' \\
&&&= 0101011000000011
\end{aligned}$$

♦

We'll see two applications of "polynomial concatenated with dot product" codes in Chapter 11. These codes are handy because the relative distance is very good (arbitrarily close to $1/2$) and the rate is not too bad (the codeword is only polynomially longer than the message):

Theorem 9.24. *For all $q = 2^\ell$ and $\varepsilon \geq 1/2q$, there exists a binary code with relative distance $\geq 1/2-\varepsilon$, message length $\ell\lfloor 2q\varepsilon\rfloor$, and codeword length q^2, and encodable in* poly q *time (given q, ε, and the message).*

Proof. For $k = \lfloor 2q\varepsilon\rfloor \geq 1$:

- The polynomial code $E_{\text{out}} = E_{q,k}\colon (\{0,1\}^\ell)^k \to (\{0,1\}^\ell)^q$ has distance $q-k+1 \geq q-k$.
- The dot product code $E_{\text{in}}\colon \{0,1\}^\ell \to \{0,1\}^q$ has distance $q/2$.

Concatenating them yields a binary code $E\colon \{0,1\}^{\ell k} \to \{0,1\}^{q^2}$ with distance $\geq (q-k)\cdot(q/2)$ and thus relative distance $\geq 1/2 - k/2q \geq 1/2-\varepsilon$. Encoding is straightforward to do in poly q time. We can find a degree-ℓ irreducible polynomial (for defining $\mathbb{F}_q$) in poly q time by brute force (trying every possibility, and checking whether it's irreducible by trying all possible factors). ∎

For one of our applications, we need to know a little more about these codes. For one thing, concatenation preserves linearity:

Lemma 9.25. *If $E_{\text{out}}\colon \mathbb{F}_{2^\ell}^k \to \mathbb{F}_{2^\ell}^n$ and $E_{\text{in}}\colon \mathbb{Z}_2^\ell \to \mathbb{Z}_2^h$ are linear then $E = E_{\text{in}} \circ E_{\text{out}}$ is linear.*

Proof. Assume E_{out} is linear (over $\mathbb{F}_{2^\ell}$) and E_{in} is linear (over $\mathbb{Z}_2$). For all $m_1, m_2 \in \mathbb{F}_{2^\ell}^k$:

$$
\begin{aligned}
E(m_1' + m_2') &= E((m_1+m_2)') && \text{(Observation 9.21)}\\
&= \big(E_{\text{in}}(E_{\text{out}}(m_1+m_2)_1),\ \ldots\big)' && \text{(definition of } E)\\
&= \big(E_{\text{in}}(E_{\text{out}}(m_1)_1 + E_{\text{out}}(m_2)_1),\ \ldots\big)' && (E_{\text{out}} \text{ is linear})\\
&= \big(E_{\text{in}}(E_{\text{out}}(m_1)_1) + E_{\text{in}}(E_{\text{out}}(m_2)_1),\ \ldots\big)' && (E_{\text{in}} \text{ is linear})\\
&= \big(E_{\text{in}}(E_{\text{out}}(m_1)_1),\ \ldots\big)' + \big(E_{\text{in}}(E_{\text{out}}(m_2)_1),\ \ldots\big)' && \text{(Observation 9.21)}\\
&= E(m_1') + E(m_2') && \text{(definition of } E)
\end{aligned}
$$

Thus E is linear (over $\mathbb{Z}_2$). ∎

The other property we need is that every pair of codewords has relative distance not only $\geq 1/2-\varepsilon$ but also $\leq 1/2+\varepsilon$: A linear binary code is *ε-balanced* iff each nonzero message's codeword has relative weight within $\pm\varepsilon$ of $1/2$. The following strengthens Theorem 9.24 by noting the linearity and ε-balanced properties of "polynomial concatenated with dot product" codes.

Theorem 9.26. *For all $q = 2^\ell$ and $\varepsilon \geq 1/2q$, there exists an ε-balanced linear binary code with message length $\ell\lfloor 2q\varepsilon\rfloor$ and codeword length q^2, and encodable in* poly q *time (given q, ε, and the message).*

Proof. The code E from the proof of Theorem 9.24 is linear by Lemma 9.25, since E_{out} and E_{in} are linear. For every $m' \neq 0^{\ell k}$, $E(m')$ has relative weight $\geq 1/2-\varepsilon$ since E has relative distance $\geq 1/2-\varepsilon$. Furthermore, $E(m')$ has relative weight $\leq 1/2 \leq 1/2+\varepsilon$ since it consists of dot product codewords, each of which has relative weight 0 or $1/2$. ∎

Exercises

9.1 Show that for binary codes, decoding from $< d$ erasures is no harder than decoding from $< d/2$ bit flips: Suppose $E\colon \{0,1\}^k \to \{0,1\}^n$ has distance d and $D\colon \{0,1\}^n \to \{0,1\}^k$ decodes if $< d/2$ many bit flips occur. Use D (and E) to design $D'\colon \{0,1,\bot\}^n \to \{0,1\}^k$ that decodes if $< d$ many erasures occur.

9.2 Every binary code with distance d can be decoded from $< d/2$ bit flips. Prove that *no* binary code with distance d can be decoded from $\leq \lceil d/2 \rceil$ bit flips: For every $E\colon \{0,1\}^k \to \{0,1\}^n$ with $\text{dist}(E) = d \geq 1$ and every $D\colon \{0,1\}^n \to \{0,1\}^k$, there exist $m \in \{0,1\}^k$ and $r \in \{0,1\}^n$ such that $\text{dist}\big(r, E(m)\big) \leq \lceil d/2 \rceil$ but $D(r) \neq m$ (decoding fails).

9.3 (a) Consider the following linear code $E\colon \{0,1\}^k \to \{0,1\}^{2k}$ where $k \geq 3$: The codeword $E(m)$ consists of m and the parities of all adjacent pairs of bits of m, where m's first and last bits are considered adjacent (wrap around). What is $\text{dist}(E)$? What is the generator matrix when $k = 4$? (You may pick any order for the columns.)

(b) Consider the following linear code $E\colon \{0,1\}^k \to \{0,1\}^{k(k+1)/2}$ where $k \geq 3$: The codeword $E(m)$ consists of m and the parities of all pairs of bits of m. What is $\text{dist}(E)$? What is the generator matrix when $k = 4$? (You may pick any order for the columns.)

9.4 For any code $E\colon \{0,1\}^k \to \{0,1\}^n$, define the code $E_\oplus\colon \{0,1\}^k \to \{0,1\}^{n+1}$ where $E_\oplus(m)$ is $E(m)$ followed by the bit $\oplus(E(m))$. That is, we append a parity bit to each codeword. Prove that if $\text{dist}(E)$ is odd then $\text{dist}(E_\oplus) = \text{dist}(E) + 1$.

9.5 Generalize Lemma 9.4 to prove that a ball of radius $d \leq n(1 - 1/q)$ in $\mathbb{Z}_q^n$ has size $\leq (q^n)^{H_q(d/n)}$ where H_q is the *q-ary entropy function*:

$$H_q(p) = \begin{cases} p\log_q(1/p) + (1-p)\log_q(1/(1-p)) + p\log_q(q-1) & \text{if } 0 < p < 1 \\ 0 & \text{if } p = 0 \\ \log_q(q-1) & \text{if } p = 1 \end{cases}$$

9.6 Give a slightly simplified proof of Theorem 9.7 for the case of linear codes: If $E\colon \{0,1\}^k \to \{0,1\}^n$ is linear and has distance $d > n/2$, then $2^k \leq 1/(1 - n/2d)$. Hint: Count the number of pairs (m, i) such that $E(m)_i = 1$ in two different ways.

9.7 Generalize Theorem 9.7 to prove that if $E\colon \mathbb{Z}_q^k \to \mathbb{Z}_q^n$ has distance $d > n(1 - 1/q)$, then $q^k \leq 1/(1 - n(1 - 1/q)/d)$. Hint: Corollary A.27 may be useful.

9.8 (a) Prove that a ball of radius $d \leq n/2$ in $\{0,1\}^n$ has size $\geq (2^n)^{H(p)}/(n+1)$ where $p = d/n$. (Recall the upper bound $\leq (2^n)^{H(p)}$ from Lemma 9.4.) Hint:

$$\tbinom{n}{d}p^d(1-p)^{n-d} \;\leq\; \text{size of ball}\big/(2^n)^{H(p)} \;\leq\; \textstyle\sum_{i=0}^{n}\tbinom{n}{i}p^i(1-p)^{n-i} \;=\; 1$$

Show that the $i = d$ summand is the largest in the summation by examining the ratios of consecutive summands.

(b) Prove that a family of binary codes with relative distance $\geq p$ must have rate $\leq 1 - H(p/2) + o(1)$, where $o(1)$ represents a function that goes to 0 as the codeword length goes to ∞. (This beats Theorem 9.6 since $H(p/2) \geq p$.) Hint: Balls of relative radius $< p/2$ centered at codewords must be disjoint.

(c) Prove that a family of binary codes with relative distance $\geq 1/2-\varepsilon$ (where $\varepsilon > 0$) must have rate $\leq 1-H(1/2-\sqrt{\varepsilon})+o(1)$. Hint: Use Exercise 9.8.a and Theorem 9.8 to count the following in two different ways: The number of (codeword, received word) pairs within relative distance $1/2-\sqrt{\varepsilon}$. (By the way, this beats Exercise 9.8.b for small ε, but a tightened-up version of Theorem 9.8 improves the rate bound to $1-H(1/2-\sqrt{\varepsilon/2})+o(1)$, which beats Exercise 9.8.b for all ε.)

9.9 Give a detailed proof of Lemma 9.11. This is like the binary setting (Lemma 9.1 and Lemma 9.2), but scalar multiplication is now relevant.

9.10 With the polynomial code $E_{7,4}$, encode the message $M = (1,0,4,1) = x^3 + 4x + 1$.

9.11 With the polynomial code $E_{11,4}$, decode the received word

$$r = (0,\bot,3,\bot,0,\bot,\bot,1,\bot,\bot,\bot)$$

using the erasure decoder from Theorem 9.13. Hint: It's unnecessary to compute any indicator polynomial that will get multiplied by 0.

9.12 Consider the field $\mathbb{F}_8 = \{0,1\}^3$ defined with the irreducible polynomial $P = x^3 + x^2 + 1$. Calculate $110 - 011$, and $110 \cdot 011$, and $101 \cdot 111$, and $100/111$.

9.13 For the pairwise uniform hash function from Lemma 8.4, we can use the field $\mathbb{F}_{2^\ell} = \{0,1\}^\ell$ instead of the field $\mathbb{Z}_p$:

$$h\colon (\{0,1\}^\ell)^2 \times \{0,1\}^\ell \to \{0,1\}^\ell \qquad \text{defined by} \qquad h_{a,b}(u) = a \cdot u + b$$

Tweak this to obtain a pairwise uniform hash function $h\colon (\{0,1\}^{\max(m,n)})^2 \times \{0,1\}^n \to \{0,1\}^m$ for any m and n (not necessarily $m = n$). In terms of m and n, when does this use fewer random bits than the diagonal-constant construction from Lemma 8.8?

9.14 (a) Prove that every $b \in \mathbb{F}_{2^\ell}$ has an $\ell \times \ell$ matrix G_b over $\mathbb{Z}_2$ such that $aG_b = a \cdot b$ for all $a \in \mathbb{F}_{2^\ell}$, where aG_b is vector-matrix multiplication over $\mathbb{Z}_2$, and $a \cdot b$ is field multiplication in $\mathbb{F}_{2^\ell}$.

(b) Lemma 9.22 says that if $E\colon \mathbb{F}_{2^\ell}^k \to \mathbb{F}_{2^\ell}^n$ is linear then $E'\colon \mathbb{Z}_2^{\ell k} \to \mathbb{Z}_2^{\ell n}$ is linear. Explain how to obtain the generator matrix of E' from the generator matrix of E .

9.15 Recall polynomial codes that use a bit string field as the alphabet (§9.5.2).

(a) With $E_{4,3}$, encode the message $M = (11, 01, 00)$.

(b) With $E_{4,2}$, decode the received word $r = (10, \bot, \bot, 01)$ using the erasure decoder from Theorem 9.13.

9.16 Adjust the proof of Theorem 9.23 to show that for every constant $c < 1/2$, there exists an asymptotically good, poly-time encodable family of binary codes with rate $\geq c$.

9.17 Suppose $E_{\text{out}}\colon (\{0,1\}^\ell)^k \to (\{0,1\}^\ell)^n$ has a poly-time decoder $D_{\text{out}}\colon (\{0,1\}^\ell)^n \to (\{0,1\}^\ell)^k$ that handles $< d_{\text{out}}/2$ symbol changes. Suppose $E_{\text{in}}\colon \{0,1\}^\ell \to \{0,1\}^h$ has a poly-time decoder $D_{\text{in}}\colon \{0,1\}^h \to \{0,1\}^\ell$ that handles $< d_{\text{in}}/2$ bit flips. Show how to combine D_{out} and D_{in} to get a poly-time decoder for the concatenated code $E_{\text{in}} \circ E_{\text{out}}$ that handles $< d_{\text{out}} d_{\text{in}}/4$ bit flips.

9.18 In the proof of Theorem 9.24, we saw that the concatenation of the polynomial code $E_{q,k}$ and the dot product code has distance $\geq (q-k+1)\cdot(q/2)$. Prove that it has distance exactly $(q-k+1)\cdot(q/2)$.

9.19 With the dot product code, the message is treated as coefficients of a multivariate polynomial over $\mathbb{Z}_2$ of total degree ≤ 1, and the codeword is this polynomial's evaluations on all assignments. Let's generalize this to larger total degrees. For any integers $1 \leq e \leq \ell$, we define a code $E\colon \{0,1\}^k \to \{0,1\}^n$ with $k = \sum_{i=0}^{e} \binom{\ell}{i}$ and $n = 2^\ell$: The message M is treated as coefficients of an ℓ-variate polynomial over $\mathbb{Z}_2$ of total degree $\leq e$ and which is multilinear (every individual degree is ≤ 1):

$$M(x) = \sum_{S\subseteq[\ell]:|S|\leq e} M_S \cdot \prod_{j\in S} x_j$$

(The coefficient M_S is the message's Sth bit.) The codeword contains the bit $M(a)$ for every assignment $a \in \mathbb{Z}_2^\ell$.

- **(a)** Prove E is linear.
- **(b)** Prove E has rate $\leq 1/n^{1-H(e/\ell)}$ if $e \leq \ell/2$.
- **(c)** Prove E has distance $d = n/2^e$. You may use the fact that the zero polynomial is the only multilinear polynomial over $\mathbb{Z}_2$ expressing the all-0 function.
- **(d)** For any $S \subseteq [\ell]$, any assignment a_S to the variables indexed by S, and any assignment a_{-S} to the variables not indexed by S, let a denote the combined assignment to all variables. Prove that if $|S| = e$ then for every a_{-S}, we have $M_S = \sum_{a_S} M(a)$ over $\mathbb{Z}_2$.
- **(e)** Assuming $|S| = e$, show how to recover M_S in poly n time from a received word with $< d/2$ many bit flips.
- **(f)** Design a (poly n)-time decoding algorithm for E that handles $< d/2$ many bit flips.

Notes

The theory of error correcting codes is known as "coding theory." Texts on coding theory include [357, 339, 256, 450].

The dot product code is also known as the "Hadamard code" and the "Walsh code."

The existence of asymptotically good (linear) codes (Theorem 9.3 and Theorem 9.5) is known as the "Gilbert–Varshamov bound" [187, 539, 456].

Theorem 9.6 and Theorem 9.10 are known as the "Singleton bound" [318, 277, 493]. Codes achieving this bound ($k = n-d+1$) are called "maximum distance separable (MDS)."

Theorem 9.7 is a form of the "Plotkin bound" [416].

Theorem 9.8 is a form of the "Johnson bound" [276].

Polynomial codes are also known as "Reed–Solomon codes" [436]. A polynomial code's generator matrix is known as a "Vandermonde matrix." Decoding polynomial codes from erasures is known as "Lagrange interpolation." Several poly-time algorithms are known for decoding polynomial codes from symbol changes; the one we presented (Theorem 9.14) is known as the "Berlekamp–Welch algorithm" [63].

Any field with q elements is sometimes denoted $GF(q)$ for "Galois field."

There exists a deterministic algorithm that, given ℓ, finds a degree-ℓ irreducible polynomial over $\mathbb{Z}_2$ in poly ℓ time [490]. A proof of Theorem 9.19.*(ii)* ($x^{2\cdot 3^e} + x^{3^e} + 1$ is irreducible over $\mathbb{Z}_2$) appears in [339, Theorem 1.1.28].

Flattened augmented polynomial codes (Theorem 9.23) are known as "Justesen codes" [280].

In Theorem 9.26 we constructed a poly-time encodable ε-balanced linear binary code with codeword length $O\big((\text{message length}/\varepsilon)^2\big)$. Such codes can be constructed with codeword length $O\big(\text{message length}/\varepsilon^{2+o(1)}\big)$ (not squaring the message length) [511].

Exercise 9.8.b is known as the "sphere-packing bound" or "Hamming bound" [231]. Exercise 9.8.c is known as the "Elias–Bassalygo bound" [49, 485, 486].

Exercise 9.19 is about "Reed–Muller codes" [379, 435].

Chapter 10

Heuristics

So far, we focused on *worst-case* complexity, where algorithms must be correct and efficient on all valid inputs—even on weird, contrived inputs that don't arise in practice. This chapter is on *average-case* complexity, where algorithms—called *heuristics*—are correct and efficient on "typical" inputs. We consider typically-correct, always-efficient heuristics (though always-correct, typically-efficient heuristics are also interesting), and we focus on time efficiency. For complexity theory, "typical" means "sampled from some probability distribution over inputs." Heuristics get a random *input*, whereas randomized algorithms (Chapter 7) produce a random *output*.

10.1 Distributional Problems

An input size N is *valid* for a problem A iff A has at least one valid input of size N.

Definition. A *distributional problem* is a pair (A, D) where A is a computational problem and D is an infinite family of distributions: For every valid N, D_N is a distribution over valid inputs of size N. If A is a decision problem, we say (A, D) is a distributional decision problem.

A *heuristic* for (A, D) with error probability ε is a deterministic program Π such that for every valid N, $\mathbf{Pr}_{x \sim D_N}\big[\Pi(x) \text{ errs}\big] \leq \varepsilon$. A heuristic's time efficiency is the maximum running time over all valid inputs of size N, including inputs on which it errs. ◀

$D_N(x)$ is intended to be the likelihood of encountering input x in reality. People often design heuristics without even specifying the input distribution, let alone proving that the heuristic works with respect to the distribution. The philosophy is that if experiments demonstrate the heuristic working on real-world inputs, then these inputs are presumably drawn from some reasonable underlying distribution. For complexity theory, proving "typical correctness" requires identifying the input distribution.

We could say a heuristic solves a promise problem version of A, where inputs on which the heuristic errs are declared invalid. But different heuristics for the same distributional problem may err on different inputs.

10.1.1 Heuristic for Independent Sets

Since Independent Set is NP-complete, we don't expect to design a poly-time algorithm that solves it on all possible inputs. But the proof of NP-completeness (§2.4) only involves inputs of a specific form, deliberately designed to trip up algorithms. Maybe we're unlikely to encounter such inputs "in the wild." This raises hope for solving Independent Set efficiently on inputs that arise in practice. Let's consider the search version:

INDEPENDENT SET SEARCH	(10.1)
Input: Undirected graph G, nonnegative integer k	
Output: An independent set of size $\geq k$ in G, or report that no such set exists	

We use the adjacency matrix encoding, so the input size N determines the number of nodes n. Suppose D_N is the following distribution over inputs (G,k):

- G is uniformly random over all $2^{\binom{n}{2}}$ possible n-node graphs: For each of the $\binom{n}{2}$ possible edges, a fair coin toss determines whether G contains that edge.
- $k = \lfloor \log n \rfloor - 3$ is a fixed value slightly below $\log n$. In this section, it matters that logs are base 2. (We won't worry about the finitely many graphs with $\lfloor \log n \rfloor \leq 3$.)

This isn't necessarily the distribution on inputs we'd expect in realistic scenarios, but it's good as an example.

We can solve INDEPENDENT SET SEARCH on such inputs in $N^{O(\log N)}$ time by brute force over all $\binom{n}{k}$ sets of k nodes. But our boss complains that it's too slow. Can we solve it faster if we forgo correctness on all graphs, and are content with correctness on most graphs?

Theorem 10.1. (INDEPENDENT SET SEARCH, D) *has a poly-time heuristic with error probability* 1/8.

Proof idea. We iterate through all the nodes, greedily selecting (and committing to) any node that has no edges to previously selected nodes. Since the edges are random, we probably select almost $\log n$ nodes before running out of nodes. This is because each selected node probably has edges to—and thus rules out—only about half of the remaining nodes. This heuristic isn't always correct: The graph might have a large independent set even if the heuristic doesn't find one. For example, a selected node might have edges to—and thus rule out—all remaining nodes. ■

Proof. On input (G,k) where $G = (V,E)$ and $V = \{1,2,\ldots,n\}$:

Heuristic for INDEPENDENT SET SEARCH (10.2)

```
initialize S ← {1}
for v ← 2,3,...,n:
    if {u,v} ∉ E for every u ∈ S: update S ← S ∪ {v}
if |S| ≥ k: output S
else: reject
```

This maintains the invariant that S is an independent set in G. Thus, if it doesn't reject, the heuristic correctly outputs an independent set of size $\geq k$. We claim that the heuristic rejects with probability $\leq 1/8$. For the analysis, it helps to imagine a process that samples a random graph one node at a time and continues indefinitely, rather than stopping at n nodes:

Algorithm to sample a random graph with an unlimited number of nodes (10.3)

```
for v ← 2,3,...:
    for u ← 1,2,...,v−1:
        toss a fair coin to determine whether {u,v} ∈ E
```

Imagine running the heuristic for as long as it takes to reach $|S| = k$, even if this goes beyond the graph's first n nodes. Let the random variable X be the value of the kth node added to S, in other words, the total number of nodes inspected until reaching $|S| = k$. Then $X = X_0 + X_1 + \cdots + X_{k-1}$ where $X_0 = 1$ and for $j > 0$:

$$X_j = ((j+1)\text{st node added to } S) - (j\text{th node added to } S)$$

That is, X_j is the number of nodes inspected after reaching $|S| = j$, until reaching $|S| = j+1$. After reaching $|S| = j$ and before reaching $|S| = j+1$, each node has probability 2^{-j} of being added to S. If we repeatedly toss a coin with heads probability 2^{-j}, then X_j is the number of tosses until the first heads. Thus X_j is a geometric random variable with expectation 2^j (Lemma A.11). By linearity of expectation and Lemma A.1:

$$\mathbf{E}[X] = \sum_{j=0}^{k-1} \mathbf{E}[X_j] = \sum_{j=0}^{k-1} 2^j = 2^k - 1 \leq 2^{\log n - 3} = n/8$$

By Lemma 7.13, $\mathbf{Pr}[\text{heuristic rejects}] = \mathbf{Pr}[X > n] \leq \mathbf{E}[X]/n \leq 1/8$. ■

Claim 10.2. *With probability $\geq 7/8$, a uniformly random n-node graph has no independent set of size $\geq 2\log n + 3$.*

Proof. Each of the $\binom{n}{k}$ many sets of k nodes has probability $1/2^{\binom{k}{2}}$ of being independent, so for $k = \lceil 2\log n + 3 \rceil$, by a union bound:

$$\begin{aligned} \mathbf{Pr}[\exists \text{ an independent set of size } k] &\leq \sum_{S:|S|=k} \mathbf{Pr}[S \text{ is independent}] = \binom{n}{k}/2^{\binom{k}{2}} \\ &\leq n^k/2^{k(k-1)/2} = 2^{k(\log n - (k-1)/2)} \leq 2^{-k} \leq 1/8 \end{aligned}$$ ■

It's also known (but we won't prove it) that a uniformly random n-node graph has an independent set of size $(2 - o(1))\log n$ with high probability. The situation is awkward for k between roughly $\log n$ and $2\log n$: No poly-time heuristic is known to find an independent set of size k, even though such a set exists (for most graphs)! Our shortsighted heuristic for $k < \log n$ commits to nodes without considering their impact on the options for subsequent nodes. It's plausible—but unknown—that a more careful poly-time heuristic could find an independent set of size $1.01\log n$ with high probability.

We also have a heuristic for the INDEPENDENT SET decision problem, when G is uniformly random and k is uniformly random from $\{1, 2, \ldots, \lfloor 4\log n \rfloor\}$ (and G and k are independent): Just accept iff $k \leq 2\log n$. For most values of k (except around $2\log n$), this heuristic is correct for most G. Thus it has low error probability on random input (G, k), despite not even looking at G.

10.1.2 Complexity Classes

Definition. For every function $\varepsilon(N) \geq 0$, $\mathsf{HEUR}_\varepsilon\mathsf{P}$ is the set of all distributional decision problems for which there exists a poly-time heuristic with error probability $\varepsilon(N)$. ◄

Unlike randomized algorithms, a heuristic's success probability isn't generally amenable to amplification: Solving some inputs correctly might not help with solving other inputs correctly. Also, $(A, D) \in \mathsf{HEUR}_0\mathsf{P}$ doesn't necessarily imply $A \in \mathsf{P}$, because the heuristic might err on valid inputs that have probability 0 under D_N.

A randomized heuristic has two sources of randomness—the input and the heuristic's internal coin tosses—and thus has two kinds of error probability.

Definition. A randomized heuristic Π for a distributional problem (A, D) has *input error probability* $\varepsilon(N)$ with respect to *output error probability* $\delta(N)$ iff for every valid N:

$$\mathbf{Pr}_{x\sim D_N}\Big[\mathbf{Pr}_r\big[\Pi(x;r)\text{ errs}\big] > \delta(N)\Big] \le \varepsilon(N)$$

$\mathsf{HEUR}_\varepsilon\mathsf{BPP}$ is the set of all distributional decision problems for which there exists a poly-time randomized heuristic with input error probability $\varepsilon(N)$ with respect to output error probability 1/3. ◄

If A is a decision problem, then standard amplification (§ 7.3.2) decreases the output error probability (so the choice of $\delta(N) = 1/3$ is immaterial) but not the input error probability. Also note that $\delta(N) < \mathbf{Pr}_r\big[\Pi(x;r)\text{ accepts}\big] < 1 - \delta(N)$ is allowed on a valid input x (unlike with BPP), and such an x would count toward the input error probability.

Defining nonuniform heuristics is straightforward.

Definition. For every function $\varepsilon(N) \ge 0$, $\mathsf{HEUR}_\varepsilon\mathsf{P/poly}$ is the set of all distributional decision problems (A, D) for which there exists a poly-time advice-taking heuristic Π and a sequence of poly-size advice $a_1, a_2, \dots$ such that for every valid N, $\mathbf{Pr}_{x\sim D_N}\big[\Pi(x;a_N)\text{ errs}\big] \le \varepsilon(N)$. ◄

Poly-time nonuniform heuristics are equivalent to poly-size circuit family heuristics, just like how poly-size circuit families characterize $\mathsf{P/poly}$ (Theorem 5.12).

$\mathsf{HEUR}_\varepsilon\mathsf{BPP} \subseteq \mathsf{HEUR}_\varepsilon\mathsf{P/poly}$ by the same proof as $\mathsf{BPP} \subseteq \mathsf{P/poly}$ (Theorem 7.9): We decrease the output error probability enough that a single outcome of Π's coin tosses r works for all size-N inputs (that originally had output error probability $\le 1/3$), and we hardcode this r as the advice a_N. Thus we can turn "randomized average-case" into "deterministic nonuniform average-case" with roughly a factor N time overhead due to amplification. With no overhead, we can turn "randomized worst-case" into "deterministic nonuniform average-case":

Lemma 10.3. *For any distributional problem (A, D), if A has an ε-error $O(T)$-time randomized program, then (A, D) has an ε-error $O(T)$-time nonuniform heuristic (with $O(T)$ words of advice).*

Proof. Let Π be the randomized program for A. For every valid N, and random $x \sim D_N$ and r:

$$\min_r\Big(\mathbf{Pr}_x\big[\Pi(x;r)\text{ errs}\big]\Big) \;\le\; \mathbf{Pr}_{x,r}\big[\Pi(x;r)\text{ errs}\big] \;\le\; \max_{\text{valid }x}\mathbf{Pr}_r\big[\Pi(x;r)\text{ errs}\big] \;\le\; \varepsilon(N)$$

Thus for some outcome r, $\mathbf{Pr}_x\big[\Pi(x;r)\text{ errs}\big] \le \varepsilon(N)$. With such r as advice, Π becomes an ε-error deterministic nonuniform heuristic for (A, D). ■

The same thing works if the randomized program was already nonuniform. This means that in the nonuniform setting, to prove a randomized worst-case lower bound, it suffices to prove a deterministic average-case lower bound with respect to an input distribution of our choosing. This provides another motivation for average-case complexity and will be useful for nonuniform lower bounds in Part IV.

10.2 Average-Case Analogue of P Versus NP

10.2.1 Formulating the Question

Does all of NP have efficient heuristics? It's a "syntax error" to ask whether $\mathsf{NP} \subseteq \mathsf{HEUR}_{1/3}\mathsf{P}$, since the latter class contains distributional problems and the former doesn't. It would be overkill to ask whether $(A, D) \in \mathsf{HEUR}_{1/3}\mathsf{P}$ for all $A \in \mathsf{NP}$ and literally all D. We only care about "realistic" D. It's reasonable to suppose nature is like a poly-time algorithm, so inputs that arise naturally are samplable by such algorithms:

Definition. PSAMP is the set of all families D (where D_N is a distribution over $(\{0,1\}^{W_N})^N$) for which there exists a randomized program that, given input N and W_N, outputs a sample from D_N in poly$N$ time. For any class $\mathcal{C}$ of decision problems, $(\mathcal{C}, \mathsf{PSAMP})$ is the set of all (A, D) such that $A \in \mathcal{C}$ and $D \in \mathsf{PSAMP}$. ◄

(If A's word size is log-bounded, then a sampler can compute W_N from N on its own. Commonplace problems have efficiently constructible word sizes, but that's not required, so we include W_N in the sampler's input.)

$(\mathsf{NP}, \mathsf{PSAMP}) \subseteq \mathsf{HEUR}_{1/3}\mathsf{P}$ is a reasonable average-case analogue of $\mathsf{NP} \subseteq \mathsf{P}$, though it's sensitive to the exact choice of input error probability. It's conceivable that $(\mathsf{NP}, \mathsf{PSAMP}) \subseteq \mathsf{HEUR}_{1/3}\mathsf{P}$ (NP is "average-case easy") even if $\mathsf{NP} \not\subseteq \mathsf{P}$ (NP is "worst-case hard"), which would mean that only "atypical" inputs require large running time. But most researchers conjecture that NP is "average-case hard."

For a total decision problem A with word size W_N, the uniform distribution U_N over all inputs $(\{0,1\}^{W_N})^N$ calls attention to A's encoding details, and it's often not how inputs are distributed in practice. Nevertheless, the uniform distribution captures many issues in average-case complexity and is simpler to study than arbitrary samplable distributions.

Definition. For every class $\mathcal{C}$ of total decision problems, $(\mathcal{C}, \mathsf{U})$ is the set of all (A, U) such that $A \in \mathcal{C}$ and U is the family of uniform distributions. ◄

U might not be ideal for individual problems, but it's as general as PSAMP for NP as a whole: If $(\mathsf{NP}, \mathsf{U}) \subseteq \mathsf{HEUR}_{1/N^c}\mathsf{BPP}$ for all c, then $(\mathsf{NP}, \mathsf{PSAMP}) \subseteq \mathsf{HEUR}_{1/N^c}\mathsf{BPP}$ for all c. We won't prove or use this theorem, but it partially justifies our focus on the uniform distribution later in this chapter. The proof is a sophisticated application of pairwise uniform hashing.

10.2.2 Decision Versus Search

$\mathsf{P} = \mathsf{NP}$ concerns decision problems but implies that NP search problems are solvable in poly time, by search-to-decision reductions. An average-case analogue holds for a subtler reason.

Suppose $A \in \mathsf{NP}$ by a verifier V with time efficiency $\le T = eN^d$ (for integers e, d) and word size W. On a valid input x of size N, the potential witnesses are elements of $(\{0,1\}^W)^T = \{0,1\}^n$ where $n = TW$.

Find Witness for V (call this problem B)	(10.4)
Input: Valid input x to A	
Output: $w \in \{0,1\}^n$ such that $V(x; w)$ accepts, or report that no such w exists	

An NP *search problem* is a problem of this form.

Theorem 10.4. *If* $(\mathsf{NP}, \mathsf{PSAMP}) \subseteq \mathsf{HEUR}_{1/N^c}\mathsf{P}$ *for all* c, *then for every* NP *search problem* B, *all* $D \in \mathsf{PSAMP}$, *and all* c, (B, D) *has a poly-time randomized heuristic with input error probability* $1/N^c$ *with respect to output error probability* $1/2^{N^c}$.

Proof idea. We design a heuristic for (B, D) that queries a heuristic oracle for some $(C, E) \in$ (NP, PSAMP). Standard search-to-decision reductions find a witness bit-by-bit, repeatedly querying the oracle to find the next bit. The set of queries that actually occur is a tiny fraction of all possible queries: $O(n)$ out of $O(2^n)$. If we consider the uniform distribution over all possible queries, then a heuristic oracle might err on just the queries that would mess up the reduction. If we consider a distribution over just the actual queries, then a low-error heuristic would answer all queries correctly, for typical inputs. But then sampling the distribution would be as hard as answering the queries, since each query depends on the answers to previous ones. The reduction is adaptive, so the actual queries aren't "typical"—they deliberately home in on thorny spots.

We need a non-adaptive search-to-decision reduction, where the queries depend only on the input (not on answers to other queries) and can thus be sampled efficiently. How about: For each index i, we ask the oracle whether there exists a witness w with $w_i = 1$. Unfortunately, the answers to these queries might not refer to the same witness as each other: There might exist a witness whose first bit is 1, and another witness whose second bit is 1, but no witness whose first two bits are both 1. This trouble disappears if there's only one witness, so we use hashing to isolate a unique witness (§8.3). ■

Proof. Suppose $A \in$ NP by a verifier V, and $B =$ FIND WITNESS FOR V as defined above.

For each $m \in [n+1]$, let $h^m\colon \{0,1\}^{3n+1} \times \{0,1\}^n \to \{0,1\}^m$ be the pairwise uniform hash function from Lemma 8.9. Actually, h^m only needs $2m+n-1$ random bits, but we round it up to $2(n+1)+n-1 = 3n+1$ (ignoring extra random bits) so the input size doesn't depend on m.

(call this problem C, with input size M)	(10.5)
Input: x, m, r, i where x is a valid input of size N to A, $m \in [n+1]$, $r \in \{0,1\}^{3n+1}$, and $i \in [n]$	
Output: Does there exist $w \in \{0,1\}^n$ such that $V(x; w)$ accepts and $h^m_r(w) = 0^m$ and $w_i = 1$?	

$C \in$ NP by a verifier V' where $V'(x, m, r, i; w)$ reads w's first n bits and accepts iff $V(x; w)$ accepts and $h^m_r(w) = 0^m$ and $w_i = 1$. Define a family $E \in$ PSAMP of distributions over valid inputs to C: To sample $(x, m, r, i) \sim E_M$, we sample $x \sim D_N$ and independently sample uniformly random m, r, i. Since $(C, E) \in$ (NP, PSAMP), we have $(C, E) \in \mathsf{HEUR}_{1/M^{c+3}}\mathsf{P}$ by a heuristic Π.

Consider this poly-time randomized heuristic Π' for (B, D):

Search heuristic using a decision heuristic (10.6)

```
Π′(x):
    sample uniformly random m ∈ [n+1] and r ∈ {0,1}^{3n+1}
    for each i ∈ [n]: let a_i ← Π(x, m, r, i)
    define a = a_1 a_2 ··· a_n
    if V(x; a) accepts: output a
    else: reject
```

Say (x, m, r) is *bad* if there exists $i \in [n]$ such that $\Pi(x, m, r, i)$ errs, and is *good* otherwise. Say x is *bad* if $\mathbf{Pr}_{m,r}\big[(x, m, r) \text{ is bad}\big] > 1/10n$, and is *good* otherwise. Then $\mathbf{Pr}_x\big[x \text{ is bad}\big] \le 1/N^c$

since otherwise, by the chain rule,

$$\begin{aligned}
\mathbf{Pr}_{x,m,r,i}\big[\Pi(x,m,r,i) \text{ errs}\big] \;&\geq\; \mathbf{Pr}_{x,m,r,i}\big[x \text{ is bad and } (x,m,r) \text{ is bad and } \Pi(x,m,r,i) \text{ errs}\big] \\
&\geq\; \mathbf{Pr}_x\big[x \text{ is bad}\big]\cdot \\
&\quad\;\; \mathbf{Pr}_{x,m,r}\big[(x,m,r) \text{ is bad} \,\big|\, x \text{ is bad}\big]\cdot \\
&\quad\;\; \mathbf{Pr}_{x,m,r,i}\big[\Pi(x,m,r,i) \text{ errs} \,\big|\, x \text{ is bad and } (x,m,r) \text{ is bad}\big] \\
&\geq\; \mathbf{Pr}_x\big[x \text{ is bad}\big]\cdot \\
&\quad\;\; \min\nolimits_{\text{bad } x} \mathbf{Pr}_{m,r}\big[(x,m,r) \text{ is bad}\big]\cdot \\
&\quad\;\; \min\nolimits_{\text{bad } (x,m,r)} \mathbf{Pr}_i\big[\Pi(x,m,r,i) \text{ errs}\big] \\
&>\; \tfrac{1}{N^c}\cdot\tfrac{1}{10n}\cdot\tfrac{1}{n} \\
&>\; 1/M^{c+3}
\end{aligned}$$

where $M \geq n \geq N$ is the common size of the inputs $(x,m,r,i) \sim E_M$.

If $A(x) = 0$, so $V(x;w)$ rejects for all w, then of course $\mathbf{Pr}_{m,r}\big[\Pi'(x;m,r) \text{ rejects}\big] = 1$.

Consider any good x with $A(x) = 1$, so $V(x;w)$ accepts for some w. Say (x,m,r) is *isolating* iff $h_r^m(w) = 0^m$ for exactly one w such that $V(x;w)$ accepts. The proof of Theorem 8.10 showed:

$$\mathbf{Pr}_{m,r}\big[(x,m,r) \text{ is isolating}\big] \;\geq\; \tfrac{1}{n+1}\cdot\tfrac{2}{9} \;\geq\; 1/5n$$

Thus:

$$\begin{aligned}
\mathbf{Pr}_{m,r}\big[(x,m,r) \text{ is isolating and good}\big] \;&\geq\; \mathbf{Pr}_{m,r}\big[(x,m,r) \text{ is isolating}\big] - \mathbf{Pr}_{m,r}\big[(x,m,r) \text{ is bad}\big] \\
&\geq\; 1/5n - 1/10n \;=\; 1/10n
\end{aligned}$$

Suppose (x,m,r) is isolating and good. Consider the unique w such that $V(x;w)$ accepts and $h_r^m(w) = 0^m$. We have $w_i = C(x,m,r,i)$ for each i:

- If $w_i = 1$ then $C(x,m,r,i) = 1$ trivially.
- If $w_i = 0$ then $C(x,m,r,i) = 0$ by the uniqueness of w.

Since (x,m,r) is good, we have $a_i = \Pi(x,m,r,i) = C(x,m,r,i) = w_i$ for each i, so $\Pi'(x;m,r)$ correctly outputs $a = w$.

In summary, if $A(x) = 1$ and x is good:

$$\mathbf{Pr}_{m,r}\big[\Pi'(x;m,r) \text{ succeeds}\big] \;\geq\; \mathbf{Pr}_{m,r}\big[(x,m,r) \text{ is isolating and good}\big] \;\geq\; 1/10n$$

By amplification (run Π' repeatedly until it finds an a such that $V(x;a)$ accepts), we decrease the output error probability from $1 - 1/10n$ to $1/2^{N^c}$ with $\operatorname{poly} N$ time overhead. Letting Π'' be this amplified heuristic for (B,D), with internal randomness q:

$$\mathbf{Pr}_{x\sim D_N}\Big[\mathbf{Pr}_q\big[\Pi''(x;q) \text{ errs}\big] > 1/2^{N^c}\Big] \;\leq\; \mathbf{Pr}_{x\sim D_N}\big[x \text{ is bad}\big] \;\leq\; 1/N^c \qquad \blacksquare$$

Theorem 10.4 also holds with $\mathsf{HEUR}_{1/N^c}\mathsf{BPP}$ in place of $\mathsf{HEUR}_{1/N^c}\mathsf{P}$, by absorbing (C,E)'s heuristic's output error probability into (B,D)'s heuristic's output error probability. We just avoided that distraction in Theorem 10.4.

10.3 Worst-Case Versus Average-Case

Theorem 10.5. *If* $\mathsf{PSPACE} \neq \mathsf{BPP}$ *then* $(\mathsf{PSPACE}, \mathsf{U}) \nsubseteq \mathsf{HEUR}_{1/N^2}\mathsf{P}$.

If we believe the default conjecture $\mathsf{PSPACE} \neq \mathsf{BPP}$, we should expect that some PSPACE problems are beyond the reach of not only fast algorithms, but fast heuristics. This is not all doom and gloom: "Average-case intractable" problems are useful for derandomization (Chapter 11) and cryptography (Chapter 12).

Proof idea. The contrapositive is that $(\mathsf{PSPACE}, \mathsf{U}) \subseteq \mathsf{HEUR}_{1/N^2}\mathsf{P}$ implies $\mathsf{PSPACE} = \mathsf{BPP}$: If every PSPACE problem can be solved quickly on most inputs, then every PSPACE problem can be solved quickly on all inputs. This doesn't say that for every $A \in \mathsf{PSPACE}$, we could turn any fast heuristic for A into a fast algorithm for A. Rather, we design a *worst-case to average-case reduction*: For every $A \in \mathsf{PSPACE}$, there exists $B \in \mathsf{PSPACE}$ such that we could turn any fast heuristic for B into a fast algorithm for A. The basic idea is to use error correcting codes (Chapter 9).

message	$A \in \mathsf{PSPACE}$		$A \in \mathsf{BPP}$	message
encoder	$\Downarrow$		$\Uparrow$	decoder
codeword	$B \in \mathsf{PSPACE}$	$\Rightarrow$ channel	$(B, U) \in \mathsf{HEUR}_{1/N^2}\mathsf{P}$	received word

- The message is A's truth table, indexed by inputs of some size.
- The codeword is B's truth table, indexed by somewhat larger inputs. The encoder turns the poly-space algorithm for A into a poly-space algorithm for B.
- The received word is the heuristic's truth table. Bit flips occur at inputs where the heuristic errs.
- To recover the message, we run the decoder and use the heuristic to get individual bits of the received word. The decoder turns the heuristic for B into an algorithm for A.

The decoder is an oracle reduction from A to B that withstands erroneous answers to some queries. The catch is that ordinary decoders recover the entire message by reading the entire received word, both of which are now exponentially long truth tables. To solve A in poly time on any particular input, we only need to recover one message bit, and we can only afford to read a few received word bits. *Query* means reading the received word bit at a particular index, which corresponds to running the heuristic on a particular input (querying the reduction's oracle). We need a *locally decodable* code: Each individual message bit can be recovered with just a few queries. The decoder is randomized, so we get $A \in \mathsf{BPP}$ rather than $A \in \mathsf{P}$. ■

We prove the theorem after defining and analyzing suitable locally decodable codes.

What about NP? It's unknown whether there exists a constant c such that if $\mathsf{NP} \nsubseteq \mathsf{BPP}$ then $(\mathsf{NP}, \mathsf{U}) \nsubseteq \mathsf{HEUR}_{1/N^c}\mathsf{P}$. Somewhat weaker theorems in this vein have been proven, after a long time and considerable effort. The question for NP is more difficult than the question for PSPACE because the encoding of locally decodable codes cannot ensure that $B \in \mathsf{NP}$ if $A \in \mathsf{NP}$.

10.3.1 Locally Decodable Codes

Definition. A code $E\colon \{0,1\}^k \to \{0,1\}^n$ is *locally decodable*

from b bit flips, using t queries, with error probability ε

iff there exists a randomized algorithm D that takes as input a message index $i \in [k]$ and received word $r \in \{0,1\}^n$, such that for

- every message $m \in \{0,1\}^k$, and
- every received word $r \in \{0,1\}^n$ with $\mathrm{dist}(r, E(m)) \le b$, and
- every message index $i \in [k]$:

$\mathbf{Pr}[D(i,r) = m_i] \ge 1 - \varepsilon$, and $D(i,r)$ always reads (queries) at most t many bits of r.

The definition of q-ary locally decodable codes is analogous. Reading a symbol of r counts as one query. ◀

The decoder D may be nonuniform (tailored to the specific code E), and its time efficiency doesn't matter. But usually we want a uniform (polylog k)-time local decoding algorithm for a family of codes.

Recall the dot product code $E\colon \{0,1\}^k \to \{0,1\}^n$ (§ 9.1.2). The $n = 2^k$ many bits of the codeword $E(m)$ are the dot products (over $\mathbb{Z}_2$) of the message m with all $x \in \{0,1\}^k$: $E(m)_x = m \odot x$. Viewing m as coefficients of a k-variate polynomial $\sum_{i=1}^k m_i x_i$ over $\mathbb{Z}_2$, $E(m)$ is the polynomial's evaluations on all $x \in \{0,1\}^k$. For example, if $m = 1101$ then the polynomial is $1x_1 + 1x_2 + 0x_3 + 1x_4 = x_1 + x_2 + x_4$.

Theorem 10.6. *For every ε, the dot product code is locally decodable from $n\varepsilon/2$ bit flips, using 2 queries, with error probability ε.*

Proof idea. The decoder in §9.1.2 is actually a local decoder that we derandomized by brute force. ■

Proof. For each $i \in [k]$, let $e^i \in \{0,1\}^k$ have a 1 at index i and 0s everywhere else, so $m \odot e^i = m_i$ for every message $m \in \{0,1\}^k$.

Local decoder for the dot product code	(10.7)
$D(i,r)$:	
pick $x \in \{0,1\}^k$ uniformly at random	
output $r_x \oplus r_{x \oplus e^i}$	

For

- every message $m \in \{0,1\}^k$, and
- every received word $r \in \{0,1\}^n$ with $\mathrm{dist}(r, E(m)) \le n\varepsilon/2$, and
- every message index $i \in [k]$:

Say $x \in \{0,1\}^k$ is *good* if $r_x = m \odot x$ and $r_{x\oplus e^i} = m \odot (x \oplus e^i)$ (that is, coordinates x and $x \oplus e^i$ are not bit flips), and say x is *bad* otherwise. If x is good then:

$$D(i,r;x) \;=\; r_x \oplus r_{x\oplus e^i} \;=\; (m \odot x) \oplus \big(m \odot (x \oplus e^i)\big) \;=\; m \odot \big(x \oplus (x \oplus e^i)\big) \;=\; m \odot e^i \;=\; m_i$$

By a union bound and the fact that $x \oplus e^i$ is also uniformly distributed:

$$\begin{aligned}\mathbf{Pr}\big[D(i,r;x) \ne m_i\big] \;\le\; \mathbf{Pr}[x \text{ is bad}] \;&\le\; \mathbf{Pr}\big[r_x \ne m \odot x\big] + \mathbf{Pr}\big[r_{x\oplus e^i} \ne m \odot (x \oplus e^i)\big] \\ &\le\; \varepsilon/2 + \varepsilon/2 \;=\; \varepsilon\end{aligned}$$

■

10.3.2 Multilinear Codes

Recall these codes, where the codeword is the message polynomial's evaluations on all points:

- Polynomial codes (§9.3) aren't locally decodable but have good rate.
  The message polynomial has 1 variable and "medium" degree.
- Dot product codes (§10.3.1) are locally decodable but have poor rate.
  The message polynomial has a "medium" number of variables and total degree 1.

To get the best of both worlds, we define analogous codes using a medium number of variables (for local decodability) and medium total degree (for decent rate).

It's convenient, but not crucial, for the message polynomial to be *multilinear*, meaning each variable has individual degree ≤ 1. A d-variate multilinear polynomial automatically has total degree $\leq d$. (Here, d stands for "degree" or "dimension," not "distance.") We use any finite field $\mathbb{F}$, such as $\mathbb{Z}_p$ (for prime p) or $\mathbb{F}_{2^\ell}$ (§9.4).

Instead of viewing the message as a polynomial's coefficients, we view it as a polynomial's evaluations on just the points $\{0,1\}^d$. The codeword is the polynomial's evaluations on all the points $\mathbb{F}^d$. The evaluations on $\{0,1\}^d$ uniquely determine a multilinear polynomial:

- This is a multivariate analogue of interpolating a univariate polynomial given its values on "degree + 1" many points (Theorem 9.13). Now, each variable has individual degree 1 and two points $\{0,1\}$.
- This is an algebraic analogue of constructing a DNF given a boolean function's truth table (Lemma 2.9). Now, $+$ and $\cdot$ play the roles of $\vee$ and $\wedge$, respectively.

Definition. For every integer $d \geq 1$ and finite field $\mathbb{F}$ of size q, the *multilinear code* $E\colon \mathbb{F}^k \to \mathbb{F}^n$ is as follows:

- The message of length $k = 2^d$ is the table of a function $m\colon \{0,1\}^d \to \mathbb{F}$.
- The codeword of length $n = q^d$ is the table of a function $P\colon \mathbb{F}^d \to \mathbb{F}$.

$P(x_1,\dots,x_n)$ is the multilinear polynomial $\sum_{b\in\{0,1\}^d} m(b)\big(\prod_{i:b_i=1} x_i\big)\big(\prod_{i:b_i=0}(1-x_i)\big)$. ◀

Claim 10.7. *With the multilinear code, $P(a) = m(a)$ for every assignment $a \in \{0,1\}^d$.*

Proof. Plug $x = a$ into P. The $b = a$ summand is

$$m(a)\big(\textstyle\prod_{i:a_i=1} a_i\big)\big(\prod_{i:a_i=0}(1-a_i)\big) \;=\; m(a)$$

because every factor after $m(a)$ is 1. Each $b \neq a$ summand is

$$m(b)\big(\textstyle\prod_{i:b_i=1} a_i\big)\big(\prod_{i:b_i=0}(1-a_i)\big) \;=\; 0$$

because for some $i \in [d]$, either $b_i = 1$ and $a_i = 0$ (giving a factor of $a_i = 0$) or $b_i = 0$ and $a_i = 1$ (giving a factor of $1 - a_i = 0$). ■

Example. With $d = 2$ and $\mathbb{F} = \mathbb{Z}_3$, consider the multilinear code $E\colon \mathbb{Z}_3^4 \to \mathbb{Z}_3^9$. The left side of Figure 10.1 shows the message (1, 0, 1, 2). Let's encode it:

$$\begin{aligned}
P(x_1,x_2) &= 1\cdot(1-x_1)(1-x_2) && +\ 0\cdot(1-x_1)x_2 && +\ 1\cdot x_1(1-x_2) && +\ 2\cdot x_1x_2\\
&= 1\cdot(x_1x_2+2x_1+2x_2+1) && +\ 0\cdot(2x_1x_2+x_2) && +\ 1\cdot(2x_1x_2+x_1) && +\ 2\cdot x_1x_2\\
&= 2x_1x_2+2x_2+1
\end{aligned}$$

The right side of Figure 10.1 shows the codeword $E(1, 0, 1, 2) = (1, 0, 2, 1, 2, 0, 1, 1, 1)$. The gray entries are where the message appears directly in the codeword. ♦

x_1	0	0	1	1
x_2	0	1	0	1
message m	1	0	1	2

x_1	0	0	0	1	1	1	2	2	2
x_2	0	1	2	0	1	2	0	1	2
codeword P	1	0	2	1	2	0	1	1	1

Figure 10.1: Example message and codeword for the multilinear code

The multilinear code's exact relative distance isn't important, but it's $\geq 1-d/q$ by Lemma 7.1 (which we stated for prime fields, but holds for all finite fields): A nonzero d-variate polynomial of total degree $\leq d$ has $\leq dq^{d-1}$ roots, so distinct d-variate polynomials of total degree $\leq d$ differ on $\geq q^d - dq^{d-1} = (1-d/q)q^d$ points.

To prepare for describing and analyzing the local decoder, we need some tools.

The *parameterized line* with *anchor* $a \in \mathbb{F}^d$ and *direction* $b \in \mathbb{F}^d$ is the function $L: \mathbb{F} \to \mathbb{F}^d$ defined by $L(z) = a + z \cdot b$, where z is the *parameter* and $\cdot$ is scalar-vector multiplication. For $d = 2$ and $\mathbb{F} = \mathbb{R}$ (not finite, but easier to visualize), we would take the ordinary number line and draw it in the plane by putting 0 at a, and 1 at $a + b$, and 2 at $a + 2b$, and so on (Figure 10.2).

Claim 10.8. *If $P: \mathbb{F}^d \to \mathbb{F}$ is a multilinear polynomial and $L: \mathbb{F} \to \mathbb{F}^d$ is a parameterized line, then the composition $P \circ L: \mathbb{F} \to \mathbb{F}$ is a univariate polynomial of degree $\leq d$.*

Proof. If P has canonical form $P(x_1, \ldots, x_d) = \sum_{S \subseteq [d]} P_S \prod_{i \in S} x_i$ (where each $P_S \in \mathbb{F}$ is a coefficient) and $L(z) = a + z \cdot b = (a_1 + zb_1, \ldots, a_d + zb_d)$, then:

$$(P \circ L)(z) = P(L(z)) = \textstyle\sum_{S \subseteq [d]} P_S \prod_{i \in S}(a_i + zb_i)$$

$$\begin{aligned} \deg(P \circ L) &\leq \max_S\big(\deg(\textstyle\prod_{i \in S}(a_i + zb_i))\big) = \max_S\big(\textstyle\sum_{i \in S} \deg(a_i + zb_i)\big) \\ &\leq \max_S\big(\textstyle\sum_{i \in S} 1\big) = \max_S(|S|) \leq d \end{aligned}$$

■

In fact, this argument shows that if P is any polynomial (not necessarily multilinear) and L is a parameterized line, then $\deg(P \circ L) \leq$ total degree of P.

Example. In $\mathbb{Z}_3^2$, the parameterized line with anchor $a = (1, 1)$ and direction $b = (1, 2)$ is:

$$L(z) = a + z \cdot b = (1,1) + z \cdot (1,2) = (z+1,\ 2z+1)$$

Thus $L(0) = (1, 1)$ and $L(1) = (2, 0)$ and $L(2) = (0, 2)$. Recall the polynomial from our earlier example:

$$P(x_1, x_2) = 2x_1x_2 + 2x_2 + 1$$

The composition is:

$$(P \circ L)(z) = P(L(z)) = 2(z+1)(2z+1) + 2(2z+1) + 1 = z^2 + z + 2$$

Thus, consistent with our earlier example:

$$\begin{aligned} (P \circ L)(0) &= 2 = P(1,1) \\ (P \circ L)(1) &= 1 = P(2,0) \\ (P \circ L)(2) &= 2 = P(0,2) \end{aligned}$$

♦

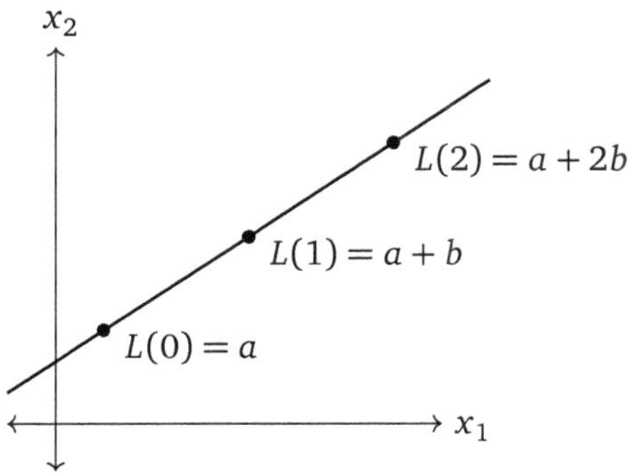

Figure 10.2: Parameterized line with anchor a and direction b, visualized in $d = 2$ dimensions

Claim 10.9. *For every $a \in \mathbb{F}^d$ and every $z \in \mathbb{F} \setminus \{0\}$, if $b \in \mathbb{F}^d$ is uniformly random then $L(z) \in \mathbb{F}^d$ is uniformly random, where L is the parameterized line with anchor a and direction b.*

Proof. For every $c \in \mathbb{F}^d$, we have $\mathbf{Pr}\big[L(z) = c\big] = q^{-d}$ because $L(z) = c$ holds (that is, $a_i + z b_i = c_i$ for each $i \in [d]$) for exactly one of the q^d many outcomes b, namely $b_i = (c_i - a_i)/z$ for each $i \in [d]$. ■

(Note that $L(z)$ for different z are not independent of each other.)

Theorem 10.10. *For any integer $d \geq 1$ and finite field $\mathbb{F}$ of size $q \geq d + 2$, the multilinear code is locally decodable from $q^d/3(d+1)$ symbol changes, using $d+1$ queries, with error probability $1/3$.*

Proof idea. Given any assignment a, we want to recover the message's value $m(a)$—which is also the codeword's value $P(a)$—from the received word r, which agrees with P at most points but might disagree at a. We query r at some points on a random line that passes through a. This is "local" since a 1-dimensional line has far fewer points than the whole d-dimensional space. Probably, the queries along the random line will miss the points where r and P disagree. In that case, we recover P along the whole line—in particular, at a—using the algorithm for Decoding Polynomial Codes from Erasures (Theorem 9.13) since P is effectively a low-degree univariate polynomial along the line. ■

Proof. Here's the local decoder:

Local decoder for the multilinear code	(10.8)

given message index $a \in \{0,1\}^d$ and received word $r : \mathbb{F}^d \to \mathbb{F}$:
  sample $b \in \mathbb{F}^d$ uniformly at random
  let $L : \mathbb{F} \to \mathbb{F}^d$ be the parameterized line with anchor a and direction b
  let $Z \subseteq \mathbb{F} \setminus \{0\}$ be an arbitrary set of size $d+1$ (which exists since $q \geq d+2$)
  for each $z \in Z$: query $r(L(z))$
  interpolate to find a polynomial Q of degree $\leq d$ such that $Q(z) = r(L(z))$ for all $z \in Z$
  output $Q(0)$

For

- every message $m\colon \{0,1\}^d \to \mathbb{F}$ with codeword $P\colon \mathbb{F}^d \to \mathbb{F}$, and
- every received word $r\colon \mathbb{F}^d \to \mathbb{F}$ with $\text{dist}(r,P) \le q^d/3(d+1)$, and
- every message index $a \in \{0,1\}^d$:

$$\begin{aligned}
\mathbf{Pr}_b\big[\text{decoder outputs } m(a)\big] &\ge \mathbf{Pr}_b\big[Q = P\circ L\big] && \text{(Claim 10.7)}\\
&\ge \mathbf{Pr}_b\big[r(L(z)) = P(L(z)) \text{ for all } z\in Z\big] && \text{(Claim 10.8)}\\
&\ge 1-\textstyle\sum_{z\in Z}\mathbf{Pr}_b\big[r(L(z))\ne P(L(z))\big] && \text{(union bound)}\\
&\ge 1-\textstyle\sum_{z\in Z} 1/3(d+1) && \text{(Claim 10.9)}\\
&= 2/3
\end{aligned}$$

In more detail:

- If $Q = P\circ L$ then the decoder correctly outputs $Q(0) = P(L(0)) = P(a) = m(a)$.
- If $r(L(z)) = P(L(z))$ for all $z \in Z$, then $Q = P\circ L$ since $\deg(Q) \le d$ and $\deg(P\circ L)\le d$ and they agree on the $d+1$ points $z \in Z$.
- $\mathbf{Pr}_b\big[r(L(z)) \ne P(L(z))\big] = \text{dist}(r,P)/q^d \le 1/3(d+1)$ for each $z \in Z$ because $L(z)$ is uniformly random. ■

10.3.3 Adjusted Multilinear Codes

We modify the multilinear code into a binary code whose message length and codeword length are powers of 2, and we observe that this code is space-efficiently encodable and time-efficiently locally decodable.

Theorem 10.11. *For all $K \ge 1$, there exist $N \in \text{poly}\,K$ and a binary code such that:*

- *The message of length 2^K is the table of a function $m\colon \{0,1\}^K \to \{0,1\}$.*
- *The codeword of length 2^N is the table of a function $c\colon \{0,1\}^N \to \{0,1\}$.*
- *It's encodable in* poly K *space.*
- *It's locally decodable in* poly K *time from $2^N/N^2$ bit flips, with error probability* $1/3$.
- *N can be computed from K, and vice versa, in* poly K *time.*

Proof idea. Consider a multilinear code E over the field $\mathbb{F} = \mathbb{F}_{2^\ell}$. Flattening E would yield a binary code by flattening both the message and the codeword (§9.5.1). Instead of flattening the message, it's simpler to just restrict E to messages that only contain 0s and 1s (corresponding to the field elements $0\cdots00$ and $0\cdots01$). Flattening the codeword would multiply its length by ℓ, which might not be a power of 2. To fix this, we insert 0s to pad each coordinate of the codeword $E(m)$ from ℓ bits to ℓ^* bits, for the smallest $\ell^* \ge \ell$ that's a power of 2. For example, if $\ell = 3$ and $\ell^* = 4$, then padding and flattening a codeword $(101, 010, 011, \ldots)$ would yield $(1010, 0100, 0110, \ldots)' = 101001000110\cdots$. ■

Proof (ancillary). Now, K plays the role of d from §10.3.2. For any K, consider the smallest $\ell \ge \log(K+2)$ of the form $2\cdot 3^e$ for defining $\mathbb{F} = \mathbb{F}_q$ where $q = 2^\ell \ge K+2$ using Theorem 9.19.*(ii)*. Consider the multilinear code E with message $m\colon \{0,1\}^K \to \mathbb{F}$ and codeword $P\colon \mathbb{F}^K \to \mathbb{F}$. For the smallest $\ell^* \ge \ell$ that's a power of 2, define $N = \ell K + \log(\ell^*)$ and a code E^* with message

$m\colon \{0,1\}^K \to \{0,1\}$ and codeword $c\colon \{0,1\}^N \to \{0,1\}$. Intuitively, c is the "padded and flattened" version of P. Viewing it as $c\colon \mathbb{F}^K \times [\ell^*] \to \{0,1\}$ (with "unflattened" domain):

$$c(x,j) = \begin{cases} j\text{th bit of } P(x) & \text{if } j \le \ell \\ 0 & \text{if } j > \ell \end{cases}$$

Here's a straightforward encoder for E^*, using the definitions of P and c.

Encoder for the adjusted multilinear code (10.9)

$E^*(m)$ where $m\colon \{0,1\}^K \to \{0,1\}$ is a message:
  for each codeword index $(x,j) \in \mathbb{F}^K \times [\ell^*]$:
    initialize $sum \leftarrow 0$
    for each $b \in \{0,1\}^K$:
      evaluate $summand \leftarrow m(b)\big(\prod_{i\,:\,b_i=1} x_i\big)\big(\prod_{i\,:\,b_i=0}(1-x_i)\big)$ in $\mathbb{F}$
      update $sum \leftarrow sum + summand$ in $\mathbb{F}$
    if $j \le \ell$: output jth bit of sum
    else: output 0

After the b loop, $sum = P(x)$, so this algorithm outputs $c(x,j)$. It uses poly$K$ space because it reuses the space to evaluate $summand$ in each iteration.

Here's a local decoder D^* for E^*, using the local decoder D for E from Theorem 10.10.

Local decoder for the adjusted multilinear code (10.10)

$D^*(a,r^*)$ where $a \in \{0,1\}^K$ is a message index and $r^*\colon \mathbb{F}^K \times [\ell^*] \to \{0,1\}$ is a received word:
  define $r\colon \mathbb{F}^K \to \mathbb{F}$ by $r(x) = r^*(x,1)r^*(x,2)\cdots r^*(x,\ell)$
  run $D(a,r)$:
    when it queries $r(x)$: do the ℓ queries $r^*(x,1), r^*(x,2), \ldots, r^*(x,\ell)$ to obtain $r(x)$
  output whatever $D(a,r)$ outputs

Consider any m, r^*, a with $\text{dist}(r^*,c) \le 2^N/N^2$. Each bit flip between r^* and c results in at most one symbol change between r and P, so

$$\text{dist}(r,P) \le \text{dist}(r^*,c) \le 2^N/N^2 = q^K\ell^*/N^2 \le q^K/3(K+1)$$

since $\ell^* \le 2\ell \le 6\log(K+2)$ and $N \ge K$ and thus $\ell^*/N^2 \le 1/3(K+1)$ for large enough K. It follows that:

$$\mathbf{Pr}\big[D^*(a,r^*) = m(a)\big] = \mathbf{Pr}\big[D(a,r) = m(a)\big] \ge 2/3$$

Running D takes poly$K$ time (including the polynomial interpolation algorithm from §9.3.3), which gets multiplied by $O(\ell) = O(\log K)$ since each symbol query becomes ℓ bit queries. This also means D^* makes only poly$K$ queries. Specifically, D^* makes $(K+1)\ell$ bit queries since D makes $K+1$ symbol queries. ■

10.3.4 Worst-Case to Average-Case Reductions

We now prove that if $\mathsf{PSPACE} \neq \mathsf{BPP}$ then $(\mathsf{PSPACE}, \mathsf{U}) \not\subseteq \mathsf{HEUR}_{1/N^2}\mathsf{P}$.

Proof of Theorem 10.5. We prove the contrapositive. Assume $(\mathsf{PSPACE}, \mathsf{U}) \subseteq \mathsf{HEUR}_{1/N^2}\mathsf{P}$. For any $A \in \mathsf{PSPACE}$, we prove that $A \in \mathsf{BPP}$. We may assume $A\colon \{0,1\}^+ \to \{0,1\}$ is a total decision problem with word size 1; we explain why at the end of the proof. We define a total decision problem $B\colon \{0,1\}^+ \to \{0,1\}$.

Denote A's input by $x \in \{0,1\}^K$ and B's input by $y \in \{0,1\}^N$. For each K, consider the number N, encoder E, and local decoder D from Theorem 10.11 (so E and D are what we called E^* and D^* in that proof).

- Use $A_K\colon \{0,1\}^K \to \{0,1\}$ as the message.
- Let $B_N\colon \{0,1\}^N \to \{0,1\}$ be the codeword $E(A_K)$.

For other N (not associated with any K in Theorem 10.11), let B_N be the constant 0 function.

Since $A \in \mathsf{PSPACE}$ by a program Π_A, we have $B \in \mathsf{PSPACE}$ by a program Π_B that runs the encoder E:

Algorithm for B using an encoder (10.11)

```
Π_B(y) where y ∈ {0,1}^N:
    find the associated K, or output 0 if there's no such K
    run E(A_K):
        when it reads A_K(x): run Π_A(x)
    output the bit at index y of E(A_K)'s output
```

$\Pi_B(y)$ outputs $B_N(y)$ by definition, and it uses $\operatorname{poly} K \leq \operatorname{poly} N$ space because E uses $\operatorname{poly} K$ space, and an additional $\operatorname{poly} K$ space can be reused by all runs of Π_A.

Now, since $(B, U) \in \mathsf{HEUR}_{1/N^2}\mathsf{P}$ by a heuristic Π'_B, we have $A \in \mathsf{BPP}$ by a randomized program Π'_A that runs the local decoder D with the table of Π'_B as the received word $r\colon \{0,1\}^N \to \{0,1\}$:

Randomized algorithm for A using a local decoder (10.12)

```
Π'_A(x) where x ∈ {0,1}^K:
    find the associated N
    run D(x, r):
        when it queries r(y): run Π'_B(y)
    output whatever D(x, r) outputs
```

Since Π'_B has error probability $1/N^2$, we have $\operatorname{dist}(r, B_N) \leq 2^N/N^2$, so for every x, $\mathbf{Pr}\big[\Pi'_A(x) = A_K(x)\big] = \mathbf{Pr}\big[D(x,r) = A_K(x)\big] \geq 2/3$. Also, Π'_A takes $\operatorname{poly} K$ time because D takes $\operatorname{poly} K$ time, and each of the $\operatorname{poly} K$ many runs of Π'_B takes $\operatorname{poly} N \leq \operatorname{poly} K$ time.

What if A is not total or has word size > 1? We may assume Π_A uses $\operatorname{poly} K$ space and halts even on invalid inputs. So if we define a total decision problem A' with the same log-bounded word size as Π_A, such that $A'(x) = \Pi_A(x)$ for all x, then $A' \in \mathsf{PSPACE}$. We turn A' into a total decision problem A'' with word size 1 by splitting each input word into single-bit words, and we have $A'' \in \mathsf{PSPACE}$ also. Thus $A'' \in \mathsf{BPP}$, so $A' \in \mathsf{BPP}$, so $A \in \mathsf{BPP}$ since any randomized program that solves A' also solves A. ■

Theorem 10.5 holds with $\mathsf{HEUR}_{1/N^2}\mathsf{BPP}$ in place of $\mathsf{HEUR}_{1/N^2}\mathsf{P}$, by absorbing Π'_B's output error probability into Π'_A's error probability. A nonuniform version also holds: If $(\mathsf{PSPACE}, \mathsf{U}) \subseteq \mathsf{HEUR}_{1/N^2}\mathsf{P/poly}$ then $\mathsf{PSPACE} \subseteq \mathsf{P/poly}$, because we can use Π'_B's advice as Π'_A's advice to conclude $A \in \mathsf{BPP/poly}$, and $\mathsf{BPP/poly} = \mathsf{P/poly}$ just like $\mathsf{BPP} \subseteq \mathsf{P/poly}$ (Theorem 7.9).

10.4 Hardness Amplification

In the previous section, we turned any "worst-case hard" problem into a "mildly average-case hard" problem, for which every efficient algorithm errs on not just one input, but a significant fraction of inputs. Now, we keep the ball rolling by turning any "mildly average-case hard" problem into a "strongly average-case hard" problem, for which every efficient algorithm errs on almost half the inputs. This is called *hardness amplification* (modifying problems to increase input error probability) in contrast to the amplification from §7.3 (modifying algorithms to decrease output error probability).

Theorem 10.12. *If* $(\mathsf{PSPACE}, \mathsf{U}) \not\subseteq \mathsf{HEUR}_{1/N^c}\mathsf{P/poly}$ *for some constant c, then* $(\mathsf{PSPACE}, \mathsf{U}) \not\subseteq \mathsf{HEUR}_{1/2-1/N^d}\mathsf{P/poly}$ *for every constant d.*

We won't use the perspective of error correcting codes, but it helps explain the presence of nonuniformity: Binary codes can't have relative distance $> 1/2$ (Theorem 9.7), so decoders can't handle $1/4$ fraction of bit flips, so we wouldn't expect to amplify hardness to $\varepsilon = 1/4$. Getting to $\varepsilon \approx 1/2$ is possible by list decoding (§9.2.3): Not too many codewords agree with the received word on significantly more than half the bits, so nonuniform advice can pick out the right codeword from the list.

10.4.1 Xor Lemma

We use bounded-fan-in circuits since we're considering nonuniform time complexity. We let C denote both a circuit and the function $C\colon \{0,1\}^m \to \{0,1\}$ it computes. For convenience, we now define a circuit's size as the number of $\wedge$ gates and $\vee$ gates (not counting $\neg$ gates or input nodes); this doesn't matter since we can push all $\neg$ gates to the input nodes while only doubling the number of $\wedge$ and $\vee$ gates (§5.2.2). We view circuits as heuristics with respect to the uniform distribution over inputs:

Definition. For every $f\colon \{0,1\}^m \to \{0,1\}$ and $s > 0$ and $0 < \alpha < 1$, say f is *(s,α)-easy* if there exists a circuit $C\colon \{0,1\}^m \to \{0,1\}$ of size $\le s$ such that for uniformly random $x \in \{0,1\}^m$:

$$\mathbf{Pr}_x\big[C(x) = f(x)\big] \ \ge\ (1+\alpha)/2$$

Otherwise, f is *(s,α)-hard.* ◀

This α (lower-case Greek alpha) measures how much better than $1/2$ the success probability is. In $\mathsf{HEUR}_\varepsilon\mathsf{P/poly}$, the error probability ε corresponds to $(1-\alpha)/2$. Note that $\alpha = 0$ is trivial (since a constant 0 or constant 1 circuit succeeds on at least half the inputs) and $\alpha = 1$ corresponds to worst-case complexity.

To prove Theorem 10.12, we turn a mildly hard function $f\colon \{0,1\}^m \to \{0,1\}$ (with α close to 1) into a strongly hard function (with α close to 0). A natural candidate is the parity (xor) of several copies of f on separate inputs. Define $f^{\oplus k}\colon (\{0,1\}^m)^k \to \{0,1\}$ by:

$$f^{\oplus k}(x_1, x_2, \ldots, x_k) \ =\ f(x_1) \oplus f(x_2) \oplus \cdots \oplus f(x_k)$$

Parity is utterly sensitive: Flipping a single coordinate always flips the output, regardless of the other coordinates. This instability is good for amplifying hardness: If we're unsure about even a single $f(x_i)$, then "all bets are off" for computing the parity. And with moderately many coordinates, botching at least one of them becomes very likely.

We'll turn a mild lower bound for f into a strong lower bound for $f^{\oplus k}$. But first, to see how strong we should aim for, let's turn an upper bound for f into an upper bound for $f^{\oplus k}$.

Lemma 10.13. *If f is (s,α)-easy, then for all k, $f^{\oplus k}$ is $\big(sk+3k,\ \alpha^k\big)$-easy.*

Proof idea. To compute $f^{\oplus k}(x_1,\ldots,x_k)$, we compute each $f(x_i)$ and output the parity of these k bits. If the success probability for computing f is $(1+\alpha)/2$, then the probability of succeeding on all k coordinates is only $((1+\alpha)/2)^k$, which is close to 0, not greater than 1/2. But we don't need to succeed on all k coordinates, because an even number of errors would cancel each other out in the parity. Thus erring overall is like getting an odd number of tails in k tosses of a biased coin. Lemma A.13 analyzes this probability. ∎

It's helpful to change the codomain from $\{0,1\}$ to $\{1,-1\}$ by replacing each bit $b\in\{0,1\}$ with $(-1)^b\in\{1,-1\}$, so 1 becomes -1, and 0 becomes 1. Thus we consider circuits $C\colon\{0,1\}^m\to\{1,-1\}$ trying to compute functions $f\colon\{0,1\}^m\to\{1,-1\}$. Keep in mind that for every random variable X taking values in $\{1,-1\}$,

$$\mathbf{E}[X] \;=\; 2\mathbf{Pr}[X=1]-1 \qquad \text{and} \qquad \mathbf{Pr}[X=1] \;=\; (1+\mathbf{E}[X])/2$$

because by the definition of expectation:

$$\mathbf{E}[X] \;=\; 1\cdot\mathbf{Pr}[X=1]+(-1)\cdot\mathbf{Pr}[X=-1] \;=\; \mathbf{Pr}[X=1]-(1-\mathbf{Pr}[X=1])$$

Claim 10.14. *$f\colon\{0,1\}^m\to\{1,-1\}$ is (s,α)-easy iff there exists a circuit $C\colon\{0,1\}^m\to\{1,-1\}$ of size $\le s$ such that $\mathbf{E}_x\big[C(x)f(x)\big]\ge\alpha$.*

Proof of Claim 10.14. For every circuit C, we have $\mathbf{Pr}_x\big[C(x)=f(x)\big]=\mathbf{Pr}_x\big[C(x)f(x)=1\big]=\big(1+\mathbf{E}_x\big[C(x)f(x)\big]\big)/2$, so $\mathbf{Pr}_x\big[C(x)=f(x)\big]\ge(1+\alpha)/2$ iff $\mathbf{E}_x\big[C(x)f(x)\big]\ge\alpha$. ∎

A benefit of the $\{1,-1\}$ perspective is that xor becomes multiplication: $(-1)^{a\oplus b}=(-1)^a(-1)^b$ for all bits a,b. Thus for $f\colon\{0,1\}^m\to\{1,-1\}$:

$$f^{\oplus k}(x_1,\ldots,x_k) \;=\; \textstyle\prod_{i=1}^k f(x_i)$$

This lets us exploit how expectation interacts with multiplication: We can factor out constants (linearity of expectation), and the expectation of a product of fully independent random variables equals the product of their expectations (Lemma A.12).

Proof of Lemma 10.13. If f is (s,α)-easy, then $\mathbf{E}_x\big[C(x)f(x)\big]\ge\alpha$ for some circuit C of size $\le s$ (Claim 10.14). Define a circuit $C^{\oplus k}\colon(\{0,1\}^m)^k\to\{1,-1\}$ that applies copies of C to all k components of the input and then outputs the parity of the resulting k bits:

$$C^{\oplus k}(x_1,\ldots,x_k) \;=\; \textstyle\prod_{i=1}^k C(x_i)$$

The k copies of C have size $\le sk$, and computing the parity takes $\le 3k$ many $\wedge$ and $\vee$ gates, so $C^{\oplus k}$ has size $\le sk+3k$. Since $x_1,\ldots,x_k$ are fully independent:

$$\begin{aligned}\mathbf{E}_{x_1,\ldots,x_k}\Big[C^{\oplus k}(x_1,\ldots,x_k)f^{\oplus k}(x_1,\ldots,x_k)\Big] &= \mathbf{E}_{x_1,\ldots,x_k}\Big[\textstyle\prod_{i=1}^k C(x_i)f(x_i)\Big]\\ &= \textstyle\prod_{i=1}^k \mathbf{E}_{x_i}\big[C(x_i)f(x_i)\big] \;\ge\; \prod_{i=1}^k \alpha \;=\; \alpha^k\end{aligned}$$

Thus $f^{\oplus k}$ is $\big(sk+3k,\ \alpha^k\big)$-easy (Claim 10.14). ∎

Circuits for $f^{\oplus k}$ don't have to treat the k input components separately. The components could jointly influence a computation in arbitrary ways. It's conceivable some circuit could do better than α^k, but this feels unlikely because the components are sampled independently. Since parity is so unforgiving, it's hard to imagine doing much better than the trivial circuit from Lemma 10.13. But proving that it's indeed impossible is far from straightforward. Here is this section's titular "xor lemma":

Lemma 10.15. *If f is (s,α)-hard, then for all k and small enough $\delta > 0$, $f^{\oplus k}$ is $\big(s\delta^3(1-\alpha)^3, \alpha^k + \delta\big)$-hard.*

Proof idea. Compared to Lemma 10.13, $\alpha^k + \delta$ is as expected, but $s\delta^3(1-\alpha)^3$ is disappointing. We wanted the circuit size to go *up* (by a factor k), but instead it goes *down* because we prove the contrapositive by reduction: We turn a hypothetical circuit achieving $\alpha^k + \delta$ for $f^{\oplus k}$ into a circuit achieving α for f. The latter circuit contains the hypothetical circuit (several copies of it, in fact) and is therefore larger. Thus $f^{\oplus k}$ is harder than f in terms of success probability, but the hardness is only known to hold against smaller circuits. The loss in circuit size is the price we pay for using reductions. A version where the circuit size goes up may be true, but nobody knows how to prove it. Fortunately, this doesn't matter for proving Theorem 10.12, since the loss is only polynomial as long as $\delta \geq 1/\text{poly}$ and $\alpha \leq 1 - 1/\text{poly}$.

The case $k = 2$ already captures the challenge of amplifying hardness. As a warmup, consider the worst-case setting: How could we use a circuit $C(x_1, x_2)$ that computes $f(x_1) \oplus f(x_2)$ on all inputs to compute f on all inputs?

- For any x_1, we can contract C with x_1 hardwired to obtain a circuit C_{x_1}. If $f(x_1) = 0$ then $C_{x_1}(x_2) = C(x_1, x_2) = 0 \oplus f(x_2) = f(x_2)$. Similarly, if $f(x_1) = 1$ then $\neg C_{x_1}(x_2) = f(x_2)$. Thus either C_{x_1} or $\neg C_{x_1}$ computes f on all inputs x_2.
- The previous bullet also yields a roundabout, overkill way to compute f on all inputs x_1: Check which of C_{x_1} or $\neg C_{x_1}$ computes $f(x_2)$. If C_{x_1} does, then $f(x_1) = 0$. If $\neg C_{x_1}$ does, then $f(x_1) = 1$.

This generalizes to the average-case setting. If C computes $f^{\oplus 2}$ on some fraction of inputs, then at least one of these approaches computes f on an even better fraction of inputs:

- Compute $f(x_2)$ using either C_{x_1} or $\neg C_{x_1}$ for some x_1.
- Compute $f(x_1)$ by checking which of C_{x_1} or $\neg C_{x_1}$ is better at computing $f(x_2)$: If C_{x_1} is better, output 0. If $\neg C_{x_1}$ is better, output 1.

The second approach seems crazy: It evaluates C_{x_1} on every x_2 (exponentially many) and compares the result to $f(x_2)$, which we don't have since we don't know how to compute f (that's the whole point, after all). Key insight: It suffices to estimate how well C_{x_1} computes $f(x_2)$ by using a small sample of x_2 inputs, rather than all x_2. Since this sample of x_2s is shared by all x_1s, we can hardwire the values $f(x_2)$ as nonuniform advice, rather than try to compute them. ∎

Proof of Theorem 10.12. Assuming $(\mathsf{PSPACE}, \mathsf{U}) \subseteq \mathsf{HEUR}_{1/2-1/N^d}\mathsf{P/poly}$ for some d, we prove that $(\mathsf{PSPACE}, \mathsf{U}) \subseteq \mathsf{HEUR}_{1/N^c}\mathsf{P/poly}$ for every c. Consider any total $A \in \mathsf{PSPACE}$ and any integer c. Like in § 10.3.4, we may assume $A\colon \{0,1\}^+ \to \{0,1\}$ has word size 1. We define a total decision problem $B\colon \{0,1\}^+ \to \{0,1\}$. For each input size M, consider $A_M\colon \{0,1\}^M \to \{0,1\}$ and let $k = M^{c+1}$. Define $B_N\colon \{0,1\}^N \to \{0,1\}$ by $B_N = A_M^{\oplus k}$ for $N = Mk = M^{c+2}$. For other N, let B_N be the constant 0 function.

Since $A \in \mathsf{PSPACE}$ by a program Π, we have $B \in \mathsf{PSPACE}$ by a program that, on input $(x_1, \ldots, x_k) \in (\{0,1\}^M)^k$, runs $\Pi(x_i)$ for each $i \in [k]$ and outputs the parity of these k bits.

Thus $(B,U) \in \mathsf{HEUR}_{(1-2/N^d)/2}\mathsf{P/poly}$, so there exist constants a,b such that B_N is $(aN^b, 2/N^d)$-easy for each $N = Mk = M^{c+2}$. Define $\alpha = 1-2/M^c$ and $\delta = 1/N^d$ and:

$$s = aN^b/\delta^3(1-\alpha)^3 = O\big(N^b N^{3d} M^{3c}\big) = O\big(M^{(c+2)(b+3d)+3c}\big) \in \text{poly}\,M$$

For large enough M, we have

$$\alpha^k \le \mathrm{e}^{-(2/M^c)k} = \mathrm{e}^{-2M} \le 1/M^{(c+2)d} = 1/N^d$$

and so $\alpha^k+\delta \le 2/N^d$. Hence B_N is $\big(s\delta^3(1-\alpha)^3,\ \alpha^k+\delta\big)$-easy, so A_M is (s,α)-easy (Lemma 10.15). Thus $(A,U) \in \mathsf{HEUR}_{1/M^c}\mathsf{P/poly}$. ■

10.4.2 Proof of the Xor Lemma

The bulk of the work is to prove a two-function version. For $f\colon \{0,1\}^m \to \{0,1\}$ and $g\colon \{0,1\}^n \to \{0,1\}$, define $f \oplus g\colon \{0,1\}^m \times \{0,1\}^n \to \{0,1\}$ by $(f\oplus g)(x,y) = f(x) \oplus g(y)$. We treat f and g asymmetrically on purpose:

Lemma 10.16. *If f is (s,α)-hard and g is (t,β)-hard, then for all small enough $\gamma > 0$, $f \oplus g$ is $\big(\min(s\gamma^3,t),\ \alpha\beta+\gamma\big)$-hard.*

Proof of Lemma 10.15. Define $\gamma = \delta(1-\alpha)$ and $t = s\gamma^3$. Starting with $f^{\oplus 1} = f$, we iteratively define $f^{\oplus i} = f \oplus f^{\oplus(i-1)}$ for each $i \leftarrow 2,\dots,k$. We claim this maintains the invariant that $f^{\oplus i}$ is $\big(t,\ \alpha^i+\delta\big)$-hard: This holds for the base case $i=1$ by the assumption that f is (s,α)-hard and $s \ge t$ and $\alpha \le \alpha^1+\delta$. Assuming the invariant holds for $i-1$, it holds for i by Lemma 10.16: If f is (s,α)-hard and $f^{\oplus(i-1)}$ is $\big(t,\ \alpha^{i-1}+\delta\big)$-hard, then $f^{\oplus i} = f \oplus f^{\oplus(i-1)}$ is $\big(\min(s\gamma^3,t),\ \alpha(\alpha^{i-1}+\delta)+\gamma\big) = \big(t,\ \alpha^i+\delta\big)$-hard. ■

Proof of Lemma 10.16 (ancillary). We use codomain $\{1,-1\}$. For $f\colon \{0,1\}^m \to \{1,-1\}$ and $g\colon \{0,1\}^n \to \{1,-1\}$, define $(fg)(x,y) = f(x)g(y)$ so fg corresponds to $f \oplus g$.

We prove the contrapositive. Suppose fg is $\big(\min(s\gamma^3,t),\ \alpha\beta+\gamma\big)$-easy, so for some circuit $C\colon \{0,1\}^m \times \{0,1\}^n \to \{1,-1\}$ of size $\le \min(s\gamma^3,t)$,

$$\mathbf{E}_{x,y}\big[C(x,y)f(x)g(y)\big] \ge \alpha\beta+\gamma$$

by Claim 10.14. We prove that either f is (s,α)-easy or g is (t,β)-easy.

Define $h(x,y) = C(x,y)g(y)$ and $H(x) = \mathbf{E}_y\big[h(x,y)\big]$.

Case 1. Assuming $|H(x)| \ge \beta$ for some x, we show that g is (t,β)-easy.

Contracting C with this x hardwired (§5.2.2) yields a circuit $C_x\colon \{0,1\}^n \to \{1,-1\}$ of size $\le$ (size of C) $\le t$ such that $C_x(y) = C(x,y)$. Since $H(x) = \mathbf{E}_y\big[C_x(y)g(y)\big]$, either

$$\mathbf{E}_y\big[C_x(y)g(y)\big] \ge \beta \quad \text{or} \quad \mathbf{E}_y\big[-C_x(y)g(y)\big] \ge \beta$$

and so either C_x or $-C_x$ shows that g is (t,β)-easy. (We're assuming the extra $\neg$ gate for $-C_x$ doesn't count toward the size.)

Case 2. Assuming $|H(x)| < \beta$ for all x, we show that f is (s,α)-easy. Note that:

$$\mathbf{E}_x\big[H(x)f(x)\big] = \mathbf{E}_x\big[\mathbf{E}_y\big[C(x,y)g(y)\big]f(x)\big] = \mathbf{E}_{x,y}\big[C(x,y)f(x)g(y)\big] \geq \alpha\beta + \gamma$$

We have $\big|H(x)/\beta\big| < 1$ for all x, and $\mathbf{E}_x\big[\big(H(x)/\beta\big)f(x)\big] \geq \alpha + \gamma/\beta \geq \alpha$. Thus the function $H(x)/\beta$ is almost what we want, except it isn't a small circuit and doesn't have codomain $\{1,-1\}$.

- To make it a small circuit, we average $h(x,y)$ over a few y rather than all y, with the values $g(y)$ hardwired (as nonuniform advice).
- To make it have codomain $\{1,-1\}$, we round values above some threshold to 1, and round values below the threshold to -1.

Define "few" as $\ell = \lceil \frac{16}{\gamma^2} \ln \frac{8}{\gamma} \rceil$.

- For any tuple $Y = (y_1,\ldots,y_\ell) \in (\{0,1\}^n)^\ell$, define

$$H_Y(x) = \mathbf{E}_j\big[h(x,y_j)\big] \text{ where } j \in [\ell] \text{ is uniformly random}$$

  unless that value is $> \beta$ or $< -\beta$, in which case define $H_Y(x)$ as β or $-\beta$, respectively.
- For any threshold $-\beta \leq r \leq \beta$, define:

$$H_{Y,r}(x) = \begin{cases} \beta & \text{if } H_Y(x) \geq r \\ -\beta & \text{if } H_Y(x) < r \end{cases}$$

Here's the technical heart, which we prove at the end of this section:

Claim 10.17. *For each x, $\mathbf{E}_{Y,r}\big[H_{Y,r}(x)\big]$ is within $\pm\gamma$ of $H(x)$, where Y,r are uniformly random.*

Thus for each x, we have $\mathbf{E}_{Y,r}\big[H_{Y,r}(x)\big]f(x) \geq H(x)f(x) - \gamma$:

- If $f(x) = 1$ then this follows from $\mathbf{E}_{Y,r}\big[H_{Y,r}(x)\big] \geq H(x) - \gamma$.
- If $f(x) = -1$ then this follows from $\mathbf{E}_{Y,r}\big[H_{Y,r}(x)\big] \leq H(x) + \gamma$.

$$\begin{aligned}\mathbf{E}_{Y,r}\big[\mathbf{E}_x\big[H_{Y,r}(x)f(x)\big]\big] = \mathbf{E}_x\big[\mathbf{E}_{Y,r}\big[H_{Y,r}(x)\big]f(x)\big] \geq \mathbf{E}_x\big[H(x)f(x) - \gamma\big] &\geq (\alpha\beta + \gamma) - \gamma \\ &= \alpha\beta\end{aligned}$$

By the probabilistic method (Lemma A.15), there exists Y,r such that $\mathbf{E}_x\big[H_{Y,r}(x)f(x)\big] \geq \alpha\beta$ and thus $\mathbf{E}_x\big[\big(H_{Y,r}(x)/\beta\big)f(x)\big] \geq \alpha$. To conclude that f is (s,α)-easy, we show that $H_{Y,r}(x)/\beta \in \{1,-1\}$ is computed by a circuit of size $\leq s$. We have:

$$H_{Y,r}(x)/\beta = 1 \iff H_Y(x) \geq r \iff \mathbf{E}_j\big[h(x,y_j)\big] \geq r \iff \textstyle\sum_{j=1}^{\ell} h(x,y_j) \geq \ell r$$

(The middle $\iff$ used $|r| \leq \beta$.) For each j, we compute $h(x,y_j)$ using a copy of $C(x,y_j)$ (contracted with y_j hardwired), negated if $g(y_j) = -1$. Then, we sum these values and compare the sum to $\lceil \ell r \rceil$, using at most $10\ell \log \ell$ gates. In total, this circuit has size

$$\leq (\text{size of } C) \cdot \ell + 10\ell \log \ell \leq (\text{size of } C)/\gamma^3 \leq s$$

assuming $\gamma \leq 10^{-5}$. ■

Proof of Claim 10.17 (ancillary). Consider any x. For brevity, we suppress x from the notation. We want to show that $\mathbf{E}_{Y,r}\big[H_{Y,r}\big]$ is within $\pm\gamma$ of H, where by definition:

$$\begin{aligned} H &= \mathbf{E}_y\big[h(y)\big], \text{ with } |H| < \beta \\ H_Y &= \mathbf{E}_j\big[h(y_j)\big] \text{ clipped so that } |H_Y| \le \beta \\ H_{Y,r} &= \beta \text{ or } -\beta, \text{ indicating whether } H_Y \ge r \end{aligned}$$

First, we show $\mathbf{E}_r\big[H_{Y,r}\big] = H_Y$ for each Y:

$$\mathbf{E}_r\big[H_{Y,r}\big] = \mathbf{Pr}_r\big[H_{Y,r} = \beta\big]\cdot\beta + \mathbf{Pr}_r\big[H_{Y,r} = -\beta\big]\cdot(-\beta) = \tfrac{H_Y-(-\beta)}{2\beta}\cdot\beta + \tfrac{\beta-H_Y}{2\beta}\cdot(-\beta) = H_Y$$

Say Y is *good* iff H_Y is within $\pm\gamma/2$ of H. Then

$$\mathbf{Pr}_Y\big[Y \text{ is good}\big] \ge \mathbf{Pr}_Y\Big[\mathbf{E}_j\big[h(y_j)\big] \text{ is within } \pm\gamma/2 \text{ of } \mathbf{E}_y\big[h(y)\big]\Big] \ge 1-\gamma/4$$

by Corollary 7.21, since sampling y is like tossing a coin where heads means $h(y)=1$: With ℓ tosses, the following are within $\pm\gamma/4$ of each other with probability $\ge 1-\gamma/4$:

$$\begin{aligned} \text{fraction of tosses that are heads} &= \mathbf{Pr}_j\big[h(y_j)=1\big] = \big(1+\mathbf{E}_j\big[h(y_j)\big]\big)/2 \\ \text{heads probability} &= \mathbf{Pr}_y\big[h(y)=1\big] = \big(1+\mathbf{E}_y\big[h(y)\big]\big)/2 \end{aligned}$$

By the law of total expectation:

$$\begin{aligned} \mathbf{E}_{Y,r}\big[H_{Y,r}\big] &= \mathbf{Pr}_Y\big[Y \text{ is good}\big]\cdot\mathbf{E}_{Y,r}\big[H_{Y,r}\,\big|\,Y \text{ is good}\big] + \mathbf{Pr}_Y\big[Y \text{ is bad}\big]\cdot\mathbf{E}_{Y,r}\big[H_{Y,r}\,\big|\,Y \text{ is bad}\big] \\ &\le \mathbf{Pr}_Y\big[Y \text{ is good}\big]\cdot\max_{\text{good }Y}\mathbf{E}_r\big[H_{Y,r}\big] + \mathbf{Pr}_Y\big[Y \text{ is bad}\big]\cdot\max_{\text{bad }Y}\mathbf{E}_r\big[H_{Y,r}\big] \\ &= \big(1-\mathbf{Pr}_Y\big[Y \text{ is bad}\big]\big)\cdot\max_{\text{good }Y}(H_Y) + \mathbf{Pr}_Y\big[Y \text{ is bad}\big]\cdot\max_{\text{bad }Y}(H_Y) \\ &= \max_{\text{good }Y}(H_Y) + \mathbf{Pr}_Y\big[Y \text{ is bad}\big]\cdot\big(\max_{\text{bad }Y}(H_Y) - \max_{\text{good }Y}(H_Y)\big) \\ &\le (H+\gamma/2) + (\gamma/4)\cdot(2\beta) \\ &\le H+\gamma \end{aligned}$$

Symmetrically, $\mathbf{E}_{Y,r}\big[H_{Y,r}\big] \ge H-\gamma$. ■

10.4.3 Asymptotics

By chaining together "worst-case to mild-average-case to strong-average-case" reductions:

Corollary 10.18. *If* $\mathsf{PSPACE} \not\subseteq \mathsf{P/poly}$ *then* $(\mathsf{PSPACE},\mathsf{U}) \not\subseteq \mathsf{HEUR}_{1/2-1/N^d}\mathsf{P/poly}$ *for every* d.

Proof. If $\mathsf{PSPACE} \not\subseteq \mathsf{P/poly}$ then $(\mathsf{PSPACE},\mathsf{U}) \not\subseteq \mathsf{HEUR}_{1/N^2}\mathsf{P/poly}$ by the variant of Theorem 10.5 noted at the end of §10.3.4, and thus $(\mathsf{PSPACE},\mathsf{U}) \not\subseteq \mathsf{HEUR}_{1/2-1/N^d}\mathsf{P/poly}$ by Theorem 10.12. ■

Chapter 11 has an application of the following variant of Corollary 10.18. The proof is more involved and is beyond the scope of this book. Recall $\mathsf{E} = \mathsf{TIME}[2^{O(N)}]$ is not robust with respect to input encodings. Restricting our attention to problems with word size 1 alleviates that issue.

Theorem 10.19. *If* E *contains a total* $A\colon \{0,1\}^+ \to \{0,1\}$ *with circuit size complexity* $2^{\Omega(N)}$*, then* E *contains a total* $B\colon \{0,1\}^+ \to \{0,1\}$ *such that* B_N *is* $(2^{cN}, 2^{-cN})$*-hard for some constant* $c > 0$ *and all large enough* N.

Compared to Corollary 10.18, Theorem 10.19 involves E rather than PSPACE, and exponential rather than polynomial circuit size. Another difference is that a "big-Ω" lower bound holds for all large enough N, whereas a "not big-O" lower bound holds for infinitely many N:

Corollary 10.18:

- Assumption: Every too-small circuit family fails for infinitely many N.
- Conclusion: Every too-small circuit family fails badly for infinitely many N.

Theorem 10.19:

- Assumption: Every too-small circuit family fails for all large enough N.
- Conclusion: Every too-small circuit family fails extremely badly for all large enough N.

The above differences between Corollary 10.18 and Theorem 10.19 have only minor impacts on the proof. The major difference is that in Theorem 10.19, the error probability is extremely close to $1/2$. One way to achieve this uses a significantly souped-up xor lemma. Another way bypasses the xor lemma and instead strengthens the locally decodable code from § 10.3 to be locally list decodable, so the decoder yields a small list containing the correct message even when a $1/2 - 1/2^{\Omega(N)}$ fraction of the $2^{O(N)}$ many codeword bits get flipped.

Exercises

10.1 Recall the heuristic for INDEPENDENT SET SEARCH (Theorem 10.1). Prove that with probability $\geq 3/4$, this heuristic doesn't find an independent set of size $\geq \log n + 3$ (even though it's known that such a set exists with high probability).

10.2 Prove (DIRECTED REACHABILITY SEARCH, D) has a log-space heuristic with error probability $2^{-\Omega(n)}$, assuming the adjacency matrix encoding (so the input size N determines the number of nodes n), where D_N is this distribution over inputs (G, s, t): G is uniformly random over all $2^{n(n-1)}$ possible n-node directed graphs (with no self-loops or multi-edges), and s is node 1, and t is node n.

10.3 Consider the uniform distribution over n-variable m-clause 3-CNFs: For each of the m clauses independently, sample one of the $\binom{n}{3}$ sets of 3 variables uniformly at random, and sample one of the 8 possible patterns of negations uniformly at random. Prove that if $m \geq 5.2n$ then $\mathbf{Pr}[\text{the CNF is satisfiable}] \leq 2^{-\Omega(n)}$.

10.4 A randomized heuristic Π for a distributional problem (A, D) has *overall error probability* $\varepsilon(N)$ iff for every valid N, $\mathbf{Pr}_{x \sim D_N,\, r}\big[\Pi(x; r) \text{ errs}\big] \leq \varepsilon(N)$.

(a) Prove that if Π has input error probability ε with respect to output error probability δ, then Π has overall error probability $1 - (1-\varepsilon)(1-\delta) \leq \varepsilon + \delta$.

(b) Prove that if Π has overall error probability ε, then Π has input error probability $\sqrt{\varepsilon}$ with respect to output error probability $\sqrt{\varepsilon}$.

10.5 With inspiration from average-case search-to-decision reductions for NP (Theorem 10.4), design parallel search-to-decision reductions for NP: Prove that if $\mathsf{NP} \subseteq \mathsf{NC}^1/\mathsf{poly}$ then every NP search problem has an $\mathsf{NC}^1/\mathsf{poly}$-type circuit family.

10.6 With $d = 2$ and $\mathbb{F} = \mathbb{F}_4$ (defined with the irreducible polynomial $x^2 + x + 1$), consider the multilinear code $E\colon \mathbb{F}^4 \to \mathbb{F}^{16}$. Encode the message (00, 11, 01, 00) shown in Figure 10.3.

10.7 With $d = 3$ and $\mathbb{F} = \mathbb{Z}_5$, consider the multilinear code $E\colon \mathbb{F}^8 \to \mathbb{F}^{125}$.

x_1	00	00	01	01
x_2	00	01	00	01
message m	00	11	01	00

Figure 10.3: Message for Exercise 10.6

(a) Find the canonical form of the codeword polynomial P for the message $m\colon \{0,1\}^3 \to \mathbb{F}$ where $m(010) = 3$ and $m(a) = 0$ for all other a.

(b) Find all the points on the parameterized line L with anchor $a = (4,2,3)$ and direction $b = (1,2,0)$.

(c) Find the canonical form of the polynomial $P \circ L$ for the P from Exercise 10.7.a and the L from Exercise 10.7.b.

10.8 For any integer $d \geq 1$ and finite field $\mathbb{F}$ of size q, recall the multilinear code E: The message is $m\colon \{0,1\}^d \to \mathbb{F}$ and the codeword is $P\colon \mathbb{F}^d \to \mathbb{F}$ such that P is a multilinear polynomial and $P(a) = m(a)$ for all $a \in \{0,1\}^d$.

Say that a decoder *handles δ corruption* if it works whenever $\leq \delta$ fraction of received word coordinates are symbol changes.

E has relative distance $\geq 1 - d/q$, so handling $< (1-d/q)/2$ corruption is possible in principle. The local decoder from Theorem 10.10 only handles $1/3(d+1)$ corruption (using $d+1$ queries, with error probability $1/3$). Now, you'll design and analyze local decoders that handle much closer to $(1-d/q)/2$ corruption.

(a) Prove that handling $(1-d/q)/6 - 1/q$ corruption is possible using q queries, with error probability $1/3$. Hint: Apply the algorithm for Decoding Polynomial Codes from Symbol Changes (Theorem 9.14).

(b) For any $a, b, c \in \mathbb{F}^d$, the *parameterized parabola* is the function $L\colon \mathbb{F} \to \mathbb{F}^d$ defined by $L(z) = a + z \cdot b + z^2 \cdot c$, where $\cdot$ is scalar-vector multiplication. (Previously L stood for "line," and we keep the same notation for parabolas.) Prove that if $P\colon \mathbb{F}^d \to \mathbb{F}$ is a multilinear polynomial and $L\colon \mathbb{F} \to \mathbb{F}^d$ is a parameterized parabola, then $P \circ L\colon \mathbb{F} \to \mathbb{F}$ is a univariate polynomial of degree $\leq 2d$.

(c) Prove that for every $a \in \mathbb{F}^d$, this randomized hash function is pairwise uniform:

$$h^a\colon (\mathbb{F}^d)^2 \times (\mathbb{F} \setminus \{0\}) \to \mathbb{F}^d \qquad \text{defined by} \qquad h^a_{b,c}(z) = L(z)$$

where L is the parameterized parabola associated with $a, b, c \in \mathbb{F}^d$.

(d) Prove that for the multilinear code, handling $(1 - 2d/q)/2 - \sqrt{3/q}$ corruption (which is $\approx 1/2$ corruption if d/q is small enough) is possible using q queries, with error probability $1/3$. Hint: This is like Exercise 10.8.a but using parabolas instead of lines, and using the hash mixing lemma to analyze the error probability.

(e) Now, consider erasure decoding for the multilinear code. Handling $< 1 - d/q$ corruption (fraction of erased coordinates) is possible in principle. Prove that handling $1 - 2d/(q-1) - \sqrt{4/q}$ corruption (which is ≈ 1 corruption if d/q is small enough) is possible using q queries, with error probability $1/3$. Hint: This is like Exercise 10.8.d but using the algorithm for Decoding Polynomial Codes from Erasures (Theorem 9.13).

10.9 Prove that if $(\mathsf{PSPACE}, \mathsf{U}) \subseteq \mathsf{HEUR}_{0.01}\mathsf{P}$ then $\mathsf{PSPACE} = \mathsf{BPP}$. To do this, combine Exercise 9.17 and Exercise 10.8.a to show that the concatenation of the multilinear code over $\mathbb{F}_{2^\ell}$ and the dot product code fulfills Theorem 10.11 except the local decoder handles $2^N/100$ bit flips rather than just $2^N/N^2$ bit flips.

10.10 In this exercise, you'll deduce the xor lemma as a corollary of another lemma, which you're not asked to prove: Every mildly average-case hard function has a "hardcore" subset of inputs on which the function is strongly average-case hard.

For any $f\colon \{0,1\}^m \to \{0,1\}$ and nonempty $H \subseteq \{0,1\}^m$ (H stands for "hardcore") and $s > 0$ and $0 < \alpha < 1$, say f is *(H,s,α)-easy* iff there exists a circuit $C\colon \{0,1\}^m \to \{0,1\}$ of size $\le s$ such that $\mathbf{Pr}_{x \in H}\big[C(x) = f(x)\big] \ge (1+\alpha)/2$ where $x \in H$ is uniformly random. Thus, (s,α)-easy means $(\{0,1\}^m, s, \alpha)$-easy.

It's known that if f is (s,α)-hard, then for all $\delta > 0$, there exists $H \subseteq \{0,1\}^m$ such that $|H|/2^m \ge (1-\alpha)/2$ and f is $\big(H,\, cs\delta^2(1-\alpha)^2,\, \delta\big)$-hard, where $c > 0$ is some constant.

Use this lemma to deduce the following version of the xor lemma (which is quantitatively slightly different from Lemma 10.15): If f is (s,α)-hard, then for all k and $\delta > 0$, $f^{\oplus k}$ is $\big(cs\delta^2(1-\alpha)^2,\, 2((1+\alpha)/2)^k + \delta\big)$-hard.

Hint: Partition $(\{0,1\}^m)^k$ according to the index of the first component that's in H.

10.11 Assuming every small circuit for $f\colon \{0,1\}^m \to \{0,1\}$ errs on at least a modest fraction of inputs, the xor lemma says that every small circuit for $f^{\oplus k}$ errs on almost half the inputs. Now, you'll prove that every small circuit for $f^k\colon (\{0,1\}^m)^k \to \{0,1\}^k$ errs on almost all inputs, where

$$f^k(x_1, x_2, \ldots, x_k) \;=\; \big(f(x_1), f(x_2), \ldots, f(x_k)\big)$$

is the concatenation (rather than xor) of the evaluations of f on all input components. Specifically: If f is (s,α)-hard, then for all k and small enough $\delta > 0$,

$$\mathbf{Pr}_{x_1,\ldots,x_k}\big[C(x_1,\ldots,x_k) = f^k(x_1,\ldots,x_k)\big] \;<\; \alpha^{k/3} + \delta + 2\cdot 0.95^k$$

for every circuit C of size $\le s\delta^3(1-\alpha)^3 - 3k$. Hint: Use the random subsum principle to show that if this were false, then the parity of a (randomly chosen) subset of $\ell \ge k/3$ output coordinates of C would compute $f^{\oplus \ell}$ on a high enough fraction of inputs to contradict the xor lemma. Use Lemma 9.4 to bound the probability that a uniformly random subset is too small.

Notes

The heuristic for INDEPENDENT SET SEARCH (Theorem 10.1), and the theorem that most n-node graphs have an independent set of size $(2 - o(1))\log n$, are due to [221]. For a survey about heuristics on random graphs, see [177].

For surveys about average-case complexity theory, see [260, 78]. This theory originated in [332], which showed that $(\mathsf{NP}, \mathsf{U})$ has "average-case complete" problems, albeit not very natural ones. The theorem that if $(\mathsf{NP}, \mathsf{U}) \subseteq \mathsf{HEUR}_{1/N^c}\mathsf{BPP}$ for all c, then $(\mathsf{NP}, \mathsf{PSAMP}) \subseteq \mathsf{HEUR}_{1/N^c}\mathsf{BPP}$ for all c is due to [262].

The average-case search-to-decision reduction for NP (Theorem 10.4) is due to [58].

Local decodability of the multilinear code is implicit in [54, 340]. The applicability to worst-case to average-case reductions for PSPACE is due to [39, 40].

For a survey about locally decodable codes, see [573]. Surprising upper bounds are known for the codeword length of 3-query locally decodable codes [155]. For lower bounds on the codeword length of locally decodable codes, see [297, 300, 21].

The xor lemma (Lemma 10.15) is due to Levin [333] but is widely known as "Yao's xor lemma." Other proofs are known [204, 259, 265]. Hardness amplification for "zero-sided-error" heuristics is also possible [77, 553].

The two proofs of Theorem 10.19 mentioned in §10.4.3 are due to [265, 509].

Though standard formulations of the conjecture "if NP is worst-case hard, then NP is average-case hard" remain open, somewhat weaker theorems in this vein are known [243]. Also, [161, 79] proved a barrier to confirming the above conjecture: NP can't have worst-case to average-case reductions of the kind PSPACE has, unless $\mathsf{NP} \subseteq \mathsf{coNP/poly}$ and thus PH collapses by Exercise 5.5. One formulation of the conjecture is that $\mathsf{P} \neq \mathsf{NP}$ implies $(\mathsf{NP}, \mathsf{PSAMP}) \nsubseteq \mathsf{HEUR}_{0.1}\mathsf{P}$, which would mean there exist $A \in \mathsf{NP}$ and $D \in \mathsf{PSAMP}$ such that every poly-time heuristic Π for A errs with probability > 0.1 over D_N for infinitely many N. Though this remains open, it is known that $\mathsf{P} \neq \mathsf{NP}$ implies a similar thing but where D depends on Π (that is, $\forall \Pi\ \exists D$ instead of $\exists D\ \forall \Pi$) [228].

Hardness amplification within NP is possible [401, 242, 349, 217], akin to (but more difficult than) the xor lemma we used for PSPACE.

Exercise 10.8 is due to [185, 186].

The proof of the xor lemma in Exercise 10.10 is due to [259] and has connections to computational learning theory [313].

Exercise 10.11 is due to [551]. Other proofs of such a "direct product lemma" (without going through the xor lemma) are known [204, 265].

Chapter 11

Pseudorandomness

We usually assume randomized algorithms can access an unlimited number of uniformly random bits. But in the real world, randomness is a resource, not to be taken for granted. Random bits from a physical source may be limited in number (low quantity) and not uniformly distributed (low quality). This chapter is about two kinds of algorithms for bridging the gap between real random sources and the ideal random sources assumed by randomized algorithms:

- A *randomness extractor* improves the quality. If a random source yields d bits containing "only $h < d$ bits worth of randomness," then an extractor turns this into almost h bits that are essentially uniformly distributed.
- A *pseudorandom generator* improves the quantity. Given a short but uniformly random bit string (such as an extractor's output), a pseudorandom generator stretches it to a long bit string that, although not uniformly distributed (since randomness can't be created out of thin air), is "as good as uniform" for the purpose of running efficient randomized algorithms.

We'll also see a surprising connection between these two seemingly disparate tools.

11.1 Statistical Distance and Pseudorandom Generators

11.1.1 Statistical Distance

A distribution over a finite sample space S is a function $D\colon S \to \mathbb{R}_{\geq 0}$ such that $\sum_{s\in S} D(s) = 1$, where $D(s) = \mathbf{Pr}_D[s]$ is the probability of outcome s. The probability of an event $E \subseteq S$ is $D(E) = \sum_{s\in E} D(s) = \mathbf{Pr}_D[E]$. Here's an important measure of the closeness of two distributions:

Definition. The *statistical distance* between distributions D_0 and D_1 over S is:

$$\Delta(D_0, D_1) \;=\; \max_{E\subseteq S}\big(\big|D_0(E) - D_1(E)\big|\big) \qquad \blacktriangleleft$$

This Δ (capital Greek delta) is not the Δ from §7.7.2.

Being close in statistical distance means each event E has approximately the same probabilities under the two distributions: $D_0(E)$ and $D_1(E)$ are within $\pm\Delta(D_0, D_1)$ of each other. Note that $0 \leq \Delta(D_0, D_1) \leq 1$ and $\Delta(D_0, D_1) = \Delta(D_1, D_0)$. The definition of $\Delta(D_0, D_1)$ involves $2^{|S|}$ many events, but the following lemma makes it easier to compute:

Lemma 11.1. *For all distributions D_0 and D_1 over S:*

$$\begin{aligned}\Delta(D_0, D_1) &= D_0(E) - D_1(E) \textit{ where } E = \big\{s : D_0(s) > D_1(s)\big\}\\ &= \tfrac{1}{2}\textstyle\sum_{s\in S}\big|D_0(s) - D_1(s)\big|\end{aligned}$$

s	a	b	c	d	e
$D_0(s)$	0.35	0.25	0.15	0.10	0.15
$D_1(s)$	0.15	0.20	0.15	0.20	0.30

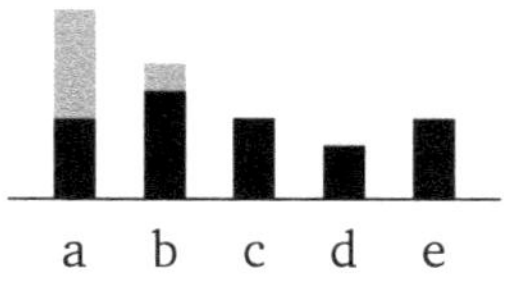

Figure 11.1: Two example distributions and their superimposed histograms

Proof. An event E that maximizes $D_0(E) - D_1(E) = \sum_{s \in E}\big(D_0(s) - D_1(s)\big)$ (without absolute value) is $E = \{s : D_0(s) > D_1(s)\}$, corresponding to all the positive contributions. An event E' that maximizes $-\big(D_0(E') - D_1(E')\big) = D_1(E') - D_0(E')$ is $E' = \overline{E} = \{s : D_0(s) \le D_1(s)\}$ (including s such that $D_0(s) = D_1(s)$ doesn't affect anything). These two quantities are equal because:

$$\big(D_0(E) - D_1(E)\big) - \big(D_1(\overline{E}) - D_0(\overline{E})\big) \;=\; D_0(S) - D_1(S) \;=\; 1 - 1 \;=\; 0$$

Thus $\Delta(D_0, D_1) = D_0(E) - D_1(E) = D_1(\overline{E}) - D_0(\overline{E})$. Also:

$$\begin{aligned}
\textstyle\sum_{s \in S} \big|D_0(s) - D_1(s)\big| &= \textstyle\sum_{s \in E}\big(D_0(s) - D_1(s)\big) + \sum_{s \in \overline{E}}\big(D_1(s) - D_0(s)\big) \\
&= \big(D_0(E) - D_1(E)\big) + \big(D_1(\overline{E}) - D_0(\overline{E})\big) \\
&= \Delta(D_0, D_1) + \Delta(D_0, D_1)
\end{aligned}$$

■

Example. Figure 11.1's left side shows two distributions D_0 and D_1 over $S = \{\mathrm{a}, \mathrm{b}, \mathrm{c}, \mathrm{d}, \mathrm{e}\}$. Figure 11.1's right side shows a dark gray histogram of D_0 and a light gray histogram of D_1, superimposed so the overlap is black. We have $E = \{s : D_0(s) > D_1(s)\} = \{\mathrm{a}, \mathrm{b}\}$ and $\Delta(D_0, D_1) = 0.25$:

The dark gray (but non-black) area is:

$$D_0(E) - D_1(E) \;=\; (0.35 + 0.25) - (0.15 + 0.20) \;=\; 0.25$$

The light gray (but non-black) area, including c's empty contribution, is:

$$D_1(\overline{E}) - D_0(\overline{E}) \;=\; (0.15 + 0.20 + 0.30) - (0.15 + 0.10 + 0.15) \;=\; 0.25$$

The sum of the dark gray and light gray areas is $\sum_{s \in S}\big|D_0(s) - D_1(s)\big| = 2 \cdot 0.25$. ♦

The following lemma is called the *triangle inequality* by analogy with the fact that in a triangle with vertices v_0, v_1, v_2, one side's length is at most the sum of the other two sides' lengths:

(distance between v_0 and v_2) $\le$ (distance between v_0 and v_1) + (distance between v_1 and v_2)

Lemma 11.2. *For all distributions D_0, D_1, D_2 over S, we have $\Delta(D_0, D_2) \le \Delta(D_0, D_1) + \Delta(D_1, D_2)$.*

Proof. For every event E:

$$\begin{aligned}
\big|D_0(E) - D_2(E)\big| &= \big|\big(D_0(E) - D_1(E)\big) + \big(D_1(E) - D_2(E)\big)\big| \\
&\le \big|D_0(E) - D_1(E)\big| + \big|D_1(E) - D_2(E)\big)\big| && \text{(Lemma A.28)} \\
&\le \Delta(D_0, D_1) + \Delta(D_1, D_2)
\end{aligned}$$

■

Here's another characterization of statistical distance. Suppose we toss a fair coin to pick whether to generate a sample from D_0 or from D_1. Then, we show someone the sample and ask them to guess whether it came from D_0 or from D_1. Statistical distance measures how much better their success probability can be than $1/2$ (a blind guess):

Lemma 11.3. *For any distributions D_0 and D_1 over S, define a joint distribution D over $\{0,1\} \times S$ by $D(i,s) = D_i(s)/2$ (sampling uniform $i \in \{0,1\}$ and then $s \sim D_i$). Then:*

$$\max_{f:S\to\{0,1\}}\big(\mathbf{Pr}_{(i,s)\sim D}[f(s)=i]\big) = \big(1+\Delta(D_0,D_1)\big)/2$$

Proof. Every $f: S \to \{0,1\}$ corresponds to an event $E = \{s : f(s) = 1\}$. By the law of total probability:

$$\begin{aligned}\mathbf{Pr}_{(i,s)\sim D}[f(s)=i] &= \mathbf{Pr}_i[i=0]\cdot\mathbf{Pr}_{s\sim D_0}[f(s)=0]+\mathbf{Pr}_i[i=1]\cdot\mathbf{Pr}_{s\sim D_1}[f(s)=1]\\ &= \tfrac{1}{2}\cdot D_0(\overline{E})+\tfrac{1}{2}\cdot D_1(E)\\ &= \big(1-D_0(E)+D_1(E)\big)/2\end{aligned}$$

So $\max_{f:S\to\{0,1\}}\big(\mathbf{Pr}_{(i,s)\sim D}[f(s)=i]\big) = \big(1+\max_{E\subseteq S}(D_1(E)-D_0(E))\big)/2 = \big(1+\Delta(D_0,D_1)\big)/2$. ■

11.1.2 Indistinguishability

Every function $f: S \to \{0,1\}$ corresponds to an event $E = \{s : f(s) = 1\}$, so $\mathbf{Pr}[f(D)=1] = \mathbf{Pr}_{s\sim D}[f(s)=1] = D(E)$ for any distribution D over S. Rephrasing the definition of statistical distance:

$$\Delta(D_0,D_1) = \max_{f:S\to\{0,1\}}\big(\big|\mathbf{Pr}[f(D_0)=1]-\mathbf{Pr}[f(D_1)=1]\big|\big)$$

If $\Delta(D_0,D_1) \le \varepsilon$, we say D_0 and D_1 are *ε-indistinguishable* because every f can hardly distinguish whether its input comes from D_0 or D_1:

$$\forall f: S\to\{0,1\}:\ \ \mathbf{Pr}[f(D_0)=1] \text{ and } \mathbf{Pr}[f(D_1)=1] \text{ are within } \pm\varepsilon$$

We generalize this by considering only some functions f, rather than all possible f:

Definition. For every set F of functions $f: S \to \{0,1\}$, and distributions D_0 and D_1 over S:

$$\Delta_F(D_0,D_1) = \max_{f\in F}\big(\big|\mathbf{Pr}[f(D_0)=1]-\mathbf{Pr}[f(D_1)=1]\big|\big)$$

If $\Delta_F(D_0,D_1) \le \varepsilon$, we say D_0 and D_1 are *ε-indistinguishable by F* because:

$$\forall f\in F:\ \ \mathbf{Pr}[f(D_0)=1] \text{ and } \mathbf{Pr}[f(D_1)=1] \text{ are within } \pm\varepsilon$$ ◀

This definition plays a vital role in cryptography (Chapter 12).

Note that $\Delta_F(D_0,D_1) \le \Delta(D_0,D_1)$.

Example. Figure 11.2 shows two distributions D_0 and D_1 over $S = \{\mathrm{a},\mathrm{b},\mathrm{c}\}$ and a set of functions $F = \{g,h\}$. We calculate:

$$\begin{aligned}\big|\mathbf{Pr}[g(D_0)=1]-\mathbf{Pr}[g(D_1)=1]\big| &= |0.1-0.3| &&= 0.2\\ \big|\mathbf{Pr}[h(D_0)=1]-\mathbf{Pr}[h(D_1)=1]\big| &= |(0.1+0.5)-(0.3+0.2)| &&= 0.1\end{aligned}$$

Thus $\Delta_F(D_0,D_1) = \max(0.2, 0.1) = 0.2$. But $\Delta(D_0,D_1) = 0.3$ because $s = \mathrm{b}$ is the only outcome with $D_0(s) > D_1(s)$, and we have $D_0(\mathrm{b}) - D_1(\mathrm{b}) = 0.3$. Thus D_0 and D_1 are 0.2-indistinguishable by F but only 0.3-indistinguishable. ♦

s	$D_0(s)$	$D_1(s)$	$g(s)$	$h(s)$
a	0.1	0.3	1	1
b	0.5	0.2	0	1
c	0.4	0.5	0	0

Figure 11.2: Example distributions and functions

11.1.3 Pseudorandom Generators

A pseudorandom generator is a function $G\colon \{0,1\}^\ell \to \{0,1\}^n$ where $\ell < n$, which "stretches" a uniformly random ℓ-bit *seed* s to a "pseudorandom" n-bit string $G(s)$. Letting U_ℓ and U_n be the uniform distributions over $\{0,1\}^\ell$ and $\{0,1\}^n$, we want the distribution $G(U_\ell)$ to be indistinguishable from U_n, so the former can be used where the latter is expected. This would let us simulate n random bits using only ℓ random bits.

Indistinguishability in terms of statistical distance would mean G "fools" every function $f\colon \{0,1\}^n \to \{0,1\}$, in the sense that f outputs 1 with approximately the same probability whether its input is sampled from $G(U_\ell)$ (pseudorandom) or from U_n (truly random). This is impossible if $\ell < n$: Defining $f\colon \{0,1\}^n \to \{0,1\}$ by $f(x) = 1$ iff $x = G(s)$ for at least one s, we have $\mathbf{Pr}\big[f(G(U_\ell)) = 1\big] = 1$ but $\mathbf{Pr}\big[f(U_n) = 1\big] \le 2^\ell/2^n \le 1/2$, so f is not fooled.

For our purposes, it's enough to fool efficiently computable functions f rather than all f. Staying abstract for now, let F be a set of functions $f\colon \{0,1\}^n \to \{0,1\}$ that we consider efficiently computable (perhaps by circuits of size n^3, or by branching programs of size n^4).

Definition. We say $G\colon \{0,1\}^\ell \to \{0,1\}^n$ *ε-fools* $f\colon \{0,1\}^n \to \{0,1\}$ iff $\mathbf{Pr}\big[f(G(U_\ell)) = 1\big]$ and $\mathbf{Pr}\big[f(U_n) = 1\big]$ are within $\pm\varepsilon$.

G is an *ε-pseudorandom generator* (ε-PRG) for a set of functions F iff G ε-fools every $f \in F$, in other words, $G(U_\ell)$ and U_n are ε-indistinguishable by F. ◀

In practice, a "pseudorandom number generator" takes a seed of one or more hardware-generated random numbers, and deterministically stretches it to a long sequence of numbers. Typical generators (such as in `java.util.Random` and Python's `random` module) fool certain statistical tests, such as whether the sequence contains approximately as many odd numbers as even numbers—a pseudorandom sequence should have this property with high probability since a truly random sequence does. Now, F corresponds to the tests we care about. For derandomization and cryptography (the main applications of pseudorandom generators in complexity theory), F corresponds to *all* efficient algorithms, not just common statistical tests. This is why programming languages have special "not fooling around" generators for cryptographic use (such as in `java.security.SecureRandom` and Python's `secrets` module).

Example. Let F contain all n functions of the form $f(x_1x_2\cdots x_n) = x_i$ (positive literals). Fooling these functions means each individual bit is equally likely to be 0 or 1. Let $G\colon \{0,1\} \to \{0,1\}^n$ output n copies of the seed bit: $G(s) = ss\cdots s$. This G is a 0-PRG for F because if $f(x) = x_i$:

$$\mathbf{Pr}\big[f(G(U_1)) = 1\big] \;=\; \mathbf{Pr}_{s\sim U_1}[s = 1] \;=\; 1/2 \;=\; \mathbf{Pr}_{u\sim U_n}[u_i = 1] \;=\; \mathbf{Pr}\big[f(U_n) = 1\big]$$

This G also 0-fools negative literals. (In general, if G ε-fools f, then G ε-fools $\overline{f}$.) Also, a constant function ($f(x) = 0$ for all x, or $f(x) = 1$ for all x) is trivially 0-fooled by every G. So this G is a 0-PRG with seed length 1 for all literals and constants.

A function expressed by a positive literal x_i is a *dictatorship*: If x_j is person j's "vote," then the outcome is simply the vote of person i (the dictator). A function expressed by a negative literal $\overline{x_i}$ is an *anti-dictatorship*. A more general kind of regime is a *d-junta*—a function that depends on at most d of its variables. Thus 1-juntas are precisely the literals (dictatorships and anti-dictatorships) and constants, from the previous paragraph.

Now, we design a 0-PRG for 2-juntas. Define $k = \lceil \log n \rceil$ and let $h\colon \{0,1\}^{k+1} \times \{0,1\}^k \to \{0,1\}$ be the pairwise uniform hash function from Lemma 8.7. Identifying $[n]$ with a subset of $\{0,1\}^k$ and ignoring the rest of $\{0,1\}^k$, we view the hash function as $h\colon \{0,1\}^{k+1} \times [n] \to \{0,1\}$. Define $G\colon \{0,1\}^{k+1} \to \{0,1\}^n$ by $G(s) = \big(h_s(1), h_s(2), \ldots, h_s(n)\big)$. Among the n bits of $G(U_{k+1})$, each pair is uniformly distributed over $\{0,1\}^2$. If $f\colon \{0,1\}^n \to \{0,1\}$ depends on at most two variables, in other words, $f(x) = f'(x_i x_j)$ for some $i \neq j$ and some $f'\colon \{0,1\}^2 \to \{0,1\}$, then

$$\mathbf{Pr}\big[f(G(U_{k+1})) = 1\big] \;=\; \mathbf{Pr}\big[f'(U_2) = 1\big] \;=\; \mathbf{Pr}\big[f(U_n) = 1\big]$$

since $\big(G(s)_i, G(s)_j\big) = \big(h_s(i), h_s(j)\big) \sim U_2$ when $s \sim U_{k+1}$. ♦

Theorem 11.4. *For every nonempty F and $0 < \varepsilon \leq 1/2$, there exists an ε-pseudorandom generator for F with seed length $\ell = \lfloor \log_2(\ln(2|F|)/\varepsilon^2) \rfloor + 1 = O\big(\log(\log(|F|)/\varepsilon)\big)$ (assuming $\ell < n$).*

Proof. We use the probabilistic method. Sample $G\colon \{0,1\}^\ell \to \{0,1\}^n$ uniformly at random: For each $s \in \{0,1\}^\ell$ independently, sample $G(s) \sim U_n$. Consider any $f \in F$. For each $s \in \{0,1\}^\ell$, imagine a coin toss where heads means $f(G(s)) = 1$. These 2^ℓ coin tosses are fully independent, and each has heads probability $p = \mathbf{Pr}\big[f(U_n) = 1\big]$. For any outcome G, the fraction of tosses that are heads is $\mathbf{Pr}\big[f(G(U_\ell)) = 1\big]$. Thus G ε-fools f iff the fraction of heads is within $\pm\varepsilon$ of p.

$$\begin{aligned}
\mathbf{Pr}_G\big[G \text{ isn't an } \varepsilon\text{-PRG for } F\big] &= \mathbf{Pr}_G\big[G \text{ doesn't } \varepsilon\text{-fool some } f \in F\big] \\
&\leq \textstyle\sum_{f \in F} \mathbf{Pr}_G\big[G \text{ doesn't } \varepsilon\text{-fool } f\big] && \text{(union bound)} \\
&\leq \textstyle\sum_{f \in F} 2e^{-\varepsilon^2 2^\ell} && \text{(Lemma 7.20)} \\
&< \textstyle\sum_{f \in F} 1/|F| && \text{(definition of } \ell\text{)} \\
&= 1
\end{aligned}$$

■

In this case, $\ell = O\big(\log(\log(|F|)/\varepsilon)\big)$ means there exists a constant $c > 0$ such that $\ell \leq c \cdot \log\big((\log|F|)/\varepsilon\big)$ if $|F| \geq 2$ and $0 < \varepsilon \leq 1/2$.

Example. Suppose F is all functions computed by size-n^3 circuits (say, bounded-fan-in circuits with $\leq n^3$ nodes). Then $|F| \leq 2^{O(n^3 \log n)} \leq 2^{\mathrm{poly}\, n}$ because in such a circuit's encoding, each node has $O(\log n)$ bits to specify its type and its inneighbors. By Theorem 11.4, there exists an ε-PRG for F with seed length $O\big(\log(\mathrm{poly}(n)/\varepsilon)\big) = O\big(\log(n/\varepsilon)\big)$. ♦

The proof of Theorem 11.4 is nonconstructive: It doesn't describe any particular ε-PRG for F, and there's no guarantee that such a G is efficiently computable. We usually measure efficiency in terms of input size, but here we measure it in terms of G's output size n.

Typically, a set of functions to fool is actually an infinite *family* of sets, parameterized by n. For example, "2-juntas" means $F_2, F_3, F_4, \ldots$ where F_n contains all 2-juntas on n variables. We designed $G_2, G_3, G_4, \ldots$ where G_n is a 0-PRG for F_n. We collect these into a single generator G where $G(n;s) = G_n(s)$, which is computed by a uniform program running in poly n time (with $O(\log n)$-bounded word size). Here, n is the output size, and the input $(n;s)$ is $O(\log n)$ bits.

A set of functions may have additional parameters besides n. Circuits are parameterized by the number of input variables n and the size m: $F_{n,m}$ contains all functions $f: \{0,1\}^n \to \{0,1\}$ computed by bounded-fan-in circuits with $\le m$ nodes. For all n, m, and $\varepsilon > 0$, suppose $G_{n,m,\varepsilon}$ is an ε-PRG for $F_{n,m}$ with seed length $\ell_{n,m,\varepsilon}$. We collect these into a single generator G where $G(n,m,\varepsilon;s) = G_{n,m,\varepsilon}(s)$. The time efficiency (and word size) of a uniform program computing G would depend on the parameters n, m, ε.

11.1.4 Derandomization

Like time and space efficiencies, a program's *randomness efficiency* (with respect to a problem) is the function $R: \mathbb{N}_+ \to \mathbb{N}$ where $R(N)$ is the maximum number of random bits used on any valid input of size N. Pseudorandom generators let us improve randomness efficiency at some cost in time or space efficiency.

Suppose a decision problem A has a $1/3$-error randomized program Π that uses at most n random bits on valid inputs x of size N. For each x, the function $f_x: \{0,1\}^n \to \{0,1\}$ defined by $f_x(r) = \Pi(x;r)$ captures how the output depends on the randomness. If a generator $G_N: \{0,1\}^\ell \to \{0,1\}^n$ ε-fools f_x for every valid x of size N, then we can use $G_N(U_\ell)$ in place of U_n for the randomness. Letting Π' be a randomized program where $\Pi'(x;s)$ computes $r \leftarrow G_N(s)$ and runs $\Pi(x;r)$:

$$\mathbf{Pr}\big[\Pi'(x;U_\ell) \neq A(x)\big] \;=\; \mathbf{Pr}\big[f_x(G_N(U_\ell)) \neq A(x)\big] \;\le\; \mathbf{Pr}\big[f_x(U_n) \neq A(x)\big] + \varepsilon \;\le\; 1/3 + \varepsilon$$

If Π and G_N are both efficient, so is Π'. By paying a small price in error probability, we decreased the number of random bits from n to ℓ.

To decrease the number of random bits to zero (*full derandomization*), we can be more proactive: Instead of picking a random seed and hoping it's good, we try all possible seeds. Let Π'' be this deterministic program:

Full derandomization using a pseudorandom generator (11.1)

$\Pi''(x)$:
  for each $s \in \{0,1\}^\ell$:
    compute $r \leftarrow G_N(s)$
    run $\Pi(x;r)$
  accept iff a majority of the runs of Π accepted

If $\varepsilon < 1/6$ then $\Pi''(x) = A(x)$ because $\Pi(x; G_N(s)) = A(x)$ for most s:

$$\mathbf{Pr}\big[f_x(G_N(U_\ell)) \neq A(x)\big] \;\le\; \mathbf{Pr}\big[f_x(U_n) \neq A(x)\big] + \varepsilon \;\le\; 1/3 + \varepsilon \;<\; 1/2$$

Iterating over all s incurs a factor 2^ℓ time overhead, which is a poly$N$ factor if $\ell \le O(\log N)$. Thus logarithmic seed length is the ultimate goal for PRG constructions.

We can turn poly-time randomized programs into poly-size circuits, so fooling poly-size circuits suffices to derandomize BPP. We can turn log-space randomized programs into poly-size streaming branching programs, so fooling poly-size streaming branching programs suffices to derandomize BPL. Let's formalize these two facts.

Lemma 11.5. P = BPP *if there exists a $1/7$-pseudorandom generator for n-variable m-node circuits with seed length $O\big(\log(nm)\big)$ and computable in time* poly(nm).

Proof. It suffices to show CIRCUIT GAP MAJORITY $\in$ P since it's BPP-complete (Lemma 7.39). Say $G_{n,m}\colon \{0,1\}^\ell \to \{0,1\}^n$ is a 1/7-PRG for n-variable m-node circuits. Given such a circuit C, we evaluate $C(G_{n,m}(s))$ for every $s \in \{0,1\}^\ell$ and accept iff a majority of the evaluations accepted. This takes poly(nm) time since computing $G_{n,m}(s)$ and evaluating C both take poly(nm) time, and there are $2^\ell = 2^{O(\log(nm))} = \text{poly}(nm)$ possibilities of s. This is correct since:

$$\mathbf{Pr}\big[C(U_n)=1\big] \geq 2/3 \Rightarrow \mathbf{Pr}\big[C(G_{n,m}(U_\ell))=1\big] \geq 2/3 - 1/7 > 1/2$$
$$\mathbf{Pr}\big[C(U_n)=1\big] \leq 1/3 \Rightarrow \mathbf{Pr}\big[C(G_{n,m}(U_\ell))=1\big] \leq 1/3 + 1/7 < 1/2$$

■

Lemma 11.6. L = BPL *if there exists a* 1/7*-pseudorandom generator for length-n width-w streaming branching programs with seed length* $O(\log(nw))$ *and computable in space* $O(\log(nw))$.

Proof. It suffices to show STREAMING BRANCHING PROGRAM GAP MAJORITY $\in$ L since it's BPL-complete (Lemma 7.40). Say $G_{n,w}\colon \{0,1\}^\ell \to \{0,1\}^n$ is a 1/7-PRG for length-n width-w streaming branching programs. Given such a streaming branching program B, we evaluate $B(G_{n,w}(s))$ for every $s \in \{0,1\}^\ell$ and accept iff a majority of the evaluations accepted. This takes $O(\log(nw))$ space since computing $G_{n,w}(s)$ and evaluating B both take $O(\log(nw))$ space, and remembering s takes $\ell = O(\log(nw))$ space. This is correct since:

$$\mathbf{Pr}\big[B(U_n)=1\big] \geq 2/3 \Rightarrow \mathbf{Pr}\big[B(G_{n,w}(U_\ell))=1\big] \geq 2/3 - 1/7 > 1/2$$
$$\mathbf{Pr}\big[B(U_n)=1\big] \leq 1/3 \Rightarrow \mathbf{Pr}\big[B(G_{n,w}(U_\ell))=1\big] \leq 1/3 + 1/7 < 1/2$$

■

By Theorem 11.4, PRGs for Lemma 11.5 and Lemma 11.6 exist if we ignore the computability requirement. The whole challenge is to find *explicit* such PRGs, which are efficiently computable.

11.2 Fooling Parities, Clauses, and Terms

11.2.1 Fooling Parities

For a set of indices $I \subseteq [n]$, the function $\oplus_I\colon \{0,1\}^n \to \{0,1\}$ outputs the parity of the input bits indexed by I, in other words, the dot product (over $\mathbb{Z}_2$) of I's characteristic bit string and the input. For example, $\oplus_{\{2,3,5\}}(x_1x_2x_3x_4x_5) = x_2 \oplus x_3 \oplus x_5 = 01101 \odot x$.

An *ε-bias generator* (or *small-bias generator* when ε is unspecified) is an ε-pseudorandom generator for the set of all parity functions $F = \{\oplus_I : I \subseteq [n]\}$. We may ignore $\oplus_\emptyset$, which is the constant 0 function and is automatically 0-fooled. For every $I \neq \emptyset$, we have $\mathbf{Pr}\big[\oplus_I(U_n)=1\big] = 1/2$ by the random subsum principle, so $G\colon \{0,1\}^\ell \to \{0,1\}^n$ ε-fools $\oplus_I$ iff $\mathbf{Pr}\big[\oplus_I(G(U_\ell)) = 1\big]$ is within $\pm\varepsilon$ of 1/2. Thus, G is an ε-bias generator iff in the pseudorandom string $G(U_\ell)$, every nonempty set of bit positions is almost equally likely to have an odd or an even number of 1s.

Since $|F| = 2^n$, there exists an ε-bias generator with seed length $O(\log(n/\varepsilon))$ by Theorem 11.4. We construct an explicit ε-bias generator with the same seed length (up to a constant factor).

Theorem 11.7. *There exists an n-bit ε-bias generator with seed length* $O(\log(n/\varepsilon))$ *and computable in time* $n\,\text{polylog}(n/\varepsilon)$.

Proof. Recall from §9.4 that $\mathbb{F}_{2^\ell}$ is a finite field with elements $\{0,1\}^\ell$, where addition is bitwise xor (vector addition in $\mathbb{Z}_2^\ell$). Let $\ell \geq \log(n/2\varepsilon)$ be the least integer for defining $\mathbb{F}_{2^\ell}$ with the simple irreducible polynomial from Theorem 9.19.*(ii)*.

Define $G\colon (\{0,1\}^\ell)^2 \to \{0,1\}^n$ by $G(a,b)_i = a^i \odot b \in \{0,1\}$ for each index $i \in \{0,\ldots,n-1\}$, where a^i uses multiplication in $\mathbb{F}_{2^\ell}$, and $\odot$ is the dot product over $\mathbb{Z}_2$. This has seed length $2\ell = O\big(\log(n/\varepsilon)\big)$ and is computable in time $n\,\mathrm{polylog}(n/\varepsilon)$, because each field multiplication and each dot product takes time $\mathrm{poly}\,\ell = \mathrm{polylog}(n/\varepsilon)$, and it takes $O(n)$ such operations to compute all the powers of a and their dot products with b.

To see that G is an ε-bias generator, consider any nonempty $I \subseteq [n]$ and let P be the nonzero polynomial $\sum_{i\in I} x^i$ over $\mathbb{F}_{2^\ell}$.

$$\begin{aligned}
\oplus_I(G(a,b)) &= \textstyle\sum_{i\in I} G(a,b)_i && (\textstyle\sum \text{ is over } \mathbb{Z}_2)\\
&= \textstyle\sum_{i\in I}(a^i \odot b) && (\text{definition of } G)\\
&= \big(\textstyle\sum_{i\in I} a^i\big)\odot b && (\text{linearity of dot product, } \textstyle\sum \text{ is over } \mathbb{F}_{2^\ell})\\
&= P(a)\odot b && (\text{definition of } P)
\end{aligned}$$

For a uniformly random seed (a,b):

$$\begin{aligned}
\mathbf{Pr}\big[\oplus_I(G(a,b))=1\big] &= \mathbf{Pr}\big[P(a)\odot b = 1\big]\\
&= \mathbf{Pr}\big[P(a)\neq 0^\ell\big]\cdot \mathbf{Pr}\big[P(a)\odot b = 1 \;\big|\; P(a)\neq 0^\ell\big] && (\text{chain rule})\\
&= \mathbf{Pr}\big[P(a)\neq 0^\ell\big]/2 && (\text{random subsum principle})
\end{aligned}$$

Since P is nonzero and has degree $< n$, it has $< n$ many roots (Theorem A.20), so:

$$1-2\varepsilon \;\le\; 1-n/2^\ell \;\le\; \mathbf{Pr}\big[P(a)\neq 0^\ell\big] \;\le\; 1$$

Thus $1/2-\varepsilon \;\le\; \mathbf{Pr}\big[\oplus_I(G(U_{2\ell}))=1\big] \;\le\; 1/2 \;\le\; 1/2+\varepsilon$. ∎

We actually already constructed this generator, at the culmination of Chapter 9, because ε-bias generators are just ε-balanced linear binary error correcting codes in disguise! To align parameter names, we use n for a code's message length here.

Lemma 11.8. *Consider any $G\colon \{0,1\}^\ell \to \{0,1\}^n$ and linear code $E\colon \{0,1\}^n \to \{0,1\}^{2^\ell}$ with generator matrix H, such that $G(s)$ is H's column indexed by $s \in \{0,1\}^\ell$. Then G is an ε-bias generator iff E is ε-balanced.*

Proof. The characteristic bit string of any nonempty $I \subseteq [n]$ is a nonzero message $m \in \{0,1\}^n$. For every seed $s \in \{0,1\}^\ell$, we have $\oplus_I(G(s)) = m \odot G(s) = (mH)_s = E(m)_s$. Thus:

$$\mathbf{Pr}\big[\oplus_I(G(U_\ell))=1\big] \;=\; \mathbf{Pr}_{s\sim U_\ell}\big[E(m)_s = 1\big] \;=\; \text{relative weight of } E(m)$$

So G ε-fools $\oplus_I$ iff $E(m)$ has relative weight within $\pm\varepsilon$ of $1/2$. Since this holds for all nonempty I and corresponding nonzero m, the lemma follows. ∎

We can turn an ε-balanced linear binary code with generator matrix H into an ε-bias generator G (or vice versa) by defining $G(s) = s$th column of H. The concatenation of the polynomial code with the dot product code is ε-balanced and linear (Theorem 9.26), with an $n \times 2^{2\ell}$ generator matrix where $n = \ell\lfloor 2^{\ell+1}\varepsilon\rfloor$, so we get an ε-bias generator with seed length $2\ell = O\big(\log(n/\varepsilon)\big)$. The construction from Theorem 11.7 is a streamlined version of this, where the polynomial code's message is a polynomial whose coefficients are just 0s and 1s, rather than arbitrary field elements.

11.2.2 Derandomizing Matrix Multiplication Verification

ε-bias generators derandomize both parts of the random subsum principle (Lemma 7.2):

Observation 11.9. *Assuming* $G\colon \{0,1\}^\ell \to \{0,1\}^n$ *is an* ε*-bias generator:*

(i) $\mathbf{Pr}_{s\sim U_\ell}\big[v \odot G(s) = 0\big]$ *is within* $\pm\varepsilon$ *of* $1/2$ *for all* $v \neq 0^n$.

(ii) $\mathbf{Pr}_{s\sim U_\ell}\big[v \odot G(s) = w \odot G(s)\big]$ *is within* $\pm\varepsilon$ *of* $1/2$ *for all* $v \neq w$.

Proof. *(i)* is by the definition of ε-bias generators. *(ii)* follows from *(i)* because

$$\mathbf{Pr}_{s\sim U_\ell}\big[v \odot G(s) = w \odot G(s)\big] \;=\; \mathbf{Pr}_{s\sim U_\ell}\big[(v \ominus w) \odot G(s) = 0\big]$$

is within $\pm\varepsilon$ of $1/2$ since $v \ominus w \neq 0^n$. ■

As an application, we derandomize the algorithm for MATRIX MULTIPLICATION VERIFICATION $\in$ coRTIME$[N]$ (§7.1.4), which had randomness efficiency $n = \Omega(\sqrt{N})$.

Theorem 11.10. MATRIX MULTIPLICATION VERIFICATION $\in$ coRTIME$[N]$ *by an algorithm with randomness efficiency* $O(\log N)$.

Proof. Given $n \times n$ matrices A, B, C over $\mathbb{Z}_2$, the algorithm from §7.1.4 samples a column vector $x \sim U_n$, computes $A(Bx) = (AB)x$ and Cx, and accepts iff $(AB)x = Cx$. We replace $x \sim U_n$ with the output of the $1/3$-bias generator $G\colon \{0,1\}^\ell \to \{0,1\}^n$ from Theorem 11.7. The new algorithm samples $s \sim U_\ell$, computes $y \leftarrow G(s)$ and $A(By) = (AB)y$ and Cy, and accepts iff $(AB)y = Cy$. If $AB = C$ then this accepts with probability 1. If $AB \neq C$ then some row i of AB is different from row i of C, so by Observation 11.9.*(ii)* applied to the vectors $(AB)_i \neq C_i$:

$$\mathbf{Pr}[\text{algorithm accepts}] \;\leq\; \mathbf{Pr}_{s\sim U_\ell}\big[(AB)_i \odot G(s) = C_i \odot G(s)\big] \;\leq\; 1/2 + 1/3 \;=\; 5/6$$

This one-sided-error algorithm has randomness efficiency $\ell = O\big(\log(3n)\big) = O(\log N)$ and time efficiency $O(N)$ since computing $y \leftarrow G(s)$ takes $n\,\mathrm{polylog}(3n) = o(N)$ time, and computing $A(By)$ and Cy take $O(n^2) = O(N)$ time. By amplification, we decrease the error probability from $5/6$ to $1/3$ with constant factor losses in the randomness and time efficiencies. ■

11.2.3 Fooling Clauses and Terms

ε-bias generators are designed to fool parities, but as a bonus, they also fool clauses and terms:

Theorem 11.11. *Every* ε*-bias generator is a* 2ε*-pseudorandom generator for clauses and terms.*

Proof idea. We express any clause or term as a linear combination (over $\mathbb{R}$) of parities. The linear combination's coefficients determine how well a PRG that fools each parity also fools the clause or term. ■

Proof. Let $G\colon \{0,1\}^\ell \to \{0,1\}^n$ be an ε-bias generator. We show that G 2ε-fools clauses, which automatically implies that G 2ε-fools terms, since terms are negations of clauses.

First, we show that G 2ε-fools the $\vee$ function on all n variables: $\vee(x) = x_1 \vee x_2 \vee \cdots \vee x_n$. By the random subsum principle, for all $x \in \{0,1\}^n$ and uniformly random $y \in \{0,1\}^n$:

$$\vee(x) = 1 \;\Rightarrow\; \mathbf{Pr}_y[x \odot y = 1] = 1/2$$
$$\vee(x) = 0 \;\Rightarrow\; \mathbf{Pr}_y[x \odot y = 1] = 0$$

Viewing y as the characteristic bit string of a uniformly random $I \subseteq [n]$:

$$\vee(x) = 2\mathbf{Pr}_y[x \odot y = 1] = 2\mathbf{E}_y[x \odot y] = 2\mathbf{E}_I\big[\oplus_I(x)\big] = \tfrac{2}{2^n}\sum_I \oplus_I(x)$$

It follows that:

$$\begin{aligned}
&\Big|\mathbf{Pr}\big[\vee(G(U_\ell)) = 1\big] - \mathbf{Pr}\big[\vee(U_n) = 1\big]\Big| \\
={}& \Big|\mathbf{E}\big[\vee(G(U_\ell))\big] - \mathbf{E}\big[\vee(U_n)\big]\Big| \\
={}& \Big|\mathbf{E}\big[\tfrac{2}{2^n}\textstyle\sum_I \oplus_I(G(U_\ell))\big] - \mathbf{E}\big[\tfrac{2}{2^n}\textstyle\sum_I \oplus_I(U_n)\big]\Big| \\
={}& \tfrac{2}{2^n}\Big|\textstyle\sum_I\Big(\mathbf{E}\big[\oplus_I(G(U_\ell))\big] - \mathbf{E}\big[\oplus_I(U_n)\big]\Big)\Big| && \text{(linearity of expectation)} \\
\le{}& \tfrac{2}{2^n}\textstyle\sum_I\Big|\mathbf{E}\big[\oplus_I(G(U_\ell))\big] - \mathbf{E}\big[\oplus_I(U_n)\big]\Big| && \text{(Lemma A.28)} \\
\le{}& \tfrac{2}{2^n}\textstyle\sum_I \varepsilon && (G\ \varepsilon\text{-fools each } \oplus_I) \\
={}& 2\varepsilon
\end{aligned}$$

Likewise, G 2ε-fools the $\vee$ of any subset of variables (clauses with only positive literals): For $J \subseteq [n]$, we have $\vee_J(x) = \bigvee_{j\in J} x_j = \frac{2}{2^{|J|}}\sum_{I\subseteq J} \oplus_I(x)$. A clause with at least one negative literal is the same linear combination of parity functions, but where $\oplus_I$ is applied to the literals indexed by I. A parity of literals is either a negated parity of variables (if an odd number of literals are negative) or an unnegated parity of variables (if an even number of literals are negative), both of which are ε-fooled by G, so the same analysis shows that the clause is 2ε-fooled. ■

Example.

$$\begin{aligned}
I ={}& \quad \emptyset \quad \{2\} \quad \{3\} \quad \{5\} \qquad \{2,3\} \qquad \{2,5\} \qquad \{3,5\} \qquad \{2,3,5\} \\
\overline{x_2} \vee \overline{x_3} \vee \overline{x_5} ={}& \tfrac{2}{2^3}\big(0 + \overline{x_2} + \overline{x_3} + \overline{x_5} + (\overline{x_2} \oplus \overline{x_3}) + (\overline{x_2} \oplus \overline{x_5}) + (\overline{x_3} \oplus \overline{x_5}) + (\overline{x_2} \oplus \overline{x_3} \oplus \overline{x_5})\big) \\
={}& \tfrac{1}{4}\big(\quad \overline{x_2} + \overline{x_3} + \overline{x_5} + (x_2 \oplus x_3) + (x_2 \oplus x_5) + (x_3 \oplus x_5) + (\overline{x_2 \oplus x_3 \oplus x_5})\big)
\end{aligned}$$ ♦

The proof of Theorem 11.11 is at the tip of an iceberg called *harmonic analysis* of boolean functions, which we touch on in §14.4.4.

11.3 Fooling Space-Efficient Computations

Next, we design a pseudorandom generator that fools poly-size streaming branching programs and thus fools log-space randomized programs (§7.8.1). This PRG has "log squared" seed length and is computable in log space (not counting the space to store the seed). En route, we'll see how to "recycle" randomness using pairwise uniform hash functions.

This section culminates with a proof of $\mathsf{BPL} \subseteq \mathsf{TISP}[\mathrm{poly}\,N, \log^2 N]$. Similar but more complicated techniques yield $\mathsf{BPL} \subseteq \mathsf{L}^{1.5}$. It's unknown whether $\mathsf{BPL} \subseteq \mathsf{TISP}[\mathrm{poly}\,N, \log^{1.5} N]$ or whether there exists a log-space computable PRG with seed length $O(\log^{1.5} N)$ for streaming branching programs.

y	$f(y)$
00	10
01	11
10	10
11	00

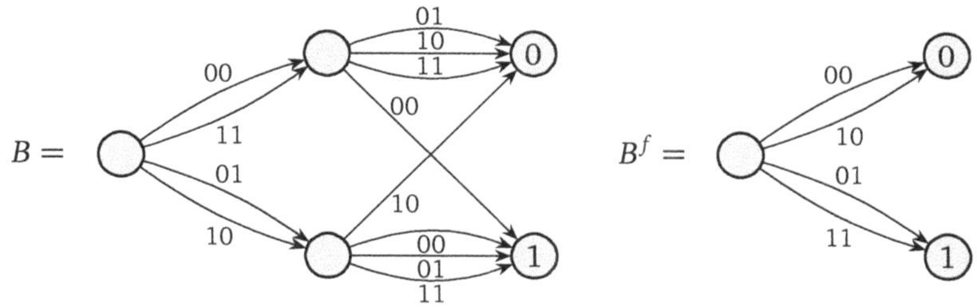

Figure 11.3: Example of bypassing one layer of a streaming branching program

11.3.1 Eliminating One Layer

Consider length-n block-size-b streaming branching programs, with the input sampled uniformly at random from $(\{0,1\}^b)^n$. To "derandomize" a streaming branching program, we want to turn it into one with fewer layers (and thus less randomness) but approximately the same acceptance probability. Say two streaming branching programs B and B' are *ε-close* if $\big|\mathbf{Pr}[B \text{ accepts}] - \mathbf{Pr}[B' \text{ accepts}]\big| \leq \varepsilon$, and say B and B' are *ε-far* otherwise.

As a warmup, consider length 2. Suppose B is a length-2 block-size-b streaming branching program and $f\colon \{0,1\}^b \to \{0,1\}^b$ is a function. Define a length-1 block-size-b streaming branching program B^f by deleting the middle layer and using f to reroute the middle layer's incoming edges directly to the output layer: For each $y \in \{0,1\}^b$, the path labeled $(y, f(y))$ in B becomes the edge labeled y in B^f (bypassing B's middle layer). Figure 11.3 shows an example.

Pairwise uniform hash functions (§8.1) work well for this:

Lemma 11.12. *For every length-2 width-w block-size-b streaming branching program B, every pairwise uniform $h\colon R \times \{0,1\}^b \to \{0,1\}^b$, and all $\varepsilon > 0$:*

$$\mathbf{Pr}_r\big[B \text{ and } B^{h_r} \text{ are } \varepsilon\text{-far}\big] \;\leq\; w^3/2^b\varepsilon^2$$

B^{h_r} uses less randomness than B does, because it has fewer layers and the same block size. This seems like "robbing Peter to pay Paul" because it introduces r, which is another source of randomness. The benefit is that we'll use a single r to eliminate many layers in a long streaming branching program, achieving an overall savings in randomness.

Proof idea for Lemma 11.12. Consider any node j in B's middle layer. The start node might have many edges to j, but once the computation reaches j, it "forgets" which edge it took. So we can sample an outgoing edge from j by "recycling" the randomness used to sample the incoming edge, instead of using fresh randomness. It's OK if the outgoing edge isn't uniformly distributed, as long as it goes to the accept node with approximately the same probability as a uniformly random edge would. The latter property follows from hash mixing (§8.5.1): The fraction of incoming edges that hash to "accepting" outgoing edges is approximately the fraction of outgoing edges that are accepting. ∎

Let's tailor the hash mixing lemma to our purpose. For any $f\colon \{0,1\}^b \to \{0,1\}^b$ and $Y, Z \subseteq \{0,1\}^b$ and $\varepsilon > 0$, say f is *(Y,Z,ε)-good* if

$$\Big|\mathbf{Pr}_y\big[y \in Y \text{ and } f(y) \in Z\big] - \mathbf{Pr}_{y,z}\big[y \in Y \text{ and } z \in Z\big]\Big| \;\leq\; \varepsilon$$

where y and z are uniform over $\{0,1\}^b$, and say f is *(Y,Z,ε)-bad* otherwise.

Lemma 11.13. *For every pairwise uniform $h: R \times \{0,1\}^b \to \{0,1\}^b$, all $Y, Z \subseteq \{0,1\}^b$, and all $\varepsilon > 0$:*

$$\mathbf{Pr}_r\big[h_r \text{ is } (Y,Z,\varepsilon)\text{-bad}\big] \le 1/2^b\varepsilon^2$$

Proof of Lemma 11.13. If $Y = \emptyset$ then every f is $(Y,Z,0)$-good since $\mathbf{Pr}_y\big[y \in Y \text{ and } f(y) \in Z\big] = 0 = \mathbf{Pr}_{y,z}\big[y \in Y \text{ and } z \in Z\big]$, so $\mathbf{Pr}_r\big[h_r \text{ is } (Y,Z,\varepsilon)\text{-bad}\big] = 0$. If $Y \ne \emptyset$ then by the chain rule:

$$\begin{aligned}
\mathbf{Pr}_r\big[h_r \text{ is } (Y,Z,\varepsilon)\text{-bad}\big] &= \mathbf{Pr}_r\Big[\Big|\mathbf{Pr}_y\big[h_r(y) \in Z \,\big|\, y \in Y\big] - \mathbf{Pr}_z\big[z \in Z\big]\Big| \cdot \mathbf{Pr}_y\big[y \in Y\big] > \varepsilon\Big] \\
&\le |Z|/|Y|2^b\big(\varepsilon/\mathbf{Pr}_y\big[y \in Y\big]\big)^2 && \text{(Lemma 8.15)} \\
&= |Y|\,|Z|/2^{3b}\varepsilon^2 \\
&\le 1/2^b\varepsilon^2
\end{aligned}$$

■

Proof of Lemma 11.12. For each node j in B's middle layer:

- Let $Y_j \subseteq \{0,1\}^b$ be the labels of edges from the start node to j.
- Let $Z_j \subseteq \{0,1\}^b$ be the labels of edges from j to the accept node.

If some $f: \{0,1\}^b \to \{0,1\}^b$ is $(Y_j, Z_j, \varepsilon/w)$-good, then intuitively, "accepting via j" is approximately equally likely in B and B^f. If f is $(Y_j, Z_j, \varepsilon/w)$-good for every j, then

$$\begin{aligned}
\mathbf{Pr}_{y,z}\big[B(y,z) \text{ accepts}\big] &= \textstyle\sum_j \mathbf{Pr}_{y,z}\big[y \in Y_j \text{ and } z \in Z_j\big] \\
&\le \textstyle\sum_j\big(\mathbf{Pr}_y\big[y \in Y_j \text{ and } f(y) \in Z_j\big] + \varepsilon/w\big) \\
&= \textstyle\sum_j \mathbf{Pr}_y\big[y \in Y_j \text{ and } f(y) \in Z_j\big] + \sum_j \varepsilon/w \\
&\le \mathbf{Pr}_y\big[B^f(y) \text{ accepts}\big] + \varepsilon
\end{aligned}$$

and similarly $\mathbf{Pr}_{y,z}\big[B(y,z) \text{ accepts}\big] \ge \mathbf{Pr}_y\big[B^f(y) \text{ accepts}\big] - \varepsilon$, so B and B^f are ε-close.

$$\begin{aligned}
\mathbf{Pr}_r\big[B \text{ and } B^{h_r} \text{ are } \varepsilon\text{-far}\big] &\le \mathbf{Pr}_r\big[h_r \text{ is } (Y_j, Z_j, \varepsilon/w)\text{-bad for some } j\big] \\
&\le \textstyle\sum_j \mathbf{Pr}_r\big[h_r \text{ is } (Y_j, Z_j, \varepsilon/w)\text{-bad}\big] && \text{(union bound)} \\
&\le \textstyle\sum_j 1/2^b(\varepsilon/w)^2 && \text{(Lemma 11.13)} \\
&\le w^3/2^b\varepsilon^2
\end{aligned}$$

■

Now, we generalize this from length 2 to length $n \ge 2$. Suppose B is a length-n block-size-b streaming branching program, and ℓ is an interior layer (not the start or output layer), and $f: \{0,1\}^b \to \{0,1\}^b$ is a function. Define a length-$(n-1)$ block-size-b streaming branching program $B^{\ell \to f}$ by deleting layer ℓ and using f to reroute its incoming edges directly to the next layer: For each node i in layer $\ell - 1$ and each $y \in \{0,1\}^b$, the edge labeled y from i in $B^{\ell \to f}$ goes to the node reached by the path labeled $(y, f(y))$ from i in B. That is, a path labeled $(y, f(y))$ from layer $\ell - 1$ to layer $\ell + 1$ in B becomes an edge labeled y in $B^{\ell \to f}$ (bypassing layer ℓ of B).

Lemma 11.14. *For every width-w block-size-b streaming branching program B, every interior layer ℓ, every pairwise uniform $h: R \times \{0,1\}^b \to \{0,1\}^b$, and all $\varepsilon > 0$:*

$$\mathbf{Pr}_r\big[B \text{ and } B^{\ell \to h_r} \text{ are } \varepsilon\text{-far}\big] \le w^7/2^b\varepsilon^2$$

Proof. For each triple of nodes (i, j, k) in layers $(\ell - 1, \ell, \ell + 1)$ in B:

- Let $Y_{i,j} \subseteq \{0,1\}^b$ be the labels of edges from i to j.
- Let $Z_{j,k} \subseteq \{0,1\}^b$ be the labels of edges from j to k.
- Let p_i be the probability that a random walk from the start node reaches i. (If i is the start node then $p_i = 1$.)
- Let q_k be the probability that a random walk from k reaches the accept node. (If k is the accept node then $q_k = 1$. If k is the reject node then $q_k = 0$.)

If f is $(Y_{i,j}, Z_{j,k}, \varepsilon/w^2)$-good for every (i,j,k), then by the chain rule,

$$\begin{aligned}
\mathbf{Pr}\big[B \text{ accepts}\big] &= \textstyle\sum_{i,j,k} \mathbf{Pr}\big[B \text{ visits } i,j,k \text{ and accepts}\big] \\
&= \textstyle\sum_{i,j,k} \mathbf{Pr}\big[B \text{ visits } i\big] \cdot \mathbf{Pr}\big[B \text{ visits } j,k \,\big|\, B \text{ visits } i\big] \cdot \mathbf{Pr}\big[B \text{ accepts} \,\big|\, B \text{ visits } i,j,k\big] \\
&= \textstyle\sum_{i,j,k} p_i \cdot \mathbf{Pr}_{y,z}\big[y \in Y_{i,j} \text{ and } z \in Z_{j,k}\big] \cdot q_k \\
&\le \textstyle\sum_{i,j,k} p_i \cdot \big(\mathbf{Pr}_y\big[y \in Y_{i,j} \text{ and } f(y) \in Z_{j,k}\big] + \varepsilon/w^2\big) \cdot q_k \\
&= \big(\textstyle\sum_{i,j,k} p_i \cdot \mathbf{Pr}_y\big[y \in Y_{i,j} \text{ and } f(y) \in Z_{j,k}\big] \cdot q_k\big) + \big(\textstyle\sum_{i,j,k} p_i \cdot (\varepsilon/w^2) \cdot q_k\big) \\
&= \mathbf{Pr}\big[B^{\ell\to f} \text{ accepts}\big] + \big(\textstyle\sum_i p_i\big) \cdot \big(\textstyle\sum_j \varepsilon/w^2\big) \cdot \big(\textstyle\sum_k q_k\big) \\
&\le \mathbf{Pr}\big[B^{\ell\to f} \text{ accepts}\big] + \varepsilon \qquad \text{(since } \textstyle\sum_i p_i \le 1 \text{ and } \textstyle\sum_k q_k \le w\text{)}
\end{aligned}$$

and similarly $\mathbf{Pr}\big[B \text{ accepts}\big] \ge \mathbf{Pr}\big[B^{\ell\to f} \text{ accepts}\big] - \varepsilon$, so B and $B^{\ell\to f}$ are ε-close.

$$\begin{aligned}
\mathbf{Pr}_r\big[B \text{ and } B^{\ell\to h_r} \text{ are } \varepsilon\text{-far}\big] &\le \mathbf{Pr}_r\big[h_r \text{ is } (Y_{i,j}, Z_{j,k}, \varepsilon/w^2)\text{-bad for some } (i,j,k)\big] \\
&\le \textstyle\sum_{i,j,k} \mathbf{Pr}_r\big[h_r \text{ is } (Y_{i,j}, Z_{j,k}, \varepsilon/w^2)\text{-bad}\big] \qquad \text{(union bound)} \\
&\le \textstyle\sum_{i,j,k} 1/2^b(\varepsilon/w^2)^2 \qquad \text{(Lemma 11.13)} \\
&\le w^7/2^b\varepsilon^2
\end{aligned}$$

■

11.3.2 Eliminating All Layers

We use the process from §11.3.1 repeatedly to eliminate multiple layers of a streaming branching program. If the eliminated layers are nonadjacent, then they don't interfere with each other and can therefore share a common sample of the hash function. So we eliminate every other layer in "one fell swoop." Having exhausted that sample's potential, we use a fresh sample of the hash function (independent of the first sample) to eliminate every other layer in the resulting streaming branching program, and so on. Let's formalize this.

Assume n is even. Suppose B is a length-n block-size-b streaming branching program and $f\colon \{0,1\}^b \to \{0,1\}^b$ is a function. Define a length-$n/2$ block-size-b streaming branching program B^f by using f to bypass each even-index layer as in §11.3.1.

Lemma 11.15. *For every length-n width-w block-size-b streaming branching program B where n is even, every pairwise uniform $h\colon R \times \{0,1\}^b \to \{0,1\}^b$, and all $\varepsilon > 0$:*

$$\mathbf{Pr}_r\big[B \text{ and } B^{h_r} \text{ are } \varepsilon\text{-far}\big] \le n^3 w^7/2^b\varepsilon^2$$

Proof. Obtain B^{h_r} from B by first eliminating layer n, then eliminating layer $n-2$, then layer $n-4$, and so on. Formally, define streaming branching programs $B_0, B_1, B_2, \ldots, B_{n/2}$ where $B_0 = B$ and $B_{m+1} = (B_m)^{(n-2m)\to h_r}$ for each $m < n/2$, and thus $B_{n/2} = B^{h_r}$. The proof of Lemma 11.14 shows that for each $m < n/2$:

$$\mathbf{Pr}_r\big[B_m \text{ and } B_{m+1} \text{ are } \varepsilon/n\text{-far}\big] \le w^7/2^b(\varepsilon/n)^2$$

A subtlety is that B_m depends on r, whereas the statement of Lemma 11.14 is for a streaming branching program that doesn't depend on r. Fortunately, that doesn't matter since B_m matches B up to layer $n-2m+1$, so B_m's dependence on r only affects the q_k values, which don't matter in the proof of Lemma 11.14.

If B_m and B_{m+1} are ε/n-close for each $m < n/2$, then $B_0 = B$ and $B_{n/2} = B^{h_r}$ are $(n/2)\cdot(\varepsilon/n)$-close and thus ε-close. (We sacrifice a factor 2 to make the notation tidier.) Hence:

$$\begin{aligned}\mathbf{Pr}_r\big[B \text{ and } B^{h_r} \text{ are } \varepsilon\text{-far}\big] &\le \mathbf{Pr}_r\big[B_m \text{ and } B_{m+1} \text{ are } \varepsilon/n\text{-far for some } m < n/2\big] \\ &\le \textstyle\sum_{m<n/2} \mathbf{Pr}_r\big[B_m \text{ and } B_{m+1} \text{ are } \varepsilon/n\text{-far}\big] \qquad \text{(union bound)} \\ &\le \textstyle\sum_{m<n/2} w^7/2^b(\varepsilon/n)^2 \\ &\le n^3w^7/2^b\varepsilon^2 \end{aligned}$$

■

Now, assume $n = 2^d$ is a power of 2. Suppose B is a length-n block-size-b streaming branching program and $f_1, f_2, \ldots, f_d \colon \{0,1\}^b \to \{0,1\}^b$ are functions. Define a length-1 block-size-b streaming branching program $B^{f_1,f_2,\ldots,f_d}$ by using f_1 to bypass half the layers of B, then using f_2 to bypass half the layers of the resulting streaming branching program, and so on:

$$B^{f_1,f_2,\ldots,f_d} = \Big(\cdots\Big(\big((B^{f_1})^{f_2}\big)^{f_3}\Big)\cdots\Big)^{f_d}$$

Lemma 11.16. *For every length-n width-w block-size-b streaming branching program B where $n = 2^d$ is a power of 2, every pairwise uniform $h\colon R \times \{0,1\}^b \to \{0,1\}^b$, and all $\varepsilon > 0$:*

$$\mathbf{Pr}_{r_1,\ldots,r_d}\big[B \text{ and } B^{h_{r_1},\ldots,h_{r_d}} \text{ are } \varepsilon\text{-far}\big] \le d^3n^3w^7/2^b\varepsilon^2$$

Proof. Define streaming branching programs $B_0, B_1, B_2, \ldots, B_d$ (different from in the proof of Lemma 11.15) where $B_0 = B$ and $B_{c+1} = (B_c)^{h_{r_{c+1}}}$ for each $c < d$, and thus $B_d = B^{h_{r_1},\ldots,h_{r_d}}$. Note that B_c has length $n/2^c$. If B_c and B_{c+1} are ε/d-close for each $c < d$, then $B_0 = B$ and $B_d = B^{h_{r_1},\ldots,h_{r_d}}$ are ε-close. Hence:

$$\begin{aligned} &\mathbf{Pr}_{r_1,\ldots,r_d}\big[B \text{ and } B^{h_{r_1},\ldots,h_{r_d}} \text{ are } \varepsilon\text{-far}\big] \\ \le\ &\mathbf{Pr}_{r_1,\ldots,r_d}\big[B_c \text{ and } B_{c+1} \text{ are } \varepsilon/d\text{-far for some } c < d\big] \\ \le\ &\textstyle\sum_{c<d} \mathbf{Pr}_{r_1,\ldots,r_d}\big[B_c \text{ and } B_{c+1} \text{ are } \varepsilon/d\text{-far}\big] \qquad \text{(union bound)} \\ \le\ &\textstyle\sum_{c<d} (n/2^c)^3w^7/2^b(\varepsilon/d)^2 \qquad \text{(Lemma 11.15)} \\ \le\ &d^3n^3w^7/2^b\varepsilon^2 \end{aligned}$$

■

11.3.3 Pseudorandom Generator

Let $h\colon \{0,1\}^{3b-1} \times \{0,1\}^b \to \{0,1\}^b$ be the pairwise uniform hash function from Lemma 8.9, which is computable in $O(b)$ space. We recursively define $G_d \colon (\{0,1\}^{3b-1})^d \times \{0,1\}^b \to (\{0,1\}^b)^n$ where $n = 2^d$:

Pseudorandom generator to fool streaming branching programs (11.2)

$G_d(r_1, \ldots, r_d, s)$:
  if $d = 0$: output s
  else: call $G_{d-1}(r_1, \ldots, r_{d-1}, s)$ and then call $G_{d-1}(r_1, \ldots, r_{d-1}, h_{r_d}(s))$

$$G_1(r_1,s) = (\; s,\; h_{r_1}(s)\;)$$

$$G_2(r_1,r_2,s) = (\; s,\; h_{r_1}(s),\; h_{r_2}(s),\; h_{r_1}(h_{r_2}(s))\;)$$

$$G_3(r_1,r_2,r_3,s) = (\; s,\; h_{r_1}(s),\; h_{r_2}(s),\; h_{r_1}(h_{r_2}(s)),\; h_{r_3}(s),\; h_{r_1}(h_{r_3}(s)),\; h_{r_2}(h_{r_3}(s)),\; h_{r_1}(h_{r_2}(h_{r_3}(s)))\;)$$

Figure 11.4: Demonstration of the recursive pseudorandom generator

Figure 11.4 shows this for $d \in \{1,2,3\}$. There's an iterative algorithm to compute $G_d(r_1,\ldots,r_d,s)$ in $O(b+d)$ space, not counting the space to store the seed $(r_1,\ldots,r_d,s)$: To obtain the output's ith component, the locations of 1s in i's binary representation say which samples of h to apply.

Iterative algorithm to evaluate G_d (11.3)

```
for i ← 0,...,n−1:
    let u ← s
    let i_{d−1} ··· i_0 be i's binary representation
    for j ← d−1,...,0:
        if i_j = 1: update u ← h_{r_{j+1}}(u)
    output u
```

Claim 11.17. *For every length-n width-w block-size-b streaming branching program B where $n = 2^d$, and for all $r_1,\ldots,r_d,s$:*

$$B\big(G_d(r_1,\ldots,r_d,s)\big) \;=\; B^{h_{r_1},\ldots,h_{r_d}}(s)$$

Proof. Define streaming branching programs $B_0,B_1,B_2,\ldots,B_d$ where $B_0 = B$ and $B_c = (B_{c-1})^{h_{r_c}}$ for each $c > 0$, and thus $B_d = B^{h_{r_1},\ldots,h_{r_d}}$. We prove that the recursive definition of G_d maintains the invariant that for every edge in B_c, say from node i to node k with label $s \in \{0,1\}^b$, the path in B labeled $G_c(r_1,\ldots,r_c,s)$ from i leads to k. This holds by definition for the base cases when $c = 0$ since $G_0(s) = s$. To see that G_c maintains the invariant when $c > 0$, assume the invariant holds for G_{c-1}. Consider an edge in B_c labeled s from i to k. This means B_{c-1} has an edge labeled s from i to some node j, and an edge labeled $h_{r_c}(s)$ from j to k. By the invariant, the path in B labeled $G_{c-1}(r_1,\ldots,r_{c-1},s)$ from i leads to j, and the path in B labeled $G_{c-1}(r_1,\ldots,r_{c-1},h_{r_c}(s))$ from j leads to k. Thus the path in B labeled $G_c(r_1,\ldots,r_c,s) = \big(G_{c-1}(r_1,\ldots,r_{c-1},s),\ G_{c-1}(r_1,\ldots,r_{c-1},h_{r_c}(s))\big)$ from i leads to k. In conclusion, the edge in $B_d = B^{h_{r_1},\ldots,h_{r_d}}$ labeled s goes from the start node to the accept node iff the path in B labeled $G_d(r_1,\ldots,r_d,s)$ leads from the start node to the accept node. ∎

Lemma 11.18. *If $b \geq \log(8d^3n^3w^7/\varepsilon^3)$ then G_d is an ε-pseudorandom generator for length-n width-w block-size-b streaming branching programs where $n = 2^d$.*

Proof. Consider any such streaming branching program B. Let E be the event that B and $B^{h_{r_1},\dots,h_{r_d}}$ are $\varepsilon/2$-far, so $\mathbf{Pr}_{r_1,\dots,r_d}[E] \leq d^3n^3w^7/2^b(\varepsilon/2)^2 \leq \varepsilon/2$ (Lemma 11.16). By Claim 11.17 and the law of total probability,

$$\begin{aligned}
\mathbf{Pr}_{r_1,\dots,r_d,s}\big[B\big(G_d(r_1,\dots,r_d,s)\big) \text{ accepts}\big] &= \mathbf{Pr}_{r_1,\dots,r_d,s}\big[B^{h_{r_1},\dots,h_{r_d}}(s) \text{ accepts}\big] \\
&= \mathbf{Pr}_{r_1,\dots,r_d,s}\big[B^{h_{r_1},\dots,h_{r_d}}(s) \text{ accepts} \,\big|\, E\big] \cdot \mathbf{Pr}_{r_1,\dots,r_d}\big[E\big] + \\
&\quad\ \mathbf{Pr}_{r_1,\dots,r_d,s}\big[B^{h_{r_1},\dots,h_{r_d}}(s) \text{ accepts} \,\big|\, \overline{E}\big] \cdot \mathbf{Pr}_{r_1,\dots,r_d}\big[\overline{E}\big] \\
&\leq 1 \cdot (\varepsilon/2) + \big(\mathbf{Pr}_u\big[B(u) \text{ accepts}\big] + \varepsilon/2\big) \cdot 1 \\
&= \mathbf{Pr}_u\big[B(u) \text{ accepts}\big] + \varepsilon
\end{aligned}$$

and similarly $\mathbf{Pr}_{r_1,\dots,r_d,s}\big[B\big(G_d(r_1,\dots,r_d,s)\big) \text{ rejects}\big] \leq \mathbf{Pr}_u\big[B(u) \text{ rejects}\big] + \varepsilon$, so:

$$\Big|\mathbf{Pr}_{r_1,\dots,r_d,s}\big[B\big(G_d(r_1,\dots,r_d,s)\big) \text{ accepts}\big] - \mathbf{Pr}_u\big[B(u) \text{ accepts}\big]\Big| \leq \varepsilon$$ ■

Lemma 11.18 assumes n is a power of 2 and the block size b is moderately large. What if n can be anything and $b = 1$?

Theorem 11.19. *There exists an ε-pseudorandom generator for length-n width-w streaming branching programs with seed length $O\big(\log(nw/\varepsilon) \cdot \log n\big)$ and computable in space $O\big(\log(nw/\varepsilon)\big)$.*

First, some observations: We can increase any streaming branching program's length by appending dummy layers (Figure 11.5). To convert a length-bn width-w streaming branching program to a length-n width-w block-size-b streaming branching program, we partition the non-output layers into n groups of b consecutive layers, and replace each group with a single layer, where each length-b path through the group becomes a single edge (Figure 11.6).

Proof of Theorem 11.19. Consider any such streaming branching program B. For some b and d (to be determined), append dummy layers to increase the length to $b2^d$, then convert this to a length-2^d width-w block-size-b streaming branching program B'. By Lemma 11.18, if $b \geq \log\big(8d^3(2^d)^3w^7/\varepsilon^3\big)$ then G_d ε-fools B' and thus G_d's first n output bits ε-fool B.

Let $d = \lceil \log n \rceil$ and $b = \big\lceil \log\big(64d^3n^3w^7/\varepsilon^3\big)\big\rceil = O\big(\log(nw/\varepsilon)\big)$. We have $2^d \leq 2n$ and thus $b \geq \log\big(8d^3(2^d)^3w^7/\varepsilon^3\big)$. So by truncating G_d's output to the first n bits, we have an ε-PRG for length-n width-w streaming branching programs with seed length $(3b-1)d + b = O\big(\log(nw/\varepsilon) \cdot \log n\big)$ and computable in space $O\big(\log(nw/\varepsilon)\big)$. ■

Corollary 11.20. *Every problem in* BPL *has a two-sided-error randomized program that uses only $O(\log^2 N)$ random bits and $O(\log N)$ space except for the space to store the random bits.*

Proof. Suppose $A \in$ BPL and x is a valid input of size N. Let B_x be the length-n width-w streaming branching program from Corollary 7.35, and let $\varepsilon = 1/7$. Let G be the PRG with these parameters from Theorem 11.19. Consider a program that plugs a uniformly random seed into G, simulates B_x on G's output, and accepts iff B_x accepts. This solves A with error probability $\leq 1/3 + 1/7 \leq 0.48$. Since G has seed length $O\big(\log(nw/\varepsilon) \cdot \log n\big) = O(\log^2 N)$ and is computable in space $O\big(\log(nw/\varepsilon)\big) = O(\log N)$, and since obtaining and simulating B_x takes $O(\log N)$ space, this program uses $O(\log^2 N)$ space for the seed and $O(\log N)$ space for everything else. ■

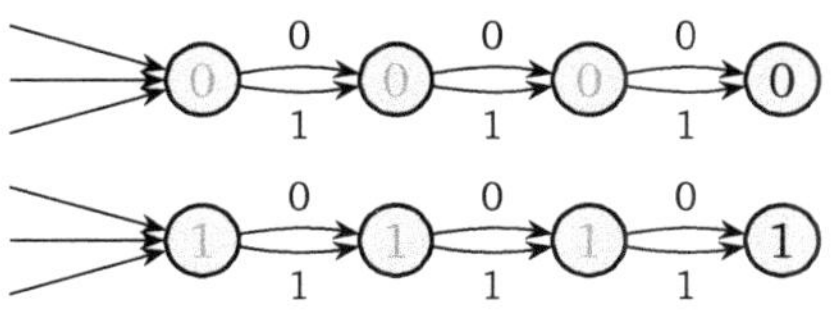

Figure 11.5: Example of increasing the length by 3

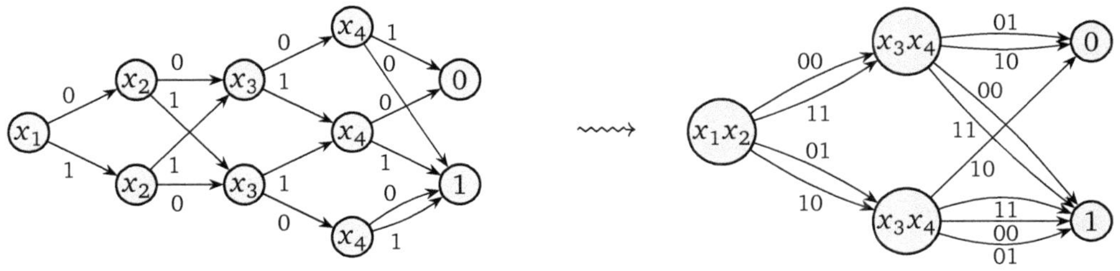

Figure 11.6: Example of changing the block size from 1 to $b = 2$

11.3.4 Time-Space-Efficient Derandomization

Theorem 11.21. $\mathsf{BPL} \subseteq \mathsf{TISP}[\text{poly} N, \log^2 N]$.

Proof idea. For full derandomization, we would normally iterate over all possible seeds of a PRG. The PRG used in Corollary 11.20 has seed length $O(\log^2 N)$, so this would take time $2^{O(\log^2 N)} = N^{O(\log N)}$. Instead, we exploit the details of this particular PRG. We examine the polynomially many possibilities of r_1 to find one that "works," and we commit to it. Then, we examine the polynomially many possibilities of r_2 to find one that "works" (given the r_1 we already picked), and we commit to this r_2. And so on, to find $r_3, \ldots, r_d$. ■

Proof (ancillary). Suppose $A \in \mathsf{BPL}$ and x is a valid input of size N. Let B_x be the length-n width-w streaming branching program from Corollary 7.35. Let $\varepsilon = 1/7$ and $d = \lceil \log n \rceil$ and $b = \lceil \log(8d^2n^3w^7/\varepsilon^2) \rceil = O(\log(nw/\varepsilon)) = O(\log N)$. Convert B_x to a length-2^d width-w block-size-b streaming branching program, which we name B for convenience. Let $h\colon \{0,1\}^{3b-1} \times \{0,1\}^b \to \{0,1\}^b$ be the pairwise uniform hash function from Lemma 8.9.

To solve A deterministically, first find $r_1, \ldots, r_d$ such that B and $B^{h_{r_1},\ldots,h_{r_d}}$ are ε-close, so:

$$\mathbf{Pr}_s\big[B^{h_{r_1},\ldots,h_{r_d}}(s) \neq A(x)\big] \leq \mathbf{Pr}_u\big[B(u) \neq A(x)\big] + \varepsilon \leq 1/3 + \varepsilon < 1/2$$

Then, compute $\mathbf{Pr}_s\big[B^{h_{r_1},\ldots,h_{r_d}}(s) \text{ accepts}\big]$ by iterating over all possible $s \in \{0,1\}^b$ and evaluating $B^{h_{r_1},\ldots,h_{r_d}}(s) = B(G_d(r_1, \ldots, r_d, s))$ (Claim 11.17), and accept iff this probability is $> 1/2$. It takes $O(bd) = O(\log^2 N)$ space to store $r_1, \ldots, r_d$, and $O(\log N)$ space and poly$N$ time to compute $\mathbf{Pr}_s\big[B^{h_{r_1},\ldots,h_{r_d}}(s) \text{ accepts}\big]$.

To find such $r_1, \ldots, r_d$:

- First, find r_1 such that $B_0 = B$ and $B_1 = (B_0)^{h_{r_1}}$ are ε/d-close.
- Then, find r_2 such that B_1 and $B_2 = (B_1)^{h_{r_2}}$ are ε/d-close.
- Then, find r_3 such that B_2 and $B_3 = (B_2)^{h_{r_3}}$ are ε/d-close.
- And so on.

This ensures that $B_0 = B$ and $B_d = B^{h_{r_1},\dots,h_{r_d}}$ are ε-close.

To find such an r_1: For any even layer ℓ and nodes (i,j,k) in layers $(\ell-1,\ell,\ell+1)$ in B, let $Y_{i,j} \subseteq \{0,1\}^b$ be the labels of edges from i to j, and let $Z_{j,k} \subseteq \{0,1\}^b$ be the labels of edges from j to k. The proofs of Lemma 11.14 and Lemma 11.15 show that if h_{r_1} is $(Y_{i,j}, Z_{j,k}, \varepsilon/d2^d w^2)$-good for all such ℓ and (i,j,k) (the "desired property"), then B and $B^{h_{r_1}}$ are ε/d-close. By Lemma 11.13:

$$\mathbf{Pr}_{r_1}\left[h_{r_1} \text{ is } (Y_{i,j}, Z_{j,k}, \varepsilon/d2^d w^2)\text{-bad}\right] \le 1/2^b(\varepsilon/d2^d w^2)^2 = d^2(2^d)^2 w^4/2^b\varepsilon^2$$

By a union bound, the probability that a uniformly random r_1 doesn't have the desired property is

$$\le 2^d w^3 \cdot d^2(2^d)^2 w^4/2^b\varepsilon^2 = d^2(2^d)^3 w^7/2^b\varepsilon^2 < 8d^2n^3w^7/2^b\varepsilon^2 \le 1$$

since $2^d < 2n$ and $b \ge \log(8d^2n^3w^7/\varepsilon^2)$. Thus an r_1 with the desired property exists. To find such an r_1, try every possibility of r_1 and check whether h_{r_1} is $(Y_{i,j}, Z_{j,k}, \varepsilon/d2^d w^2)$-good for all relevant ℓ and (i,j,k). It takes $O(\log N)$ space and poly$N$ time to iterate over all r_1 and ℓ and (i,j,k) and to compute $\mathbf{Pr}_y\left[y \in Y_{i,j} \text{ and } h_{r_1}(y) \in Z_{j,k}\right]$ and $\mathbf{Pr}_{y,z}\left[y \in Y_{i,j} \text{ and } z \in Z_{j,k}\right]$ by iterating over all $y \in \{0,1\}^b$ and $z \in \{0,1\}^b$.

After finding $r_1, \dots, r_c$, find r_{c+1} in the same way. The catch: We must be able to check—in $O(\log N)$ space and poly$N$ time—whether $y \in Y_{i,j}$ and $z \in Z_{j,k}$ for any i,j,k,y,z, where the sets $Y_{i,j}$ and $Z_{j,k}$ are defined with respect to B_c. For this, it suffices to obtain the encoding of B_c in $O(\log N)$ space. The set of nodes in B_c depends only on B and c. For any node i and label $s \in \{0,1\}^b$, the edge in B_c from i labeled s goes to the same node that the path in B from i labeled $G_c(r_1, \dots, r_c, s)$ leads to (see the proof of Claim 11.17), which is computable in $O(\log N)$ space since G_c is.

In summary, we need $O(\log^2 N)$ space for storing $r_1, \dots, r_d$, and $O(\log N)$ space and poly$N$ time for everything else. Thus $A \in \mathsf{TISP}[\text{poly}N, \log^2 N]$. ■

11.4 Fooling Time-Efficient Computations

This is a landmark in complexity theory:

Theorem 11.22. $\mathsf{P} = \mathsf{BPP}$ *if* E *contains a total* $A\colon \{0,1\}^+ \to \{0,1\}$ *with circuit size complexity* $2^{\Omega(N)}$.

The assumption that some A has time complexity $2^{O(N)}$ and circuit size complexity $2^{\Omega(N)}$ is a "strong time hierarchy conjecture."

- By a uniform hierarchy theorem, some A has time complexity $2^{O(N)}$ and $2^{\Omega(N)}$. (See §4.2.2 and Exercise 4.7.)
- By a nonuniform hierarchy theorem, some A has circuit size complexity $2^{O(N)}$ and $2^{\Omega(N)}$. (See §5.2.4.)

Theorem 11.22 needs the uniform upper bound and the nonuniform lower bound simultaneously (for the same A). It assumes we can't always trade uniformity for speed. Many researchers believe such a hierarchy theorem is true and therefore that $\mathsf{P} = \mathsf{BPP}$.

It matters that the circuit size complexity is $2^{\Omega(N)}$ rather than "not $2^{o(N)}$". The latter would mean A is hard for infinitely many N, which would only let us derandomize programs for infinitely many N, whereas $\mathsf{P} = \mathsf{BPP}$ requires the derandomization to work for all N.

Theorem 11.22 is proven by using A to construct a pseudorandom generator family that fools poly-size circuits, has log seed length, and is poly-time computable, which implies $\mathsf{P} = \mathsf{BPP}$ (Lemma 11.5). Constructing such a PRG actually requires the strong time hierarchy conjecture: If $G\colon \{0,1\}^\ell \to \{0,1\}^n$ is a $1/7$-PRG for size-n^c circuits with $\ell = d\log n$ and computable in time $O(n^e)$ (for integers c, d, e), then $g\colon \{0,1\}^{\ell+1} \to \{0,1\}$ defined by

$$g(x) = 1 \iff \big(\exists s \in \{0,1\}^\ell\colon \text{the first } \ell+1 \text{ bits of } G(s) \text{ are } x\big)$$

is computable in time $2^\ell \cdot O(n^e) = 2^{O(\ell)}$ (by brute force) but has no circuit of size $n^c = 2^{\Omega(\ell)}$, because G wouldn't fool such a circuit C applied to the first $\ell+1$ bits of an n-bit input:

$$\mathbf{Pr}\big[C(G(U_\ell)) = 1\big] - \mathbf{Pr}\big[C(U_n) = 1\big] \;\ge\; 1 - 2^\ell/2^{\ell+1} \;=\; 1/2 \;>\; 1/7$$

In other words, we can't construct a PRG that yields $\mathsf{P} = \mathsf{BPP}$ without also proving an exponential circuit size lower bound for E. Theorem 11.22 is the converse. It's conceivable, however, that we could prove $\mathsf{P} = \mathsf{BPP}$ without using a PRG.

We won't fully prove Theorem 11.22. In this section, we prove a somewhat weaker version that assumes A is not just worst-case hard, but average-case hard.

Since s stands for "seed," we denote circuit size by t, for "time." As in §10.4, a size-t circuit has bounded fan-in and $\le t$ many $\wedge$ and $\vee$ gates (not counting $\neg$ gates or input nodes—a convenient but immaterial convention). Let "(t,ε)-PRG" mean "ε-PRG for size-t circuits." Say $g\colon \{0,1\}^m \to \{0,1\}$ is (t,ε)-*hard* iff for every size-t circuit $C\colon \{0,1\}^m \to \{0,1\}$, $\mathbf{Pr}_{x\sim U_m}\big[C(x) = g(x)\big] \le (1+\varepsilon)/2$. The definition of (t,ε)-hard in §10.4 had $<$, but now we change it to $\le$ for convenience.

Theorem 11.23. $\mathsf{P} = \mathsf{BPP}$ *if* E *contains a total* $A\colon \{0,1\}^+ \to \{0,1\}$ *such that* A_N *is* $(2^{cN}, 2^{-cN})$-*hard for some constant* $c > 0$ *and all large enough* N.

Theorem 11.22 follows by combining Theorem 11.23 with the worst-case to strong-average-case reduction of Theorem 10.19 (which we didn't prove).

11.4.1 Warmup

Let's use an average-case hard function to construct a pseudorandom generator with one bit of stretch. This might not sound impressive, but we use it for cryptography in Chapter 12.

Lemma 11.24. *If* $g\colon \{0,1\}^\ell \to \{0,1\}$ *is* $(t, 2\varepsilon)$-*hard, then* $G\colon \{0,1\}^\ell \to \{0,1\}^{\ell+1}$ *defined by* $G(s) = (s, g(s))$ *is a* (t,ε)-*PRG.*

Proof idea. We prove the contrapositive by a reduction from average-case solving g to distinguishing G's output from uniform. Suppose some circuit distinguishes $G(U_\ell)$ from $U_{\ell+1}$. This circuit takes an input $(s,b) \in \{0,1\}^\ell \times \{0,1\}$, and intuitively, its output indicates whether it thinks $b = g(s)$. Here's a heuristic for g on input s: Randomly guess the value of $g(s)$ and ask the circuit whether it thinks the guess is correct. If it does, output the guess. If it doesn't, output the opposite bit. This proof was foreshadowed by Lemma 11.3. ■

Proof. Suppose G isn't a (t,ε)-PRG, so for some size-t circuit $C\colon \{0,1\}^{\ell+1} \to \{0,1\}$:

$$\mathbf{Pr}\big[C(G(U_\ell)) = 1\big] - \mathbf{Pr}\big[C(U_{\ell+1}) = 1\big] \;>\; \varepsilon$$

(By definition, the inequality's left side should be inside absolute value bars. But we assume C has already been negated if necessary to remove the absolute value bars.) This means:

$$\mathbf{Pr}_s\big[C(s,g(s))=1\big]-\mathbf{Pr}_{s,b}\big[C(s,b)=1\big] \;>\; \varepsilon$$

By the law of total probability:

$$\begin{aligned}\mathbf{Pr}_{s,b}\big[C(s,b)=1\big] \;&=\; \mathbf{Pr}_{s,b}\big[b=g(s)\big]\cdot\mathbf{Pr}_{s,b}\big[C(s,b)=1\,\big|\,b=g(s)\big]+\\ &\quad\;\mathbf{Pr}_{s,b}\big[b=\overline{g(s)}\big]\cdot\mathbf{Pr}_{s,b}\big[C(s,b)=1\,\big|\,b=\overline{g(s)}\big]\\ &=\; \tfrac{1}{2}\cdot\mathbf{Pr}_s\big[C(s,g(s))=1\big]+\tfrac{1}{2}\cdot\mathbf{Pr}_s\big[C(s,\overline{g(s)})=1\big]\end{aligned}$$

Combining these yields:

$$\mathbf{Pr}_s\big[C(s,g(s))=1\big]-\mathbf{Pr}_s\big[C(s,\overline{g(s)})=1\big] \;>\; 2\varepsilon$$

For each bit b (the "guess"), define a circuit $C'_b\colon \{0,1\}^{\ell}\to\{0,1\}$ such that:

$$C'_b(s) \;=\; \begin{cases} b & \text{if } C(s,b)=1\\ \overline{b} & \text{if } C(s,b)=0\end{cases}$$

C'_1 is C with the last input bit hardwired to 1, and C'_0 is C with the last input bit hardwired to 0 and with the output negated. Thus C'_1 and C'_0 are size-t circuits. Using the law of total probability:

$$\begin{aligned}\max_b\Big(\mathbf{Pr}_s\big[C'_b(s)=g(s)\big]\Big) \;&\geq\; \mathbf{Pr}_{s,b}\big[C'_b(s)=g(s)\big]\\ &=\; \mathbf{Pr}_{s,b}\big[b=g(s)\big]\cdot\mathbf{Pr}_{s,b}\big[C'_b(s)=g(s)\,\big|\,b=g(s)\big]+\\ &\quad\;\mathbf{Pr}_{s,b}\big[b=\overline{g(s)}\big]\cdot\mathbf{Pr}_{s,b}\big[C'_b(s)=g(s)\,\big|\,b=\overline{g(s)}\big]\\ &=\; \tfrac{1}{2}\cdot\mathbf{Pr}_s\big[C'_{g(s)}(s)=g(s)\big]+\tfrac{1}{2}\cdot\mathbf{Pr}_s\big[C'_{\overline{g(s)}}(s)=g(s)\big]\\ &=\; \Big(\mathbf{Pr}_s\big[C(s,g(s))=1\big]+\mathbf{Pr}_s\big[C(s,\overline{g(s)})=0\big]\Big)/2\\ &=\; \Big(1+\mathbf{Pr}_s\big[C(s,g(s))=1\big]-\mathbf{Pr}_s\big[C(s,\overline{g(s)})=1\big]\Big)/2\\ &>\; (1+2\varepsilon)/2\end{aligned}$$

Thus $\mathbf{Pr}_s\big[C'_b(s)=g(s)\big]>(1+2\varepsilon)/2$ for some b, so g is $(t,2\varepsilon)$-easy. ■

11.4.2 Predicting Versus Distinguishing

Let D be a distribution over $\{0,1\}^n$. A *distinguisher* is a function that, given a sample from either D or the uniform distribution U_n, tries to determine which distribution it came from. A *predictor* is a function that, given the first $i-1$ bits of a sample from D, tries to predict the ith bit. Generalizing Lemma 11.24, we turn any distinguisher into a predictor:

Lemma 11.25. *For every distribution D over $\{0,1\}^n$, if $f\colon\{0,1\}^n\to\{0,1\}$ is such that*

$$\Big|\mathbf{Pr}\big[f(D)=1\big]-\mathbf{Pr}\big[f(U_n)=1\big]\Big| \;>\; \varepsilon$$

then there exist $i\in[n]$ and $f'\colon\{0,1\}^{i-1}\to\{0,1\}$ (a constant if $i=1$) such that

$$\mathbf{Pr}_{x\sim D}\big[f'(x_{<i})=x_i\big] \;>\; 1/2+\varepsilon/n$$

and $f'(x_{<i})=f(x_{<i},y_{\geq i})\oplus b$ for some hardwired $y_{\geq i}\in\{0,1\}^{n-i+1}$ and bit b.

Proof idea. We use a *hybrid argument*. For each $i \in \{0, 1, \ldots, n\}$, define the distribution D^i over $\{0,1\}^n$ that samples the first i bits according to D and the remaining bits according to U_n (so D^i is a hybrid of D and U_n). The sequence of distributions $D^n, D^{n-1}, \ldots, D^1, D^0$ interpolates between $D = D^n$ and $U_n = D^0$. If a function ε-distinguishes D and U_n, then it ε/n-distinguishes some adjacent pair D^i and D^{i-1} in this sequence. Turning this distinguisher into a predictor for the ith bit is like Lemma 11.24. ∎

Proof. Assume $\mathbf{Pr}\big[f(D) = 1\big] - \mathbf{Pr}\big[f(U_n) = 1\big] > \varepsilon$ (otherwise replace f with $\overline{f}$ throughout). Consider a joint probability space where $x \sim D$ and $y \sim U_n$ are sampled independently. Letting $p_i = \mathbf{Pr}\big[f(x_{\le i}, y_{>i}) = 1\big]$, so $p_n = \mathbf{Pr}\big[f(D) = 1\big]$ and $p_0 = \mathbf{Pr}\big[f(U_n) = 1\big]$, we have:

$$(p_n - p_{n-1}) + (p_{n-1} - p_{n-2}) + \cdots + (p_2 - p_1) + (p_1 - p_0) \;=\; p_n - p_0 \;>\; \varepsilon$$

Thus there exists $i \in [n]$ such that $p_i - p_{i-1} > \varepsilon/n$, in other words:

$$\mathbf{Pr}\big[f(x_{\le i}, y_{>i}) = 1\big] - \mathbf{Pr}\big[f(x_{<i}, y_{\ge i}) = 1\big] \;>\; \varepsilon/n$$

By the law of total probability:

$$\begin{aligned}
\mathbf{Pr}\big[f(x_{<i}, y_{\ge i}) = 1\big] \;&=\; \mathbf{Pr}\big[y_i = x_i\big] \cdot \mathbf{Pr}\big[f(x_{<i}, y_{\ge i}) = 1 \,\big|\, y_i = x_i\big] + \\
&\;\; \mathbf{Pr}\big[y_i = \overline{x_i}\big] \cdot \mathbf{Pr}\big[f(x_{<i}, y_{\ge i}) = 1 \,\big|\, y_i = \overline{x_i}\big] \\
&=\; \tfrac{1}{2} \cdot \mathbf{Pr}\big[f(x_{<i}, x_i, y_{>i}) = 1\big] + \tfrac{1}{2} \cdot \mathbf{Pr}\big[f(x_{<i}, \overline{x_i}, y_{>i}) = 1\big]
\end{aligned}$$

Combining these yields:

$$\mathbf{Pr}\big[f(x_{<i}, x_i, y_{>i}) = 1\big] - \mathbf{Pr}\big[f(x_{<i}, \overline{x_i}, y_{>i}) = 1\big] \;>\; 2\varepsilon/n$$

For each $y_{\ge i} \in \{0,1\}^{n-i+1}$, define $f'_{y_{\ge i}} : \{0,1\}^{i-1} \to \{0,1\}$ by:

$$f'_{y_{\ge i}}(x_{<i}) \;=\; \begin{cases} y_i & \text{if } f(x_{<i}, y_{\ge i}) = 1 \\ \overline{y_i} & \text{if } f(x_{<i}, y_{\ge i}) = 0 \end{cases}$$

That is, $f'_{y_{\ge i}}(x_{<i}) = f(x_{<i}, y_{\ge i}) \oplus \overline{y_i}$. Using the law of total probability:

$$\begin{aligned}
\max_y \Big(\mathbf{Pr}_x\big[f'_{y_{\ge i}}(x_{<i}) = x_i\big]\Big) \;&\ge\; \mathbf{Pr}_{x,y}\big[f'_{y_{\ge i}}(x_{<i}) = x_i\big] \\
&=\; \mathbf{Pr}\big[y_i = x_i\big] \cdot \mathbf{Pr}\big[f'_{y_{\ge i}}(x_{<i}) = x_i \,\big|\, y_i = x_i\big] + \\
&\;\; \mathbf{Pr}\big[y_i = \overline{x_i}\big] \cdot \mathbf{Pr}\big[f'_{y_{\ge i}}(x_{<i}) = x_i \,\big|\, y_i = \overline{x_i}\big] \\
&=\; \tfrac{1}{2} \cdot \mathbf{Pr}\big[f(x_{<i}, x_i, y_{>i}) = 1\big] + \tfrac{1}{2} \cdot \mathbf{Pr}\big[f(x_{<i}, \overline{x_i}, y_{>i}) = 0\big] \\
&=\; \Big(1 + \mathbf{Pr}\big[f(x_{<i}, x_i, y_{>i}) = 1\big] - \mathbf{Pr}\big[f(x_{<i}, \overline{x_i}, y_{>i}) = 1\big]\Big)/2 \\
&>\; (1 + 2\varepsilon/n)/2
\end{aligned}$$

Thus $\mathbf{Pr}_x\big[f'_{y_{\ge i}}(x_{<i}) = x_i\big] > (1 + 2\varepsilon/n)/2$ for some $y_{\ge i}$, so $f'_{y_{\ge i}}$ fulfills the statement of the lemma. ∎

11.4.3 Pseudorandom Generator

In § 11.4.1, we turned an average-case hard function g into a PRG with one bit of stretch, by applying g once. To get a PRG with much bigger stretch, we apply g many times, to different parts of the seed. These parts must overlap somewhat, to keep the seed short. As long as the overlaps aren't too large, this PRG still works.

An *(ℓ,m,n)-system* is a tuple $(H_1,H_2,\dots,H_n)$ such that $H_i \subseteq [\ell]$ and $|H_i| = m$ for all $i \in [n]$. For any such system and $g\colon \{0,1\}^m \to \{0,1\}$, define $G\colon \{0,1\}^\ell \to \{0,1\}^n$ by

$$G(s) = \big(g(s_{H_1}), g(s_{H_2}), \dots, g(s_{H_n})\big)$$

where s_{H_i} is the bits of s indexed by H_i. For example, $s_{\{2,4,5\}} = s_2 s_4 s_5 \in \{0,1\}^3$. See Figure 11.7.

Lemma 11.26. *Define $G\colon \{0,1\}^\ell \to \{0,1\}^n$ by $G(s)_i = g(s_{H_i})$ for some $g\colon \{0,1\}^m \to \{0,1\}$ and (ℓ,m,n)-system $(H_1,\dots,H_n)$. If $f\colon \{0,1\}^n \to \{0,1\}$ is such that*

$$\Big|\mathbf{Pr}\big[f(G(U_\ell)) = 1\big] - \mathbf{Pr}\big[f(U_n) = 1\big]\Big| > \varepsilon$$

then there exists $f^*\colon \{0,1\}^m \to \{0,1\}$ such that

$$\mathbf{Pr}_{z\sim U_m}\big[f^*(z) = g(z)\big] > 1/2 + \varepsilon/n$$

and for some $i \in [n]$, using H_i to index z's bits,

$$f^*(z) = f\Big(g_1\big(z_{H_i\cap H_1}\big), \dots, g_{i-1}\big(z_{H_i\cap H_{i-1}}\big), y_{\ge i}\Big) \oplus b$$

for some functions $g_j\colon \{0,1\}^{|H_i\cap H_j|} \to \{0,1\}$ (for $j < i$) and $y_{\ge i} \in \{0,1\}^{n-i+1}$ and bit b.

Proof. By Lemma 11.25 with $D = G(U_\ell)$, there exist $i \in [n]$ and $f'\colon \{0,1\}^{i-1} \to \{0,1\}$ such that for $s \sim U_\ell$ and $x = G(s)$,

$$\mathbf{Pr}\big[f'(x_{<i}) = x_i\big] > 1/2 + \varepsilon/n$$

and $f'(x_{<i}) = f(x_{<i}, y_{\ge i}) \oplus b$ for some $y_{\ge i} \in \{0,1\}^{n-i+1}$ and bit b. That is, since $x_j = g(s_{H_j})$ for each $j \in [n]$:

$$\mathbf{Pr}\Big[f'\big(g(s_{H_1}), \dots, g(s_{H_{i-1}})\big) = g(s_{H_i})\Big] > 1/2 + \varepsilon/n$$

Splitting s into $z = s_{H_i}$ and $a = s_{[\ell]\setminus H_i}$, there exists an outcome a such that the above inequality holds for $z \sim U_m$. With this a hardwired, $g(s_{H_j}) = g_j\big(z_{H_i\cap H_j}\big)$ for some function g_j. Thus for

$$f^*(z) = f'\Big(g_1\big(z_{H_i\cap H_1}\big), \dots, g_{i-1}\big(z_{H_i\cap H_{i-1}}\big)\Big)$$

we have $\mathbf{Pr}\big[f^*(z) = g(z)\big] > 1/2 + \varepsilon/n$. See Figure 11.8. ∎

We want to show that if g is average-case hard, then G is a good PRG. For the contrapositive, if f is efficient, then f^* should be efficient too. Why would the functions $g_j\colon \{0,1\}^{|H_i\cap H_j|} \to \{0,1\}$ that appear in f^* be efficient? If $H_i \cap H_j$ is small, then brute forcing g_j is efficient enough. A *(k,ℓ,m,n)-system* is an (ℓ,m,n)-system $(H_1,\dots,H_n)$ such that $|H_i \cap H_j| \le k$ for all pairs $i \ne j$.

Lemma 11.27. *$G\colon \{0,1\}^\ell \to \{0,1\}^n$ defined by $G(s)_i = g(s_{H_i})$ is a (t,ε)-PRG if $g\colon \{0,1\}^m \to \{0,1\}$ is $\big(t + 3n2^k,\ 2\varepsilon/n\big)$-hard and $(H_1,\dots,H_n)$ is a (k,ℓ,m,n)-system.*

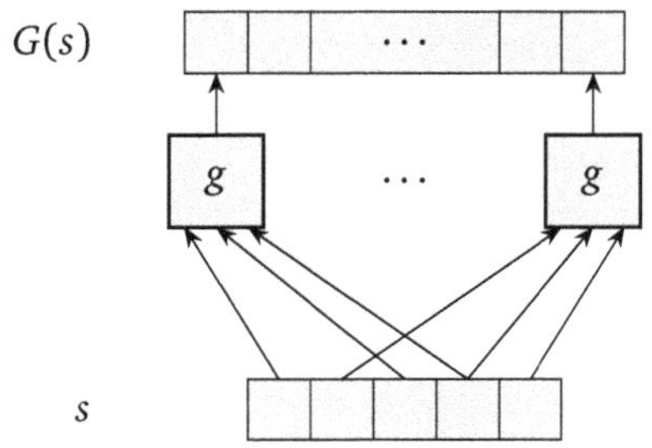

Figure 11.7: Example G from Lemma 11.26 with $H_1 = \{1,3,4\}$ and $H_n = \{2,4,5\}$

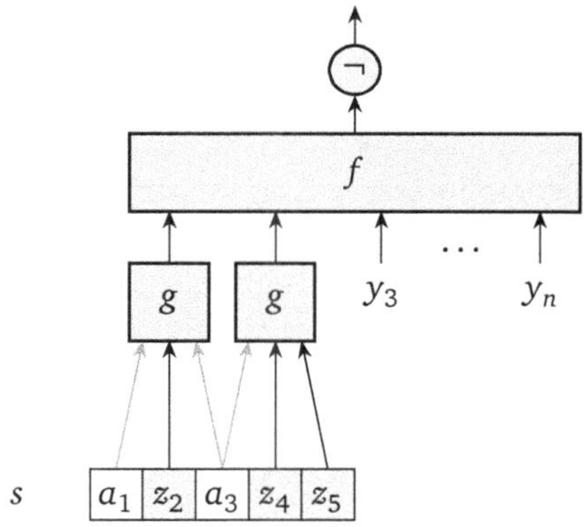

Figure 11.8: Example f^* from Lemma 11.26 with $b = 1$, $i = 3$, $H_1 = \{1,2,3\}$, $H_2 = \{3,4,5\}$, and $H_3 = \{2,4,5\}$

Proof. Suppose G isn't a (t,ε)-PRG. For some size-t circuit $C\colon \{0,1\}^n \to \{0,1\}$:

$$\Big|\mathbf{Pr}\big[C(G(U_\ell)) = 1\big] - \mathbf{Pr}\big[C(U_n) = 1\big]\Big| \;>\; \varepsilon$$

Using C as f in Lemma 11.26, we obtain $f^*\colon \{0,1\}^m \to \{0,1\}$ such that:

$$\mathbf{Pr}_{z\sim U_m}\big[f^*(z) = g(z)\big] \;>\; (1 + 2\varepsilon/n)/2$$

To conclude that g is $\big(t+3n2^k,\, 2\varepsilon/n\big)$-easy, we design a size-$(t+3n2^k)$ circuit C^* that computes:

$$f^*(z) \;=\; f\Big(g_1\big(z_{H_i\cap H_1}\big), \ldots, g_{i-1}\big(z_{H_i\cap H_{i-1}}\big), y_{\geq i}\Big) \oplus b$$

We start with C. The size doesn't increase when we hardwire $y_{\geq i}$ (and contract) and negate the output if $b = 1$. For each $j < i$ (of which there are $< n$), we substitute into C's jth input bit a circuit for g_j of size $\leq 3\cdot 2^{|H_i\cap H_j|} \leq 3\cdot 2^k$, from the proof of Theorem 5.7. ■

Lemma 11.28. *A (k,ℓ,m,n)-system exists if $n \leq (k\ell/em^2)^k$ and ℓ is divisible by m. Moreover, such a system can be found in time* $\mathrm{poly}(n2^\ell)$ *given k,ℓ,m,n as input.*

We prove Lemma 11.28 in §11.4.4.

Proof of Theorem 11.23. Assume E contains a total $A\colon \{0,1\}^+ \to \{0,1\}$ such that A_N is $(2^{cN}, 2^{-cN})$-hard for some constant $c > 0$ and all large enough N. To conclude that $\mathsf{P} = \mathsf{BPP}$, it suffices to design a $(t,1/7)$-PRG with seed length $O(\log t)$ and computable in time $\mathrm{poly}\, t$, for all large enough $t \geq n$ (Lemma 11.5). Define:

$$d \;=\; \lceil 1/c\rceil \qquad k \;=\; \lceil \log(4t)\rceil \qquad m \;=\; 2dk \qquad \ell \;=\; 12dm$$

Let $g = A_m\colon \{0,1\}^m \to \{0,1\}$, which is $(2^{cm}, 2^{-cm})$-hard and thus $\big(t+3n2^k,\, 2/7n\big)$-hard since:

$$t+3n2^k \;\leq\; 4t2^k \;\leq\; 2^k2^k \;=\; 2^{m/d} \;\leq\; 2^{cm} \qquad\qquad 2/7n \;\geq\; 1/4t \;\geq\; 2^{-k} \;\geq\; 2^{-cm}$$

There exists a (k,ℓ,m,n)-system $(H_1,\ldots,H_n)$ since $n \leq t \leq 2^k \leq (k\ell/em^2)^k$ (Lemma 11.28). Thus G is a $(t,1/7)$-PRG (Lemma 11.27) with seed length $\ell = 24d^2\lceil\log(4t)\rceil = O(\log t)$ and computable in time $\mathrm{poly}(n2^\ell) + n2^{O(m)} \leq \mathrm{poly}\, t$:

Algorithm to evaluate the pseudorandom generator G (11.4)

$G(n,t;s)$:
  compute k,m,ℓ
  compute $(H_1,\ldots,H_n)$ in time poly$(n2^\ell)$ (Lemma 11.28)
  for each $i \in [n]$:
    compute and output $g(s_{H_i})$ using the $2^{O(m)}$-time program for $A \in \mathsf{E}$

■

11.4.4 Set System

Proof idea for Lemma 11.28. We prove such a system exists using the probabilistic method: A random system (from a suitable distribution) has the desired properties with positive probability. To find such a system algorithmically, brute force over all tuples $(H_1,\ldots,H_n)$ would be too slow. Instead, we use "greedy brute force": After finding and committing to $(H_1,\ldots,H_{i-1})$, we use brute force over all possible H_i. Regardless of $(H_1,\ldots,H_{i-1})$, a random H_i has small enough intersections with all prior H_j with positive probability. So we need not reconsider our choice of $(H_1,\ldots,H_{i-1})$. ■

To optimize the parameters, we use a concentration bound similar to Lemma 7.20 but actually simpler to prove. We prove it at the end of this section.

Lemma 11.29. *If X is the number of heads in m tosses of a coin with heads probability p, then* $\mathbf{Pr}[X > k] \le (epm/k)^k$ *for all k.*

Proof of Lemma 11.28 (ancillary). Since ℓ is divisible by m, we can partition $[\ell]$ into m *intervals* of size ℓ/m each. It's helpful to restrict our attention to subsets of $[\ell]$ that are *structured*, meaning they contain exactly one element from each of the m intervals. We claim that the following algorithm finds a tuple of structured sets $(H_1,\ldots,H_n)$ such that $|H_i \cap H_j| \le k$ for all pairs $i \ne j$.

Algorithm to find a set system with small pairwise intersections (11.5)

for $i \leftarrow 1,\ldots,n$:
  for every structured set H:
    if $|H \cap H_j| \le k$ for all $j < i$:
      let $H_i \leftarrow H$ and continue to the next i

To prove the algorithm doesn't get stuck in iteration i, we use the probabilistic method to show such an H_i exists. Consider a uniformly random structured set H: For each interval independently, pick a uniformly random element to put in H. For each $j < i$, the random variable $|H \cap H_j|$ is the number of heads in m tosses of a coin with heads probability $p = m/\ell$, where "ath toss is heads" means "H contains the same element as H_j in the ath interval."

$$\begin{aligned}
\mathbf{Pr}\big[|H \cap H_j| > k \text{ for some } j < i\big] &\le \textstyle\sum_{j<i} \mathbf{Pr}\big[|H \cap H_j| > k\big] && \text{(union bound)}\\
&\le \textstyle\sum_{j<i} (epm/k)^k && \text{(Lemma 11.29)}\\
&\le (i-1)/n && \text{(assumption on } n)\\
&< 1
\end{aligned}$$

So there exists a structured set H_i such that $|H_i \cap H_j| \le k$ for all $j < i$.

There are n iterations of i, at most 2^ℓ iterations of H, and at most n iterations of j. Checking whether $|H \cap H_j| \le k$ and updating H take poly ℓ time. Thus the overall running time is $\le n \cdot 2^\ell \cdot n \cdot \text{poly}\,\ell \le \text{poly}(n2^\ell)$. ■

Proof of Lemma 11.29 (ancillary). Assume $k > pm$ since otherwise $\mathbf{Pr}[X > k] \le 1$ is trivial. Let $X = X_1 + \cdots + X_m$ where X_i indicates whether the ith toss is heads. For $b = k/pm > 1$, we have $\mathbf{Pr}[X > k] = \mathbf{Pr}\big[b^X > b^k\big] \le \mathbf{E}\big[b^X\big]/b^k$ (Lemma 7.13, since $b^X \ge 0$). We have $\mathbf{E}\big[b^X\big] = \mathbf{E}\big[b^{X_1} \cdots b^{X_m}\big] = \mathbf{E}\big[b^{X_1}\big] \cdots \mathbf{E}\big[b^{X_m}\big]$ since $X_1, \ldots, X_m$ are fully independent and thus $b^{X_1}, \ldots, b^{X_m}$ are fully independent (Lemma A.12). For each i:

$$\mathbf{E}\big[b^{X_i}\big] = \mathbf{Pr}[X_i = 0] \cdot b^0 + \mathbf{Pr}[X_i = 1] \cdot b^1 = (1-p) \cdot 1 + p \cdot b \le 1 + pb = 1 + k/m \le \mathrm{e}^{k/m}$$

Combining everything, $\mathbf{Pr}[X > k] \le (\mathrm{e}^{k/m})^m / b^k = (\mathrm{e}/b)^k$. ■

11.5 Extracting Randomness

11.5.1 Extractors and Min-Entropy

A "crude" source of randomness is a distribution D over $\{0,1\}^d$. A "pure" source of randomness is the uniform distribution U_n over $\{0,1\}^n$. What if we want a pure source but only have a crude source? Given a sample $r \sim D$, suppose we apply some function $E\colon \{0,1\}^d \to \{0,1\}^n$ which we menacingly call an *extractor*. The idea is for $E(r)$ to "extract" whatever randomness r "contains" and distill it into a uniformly distributed string: We want the distribution $E(D)$ to be U_n. Figure 11.9 shows an example of a crude source D on $d = 2$ bits and a function E that extracts $n = 1$ uniformly distributed bit from it.

How should we quantify the amount of extractable randomness D contains? For starters, it's between 0 bits (if D is constant) and d bits (if D is uniform). For every $r \in \{0,1\}^d$, $\mathbf{Pr}_{E(D)}\big[E(r)\big] = \sum_{q\,:\,E(q)=E(r)} D(q) \ge D(r)$ regardless of E. If we want $E(D) = U_n$, then every outcome under D must have probability $\le 2^{-n}$ since every outcome under U_n has probability 2^{-n}. Thus D's most probable outcome is a "sticking point" that limits the number of bits we can hope to extract. Although E can combine low-probability outcomes into a single high-probability outcome, it can't do the reverse.

Example. Suppose $D(0^d) = 1/2$ and $D(r) = 1/2(2^d - 1)$ for all $r \ne 0^d$. Thus D is uniform except for an extreme outlier. Though D seems to contain plenty of randomness outside the pesky outcome 0^d, that randomness is unfortunately not extractable. If the crude source gives us 0^d, we must do something with it—we can't request a replacement sample. The best we can do is extract one bit with $E(0^d) = 0$ and $E(r) = 1$ for all $r \ne 0^d$. ♦

The *min-entropy* of a distribution D over sample space S is $\log_2\big(1/\max_{r \in S} D(r)\big)$. Thus D has min-entropy $\ge h$ iff $D(r) \le 2^{-h}$ for every $r \in S$. The uniform distribution over $\{0,1\}^d$ has min-entropy d, so "bits" are the unit of min-entropy. Other definitions of entropy also measure "how random" a distribution is. (The binary entropy function from §9.2.1 is related to one of them.) "Min"-entropy has the smallest value among these definitions.

Perfectly achieving $E(D) = U_n$ is often too much to ask for. Instead, we allow $E(D)$ and U_n to be within some $\varepsilon \ge 0$ in statistical distance (§11.1.1).

We'd like an extractor to be general-purpose, meaning it doesn't know which distribution D it's extracting from, like how a PRG doesn't know which function f it's fooling. A tentative definition

r	$D(r)$	$E(r)$
00	0.3	0
01	0.1	1
10	0.4	1
11	0.2	0

$$\mathbf{Pr}_{E(D)}[0] = 0.3+0.2 = 0.5$$
$$\mathbf{Pr}_{E(D)}[1] = 0.1+0.4 = 0.5$$

Figure 11.9: Example of a crude source and an extractor for it

is that $E\colon \{0,1\}^d \to \{0,1\}^n$ is an (h,ε)-extractor iff $\Delta\big(E(D), U_n\big) \le \varepsilon$ for every distribution D over $\{0,1\}^d$ with min-entropy $\ge h$. We have four parameters d, n, h, ε. Keep in mind that $n \le h \le d$ and we want n close to h (so randomness doesn't go to waste) and d much larger than h (because extraction is more challenging when the randomness is "hidden" within more bits) and ε close to 0. Also, E doesn't try to figure out how much randomness to extract after seeing the sample—the parameters are all fixed in advance.

Unfortunately, this tentative definition is unachievable if $h \le d-1$ and $\varepsilon < 1/2$: For any $E\colon \{0,1\}^d \to \{0,1\}$, consider the uniform distribution D over the larger of the two sets $E^{-1}(0)$ and $E^{-1}(1)$. This D has min-entropy $\ge d-1 \ge h$ since $D(r) \le 1/2^{d-1}$ for all r, but $E(D)$ is a constant, which has statistical distance $1/2$ from U_1. This is like how a PRG with seed length < output length can't ε-fool every f (§11.1.3).

There are two ways to circumvent this. We study one way in §11.6. The other way is to assume D comes from some restricted set of possible distributions, rather than try to extract from literally every D with high min-entropy. This is like how PRGs only fool functions from some set F. Now, we study extractors for an important restricted set of distributions—those composed of two independent parts.

11.5.2 Extracting from Independent Sources

What if we can access two crude sources of randomness, which have high min-entropy and are independent of each other? Independence enables extraction because the sources can't collude to thwart an extractor. If D_1 and D_2 are distributions over $\{0,1\}^d$, let (D_1, D_2) denote the joint distribution over $\{0,1\}^d \times \{0,1\}^d$ where D_1 and D_2 are sampled independently.

Claim 11.30. *The min-entropy of (D_1, D_2) is the sum of the min-entropies of D_1 and D_2.*

Proof. If D_1 and D_2 have min-entropies h_1 and h_2, then $D = (D_1, D_2)$ has min-entropy $\ge h_1 + h_2$ because $D(r_1, r_2) = D_1(r_1) \cdot D_2(r_2) \le 2^{-h_1} \cdot 2^{-h_2} = 2^{-(h_1+h_2)}$ for all r_1 and r_2, and D has min-entropy $\le h_1 + h_2$ because there exist r_1 and r_2 such that $D_1(r_1) = 2^{-h_1}$ and $D_2(r_2) = 2^{-h_2}$ and thus $D(r_1, r_2) = D_1(r_1) \cdot D_2(r_2) = 2^{-(h_1+h_2)}$. ■

Definition. A *two-source (h,ε)-extractor* is a function $E\colon \{0,1\}^d \times \{0,1\}^d \to \{0,1\}^n$ such that for all distributions D_1 and D_2 over $\{0,1\}^d$ where (D_1, D_2) has min-entropy $\ge h$:

$$\Delta\big(E(D_1, D_2), U_n\big) \le \varepsilon$$

d is the *individual source length*, n is the *output length*, and ε is the *error*. ◀

Theorem 11.31. *$E\colon \{0,1\}^d \times \{0,1\}^d \to \{0,1\}$ defined by $E(r_1, r_2) = r_1 \odot r_2$ (the dot product over $\mathbb{Z}_2$) is a two-source $\big(d + 2\log(1/2\varepsilon), \varepsilon\big)$-extractor for all $\varepsilon > 0$.*

Proof. Consider any distributions D_1 and D_2 over $\{0,1\}^d$ with min-entropies h_1 and h_2 such that (D_1, D_2) has min-entropy $h_1 + h_2 \geq d + 2\log(1/2\varepsilon)$ (Claim 11.30). View E as a $2^d \times 2^d$ matrix with rows and columns indexed by $\{0,1\}^d$. Define the $2^d \times 2^d$ matrix M by:

$$M(r_1, r_2) \;=\; (-1)^{E(r_1, r_2)} \;=\; 1 - 2E(r_1, r_2)$$

View D_1 as a 1×2^d row vector, and D_2 as a $2^d \times 1$ column vector, and consider matrix arithmetic over $\mathbb{R}$.

$$\begin{aligned}
2\Delta\big(E(D_1, D_2), U_1\big) &= 2\big|1/2 - \mathbf{Pr}\big[E(D_1, D_2) = 1\big]\big| \\
&= \big|1 - 2\mathbf{E}\big[E(D_1, D_2)\big]\big| \\
&= \big|\mathbf{E}\big[M(D_1, D_2)\big]\big| && \text{(linearity of expectation)} \\
&= \big|\textstyle\sum_{r_1, r_2} D_1(r_1) M(r_1, r_2) D_2(r_2)\big| \\
&= \big|D_1 M D_2\big| \\
&\leq \sqrt{(D_1 \cdot D_1)(MD_2 \cdot MD_2)} && \text{(Theorem A.26 for } D_1 \cdot (MD_2))
\end{aligned}$$

We have

$$D_1 \cdot D_1 \;=\; \textstyle\sum_{r_1} D_1(r_1)^2 \;\leq\; \big(\max_{r_1} D_1(r_1)\big) \sum_{r_1} D_1(r_1) \;=\; 2^{-h_1}$$

and $D_2 \cdot D_2 \leq 2^{-h_2}$. We prove below that $M^\top M = 2^d I$ where I is the $2^d \times 2^d$ identity matrix (and $M^\top$ is M's transpose), which implies:

$$MD_2 \cdot MD_2 \;=\; (MD_2)^\top (MD_2) \;=\; D_2^\top M^\top M D_2 \;=\; D_2^\top (2^d I) D_2 \;=\; 2^d (D_2 \cdot D_2) \;\leq\; 2^d 2^{-h_2}$$

Combining everything:

$$2\Delta\big(E(D_1, D_2), U_1\big) \;\leq\; \sqrt{2^{-h_1} 2^d 2^{-h_2}} \;=\; 2^{(d - h_1 - h_2)/2} \;\leq\; 2^{(d - (d + 2\log(1/2\varepsilon)))/2} \;=\; 2\varepsilon$$

Thus $\Delta\big(E(D_1, D_2), U_1\big) \leq \varepsilon$, so E is a two-source $\big(d + 2\log(1/2\varepsilon), \varepsilon\big)$-extractor.

Now, we prove that $M^\top M = 2^d I$. The entry at row q and column s of $M^\top M$ is the dot product (over $\mathbb{R}$) of row q of $M^\top$ (which is column q of M) and column s of M:

$$(M^\top M)(q, s) \;=\; \textstyle\sum_r M(r, q) M(r, s) \;=\; \sum_r (-1)^{r \odot q} (-1)^{r \odot s} \;=\; \sum_r (-1)^{(r \odot q) \oplus (r \odot s)}$$

If $q = s$, this is $\sum_r (-1)^0 = 2^d$. If $q \neq s$, this is 0 because half the summands are 1 and the other half are -1 by the random subsum principle: $(r \odot q) \oplus (r \odot s) = 0$ for exactly half of all r. ■

The following corollary has an application to communication protocols in Chapter 17. A binary matrix is *ε-balanced* iff the fraction of entries that are 1s is within $\pm\varepsilon$ of $1/2$.

Corollary 11.32. *In the matrix E with rows and columns indexed by $\{0,1\}^d$ defined by $E(r_1, r_2) = r_1 \odot r_2$ (the dot product over $\mathbb{Z}_2$), every submatrix with $\geq 2^d/4\varepsilon^2$ many entries is ε-balanced.*

Proof. Consider any set $A_1 \subseteq \{0,1\}^d$ of row indices and set $A_2 \subseteq \{0,1\}^d$ of column indices such that the $A_1 \times A_2$ submatrix has $|A_1||A_2| \geq 2^d/4\varepsilon^2$ entries. Let D_1 and D_2 be the uniform distributions over A_1 and A_2. Then (D_1, D_2) is uniform over $A_1 \times A_2$ and has min-entropy $\log(|A_1||A_2|) \geq d + 2\log(1/2\varepsilon)$. By Theorem 11.31, $\Delta\big(E(D_1, D_2), U_1\big) \leq \varepsilon$, which means the $A_1 \times A_2$ submatrix is ε-balanced. ■

Corollary 11.32 is related to Theorem A.14, which says for every $n \geq 2$, there exists an $n \times n$ binary matrix with no monochromatic $k \times k$ submatrix where $k = \lceil 2 \log n \rceil$, and monochromatic means "all entries are the same." For every even d and $n = 2^d$, the $n \times n$ binary matrix from Corollary 11.32 has no monochromatic $k \times k$ submatrix where $k = \sqrt{n} + 1$, because every $k \times k$ submatrix has $k^2 > 2^d / 4\varepsilon^2$ many entries for some $\varepsilon < 1/2$ and is thus ε-balanced and therefore not monochromatic. This is worse than Theorem A.14 because $\sqrt{n} + 1 > \lceil 2 \log n \rceil$ (unless n is tiny). But it has the advantage that we know what the matrix is, unlike Theorem A.14, which shows such a matrix exists nonconstructively.

Back to the topic of extractors, Theorem 11.31 seems meager because it only extracts one bit and requires the total min-entropy to be more than half the total source length of $2d$. The latter is unavoidable because a two-source extractor handling total min-entropy less than the individual source length would yield an extractor according to the tentative definition from § 11.5.1—by just hardwiring the 2nd source to 0^d (or anything)—contradicting the impossibility of extracting from arbitrary sources.

However, two-source extraction is possible with much lower min-entropy if we require both sources to have individual min-entropy $\geq h/2$, rather than just total min-entropy $\geq h$. This is not difficult to achieve nonconstructively (see Exercise 11.19, which is related to § 11.6.3). Constructing poly-time computable two-source extractors for significantly lower individual min-entropy than Theorem 11.31 was a major open question for a long time. A research triumph finally yielded such extractors for individual min-entropy $O(\log d)$.

11.6 Seeded Extractors

11.6.1 Definition and Results

Seeded extractors overcome the impossibility of extracting from arbitrary high-min-entropy crude sources (§ 11.5.1) by using a short, uniformly distributed *seed* that's independent of the crude source. (The extractors from § 11.5 are called *seedless* or *deterministic*.)

Definition. An (h, ε)-*extractor* is a function $E \colon \{0,1\}^d \times \{0,1\}^\ell \to \{0,1\}^n$ such that for every distribution D over $\{0,1\}^d$ with min-entropy $\geq h$:

$$\Delta\big(E(D, U_\ell), U_n\big) \leq \varepsilon$$

d is the *source length*, ℓ is the *seed length*, n is the *output length*, and ε is the *error*. ◂

The seed comes from a pure source U_ℓ, which seems like cheating because the whole point of extraction is that we don't already have a pure source. Seeded extractors could just ignore the crude source and output the seed itself. But they're interesting when the seed contains much less randomness than the crude source ($\ell < h$). Seeded extractors are like yogurt recipes that require some preexisting yogurt as a "starter" to help turn the other ingredients into more yogurt. Injecting a little pure randomness into the mix can help turn a lot of crude randomness into a lot of pure randomness.

If we don't even have enough pure randomness available for the seed, we can do brute force over all possible seeds, like in § 11.1.4: Suppose a decision problem A has a $1/12$-error randomized program Π that uses at most n pure random bits on valid inputs x of size N. Suppose $E \colon \{0,1\}^d \times \{0,1\}^\ell \to \{0,1\}^n$ is an efficiently computable $(h, 1/12)$-extractor. Let Π' be this randomized program:

Purifying randomness using a seeded extractor (11.6)

$\Pi'(x;r)$:
 for each $s \in \{0,1\}^\ell$:
  compute $q \leftarrow E(r,s)$
  run $\Pi(x;q)$
 accept iff a majority of the runs accepted

Π' solves A on inputs of size N with error probability $1/3$ even when the randomness $r \in \{0,1\}^d$ comes from any D with min-entropy $\geq h$:

$$\begin{aligned}\mathbf{Pr}\big[\Pi'(x;D) \neq A(x)\big] &\leq \mathbf{Pr}_{r\sim D}\big[\mathbf{Pr}\big[\Pi(x;E(r,U_\ell)) \neq A(x)\big] \geq 1/2\big] \\ &\leq 2\cdot \mathbf{Pr}\big[\Pi(x;E(D,U_\ell)) \neq A(x)\big] \\ &\leq 2\cdot \big(\mathbf{Pr}\big[\Pi(x;U_n) \neq A(x)\big] + 1/12\big) \\ &\leq 2\cdot(1/12+1/12) \\ &= 1/3\end{aligned}$$

The loop over s incurs a factor 2^ℓ time overhead, so minimizing the seed length is important.

It's possible to extract *all* the min-entropy using a fairly short seed:

Theorem 11.33. *For all $d \geq n$ and $0 < \varepsilon \leq 1/2$, there exists an (n,ε)-extractor with source length d, seed length $\lceil \log(d/\varepsilon^2) \rceil + 2$, and output length n.*

We prove this in § 11.6.3 after covering some necessary tools in § 11.6.2. The proof nonconstructively shows that most functions E are good seeded extractors, without identifying any particular such E or guaranteeing that such an E is efficiently computable. This is like the nonconstructive proof that PRGs with small seed length exist (Theorem 11.4).

It's more challenging to construct a poly-time computable seeded extractor. (Technically, we mean an infinite family of seeded extractors computable by a uniform poly-time program.) The next theorem comes somewhat close to the parameters of Theorem 11.33: We can efficiently extract n bits of pure randomness from n^b bits worth of randomness (for arbitrarily small $b > 1$) hidden within an n^c-bit crude source (for arbitrarily large c) using a $O(\log n)$-bit pure seed.

Theorem 11.34. *For all constants $1 < b < c$ and $\varepsilon > 0$ and all large enough n, there exists an (n^b,ε)-extractor with source length n^c, seed length $O(\log n)$, and output length n, and computable in time* poly n.

We prove this in §11.6.4. Even better poly-time seeded extractors are known, but are beyond the scope of this book.

Informally, poly-time computable functions are "pseudorandom" when they have certain properties that random functions have with high probability, such as being a good pseudorandom generator (Theorem 11.4), extractor (Theorem 11.33), or linear error correcting code (Theorem 9.5). The probabilistic method shows that functions with these properties exist, but doesn't explicitly describe a specific such function. "Poly-time computable" formalizes the word "explicit."

11.6.2 Mixtures

If $D_1, \dots, D_m$ are distributions over S, and C is a distribution over $[m]$ (C stands for "coefficients"), then the *mixture* is the distribution D over S defined by $D(r) = \sum_{i=1}^{m} C(i) \cdot D_i(r)$. To sample $r \sim D$, we sample $i \sim C$ and then $r \sim D_i$. We abbreviate this as $D = \sum_i C(i) \cdot D_i$. Formally, D is a distribution because $\sum_{r \in S} D(r) = \sum_i C(i) \cdot \sum_{r \in S} D_i(r) = \sum_i C(i) \cdot 1 = 1$.

A mixture of distributions that are close to uniform is close to uniform:

Lemma 11.35. *Suppose $D = \sum_i C(i) \cdot D_i$ is a mixture of distributions over S, and U is the uniform distribution over S. If $\Delta(D_i, U) \le \varepsilon$ for each i, then $\Delta(D, U) \le \varepsilon$.*

Proof. For every event $A \subseteq S$:

$$\begin{aligned}
\left|D(A) - U(A)\right| &= \left|\left(\textstyle\sum_i C(i) \cdot D_i(A)\right) - U(A)\right| && \text{(law of total probability)} \\
&= \left|\textstyle\sum_i C(i) \cdot \left(D_i(A) - U(A)\right)\right| \\
&\le \textstyle\sum_i C(i) \cdot \left|D_i(A) - U(A)\right| && \text{(Lemma A.28)} \\
&\le \textstyle\sum_i C(i) \cdot \varepsilon && (\Delta(D_i, U) \le \varepsilon) \\
&= \varepsilon
\end{aligned}$$

■

A *k-flat* distribution is a uniform distribution U_A over an event $A \subseteq S$ of size $|A| = k$. That is, U_A assigns probability $1/k$ to each $r \in A$ and probability 0 to each $r \notin A$. Thus U_A has min-entropy $\log k$.

Lemma 11.36. *For every distribution D and integer $k \ge 1$, D has min-entropy $\ge \log k$ iff D is a mixture of k-flat distributions.*

Proof. $\Leftarrow$: Suppose $D = \sum_{A \subseteq S : |A| = k} C(A) \cdot U_A$ is a mixture of k-flat distributions. For every $r \in S$, we have $D(r) = \sum_A C(A) \cdot U_A(r) \le \sum_A C(A) \cdot (1/k) = 1/k$ since each $U_A(r) \in \{0, 1/k\}$. Thus D has min-entropy $\ge \log k$.

$\Rightarrow$: Suppose D has min-entropy $\ge \log k$. A *half-open interval* is a set of real numbers $[a, b) = \{x : a \le x < b\}$ with endpoints $a < b$ and length $b - a$. Partition $[0, 1)$ into half-open intervals, where each $r \in S$ has an associated half-open interval of length $D(r) \le 1/k$ (ignoring any r with $D(r) = 0$). For each $x \in [0, 1)$, let r_x be the element of S whose interval contains x. For each $y \in [0, 1/k)$, let $B_y = \{y, y + 1/k, y + 2/k, \dots, y + (k-1)/k\} \subseteq [0, 1)$ and $A_y = \{r_x : x \in B_y\} \subseteq S$. The B_y sets partition $[0, 1)$. Since the k points in B_y are spaced $1/k$ apart, no two of them are in the same r's interval, so $|A_y| = k$. Letting $\equiv$ mean "equivalent to":

$$\begin{aligned}
\text{sample } r \sim D &\equiv \text{sample } \underbrace{\text{uniform } x \in [0,1)} \text{ and let } r = r_x \\
&\equiv \text{sample } \overbrace{\text{uniform } y \in [0, 1/k) \text{ and } \underbrace{\text{uniform } x \in B_y \text{ and let } r = r_x}} \\
&\equiv \text{sample uniform } y \in [0, 1/k) \text{ and } \overbrace{\text{uniform } r \in A_y}
\end{aligned}$$

Thus D is the mixture of the k-flat distributions U_{A_y} over uniformly random $y \in [0, 1/k)$. The uniform distribution over $[0, 1/k)$ isn't discrete, but we can accomplish the same thing with a discrete distribution by partitioning $[0, 1/k)$ into finitely many half-open intervals such that A_y is the same for all y in each interval.

■

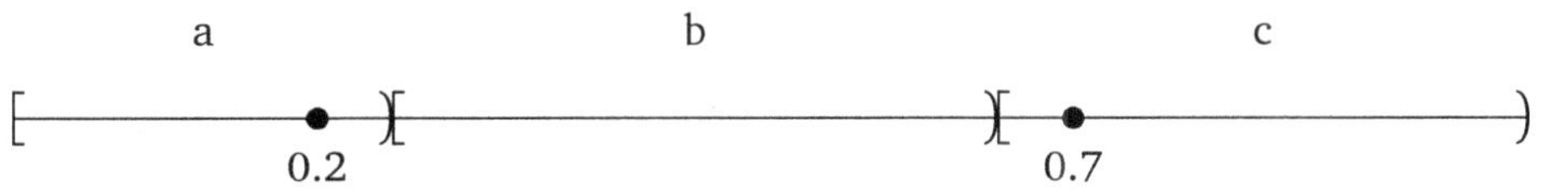

$$D = \tfrac{0.15-0}{0.5} \cdot U_{\{a,b\}} + \tfrac{0.25-0.15}{0.5} \cdot U_{\{a,c\}} + \tfrac{0.5-0.25}{0.5} \cdot U_{\{b,c\}}$$
$$= 0.3 \cdot U_{\{a,b\}} + 0.2 \cdot U_{\{a,c\}} + 0.5 \cdot U_{\{b,c\}}$$

r	a	b	c
$U_{\{a,b\}}(r)$	0.5	0.5	0
$U_{\{a,c\}}(r)$	0.5	0	0.5
$U_{\{b,c\}}(r)$	0	0.5	0.5

Figure 11.10: Example demonstrating the proof of Lemma 11.36

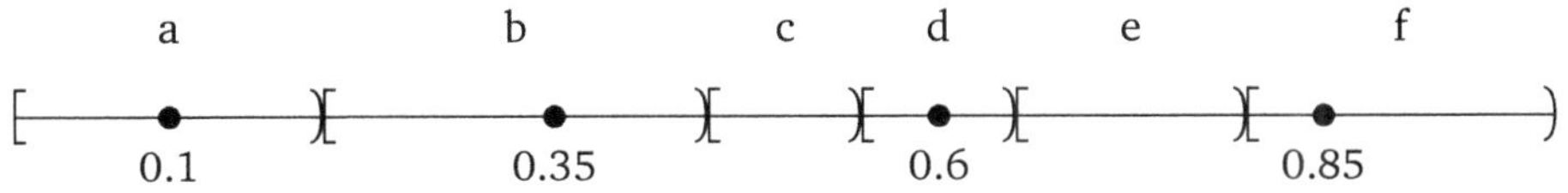

Figure 11.11: Another example demonstrating the proof of Lemma 11.36

Example. Let $S = \{a, b, c\}$ and $k = 2$. The distribution D defined by $D(a) = 0.25$, $D(b) = 0.4$, $D(c) = 0.35$ has min-entropy $\geq 1 = \log k$ since each outcome has probability $\leq 1/2 = 1/k$. The top of Figure 11.10 shows $[0, 1)$ partitioned into $[0, 0.25)$ for a, and $[0.25, 0.65)$ for b, and $[0.65, 1)$ for c. The dots are $B_{0.2} = \{0.2, 0.7\}$, which lie in the intervals corresponding to $A_{0.2} = \{a, c\}$. Starting at $y = 0$, we have $A_0 = \{a, b\}$. As we slide y to the right, A_y remains $\{a, b\}$ until $y = 0.15$, at which point $y + 1/2$ leaves b's interval and enters c's interval. Then A_y remains $\{a, c\}$ until $y = 0.25$, at which point $y + 0/2$ leaves a's interval and enters b's interval. Then A_y remains $\{b, c\}$ for the rest of $y < 0.5$. The bottom of Figure 11.10 shows how D is decomposed into a mixture of 2-flat distributions. ♦

Example. Let $S = \{a, b, c, d, e, f\}$ and $k = 4$. The distribution D defined by $D(a) = 0.2$, $D(b) = 0.25$, $D(c) = 0.1$, $D(d) = 0.1$, $D(e) = 0.15$, $D(f) = 0.2$ has min-entropy $\geq 2 = \log k$ since each outcome has probability $\leq 1/4 = 1/k$. Figure 11.11 shows $[0, 1)$ partitioned into half-open intervals for the elements of S. The dots are $B_{0.1} = \{0.1, 0.35, 0.6, 0.85\}$, which lie in the intervals corresponding to $A_{0.1} = \{a, b, d, f\}$. ♦

11.6.3 Nonconstructive Existence

Proof idea for Theorem 11.33. We use the probabilistic method: A random function E is an (n, ε)-extractor with positive probability. We can't do a union bound over all infinitely many distributions with min-entropy $\geq n$, but by Lemma 11.35 and Lemma 11.36, we can just worry about finitely many flat distributions. The calculation is like in the proof that PRGs exist (Theorem 11.4). ■

Lemma 11.37. *$E\colon \{0,1\}^d \times \{0,1\}^\ell \to \{0,1\}^n$ is a $(\log k, \varepsilon)$-extractor iff for every k-flat distribution U_A over $\{0,1\}^d$:*

$$\Delta\big(E(U_A, U_\ell), U_n\big) \leq \varepsilon$$

Proof of Lemma 11.37. $\Rightarrow$: This is because k-flat distributions have min-entropy $\log k$.

$\Leftarrow$: Consider any distribution D over $\{0,1\}^d$ with min-entropy $\geq \log k$. By Lemma 11.36,

$$D = \sum_{A \subseteq \{0,1\}^d : |A|=k} C(A) \cdot U_A$$

is a mixture of k-flat distributions. Then $E(D, U_\ell)$ is the mixture $\sum_A C(A) \cdot E(U_A, U_\ell)$ because:

$$\begin{aligned} \text{sample } q \sim E(D,U_\ell) &\equiv \text{sample } \underbrace{r \sim D}_{} \text{ and } s \sim U_\ell \text{ and let } q = E(r,s) \\ &\equiv \text{sample } \overbrace{A \sim C \text{ and } r \sim U_A} \underbrace{\text{ and } s \sim U_\ell \text{ and let } q = E(r,s)} \\ &\equiv \text{sample } A \sim C \text{ and } \overbrace{q \sim E(U_A, U_\ell)} \end{aligned}$$

Since $\Delta\big(E(U_A, U_\ell),\, U_n\big) \leq \varepsilon$ for each A by assumption, $\Delta\big(E(D, U_\ell),\, U_n\big) \leq \varepsilon$ (Lemma 11.35). ∎

Proof of Theorem 11.33. Let $\ell = \lceil \log(d/\varepsilon^2) \rceil + 2$. Sample $E\colon \{0,1\}^d \times \{0,1\}^\ell \to \{0,1\}^n$ uniformly at random: For each $(r,s) \in \{0,1\}^d \times \{0,1\}^\ell$ independently, sample $E(r,s) \sim U_n$.

Let $h = n$. This notation conceptually distinguishes the min-entropy h from the output length n, even though they're equal here.

Consider any $A \subseteq \{0,1\}^d$ with $|A| = 2^h$ and any $f\colon \{0,1\}^n \to \{0,1\}$. For each $(r,s) \in A \times \{0,1\}^\ell$, imagine a coin toss where heads means $f(E(r,s)) = 1$. These $2^{h+\ell}$ coin tosses are fully independent, and each has heads probability $p = \mathbf{Pr}\big[f(U_n) = 1\big]$. For any outcome E, the fraction of tosses that are heads is $\mathbf{Pr}\big[f(E(U_A, U_\ell)) = 1\big]$, and by Lemma 7.20:

$$\mathbf{Pr}_E\big[\text{fraction of heads isn't within } \pm\varepsilon \text{ of } p\big] \leq 2e^{-\varepsilon^2 2^{h+\ell}} < 2^{1-\varepsilon^2 2^{h+\ell}} \leq 2^{1-4d2^h}$$

Thus:

$$\begin{aligned} &\mathbf{Pr}_E\big[E \text{ isn't an } (h,\varepsilon)\text{-extractor}\big] \\ =\; &\mathbf{Pr}_E\big[\Delta\big(E(U_A, U_\ell),\, U_n\big) > \varepsilon \text{ for some } 2^h\text{-flat } U_A\big] && \text{(Lemma 11.37)} \\ =\; &\mathbf{Pr}_E\Big[\big|\mathbf{Pr}\big[f(E(U_A, U_\ell)) = 1\big] - p\big| > \varepsilon \text{ for some } 2^h\text{-flat } U_A \text{ and some } f\Big] \\ \leq\; &\textstyle\sum_{A,f} \mathbf{Pr}_E\Big[\big|\mathbf{Pr}\big[f(E(U_A, U_\ell)) = 1\big] - p\big| > \varepsilon\Big] && \text{(union bound)} \\ <\; &\textstyle\sum_{A,f} 2^{1-4d2^h} \\ =\; &\tbinom{2^d}{2^h} \cdot 2^{2^n} \cdot 2^{1-4d2^h} \\ \leq\; &2^{d2^h + 2^h + 1 - 4d2^h} && \text{(since } \tbinom{2^d}{2^h} \leq (2^d)^{2^h} \text{ and } n = h\text{)} \\ <\; &1 \end{aligned}$$

Thus there exists an (h,ε)-extractor $E\colon \{0,1\}^d \times \{0,1\}^\ell \to \{0,1\}^n$. ∎

11.6.4 Extractors via Pseudorandom Generators

Now, we prove Theorem 11.34 by designing a poly-time computable extractor for small poly min-entropy and large poly source length, with log seed length.

This extractor is closely related to the PRG from § 11.4. This is surprising since that PRG fools small circuits and assumes E contains an average-case hard problem, whereas the extractor doesn't involve circuits and works without unproven assumptions. The connection between extractors and pseudorandom generators is a great plot twist for ending Part II.

The connection is based on the following technique for analyzing extractors:

Lemma 11.38. *Consider any* $E\colon \{0,1\}^d \times \{0,1\}^\ell \to \{0,1\}^n$. *Suppose for every* $f\colon \{0,1\}^n \to \{0,1\}$, *at most* B *many* $r \in \{0,1\}^d$ *are bad in the sense that:*

$$\left|\mathbf{Pr}\big[f(E(r,U_\ell))=1\big]-\mathbf{Pr}\big[f(U_n)=1\big]\right| \;>\; \gamma$$

Then E *is an* $(h,\, \gamma + B/2^h)$*-extractor for all* h.

Proof. Consider any distribution D over $\{0,1\}^d$ with min-entropy $\geq h$. To prove that $\Delta\big(E(D,U_\ell), U_n\big) \leq \gamma + B/2^h$, we consider any $f\colon \{0,1\}^n \to \{0,1\}$ and prove that

$$\left|\mathbf{Pr}\big[f(E(D,U_\ell))=1\big]-p\right| \;\leq\; \gamma + B/2^h$$

where $p = \mathbf{Pr}\big[f(U_n)=1\big]$. We have $\mathbf{Pr}_{r\sim D}\big[r \text{ is bad}\big] \leq B/2^h$ since $D(r) \leq 1/2^h$ for each bad r, of which there are $\leq B$. By the law of total probability:

$$\begin{aligned}\mathbf{Pr}\big[f(E(D,U_\ell))=1\big] &\leq \mathbf{Pr}_{r\sim D}\big[r \text{ is good}\big]\cdot \max_{\text{good } r} \mathbf{Pr}\big[f(E(r,U_\ell))=1\big] + \\ &\quad\; \mathbf{Pr}_{r\sim D}\big[r \text{ is bad}\big]\;\; \cdot \max_{\text{bad } r}\; \mathbf{Pr}\big[f(E(r,U_\ell))=1\big] \\ &\leq 1\cdot(p+\gamma)+(B/2^h)\cdot 1 \\ &= p+(\gamma+B/2^h)\end{aligned}$$

Applying this to $\overline{f}$ shows that $\mathbf{Pr}\big[f(E(D,U_\ell))=1\big] \geq p-(\gamma+B/2^h)$. ■

In the statement of Lemma 11.38, f distinguishes the distribution $E(r,U_\ell)$ from U_n, like how f may distinguish a PRG's output $G(U_\ell)$ from U_n. In §11.4, we turned any $g\colon \{0,1\}^m \to \{0,1\}$ into $G(U_\ell)$ and turned any small circuit distinguisher f into a small circuit heuristic for g. Now, we similarly turn any $r \in \{0,1\}^d$ into $E(r,U_\ell)$ and note that the distinguisher-to-heuristic conversion is "black box": It works for all f (not just small circuits), yielding a heuristic that's a modified version of f. Now, we care about the "amount of nonuniform advice" the conversion needs, since this relates to the B in Lemma 11.38. We first encode r with an error correcting code, like we encoded truth tables for worst-case to average-case reductions (§10.3), but now the code need not be locally decodable. Let's flesh out this idea.

In Chapter 9, we denoted a code by E ("encoder"), but now we denote it C ("code") since E stands for "extractor." Also, d,k,ℓ,m,n,r now stand for different things than in Chapter 9.

Recall that an (ℓ,m,n)-system is a tuple $(H_1,\ldots,H_n)$ such that $H_i \subseteq [\ell]$ and $|H_i| = m$ for all $i \in [n]$. If $|H_i \cap H_j| \leq k$ for all pairs $i \neq j$, then we call $(H_1,\ldots,H_n)$ a (k,ℓ,m,n)-system.

Lemma 11.39. *Let* $C\colon \{0,1\}^d \to \{0,1\}^{2^m}$ *be an error correcting code with relative distance* $\geq 1/2-\delta$, *and view a codeword as* $g\colon \{0,1\}^m \to \{0,1\}$. *Let* $(H_1,\ldots,H_n)$ *be a* (k,ℓ,m,n)*-system. Define* $E\colon \{0,1\}^d \times \{0,1\}^\ell \to \{0,1\}^n$ *by* $E(r,s)_i = g(s_{H_i})$ *where* $g = C(r)$. *Then* E *is an* $\big(h,\, n\sqrt{\delta} + 2^{2n2^k}/\delta 2^h\big)$*-extractor for all* h.

Proof. By Lemma 11.38, it suffices to show that for every $f\colon \{0,1\}^n \to \{0,1\}$, at most $2^{2n2^k}/\delta$ many $r \in \{0,1\}^d$ are bad in the sense that:

$$\left|\mathbf{Pr}\big[f(E(r,U_\ell))=1\big]-\mathbf{Pr}\big[f(U_n)=1\big]\right| \;>\; n\sqrt{\delta}$$

If r is bad, then by Lemma 11.26 with $G\colon \{0,1\}^\ell \to \{0,1\}^n$ defined by $G(s) = E(r,s)$, there exists $f^*\colon \{0,1\}^m \to \{0,1\}$ such that

$$\mathbf{Pr}_{z\sim U_m}\big[f^*(z)=g(z)\big] \;>\; 1/2+(n\sqrt{\delta})/n \;=\; 1/2+\sqrt{\delta}$$

so g is in the ball of relative radius $1/2 - \sqrt{\delta}$ centered at f^*, and furthermore f^* is determined by these things:

$$\begin{array}{ll} i \in [n] & (n \text{ possibilities}) \\ g_1 \colon \{0,1\}^{|H_i \cap H_1|} \to \{0,1\} & (2^{2^{|H_i \cap H_1|}} \leq 2^{2^k} \text{ possibilities}) \\ \vdots & \vdots \\ g_{i-1} \colon \{0,1\}^{|H_i \cap H_{i-1}|} \to \{0,1\} & (2^{2^{|H_i \cap H_{i-1}|}} \leq 2^{2^k} \text{ possibilities}) \\ y_{\geq i} \in \{0,1\}^{n-i+1} & (2^{n-i+1} \leq 2^n \text{ possibilities}) \\ b \in \{0,1\} & (2 \text{ possibilities}) \end{array}$$

The number of possibilities of f^* is:

$$\leq n \cdot 2^{2^k} \cdots 2^{2^k} \cdot 2^n \cdot 2 \leq 2^{\log n + (n-1)2^k + n + 1} \leq 2^{2n2^k}$$

By Theorem 9.8 (on list decoding), for any f^*, at most $1/\delta$ many r are such that $g = C(r)$ is in the ball of relative radius $1/2 - \sqrt{\delta}$ centered at f^*. In total:

$$\text{number of bad } r \leq (\text{number of } f^*) \cdot (\text{number of bad } r \text{ per } f^*) \leq 2^{2n2^k}/\delta$$ ■

Proof idea for Theorem 11.34. We want to extract n bits from a crude source with min-entropy n^b (for small $b > 1$) and length n^c (for large c) using seed length $\ell = O(\log n)$. We use the code from Theorem 9.24 and the set system from Lemma 11.28 and crunch the parameters in Lemma 11.39. Ignoring the minor influence of ε and δ:

- $k \approx (b-1)\log n$ to handle min-entropy n^b.
- $m \approx 2c \log n$ so the source length is n^c.
- $\ell \approx a \log n$ for a large enough constant a to achieve the desired output length:

$$n \approx (k\ell/em^2)^k \approx \left((b-1)a/e(2c)^2\right)^{(b-1)\log n} \approx 2^{\log n}$$ ■

Proof of Theorem 11.34 (ancillary). Define:

$$\delta = (\varepsilon/2n)^2 \qquad m = 2\lceil \log(n^c/\delta) \rceil \qquad q = 2^{m/2}$$

There exists a code $C \colon \{0,1\}^d \to \{0,1\}^{2^m}$ with relative distance $\geq 1/2 - \delta$, message length $d = (m/2)\lfloor 2q\delta \rfloor \geq \lfloor q\delta \rfloor \geq n^c$, and codeword length $q^2 = 2^m$ (Theorem 9.24). Define:

$$k = \left\lfloor \log\left(n^{b-1} + \log(\delta\varepsilon/2)/n\right) \right\rfloor - 1 \qquad \ell = m\left\lceil (3m/k) n^{1/k} \right\rceil$$

There exists a (k, ℓ, m, n)-system $(H_1, \ldots, H_n)$ since $n \leq (k\ell/em^2)^k$ (Lemma 11.28). Thus E is an $\left(h,\, n\sqrt{\delta} + 2^{2n2^k}/\delta 2^h\right)$-extractor for all h (Lemma 11.39). It has source length $d \geq n^c$ and output length n. The error is $\leq \varepsilon/2 + \varepsilon/2 = \varepsilon$ if $h = n^b$. The seed length is $\ell = O(\log n)$ because $m = O(\log n)$ and $k = \Omega(\log n)$ and $n^{1/k} = O(1)$ since $\log(n^{1/k}) = (\log n)/k = (\log n)/\Omega(\log n) = O(1)$. Also, E is computable in time poly n because C is encodable in time poly q = poly n, and $(H_1, \ldots, H_n)$ can be found in time poly$(n2^\ell)$ = poly n, and the rest of E's definition is straightforward. ■

Exercises

11.1 Prove that for all distributions D_0 and D_1 over S and every function $f: S \to T$, we have $\Delta\big(f(D_0), f(D_1)\big) \le \Delta(D_0, D_1)$. That is, functions can only bring distributions closer together, not push them farther apart.

11.2 Prove that for all distributions D_0 and D_1 over S, $\mathbf{Pr}_{s \sim D_1}\big[D_1(s) < D_0(s)/2\big] \le \Delta(D_0, D_1)$.

11.3 Prove that a pseudorandom generator works even when its seed is statistically close to uniform rather than perfectly uniform (say, the seed is an extractor's output): Suppose $G: \{0,1\}^\ell \to \{0,1\}^n$ is an ε-PRG for a set F of functions, and D is a distribution over $\{0,1\}^\ell$ such that $\Delta(D, U_\ell) \le \delta$. Prove that $G(D)$ and U_n are $(\delta + \varepsilon)$-indistinguishable by F.

11.4 In this exercise, you'll design pseudorandom generators that fool decision trees.

(a) As a warmup, prove that if $G: \{0,1\}^\ell \to \{0,1\}^n$ is an $(\varepsilon/2^{n+1})$-bias generator, then $\Delta\big(G(U_\ell), U_n\big) \le \varepsilon$.

(b) Prove that if $G: \{0,1\}^\ell \to \{0,1\}^n$ is an $(\varepsilon/2m)$-bias generator, then G is an ε-PRG for decision trees with $\le m$ leaves. (This subsumes Exercise 11.4.a since every $f: \{0,1\}^n \to \{0,1\}$ has a decision tree with 2^n leaves.) Hint: Theorem 6.21.

(c) Design a poly-time computable 0-PRG $G: \{0,1\}^k \to \{0,1\}^n$ for d-juntas—and therefore also for depth-d decision trees—with seed length $k = O(d \log n)$. Furthermore, G should be linear in the sense that $G(s) = sH$ for some $k \times n$ matrix H over $\mathbb{Z}_2$, viewing s as a $1 \times k$ vector and $G(s)$ as a $1 \times n$ vector. Hint: This is essentially Exercise 8.2 but with a bit string field instead of a prime field.

(d) Prove that if $G_1: \{0,1\}^\ell \to \{0,1\}^k$ is an ε-bias generator and $G_2: \{0,1\}^k \to \{0,1\}^n$ is a linear 0-PRG for d-juntas (as in Exercise 11.4.c), then $G_2 \circ G_1: \{0,1\}^\ell \to \{0,1\}^n$ is an ε-PRG for parities of at most d variables ($\oplus_I$ where $|I| \le d$).

(e) Combine Theorem 11.7, Exercise 11.4.c, and Exercise 11.4.d to obtain an ε-PRG for parities of at most d out of n variables with seed length $O\big(\log(d/\varepsilon) + \log\log n\big)$ and computable in time $\mathrm{poly}\big(n \log(1/\varepsilon)\big)$.

(f) Conclude that there exists an ε-PRG for n-variable depth-d decision trees (in particular, d-juntas) with seed length $O\big(d + \log(1/\varepsilon) + \log\log n\big)$ and computable in time $\mathrm{poly}\big(n \log(1/\varepsilon)\big)$.

11.5 In this exercise, you'll show that pseudorandom generators for space-efficient computations can be used for randomness-efficient amplification of time-efficient computations (§8.5.2). The connection is that the usual amplification method—which runs the original computation repeatedly—only needs small space to remember how many runs accepted (it need not remember which runs accepted).

(a) Suppose a decision problem A has a 1/3-error randomized program Π using $\le b$ random bits on every valid input x of size N. Suppose $n \ge 18 \ln(2/\varepsilon)$ is odd and $G: \{0,1\}^\ell \to (\{0,1\}^b)^n$ is an $\varepsilon/2$-PRG for length-n width-n block-size-b streaming branching programs. Prove that the following randomized program solves A on inputs of size N with error probability ε and only ℓ random bits.

Two-sided-error randomness-efficient amplification using a PRG (11.7)

$\Pi'(x)$:
  sample $s \sim U_\ell$
  compute $(q_1, \ldots, q_n) \leftarrow G(s)$
  for each $i \in [n]$: run $\Pi(x; q_i)$
  accept iff a majority of the runs accepted

(b) Show that the PRG G_d defined in § 11.3.3 yields randomness-efficient amplification of one-sided-error randomized programs, by a proof that uses hash mixing (Lemma 11.13) but is otherwise much simpler than the proof that G_d is a PRG: Suppose a decision problem A has a 1/3-one-sided-error randomized program Π using $\leq b$ random bits on every valid input x of size N. With ordinary amplification, achieving one-sided error probability 3^{-n} would take bn random bits. Consider $G_d : (\{0,1\}^{3b-1})^d \times \{0,1\}^b \to (\{0,1\}^b)^n$ where $n = 2^d$ from §11.3.3. Prove that the following randomized program solves A on inputs of size N with one-sided error probability $3^{-n} + (d+4)2^{-b/3}$ and only $(3b-1)d + b = O(bd)$ random bits.

One-sided-error randomness-efficient amplification using a PRG (11.8)

$\Pi'(x)$:
  sample $(r_1, \ldots, r_d, s)$ uniformly from $(\{0,1\}^{3b-1})^d \times \{0,1\}^b$
  compute $(q_1, \ldots, q_n) \leftarrow G_d(r_1, \ldots, r_d, s)$
  for each $i \in [n]$: run $\Pi(x; q_i)$
  accept iff at least one run accepted

Hint: Suppose $A(x) = 1$. Say $(r_1, \ldots, r_d, s)$ is *bad* iff $\Pi(x; q_i)$ rejects for every component q_i of $G_d(r_1, \ldots, r_d, s)$. Say $(r_1, \ldots, r_d)$ is *bad* iff $\mathbf{Pr}_s\big[(r_1, \ldots, r_d, s) \text{ is bad}\big] > 3^{-2^d} + 4 \cdot 2^{-b/3}$. Show that G_d's recursive definition maintains the invariant that $\mathbf{Pr}_{r_1,\ldots,r_d}\big[(r_1, \ldots, r_d) \text{ is bad}\big] \leq d2^{-b/3}$.

11.6 For any $G\colon \{0,1\}^\ell \to \{0,1\}^n$ and $a \in \{0,1\}^n$, define $G_a\colon \{0,1\}^\ell \to \{0,1\}^n$ by $G_a(s) = G(s) \oplus a$. Prove that if G is an ε-PRG for size-t circuits (with $\leq t$ many $\wedge$ and $\vee$ gates), then $G(U_\ell)$ and $G_a(U_\ell)$ are 2ε-indistinguishable by size-t circuits. Hint: First, prove G_a is an ε-PRG for size-t circuits.

11.7 Lemma 11.25 says "distinguishers yield predictors." Prove a converse showing that "predictors yield distinguishers": For every distribution D over $\{0,1\}^n$, if $i \in [n]$ and $f\colon \{0,1\}^{i-1} \to \{0,1\}$ are such that

$$\mathbf{Pr}_{x \sim D}\big[f(x_{<i}) = x_i\big] \; > \; 1/2 + \varepsilon$$

then $f'\colon \{0,1\}^n \to \{0,1\}$ defined by $f'(x) = f(x_{<i}) \oplus x_i$ is such that:

$$\Big|\mathbf{Pr}\big[f'(D) = 1\big] - \mathbf{Pr}\big[f'(U_n) = 1\big]\Big| \; > \; \varepsilon$$

11.8 For this exercise, redefine "(t,ε)-hard" and "(t,ε)-PRG" to be for t-node branching programs (ordinary, not streaming) instead of circuits. Prove an analogue of Theorem 11.23: If E contains a total $A\colon \{0,1\}^+ \to \{0,1\}$ such that A_N is $(2^{cN}, 2^{-cN})$-hard for some constant $c > 0$ and all large enough N, then there exists a $(t, 1/7)$-PRG with seed length $O(\log t)$ and computable in time poly t, for all large enough $t \geq n$, and therefore BP*L $\subseteq$ P. Here, BP*L (from Exercise 7.15) is the variant of BPL allowing "read-rand Reg[i] $\leftarrow$ Rand[Reg[j]]" instead of "read-rand Reg[i]" (and not counting the randomness toward the space).

11.9 Prove that for every constant $c < 1$ and all large enough n, there does not exist an $(n, 1/2)$-PRG with seed length $\leq c \log n$ for n-variable circuits.

11.10 Prove that if P = NP, then there exists a $(t, 1/7)$-PRG with seed length $O(\log t)$ and computable in time poly t, for all large enough $t \geq n$. Hint: Use Exercise 5.15 and Theorem 10.19.

11.11 In this exercise, you'll prove that PRGs for monotone circuits automatically fool nonmonotone circuits with slightly worse parameters.

(a) Prove that for every size-t nonmonotone circuit $C\colon \{0,1\}^n \to \{0,1\}$ and every $k \in \{0,\ldots,n\}$, some size-$O(t + n^2 \log^2 n)$ monotone circuit $C_k\colon \{0,1\}^n \to \{0,1\}$ agrees with C on all weight-k inputs. Hint: The threshold function $T_k^m\colon \{0,1\}^m \to \{0,1\}$, defined by $T_k^m(x) = 1$ iff weight$(x) \geq k$, has a size-$O(m \log^2 m)$ monotone circuit derived from a sorting network, as in Exercise 5.16.

(b) Prove that for some constant c, every $\varepsilon/2(n+1)$-PRG for size-$c(t + n^2 \log^2 n)$ monotone circuits is an ε-PRG for size-t (nonmonotone) circuits. Hint: For any nonmonotone circuit C, the relevant monotone circuits are (for all k) T_k^n and $C'_k\colon \{0,1\}^n \to \{0,1\}$ defined by:

$$C'_k(x) = \begin{cases} C(x) & \text{if weight}(x) = k \\ 1 & \text{if weight}(x) > k \\ 0 & \text{if weight}(x) < k \end{cases}$$

11.12 Suppose $\mathbb{F}$ is a field of size m. For all $1 \leq k < m$, use univariate polynomials of degree $\leq k$ over $\mathbb{F}$ to design a structured (k, ℓ, m, n)-system where $\ell = m^2$ and $n = m^{k+1}$. How does this compare to Lemma 11.28?

11.13 A *bit-fixing source* with min-entropy h is a distribution over $\{0,1\}^d$ such that the bits indexed by some $I \subseteq [d]$ with $|I| = h$ are uniformly random, and the other bits are constants ("fixed"). This exercise is about deterministic extractors with error $\varepsilon = 0$ for bit-fixing sources.

(a) Show how to extract 1 bit from bit-fixing sources with min-entropy ≥ 1.

(b) Show how to extract 2 bits from bit-fixing sources with min-entropy $> d/2$, assuming d is even.

(c) Show how to extract 2 bits from bit-fixing sources with min-entropy $> d/3$, assuming d is divisible by 3. Hint: Lemma 8.5.

11.14 Recall that deterministic extractors may exist if we restrict the set of allowed crude sources. One natural restriction is that the source is samplable by a time-efficient algorithm, say a small circuit. (Real-world sources of randomness are generated by physical processes, which are reasonable to model as efficient algorithms.) Such a circuit takes uniformly random input bits and outputs a sample from a distribution D over $\{0,1\}^d$.

Prove that uniform poly-time extraction from poly-size circuit samplers would require a "strong time hierarchy conjecture" with a uniform upper bound and nonuniform lower bound: If $E\colon \{0,1\}^+ \to \{0,1\}$ is in P and for some constant $c > 1$ and all large enough d, $E_d\colon \{0,1\}^d \to \{0,1\}$ is a $(d-1, 1/5)$-extractor for size-d^c circuit samplers, then E has circuit size complexity $\Omega(d^c)$.

11.15 In this exercise, you'll prove that deterministic extractors for independent sources also extract from sources with space-efficient samplers. We model such a sampler as a layered dag with each edge labeled 0 or 1 (multi-edges allowed), with only the start node in the first layer, and with only the last layer containing a sink. Assuming there are $d+1$ layers, it samples from a distribution over $\{0,1\}^d$ by outputting the edge labels along a random walk from the start node. Space corresponds to the log of the number of nodes.

(a) Suppose $D = \sum_i C(i) \cdot D_i$ is a mixture of distributions over S, and U is the uniform distribution over S. Prove that if $\mathbf{Pr}_{i \sim C}\big[\Delta(D_i, U) > \varepsilon\big] \le \delta$, then $\Delta(D, U) \le \delta + \varepsilon$.

(b) Prove that if $D = \sum_{i=1}^m C(i) \cdot D_i$ is a mixture of m distributions over S, and D has min-entropy $\ge h + \log(m/\delta)$, then $\mathbf{Pr}_{i \sim C}\big[D_i \text{ has min-entropy} < h\big] \le \delta$.

(c) Suppose T is a set of distributions over $\{0,1\}^d$, and $E\colon \{0,1\}^d \to \{0,1\}^n$ is an (h, ε)-extractor for T, meaning that $\Delta\big(E(D), U_n\big) \le \varepsilon$ for every $D \in T$ with min-entropy $\ge h$. Prove E is an $\big(h + \log(m/\delta),\, \delta + \varepsilon\big)$-extractor for mixtures of at most m distributions from T.

(d) Prove that if d is even and $E\colon \{0,1\}^{d/2} \times \{0,1\}^{d/2} \to \{0,1\}^n$ is a two-source (h, ε)-extractor, then E is an $\big(h + \log(m/\delta),\, \delta + \varepsilon\big)$-extractor for m-node samplers.

(e) Show that there exists a poly-time computable $\big(d/2 + \log(2m/\gamma^3),\, \gamma\big)$-extractor with output length 1 for m-node samplers with even source length d.

11.16 Prove that if D is a mixture of two distributions D_1 and D_2 over S, then $\Delta(D_1, D_2) = \Delta(D_1, D) + \Delta(D, D_2)$, so the triangle inequality (Lemma 11.2) is tight.

11.17 Recall Lemma 11.35: A mixture of distributions that are close to uniform is close to uniform. Now, you'll prove that a mixture of few distributions that are far from uniform is far from uniform.

(a) Suppose D is a mixture of two distributions D_1 and D_2 over S, and U is the uniform distribution over S. Prove that if $\Delta(D_1, U) \ge 1 - \delta$ and $\Delta(D_2, U) \ge 1 - \varepsilon$, then $\Delta(D, U) \ge 1 - \delta - \varepsilon$.

(b) Suppose D is a mixture of n distributions $D_1, \ldots, D_n$ over S, and U is the uniform distribution over S. Prove that if $\Delta(D_i, U) \ge 1 - \varepsilon$ for each i, then $\Delta(D, U) \ge 1 - n\varepsilon$.

11.18 Use the proof of Lemma 11.36 to express the distribution D over $S = \{\mathrm{a}, \mathrm{b}, \mathrm{c}, \mathrm{d}\}$ defined by $D(\mathrm{a}) = 1/4$, $D(\mathrm{b}) = 1/6$, $D(\mathrm{c}) = 1/3$, $D(\mathrm{d}) = 1/4$ as a mixture of 3-flat distributions.

11.19 A *two-source (h_1, h_2, ε)-extractor* is a function $E\colon \{0,1\}^d \times \{0,1\}^d \to \{0,1\}^n$ such that for all distributions D_1 and D_2 over $\{0,1\}^d$ with min-entropies $\ge h_1$ and $\ge h_2$ respectively:

$$\Delta\big(E(D_1, D_2), U_n\big) \le \varepsilon$$

(a) Prove that $E\colon \{0,1\}^d \times \{0,1\}^d \to \{0,1\}^n$ is a two-source $\big(\log k, \log k, \varepsilon\big)$-extractor iff for all k-flat distributions U_{A_1} and U_{A_2}:

$$\Delta\big(E(U_{A_1}, U_{A_2}), U_n\big) \le \varepsilon$$

(b) Prove that for all $0 < \varepsilon \leq 1/2$ and integers $h \leq d \leq \varepsilon^2 2^h/4$, there exists a two-source (h,h,ε)-extractor with individual source length d and output length $n = \lfloor 2h - \log(1/\varepsilon^2) \rfloor - 2$.

11.20 A *strong seeded* (h,ε)*-extractor* is a function $E\colon \{0,1\}^d \times \{0,1\}^\ell \to \{0,1\}^n$ such that for every distribution D over $\{0,1\}^d$ with min-entropy $\geq h$,

$$\Delta\big((E(D,U_\ell),U_\ell),\,(U_n,U_\ell)\big) \;\leq\; \varepsilon$$

where $(E(D,U_\ell),U_\ell)$ means $(E(r,s),s)$ where $r \sim D$ and $s \sim U_\ell$. Compared to ordinary (non-strong) seeded extractors, the output distribution must be close to uniform even if the seed is included in the output. The seed s is reusable because it's "as good as independent" of $E(r,s)$. Strong seeded extractors make sense even when the seed contains more randomness than the source, because the seed's randomness is "preserved." The seed is like a catalyst in a chemical reaction—a substance that facilitates the reaction but ultimately appears as if it didn't participate in the reaction. In this exercise, you'll prove that pairwise avoiding hash functions are strong seeded extractors.

(a) The *collision probability* of a distribution D over S is $\sum_{r\in S} D(r)^2$ (the probability that two independent samples from D are equal). Prove that if D has collision probability p, then $\Delta(D,U) \leq \frac{1}{2}\sqrt{|S|p-1}$ where U is the uniform distribution over S. Hint: Apply Theorem A.26 to the vectors $D-U$ and C where:

$$C(r) \;=\; \begin{cases} 1 & \text{if } D(r) \geq U(r) \\ -1 & \text{if } D(r) < U(r) \end{cases}$$

(b) Let $H\colon \{0,1\}^\ell \times \{0,1\}^d \to \{0,1\}^n$ be a pairwise avoiding hash function. Prove that if $n \leq h - 2\log(1/\varepsilon)$ then $E\colon \{0,1\}^d \times \{0,1\}^\ell \to \{0,1\}^n$ defined by $E(r,s) = H(s,r)$ is a strong seeded (h,ε)-extractor.

11.21 Recall the definition of strong seeded extractors from Exercise 11.20.

(a) Prove that if $\Delta\big((E(D,U_\ell),U_\ell),\,(U_n,U_\ell)\big) \leq \varepsilon$ then:

$$\mathbf{Pr}_{s\sim U_\ell}\big[\Delta\big(E(D,s),\,U_n\big) > \sqrt{\varepsilon}\big] \;\leq\; \sqrt{\varepsilon}$$

(b) Prove that if $\mathbf{Pr}_{s\sim U_\ell}\big[\Delta\big(E(D,s),\,U_n\big) > \gamma\big] \leq \delta$ then:

$$\Delta\big((E(D,U_\ell),U_\ell),\,(U_n,U_\ell)\big) \;\leq\; \gamma+\delta$$

Notes

For surveys on pseudorandom generators and extractors, see [530, 480, 114, 120, 241].

Statistical distance is also known as "total variation distance."

ε-bias generators were introduced by [384, 411]. The construction from Theorem 11.7 is due to [17]. If G is an ε-bias generator, then $G'(s_1,\ldots,s_d) = G(s_1) \oplus \cdots \oplus G(s_d)$ fools polynomials of total degree d over $\mathbb{Z}_2$ [547].

The PRG for space-efficient computations (§ 11.3) is known as "Nisan's generator" [394]. $\mathsf{BPL} \subseteq \mathsf{TISP}[\text{poly}\,N, \log^2 N]$ (Theorem 11.21) is due to [396]. An alternative PRG for space-efficient computations using "expander graphs" instead of pairwise uniform hashing is due to

[264]. The seed length of Theorem 11.19 for width-w streaming branching programs can be improved for width 2 (just using an ε-bias generator) [75, 241] and for width 3 [363].

The PRG for time-efficient computations based on average-case hardness (§11.4) is known as the "Nisan–Wigderson generator" [398]. The PRG based on worst-case hardness (Theorem 11.22) is due to [265], with different proofs due to [509, 481]. Derandomization with very low time overhead is also possible under certain hardness assumptions [119].

Pseudorandom generators imply derandomization, but not necessarily the converse. However, $\mathsf{P} = \mathsf{BPP}$ iff there exists a "targeted pseudorandom generator" which is told (as part of the input) which circuit it's supposed to fool (and has log seed length and is poly-time computable) [197, 200].

Pseudorandom generators are for derandomizing two-sided-error algorithms. "Hitting set generators" are the analogue for one-sided error. But there are techniques for using hitting set generators to derandomize two-sided-error algorithms anyway, for both time [206] and space [121].

The "dot product" two-source extractor (Theorem 11.31) is due to [125]. Much better two-source extractors (but where the min-entropy bound applies to each source individually) are due to [116, 336].

[399] initiated the study of seeded extractors and used them to prove that if $A \in \mathsf{BPL}$ by a program with randomness efficiency polylog N, then $A \in \mathsf{L}$. The seeded extractor based on PRGs (Theorem 11.34) is due to [522]. Poly-time computable seeded extractors that are essentially as good as the nonconstructive seeded extractors from Theorem 11.33 are known [227].

Exercise 11.4 is due to [384]. Exercise 11.5.b is due to [351]. Exercise 11.11 is due to [289]. Exercise 11.13 is due to [127]. Exercise 11.17 is due to [550]. Exercise 11.20 is the "leftover hash lemma" and is due to [240].

Extractors for bit-fixing sources (as in Exercise 11.13) were studied in [286, 181]. Extractors for circuit samplers (as in Exercise 11.14) were studied in [524, 548]. Extractors for space-efficient samplers (as in Exercise 11.15) were studied in [285, 115].

Part III

SCOPE OF COMPLEXITY

Chapter 12

Cryptography

Cryptography is a vital component of computer security. Cryptography is about secure communication over a channel where an adversary can observe, and possibly interfere with, the communication. This has several "dimensions":

- Goals: One goal of cryptography is *confidentiality*—the adversary shouldn't learn anything about the message being transmitted. To achieve this, the sender *encrypts* the message in a way that the intended receiver can *decrypt* but the adversary cannot. Another goal of cryptography is *authenticity*—the adversary shouldn't be able to impersonate the sender or tamper with the message without being detected.
- Attack scenarios: What is the adversary capable of? A passive adversary may just eavesdrop on the communication channel. A more active adversary may trick the sender into encrypting a message of the adversary's choice, for example. Choosing a cryptographic protocol involves judging what kind of adversaries pose a realistic threat. There's a tradeoff—protocols that withstand stronger adversaries are generally less efficient.
- Private versus public keys: Decryption requires a *key*—a secret piece of information analogous to a physical key for unlocking a box containing the message. In the *private* (or *symmetric*) key setting, the sender uses an identical key for encryption. In the *public* (or *asymmetric*) key setting, the encryption key is different and is made public, so anyone can send an encrypted message to the receiver who possesses the secret decryption key.

Entire books are devoted to exploring all combinations of these aspects. This chapter focuses on private-key encryption with a passive eavesdropper. This tip of the iceberg showcases how computational complexity puts cryptography on a firm foundation:

- Precise definitions: To know that a cryptographic protocol is secure, we must first know what that even means. Intuition won't cut it. Given what's at stake (financial information, government intelligence, and so forth), we need mathematical precision. "Theoretically unbreakable" protocols are often impractical and overkill. Protocols that are secure against somewhat efficient adversaries—say, computations taking only a thousand years—are practical and secure enough. Cryptography harnesses what efficient computations *can't* do—the upside of intractability.
- Rigorous proofs: Cryptography has a long history of protocols that seemed secure but were later broken, sometimes with disastrous consequences. For example, attackers exposed millions of credit card numbers by exploiting flaws in the RC4 encryption used in Wired Equivalent Privacy (WEP) for Wi-Fi security. We want to be sure that a cryptographic protocol is secure not just against known types of attacks, but against literally any adversary modeled as a somewhat efficient computation. This would preclude any unanticipated attacks. These proofs involve several tools from Part II.

- Formal assumptions: Proving security against somewhat efficient adversaries would require proving that certain computational problems are intractable. Cryptography requires even stronger intractability assumptions than $\mathsf{P} \neq \mathsf{NP}$. Thus unconditional proofs of security are unattainable for the foreseeable future. But we can give conditional proofs, showing that a protocol is secure *assuming* the conjecture that a certain simple, well-studied problem is average-case hard. Such proofs are by reduction: We could turn a hypothetical security-breaching adversary into a heuristic for the simple problem. This is better than just assuming the protocol is secure, because if the conjecture has been vetted by experts and withstood considerable effort at designing heuristics, then we can be confident in protocols based on that conjecture.

Besides the obvious motivation from computer security, cryptography has other benefits for computational complexity: Pseudorandom functions (§12.4) are integral parts of many cryptographic protocols, but they're also useful for showing the intractability of some problems where NP-completeness isn't known to apply (§12.5). They also help explain the limitations of machine learning (§13.7) and of circuit lower bound techniques (§18.7).

12.1 Perfectly Secure Encryption

12.1.1 Syntax

The sender, receiver, and adversary have monikers: Alice (A) wants to send Bob (B) a message over a channel observed by Eve the Evil Eavesdropper. Alice encrypts the message to get a *ciphertext*, which she sends over the channel. Bob decrypts the ciphertext to recover the original message. Since Eve sees the ciphertext, why couldn't she decrypt it like Bob does? Because encryption and decryption use a key that Alice and Bob know but Eve doesn't. See Figure 12.1.

History has shown it's unwise to assume Eve doesn't know how the encryption and decryption algorithms work. In fact, these algorithms should be public so they can be extensively tested. The key should encapsulate everything Eve doesn't know about encryption and decryption. Keeping the key secret requires physical security: Alice and Bob could meet in person ahead of time to agree on the key, or one of them could send the key by a courier with a briefcase handcuffed to their wrist. (Public-key encryption is another option, which is beyond the scope of this book.)

A *private-key encryption scheme* is a pair of functions:

- Encryption: $E\colon \{0,1\}^\ell \times \{0,1\}^n \to \{0,1\}^c$
- Decryption: $D\colon \{0,1\}^\ell \times \{0,1\}^c \to \{0,1\}^n$

ℓ is the *key length*, n is the *message length*, and c is the *ciphertext length*.

- Alice encrypts a message $m \in \{0,1\}^n$ using a key $k \in \{0,1\}^\ell$ to get a ciphertext $E(k,m) \in \{0,1\}^c$, which we also write as $E_k(m)$.
- Bob decrypts a ciphertext $x \in \{0,1\}^c$ using a key $k \in \{0,1\}^\ell$ to get a message $D(k,x) \in \{0,1\}^n$, which we also write as $D_k(x)$.

We must have $D_k(E_k(m)) = m$ for all m and k: Bob gets the original message if he decrypts the ciphertext using the same key Alice used to encrypt the message. We assume Bob always receives whatever ciphertext Alice sent—Eve can't tamper with it, and there's no accidental corruption as there is with error correcting codes (Chapter 9).

In theory, we consider infinite families of private-key encryption schemes, parameterized by n. We assume that ℓ and c are $(\operatorname{poly} n)$-time computable functions of n, and that $E(n;k,m)$

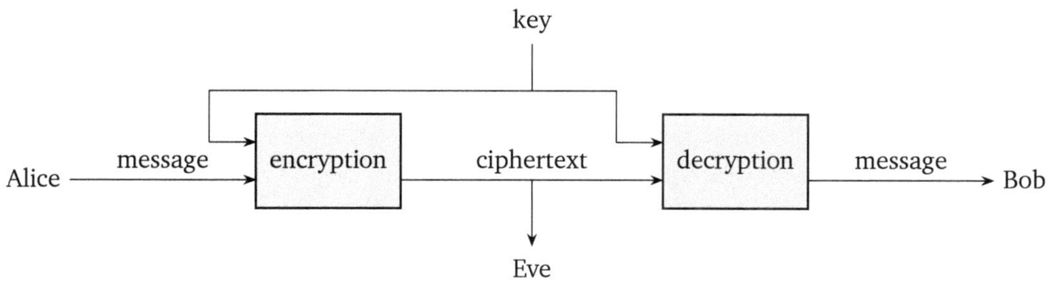

Figure 12.1: Private-key encryption scheme

and $D(n; k, x)$ are computable by uniform, deterministic (poly n)-time programs. (Handling more active adversaries may require randomized encryption, but deterministic encryption is good enough for the setting we consider.) With this in mind, we generally consider a single, unspecified n. This chapter typically has $c = n$ even though that's not mandatory.

With the syntax established, we move on to semantics: What does it mean for an encryption scheme to be secure?

12.1.2 Security

"Secret" means "random." The secret key must be random because if Alice and Bob pick it in a deterministic way, then Eve could obtain the key in the same way. We assume the key is sampled from U_ℓ, the uniform distribution over $\{0,1\}^\ell$. It's essential to use a pure source of randomness for the key. Real-world cryptosystems have been broken because the key wasn't as random as it was assumed to be.

Perfect security for private-key encryption means *Eve cannot learn anything about the message.* This is more subtle than it seems at first glance.

- *Cannot* means we must consider literally anything Eve could do with the ciphertext, not only foreseeable types of attacks.
- *Learn* means after seeing the ciphertext, Eve would know something about the message that she didn't know before. Eve might have any prior information—perhaps that the message is formatted as a bank account number, or that it's either "buy" or "sell." An encryption scheme should be applicable in any context, regardless of Eve's prior knowledge.
- *Anything* means any function of the message whatsoever. Preventing Eve from learning the whole message or even part of the message isn't enough. For example, it's unacceptable if Eve can sometimes determine whether the bank account number is divisible by 3.

This boils down to a simple definition:

Definition. A private-key encryption scheme (E, D) with key length ℓ is *perfectly secure* iff the distributions $E_{U_\ell}(m)$ are identical for all messages m. ◄

This means the distribution over ciphertexts doesn't depend on the message. Thus for any distribution over messages (representing Eve's prior knowledge), the ciphertext is independent of the message. Anything Eve can do after seeing the ciphertext, she could have done without seeing it, by just sampling a ciphertext on her own. She learns nothing.

Another perspective on perfect security is analogous to Lemma 11.3: If we toss a fair coin to pick which of two messages to encrypt, and show Eve the ciphertext and ask her to guess which message was encrypted, then her success probability is the same as a blind guess, no matter how smart (or dumb!) she is.

Lemma 12.1. *A private-key encryption scheme (E, D) with key length ℓ and ciphertext length c is perfectly secure iff for every pair of messages $m_0 \neq m_1$ and every function $f: \{0,1\}^c \to \{0,1\}$, we have $\mathbf{Pr}_{i \sim U_1, k \sim U_\ell}\big[f(E_k(m_i)) = i\big] = 1/2$.*

Proof. $\Rightarrow$: Suppose (E, D) is perfectly secure, and consider any $m_0 \neq m_1$ and f. By the law of total probability,

$$\begin{aligned}\mathbf{Pr}_{i,k}\big[f(E_k(m_i)) = i\big] &= \mathbf{Pr}_i[i=0] \cdot \mathbf{Pr}_k\big[f(E_k(m_0)) = 0\big] + \mathbf{Pr}_i[i=1] \cdot \mathbf{Pr}_k\big[f(E_k(m_1)) = 1\big] \\ &= \tfrac{1}{2} \cdot \big(1 - \mathbf{Pr}_k\big[f(E_k(m_0)) = 1\big]\big) + \tfrac{1}{2} \cdot \mathbf{Pr}_k\big[f(E_k(m_1)) = 1\big] \\ &= 1/2\end{aligned}$$

since $\mathbf{Pr}_k\big[f(E_k(m_0)) = 1\big] = \mathbf{Pr}_k\big[f(E_k(m_1)) = 1\big]$ because $E_{U_\ell}(m_0)$ and $E_{U_\ell}(m_1)$ are the same distribution.

$\Leftarrow$: Suppose (E, D) is not perfectly secure, so there exist $m_0 \neq m_1$ such that $E_{U_\ell}(m_0)$ and $E_{U_\ell}(m_1)$ are different distributions and therefore $\mathbf{Pr}_k\big[f(E_k(m_0)) = 1\big] \neq \mathbf{Pr}_k\big[f(E_k(m_1)) = 1\big]$ for some f. Like in the $\Rightarrow$ direction:

$$\mathbf{Pr}_{i,k}\big[f(E_k(m_i)) = i\big] = \big(1 - \mathbf{Pr}_k\big[f(E_k(m_0)) = 1\big] + \mathbf{Pr}_k\big[f(E_k(m_1)) = 1\big]\big)/2 \neq 1/2 \qquad \blacksquare$$

12.1.3 One-Time Pad and Key Length

In the *one-time pad* private-key encryption scheme, the message, key, and ciphertext all have length n. Encryption and decryption are both just bitwise-xor with the key:

$$E_k(m) = m \oplus k \qquad\qquad D_k(x) = x \oplus k$$

Decryption succeeds because:

$$D_k(E_k(m)) = (m \oplus k) \oplus k = m \oplus (k \oplus k) = m \oplus 0^n = m$$

The one-time pad is perfectly secure since $E_{U_n}(m) = U_n$ for every message m. This is because for every ciphertext x:

$$\mathbf{Pr}_k\big[E_k(m) = x\big] = \mathbf{Pr}_k\big[k = m \oplus x\big] = 2^{-n}$$

The "one-time" pad is only secure if the key is only used once: If Alice encrypts two messages m_0, m_1 with the same k, then Eve can xor the ciphertexts together to get $(m_0 \oplus k) \oplus (m_1 \oplus k) = m_0 \oplus m_1$, which reveals information about the relationship between the two messages.

A big drawback of the one-time pad is that the key is as long as the message. If Alice wants to send Bob a gigabyte, then they need a gigabyte-long key, which is likely impractical to obtain. The key must be pure random bits, which are not easy to come by (Chapter 11). Unfortunately, it's impossible to do better than the one-time pad in this regard:

Theorem 12.2. *For every perfectly secure private-key encryption scheme, the key is at least as long as the message.*

Proof. Consider any private-key encryption scheme (E,D) where the key length ℓ is less than the message length n. Pick any key k_0 and message m_0 (it doesn't matter which) and let $x = E_{k_0}(m_0)$. The number of messages m_1 such that $D_{k_1}(x) = m_1$ for some k_1 is at most the number of possible keys, which is less than the number of possible messages. Thus there exists m_1 such that $D_{k_1}(x) \neq m_1$ for all k_1 and therefore $E_{k_1}(m_1) \neq x$ for all k_1. We have

$$\mathbf{Pr}\big[E_{U_\ell}(m_0) = x\big] \neq 0 = \mathbf{Pr}\big[E_{U_\ell}(m_1) = x\big]$$

so the distributions $E_{U_\ell}(m_0)$ and $E_{U_\ell}(m_1)$ are different. Hence (E,D) is not perfectly secure. ■

12.2 Computationally Secure Encryption

To make encryption practical, keys should be significantly shorter than messages. This requires sacrificing perfect security (Theorem 12.2). That's OK because perfect security is overkill: Breaking an encryption scheme just needs to be extremely impractical, not absolutely impossible. We define this relaxation of perfect security and construct such encryption schemes using pseudorandom generators. The syntax of private-key encryption schemes is unchanged from §12.1.1.

12.2.1 Security

Eve is an algorithm whose input is a ciphertext. We only worry about somewhat time-efficient Eves. If Eve takes a thousand years to break our encryption, then presumably it wouldn't matter anymore. We might as well assume Eve is nonuniform, in case she made extraordinary preparations for the moment she observes the ciphertext. So we model Eve as a bounded-fan-in circuit, whose size approximately corresponds to a nonuniform program's time efficiency (§5.3). As in §10.4 and §11.4, we define a bounded-fan-in circuit's size as the number of $\wedge$ gates and $\vee$ gates (not counting $\neg$ gates or input nodes)—this doesn't matter since we can push all $\neg$ gates to the input nodes while only doubling the number of $\wedge$ and $\vee$ gates (§5.2.2). We denote circuit size by t ("time") since s stands for "seed" later.

Computational security means the ciphertext distributions for different messages are ε-indistinguishable by size-t circuits, as defined in §11.1.2:

Definition. A private-key encryption scheme (E,D) with key length ℓ and ciphertext length c is (t,ε)-*secure* iff for every pair of messages $m_0 \neq m_1$, the distributions $E_{U_\ell}(m_0)$ and $E_{U_\ell}(m_1)$ are (t,ε)-*indistinguishable*, meaning for every size-t circuit $C\colon \{0,1\}^c \to \{0,1\}$:

$$\mathbf{Pr}\big[C(E_{U_\ell}(m_0)) = 1\big] \text{ and } \mathbf{Pr}\big[C(E_{U_\ell}(m_1)) = 1\big] \text{ are within } \pm\varepsilon$$ ◀

If t and ε are functions of n, then an encryption scheme family (E^1,D^1), (E^2,D^2), (E^3,D^3), ... is (t,ε)-*secure* iff (E^n,D^n) is $(t(n),\varepsilon(n))$-secure for every n. An encryption scheme family is $(\operatorname{poly} n, \operatorname{negl} n)$-secure—or *computationally secure*—iff for every function $t \in \operatorname{poly} n = n^{O(1)}$, there exists a function $\varepsilon \in \operatorname{negl} n = 1/n^{\omega(1)}$ such that the family is (t,ε)-secure. Here, $\operatorname{negl} n$ is the set of all *negligible* functions, which go to 0 faster than any inverse polynomial. Thus, computationally secure means for all a and b, there exists n_0 such that for all $n \geq n_0$, (E^n,D^n) is $(n^a, 1/n^b)$-secure: Running a nonuniform poly-time computation on the ciphertext hardly helps Eve at all. Eve is only "somewhat" efficient because a is arbitrarily large. (For $n = 30$ and $a = 20$, an attack running in time 30^{20} is not a realistic concern.) Since b is arbitrarily large, a $1/n^b$ difference in distinguishing probability would not be noticeable in practice.

Now, we characterize computational security like we did for perfect security (Lemma 12.1): If we toss a fair coin to pick which of two messages to encrypt, and show Eve the ciphertext and ask her to guess which message was encrypted, then her success probability is at most negligibly better than a blind guess.

Lemma 12.3. *A private-key encryption scheme (E,D) with key length ℓ and ciphertext length c is (t,ε)-secure iff for every pair of messages $m_0 \neq m_1$ and every size-t circuit $C\colon \{0,1\}^c \to \{0,1\}$, we have $\mathbf{Pr}_{i\sim U_1,k\sim U_\ell}\big[C(E_k(m_i)) = i\big] \leq (1+\varepsilon)/2$.*

Proof. $\Rightarrow$: Suppose (E,D) is (t,ε)-secure, and consider any $m_0 \neq m_1$ and C. By the law of total probability:

$$\begin{aligned}
\mathbf{Pr}_{i,k}\big[C(E_k(m_i)) = i\big] &= \mathbf{Pr}_i[i=0]\cdot\mathbf{Pr}_k\big[C(E_k(m_0)) = 0\big] + \mathbf{Pr}_i[i=1]\cdot\mathbf{Pr}_k\big[C(E_k(m_1)) = 1\big] \\
&= \tfrac{1}{2}\cdot\big(1-\mathbf{Pr}_k\big[C(E_k(m_0)) = 1\big]\big) + \tfrac{1}{2}\cdot\mathbf{Pr}_k\big[C(E_k(m_1)) = 1\big] \\
&\leq \tfrac{1}{2} + \tfrac{1}{2}\cdot\Big|\mathbf{Pr}_k\big[C(E_k(m_0)) = 1\big] - \mathbf{Pr}_k\big[C(E_k(m_1)) = 1\big]\Big| \\
&\leq (1+\varepsilon)/2
\end{aligned}$$

$\Leftarrow$: Suppose (E,D) is not (t,ε)-secure, so there exist $m_0 \neq m_1$ and C such that:

$$\Big|\mathbf{Pr}_k\big[C(E_k(m_0)) = 1\big] - \mathbf{Pr}_k\big[C(E_k(m_1)) = 1\big]\Big| > \varepsilon$$

Swapping m_0 and m_1 if necessary, we may assume:

$$\mathbf{Pr}_k\big[C(E_k(m_1)) = 1\big] - \mathbf{Pr}_k\big[C(E_k(m_0)) = 1\big] > \varepsilon$$

Like in the $\Rightarrow$ direction:

$$\mathbf{Pr}_{i,k}\big[C(E_k(m_i)) = i\big] = \Big(1-\mathbf{Pr}_k\big[C(E_k(m_0)) = 1\big] + \mathbf{Pr}_k\big[C(E_k(m_1)) = 1\big]\Big)/2 > (1+\varepsilon)/2 \qquad \blacksquare$$

12.2.2 Stream Ciphers

We prove that the one-time pad is computationally secure if we bitwise-xor with a pseudorandom string instead of a truly random string. The benefit is that the key is much shorter. We use the key as the seed in a pseudorandom generator (PRG), and we encrypt and decrypt by bitwise-xoring with the PRG's output. This kind of encryption scheme is called a *stream cipher* (imagining the PRG's output as a "stream" of bits).

As in §11.4, a (t,ε)-PRG is a function $G\colon \{0,1\}^\ell \to \{0,1\}^n$ such that the distributions $G(U_\ell)$ and U_n are (t,ε)-indistinguishable, meaning for every size-t circuit $C\colon \{0,1\}^n \to \{0,1\}$:

$$\mathbf{Pr}\big[C(G(U_\ell)) = 1\big] \text{ and } \mathbf{Pr}\big[C(U_n) = 1\big] \text{ are within } \pm\varepsilon$$

Theorem 12.4. *If $G\colon \{0,1\}^\ell \to \{0,1\}^n$ is a $(t,\varepsilon/2)$-PRG, then the private-key encryption scheme with key length ℓ, message length n, and ciphertext length n defined by*

$$E_k(m) = m \oplus G(k) \qquad\qquad D_k(x) = x \oplus G(k)$$

is (t,ε)-secure.

Decryption succeeds for the same reason as the one-time pad. We offer two perspectives on why (E,D) is (t,ε)-secure:

First proof. Consider any messages $m_0 \neq m_1$ and size-t circuit C. For each $i \in \{0,1\}$, define a circuit $C_i\colon \{0,1\}^n \to \{0,1\}$ by $C_i(y) = C(m_i \oplus y)$, which is C with $\neg$ gates added to the input variables that m_i assigns 1. We're not counting $\neg$ gates toward the size, so C_i has size t. We have $\mathbf{Pr}\big[C_0(U_n)=1\big] = \mathbf{Pr}\big[C(U_n)=1\big] = \mathbf{Pr}\big[C_1(U_n)=1\big]$ since $m_0 \oplus U_n$ and $m_1 \oplus U_n$ are the same as U_n. The two probabilities we care about are both within $\pm\varepsilon/2$ of $\mathbf{Pr}\big[C(U_n)=1\big]$, so they're within $\pm\varepsilon$ of each other:

$$\begin{aligned}
&\Big|\mathbf{Pr}\big[C(E_{U_\ell}(m_0))=1\big]-\mathbf{Pr}\big[C(E_{U_\ell}(m_1))=1\big]\Big|\\
=\;&\Big|\mathbf{Pr}\big[C(m_0\oplus G(U_\ell))=1\big]-\mathbf{Pr}\big[C(m_1\oplus G(U_\ell))=1\big]\Big|\\
\le\;&\Big|\mathbf{Pr}\big[C(m_0\oplus G(U_\ell))=1\big]-\mathbf{Pr}\big[C(U_n)=1\big]\Big|+\Big|\mathbf{Pr}\big[C(U_n)=1\big]-\mathbf{Pr}\big[C(m_1\oplus G(U_\ell))=1\big]\Big|\\
=\;&\Big|\mathbf{Pr}\big[C_0(G(U_\ell))=1\big]-\mathbf{Pr}\big[C_0(U_n)=1\big]\Big|+\Big|\mathbf{Pr}\big[C_1(U_n)=1\big]-\mathbf{Pr}\big[C_1(G(U_\ell))=1\big]\Big|\\
\le\;&\varepsilon/2+\varepsilon/2
\end{aligned}$$

■

Second proof. We prove the contrapositive by giving a reduction from "breaking" the PRG to breaking the encryption scheme in the sense of Lemma 12.3.

Suppose (E,D) is not (t,ε)-secure, so there exist messages $m_0 \neq m_1$ and a size-t circuit C such that $\mathbf{Pr}_{i\sim U_1,k\sim U_\ell}\big[C(E_k(m_i)) = i\big] > (1+\varepsilon)/2$. Consider an algorithm that takes input $y \in \{0,1\}^n$, samples $i \sim U_1$, evaluates $C(m_i \oplus y)$, and accepts iff C outputs i (Eve guesses right).

- If $y \sim G(U_\ell)$, this simulates the security experiment for the stream cipher (Lemma 12.3) and thus accepts with probability $> 1/2+\varepsilon/2$.
- If $y \sim U_n$, this simulates the security experiment for the one-time pad (Lemma 12.1) and thus accepts with probability $1/2$.

These two probabilities differ by $> \varepsilon/2$, so they differ by $> \varepsilon/2$ conditioned on some outcome of $i \in \{0,1\}$. Thus the circuit $C'(y) = C(m_i \oplus y) \oplus \bar{i}$ shows that G is not a $(t,\varepsilon/2)$-PRG:

$$\mathbf{Pr}\big[C'(G(U_\ell))=1\big]-\mathbf{Pr}\big[C'(U_n)=1\big] \;>\; \varepsilon/2$$

■

We use the same kind of pseudorandom generators for stream ciphers as for derandomization (§11.4) but with different parameters. Suppose a PRG is $O(n^a)$-time computable and fools size-n^b circuits:

- $a > b$ for derandomization: The PRG may use more resources than the circuits it fools. Achieving $\mathsf{P} = \mathsf{BPP}$ requires seed length $O(\log n)$.
- $a < b$ for stream ciphers: The PRG uses less resources than the circuits it fools. ("Pick on someone your own size, or larger.") Alice and Bob don't want to spend more time than necessary, but Eve might be quite patient. Seed length n^d for a small constant $d > 0$ is good enough—we don't want the bare minimum $O(\log n)$ since then Eve could do brute force over all seeds.

12.2.3 Necessity of Complexity Assumptions

At the beginning of §11.4, we showed that PRGs that yield $\mathsf{P} = \mathsf{BPP}$ would also imply that some problem in E has exponential circuit size complexity. The same argument shows that PRGs that yield stream ciphers would also imply that some problem in NP has superpolynomial circuit size complexity and thus $\mathsf{P} \neq \mathsf{NP}$. So proving that a stream cipher is computationally secure is hopeless until we prove $\mathsf{P} \neq \mathsf{NP}$. Maybe we could prove that another encryption scheme (not based on PRGs) is computationally secure without assuming $\mathsf{P} \neq \mathsf{NP}$? Unfortunately, no:

Theorem 12.5. *If there exists a computationally secure, poly-time computable, private-key encryption scheme family with shorter keys than messages (and with ciphertexts the same length as messages), then some problem in* NP *has circuit size complexity* $N^{\omega(1)}$ *and thus* $\mathsf{P} \neq \mathsf{NP}$.

The assumption that ciphertexts are the same length as messages is for convenience; the same proof can handle longer ciphertexts.

Proof idea. We show that if keys are shorter than messages, then there exist two messages such that encrypting one of them probably yields a ciphertext that couldn't have come from the other one. Thus we can break the encryption scheme by checking whether the ciphertext could have come from the latter message. This is an NP problem—the encryption key is the witness. If we can solve the NP problem efficiently, we can break the encryption scheme efficiently. ■

Proof. We prove the contrapositive. Assume no problem in NP has circuit size complexity $N^{\omega(1)}$. This means for every $A \in \mathsf{NP}$, there exist constants d and e such that A_N has a size-dN^e circuit for infinitely many N.

Consider any poly-time computable, private-key encryption scheme family (E^1, D^1), ... with message length n, key length $\ell(n) < n$, and ciphertext length n. Abbreviate $E^n, D^n, \ell(n)$ as E, D, ℓ. To show the family is not computationally secure, we show that for infinitely many n, there exist messages $m_0 \neq m_1$ and a poly-size circuit that distinguishes the distributions $E_{U_\ell}(m_0)$ and $E_{U_\ell}(m_1)$.

(call this problem A)	(12.1)
Input: Ciphertext $x \in \{0,1\}^n$	
Output: Does there exist a key $k \in \{0,1\}^\ell$ such that $E_k(0^n) = x$?	

(Nothing is special about 0^n; we could use any message.) $A \in \mathsf{NP}$ by a verifier V where $V(x;k) = 1$ iff $E_k(0^n) = x$, using E's poly-time program. Thus A_n has a size-dn^e circuit C for infinitely many n. Consider any such n. We claim that C distinguishes $E_{U_\ell}(m_0)$ and $E_{U_\ell}(m_1)$ for $m_0 = 0^n$ and some $m_1 \neq m_0$. We have $\mathbf{Pr}\big[C(E_{U_\ell}(m_0)) = 1\big] = 1$. We prove $\mathbf{Pr}\big[C(E_{U_\ell}(m_1)) = 1\big] \leq 1/2$ for some m_1 (necessarily $\neq m_0$) using the probabilistic method. Consider $m_1 \sim U_n$. For every k, $\mathbf{Pr}_{m_1}\big[C(E_k(m_1)) = 1\big] \leq 2^\ell/2^n \leq 1/2$ because encrypting the 2^n messages m_1 with the same key k yields 2^n different ciphertexts (otherwise decryption wouldn't always work), of which $\leq 2^\ell$ are 1-inputs of A. There exists m_1 such that $\mathbf{Pr}_k\big[C(E_k(m_1)) = 1\big] \leq 1/2$ because:

$$\min\nolimits_{m_1}\Big(\mathbf{Pr}_k\big[C(E_k(m_1)) = 1\big]\Big) \leq \max\nolimits_k\Big(\mathbf{Pr}_{m_1}\big[C(E_k(m_1)) = 1\big]\Big) \leq 1/2$$ ■

$\mathsf{P} \neq \mathsf{NP}$ is necessary, but not known to be sufficient, for nontrivial encryption. It would be great to base an encryption scheme's security on decades of confidence that NP-complete problems can't (or at least won't) be solved in poly time. But nobody knows how to do that.

- $\mathsf{P} \neq \mathsf{NP}$ is about worst-case complexity: No poly-time algorithm solves an NP-complete problem on *all* inputs.

- Cryptography is like average-case complexity: It's not enough that no poly-time algorithm *always* breaks an encryption scheme. (If Eve learns someone's bank account information, it's no consolation knowing that a different key would have prevented that.)

How about basing encryption schemes on an average-case analogue of $\mathsf{P} \neq \mathsf{NP}$ such as $(\mathsf{NP}, \mathsf{U}) \not\subseteq \mathsf{HEUR}_{1/3}\mathsf{P/poly}$ (Chapter 10)? This is also open but is in the right direction. Next, we'll see the specific kind of average-case complexity assumptions that suffice for private-key encryption.

12.3 Pseudorandom Generators from One-Way Functions

One-way functions are easy to compute (given a preimage, find the image) but average-case hard to invert (given an image, find a preimage). A mega-theorem is that essentially all of computationally secure private-key cryptography is equivalent to the existence of one-way functions. We prove part of this mega-theorem.

12.3.1 One-Way Functions

First, we define *one-way permutations* since they're simpler. Here, permutation means bijection—a function where each codomain element has exactly one preimage.

Definition. $f\colon \{0,1\}^n \to \{0,1\}^n$ is a (t,ε)-*one-way permutation (OWP)* iff f is a bijection and for every size-t circuit $C\colon \{0,1\}^n \to \{0,1\}^n$:

$$\mathbf{Pr}_{x\sim U_n}\big[C(f(x)) = x\big] \leq \varepsilon \qquad \blacktriangleleft$$

If f isn't a permutation, we may have $f(x') = f(x)$ for some $x' \neq x$. Given $f(x)$, C can't know which preimage is "intended." We say C succeeds if it finds any x' with $f(x') = f(x)$.

Definition. $f\colon \{0,1\}^n \to \{0,1\}^n$ is a (t,ε)-*one-way function (OWF)* iff for every size-t circuit $C\colon \{0,1\}^n \to \{0,1\}^n$:

$$\mathbf{Pr}_{x\sim U_n}\big[f(C(f(x))) = f(x)\big] \leq \varepsilon \qquad \blacktriangleleft$$

We consider infinite families of OWPs or OWFs, parameterized by n and computed by uniform, deterministic, poly-time programs. Like with encryption schemes, a function family is $(\operatorname{poly} n, \operatorname{negl} n)$-one-way—or simply *one-way* for short—iff for every $t \in \operatorname{poly} n$, there exists $\varepsilon \in \operatorname{negl} n$ such that for all n, the family's nth function is $(t(n), \varepsilon(n))$-one-way. Inverting a function family is a search problem. Inverting a permutation family is a function problem.

MULTIPLICATION is conjectured to be a one-way function family. The input is two binary numbers x (first $n/2$ bits) and y (last $n/2$ bits), and the output is the product xy. (If n is odd then x is $\lceil n/2 \rceil$ bits and y is $\lfloor n/2 \rfloor$ bits, but let's ignore that.) Inverting MULTIPLICATION means factoring xy into two $n/2$-bit numbers, which don't have to be the original x and y. Factoring is too easy if we're allowed to find factors that aren't $n/2$ bits: With probability 3/4, either x or y is even, so xy is even and we can factor xy into $2\cdot(xy/2)$ (where $xy/2$ could be $n-1$ bits). When the output must be two $n/2$-bit numbers, nobody knows a poly-time factoring algorithm that succeeds with nonnegligible probability. Subexponential-time algorithms are known, though.

Candidate one-way permutation families are not as simple to come by, though number theory provides some candidates if we make syntactic adjustments to the definition.

A major theorem—beyond the scope of this book—is that OWFs yield cryptographic PRGs. *Cryptographic* means $(\operatorname{poly} n, \operatorname{negl} n)$ as needed for computationally secure stream ciphers, as opposed to the parameters needed for derandomization.

x	$f(x)$	$h(x)$
000	011	0
001	101	1
010	000	1
011	111	0
100	100	1
101	001	0
110	010	0
111	110	1

y	$h(f^{-1}(y))$
000	1
001	0
010	0
011	0
100	1
101	1
110	1
111	0

Figure 12.2: Example permutation f with a bit h, illustrating the syntax of hardcore bits

Theorem 12.6. *If a poly-time computable one-way function family exists, then for all $d > 0$, a poly-time computable cryptographic pseudorandom generator family with seed length n^d exists.*

We prove a weaker version: OWPs yield cryptographic PRGs.

Theorem 12.7. *If a poly-time computable one-way permutation family exists, then for all $d > 0$, a poly-time computable cryptographic pseudorandom generator family with seed length n^d exists.*

Here's a bird's eye view of the proof of Theorem 12.7:

- § 12.3.3: We turn any OWP into an OWP that has a "hardcore bit." This means given $f(x)$, it's average-case hard not only to compute x, but even to compute a certain single bit $h(x)$ of information about x.
- § 12.3.2: We turn any OWP with a hardcore bit into a cryptographic PRG. This is related to turning average-case hardness into pseudorandomness (§ 11.4).

Definition. $h\colon \{0,1\}^n \to \{0,1\}$ is a (t,ε)-*hardcore bit* for a permutation $f\colon \{0,1\}^n \to \{0,1\}^n$ iff for every size-t circuit $C\colon \{0,1\}^n \to \{0,1\}$:

$$\mathbf{Pr}_{x\sim U_n}\big[C(f(x)) = h(x)\big] \le (1+\varepsilon)/2$$ ◀

If f is a permutation then $f(U_n) = U_n$. So h is a (t,ε)-hardcore bit for f iff $h \circ f^{-1}\colon \{0,1\}^n \to \{0,1\}$ is (t,ε)-*hard*, meaning for every size-t circuit $C\colon \{0,1\}^n \to \{0,1\}$:

$$\mathbf{Pr}_{y\sim U_n}\big[C(y) = h(f^{-1}(y))\big] \le (1+\varepsilon)/2$$

The definition of (t,ε)-hard in § 10.4 has $<$, but we use the version with $\le$ for convenience, as in § 11.4.

Example. To illustrate the syntax, Figure 12.2 shows an example of f, h, and $h \circ f^{-1}$. This f is a permutation since all eight bit strings show up exactly once in the $f(x)$ column. The table for $h \circ f^{-1}$ is the $f(x)$ and $h(x)$ columns sorted according to $f(x)$. ♦

12.3.2 Pseudorandomness from Hardcore Bits

First, we show that a hardcore bit yields a PRG with a meager one bit of stretch. We essentially already proved this in § 11.4.1.

Lemma 12.8. *If* $h\colon \{0,1\}^\ell \to \{0,1\}$ *is a* $(t, 2\varepsilon)$*-hardcore bit for a permutation* $f\colon \{0,1\}^\ell \to \{0,1\}^\ell$*, then* $G\colon \{0,1\}^\ell \to \{0,1\}^{\ell+1}$ *defined by* $G(s) = (f(s), h(s))$ *is a* (t,ε)*-PRG.*

Proof. Since $h \circ f^{-1}$ is $(t, 2\varepsilon)$-hard, Lemma 11.24 says $G'\colon \{0,1\}^\ell \to \{0,1\}^{\ell+1}$ defined by $G'(r) = (r, h(f^{-1}(r)))$ is a (t,ε)-PRG. The distributions $G(U_\ell)$ and $G'(U_\ell)$ are the same because f is a permutation, so $G(U_\ell)$ and $U_{\ell+1}$ are (t,ε)-indistinguishable since $G'(U_\ell)$ and $U_{\ell+1}$ are. Thus G is also a (t,ε)-PRG. ■

Why use a hardcore bit instead of directly applying Lemma 11.24 with an arbitrary $(t, 2\varepsilon)$-hard function? Because for cryptography, computing G should be faster than t—the PRG uses less resources than a distinguisher. (For derandomization, computing G can be somewhat slower than t—the PRG uses more resources than a distinguisher.) In this case, $(f(s), h(s))$ is computable in fixed-degree poly time, while $h(f^{-1}(r))$ isn't computable in any-degree poly time. Decomposing an average-case hard function into "OWP with hardcore bit" speeds up the PRG without hurting its pseudorandomness.

Next, we prove that any PRG with one bit of stretch can "pull itself up by its bootstraps" to achieve any polynomial amount of stretch, with only minor degradation of the pseudorandomness. For any $G\colon \{0,1\}^\ell \to \{0,1\}^{\ell+1}$ and $n \geq 1$, define $G^n\colon \{0,1\}^\ell \to \{0,1\}^n$ iteratively as follows (see Figure 12.3):

Poly-stretch PRG using a 1-bit-stretch PRG (12.2)

```
G^n(s_0):
    for i ← 1, 2, ..., n:
        let s_i and z_i be the first ℓ bits and last bit (respectively) of G(s_{i-1})
    output z_1 z_2 ··· z_n
```

Example. Let's apply Lemma 12.8 to the example from the end of §12.3.1 to obtain $G\colon \{0,1\}^3 \to \{0,1\}^4$, and then define $G^5\colon \{0,1\}^3 \to \{0,1\}^5$.

$G(000) = 0110 \quad G(011) = 1110 \quad G(111) = 1101 \quad G(110) = 0100 \quad G(010) = 0001$

$G^5(000) = 00101$ is the concatenation of the last bit of each of those five strings. ♦

Lemma 12.9. *If* $G\colon \{0,1\}^\ell \to \{0,1\}^{\ell+1}$ *is a* $(t + nt', \varepsilon/n)$*-PRG computed by a size-*t' *circuit, then* G^n *is a* (t,ε)*-PRG.*

Proof idea. We use a *hybrid argument* (like for turning distinguishers into predictors in §11.4.2): We define a sequence of hybrid distributions that interpolate between $G^n(U_\ell)$ and U_n. A circuit that ε-distinguishes those two distributions ("breaking" G^n) ε/n-distinguishes some adjacent pair of distributions in the sequence. By slightly reorganizing this pair of distributions, we get a circuit that ε/n-distinguishes $G(U_\ell)$ and $U_{\ell+1}$ ("breaking" G). ■

Proof. Assuming G has a size-t' circuit and G^n is not a (t,ε)-PRG, we prove that G is not a $(t + nt', \varepsilon/n)$-PRG. Let $C\colon \{0,1\}^n \to \{0,1\}$ be a size-t circuit such that

$$\mathbf{Pr}\big[C(G^n(U_\ell)) = 1\big] - \mathbf{Pr}\big[C(U_n) = 1\big] > \varepsilon$$

(assuming C has already been negated if necessary to remove the absolute value bars). Letting $p_i = \mathbf{Pr}\big[C(U_i, G^{n-i}(U_\ell)) = 1\big]$, so $p_0 = \mathbf{Pr}\big[C(G^n(U_\ell)) = 1\big]$ and $p_n = \mathbf{Pr}\big[C(U_n) = 1\big]$:

$$(p_0 - p_1) + (p_1 - p_2) + \cdots + (p_{n-2} - p_{n-1}) + (p_{n-1} - p_n) = p_0 - p_n > \varepsilon$$

Thus there exists $i \in [n]$ such that $p_{i-1} - p_i > \varepsilon/n$.

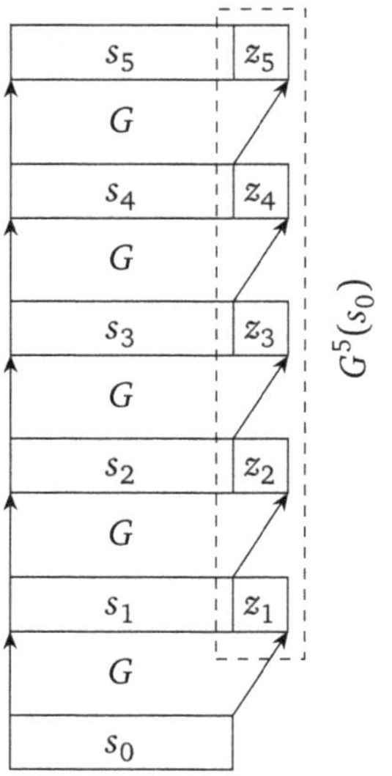

Figure 12.3: Defining G^5 from G

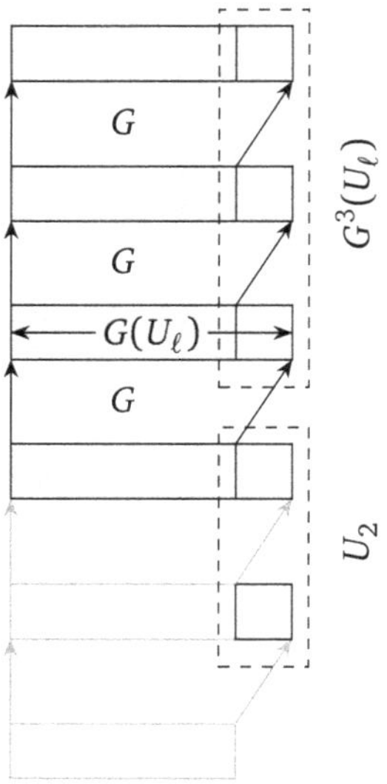

Figure 12.4: Using $G(U_\ell)$ to simulate hybrid $i-1=2$

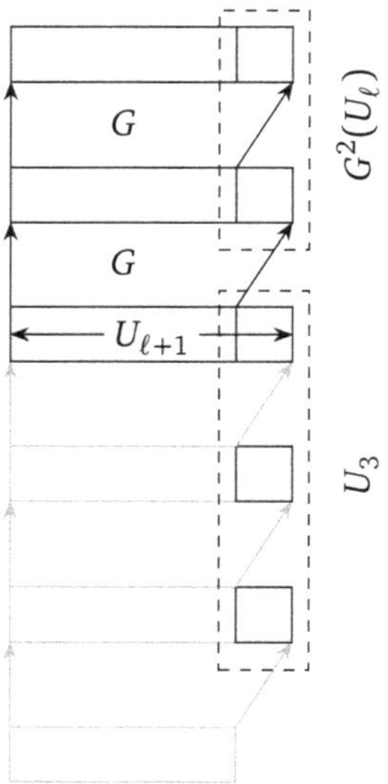

Figure 12.5: Using $U_{\ell+1}$ to simulate hybrid $i=3$

- We have a circuit C that ε/n-distinguishes $(U_{i-1}, G^{n-i+1}(U_\ell))$ and $(U_i, G^{n-i}(U_\ell))$.
- We want a circuit C' that ε/n-distinguishes $G(U_\ell)$ and $U_{\ell+1}$.

We translate between these pairs of distributions using this function:

$$f\colon \{0,1\}^{i-1} \times \{0,1\}^{\ell} \times \{0,1\} \to \{0,1\}^n \qquad \text{defined by} \qquad f(u,s,z) = (u, z, G^{n-i}(s))$$

- $f(U_{i-1}, G(U_\ell)) = (U_{i-1}, G^{n-i+1}(U_\ell))$ as Figure 12.4 illustrates. This is because sampling $(s,z) \sim G(U_\ell)$ and outputting $(z, G^{n-i}(s))$ is the same as sampling $s_0 \sim U_\ell$ and outputting $G^{n-i+1}(s_0)$, since $(s,z) \sim G(U_\ell)$ is equivalent to the first iteration of $G^{n-i+1}(s_0)$.
- $f(U_{i-1}, U_{\ell+1}) = (U_i, G^{n-i}(U_\ell))$ as Figure 12.5 illustrates.

$$\begin{aligned} &\mathbf{Pr}\big[C(f(U_{i-1}, G(U_\ell))) = 1\big] - \mathbf{Pr}\big[C(f(U_{i-1}, U_{\ell+1})) = 1\big] \\ =\ &\mathbf{Pr}\big[C(U_{i-1}, G^{n-i+1}(U_\ell)) = 1\big] - \mathbf{Pr}\big[C(U_i, G^{n-i}(U_\ell)) = 1\big] \ = \ p_{i-1} - p_i \ > \ \varepsilon/n \end{aligned}$$

So for some $u \in \{0,1\}^{i-1}$, defining $C'(y) = C(f(u,y))$:

$$\mathbf{Pr}\big[C'(G(U_\ell)) = 1\big] - \mathbf{Pr}\big[C'(U_{\ell+1}) = 1\big] \ > \ \varepsilon/n$$

C' is a size-$(t + nt')$ circuit consisting of C and at most n copies of the size-t' circuit for G (to implement f). Therefore G is not a $(t + nt',\ \varepsilon/n)$-PRG. ■

12.3.3 Hardcore Bits for One-Way Permutations

Lemma 12.10. *For any permutation $f\colon \{0,1\}^n \to \{0,1\}^n$, define the permutation $f'\colon (\{0,1\}^n)^2 \to (\{0,1\}^n)^2$ by $f'(x,r) = (f(x), r)$, and define $h\colon (\{0,1\}^n)^2 \to \{0,1\}$ by $h(x,r) = x \odot r$ (the dot product over $\mathbb{Z}_2$). If f is $\big(tn^3/\varepsilon^3,\ \varepsilon^3/520n\big)$-one-way, then h is a (t,ε)-hardcore bit for f'.*

Proof idea. We prove the contrapositive by reduction: Assuming a circuit C computes $h(x,r)$ from $f'(x,r)$ with probability somewhat $> 1/2$, we want to use C to compute x from $f(x)$ with probability somewhat > 0.

This is related to decoding the dot product code (§9.1.2): For a message x, the codeword's rth bit is $x \odot r$, and the received word's rth bit is $C(f(x),r)$. When the received word matches the codeword on somewhat $> 1/2$ fraction of all r, our goal is to recover the entire message x. (Beware: n, x, r denote different things than in §9.1.2.)

The decoder from §9.1.2 is too slow (it reads all 2^n bits of the received word) and requires the received word to match the codeword on $> 3/4$ of all r. But let's review the idea: Let $e^i \in \{0,1\}^n$ have a 1 at index i and 0s everywhere else. If for some r, we knew both the rth and $(r \oplus e^i)$th codeword bits, we could xor them to get the ith message bit:

$$\big(x \odot r\big) \oplus \big(x \odot (r \oplus e^i)\big) \;=\; x \odot \big(r \oplus (r \oplus e^i)\big) \;=\; x \odot e^i \;=\; x_i$$

The local decoder from §10.3.1 fixes the speed issue by picking a single r randomly (instead of using all r), but the distance issue remains: If the received word is correct on a random r with probability somewhat $> 1/2$, and similarly for $r \oplus e^i$, then it's correct on both with probability somewhat > 0, which isn't good enough since we need to get x's other bits too.

Idea: If we magically knew $x \odot r$, we could just consult the received word to get $x \odot (r \oplus e^i)$ with probability somewhat $> 1/2$. Then we could amplify to get x_i with high probability, and do a union bound over i to get all of x. Maybe just randomly guessing the value of $x \odot r$ is OK, since recovering x with low (but not too low) probability is OK? Unfortunately, the amplification would require guessing $x \odot r$ for many r, and the probability of correctly guessing all those bits would be too low.

To get by with sampling only a few r, we do randomness-efficient amplification using a pairwise uniform hash function (§8.5.2). We only guess $x \odot r$ for the original sampled strings r, not guess $x \odot r$ for all the other r (obtained from the hash function), because we can "extrapolate" the latter from the former if the hash function is linear over $\mathbb{Z}_2$. Now, the probability of correctly guessing all the needed bits is not too low.

In the proof, $(a_1, \dots, a_k)$ are the original sampled strings, and $(b_1, \dots, b_k)$ are the guesses for $(x \odot a_1, \dots, x \odot a_k)$. The algorithm is effectively a *local list decoder* for the dot product code. The list entries correspond to possibilities of the tuple $(b_1, \dots, b_k)$. ■

Proof. Suppose h is not (t, ε)-hardcore for f'. Let $C\colon (\{0,1\}^n)^2 \to \{0,1\}$ be a size-t circuit such that:

$$\mathbf{Pr}_{x \sim U_n,\, r \sim U_n}\big[C(f(x),r) = x \odot r\big] \;>\; 1/2 + \varepsilon/2$$

We'll show that f is not $\big(tn^3/\varepsilon^3,\ \varepsilon^3/520n\big)$-one-way. Define $k = \big\lceil \log(32n/\varepsilon^2 + 1)\big\rceil$.

- For a tuple $a = (a_1, \dots, a_k) \in (\{0,1\}^n)^k$ and a set $J \subseteq [k]$, let $a_J = \bigoplus_{j \in J} a_j \in \{0,1\}^n$ be the bitwise xor of the strings indexed by J.
- For a tuple $b = (b_1, \dots, b_k) \in \{0,1\}^k$ and a set $J \subseteq [k]$, let $b_J = \bigoplus_{j \in J} b_j \in \{0,1\}$ be the xor of the bits indexed by J.

Let $e^i \in \{0,1\}^n$ have a 1 at index i and 0s everywhere else. Consider this randomized algorithm that takes input $y \in \{0,1\}^n$ and randomness $a \sim (U_n)^k$ and $b \sim (U_1)^k$:

Randomized algorithm to invert f (12.3)

$\Pi(y; a, b)$:
  for each $i \in [n]$:
    for each nonempty $J \subseteq [k]$: let $vote_J \leftarrow C(y, a_J \oplus e^i) \oplus b_J$
    let $z_i \leftarrow$ majority bit among $vote_J$ over all nonempty $J \subseteq [k]$
  output $z_1 \cdots z_n$

We claim that $\mathbf{Pr}_{x,a,b}\big[\Pi(f(x); a, b) = x\big]$ is not too small:

- Define $R_x = \{r \in \{0,1\}^n : C(f(x), r) = x \odot r\}$. Say x is *good* iff $\mathbf{Pr}_r\big[r \in R_x\big] > 1/2 + \varepsilon/4$. Then $\mathbf{Pr}_x\big[x \text{ is good}\big] > \varepsilon/4$ since otherwise:

$$\begin{aligned}\mathbf{Pr}_{x,r}\big[r \in R_x\big] \;\le\; \mathbf{Pr}_x\big[x \text{ is good}\big] + \mathbf{Pr}_{x,r}\big[r \in R_x \,\big|\, x \text{ is bad}\big] \;&\le\; \varepsilon/4 + (1/2 + \varepsilon/4)\\ &=\; 1/2 + \varepsilon/2\end{aligned}$$

- $H\colon (\{0,1\}^n)^k \times \{\text{nonempty subsets of } [k]\} \to \{0,1\}^n$ defined by $H(a, J) = a_J$ is a pairwise uniform hash function (Lemma 8.6): Using $a_1, \ldots, a_k$ as columns of an $n \times k$ matrix A, and identifying J with a nonzero $k \times 1$ vector u (its characteristic bit string), we have $a_J = Au$.
- Define $R_{x,i} = \{r : r \oplus e^i \in R_x\}$. If x is good then by hash mixing (Lemma 8.15), with probability $\ge 1 - 1/(2^k - 1)(\varepsilon/4)^2 \ge 1 - 1/2n$ over a, the fraction of nonempty sets J such that $a_J \in R_{x,i}$ is within $\pm\varepsilon/4$ of $|R_{x,i}|/2^n = |R_x|/2^n > 1/2 + \varepsilon/4$ and is thus $> 1/2$.
- Say a is *good* (with respect to x) iff for all i, we have $a_J \in R_{x,i}$ for a majority of nonempty J. For any good x, we have $\mathbf{Pr}_a\big[a \text{ is good}\big] \ge 1/2$ because by a union bound:

$$\mathbf{Pr}_a\big[a \text{ is bad}\big] \;\le\; \textstyle\sum_{i \in [n]} \mathbf{Pr}_a\big[a_J \notin R_{x,i} \text{ for a majority of nonempty } J\big] \;\le\; n/2n \;=\; 1/2$$

- Say b is *good* (with respect to x and a) iff $b_j = x \odot a_j$ for all $j \in [k]$. If b is good then $b_J = x \odot a_J$ for all $J \subseteq [k]$ because by linearity:

$$b_J \;=\; \textstyle\bigoplus_{j \in J} b_j \;=\; \bigoplus_{j \in J}(x \odot a_j) \;=\; x \odot \big(\bigoplus_{j \in J} a_j\big) \;=\; x \odot a_J$$

  For any x and a, we have $\mathbf{Pr}_b\big[b \text{ is good}\big] = 1/2^k \ge 1/2^{\log(32n/\varepsilon^2+1)+1} \ge \varepsilon^2/65n$.
- For any x, good a, good b, and i,

$$\begin{aligned}vote_J \;=\; C(f(x), a_J \oplus e^i) \oplus b_J \;&=\; \big(x \odot (a_J \oplus e^i)\big) \oplus \big(x \odot a_J\big)\\ &=\; x \odot \big((a_J \oplus e^i) \oplus a_J\big) \;=\; x \odot e^i \;=\; x_i\end{aligned}$$

  for a majority of nonempty J, and thus $z_i = x_i$. Hence for any x, good a, and good b, we have $\Pi(f(x); a, b) = x$.
- Combining everything using the chain rule:

$$\begin{aligned}&\mathbf{Pr}_{x,a,b}\big[\Pi(f(x); a, b) = x\big]\\ \ge\;& \mathbf{Pr}_{x,a,b}\big[x, a, b \text{ are all good}\big]\\ =\;& \mathbf{Pr}_x\big[x \text{ is good}\big] \cdot \mathbf{Pr}_{x,a}\big[a \text{ is good} \,\big|\, x \text{ is good}\big] \cdot \mathbf{Pr}_{x,a,b}\big[b \text{ is good} \,\big|\, x, a \text{ are both good}\big]\\ \ge\;& \mathbf{Pr}_x\big[x \text{ is good}\big] \cdot \min_{\text{good } x} \mathbf{Pr}_a\big[a \text{ is good}\big] \cdot \min_{x,a} \mathbf{Pr}_b\big[b \text{ is good}\big]\\ >\;& \tfrac{\varepsilon}{4} \cdot \tfrac{1}{2} \cdot \tfrac{\varepsilon^2}{65n}\\ =\;& \varepsilon^3/520n\end{aligned}$$

For some a and b, $\mathbf{Pr}_x\big[\Pi(f(x);a,b) = x\big] > \varepsilon^3/520n$. We implement $\Pi(y;a,b)$ as a circuit $C'(y)$, so $\mathbf{Pr}_x\big[C'(f(x)) = x\big] > \varepsilon^3/520n$. Thus f is not $\big(tn^3/\varepsilon^3,\ \varepsilon^3/520n\big)$-one-way, because C' has size $n \cdot 2^k \cdot (t+10k) \leq tn^3/\varepsilon^3$ since $2^k \leq 65n/\varepsilon^2$ and (for convenience) we sloppily bound the cost of adding $vote_J$ to the running sum by $10k \leq n/65\varepsilon$. ■

12.3.4 Putting It All Together

Proof of Theorem 12.7 (ancillary). Assume a poly-time computable one-way permutation family $f_1, f_2, f_3, \ldots$ exists. Consider any $d > 0$ and assume $d = 1/(\text{an integer})$. We construct a poly-time computable cryptographic PRG family $G_1, G_2, G_3, \ldots$ with seed length $\leq n^d$. Consider any large enough n, and let $m = \lfloor n^d/2 \rfloor$. Starting with $f_m\colon \{0,1\}^m \to \{0,1\}^m$:

- Define $f'\colon \{0,1\}^{2m} \to \{0,1\}^{2m}$ and $h\colon \{0,1\}^{2m} \to \{0,1\}$ from f_m as in Lemma 12.10.
- Define $G\colon \{0,1\}^{2m} \to \{0,1\}^{2m+1}$ from f' and h as in Lemma 12.8.
- Define $G_n = G^n\colon \{0,1\}^{2m} \to \{0,1\}^n$ from G as in Lemma 12.9.

G_n is poly-time computable and has seed length $2m \leq n^d$. If this isn't a $(\operatorname{poly} n, \operatorname{negl} n)$-PRG family, then for some e and infinitely many n, G_n isn't an $(n^e, 1/n^e)$-PRG, and furthermore, e is large enough that G has a size-n^e circuit. For such n:

- G isn't an $(n^e + n^{e+1},\ 1/n^{e+1})$-PRG, by Lemma 12.9.
- h isn't $(n^e + n^{e+1},\ 2/n^{e+1})$-hardcore for f', by Lemma 12.8.
- f_m isn't $\big((n^e + n^{e+1})m^3(n^{e+1}/2)^3,\ (2/n^{e+1})^3/520m\big)$-one-way, by Lemma 12.10.

Since $n \in \operatorname{poly} m$, this shows that $f_1, f_2, f_3, \ldots$ isn't $(\operatorname{poly} m, \operatorname{negl} m)$-one-way. ■

12.3.5 Commitment Schemes

Suppose Alice puts a message on paper in an opaque lockbox, locks the box, and gives it to Bob. Later, Alice gives the key to Bob, who unlocks the box and reads the message. In the meantime:

- *Hiding*: Bob learns nothing about the message, since the box is locked and opaque.
- *Binding*: Alice can't change the message without Bob detecting it, since Bob has the box. Alice *committed* to the message—she can't pretend she had put something else in the box.

A *commitment scheme* simulates this over a digital communication channel. This could be used to implement a sealed-bid auction. We'll also see an application of commitment schemes in §15.4.

This setting has no external adversary.

- Alice views Bob as the adversary for the hiding property.
- Bob views Alice as the adversary for the binding property.

Private-key encryption schemes yield the hiding property: The key is analogous to the lockbox's physical key. Alice samples the key by herself (without sharing it with Bob yet) and uses it to encrypt the message.

- *Commit phase*: Alice sends the ciphertext to Bob, who learns nothing about the message.
- *Reveal phase*: Later, Alice sends the key to Bob, who uses it to decrypt the ciphertext.

But private-key encryption schemes don't necessarily yield the binding property: For example, using a stream cipher, Alice could send the ciphertext $x = m \oplus G(k)$ (with message m, key k, and PRG G) in the commit phase, but then send some $k' \neq k$ in the reveal phase, thereby claiming the message was $m' = x \oplus G(k')$ all along. Bob wouldn't be able to tell. The issue is that a single ciphertext could decrypt to different messages (using different keys). For binding, we need an encryption scheme where this doesn't happen.

Now, we define commitment schemes that are computationally hiding (against efficient Bobs) and perfectly binding (against all Alices). Commitment schemes that are perfectly hiding (against all Bobs) and computationally binding (against efficient Alices) also make sense but are more complicated to construct. The best of both worlds—perfectly hiding and perfectly binding—is impossible because with a perfectly binding commitment scheme, a ciphertext can only correspond to one message, which Bob could find by brute forcing over all keys.

For the definition, we slightly generalize the syntax of encryption schemes so the decryption function D has codomain $\{0,1\}^n \cup \{\bot\}$ (instead of $\{0,1\}^n$): $D_k(x) = \bot$ means x is an invalid ciphertext for key k—there's no message m such that $E_k(m) = x$. Bob shouldn't be duped by an invalid x sent by an untrustworthy Alice.

Definition. A *(t,ε)-hiding, perfectly binding commitment scheme* is a (t,ε)-secure private-key encryption scheme (E,D) for which there do not exist x,k,k' such that $\bot \neq D_k(x) \neq D_{k'}(x) \neq \bot$. A *bit commitment scheme* has message length 1. ◀

In particular, a bit commitment scheme with key length ℓ is (t,ε)-hiding iff $E_{U_\ell}(0)$ and $E_{U_\ell}(1)$ are (t,ε)-indistinguishable, and is perfectly binding iff there do not exist x,k,k' such that $D_k(x)=0$ and $D_{k'}(x)=1$.

Theorem 12.11. *If $h\colon \{0,1\}^\ell \to \{0,1\}$ is a (t,ε)-hardcore bit for a permutation $f\colon \{0,1\}^\ell \to \{0,1\}^\ell$, then the following is a (t,ε)-hiding, perfectly binding bit commitment scheme:*

$$E\colon \{0,1\}^\ell \times \{0,1\} \to \{0,1\}^{\ell+1} \qquad \textit{defined by} \qquad E_k(m) = \big(f(k),\, h(k)\oplus m\big)$$

$$D\colon \{0,1\}^\ell \times \{0,1\}^{\ell+1} \to \{0,1,\bot\} \qquad \textit{defined by} \qquad D_k(x) = \begin{cases} h(k)\oplus x_{\ell+1} & \textit{if } f(k) = x_1\cdots x_\ell \\ \bot & \textit{otherwise} \end{cases}$$

Proof idea. Hiding: Distinguishing $\big(f(k), h(k)\oplus 0\big)$ from $\big(f(k), h(k)\oplus 1\big)$ (for $k \sim U_\ell$) is tantamount to computing $h(k)$ from $f(k)$, so if the latter is hard then the former is hard. Binding: The presence of $f(k)$ in the ciphertext ensures that only one key leads to a valid decryption. ■

Proof. For all m and k, we have $D_k(E_k(m)) = h(k)\oplus\big(h(k)\oplus m\big) = m$.

Hiding: We argue that (E,D) is a (t,ε)-secure private-key encryption scheme. $G\colon \{0,1\}^\ell \to \{0,1\}^{\ell+1}$ defined by $G(k) = (f(k), h(k))$ is a $(t,\varepsilon/2)$-PRG (Lemma 12.8), so G's associated stream cipher is (t,ε)-secure (Theorem 12.4). Since $E_k(m) = 0^\ell m \oplus G(k)$, in other words, E encrypts m by using the stream cipher to encrypt $0^\ell m$, (E,D) is also (t,ε)-secure.

Binding: There do not exist x,k,k' such that $\bot \neq D_k(x) \neq D_{k'}(x) \neq \bot$, because $D_k(x) \neq \bot \neq D_{k'}(x)$ would imply $f(k) = x_1\cdots x_\ell = f(k')$ and thus $k = k'$ since f is a permutation, and therefore $D_k(x) = D_{k'}(x)$. ■

12.4 Pseudorandom Functions

A PRG produces polynomially many pseudorandom bits that are indistinguishable from truly random bits. A pseudorandom function (PRF) is effectively a beefed up PRG that produces exponentially many pseudorandom bits that are indistinguishable from truly random bits. A PRF uses poly seed length and generates individual pseudorandom bits "on demand" in poly time.

Indistinguishability holds against poly-time computations that adaptively pick and choose which (of the exponentially many) bits to examine.

PRFs let us access a ton of pseudorandomness at very low cost. This makes them powerful and flexible tools in cryptography and beyond, as we'll see in § 12.5. They're a theoretical model for the ubiquitous tool AES (Advanced Encryption Standard) and its predecessor DES (Data Encryption Standard).

12.4.1 Definition

A *seeded function* is a function $F\colon \{0,1\}^\ell \times \{0,1\}^n \to \{0,1\}^b$. Given a seed $s \in \{0,1\}^\ell$, define $F_s\colon \{0,1\}^n \to \{0,1\}^b$ by $F_s(x) = F(s,x)$. Figure 12.6 shows an example with $\ell = n = 2$ and $b = 1$. Turning our head 90 degrees, the output column of F_s's table is a tuple of 2^n many blocks of b bits each, so b stands for *block length*. (Randomized hash functions and encryption/decryption functions are examples of seeded functions.)

- A seeded function F yields a distribution F_{U_ℓ} over functions $f\colon \{0,1\}^n \to \{0,1\}^b$:

$$f \sim F_{U_\ell} \quad \text{means} \quad f = F_s \text{ for } s \sim U_\ell$$

- Let $U_{n\to b}$ denote the uniform distribution over all functions $f\colon \{0,1\}^n \to \{0,1\}^b$:

$$f \sim U_{n\to b} \quad \text{means} \quad f(x) \sim U_b \text{ independently for all } x$$

F being pseudorandom means F_{U_ℓ} and $U_{n\to b}$ are "indistinguishable." Given as input a function $f\colon \{0,1\}^n \to \{0,1\}^b$ (sampled from either F_{U_ℓ} or $U_{n\to b}$), a distinguisher won't have time to examine all 2^n blocks. Instead of getting the input f in the traditional way, a distinguisher now has oracle access to f: It chooses an $x \in \{0,1\}^n$ and queries the oracle to get $f(x)$. Then, it may choose another x for a second query—which may depend on the first query's answer—and so on. This is like how an oracle reduction adaptively queries its oracle. We model a nonuniform distinguisher as an *oracle circuit* C:

- There are *oracle gates* in addition to $\wedge$, $\vee$, and $\neg$ gates. If an oracle gate's n incoming wires carry $x \in \{0,1\}^n$, then its b outgoing wires carry $f(x) \in \{0,1\}^b$. Outgoing wires may be split.
- There are no ordinary input nodes. Constant nodes labeled 0 and 1 are allowed since oracle gates can't be contracted.
- The output is denoted $C(f) \in \{0,1\}$ and is designated as one $\wedge$, $\vee$, or $\neg$ gate or constant node or outgoing wire of an oracle gate.
- For convenience, we define an oracle circuit's size as the number of $\wedge$, $\vee$, and oracle gates (not counting $\neg$ gates or constant nodes). Like with ordinary circuits, we can push $\neg$ gates to the oracle gates' outputs while only doubling the number of $\wedge$ and $\vee$ gates.

Figure 12.7 shows an example. The goal is that every small oracle circuit C can hardly tell whether its oracle is $f \sim F_{U_\ell}$ or $f \sim U_{n\to b}$. Though f is sampled randomly, the same f is used for all oracle gates when evaluating C. So if C makes the same query x more than once during the computation, it will get the same answer $f(x)$. In particular, for $C(F_{U_\ell})$, all oracle gates are F_s for the same seed $s \sim U_\ell$.

Definition. $F\colon \{0,1\}^\ell \times \{0,1\}^n \to \{0,1\}^b$ is a (t,ε)*-pseudorandom function (PRF)* iff for every size-t oracle circuit C where oracle gates have n incoming wires and b outgoing wires:

$$\mathbf{Pr}\big[C(F_{U_\ell}) = 1\big] \text{ and } \mathbf{Pr}\big[C(U_{n\to b}) = 1\big] \text{ are within } \pm\varepsilon \qquad ◀$$

s	x	$F(s,x)$
00	00	1
00	01	0
00	10	0
00	11	1
01	00	0
01	01	0
01	10	1
01	11	1
10	00	1
10	01	1
10	10	0
10	11	1
11	00	0
11	01	1
11	10	0
11	11	0

x	$F_{00}(x)$
00	1
01	0
10	0
11	1

x	$F_{01}(x)$
00	0
01	0
10	1
11	1

x	$F_{10}(x)$
00	1
01	1
10	0
11	1

x	$F_{11}(x)$
00	0
01	1
10	0
11	0

Figure 12.6: Example seeded function $F\colon \{0,1\}^2 \times \{0,1\}^2 \to \{0,1\}$

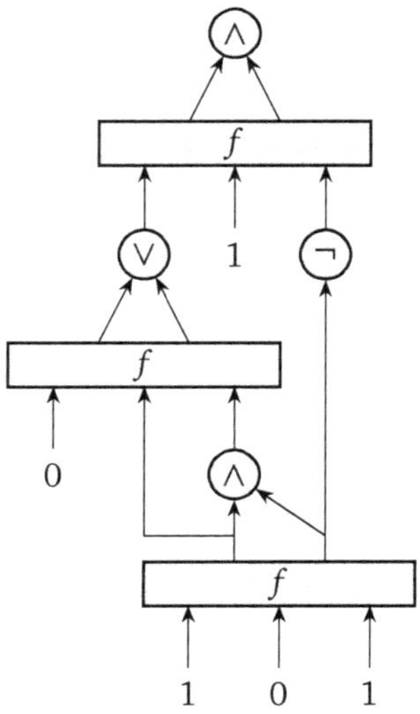

Figure 12.7: Example oracle circuit with oracle $f\colon \{0,1\}^3 \to \{0,1\}^2$

The block size b is not especially important. To decrease the block size while preserving (t,ε)-pseudorandomness, we can just discard some bits from each block. To increase the block size, say from 1 to $b = 2^e$, we can turn $F\colon \{0,1\}^\ell \times \{0,1\}^n \to \{0,1\}$ into $F'\colon \{0,1\}^\ell \times \{0,1\}^{n-e} \to \{0,1\}^b$ where $F'_s(x)$ is the values of F_s on all e-bit extensions of x. If F is a (tb,ε)-PRF, then F' is a (t,ε)-PRF because we could turn a distinguisher for F' into a distinguisher for F by replacing each oracle gate with b oracle gates (with constants for their last e incoming bits) to get the block's bits individually.

For a pseudorandom function family parameterized by n, *poly-time* means $(\operatorname{poly} n)$-time (and the seed length $\ell(n)$ and block size $b(n)$ are in $\operatorname{poly} n$), and *cryptographic* means $(\operatorname{poly} n, \operatorname{negl} n)$ as in §12.3.1.

12.4.2 Constructing Pseudorandom Functions

Here's a recipe to turn PRGs into PRFs. For any *length-doubling* function $G\colon \{0,1\}^\ell \to \{0,1\}^{2\ell}$:

- Define $G_0\colon \{0,1\}^\ell \to \{0,1\}^\ell$ by $G_0(s) =$ left half of $G(s)$.
- Define $G_1\colon \{0,1\}^\ell \to \{0,1\}^\ell$ by $G_1(s) =$ right half of $G(s)$.

For any n, define the seeded function $F\colon \{0,1\}^\ell \times \{0,1\}^n \to \{0,1\}^\ell$ by:

$$F_s(x_1 \cdots x_n) \;=\; G_{x_n}(G_{x_{n-1}}(\cdots G_{x_3}(G_{x_2}(G_{x_1}(s)))\cdots))$$

Figure 12.8 illustrates F_s as a depth-n binary tree where each node's label is a string in $\{0,1\}^\ell$:

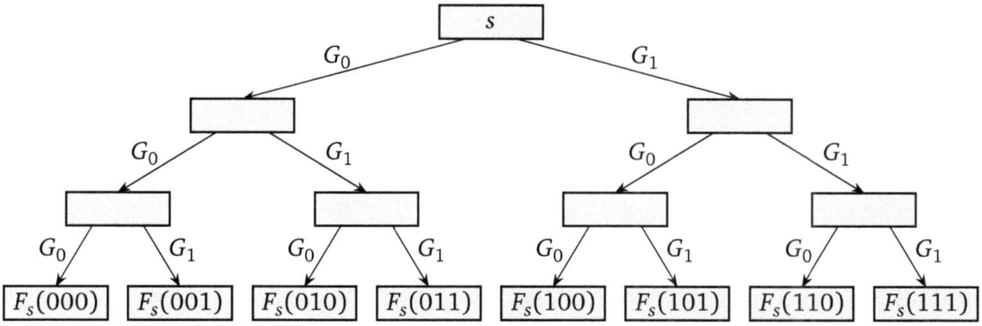

Figure 12.8: Constructing a PRF from a length-doubling PRG

s	$G(s)$	$G_0(s)$	$G_1(s)$
00	1001	10	01
01	0010	00	10
10	1100	11	00
11	0111	01	11

x	$F_{01}(x)$
000	$G_0(G_0(G_0(01))) = 11$
001	$G_1(G_0(G_0(01))) = 00$
010	$G_0(G_1(G_0(01))) = 00$
011	$G_1(G_1(G_0(01))) = 10$
100	$G_0(G_0(G_1(01))) = 01$
101	$G_1(G_0(G_1(01))) = 11$
110	$G_0(G_1(G_1(01))) = 10$
111	$G_1(G_1(G_1(01))) = 01$

Figure 12.9: Example of constructing $F_{01}\colon \{0,1\}^3 \to \{0,1\}^2$ from $G\colon \{0,1\}^2 \to \{0,1\}^4$

- The root's label is the seed s.
- An internal node labeled r has left child labeled $G_0(r)$ and right child labeled $G_1(r)$.
- Therefore, the leaf reached by the path corresponding to x (go left when $x_i = 0$, go right when $x_i = 1$) is labeled $F_s(x)$.

Figure 12.9 shows an example.

Theorem 12.12. *If $G\colon \{0,1\}^\ell \to \{0,1\}^{2\ell}$ is computed by a size-t' circuit and is a $\left(t^2t'\ell n,\ \varepsilon/nt\right)$-PRG, then $F\colon \{0,1\}^\ell \times \{0,1\}^n \to \{0,1\}^\ell$ defined above is a (t,ε)-PRF.*

First, we need a lemma. If D is a distribution, then D^q denotes q many fully independent samples from D. (In the proof of Theorem 12.12, q will correspond to "number of queries.")

Lemma 12.13. *If D_0 and D_1 are $(t,\varepsilon/q)$-indistinguishable distributions, then D_0^q and D_1^q are (t,ε)-indistinguishable.*

Proof of Lemma 12.13. We prove the contrapositive by a hybrid argument. Suppose D_0^q and D_1^q aren't (t,ε)-indistinguishable. Let C be a size-t circuit such that

$$\mathbf{Pr}\left[C(D_0^q) = 1\right] - \mathbf{Pr}\left[C(D_1^q) = 1\right] \ > \ \varepsilon$$

(assuming C has already been negated if necessary to remove the absolute value bars). Letting $p_i = \mathbf{Pr}\left[C(D_0^{q-i}, D_1^i) = 1\right]$, so $p_0 = \mathbf{Pr}\left[C(D_0^q) = 1\right]$ and $p_q = \mathbf{Pr}\left[C(D_1^q) = 1\right]$, we have:

$$(p_0 - p_1) + (p_1 - p_2) + \cdots + (p_{q-2} - p_{q-1}) + (p_{q-1} - p_q) \ = \ p_0 - p_q \ > \ \varepsilon$$

Thus there exists $i \in [q]$ such that $p_{i-1} - p_i > \varepsilon/q$, which means:

$$\mathbf{Pr}\big[C(D_0^{q-i}, D_0, D_1^{i-1}) = 1\big] - \mathbf{Pr}\big[C(D_0^{q-i}, D_1, D_1^{i-1}) = 1\big] \;>\; \varepsilon/q$$

For some outcome of $r_{\leq q-i} \sim D_0^{q-i}$ and $r_{\geq q-i+2} \sim D_1^{i-1}$, contracting C with $r_{\leq q-i}$ and $r_{\geq q-i+2}$ plugged in yields a size-t circuit $C'(r_{q-i+1})$ such that:

$$\begin{aligned} &\mathbf{Pr}\big[C'(D_0) = 1\big] - \mathbf{Pr}\big[C'(D_1) = 1\big] \\ =\; &\mathbf{Pr}\big[C(r_{\leq q-i}, D_0, r_{\geq q-i+2}) = 1\big] - \mathbf{Pr}\big[C(r_{\leq q-i}, D_1, r_{\geq q-i+2}) = 1\big] \;>\; \varepsilon/q \end{aligned}$$

Thus D_0 and D_1 aren't $(t, \varepsilon/q)$-indistinguishable. ■

Proof of Theorem 12.12. Assuming G has a size-t' circuit and F isn't a (t, ε)-PRF, we prove that G isn't a $\big(t^2 t' \ell n,\ \varepsilon/nt\big)$-PRG. Let C be a size-t oracle circuit such that

$$\mathbf{Pr}\big[C(F_{U_\ell}) = 1\big] - \mathbf{Pr}\big[C(U_{n\to\ell}) = 1\big] \;>\; \varepsilon$$

(assuming C has already been negated if necessary to remove the absolute value bars). In the tree representing F_s, let level 0 be the root and level n be the leaves. For each $i \in \{0, 1, \ldots, n\}$, define a distribution L_i over functions $f : \{0,1\}^n \to \{0,1\}^\ell$:

- Fill level i's nodes with independent samples from U_ℓ.
- Fill levels $i+1, \ldots, n$ using G as usual.
- Let $f(x)$ be the label of the leaf corresponding to x.

Thus L_0 is F_{U_ℓ}, and L_n is $U_{n\to\ell}$. Letting $p_i = \mathbf{Pr}\big[C(L_i) = 1\big]$, so $p_0 = \mathbf{Pr}\big[C(F_{U_\ell}) = 1\big]$ and $p_n = \mathbf{Pr}\big[C(U_{n\to\ell}) = 1\big]$, we have:

$$(p_0 - p_1) + (p_1 - p_2) + \cdots + (p_{n-2} - p_{n-1}) + (p_{n-1} - p_n) \;=\; p_0 - p_n \;>\; \varepsilon$$

Thus there exists $i \in [n]$ such that $p_{i-1} - p_i > \varepsilon/n$.

First attempt at completing the proof: We'll show that distinguishing L_{i-1} and L_i lets us distinguish $G(U_\ell)^q$ and $U_{2\ell}^q$ where $q = 2^{i-1}$, which lets us distinguish $G(U_\ell)$ and $U_{2\ell}$ by Lemma 12.13. (Never mind the parameters for now.) Given a sample $(r_1, \ldots, r_q)$ from either $G(U_\ell)^q$ or $U_{2\ell}^q$, we turn it into a sample f from either L_{i-1} or L_i as follows:

- Fill level i's nodes (from left to right) with r_1's left half, r_1's right half, r_2's left half, r_2's right half, r_3's left half, and so on.
- Fill levels $i+1, \ldots, n$ using G as usual.
- Let $f(x)$ be the label of the leaf corresponding to x.

Thus:

- $(r_1, \ldots, r_q) \sim G(U_\ell)^q$ becomes $f \sim L_{i-1}$, as Figure 12.10 illustrates.
- $(r_1, \ldots, r_q) \sim U_{2\ell}^q$ becomes $f \sim L_i$, as Figure 12.11 illustrates.

To distinguish $G(U_\ell)^q$ and $U_{2\ell}^q$, we turn $(r_1, \ldots, r_q)$ into f and use $C(f)$ to distinguish L_{i-1} and L_i. A straightforward implementation of this idea has poor parameters since q may be exponentially large. We can't afford to touch all the nodes in level i. Fortunately, neither can C. To fix this attempt, we redefine q to be the number of oracle gates in C, and we use $(r_1, \ldots, r_q)$ only for the level-i nodes that are relevant to the queries made by $C(f)$. This is subtle since C's queries may depend on the answers to previous queries, which depend on $(r_1, \ldots, r_q)$. But we can make it work: To distinguish $G(U_\ell)^q$ and $U_{2\ell}^q$, we assign $(r_1, \ldots, r_q)$ to level-i sibling pairs "on the fly":

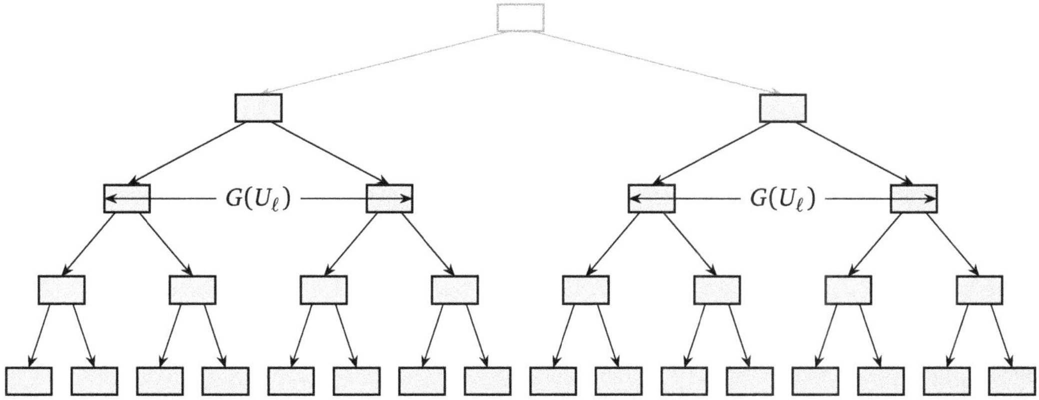

Figure 12.10: Using independent copies of $G(U_\ell)$ to simulate hybrid $i-1=1$

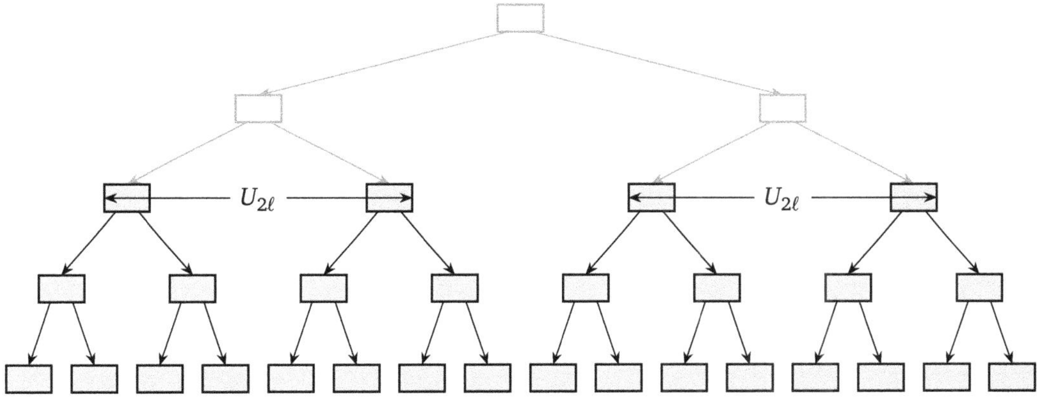

Figure 12.11: Using independent copies of $U_{2\ell}$ to simulate hybrid $i=2$

- If C's first query is x, we assign r_1's two halves to the nodes corresponding to $x_1 \cdots x_{i-1}0$ and $x_1 \cdots x_{i-1}1$, and answer the query by repeatedly evaluating G to reach x's leaf.
- If C's second query is y, we first check whether $y_1 \cdots y_i$ leads to one of the r_1 nodes. If so, we answer the query as usual, starting from the relevant half of r_1. If not, we assign r_2's two halves to the nodes corresponding to $y_1 \cdots y_{i-1}0$ and $y_1 \cdots y_{i-1}1$, and then answer the query.
- If C's third query is z and only r_1 has been assigned so far, we handle the query in the same way we handled the second query, possibly assigning r_2 in the process. If both r_1 and r_2 were already assigned, we first check whether $z_1 \cdots z_i$ leads to an r_1 or r_2 node. If so, we answer the query as usual. If not, we assign r_3's two halves to the nodes corresponding to $z_1 \cdots z_{i-1}0$ and $z_1 \cdots z_{i-1}1$, and then answer the query.

And so on. C's queries touch $\leq q$ many level-i sibling pairs, so we won't run out of samples in $(r_1, \ldots, r_q)$. Calling this distinguisher C', we have:

$$\mathbf{Pr}\big[C'(G(U_\ell)^q)=1\big]-\mathbf{Pr}\big[C'(U_{2\ell}^q)=1\big] \;=\; \mathbf{Pr}\big[C(L_{i-1})=1\big]-\mathbf{Pr}\big[C(L_i)=1\big] \;>\; \varepsilon/n$$

For each r_i, C' remembers which sibling pair r_i was assigned to, if any. For each query x, C' compares $x_1 \cdots x_i$ to the assignments so far to see if the corresponding level-i node already has a value or if a fresh r_i should be assigned ($\le 20q(\ell+n) \le 20t(\ell+n)$ gates per query), and then C' repeatedly evaluates G to reach x's leaf ($\le n(t'+10\ell)$ gates per query, including copies of G's circuit and muxes). In total, C' has size $\le t\big(20t(\ell+n)+n(t'+10\ell)\big) \le t^2t'\ell n$ (for simplicity).

In conclusion, $G(U_\ell)^q$ and $U_{2\ell}^q$ are $\big(t^2t'\ell n,\, \varepsilon/n\big)$-distinguishable. By Lemma 12.13, $G(U_\ell)$ and $U_{2\ell}$ are $\big(t^2t'\ell n,\, \varepsilon/nt\big)$-distinguishable since $q \le t$. ■

Upshot: We can make any poly-time computable cryptographic PRG family length-doubling and turn it into a poly-time computable cryptographic PRF family with any seed length $\ell = n^{\Omega(1)}$.

12.4.3 Pseudorandom Permutations

Some applications in cryptography benefit from *pseudorandom permutations (PRPs)*, also known as *block ciphers*, which are pseudorandom functions where $F_s\colon \{0,1\}^n \to \{0,1\}^n$ is a bijection for every seed s. AES, and previously DES, are widely used block ciphers in practice. For example, with one setting of parameters, AES is a seeded permutation $F\colon \{0,1\}^{256} \times \{0,1\}^{128} \to \{0,1\}^{128}$ that's conjectured to be a (t,ε)-PRP for some enormous t and some tiny ε.

We won't discuss applications that require PRPs, but we mention how to construct PRPs from PRFs. For any function $f\colon \{0,1\}^n \to \{0,1\}^n$, define $f'\colon (\{0,1\}^n)^2 \to (\{0,1\}^n)^2$ by:

$$f'(x,y) = (y, x \oplus f(y))$$

f' is guaranteed to be a permutation because it's invertible: Given (y,z), we can recover $(x,y) = (z \oplus f(y), y)$ such that $f'(x,y) = \big(y, (z \oplus f(y)) \oplus f(y)\big) = (y,z)$. If f is poly-time computable, then f' is poly-time computable and poly-time invertible.

For any seeded function $F\colon \{0,1\}^\ell \times \{0,1\}^n \to \{0,1\}^n$, define $F'\colon \{0,1\}^\ell \times (\{0,1\}^n)^2 \to (\{0,1\}^n)^2$ by $(F')_s = (F_s)'$. Unfortunately, F' is definitely not pseudorandom: If we pick any (x,y) and query $(a,b) \leftarrow f(x,y)$:

- $f \sim F'_{U_\ell}$ has $a = y$ with probability 1.
- $f \sim U_{2n\to 2n}$ has $a = y$ with probability 2^{-n}.

Let's "double down" on this idea by sampling several independent seeds and composing the associated permutations: The k-round version is $F'^k\colon (\{0,1\}^\ell)^k \times (\{0,1\}^n)^2 \to (\{0,1\}^n)^2$ defined by $(F'^k)_{s_1,\ldots,s_k} = F'_{s_k} \circ \cdots \circ F'_{s_1}$, as Figure 12.12 illustrates with $k=3$.

The two-round version is still not pseudorandom (Exercise 12.13). Fortunately, three rounds yield a PRP if F is a PRF, but the proof is beyond the scope of this book. DES (but not AES) uses this template with 16 rounds.

12.5 Applications of Pseudorandom Functions

12.5.1 Arbitrary Length Messages and Multiple Encryptions

Here are two issues with encryption schemes as defined in §12.1 and §12.2:

(i) They only handle messages of a particular length.
(ii) They can only be used once without sampling a fresh key.

We adapt stream ciphers (§12.2.2) to address these issues: Alice and Bob agree on a key k for the seed of a PRG $G\colon \{0,1\}^\ell \to \{0,1\}^n$. To send Bob a sequence of messages of varying lengths $n_1, n_2, n_3, \ldots$, Alice xors the first message with $G(k)$'s first n_1 bits, and xors the second message

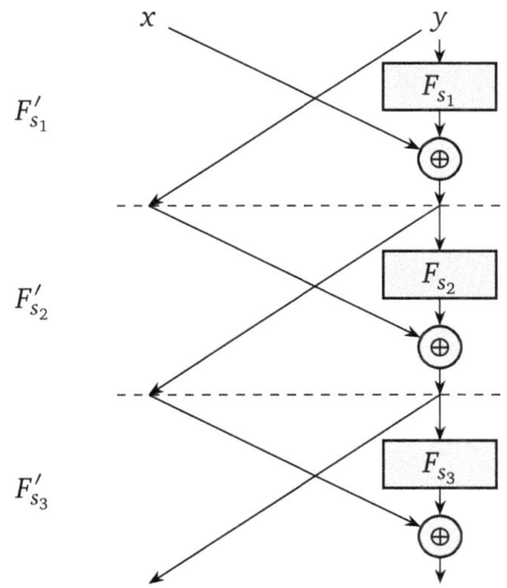

Figure 12.12: Turning a seeded function into a 3-round seeded permutation

with $G(k)$'s next n_2 bits (indices $n_1+1,\ldots,n_1+n_2$), and so on. The concatenation of the messages is like one big message. Now, we have two further issues:

(iii) The total length of all messages is limited by G's output length (unless a fresh key is sampled).

(iv) Alice and Bob must maintain *state*: They must remember how many bits were already transmitted, so they're "on the same page" about which portion of $G(k)$ to use next.

Pseudorandom functions provide exponentially many pseudorandom bits—effectively limitless for practical purposes—resolving issue *(iii)*. Maintaining state is not always problematic, but sometimes *stateless* encryption schemes are preferable. To resolve *(iv)*, Alice can randomly pick which contiguous portion of the pseudorandom bits to use, and tell Bob (as part of the ciphertext) which portion she picked. Eve also sees which portion is being used, but it doesn't matter since she's still clueless about those pseudorandom bits. Eve could learn something if multiple messages happen to use overlapping portions, but that's exceedingly unlikely since Alice picks the portions randomly. So Alice doesn't bother remembering which portions she already picked. The tradeoff for statelessness is that Alice needs extra randomness, but this is often acceptable in practice.

Let's formalize this. We update the syntax of encryption schemes to allow randomized encryption and arbitrary length messages:

- Encryption: $E\colon \{0,1\}^\ell \times \{0,1\}^n \times \{0,1\}^+ \to \{0,1\}^+$
- Decryption: $D\colon \{0,1\}^\ell \times \{0,1\}^+ \to \{0,1\}^+$

Now, n is the length of Alice's private random string.

- Alice encrypts a message $m \in \{0,1\}^+$ using a key $k \in \{0,1\}^\ell$ and an *initialization vector* $r \in \{0,1\}^n$ to get a ciphertext $E(k,r,m) = E_{k,r}(m) \in \{0,1\}^+$.
- Bob decrypts a ciphertext $x \in \{0,1\}^+$ using a key $k \in \{0,1\}^\ell$ to get a message $D(k,x) = D_k(x) \in \{0,1\}^+$.

We must have $D_k(E_{k,r}(m)) = m$ for all k, r, and m.

The *counter mode (CTR)* encryption scheme uses a pseudorandom function $F\colon \{0,1\}^\ell \times \{0,1\}^n \to \{0,1\}$ (but can be adapted to other block sizes) and treats the initialization vector as a binary number $r \in \{0,1,\ldots,2^n-1\}$:

- To encrypt a message m of length n_1:

$$E_{k,r}(m) \;=\; \big(r,\; m \oplus \big(F_k(r),\, F_k(r+1),\, F_k(r+2),\, \ldots,\, F_k(r+n_1-1)\big)\big)$$

- To decrypt a ciphertext (r,x) of length $n+n_1$:

$$D_k(r,x) \;=\; x \oplus \big(F_k(r),\, F_k(r+1),\, F_k(r+2),\, \ldots,\, F_k(r+n_1-1)\big)$$

The arithmetic is mod 2^n, so $r+i$ means $(r+i) \bmod 2^n$. If F is a cryptographic PRF, then counter mode is secure for polynomially many messages of polynomial lengths:

Theorem 12.14. *With the counter mode encryption scheme, if F is a (t,ε)-PRF, then for*

- *every sequence of messages $m_1, m_2, \ldots, m_h$ of lengths $n_1, n_2, \ldots, n_h$,*
- *every sequence of messages $m'_1, m'_2, \ldots, m'_h$ of the same lengths $n_1, n_2, \ldots, n_h$, and*
- *every size-$(t-n_1-\cdots-n_h)$ circuit $C\colon \{0,1\}^{hn+n_1+\cdots+n_h} \to \{0,1\}$,*

$\mathbf{Pr}\big[C\big(E_{k,r_1}(m_1),\, \ldots,\, E_{k,r_h}(m_h)\big) = 1\big]$ *(where $k \sim U_\ell$, $r_1 \sim U_n$, $\ldots$, $r_h \sim U_n$) is within $\pm\big(2\varepsilon + (n_1+\cdots+n_h)h/2^n\big)$ of the same probability with $m'_1, \ldots, m'_h$ in place of $m_1, \ldots, m_h$.*

Proof (ancillary). Say an outcome $q = (r_1, \ldots, r_h)$ is *good* iff the intervals $\{r_1, \ldots, r_1+n_1-1\}$, $\ldots$, $\{r_h, \ldots, r_h+n_h-1\}$ are pairwise disjoint. For any $i<j$, $\mathbf{Pr}\big[i\text{th and } j\text{th intervals overlap}\big] \le (n_i+n_j)/2^n$, so by a union bound:

$$\mathbf{Pr}_q\big[q \text{ is bad}\big] \;\le\; \tfrac{1}{2}\textstyle\sum_{i=1}^{h}\sum_{j=1}^{h}(n_i+n_j)/2^n \;=\; (n_1+\cdots+n_h)h/2^n$$

The rest of the proof is similar to our first proof of Theorem 12.4. For each $q = (r_1, \ldots, r_h)$, consider an oracle circuit C_q such that

$$C_q(f) \;=\; C\Big(\big(r_1,\; m_1 \oplus \big(f(r_1), \ldots, f(r_1+n_1-1)\big)\big),\; \ldots,\; \big(r_h,\; m_h \oplus \big(f(r_h), \ldots, f(r_h+n_h-1)\big)\big)\Big)$$

and an analogous oracle circuit C'_q using $m'_1, \ldots, m'_h$. Each C_q and C'_q has size $\le t$ because it has C and $n_1+\cdots+n_h$ many oracle gates and some $\neg$ gates and constants. If q is good then:

$$C_q(U_{n\to 1}) \;=\; C\big((r_1,\, U_{n_1}),\; \ldots,\; (r_h,\, U_{n_h})\big) \;=\; C'_q(U_{n\to 1})$$

Putting everything together:

$$\begin{aligned}
&\Big|\mathbf{Pr}_{k,q}\big[C\big(E_{k,r_1}(m_1), \ldots, E_{k,r_h}(m_h)\big)=1\big] - \mathbf{Pr}_{k,q}\big[C\big(E_{k,r_1}(m'_1), \ldots, E_{k,r_h}(m'_h)\big)=1\big]\Big| \\
&= \Big|\mathbf{Pr}_{k,q}\big[C_q(F_k)=1\big] - \mathbf{Pr}_{k,q}\big[C'_q(F_k)=1\big]\Big| \\
&\le \mathbf{E}_q\Big|\mathbf{Pr}\big[C_q(F_{U_\ell})=1\big] - \mathbf{Pr}\big[C'_q(F_{U_\ell})=1\big]\Big| \\
&\le \max\nolimits_{\text{good } q}\Big|\mathbf{Pr}\big[C_q(F_{U_\ell})=1\big] - \mathbf{Pr}\big[C'_q(F_{U_\ell})=1\big]\Big| + \mathbf{Pr}_q\big[q \text{ is bad}\big] \\
&\le \max\nolimits_{\text{good } q}\Big(\Big|\mathbf{Pr}\big[C_q(F_{U_\ell})=1\big] - \mathbf{Pr}\big[C_q(U_{n\to 1})=1\big]\Big| + \\
&\qquad\qquad \Big|\mathbf{Pr}\big[C'_q(U_{n\to 1})=1\big] - \mathbf{Pr}\big[C'_q(F_{U_\ell})=1\big]\Big|\Big) + \mathbf{Pr}_q\big[q \text{ is bad}\big] \\
&\le \max\nolimits_{\text{good } q}(\varepsilon+\varepsilon) + (n_1+\cdots+n_h)h/2^n
\end{aligned}$$

∎

There are other modes (ways of turning PRFs into encryption schemes), but counter mode has several advantages:

- Each ciphertext bit (ith bit of x) = (ith bit of m) $\oplus F_k(r + i - 1)$ can be encrypted and decrypted independently of the other bits. Thus, encryption and decryption can be parallelized, and Bob can get any message bit without needing to decrypt the other bits.
- Alice can pick r and compute the pseudorandom bits $F_k(r), F_k(r + 1), \ldots$ ahead of time, so encryption will be lightning fast once the message is available.
- Counter mode remains secure even if Eve tricks Alice into encrypting messages of Eve's choice—a *chosen plaintext attack*. ("Plaintext" means "message.") Intuitively, this is because the intervals Alice picks for encrypting Eve's chosen messages probably won't overlap the intervals for other messages. We won't prove this, but Exercise 12.14 is related.

Stream ciphers have few advantages except for being slightly more efficient. In practice, block ciphers such as AES are usually preferred over stream ciphers.

12.5.2 Message Authentication

So far we considered *confidentiality*—the adversary shouldn't learn anything about the message. Another goal of cryptography is *authenticity*—Bob should be able to verify that a transmission that's ostensibly from Alice is authentic, meaning Alice really did send exactly that. An adversary shouldn't be able to impersonate Alice or tamper with the transmission without Bob detecting it.

It's tempting to assume that confidentiality implies authenticity, because if the adversary can't discern anything from the ciphertext, then she can't meaningfully modify it. But that's wrong. Stream ciphers don't ensure authenticity at all: If the adversary tampers with the ciphertext by flipping the first bit (say), then the message's first bit would also be flipped, and Bob would have no idea that's not what Alice intended.

Message authentication codes (MACs) are to authenticity as encryption schemes are to confidentiality. A MAC is a seeded function $F: \{0,1\}^\ell \times \{0,1\}^n \to \{0,1\}^b$ where ℓ is the *key length*, n is the *message length*, and b is the *tag length*.

- Alice and Bob agree on a uniformly random key $k \in \{0,1\}^\ell$ beforehand.
- Given message $m \in \{0,1\}^n$, Alice computes the *tag* $a = F(k,m) = F_k(m) \in \{0,1\}^b$ and sends the pair (m, a).
- Upon receiving message $m \in \{0,1\}^n$ with tag $a \in \{0,1\}^b$, Bob computes $F_k(m)$ and accepts iff $a = F_k(m)$, indicating he's convinced m was really a message from Alice.

Intuitively, security means the tag $F_k(m)$ is like a signature that only someone who knows the key could have produced. The adversary can't forge a tag on any message that Alice hasn't already sent. (In fact, the public-key counterparts of MACs are called *digital signatures*.)

Alice and Bob should be able to keep using the same key to authenticate multiple messages. This unfortunately enables *replay attacks*: After observing an authentic transmission (m, a) from Alice, the adversary can impersonate Alice and retransmit (m, a) to Bob, who again verifies that $a = F_k(m)$. Bob is confident that Alice indeed sent (m, a) at least once, but can't be sure how many times Alice actually intended to send (m, a). Replay attacks are a separate security concern that MACs don't defend against. Other security concerns that MACs don't address include the adversary re-ordering transmissions or preventing Bob from receiving a transmission.

Before attempting a forgery, the adversary can see whatever authentic (message, tag) pairs Alice sends. We also want to defend against an active adversary who can influence Alice to generate tags for messages of the adversary's choice. (The adversary might be Alice's coworker, for example.) The adversary picks a message and observes the tag Alice generates for it, and then the adversary picks another message (possibly depending on the first tag) and sees its tag, and so on. We model the adversary as an oracle circuit C that outputs a pair $(m,a) \in \{0,1\}^n \times \{0,1\}^b$ and has oracle gates representing $F_k\colon \{0,1\}^n \to \{0,1\}^b$. The output is a *forgery* iff $a = F_k(m)$ (Bob would accept it) and m differs from all queries made by $C(F_k)$ (a replay isn't a forgery).

Definition. A message authentication code F with key length ℓ is (t,ε)*-unforgeable* iff for every size-t oracle circuit C, $\mathbf{Pr}\big[C(F_{U_\ell}) \text{ is a forgery}\big] \le \varepsilon$. ◂

Pseudorandom functions are message authentication codes:

Theorem 12.15. *If $F\colon \{0,1\}^\ell \times \{0,1\}^n \to \{0,1\}^b$ is a $\big(t(4n+1)+4b,\ \varepsilon - 2^{-b}\big)$-PRF, then F is a (t,ε)-unforgeable MAC.*

Proof. Suppose F isn't a (t,ε)-unforgeable MAC, so $\mathbf{Pr}\big[C(F_{U_\ell}) \text{ is a forgery}\big] > \varepsilon$ for some size-t oracle circuit C. Define an oracle circuit C' such that $C'(f) = 1$ iff $C(f)$ is a forgery: Letting $(m,a) = C(f)$, we have $C'(f) = 1$ iff $a = f(m)$ and m is *new*, meaning that m differs from all queries made by $C(f)$. We have $\mathbf{Pr}\big[C'(F_{U_\ell}) = 1\big] > \varepsilon$ by assumption, and

$$\begin{aligned}\mathbf{Pr}\big[C'(U_{n\to b}) = 1\big] &= \mathbf{Pr}_{f\sim U_{n\to b}}\big[a = f(m) \text{ and } m \text{ is new}\big]\\ &\le \mathbf{Pr}_{f\sim U_{n\to b}}\big[a = f(m) \,\big|\, m \text{ is new}\big] \;=\; 2^{-b}\end{aligned}$$

since $f(m)$ is uniform and independent of a if m is new. It follows that:

$$\Big|\mathbf{Pr}\big[C'(F_{U_\ell}) = 1\big] - \mathbf{Pr}\big[C'(U_{n\to b}) = 1\big]\Big| \;>\; \varepsilon - 2^{-b}$$

Thus F isn't a $\big(t(4n+1)+4b,\ \varepsilon-2^{-b}\big)$-PRF, since C' has size $\le t+1+(4b-1)+t(4n-1)+t = t(4n+1)+4b$ because: C has size $\le t$. The final query $f(m)$ is one oracle gate. Checking $a = f(m)$ takes $4b-1$ many $\wedge$ and $\vee$ gates. For each of the $\le t$ many queries of $C(f)$, checking whether it equals m takes $4n-1$ many $\wedge$ and $\vee$ gates. "And"ing together the "$a = f(m)$" and "$m \ne$ previous query" checks takes $\le t$ gates. ■

Directly using PRFs as MACs is not especially practical, but at least Theorem 12.15 demonstrates that message authentication is possible in principle. Other MAC constructions are more efficient and handle arbitrary length messages.

MACs provide no confidentiality at all, since the adversary sees the message m. To achieve confidentiality and authenticity simultaneously (as typically desired in practice), we can encrypt the message and then authenticate the ciphertext: Using an encryption scheme $E\colon \{0,1\}^{\ell_1} \times \{0,1\}^n \to \{0,1\}^c$ and $D\colon \{0,1\}^{\ell_1} \times \{0,1\}^c \to \{0,1\}^n$ and a MAC $F\colon \{0,1\}^{\ell_2} \times \{0,1\}^c \to \{0,1\}^b$:

- Alice and Bob agree on two independent keys $k_1 \sim U_{\ell_1}$ and $k_2 \sim U_{\ell_2}$ beforehand.
- Given message $m \in \{0,1\}^n$, Alice computes $x = E_{k_1}(m)$ and $a = F_{k_2}(x)$ and sends (x,a).
- Upon receiving ciphertext $x \in \{0,1\}^c$ with tag $a \in \{0,1\}^b$, Bob verifies that $a = F_{k_2}(x)$ and if so, computes $m = D_{k_1}(x)$.

This combination achieves confidentiality and authenticity if (E,D) and F do (but we won't argue this formally). Using independent keys is important. In general, secure cryptographic tools can become insecure if combined improperly, such as using the same key for two purposes.

12.5.3 Minimum Circuit Size Problem

A fundamental goal of digital logic synthesis is to find a smallest circuit that computes a given function. Many heuristics are used by computer-aided design (CAD) tools in practice, but the general problem is not known to have a poly-time algorithm. Here's a decision version:

Minimum Circuit Size Problem (or MCSP for short)	(12.4)
Input: Truth table of a function $g\colon \{0,1\}^m \to \{0,1\}$, and $t \in [2^{m+2}]$	
Output: Does g have a bounded-fan-in circuit with $\le t$ many $\wedge$, $\vee$, and $\neg$ gates?	

Every g has a size-2^{m+2} circuit (Theorem 5.7). MCSP $\in$ NP where the witness is a size-t circuit for g: The verifier evaluates the circuit on every $x \in \{0,1\}^m$ and checks that it agrees with $g(x)$. This takes time poly M where $M = O(2^m)$ is MCSP's input size.

MCSP is a candidate NP-intermediate problem: It's neither known to be in P nor known to be NP-complete. We give evidence that MCSP $\notin$ P by proving that this follows from the existence of pseudorandom functions (which follows from the existence of one-way functions). There's no strong evidence for or against MCSP being NP-complete. But proving that MCSP is NP-complete would be extremely challenging because it's known to imply EXP $\neq$ ZPP (which is a major open question in the vein of P versus NP). The version of MCSP where g is a partial function is known to be NP-hard under randomized reductions; this is difficult to prove and was an open question for a long time. It's unknown whether MCSP has a search-to-decision reduction; proving that it does is a necessary step toward proving that it's NP-complete, since all NP-complete problems have search-to-decision reductions (Exercise 2.15).

Theorem 12.16. *If there exists a poly-time computable cryptographic PRF family, then* MCSP $\notin$ P/poly.

Proof idea. A pseudorandom function has a small circuit. A uniformly random function probably doesn't. An MCSP algorithm could distinguish these cases and thus "break" any pseudorandom function. ■

Proof. Assume MCSP $\in$ P/poly. Consider any (poly n)-time computable seeded function family $F^1, F^2, \ldots$ where $F^n\colon \{0,1\}^{\ell(n)} \times \{0,1\}^n \to \{0,1\}$. We show that it's not a (poly n, negl n)-PRF family. (We may assume a PRF has block size 1.)

Consider any large enough n. Abbreviate F^n as F and $\ell(n)$ as ℓ. Since the family is (poly n)-time computable, F has a size-t circuit where $t = n^d$ for a constant d. Contracting this circuit yields a size-t circuit for F_s for each seed $s \in \{0,1\}^\ell$.

Let $m = \lceil \log(t^2) \rceil$. Let M be the size of inputs to MCSP where $g\colon \{0,1\}^m \to \{0,1\}$. Since MCSP $\in$ P/poly, MCSP_M has a size-M^e circuit B for a constant e.

Consider an oracle circuit C with oracle $f\colon \{0,1\}^n \to \{0,1\}$, where $C(f)$ queries $f(x0^{n-m})$ for every $x \in \{0,1\}^m$, treats the answers as the truth table of a function $f'\colon \{0,1\}^m \to \{0,1\}$, and evaluates $B(f', t)$. We have $\mathbf{Pr}\big[C(F_{U_\ell}) = 1\big] = 1$ since for each seed s, F_s has a size-t circuit and therefore so does F'_s. We have $\mathbf{Pr}\big[C(U_{n\to 1}) = 1\big] \le 2^{3t\log t}/2^{2^m} < 1/2$ since by the proof of Theorem 5.8, at most $2^{3t\log t}$ of the 2^{2^m} many functions f' have size-t circuits. It follows that:

$$\Big|\mathbf{Pr}\big[C(F_{U_\ell}) = 1\big] - \mathbf{Pr}\big[C(U_{n\to 1}) = 1\big]\Big| > 1/2$$

C has size $2^m + M^e \le n^{3de}$. Therefore F isn't an $(n^{3de}, 1/2)$-PRF. ■

MCSP is a prototypical problem in *meta complexity*, which is about the complexity of determining the complexity of a function that's given as input (for various measures of complexity).

Exercises

12.1 Suppose we relax the definition of perfect security: A private-key encryption scheme (E, D) with key length ℓ is *ε-secure* iff for every pair of messages $m_0 \neq m_1$, the distributions $E_{U_\ell}(m_0)$ and $E_{U_\ell}(m_1)$ are ε-indistinguishable in statistical distance (§11.1.2).

Prove that for every ε-secure private-key encryption scheme with $\varepsilon < 1/2$, the key is at least as long as the message.

12.2 Prove that composing cryptographic pseudorandom generators yields a cryptographic pseudorandom generator. Specifically: If $G_1\colon \{0,1\}^\ell \to \{0,1\}^m$ is a $(t+t', \varepsilon/2)$-PRG and $G_2\colon \{0,1\}^m \to \{0,1\}^n$ is a $(t, \varepsilon/2)$-PRG and G_2 is computed by a size-t' circuit, then $G_2 \circ G_1\colon \{0,1\}^\ell \to \{0,1\}^n$ is a (t, ε)-PRG.

12.3 Prove that if there exists a poly-time computable $(\operatorname{poly} n, \operatorname{negl} n)$-one-way function family, then $\mathsf{P} \neq \mathsf{NP}$.

12.4 Prove that cryptographic pseudorandom generators are one-way functions. (We relax the definition of OWFs so the output may be longer than the input. This doesn't matter since we could append dummy bits to make the input as long as the output while preserving one-way-ness.) Specifically: If $G\colon \{0,1\}^\ell \to \{0,1\}^{2\ell}$ is a $\left(t + t' + 8\ell, \varepsilon - 2^{-\ell}\right)$-PRG computed by a size-$t'$ circuit, then G is a (t, ε)-OWF.

12.5 Prove that if $f\colon \{0,1\}^n \to \{0,1\}^n$ is a $(t+t', \varepsilon)$-OWP computed by a size-t' circuit, then $f \circ f$ is a (t, ε)-OWP.

12.6 Prove that permutations with hardcore bits are automatically one-way. Specifically: If a permutation $f\colon \{0,1\}^n \to \{0,1\}^n$ and $h\colon \{0,1\}^n \to \{0,1\}$ are computed by size-t' circuits, and h is a $\left(t + 2t' + 4n, \varepsilon\right)$-hardcore bit for f, then f is (t, ε)-one-way.

12.7 For $G\colon \{0,1\}^2 \to \{0,1\}^3$ in Figure 12.13, write the table of $G^4\colon \{0,1\}^2 \to \{0,1\}^4$ from Lemma 12.9, and write the table of the hybrid distribution $(U_1, G^3(U_2))$ (that is, every outcome's probability) from the proof of Lemma 12.9.

12.8 By Lemma 12.8 and Lemma 12.9, if $h\colon \{0,1\}^\ell \to \{0,1\}$ is a $\left(t + nt', 2\varepsilon/n\right)$-hardcore bit for a permutation $f\colon \{0,1\}^\ell \to \{0,1\}^\ell$, and $G\colon \{0,1\}^\ell \to \{0,1\}^{\ell+1}$ defined by $G(s) = (f(s), h(s))$ is computed by a size-t' circuit, then $G^n\colon \{0,1\}^\ell \to \{0,1\}^n$ is a (t, ε)-PRG. Give a streamlined proof of this using Lemma 11.25 (predicting versus distinguishing).

12.9 Give a streamlined proof that the bit commitment scheme from Theorem 12.11 is (t, ε)-hiding (without invoking Lemma 11.24, Lemma 12.8, or Theorem 12.4).

12.10 Here's another way to construct a computationally hiding, perfectly binding bit commitment scheme, but with the caveat that Bob sends Alice a uniformly random string a ahead of time, and the binding property only holds with high probability over a. Suppose $G\colon \{0,1\}^\ell \to \{0,1\}^{3\ell}$ is a $(t, \varepsilon/2)$-PRG. Bob sends Alice $a \sim U_{3\ell}$ ahead of time.

s	$G(s)$
00	100
01	001
10	110
11	001

Figure 12.13: Function for Exercise 12.7

s	$G(s)$
00	0011
01	1000
10	1101
11	0110

Figure 12.14: Function for Exercise 12.12

- Commit phase: Given message $m \in \{0,1\}$, Alice samples $k \sim U_\ell$ and sends Bob:

$$x = E_{a,k}(m) = \begin{cases} G(k) & \text{if } m = 0 \\ G(k) \oplus a & \text{if } m = 1 \end{cases}$$

- Reveal phase: Alice sends k to Bob, who computes:

$$D_{a,k}(x) = \begin{cases} 0 & \text{if } x = G(k) \\ 1 & \text{if } x = G(k) \oplus a \\ \perp & \text{otherwise} \end{cases}$$

(The first two cases might both hold if $a = 0^{3\ell}$, but the error probability analysis will cover that anyway.)

(a) Prove that with probability 1 over a, this is (t,ε)-hiding: $E_{a,U_\ell}(0)$ and $E_{a,U_\ell}(1)$ are (t,ε)-indistinguishable. (This is essentially Exercise 11.6.)

(b) Prove that with probability $\geq 1 - 2^{-\ell}$ over a, this is perfectly binding: There do not exist x, k, k' such that $D_{a,k}(x) = 0$ and $D_{a,k'}(x) = 1$.

12.11 Prove that a pseudorandom function's seed can't be too short: If $\ell \leq \log t - \log\log t - 1$ and $\ell < 2^n$, then no $F\colon \{0,1\}^\ell \times \{0,1\}^n \to \{0,1\}$ is a $(t, 1/3)$-PRF.

12.12 For $G\colon \{0,1\}^2 \to \{0,1\}^4$ in Figure 12.14, write the table of $F_{11}\colon \{0,1\}^3 \to \{0,1\}^2$ defined using the PRF construction from §12.4.2.

12.13 Prove that for every seeded function $F\colon \{0,1\}^\ell \times \{0,1\}^n \to \{0,1\}^n$, the two-round seeded permutation F'^2 defined in §12.4.3 is *not* a $(5n, 1/2)$-PRP. Hint: Make two queries (x,y) and (x',y) where $x \neq x'$.

12.14 In a *chosen plaintext attack (CPA)*, Eve somehow gets an unwitting Alice to encrypt messages of Eve's choice. Let's consider a slightly simplified setting:

- Eve sees an unknown message's ciphertext.
- Based on that, Eve chooses a message and somehow gets Alice to encrypt it using the same key as the first encryption.
- Eve sees that message's ciphertext.

Eve wants to learn something about the unknown message. (In general, Eve could "request" encryptions of even more messages of her choice, but the idea is the same.)

A deterministic encryption scheme (with no randomness besides the key) can't be secure against chosen plaintext attacks, because if Eve sees the same ciphertext again, she would know it was the same message as before. We consider randomized encryption schemes like in §12.5.1. For simplicity, we assume the extra randomness and the message have the same length n (but this doesn't matter).

- Encryption: $E\colon \{0,1\}^\ell \times \{0,1\}^n \times \{0,1\}^n \to \{0,1\}^c$ $\quad E(k,r,m) = E_{k,r}(m)$
- Decryption: $D\colon \{0,1\}^\ell \times \{0,1\}^c \to \{0,1\}^n$ $\quad D(k,x) = D_k(x)$

(E,D) is (t,ε)-*CPA-secure* iff for

- every pair of messages $m_0 \neq m_1$,
- every size-t circuit $B\colon \{0,1\}^c \to \{0,1\}^n$ (choosing a message based on the first ciphertext), and
- every size-t circuit $C\colon \{0,1\}^{2c} \to \{0,1\}$,

$\mathbf{Pr}\big[C\big(E_{k,r}(m_0),\, E_{k,r'}(B(E_{k,r}(m_0)))\big) = 1\big]$ (where $k \sim U_\ell$, $r \sim U_n$, $r' \sim U_n$) is within $\pm\varepsilon$ of the same probability with m_1 in place of m_0.

Consider the following randomized encryption scheme with ciphertext length $c = 2n$ using a pseudorandom function $F\colon \{0,1\}^\ell \times \{0,1\}^n \to \{0,1\}^n$:

$$E_{k,r}(m) \;=\; (r,\, m \oplus F_k(r)) \qquad\qquad D_k(r,x) \;=\; x \oplus F_k(r)$$

Prove that if F is a $\big(2t+3n+2,\, (\varepsilon - 2^{-n})/2\big)$-PRF, then this is (t,ε)-CPA-secure.

12.15 We considered perfect security for encryption schemes in § 12.1. Here's a version of perfect security for message authentication codes.

A MAC $F\colon \{0,1\}^\ell \times \{0,1\}^n \to \{0,1\}^b$ is *one-time perfectly unforgeable* iff for every message $m \in \{0,1\}^n$ and every function $g\colon \{0,1\}^b \to \{0,1\}^n \times \{0,1\}^b$,

$$\mathbf{Pr}\big[g(F_{U_\ell}(m)) \text{ is a forgery}\big] \;\le\; 2^{-b}$$

where *forgery* means that $(m',a') = g(F_k(m))$ satisfies $a' = F_k(m')$ and $m' \neq m$. In other words, if Alice only generates one authentic tag (for a message m of the adversary's choice), then the adversary can't (regardless of her resources) make a forgery with probability any higher than if she just blindly guessed a random tag for a new message. Prove that pairwise uniform hash functions are one-time perfectly unforgeable MACs.

12.16 Assuming $F\colon \{0,1\}^\ell \times \{0,1\}^n \to \{0,1\}^b$ is a message authentication code, we might try modifying it to handle messages of length $2n$ by defining $F'\colon (\{0,1\}^\ell)^2 \times (\{0,1\}^n)^2 \to (\{0,1\}^b)^2$ by $F'_{k_1,k_2}(m_1,m_2) = \big(F_{k_1}(m_1), F_{k_2}(m_2)\big)$. Prove that for every $\varepsilon < 1$, F' is *not* $(2,\varepsilon)$-unforgeable.

Notes

Texts covering the complexity-theoretic foundations of cryptography include [194, 195, 451, 513, 296].

Basing cryptography on computational complexity, with precise definitions and rigorous proofs, originated in [207].

The theorem that one-way functions imply cryptographic pseudorandom generators is due to [240], and a much simpler proof is in [362]. The necessity of one-way functions for much of private-key cryptography is due to [263].

Constructing arbitrary stretch PRGs from OWPs with hardcore bits (§12.3.2) is due to [570, 72]. Hardcore bits for one-way permutations (Lemma 12.10) is known as the "Goldreich–Levin theorem" [202]. (Hardcore bits are unrelated to the hardcore sets of Exercise 10.10.)

Constructing pseudorandom functions from pseudorandom generators (Theorem 12.12) is due to [201]. For a survey on pseudorandom functions and their applications, see [76]. The theorem that pseudorandom functions imply pseudorandom permutations (§ 12.4.3) is due to [350], and the construction is known as a "Feistel cipher/network." An oracle circuit C with oracle function f is often denoted C^f instead of $C(f)$.

The survey [260] identified five possible "worlds":

- *Algorithmica*: NP is worst-case easy ($\mathsf{P} = \mathsf{NP}$ or perhaps $\mathsf{NP} \subseteq \mathsf{BPP}$).
- *Heuristica*: NP is worst-case hard but average-case easy.
- *Pessiland*: NP is average-case hard but one-way functions don't exist. (This is the most pessimistic possibility because we get neither the advantage of solving NP-complete problems nor the advantage of cryptography.)
- *Minicrypt*: One-way functions exist (so private-key cryptography is possible) but public-key cryptography is impossible.
- *Cryptomania*: Public-key cryptography is possible.

It's unknown which "world" is reality, but most researchers believe we live in Cryptomania.

MCSP $\notin \mathsf{P/poly}$ if pseudorandom functions exist (Theorem 12.16) is due to [281]. The theorem that if MCSP is NP-complete then $\mathsf{EXP} \neq \mathsf{ZPP}$ is due to [382]. The theorem that the partial function version of MCSP is NP-hard under randomized reductions is due to [244].

Exercise 12.10 is due to [385].

Chapter 13

Learning

Computational learning theory addresses foundational questions about machine learning. In this setting, an algorithm's goal is to learn an unknown function, given partial information about that function. What exactly does "learning" mean? How can we prove that an algorithm learns successfully? Which kinds of functions can be learned efficiently?

13.1 Probably Approximately Correct Learners

13.1.1 Basic Framework

We consider classification in supervised machine learning.

- *Classification* means the unknown function has codomain $\{0,1\}$, or sometimes another finite set. (With *regression*, the codomain is $\mathbb{R}$.) We call such a function a *concept* $c\colon X \to \{0,1\}$. Often, the domain X is a cartesian product whose coordinates are called *features*.
- *Supervised* means an algorithm is given *training data* consisting of *labeled examples*, which are input-output pairs $(x, c(x))$ of the target concept: x is an example, and $c(x)$ is its label. If $c(x) = 1$ then x is a *positive* example. If $c(x) = 0$ then x is a *negative* example. We use superscripts to index training examples, so the training data is $(x^1, c(x^1)), \ldots, (x^m, c(x^m))$.
- *Learning* means an algorithm produces a *hypothesis* $h\colon X \to \{0,1\}$, which is its "best guess" for c. We want h to have *predictive power*, meaning that $h(y) = c(y)$ for a future unlabeled example y that wasn't part of the training data. Thus h is useful as a proxy for c. (In machine learning lingo, h may be called a "model.")

For example, suppose we want to determine whether a patient has a particular disease, based on the outcomes of three relevant lab tests. Assuming for simplicity that the "right diagnosis" depends only on these three features, there's an underlying concept $c\colon \text{Test}_1 \times \text{Test}_2 \times \text{Test}_3 \to \{0,1\}$. The training data consists of labeled examples $(x, c(x))$ where x is a previous patient's features, and $c(x)$ indicates whether that patient actually had the disease (positive example) or not (negative example). A learning algorithm formulates a hypothesis h, which makes a prediction $h(y)$ about whether a new patient with features y has the disease.

Other applications of classification in supervised machine learning include spam detection in email, fraud detection in financial transactions, sentiment analysis in text, and face recognition in images.

For simplicity, this chapter assumes each feature is boolean: $X = \{0,1\}^n$. Choosing appropriate features for different applications is a separate issue, which we won't address.

If $(y, c(y))$ wasn't in the training data, then a learner seemingly has no information about $c(y)$ and thus can't predict it. To reconcile this with machine learning's success in practice, we need assumptions that relate $(y, c(y))$ with the training data $(x^1, c(x^1)), \ldots, (x^m, c(x^m))$:

- To relate y with $x^1,\ldots,x^m$, we assume $x^1,\ldots,x^m$ and y are all independently sampled from the same distribution D (which represents how examples are distributed in some practical scenario). This means y probably won't "come out of left field." In *distribution-free* learning (a misnomer since there is, in fact, a distribution), D could be any distribution, and the learner doesn't know what D is. (Learning under specific, known distributions—such as the uniform one—is also interesting, but we won't consider it.)
- To relate $c(y)$ with $c(x^1),\ldots,c(x^m)$, we assume that instead of being completely arbitrary, c comes from some *concept class* C (which represents what concepts might arise in some practical scenario). This means c isn't unexpectedly weird. The learner knows what C is.

This potent combination of assumptions makes learning possible. For example, consider optical character recognition (OCR). Say examples in $\{0,1\}^n$ are $\sqrt{n}\times\sqrt{n}$ arrays of black and white pixels, and the target concept $c\colon \{0,1\}^n \to \{0,1\}$ is such that $c(x)=1$ iff x depicts the letter "A". The training data contains various positive examples ("A"s) and negative examples (non-"A"s). Assume the concept is unambiguous and the training data has no errors.

- D would be the distribution of image fragments the OCR software encounters. There's no need to specify D, since a learner should work for any D. The point is that the training data is representative of the kind of examples the hypothesis will need to handle, so the learner won't waste effort anticipating examples that are unlikely to arise.
- C should contain every concept that might classify images into "A" versus non-"A". This seems somewhat circular since the whole point of learning is that we don't already know such a concept. But it's intuitively clear that the "A" versus non-"A" concept is not unusually complicated, so it should be efficiently computable, say by a size-n^4 circuit. Letting C correspond to size-n^4 circuits ought to cover it. In general, we may presume the concept obeys more specific constraints, which could make learning easier. In practice, people often don't specify a concept class or formally prove that a learning algorithm is correct: If experiments demonstrate the hypothesis working, that's good enough. Computational learning theory aims to explain why machine learning works in practice.

Since $x^1,\ldots,x^m$ are random and y is random, we have two parameters $0<\delta,\varepsilon\le 1/2$ for the two kinds of error probability.

Definition. A *concept class* is a set C of functions $c\colon \{0,1\}^n \to \{0,1\}$. A (δ,ε)-*PAC (probably approximately correct) learner* for C is a function $L\colon \big(\{0,1\}^n \times \{0,1\}\big)^m \to C$ such that for every concept $c \in C$ and every distribution D over $\{0,1\}^n$:

$$\mathbf{Pr}_{(x^1,\ldots,x^m)\sim D^m}\left[\begin{array}{l}\mathbf{Pr}_{y\sim D}\big[h(y)=c(y)\big] \ge 1-\varepsilon \\ \text{where } h = L\big((x^1,c(x^1)),\ldots,(x^m,c(x^m))\big)\end{array}\right] \ge 1-\delta$$

- $1-\delta$ is the *confidence*, corresponding to "probably" in "PAC."
- $1-\varepsilon$ is the *accuracy*, corresponding to "approximately" in "PAC." ◀

PAC is pronounced "pack."

13.1.2 Learning Thresholds

Viewing $\{0,1\}^n$ as binary numbers $\{0,1,\ldots,2^n-1\}$, a *threshold function* evaluates to 1 on numbers that are $\ge$ some threshold. Let $C=\big\{c_a : a\in\{0,1\}^n\big\}$ be the concept class of threshold functions, where $c_a\colon \{0,1\}^n \to \{0,1\}$ is defined by $c_a(x)=1$ iff $x \ge a$.

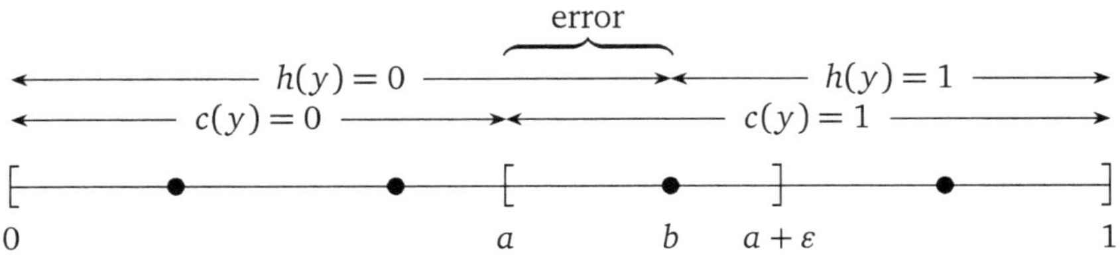

Figure 13.1: Learning thresholds, imagining the interval is $[0,1]$ instead of $\{0,1,\ldots,2^n-1\}$

Example. Suppose $n=3$ and the target concept is $c=c_a$ for some unknown $a \in \{0,1,\ldots,7\}$. Training data $(6,1)$, $(2,0)$, $(5,1)$, $(0,0)$ would tell us a is ≤ 6, >2, ≤ 5, >0. Thus c is either c_3, c_4, or c_5, but we don't know which. Our learning algorithm could pick any of those for the hypothesis h, but for simplicity, it will pick the one with the largest threshold, c_5 (corresponding to the smallest positive training example).

By the way, a learner need not behave in any particular way if the training data doesn't come from a concept in C. The training data is promised to be valid. For threshold functions, $(3,1)$, $(4,0)$ would be invalid, for example. ♦

PAC learner for threshold functions (13.1)

$L\big((x^1,c(x^1)),\ldots,(x^m,c(x^m))\big)$:
  if $c(x^i)=1$ for some i: let b be the minimum x^i such that $c(x^i)=1$
  else: let $b=2^n-1$
  output the hypothesis $h=c_b$

Theorem 13.1. *If $m \geq \frac{1}{\varepsilon}\ln\frac{1}{\delta}$ then L is a (δ,ε)-PAC learner for C.*

Proof idea. Imagine the interval $\{0,1,\ldots,2^n-1\}$ is actually the continuous interval $[0,1] = \{x : 0 \leq x \leq 1\}$ and D is the uniform continuous distribution over $[0,1]$. The target concept $c=c_a$ divides $[0,1]$ into $\geq a$ and $<a$. The hypothesis $h=c_b$ divides $[0,1]$ into $\geq b$ and $<b$. Thus h misclassifies y iff $a \leq y < b$. See Figure 13.1, in which the dots represent training examples. With probability $\geq 1-\delta$ over the training examples, at least one training example falls in the interval $[a,a+\varepsilon]$, and thus $b \in [a,a+\varepsilon]$, in which case h misclassifies a random y with probability $\leq \varepsilon$. ■

Proof. Consider any target concept $c=c_a$ and any distribution D over $\{0,1\}^n$. Note that $b \geq a$ since $c(b)=1$. Here's some notation: For any $a' \geq a$, let $[a,a'] = \{a,a+1,\ldots,a'\}$, and for any $a'<a$, let $[a,a']=\emptyset$. If $D([a,2^n-1]) \leq \varepsilon$ then $\mathbf{Pr}_{y\sim D}\big[h(y)\neq c(y)\big] = D([a,b-1]) \leq D([a,2^n-1]) \leq \varepsilon$ with probability 1 over $(x^1,\ldots,x^m)\sim D^m$. Otherwise, consider the smallest $a' \geq a$ such that $D([a,a'])>\varepsilon$. If $b \in [a,a']$ then $\mathbf{Pr}_{y\sim D}\big[h(y)\neq c(y)\big] = D([a,b-1]) \leq D([a,a'-1]) \leq \varepsilon$. Thus:

$$
\begin{aligned}
& \mathbf{Pr}_{(x^1,\ldots,x^m)\sim D^m}\Big[\mathbf{Pr}_{y\sim D}\big[h(y)=c(y)\big] < 1-\varepsilon\Big] \\
\leq\; & \mathbf{Pr}_{(x^1,\ldots,x^m)\sim D^m}\big[b \notin [a,a']\big] \\
\leq\; & \mathbf{Pr}_{(x^1,\ldots,x^m)\sim D^m}\big[\forall i : x^i \notin [a,a']\big] \\
=\; & \textstyle\prod_{i=1}^m \mathbf{Pr}_{x^i\sim D}\big[x^i \notin [a,a']\big] && (x^1,\ldots,x^m \text{ are independent}) \\
=\; & \textstyle\prod_{i=1}^m (1-D([a,a']))
\end{aligned}
$$

$$\begin{aligned} &\leq (1-\varepsilon)^m \\ &\leq e^{-\varepsilon m} && \text{(Fact 7.6)} \\ &\leq \delta \end{aligned}$$

■

13.1.3 Learning Points

A *point function* evaluates to 1 on exactly one input (one "point"). Let $C = \{c_a : a \in \{0,1\}^n\}$ be the concept class of point functions, where $c_a \colon \{0,1\}^n \to \{0,1\}$ is defined by $c_a(x) = 1$ iff $x = a$.

PAC learner for point functions (13.2)

$L((x^1, c(x^1)), \ldots, (x^m, c(x^m)))$:
  if $c(x^i) = 1$ for some i: let $b = x^i$
  else: pick any $b \notin \{x^1, \ldots, x^m\}$
  output the hypothesis $h = c_b$

Theorem 13.2. *If* $m \geq \frac{2}{\varepsilon} \ln \frac{2}{\delta\varepsilon}$ *then* L *is a* (δ, ε)*-PAC learner for* C.

Proof idea. Assume the target concept c evaluates to 1 on a unique point a. The learner's goal is to find a point b that's either a or "almost as good as a."

- Suppose $D(a)$ is not tiny. Then probably a will show up in the training data and the learner will see $c(x^i) = 1$, which is a dead giveaway that $x^i = a$.
- Suppose $D(a)$ is tiny. Then it doesn't matter if the hypothesis errs on a. The hypothesis would also err on b, so we want $D(b)$ to be tiny as well. If m is large enough, the training examples will probably include *all* y for which $D(y)$ is not tiny. Thus we can pick any b that's different from all training examples. ■

Proof. Consider any target concept $c = c_a$ and any distribution D over $\{0,1\}^n$.

- If $b = a$ then $\mathbf{Pr}_{y\sim D}[h(y) = c(y)] = 1$ since the hypothesis $h = c_b$ is the target concept $c = c_a$.
- If $b \neq a$ then $\mathbf{Pr}_{y\sim D}[h(y) = c(y)] = 1 - D(a) - D(b)$ since $h(a) = 0$ and $c(a) = 1$, and $h(b) = 1$ and $c(b) = 0$, and $h(y) = c(y) = 0$ for all $y \notin \{a, b\}$.

Say $y \in \{0,1\}^n$ is *heavy* iff $D(y) > \varepsilon/2$. We claim that if every heavy y is in $\{x^1, \ldots, x^m\}$, then $\mathbf{Pr}_{y\sim D}[h(y) = c(y)] \geq 1 - \varepsilon$:

- If $a \in \{x^1, \ldots, x^m\}$ then $b = a$ and $\mathbf{Pr}_{y\sim D}[h(y) = c(y)] = 1$.
- If $a \notin \{x^1, \ldots, x^m\}$ then $b \notin \{x^1, \ldots, x^m\}$, so either $b \neq a$ and $\mathbf{Pr}_{y\sim D}[h(y) = c(y)] \geq 1 - \varepsilon/2 - \varepsilon/2$ since neither a nor b is heavy, or $b = a$ and $\mathbf{Pr}_{y\sim D}[h(y) = c(y)] = 1$ by sheer luck.

Thus:

$$\begin{aligned} &\mathbf{Pr}_{(x^1,\ldots,x^m)\sim D^m}\Big[\mathbf{Pr}_{y\sim D}[h(y) = c(y)] < 1 - \varepsilon\Big] \\ \leq\ &\mathbf{Pr}_{(x^1,\ldots,x^m)\sim D^m}\big[\text{some heavy } y \text{ is not in } \{x^1, \ldots, x^m\}\big] && \text{(above claim)} \\ \leq\ &\textstyle\sum_{\text{heavy } y} \mathbf{Pr}_{(x^1,\ldots,x^m)\sim D^m}\big[\forall i : x^i \neq y\big] && \text{(union bound)} \end{aligned}$$

$$
\begin{aligned}
&= \textstyle\sum_{\text{heavy } y} \prod_{i=1}^{m} \mathbf{Pr}_{x^i \sim D}\big[x^i \neq y\big] && (x^1,\ldots,x^m \text{ are independent})\\
&= \textstyle\sum_{\text{heavy } y} \prod_{i=1}^{m} (1-D(y))\\
&\leq \textstyle\sum_{\text{heavy } y} (1-\varepsilon/2)^m\\
&\leq \textstyle\sum_{\text{heavy } y} \mathrm{e}^{-m\varepsilon/2} && \text{(Fact 7.6)}\\
&\leq (2/\varepsilon)\mathrm{e}^{-m\varepsilon/2} && (\leq 2/\varepsilon \text{ many } y \text{ are heavy})\\
&\leq \delta
\end{aligned}
$$

■

13.1.4 Learning Dictatorships

A *dictatorship* is a function expressed by a positive literal. Let $C = \{c_a : a \in [n]\}$ be the concept class of dictatorships, where $c_a\colon \{0,1\}^n \to \{0,1\}$ is defined by $c_a(x) = x_a$. If x_j is person j's "vote," then the outcome is simply the vote of person a (the dictator). (A negative literal expresses an *anti-dictatorship*.)

PAC learner for dictatorships (13.3)

$L\big((x^1, c(x^1)), \ldots, (x^m, c(x^m))\big)$:
  for $j \leftarrow 1, \ldots, n$:
    if $x^i_j = c(x^i)$ for every $i \in [m]$:
      let $b = j$ and output the hypothesis $h = c_b$

Example. Let's run $L\big((00010,0),\ (10101,1),\ (10010,0)\big)$.

- $c(x)$ can't be x_1, because $x^3_1 = 1$ but $c(x^3) = 0$.
- $c(x)$ can't be x_2, because $x^2_2 = 0$ but $c(x^2) = 1$.
- $c(x)$ might be x_3, because $x^1_3 = 0 = c(x^1)$ and $x^2_3 = 1 = c(x^2)$ and $x^3_3 = 0 = c(x^3)$.

Also, $c(x)$ can't be x_4 but might be x_5. It wouldn't matter if L outputs c_5 instead of c_3. ◆

Theorem 13.3. *If $m \geq \frac{1}{\varepsilon} \ln \frac{n}{\delta}$ then L is a (δ, ε)-PAC learner for C.*

Proof idea. Assume the target concept is some literal x_a. The learner's goal is to find a literal x_b such that D is mostly concentrated on examples where x_b and x_a have the same value. So the learner finds an x_b such that for all training examples, x_b and x_a have the same value. The training examples are probably representative of D. ■

Proof. Consider any target concept $c = c_a$ and any distribution D over $\{0,1\}^n$. Certainly, L outputs a hypothesis, because if L hasn't halted before the $j = a$ iteration, then it would output $h = c_a$. Say $j \in [n]$ is *bad* iff $\mathbf{Pr}_{y \sim D}\big[y_j = y_a\big] < 1 - \varepsilon$. Then:

$$
\begin{aligned}
&\mathbf{Pr}_{(x^1,\ldots,x^m)\sim D^m}\Big[\mathbf{Pr}_{y\sim D}\big[h(y) = c(y)\big] < 1-\varepsilon\Big]\\
&= \mathbf{Pr}_{(x^1,\ldots,x^m)\sim D^m}\big[b \text{ is bad}\big]\\
&\leq \mathbf{Pr}_{(x^1,\ldots,x^m)\sim D^m}\big[\exists \text{ bad } j \text{ such that } \forall i:\ x^i_j = c(x^i)\big]\\
&\leq \textstyle\sum_{\text{bad } j} \mathbf{Pr}_{(x^1,\ldots,x^m)\sim D^m}\big[\forall i:\ x^i_j = c(x^i)\big] && \text{(union bound)}\\
&= \textstyle\sum_{\text{bad } j} \prod_{i=1}^{m} \mathbf{Pr}_{x^i\sim D}\big[x^i_j = x^i_a\big] && (x^1,\ldots,x^m \text{ are independent})
\end{aligned}
$$

$$\leq \textstyle\sum_{\text{bad } j}(1-\varepsilon)^m$$
$$\leq ne^{-\varepsilon m} \qquad \text{(Fact 7.6)}$$
$$\leq \delta$$
■

13.1.5 General Framework

Sometimes, learning is easier if the learner can produce a hypothesis h that's not necessarily in the concept class C, but in a larger *hypothesis class* $H \supseteq C$. For example, if the target concept is a size-n^2 circuit c, and the learner finds a size-n^3 circuit h such that $\mathbf{Pr}_{y\sim D}[h(y) = c(y)] \geq 1-\varepsilon$, then h is still useful for predictions. Ideally, we'd like a size-n^2 circuit because it's faster to evaluate. But refusing to use a size-n^3 circuit would "let perfect be the enemy of good." This extra flexibility may drastically speed up learning. We'll see a situation like this in §13.3.

Proper learning means $H = C$. Our learners for threshold functions, point functions, and dictatorships were proper. The general definition allows *improper* learning, in which $h \in H \supseteq C$ (but still $c \in C$):

Definition. A (δ,ε)-*PAC learner* for (C,H) is a function $L\colon (\{0,1\}^n \times \{0,1\})^m \to H$ such that for every concept $c \in C$ and every distribution D over $\{0,1\}^n$:

$$\mathbf{Pr}_{(x^1,\ldots,x^m)\sim D^m}\left[\begin{array}{l}\mathbf{Pr}_{y\sim D}[h(y) = c(y)] \geq 1-\varepsilon \\ \text{where } h = L((x^1,c(x^1)),\ldots,(x^m,c(x^m)))\end{array}\right] \geq 1-\delta$$
◄

We want learners to be efficient uniform programs, so we consider infinite *families* of concept classes and hypothesis classes, parameterized by n:

- A concept class family is $C_1, C_2, C_3, \ldots$ where C_n is a set of functions $c\colon \{0,1\}^n \to \{0,1\}$.
- A hypothesis class family is $H_1, H_2, H_3, \ldots$ where $H_n \supseteq C_n$ is a set of functions $h\colon \{0,1\}^n \to \{0,1\}$.

Furthermore, hypotheses must have an encoding (or "representation"), which is normally clear from context. For example, if H_n is all size-n^3 circuits, then a learner would output h's natural encoding (a graph of gates and wires) as opposed to h's truth table. A single truth table might have multiple encodings. For example, different size-n^3 circuits might compute the same function as each other.

A learner is a uniform program L such that:

- L takes as input n, δ, ε.
- L can call an oracle (with no arguments) that returns a fresh labeled example $(x, c(x))$ where $x \sim D$, for some concept $c \in C_n$ and distribution D over $\{0,1\}^n$. The maximum number of oracle calls corresponds to m.
- L outputs an encoding of a hypothesis $h \in H_n$.
- L implements a (δ,ε)-PAC learner for (C_n, H_n).
- L's time efficiency and word size depend on n, δ, ε. "Poly" time means polynomial in n, $\frac{1}{\varepsilon}$, and $\frac{1}{\delta}$, though we show in §13.5.1 that the dependence on δ can be $\log \frac{1}{\delta}$ without loss of generality.

We often eschew the uniform framework's formalities and just use the concrete definition where n, δ, ε are fixed and arbitrary. It will always be clear that a concrete learner $L\colon (\{0,1\}^n \times \{0,1\})^m \to H$ can be cast in the uniform framework.

13.2 Consistent Learners

13.2.1 Consistent Learners Are PAC Learners

Definition. Consider any concept class C and hypothesis class $H \supseteq C$. An *m-consistent learner* for (C,H) is a function $L\colon \big(\{0,1\}^n \times \{0,1\}\big)^m \to H$ such that for every concept $c \in C$ and every tuple $(x^1,\ldots,x^m)$, $L\big((x^1,c(x^1)),\ldots,(x^m,c(x^m))\big)$ outputs a hypothesis $h \in H$ *consistent* with the training data, meaning that $h(x^i) = c(x^i)$ for every $i \in [m]$. ◄

Our learners for threshold functions, point functions, and dictatorships (§ 13.1) were consistent, and we proved they were also PAC. This is no coincidence: Given enough training data, every consistent learner is a PAC learner. This is perhaps surprising since PAC learning and consistent learning have different goals:

- PAC learning: The hypothesis should succeed on a future example. Success on the training examples doesn't matter.
- Consistent learning: The hypothesis should succeed on the training examples. Success on a future example doesn't matter.

Success on training examples is related to success on future examples, since all examples are sampled from the same distribution. The past is the best predictor of the future. Here's a technique to design a PAC learner without even thinking about probabilities:

(i) Design an m-consistent learner L for arbitrary m.
(ii) Apply a general theorem that says how big m should be to ensure L is a (δ,ε)-PAC learner.

In § 13.2.2 and § 13.2.3 we'll see more examples of *(i)*. Now, we prove a simple theorem for *(ii)*. (We refine this theorem in § 13.4.) Our bound on m depends on the number of possible hypotheses $|H|$. This is theoretical confirmation of the practical adage that "simple" hypotheses are less likely to overfit the training data:

- A complicated hypothesis may be tantamount to a lookup table of the training data, with little predictive power.
- A simple hypothesis must capture an actual pattern in the training data, and this pattern should apply to other examples too.

"Simple" means $|H|$ is small, so each hypothesis has a short description with $\approx \log|H|$ bits. If we allow more complicated hypotheses, then we need more training data to prevent overfitting.

Theorem 13.4. *If $m \geq \frac{1}{\varepsilon}\ln\frac{|H|}{\delta}$ then every m-consistent learner for (C,H) is a (δ,ε)-PAC learner for (C,H).*

Proof idea. A labeled example $(x^i,c(x^i))$ rules out every hypothesis h with $h(x^i) \neq c(x^i)$. A bad hypothesis will probably be ruled out by at least one labeled example. Enough training data will probably eliminate *all* bad hypotheses from contention. Then whichever consistent hypothesis the learner outputs, it will be good. This is essentially the proof of Theorem 13.3 (for dictatorships) but more abstract since we don't have a particular H in mind. ■

Proof. Assume $m \geq \frac{1}{\varepsilon}\ln\frac{|H|}{\delta}$ and L is an m-consistent learner for (C,H). Consider any concept $c \in C$ and distribution D over $\{0,1\}^n$. Say a hypothesis $h \in H$ is *bad* iff $\mathbf{Pr}_{y\sim D}\big[h(y) = c(y)\big] <$

$1-\varepsilon$. Then:

$$
\begin{aligned}
&\mathbf{Pr}_{(x^1,\dots,x^m)\sim D^m}\big[L\big((x^1,c(x^1)),\dots,(x^m,c(x^m))\big) \text{ is bad}\big] \\
\le\ &\mathbf{Pr}_{(x^1,\dots,x^m)\sim D^m}\big[\exists \text{ bad } h \text{ consistent with } (x^1,c(x^1)),\dots,(x^m,c(x^m))\big] \\
\le\ &\textstyle\sum_{\text{bad } h} \mathbf{Pr}_{(x^1,\dots,x^m)\sim D^m}\big[\forall i:\ h(x^i)=c(x^i)\big] && \text{(union bound)} \\
=\ &\textstyle\sum_{\text{bad } h} \prod_{i=1}^m \mathbf{Pr}_{x^i\sim D}\big[h(x^i)=c(x^i)\big] && (x^1,\dots,x^m \text{ are independent}) \\
\le\ &\textstyle\sum_{\text{bad } h}(1-\varepsilon)^m \\
\le\ &|H|\mathrm{e}^{-\varepsilon m} && \text{(Fact 7.6)} \\
\le\ &\delta
\end{aligned}
$$

Thus L is a (δ,ε)-PAC learner for (C,H). ■

13.2.2 Learning Terms

A *term* is a conjunction (and) of literals corresponding to distinct variables, for example $\overline{x_2}\wedge x_4\wedge\overline{x_5}$. For practical motivation, perhaps a concept diagnoses a disease based on features representing outcomes of medical tests: $\overline{x_2}\wedge x_4\wedge\overline{x_5}$ means for a positive diagnosis, tests 2 and 5 must be negative, and test 4 must be positive, and tests 1 and 3 are irrelevant.

A term's width is its number of literals. Width-n terms express point functions. Width-1 terms (literals) express dictatorships and anti-dictatorships. A width-0 term always evaluates to 1.

Let C be the concept class of all terms on n variables. We have $|C|=3^n$ because each variable has 3 possibilities: positive literal, negative literal, or absent. For any m, we now design a proper m-consistent learner for C. By Theorem 13.4, this is a proper (δ,ε)-PAC learner for C if $m\ge\frac{1}{\varepsilon}\ln\frac{3^n}{\delta}=\frac{1}{\varepsilon}\big(n\ln 3+\ln\frac{1}{\delta}\big)$.

The idea is to include all the literals we can while being consistent with the positive examples. This ensures that we include all the target concept's literals and are thus consistent with the negative examples as well.

Consistent learner for terms (13.4)

$L\big((x^1,c(x^1)),\dots,(x^m,c(x^m))\big)$:
  if $c(x^i)=1$ for at least one i:
    form the binary matrix whose rows are the strings x^i such that $c(x^i)=1$
    for each $j\in[n]$:
      if column j is all-1: include the literal x_j in the term h
      if column j is all-0: include the literal $\overline{x_j}$ in the term h
    output h
  else:
    find a $b\in\{0,1\}^n\setminus\{x^1,\dots,x^m\}$
    output the width-n term h such that $h(x)=1$ iff $x=b$

Example. Suppose $n=5$ and $c=x_1\wedge\overline{x_3}$. To run

$$L\big((10011,1),\ (11011,1),\ (10101,0),\ (11010,1)\big)$$

we ignore $x^3=10101$ since $c(x^3)=0$, and we form this matrix:

$$\begin{bmatrix}x^1\\x^2\\x^4\end{bmatrix}=\begin{bmatrix}1&0&0&1&1\\1&1&0&1&1\\1&1&0&1&0\end{bmatrix}$$

(1) Include x_1 since column 1 is all-1.
(2) Exclude x_2 and $\overline{x_2}$ since column 2 has a 0 and a 1.
(3) Include $\overline{x_3}$ since column 3 is all-0.
(4) Include x_4 since column 4 is all-1.
(5) Exclude x_5 and $\overline{x_5}$ since column 5 has a 0 and a 1.

The hypothesis $h = x_1 \wedge \overline{x_3} \wedge x_4$ and the concept $c = x_1 \wedge \overline{x_3}$ are different, but they agree on the training examples.

If we instead run $L\big((01010,0), (11100,0), (00101,0)\big)$, we could pick $b = 00110$ (or many other possibilities) and output the hypothesis $h = \overline{x_1} \wedge \overline{x_2} \wedge x_3 \wedge x_4 \wedge \overline{x_5}$. ♦

Why is the hypothesis h guaranteed to be consistent with the training data? First, suppose $c(x^i) = 1$ for at least one i. Then for all i:

- If $c(x^i) = 1$ then $h(x^i) = 1$ because for every $j \in [n]$:
  - If x_j is in h then column j is all-1, so $x^i_j = 1$.
  - If $\overline{x_j}$ is in h then column j is all-0, so $x^i_j = 0$.
- If $c(x^i) = 0$ then since the learner ignores x^i and doesn't "try" to ensure $h(x^i) = 0$, it's perhaps surprising that indeed $h(x^i) = 0$. But this holds because h includes all of c's literals (and possibly more):
  - If x_j is in c then column j is all-1, so x_j is in h.
  - If $\overline{x_j}$ is in c then column j is all-0, so $\overline{x_j}$ is in h.

  If $c(x^i) = 0$ then some literal in c—and hence in h—evaluates to 0 on x^i, so $h(x^i) = 0$.

Now, suppose $c(x^i) = 0$ for all i. A hypothesis that always evaluates to 0 would be consistent with the training data, but no term always evaluates to 0. Instead, the learner's hypothesis h is a term consistent with the training data, assuming $b \in \{0,1\}^n \setminus \{x^1, \dots, x^m\}$ exists. Such a b indeed exists because if it didn't, then the term c would always evaluate to 0. For every i, we have $x^i \neq b$ and thus $h(x^i) = 0 = c(x^i)$.

13.2.3 Learning Decision Lists

A *decision list* is a decision tree (§5.5.1) in which each internal node (reading an input variable) has at least one child that's a leaf (output node). We draw decision lists horizontally for convenience. Each internal node is specified by (j, a, b) where x_j is the variable being read, $a \in \{0,1\}$ is the label of the edge to a leaf child, and $b \in \{0,1\}$ is that leaf's label: "If $x_j = a$ then output b." The last internal node has two leaf children: One of them is determined by (j, a, b) as usual. The other is considered the decision list's *terminal* node and automatically outputs the opposite of its sibling (otherwise their parent would be pointless). As a corner case, a decision list may have just one node, which is simultaneously the root and the terminal leaf.

Example. Figure 13.2 shows a decision list on $n = 6$ variables. It's like a highway with exits. Each input drives down the highway and gets off at some exit. Letting $c\colon \{0,1\}^6 \to \{0,1\}$ be this decision list's function:

- $c(001011) = 1$ because $x_2 = 0$ and $x_4 = 0$, so 001011 gets off the highway at the x_4 exit, leading to a leaf labeled 1.
- $c(101101) = 0$ because $x_2 = 0$ and $x_4 = 1$ and $x_1 = 1$ and $x_6 = 1$, so 101101 takes the x_6 exit.

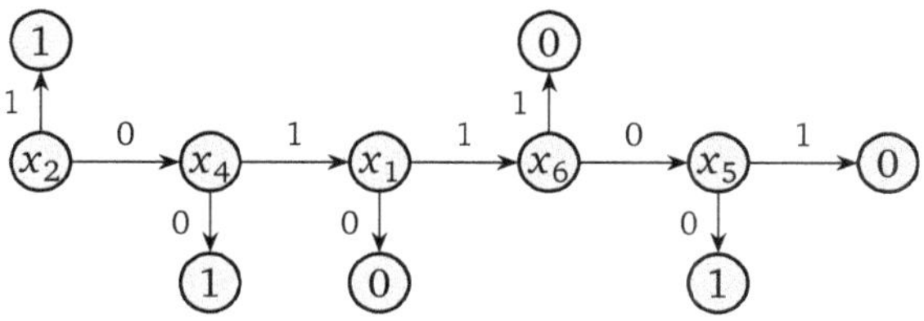

Figure 13.2: Example decision list

- $c(100110) = 0$ because 100110 stays on the highway until the terminal "end of the road" leaf, which is labeled 0.

This decision list's "(j, a, b) representation" is $(2, 1, 1)$, $(4, 0, 1)$, $(1, 0, 0)$, $(6, 1, 0)$, $(5, 0, 1)$. ♦

Decision lists are more general than the other concept classes we've studied so far. Terms are equivalent to decision lists where only the terminal leaf outputs 1. Decision lists can compute threshold functions by reading the bits from most to least significant: The first index j such that $x_j \neq a_j$ determines whether or not $x \geq a$.

Let C be the concept class of all decision lists on n variables. We have $|C| \leq 2 + \sum_{k=1}^{n}(4n)^k \leq 2(4n)^n$ because two decision lists have only one node, and at most $(4n)^k$ decision lists have $k \geq 1$ internal nodes, since each internal node has $n \cdot 2 \cdot 2$ possibilities of (j, a, b). (This overcounts because it allows rereading variables and because different decision lists may compute the same function.) For any m, we now design a proper m-consistent learner for C. By Theorem 13.4, this is a proper (δ, ε)-PAC learner for C if $m \geq \frac{1}{\varepsilon} \ln \frac{2(4n)^n}{\delta} = \frac{1}{\varepsilon}\left(n \ln(4n) + \ln \frac{2}{\delta}\right)$. To motivate the algorithm, we demonstrate it with an example first.

Example. Suppose $n = 3$ and the training data is shown at the top of Figure 13.3. Let's find a decision list h consistent with this. The root can't be terminal, since the training examples are not all negative and not all positive. We try all possible (j, a, b) for the root until we find one consistent with the relevant training data:

> $(1, 0, 0)$ doesn't work because $c(001) = 1$. $(1, 0, 1)$ doesn't work because $c(010) = 0$.
> $(1, 1, 0)$ doesn't work because $c(101) = 1$. $(1, 1, 1)$ doesn't work because $c(100) = 0$.
> $(2, 0, 0)$ doesn't work because $c(001) = 1$. $(2, 0, 1)$ doesn't work because $c(100) = 0$.
> $(2, 1, 0)$ works because $c(010) = 0$ and $c(011) = 0$ are the only training examples with $x_2 = 1$.

See the second part of Figure 13.3, which shows the remaining training examples in black. The next node can't be terminal, since the remaining training examples are not all negative and not all positive. So we look for another (j, a, b):

> $(1, 0, 0)$ still doesn't work because $c(001) = 1$.
> $(1, 0, 1)$ didn't work before, but both problematic training examples $c(010) = 0$ and $c(011) = 0$ have been taken care of. It works now because $c(001) = 1$ is the only remaining training example with $x_1 = 0$.

See the third part of Figure 13.3. The next node can't be terminal, since the remaining training examples are not all negative and not all positive.

> $(3, 0, 0)$ works because $c(100) = 0$ is the only remaining training example with $x_3 = 0$.

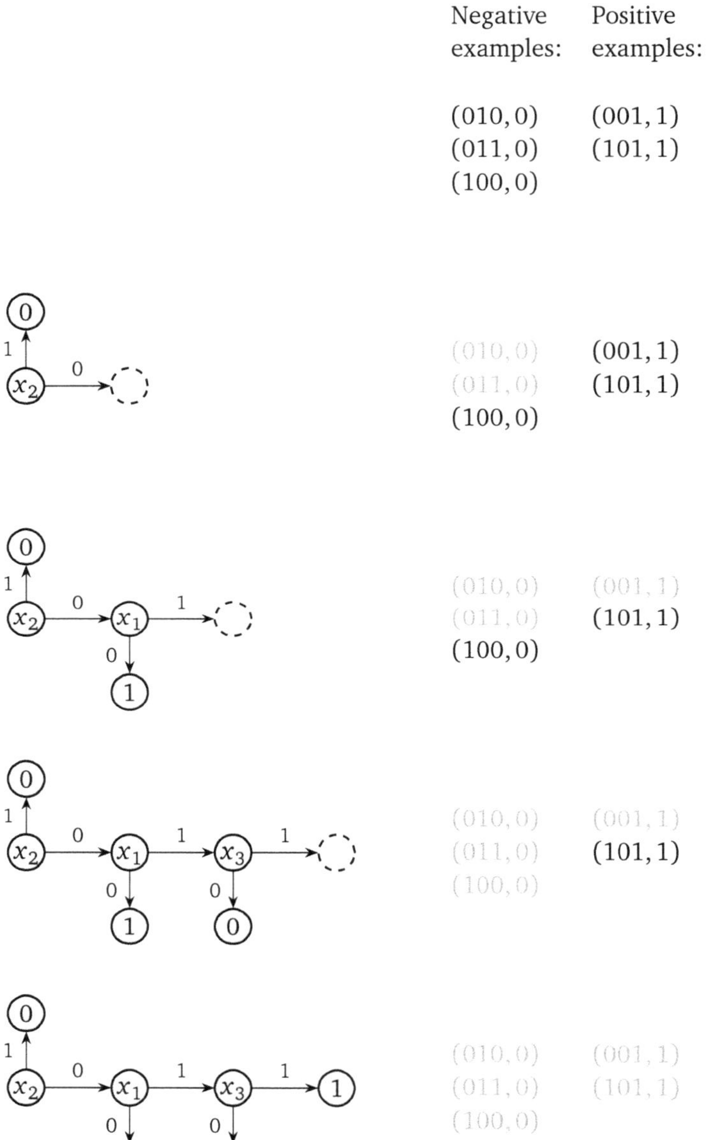

Figure 13.3: Demonstration of learning a decision list

See the fourth part of Figure 13.3. The next node is terminal and labeled 1, since all remaining training examples are positive. The last part of Figure 13.3 shows the finished hypothesis. ♦

This greedy algorithm finds the "(j,a,b) representation" of a decision list h consistent with the training data, assuming such a decision list exists:

Consistent learner for decision lists (13.5)

$L((x^1,c(x^1)),\ldots,(x^m,c(x^m)))$:
initialize $I \leftarrow [m]$
repeat:
if $c(x^i)$ is the same for all $i \in I$:
append to h a terminal node with this common label, let $I \leftarrow \emptyset$, and halt
find a (j,a,b) such that: $c(x^i) = b$ for all $i \in I$ with $x^i_j = a$, and such an i exists
append (j,a,b) to h
remove from I all i such that $x^i_j = a$

It builds h from left to right, committing to nodes as it goes, and remembering the set I of indices of remaining training examples (which are "still on the highway"). Each iteration asks, "If we read x_j next and have the a edge go to a leaf, would all the relevant training examples agree on which value b to output at that leaf?" This learner L maintains the invariant that for every i:

- If $i \in I$ then $h(x^i)$ doesn't output anything yet.
- If $i \notin I$ then $h(x^i)$ already outputs $c(x^i)$.

Nothing appended to h in subsequent iterations can undo what h achieved so far. Thus if L halts, then h is consistent with all the training data. If L finds a suitable (j,a,b) in each iteration (it doesn't get stuck), then it halts since I shrinks in each iteration.

We just need to argue that if the training data comes from a decision list c, then L never gets stuck (even if it doesn't always pick the same (j,a,b) as c has). This holds because c's first (j,a,b) is always a suitable option ($c(x^i) = b$ for all $i \in [m]$ with $x^i_j = a$) until L picks it, after which c's second (j,a,b) is always a suitable option until L picks it, and so on. Every choice L makes is safe—L can't get stuck later due to an unfortunate choice earlier. Another way to say it: If the algorithm got stuck, then there wouldn't exist a decision list for the remaining training data, so there wouldn't exist a decision list for all the training data to begin with.

13.3 Time Complexity

If there are at most an exponential number of hypotheses, then a polynomial amount of training data suffices for PAC learning by a brute force consistent learner (Theorem 13.4). But brute force generally takes exponential time. In §13.2, we designed poly-time learners for terms and decision lists. This section covers techniques for showing that concept classes have poly-time PAC learners, or giving evidence that they don't.

13.3.1 Reductions

In general, reductions are tools for relating the complexities of different problems: If "that" has an efficient algorithm, then so does "this" (and if "this" doesn't have an efficient algorithm, then neither does "that"). Here's a formulation of reductions for PAC learning.

Definition. Suppose $C \subseteq H$ are classes of functions on $\{0,1\}^n$, and $C' \subseteq H'$ are classes of functions on $\{0,1\}^{n'}$. A *learning reduction* from (C,H) to (C',H') consists of three functions:

- $F_{\text{ex}}: \{0,1\}^n \to \{0,1\}^{n'}$.
- $F_{\text{con}}: C \to C'$ such that for all $c \in C$ and $x \in \{0,1\}^n$, we have $c(x) = c'(x')$ where $c' = F_{\text{con}}(c)$ and $x' = F_{\text{ex}}(x)$.
- $F_{\text{hyp}}: H' \to H$ such that for all $h' \in H'$ and $y \in \{0,1\}^n$, we have $h(y) = h'(y')$ where $h = F_{\text{hyp}}(h')$ and $y' = F_{\text{ex}}(y)$. ◀

Lemma 13.5. *If $(F_{\text{ex}}, F_{\text{con}}, F_{\text{hyp}})$ is a learning reduction from (C,H) to (C',H') and $L': \big(\{0,1\}^{n'} \times \{0,1\}\big)^m \to H'$ is a (δ,ε)-PAC learner for (C',H'), then $L: \big(\{0,1\}^n \times \{0,1\}\big)^m \to H$ is a (δ,ε)-PAC learner for (C,H) where:*

$$L\big((x^1,c(x^1)),\dots,(x^m,c(x^m))\big) = F_{\text{hyp}}\big(L'\big((F_{\text{ex}}(x^1),c(x^1)),\dots,(F_{\text{ex}}(x^m),c(x^m))\big)\big)$$

Proof. For any concept $c \in C$ and distribution D over $\{0,1\}^n$, consider the concept $c' = F_{\text{con}}(c) \in C'$ and distribution $D' = F_{\text{ex}}(D)$ over $\{0,1\}^{n'}$. Suppose L is given training data:

$$(x^1,c(x^1)),\dots,(x^m,c(x^m)) \text{ where } (x^1,\dots,x^m) \sim D^m$$

For each $x^i \sim D$, let $x^{i\prime} = F_{\text{ex}}(x^i) \sim D'$ and note that $c(x^i) = c'(x^{i\prime})$. So L feeds L' training data:

$$(x^{1\prime},c'(x^{1\prime})),\dots,(x^{m\prime},c'(x^{m\prime})) \text{ where } (x^{1\prime},\dots,x^{m\prime}) \sim (D')^m$$

Then, L' produces a hypothesis h', and L produces the hypothesis $h = F_{\text{hyp}}(h')$. With probability $\geq 1-\delta$, h' is good, meaning that $\mathbf{Pr}_{y'\sim D'}\big[h'(y') = c'(y')\big] \geq 1-\varepsilon$. For $y \sim D$, let $y' = F_{\text{ex}}(y) \sim D'$ and note that $h(y) = h'(y')$ and $c(y) = c'(y')$. Thus $\mathbf{Pr}_{y\sim D}\big[h(y) = c(y)\big] = \mathbf{Pr}_{y'\sim D'}\big[h'(y') = c'(y')\big]$, so h is good if h' is good. ■

Corollary 13.6. *Suppose $C, H, C', H', F_{\text{ex}}, F_{\text{con}}, F_{\text{hyp}}$ are infinite families. If F_{ex} and F_{hyp} (but not necessarily F_{con}) are poly-time computable and (C',H') has a uniform poly-time PAC learner, then (C,H) has a uniform poly-time PAC learner (in the sense of §13.1.5).* ■

An algorithm for F_{hyp} takes an encoding of h' (not its truth table) and outputs an encoding of h. When $C = H$ and $C' = H'$ (proper learning on both sides), we abbreviate "from (C,H) to (C',H')" as "from C to C'".

For illustration, suppose C is the concept class of literals (dictatorships and anti-dictatorships) on n variables, and C' is the concept class of positive literals (dictatorships) on $n' = 2n$ variables. We design a learning reduction from C to C' and so obtain a poly-time proper PAC learner for C from our poly-time proper PAC learner for C' (§13.1.4). Denote strings in $\{0,1\}^n$ by $x = x_1 \cdots x_n$ and strings in $\{0,1\}^{n'}$ by $xw = x_1 \cdots x_n w_1 \cdots w_n$. Define $x' = F_{\text{ex}}(x) = x\overline{x}$ where $\overline{x}$ is the bitwise negation of x, and define $c' = F_{\text{con}}(c)$ and $h = F_{\text{hyp}}(h')$ by:

$$c' = \begin{cases} x_j & \text{if } c = x_j \\ w_j & \text{if } c = \overline{x_j} \end{cases} \qquad\qquad h = \begin{cases} x_j & \text{if } h' = x_j \\ \overline{x_j} & \text{if } h' = w_j \end{cases}$$

We have $c(x) = c'(x')$ and $h(x) = h'(x')$ since $w_j = \overline{x_j}$ for all x. Figure 13.4 shows an example.

Corollary 13.6 says: If (C',H') is poly-time PAC learnable, then (C,H) is poly-time PAC learnable. The contrapositive is: If (C,H) isn't poly-time PAC learnable, then (C',H') isn't poly-time PAC learnable. In § 13.7.1 we'll see evidence that (size-n^d circuits, size-n^e circuits) isn't

x	c: $\overline{x_1}$
00	1
01	1
10	0
11	0

$\rightsquigarrow$

$x\ w$	c': w_1	h': x_2
0000	0	0
0001	0	0
0010	1	0
0011	1	0
0100	0	1
0101	0	1
0110	1	1
0111	1	1
1000	0	0
1001	0	0
1010	1	0
1011	1	0
1100	0	1
1101	0	1
1110	1	1
1111	1	1

$\rightsquigarrow$

x	h: x_2
00	0
01	1
10	0
11	1

Figure 13.4: Learning reduction from literals to positive literals

poly-time PAC learnable for $d \le e$. Maybe learning monotone circuits (without $\neg$ gates) is easier? Unfortunately no, because we can "learning reduce" from $(C,H) =$ (size-n^d circuits, size-n^e circuits) to $(C',H') =$ (size-$2n^d$ monotone circuits, size-n^e circuits) on $n' = 2n$ variables, like we did for literals (assuming for convenience that a bounded-fan-in circuit's size is its number of $\wedge$ and $\vee$ gates): Denote strings in $\{0,1\}^n$ by $x = x_1 \cdots x_n$ and strings in $\{0,1\}^{n'}$ by $xw = x_1 \cdots x_n w_1 \cdots w_n$. Define $x' = x\overline{x}$. For a size-n^d circuit c, define a size-$2n^d$ monotone circuit c' by pushing all $\neg$ gates to the input variables (which at most doubles the number of $\wedge$ and $\vee$ gates) and replacing $\neg x_j$ with the variable w_j. For a size-n^e circuit h', define a size-n^e circuit h by replacing w_j with $\neg x_j$. We have $c(x) = c'(x')$ and $h(x) = h'(x')$. This is similar to Circuit Evaluation $\le_\ell^m$ Monotone Circuit Evaluation (Theorem 5.16).

As another illustration, suppose C is the concept class of 3-CNFs on n variables, and C' is the concept class of terms on $n' = 2^3\binom{n}{3} = O(n^3)$ variables. We design a learning reduction from C to C' and so obtain a poly-time proper PAC learner for C from our poly-time proper PAC learner for C' (§13.2.2). For each $x \in \{0,1\}^n$, the bits of $x' \in \{0,1\}^{n'}$ are the values of all possible width-3 clauses on x. For example, if $x = 1010$ then the bit of x' corresponding to the clause $x_2 \vee \overline{x_3} \vee \overline{x_4}$ is $0 \vee \overline{1} \vee \overline{0} = 1$. There are n' width-3 clauses since there are $\binom{n}{3}$ sets of 3 distinct variables and 2^3 patterns of negations for those 3 variables. For a 3-CNF c, define a term c' containing the positive literals corresponding to the clauses of c. For a term h', define a 3-CNF h:

- For each positive literal in h', include in h the associated clause.
- For each negative literal in h', consider the unnegated variable's associated clause, and include in h the $2^3 - 1$ clauses that collectively express that clause's negation.

We have $c(x) = c'(x')$ and $h(x) = h'(x')$. The same technique "learning reduces" from k-CNFs to terms in poly time, for any constant k. (In practice, this technique is used for reducing from polynomial regression to linear regression.)

13.3.2 Proper Versus Improper Learning

Improper learning is sometimes much faster than proper learning:

Theorem 13.7. *The concept class of 3-term DNFs has a poly-time PAC learner using the hypothesis class of 3-CNFs, but has no poly-time proper PAC learner unless* $\mathsf{NP} = \mathsf{RP}$.

This also holds for k-term DNFs and k-CNFs for every constant $k \geq 2$. We just prove the $k = 3$ case using the following two lemmas, which we prove afterward.

Lemma 13.8. *Every 3-term DNF on $n \geq 3$ variables is equivalent to some 3-CNF.*

For any concept class family $C = (C_1, C_2, C_3, \ldots)$, define this decision problem:

CONSISTENCY FOR C	(13.6)
Input: n, m, and $\big((x^1,z^1),\ldots,(x^m,z^m)\big) \in \big(\{0,1\}^n \times \{0,1\}\big)^m$	
Output: Does there exist a concept $c \in C_n$ consistent with $(x^1,z^1),\ldots,(x^m,z^m)$?	

Lemma 13.9. CONSISTENCY FOR 3-TERM DNFs *is* NP*-complete.*

Proof of Theorem 13.7. The poly-time proper PAC learner for 3-CNFs from the end of § 13.3.1 is a poly-time PAC learner for (3-term DNFs, 3-CNFs) by Lemma 13.8: A learner is oblivious to the concept's representation, so training data from a 3-term DNF might as well come from an equivalent 3-CNF. Thus the learner probably finds a 3-CNF hypothesis that approximates the 3-term DNF concept.

Now, we argue that if there exists a poly-time proper PAC learner for 3-term DNFs, then CONSISTENCY FOR 3-TERM DNFs $\in \mathsf{RP}$, which implies $\mathsf{NP} = \mathsf{RP}$ by Lemma 13.9. On input $n, m, (x^1,z^1),\ldots,(x^m,z^m)$, we run the learner with $\delta = 1/3$ and $\varepsilon = 1/2m$, but we don't directly feed it $(x^1,z^1),\ldots,(x^m,z^m)$ as the training data. (In fact, this m might not be the number of training examples the learner wants.) Instead, for each training example, we independently sample a uniformly random $i \in [m]$ and give the learner (x^i,z^i). We also clock the learner so it halts in $\mathrm{poly}(nm/\varepsilon) = \mathrm{poly}(nm)$ time even if the training data is not consistent with any 3-term DNF. When the learner produces a 3-term DNF hypothesis h, we check whether h is consistent with $(x^1,z^1),\ldots,(x^m,z^m)$, and we accept iff it is.

If no 3-term DNF is consistent with $(x^1,z^1),\ldots,(x^m,z^m)$, then the algorithm certainly rejects.

If some 3-term DNF c is consistent with $(x^1,z^1),\ldots,(x^m,z^m)$, then the algorithm simulates the learner with concept c and with distribution D defined as x^i for uniformly random $i \in [m]$. Thus with probability $\geq 1 - \delta = 2/3$, the learner produces h such that:

$$\mathbf{Pr}_{y\sim D}\big[h(y) = c(y)\big] \;=\; \mathbf{Pr}_{i\in[m]}\big[h(x^i) = z^i\big] \;\geq\; 1 - \varepsilon \;>\; 1 - 1/m$$

In this case, $h(x^i) = z^i$ for all $i \in [m]$, so h is consistent with $(x^1,z^1),\ldots,(x^m,z^m)$ and the algorithm accepts. ■

Proof idea for Lemma 13.8. For every binary matrix, there exists an all-1 column iff for every way of choosing one entry from each column, at least one chosen entry is 1. For any 3-term k-DNF φ, consider the $k \times 3$ matrix of literals where the entry in row i and column j is the ith literal in the jth term of φ. If we plug in an assignment, this is a binary matrix. Then φ is satisfied (there exists an all-1 column) iff ψ is satisfied, where ψ is a 3-CNF whose clauses correspond to all ways of choosing one literal from each column. In general, φ's terms might not have the same widths, and ψ's "clauses" might have repeated variables, but those are minor issues. ■

Proof of Lemma 13.8. Let $\varphi = T_1 \vee T_2 \vee T_3$ be an n-variable 3-term DNF. View each term as a set of literals. If some term is empty, then φ always evaluates to 1, so φ is equivalent to a 3-CNF with no clauses. Now, assume each term is nonempty. Define $\psi = \bigwedge_{\ell_1 \in T_1,\, \ell_2 \in T_2,\, \ell_3 \in T_3} (\ell_1 \vee \ell_2 \vee \ell_3)$. Then φ and ψ are equivalent because for each $a \in \{0,1\}^n$, $\varphi(a) = 1$ iff $\psi(a) = 1$:

$\Rightarrow$: If some term T_j in φ is satisfied, then each $(\ell_1 \vee \ell_2 \vee \ell_3)$ in ψ is satisfied since ℓ_j is satisfied.

$\Leftarrow$: If all terms in φ are unsatisfied, then there exist unsatisfied literals $\ell_1 \in T_1$, $\ell_2 \in T_2$, $\ell_3 \in T_3$, and thus $(\ell_1 \vee \ell_2 \vee \ell_3)$ in ψ is unsatisfied.

If ψ isn't a 3-CNF, we can turn it into an equivalent 3-CNF:

(i) If any $(\ell_1 \vee \ell_2 \vee \ell_3)$ contains opposite literals, say $\ell_1 = \overline{\ell_2}$, then delete $(\ell_1 \vee \ell_2 \vee \ell_3)$ since it always evaluates to 1.

(ii) If any $(\ell_1 \vee \ell_2 \vee \ell_3)$ contains duplicate literals, then delete the duplicates so only one of each distinct literal remains. Now, the whole formula is a conjunction of clauses (in which literals correspond to distinct variables), so it's a CNF.

(iii) If any clause C has width < 3, replace it with the two clauses $(C \vee x_i) \wedge (C \vee \overline{x_i})$ where x_i is some variable not in C (which exists since $n \geq 3$). This updated CNF is equivalent by the proof of Claim 2.12. Repeat this until all clauses have width 3. ■

Example. Let's turn $(x_1 \wedge x_2) \vee (x_2 \wedge \overline{x_3}) \vee (\overline{x_1} \wedge x_3)$ into a 3-CNF:

$$\begin{aligned}
&(x_1 \vee x_2 \vee \overline{x_1}) \wedge (x_1 \vee x_2 \vee x_3) \wedge (x_1 \vee \overline{x_3} \vee \overline{x_1}) \wedge (x_1 \vee \overline{x_3} \vee x_3) \wedge \\
&(x_2 \vee x_2 \vee \overline{x_1}) \wedge (x_2 \vee x_2 \vee x_3) \wedge (x_2 \vee \overline{x_3} \vee \overline{x_1}) \wedge (x_2 \vee \overline{x_3} \vee x_3) \\
= {}&(x_1 \vee x_2 \vee x_3) \wedge (x_2 \vee x_2 \vee \overline{x_1}) \wedge (x_2 \vee x_2 \vee x_3) \wedge (x_2 \vee \overline{x_3} \vee \overline{x_1}) && \text{(step } (i)\text{)} \\
= {}&(x_1 \vee x_2 \vee x_3) \wedge (x_2 \vee \overline{x_1}) \wedge (x_2 \vee x_3) \wedge (x_2 \vee \overline{x_3} \vee \overline{x_1}) && \text{(step } (ii)\text{)} \\
= {}&(x_1 \vee x_2 \vee x_3) \wedge (x_2 \vee \overline{x_1} \vee x_3) \wedge (x_2 \vee \overline{x_1} \vee \overline{x_3}) \wedge \\
&(x_2 \vee x_3 \vee x_1) \wedge (x_2 \vee x_3 \vee \overline{x_1}) \wedge (x_2 \vee \overline{x_3} \vee \overline{x_1}) && \text{(step } (iii)\text{)} \\
= {}&(x_1 \vee x_2 \vee x_3) \wedge (\overline{x_1} \vee x_2 \vee x_3) \wedge (\overline{x_1} \vee x_2 \vee \overline{x_3})
\end{aligned}$$

In the last step, we put variables in ascending order and deleted duplicate clauses. ♦

Proof of Lemma 13.9. Let A be CONSISTENCY FOR 3-TERM DNFs. We have $A \in \mathsf{NP}$ since given a 3-term DNF as a witness, a poly-time verifier can check whether it's consistent with the training data. Since GRAPH 3-COLORING is NP-complete (Theorem 2.25), it suffices to show GRAPH 3-COLORING $\leq_p^m A$. Map G to an input to A as follows. Assume G has n nodes, numbered $1, \ldots, n$. We use the same n in the input to A, so an example $x = x_1 \cdots x_n$ has bits indexed by G's nodes.

- For each node v in G, we have a positive example with 0 at index v and 1s elsewhere.
- For each edge $\{v, w\}$ in G, we have a negative example with 0s at indices v and w and 1s elsewhere.

To show this poly-time mapping reduction is correct, we argue that G has a proper 3-coloring iff there exists a 3-term DNF consistent with the training data:

$\Rightarrow$: Assume G has a proper 3-coloring. Define a 3-term DNF $\varphi = T_{\text{red}} \vee T_{\text{green}} \vee T_{\text{blue}}$ where:

$$T_{\text{red}} = \bigwedge_{\text{non-red nodes } u} x_u \qquad T_{\text{green}} = \bigwedge_{\text{non-green nodes } u} x_u \qquad T_{\text{blue}} = \bigwedge_{\text{non-blue nodes } u} x_u$$

φ is consistent with the training data because:

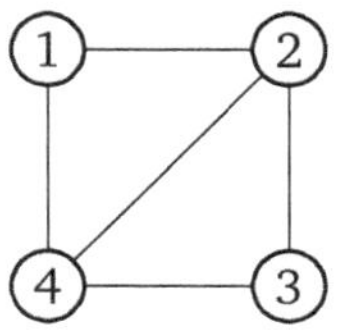

(0111, 1)	(0011, 0)
(1011, 1)	(0110, 0)
(1101, 1)	(1001, 0)
(1110, 1)	(1010, 0)
	(1100, 0)

Figure 13.5: Reducing GRAPH 3-COLORING to CONSISTENCY FOR 3-TERM DNFs

- Each node v's positive example satisfies φ: If v is red (say) then T_{red} is satisfied since $x_u = 1$ for every non-red node u.
- Each edge $\{v, w\}$'s negative example doesn't satisfy φ: T_{red} is unsatisfied since $x_v = x_w = 0$ and either v or w is non-red. Similarly, T_{green} and T_{blue} are unsatisfied.

$\Leftarrow$: Assume $\varphi = T_{\text{red}} \vee T_{\text{green}} \vee T_{\text{blue}}$ is a 3-term DNF consistent with the training data.

- Each node v's positive example satisfies φ. Color v red if T_{red} is satisfied, green if T_{green} is satisfied, or blue if T_{blue} is satisfied. If more than one term is satisfied, it doesn't matter which of the corresponding colors v is assigned.
- We claim that each edge $\{v, w\}$ is multicolored and thus the color assignment is proper. Suppose for contradiction v and w are both red (say). Then T_{red} doesn't contain the literal x_v since v's example has $x_v = 0$ and satisfies T_{red}. Similarly, T_{red} doesn't contain the literal x_w or the literal $\overline{x_u}$ for any $u \notin \{v, w\}$. This means $\{v, w\}$'s negative example satisfies T_{red} and thus φ. Thus φ is inconsistent with the training data. ■

Example. Given the graph on the left of Figure 13.5, the reduction yields the training data on the right.

$\Rightarrow$: If nodes 1 and 3 are red, 2 is green, and 4 is blue, then

$$\varphi = T_{\text{red}} \vee T_{\text{green}} \vee T_{\text{blue}} = (x_2 \wedge x_4) \vee (x_1 \wedge x_3 \wedge x_4) \vee (x_1 \wedge x_2 \wedge x_3)$$

is consistent with the training data.

$\Leftarrow$: The 3-term DNF

$$\varphi = T_{\text{red}} \vee T_{\text{green}} \vee T_{\text{blue}} = (x_1 \wedge \overline{x_2} \wedge x_3 \wedge x_4) \vee (x_1 \wedge x_2 \wedge x_3 \wedge \overline{x_4}) \vee (x_2 \wedge x_4)$$

is consistent with the training data. We color node 2 red since its example satisfies T_{red}, color 4 green since its example satisfies T_{green}, and color 1 and 3 blue since their examples satisfy T_{blue}. This is a proper 3-coloring. ♦

13.4 Sample Complexity

Consider any concept class C and hypothesis class $H \supseteq C$. The *sample complexity* of (δ, ε)-PAC learning (C, H) is the minimum number of training examples m used by any such learner. Training data is a valuable resource—it may be costly to come by. In this section, we ignore time efficiency and just ask how much training data is necessary for PAC learning.

By Theorem 13.4, the sample complexity is $\leq \lceil \frac{1}{\varepsilon} \ln \frac{|C|}{\delta} \rceil$ because a brute force proper consistent learner with that much training data is a (δ, ε)-PAC learner. But sometimes the sample complexity is even lower. For learning threshold functions (Theorem 13.1) and point functions (Theorem 13.2), the amount of training data didn't even depend on $|C|$, because those classes are somehow "simpler" than the number of concepts $|C|$ suggests. This section quantifies how "simple" any class is for the purpose of PAC learning: Sample complexity is essentially determined by the so-called *VC dimension* of C. ("VC" are the initials of two people who published a paper on the topic. This book's author would prefer a more descriptive name, but "VC dimension" is thoroughly entrenched, with no recognized alternative.)

If δ and ε are constants and C has VC dimension d, then the sample complexity is $O(d)$ for proper learning (§ 13.4.4) and $\Omega(d)$ even for improper learning (§ 13.4.5). Improper learners are sometimes more time-efficient than proper ones, but they never have much advantage in sample efficiency. The upshot is that if we just care about sample complexity, then we need not design a learning algorithm—we can just analyze the concept class's VC dimension and give approximately that many training examples to a brute force proper consistent learner. No other approach works with much less training data.

13.4.1 VC Dimension

Definition.

- For any concept $c\colon \{0,1\}^n \to \{0,1\}$ and set $S \subseteq \{0,1\}^n$, define $c_S\colon S \to \{0,1\}$ by $c_S(x) = c(x)$ for each $x \in S$ (just restricting c to domain S). As a corner case, we count $c_\emptyset\colon \emptyset \to \{0,1\}$ as a unique function.
- For any concept class C and set S, define $C_S = \{c_S : c \in C\}$. We could have $|C_S| < |C|$, because c_S and c'_S could be the same element of C_S (that is, $c(x) = c'(x)$ for every $x \in S$) even if c and c' are distinct elements of C. As a corner case, $|C_\emptyset| = 1$.
- Say C *shatters* S iff $|C_S| = 2^{|S|}$, in other words, C_S contains all possible functions $f\colon S \to \{0,1\}$. Note that a shattered set's subsets (including $\emptyset$) are also shattered.
- Define C's *growth function* $g_C\colon \mathbb{N} \to \mathbb{N}$ by $g_C(m) = \max_{S\,:\,|S|=m} |C_S|$.
- Define C's *VC dimension* as the size of a largest set that C shatters, in other words, the maximum m such that $g_C(m) = 2^m$. ◄

There are two parts to proving that C has VC dimension d:

- VC dimension $\geq d$ means:

$$\big(\exists S \subseteq \{0,1\}^n \text{ of size } d\big)\ \big(\forall f\colon S \to \{0,1\}\big)\ \big(\exists c \in C\big)\ \big(\forall x \in S\big):\ \ c(x) = f(x)$$

  To prove this, we must exhibit a size-d set S and argue that S is shattered, by considering any f and exhibiting a concept c that agrees with f on S.

- VC dimension $\leq d$ means:

$$\big(\forall S \subseteq \{0,1\}^n \text{ of size } d+1\big)\ \big(\exists f\colon S \to \{0,1\}\big)\ \big(\forall c \in C\big)\ \big(\exists x \in S\big):\ \ c(x) \neq f(x)$$

  To prove this, we must consider any size-$(d+1)$ set S and argue that S is not shattered, by exhibiting an f and showing that every concept c disagrees with f on an element of S.

Every C has VC dimension $\leq \log|C|$ because if C shatters S, then $2^{|S|} = |C_S| \leq |C|$.

x	C
00	0 1 0 1 1 1
01	0 0 0 1 0 0
10	0 0 1 0 1 0
11	0 1 0 1 1 0

x	$C_{\{00,01\}}$
00	0 1 0 1 1 1
01	0 0 0 1 0 0
10	0 0 1 0 1 0
11	0 1 0 1 1 0

x	$C_{\{00,10\}}$
00	0 1 0 1 1 1
01	0 0 0 1 0 0
10	0 0 1 0 1 0
11	0 1 0 1 1 0

Figure 13.6: Example for demonstrating shattering, VC dimension, and growth function

Example. See Figure 13.6. On the left is a concept class C containing six concepts, with $n = 2$. This C shatters each size-1 set $S \subseteq \{0,1\}^2$ because each row (on the table's right side) contains at least one 0 and at least one 1. How about size-2 sets? The middle table shows that C doesn't shatter $\{00,01\}$ because on those two rows (shown in black), the table's right side has only three of the four possible functions—it's missing the function f with $f(00) = 0$ and $f(01) = 1$. The last table shows that C shatters $\{00,10\}$ because on those two rows, the table's right side has all four possible functions $f\colon \{00,10\} \to \{0,1\}$.

$$\left|C_{\{00,01\}}\right| = 3 \quad \left|C_{\{00,10\}}\right| = 4 \quad \left|C_{\{00,11\}}\right| = 3 \quad \left|C_{\{01,10\}}\right| = 3 \quad \left|C_{\{01,11\}}\right| = 3 \quad \left|C_{\{10,11\}}\right| = 4$$

Shattering a size-3 set would require $2^3 = 8$ distinct concepts, but C only has 6 concepts. Since no size-3 set is shattered, but some size-2 set is shattered, C has VC dimension 2. Trivially, $|C_S| \le |C| = 6$ for every size-3 set S, but in this case actually $|C_S| \le 5$ for every size-3 set S:

$$\left|C_{\{00,01,10\}}\right| = 5 \qquad \left|C_{\{00,01,11\}}\right| = 4 \qquad \left|C_{\{00,10,11\}}\right| = 5 \qquad \left|C_{\{01,10,11\}}\right| = 5$$

Also, $\left|C_{\{00,01,10,11\}}\right| = |C| = 6$. In summary, C's growth function is:

$$g_C(0) = 1 \qquad g_C(1) = 2 \qquad g_C(2) = 4 \qquad g_C(3) = 5 \qquad g_C(4) = 6$$

♦

13.4.2 VC Dimension of Important Classes

Let's revisit the concept classes we studied in §13.1 and §13.2.

Lemma 13.10. *The class of threshold functions has VC dimension* 1.

Proof. Viewing $\{0,1\}^n$ as binary numbers $\{0,1,\ldots,2^n-1\}$, let $C = \{c^a : a \in \{0,1,\ldots,2^n-1\}\}$ be the class of threshold functions, where $c^a(x) = 1$ iff $x \ge a$. (In §13.1.2, c^a was called c_a.) The VC dimension is ≥ 1 because $\{0\}$ is shattered: $c^0(0) = 1$ and $c^1(0) = 0$. The VC dimension is ≤ 1 because for all $b < b'$, $\{b, b'\}$ is not shattered: There's no a such that $c^a(b) = 1$ and $c^a(b') = 0$. ∎

Lemma 13.11. *The class of point functions has VC dimension* 1.

Proof. Let $C = \{c^a : a \in \{0,1\}^n\}$ be the class of point functions, where $c^a(x) = 1$ iff $x = a$. (In §13.1.3, c^a was called c_a.) The VC dimension is ≥ 1 because for some b (in fact, for all b), $\{b\}$ is shattered: $c^b(b) = 1$ and $c^a(b) = 0$ for $a \ne b$. The VC dimension is ≤ 1 because for all $b \ne b'$, $\{b, b'\}$ is not shattered: There's no a such that $c^a(b) = c^a(b') = 1$. ∎

x	x_1	x_2	x_3	x_4
0000	0	0	0	0
0001	0	0	0	1
0010	0	0	1	0
0011	0	0	1	1
0100	0	1	0	0
0101	0	1	0	1
0110	0	1	1	0
0111	0	1	1	1
1000	1	0	0	0
1001	1	0	0	1
1010	1	0	1	0
1011	1	0	1	1
1100	1	1	0	0
1101	1	1	0	1
1110	1	1	1	0
1111	1	1	1	1

Figure 13.7: Set shattered by dictatorships

x_1	x_1	$\overline{x_1}$	
0	0	1	1
1	1	0	1

Figure 13.8: Concept class of terms for $n = 1$

x	$x_1 \wedge x_2 \wedge x_3$	$x_1 \wedge x_2$	$x_1 \wedge x_3$	x_1	$x_2 \wedge x_3$	x_2	x_3		...
000	0	0	0	0	0	0	0	1	...
001	0	0	0	0	0	0	1	1	...
010	0	0	0	0	0	1	0	1	...
011	0	0	0	0	1	1	1	1	...
100	0	0	0	1	0	0	0	1	...
101	0	0	1	1	0	0	1	1	...
110	0	1	0	1	0	1	0	1	...
111	1	1	1	1	1	1	1	1	...

Figure 13.9: Set shattered by terms

Lemma 13.12. *The class of dictatorships has VC dimension* $\lfloor \log n \rfloor$.

Proof. Let C be the class of dictatorships on n variables. The VC dimension is automatically $\leq \lfloor \log |C| \rfloor = \lfloor \log n \rfloor$. The VC dimension is $\geq \lfloor \log n \rfloor$ because there exists a $\lfloor \log n \rfloor \times n$ binary matrix with all $2^{\lfloor \log n \rfloor} \leq n$ possible columns, and this matrix's rows are a shattered set. Figure 13.7 shows an example with $n = 4$ and $\lfloor \log n \rfloor = 2$, using this matrix:

$$\begin{bmatrix} 0 & 0 & 1 & 1 \\ 0 & 1 & 0 & 1 \end{bmatrix}$$

Note that the table's right side is a copy of its left side. ■

Lemma 13.13. *The class of terms has VC dimension n.*

Proof. Assume $n \geq 2$, because if $n = 1$ then the VC dimension is evidently 1 (Figure 13.8).

First, we prove the VC dimension is $\geq n$. Consider the size-n set of all weight-$(n-1)$ strings $S = \{x^1, \ldots, x^n\}$ where x^i has a 0 at index i and 1s elsewhere. This S is shattered: For every $f : S \to \{0,1\}$, the term $c^f(x) = \bigwedge_{i : f(x^i)=0} x_i$ agrees with f on S because:

- If $f(x^i) = 0$ then $c^f(x^i) = 0$ because c^f contains the literal x_i and $x^i_i = 0$.
- If $f(x^i) = 1$ then $c^f(x^i) = 1$ because for every literal x_j of c^f, we have $j \neq i$ and $x^i_j = 1$.

Figure 13.9 illustrates this for $n = 3$.

Now, we prove the VC dimension is $\leq n$. Suppose for contradiction there exists a size-$(n+1)$ shattered set $S = \{x^1, \ldots, x^{n+1}\}$ (unrelated to the previous paragraph's S). In particular, for each $i \in [n+1]$, there exists a term c^i such that $c^i(x^i) = 0$ and $c^i(x^j) = 1$ for all $j \neq i$.

- Since $c^i(x^i) = 0$, c^i contains a literal ℓ^i such that $\ell^i(x^i) = 0$.
- Since $c^i(x^j) = 1$ for all $j \neq i$, we have $\ell^i(x^j) = 1$.

There are only n variables, so by the pigeonhole principle, there exist distinct indices $i \neq i'$ such that ℓ^i and $\ell^{i'}$ have the same variable x_k.

- If ℓ^i and $\ell^{i'}$ are the same literal—both x_k or both $\overline{x_k}$—then we have the contradiction $\ell^i(x^i) = 0$ and $\ell^{i'}(x^i) = 1$.
- If ℓ^i and $\ell^{i'}$ are opposite literals—say $\ell^i = x_k$ and $\ell^{i'} = \overline{x_k}$—then for some $j \in [n+1] \setminus \{i, i'\}$ (which exists since $n \geq 2$) we have the contradiction $\ell^i(x^j) = 1 = \ell^{i'}(x^j)$. ■

The class of decision lists has VC dimension $n + 1$ (Exercise 13.18).

A *halfspace* is a function $c\colon \{0,1\}^n \to \{0,1\}$ of the form: $c(x) = 1$ iff $w \cdot x \geq \theta$, where $w \in \mathbb{R}^n$ is a tuple of *weights* (coefficients) and $\theta \in \mathbb{R}$ (lower-case Greek theta) is a *threshold*, and the dot product $w \cdot x = \sum_{i=1}^{n} w_i x_i$ is over $\mathbb{R}$. Halfspaces are building blocks for neural networks and so play an important role in machine learning. They're called "half"spaces because they partition the expanded domain $\mathbb{R}^n$ into two "halves": all x with $w \cdot x \geq \theta$, and all x with $w \cdot x < \theta$. The boundary (all x with $w \cdot x = \theta$) is a line when $n = 2$ (see Figure 13.10 and Figure 13.11), a plane when $n = 3$, and is generally called an *affine hyperplane*. (Halfspaces are also called *linear threshold functions* or sometimes *perceptrons*. But confusingly, "perceptron" also refers to a particular learning algorithm.) Poly-time proper consistent learning of halfspaces is possible by a technique called linear programming, which we won't cover.

Lemma 13.14. *The class of halfspaces has VC dimension* $n + 1$.

Proof (ancillary). First, we prove the VC dimension is $\geq n + 1$. Consider the size-$(n + 1)$ set $S = \{x^0, x^1, \ldots, x^n\} \subseteq \{0,1\}^n$ where x^0 is the all-0 string and for each $i \in [n]$, x^i has a 1 at index i and 0s elsewhere. To see that S is shattered, consider any $f\colon S \to \{0,1\}$:

- If $f(x^0) = 0$ then f agrees with the halfspace "$\sum_{i\,:\,f(x^i)=1} x_i \geq 1$", that is, "$w \cdot x \geq \theta$" where $w_i = f(x^i)$ and $\theta = 1$.
- If $f(x^0) = 1$ then f agrees with the halfspace "$\sum_{i\,:\,f(x^i)=0} x_i \leq 0$", that is, "$w \cdot x \geq \theta$" where $w_i = f(x^i) - 1$ and $\theta = 0$.

Now, we prove the VC dimension is $\leq n+1$. Consider any size-$(n+2)$ set $S = \{x^1, \ldots, x^{n+2}\} \subseteq \{0,1\}^n$ (unrelated to the previous paragraph's S). We claim that S is not shattered. Let $a^i \in \{0,1\}^{n+1}$ be x^i with a 1 appended. View $a^1, \ldots, a^{n+2}$ as columns of an $(n+1) \times (n+2)$ matrix A over $\mathbb{R}$ (whose last row is all 1s). There exists a nonzero column vector $z \in \mathbb{R}^{n+2}$ such that Az is all 0s (Theorem A.29). We have $\sum_{i=1}^{n+2} z_i = (Az)_{n+1} = 0$. The entries of z aren't all ≥ 0, since they sum to 0 but aren't all 0. Define $f\colon S \to \{0,1\}$ by $f(x^i) = 1$ iff $z_i \geq 0$. Suppose for contradiction that some halfspace "$w \cdot x \geq \theta$" agrees with f on S.

- For each i with $z_i \geq 0$, we have $w \cdot x^i \geq \theta$ and thus $z_i(w \cdot x^i) \geq z_i \theta$.
- For each i with $z_i < 0$, we have $w \cdot x^i < \theta$ and thus $z_i(w \cdot x^i) > z_i \theta$.

The contradiction is

$$\begin{aligned} 0 = w \cdot (00\cdots0) = w \cdot (Az)_{1,\ldots,n} = w \cdot \textstyle\sum_{i=1}^{n+2} z_i x^i &= \textstyle\sum_{i=1}^{n+2} z_i (w \cdot x^i) \\ &> \textstyle\sum_{i=1}^{n+2} z_i \theta = 0\theta = 0 \end{aligned}$$

where the inequality is $>$ for some i and $\geq$ for each i. ■

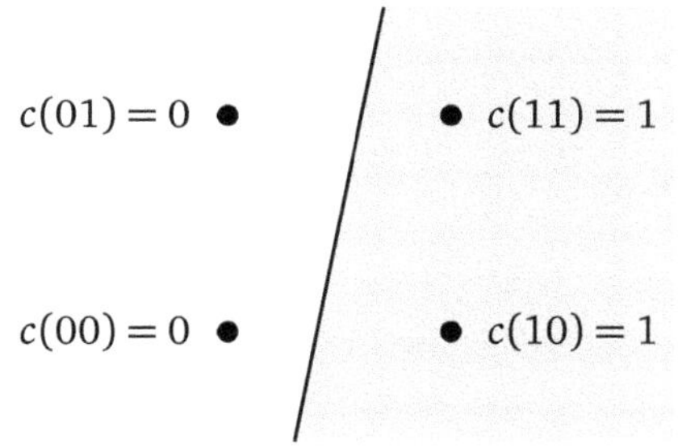

Figure 13.10: Halfspace "$5x_1 - 1x_2 \geq 2$"

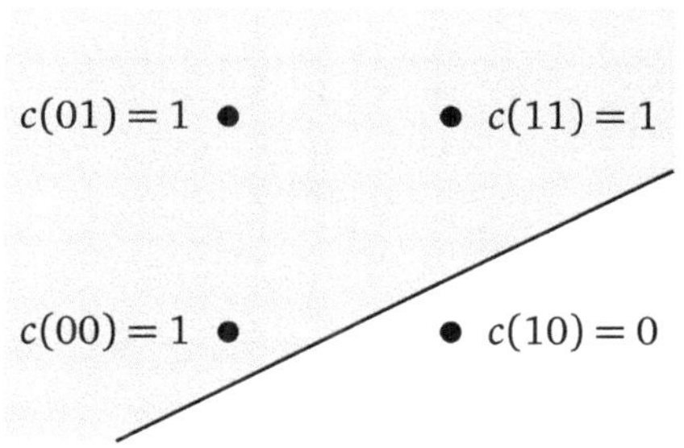

Figure 13.11: Halfspace "$-2x_1 + 4x_2 \geq -1$"

13.4.3 Growth Function

Lemma 13.15. *If a concept class C has VC dimension d, then $g_C(m) \leq (em/d)^d$ for all $m > d$.*

Thus the growth function has two phases: It's exponential (2^m) for $m \leq d$, then switches to a degree-d polynomial for $m > d$.

Lemma 13.16. *Every concept class C shatters at least $|C|$ many sets (including $\emptyset$).*

Proof of Lemma 13.15. Assume C has VC dimension d. Consider any set $S \subseteq \{0,1\}^n$ of size $m > d$. By Lemma 13.16, C_S shatters at least $|C_S|$ many sets, which means C shatters at least $|C_S|$ many subsets of S. Since every set that C shatters has size $\leq d$:

$$|C_S| \;\leq\; (\text{number of subsets of } S \text{ of size} \leq d) \;=\; \tbinom{m}{0} + \tbinom{m}{1} + \cdots + \tbinom{m}{d}$$

It's not tricky to see the latter quantity is $O(m^d)$, but let's go for a more precise bound:

$$\begin{aligned}
(d/m)^d \textstyle\sum_{i=0}^{d} \binom{m}{i} &\leq \textstyle\sum_{i=0}^{d} \binom{m}{i}(d/m)^i && (d/m < 1)\\
&\leq \textstyle\sum_{i=0}^{m} \binom{m}{i}(d/m)^i 1^{m-i} \\
&= (1 + d/m)^m && \text{(binomial formula)}\\
&\leq (e^{d/m})^m && \text{(Fact 7.6)}\\
&= e^d
\end{aligned}$$

Dividing both sides by $(d/m)^d$ shows that $|C_S| \leq (em/d)^d$. ■

Proof of Lemma 13.16. First, some definitions: Consider any set S of size ≥ 2 and any $y \in S$, and let $T = S \setminus \{y\}$. For any $c\colon T \to \{0,1\}$ and any $b \in \{0,1\}$, define $c^{y\to b}\colon S \to \{0,1\}$ by $c^{y\to b}(y) = b$ and $c^{y\to b}(x) = c(x)$ for each $x \neq y$. For any class C of functions with domain S:

- Note that $C_T = \{c\colon T \to \{0,1\} : c^{y\to 0} \in C \text{ or } c^{y\to 1} \in C\}$.
- Define $C_T^* = \{c\colon T \to \{0,1\} : c^{y\to 0} \in C \text{ and } c^{y\to 1} \in C\}$.

See Figure 13.12 for an example. We design a recursive subroutine that maintains the invariant that for every class C, find-shattered(C) returns a set containing $|C|$ many sets that C shatters.

x	C					
00	0	0	1	1	0	1
01	1	1	0	0	0	1
10	0	0	1	1	1	0
11	0	1	0	1	0	1

x	C_T			
00	0	1	0	1
01	1	0	0	1
10	0	1	1	0

x	C_T^*	
00	0	1
01	1	0
10	0	1

Figure 13.12: Removing $y = 11$ from a concept class's domain $S = \{00, 01, 10, 11\}$

Algorithm to find many shattered sets (13.7)

find-shattered(C):
  let S be the domain of the functions in C
  if $|S| = 1$: return $\emptyset$ if $|C| = 0$, or $\{\emptyset\}$ if $|C| = 1$, or $\{\emptyset, S\}$ if $|C| = 2$
  pick any $y \in S$, and let $T = S \setminus \{y\}$
  return find-shattered$(C_T) \cup \{U \cup \{y\} : U \in$ find-shattered$(C_T^*)\}$

The invariant holds for the base cases when $|S| = 1$ by definition. (Recall that if $C \neq \emptyset$ then C shatters $\emptyset$.) To see that the invariant is maintained for C when $|S| > 1$, assume it holds for C_T and C_T^*. We have

$$\left|\text{find-shattered}(C)\right| = \left|\text{find-shattered}(C_T)\right| + \left|\text{find-shattered}(C_T^*)\right| = |C_T| + |C_T^*| = |C|$$

where the last equality holds because:

- Each $c \in C_T^*$ contributes 1 to $|C_T|$ and 1 to $|C_T^*|$ and 2 to $|C|$.
- Each $c \in C^T \setminus C_T^*$ contributes 1 to $|C_T|$ and 0 to $|C_T^*|$ and 1 to $|C|$.

C shatters every set in find-shattered(C) because:

- If $U \in$ find-shattered(C_T), then C_T shatters U, and C shatters U.
- If $U \in$ find-shattered(C_T^*), then C_T^* shatters U, and we claim that C shatters $U \cup \{y\}$. Consider any $f : U \cup \{y\} \to \{0, 1\}$. Let $b = f(y)$. Some $c \in C_T^*$ agrees with f_U, so $c^{y \to b} \in C$ agrees with f, because $c^{y \to b}(y) = b = f(y)$ and for all $x \in U$, we have $c^{y \to b}(x) = c(x) = f_U(x) = f(x)$. ■

13.4.4 Sample Complexity Upper Bound

Now, we prove a refined version of Theorem 13.4. If a hypothesis class H is large but has small VC dimension d, then the following theorem more tightly bounds the amount of training data sufficient for PAC learning—roughly $O(d)$ instead of $O(\log |H|)$.

Theorem 13.17. *If H has VC dimension d and $m \geq \frac{18}{\varepsilon}\left(d \log \frac{1}{\varepsilon} + \log \frac{1}{\delta}\right)$ then every m-consistent learner for (C, H) is a (δ, ε)-PAC learner for (C, H).*

Since C's VC dimension is no larger than H's, we might as well let $H = C$ if we only care about sample complexity. Theorem 13.17 allows improper learners since they might be faster than proper learners despite using more training data.

Proof idea. The idea behind Theorem 13.4 was that each bad hypothesis has low probability of being consistent with the random training data, and we did a union bound over all bad hypotheses, of which there are $\leq |H|$. Now, on the m training examples, H collapses to a set H_S

of $\leq g_H(m)$ many distinct functions, which is far less than $|H|$ by Lemma 13.15. We'd like to do a union bound over these $g_H(m)$ distinct functions. The catch is that H_S depends on the random training examples, but a simple union bound would assume it doesn't. The idea to circumvent this circular reasoning involves imagining an enlarged tuple of training examples, fixing H_S with respect to all these examples, and then randomly selecting which of them to use for the "real" training data. That way, the real examples are random even though H_S is fixed. ∎

Proof (ancillary). Assume H has VC dimension d and $m \geq \frac{18}{\varepsilon}\big(d \log \frac{1}{\varepsilon} + \log \frac{1}{\delta}\big)$ and L is an m-consistent learner for (C, H). Consider any concept $c \in C$ and distribution D over $\{0,1\}^n$. Say a hypothesis $h \in H$ is *bad* iff $\mathbf{Pr}_{y \sim D}\big[h(y) = c(y)\big] < 1 - \varepsilon$.

Consider an expanded random experiment in which we sample $(x^1, \ldots, x^{2m}) \sim D^{2m}$ and a uniformly random permutation $q\colon [2m] \to [2m]$. The original random experiment $(x^1, \ldots, x^m) \sim D^m$ is equivalent to $(x^{q(1)}, \ldots, x^{q(m)})$ in the expanded experiment.

- Let $t = \big((x^1, c(x^1)), \ldots, (x^{2m}, c(x^{2m}))\big)$ be all the training data.
- Let $t^q = \big((x^{q(1)}, c(x^{q(1)})), \ldots, (x^{q(2m)}, c(x^{q(2m)}))\big)$ be the permuted training data.
- Let $t^{q,\text{left}}$ and $t^{q,\text{right}}$ be the first m and last m components of t^q.
- Recall h is *inconsistent* with $t^{q,\text{left}}$ iff $h(x^{q(i)}) \neq c(x^{q(i)})$ for at least one $i \in [m]$.
- Say h is *very inconsistent* with t iff $h(x^i) \neq c(x^i)$ for $> m\varepsilon/2$ many $i \in [2m]$.
- Let A be the event that some bad $h \in H$ is consistent with $t^{q,\text{left}}$.
- Let B be the event that some $h \in H$ is consistent with $t^{q,\text{left}}$ but very inconsistent with t.

Lemma 13.18. $\mathbf{Pr}[B \mid A] \geq 1/2$.

Lemma 13.19. $\mathbf{Pr}[B] \leq \delta/2$.

These lemmas will finish the proof of Theorem 13.17 since $\mathbf{Pr}[B \mid A] \leq \mathbf{Pr}[B]/\mathbf{Pr}[A]$ implies

$$\mathbf{Pr}\big[L(t^{q,\text{left}}) \text{ is bad}\big] \;\leq\; \mathbf{Pr}[A] \;\leq\; \mathbf{Pr}[B]/\mathbf{Pr}[B \mid A] \;\leq\; (\delta/2)/(1/2) \;=\; \delta$$

and thus L is a (δ, ε)-PAC learner for (C, H). ∎

We need a concentration bound similar to Lemma 11.29 but bounding the probability of getting too few heads (rather than too many). We prove it at the end of this section.

Lemma 13.20. *If X is the number of heads in m tosses of a coin with heads probability p, then* $\mathbf{Pr}[X < mp/2] \leq 0.9^{mp}$.

Proof of Lemma 13.18 (ancillary). Condition on any outcome of q and $(x^{q(1)}, \ldots, x^{q(m)})$ such that A holds. Then $(x^{q(m+1)}, \ldots, x^{q(2m)})$ is still distributed according to D^m. Consider some bad h consistent with $t^{q,\text{left}}$. For each $i \in \{m+1, \ldots, 2m\}$, imagine a coin toss where heads means $h(x^{q(i)}) \neq c(x^{q(i)})$. Since h is bad, the heads probability p is $> \varepsilon$. Let X be the number of heads among these m tosses. Conditioned on the arbitrary outcome of q and $(x^{q(1)}, \ldots, x^{q(m)})$ such that A holds:

$$\begin{aligned}
\mathbf{Pr}\big[\overline{B}\big] &\leq \mathbf{Pr}_{x^{q(m+1)}, \ldots, x^{q(2m)}}\big[h \text{ is not very inconsistent with } t\big] \\
&= \mathbf{Pr}[X \leq m\varepsilon/2] \;\leq\; \mathbf{Pr}[X < mp/2] \;\leq\; 0.9^{mp} \;\leq\; 0.9^{m\varepsilon} \qquad \text{(Lemma 13.20)} \\
&\leq 1/2
\end{aligned}$$

∎

Proof of Lemma 13.19 (ancillary). Condition on any outcome of $(x^1,\ldots,x^{2m})$. For any h that's very inconsistent with t, letting $k > m\varepsilon/2$ be the number of $i \in [2m]$ such that $h(x^i) \neq c(x^i)$:

$$\begin{aligned}
\mathbf{Pr}_q\big[h \text{ is consistent with } t^{q,\text{left}}\big] &= \mathbf{Pr}_q\big[\forall i \le m:\ h(x^{q(i)}) = c(x^{q(i)})\big] \\
&= \mathbf{Pr}_q\big[\forall i \text{ such that } h(x^i) \neq c(x^i):\ q^{-1}(i) > m\big] \\
&= \frac{m(m-1)(m-2)\cdots(m-k+1)}{2m(2m-1)(2m-2)\cdots(2m-k+1)} \\
&\le (1/2)^k \\
&< 2^{-m\varepsilon/2}
\end{aligned}$$

Define $S = \{x^1,\ldots,x^{2m}\}$, which has size $|S| \le 2m$. By Lemma 13.15, the number of distinct functions h_S is $\le g_H(|S|) \le g_H(2m) \le (\mathrm{e}2m/d)^d$. Conditioned on the arbitrary outcome of $(x^1,\ldots,x^{2m})$:

$$\begin{aligned}
\mathbf{Pr}[B] &= \mathbf{Pr}_q\big[\exists\ h_S \text{ very inconsistent with } t \text{ such that } h_S \text{ is consistent with } t^{q,\text{left}}\big] \\
&\le \textstyle\sum_{h_S \text{ very inconsistent with } t} \mathbf{Pr}_q\big[h_S \text{ is consistent with } t^{q,\text{left}}\big] \qquad \text{(union bound)} \\
&\le (\mathrm{e}2m/d)^d 2^{-m\varepsilon/2} \\
&\le \delta/2
\end{aligned}$$

The last inequality needs elaboration. First, assume m is exactly $\frac{18}{\varepsilon}\big(d\log\frac{1}{\varepsilon} + \log\frac{1}{\delta}\big)$:

$$2^{-m\varepsilon/2} = 2^{-9(d\log\frac{1}{\varepsilon}+\log\frac{1}{\delta})} = \varepsilon^{9d}\delta^9$$

$$(\mathrm{e}2m/d)^d = \Big(\tfrac{36\mathrm{e}}{\varepsilon}\big(\log\tfrac{1}{\varepsilon} + \log\tfrac{1}{\delta^{1/d}}\big)\Big)^d \le \Big(\tfrac{100}{\varepsilon}\cdot\tfrac{1}{\varepsilon}\cdot\tfrac{1}{\delta^{1/d}}\Big)^d = \Big(\tfrac{100}{\varepsilon^2}\Big)^d\cdot\tfrac{1}{\delta}$$

Multiplying these yields $(100\varepsilon^7)^d\delta^8 \le \delta^8 \le \delta/2$ since $\varepsilon,\delta \le 1/2$. If we increase m, then the inequality still holds since $2^{m\varepsilon/2}$ (with no $-$ sign in the exponent) grows faster than $(\mathrm{e}2m/d)^d$. ■

Proof of Lemma 13.20 (ancillary). Let $X = X_1 + \cdots + X_m$ where X_i indicates whether the ith toss is heads. For $b = 1/2$, we have $\mathbf{Pr}[X < mp/2] = \mathbf{Pr}\big[b^X > b^{mp/2}\big] \le \mathbf{E}\big[b^X\big]/b^{mp/2}$ (Lemma 7.13, since $b^X \ge 0$). We have $\mathbf{E}\big[b^X\big] = \mathbf{E}\big[b^{X_1}\cdots b^{X_m}\big] = \mathbf{E}\big[b^{X_1}\big]\cdots\mathbf{E}\big[b^{X_m}\big]$ since $X_1,\ldots,X_m$ are fully independent and thus $b^{X_1},\ldots,b^{X_m}$ are fully independent (Lemma A.12). For each i:

$$\mathbf{E}\big[b^{X_i}\big] = \mathbf{Pr}[X_i = 0]\cdot b^0 + \mathbf{Pr}[X_i = 1]\cdot b^1 = (1-p)\cdot 1 + p\cdot b = 1 + (b-1)p \le \mathrm{e}^{(b-1)p}$$

Combining everything, $\mathbf{Pr}[X < mp/2] \le (\mathrm{e}^{(b-1)p})^m/b^{mp/2} = (\mathrm{e}^{b-1}/b^{1/2})^{mp} \le 0.9^{mp}$. ■

13.4.5 Sample Complexity Lower Bound

Assuming δ and ε are constants and C has VC dimension d: By Theorem 13.17, $O(d)$ training examples suffice for proper PAC learning. Now, we prove that $\Omega(d)$ training examples are necessary for PAC learning, even if H contains all possible functions. Thus the sample complexity is $\Theta(d)$.

Theorem 13.21. *If C has VC dimension d, then every $(1/5,1/5)$-PAC learner for (C,H) uses at least $d/5$ training examples.*

Proof idea. On a shattered set S, the concept could be literally any function. Thus if the training examples come from S, then a learner has no information whatsoever about the concept on examples in S that aren't in the training data. For the hypothesis to succeed on most of S, the training data must cover a significant fraction of S. ■

Proof. Assume C has VC dimension d. Consider any $L\colon \big(\{0,1\}^n \times \{0,1\}\big)^m \to H$ with $m < d/5$. We claim that L isn't a $(1/5, 1/5)$-PAC learner for (C,H). That is, there exist a concept $c \in C$ and a distribution D over $\{0,1\}^n$ such that:

$$\mathbf{Pr}_{(x^1,\dots,x^m)\sim D^m}\left[\begin{array}{l}\mathbf{Pr}_{y\sim D}\big[h(y)=c(y)\big] \ge 4/5 \\ \text{where } h = L\big((x^1,c(x^1)),\dots,(x^m,c(x^m))\big)\end{array}\right] < 4/5$$

Let $S \subseteq \{0,1\}^n$ be a size-d set that C shatters. Let D be the uniform distribution over S. We use the probabilistic method to show the existence of c. Since C_S is the set of all functions $f\colon S \to \{0,1\}$, we can sample a uniformly random $f\colon S \to \{0,1\}$ and let $c \in C$ be such that $c_S = f$. In other words, we toss a fair coin d times to specify $c(x)$ for all $x \in S$, and then we define $c(x)$ for all $x \notin S$ in such a way that $c \in C$. This distribution of c ensures that if $y \in S$ wasn't in the training data, then h can't do better than a blind guess. Specifically, for every $(x^1,\dots,x^m) \in S^m$,

$$\begin{aligned}\mathbf{Pr}_{c,y}\big[h(y)\ne c(y)\big] &\ge \mathbf{Pr}_{c,y}\big[y \notin \{x^1,\dots,x^m\} \text{ and } h(y)\ne c(y)\big]\\ &= \mathbf{Pr}_{y}\big[y \notin \{x^1,\dots,x^m\}\big]\cdot \mathbf{Pr}_{c,y}\big[h(y)\ne c(y)\,\big|\, y\notin\{x^1,\dots,x^m\}\big]\\ &\ge (1-m/d)\cdot(1/2)\\ &> 2/5\end{aligned}$$

since $h(y)$ depends only on $c(x^1),\dots,c(x^m)$ and so is independent of $c(y)$ if $y \in S \setminus \{x^1,\dots,x^m\}$. Therefore:

$$\min_c\Big(\mathbf{E}_{x^1,\dots,x^m}\Big[\mathbf{Pr}_y\big[h(y)=c(y)\big]\Big]\Big) \le \max_{(x^1,\dots,x^m)\in S^m}\Big[\mathbf{Pr}_{c,y}\big[h(y)=c(y)\big]\Big] < 3/5$$

Thus there exists a concept $c \in C$ such that:

$$\mathbf{E}_{x^1,\dots,x^m}\Big[\mathbf{Pr}_y\big[h(y)=c(y)\big]\Big] < 3/5$$

By Lemma 7.13:

$$\mathbf{Pr}_{x^1,\dots,x^m}\Big[\mathbf{Pr}_y\big[h(y)=c(y)\big]\ge 4/5\Big] < (3/5)/(4/5) = 3/4 < 4/5$$ ■

Exercise 13.22 generalizes this lower bound from $\Omega(d)$ (for constant ε) to $\Omega(\frac{d}{\varepsilon})$. Thus the upper bound of Theorem 13.17 is tight within a $O(\log\frac{1}{\varepsilon})$ factor (for constant δ).

13.5 Amplification and Boosting

A uniform PAC learner (§ 13.1.5) works for any parameters δ and ε given as input. What if we have a PAC learner that only works for some particular δ and ε?

- *Amplification* (§ 13.5.1) means improving the confidence $1-\delta$.
- *Boosting* (§ 13.5.2) means improving the accuracy $1-\varepsilon$.

Boosting is trickier than amplification.

13.5.1 Amplifying Confidence

For any learner $L\colon \big(\{0,1\}^n \times \{0,1\}\big)^m \to H$, we define a learner $L'\colon \big(\{0,1\}^n \times \{0,1\}\big)^{m'} \to H$ and prove that L' has much better confidence and only slightly worse accuracy. The idea is to run L several times—with fresh training data for each run—and pick the "best" of the resulting candidate hypotheses. If L is a $(1/2, \varepsilon)$-PAC learner for (C, H), then with high probability, at least one candidate hypothesis h has error $\mathbf{Pr}_{y\sim D}\big[h(y) \neq c(y)\big] \leq \varepsilon$. If we could somehow determine each candidate hypothesis's error, we could simply pick the one with lowest error. We accomplish something almost as good using an idea reminiscent of cross-validation in machine learning: We estimate each candidate hypothesis's error using an extra group of training data for *validation* (not for training L). With high probability, the fraction of validation examples on which h errs (the *empirical error*) approximates h's actual error. The candidate h with lowest empirical error might not have the lowest actual error, but it's good enough.

The training data of L' has $m' = tm + v$ labeled examples, where:

$$\begin{aligned} t &= \text{number of training runs of } L \\ m &= \text{number of training examples per run of } L \\ v &= \text{number of validation examples} \end{aligned}$$

We denote the examples:

$$\underbrace{x^{1,1},\ldots,x^{1,m}}_{\text{training } L},\ \underbrace{x^{2,1},\ldots,x^{2,m}}_{\text{training } L},\ \ldots,\ \underbrace{x^{t,1},\ldots,x^{t,m}}_{\text{training } L},\ \underbrace{y^{1},\ldots,y^{v}}_{\text{validation}}$$

Amplified PAC learner (13.8)

L':

for each $i \in [t]$: let $h^i \leftarrow L\big((x^{i,1}, c(x^{i,1})), \ldots, (x^{i,m}, c(x^{i,m}))\big)$
output whichever h^i has $h^i(y^j) \neq c(y^j)$ for the fewest indices $j \in [v]$

Theorem 13.22. *If L is a $(1/2, \varepsilon)$-PAC learner for (C, H) and $t \geq \log \frac{2}{\delta}$ and $v \geq \frac{4}{\gamma^2} \ln \frac{4t}{\delta}$, then L' is a $(\delta, \varepsilon + \gamma)$-PAC learner for (C, H).*

Proof. Consider any concept $c \in C$ and distribution D over $\{0,1\}^n$. For any hypothesis $h \in H$, define $\varepsilon_h = \mathbf{Pr}_{y\sim D}\big[h(y) \neq c(y)\big]$ (the actual error) and $\beta_h =$ fraction of $j \in [v]$ with $h(y^j) \neq c(y^j)$ (the empirical error, which is a random variable depending on the outcome of $y^1, \ldots, y^v$).

- For each $i \in [t]$, consider a coin toss where heads means $\varepsilon_{h^i} \leq \varepsilon$, so the heads probability is $\geq 1/2$. If $t \geq \log \frac{2}{\delta}$ then with probability $\geq 1 - 1/2^t \geq 1 - \delta/2$, at least one toss is heads.
- For each $i \in [t]$, after h^i is produced, β_{h^i} is the fraction of tails among v tosses of a coin with tails probability ε_{h^i}. If $v \geq \frac{4}{\gamma^2} \ln \frac{4t}{\delta}$ then $\big|\beta_{h^i} - \varepsilon_{h^i}\big| \leq \gamma/2$ with probability $\geq 1 - \delta/2t$ (Corollary 7.21). By a union bound, this holds for all $i \in [t]$ simultaneously with probability $\geq 1 - \delta/2$.

So with probability $\geq (1-\delta/2)(1-\delta/2) \geq 1-\delta$ over all training data of L', the following hold:

(i) $\varepsilon_{h^i} \leq \varepsilon$ for some i.
(ii) $\beta_{h^i} \leq \varepsilon_{h^i} + \gamma/2$ for all i.
(iii) $\beta_{h^i} \geq \varepsilon_{h^i} - \gamma/2$ for all i.

(i) and *(ii)* imply that L' outputs some h^i with $\beta_{h^i} \leq \varepsilon + \gamma/2$. (It doesn't necessarily output the h^i with $\varepsilon_{h^i} \leq \varepsilon$ from *(i)*.) Then *(iii)* implies that $\varepsilon_{h^i} \leq \varepsilon + \gamma$. ∎

13.5.2 Boosting Accuracy

A (δ, ε)-PAC learner L for (C, H) might never produce a hypothesis h whose error $\mathbf{Pr}_{y \sim D}\big[h(y) \neq c(y)\big]$ is any better than ε. To design a (δ', ε')-PAC learner where $\varepsilon' < \varepsilon$, we use L to obtain several hypotheses and combine them into a hypothesis h' from a somewhat larger class H'. A simple example: If we could coax L to produce three hypotheses h^1, h^2, h^3 that each err on a third of all possible examples, and these thirds were disjoint from each other, then $h' = \text{MAJORITY}(h^1, h^2, h^3)$ would be correct on every example x, since two of $h^1(x), h^2(x), h^3(x)$ would equal $c(x)$.

To make L produce hypotheses that err on different examples, we exploit the fact that L works for every distribution over examples. We get h^1 by simulating L with some distribution D_1. Then, we get h^2 by simulating L with a different distribution D_2 that gives higher probability to examples on which h^1 errs, and so on. This steers L toward examples that need more attention. To simulate L with different distributions, we pick and choose which of our training examples to give L. This is the general strategy of boosting.

We now describe a widely used algorithm called AdaBoost ("adaptive boosting"). A common technique in practice is to design a simple learner that works somewhat well (better than blind guessing), and improve its accuracy by applying AdaBoost "off the shelf." Here's the basic setup for the boosted learner L':

- L' is a consistent learner for an arbitrarily large number m of training examples. Thus L' is automatically a PAC learner with arbitrarily small error ε' (§13.4.4).
- Actually, L' is a *randomized* (δ^*, m)-consistent learner, which means with probability $\geq 1 - \delta^*$ over its internal randomness, L' finds a hypothesis consistent with its training data. This implies L' is a *randomized* (δ', ε')-PAC learner (where $\delta' > \delta^*$), which means with probability $\geq 1 - \delta'$ over its training data and its internal randomness, L' finds a hypothesis that has error $\leq \varepsilon'$. We need L' to be randomized since it feeds L training data sampled randomly from its own training data.
- The new hypothesis class H' consists of halfspaces (§13.4.2) applied to hypotheses from H: Letting H^* be the class of t-variable halfspaces, define:

$$H' = \big\{h' : h'(x) = h^*\big(h^1(x), \ldots, h^t(x)\big) \text{ for some } h^* \in H^* \text{ and } h^1, \ldots, h^t \in H\big\}$$

  The parameter t is the number of runs of L. A halfspace is like a "weighted majority": Lower-error hypotheses of L will carry more weight in the combined hypothesis h'. We have $H \subseteq H'$ since h^* can be a dictatorship.
- For convenience in analyzing L', we change the codomain of concepts and hypotheses from $\{0,1\}$ to $\{-1,1\}$. We use a halfspace $h^*\colon \{-1,1\}^t \to \{-1,1\}$ of the form $h^*(a_1, \ldots, a_t) = \text{sign}\big(w_1 a_1 + \cdots + w_t a_t\big)$ where $\text{sign}(a) = 1$ if $a \geq 0$ and $\text{sign}(a) = -1$ if $a < 0$. The w_i coefficients are weights.
- We let $i \in [t]$ index the runs of L, and $j \in [m]$ index the training examples $x^1, \ldots, x^m$ of L'. (We don't need notation for the number of training examples L uses.) For each $i \in [t]$, L' constructs a distribution J_i over the indices $[m]$ of training examples. This induces a distribution $D_i = x^{J_i}$ over the training examples (x^j where $j \sim J_i$).

For any learner L and parameters t and m, we define the randomized learner L':

AdaBoost (13.9)

```
L'((x^1, c(x^1)), ..., (x^m, c(x^m))) :
    for each j ∈ [m]: let J_1(j) ← 1/m
    for i ← 1, ..., t:
        obtain hypothesis h^i ∈ H by running L with concept c and distribution D_i = x^{J_i}:
            for each training example of L: use (x^j, c(x^j)) for an independent j ~ J_i
        define E_i = {j ∈ [m] : h^i(x^j) ≠ c(x^j)}
        if E_i = ∅: halt and output h^i
        compute ε_i ← J_i(E_i) = Σ_{j∈E_i} J_i(j)
        for each j ∈ E_i: let J_{i+1}(j) ← J_i(j)/2ε_i
        for each j ∈ \overline{E_i}: let J_{i+1}(j) ← J_i(j)/2(1 − ε_i)
    output the hypothesis h' = sign(Σ_{i=1}^t w_i h^i) where w_i = ½ ln((1−ε_i)/ε_i)
```

- $\varepsilon_i = \mathbf{Pr}_{y\sim D_i}\left[h^i(y) \neq c(y)\right]$ is the error of hypothesis h^i under distribution D_i.
- J_{i+1} is J_i but rebalanced so the error event E_i has probability exactly $1/2$: We had $J_i(E_i) = \varepsilon_i$, and we divide the probabilities of outcomes in E_i by $2\varepsilon_i$, so now $J_{i+1}(E_i) = \varepsilon_i/2\varepsilon_i = 1/2$. Also $J_i(\overline{E_i}) = 1-\varepsilon_i$ and $J_{i+1}(\overline{E_i}) = (1-\varepsilon_i)/2(1-\varepsilon_i) = 1/2$.
- L' maintains the invariant that J_i is indeed a distribution over $[m]$ (the probabilities sum to 1), and $J_i(j) > 0$ for all j, and $\varepsilon_i > 0$, unless L' halts with $E_i = \emptyset$.
- If ε_i is small then w_i is large: It makes sense that a better h^i gets more weight in h'.

Theorem 13.23. *If L is a (δ,ε)-PAC learner for (C,H) where $0 < \varepsilon < 1/2$, and if $t \geq \frac{1}{2\gamma^2}\ln m$ where $\gamma = 1/2-\varepsilon$, then L' is a randomized $(t\delta, m)$-consistent learner for (C,H').*

"AdaBoost" stands for "adaptive boosting" because the algorithm doesn't need to know ε (which is generally hard to determine in practice): It could "adapt" to any unknown ε by simply running for as many iterations as it takes to get h' consistent with the training data (rather than specifying t from the outset).

Proof of Theorem 13.23 (ancillary). In iteration i, we have $\mathbf{Pr}[\varepsilon_i \leq \varepsilon] \geq 1-\delta$ since L is a (δ,ε)-PAC learner. By a union bound, $\mathbf{Pr}\left[\varepsilon_i \leq \varepsilon \text{ for all } i\right] \geq 1-t\delta$. Henceforth assume $\varepsilon_i \leq \varepsilon$ for all i. We argue that L' outputs a hypothesis consistent with $(x^1, c(x^1)), \ldots, (x^m, c(x^m))$. This is true by definition if L' halts early and outputs h^i. Now, assume L' outputs h' at the end. Consider any $j \in [m]$. We argue that $h'(x^j) = c(x^j)$, in other words, $h'(x^j)c(x^j) = 1$ (since the codomain is $\{-1,1\}$). To show $\text{sign}\left(\sum_{i=1}^t w_i h^i(x^j)\right)c(x^j) = 1$, it suffices to show $\left(\sum_{i=1}^t w_i h^i(x^j)\right)c(x^j) > 0$, in other words, $e^{-\sum_{i=1}^t w_i h^i(x^j)c(x^j)} < 1$.

First, we claim that for all $i \in [t]$, $e^{-w_i h^i(x^j)c(x^j)} = z_i J_{i+1}(j)/J_i(j)$ where $z_i = 2\sqrt{\varepsilon_i(1-\varepsilon_i)}$:

- If $j \in E_i$: $e^{-w_i h^i(x^j)c(x^j)} = e^{w_i} = \sqrt{(1-\varepsilon_i)/\varepsilon_i} = z_i/2\varepsilon_i = z_i J_{i+1}(j)/J_i(j)$
- If $j \in \overline{E_i}$: $e^{-w_i h^i(x^j)c(x^j)} = e^{-w_i} = \sqrt{\varepsilon_i/(1-\varepsilon_i)} = z_i/2(1-\varepsilon_i) = z_i J_{i+1}(j)/J_i(j)$

Defining $\gamma_i = 1/2-\varepsilon_i$, we have $\gamma_i \geq 1/2-\varepsilon = \gamma > 0$ and:

$$z_i = \sqrt{1-4\gamma_i^2} < \sqrt{e^{-4\gamma_i^2}} = e^{-2\gamma_i^2} \leq e^{-2\gamma^2}$$

Therefore, using $J_1(j) = 1/m$ and $J_{t+1}(j) \leq 1$:

$$\begin{aligned} e^{-\sum_{i=1}^t w_i h^i(x^j)c(x^j)} &= \prod_{i=1}^t e^{-w_i h^i(x^j)c(x^j)} = \prod_{i=1}^t z_i J_{i+1}(j)/J_i(j) \\ &= z_1 \cdots z_t J_{t+1}(j)/J_1(j) \leq z_1 \cdots z_t m < \left(e^{-2\gamma^2}\right)^t m \leq 1 \end{aligned}$$

■

Lemma 13.24. *If H has VC dimension d and H^* is the class of t-variable halfspaces, then H' has VC dimension $< 4dt\log t$ (assuming $t \geq 100$).*

Proof (ancillary). Consider any $S \subseteq \{0,1\}^n$ of size $m = 4dt\log t$. To show that H' doesn't shatter S, we show $|H'_S| < 2^m$. For each $i \in [t]$, there are $|H_S| \leq g_H(m) \leq (em/d)^d$ possibilities of h^i_S with $h^i \in H$ (Lemma 13.15). Thus there are $\leq (em/d)^{dt}$ possibilities of the tuple $(h^1_S,\ldots,h^t_S)$. For each such possibility, the set $S^* = \{(h^1(x),\ldots,h^t(x)) : x \in S\} \subseteq \{0,1\}^t$ has size $\leq m$, so there are $|H^*_{S^*}| \leq g_{H^*}(m) \leq (em/(t+1))^{t+1}$ possibilities of $h^*_{S^*}$ with $h^* \in H^*$ (Lemma 13.15) since H^* has VC dimension $t+1$ (Lemma 13.14). Thus there are $|H'_S| \leq (em/d)^{dt}(em/(t+1))^{t+1}$ possibilities of h'_S where $h'(x) = h^*\big(h^1(x),\ldots,h^t(x)\big)$. To conclude that $|H'_S| < 2^m$, by taking the log of both sides, we need to show m is large enough that:

$$dt\log(em/d) + (t+1)\log(em/(t+1)) < m$$

We have:

$$\begin{aligned} dt\log(em/d) &< dt\log(11t\log t) &&< 2dt\log t = m/2 \\ (t+1)\log(em/(t+1)) &< (t+1)\log(11d\log t) &&< 2dt\log t = m/2 \end{aligned}$$

■

Combining everything, we have a roadmap for turning a (δ,ε)-PAC learner L for (C,H) into a randomized (δ',ε')-PAC learner L' for (C,H'), where ε' is arbitrarily close to 0 and δ' is somewhat greater than δ (which doesn't matter since we can amplify confidence by Theorem 13.22):

- We turn L into a randomized consistent learner L' for (C,H') with arbitrarily large m (Theorem 13.23).
- Thus L' is a randomized PAC learner for (C,H') with arbitrarily small ε' (by a randomized version of Theorem 13.17).
- The relationship between m and ε' depends on the VC dimension d' of H', which is not too large (Lemma 13.24).

Glossing over lower-order factors, the number of training examples for L' should be:

$$m \approx d'/\varepsilon' \approx dt/\varepsilon' \approx d(\ln m)/\gamma^2\varepsilon'$$

There's a circular dependence here: Increasing m also increases t (the number of invocations of L), which enlarges H' and thus increases d', raising the target even higher for m. Fortunately, this is achievable since the right side only depends logarithmically on m. We won't wrestle with the parameters, but the upshot is that m and t only need to be polynomial in d, $1/\gamma$, and $1/\varepsilon'$.

13.6 Exact Learners

Exact learning is kind of like PAC learning with $\varepsilon = 0$. The goal is to find a hypothesis h that agrees with the target concept c on all possible examples. Now, there's no distribution over examples. An exact learner need not find the encoding of c. For example, if C is size-n^2 circuits and H is size-n^3 circuits, then it's enough to find the encoding of a size-n^3 circuit h that computes the same function as the unknown size-n^2 circuit c.

13.6.1 Active Learning with Queries

An ordinary passive learner (as we've studied so far) receives training data that it has no influence over, and then it throws a hypothesis over the wall. Exact learning requires a more active learner, that solicits help during its computation. We consider two kinds of queries an active learner could make:

- *Membership query*: The learner chooses an example x and requests the label $c(x)$. (It asks whether x is a member of the set of all positive examples.) Then, it can make another query that depends on the first query's label, and so on. (This is like adaptive oracle queries in reductions between computational problems.)
- *Equivalence query*: The learner produces a tentative hypothesis $h \in H$ and is either told that h is equivalent to the target concept $c \in C$ (that is, $h(x) = c(x)$ for all x) or given a *counterexample* x such that $h(x) \neq c(x)$. If h is equivalent to c then the learner is done; otherwise it may make more queries. The oracle is like a teacher who confirms that a hypothesis is right or gives feedback about why it's wrong.

In practice, a human expert could provide the labels for membership queries. It's less realistic for a human to answer equivalence queries. But we claim that exact learners with equivalence queries yield PAC learners without equivalence queries, so this provides a technique for designing PAC learners.

Specifically, if hypotheses in H can be evaluated in poly time, then we can turn a poly-time exact learner with equivalence queries into a poly-time consistent learner (which is also a poly-time PAC learner, assuming H has poly VC dimension): Given training data $(x^1, c(x^1)), \ldots, (x^m, c(x^m))$, we run the exact learner and whenever it makes an equivalence query h, we check whether h is consistent with the training data (by evaluating h on each of $x^1, \ldots, x^m$). If so, we halt and output h. If not, then one of $x^1, \ldots, x^m$ is a counterexample, which we give the exact learner in response to its query. If the exact learner runs to completion, it finds an h that's equivalent to c and is therefore consistent with the training data.

In the same way, we can turn a poly-time exact learner with membership queries and equivalence queries into a poly-time consistent learner with membership queries. The latter learner is also a poly-time PAC learner with membership queries (assuming H has poly VC dimension) because the membership queries have no bearing on the "consistent is PAC" analysis of Theorem 13.17.

13.6.2 Equivalence Queries Only

An equivalence query is a *success* when h is equivalent to c, and is a *mistake* otherwise. A *k-mistake learner* for (C, H) is a deterministic algorithm that receives no training data, makes equivalence queries (but not membership queries), and succeeds after at most k mistakes, no matter which counterexample it's given for each mistake. The counterexamples serve as the training data. This is the *mistake bound* model.

Another perspective: The learner's tentative hypothesis can be used for predictions until a counterexample is found. The learner then updates the hypothesis, which is used until a counterexample for this new hypothesis is found, and so on. After seeing only k counterexamples, the learner's hypothesis will make flawless predictions.

We start by illustrating two basic learning techniques with the concept classes from §13.1.

x	B							$\text{MAJ}_B(x)$
00	0	1	1	0	1	0	0	0
01	0	1	0	1	1	0	1	1
10	1	1	0	1	0	0	1	1
11	0	0	0	0	0	1	1	0

x	B							$\text{MAJ}_B(x)$
00	0	1	1	0	1	0	0	1
01	0	1	0	1	1	0	1	0
10	1	1	0	1	0	0	1	0
11	0	0	0	0	0	1	1	0

x	B							$c(x)$
00	0	1	1	0	1	0	0	1
01	0	1	0	1	1	0	1	1
10	1	1	0	1	0	0	1	0
11	0	0	0	0	0	1	1	0

Figure 13.13: Demonstration of the halving algorithm, with dashed boxes around counterexamples, and with gray columns removed from B

Brute force proper learning. Every concept class C has a proper $(|C|-1)$-mistake learner that doesn't even heed the counterexamples:

Brute force mistake bound learner (13.10)

for each hypothesis $h \in C$ in any order:
 do an equivalence query with hypothesis h
 if success: output hypothesis h

If the first $|C|-1$ queries are mistakes, then the last query must be a success. Brute force makes $\le 2^n - 1$ mistakes for threshold functions and point functions, and $\le n-1$ mistakes for dictatorships. For threshold functions, we'll see a better learner. But for point functions and dictatorships, we prove that this braindead learner is actually optimal: Proper k-mistake learners require $k \ge 2^n - 1$ for point functions and $k \ge n-1$ for dictatorships—counterexamples are useless in these cases.

Halving. With brute force, each mistake rules out one concept. With the *halving* algorithm, each mistake rules out half of the remaining concepts. To achieve this, we heed the counterexamples and resort to improper learning, with the hypothesis class of all majorities of sets of concepts: For any concept class C, let $H = \{\text{MAJ}_B : B \subseteq C\}$ where $\text{MAJ}_B(x) = 1$ iff $b(x) = 1$ for at least half of all concepts $b \in B$. Here's a $\lfloor \log |C| \rfloor$-mistake learner for (C, H):

Halving mistake bound learner (13.11)

initialize $B \leftarrow C$
repeat:
 do an equivalence query with hypothesis MAJ_B
 if success: output hypothesis MAJ_B
 else given counterexample $a \in \{0,1\}^n$: remove from B every b with $b(a) = \text{MAJ}_B(a)$

Figure 13.13 demonstrates a run of this algorithm.

Consider any target concept c. For each mistake, the counterexample a says $c(a) = \overline{\text{MAJ}_B(a)}$. The learner removes from B all concepts b such that $b(a) \ne c(a)$. Thus it maintains the invariant that B is the set of all concepts that remain in contention (they're consistent with all the counterexamples so far). In particular, $c \in B$.

The learner also maintains the invariant that $|B| \le |C|/2^i$ after i iterations, because for each mistake, at least half of all $b \in B$ have $b(a) = \text{MAJ}_B(a)$ (by definition of MAJ_B) and so get removed from B. After $\lfloor \log |C| \rfloor$ mistakes, we have $|B| \le |C|/2^{\lfloor \log |C| \rfloor} < 2$ and thus $|B| = 1$. Then the only remaining concept in B is MAJ_B, which must be the target concept c.

Halving is mistake-efficient but not necessarily time-efficient, since it still explicitly considers all concepts in C.

Halving makes $\le n$ mistakes for threshold functions and point functions, and $\le \lfloor \log n \rfloor$ mistakes for dictatorships. For threshold functions and dictatorships, we prove that halving is optimal: Even if the hypothesis class contains all possible functions, k-mistake learners require $k \ge n$ for threshold functions and $k \ge \lfloor \log n \rfloor$ for dictatorships. But for point functions, halving is overkill: We can do an equivalence query with the all-0 function as the hypothesis, and the counterexample will be the target point, so only one mistake is made.

For threshold functions, halving is actually a proper learner, because a "majority of threshold functions" is a threshold function. Halving is just binary search in this setting. Identifying $\{0,1\}^n$ with $\{0,1,\ldots,2^n-1\}$, the target concept is $c(x) =$ "$x \ge t$", which means $c(x) = 1$ iff $x \ge t$, for some unknown threshold $t \in \{0,1,\ldots,2^n-1\}$.

Halving mistake bound learner for threshold functions (13.12)

```
initialize ℓ ← 0 and u ← 2^n − 1
repeat:
    let m ← ⌊(ℓ + u)/2⌋
    do an equivalence query with hypothesis "x ≥ m"
    if success: output hypothesis "x ≥ m"
    else given counterexample a ∈ {ℓ, ..., u − 1}:
        if a < m: update u ← a
        if a ≥ m: update ℓ ← a + 1
```

In each iteration, the learner considers thresholds ℓ ("lower"), u ("upper"), and m ("middle"). It maintains the invariant that $\ell \le t \le u$, and $\{\ell,\ldots,u\}$ corresponds to the set B of remaining concepts. The hypothesis "$x \ge m$" is MAJ_B, and any counterexample a eliminates at least half of the remaining concepts. We must have $a \in \{\ell,\ldots,u-1\}$ since the hypothesis "$x \ge m$" and concept "$x \ge t$" agree on all other examples (both are 0 for $x < \ell$ and 1 for $x \ge u$). After n mistakes, only one concept would remain ($\ell = u = m = t$), ensuring success.

In summary: For threshold functions, binary search (halving) is a proper learner and is optimal even among improper learners. For dictatorships, brute force is an optimal proper learner, and halving is an optimal improper learner.

Monotone terms. A monotone term is a conjunction of positive literals, for example $x_2 \wedge x_4 \wedge x_5$. There are 2^n many distinct monotone terms on n variables. The empty monotone term expresses the constant 1 function.

For the concept class of monotone terms, brute force is proper but makes $2^n - 1$ mistakes, and halving makes only n mistakes but is improper. We can get the best of both worlds. Here's a proper n-mistake learner, which we soon prove is optimal even among improper learners:

Mistake bound learner for monotone terms (13.13)

initialize $h \leftarrow x_1 \wedge x_2 \wedge \cdots \wedge x_n$
repeat:
  do an equivalence query with hypothesis h
  if success: output hypothesis h
  else given counterexample $a \in \{0,1\}^n$: remove from h every literal x_j with $a_j = 0$

Consider any target concept c. We claim this learner maintains the invariant that h contains all literals of c and that h has at most $n-i$ literals after iteration i. The invariant holds at the beginning. Suppose the invariant holds right before iteration i and that h is a mistake. This implies that $c(a) = 1$ and $h(a) = 0$.

- $c(a) = 1$ implies that if $a_j = 0$ then x_j isn't in c and is therefore safe to remove from h. So h continues to contain all literals of c.
- $h(a) = 0$ implies that $a_j = 0$ for at least one of h's literals x_j, which gets removed. So h goes from at most $n-i+1$ literals to at most $n-i$ literals.

Thus the invariant is maintained. After n mistakes, h would be empty (at most $n-n$ literals) and therefore equal c since h contains all literals of c.

13.6.3 Lower Bounds for Equivalence Queries

The *mistake complexity* of exactly learning (C,H) is the minimum k such that there exists a k-mistake learner for (C,H). We characterize mistake complexity with a game between an eager learner and a sadistic teacher who begrudgingly provides counterexamples but tries to delay the learner's success for as long as possible. No target concept is fixed in advance; rather, the game maintains a set B (initially C) of remaining possibilities for the target concept. In each round, the learner picks a hypothesis $h \in H$, and then the teacher picks an $a \in \{0,1\}^n$ and removes from B every concept b with $b(a) = h(a)$. This informs the learner that a is a counterexample for whatever the target concept may be. The teacher is not allowed to pick an a that would remove all of B. The game ends when only one concept remains in B. For some parameter k, the learner wins iff the game ends after $\le k$ rounds.

- The mistake complexity is $\le k$ iff there exists a learner strategy that guarantees the game ends after $\le k$ rounds.
- The mistake complexity is $> k$ iff there exists a teacher strategy that guarantees the game lasts for $> k$ rounds. (After round k, at least two concepts remain in B.)

To prove a lower bound on mistake complexity, we design a teacher strategy that prolongs the game. Intuitively, the teacher should pick counterexamples that remove as little of B as possible.

For point functions, brute force is an optimal proper learner:

Theorem 13.25. *If $C = H$ is the class of point functions, then the mistake complexity is $2^n - 1$.*

Proof. We already showed the mistake complexity is $\le 2^n - 1$. To show it's $> 2^n - 2$, we exhibit a teacher strategy that makes the game last for $> 2^n - 2$ rounds. When the learner picks a hypothesis h, the teacher picks the unique a such that $h(a) = 1$. This eliminates only h itself, because $b(a) = 0$ for all other concepts b. After round $2^n - 2$, at least two of the 2^n concepts remain, so the game is not over. ∎

For dictatorships, brute force is an optimal proper learner:

Theorem 13.26. *If $C = H$ is the class of dictatorships, then the mistake complexity is $n-1$.*

Proof. We already showed the mistake complexity is $\leq n-1$. To show it's $> n-2$, we exhibit a teacher strategy that makes the game last for $> n-2$ rounds. When the learner picks a hypothesis x_i, the teacher picks the a such that $a_i = 1$ and $a_j = 0$ for all $j \neq i$. This eliminates only x_i. After round $n-2$, at least two of the n concepts remain, so the game is not over. (This is the same as in Theorem 13.25, noting that dictatorships are point functions on the restricted domain of all weight-1 strings.) ■

Lemma 13.27. *If C has VC dimension d and $H \supseteq C$, then the mistake complexity is $\geq d$.*

Proof. We exhibit a teacher strategy that makes the game last for $> d-1$ rounds. Consider a size-d set $S \subseteq \{0,1\}^n$ shattered by C. The teacher ignores the learner's hypotheses and just picks the elements of S as counterexamples in any order, say $a^1, a^2, \ldots, a^d$. Suppose the learner picks hypotheses $h^1, h^2, \ldots, h^{d-1}$ in the first $d-1$ rounds. Since C shatters S, there exist concepts $b^0, b^1 \in C$ such that $b^0(a^i) = b^1(a^i) = \overline{h^i(a^i)}$ for all $i \leq d-1$ and $b^0(a^d) = 0$ and $b^1(a^d) = 1$. Thus b^0 and b^1 remain in B after round $d-1$ and are distinct, so the game is not over. ■

For dictatorships, halving is an optimal improper learner:

Corollary 13.28. *If C is the class of dictatorships and $H \supseteq C$, then the mistake complexity is $\lfloor \log n \rfloor$.*

Proof. We already showed the mistake complexity is $\leq \lfloor \log n \rfloor$. It's $\geq \lfloor \log n \rfloor$ by Lemma 13.27 since C has VC dimension $\lfloor \log n \rfloor$ (Lemma 13.12). ■

For monotone terms, the proper learner from § 13.6.2 is optimal even among improper learners:

Corollary 13.29. *If C is the class of monotone terms and $H \supseteq C$, then the mistake complexity is n.*

Proof. We already showed the mistake complexity is $\leq n$. It's $\geq n$ by Lemma 13.27 since C has VC dimension n: In the proof that the class of terms has VC dimension n (Lemma 13.13), the size-n set shattered by terms is actually shattered by monotone terms. ■

For threshold functions, binary search is a proper learner and is optimal even among improper learners:

Theorem 13.30. *If C is the class of threshold functions and $H \supseteq C$, then the mistake complexity is n.*

Proof. We already showed the mistake complexity is $\leq n$. To show it's $> n-1$, we exhibit a teacher strategy that makes the game last for $> n-1$ rounds. The teacher maintains the invariant that after round i, the set B of remaining concepts corresponds to 2^{n-i} many consecutive thresholds. When the learner picks a hypothesis h in round i, the teacher disregards h and picks a to be the (2^{n-i})th smallest threshold among the 2^{n-i+1} many remaining thresholds. If $h(a) = 0$, B's upper half is eliminated. If $h(a) = 1$, B's lower half is eliminated. After round $n-1$, B has $2^{n-(n-1)} = 2$ remaining concepts, so the game is not over. ■

13.6.4 Membership and Equivalence Queries

A major open question is whether poly-size DNFs are poly-time PAC learnable (even improperly, by poly-size circuits). Learning DNFs reduces to learning monotone DNFs in the same way that learning circuits reduces to learning monotone circuits (§ 13.3.1). So it's also open whether poly-size monotone DNFs are poly-time PAC learnable. We now prove that poly-size monotone DNFs are poly-time PAC learnable with membership queries. (Unfortunately, this doesn't imply that poly-size general DNFs are poly-time PAC learnable with membership queries, because the reduction doesn't handle membership queries.) As explained in § 13.6.1, it suffices to prove that poly-size monotone DNFs are poly-time exactly learnable with membership and equivalence queries. These two types of queries are a potent combination.

Definition. In this section, b and c denote bit strings, not concepts.

- For $a, b \in \{0,1\}^n$, say $a \subseteq b$ iff $\{i : a_i = 1\} \subseteq \{i : b_i = 1\}$. That is, we overload "$\subseteq$" by viewing subsets of $[n]$ as their characteristic bit strings. Let $a \subsetneq b$ mean $a \subseteq b$ and $a \neq b$. For example, $10010 \subsetneq 11011$ and $01 \not\subseteq 10$. If $a \subseteq b$ and $b \subseteq c$, then $a \subseteq c$.
- A function $f\colon \{0,1\}^n \to \{0,1\}$ is *monotone* iff $f(a) \leq f(b)$ for all a, b such that $a \subseteq b$. In other words, flipping input bits from 0 to 1 never flips the output from 1 to 0. Every monotone circuit with one output node computes a monotone function.
- For each $a \in \{0,1\}^n$, define the monotone term $T_a(x_1 \cdots x_n) = \bigwedge_{i : a_i = 1} x_i$. For example, $T_{01101} = x_2 \wedge x_3 \wedge x_5$. Note that $T_a(b) = 1$ iff $a \subseteq b$.
- For a monotone $f\colon \{0,1\}^n \to \{0,1\}$: A *1-input* is a b such that $f(b) = 1$. A *minimal 1-input* is a 1-input b such that $f(a) = 0$ for all $a \subsetneq b$. A *minimal term* is T_b for a minimal 1-input b.
- A *t-term monotone DNF* is a disjunction of t or fewer monotone terms. ◀

Lemma 13.31. *For every monotone $f\colon \{0,1\}^n \to \{0,1\}$:*

(i) For every 1-input $c \in \{0,1\}^n$, there exists a minimal 1-input $b \subseteq c$.
(ii) The monotone DNF $\varphi = \bigvee_{\text{minimal 1-input } b} T_b$ (consisting of f's minimal terms) expresses f.
(iii) Every monotone DNF expressing f contains f's minimal terms.
(iv) f has a t-term monotone DNF iff f has at most t many minimal 1-inputs.

To express a monotone f with a monotone DNF, the minimal terms are necessary by *(iii)* and sufficient by *(ii)*. Thus every monotone f has a unique smallest monotone DNF, consisting of f's minimal terms.

Example. The monotone function f in Figure 13.14 has minimal 1-inputs 010 and 101 and minimal terms x_2 and $x_1 \wedge x_3$, so f's unique smallest monotone DNF is $(x_2) \vee (x_1 \wedge x_3)$. ◆

Proof of Lemma 13.31. *(i)*: A 1-input $b \subseteq c$ of least weight (with the fewest 1s) is a minimal 1-input. As an alternative proof, the following algorithm finds a minimal 1-input $b \subseteq c$:

Algorithm to find a minimal 1-input (13.14)

initialize $b \leftarrow c$
for $i \leftarrow 1, \ldots, n$:
  if $b_i = 1$ and b would remain a 1-input after flipping b_i to 0: flip b_i to 0

x	$f(x)$
000	0
001	0
010	1
011	1
100	0
101	1
110	1
111	1

Figure 13.14: Monotone function f with minimal 1-inputs highlighted

This maintains the invariant that $b \subseteq c$ and $f(b) = 1$. To see that the final b is a minimal 1-input, consider any $a \subsetneq b$. Consider the least i such that $a_i = 0$ and $b_i = 1$. In iteration i, the algorithm didn't flip b_i to 0, because the resulting string b' would be a 0-input. Since $a \subseteq b'$ and f is monotone, we have $f(a) \leq f(b') = 0$, so $f(a) = 0$.

(ii): For all $c \in \{0,1\}^n$, we show that $\varphi(c) = 1$ iff $f(c) = 1$: If $f(c) = 1$ then $b \subseteq c$ for some minimal 1-input b by *(i)*, so $T_b(c) = 1$ and thus $\varphi(c) = 1$. If $\varphi(c) = 1$ then $T_b(c) = 1$ for some minimal 1-input b, so $b \subseteq c$ and thus $1 = f(b) \leq f(c)$ since f is monotone, so $f(c) = 1$.

(iii): Consider any monotone DNF ψ expressing f, and consider any minimal 1-input b. Since $f(b) = 1$, we have $\psi(b) = 1$. Therefore ψ contains a monotone term T_a for some $a \in \{0,1\}^n$ such that $T_a(b) = 1$ and thus $a \subseteq b$. Since $T_a(a) = 1$, we have $\psi(a) = 1$ and thus $f(a) = 1$. Since b is a minimal 1-input, we have $a = b$. Thus ψ contains T_b.

(iv): The $\Leftarrow$ direction follows from *(ii)*. The $\Rightarrow$ direction follows from *(iii)*. ■

Theorem 13.32. *For the concept class of n-variable t-term monotone DNFs, there exists a* poly(nt)*-time proper exact learner with membership and equivalence queries.*

Proof idea. By Lemma 13.31, it suffices to find the target monotone DNF's minimal 1-inputs, one by one. We use an equivalence query's counterexample as a "foothold" and then use membership queries to "home in on" another minimal 1-input. ■

Proof. The target concept is a t-term monotone DNF φ.

- Membership query: The learner can pick any $a \in \{0,1\}^n$ and get $\varphi(a)$.
- Equivalence query: The learner can pick any t-term monotone DNF hypothesis ψ, find out whether ψ is equivalent to φ, and if not, get some $a \in \{0,1\}^n$ such that $\psi(a) \neq \varphi(a)$.

Assume $\varphi = \bigvee_{\text{minimal 1-input } b} T_b$ (Lemma 13.31). For any $S \subseteq \{0,1\}^n$, define $\psi_S = \bigvee_{b \in S} T_b$.

Exact learner for monotone DNFs	(13.15)

```
initialize S ← ∅
repeat:
    do an equivalence query with hypothesis ψ_S = ⋁_{b∈S} T_b
    if success: output hypothesis ψ_S
    else given counterexample c ∈ {0,1}^n:
        initialize b ← c
        for i ← 1,...,n:
            if b_i = 1:
                let b' ← b but with b'_i ← 0
                do a membership query with b'
                if φ(b') = 1: update b ← b'
        add b to S
```

In every iteration of the outer loop, this learner L finds another minimal 1-input and adds it to S. Once L has found all minimal 1-inputs, ψ_S is φ. Specifically, L maintains the invariant that each string in S is a minimal 1-input of φ (so each term in ψ_S is in φ) and $|S| = k$ after k iterations. To see that the invariant is maintained, suppose it holds at the beginning of an iteration and that ψ_S is a mistake. Since $\psi_S(c) \neq \varphi(c)$, we have $\psi_S(c) = 0$ and $\varphi(c) = 1$ (because if a term of ψ_S evaluates to 1, then the same term of φ would evaluate to 1). Since $\varphi(c) = 1$, the proof of Lemma 13.31.*(i)* shows that L adds a minimal 1-input $b \subseteq c$ to S. Since $\psi_S(c) = 0$ (before adding b to S) and $b \subseteq c$, it follows that b wasn't already in S, so $|S|$ increases.

For each of the $\leq t$ many minimal 1-inputs, L makes one equivalence query mistake and $\leq n$ membership queries. Thus L makes $\leq t$ equivalence query mistakes and $\leq nt$ membership queries. Also, L runs in poly(nt) time. ■

13.7 Learning Circuits

This chapter's grand finale is about the prospect of learning poly-size circuits. The prevailing conjecture is that poly-size circuits aren't poly-time PAC learnable (even improperly, by larger poly-size circuits). If P = NP, then poly-size circuits are poly-time properly PAC learnable: Given $(x^1, c(x^1)), \ldots, (x^m, c(x^m))$ for some size-n^d circuit concept c, we can find a size-n^d circuit hypothesis h consistent with the training data using a search-to-decision reduction to an NP problem. We consider two questions related to that observation:

- Converse: Does P ≠ NP imply that poly-size circuits aren't poly-time PAC learnable? This is an open question, but we prove something almost as strong in § 13.7.1, replacing the P ≠ NP assumption with a standard cryptographic assumption. The connection between learning and cryptography is perhaps an intriguing surprise.
- Strengthening: Does P = NP imply that poly-size circuits are poly-time exactly learnable with equivalence queries? The answer is yes in the improper setting, though we only prove a randomized version in § 13.7.2. This is an application of sampling random NP witnesses using hashing (§ 8.4).

13.7.1 Cryptographic Hardness of PAC Learning

We prove that poly-size circuits aren't poly-time PAC learnable, assuming cryptographic pseudorandom functions exist (which is the case if one-way functions exist). Recall from §12.4.1 that a seeded function $F\colon \{0,1\}^\ell \times \{0,1\}^n \to \{0,1\}$ is a (t,ε)-pseudorandom function (PRF) iff every size-t oracle circuit A (where each oracle gate has n incoming wires and one outgoing wire) can't distinguish by more than ε whether its oracle is $F_s\colon \{0,1\}^n \to \{0,1\}$ where $F_s(x) = F(s,x)$ for a uniformly random seed $s \in \{0,1\}^\ell$, or is a uniformly random function $f\colon \{0,1\}^n \to \{0,1\}$. That is, $\mathbf{Pr}\big[A(F_{U_\ell}) = 1\big]$ and $\mathbf{Pr}\big[A(U_{n\to 1}) = 1\big]$ are within $\pm\varepsilon$, where U_ℓ is the uniform distribution over $\{0,1\}^\ell$, and $U_{n\to 1}$ is the uniform distribution over all $f\colon \{0,1\}^n \to \{0,1\}$. (We don't call the circuit C because C stands for "concept class" in this chapter.) A PRF family is cryptographic iff for every polynomial $t(n) = n^{O(1)}$, there exists a negligible $\varepsilon(n) = 1/n^{\omega(1)}$ such that the family consists of a $(t(n),\varepsilon(n))$-PRF for all n.

Theorem 13.33. *If there exists a poly-time computable cryptographic PRF family, then for some d and all e, there does not exist a poly-time PAC learner for (size-n^d circuits, size-n^e circuits).*

Proof idea. If poly-size circuits can't break the PRF, then poly-size circuits can't be PAC learned. We prove this by reduction: A PAC learner could be used to break the PRF. Given oracle access to some $f\colon \{0,1\}^n \to \{0,1\}$, our distinguisher treats f as a concept, tries to learn f, and tests whether it has learned f: It feeds the learner random training data $(x^1, f(x^1)),\dots,(x^m, f(x^m))$ and accepts iff the resulting hypothesis h succeeds on another random example y.

If f is the PRF with any seed plugged in, then f can be learned: Since the PRF is poly-time computable, f is indeed a concept (a poly-size circuit), so our distinguisher simulates the learner on valid training data. With high probability over $x^1,\dots,x^m$, we have $h(y) = f(y)$ with high probability over y. Thus the distinguisher accepts with high overall probability.

If f is a uniformly random function, then f can't be learned: Unless y happens to be one of the training examples (which happens with low probability over y), $f(y)$ is independent of everything else and hence equals $h(y)$ with probability $1/2$ over f. Thus the distinguisher accepts with overall probability not much more than $1/2$. ■

We prove the following concrete version. The same argument yields the general uniform version (Theorem 13.33).

Theorem 13.34. *If there exists an $(n^{20}, 1/8)$-PRF computed by a size-n^3 circuit, then there does not exist a $(1/8,1/8)$-PAC learner for (size-n^3 circuits, size-n^9 circuits) computed by a size-n^9 circuit.*

Proof. We prove the contrapositive. Suppose $L\colon \big(\{0,1\}^n \times \{0,1\}\big)^m \to H$ is a $(1/8,1/8)$-PAC learner for $(C,H) =$ (size-n^3 circuits, size-n^9 circuits) computed by a size-n^9 circuit. Consider any $F\colon \{0,1\}^\ell \times \{0,1\}^n \to \{0,1\}$ computed by a size-n^3 circuit. We claim F isn't an $(n^{20}, 1/8)$-PRF. For any $(x^1,\dots,x^m,y) \in (\{0,1\}^n)^{m+1}$, define an oracle circuit with oracle $f\colon \{0,1\}^n \to \{0,1\}$:

Oracle circuit to break a pseudorandom function using a PAC learner (13.16)

$A_{x^1,\dots,x^m,y}(f)$:
  query f on each of $x^1,\dots,x^m,y$
  evaluate $L\big((x^1,f(x^1)),\dots,(x^m,f(x^m))\big)$ to get the encoding of a size-n^9 circuit h
  evaluate $h(y)$
  output 1 iff $h(y) = f(y)$

For each seed $s \in \{0,1\}^\ell$, F_s is computed by a size-n^3 circuit (a contraction of F's circuit). If we sample $x^1,\dots,x^m,y$ uniformly at random, then $A_{x^1,\dots,x^m,y}(F_s)$ simulates giving L training data for the concept $c = F_s \in C$ with the uniform distribution $D = U_n$, and testing whether the hypothesis $h \in H$ succeeds on y. Say h is *good* iff $\mathbf{Pr}_y\big[h(y) = c(y)\big] \geq 7/8$. Since L is a $(1/8,1/8)$-PAC learner for (C,H):

$$\mathbf{Pr}\big[A_{U_n^{m+1}}(F_s)=1\big] \geq \mathbf{Pr}\big[h \text{ is good}\big]\cdot\mathbf{Pr}\big[h(y)=c(y)\,\big|\,h \text{ is good}\big] \geq (7/8)\cdot(7/8) > 6/8$$

When $f \sim U_{n\to 1}$, if $y \notin \{x^1,\dots,x^m\}$ then $f(y)$ is an independent uniformly random bit and thus $\mathbf{Pr}\big[h(y)=f(y)\big]=1/2$ conditioned on this event. Since $m \leq n^9 < 2^n/8$:

$$\begin{aligned}\mathbf{Pr}\big[A_{U_n^{m+1}}(U_{n\to 1})=1\big] &\leq \mathbf{Pr}\big[y\in\{x^1,\dots,x^m\}\big]+\mathbf{Pr}\big[h(y)=f(y)\,\big|\,y\notin\{x^1,\dots,x^m\}\big]\\ &\leq m/2^n+1/2 < 5/8\end{aligned}$$

Combining everything:

$$\begin{aligned}&\mathbf{E}_{x^1,\dots,x^m,y}\Big[\mathbf{Pr}\big[A_{x^1,\dots,x^m,y}(F_{U_\ell})=1\big]-\mathbf{Pr}\big[A_{x^1,\dots,x^m,y}(U_{n\to1})=1\big]\Big]\\ =\;&\mathbf{Pr}\big[A_{U_n^{m+1}}(F_{U_\ell})=1\big]-\mathbf{Pr}\big[A_{U_n^{m+1}}(U_{n\to1})=1\big] > 6/8-5/8 = 1/8\end{aligned}$$

So $\mathbf{Pr}\big[A_{x^1,\dots,x^m,y}(F_{U_\ell}) = 1\big]-\mathbf{Pr}\big[A_{x^1,\dots,x^m,y}(U_{n\to1}) = 1\big] > 1/8$ for some outcome $x^1,\dots,x^m,y$. Also, $A_{x^1,\dots,x^m,y}$ has size $\leq n^{20}$ since it has $m+1 \leq n^9+1$ oracle gates, and L's circuit has size $\leq n^9$, and $h(y)$ can be evaluated in $O(n^9)$ time (Lemma 5.10) and thus by a circuit of size $(n^9)^2 \operatorname{polylog} n \leq n^{19}$ (Theorem 5.11). Therefore F isn't an $(n^{20},1/8)$-PRF. ■

Bonus observation: This proof shows that PRFs imply that circuits can't be efficiently PAC learned even when the learner knows D is the uniform distribution over examples, and even when the learner can use membership queries (§ 13.6.1). Membership queries would become additional, adaptive oracle gates in the distinguisher, which is still fine for breaking the PRF.

13.7.2 Exact Learning

We conclude the chapter by proving that if $\mathsf{NP} \subseteq \mathsf{BPP}$, then the concept class of poly-size circuits has a poly-time improper randomized exact learner with equivalence queries.

Halving (§13.6.2) is a generic approach to exact learning with equivalence queries. Halving is mistake-efficient but generally time-inefficient since the hypotheses can be huge: Each hypothesis computes the majority value of an arbitrary subset—potentially all—of the concepts. For example, if concepts are size-n^d circuits, then the halving algorithm's first hypothesis computes the majority value of all (exponentially many) size-n^d circuits. The first step toward making halving feasible is to restrict it to small hypotheses, which compute the majority value of only a few concepts. The tradeoff is that the learner uses randomness: A few randomly selected concepts are probably "representative" of all the concepts. We now define and analyze this generic *randomized halving* algorithm, as a warmup for our learner for poly-size circuits.

Deterministic halving makes $\log|C|$ mistakes, and each hypothesis combines up to $|C|$ concepts. Randomized halving makes $O(\log|C|)$ mistakes (almost as good!), and each hypothesis combines up to $O(n+\log\log|C|+\log\frac{1}{\delta})$ concepts (much better!), where δ is the error probability.

For a *randomized* (δ,k)*-mistake learner*, with probability $\geq 1-\delta$ over its internal randomness, it makes at most k mistakes no matter which counterexamples are provided. With the remaining probability, the learner may either abort (output nothing) or succeed after more mistakes. We now consider hypotheses that compute majorities of tuples—rather than sets—of concepts:

- Recall that for any set $B \subseteq C$, we defined the hypothesis $\textsc{Maj}_B$ by $\textsc{Maj}_B(x) = 1$ iff $b(x) = 1$ for at least half of all $b \in B$.
- Now, for any tuple $\beta = (b^1, b^2, \ldots, b^\ell) \in C^\ell = C \times C \times \cdots \times C$, we define the hypothesis $\textsc{Maj}_\beta$ by $\textsc{Maj}_\beta(x) = 1$ iff $b^j(x) = 1$ for at least half of all $j \in [\ell]$.

Lemma 13.35. *For every concept class C, there exists a randomized (δ, k)-mistake learner for (C, H) where $k = \lfloor \log_{3/2} |C| \rfloor$ and $H = \{\textsc{Maj}_\beta : \beta \in C^\ell\}$ assuming $\ell \geq 36 \ln \frac{2k2^n}{\delta}$.*

Proof.

Randomized halving mistake bound learner (13.17)

initialize $B \leftarrow C$
repeat:
  sample $\beta \in B^\ell$ uniformly at random
  do an equivalence query with hypothesis $\textsc{Maj}_\beta$
  if success: output hypothesis $\textsc{Maj}_\beta$
  else given counterexample $a \in \{0,1\}^n$: remove from B every b with $b(a) = \textsc{Maj}_\beta(a)$

Consider any target concept c. For each mistake, the counterexample a says $c(a) = \overline{\textsc{Maj}_\beta(a)}$. The learner removes from B every b with $b(a) \neq c(a)$. Thus it maintains the invariant that $c \in B$.

We claim that with probability $\geq 1 - \delta$, the learner maintains the invariant that $|B| \leq |C|(2/3)^i$ after i iterations. In that event, after $k = \lfloor \log_{3/2} |C| \rfloor$ mistakes, we have $|B| \leq |C|(2/3)^k < |C|(2/3)^{(\log_{3/2}|C|)-1} = 3/2$ and thus $|B| = 1$. Then the learner succeeds because $\textsc{Maj}_\beta$ equals the only remaining concept in B, which must be the target concept c.

To prove the claim, by a union bound it suffices to show that in each iteration in which $|B| > 1$, with probability $\geq 1 - \delta/k$ over β, the learner either succeeds or removes $\geq 1/3$ fraction of B. Consider any such iteration. For each $x \in \{0,1\}^n$, let p_x be the fraction of $b \in B$ with $b(x) = 1$, and let q_x be the fraction of $j \in [\ell]$ with $b^j(x) = 1$, so q_x is a random variable that depends on the outcome of $\beta = (b^1, \ldots, b^\ell)$. Then q_x is the fraction of heads among ℓ tosses of a coin with heads probability p_x. Since $\ell \geq 36 \ln \frac{2k2^n}{\delta}$, with probability $\geq 1 - \delta/k2^n$ we have $|q_x - p_x| \leq 1/6$ (Corollary 7.21). By a union bound, with probability $\geq 1 - \delta/k$ we have $|q_x - p_x| \leq 1/6$ for all x simultaneously. Assume the latter event occurs, and consider any counterexample a. We have $b^j(a) = \textsc{Maj}_\beta(a)$ for $\geq 1/2$ fraction of all $j \in [\ell]$ (by definition of $\textsc{Maj}_\beta$) and thus $b(a) = \textsc{Maj}_\beta(a)$ for $\geq 1/2 - 1/6 = 1/3$ fraction of all $b \in B$, since $|q_a - p_a| \leq 1/6$. Thus $\geq 1/3$ fraction of B is removed. ■

Theorem 13.36. *If* NP $\subseteq$ BPP *then for every integer $d \geq 1$, there exists a poly-time randomized $(2^{-n}, \text{poly}\, n)$-mistake learner for (size-n^d circuits, size-n^{d+2} circuits).*

Proof idea. Randomized halving reins in the hypothesis class, but how can we efficiently sample random elements of B? We can sample random NP witnesses in poly time using an NP oracle (§8.4.2). The remaining concepts in B are witnesses for a verifier that checks whether a circuit is consistent with the "training data" from the counterexamples so far.

The analysis is like the proof of Lemma 13.35. Two inconsequential issues arise:

- The sampler's distribution is approximately (not perfectly) uniform over B.
- Different circuits may correspond to the same function (concept). A counterexample rules out 1/3 of the circuits, not necessarily 1/3 of the functions they compute. ■

Proof (ancillary). Consider any n. Let C be the concept class of size-n^d circuits $c\colon \{0,1\}^n \to \{0,1\}$. Different size-$n^d$ circuits may compute the same function as each other, but are considered different elements of C. Let H be the hypothesis class of size-n^{d+2} circuits h. Let $\delta = 2^{-n}$ and $k = \lfloor \log_{3/2}((4(n^d)^2)^{n^d}) \rfloor \geq \lfloor \log_{3/2}|C| \rfloor$ and $\ell = \lceil 144 \ln \frac{4k2^n}{\delta} \rceil$. (To avoid the issue of computing natural log in our model, we could round ln up to $\log_2$.)

The learner maintains the tuple $\alpha = \big((a^1, c(a^1)), (a^2, c(a^2)), \ldots\big)$ of correctly labeled counterexamples so far, where $c \in C$ is the target concept. A concept b is consistent with α iff $b(a^i) = c(a^i)$ for all i. Let $B_\alpha = \{b \in C : b \text{ is consistent with } \alpha\}$ be the remaining concepts.

We claim that if NP ⊆ BPP then there exists a poly-time randomized program Π such that if $B_\alpha \neq \emptyset$, then $\Pi(\alpha)$ aborts with probability $\leq \delta/2(k+1)\ell$ and conditioned on not aborting, it outputs a sample from a distribution D_α that's approximately uniform over B_α: $D_\alpha(b) \leq 5/4|B_\alpha|$ for each $b \in B_\alpha$, and $D_\alpha(b) = 0$ for each $b \notin B_\alpha$. This follows from Theorem 8.14: $\Pi(\alpha)$ constructs a poly-size circuit A_α such that $A_\alpha(b) = 1$ iff $b \in B_\alpha$. (A_α checks that b encodes a size-n^d circuit, evaluates $b(a^i)$ for all i, and outputs 1 iff $b(a^i) = c(a^i)$ for all i.) Then, $\Pi(\alpha)$ runs a fully poly-time randomized program for Circuit Sat Approximate Sampling on input $\big(A_\alpha, 1/5, \delta/2(k+1)\ell\big)$. For each $b \in B_\alpha$, $\mathbf{Pr}\big[\Pi(\alpha) = b\big] \leq 6/5|B_\alpha|$ and so $D_\alpha(b) \leq \big(6/5|B_\alpha|\big)/\big(1 - \delta/2(k+1)\ell\big) \leq 5/4|B_\alpha|$. This proves the claim.

D_α^ℓ is the distribution over B_α^ℓ where each coordinate is an independent sample from D_α.

Here's a randomized (δ, k)-mistake learner for (C, H).

Randomized exact learner for circuits assuming NP ⊆ BPP (13.18)

```
initialize α ← empty tuple
compute k and ℓ
repeat k + 1 times:
    sample β ~ D_α^ℓ by running Π(α) ℓ times (and aborting if any run aborts)
    construct a circuit h ∈ H that computes MAJ_β
    do an equivalence query with hypothesis h
    if success: output hypothesis h
    else given counterexample a ∈ {0,1}^n: append (a, ¬h(a)) to α
abort
```

Consider any target concept c. For each mistake, the counterexample a says $c(a) = \overline{h(a)}$. Thus the learner maintains the invariant that c is consistent with α, in other words, $c \in B_\alpha$.

The learner runs Π at most $(k+1)\ell$ times, each of which has probability $\leq \delta/2(k+1)\ell$ of aborting. By a union bound, with probability $\geq 1 - \delta/2$, no run of Π aborts. Henceforth, we condition on the latter event and show that the learner succeeds after $\leq k$ mistakes with probability $\geq 1 - \delta/2$. This implies the overall probability of success after $\leq k$ mistakes is $\geq (1-\delta/2)(1-\delta/2) \geq 1-\delta$.

We claim that with probability $\geq 1 - \delta/2$, the learner maintains the invariant that $|B_\alpha| \leq |C|(2/3)^i$ after i iterations. In that event, after $k \geq \lfloor \log_{3/2}|C| \rfloor$ mistakes, we have $|B_\alpha| \leq |C|(2/3)^k < 3/2$ and thus $|B_\alpha| = 1$. Then the learner succeeds because h is equivalent to the only remaining concept in B_α, which must be the target concept c.

To prove the claim, by a union bound it suffices to show that in each iteration in which $|B_\alpha| > 1$, with probability $\geq 1 - \delta/2k$ over β, the learner either succeeds or has $|B_{\alpha'}| \leq |B_\alpha| \cdot 2/3$ where α and α' are from before and after the iteration, respectively. Consider any such iteration. For each $x \in \{0,1\}^n$, let $p_x = \mathbf{Pr}_{b \sim D_\alpha}\big[b(x) = 1\big]$, and let q_x be the fraction of $j \in [\ell]$ with $b^j(x) = 1$, so q_x is a random variable that depends on the outcome of $\beta = (b^1, \ldots, b^\ell)$. Then q_x

is the fraction of heads among ℓ tosses of a coin with heads probability p_x. Since $\ell \geq 144 \ln \frac{4k2^n}{\delta}$, with probability $\geq 1-\delta/2k2^n$ we have $|q_x - p_x| \leq 1/12$ (Corollary 7.21). By a union bound, with probability $\geq 1-\delta/2k$ we have $|q_x - p_x| \leq 1/12$ for all x simultaneously. Assume the latter event occurs, and consider any counterexample a. We have $b^j(a) = h(a)$ for $\geq 1/2$ fraction of all $j \in [\ell]$ (by definition of MAJ_β) and thus $\mathbf{Pr}_{b\sim D_\alpha}\big[b(a) = h(a)\big] \geq 1/2 - 1/12 = 5/12$, since $|q_a - p_a| \leq 1/12$. Therefore the fraction of B_α that's not in $B_{\alpha'}$ is:

$$\textstyle\sum_{b\in B_\alpha : b(a)=h(a)} 1/|B_\alpha| \;\geq\; \sum_{b\in B_\alpha : b(a)=h(a)} D_\alpha(b)\cdot 4/5 \;=\; \mathbf{Pr}_{b\sim D_\alpha}\big[b(a)=h(a)\big]\cdot 4/5 \;\geq\; 1/3$$

The learner runs in poly n time since $k \in \text{poly}\, n$ and $\ell \in \text{poly}\, n$. We have $h \in H$ in each iteration since h consists of ℓ size-n^d circuits plus $\leq 10\ell \log \ell$ gates and wires to compute the majority, and thus h has size $\leq \ell n^d + 10\ell \log \ell \leq O(nn^d + n \log n) \leq n^{d+2}$ since $\ell \leq O(n)$. ■

If $\mathsf{P} = \mathsf{NP}$ then $\mathsf{P} = \mathsf{PH}$ (Theorem 4.21), in which case this learner can be derandomized along the lines of $\mathsf{BPP} \subseteq \mathsf{PH}$ (Theorem 7.10). We won't go through the details.

Exercises

13.1 Viewing $\{0,1\}^n$ as binary numbers $\{0,1,\ldots,2^n-1\}$, let $C = \{c_{\ell,u} : \ell, u \in \{0,1\}^n\}$ be the concept class of *interval functions*, where $c_{\ell,u}\colon \{0,1\}^n \to \{0,1\}$ is defined by $c_{\ell,u}(x) = 1$ iff $\ell \leq x \leq u$. (If $u = 2^n - 1$ then $c_{\ell,u}$ is a threshold function. If $\ell = u$ then $c_{\ell,u}$ is a point function. If $\ell > u$ then $c_{\ell,u}$ is the constant-0 function.)

- **(a)** Design a proper m-consistent learner for C (for arbitrary m).
- **(b)** According to Theorem 13.4, how much training data suffices for a consistent learner to be a (δ,ε)-PAC learner for C?
- **(c)** Prove that in fact, if $m \geq \frac{2}{\varepsilon} \ln \frac{2}{\delta}$ then your learner from Exercise 13.1.a is a (δ,ε)-PAC learner for C.

13.2 For any $S \subseteq \{0,1\}^n$, define the concept $c^S\colon \{0,1\}^n \to \{0,1\}$ by $c^S(x) = 1$ iff $x \in S$.

- **(a)** For a parameter k, consider the class $C = \{c^S : |S| \leq k\}$ of concepts that evaluate to 1 on at most k examples. Design a proper m-consistent learner for C (for arbitrary m), and prove that if $m \geq \frac{k}{\varepsilon} \ln \frac{k}{\delta}$ then your learner is a (δ,ε)-PAC learner for C.
- **(b)** For a parameter k, consider the class $C = \{c^S : |S| = k\}$ of concepts that evaluate to 1 on exactly k examples. Design a proper m-consistent learner for C (for arbitrary m), and prove that if $m \geq \frac{2k}{\varepsilon} \ln \frac{2k}{\delta\varepsilon}$ then every m-consistent learner for C is a (δ,ε)-PAC learner for C. (When $k = 1$, this matches Theorem 13.2 for point functions.)

13.3 An *m-nearly consistent learner* for (C,H) is a function $L\colon \big(\{0,1\}^n \times \{0,1\}\big)^m \to H$ such that for every concept $c \in C$ and every tuple $(x^1,\ldots,x^m)$, $L\big((x^1,c(x^1)),\ldots,(x^m,c(x^m))\big)$ outputs a hypothesis $h \in H$ *nearly consistent* with the training data, meaning that $h(x^i) = c(x^i)$ for all except possibly one index $i \in [m]$. Prove that if $m \geq \frac{2}{\varepsilon} \ln \frac{|H|}{\delta\varepsilon} + 1$ then every m-nearly consistent learner for (C,H) is a (δ,ε)-PAC learner for (C,H).

13.4 Run the algorithm from §13.2.2 to find a term consistent with this training data:

$$(001100,1),\ (000101,0),\ (101100,1),\ (001110,1),\ (101010,0),\ (100100,1)$$

13.5 Run the algorithm from §13.2.3 to find a decision list consistent with this training data:

$$(0010,0),\ (1111,0),\ (0101,1),\ (0110,1),\ (1010,1)$$

13.6 Find a decision list that computes the threshold function defined by $c_a(x) = 1$ iff $x \geq a$ where $a = 010110$.

13.7 Prove that for every $c\colon \{0,1\}^n \to \{0,1\}$, there exists a decision list for c iff for every nonempty $S \subseteq \{0,1\}^n$, either c is constant on S or there exist $b \in \{0,1\}$ and a literal ℓ that accepts a string in $S \cap c^{-1}(b)$ but none in $S \cap c^{-1}(\overline{b})$.

13.8 Design a poly-time proper m-consistent learner (for arbitrary m) for the concept class of 2-term DNFs in which at least one variable appears positively in one term and negatively in the other term. (There's no such learner for arbitrary 2-term DNFs unless $\mathsf{NP} = \mathsf{RP}$.)

13.9 Prove that every concept class C has a learning reduction to the concept class of dictatorships on $|C|$ variables.

13.10 (a) Let C be the concept class of point functions and the constant-0 function on n variables. Let C' be the concept class of point functions on $n+1$ variables. Exhibit a learning reduction from C to C'.

(b) Let C be any concept class such that for some concepts $c^1, c^2 \in C$ and some examples x^1, x^2, we have $c^1(x^1) = 0$ and $c^1(x^2) = c^2(x^1) = c^2(x^2) = 1$. Let C' be the concept class of point functions on some number of variables (it doesn't matter how many). Prove that there does not exist a learning reduction from C to C'.

13.11 Prove that every 4-clause CNF on $n \geq 4$ variables is equivalent to some 4-DNF.

13.12 (a) Prove that unless $\mathsf{NP} = \mathsf{RP}$, there's no poly-time proper PAC learner for the concept class $C = \{c_I\colon \{0,1\}^n \times [n] \to \{0,1\} : I \subseteq [n]\}$ where $c_I(x,t) = 1$ iff $\sum_{i \in I} x_i \geq t$. Hint: Prove INDEPENDENT SET $\leq_p^m$ CONSISTENCY FOR C.

(b) Prove that unless $\mathsf{NP} = \mathsf{RP}$, there's no poly-time proper PAC learner for the concept class $C = \{c_{I,t}\colon \{0,1\}^n \to \{0,1\} : I \subseteq [n] \text{ and } t \in [n]\}$ where $c_{I,t}(x) = 1$ iff $\sum_{i \in I} x_i \geq t$. (These are halfspaces with boolean weights.) Hint: Start with the idea from Exercise 13.12.a. On input (G,k), create k extra variables (besides G's nodes) and extra training examples to enforce $t = k$.

13.13 Find the VC dimension and growth function of the concept class in Figure 13.15.

13.14 Find the VC dimension of the class of interval functions from Exercise 13.1.

13.15 Find the VC dimension of the class of literals (dictatorships and anti-dictatorships) on n variables.

13.16 Prove that if there exists a learning reduction from C to C', then C's VC dimension is at most C''s VC dimension.

13.17 Prove that the parity function $\oplus(x) = x_1 \oplus x_2 \oplus \cdots \oplus x_n$ is not a halfspace if $n \geq 2$.

13.18 Prove that the class of decision lists on n variables has VC dimension $n+1$.

(a) Prove the VC dimension is $\geq n+1$. Hint: Terms and clauses are special cases of decision lists. Show that the set S from the corresponding result for halfspaces (Lemma 13.14) is also shattered by decision lists.

x	C				
00	0	1	0	0	1
01	1	1	1	0	1
10	0	0	1	0	0
11	1	0	1	1	1

Figure 13.15: Concept class for Exercise 13.13

x	C				
00	0	1	1	0	1
01	1	0	0	1	0
10	1	1	0	1	0
11	0	0	1	1	0

Figure 13.16: Concept class for Exercise 13.20

(b) Prove the VC dimension is $\le n+1$. Hint: Show that every decision list is equivalent to a halfspace. Then, apply Lemma 13.14.

13.19 In §13.4.3 we proved that if a concept class C has VC dimension d, then $g_C(m) \le \binom{m}{0} + \binom{m}{1} + \cdots + \binom{m}{d}$ for all $m > d$. Prove this is tight: For every $n > \log d$, there exists a class C of concepts $c\colon \{0,1\}^n \to \{0,1\}$ with VC dimension d and $g_C(m) = \binom{m}{0} + \binom{m}{1} + \cdots + \binom{m}{d}$ for all $m > d$.

13.20 Recall the recursive algorithm for finding $|C|$ many sets shattered by a concept class C (Lemma 13.16). For the C in Figure 13.16, find C_T and C_T^* when $y = 11$ and $T = \{00, 01, 10\}$. After find-shattered(C_T) returns $\{\emptyset, \{00\}, \{10\}\}$ and find-shattered(C_T^*) returns $\{\emptyset, \{00\}\}$, what does find-shattered(C) return?

13.21 Consider any concept class C. For some parameter t, define C' as the concept class of all conjunctions of t concepts from C. That is, $c' \in C'$ iff $c'(x) = c^1(x) \wedge c^2(x) \wedge \cdots \wedge c^t(x)$ for some $c^1, \dots, c^t \in C$. Prove that if C has VC dimension d, then C' has VC dimension $< 2dt \log(3t)$. Hint: Use Lemma 13.15.

13.22 Prove that if a concept class C has VC dimension $d \ge 2$ and $\varepsilon < 0.1$, then every $(0.01, \varepsilon)$-PAC learner for (C, H) uses at least $0.01d/\varepsilon$ training examples.

Hint: Adapt the proof of Theorem 13.21. Consider a size-d shattered set S, and let $z \in S$ be an arbitrary distinguished element. Define the distribution D by $D(z) = 1 - 10\varepsilon$ and $D(y) = 10\varepsilon/(d-1)$ for all $y \in S \setminus \{z\}$. Let D' be the uniform distribution over $S \setminus \{z\}$. Show that achieving $\mathbf{Pr}_{y\sim D}\big[h(y) = c(y)\big] \ge 1 - \varepsilon$ requires achieving $\mathbf{Pr}_{y\sim D'}\big[h(y) = c(y)\big] \ge 0.9$, and that probably only a $O(\varepsilon)$ fraction of the training examples are $\neq z$, so $\Omega(1/\varepsilon)$ times as much training data is needed compared to Theorem 13.21.

13.23 Regarding AdaBoost (Theorem 13.23): Suppose we're content with L' finding a hypothesis that agrees with the target concept on $\ge 1 - \beta$ fraction of the training examples (rather than all of them). Prove that $t \ge \frac{1}{2\gamma^2} \ln \frac{1}{\beta}$ iterations of AdaBoost suffice for this.

13.24 Prove that every class C of concepts $c\colon \{0,1\}^n \to \{0,1\}$ has a proper 2^n-mistake learner.

13.25 In §13.6.1 we described how to turn an exact learner with equivalence queries into a consistent learner, which is automatically a PAC learner. Here's a more direct way to turn an exact learner with equivalence queries into a PAC learner. Suppose L is a k-mistake learner for (C, H). For any $\ell \ge \frac{1}{\varepsilon} \ln \frac{k}{\delta}$ and $m = k\ell$, define a learner L' that takes m labeled examples $(x^{i,j}, c(x^{i,j}))$ for $i \in [k]$ and $j \in [\ell]$:

PAC learner using a mistake bound learner	(13.19)
initialize $h \leftarrow L$'s first hypothesis	
for $i \leftarrow 1,\dots,k$:	
if $h(x^{i,j}) = c(x^{i,j})$ for all $j \in [\ell]$: halt and output h	
else: give L some counterexample $x^{i,j}$ and update $h \leftarrow L$'s next hypothesis	
output h	

Prove L' is a (δ, ε)-PAC learner for (C, H).

13.26 Let C be the concept class of terms on n variables.

(a) Prove that for every $H \supseteq C$ that doesn't contain the constant 0 function, the mistake complexity of (C, H) is either $2^n - 1$ or 2^n. You may use Exercise 13.24.

(b) Prove that for every $H \supseteq C$ that contains the constant 0 function, the mistake complexity of (C, H) is either n or $n+1$.

13.27 Prove that the concept class of decision lists on n variables has mistake complexity $O(n^2)$. Hint: Imagine that a decision list is a permutation of all $4n+2$ possible "items": the $4n$ triples (j, a, b) and the 2 terminals (output 0 or output 1). The part of the permutation after the first terminal node wouldn't really exist, but we imagine it exists (and is never reached) for convenience. Also imagine that the items are partitioned into contiguous "levels" for specifying and analyzing the learner. (The levels don't affect the decision list's behavior.) The start item is in level 1. Levels may be empty. The learner begins with an arbitrary permutation and with all items in level 1. For each counterexample, it moves the item that caused the erroneous output to the next level. Prove this is a $O(n^2)$-mistake learner.

13.28 Prove that if there exists a learning reduction from (C, H) to (C', H'), then (C, H)'s mistake complexity is at most (C', H')'s mistake complexity.

13.29 The "membership + equivalence" complexity of exactly learning (C, H) is the minimum k such that there exists an exact learner whose total number of membership queries and equivalence query mistakes is always $\leq k$. Now, you'll develop and apply a technique for lower bounding this complexity, similar to the technique in §13.6.3.

(a) Formulate a game between a learner and a teacher, such that the complexity is $\leq k$ iff there exists a learner strategy that guarantees the game ends after $\leq k$ rounds.

(b) Prove that if $C = H$ is the class of point functions, then the complexity is $\geq 2^n - 1$. Membership queries have no advantage over equivalence queries here.

(c) Prove that if C is the class of dictatorships and $H \supseteq C$, then the complexity is $\geq \lfloor \log n \rfloor$. Membership queries have no advantage over equivalence queries here.

(d) Prove that if C is the class of threshold functions and $H \supseteq C$, then the complexity is $\geq n$. Membership queries have no advantage over equivalence queries here.

13.30 Recall that an equivalence query asks whether $\{x : h(x) = 1\} = \{x : c(x) = 1\}$ and if not, asks for a counterexample x such that $h(x) \neq c(x)$.

(a) A *subset query* asks whether $\{x : h(x) = 1\} \subseteq \{x : c(x) = 1\}$ and if not, asks for a counterexample x such that $h(x) = 1$ and $c(x) = 0$. A *superset query* asks whether $\{x : h(x) = 1\} \supseteq \{x : c(x) = 1\}$ and if not, asks for a counterexample x such that $h(x) = 0$ and $c(x) = 1$. Show that any equivalence query can be simulated with a subset query along with a superset query.

(b) A *weak subset query* asks whether $\{x : h(x) = 1\} \subseteq \{x : c(x) = 1\}$. A *weak superset query* asks whether $\{x : h(x) = 1\} \supseteq \{x : c(x) = 1\}$. Show that any subset query with hypothesis class $H = \{n\text{-variable size-}s\text{ circuits}\}$ can be simulated with $n+1$ weak subset queries with hypothesis class $H' = \{n\text{-variable size-}(s+10n)\text{ circuits}\}$ (and similarly for superset). Thus, weak subset and weak superset queries together are essentially as powerful as equivalence queries.

13.31 Define $\text{MAJ}: \{0,1\}^3 \to \{0,1\}$ by $\text{MAJ}(x) = 1$ iff $x_1 + x_2 + x_3 \geq 2$. Define the monotone function $f: \{0,1\}^6 \to \{0,1\}$ by $f(x) = \text{MAJ}(x_1x_2x_3) \wedge \text{MAJ}(x_4x_5x_6)$. What are f's minimal 1-inputs? What is f's unique smallest monotone DNF?

13.32 Prove that the class of all n-variable monotone functions has VC dimension $\binom{n}{\lfloor n/2 \rfloor}$. For upper bounding the VC dimension, you may use (without proving it) the following standard theorem in combinatorics: For every set Z of more than $\binom{n}{\lfloor n/2 \rfloor}$ subsets of $[n]$, there exist distinct $A, B \in Z$ such that $A \subseteq B$. Hint: You may also use Lemma 13.31 and may refer to the proof of Lemma 13.13 for inspiration.

13.33 Prove that the concept class of n-variable t-term DNFs has a $\text{poly}(n^{\log(t/\varepsilon)} \log \frac{1}{\delta})$-time improper (δ, ε)-PAC learner that works for the uniform distribution $D = U_n$ on $\{0,1\}^n$ (but not necessarily for other distributions). Specifically, prove that the following learner works. Let $k = \lfloor \log(2t/\varepsilon) \rfloor$ and $K = n^k$. Assuming $8 \leq k \leq n$, at most K terms have width $\leq k$ (similar to the proof of Lemma 13.15). The learner takes $m \geq \frac{2K}{\varepsilon} \ln \frac{K}{\delta}$ training examples $(x^1, \varphi(x^1)), \ldots, (x^m, \varphi(x^m))$ where φ is the target t-term DNF concept and each $x^i \sim U_n$. The learner outputs the DNF hypothesis ψ which is the disjunction of all terms T of width $\leq k$ for which no training example has $T(x^i) = 1$ and $\varphi(x^i) = 0$. (This is improper because there may be more than t such terms.) Hint: Error with $\psi(y) = 0$ and $\varphi(y) = 1$ is due to terms of width $> k$ in φ but not in ψ. Error with $\psi(y) = 1$ and $\varphi(y) = 0$ is due to terms of width $\leq k$ in ψ but not in φ.

13.34 This exercise is about the complexity of computing the VC dimension of a concept class C that's given as input. Here, C consists of concepts $c^a: \{0,1\}^n \to \{0,1\}$ indexed by strings $a \in \{0,1\}^\ell$. If $a \neq a'$, then c^a and $c^{a'}$ are allowed to be the same function.

(a) Prove that the following problem is in $\mathsf{NP} \cap \mathsf{TIME}[N^{O(\log N)}]$.

TRUTH TABLE VC DIMENSION	(13.20)
Input:	Concept class C specified by each concept's truth table, namely the bit $c^a(b)$ for each $a \in \{0,1\}^\ell$ and $b \in \{0,1\}^n$, and positive integer $d \leq \ell$
Output:	Is C's VC dimension $\geq d$?

(b) Prove that the following problem is $\Sigma_3\mathsf{P}$-complete.

Succinct VC Dimension	(13.21)
Input:	Concept class C specified by a circuit E such that $E(a,b) = c^a(b)$ for each $a \in \{0,1\}^\ell$ and $b \in \{0,1\}^n$, and positive integer $d \le \ell$
Output:	Is C's VC dimension $\ge d$?

To prove Σ_3P-hardness, reduce from the following problem, which is known to be Σ_3P-complete (analogous to Exercise 4.14.a).

Adjusted Σ_3Sat	(13.22)
Input:	CNF $\varphi(x,y,z)$ with three groups of k variables each, where k is a power of 2
Output:	Does there exist $x \in \{0,1\}^k$ such that for all $y \in \{0,1\}^k \setminus \{0^k\}$, there exists $z \in \{0,1\}^k$ such that φ is satisfied?

("Adjusted" refers to the size of each variable group being a power of 2, and to the domain of $\forall y$ being nonzero assignments, which are minor but useful details.) Hint: Map φ to (E,d) as follows: Let $\ell = 3k$ and view $a = (x,y,z) \in (\{0,1\}^k)^3$. Let $n = k + \log k$ and view $b = (w,i) \in \{0,1\}^k \times [k]$. Let $E(a,b) = 1$ iff $w = x$ and $y_i = 1$ and $\varphi(x,y,z) = 1$. Let $d = k$. Prove that this mapping reduction works.

Notes

Computational learning theory was introduced by [536]. A standard text on the subject is [299].

Consistent learning is also called "empirical risk minimization (ERM)."

Theorem 13.4 (consistent learners with enough training data are PAC learners) is due to [73] and is regarded as a formulation of "Occam's razor."

The algorithm for learning decision lists (§ 13.2.3) is due to [444].

Learning reductions (§ 13.3.1) were introduced by [415].

NP-hardness of properly learning k-term DNFs for $k \ge 2$ (Theorem 13.7 for $k = 3$) is due to [414].

VC dimension was introduced by Vapnik and Chervonenkis [538]. The lemma that C's growth function is bounded by a polynomial whose degree is C's VC dimension (Lemma 13.15) is known as the "Sauer–Shelah lemma" and is due to [538, 461, 487]. Lemma 13.16 is due to [406].

The sample complexity upper bound in terms of VC dimension (Theorem 13.17) is due to [74]. The $\log \frac{1}{\varepsilon}$ factor can be removed from the upper bound in the setting of improper randomized learning [232, 326]. The sample complexity lower bound in terms of VC dimension (Theorem 13.21 and Exercise 13.22) is due to [156].

AdaBoost (Theorem 13.23) is due to [175].

The mistake bound model (§ 13.6.2) is also called the "online mistake bound model," where "online" refers not to the internet, but to how the algorithm must repeatedly produce some output (a tentative hypothesis, in this case) before receiving subsequent input (counterexamples). A characterization of mistake complexity (for exact learning with equivalence queries) is in [342].

The exact learner for poly-size monotone DNFs with membership and equivalence queries (Theorem 13.32) is due to [26]. Minimal terms are also called "prime implicants."

The improper exact learner for poly-size circuits with equivalence queries and an NP oracle (Theorem 13.36) is due to [94].

This chapter focused on the *realizable* setting, in which the target concept c comes from a known class C and the label of each training example x^i is guaranteed to be $c(x^i)$. In the *agnostic* setting, c might not come from a specific concept class, but the learner still tries to find a hypothesis that's as good as possible. In the *noisy* setting, random noise may corrupt the labels of training examples, so with some probability, x^i's label might not be $c(x^i)$. These generalizations of PAC learning reflect practical issues in machine learning.

Exercise 13.7 is due to [213]. Exercise 13.12.b is due to [414]. The combinatorial theorem mentioned in Exercise 13.32 is known as "Sperner's theorem" [502]. Exercise 13.33 is due to [544]. Exercise 13.34.b is due to [465].

Quasi-polynomial-time improper learning of poly-size DNFs under the uniform distribution (Exercise 13.33) can be improved to polynomial time with membership queries, using techniques related to boosting (§ 13.5.2) and to hardcore bits (§ 12.3.3) [269]. For the fastest known distribution-free PAC learner for DNFs (without membership queries), see [314]. Under a cryptographic assumption, membership queries don't help for PAC learning DNFs [27].

Chapter 14

Optimization

In an optimization problem, the goal is to output not just any solution, but a "best" solution. Optimization is prevalent in engineering, machine learning, operations research, finance, and other fields. Here are some practical example scenarios:

- A ridesharing or food delivery company determines which drivers to dispatch to which customers, to minimize customers' waiting times.
- A university determines which courses to offer, and when and where and taught by whom, to maximize students' enrollment in courses they need.
- A manufacturing company determines where to build factories, to minimize transportation costs and so forth.
- A producer of integrated circuits determines how to arrange components on a chip, to maximize things like speed, reliability, and energy efficiency.

Definition. An *optimization problem* associates two things to each valid input x:

- A nonempty set F_x of *feasible solutions*.
- An *objective function* $f_x : F_x \to \mathbb{R}_{\geq 0}$, which assigns a nonnegative *objective value* $f_x(s)$ to each feasible solution s.

There are two kinds of optimization problems:

- *Minimization*: The goal is to output a feasible solution of smallest objective value.
- *Maximization*: The goal is to output a feasible solution of largest objective value. ◀

Feasible means a solution must obey certain constraints specified by x. For example: In the ridesharing application, assigning a driver to two customers without sufficient time to travel between them would be infeasible. In the course scheduling application, assigning two courses to the same room with overlapping times would be infeasible.

Many interesting optimization problems have an NP-complete decision problem analogue: Given x and k, does there exist a feasible solution with objective value $\leq k$ (for minimization) or $\geq k$ (for maximization)? Such optimization problems are NP-hard (assuming objective functions are poly-time computable), so presumably poly-time algorithms for them are not forthcoming.

Approximation algorithms cope with NP-hardness by finding a feasible solution that's "almost optimal," meaning its objective value is not too far from the best possible. In practice, there's a time-quality tradeoff: Eking out a slightly better solution might not be worth a big slowdown. (We saw in Chapter 10 that heuristics cope with NP-hardness by sacrificing the output's correctness on some inputs. In contrast, approximation algorithms sacrifice the output's quality on all inputs.) Some NP-hard optimization problems are more amenable to approximation than others: Some can be approximated very well in poly time, while for others, achieving even a modest approximation remains NP-hard.

14.1 Approximation Algorithms

For any optimization problem, any algorithm that always outputs a feasible solution, and any valid input x:

- ALG denotes the objective value of the solution output by the algorithm.
- OPT denotes the objective value of an optimal solution:

$$\begin{aligned} OPT &= \min_{s \in F_x} f_x(s) \quad \text{for minimization} \\ OPT &= \max_{s \in F_x} f_x(s) \quad \text{for maximization} \end{aligned}$$

The closer ALG is to OPT, the better. It's common to measure the closeness as a ratio. A c-*approximation* algorithm achieves:

$$\begin{aligned} ALG &\leq c \cdot OPT \quad \text{for minimization, where } 1 < c < \infty \\ ALG &\geq c \cdot OPT \quad \text{for maximization, where } 0 < c < 1 \end{aligned}$$

The closer c is to 1, the better. (Sometimes people call this a $1/c$-approximation.)

Proving that an algorithm achieves some approximation ratio c is often tricky because we don't know OPT. How can we compare the algorithm's solution to an optimal solution, when the whole point is that we can't find the latter? In this section, we design poly-time approximation algorithms that exemplify a few analysis techniques.

14.1.1 Min Node Cover

Node Cover is NP-complete (Corollary 2.18), so we don't expect a poly-time exact algorithm for the optimization version:

Min Node Cover	(14.1)
Input:	Undirected graph G
Output:	A node cover for G with as few nodes as possible

A feasible solution is any node cover S for G, and its objective value is $|S|$.

Theorem 14.1. Min Node Cover *has a poly-time* 2*-approximation algorithm.*

Proof idea. To show $ALG \leq 2 \cdot OPT$, we'll identify a number d such that $ALG \leq 2 \cdot d$ and $OPT \geq d$. If we find d many edges in G that are disjoint from one another, then every feasible solution must contain a node from each of these edges, so $OPT \geq d$. This provides inspiration for an algorithm: For each edge that hasn't yet been covered, we must include *at least one* of its endpoints. Perhaps surprisingly, we include *both*. This is a feature, not a bug! It ensures that we get a node cover by the end, with at most twice as many nodes as necessary. ■

Proof. The input is $G = (V, E)$.

Approximation algorithm for Min Node Cover (14.2)

initialize $S \leftarrow \emptyset$
for each edge $\{u, v\} \in E$ (in arbitrary order):
    if $u \notin S$ and $v \notin S$: add both u and v to S
output S

First, we prove that the algorithm outputs a node cover. Consider any edge $\{u, v\} \in E$. In this edge's iteration, if $u \in S$ or $v \in S$ then we still have $u \in S$ or $v \in S$ at the end (since nodes are never removed from S), and if $u \notin S$ and $v \notin S$ then u and v are added to S. Either way, the final S covers the edge $\{u, v\}$.

Now, we prove that $ALG \leq 2 \cdot OPT$. Let $D \subseteq E$ be the set of edges whose endpoints the algorithm puts in S. Note that $ALG = |S| = 2 \cdot |D|$. We have $|D| \leq OPT$ because the edges in D have no endpoints in common with each other, and every node cover contains at least one endpoint from each edge in D. ■

On some inputs, this algorithm does better than a factor of 2. For example, it outputs an optimal solution on the triangle graph. But on some other inputs, this algorithm's solution is really a factor of 2 worse than the optimum. For example, if G is just disjoint edges, then $OPT = |E|$ and $ALG = |V| = 2 \cdot |E|$. So analyzing this algorithm more carefully wouldn't improve its approximation ratio. This doesn't preclude a different algorithm achieving a better ratio. However, assuming a conjecture somewhat stronger than P ≠ NP, Min Node Cover has no poly-time c-approximation algorithm for any constant $c < 2$.

14.1.2 Min Set Cover

A *set system* is a tuple $S = (S_1, \ldots, S_n)$ of subsets of $[m] = \{1, \ldots, m\}$ such that S covers $[m]$, which means $\bigcup_{i \in [n]} S_i = [m]$. A *set cover* for S is a subtuple of S that still covers $[m]$: A set cover corresponds to indices $I \subseteq [n]$ such that $\bigcup_{i \in I} S_i = [m]$, in other words, for every $r \in [m]$ there exists $i \in I$ such that $r \in S_i$. We want to minimize $|I|$ (the number of sets we pick from S).

Min Set Cover	(14.3)
Input: Set system S	
Output: A set cover for S with as few sets as possible	

A feasible solution is any set cover I for S, and its objective value is $|I|$.

Example. Suppose $m = 6$ and:

$$S_1 = \{1,2,4,5\} \qquad S_2 = \{2,3,5\} \qquad S_3 = \{1,3,4\} \qquad S_4 = \{1,2,6\} \qquad S_5 = \{2,5,6\}$$

One feasible solution is $I = \{1,2,4\}$ since $S_1 \cup S_2 \cup S_4 = [6]$. Another is $I = \{3,5\}$ since $S_3 \cup S_5 = [6]$. The latter feasible solution is better since it uses only two sets instead of three. It's optimal since no single set S_i covers $[6]$. ◆

A possible practical motivation: A company has m different responsibilities and n job candidates, and S_i is the set of responsibilities candidate i can handle. We'd like to hire as few candidates as possible so all responsibilities are covered.

Min Node Cover is equivalent to the special case of Min Set Cover where each element of $[m]$ is in exactly two of the sets $S_1, \ldots, S_n$: Elements of $[m]$ correspond to edges, and S_v corresponds to the set of edges incident to node v. Thus Min Set Cover is NP-hard since Min Node Cover is.

Theorem 14.2. MIN SET COVER *has a poly-time* $\lceil \ln m \rceil$*-approximation algorithm.*

Proof idea. To cover all elements of $[m]$ using few sets from S, it's intuitively good to choose sets that cover many elements. This suggests a greedy algorithm: Repeatedly choose whichever set S_i covers the most remaining elements (that weren't covered by previously chosen sets). To compare this algorithm's solution to an (unknown) optimal solution, we note that in each step, one of the *OPT* many sets from an optimal solution would cover $\geq 1/OPT$ fraction of the algorithm's remaining elements, so the algorithm makes at least that much progress. ■

Proof. The input is a set system $S = (S_1, \ldots, S_n)$ over $[m]$. This algorithm maintains the invariant that $R = [m] \setminus \bigcup_{i \in I} S_i$ is the set of remaining (not yet covered) elements:

Greedy approximation algorithm for MIN SET COVER	(14.4)

initialize $I \leftarrow \emptyset$ and $R \leftarrow [m]$
while $R \neq \emptyset$:
    pick i with the largest $\lvert S_i \cap R \rvert$
    add i to I, and remove $S_i \cap R$ from R
output I	

We claim that for every iteration, $|R'| \leq |R|(1 - 1/OPT)$ where R is from the beginning of the iteration, and R' denotes the updated R after the iteration. Let $J \subseteq [n]$ be an optimal solution. Since $\bigcup_{j \in J} S_j = [m]$ contains all of R, there exists $j \in J$ such that S_j contains $\geq 1/|J| = 1/OPT$ fraction of R, in other words, $|S_j \cap R| \geq |R|/OPT$. Whichever i the algorithm picks is no worse than j, so $|R'| = |R| - |S_i \cap R| \leq |R| - |R|/OPT$. This proves the claim.

Hence, the algorithm maintains the invariant that $|R| \leq m(1 - 1/OPT)^{|I|}$ because initially $|R| = m$, and $|R|$ gets multiplied by $\leq 1 - 1/OPT$ in each iteration, and the number of iterations is $|I|$. After $\lceil \ln m \rceil \cdot OPT$ many iterations,

$$|R| \;\leq\; m(1 - 1/OPT)^{\lceil \ln m \rceil \cdot OPT} \;\leq\; m(\mathrm{e}^{-1/OPT})^{\lceil \ln m \rceil \cdot OPT} \;=\; m\mathrm{e}^{-\lceil \ln m \rceil} \;<\; m\mathrm{e}^{-\ln m} \;=\; 1$$

by Fact 7.6, so the algorithm would halt because $|R| = 0$. At the end, I is a set cover since $\bigcup_{i \in I} S_i = [m] \setminus R = [m]$, and we have $ALG = |I| \leq \lceil \ln m \rceil \cdot OPT$. ■

If $\mathsf{P} \neq \mathsf{NP}$ then MIN SET COVER has no poly-time $c(\ln m)$-approximation algorithm for any constant $c < 1$, though this is very difficult to prove.

14.1.3 MAX *k*-SAT

SATISFIABILITY is "all or nothing": Either all clauses can be satisfied simultaneously, or not. But trying to maximize the number of satisfied clauses may be preferable to giving up if we don't manage to satisfy them all.

MAX *k*-SAT	(14.5)
Input: k-CNF formula φ	
Output: An assignment satisfying as many clauses of φ as possible	

A feasible solution is any assignment to φ's variables, and its objective value is the number of clauses of φ that it satisfies.

Lemma 14.3. *For every k-CNF, some assignment satisfies $\geq 1-2^{-k}$ fraction of the clauses.*

Proof. We use the probabilistic method. Let $\varphi = C_1 \wedge \cdots \wedge C_m$ be a k-CNF. Consider a uniformly random assignment. For each $i \in [m]$, let Y_i be the indicator random variable for C_i being unsatisfied. Then $\mathbf{E}[Y_i] = \mathbf{Pr}[C_i \text{ is unsatisfied}] = 2^{-k}$ since of the 2^k many assignments to the k variables in C_i, one of them doesn't satisfy C_i. The number of unsatisfied clauses is $Y = Y_1 + \cdots + Y_m$. By linearity of expectation, $\mathbf{E}[Y] = \mathbf{E}[Y_1] + \cdots + \mathbf{E}[Y_m] = 2^{-k}m$. By Lemma A.15, $Y(a) \leq 2^{-k}m$ for some assignment a, so a satisfies $\geq 1-2^{-k}$ fraction of φ's clauses. ■

Of course, an assignment satisfying $\geq 1-2^{-k}$ fraction of the clauses is within a factor $1-2^{-k}$ of optimal. Such an assignment exists, but how can we find one efficiently and deterministically?

Theorem 14.4. Max k-Sat *has a poly-time $(1-2^{-k})$-approximation algorithm.*

Proof idea. We derandomize the proof of Lemma 14.3 using the *method of conditional expectations*. This resembles a search-to-decision reduction for Sat (§2.3.5): We find an assignment bit-by-bit, somehow determining a "safe" bit to commit to in each step. Letting # mean "number of":

Method of conditional expectations for Max k-Sat	(14.6)
if $\mathbf{E}_{x_2x_3\cdots}\big[\#\text{ clauses unsatisfied by } 1x_2x_3x_4\cdots\big] \leq 2^{-k}m$ then let $a_1 \leftarrow 1$, else let $a_1 \leftarrow 0$ if $\mathbf{E}_{x_3x_4\cdots}\big[\#\text{ clauses unsatisfied by } a_1 1x_3x_4\cdots\big] \leq 2^{-k}m$ then let $a_2 \leftarrow 1$, else let $a_2 \leftarrow 0$ if $\mathbf{E}_{x_4x_5\cdots}\big[\#\text{ clauses unsatisfied by } a_1a_2 1x_4\cdots\big] \leq 2^{-k}m$ then let $a_3 \leftarrow 1$, else let $a_3 \leftarrow 0$ ⋮	

We can compute these expectations in poly time: For a uniformly random assignment to a CNF ψ (which is a contraction of φ and is not necessarily a k-CNF),

$$\mathbf{E}\big[\#\text{ unsatisfied clauses in } \psi\big] \;=\; \textstyle\sum_{\text{clause } C \text{ in } \psi} \mathbf{Pr}\big[C \text{ is unsatisfied}\big] \;=\; \textstyle\sum_{\text{clause } C \text{ in } \psi} 2^{-\text{width of } C}$$

by the same reasoning as in Lemma 14.3. ■

Proof. The input is an n-variable m-clause k-CNF φ.

Approximation algorithm for Max k-Sat	(14.7)

initialize $a \leftarrow **\cdots*$ (partial assignment to φ's variables)
for $i \leftarrow 1,2,\ldots,n$:
    let b be a except $b_i = 1$
    compute $\mathbf{E}\big[\#\text{ unsatisfied clauses in } \varphi\vert_b\big] = \sum_{\text{clause } C \text{ in } \varphi\vert_b} 2^{-\text{width of } C}$
    if this is $\leq 2^{-k}m$: update $a_i \leftarrow 1$
    else: update $a_i \leftarrow 0$
output a	

We claim that this outputs an assignment satisfying $ALG \geq (1-2^{-k})m$ clauses of φ. Trivially $OPT \leq m$, so $ALG \geq (1-2^{-k})\cdot OPT$. It suffices to show that this algorithm maintains the invariant that $\mathbf{E}\big[\#\text{ unsatisfied clauses in } \varphi\vert_a\big] \leq 2^{-k}m$, because then at the end:

$$\#\text{ clauses in } \varphi \text{ unsatisfied by } a \;=\; \mathbf{E}\big[\#\text{ unsatisfied clauses in } \varphi\vert_a\big] \;\leq\; 2^{-k}m$$

(That $\mathbf{E}$ has no randomness since a has no remaining unassigned variables at the end, and $\varphi|_a$ only has width-0 clauses corresponding to φ's unsatisfied clauses.) The invariant holds at the beginning by the proof of Lemma 14.3. To see that the invariant is maintained, assume it holds at the beginning of iteration i. Let b and b' be a except $b_i = 1$ and $b'_i = 0$. By the law of total expectation (§A.3.2):

$$\begin{aligned}
2^{-k}m &\geq \mathbf{E}\big[\#\text{ unsatisfied clauses in } \varphi|_a\big] \\
&= \mathbf{E}\big[\#\text{ unsatisfied clauses in } \varphi|_a \,\big|\, x_i = 1\big] \cdot \mathbf{Pr}[x_i = 1] + \\
&\quad\; \mathbf{E}\big[\#\text{ unsatisfied clauses in } \varphi|_a \,\big|\, x_i = 0\big] \cdot \mathbf{Pr}[x_i = 0] \\
&= \mathbf{E}\big[\#\text{ unsatisfied clauses in } \varphi|_b\,\big] \cdot \tfrac{1}{2} + \\
&\quad\; \mathbf{E}\big[\#\text{ unsatisfied clauses in } \varphi|_{b'}\big] \cdot \tfrac{1}{2}
\end{aligned}$$

(The last equality holds because a clause in $\varphi|_a$ is unsatisfied by an assignment consistent with b iff the corresponding clause in $\varphi|_b$ is unsatisfied, and similarly for b'.) So one of these cases happens:

- $\mathbf{E}\big[\#\text{ unsatisfied clauses in } \varphi|_b\,\big] \leq 2^{-k}m$ and the algorithm updates $a \leftarrow b$.
- $\mathbf{E}\big[\#\text{ unsatisfied clauses in } \varphi|_{b'}\big] \leq 2^{-k}m$ and the algorithm updates $a \leftarrow b'$.

Either way, the invariant is maintained. ■

We get a 0.75-approximation for MAX 2-SAT, a 0.875-approximation for MAX 3-SAT, a 0.9375-approximation for MAX 4-SAT, and so on. (MAX 2-SAT is NP-hard even though 2-SAT $\in$ P—see Exercise 2.30.e and Exercise 2.12.) Surprisingly, MAX 2-SAT has a sophisticated poly-time 0.94-approximation algorithm (beyond the scope of this book). But for each $k \geq 3$, the approximation ratio of $1 - 2^{-k}$ for MAX k-SAT can't be improved unless P = NP (§14.2).

14.1.4 MAX EDGE DISJOINT PATHS

Suppose a directed graph represents a communication network, and we have some "connection requests": For some nodes $s_1, t_1, s_2, t_2, \ldots$ called *terminals*, we want a path to route data from s_1 to t_1, and a path to route data from s_2 to t_2, and so on. We must not overload any edge. Let's consider the simple setting where the chosen paths must be *edge disjoint* from each other—no two of them have any edge in common. If we don't fulfill all the connection requests, we'd still like to fulfill as many as we can. This problem has practical applications for routing in high-speed networks and for VLSI (very large scale integrated) circuit layout.

MAX EDGE DISJOINT PATHS	(14.8)
Input: Directed graph G, pairs of nodes $(s_1, t_1), (s_2, t_2), \ldots, (s_k, t_k)$	
Output: A path from s_i to t_i for as many $i \in [k]$ as possible, such that these paths are edge disjoint	

A feasible solution is any set of indices $I \subseteq [k]$ along with edge disjoint paths from s_i to t_i for all $i \in I$, and its objective value is $|I|$.

The decision version is NP-complete (Exercise 2.31.b). The approximation ratio we achieve in poly time is meager but better than nothing:

Theorem 14.5. MAX EDGE DISJOINT PATHS *has a poly-time* $1/O(\sqrt{m})$*-approximation algorithm, where* m *is the number of edges in the input graph.*

Proof idea. Intuitively, we should favor shorter paths because longer paths have more potential to interfere with other paths and thereby obstruct us from connecting more pairs of terminals. This suggests a greedy algorithm: Find a shortest path for each pair of terminals, choose the shortest of these paths, remove this path's edges from the graph (ensuring subsequent paths are edge disjoint from this one), and repeat with the remaining pairs of terminals, until no new path is found. Extended breadth-first search finds shortest paths in poly time (§1.1.2).

To analyze the algorithm's approximation ratio, we show that an optimal solution can't connect too many more pairs of terminals than the algorithm's solution does: An optimal solution can't use too many long paths because the graph only has m edges, and it can't use too many short paths that the algorithm doesn't use. ■

Proof. The input is a directed graph G and pairs of nodes $(s_1, t_1), \ldots, (s_k, t_k)$. For any directed graph H and nodes s and t, let $\text{dist}_H(s,t)$ be the distance (length of a shortest path) from s to t in H, or ∞ if t is unreachable from s in H. Extended BFS computes $\text{dist}_H(s,t)$ and a corresponding shortest path in poly time.

Approximation algorithm for MAX EDGE DISJOINT PATHS	(14.9)

initialize $I \leftarrow \emptyset$ and $H \leftarrow G$
while $I \neq [k]$:
    compute $\text{dist}_H(s_i, t_i)$ for each $i \notin I$
    if $\text{dist}_H(s_i, t_i) = \infty$ for all $i \notin I$: break out of loop
    add to I an i with smallest $\text{dist}_H(s_i, t_i)$, and let P_i be a corresponding shortest path
    remove P_i's edges from H
output I and P_i for each $i \in I$	

Consider an optimal solution $J \subseteq [k]$ with edge disjoint paths Q_j from s_j to t_j for all $j \in J$. Thus $OPT = |J|$ and $ALG = |I|$ at the end. We claim that $|J| \leq (2\sqrt{m}+1) \cdot |I|$, which means $ALG \geq OPT/(2\sqrt{m}+1)$. First, note that if $|I| = 0$ then no t_i is reachable from s_i in G, and thus $|J| = 0$. So assume $|I| \geq 1$. Say a path is *long* if it has $\geq \sqrt{m}$ many edges, and is *short* otherwise. Partition J into three parts:

- $j \in J \cap I$: There are $\leq |I|$ many such j.
- $j \in J \setminus I$ such that Q_j is long: There are $\leq \sqrt{m}$ many such j because these Q_j are edge disjoint from each other, and G only has m edges. (If there were $> \sqrt{m}$ many such j, then G would have $> \sqrt{m} \cdot \sqrt{m} = m$ edges.)
- $j \in J \setminus I$ such that Q_j is short: We claim there are $\leq \sqrt{m} \cdot |I|$ many such j. First, observe that each such Q_j shares an edge with at least one short P_i, because if such a Q_j were edge disjoint from all short P_i, then the algorithm would have chosen this short Q_j before choosing any long P_i or halting (contradicting the assumption that $j \notin I$). There are $\leq |I|$ many short P_i, each of which shares edges with $< \sqrt{m}$ many short Q_j with $j \in J \setminus I$ (since those Q_j are edge disjoint from each other, and P_i has $< \sqrt{m}$ edges).

In summary, $|J| \leq |I| + \sqrt{m} + \sqrt{m} \cdot |I| \leq (2\sqrt{m}+1) \cdot |I|$ since $|I| \geq 1$. ■

Example. Figure 14.1 shows an example input: $ALG = 1$ (shown on the left) because the algorithm chooses the length-4 path from s_1 to t_1, which blocks the length-5 paths from s_i to t_i for $i \in \{2,3,4,5\}$. But $OPT = 4$ (shown on the right) because the latter paths are edge disjoint.

We generalize this example to have a length-$(k-1)$ path from s_1 to t_1, which overlaps length-k

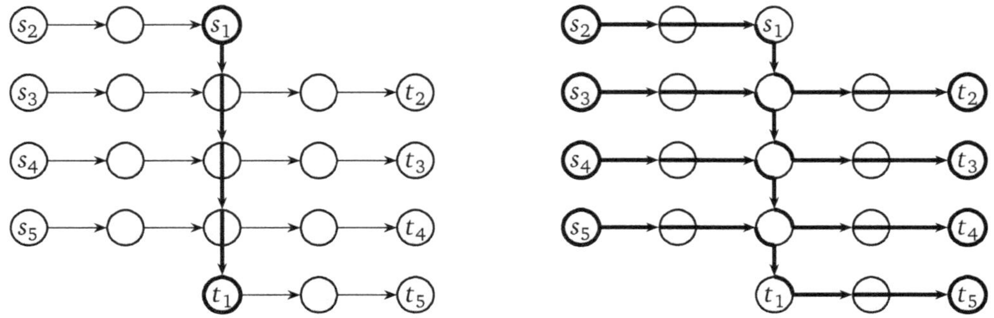

Figure 14.1: Example for the MAX EDGE DISJOINT PATHS approximation algorithm

edge disjoint paths from s_i to t_i for $i \in \{2, \ldots, k\}$. Since the graph has $m \leq k^2$ edges and $ALG = 1$ and $OPT = k-1 \geq \sqrt{m}-1$, our algorithm's approximation ratio is no better than $1/(\sqrt{m}-1)$. ♦

The analysis of the greedy algorithm's approximation ratio can be improved somewhat (Exercise 14.12), but the example shows that analyzing this algorithm even more carefully wouldn't significantly improve its approximation ratio. This doesn't preclude a different algorithm achieving a better ratio. However, it's known that ratio $1/m^d$ can't be achieved in poly time for any constant $d < 1/2$ unless $\mathsf{P} = \mathsf{NP}$ (§ 14.2). The greedy algorithm is essentially the best possible.

14.2 Hardness of Approximation

We present tools for proving that particular optimization problems are hard to approximate, meaning they don't have poly-time algorithms with certain approximation ratios, assuming $\mathsf{P} \neq \mathsf{NP}$.

- *Gap-introducing reductions* (§ 14.2.1) imply that if an optimization problem is hard to solve exactly, then it's hard to solve even approximately.
- *Gap-preserving reductions* (§ 14.2.2) translate hardness of approximating one problem to hardness of approximating another problem.
- *Gap-amplifying reductions* (§ 14.2.3) imply that if a problem is hard to approximate with a certain ratio, then it's hard to approximate even with some weaker ratio.

A cornerstone of this topic is a very deep theorem: 3-SAT remains NP-complete even when the 3-CNF is promised to be either satisfiable or "very unsatisfiable," meaning that every assignment falsifies not just one clause, but a constant fraction of the clauses.

14.2.1 Gap-Introducing Reductions

For an optimization problem B and nonnegative parameters α and β—which may depend on input parameters such as the number of clauses in a CNF or the number of nodes or edges in a graph—we define a promise decision problem:

(α,β)-GAP B	(14.10)
Input:	Valid input to B
Output:	If B is a minimization problem: 1 if $OPT \le \alpha$, 0 if $OPT > \beta$, undefined otherwise If B is a maximization problem: 1 if $OPT \ge \alpha$, 0 if $OPT < \beta$, undefined otherwise

For minimization: $OPT \le \alpha$ means some feasible solution has objective value $\le \alpha$.
$OPT > \beta$ means every feasible solution has objective value $> \beta$.

For maximization: $OPT \ge \alpha$ means some feasible solution has objective value $\ge \alpha$.
$OPT < \beta$ means every feasible solution has objective value $< \beta$.

"GAP" refers to inputs that are invalid for this decision problem because $\alpha < OPT \le \beta$ for minimization, or $\beta \le OPT < \alpha$ for maximization.

Lemma 14.6. *If B has a poly-time β/α-approximation algorithm, then (α,β)-GAP $B \in$ P, assuming that the objective value of a given feasible solution for a given input y can be computed in poly time, and that β can be computed from y in poly time.*

Proof. This runs in poly time:

```
Algorithm for (α, β)-GAP B                                        (14.11)
on input y:
    run the approximation algorithm for B on input y to get a feasible solution s
    compute ALG = s's objective value, and compute β
    accept iff ALG ≤ β for minimization, or ALG ≥ β for maximization
```

For minimization: If $OPT \le \alpha$ then $ALG \le (\beta/\alpha)\cdot OPT \le \beta$ and the algorithm accepts.
If $OPT > \beta$ then $ALG \ge OPT > \beta$ and the algorithm rejects.

For maximization: If $OPT \ge \alpha$ then $ALG \ge (\beta/\alpha)\cdot OPT \ge \beta$ and the algorithm accepts.
If $OPT < \beta$ then $ALG \le OPT < \beta$ and the algorithm rejects. ■

Definition. An (α,β)*-gap-introducing reduction* from a decision problem A to an optimization problem B is a mapping reduction from A to (α,β)-GAP B. ◄

A poly-time reduction of this type implies that if $A \notin$ P then (α,β)-GAP $B \notin$ P and therefore B has no poly-time β/α-approximation algorithm (assuming the objective function and β are poly-time computable).

3-SAT is the same as (m,m)-GAP MAX 3-SAT, where m is the number of clauses. What if we enlarge the gap from nothing to a constant factor? How hard is approximating MAX 3-SAT? Recall $(m,(7/8)m)$-GAP MAX 3-SAT $\in$ P since it doesn't even have 0-inputs (Lemma 14.3), and in fact, MAX 3-SAT has a poly-time 7/8-approximation algorithm (Theorem 14.4). But achieving a ratio better than 7/8 is as hard as achieving a ratio of 1:

Theorem 14.7. *For every constant $c > 7/8$, (m,cm)-GAP MAX 3-SAT (with m clauses) is NP-complete, so MAX 3-SAT has no poly-time c-approximation algorithm unless P = NP.*

This theorem is a tour de force and a major landmark in computational complexity. It's very difficult to prove, so we won't, but we provide some perspective on the proof in §14.4.

NP-hardness of 3-SAT means for every $A \in \mathsf{NP}$, there exists a poly-time reduction that maps x to a 3-CNF φ such that:

$$A(x)=1 \Rightarrow OPT(\varphi) \geq m \quad \text{(some assignment satisfies all clauses)}$$
$$A(x)=0 \Rightarrow OPT(\varphi) < m \quad \text{(no assignment satisfies all clauses)}$$

Theorem 14.7 strengthens this to:

$$A(x)=1 \Rightarrow OPT(\varphi) \geq m \quad \text{(some assignment satisfies all clauses)}$$
$$A(x)=0 \Rightarrow OPT(\varphi) < cm \quad \text{(no assignment satisfies even a } c \text{ fraction of all clauses)}$$

We already know A has a poly-time mapping reduction to 3-SAT, in other words, a poly-time (m,m)-gap-introducing reduction to MAX 3-SAT. Theorem 14.7 strengthens (m,m) to (m,cm). Chapter 2's proof that 3-SAT is NP-hard doesn't yield this stronger statement, even for $c=0.999$. Why not? Letting V be a verifier for A, the reduction produces a CNF $\varphi = \varphi_{\text{transcript}} \wedge \varphi_{\text{accept}}$ (subsequently transformed to a 3-CNF) with variable groups x, w, y, where $\varphi_{\text{transcript}}$ checks that y is the transcript of $V(x;w)$, and φ_{accept} checks that y's last row is an accept configuration. There are only $O(1)$ clauses in φ_{accept}, so even when $A(x)=0$, we have $OPT \geq m-O(1)$ (not $< cm$): Assign w arbitrarily, and let y be the transcript of $V(x;w)$. This satisfies $\varphi_{\text{transcript}}$, so only φ_{accept} is unsatisfied. To introduce a constant factor gap, we must encode transcripts differently, so a constant fraction of the clauses will notice if the assignment doesn't represent an accepting transcript. This is a major challenge since computation is generally fragile—a single flipped bit anywhere might derail a computation. It's no surprise that the proof of Theorem 14.7 involves error correcting codes (Chapter 9).

When we can restrict our attention to inputs with $OPT \leq O(1)$, we automatically get a constant factor gap. This happens with MAX EDGE DISJOINT PATHS: It's NP-complete to distinguish $OPT \geq 2$ from $OPT \leq 1$ because the decision version remains NP-complete even for $k=2$.

TWO EDGE DISJOINT PATHS	(14.12)
Input:	Directed graph G, pairs of nodes (s_1,t_1) and (s_2,t_2)
Output:	Do there exist edge disjoint paths from s_1 to t_1 and from s_2 to t_2?

Theorem 14.8. TWO EDGE DISJOINT PATHS *is* NP-*complete. Thus, for every constant* $c > 1/2$, $(2,2c)$-GAP MAX EDGE DISJOINT PATHS *is* NP-*complete, so* MAX EDGE DISJOINT PATHS *has no poly-time* c*-approximation algorithm unless* P = NP.

We won't prove Theorem 14.8, which involves a tricky but still elementary gadget reduction. It's not nearly as deep as Theorem 14.7.

14.2.2 Gap-Preserving Reductions

Definition. An $(\alpha,\beta,\gamma,\delta)$*-gap-preserving reduction* from an optimization problem A to an optimization problem B is a mapping reduction from (α,β)-GAP A to (γ,δ)-GAP B. It maps x to y such that:

If A and B are both minimization:
$$OPT_A(x) \leq \alpha \Rightarrow OPT_B(y) \leq \gamma$$
$$OPT_A(x) > \beta \Rightarrow OPT_B(y) > \delta$$

If A and B are both maximization: $OPT_A(x) \ge \alpha \Rightarrow OPT_B(y) \ge \gamma$
$OPT_A(x) < \beta \Rightarrow OPT_B(y) < \delta$

If A is min and B is max: $OPT_A(x) \le \alpha \Rightarrow OPT_B(y) \ge \gamma$
$OPT_A(x) > \beta \Rightarrow OPT_B(y) < \delta$

If A is max and B is min: $OPT_A(x) \ge \alpha \Rightarrow OPT_B(y) \le \gamma$
$OPT_A(x) < \beta \Rightarrow OPT_B(y) > \delta$ ◀

The gap δ/γ need not equal the gap β/α, so "preserving" is a slightly misleading term. The point is that we're cognizant of the gap and can argue that the reduction doesn't degrade the gap too much. A poly-time reduction of this type translates NP-hardness of approximating A to NP-hardness of approximating B.

Some standard reductions between NP-complete problems don't preserve gaps at all, while others preserve gaps fairly well. Here are examples of the latter.

MAX INDEPENDENT SET	(14.13)
Input: Undirected graph G	
Output: An independent set in G with as many nodes as possible	

Lemma 14.9. *For every constant $c > 7/8$, there exists a poly-time $(m, cm, n/3, cn/3)$-gap-preserving reduction from* MAX 3-SAT *(with m clauses) to* MAX INDEPENDENT SET *(with n nodes).*

Proof. The reduction from 3-SAT to INDEPENDENT SET in §2.4.2 maps φ to (G, k) as follows: If φ has m clauses, then G has $n = 3m$ nodes. Each clause in φ corresponds to a triangle gadget in G whose three nodes represent the clause's literals. Also, G has "inter-clause" edges between all pairs of nodes representing opposite literals (x_i and $\overline{x_i}$). Finally, $k = m = n/3$. We proved that φ is satisfiable iff G has an independent set of size $\ge k$.

For the $(m, cm, n/3, cn/3)$-gap-preserving reduction, we just map φ to G. (The input to MAX INDEPENDENT SET has no k.) We claim that:

(i) $OPT(\varphi) \ge m \Rightarrow OPT(G) \ge m$
(ii) $OPT(\varphi) < cm \Rightarrow OPT(G) < cm$

(We omit the subscript of OPT when the problem is clear from context.)

(i): For any assignment satisfying all m clauses, let S be a set of nodes corresponding to one satisfied literal from each clause. This S is an independent set of size m.

(ii): It suffices to show $OPT(\varphi) \ge OPT(G)$. Consider any independent set S of size $OPT(G)$. The triangle edges ensure S's nodes are all in different clause gadgets. The inter-clause edges ensure for each variable x_i, S has either no x_i nodes or no $\overline{x_i}$ nodes. For each x_i, assign $x_i = 0$ if S has no x_i nodes, and assign $x_i = 1$ if S has no $\overline{x_i}$ nodes. If S has neither x_i nor $\overline{x_i}$ nodes, then it doesn't matter how we assign x_i. This assignment satisfies the $OPT(G)$ many clauses whose gadgets contain a node of S, since every node in S represents a satisfied literal. ■

Corollary 14.10. *For every constant $c > 7/8$, $(n/3, cn/3)$-*GAP MAX INDEPENDENT SET *(with n nodes) is* NP*-complete, so* MAX INDEPENDENT SET *has no poly-time c-approximation algorithm unless* P = NP.

Proof. By Theorem 14.7 and Lemma 14.9. ■

That reduction was max-to-max. Here's a max-to-min reduction.

Lemma 14.11. *For every constant $c > 7/8$, there exists a poly-time $(n/3,\ cn/3,\ 2n/3,\ (1-c/3)n)$-gap-preserving reduction from* MAX INDEPENDENT SET *(with n nodes) to* MIN NODE COVER *(with n nodes).*

Proof. Map G to itself. For every subset S of nodes, S is an independent set iff $\overline{S}$ is a node cover (Claim 2.17). This implies $OPT' = n - OPT$ where OPT is the maximum independent set size and OPT' is the minimum node cover size. Thus:

(i) $OPT \geq n/3 \Rightarrow OPT' \leq 2n/3$

(ii) $OPT < cn/3 \Rightarrow OPT' > (1-c/3)n$ ■

Corollary 14.12. *For every constant $c < 17/16 = 1.0625$, $(2n/3, c2n/3)$-*GAP MIN NODE COVER *(with n nodes) is* NP*-complete, so* MIN NODE COVER *has no poly-time c-approximation algorithm unless* P = NP.

Proof. By Corollary 14.10 and Lemma 14.11 since $(1-(7/8)/3)\,/\,(2/3) = 17/16$. ■

For comparison, MIN NODE COVER has a poly-time 2-approximation algorithm (Theorem 14.1) and is known (by a very difficult proof) to have no poly-time c-approximation algorithm for any constant $c < \sqrt{2} \approx 1.414$ unless P = NP.

Lemma 14.13. *For all constants $k \geq 3$ and $c > 1 - 2^{-k}$ and $c' = 1 - (1-c)/2$, there exists a poly-time $(m,\ cm,\ m',\ c'm')$-gap-preserving reduction from* MAX k-SAT *(with m clauses) to* MAX $(k+1)$-SAT *(with m' clauses).*

Proof. Map an m-clause k-CNF $\varphi(x)$ to an m'-clause $(k+1)$-CNF $\varphi'(x,y)$ where $m' = 2m$ and y is a single new variable, by replacing each width-k clause C with two width-$(k+1)$ clauses $(C \vee y) \wedge (C \vee \overline{y})$ (like Claim 2.12). We claim that

(i) $OPT \geq m \Rightarrow OPT' \geq m'$

(ii) $OPT < cm \Rightarrow OPT' < c'm'$

where OPT and OPT' are for φ and φ' respectively.

(i): Any assignment to x that satisfies all clauses of φ, together with an arbitrary assignment to y, also satisfies all clauses of φ'.

(ii): Suppose $OPT' \geq c'm'$. Consider any assignment to x, y satisfying $\geq c'm'$ clauses of φ'. Since $\leq (1-c')m' = (1-c)m$ clauses of φ' are falsified, $\leq (1-c)m$ clauses of φ have at least one of their two associated clauses of φ' falsified. Thus $\geq cm$ clauses of φ have both associated clauses of φ' satisfied. These clauses of φ are satisfied by the assignment to x (ignoring y), so $OPT \geq cm$. ■

Corollary 14.14. *For all constants $k \geq 3$ and $c > 1 - 2^{-k}$, (m, cm)-*GAP MAX k-SAT *(with m clauses) is* NP*-complete, so* MAX k-SAT *has no poly-time c-approximation algorithm unless* P = NP.

Proof. This holds for $k = 3$ by Theorem 14.7. If it holds for some k, then it also holds for $k+1$: Lemma 14.13 implies that for every constant $c' > 1 - 2^{-(k+1)}$ and $c = 1 - 2(1-c') > 1 - 2^{-k}$, if (m, cm)-GAP MAX k-SAT is NP-complete then so is $(m', c'm')$-GAP MAX $(k+1)$-SAT. ■

We can also decrease the width without degrading the gap a lot (pretending we don't know Theorem 14.7):

Lemma 14.15. *For all constants $k > 3$ and $c > 1-2^{-k}$ and $c' = 1-(1-c)/(k-2)$, there exists a poly-time $(m, cm, m', c'm')$-gap-preserving reduction from* Max k-Sat *(with m clauses) to* Max 3-Sat *(with m' clauses).*

Proof. Map an m-clause k-CNF $\varphi(x)$ to an m'-clause 3-CNF $\varphi'(x, y)$ where $m' = (k-2)m$ and y is a group of new variables, by replacing each width-k clause $C(x)$ with a group $C'(x, y_C)$ of $k-2$ width-3 clauses using a group of fresh variables y_C (part of y), as in Theorem 2.11 and Claim 2.13. For every C and every assignment to x, we have $C(x) = 1 \iff \big(\exists y_C : C'(x, y_C) = 1\big)$. We claim that

$$\text{(i)}\quad OPT \geq m \;\Rightarrow\; OPT' \geq m'$$
$$\text{(ii)}\quad OPT < cm \;\Rightarrow\; OPT' < c'm'$$

where OPT and OPT' are for φ and φ' respectively.

(i): Any assignment to x that satisfies all clauses of φ, together with some assignment to y, also satisfies all clauses of φ'.

(ii): Suppose $OPT' \geq c'm'$. Consider any assignment to x, y satisfying $\geq c'm'$ clauses of φ'. Since $\leq (1-c')m' = (1-c)m$ clauses of φ' are falsified, $\leq (1-c)m$ clauses of φ have at least one of their $k-2$ associated clauses of φ' falsified. Thus $\geq cm$ clauses of φ have all $k-2$ of their associated clauses of φ' satisfied. These clauses of φ are satisfied by the assignment to x (ignoring y), so $OPT \geq cm$. ■

Corollary 14.16. *For all constants $k > 3$ and $c > 1-2^{-k}$ and $c' = 1-(1-c)/(k-2)$, if (m, cm)-*Gap Max k-Sat *(with m clauses) is* NP*-complete, then so is $(m', c'm')$-*Gap Max 3-Sat *(with m' clauses).* ■

14.2.3 Gap-Amplifying Reductions

Definition. An $(\alpha, \beta, \gamma, \delta)$-*gap-amplifying reduction* for an optimization problem A is a mapping reduction from (α, β)-Gap A to (γ, δ)-Gap A. It maps x to y such that:

If A is minimization:
$$OPT(x) \leq \alpha \;\Rightarrow\; OPT(y) \leq \gamma$$
$$OPT(x) > \beta \;\Rightarrow\; OPT(y) > \delta$$

If A is maximization:
$$OPT(x) \geq \alpha \;\Rightarrow\; OPT(y) \geq \gamma$$
$$OPT(x) < \beta \;\Rightarrow\; OPT(y) < \delta$$

The gap δ/γ should be wider than the gap β/α (that is, $\delta/\gamma > \beta/\alpha$ for minimization, or $\delta/\gamma < \beta/\alpha$ for maximization). ◄

A poly-time reduction of this type shows that if approximating A is somewhat hard, then approximating A is actually even harder (in terms of the approximation ratio).

Lemma 14.17. *For all $\alpha > \beta$ and every integer $\ell > 1$, there exists a poly-time $(\alpha, \beta, \alpha^\ell, \beta^\ell)$-gap-amplifying reduction for* Max Independent Set.

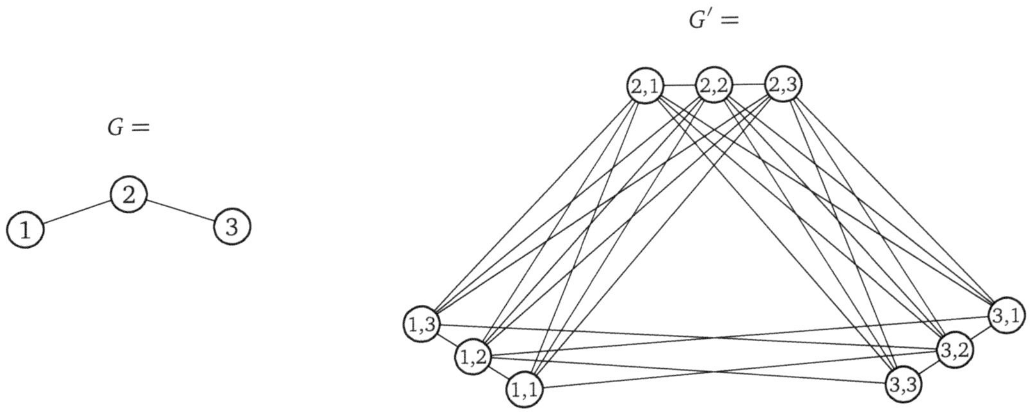

Figure 14.2: Example of the gap-amplifying reduction for MAX INDEPENDENT SET with $\ell = 2$

Proof. Map $G = (V, E)$ to $G' = (V', E')$ where $V' = V^\ell$ is the set of all ℓ-tuples of nodes from V, and:

$$\{(v_1, \ldots, v_\ell), (w_1, \ldots, w_\ell)\} \in E' \iff \big(\exists i \in [\ell] : \{v_i, w_i\} \in E\big)$$

This takes poly time since ℓ is a constant. We claim that

(i) $OPT \geq \alpha \Rightarrow OPT' \geq \alpha^\ell$

(ii) $OPT < \beta \Rightarrow OPT' < \beta^\ell$

where OPT and OPT' are for G and G' respectively. It suffices to prove $OPT' = OPT^\ell$.

$OPT' \geq OPT^\ell$: If $S \subseteq V$ is a largest independent set in G, then $S^\ell \subseteq V'$ is an independent set in G'. Thus $OPT' \geq |S^\ell| = |S|^\ell = OPT^\ell$.

$OPT' \leq OPT^\ell$: Suppose $S' \subseteq V'$ is a largest independent set in G'. For each $i \in [\ell]$, let $S_i = \{v_i : (v_1, \ldots, v_\ell) \in S'\} \subseteq V$ be the set of all nodes in G that appear in the ith coordinate of nodes in S'. Each S_i is an independent set in G because for all nodes $v, w \in S_i$, we have $v = v_i$ and $w = w_i$ for some nodes $(v_1, \ldots, v_\ell), (w_1, \ldots, w_\ell) \in S'$, and since S' is independent, we have $\{(v_1, \ldots, v_\ell), (w_1, \ldots, w_\ell)\} \notin E'$ and therefore $\{v_i, w_i\} \notin E$ by the definition of E'. Let S be the largest of the sets S_i over all $i \in [\ell]$. Since $S' \subseteq S_1 \times \cdots \times S_\ell$, we have $|S'| \leq |S_1| \cdots |S_\ell| \leq |S|^\ell$. Thus $OPT \geq |S| \geq |S'|^{1/\ell} = (OPT')^{1/\ell}$. ∎

Example. Figure 14.2 shows an example G and G' with $\ell = 2$. The largest independent set in G is $\{1, 3\}$. The largest independent set in G' is $\{1, 3\}^2 = \{(1,1), (1,3), (3,1), (3,3)\}$. ♦

Corollary 14.18. *For every constant $c > 0$,* MAX INDEPENDENT SET *has no poly-time c-approximation algorithm unless* $\mathsf{P} = \mathsf{NP}$.

Proof. For any constant $c > 0$, let $\ell > 1$ be an integer such that $c^{1/\ell} > 7/8$. By Corollary 14.10, (α, β)-GAP MAX INDEPENDENT SET is NP-complete for some $\beta/\alpha = c^{1/\ell}$. By Lemma 14.17, $(\alpha^\ell, \beta^\ell)$-GAP MAX INDEPENDENT SET is NP-complete. We have $\beta^\ell/\alpha^\ell = (\beta/\alpha)^\ell = c$. ∎

It's known—but difficult to prove—that for every constant $d < 1$, MAX INDEPENDENT SET (with n nodes) has no poly-time $1/n^d$-approximation algorithm unless $\mathsf{P} = \mathsf{NP}$. Thus the trivial

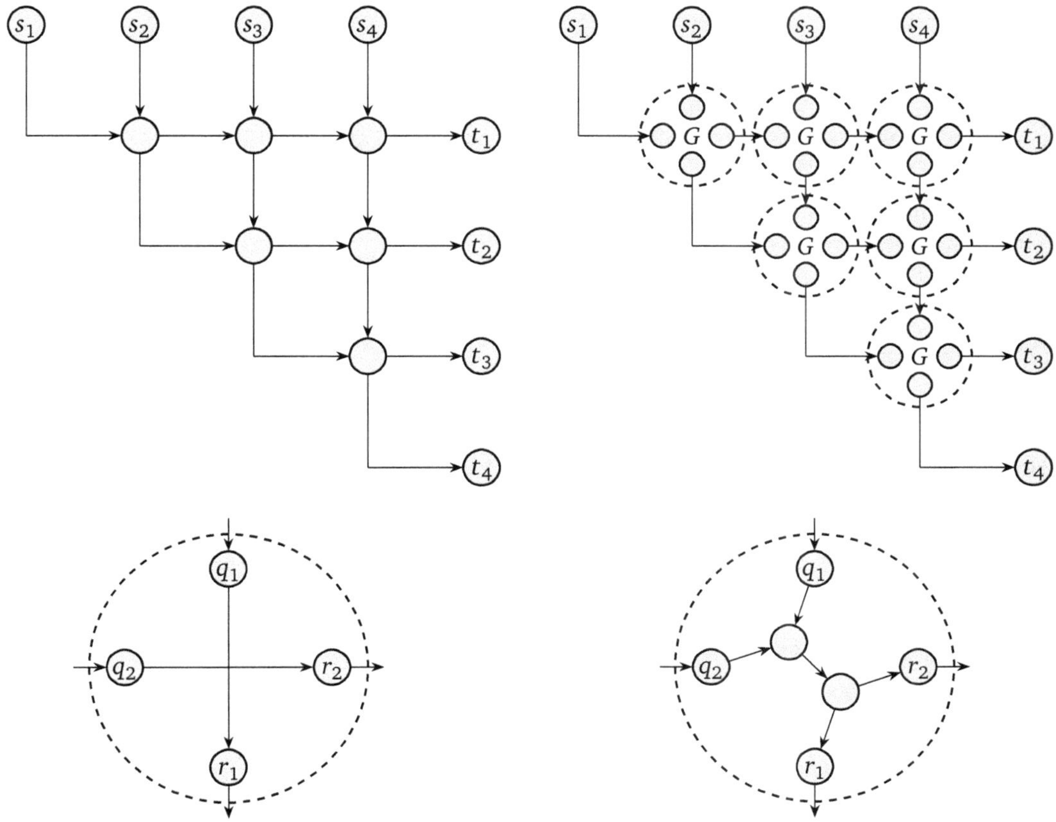

Figure 14.3: Example of the gap-amplifying reduction for MAX EDGE DISJOINT PATHS with $k = 4$

algorithm that just outputs a single node—achieving an approximation ratio of $1/n$—is essentially the best possible if $\mathsf{P} \neq \mathsf{NP}$.

Recall Theorem 14.8: TWO EDGE DISJOINT PATHS is NP-complete, so for every constant $c > 1/2$, MAX EDGE DISJOINT PATHS has no poly-time c-approximation algorithm unless $\mathsf{P} = \mathsf{NP}$. We now amplify the gap from $1/2$ to almost $1/\sqrt{m}$, implying that the approximation algorithm from Theorem 14.5 is essentially the best possible if $\mathsf{P} \neq \mathsf{NP}$.

Theorem 14.19. *For every constant $d < 1/2$,* MAX EDGE DISJOINT PATHS *(with m edges) has no poly-time $1/m^d$-approximation algorithm unless* $\mathsf{P} = \mathsf{NP}$.

Proof idea. We design essentially a gap-amplifying reduction from gap $c > 1/2$ to gap $1/m^d$ for $d < 1/2$, except that we only reduce from the special case with two pairs of terminals (TWO EDGE DISJOINT PATHS).

For starters, observe that the input in the upper left of Figure 14.3 has edge disjoint paths for all k pairs of terminals: There's a unique path from s_1 to t_1, and a unique path from s_2 to t_2 that's edge disjoint from the first path, and a unique path from s_3 to t_3 that's edge disjoint from the first two paths, and so on.

As shown in the upper right of Figure 14.3, we replace each nonterminal node with a graph G and attach the four incident edges to four designated nodes of G. If G has edge disjoint paths from top to bottom and from left to right—such as in the lower left of Figure 14.3—then the whole graph still has edge disjoint paths for all k pairs of terminals, like before. If not—such as in the lower right of Figure 14.3—then the whole graph can't have edge disjoint paths for more than one pair of terminals, since any two such paths would need to share an edge in some copy of G.

"2 versus 1" is amplified to "k versus 1". The whole graph has $m \approx k^2$ edges, so the gap becomes $1/k \approx 1/\sqrt{m}$. Actually, m also depends on the number of edges in G, but we can make this factor relatively small by choosing k large. ■

Proof. We exhibit a poly-time mapping reduction from Two Edge Disjoint Paths to $(k, k/m^d)$-Gap Max Edge Disjoint Paths (with m edges and k pairs of terminals). Since the former problem is NP-complete (Theorem 14.8), so is the latter, which implies the theorem.

Given input $(G,(q_1,r_1),(q_2,r_2))$ to Two Edge Disjoint Paths, we may assume the terminals q_1,r_1,q_2,r_2 are four distinct nodes (by creating new terminals with edges to/from the original terminals as appropriate). Assuming G has ℓ edges, define $k = \lceil \ell^{1/(1/d-2)} \rceil$, which is in poly ℓ since $d < 1/2$. Map $(G,(q_1,r_1),(q_2,r_2))$ to $(G',(s_1,t_1),\ldots,(s_k,t_k))$ as in the upper right of Figure 14.3 (which shows $k = 4$) where each copy of G has q_1 on the top, r_1 on the bottom, q_2 on the left, and r_2 on the right.

- G' has $1+2+\cdots+(k-1) = k(k-1)/2$ copies of G.
- G' has k^2 other edges since each copy of G has two outgoing edges, and each of $s_1,\ldots,s_k$ has one outgoing edge, for a total of $(k(k-1)/2)\cdot 2 + k\cdot 1 = k^2$ other edges.

Thus G' has $m = \ell k(k-1)/2 + k^2 < \ell k^2$ edges. Since $\ell \le k^{1/d-2}$, we have $m < k^{1/d}$ and thus $m^d < k$. We claim that

(i) $OPT \geq 2 \Rightarrow OPT' \geq k$

(ii) $OPT \leq 1 \Rightarrow OPT' \leq 1 < k/m^d$

where OPT and OPT' are for G and G' respectively.

(i): Suppose G has edge disjoint paths from q_1 to r_1 and from q_2 to r_2. Then G' has edge disjoint paths from s_i to t_i for all i: The path from s_i goes all the way downward (using the q_1 to r_1 path in each copy of G along the way) and then rightward to t_i (using the q_2 to r_2 path in each copy of G along the way).

(ii): Suppose G' has at least two edge disjoint paths ($OPT' \geq 2$), say from s_i to t_i and from s_j to t_j, where $i < j$. Since s_i is left of s_j, and t_i is above t_j, the two paths must "cross" each other in some copy of G, with the s_i to t_i path going from q_2 to r_2, and the s_j to t_j path going from q_1 to r_1. Thus G has edge disjoint paths from q_1 to r_1 and from q_2 to r_2 ($OPT \geq 2$). ■

14.3 Label Cover

14.3.1 The Problem

The following optimization problem plays an important role in hardness of approximation. It's a constraint satisfaction problem where each constraint depends on two variables, and each variable can be assigned ("labeled") any of k possible values. We represent variables as nodes and constraints as edges in a bipartite graph, and we view an edge as a tuple (u, v) where node u is on the bipartition's left side and node v is on the right side. (Despite the similar name, this is not a variant of Node Cover or Set Cover.)

MAX k-LABEL COVER	(14.14)
Input: Bipartite graph $G = (V, E)$ where each edge e has a function $f_e\colon [k] \times [k] \to \{0,1\}$	
Output: An assignment $a\colon V \to [k]$ satisfying as many edges as possible, where $e = (u, v)$ is satisfied iff $f_e\big(a(u), a(v)\big) = 1$	

A feasible solution is any assignment a, and its objective value is the number of edges of G that it satisfies.

A MAX k-LABEL COVER input is also called a *two-prover one-round game*: A "verifier" plays against a team of two "provers." The verifier picks a uniformly random edge $e = (u, v)$ of G and sends u to one prover and v to the other prover. They respond with $a(u)$ and $a(v)$ respectively. The prover team wins iff e is satisfied. Thus OPT/m (where m is the number of edges) is the maximum probability with which the provers can win. The provers agree on a strategy $a\colon V \to [k]$ beforehand, but they can't communicate with each other after receiving u and v, so neither knows which node the other got. One prover labels the left-side nodes, and the other labels the right-side nodes.

Lemma 14.20. *For every constant $c > 7/8$ and $c' = 1 - (1 - c)/3$, there exists a poly-time $(m, cm, m', c'm')$-gap-preserving reduction from* MAX 3-SAT *(with m clauses) to* MAX 7-LABEL COVER *(with m' edges).*

Proof. Map an n-variable m-clause 3-CNF φ to G with $m' = 3m$ edges:

- The m left-side nodes correspond to φ's clauses. For each such node, identify the labels $[7]$ with the seven satisfying assignments to the clause's three variables.
- The n right-side nodes correspond to φ's variables. For each such node, identify two labels with the bits $\{0, 1\}$ and ignore the other five labels.
- For each clause C and variable x_i in C, have an edge $e = (C, x_i)$ where $f_e\big(a(C), a(x_i)\big) = 1$ iff $a(C)$ and $a(x_i)$ agree on the bit assigned to x_i.

We claim that

(i) $OPT \geq m \quad \Rightarrow OPT' \geq m'$
(ii) $OPT < cm \Rightarrow OPT' < c'm'$

where OPT and OPT' are for φ and G respectively.

(i): Suppose $OPT \geq m$. Consider any assignment to $x_1 \cdots x_n$ satisfying all clauses of φ. View it as an assignment to the right-side nodes. Since each clause is satisfied, the assignment to its three variables is a label we can assign to the associated left-side node. This yields an assignment satisfying all edges of G, so $OPT' \geq m'$.

(ii): Suppose $OPT' \geq c'm'$. Consider any assignment to G's nodes satisfying $\geq c'm'$ edges. Since $\leq (1 - c')m' = (1 - c)m$ edges are falsified, $\leq (1 - c)m$ left-side nodes have at least one of their three edges falsified. Thus $\geq cm$ left-side nodes have all three of their edges satisfied. The corresponding clauses are satisfied by the assignment to the right-side nodes (variables of φ), so $OPT \geq cm$. ■

14.3.2 Parallel Repetition

Many hardness of approximation results are proven by gap-preserving reductions from MAX k-LABEL COVER. It's useful to first amplify the gap for MAX k-LABEL COVER (at the expense of increasing the number of labels k). At a glance, this seems like one-sided-error amplification of randomized algorithms: If we run a computation ℓ times independently and accept iff all runs accept, then the acceptance probability gets raised to the power ℓ. An analogue for two-prover one-round games is: The verifier samples ℓ edges of G independently and sends their left endpoints to one prover and their right endpoints to the other prover, and the provers win iff they satisfy all ℓ edges. This is called *parallel repetition* because each prover gets a whole batch of nodes at once, and then assigns labels to all of them (as opposed to assigning a label before getting the next node). Formally, map $G = (V, E)$ with m edges and k labels to $G' = (V', E')$ with $m' = m^\ell$ edges and $k' = k^\ell$ labels:

- If V is partitioned into left nodes L and right nodes R, then V' is partitioned into left nodes L^ℓ and right nodes R^ℓ: Each node of G' is an ℓ-tuple of nodes from the same side of G.
- View labels in $[k']$ as ℓ-tuples of labels in $[k]$. Denote labels of nodes in L^ℓ and R^ℓ by $(y_1, \ldots, y_\ell) \in [k]^\ell$ and $(z_1, \ldots, z_\ell) \in [k]^\ell$ respectively.
- Each ℓ-tuple of edges $(e_1, \ldots, e_\ell) = \big((u_1, v_1), \ldots, (u_\ell, v_\ell)\big) \in E^\ell$ corresponds to an edge $e' = \big((u_1, \ldots, u_\ell), (v_1, \ldots, v_\ell)\big) \in E'$ with:

$$f_{e'}\big((y_1, \ldots, y_\ell), (z_1, \ldots, z_\ell)\big) = f_{e_1}(y_1, z_1) \wedge \cdots \wedge f_{e_\ell}(y_\ell, z_\ell)$$

OPT and OPT' are the maximum numbers of edges that can be satisfied in G and G' respectively. We have $OPT' \geq OPT^\ell$ because if $a : V \to [k]$ satisfies OPT many edges of G, then assigning $(u_1, \ldots, u_\ell)$ the label $\big(a(u_1), \ldots, a(u_\ell)\big)$ and assigning $(v_1, \ldots, v_\ell)$ the label $\big(a(v_1), \ldots, a(v_\ell)\big)$ satisfies $\geq OPT^\ell$ many edges of G' (namely, all ℓ-tuples of satisfied edges of G). We might also expect that $OPT' \leq OPT^\ell$ and therefore $OPT'/m' = (OPT/m)^\ell$. However, this doesn't always hold (Exercise 14.17), because:

- The left prover's label y_i of u_i can depend on all of $(u_1, \ldots, u_\ell)$, not just on u_i.
- The right prover's label z_i of v_i can depend on all of $(v_1, \ldots, v_\ell)$, not just on v_i.

This ability to coordinate labels across the ℓ repetitions is a major complication. The difficult-to-prove *parallel repetition theorem* says the gap is indeed amplified exponentially in ℓ if we change the exponential's base from c to some $d > c$:

Theorem 14.21. *For all constants $c < 1$ and k, there exists a constant $d < 1$ such that for all ℓ, the ℓ-fold parallel repetition is an $(m, cm, m', d^\ell m')$-gap-amplifying reduction from* MAX k-LABEL COVER *(with m edges) to* MAX k'-LABEL COVER *(with $m' = m^\ell$ edges and $k' = k^\ell$ labels).*

The gap c (which is arbitrarily close to 1) is amplified to d^ℓ (which is arbitrarily close to 0, by choosing ℓ large enough):

(i) $OPT \geq m \;\Rightarrow\; OPT' \geq m'$
(ii) $OPT < cm \;\Rightarrow\; OPT' < d^\ell m'$

As an example of how this is used, here's the outline for proving that (m, cm)-GAP MAX 3-SAT is NP-complete for every constant $c > 7/8$ (Theorem 14.7):

(1) Prove that (m, bm)-GAP MAX 3-SAT is NP-complete for some constant $b < 1$ (§14.4).
(2) Use the gap-preserving reduction to MAX 7-LABEL COVER (Lemma 14.20).
(3) Amplify the gap using parallel repetition (Theorem 14.21).
(4) Design a gap-preserving reduction to (m, cm)-GAP MAX 3-SAT for every constant $c > 7/8$.

Steps *(1)*, *(3)*, and *(4)* are each very involved.

14.3.3 Unique Games Conjecture

For some optimization problems, such as Min Set Cover, Max k-Sat for $k \geq 3$, and Max Edge Disjoint Paths, we know the best achievable approximation ratios assuming P $\neq$ NP—we have algorithms and NP-hardness results with essentially matching approximation ratios. For other problems, such as Min Node Cover and Max 2-Sat, the known algorithms and NP-hardness results don't match. Since we're assuming P $\neq$ NP anyway, maybe we can pinpoint the best approximation ratios if we assume some other general conjecture? The *unique games conjecture* is a particularly influential tool.

Max Unique k-Label Cover is like Max k-Label Cover except every $f_e : [k] \times [k] \to \{0,1\}$ must have this property:

- For each $y \in [k]$, $f_e(y,z) = 1$ holds for exactly one $z \in [k]$.
- For each $z \in [k]$, $f_e(y,z) = 1$ holds for exactly one $y \in [k]$.

In terms of the two-prover one-round game: Any prover's response uniquely determines what the other prover's response ought to be.

Theorem 14.22. (m,m)-Gap Max Unique k-Label Cover $\in$ P.

Proof. We design a poly-time algorithm to decide whether there exists an assignment satisfying all edges. This is like Graph 2-Coloring $\in$ P (Theorem 2.1): After picking a label for a node, its neighbors' labels are "forced," and then their neighbors' labels are "forced," and so on.

Algorithm for satisfiability of unique games (14.15)

```
for each connected component of G:
    pick an arbitrary node w in the component
    for each y ∈ [k]:
        clear the labels of all nodes in this component
        assign w the label y
        run BFS starting from w, assigning labels to nodes as they're discovered:
            whenever a node u causes the discovery of a node v:
                assign v the unique label to satisfy the edge between u and v
        if this assignment satisfies all edges in this component: continue to next component
    reject
accept
```

If the algorithm accepts, then G is satisfiable since the algorithm found a satisfying assignment. Conversely, if G has a satisfying assignment a, then the algorithm accepts: For each connected component, when the initial node w gets assigned $a(w)$, the algorithm maintains the invariant that every node v gets assigned $a(v)$, by the uniqueness property. Or, the algorithm might satisfy the whole component using a different label for w. Either way, the algorithm satisfies the whole component. ∎

So for (α, β)-Gap Max Unique k-Label Cover to be NP-hard, we can't have $\alpha = m$. We merely require that on 1-inputs, it's possible to satisfy most edges, rather than all edges:

Conjecture 14.23. *For all constants $c < 1$ and $d > 0$, there exists a constant k such that (cm, dm)-*Gap Max Unique k-Label Cover *(with m edges) is* NP*-complete.*

In other words, given a "unique" two-prover one-round game for which it's either possible to satisfy $\geq cm$ edges or impossible to satisfy $\geq dm$ edges, deciding which case holds should be NP-complete. The research community has much less conviction about the truth of the unique games conjecture than about P $\neq$ NP. There are reasons for both optimism and pessimism. Even if the conjecture is false, (cm, dm)-GAP MAX UNIQUE k-LABEL COVER $\notin$ P might hold, which would still be meaningful for hardness of approximation. It's known that assuming the unique games conjecture (but not known without assuming the unique games conjecture):

- The approximation ratio of 2 for MIN NODE COVER (Theorem 14.1) can't be improved (to any constant < 2) unless P $=$ NP.
- The approximation ratio achieved by the best known poly-time algorithm for MAX 2-SAT can't be improved unless P $=$ NP.

14.4 Probabilistically Checkable Proofs

For an NP problem, a witness is a proof that the input is a 1-input. Proofs are generally fragile: When a verifier program checks a witness—or a human verifier checks a proof of a theorem—any bit of the purported proof might reveal a fatal flaw, so scrutinizing every bit is essential. Or is it? Amazingly, no: If correct proofs are suitably encoded, then a verifier can just randomly "spot check" a few bits. This means proofs can always be made robust, so any flaw can be spotted "at a glance" with high probability.

These are called *probabilistically checkable proofs (PCPs)*. Unfortunately, this name highlights the drawback (the randomness) rather than the advantage (reading few bits). Perhaps *locally checkable proofs* would be a better name, by analogy with locally decodable codes (§10.3.1). In this context, "reading a bit" is called a *query* (unrelated to a reduction querying its oracle).

The deep *PCP theorem* says every problem in NP has a randomized verifier that uses only $O(\log N)$ random bits and queries only $O(1)$ bits of the purported witness. This "crown jewel" of computational complexity is essentially equivalent to the NP-hardness of approximating MAX 3-SAT, and it has a profound philosophical implication for the nature of "proof." Unfortunately, known proofs of the PCP theorem involve enormous constants that severely limit its practical utility, but it's still a conceptual watershed. We won't fully prove the PCP theorem since it's quite difficult, but we illustrate some of the ideas by proving a weaker version.

14.4.1 The PCP Theorem and Hardness of Approximation

Recall that V is a verifier for a decision problem A iff for every input x:

- Completeness: $A(x) = 1 \Rightarrow \big(\exists w:\ V(x;w) \text{ accepts}\big)$
- Soundness: $A(x) = 0 \Rightarrow \big(\forall w:\ V(x;w) \text{ doesn't accept}\big)$

V is a *randomized verifier* with completeness c and soundness s for a decision problem A iff for every input x:

- Completeness c: $A(x) = 1 \Rightarrow \big(\exists w:\ \mathbf{Pr}_r\big[V(x;w;r) \text{ accepts}\big] \geq c\big)$
- Soundness s: $A(x) = 0 \Rightarrow \big(\forall w:\ \mathbf{Pr}_r\big[V(x;w;r) \text{ accepts}\big] \leq s\big)$

We care about the number of bits V reads from r and from w on valid inputs x of size N:

- V has *randomness efficiency* $\le R(N)$ iff $V(x;w;r)$ reads only the first $\le R(N)$ bits of r.
- V has *query efficiency* $\le Q(N)$ iff $V(x;w;r)$ reads $\le Q(N)$ bits of w, nonadaptively.

There are two subtleties with how V accesses w:

- The witness segment has word size 1, so each read-witness instruction gets one bit of w.
- V must first determine all the addresses of w it will read, and then execute all its read-witness instructions in one batch. (In contrast, *adaptive* would mean the value of a bit V reads from w could influence which bit V chooses to read next from w, and so on.)

Definition. For every constant k, $\mathsf{PCP}[\log N, k]$ is the set of all decision problems for which there exists a randomized verifier with completeness 1, soundness 1/3, $O(\log N)$ randomness efficiency, $\le k$ query efficiency, $\text{poly}\, N$ time efficiency, and $O(\log N)$-bounded word size. ◀

(Saying "$O(1)$ query efficiency" would mean the constant may depend on the problem.)
The acclaimed *PCP theorem* is:

Theorem 14.24. $\mathsf{NP} = \mathsf{PCP}[\log N, k]$ *for some constant* k.

$\mathsf{PCP}[\log N, k] \subseteq \mathsf{NP}$ by brute force derandomization: Since V uses $O(\log N)$ random bits, a deterministic verifier can run V on all $2^{O(\log N)} = \text{poly}\, N$ possible outcomes of the randomness, and accept iff all runs of V accept. (The soundness and query efficiency are irrelevant.) We won't prove the difficult converse $\mathsf{NP} \subseteq \mathsf{PCP}[\log N, k]$.

The PCP theorem is essentially "NP-hardness of approximating MAX 3-SAT" in disguise. This corollary is Theorem 14.7 but with "every $c > 7/8$" replaced by "some $b < 1$":

Corollary 14.25. *For some constant* $b < 1$, (m, bm)-GAP MAX 3-SAT *(with m clauses) is* NP-*complete, so* MAX 3-SAT *has no poly-time b-approximation algorithm unless* $\mathsf{P} = \mathsf{NP}$.

Proof idea. To prove that 3-SAT is NP-complete, we turned any NP verifier into a reduction to 3-SAT. Now, we turn any $\mathsf{PCP}[\log N, k]$ verifier into a gap-introducing reduction to MAX 3-SAT. This is more straightforward because the verifier's output depends on the witness in a very restricted way. We do brute force over the $\text{poly}\, N$ many outcomes of the randomness. The approximation gap comes from the completeness versus soundness gap. ■

Proof. We prove that $(m, (1-2^{-k-1})m)$-GAP MAX k-SAT is NP-complete, where k is from Theorem 14.24. By Corollary 14.16, this implies (m, bm)-GAP MAX 3-SAT is NP-complete where $b = 1 - 2^{-k-1}/(k-2)$.

For any $A \in \mathsf{NP}$, we have $A \in \mathsf{PCP}[\log N, k]$ (Theorem 14.24). Let V be a poly-time randomized verifier for A with completeness 1, soundness 1/3, randomness efficiency $\le a \log N$ (for an integer a), and query efficiency $\le k$. We may assume V always queries exactly k different bit positions of $w \in \{0,1\}^n$ where $n = dN^e$ (for integers d, e). For each valid input x of size N and each $r \in \{0,1\}^{a \log N}$, there exist:

- A size-k set $I_{x,r} \subseteq \{0, \dots, n-1\}$ of indices of w queried by $V(x;w;r)$.
- A function $f_{x,r} \colon \{0,1\}^k \to \{0,1\}$ such that $V(x;w;r)$ accepts iff $f_{x,r}(w_{I_{x,r}}) = 1$.

Some k-CNF $\varphi_{x,r}$ expresses $f_{x,r}$ (Lemma 2.9). Assume $\varphi_{x,r}$ has n variables representing w's bits, but only depends on variables indexed by $I_{x,r}$. Thus $V(x;w;r)$ accepts iff $\varphi_{x,r}(w) = 1$.

Here's a poly-time mapping reduction from A to $(m,(1-2^{-k-1})m)$-GAP MAX k-SAT: Map x to $\varphi_x(w) = \bigwedge_r \varphi_{x,r}(w)$. This has $m \le N^a 2^k \le \text{poly}N$ clauses since there are $2^{a\log N} = N^a$ possibilities of r, and each $\varphi_{x,r}$ has $\le 2^k$ clauses.

$$
\begin{aligned}
A(x)=1 &\Rightarrow \big(\exists w:\ \mathbf{Pr}_r[\varphi_{x,r}(w)=1]\ge 1\big) && \text{(completeness 1)}\\
&\Rightarrow \big(\exists w:\ \text{all } m \text{ clauses of } \varphi_x \text{ are satisfied}\big)\\
&\Rightarrow OPT(\varphi_x)\ge m
\end{aligned}
$$

$$
\begin{aligned}
A(x)=0 &\Rightarrow \big(\forall w:\ \mathbf{Pr}_r[\varphi_{x,r}(w)=0]\ge 2/3>1/2\big) && \text{(soundness 1/3)}\\
&\Rightarrow \big(\forall w:\ \text{for} > N^a/2 \text{ many } r, \text{ at least one clause of } \varphi_{x,r} \text{ is falsified}\big)\\
&\Rightarrow \big(\forall w:\ \text{more than } N^a/2 \ge m/2^{k+1} \text{ clauses of } \varphi_x \text{ are falsified}\big)\\
&\Rightarrow OPT(\varphi_x)<(1-2^{-k-1})m
\end{aligned}
$$

■

Essentially the same argument works "in reverse" to show that NP-completeness of (m, bm)-GAP MAX 3-SAT implies the PCP theorem (Exercise 14.19).

Definition. For every constant k, PCP[poly$N$, k] is the set of all decision problems for which there exists a randomized verifier with completeness 1, soundness 1/3, poly$N$ randomness efficiency, $\le k$ query efficiency, poly$N$ time efficiency, $2^{\text{poly}N}$ witness size, and poly$N$-bounded word size. ◄

PCP[poly$N$, k] (in contrast to PCP[log$N$, k]) allows randomness efficiency poly$N$ and witness size $2^{\text{poly}N}$. The poly$N$-bounded word size is necessary since a witness segment address is now poly$N$ bits long. Unlike in §2.2.2, the time efficiency doesn't depend on the witness size here. This is a "scaled up" variant of the PCP theorem:

Theorem 14.26. NEXP = PCP[poly$N$, k] *for some constant* k.

We spend the rest of this section proving a weaker version of the PCP theorem:

Theorem 14.27. NP $\subseteq$ PCP[poly$N$, k] *for some constant* k.

14.4.2 Proof Idea for the Weak PCP Theorem

In a linear equation over $\mathbb{Z}_2$, the left side is the sum (parity) of a subset of variables—in other words, the dot product of a vector of coefficients and the vector of all variables—and the right side is either 0 or 1. For example, $x_2 \oplus x_3 \oplus x_5 = 1$ is the same as $01101 \odot x_1x_2x_3x_4x_5 = 1$.

$\mathbb{Z}_2$ LINEAR SYSTEM SAT	(14.16)
Input: A system of linear equations over $\mathbb{Z}_2$	
Output: Does there exist an assignment satisfying all the equations?	

As a warmup, we show $\mathbb{Z}_2$ LINEAR SYSTEM SAT $\in$ PCP[poly$N$, k] for some constant k. (In fact, $\mathbb{Z}_2$ LINEAR SYSTEM SAT $\in$ P since linear systems can be solved in poly time, but this is still a helpful warmup.)

Represent a system of m linear equations in n variables over $\mathbb{Z}_2$ as $Mx = d$ where M is an $m \times n$ matrix of coefficients, x is an $n \times 1$ vector of variables, and d is an $m \times 1$ vector of right sides. The ith equation is $M_i x = d_i$ where M_i is M's ith row.

To convince us the system is satisfiable, someone could provide a satisfying assignment a as the witness, but then we'd have to query every bit of the witness. We can do better. First idea: Instead of checking all equations, just check a random linear combination of them. For a uniformly random $1 \times m$ vector r, let r_i be the coefficient of the ith equation in the linear combination. The resulting equation is $(rM)x = rd$. The left side rM is a linear combination of M's rows, and the right side rd is a linear combination of d's entries. If a satisfies $Mx = d$ then a satisfies every linear combination $(rM)x = rd$, and if a doesn't satisfy $Mx = d$ then a satisfies only half of the linear combinations $(rM)x = rd$, by associativity and the random subsum principle (Lemma 7.2):

$$\mathbf{Pr}_r\big[(rM)a = rd\big] = \mathbf{Pr}_r\big[r(Ma) = rd\big] = \begin{cases} 1 & \text{if } Ma = d \\ 1/2 & \text{if } Ma \neq d \end{cases}$$

Suppose someone encodes the "message" $a \in \{0,1\}^n$ with the dot product code (§ 9.1.2) and provides as the witness the codeword $w \in \{0,1\}^{2^n}$, viewed as the table of a function $w\colon \{0,1\}^n \to \{0,1\}$ where $w(y) = y \odot a$ for all y. This would let us obtain $y \odot a$ (for any y of our choice) with a single query to w. Consider this randomized verifier:

First attempt at a PCP verifier for $\mathbb{Z}_2$ LINEAR SYSTEM SAT (14.17)

$V(M, d;\, w;\, r)$:
  accept iff $w(rM) = rd$

This computes rM and rd and queries one bit of w. It accepts iff $(rM)a = rd$, assuming $w(y) = y \odot a$ for all y.

- Completeness 1: $\big(\exists a : Ma = d\big) \Rightarrow \big(\exists a : \mathbf{Pr}_r\big[V(M,d;\, w;\, r) \text{ accepts}\big] = 1\big)$
- Soundness 1/2? $\big(\forall a : Ma \neq d\big) \Rightarrow \big(\forall a : \mathbf{Pr}_r\big[V(M,d;\, w;\, r) \text{ accepts}\big] \leq 1/2\big)$

The catch is that soundness requires $\forall w$, not $\forall a$: We can't assume the purported witness w is some a's codeword. Before handling that, let's see an example.

Example. Consider this system with $m = 4$ and $n = 3$:

$$\begin{aligned} x_1 \oplus x_2 &= 0 \\ x_2 \oplus x_3 &= 0 \\ x_1 \oplus x_3 &= 1 \\ x_1 \oplus x_2 \oplus x_3 &= 1 \end{aligned} \qquad Mx = \begin{bmatrix} 1 & 1 & 0 \\ 0 & 1 & 1 \\ 1 & 0 & 1 \\ 1 & 1 & 1 \end{bmatrix} \begin{bmatrix} x_1 \\ x_2 \\ x_3 \end{bmatrix} = \begin{bmatrix} 0 \\ 0 \\ 1 \\ 1 \end{bmatrix} = d$$

It's unsatisfiable since the first three equations say $x_1 = x_2$ and $x_2 = x_3$ and $x_1 \neq x_3$. Consider the assignment $a = 110$ and its codeword $w = 00111100$ (indexed by 000, 001, 010, 011, 100, 101, 110, 111). We have:

$$Ma = \begin{bmatrix} 1 & 1 & 0 \\ 0 & 1 & 1 \\ 1 & 0 & 1 \\ 1 & 1 & 1 \end{bmatrix} \begin{bmatrix} 1 \\ 1 \\ 0 \end{bmatrix} = \begin{bmatrix} 0 \\ 1 \\ 1 \\ 0 \end{bmatrix} \neq \begin{bmatrix} 0 \\ 0 \\ 1 \\ 1 \end{bmatrix} = d$$

If the verifier randomly picks $r = \begin{bmatrix} 1 & 1 & 0 & 0 \end{bmatrix}$, then it computes

$$rM = \begin{bmatrix} 1 & 1 & 0 & 0 \end{bmatrix} \begin{bmatrix} 1 & 1 & 0 \\ 0 & 1 & 1 \\ 1 & 0 & 1 \\ 1 & 1 & 1 \end{bmatrix} = \begin{bmatrix} 1 & 0 & 1 \end{bmatrix} \qquad rd = \begin{bmatrix} 1 & 1 & 0 & 0 \end{bmatrix} \begin{bmatrix} 0 \\ 0 \\ 1 \\ 1 \end{bmatrix} = 0$$

so the linear combination of equations $(rM)x = rd$ is $\begin{bmatrix}1 & 0 & 1\end{bmatrix}x = 0$. Next, it queries the bit

$$w(101) \;=\; (rM)a \;=\; \begin{bmatrix}1 & 0 & 1\end{bmatrix}\begin{bmatrix}1\\1\\0\end{bmatrix} \;=\; 1$$

and rejects since $(rM)a \neq rd$.

If the verifier instead randomly picks $r = \begin{bmatrix}0 & 1 & 1 & 1\end{bmatrix}$, then it computes

$$rM \;=\; \begin{bmatrix}0 & 1 & 1 & 1\end{bmatrix}\begin{bmatrix}1 & 1 & 0\\0 & 1 & 1\\1 & 0 & 1\\1 & 1 & 1\end{bmatrix} \;=\; \begin{bmatrix}0 & 0 & 1\end{bmatrix} \qquad\qquad rd \;=\; \begin{bmatrix}0 & 1 & 1 & 1\end{bmatrix}\begin{bmatrix}0\\0\\1\\1\end{bmatrix} \;=\; 0$$

so the linear combination of equations $(rM)x = rd$ is $\begin{bmatrix}0 & 0 & 1\end{bmatrix}x = 0$. Next, it queries the bit

$$w(001) \;=\; (rM)a \;=\; \begin{bmatrix}0 & 0 & 1\end{bmatrix}\begin{bmatrix}1\\1\\0\end{bmatrix} \;=\; 0$$

and accepts since $(rM)a = rd$. ♦

If $Mx = d$ is unsatisfiable, we want the acceptance probability to be small even if w isn't a dot product codeword. For this, we use the "damned if you do, damned if you don't" paradigm:

- If w is close to a codeword c corresponding to a message a, then we can treat w as a received word and recover c from it (and use c to detect that $Ma \neq d$, as before). Decoding means recovering the message a from w, and *correcting* means recovering the codeword c from w. Local decoding means recovering any bit of a using few queries to w, and *local correcting* means recovering any bit of c using few queries to w. The idea underlying the dot product code's local decoder (§10.3.1) also yields a local corrector: Say we want $c(y)$. With high probability over a uniformly random q, we have $w(y \oplus q) = c(y \oplus q)$ and $w(q) = c(q)$ and thus $w(y \oplus q) \oplus w(q) = c(y \oplus q) \oplus c(q) = c\big((y \oplus q) \oplus q\big) = c(y)$.
- If w is far from every codeword, then we can detect this and reject with moderate probability using few queries to w: By linearity, $c(s \oplus t) = c(s) \oplus c(t)$ for every codeword c and all s, t. It's natural to conjecture that if w is far from every codeword, then $w(s \oplus t) \neq w(s) \oplus w(t)$ with moderate probability over uniformly random s, t. This is indeed true, but proving it is somewhat tricky and involves new machinery, so we postpone the proof to §14.4.4. We say the dot product code is *locally testable*.

Theorem 14.28. *For every $w\colon \{0,1\}^n \to \{0,1\}$:*

$$\mathbf{Pr}_{s,t}\big[w(s \oplus t) = w(s) \oplus w(t)\big] \;\leq\; \max_{a \in \{0,1\}^n} \mathbf{Pr}_q\big[w(q) = q \odot a\big]$$

Let's use these ideas to synthesize a new randomized verifier. On input (M, d), purported witness $w\colon \{0,1\}^n \to \{0,1\}$, and randomness $(q, r, s, t) \in \{0,1\}^n \times \{0,1\}^m \times \{0,1\}^n \times \{0,1\}^n$:

PCP verifier for $\mathbb{Z}_2$ LINEAR SYSTEM SAT (14.18)

$V(M, d;\, w;\, q, r, s, t)$:
 accept iff $w(rM \oplus q) \oplus w(q) = rd$ and $w(s \oplus t) = w(s) \oplus w(t)$

Claim 14.29. *V has completeness* 1.

Proof. Suppose $Ma = d$ for some $a \in \{0,1\}^n$. Define $w\colon \{0,1\}^n \to \{0,1\}$ by $w(y) = y \odot a$ for all y. Then $\mathbf{Pr}_{q,r,s,t}\big[V(M,d;\, w;\, q,r,s,t) \text{ accepts}\big] = 1$ because by linearity:

$$w(rM \oplus q) \oplus w(q) \;=\; \big((rM \oplus q) \odot a\big) \oplus (q \odot a) \;=\; \big((rM \oplus q) \oplus q\big) \odot a \;=\; (rM)a \;=\; r(Ma) \;=\; rd$$

$$w(s \oplus t) \;=\; (s \oplus t) \odot a \;=\; (s \odot a) \oplus (t \odot a) \;=\; w(s) \oplus w(t)$$

■

Claim 14.30. *V has soundness* $5/6$.

Proof. Suppose $Ma \neq d$ for all $a \in \{0,1\}^n$. Consider any $w\colon \{0,1\}^n \to \{0,1\}$. In both of the following cases, $\mathbf{Pr}_{q,r,s,t}\big[V(M,d;\, w;\, q,r,s,t) \text{ accepts}\big] \le 5/6$:

Case 1. For some a, $\mathbf{Pr}_q\big[w(q) \neq q \odot a\big] \le 1/6$. If $r(Ma) \neq rd$ and $w(rM \oplus q) = (rM \oplus q) \odot a$ and $w(q) = q \odot a$, then $w(rM \oplus q) \oplus w(q) = r(Ma) \neq rd$ like in Claim 14.29. Thus

$$\begin{aligned}
&\mathbf{Pr}_{q,r}\big[w(rM \oplus q) \oplus w(q) = rd\big] \\
&\le \mathbf{Pr}_{q,r}\big[r(Ma) = rd \;\text{ or }\; w(rM \oplus q) \neq (rM \oplus q) \odot a \;\text{ or }\; w(q) \neq q \odot a\big] \\
&\le \mathbf{Pr}_{r}\big[r(Ma) = rd\big] + \mathbf{Pr}_{q,r}\big[w(rM \oplus q) \neq (rM \oplus q) \odot a\big] + \mathbf{Pr}_{q}\big[w(q) \neq q \odot a\big] \\
&\le 1/2 + 1/6 + 1/6 \\
&= 5/6
\end{aligned}$$

by a union bound, the random subsum principle, and the fact that $rM \oplus q$ is also uniformly random.

Case 2. For all a, $\mathbf{Pr}_q\big[w(q) \neq q \odot a\big] \ge 1/6$. Then we have $\mathbf{Pr}_{s,t}\big[w(s \oplus t) = w(s) \oplus w(t)\big] \le 5/6$ by Theorem 14.28. ■

V has soundness $5/6$ and query efficiency 5, with queries $w(rM \oplus q)$, $w(q)$, $w(s \oplus t)$, $w(s)$, $w(t)$. Running it 7 times independently and accepting iff all runs accept, the soundness is $(5/6)^7 \le 1/3$ and the query efficiency is $7 \cdot 5 = 35$. Thus $\mathbb{Z}_2$ Linear System Sat $\in \mathsf{PCP}[\text{poly}\,N, 35]$.

Instead of just linear equations, with a little more work we can handle quadratic equations, which are powerful enough to capture NP. In a quadratic equation over $\mathbb{Z}_2$, the left side is a sum (parity) of products ("and"s) of pairs of variables, and the right side is either 0 or 1. For example, $x_2x_4 \oplus x_3^2 \oplus x_1x_4 = 0$. Since $x_i = x_i^2$, we may assume there are no degree-1 monomials.

$\mathbb{Z}_2$ Quadratic System Sat	(14.19)
Input: A system of quadratic equations over $\mathbb{Z}_2$	
Output: Does there exist an assignment satisfying all the equations?	

Lemma 14.31. *$\mathbb{Z}_2$ Quadratic System Sat is* NP*-complete.*

We prove this lemma at the end of §14.4.3. So for the weak PCP theorem, it suffices to prove $\mathbb{Z}_2$ Quadratic System Sat $\in \mathsf{PCP}[\text{poly}\,N, k]$ for some constant k.

For $u \in \{0,1\}^n$ and $v \in \{0,1\}^n$, define the *tensor product* $u \otimes v \in \{0,1\}^{n^2}$ by $(u \otimes v)_{i,j} = u_i v_j$, viewing the set of indices as $[n] \times [n]$. For example:

$$(u_1, u_2, u_3) \otimes (v_1, v_2, v_3) \;=\; (u_1v_1,\; u_1v_2,\; u_1v_3,\; u_2v_1,\; u_2v_2,\; u_2v_3,\; u_3v_1,\; u_3v_2,\; u_3v_3)$$

If u and v are $n \times 1$ vectors, then $u \otimes v$ is an $n^2 \times 1$ vector.

A quadratic equation with variables $x = (x_1, \ldots, x_n)$ is a linear equation whose "variables" are the entries of $x \otimes x$. Represent a system of m quadratic equations in n variables over $\mathbb{Z}_2$ as $M(x \otimes x) = d$ where M is an $m \times n^2$ matrix of coefficients, x is an $n \times 1$ vector of variables, and d is an $m \times 1$ vector of right sides. The ith equation is $M_i(x \otimes x) = d_i$ where M_i is M's ith row.

Example. This system has $m = 2$ and $n = 2$:

$$\begin{aligned} x_1^2 \oplus x_2x_1 &= 0 \\ x_1x_2 \oplus x_2^2 &= 1 \end{aligned} \qquad M(x \otimes x) = \begin{bmatrix} 1 & 0 & 1 & 0 \\ 0 & 1 & 0 & 1 \end{bmatrix} \begin{bmatrix} x_1x_1 \\ x_1x_2 \\ x_2x_1 \\ x_2x_2 \end{bmatrix} = \begin{bmatrix} 0 \\ 1 \end{bmatrix} = d$$

It's satisfiable since $x_1 = 0$ and $x_2 = 1$ is a satisfying assignment. Of course, $x_1x_2 = x_2x_1$, so the first equation is equivalent to $x_1^2 \oplus x_1x_2 = 0$, and the second is equivalent to $x_2x_1 \oplus x_2^2 = 1$. ♦

What if we give this (M, d) to our randomized verifier for linear systems? The completeness would still be 1, by letting the witness $w\colon \{0,1\}^{n^2} \to \{0,1\}$ be the dot product codeword of the message $a \otimes a$ where a is a satisfying assignment. What about soundness? Now, $w\colon \{0,1\}^{n^2} \to \{0,1\}$ could be any function.

- The local linearity test detects if w is far from every codeword, so we might as well assume w is close to the codeword of some message $b \in \{0,1\}^{n^2}$.
- The local corrector recovers any bit of the codeword, so we might as well assume w is the exact codeword: $w(y) = y \odot b$ for all $y \in \{0,1\}^{n^2}$.

The trouble is that even if the quadratic system is unsatisfiable, we might have $Mb = d$ for some b that's not of the form $a \otimes a$, and the "linear system" verifier would accept. We need another "local check" to detect and reject when $b \neq a \otimes a$ for all a, assuming $w(y) = y \odot b$ for all y. We call this the *quadratic consistency* check.

First, observe that if $b = a \otimes a$, then $b_{i,i} = a_i^2 = a_i$ for all i. So instead of worrying about every a, we can just consider the specific a defined by $a_i = b_{i,i}$ for all i. Using few queries to w, we want to accept with probability 1 if $b = a \otimes a$, and accept with constant probability < 1 if $b \neq a \otimes a$. The next idea is to use the random subsum principle again: For uniformly random $z \in \{0,1\}^{n^2}$, $\mathbf{Pr}_z\big[z \odot b = z \odot (a \otimes a)\big]$ equals 1 if $b = a \otimes a$, and equals $1/2$ if $b \neq a \otimes a$. We can query $w(z)$ to get $z \odot b$, but unfortunately we can't get $z \odot (a \otimes a)$ by querying w.

The crucial idea is to sample z not from the uniform distribution, but from a different distribution that's good enough for soundness but lets us get $z \odot (a \otimes a)$ by querying w. For $z = u \otimes v$ for uniformly random $u, v \in \{0,1\}^n$, we prove that $\mathbf{Pr}_{u,v}\big[(u \otimes v) \odot b = (u \otimes v) \odot (a \otimes a)\big] \le 3/4$ if $b \neq a \otimes a$, and that $(u \otimes v) \odot (a \otimes a) = (u \odot a)(v \odot a) = (u' \odot b)(v' \odot b) = w(u')w(v')$ for some u' and v'.

We now assemble these ideas into a self-contained formal proof of Theorem 14.27.

14.4.3 Proof of the Weak PCP Theorem

We prove $\mathbb{Z}_2$ Quadratic System Sat $\in$ PCP[poly$N$, k] for some constant k, which implies NP $\subseteq$ PCP[poly$N$, k] since $\mathbb{Z}_2$ Quadratic System Sat is NP-complete (Lemma 14.31).

Represent a system of m quadratic equations in n variables over $\mathbb{Z}_2$ as $M(x \otimes x) = d$ where M is an $m \times n^2$ matrix of coefficients, x is an $n \times 1$ vector of variables, $x \otimes x$ is the $n^2 \times 1$ vector defined by $(x \otimes x)_{i,j} = x_i x_j$ for $(i,j) \in [n] \times [n]$, and d is an $m \times 1$ vector of right sides. The ith equation is $M_i(x \otimes x) = d_i$ where M_i is M's ith row.

On input (M, d), the purported witness is some $w\colon \{0,1\}^{n^2} \to \{0,1\}$, and the randomness is (q, r, s, t, u, v) where:

$q \in \{0,1\}^{n^2}$	(for locally correcting w)
$r \in \{0,1\}^m$	(for the linear combination of equations; r is a $1 \times m$ vector)
$s, t \in \{0,1\}^{n^2}$	(for locally testing linearity of w)
$u, v \in \{0,1\}^n$	(for checking quadratic consistency of w)

- Define $w_q\colon \{0,1\}^{n^2} \to \{0,1\}$ by $w_q(y) = w(y \oplus q) \oplus w(q)$, which is two queries to w.
- Define $u \otimes v \in \{0,1\}^{n^2}$ by $(u \otimes v)_{i,j} = u_i v_j$.
- Define $u' \in \{0,1\}^{n^2}$ by $u'_{i,i} = u_i$ and $u'_{i,j} = 0$ for $i \neq j$, and similarly define v' from v.

PCP verifier for $\mathbb{Z}_2$ QUADRATIC SYSTEM SAT (14.20)

$V(M, d;\ w;\ q, r, s, t, u, v)$:
accept iff $w_q(rM) = rd$ and $w(s \oplus t) = w(s) \oplus w(t)$ and $w_q(u \otimes v) = w_q(u')w_q(v')$

First, we record some observations that we'll use tacitly several times.

- For $a \in \{0,1\}^n$:

$$(u \otimes v) \odot (a \otimes a) \;=\; \textstyle\sum_{i,j}(u_i v_j)(a_i a_j) \;=\; \big(\sum_i u_i a_i\big)\big(\sum_j v_j a_j\big) \;=\; (u \odot a)(v \odot a)$$

- For $b \in \{0,1\}^{n^2}$ and $y \in \{0,1\}^{n^2}$, if $w(y \oplus q) = (y \oplus q) \odot b$ and $w(q) = q \odot b$ then:

$$w_q(y) \;=\; w(y \oplus q) \oplus w(q) \;=\; \big((y \oplus q) \odot b\big) \oplus (q \odot b) \;=\; \big((y \oplus q) \oplus q\big) \odot b \;=\; y \odot b$$

- For $b \in \{0,1\}^{n^2}$, if $\mathbf{Pr}_q\big[w(q) \neq q \odot b\big] \leq 1/28$ then for every $y \in \{0,1\}^{n^2}$,

$$\begin{aligned}\mathbf{Pr}_q\big[w_q(y) \neq y \odot b\big] &\leq \mathbf{Pr}_q\big[w(y \oplus q) \neq (y \oplus q) \odot b \text{ or } w(q) \neq q \odot b\big] \\ &\leq \mathbf{Pr}_q\big[w(y \oplus q) \neq (y \oplus q) \odot b\big] + \mathbf{Pr}_q\big[w(q) \neq q \odot b\big] \\ &\leq 1/28 + 1/28 \;=\; 1/14\end{aligned}$$

  by a union bound and the fact that $y \oplus q$ is also uniformly random.

Claim 14.32. *V has completeness* 1.

Proof. Suppose $M(a \otimes a) = d$ for some $a \in \{0,1\}^n$. Define $w\colon \{0,1\}^{n^2} \to \{0,1\}$ by $w(y) = y \odot b$ where $b = a \otimes a$. Then $\mathbf{Pr}_{q,r,s,t,u,v}\big[V(M, d;\ w;\ q, r, s, t, u, v) \text{ accepts}\big] = 1$ because $w_q = w$ and:

$$w(rM) \;=\; (rM)b \;=\; r(Mb) \;=\; rd$$

$$w(s \oplus t) \;=\; (s \oplus t) \odot b \;=\; (s \odot b) \oplus (t \odot b) \;=\; w(s) \oplus w(t)$$

$$w(u \otimes v) \;=\; (u \otimes v) \odot (a \otimes a) \;=\; (u \odot a)(v \odot a) \;=\; (u' \odot b)(v' \odot b) \;=\; w(u')w(v') \qquad \blacksquare$$

Claim 14.33. *V has soundness* $27/28$.

Proof. Suppose $M(a \otimes a) \neq d$ for all $a \in \{0,1\}^n$. Consider any $w\colon \{0,1\}^{n^2} \to \{0,1\}$. In all three of the following cases, $\mathbf{Pr}_{q,r,s,t,u,v}\big[V(M, d;\ w;\ q, r, s, t, u, v) \text{ accepts}\big] \leq 27/28$:

Case 1. For some a and $b = a \otimes a$, $\mathbf{Pr}_q\big[w(q) \neq q \odot b\big] \leq 1/28$. Viewing r as a $1 \times m$ vector and b as an $n^2 \times 1$ vector,

$$\begin{aligned}\mathbf{Pr}_{q,r}\big[w_q(rM) = rd\big] &\leq \mathbf{Pr}_{q,r}\big[r(Mb) = rd \text{ or } w_q(rM) \neq (rM)b\big] \\ &\leq \mathbf{Pr}_r\big[r(Mb) = rd\big] + \mathbf{Pr}_{q,r}\big[w_q(rM) \neq (rM)b\big] \\ &\leq 1/2 + 1/14 \leq 27/28\end{aligned}$$

by a union bound and the random subsum principle, since $Mb \neq d$.

Case 2. For all b (not necessarily of the form $a \otimes a$), $\mathbf{Pr}_q\big[w(q) \neq q \odot b\big] \geq 1/28$. Then we have $\mathbf{Pr}_{s,t}\big[w(s \oplus t) = w(s) \oplus w(t)\big] \leq 27/28$ by Theorem 14.28.

Case 3. For some b, $\mathbf{Pr}_q\big[w(q) \neq q \odot b\big] \leq 1/28$ but $b \neq a \otimes a$ for all a. By a union bound:

$$\begin{aligned}&\mathbf{Pr}_{q,u,v}\big[w_q(u \otimes v) = w_q(u')w_q(v')\big] \\ &\leq \mathbf{Pr}_{q,u,v}\big[(u \otimes v) \odot b = (u' \odot b)(v' \odot b) \text{ or } \\ &\qquad w_q(u \otimes v) \neq (u \otimes v) \odot b \text{ or } w_q(u') \neq u' \odot b \text{ or } w_q(v') \neq v' \odot b\big] \\ &\leq \mathbf{Pr}_{u,v}\big[(u \otimes v) \odot b = (u' \odot b)(v' \odot b)\big] + \\ &\quad \mathbf{Pr}_{q,u,v}\big[w_q(u \otimes v) \neq (u \otimes v) \odot b\big] + \mathbf{Pr}_{q,u}\big[w_q(u') \neq u' \odot b\big] + \mathbf{Pr}_{q,v}\big[w_q(v') \neq v' \odot b\big] \\ &\leq \mathbf{Pr}_{u,v}\big[(u \otimes v) \odot b = (u' \odot b)(v' \odot b)\big] + 1/14 + 1/14 + 1/14\end{aligned}$$

Consider a defined by $a_i = b_{i,i}$ for all $i \in [n]$, and let $c = a \otimes a$. We have $(u' \odot b)(v' \odot b) = (u \odot a)(v \odot a) = (u \otimes v) \odot c$. Let $b_i = (b_{i,1}, \ldots, b_{i,n})$ and $c_i = (c_{i,1}, \ldots, c_{i,n})$ for each i. Note that

$$(u \otimes v) \odot b = \textstyle\sum_{i,j} u_i v_j b_{i,j} = \sum_i u_i \sum_j v_j b_{i,j} = \sum_i u_i (v \odot b_i) = u \odot \big(v \odot b_1, \ldots, v \odot b_n\big)$$

and $(u \otimes v) \odot c = u \odot \big(v \odot c_1, \ldots, v \odot c_n\big)$. Since $b \neq c$, we have $b_i \neq c_i$ for some i. By the random subsum principle, $\mathbf{Pr}_v\big[v \odot b_i \neq v \odot c_i\big] = 1/2$. If $v \odot b_i \neq v \odot c_i$, then $\big(v \odot b_1, \ldots, v \odot b_n\big) \neq \big(v \odot c_1, \ldots, v \odot c_n\big)$ in which case $\mathbf{Pr}_u\big[(u \otimes v) \odot b \neq (u \otimes v) \odot c\big] = 1/2$ by the random subsum principle again. By the chain rule:

$$\begin{aligned}&\mathbf{Pr}_{u,v}\big[(u \otimes v) \odot b \neq (u' \odot b)(v' \odot b)\big] \\ &= \mathbf{Pr}_{u,v}\big[(u \otimes v) \odot b \neq (u \otimes v) \odot c\big] \\ &\geq \mathbf{Pr}_v\big[v \odot b_i \neq v \odot c_i\big] \cdot \mathbf{Pr}_{u,v}\big[(u \otimes v) \odot b \neq (u \otimes v) \odot c \,\big|\, v \odot b_i \neq v \odot c_i\big] \\ &= (1/2) \cdot (1/2) = 1/4\end{aligned}$$

Putting everything together, $\mathbf{Pr}_{q,u,v}\big[w_q(u \otimes v) = w_q(u')w_q(v')\big] \leq 3/4 + 3/14 = 27/28$. ■

V has soundness $27/28$ and query efficiency 11. Running it 31 times independently and accepting iff all runs accept, the soundness is $(27/28)^{31} \leq 1/3$ and the query efficiency is $31 \cdot 11 = 341$. It has $\operatorname{poly} N$ randomness efficiency, $\operatorname{poly} N$ time efficiency, $2^{\operatorname{poly} N}$ witness size, and $\operatorname{poly} N$-bounded word size. This concludes the proof of Theorem 14.27, except for the NP-completeness of $\mathbb{Z}_2$ Quadratic System Sat:

Proof of Lemma 14.31. $\mathbb{Z}_2$ Quadratic System Sat $\in$ NP because given an assignment to x as a purported witness, a poly-time verifier can plug it in and check whether all the equations are satisfied. Next, it suffices to show Circuit Sat $\leq_p^m$ $\mathbb{Z}_2$ Quadratic System Sat since Circuit Sat is NP-complete (Theorem 5.18). Map a circuit C to a system S of quadratic equations over $\mathbb{Z}_2$:

- Assume C has no $\vee$ gates, only $\wedge$ and $\neg$ gates (§5.2.2).
- For each node of C, S has a corresponding variable. Say $x_1, \ldots, x_n$ are the input variables, and $x_{n+1}, \ldots, x_{n+m}$ are the gate variables.
- For each $\neg$ gate $x_i = \neg x_j$ of C, S has the equation $x_i^2 \oplus x_j^2 = 1$ (equivalent to $x_i = x_j \oplus 1$).
- For each $\wedge$ gate $x_i = x_j \wedge x_k$ of C, S has the equation $x_i^2 \oplus x_j x_k = 0$ (equivalent to $x_i = x_j x_k$).
- For the output node x_i of C, S has the equation $x_i^2 = 1$ (equivalent to $x_i = 1$).

An assignment $(a, b) \in \{0,1\}^n \times \{0,1\}^m$ satisfies S iff a satisfies C and b is the values of all gates when evaluating $C(a)$. This poly-time mapping reduction is correct because C is satisfiable iff S is satisfiable:

$\Leftarrow$: If (a, b) satisfies S, then a satisfies C.

$\Rightarrow$: If a satisfies C, then (a, b) satisfies S, where b is the values of all gates when evaluating $C(a)$. ■

14.4.4 Harmonic Analysis and Linearity Testing

Traditionally, *harmonic analysis* is about expressing functions $f : \mathbb{R} \to \mathbb{R}$ as linear combinations of "sine waves" of varying frequencies, which are called harmonics since they correspond to different pitches in music. The linear combination's coefficients carry information about f that might be harder to glean from the values $f(x)$.

We develop a discrete analogue of harmonic analysis—for boolean functions $f : \{0,1\}^n \to \{0,1\}$—and use it to prove that the dot product code's local tester works (Theorem 14.28). Discrete harmonic analysis has many other applications in computational complexity. The role of harmonics is played by parity functions (over subsets of input variables): Their values "oscillate" between 0 and 1 as we flip individual input bits. We express any boolean function f as a linear combination (over $\mathbb{R}$) of parity functions, and the coefficients provide a useful perspective on f.

It helps to switch from $\{0,1\}$ to $\{1,-1\}$: Replace each bit $b \in \{0,1\}$ with $(-1)^b \in \{1,-1\}$, so 0 becomes 1, and 1 becomes -1. Addition in $\mathbb{Z}_2$ becomes multiplication in $\mathbb{R}$ because $(-1)^{a \oplus b} = (-1)^a(-1)^b$ for all $a, b \in \{0,1\}$. When we translate parity functions from $\{0,1\}$ to $\{1,-1\}$, they're known as *characters* for historical reasons. For any set of indices $I \subseteq [n]$:

- $\oplus_I : \{0,1\}^n \to \{0,1\}$ is the parity function defined by $\oplus_I(x) = \bigoplus_{i \in I} x_i$, and $\oplus_\emptyset$ is the constant-0 function. For example, $\oplus_{\{2,3,5\}}(x_1, x_2, x_3, x_4, x_5) = x_2 \oplus x_3 \oplus x_5$.
- $\chi_I : \{1,-1\}^n \to \{1,-1\}$ is the character defined by $\chi_I(x) = \prod_{i \in I} x_i$, and $\chi_\emptyset$ is the constant-1 function. (χ is lower-case Greek chi.) For example, $\chi_{\{2,3,5\}}(x_1, x_2, x_3, x_4, x_5) = x_2 x_3 x_5$.

Figure 14.4 shows an example parity function and the corresponding character.

For any two functions $f, g : \{1,-1\}^n \to \mathbb{R}$, define $\langle f, g \rangle = \mathbf{E}_x\big[f(x)g(x)\big]$ over uniformly random $x \in \{1,-1\}^n$. (The $\langle$ and $\rangle$ are "angle brackets.") *Linearity* means $\langle f + g, h \rangle = \langle f, h \rangle + \langle g, h \rangle$ and $\langle cf, g \rangle = c\langle f, g \rangle$ where $(f + g)(x) = f(x) + g(x)$ and $(cf)(x) = cf(x)$ for a constant $c \in \mathbb{R}$. For $f, g : \{1,-1\}^n \to \{1,-1\}$:

$$\begin{aligned}\langle f, g \rangle &= \mathbf{E}_x\big[f(x)g(x)\big] = 1\mathbf{Pr}_x\big[f(x)g(x) = 1\big] + (-1)\mathbf{Pr}_x\big[f(x)g(x) = -1\big] \\ &= \mathbf{Pr}_x\big[f(x) = g(x)\big] - \big(1 - \mathbf{Pr}_x\big[f(x) = g(x)\big]\big) \\ &= 2\mathbf{Pr}_x\big[f(x) = g(x)\big] - 1\end{aligned}$$

Thus $1 \geq \langle f, g \rangle \geq -1$ measures the "distance" between f and g when the codomain is $\{1,-1\}$:

x_1	x_2	x_3	$\oplus_{\{1,3\}}(x) = x_1 \oplus x_3$
0	0	0	0
0	0	1	1
0	1	0	0
0	1	1	1
1	0	0	1
1	0	1	0
1	1	0	1
1	1	1	0

x_1	x_2	x_3	$\chi_{\{1,3\}}(x) = x_1 x_3$
1	1	1	1
1	1	−1	−1
1	−1	1	1
1	−1	−1	−1
−1	1	1	−1
−1	1	−1	1
−1	−1	1	−1
−1	−1	−1	1

Figure 14.4: Example parity function and the corresponding character

- $\langle f, g\rangle = 1$ iff $f(x) = g(x)$ for all x.
- $\langle f, g\rangle = 0$ iff $f(x) = g(x)$ for half of all x.
- $\langle f, g\rangle = -1$ iff $f(x) = g(x)$ for no x.

Here's the "character version" of the random subsum principle:

Lemma 14.34. *$\langle \chi_I, \chi_I\rangle = 1$ and $\langle \chi_I, \chi_J\rangle = 0$ if $I \neq J$.*

Proof. $\langle \chi_I, \chi_I\rangle = \mathbf{E}_x\big[\chi_I(x)^2\big] = \mathbf{E}_x[1] = 1$ since $\chi_I(x) \in \{1, -1\}$. If $I \neq J$ then for $K = (I \smallsetminus J) \cup (J \smallsetminus I) \neq \emptyset$,

$$\chi_I(x)\chi_J(x) \;=\; \prod_{i\in I} x_i \prod_{j\in J} x_j \;=\; \prod_{i\in I\cap J} x_i^2 \prod_{k\in K} x_k \;=\; \prod_{k\in K} x_k \;=\; \chi_K(x)$$

since $x_i^2 = 1$, and therefore

$$\langle \chi_I, \chi_J\rangle \;=\; \mathbf{E}_x\big[\chi_I(x)\chi_J(x)\big] \;=\; \mathbf{E}_x\big[\chi_K(x)\big] \;=\; \prod_{k\in K} \mathbf{E}_x[x_k] \;=\; \prod_{k\in K} 0 \;=\; 0$$

since $x_1, \ldots, x_n$ are independent, and $\mathbf{Pr}_x[x_k = 1] = \mathbf{Pr}_x[x_k = -1] = 1/2$, and $K \neq \emptyset$. ■

A linear combination of characters is $\sum_{I\subseteq[n]} c_I \chi_I$ for some coefficients $c_I \in \mathbb{R}$. A character is a multilinear monomial (each variable has individual degree ≤ 1), so a linear combination of characters is a multilinear polynomial. The following fundamental lemma says f can be expressed as a multilinear polynomial in a unique way. We saw related things in §11.2.3 (clauses and terms are linear combinations of parity functions) and §10.3.2 (multilinear codes over finite fields).

Lemma 14.35. *For every $f\colon \{1, -1\}^n \to \mathbb{R}$, there exists a unique way to write f as a linear combination of characters:*

$$f \;=\; \sum_{I\subseteq[n]} \widehat{f}_I \chi_I \quad \textit{where} \quad \widehat{f}_I \;=\; \langle f, \chi_I\rangle$$

Proof. For each $a \in \{1, -1\}^n$, define $g_a\colon \{1, -1\}^n \to \mathbb{R}$ by $g_a(x) = 1$ if $x = a$, and $g_a(x) = 0$ if $x \neq a$. Then $g_a(x) = \prod_{i\in[n]}(1 + a_i x_i)/2$ because $(1 + a_i x_i)/2$ is 1 if $x_i = a_i$, and is 0 if $x_i \neq a_i$. This expression for g_a expands to a multilinear polynomial. Therefore $f = \sum_{a\in\{1,-1\}^n} f(a) g_a$ is a multilinear polynomial, since it's a linear combination of the multilinear polynomials g_a.

Now, we prove that only one multilinear polynomial expresses f, so each character's coefficient is unique. Consider any multilinear polynomial $\sum_{I\subseteq[n]} c_I \chi_I = f$. For every I, the coefficient c_I must equal $\langle f, \chi_I\rangle$ because by linearity and Lemma 14.34:

$$\langle f, \chi_I\rangle \;=\; \Big\langle \sum_{J\subseteq[n]} c_J \chi_J, \chi_I\Big\rangle \;=\; \sum_{J\subseteq[n]} c_J \langle \chi_J, \chi_I\rangle \;=\; c_I\, 1 + \sum_{J\neq I} c_J\, 0 \;=\; c_I$$ ■

Here are two ways to represent any $f\colon \{1,-1\}^n \to \mathbb{R}$:

- The 2^n many numbers $f(x)$ for all $x \in \{1,-1\}^n$.
- The 2^n many numbers $\widehat{f}_I$ for all $I \subseteq [n]$. (The caret $\widehat{\ }$ over f is called a "hat.")

(For readers familiar with linear algebra: $\langle\ ,\ \rangle$ is an inner product for the 2^n-dimensional vector space of all functions $f\colon \{1,-1\}^n \to \mathbb{R}$, and Lemma 14.34 and Lemma 14.35 say the characters are an orthonormal basis with respect to this inner product.)

Lemma 14.36. $\sum_{I\subseteq[n]} \widehat{f}_I^{\,2} = 1$ *for every* $f\colon \{1,-1\}^n \to \{1,-1\}$.

Proof. For every x, we have $f(x)^2 = 1$ since $f(x) \in \{1,-1\}$, so:

$$\begin{aligned}
1 = \mathbf{E}_x\big[f(x)^2\big] = \langle f,f\rangle &= \big\langle \textstyle\sum_I \widehat{f}_I \chi_I, \sum_J \widehat{f}_J \chi_J \big\rangle && \text{(Lemma 14.35)}\\
&= \textstyle\sum_{I,J} \widehat{f}_I \widehat{f}_J \langle \chi_I, \chi_J\rangle && \text{(linearity)}\\
&= \textstyle\sum_I \widehat{f}_I^{\,2}\, 1 + \sum_{I,J\neq I} \widehat{f}_I \widehat{f}_J\, 0 && \text{(Lemma 14.34)}\\
&= \textstyle\sum_I \widehat{f}_I^{\,2}
\end{aligned}$$

■

The *pointwise product* of two inputs $x, y \in \{1,-1\}^n$ is $xy = (x_1y_1, \ldots, x_ny_n) \in \{1,-1\}^n$. For example, $(1,1,-1,-1)(1,-1,1,-1) = (1,-1,-1,1)$. For all I:

$$\chi_I(xy) = \textstyle\prod_{i\in I} x_iy_i = \prod_{i\in I} x_i \prod_{i\in I} y_i = \chi_I(x)\chi_I(y)$$

If we switch from $\{1,-1\}$ back to $\{0,1\}$, then xy corresponds to $x \oplus y$ (bitwise xor). We're ready to prove the linearity tester's correctness, reformulated using $\{1,-1\}$ instead of $\{0,1\}$:

Theorem 14.28 (restated). *For every* $f\colon \{1,-1\}^n \to \{1,-1\}$*:*

$$\mathbf{Pr}_{x,y}\big[f(xy) = f(x)f(y)\big] \le \max_I \mathbf{Pr}_x\big[f(x) = \chi_I(x)\big]$$

Proof.

$$\begin{aligned}
&2\mathbf{Pr}_{x,y}\big[f(xy) = f(x)f(y)\big] - 1\\
&= \mathbf{E}_{x,y}\big[f(xy)f(x)f(y)\big]\\
&= \mathbf{E}_{x,y}\Big[\big(\textstyle\sum_I \widehat{f}_I \chi_I(xy)\big)\big(\sum_J \widehat{f}_J \chi_J(x)\big)\big(\sum_K \widehat{f}_K \chi_K(y)\big)\Big] && \text{(Lemma 14.35)}\\
&= \mathbf{E}_{x,y}\Big[\textstyle\sum_{I,J,K} \widehat{f}_I \widehat{f}_J \widehat{f}_K\, \chi_I(xy)\chi_J(x)\chi_K(y)\Big]\\
&= \textstyle\sum_{I,J,K} \widehat{f}_I \widehat{f}_J \widehat{f}_K\, \mathbf{E}_{x,y}\big[\chi_I(xy)\chi_J(x)\chi_K(y)\big] && \text{(linearity of expectation)}\\
&= \textstyle\sum_{I,J,K} \widehat{f}_I \widehat{f}_J \widehat{f}_K\, \mathbf{E}_{x,y}\big[\chi_I(x)\chi_I(y)\chi_J(x)\chi_K(y)\big]\\
&= \textstyle\sum_{I,J,K} \widehat{f}_I \widehat{f}_J \widehat{f}_K\, \mathbf{E}_{x}\big[\chi_I(x)\chi_J(x)\big]\mathbf{E}_y\big[\chi_I(y)\chi_K(y)\big] && \text{(x, y are independent)}\\
&= \textstyle\sum_{I,J,K} \widehat{f}_I \widehat{f}_J \widehat{f}_K\, \langle \chi_I, \chi_J\rangle\langle \chi_I, \chi_K\rangle\\
&= \textstyle\sum_I \widehat{f}_I^{\,3} && \text{(Lemma 14.34)}\\
&\le \big(\max_I \widehat{f}_I\big)\textstyle\sum_I \widehat{f}_I^{\,2}\\
&= \max_I \widehat{f}_I && \text{(Lemma 14.36)}\\
&= \max_I \langle f, \chi_I\rangle && \text{(Lemma 14.35)}\\
&= 2\max_I \mathbf{Pr}_x\big[f(x) = \chi_I(x)\big] - 1
\end{aligned}$$

■

Exercises

14.1 Prove that if P = NP, then MIN NODE COVER has a poly-time exact algorithm.

14.2 For any integer $b \geq 2$, consider the special case of MIN SET COVER where each element of $[m]$ is contained in at most b of the sets $S_1, \ldots, S_n$. Design a poly-time b-approximation algorithm by generalizing the 2-approximation algorithm for MIN NODE COVER.

14.3 **(a)** Prove that the greedy algorithm for MIN SET COVER actually achieves $ALG \leq \lceil 1 + \ln \frac{m}{OPT} \rceil \cdot OPT$. Hint: Consider the phases $|R| > OPT$ and $|R| \leq OPT$ separately.

(b) For any integer $b \geq 2$, consider the special case of MIN SET COVER where $|S_i| \leq b$ for each $i \in [n]$. Prove that the greedy algorithm is a $\lceil 1 + \ln b \rceil$-approximation algorithm using Exercise 14.3.a.

14.4 Give an example input (for arbitrarily large m) showing that the greedy algorithm for MIN SET COVER achieves no better than a $\Omega(\log m)$-approximation.

14.5 Consider the variant of MIN SET COVER where the input includes a "budget" b, and we want to cover as many elements as we can using only b subsets:

MAX SET COVERAGE	(14.21)
Input: Set system $S = (S_1, \ldots, S_n)$, integer $1 \leq b \leq n$	
Output: $I \subseteq [n]$ with $|I| = b$ such that $\left|\bigcup_{i \in I} S_i\right|$ is as large as possible	

Design a poly-time $(1 - 1/e)$-approximation algorithm for MAX SET COVERAGE, drawing inspiration from the greedy MIN SET COVER algorithm.

14.6 In § 13.2.2, we designed a poly-time proper m-consistent learner for the concept class of terms. Now, design a poly-time improper m-consistent learner for the concept class of terms of width $\leq w$, with the hypothesis class of terms of width $\leq w\lceil \ln m \rceil$, using the greedy approximation algorithm for MIN SET COVER. The learner doesn't even need to know w.

(a) Do this assuming the hypothesis class also contains the constant 0 function. Hint: Use the learner from § 13.2.2 (if at least one training example is positive), and decrease the resulting term's width by removing some literals without compromising consistency on the negative training examples. Specifically, for each literal of the resulting term, consider the subset of negative training examples on which this literal evaluates to 0.

(b) To avoid assuming the hypothesis class contains the constant 0 function: When all m training examples are negative, find a term of width $\leq \lfloor 1 + \log m \rfloor$ consistent with the training data. If $w \geq 2$, this hypothesis has width $\leq \frac{w}{2} \lfloor 1 + \log m \rfloor \leq w \lceil \ln m \rceil$. Handle $w = 1$ separately.

14.7 **(a)** Compute $\mathbf{E}\big[\#\text{ unsatisfied clauses in } \varphi|_a\big]$ where $a = 10{*}{*}{*}$ and:

$$\varphi = (\overline{x_1} \vee \overline{x_3} \vee x_5) \wedge (\overline{x_1} \vee \overline{x_2} \vee x_3) \wedge (x_3 \vee x_4 \vee \overline{x_5}) \wedge (\overline{x_1} \vee x_2 \vee \overline{x_4}) \wedge (x_2 \vee x_4 \vee x_5)$$

(b) In the proof of Theorem 14.4, we used the fact that

$$\mathbf{E}\big[\#\text{ unsatisfied clauses in } \varphi|_a \,\big|\, x_i = 1\big] = \mathbf{E}\big[\#\text{ unsatisfied clauses in } \varphi|_b\big]$$

where a is a partial assignment with $a_i = *$, and b is a except $b_i = 1$. Is the following similar equality guaranteed to hold? Why or why not?

$$\mathbf{E}\big[\#\text{ satisfied clauses in } \varphi|_a \,\big|\, x_i = 1\big] \;=\; \mathbf{E}\big[\#\text{ satisfied clauses in } \varphi|_b\big]$$

14.8 In a linear equation over $\mathbb{Z}_2$, the left side is the parity of a subset of variables, and the right side is either 0 or 1. For example, $x_2 \oplus x_5 \oplus x_7 = 1$ is such an equation.

(a) Use the probabilistic method (like in Lemma 14.3) to prove that for every system of linear equations over $\mathbb{Z}_2$ with nonempty left sides, some assignment satisfies at least half of the equations.

(b) Design a poly-time 1/2-approximation algorithm for this optimization problem:

Max $\mathbb{Z}_2$ Linear System Sat	(14.22)
Input: A system of linear equations over $\mathbb{Z}_2$	
Output: An assignment satisfying as many of the equations as possible	

Trivially $OPT \le m$ where m is the number of equations other than $0 = 1$, so it suffices to achieve $ALG \ge m/2$ by derandomizing Exercise 14.8.a.

14.9 **(a)** Use the probabilistic method (like in Lemma 14.3) to prove that for every undirected graph, some 3-color assignment multicolors at least two thirds of the edges.

(b) Design a poly-time 2/3-approximation algorithm for this optimization problem:

Max Graph 3-Coloring	(14.23)
Input: Undirected graph G	
Output: A 3-color assignment that multicolors as many edges of G as possible	

Trivially $OPT \le m$ where m is the number of edges in G, so it suffices to achieve $ALG \ge (2/3)m$ by derandomizing Exercise 14.9.a.

14.10 Consider this optimization promise problem:

Min Coloring of 3-Colorable Graphs	(14.24)
Input: Properly 3-colorable graph G	
Output: A proper coloring of G using as few colors as possible	

By assumption, $OPT \le 3$. Design a poly-time algorithm achieving $ALG \le O(\sqrt{n})$ where n is the number of nodes in G.

(a) First, design a poly-time algorithm that, given a graph where every node has degree $< d$, finds a proper d-coloring.

(b) To achieve $ALG \le O(\sqrt{n})$, use Exercise 14.10.a with $d = \lceil \sqrt{n} \rceil$, but first deal with nodes of degree $\ge d$ using the poly-time algorithm for properly 2-coloring properly 2-colorable graphs (Theorem 2.1).

14.11 Show that the following isn't even a $1/o(m)$-approximation algorithm for Max Edge Disjoint Paths. The input is an m-edge directed graph G and pairs of nodes $(s_1, t_1), \ldots, (s_k, t_k)$. We may assume each t_i is reachable from s_i.

Bad approximation algorithm for MAX EDGE DISJOINT PATHS	(14.25)
for each $i \in [k]$: use extended BFS to find a shortest path P_i from s_i to t_i in G initialize $I \leftarrow \emptyset$ for each $i \in [k]$ in increasing order of P_i's length: if P_i is edge disjoint from all P_j with $j \in I$: add i to I output I and P_i for each $i \in I$	

14.12 In Theorem 14.5, we proved that the greedy algorithm for MAX EDGE DISJOINT PATHS achieves $OPT \le ALG + \sqrt{m} \cdot (ALG+1)$. Prove it actually achieves $OPT \le ALG + \sqrt{m} \cdot \sqrt{ALG}$. Hint: Let $|P|$ denote the length of any path P. Partition $J \setminus I$ into $|I|$ many sets J_i indexed by $i \in I$, such that for each $j \in J_i$, we have $|P_i| \le |Q_j|$ and Q_j shares an edge with P_i. For each $i \in I$, define $v_i = \sqrt{\sum_{j \in J_i} |Q_j|}$. Show that $|J_i| \le v_i$, and apply Corollary A.27 to the vector with components v_i for $i \in I$.

14.13 A *shy set* in an undirected graph is a subset S of nodes such that each node in S has at most one neighbor in S. Recall that SHY SET is NP-complete (Exercise 2.20). Consider the optimization version:

MAX SHY SET	(14.26)
Input: Undirected graph G	
Output: A shy set in G with as many nodes as possible	

Prove that for every constant $c > 31/32$, MAX SHY SET has no poly-time c-approximation algorithm unless $\mathsf{P} = \mathsf{NP}$. Hint: Use a gap-preserving reduction from MAX INDEPENDENT SET.

14.14 Show that in the proofs of Lemma 14.13 and Lemma 14.15, $m - OPT = m' - OPT'$ holds.

14.15 Recall that 3-NAE SAT is NP-complete (Exercise 2.30.b and Exercise 2.30.c). Consider the optimization version:

MAX 3-NOT-ALL-EQUAL SATISFIABILITY (or MAX 3-NAE SAT for short)	(14.27)
Input: 3-NAE formula φ	
Output: An assignment satisfying as many NAE-clauses of φ as possible	

(An NAE-clause is satisfied iff its literals are not all 0 and not all 1.)

(a) Design a poly-time 3/4-approximation algorithm for MAX 3-NAE SAT.

(b) Prove that for every constant $c > 15/16$, MAX 3-NAE SAT has no poly-time c-approximation algorithm unless $\mathsf{P} = \mathsf{NP}$.

14.16 Prove that Theorem 14.19 holds even if we restrict MAX EDGE DISJOINT PATHS to strongly connected graphs: For every constant $d < 1/2$, this problem has no poly-time $1/m^d$-approximation algorithm unless $\mathsf{P} = \mathsf{NP}$.

14.17 To disprove the "perfect parallel repetition conjecture," prove that the following two-prover one-round game has $OPT \le 2$ but its 2-fold parallel repetition has $OPT' \ge 8 > 2^2$:

The verifier sends a bit u_1 to prover 1 and a bit u_2 to prover 2. Each prover responds with the index i of a prover and a bit w. The provers win iff they both pick the same i and $w = u_i$ (they're correct about which bit was given to some prover that they agree on). In other words: The graph has two left nodes and two right nodes and all four possible edges. The $k = 4$ labels are $\{1,2\} \times \{0,1\}$. Edge $(u_1, u_2) \in \{(0,0), (0,1), (1,0), (1,1)\}$ is satisfied by labels (i, w) and (j, x) iff $i = j$ and $w = x = u_i$.

14.18 Prove that the unique games conjecture is equivalent to the version where the input graph need not be bipartite: Design a poly-time $(\alpha, \beta, \alpha, 4\beta)$-gap-preserving reduction (for arbitrary $\alpha \geq 4\beta$) from the nonbipartite analogue of MAX UNIQUE k-LABEL COVER to the original bipartite version (without changing the number of edges).

14.19 We proved that Theorem 14.24 implies Corollary 14.25. Prove the converse: If (m, bm)-GAP MAX 3-SAT is NP-complete for some constant $b < 1$, then the PCP theorem holds.

14.20 **(a)** Design a poly-time exact algorithm for MAX 1-SAT.

(b) Prove that for all rational constants $c > s$, $\mathsf{PCP}_{c,s}[\log N,\ 1] \subseteq \mathsf{P}$ where the subscripts mean completeness c and soundness s (instead of the default $c = 1$ and $s = 1/3$).

14.21 Prove a variant of the PCP theorem where instead of restricting the number of queries the verifier makes to the purported witness w, we restrict the verifier to run in log space with streaming access to w. As with NL (§3.3.1), streaming means "read-witness Reg[i]" puts w's next unread word into Reg[i].

$\mathsf{NLPCP}[\log N]$ is the set of all decision problems for which there exists a randomized streaming verifier with completeness 1, soundness 1/3, $O(\log N)$ randomness efficiency, $O(\log N)$ space efficiency, and $O(\log N)$-bounded word size. Prove $\mathsf{NP} \subseteq \mathsf{NLPCP}[\log N]$.

Hint: Consider the trivial randomized verifier for SAT that views w as an assignment, picks a uniformly random clause of the input CNF, and accepts iff w satisfies that clause. This has completeness 1 and soundness $1 - 1/m$ where m is the number of clauses. To amplify the soundness, run this trivial randomized verifier repeatedly (with independent randomness for each run) and accept iff all runs accept. To make this streaming, view w as a sequence of assignments, and let successive runs use successive assignments from w. This unfortunately has poly N randomness efficiency. Instead, do randomness-efficient amplification with pairwise uniform hashing. Use Exercise 8.12 for the analysis.

14.22 Recall the quadratic consistency check from our proof of the weak PCP theorem. Now, you'll analyze a similar *cubic consistency* check.

For $u, v, w \in \{0,1\}^n$, define $u \otimes v \otimes w \in \{0,1\}^{n^3}$ by $(u \otimes v \otimes w)_{i,j,k} = u_i v_j w_k$, viewing the set of indices as $[n] \times [n] \times [n]$. Define $u' \in \{0,1\}^{n^3}$ by $u'_{i,i,i} = u_i$ and $u'_{i,j,k} = 0$ when i, j, k aren't all equal, and similarly define v' from v, and w' from w.

Prove that for every $b \in \{0,1\}^{n^3}$, if $b \neq a \otimes a \otimes a$ for all $a \in \{0,1\}^n$, then

$$\mathbf{Pr}_{u,v,w}\big[(u \otimes v \otimes w) \odot b = (u' \odot b)(v' \odot b)(w' \odot b)\big] \leq 7/8$$

over uniformly random $u, v, w \in \{0,1\}^n$.

14.23 In our proof of the weak PCP theorem, the verifier had soundness 27/28 and query efficiency 11, with intended witness $w\colon \{0,1\}^{n^2} \to \{0,1\}$ defined by $w(z) = z \odot b$ where $b = a \otimes a$ for a satisfying assignment a.

Modify this verifier to have soundness 19/20 and query efficiency 12, with intended witness (w^1, w^2) (these are superscripts, not exponents) where $w^1: \{0,1\}^n \to \{0,1\}$ is defined by $w^1(y) = y \odot a$ for a satisfying assignment a, and $w^2: \{0,1\}^{n^2} \to \{0,1\}$ is defined by $w^2(z) = z \odot b$ for $b = a \otimes a$.

Hint: The verifier needs to test linearity of w^1 as well as w^2, but it no longer needs to do local correction of w^1 when checking that w^2 is quadratically consistent with w^1.

14.24 Prove that for every constant $c > 1/2$, this optimization problem has no poly-time c-approximation algorithm unless P = NP:

Max $\mathbb{Z}_2$ Quadratic System Sat	(14.28)
Input: A system of quadratic equations over $\mathbb{Z}_2$	
Output: An assignment satisfying as many of the equations as possible	

To prove this, show that the following is an (m', cm')-gap-introducing reduction from $\mathbb{Z}_2$ Quadratic System Sat (with m equations) to Max $\mathbb{Z}_2$ Quadratic System Sat (with m' equations): Let $G: \{0,1\}^\ell \to \{0,1\}^m$ be a poly-time computable ε-bias generator (Theorem 11.7) with seed length $\ell = O(\log(m/\varepsilon))$ where $0 < \varepsilon < c - 1/2$ is a constant. Map the system $M(x \otimes x) = d$ to the system that has the same variables x and has, for each seed $s \in \{0,1\}^\ell$, the equation $(rM)(x \otimes x) = rd$ where $r = G(s)$ is a $1 \times m$ vector (of coefficients for the linear combination of equations of $M(x \otimes x) = d$).

14.25 Prove $\langle f, g\rangle = \sum_{I \subseteq [n]} \widehat{f}_I \widehat{g}_I$ for all $f, g: \{1, -1\}^n \to \mathbb{R}$.

Notes

Texts on approximation algorithms and hardness of approximation include [246, 34, 541, 565].

The greedy $\lceil \ln m \rceil$-approximation algorithm for Min Set Cover (Theorem 14.2) is due to [274, 346, 129]. NP-hardness of $c(\ln m)$-approximating Min Set Cover for $c < 1$ is due to [148].

NP-hardness of c-approximating Max 3-Sat for $c > 7/8$ (Theorem 14.7) is due to [239]. The poly-time 0.94-approximation algorithm for Max 2-Sat is due to [88], the culmination of a series of work starting with [192]. Max Sat has a poly-time 0.75-approximation algorithm [567, 191].

The $1/O(\sqrt{m})$-approximation algorithm for Max Edge Disjoint Paths (Theorem 14.5) is due to [311]. NP-completeness of Two Edge Disjoint Paths (Theorem 14.8) is due to [170]. NP-hardness of $1/m^d$-approximating Max Edge Disjoint Paths for $d < 1/2$ (Theorem 14.19) is due to [226].

NP-hardness of $1/n^d$-approximating Max Independent Set for $d < 1$ is due to [238, 579].

The parallel repetition theorem (Theorem 14.21) is due to [427], with a simplified proof due to [248].

The unique games conjecture (Conjecture 14.23) is due to [302].

The known NP-hardness of approximating Min Node Cover matches the best known poly-time algorithm's approximation ratio of 2 (Theorem 14.1) assuming the unique games conjecture [306] but is somewhat weaker without assuming this conjecture [147, 304, 146, 305].

The known NP-hardness of approximating Max 2-Sat matches the best known poly-time algorithm's approximation ratio assuming the unique games conjecture [35, 88] but is somewhat weaker without assuming this conjecture [239].

The known NP-hardness of approximating Max Cut matches the best known poly-time algorithm's approximation ratio [192, 359] assuming the unique games conjecture [303, 377] but is somewhat weaker without assuming this conjecture [523].

The PCP theorem (Theorem 14.24) is due to [29, 30], with a simplified proof due to [145].

A standard text on harmonic analysis ("Fourier analysis") of boolean functions is [402]. Local testability of the dot product code (Theorem 14.28) is due to [71]. Lemma 14.36 is known as "Parseval's theorem," and the generalization in Exercise 14.25 is known as "Plancherel's theorem."

Exercise 14.10 is due to [558].

Chapter 15

Verification

A major goal of software verification is to ascertain the correctness of a computation. Verifying correctness for all possible inputs simultaneously is often impractical or even impossible, so in computational complexity we consider verifying correctness on a single, arbitrary input. Suppose x is a valid input to a computational problem A. We personify this setup with an untrusted *prover* who claims that $A(x)$ is a particular value and tries to convince a skeptical *verifier*:

- *Completeness*: If the prover's claim is correct, then he can convince the verifier.
- *Soundness*: If the prover's claim is incorrect, then he can't convince the verifier.

The verifier should be more efficient than solving A. The prover should be not much less efficient than solving A. This framework is motivated by several practical scenarios:

- *Delegation*: The verifier lacks the computational resources to solve A himself, so he delegates (outsources) the computation to a more powerful entity (say, a cloud computing service) but doesn't trust them to run the computation correctly and to report the actual output.
- *Program checking*: A program hasn't been sufficiently vetted, so the verifier doesn't trust that it's correct. He wants to put up "guardrails" to detect if the output is erroneous. This is like a human checking their work after solving a complicated equation, by plugging in the solution to see that the equation indeed holds.

To transcend the "NP-style" verification we're accustomed to—in which the prover just sends the verifier a purported witness to check—we use two ingredients:

- *Interaction*: The verifier and prover have a back-and-forth conversation. The verifier requests specific information that would help to convince him.
- *Randomness*: The verifier presses the prover with random inquiries to keep him on his toes. It's more convincing if the prover answers inquiries that he couldn't anticipate.

We consider the verifier's efficiency in § 15.1 and § 15.2. We consider the prover's efficiency in § 15.3. We consider the relevance to cryptography in § 15.4: The prover knows some information the verifier doesn't, and he wants to convince the verifier that he knows it, but without revealing the information. This sounds paradoxical but is surprisingly achievable.

15.1 Arthur and Merlin

15.1.1 Definition

When the prover's efficiency is immaterial, the two characters have traditional names:

- King Arthur is the poly-time verifier.
- His magician advisor Merlin is the computationally unlimited prover.

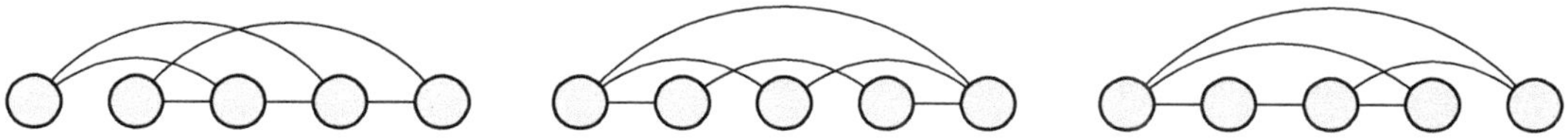

Figure 15.1: The left and middle graphs are isomorphic to each other but not to the right graph

If Merlin can exhibit a witness to convince a deterministic Arthur that $A(x) = 1$, then $A \in \mathsf{NP}$. Interaction and randomness let us transcend NP. First, consider these two features in isolation:

- Suppose Arthur and Merlin have an interactive conversation, but Arthur is deterministic. Merlin could foresee the entire conversation and send the transcript to Arthur, who could check it with no further help, rendering the interactivity pointless. We'd still just have NP.
- Suppose Arthur is randomized, but Merlin just throws a witness over the wall with no interaction. Such proof systems are presumably no more powerful than NP, since Arthur could be derandomized (Chapter 11).

Interaction plus randomness is a potent combination.

Definition. An *Arthur–Merlin proof system* for a decision problem A has this format: Both Arthur and Merlin know the input x. Arthur tosses some coins and then sends a message to Merlin, who responds instantaneously. Arthur accepts or rejects, indicating whether or not he's convinced that $A(x) = 1$.

- Completeness c: $A(x) = 1 \Rightarrow \mathbf{Pr}[\text{Merlin can make Arthur accept}] \geq c$
- Soundness s: $A(x) = 0 \Rightarrow \mathbf{Pr}[\text{Merlin can make Arthur accept}] \leq s$

By default, $c = 2/3$ and $s = 1/3$. In a poly-time proof system, Arthur tosses poly$N$ many coins and runs in poly$N$ time, and Arthur's message and Merlin's response have poly$N$ size (where N is the size of x). ◄

Merlin is omnipotent: His response can be any function of x and Arthur's message, but he can't influence the outcomes of Arthur's coin tosses. Soundness means that no matter how a devious Merlin responds, he's unlikely to dupe Arthur into believing x is a 1-input when it's not.

Now, we'll see that this single round of interaction lets Merlin convince Arthur of something surprising. In § 15.2, we'll see that multiple rounds of interaction let Merlin convince Arthur of even more astonishing things.

15.1.2 Private Coins

In this section, Merlin is not omniscient: He doesn't know the outcomes of Arthur's "private" coin tosses unless Arthur reveals them. This seemingly gives Arthur a leg up against a potentially deceitful Merlin.

We illustrate this with a problem involving graphs. Two undirected graphs are *isomorphic* (to each other) iff they're the same except possibly rearranged. "Iso" means "same," and "morph" means "form."

Example. In Figure 15.1, the left and middle graphs are isomorphic. Both consist of a length-3 cycle and a length-4 cycle that share an edge. If we rearrange the graph on the left by swapping the 1st and 3rd nodes and swapping the 4th and 5th nodes, it would look exactly like the middle graph. The left and middle graphs are not isomorphic to the graph on the right, which doesn't contain a length-3 cycle. ♦

GRAPH ISOMORPHISM	(15.1)
Input: Undirected graphs G_1 and G_2	
Output: Are G_1 and G_2 isomorphic?	

We assume G_1 and G_2 have the same number of nodes, since otherwise they're obviously nonisomorphic.

GRAPH ISOMORPHISM $\in$ NP since Merlin can show Arthur how to rearrange G_1 to make it into G_2. Many researchers conjecture GRAPH ISOMORPHISM $\in$ P. It's known, but very difficult to prove, that GRAPH ISOMORPHISM $\in \mathsf{TIME}[N^{\text{polylog}\,N}]$ (quasi-polynomial time). The complement problem GRAPH NONISOMORPHISM = $\overline{\text{GRAPH ISOMORPHISM}}$ is not known to be in NP: It's unclear how Merlin might convince Arthur that G_1 can't be rearranged to G_2. But with a little interaction and randomness, it's possible.

Theorem 15.1. GRAPH NONISOMORPHISM *has a poly-time private-coin Arthur–Merlin proof system.*

Proof idea. Young Arthur has two colors of socks but can't tell them apart since he's colorblind. For crazy sock day at school, he wants to know that the socks he's wearing are different colors. How can Merlin convince him? Arthur takes off his socks, hides them behind his back (where Merlin can't see), randomly picks one of them, shows it to Merlin, and asks which foot it was on. If the socks are indeed different colors, Merlin can always answer correctly. If the socks are identical, Merlin has no clue which sock Arthur picked, so he'll answer correctly with probability only $1/2$. Repeating this ℓ times, the probability that Merlin succeeds every time is only $1/2^\ell$ if the socks are identical.

Nonisomorphic graphs are different-colored socks. Isomorphic graphs are same-colored socks. To make two isomorphic graphs truly indistinguishable, Arthur randomly permutes the nodes. ∎

Let's formalize this. A *permutation* on $[n] = \{1,2,\ldots,n\}$ is a function $p\colon [n] \to [n]$ such that each element of $[n]$ appears exactly once among $p(1), p(2), \ldots, p(n)$. If a graph G has nodes $[n]$, and p is a permutation on $[n]$, then $p(G)$ denotes the graph with nodes $[n]$ such that each edge $\{u,v\}$ in G corresponds to the edge $\{p(u), p(v)\}$ in $p(G)$. In other words, p rearranges G so the node at index v moves to index $p(v)$. Figure 15.2 shows an example.

Suppose graphs G_1 and G_2 both have nodes $[n]$. We say G_1 is *isomorphic* to G_2, denoted $G_1 \cong G_2$, iff there exists an *isomorphism* from G_1 to G_2, which is a permutation $p\colon [n] \to [n]$ such that $p(G_1) = G_2$. An isomorphism is a witness that G_1 is isomorphic to G_2.

- *Reflexive*: $G_1 \cong G_1$ since $e(G_1) = G_1$ where e is the *identity* permutation defined by $e(v) = v$ for all $v \in [n]$.
- *Symmetric*: If $G_1 \cong G_2$ then $G_2 \cong G_1$ (and we say G_1 and G_2 are isomorphic to each other), since if $p(G_1) = G_2$ for a permutation p, then $p^{-1}(G_2) = G_1$ for the *inverse* permutation p^{-1} defined by $p^{-1}(p(v)) = v$ for all $v \in [n]$.
- *Transitive*: If $G_1 \cong G_2$ and $G_2 \cong G_3$ then $G_1 \cong G_3$, since if $p(G_1) = G_2$ and $q(G_2) = G_3$ for permutations p and q, then $(pq)(G_1) = q(p(G_1)) = G_3$ for the *composed* permutation pq defined by $(pq)(v) = q(p(v))$ for all $v \in [n]$. (This pq is sometimes denoted $q \circ p$.)

Note that $pp^{-1} = p^{-1}p = e$.

Thus we partition the set of all undirected graphs: Graphs in the same part are isomorphic, and graphs in different parts are nonisomorphic.

p

v	1	2	3	4
$p(v)$	2	4	3	1

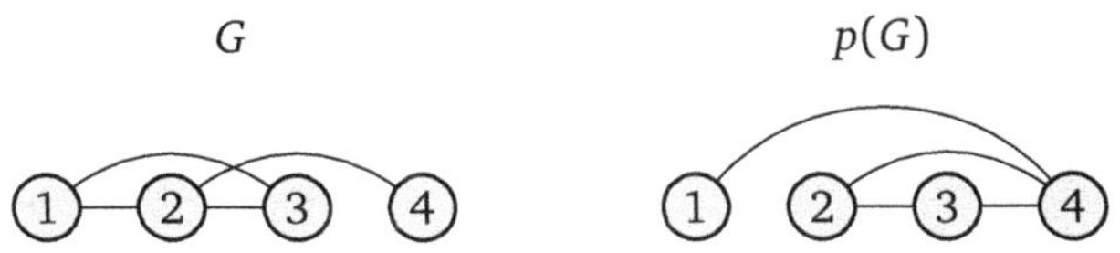

Figure 15.2: Example of applying a permutation to a graph

Proof of Theorem 15.1. On input (G_1, G_2) where G_1 and G_2 have nodes $[n]$:

Private-coin Arthur–Merlin proof system for GRAPH NONISOMORPHISM	(15.2)
Arthur picks $i \in \{1,2\}$ and a permutation $p\colon [n] \to [n]$ uniformly at random Arthur sends Merlin $p(G_i)$ Merlin responds with $j \in \{1,2\}$ Arthur accepts iff $j = i$	

Completeness 1: Suppose $G_1 \ncong G_2$. For all i and p, we have $p(G_i) \cong G_j$ for exactly one j, namely $j = i$. If Merlin responds with this j, then Arthur accepts.

Soundness 1/2: Suppose $G_1 \cong G_2$, say $q(G_1) = G_2$ for a permutation q. The distribution $p(G_1)$ is the same as the distribution $p(G_2) = p(q(G_1)) = (qp)(G_1)$ because qp is also a uniformly random permutation. It follows that $p(G_i)$ is independent of i (over random i and p), so Merlin's response j—which depends on Arthur's message $p(G_i)$—is also independent of i. Therefore Arthur's acceptance probability is:

$$\begin{aligned}
\mathbf{Pr}[j = i] &= \mathbf{Pr}[j = i = 1] + \mathbf{Pr}[j = i = 2] \\
&= \mathbf{Pr}[j = 1]\cdot\mathbf{Pr}[i = 1] + \mathbf{Pr}[j = 2]\cdot\mathbf{Pr}[i = 2] && (j \text{ and } i \text{ are independent}) \\
&= \mathbf{Pr}[j = 1]/2 + \mathbf{Pr}[j = 2]/2 && (i \text{ is uniformly distributed}) \\
&= 1/2
\end{aligned}$$

To amplify the soundness to $1/2^\ell$ (for any ℓ) while retaining completeness 1, Arthur can sample $(i_1, p_1), (i_2, p_2), \ldots, (i_\ell, p_\ell)$ independently, send Merlin $p_1(G_{i_1}), \ldots, p_\ell(G_{i_\ell})$, get responses $j_1, \ldots, j_\ell$, and accept iff $j_k = i_k$ for all $k \in [\ell]$. This is subtle since j_k can depend on all of $p_1(G_{i_1}), \ldots, p_\ell(G_{i_\ell})$, not only on $p_k(G_{i_k})$. So $j_1, \ldots, j_\ell$ might not be independent of each other, but the tuple $(j_1, \ldots, j_\ell)$ is still independent of $(i_1, \ldots, i_\ell)$. It follows that $\mathbf{Pr}\big[(j_1, \ldots, j_\ell) = (i_1, \ldots, i_\ell)\big] = 1/2^\ell$ since this holds conditioned on each particular outcome of $(j_1, \ldots, j_\ell)$. ■

15.1.3 Public Coins

In this section, Merlin is omniscient: Arthur's coin tosses are "public," visible to Merlin. Since Merlin knows what message Arthur would send (as a function of x and the coin tosses), the message might as well just be the coin tosses themselves.

The private-coin Arthur–Merlin proof system for GRAPH NONISOMORPHISM (Theorem 15.1) breaks down if Arthur can't keep i and p secret from Merlin. If Merlin sees i, that's obviously what he should respond. If Merlin sees p, he could apply p^{-1} to recover G_i.

Here is GRAPH NONISOMORPHISM redux, now with 100% less secrecy.

Theorem 15.2. GRAPH NONISOMORPHISM *has a poly-time public-coin Arthur–Merlin proof system.*

Proof idea. For each $i \in \{1,2\}$, consider the set S_i of all graphs isomorphic to G_i. Define $S = S_1 \cup S_2$. Imagine, for starters, that $|S_1| = |S_2| = K$ for some K known to Arthur.

- If $G_1 \ncong G_2$ then $S_1 \cap S_2 = \emptyset$ and hence $|S| = |S_1| + |S_2| = 2K$.
- If $G_1 \cong G_2$ then $S_1 = S_2 = S$ and hence $|S| = K$.

So Arthur knows that $|S|$ is either $2K$ or K, and Merlin wants to convince him it's $2K$. We use an idea from approximate counting of witnesses using an NP oracle (Theorem 8.12): With a pairwise uniform hash function, we hash elements of S into a set T of size $\Theta(K)$. The probability that at least one element of S hashes to a particular target t (which we arbitrarily pick to be the all-0 string) is high if $|S| = 2K$ and low if $|S| = K$. Arthur samples the hash function's random seed, and then Merlin shows him a graph $H \in S$ that hashes to t, and furthermore convinces him that $H \in S$ by exhibiting an isomorphism from H to either G_1 or G_2. Thus, with high probability, Merlin can convince Arthur iff $|S|$ is large enough.

Unfortunately, $|S_1|$ might not equal $|S_2|$, and Arthur generally wouldn't know these sizes anyway. But there's a trick for enlarging S_1 and S_2 up to a known size, without interfering with the rest of the proof. ■

An *automorphism* of a graph G with nodes $[n]$ is an isomorphism from G to itself (a permutation p such that $p(G) = G$). Intuitively, an automorphism is "a symmetry of G." Here's a result of group theory:

Lemma 15.3. *The number of graphs isomorphic to G is $n!/$(number of automorphisms of G), assuming G has nodes $[n]$.*

Proof. The division principle for counting says that if we partition a set U into equal-size parts, then the number of parts is $|U|/$(size of each part). Let's partition the set of all $n!$ permutations $q\colon [n] \to [n]$ according to $q(G)$. The parts correspond to graphs isomorphic to G, so it suffices to prove that each part's size is the number of automorphisms of G. In other words, for every graph H isomorphic to G, the number of isomorphisms from G to H equals the number of automorphisms of G. So suppose $q(G) = H$ for some permutation q. We claim that the isomorphisms from G to H are precisely the permutations pq where p is an automorphism of G. That is, for every permutation r, we have $r(G) = H$ iff $r = pq$ for some automorphism p of G:

$\Leftarrow$: If $r = pq$ for some automorphism p of G, then $r(G) = (pq)(G) = q(p(G)) = q(G) = H$.

$\Rightarrow$: If $r(G) = H$, then $(rq^{-1})(G) = q^{-1}(r(G)) = q^{-1}(H) = G$ and thus $p = rq^{-1}$ is an automorphism of G, and we have $pq = rq^{-1}q = re = r$. ■

Example. An automorphism of the graph in Figure 15.3 could either swap 1 and 2 or not (two possibilities) and either swap 4 and 5 or not (two possibilities). Since there are $2 \cdot 2 = 4$ automorphisms, $5!/4 = 30$ graphs are isomorphic to this one. ♦

Proof of Theorem 15.2. The input is (G_1, G_2) where G_1 and G_2 have nodes $[n]$. For each $i \in \{1,2\}$, define:

$$S_i = \{(H,p) : H \cong G_i \text{ and } p \text{ is an automorphism of } H\}$$

If $H \cong G_i$ then H has the same number of automorphisms as G_i, so by Lemma 15.3:

$$|S_i| = (\text{number of graphs isomorphic to } G_i) \cdot (\text{number of automorphisms of } G_i) = n!$$

Define $S = S_1 \cup S_2$.

Figure 15.3: Example graph for counting automorphisms

- If $G_1 \ncong G_2$ then $S_1 \cap S_2 = \emptyset$ and hence $|S| = |S_1| + |S_2| = 2n!$.
- If $G_1 \cong G_2$ then $S_1 = S_2 = S$ and hence $|S| = n!$.

Let $h\colon \{0,1\}^{2m+\ell-1} \times \{0,1\}^{\ell} \to \{0,1\}^m$ be the pairwise uniform hash function from Lemma 8.9:

- $\ell \in \operatorname{poly} N$ is large enough to encode elements of S as strings in $\{0,1\}^{\ell}$.
- $m = \lceil \log(8n!) \rceil = O(n \log n)$, so $8n! \le 2^m < 16n!$ and thus $1/8 \ge n!/2^m > 1/16$.

Public-coin Arthur–Merlin proof system for GRAPH NONISOMORPHISM (15.3)

Arthur sends Merlin a uniformly random seed $r \in \{0,1\}^{2m+\ell-1}$
Merlin sends Arthur some H, p, q
Arthur accepts iff the following all hold:
  H is a graph with nodes $[n]$ and $p, q\colon [n] \to [n]$ are permutations
  $q(H) \in \{G_1, G_2\}$ and $p(H) = H$
  $h_r(H, p) = 0^m$

Completeness $1.5n!/2^m$: Suppose $G_1 \ncong G_2$, so $|S| = 2n!$. By Lemma 8.11:

$$\mathbf{Pr}_r\big[h_r(H,p) = 0^m \text{ for some } (H,p) \in S\big] \;\ge\; \tfrac{2n!}{2^m}\big(1 - \tfrac{2n!}{2^m}\big) \;\ge\; 1.5n!/2^m$$

In this event, to make Arthur accept, Merlin sends such an (H,p) and a permutation q such that $q(H) \in \{G_1, G_2\}$, which exists since $H \cong G_1$ or $H \cong G_2$.

Soundness $n!/2^m$: Suppose $G_1 \cong G_2$, so $|S| = n!$. By a union bound:

$$\mathbf{Pr}_r\big[h_r(H,p) = 0^m \text{ for some } (H,p) \in S\big] \;\le\; \textstyle\sum_{(H,p)\in S} \mathbf{Pr}_r\big[h_r(H,p) = 0^m\big] \;=\; n!/2^m$$

This event holds if Arthur accepts, since "$q(H) \in \{G_1, G_2\}$ and $p(H) = H$" implies $(H,p) \in S$.

To amplify the completeness to 2/3 while keeping the soundness below 1/3, we run the above proof system multiple times in parallel (with independent randomness for each run), and have Arthur accept iff he would accept for $\ge 1.25n!/2^m$ fraction of the runs. Like in Corollary 7.22, with some constant number of runs, the probability that Merlin can make Arthur accept $\ge 1.25n!/2^m$ fraction of the runs is $\ge 2/3$ if $G_1 \ncong G_2$, and $\le 1/3$ if $G_1 \cong G_2$. ■

Using similar ideas, it's possible to turn any private-coin Arthur–Merlin proof system into a public-coin one with only polynomial loss in efficiency.

15.1.4 Complexity Classes

A public-coin Arthur–Merlin proof system is a randomized verifier $V(x;r;w)$ where x is the input, r is Arthur's coin tosses, and w is Merlin's purported witness (which depends on x and r).

Definition. AM is the set of all decision problems A for which there exists a poly-time randomized verifier V such that for every input x:

- Completeness 2/3: $A(x) = 1 \Rightarrow \mathbf{Pr}_r\big[\exists w\colon\ V(x;r;w) \text{ accepts}\big] \ge 2/3$
- Soundness 1/3: $A(x) = 0 \Rightarrow \mathbf{Pr}_r\big[\exists w\colon\ V(x;r;w) \text{ accepts}\big] \le 1/3$ ◄

Theorem 15.2 says GRAPH NONISOMORPHISM $\in$ AM. We also have a complexity class for noninteractive *Merlin–Arthur proof systems*, where Merlin sends w before Arthur samples r.

Definition. MA is the set of all decision problems A for which there exists a poly-time randomized verifier V such that for every input x:

- Completeness 2/3: $A(x)=1 \Rightarrow \exists w: \mathbf{Pr}_r\big[V(x;w;r) \text{ accepts}\big] \geq 2/3$
- Soundness 1/3: $A(x)=0 \Rightarrow \forall w: \mathbf{Pr}_r\big[V(x;w;r) \text{ accepts}\big] \leq 1/3$ ◀

NP $\subseteq$ MA (Arthur need not toss coins) and BPP $\subseteq$ MA (Arthur can ignore Merlin).

Like amplification for BPP (§7.3.2), for AM and MA we can amplify completeness and soundness from $1/2+\delta$ and $1/2-\delta$ to $1-\varepsilon$ and ε with a factor $k = O\big(\frac{1}{\delta^2}\log\frac{1}{\varepsilon}\big)$ time overhead:

- If $A \in$ MA by a randomized verifier V, define a randomized verifier V' where $V'(x;w;r_1,\ldots,r_k)$ runs $V(x;w;r_1),\ldots,V(x;w;r_k)$ and accepts iff a majority of them accept.
- If $A \in$ AM by a randomized verifier V, define a randomized verifier V' where $V'(x;r_1,\ldots,r_k;w_1,\ldots,w_k)$ runs $V(x;r_1;w_1),\ldots,V(x;r_k;w_k)$ and accepts iff a majority of them accept. This works because

$$\begin{aligned} &\mathbf{Pr}_{r_1,\ldots,r_k}\big[\exists w_1,\ldots,w_k : V'(x;r_1,\ldots,r_k;w_1,\ldots,w_k) \text{ accepts}\big] \\ =\ &\mathbf{Pr}_{r_1,\ldots,r_k}\big[\text{for a majority of } i \in [k] : \exists w_i : V(x;r_i;w_i) \text{ accepts}\big] \end{aligned}$$

which is $\geq 1-\varepsilon$ if $A(x)=1$, and $\leq \varepsilon$ if $A(x)=0$.

Theorem 15.4. MA $\subseteq$ AM.

Proof idea. We can't just swap Merlin and Arthur: If w can suddenly depend on r, Merlin might exploit this to increase Arthur's acceptance probability when $A(x)=0$. But if we first amplify the Merlin–Arthur proof system to have tiny soundness, then Merlin's advantage when w can depend on r isn't enough to push the soundness above $1/3$. We already saw this in the proof that if NP $\subseteq$ BPP then Σ_2P $\subseteq$ BPP (Theorem 7.12): We argued that Σ_2P $\subseteq$ MA $\subseteq$ AM $\subseteq$ BPP where the first and last $\subseteq$ are by the hypothesis NP $\subseteq$ BPP, and the middle $\subseteq$ is because drastic amplification lets us swap Merlin and Arthur. ∎

Proof. Suppose $A \in$ MA by a randomized verifier V with time efficiency $\leq T = cN^d$ (for integers c, d) and log-bounded word size W, so the witness is $w \in (\{0,1\}^W)^T$. By amplification, A has a poly-time randomized verifier V' with the same witness size and with completeness $2/3$ and soundness $\varepsilon = 2^{-TW}/3$. Then $A \in$ AM by a randomized verifier V'' where $V''(x;r;w)$ runs $V'(x;w;r)$:

$$\begin{aligned} A(x)=1 &\Rightarrow \exists w : \mathbf{Pr}_r\big[V'(x;w;r) \text{ accepts}\big] \geq 2/3 \\ &\Rightarrow \mathbf{Pr}_r\big[\exists w : V'(x;w;r) \text{ accepts}\big] \geq 2/3 \\ &\Rightarrow \mathbf{Pr}_r\big[\exists w : V''(x;r;w) \text{ accepts}\big] \geq 2/3 \end{aligned}$$

$$\begin{aligned} A(x)=0 &\Rightarrow \forall w : \mathbf{Pr}_r\big[V'(x;w;r) \text{ accepts}\big] \leq \varepsilon \\ &\Rightarrow \mathbf{Pr}_r\big[\exists w : V'(x;w;r) \text{ accepts}\big] \leq 2^{TW}\cdot\varepsilon = 1/3 \qquad \text{(union bound)} \\ &\Rightarrow \mathbf{Pr}_r\big[\exists w : V''(x;r;w) \text{ accepts}\big] \leq 1/3 \end{aligned}$$

∎

Theorem 15.5. *If* P = BPP *then* NP = MA.

Proof. Suppose $A \in$ MA by a randomized verifier V with time efficiency $\leq T = cN^d$ (for integers c, d) and log-bounded word size W. Consider this promise decision problem:

ARTHUR OF V (call this problem B)	(15.4)
Input: x, w where $x \in (\{0,1\}^W)^N$ is a valid input to A, and $w \in (\{0,1\}^W)^T$	
Output: 1 if $\mathbf{Pr}_r\big[V(x;w;r) \text{ accepts}\big] \geq 2/3$	
0 if $\mathbf{Pr}_r\big[V(x;w;r) \text{ accepts}\big] \leq 1/3$	
undefined otherwise	

$B \in$ BPP by a randomized program Π where $\Pi(x,w;r)$ runs $V(x;w;r)$. Assuming P = BPP, we have $B \in$ P by a deterministic program Π'. Then $A \in$ NP by a verifier V' where $V'(x;w)$ runs $\Pi'(x,w)$:

$$A(x)=1 \Rightarrow \big(\exists w:\ B(x,w)=1\big) \Rightarrow \big(\exists w:\ \Pi'(x,w) \text{ accepts}\big) \Rightarrow \big(\exists w:\ V'(x;w) \text{ accepts}\big)$$
$$A(x)=0 \Rightarrow \big(\forall w:\ B(x,w)=0\big) \Rightarrow \big(\forall w:\ \Pi'(x,w) \text{ rejects}\ \big) \Rightarrow \big(\forall w:\ V'(x;w) \text{ rejects}\ \big) \blacksquare$$

Hence, NP = MA follows from the same circuit lower bound conjecture that implies P = BPP (Theorem 11.22). A somewhat similar conjecture implies NP = AM. So many researchers suspect that NP = MA = AM, which would imply GRAPH ISOMORPHISM $\in$ NP $\cap$ coNP.

Theorem 15.6. MA $\subseteq \Sigma_2$P.

Proof idea. Since BPP $\subseteq \Sigma_2$P, we can replace Arthur's randomness with $\exists\,\forall$, and merge that $\exists$ with Merlin's $\exists$. ■

Proof. Suppose $A \in$ MA by a randomized verifier V. Consider B = ARTHUR OF $V \in$ BPP as in Theorem 15.5. Since BPP $\subseteq \Sigma_2$P (Theorem 7.10), we have $B \in \Sigma_2$P by a 2-witness verifier V':

$$B(x,w)=1 \Rightarrow \exists w_1\ \forall w_2:\ V'(x,w;w_1;w_2) \text{ accepts}$$
$$B(x,w)=0 \Rightarrow \forall w_1\ \exists w_2:\ V'(x,w;w_1;w_2) \text{ rejects}$$

Then $A \in \Sigma_2$P by a 2-witness verifier V'' where $V''(x;w,w_1;w_2)$ runs $V'(x,w;w_1;w_2)$:

$$\begin{aligned} A(x)=1 &\Rightarrow \exists w:\ B(x,w)=1 \\ &\Rightarrow \exists w\ \exists w_1\ \forall w_2:\ V'(x,w;w_1;w_2) \text{ accepts} \\ &\Rightarrow \exists w, w_1\ \ \forall w_2:\ V''(x;w,w_1;w_2) \text{ accepts} \end{aligned}$$

$$\begin{aligned} A(x)=0 &\Rightarrow \forall w:\ B(x,w)=0 \\ &\Rightarrow \forall w\ \forall w_1\ \exists w_2:\ V'(x,w;w_1;w_2) \text{ rejects} \\ &\Rightarrow \forall w, w_1\ \ \exists w_2:\ V''(x;w,w_1;w_2) \text{ rejects} \end{aligned}$$ ■

Theorem 15.7. AM $\subseteq \Pi_2$P.

Proof idea. By the same proof as BPP $\subseteq \Pi_2$P, we can replace Arthur's randomness with $\forall\,\exists$, and merge that $\exists$ with Merlin's $\exists$. ■

Proof (ancillary). Suppose $A \in \mathsf{AM}$. By amplification, A has a randomized verifier V with completeness $1 - 1/2^N$, soundness $1/3$, time efficiency $\leq T = cN^d$ (for integers c, d), and log-bounded word size W.

Merlin of V (call this problem B)	(15.5)
Input: x, r where $x \in (\{0,1\}^W)^N$ is a valid input to A, and $r \in (\{0,1\}^W)^T$	
Output: Does there exist w such that $V(x; r; w)$ accepts?	

Thus:

$$A(x) = 1 \Rightarrow \mathbf{Pr}_r\big[B(x,r) = 1\big] \geq 1 - 1/2^N$$
$$A(x) = 0 \Rightarrow \mathbf{Pr}_r\big[B(x,r) = 1\big] \leq 1/3$$

Denote $s = (s_1, \ldots, s_k)$ where each $s_i \in (\{0,1\}^W)^T$ for $k = TW \in \operatorname{poly} N$. We claim that:

$$A(x) = 1 \iff \forall s\ \exists r\ \forall i :\ B(x, r \oplus s_i) = 1$$

$\Rightarrow$: Assume $A(x) = 1$, so $\mathbf{Pr}_r\big[B(x,r) = 0\big] \leq 1/2^N$. For every s:

$$\mathbf{Pr}_r\big[\exists i :\ B(x, r \oplus s_i) = 0\big] \ \leq\ \textstyle\sum_i \mathbf{Pr}_r\big[B(x, r \oplus s_i) = 0\big] \ \leq\ \sum_i 1/2^N \ =\ k/2^N \ <\ 1$$

Thus $\forall s\ \exists r\ \forall i :\ B(x, r \oplus s_i) = 1$.

$\Leftarrow$: Assume $A(x) = 0$, so $\mathbf{Pr}_r\big[B(x,r) = 1\big] \leq 1/3$. For uniformly random s:

$$\mathbf{Pr}_s\big[\exists r\ \forall i :\ B(x, r \oplus s_i) = 1\big] \ \leq\ \textstyle\sum_r \mathbf{Pr}_s\big[\forall i :\ B(x, r \oplus s_i) = 1\big] \ =\ \sum_r \prod_i \mathbf{Pr}_{s_i}\big[B(x, r \oplus s_i) = 1\big]$$
$$\leq\ \textstyle\sum_r \prod_i 1/3 \ =\ 2^{TW}/3^k \ <\ 1$$

Thus $\exists s\ \forall r\ \exists i :\ B(x, r \oplus s_i) = 0$.

That proves the claim. Denote $w = (w_1, \ldots, w_k)$ where each $w_i \in (\{0,1\}^W)^T$. For all s and r:

$$\big(\forall i :\ B(x, r \oplus s_i) = 1\big) \iff \big(\exists w\ \forall i :\ V(x; r \oplus s_i; w_i) \text{ accepts}\big)$$

It follows that $A \in \Pi_2\mathsf{P}$ by a 2-witness verifier V' where $V'(x; s; r, w)$ runs $V(x; r \oplus s_i; w_i)$ for each i and accepts iff all of these runs accept:

$$A(x) = 1 \iff \forall s\ \exists r\ \exists w\ \forall i :\ V(x; r \oplus s_i; w_i) \text{ accepts}$$
$$\iff \forall s\ \exists r, w :\ V'(x; s; r, w) \text{ accepts}$$

■

Figure 15.4 updates the map of complexity classes from §7.10.

15.2 Interactive Proofs

15.2.1 Definition

An *interactive proof system* is like an Arthur–Merlin proof system except the interaction can continue for many rounds: Arthur sends Merlin a message, then Merlin sends Arthur a message in response, then Arthur sends another message, then Merlin responds again, and so on, until Arthur accepts or rejects.

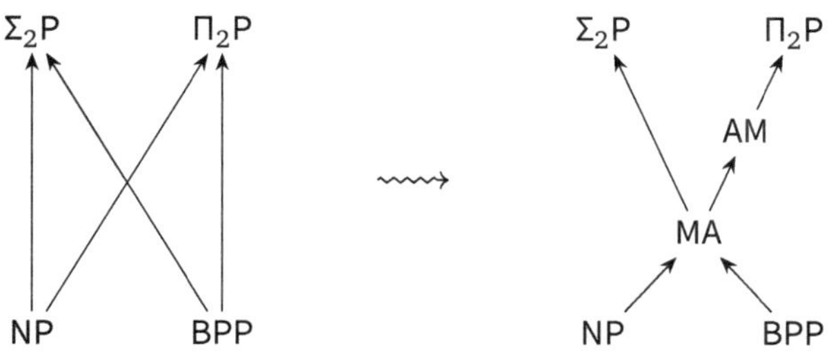

Figure 15.4: Incorporating MA and AM into the map of complexity classes

- Merlin's next message is specified by his *strategy*—an arbitrary function of the input x and the *communication history*, which is the sequence of messages so far.
- Private-coin version: Arthur's next message is a poly-time computable function of x and r (his coin tosses) and the communication history.
- Public-coin version: Arthur's next message is the outcomes of fresh coin tosses. Thus r is the concatenation of all of Arthur's messages. Merlin sees all coin tosses so far, but can't predict the outcomes of future coin tosses.

Definition. IP is the set of all decision problems A for which there exists a poly-time private-coin interactive proof system such that for every input x:

- Completeness 2/3: $A(x)=1 \Rightarrow \exists$ Merlin strategy: $\mathbf{Pr}[\text{Arthur accepts}] \geq 2/3$
- Soundness 1/3: $A(x)=0 \Rightarrow \forall$ Merlin strategy: $\mathbf{Pr}[\text{Arthur accepts}] \leq 1/3$ ◀

IP stands for "interactive proof." NP stands for "nondeterministic polynomial time," but in jest, it could retroactively stand for "noninteractive proof."

We prove one of complexity theory's most notable results:

Theorem 15.8. IP = PSPACE.

PSPACE-complete two-player games such as QSAT (§3.1) presumably aren't in NP: It's unclear how Merlin could convince a poly-time Arthur that a particular player has a winning strategy, which is an exponentially large thing. But remarkably, this is doable with some interaction and randomness. Philosophical takeaway: Although nobody knows whether black has a winning strategy in chess (for example), a deity could quickly convince a mortal of this (assuming that black can always win in a reasonable number of moves, and that the deity can't influence or predict the mortal's coin tosses).

We prove IP $\subseteq$ PSPACE in §15.2.2 (which also clarifies the definition of IP). We prove the more profound direction PSPACE $\subseteq$ IP in §15.2.4 after a warmup in §15.2.3. First, we show that interactive proof systems can be amplified, which is slightly less obvious than it might seem.

Lemma 15.9. *An interactive proof system's completeness and soundness can be amplified from* $1/2+\delta$ *and* $1/2-\delta$ *to* $1-\varepsilon$ *and* ε *with a factor* $k = O\left(\frac{1}{\delta^2}\log\frac{1}{\varepsilon}\right)$ *time overhead, in both the private-coin and public-coin settings.*

Proof. The new Arthur runs the original Arthur k times—with fresh randomness for each run—and accepts iff a majority of the runs accept.

Completeness $1-\varepsilon$: Suppose $A(x)=1$, so some Merlin strategy makes the original Arthur accept with probability $\geq 1/2+\delta$. Merlin can use this strategy in each run, so each run accepts with probability $\geq 1/2+\delta$ independently of the other runs. By Lemma 7.7 with k tosses of a coin with heads probability $\geq 1/2+\delta$, where heads means a run accepts:

$$\mathbf{Pr}[\text{new Arthur rejects}] \leq \mathbf{Pr}[\text{at most half the tosses are heads}] \leq \varepsilon$$

Soundness ε: Suppose $A(x)=0$, so every Merlin strategy makes the original Arthur accept with probability $\leq 1/2-\delta$. Consider any Merlin strategy with the new Arthur. Merlin's messages in each run may depend on prior runs—so the runs aren't independent—but that doesn't matter: Conditioned on any particular outcome of the randomness of all prior runs, the probability that a particular run accepts is $\leq 1/2-\delta$, so we can treat the run's outcome as an independent coin toss by imagining the acceptance probability is always rounded up to exactly $1/2-\delta$. By Lemma 7.7 with k tosses of a coin with heads probability $1/2-\delta$:

$$\mathbf{Pr}[\text{new Arthur accepts}] \leq \mathbf{Pr}[\text{at least half the tosses are heads}] \leq \varepsilon \qquad \blacksquare$$

15.2.2 IP ⊆ PSPACE

Lemma 15.10. IP ⊆ PSPACE.

Proof idea. We design a recursive algorithm to compute the maximum of **Pr**[Arthur accepts] over all Merlin strategies, and see whether it's $\geq 2/3$ or $\leq 1/3$. This is like solving two-player games (§3.1) except that Arthur plays randomly.

We assume every message is one bit and that Arthur and Merlin alternate: Arthur sends a bit, then Merlin sends a bit, then Arthur sends a bit, and so on. If someone wants to send a longer message, the other person can interject dummy bits. We also assume the whole conversation is always exactly n bits $a_1a_2\cdots a_n$, so Arthur's messages are $a_1a_3a_5\cdots$ and Merlin's are $a_2a_4a_6\cdots$.

First, consider the public-coin setting. Input x's *evaluation tree* has root-to-leaf paths corresponding to all conversations $a_1\cdots a_n \in \{0,1\}^n$. Stepping to a node's left child means sending the message 0, and stepping right means sending 1. A leaf's label is the bit $V(x;a_1\cdots a_n)$ that Arthur would output. An internal node's label is the maximum of **Pr**[Arthur accepts] over all Merlin strategies, pretending this node is the root. To calculate these labels from bottom to top:

- At an even-layer node v: Merlin picks the child with the larger label (breaking a tie in favor of the left child) and copies that label to v. Visualize the edge to that child as bold.
- At an odd-layer node v: Arthur picks a uniformly random child, so v's label is the average of its children's labels. Visualize both edges as bold since either could be traversed.

Figure 15.5 shows an example where Merlin has a strategy to make Arthur accept with probability 3/4. Only the bold edges are relevant for Merlin's strategy: In this example, no conversation would start with 00 (since Merlin sends 1 if Arthur sent 0), so we need not specify Merlin's strategy inside the 00 subtree.

This recursive subroutine returns the label of the node reached by the path $a_1\cdots a_{i-1}$:

Recursive algorithm to simulate a public-coin interactive proof system (15.6)

eval($a_1\cdots a_{i-1}$):
  if $i=n+1$: return $V(x;a_1\cdots a_n)$
  let $q_0 \leftarrow$ eval($a_1\cdots a_{i-1}0$) and $q_1 \leftarrow$ eval($a_1\cdots a_{i-1}1$)
  if i is even (Merlin): return $\max(q_0,q_1)$
  if i is odd (Arthur): return $q_0/2+q_1/2$

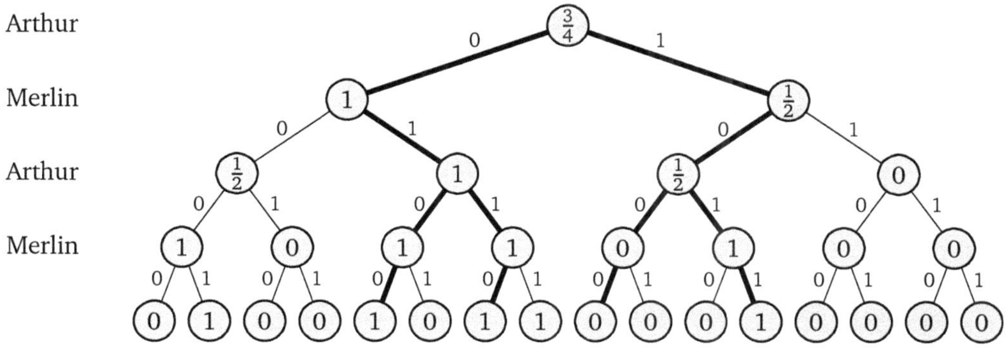

Figure 15.5: Example evaluation tree for a public-coin interactive proof system

In the private-coin setting, the only difference is that Arthur's nodes may have different distributions over their children (not all the uniform distribution). Instead of $q_0/2 + q_1/2$, we must compute q_0's and q_1's coefficients, which are the probabilities of sending 0 and 1 conditioned on the communication history. ■

Proof. Assume $A \in \mathsf{IP}$ by a poly-time private-coin interactive proof system with randomness $r \in \{0,1\}^m$ and where (without loss of generality) Arthur and Merlin strictly alternate sending one-bit messages, Arthur goes first, Merlin goes last, and every conversation is exactly n bits long, where $m, n \in \text{poly}N$. Treat Arthur's output as the "$(n+1)$st message," so the whole conversation is $a_1 \cdots a_n a_{n+1}$ where $a_1 \cdots a_n$ is the ordinary communication, and a_{n+1} is the output. For odd i, let $V(x; r; a_1 \cdots a_{i-1})$ denote the bit Arthur sends next if the communication history is $a_1 \cdots a_{i-1}$. We design subroutines that have access to the input x:

- $\text{eval}(a_1 \cdots a_{i-1})$ returns the maximum of $\mathbf{Pr}[\text{Arthur accepts}]$ conditioned on the communication history being $a_1 \cdots a_{i-1}$, over all Merlin strategies. It returns 0 if the conditioning event has probability 0. In the pseudocode, we assume any divisions by 0 evaluate to 0.
- $\text{prob}(a_1 \cdots a_i)$ returns the probability that Arthur sends $a_1 a_3 a_5 \cdots$, assuming Merlin sends $a_2 a_4 a_6 \cdots$ (that is, their communication begins $a_1 \cdots a_i$, assuming Merlin cooperates).
- $\text{reach}(r, a_1 \cdots a_i)$ returns true iff Arthur sends $a_1 a_3 a_5 \cdots$, assuming Arthur samples r and Merlin sends $a_2 a_4 a_6 \cdots$.

Recursive algorithm to simulate a private-coin interactive proof system (15.7)

$\text{eval}(a_1 \cdots a_{i-1})$:
  if $i = n+1$: return $\text{prob}(a_1 \cdots a_n 1) / \text{prob}(a_1 \cdots a_n)$
  let $q_0 \leftarrow \text{eval}(a_1 \cdots a_{i-1} 0)$ and $q_1 \leftarrow \text{eval}(a_1 \cdots a_{i-1} 1)$
  if i is even (Merlin): return $\max(q_0, q_1)$
  if i is odd (Arthur): return $\frac{p_0}{p} q_0 + \frac{p_1}{p} q_1$
    where $p_0 \leftarrow \text{prob}(a_1 \cdots a_{i-1} 0)$ and $p_1 \leftarrow \text{prob}(a_1 \cdots a_{i-1} 1)$ and $p \leftarrow p_0 + p_1$

$\text{prob}(a_1 \cdots a_i)$: return $\frac{1}{2^m}(\text{number of } r \in \{0,1\}^m \text{ such that reach}(r, a_1 \cdots a_i))$

$\text{reach}(r, a_1 \cdots a_i)$: return true iff $V(x; r; a_1 \cdots a_{j-1}) = a_j$ for every odd $j \leq i$

To compute $A(x)$, call eval(empty string) and accept if the result is $\geq 2/3$, and reject if it's $\leq 1/3$. To conclude $A \in \mathsf{PSPACE}$, we see that the subroutines use poly$N$ space:

- reach runs V at most n times, and each run takes poly$N$ time and thus poly$N$ space.
- prob loops over all $r \in \{0,1\}^m$ and reuses the same poly$N$ space to call reach for each r.
- eval has recursion depth $n+1$, and each stack frame uses poly$N$ space, so the total space is:

$$\big(\text{poly}N \text{ stack frames at a time}\big) \cdot \big(\text{poly}N \text{ bits per stack frame}\big) = \text{poly}N \text{ bits} \qquad \blacksquare$$

15.2.3 Sum-Check Protocol

It's not obvious how Merlin could convince Arthur that a CNF has no satisfying assignment. But amazingly, he can even convince Arthur of the exact number of satisfying assignments:

#SATISFIABILITY (or #SAT for short)	(15.8)
Input: CNF φ, nonnegative integer k	
Output: Does φ have exactly k satisfying assignments?	

#SAT is pronounced "sharp SAT" or "number SAT."

Theorem 15.11. #SAT $\in$ IP.

This implies coNP $\subseteq$ IP since $\overline{\text{SAT}}$ is coNP-complete and $\overline{\text{SAT}} \leq_p^m$ #SAT by mapping φ to $(\varphi, 0)$.

Proof idea. "Think outside the box." The box is the values $\{0,1\}$ we normally plug into φ's variables. Outside the box is a field of numbers including $\{0,1\}$. Plugging other field elements into φ's variables makes sense if we convert φ to a multivariate polynomial P, where $\neg$ becomes "$1-$", $\wedge$ becomes multiplication, and $\vee$ is expressed with $\wedge$ and $\neg$. This is *arithmetization*—using arithmetic to generalize logic. For example:

$$\varphi = (x_1 \vee \overline{x_2} \vee x_3) \wedge (\overline{x_3} \vee x_4 \vee \overline{x_5}) = \overline{(\overline{x_1} \wedge x_2 \wedge \overline{x_3})} \wedge \overline{(x_3 \wedge \overline{x_4} \wedge x_5)}$$
$$P = \big(1-(1-x_1)x_2(1-x_3)\big)\big(1-x_3(1-x_4)x_5\big)$$

P agrees with φ on every boolean assignment, so φ has $\sum_{(x_1,\ldots,x_n)\in\{0,1\}^n} P(x_1,\ldots,x_n)$ many satisfying assignments. The benefit of expanding $\{0,1\}$ to an ambient field is that we can "simulate" all 2^n boolean assignments simultaneously with a single assignment of field elements.

We design an interactive proof system called the *sum-check protocol*. Letting $b_0 = k$ (for consistency with subsequent notation), Merlin claims:

$$\sum_{x_1\in\{0,1\}} \sum_{x_2\in\{0,1\}} \cdots \sum_{x_n\in\{0,1\}} P(x_1, x_2, \ldots, x_n) = b_0$$

If this claim is false, Merlin wants to trick Arthur into accepting anyway. Consider the univariate polynomial that leaves x_1 as a variable instead of summing over $x_1 \in \{0,1\}$:

$$P_1(x_1) = \sum_{x_2\in\{0,1\}} \cdots \sum_{x_n\in\{0,1\}} P(x_1, x_2, \ldots, x_n)$$

Since $P_1(0) + P_1(1) = \sum_{x_1\in\{0,1\}} \sum_{x_2\in\{0,1\}} \cdots \sum_{x_n\in\{0,1\}} P(x_1, x_2, \ldots, x_n)$, Merlin claims $P_1(0) + P_1(1) = b_0$. To help convince Arthur of this, Merlin sends the coefficients of a univariate polynomial Q_1 and claims $P_1 = Q_1$. (It would take Arthur exponential time to find P_1 by himself.)

Arthur rejects if $Q_1(0)+Q_1(1) \neq b_0$. So if $P_1(0)+P_1(1) \neq b_0$ then Merlin must send some $Q_1 \neq P_1$ to have any hope of Arthur accepting. (Lies beget lies: If "$P_1(0)+P_1(1)=b_0$" was a lie, then "$P_1 = Q_1$" must be a lie.) Both polynomials have low degree, so if $P_1 \neq Q_1$ then probably $P_1(a_1) \neq Q_1(a_1)$ for a random a_1 that Arthur samples from a large enough field (as with polynomial identity testing in §7.1). Merlin couldn't predict a_1 when he picked Q_1, which gives Arthur an edge. Defining $b_1 = Q_1(a_1)$, Merlin implicitly claims $P_1(a_1) = b_1$, which is probably false if his original claim was false. Arthur has simplified the original claim by replacing $\sum_{x_1 \in \{0,1\}}$ with a single value $x_1 = a_1$. Arthur rinses and repeats with x_2 and the other variables:

$$\begin{array}{lll} & \text{claim} & \sum_{x_1\in\{0,1\}} \sum_{x_2\in\{0,1\}} \sum_{x_3\in\{0,1\}} \cdots P(x_1,x_2,x_3,\ldots,x_n) = b_0 \\ \rightsquigarrow & \text{claim} & \sum_{x_2\in\{0,1\}} \sum_{x_3\in\{0,1\}} \cdots P(a_1,x_2,x_3,\ldots,x_n) = b_1 \\ \rightsquigarrow & \text{claim} & \sum_{x_3\in\{0,1\}} \cdots P(a_1,a_2,x_3,\ldots,x_n) = b_2 \\ \vdots & & \vdots \\ \rightsquigarrow & \text{claim} & P(a_1,a_2,a_3,\ldots,a_n) = b_n \end{array}$$

Arthur backs Merlin into a corner with the claim $P(a_1,\ldots,a_n) = b_n$, which Arthur checks on his own by evaluating P. If Merlin strings Arthur along, digging himself into an ever-deeper hole, then his lies finally catch up with him when Arthur sees $P(a_1,\ldots,a_n) \neq b_n$ and reproaches him. Arthur is not angry, just disappointed. ■

Proof. We design a poly-time public-coin interactive proof system with completeness 1 and soundness $1/3$ for #SAT. The input is (φ, k) where φ is an n-variable m-clause CNF and $0 \le k \le 2^n$. The arithmetization of φ is this n-variable polynomial P:

$$\prod_{\text{clause } C \text{ in } \varphi} \Big(1 - \prod_{\text{literal } x_i \text{ in } C} (1-x_i) \prod_{\text{literal } \overline{x_i} \text{ in } C} (x_i)\Big)$$

$P(x_1,\ldots,x_n) = \varphi(x_1,\ldots,x_n)$ for every assignment in $\{0,1\}^n$. Each variable has individual degree $\le m$ in P. Consider P over the field $\mathbb{Z}_p$ for a prime number $p > \max(2^n, 3nm)$. We revisit the issue of finding p later.

Sum-check protocol for #SAT	(15.9)
let $b_0 \leftarrow k$	
for $i \leftarrow 1,\ldots,n$:	
Merlin sends the coefficients of a polynomial $Q_i(x_i)$ of degree $\le m$	
if $Q_i(0)+Q_i(1) \neq b_{i-1}$: Arthur rejects	
Arthur samples $a_i \in \mathbb{Z}_p$ uniformly at random and lets $b_i \leftarrow Q_i(a_i)$	
Arthur accepts iff $P(a_1,\ldots,a_n) = b_n$, where P is φ's arithmetization	

For the analysis, consider polynomials $P_0,\ldots,P_n$ where:

$$P_i(x_1,\ldots,x_i) = \sum_{x_{i+1}\in\{0,1\}} \sum_{x_{i+2}\in\{0,1\}} \cdots \sum_{x_n\in\{0,1\}} P(x_1,\ldots,x_i,x_{i+1},\ldots,x_n)$$

These polynomials "interpolate" between P_0, which is the number of satisfying assignments of φ, and $P_n = P$, which can be evaluated in poly time. We also define these polynomials iteratively, in reverse order, to relate them to each other:

Interpolating polynomials for the sum-check protocol (15.10)

define $P_n = P$
for $i \leftarrow n, \ldots, 1$:
  define $P_{i-1}(x_1, \ldots, x_{i-1}) = P_i(x_1, \ldots, x_{i-1}, 0) + P_i(x_1, \ldots, x_{i-1}, 1)$

With respect to a Merlin strategy, define events $E_0,\ D_1,\ E_1,\ D_2,\ E_2,\ \ldots,\ D_n,\ E_n$:

- D_i means $P_i(a_1, \ldots, a_{i-1}, x_i) = Q_i(x_i)$ and Arthur hasn't rejected by the end of iteration i.
- E_i means $P_i(a_1, \ldots, a_i) = b_i$ and Arthur hasn't rejected by the end of iteration i.

Completeness 1: Assume φ has exactly k satisfying assignments. Merlin has a strategy to ensure all the events $E_0,\ D_1,\ E_1,\ \ldots,\ D_n,\ E_n$ hold: E_0 holds because $P_0 = k = b_0$. If E_{i-1} holds then Merlin makes D_i hold by sending $Q_i(x_i) = P_i(a_1, \ldots, a_{i-1}, x_i)$ (which has degree $\leq m$ since x_i has individual degree $\leq m$ in P), and Arthur doesn't reject since:

$$Q_i(0) + Q_i(1) \ = \ P_i(a_1, \ldots, a_{i-1}, 0) + P_i(a_1, \ldots, a_{i-1}, 1) \ = \ P_{i-1}(a_1, \ldots, a_{i-1}) \ = \ b_{i-1}$$

If D_i holds then E_i holds regardless of a_i, since $P_i(a_1, \ldots, a_{i-1}, a_i) = Q_i(a_i) = b_i$. Finally, Arthur accepts since E_n holds.

Soundness 1/3: Assume φ doesn't have exactly k satisfying assignments. Consider any Merlin strategy. $\overline{E_0}$ holds because $P_0 \neq k$ over the integers implies $P_0 \neq k$ over $\mathbb{Z}_p$ since $p > 2^n \geq k$. If $\overline{E_{i-1}}$ holds then $\overline{D_i}$ holds, because if $P_i(a_1, \ldots, a_{i-1}, x_i) = Q_i(x_i)$ then Arthur rejects since:

$$Q_i(0) + Q_i(1) \ = \ P_i(a_1, \ldots, a_{i-1}, 0) + P_i(a_1, \ldots, a_{i-1}, 1) \ = \ P_{i-1}(a_1, \ldots, a_{i-1}) \ \neq \ b_{i-1}$$

$\mathbf{Pr}\big[E_i \,\big|\, \overline{D_i}\big] \leq m/p$ since $P_i(a_1, \ldots, a_{i-1}, x_i)$ and $Q_i(x_i)$ are distinct polynomials of degree $\leq m$ (Corollary A.21). Arthur accepts iff E_n holds, in which case the sequence of events $E_0,\ D_1,\ E_1,\ \ldots,\ D_n,\ E_n$ switches from not holding to holding at some step, which must be a D_i to E_i step:

$$\begin{aligned}
\mathbf{Pr}[\text{Arthur accepts}] \ = \ \mathbf{Pr}[E_n] \ &\leq \ \mathbf{Pr}\big[\exists i : \overline{D_i} \text{ and } E_i \text{ hold}\big] \\
&\leq \ \textstyle\sum_i \mathbf{Pr}\big[\overline{D_i} \text{ and } E_i \text{ hold}\big] \qquad \text{(union bound)} \\
&\leq \ \textstyle\sum_i \mathbf{Pr}\big[E_i \,\big|\, \overline{D_i}\big] \\
&\leq \ \textstyle\sum_i m/p \ = \ nm/p \ \leq \ 1/3
\end{aligned}$$

To alleviate the issue of perfectly sampling $a_i \in \mathbb{Z}_p$ using coin tosses, Arthur could instead sample a_i uniformly from a set of size $2^h > \max(2^n, 3nm)$ for some integer h. By the "prime number theorem" (which we accept as a gift from number theory), some prime p is in the range $2^h < p \leq 2^{h+1}$. Merlin sends such a p to Arthur, who confirms it using PRIMALITY TESTING $\in$ P. Another approach—for which brute force PRIMALITY TESTING is efficient enough—is for Arthur to find all primes in the range $6nm \leq p \leq (nm)^2$ and pick a uniformly random one. By the prime number theorem, that range has at least $6n$ primes. If $P_0 \neq k$ then $|P_0 - k| \leq 2^n$ has at most n prime factors, so we have $\mathbf{Pr}_p\big[P_0 = k \text{ over } \mathbb{Z}_p\big] = \mathbf{Pr}_p\big[|P_0 - k| \text{ is divisible by } p\big] \leq n/6n = 1/6$ contribution to the soundness, in addition to the $nm/p \leq 1/6$ contribution to the soundness.

Arthur runs in poly N time because the loop has n iterations, each Q_i has $m+1$ coefficients, each field element has $\log p \leq \text{poly} N$ bits, each $\mathbb{Z}_p$ arithmetic operation takes poly N time, and the expression for evaluating P has only poly N size. ■

The sum-check protocol also has a significant practical application in "SNARKs" (succinct noninteractive arguments of knowledge).

15.2.4 PSPACE $\subseteq$ IP

Theorem 15.12. PSPACE $\subseteq$ IP.

Proof idea. We design an interactive proof system for the PSPACE-complete problem QSAT. The input is an n-variable CNF φ where n is even. We replace $\exists$ with $\neg\forall\neg$:

$$\begin{aligned}\text{QSAT}(\varphi) &= \exists x_1 \quad \forall x_2 \quad \exists x_3 \quad \forall x_4 \cdots \forall x_n : \varphi(x_1,\ldots,x_n)\\ &= \neg\forall x_1 \neg \forall x_2 \neg \forall x_3 \neg \forall x_4 \cdots \neg \forall x_n : \varphi(x_1,\ldots,x_n)\\ &= \overline{\forall x_1}\quad \overline{\forall x_2}\quad \overline{\forall x_3}\quad \overline{\forall x_4} \cdots \overline{\forall x_n} : \varphi(x_1,\ldots,x_n)\end{aligned}$$

Arithmetization turns φ into a polynomial P that agrees with φ on every assignment in $\{0,1\}^n$. Replacing each $\overline{\forall x_i}\cdots$ with $1-\prod_{x_i\in\{0,1\}}(\cdots)$, we know QSAT$(\varphi)$ is:

$$1-\prod_{x_1\in\{0,1\}}\Big(1-\prod_{x_2\in\{0,1\}}\Big(1-\prod_{x_3\in\{0,1\}}\Big(\cdots\Big(1-\prod_{x_n\in\{0,1\}}P(x_1,\ldots,x_n)\Big)\cdots\Big)\Big)\Big)$$

If we ignore all the "$1-$" (which are trivial to handle), it would become:

$$\prod_{x_1\in\{0,1\}}\prod_{x_2\in\{0,1\}}\cdots\prod_{x_n\in\{0,1\}}P(x_1,\ldots,x_n)$$

Merlin could convince Arthur of this expression's value using a "product-check protocol" like the sum-check protocol. Recalling all the "$1-$", we change one line of Arthur's code and use different polynomials $P_0,\ldots,P_n$ in the analysis:

$$\text{if } Q_i(0)+Q_i(1)\neq b_{i-1} \quad\rightsquigarrow\quad \text{if } 1-Q_i(0)\cdot Q_i(1)\neq b_{i-1}$$

Interpolating polynomials for the product-check protocol (15.11)

define $P_n = P$
for $i \leftarrow n,\ldots,1$:
  define $P_{i-1}(x_1,\ldots,x_{i-1}) = 1-P_i(x_1,\ldots,x_{i-1},0)\cdot P_i(x_1,\ldots,x_{i-1},1)$

The catch is that since each $\prod$ may double the individual degrees (whereas $\sum$ doesn't increase them), Q_i would need exponentially large degree, and Arthur doesn't have time to read that many coefficients. We can fix this. Between the steps that eliminate variables one by one (and increase the individual degrees of other variables), we insert new steps that bluntly decrease the individual degrees of variables one by one, without affecting the polynomial's values on boolean assignments. Merlin convinces Arthur that this is done properly, in much the same way as he convinces Arthur that variables are eliminated properly. ∎

Linearizing a variable x_j in a polynomial means replacing x_j^d with x_j for each $d\geq 1$, throughout the polynomial's canonical form. The new polynomial agrees with the original on every assignment with $x_j\in\{0,1\}$ since $1^d=1$ and $0^d=0$ for all $d\geq 1$.

Example. Here's a univariate example:

$$x^3+4x^2+2x+8 \;\rightsquigarrow\; x+4x+2x+8 \;=\; (1+4+2)x+8 \;=\; 7x+8$$

Here's a multivariate example where we linearize x_2:

$$\begin{aligned}&\big(x_1x_3+4x_1\big)x_2^2+\big(x_1+6\big)x_2+\big(x_3^2+7\big)\\ \rightsquigarrow\;&\big(x_1x_3+4x_1\big)x_2+\big(x_1+6\big)x_2+\big(x_3^2+7\big)\\ =\;&\big((x_1x_3+4x_1)+(x_1+6)\big)x_2+\big(x_3^2+7\big)\\ =\;&\big(x_1x_3+5x_1+6\big)x_2+\big(x_3^2+7\big)\end{aligned}$$

♦

Proof of Theorem 15.12. Since QSAT is PSPACE-complete (Theorem 3.4), it suffices to prove QSAT $\in$ IP. We design a poly-time public-coin interactive proof system with completeness 1 and soundness 1/3 for QSAT. The input is an n-variable m-clause CNF φ where n is even. Let P be φ's arithmetization as in the proof of Theorem 15.11, so $P(x_1,\dots,x_n) = \varphi(x_1,\dots,x_n)$ for every assignment in $\{0,1\}^n$, and each variable has individual degree $\le m$ in P.

$$\begin{aligned}\text{QSAT}(\varphi) &= \exists x_1\ \forall x_2\ \exists x_3\ \forall x_4\ \cdots\ \forall x_n:\ \varphi(x_1,\dots,x_n)\\ &= 1-\textstyle\prod_{x_1\in\{0,1\}}\Big(1-\prod_{x_2\in\{0,1\}}\Big(1-\prod_{x_3\in\{0,1\}}\Big(\cdots\Big(1-\prod_{x_n\in\{0,1\}}P(x_1,\dots,x_n)\Big)\cdots\Big)\Big)\Big)\end{aligned}$$

Consider P over the field $\mathbb{Z}_p$ where $p \ge 3n(n+1)m$ is a prime number, which Arthur finds in poly$N$ time by brute force.

Throughout the interactive proof system, $a_1,\dots,a_n \in \mathbb{Z}_p$ keep changing values as Arthur repeatedly resamples them:

Interactive proof system for QSAT (15.12)

let $b_{0,0} \leftarrow 1$
for $i \leftarrow 1,\dots,n$:
  Merlin sends the coefficients of a polynomial $Q_{i,0}(x_i)$ of degree $\le m$
  if $1-Q_{i,0}(0)\cdot Q_{i,0}(1) \ne b_{i-1,i-1}$: Arthur rejects
  Arthur samples $a_i \in \mathbb{Z}_p$ uniformly at random and lets $b_{i,0} \leftarrow Q_{i,0}(a_i)$
  for $j \leftarrow 1,\dots,i$:
    Merlin sends the coefficients of a polynomial $Q_{i,j}(x_j)$ of degree $\le m$
    if $Q'_{i,j}(a_j) \ne b_{i,j-1}$ where $Q'_{i,j} \leftarrow Q_{i,j}$ with x_j linearized: Arthur rejects
    Arthur resamples $a_j \in \mathbb{Z}_p$ uniformly at random and lets $b_{i,j} \leftarrow Q_{i,j}(a_j)$
Arthur accepts iff $P(a_1,\dots,a_n) = b_{n,n}$, where P is φ's arithmetization

For the analysis, we define polynomials that "interpolate" between $P_{n,n} = P$ and $P_{0,0} = \text{QSAT}(\varphi) \in \{0,1\}$:

Interpolating polynomials for the interactive proof system for QSAT (15.13)

define $P_{n,n} = P$
for $i \leftarrow n,\dots,1$:
  for $j \leftarrow i,\dots,1$:
    define $P_{i,j-1} = P_{i,j}$ with x_j linearized
  define $P_{i-1,i-1}(x_1,\dots,x_{i-1}) = 1 - P_{i,0}(x_1,\dots,x_{i-1},0)\cdot P_{i,0}(x_1,\dots,x_{i-1},1)$

The polynomial $P_{i,j}$ (where $n \ge i \ge j \ge 0$) has i variables, of which the first j haven't yet been linearized. For each i, the polynomials $P_{i,i},\dots,P_{i,0}$ agree with each other on assignments in $\{0,1\}^i$. In each $P_{i,j}$, every variable has individual degree $\le m$: This holds in $P_{n,n} = P$ since φ has m clauses. Linearization makes the individual degrees ≤ 1. The definition of $P_{i-1,i-1}$ from $P_{i,0}$ at most doubles the individual degrees to $2 \le m$.

With respect to a Merlin strategy, define events

$$\underbrace{E_{0,0}}_{i=0}\quad \underbrace{D_{1,0}\quad E_{1,0}\quad D_{1,1}\quad E_{1,1}}_{i=1}\quad \underbrace{D_{2,0}\quad E_{2,0}\quad D_{2,1}\quad E_{2,1}\quad D_{2,2}\quad E_{2,2}}_{i=2}\quad \cdots\quad E_{n,n}$$

where $D_{i,j}$ and $E_{i,j}$ concern the end of inner iteration j of outer iteration i (where outer iteration 0 is the part before "for i", and inner iteration 0 is the part before "for j"):

- $D_{i,0}$ means $P_{i,0}(a_1,\ldots,a_{i-1},x_i) = Q_{i,0}(x_i)$ and Arthur hasn't rejected.
- $D_{i,j}$ for $j > 0$ means $P_{i,j}(\ldots,a_{j-1},x_j,a_{j+1},\ldots) = Q_{i,j}(x_j)$ and Arthur hasn't rejected.
- $E_{i,j}$ means $P_{i,j}(a_1,\ldots,a_i) = b_{i,j}$ and Arthur hasn't rejected.

Completeness 1: Assume $\text{QSAT}(\varphi) = 1$. Merlin has a strategy to ensure all the events hold:

- $E_{0,0}$ holds because $P_{0,0} = \text{QSAT}(\varphi) = 1 = b_{0,0}$.
- If $E_{i-1,i-1}$ holds then Merlin makes $D_{i,0}$ hold by sending $Q_{i,0}(x_i) = P_{i,0}(a_1,\ldots,a_{i-1},x_i)$ (which has degree $\le m$), and Arthur doesn't reject since:

$$\begin{aligned} 1 - Q_{i,0}(0)\cdot Q_{i,0}(1) &= 1 - P_{i,0}(a_1,\ldots,a_{i-1},0)\cdot P_{i,0}(a_1,\ldots,a_{i-1},1) \\ &= P_{i-1,i-1}(a_1,\ldots,a_{i-1}) \;=\; b_{i-1,i-1} \end{aligned}$$

- If $D_{i,0}$ holds then $E_{i,0}$ holds regardless of a_i, since $P_{i,0}(a_1,\ldots,a_{i-1},a_i) = Q_{i,0}(a_i) = b_{i,0}$.
- If $E_{i,j-1}$ holds then Merlin makes $D_{i,j}$ hold by sending $Q_{i,j}(x_j) = P_{i,j}(\ldots,a_{j-1},x_j,a_{j+1},\ldots)$ (which has degree $\le m$) so $Q'_{i,j}(x_j) = P_{i,j-1}(\ldots,a_{j-1},x_j,a_{j+1},\ldots)$, and Arthur doesn't reject since for the old a_j:

$$Q'_{i,j}(a_j) \;=\; P_{i,j-1}(\ldots,a_{j-1},a_j,a_{j+1},\ldots) \;=\; b_{i,j-1}$$

- If $D_{i,j}$ holds then $E_{i,j}$ holds regardless of the new a_j, since $P_{i,j}(\ldots,a_{j-1},a_j,a_{j+1},\ldots) = Q_{i,j}(a_j) = b_{i,j}$.

Finally, Arthur accepts since $E_{n,n}$ holds.

Soundness 1/3: Assume $\text{QSAT}(\varphi) = 0$. Consider any Merlin strategy.

- $\overline{E_{0,0}}$ holds because $P_{0,0} = \text{QSAT}(\varphi) = 0 \neq b_{0,0}$.
- If $\overline{E_{i-1,i-1}}$ holds then $\overline{D_{i,0}}$ holds because if $P_{i,0}(a_1,\ldots,a_{i-1},x_i) = Q_{i,0}(x_i)$ then Arthur rejects since:

$$\begin{aligned} 1 - Q_{i,0}(0)\cdot Q_{i,0}(1) &= 1 - P_{i,0}(a_1,\ldots,a_{i-1},0)\cdot P_{i,0}(a_1,\ldots,a_{i-1},1) \\ &= P_{i-1,i-1}(a_1,\ldots,a_{i-1}) \;\neq\; b_{i-1,i-1} \end{aligned}$$

- $\mathbf{Pr}\big[E_{i,0} \,\big|\, \overline{D_{i,0}}\big] \le m/p$ since $P_{i,0}(a_1,\ldots,a_{i-1},x_i)$ and $Q_{i,0}(x_i)$ are distinct polynomials of degree $\le m$ (Corollary A.21).
- If $\overline{E_{i,j-1}}$ holds then $\overline{D_{i,j}}$ holds because if $P_{i,j}(\ldots,a_{j-1},x_j,a_{j+1},\ldots) = Q_{i,j}(x_j)$ and therefore $P_{i,j-1}(\ldots,a_{j-1},x_j,a_{j+1},\ldots) = Q'_{i,j}(x_j)$, then Arthur rejects since for the old a_j:

$$Q'_{i,j}(a_j) \;=\; P_{i,j-1}(\ldots,a_{j-1},a_j,a_{j+1},\ldots) \;\neq\; b_{i,j-1}$$

- $\mathbf{Pr}\big[E_{i,j} \,\big|\, \overline{D_{i,j}}\big] \le m/p$ since $P_{i,j}(\ldots,a_{j-1},x_j,a_{j+1},\ldots)$ and $Q_{i,j}(x_j)$ are distinct polynomials of degree $\le m$ (Corollary A.21).

Arthur accepts iff $E_{n,n}$ holds, in which case the sequence of events switches from not holding to holding at some step, which must be a $D_{i,j}$ to $E_{i,j}$ step with $i \in \{1,\ldots,n\}$ and $j \in \{0,\ldots,i\}$:

$$\begin{aligned} \mathbf{Pr}[\text{Arthur accepts}] \;=\; \mathbf{Pr}[E_{n,n}] &\le \mathbf{Pr}\big[\exists i,j : \overline{D_{i,j}} \text{ and } E_{i,j} \text{ hold}\big] \\ &\le \textstyle\sum_{i,j} \mathbf{Pr}\big[\overline{D_{i,j}} \text{ and } E_{i,j} \text{ hold}\big] \qquad \text{(union bound)} \\ &\le \textstyle\sum_{i,j} \mathbf{Pr}\big[E_{i,j} \,\big|\, \overline{D_{i,j}}\big] \\ &\le \textstyle\sum_{i,j} m/p \;\le\; n(n+1)m/p \;\le\; 1/3 \end{aligned}$$

Arthur runs in poly N time because there are poly N iterations, each $Q_{i,j}$ has $m+1$ coefficients, each field element has $\log p \le O(\log N)$ bits, each $\mathbb{Z}_p$ arithmetic operation takes polylog N time, and the expression for evaluating P has only poly N size. ■

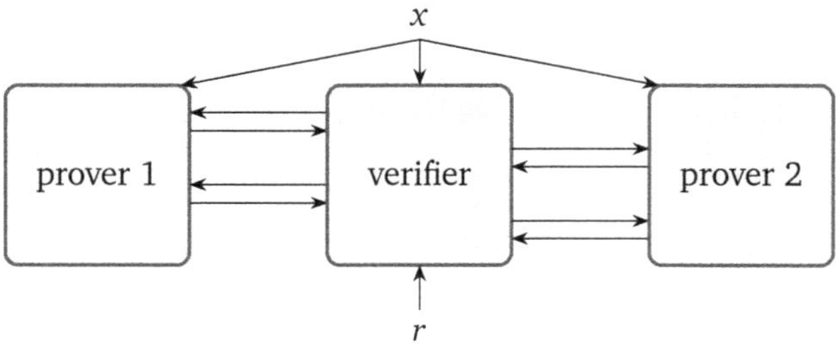

Figure 15.6: Two-prover interactive proof system

15.2.5 Multiple Provers

What if two provers are in cahoots to convince a verifier that $A(x) = 1$? If the provers see each other's messages from the verifier, then they might as well be a single, combined prover. But suppose they can't see each other's messages or communicate with each other during the execution, though they may coordinate their strategies ahead of time. The verifier can leverage this, like police interrogating suspected accomplices separately to catch inconsistencies in their stories. See Figure 15.6.

Definition. MIP is the set of all decision problems A for which there exists a poly-time private-coin two-prover interactive proof system such that for every input x:

- Completeness 2/3: $A(x) = 1 \Rightarrow \exists$ prover strategies: $\mathbf{Pr}[\text{verifier accepts}] \geq 2/3$
- Soundness 1/3: $A(x) = 0 \Rightarrow \forall$ prover strategies: $\mathbf{Pr}[\text{verifier accepts}] \leq 1/3$ ◄

Theorem 15.13. MIP = NEXP.

We prove MIP ⊆ NEXP momentarily. We won't prove NEXP ⊆ MIP, which uses similar ingredients as PSPACE ⊆ IP but is more involved.

There's a connection with probabilistically checkable proofs (PCPs). The current section doesn't depend on §14.4, where we first encountered PCPs. The following class is defined like MA, except the purported witness can be exponentially large (without counting against the time efficiency), and the verifier only reads polynomially many bits of it.

Definition. PCP is the set of all decision problems A for which there exists a poly-time randomized verifier V with witness size $2^{\text{poly} N}$, such that for every input x:

- Completeness 2/3: $A(x) = 1 \Rightarrow \exists w:\ \mathbf{Pr}_r\big[V(x; w; r) \text{ accepts}\big] \geq 2/3$
- Soundness 1/3: $A(x) = 0 \Rightarrow \forall w:\ \mathbf{Pr}_r\big[V(x; w; r) \text{ accepts}\big] \leq 1/3$ ◄

The randomness r is poly$N$ bits, and V queries (reads) poly$N$ bits of w, adaptively. We could model V's access to w in two ways:

- V could have poly-bounded word size, a witness segment (with word size 1), and instructions "read-witness Reg[i] ← Wit[Reg[j]]" to put the bit of w indexed by Reg[j]'s value into Reg[i].
- V could have log-bounded word size, a query segment, and instructions "write-query Reg[i]" to put the word from Reg[i] into the next query segment address, and "query Reg[i] ← Answer" to put the bit of w indexed by the query segment's contents into Reg[i] and erase the query segment.

We can straightforwardly amplify completeness and soundness from $1/2+\delta$ and $1/2-\delta$ to $1-\varepsilon$ and ε with a factor $O(\frac{1}{\delta^2}\log\frac{1}{\varepsilon})$ time overhead.

PCP[poly N, k] from §14.4.1 is like PCP but requires V to have completeness 1 and to query only k bits of w, nonadaptively. The "scaled up PCP theorem" says NEXP = PCP[poly N, k] for some constant k (Theorem 14.26), while a somewhat weaker version NEXP = PCP follows from NEXP $\subseteq$ MIP and the next two lemmas.

Lemma 15.14. PCP $\subseteq$ NEXP.

Proof. If $A \in$ PCP by a randomized verifier V, then $A \in$ NEXP by a verifier V' where $V'(x;w)$ runs $V(x;w;r)$ for all r and accepts iff a majority of the runs accept. V' has time efficiency $2^{\text{poly}\,N}$ since w has size $2^{\text{poly}\,N}$ and there are $2^{\text{poly}\,N}$ possibilities of r. For completeness and soundness:

$$A(x)=1 \Rightarrow \big(\exists w:\ \mathbf{Pr}_r\big[V(x;w;r)\text{ accepts}\big]>1/2\big) \Rightarrow \big(\exists w:\ V'(x;w)\text{ accepts}\big)$$
$$A(x)=0 \Rightarrow \big(\forall w:\ \mathbf{Pr}_r\big[V(x;w;r)\text{ accepts}\big]<1/2\big) \Rightarrow \big(\forall w:\ V'(x;w)\text{ rejects}\big)$$ ■

Lemma 15.15. MIP $\subseteq$ PCP.

Proof. If $A \in$ MIP by a randomized verifier V, then $A \in$ PCP by a randomized verifier V' that views w as specifying both provers' strategies, assuming the provers send 1-bit messages: $w_{j,h}$ is the bit that prover $j \in \{1,2\}$ would send given communication history h. Then $V'(x;w;r)$ runs V with randomness r, simulating the communication with both provers by making queries to w. Completeness and soundness are inherited from V. ■

Lemma 15.16. PCP $\subseteq$ MIP.

Proof idea. How about simulating a PCP verifier with an interactive proof system using a prover to answer queries to the PCP witness? A devious prover's answers might not conform to any single witness, because his answers may depend on which other queries were already made. We use a second prover to keep the first prover in check. We only make one query to the second prover, so her answer conforms to a single witness. If the first prover doesn't conform to the same witness, we have a decent chance of catching him red-handed by randomly picking one of the queries to cross-check with the second prover. ■

Proof. Suppose $A \in$ PCP by a randomized verifier V with completeness $1-2^{-N}$ and soundness 2^{-N}. Define a randomized verifier V' that interacts with provers P1 and P2: V' simulates V, and whenever V queries a bit of w, V' requests that bit from P1. If V accepts, then V' picks—uniformly at random—one of the queries it made to P1, makes the same query to P2, and accepts iff their answers to that query agree.

Completeness $1-2^{-N}$: Suppose $A(x)=1$, so $\mathbf{Pr}_r\big[V(x;w;r)\text{ accepts}\big] \geq 1-2^{-N}$ for some w. If P1 and P2 conform to one such w (given a query i, they respond with w_i), then V' accepts with probability $\geq 1-2^{-N}$.

Soundness $1-1/q+2^{-N}$ where $q \in \text{poly}\,N$ is an upper bound on how many queries V makes: Suppose $A(x)=0$, so $\mathbf{Pr}_r\big[V(x;w;r)\text{ accepts}\big] \leq 2^{-N}$ for all w. Consider any strategies for P1 and P2, and assume they always send 1-bit messages. P2's strategy corresponds to a purported witness w, where w_i is what P2 would respond if i is the query (since P2 only gets one query and can't communicate with P1). Let E be the event that V' makes some query i to P1 such that P1's response isn't w_i. If E holds, then V' rejects with probability $\geq 1/q$ since V' would discover the inconsistency between P1 and P2 for at least one of the q queries. If V' accepts and $\overline{E}$ holds, then V accepts with w.

$$\begin{aligned}\mathbf{Pr}\big[V' \text{ accepts}\big] &= \mathbf{Pr}\big[V' \text{ accepts and } E\big] + \mathbf{Pr}\big[V' \text{ accepts and } \overline{E}\big] \\ &\le \mathbf{Pr}\big[V' \text{ accepts} \,\big|\, E\big] + \mathbf{Pr}_r\big[V(x; w; r) \text{ accepts}\big] \le (1 - 1/q) + 2^{-N}\end{aligned}$$

To conclude $A \in \mathsf{MIP}$, we amplify soundness to $1/3$ while keeping completeness above $2/3$: We run V' for $10q^2 \in \text{poly} N$ times—with fresh randomness for each run—and accept iff $\ge 1 - 1/2q$ fraction of the runs accept. Like amplification of single-prover interactive proof systems (Lemma 15.9), this works because by Lemma 7.20 with $10q^2$ tosses of a coin with heads probability p and for $\gamma = 1/2q - 2^{-N}$:

$$\begin{aligned} p &= 1 - 2^{-N} &&= 1 - 1/2q + \gamma \Rightarrow \mathbf{Pr}\big[< 1 - 1/2q \text{ fraction of tosses are heads}\big] \le 1/3 \\ p &= 1 - 1/q + 2^{-N} &&= 1 - 1/2q - \gamma \Rightarrow \mathbf{Pr}\big[\ge 1 - 1/2q \text{ fraction of tosses are heads}\big] \le 1/3 \end{aligned}$$ ■

$\mathsf{MIP} = \mathsf{NEXP}$ and $\mathsf{IP} = \mathsf{PSPACE}$, so two provers are better than one (unless $\mathsf{NEXP} = \mathsf{PSPACE}$). Are three provers better than two? Nope. Define MIP_ℓ like MIP but letting the verifier interact with ℓ provers, who can't communicate with each other during the execution but may coordinate their strategies in advance (so $\mathsf{MIP}_1 = \mathsf{IP}$ and $\mathsf{MIP}_2 = \mathsf{MIP}$). In general, ℓ may depend on the input size N. We have $\mathsf{MIP}_{\text{poly} N} \subseteq \mathsf{PCP}$ (for the same reason as $\mathsf{MIP} \subseteq \mathsf{PCP}$) and $\mathsf{PCP} \subseteq \mathsf{MIP} \subseteq \mathsf{MIP}_{\text{poly} N}$ (Lemma 15.16). In summary, NEXP has many guises:

$$\mathsf{MIP}_{\text{poly} N} = \mathsf{MIP} = \mathsf{NEXP} = \mathsf{PCP} = \mathsf{PCP}[\text{poly} N, k]$$

15.3 Delegation and Program Checking

So far, we focused on the verifier's efficiency. Now, we consider the prover's efficiency, since omnipotent provers don't exist in reality. So we don't call the prover Merlin in this section.

The verifier should be more efficient than solving A from scratch. The *honest prover*—who always sends the intended message as in the completeness analysis—should be not much less efficient than solving A. Soundness should still hold against literally all provers (regardless of their efficiency). The honest prover's efficiency matters for delegation and for program checking, mentioned at the start of this chapter.

15.3.1 Efficiency of Honest Provers

Lemma 15.17. *The interactive proof system for* #SAT *from §15.2.3 has a poly-space honest prover.*

Proof. In iteration i, the honest prover sends the coefficients of:

$$Q_i(x_i) = P_i(a_1, \ldots, a_{i-1}, x_i) = \textstyle\sum_{(x_{i+1}, \ldots, x_n) \in \{0,1\}^{n-i}} P(a_1, \ldots, a_{i-1}, x_i, x_{i+1}, \ldots, x_n)$$

To find Q_i, he iterates over all $(z_{i+1}, \ldots, z_n) \in \{0,1\}^{n-i}$, obtains the coefficients of the univariate polynomial $P(a_1, \ldots, a_{i-1}, x_i, z_{i+1}, \ldots, z_n)$ by partially evaluating P, and sums all these polynomials. Remembering the current $(z_{i+1}, \ldots, z_n)$ and the running sum only takes poly space. Partially evaluating P only takes poly space, which is reused in each iteration. ■

Lemma 15.18. *The interactive proof system for* QSAT *from §15.2.4 has a poly-space honest prover.*

Proof. The proof of IP ⊆ PSPACE (Lemma 15.10) yields a poly-space algorithm to compute the maximum acceptance probability of the verifier, over all prover strategies, conditioned on any given communication history. Our interactive proof system for QSAT has completeness 1. So if QSAT(φ) = 1, then whenever the prover needs to send a message, he can try all possible messages, compute the maximum acceptance probability for each message, and pick a message that leads to acceptance probability 1. We argued that if the prover ever sends a dishonest message, then the verifier probably rejects. Thus, a message leading to acceptance probability 1 must be honest. ■

If PSPACE ⊆ P/poly then PSPACE = Σ_2P (Theorem 5.6). The following is stronger since MA ⊆ Σ_2P (Theorem 15.6).

Corollary 15.19. *If* PSPACE ⊆ P/poly *then* PSPACE = MA.

Proof. Assume PSPACE ⊆ P/poly. To show PSPACE = MA, it suffices to show QSAT ∈ MA since QSAT is PSPACE-complete (Theorem 3.4). Consider the interactive proof system for QSAT with completeness 1 and soundness 1/3 from §15.2.4.

(call this problem B)	(15.14)
Input: CNF φ such that QSAT(φ) = 1, communication history h, and index k	
Output: kth bit of honest prover's next message on input φ and communication history h	

B ∈ PSPACE (Lemma 15.18) so B ∈ P/poly by a nonuniform program Π. Assume Π runs in poly time even on invalid inputs or with wrong advice.

"Prover" and "verifier" refer to the interactive proof system for QSAT ∈ IP, while "Merlin" and "Arthur" refer to showing QSAT ∈ MA: First, Merlin sends purported advice for Π for all relevant input sizes. Then, Arthur runs the verifier and generates the prover's messages using Π with the purported advice from Merlin.

Completeness 1: If QSAT(φ) = 1 then Merlin sends Π's actual advice, so Arthur faithfully simulates the verifier's interaction with the honest prover and thus accepts with probability 1.

Soundness 1/3: If QSAT(φ) = 0 then regardless of what Merlin sends, Arthur simulates the verifier's interaction with some prover strategy and thus accepts with probability ≤ 1/3. ■

15.3.2 Delegation

For interactive proof systems to be practical, the honest prover should be time-efficient (not just space-efficient), and the verifier should be even more time-efficient. A *doubly efficient* interactive proof system has a poly-time honest prover and quasi-linear-time verifier. If the verifier seeks $A(x)$ and can wait poly time for the answer, but can't devote enough resources to run the whole computation himself, then he can delegate the computation to an untrusted prover and ask the prover to convince him of the answer. With a doubly efficient interactive proof system, the verifier only participates for a quasi-linear amount of the poly time. The verifier can be convinced that $A(x) = 1$ or that $A(x) = 0$ using an interactive proof system for A or for $\overline{A}$, respectively.

Our example of a doubly efficient interactive proof system concerns *triangles* (size-3 cliques in graphs). To convince the verifier that an n-node graph contains a triangle, the prover could find a triangle in $O(n^3)$ time by brute force (trying all sets of three nodes) and send the triangle to the verifier, who checks it in $O(1)$ time. What about convincing the verifier of the absence of triangles, or more generally, of the exact number of triangles?

#TRIANGLE	(15.15)
Input: Undirected graph G, nonnegative integer k	
Output: Does G have exactly k triangles?	

Assume $G = (V, E)$ is an n-node m-edge undirected graph (with no multi-edges or self-loops), so the adjacency list encoding has size $N \approx n + m$. No quasi-linear-time algorithm is known for #TRIANGLE, but the following algorithm is faster than brute force.

Algorithm for #TRIANGLE (15.16)

let M be G's $n \times n$ adjacency matrix
compute M^2 using a state-of-the-art MATRIX MULTIPLICATION algorithm
accept iff $k = \frac{1}{3}\sum_{\{u,v\}\in E}(M^2)_{u,v}$

The number of triangles is $\frac{1}{3}\sum_{\{u,v\}\in E}(M^2)_{u,v}$ because:

- $(M^2)_{u,v}$ is the number of length-2 walks between u and v (Lemma A.30) and is therefore the number of triangles containing the edge $\{u, v\}$.
- $\sum_{\{u,v\}\in E}(M^2)_{u,v}$ counts each triangle three times, since any of a triangle's three edges could play the role of $\{u, v\}$.

Computing M^2 takes $O(n^{2.38})$ time, and then evaluating $\frac{1}{3}\sum_{\{u,v\}\in E}(M^2)_{u,v}$ takes $O(m) \le O(n^2)$ time, so the total time is $O(n^{2.38})$. Anyway:

Theorem 15.20. #TRIANGLE *has a doubly efficient public-coin interactive proof system.*

Proof idea. We know we can turn poly-space algorithms into interactive proof systems with exponential-time honest provers. Scaling this down, we can turn log-space algorithms—such as the brute force #TRIANGLE algorithm—into interactive proof systems with poly-time honest provers. We "arithmetize" the input graph and apply the sum-check protocol to the resulting polynomial, which has roughly the same size as the graph. Almost all the verifier's work is to evaluate the polynomial once, which takes quasi-linear time. ■

Proof. We design a public-coin interactive proof system with completeness 1 and soundness 1/3 for #TRIANGLE. The input is (G, k) where $G = (V, E)$ is an n-node m-edge undirected graph (with no multi-edges or self-loops) and $0 \le k \le \binom{n}{3}$. Assume n is a power of 2 by adding degree-0 nodes if necessary. Consider the field $\mathbb{Z}_p$ for a prime $p > \max\left(\binom{n}{3}, 18\log n\right)$. Identify the set of nodes V with $\{0,1\}^{\log n}$, so a node v is a tuple of bits $(v_1, \ldots, v_{\log n})$. For each node $v \in \{0,1\}^{\log n}$, define a polynomial $R_v(x)$ where $x = (x_1, \ldots, x_{\log n})$ is a tuple of variables:

$$R_v(x) = \prod_{i:v_i=0}(1 - x_i)\prod_{i:v_i=1} x_i$$

For every boolean assignment to x, we have $R_v(x) = 1$ if $x = v$, and $R_v(x) = 0$ if $x \ne v$. Define a polynomial $S(x, y)$ where x, y are two tuples of $\log n$ variables each:

$$S(x,y) = \sum_{u<v:\{u,v\}\in E} R_u(x) \cdot R_v(y)$$

For every boolean assignment to x, y, we have $S(x, y) = 1$ if $x < y$ and $\{x, y\} \in E$, and $S(x, y) = 0$ otherwise. Define a polynomial $T(x, y, z)$ where x, y, z are three tuples of $\log n$ variables each:

$$T(x,y,z) = S(x,y) \cdot S(x,z) \cdot S(y,z)$$

For every boolean assignment to x, y, z, we have $T(x, y, z) = 1$ if $x < y < z$ and $\{x, y, z\}$ is a triangle in G, and $T(x, y, z) = 0$ otherwise. There are $\sum_{(x,y,z)\in(\{0,1\}^{\log n})^3} T(x, y, z)$ triangles in G. Every variable has individual degree 2 in T. For convenience, denote the variables in x, y, z by $(x_1, \ldots, x_{3\log n})$, by renaming $y = (x_{\log n+1}, \ldots, x_{2\log n})$ and $z = (x_{2\log n+1}, \ldots, x_{3\log n})$. Unlike in §15.2.3, n is not the number of variables here.

Interactive proof system for #TRIANGLE (15.17)

let $b_0 \leftarrow k$
for $i \leftarrow 1, \ldots, 3\log n$:
  prover sends the coefficients of a polynomial $Q_i(x_i)$ of degree ≤ 2
  if $Q_i(0) + Q_i(1) \neq b_{i-1}$: verifier rejects
  verifier samples $a_i \in \mathbb{Z}_p$ uniformly at random and lets $b_i \leftarrow Q_i(a_i)$
verifier accepts iff $T(a_1, \ldots, a_{3\log n}) = b_{3\log n}$

As in the proof of #SAT ∈ IP (Theorem 15.11), this has completeness 1 and soundness:

$$\text{(number of variables)} \cdot \text{(individual degree)}/p \;=\; (3\log n) \cdot 2/p \;\leq\; 1/3$$

In iteration i, the honest prover sends the coefficients of:

$$Q_i(x_i) \;=\; T_i(a_1, \ldots, a_{i-1}, x_i) \;=\; \sum_{(x_{i+1},\ldots,x_{3\log n})\in\{0,1\}^{3\log n - i}} T(a_1, \ldots, a_{i-1}, x_i, x_{i+1}, \ldots, x_{3\log n})$$

To find Q_i in poly$N$ time, he iterates over all $2^{3\log n - i} \leq n^3$ possibilities of $(z_{i+1}, \ldots, z_{3\log n}) \in \{0,1\}^{3\log n - i}$, obtains the coefficients of the univariate polynomial $T(a_1, \ldots, a_{i-1}, x_i, z_{i+1}, \ldots, z_{3\log n})$ by partially evaluating T, and sums all these polynomials. The verifier spends polylog$N$ time in the loop, plus N polylog$N$ time evaluating $T(a_1, \ldots, a_{3\log n})$ since the expression defining T has size $O(m \log n)$. ■

Doubly efficient interactive proof systems exist for all problems in NC $= \bigcup_i \mathsf{NC}^i$, which includes NL (Theorem 6.9) and BPL (Theorem 7.38). Doubly efficient interactive proof systems with $O(1)$ rounds of interaction exist for all problems in TISP[poly$N$, polylog$N$], which includes BPL (Theorem 11.21).

15.3.3 Program Checking

One major goal of software verification is to check whether a program actually solves the problem A it's intended to solve. Treating the program as an oracle for some problem B, we want to check whether $B = A$, in other words, $B(x) = A(x)$ for all inputs x. This is generally impossible since there are infinitely many x. In reality, we wouldn't need to run the program on all possible inputs, so maybe we should just focus on individual inputs that we care about? That is, given input x, check whether $B(x) = A(x)$ for that x. This is equivalent to solving A, which is what we're trying to check in the first place. We define a relaxed notion: Given input x, a *program checker* distinguishes between $B = A$ and $B(x) \neq A(x)$. In the "middle case" where $B \neq A$ and $B(x) = A(x)$, a program checker's determination doesn't matter:

- It's OK to say the program is incorrect, since it's incorrect on some input.
- It's OK to say the program is correct, since it's correct on the input x we care about.

A program checker may query B (run the purported program for A) on x and on any other inputs it deems helpful. Let's formalize this definition.

An *oracle program* is like an oracle reduction except it doesn't reduce to any particular problem. It has a query segment and "write-query" and "query" instructions as in §1.8.5. Let Π^B denote an oracle program Π with a decision problem B plugged in for the oracle: If the query segment contains y, then "query Reg$[i] \leftarrow$ Answer" puts $B(y)$ into Reg$[i]$ and erases the query segment (or freezes if y is an invalid input to B).

The definition involves completeness and soundness parameters $1 \geq c > s \geq 0$, but these are not about whether $A(x) = 1$ or $A(x) = 0$.

Definition. A (c,s)-*checker* for a decision problem A is a randomized oracle program Π such that for every valid input x and every decision problem B with the same valid inputs as A:

- Completeness c: $\quad B = A \quad \Rightarrow \mathbf{Pr}_r\big[\Pi^B(x;r) \text{ accepts}\big] \geq c$
- Soundness s: $\quad B(x) \neq A(x) \Rightarrow \mathbf{Pr}_r\big[\Pi^B(x;r) \text{ accepts}\big] \leq s$ ◀

First, we'll see that program checkers are equivalent to *program protectors*:

Definition. A (c,s)-*protector* for a decision problem A is a randomized oracle program Π that outputs 0, 1, or $\perp$, such that for every valid input x and every decision problem B with the same valid inputs as A:

- Completeness c: $\quad B = A \Rightarrow \mathbf{Pr}_r\big[\Pi^B(x;r) = A(x)\big] \geq c$
- Soundness s: $\quad \mathbf{Pr}_r\big[\Pi^B(x;r) = \overline{A(x)}\big] \leq s$ ◀

A program protector is a wrapper around a potentially buggy program, like a "safety harness" preventing the program from outputting the wrong bit. If a proposed program for A hasn't been vetted, we can use it anyway by plugging it into a program protector for A. If the program indeed solves A, the protected version does too (albeit with randomness). Otherwise, the protected version may output $A(x)$ or $\perp$ (meaning "don't trust that program") but is unlikely to output $\overline{A(x)}$. For some problems A, a safety harness is more efficient than any known algorithm for A.

Lemma 15.21. *A has a poly-time (c,s)-checker iff A has a poly-time (c,s)-protector.*

Proof. $\Rightarrow$: If A has a poly-time (c,s)-checker Π_{check}, then A has a poly-time (c,s)-protector Π_{protect}:

Program protector using a program checker (15.18)

```
Π^B_protect(x; r):
    query B(x)
    if Π^B_check(x; r) accepts: output B(x)
    output ⊥
```

Completeness: If $B = A$ then $B(x) = A(x)$ and:

$$\mathbf{Pr}_r\big[\Pi^B_{\text{protect}}(x;r) = A(x)\big] = \mathbf{Pr}_r\big[\Pi^B_{\text{check}}(x;r) \text{ accepts}\big] \geq c$$

Soundness: If $B(x) = A(x)$ then $\mathbf{Pr}_r\big[\Pi^B_{\text{protect}}(x;r) = \overline{A(x)}\big] = 0 \leq s$. If $B(x) \neq A(x)$ then:

$$\mathbf{Pr}_r\big[\Pi^B_{\text{protect}}(x;r) = \overline{A(x)}\big] = \mathbf{Pr}_r\big[\Pi^B_{\text{check}}(x;r) \text{ accepts}\big] \leq s$$

$\Leftarrow$: If A has a poly-time (c,s)-protector Π_{protect}, then A has a poly-time (c,s)-checker Π_{check}:

Program checker using a program protector	(15.19)
$\Pi^B_{\text{check}}(x;r)$:	
query $B(x)$	
if $\Pi^B_{\text{protect}}(x;r)$ outputs $B(x)$: accept	
reject	

Completeness: If $B = A$ then $B(x) = A(x)$ and:

$$\mathbf{Pr}_r\left[\Pi^B_{\text{check}}(x;r) \text{ accepts}\right] = \mathbf{Pr}_r\left[\Pi^B_{\text{protect}}(x;r) = A(x)\right] \geq c$$

Soundness: If $B(x) \neq A(x)$ then:

$$\mathbf{Pr}_r\left[\Pi^B_{\text{check}}(x;r) \text{ accepts}\right] = \mathbf{Pr}_r\left[\Pi^B_{\text{protect}}(x;r) = \overline{A(x)}\right] \leq s$$ ■

Lemma 15.22. *A has a poly-time* (c,s)*-checker if A and* $\overline{A}$ *have poly-time private-coin interactive proof systems with completeness c and soundness s where the honest provers are computed by poly-time oracle reductions to A.*

Proof. Assume A has such an interactive proof system with verifier V_A and honest prover P_A (which makes queries to A), and $\overline{A}$ has such an interactive proof system with verifier $V_{\overline{A}}$ and honest prover $P_{\overline{A}}$ (which makes queries to A). Here is a poly-time (c,s)-checker for A:

Program checker using interactive proof systems	(15.20)
$\Pi^B(x;r)$:	
query $B(x)$	
if $B(x) = 1$: run $V_A(x;r)$ using P_A^B to obtain the prover's messages; output the same thing	
if $B(x) = 0$: run $V_{\overline{A}}(x;r)$ using $P_{\overline{A}}^B$ to obtain the prover's messages; output the same thing	

Π^B clocks V_A, P_A, $V_{\overline{A}}$, $P_{\overline{A}}$ so they run in poly time no matter what.

Completeness: If $B = A$ then $B(x) = A(x)$ and Π^B faithfully simulates the interactive proof system (with its honest prover) for either A or $\overline{A}$, whichever has x as a 1-input, and thus accepts with probability $\geq c$.

Soundness: If $B(x) \neq A(x)$ then Π^B faithfully simulates the interactive proof system (with some prover strategy) for either A or $\overline{A}$, whichever has x as a 0-input, and thus accepts with probability $\leq s$. ■

Replacing single-prover with multi-prover interactive proof systems in Lemma 15.22 yields a characterization of program checkability (Exercise 15.16).

Theorem 15.23. *Every* PSPACE*-complete problem has a poly-time* $(1, 1/3)$*-checker.*

Proof. Suppose A is PSPACE-complete. Consider the interactive proof system for QSAT with completeness 1 and soundness $1/3$ from §15.2.4, and recall this problem $B \in$ PSPACE from the proof of Corollary 15.19:

(call this problem B)	(15.21)
Input:	CNF φ such that QSAT$(\varphi) = 1$, communication history h, and index k
Output:	kth bit of honest prover's next message on input φ and communication history h

- $A \le_p^m$ QSAT since $A \in$ PSPACE and QSAT is PSPACE-hard.
- $B \le_p^m A$ since $B \in$ PSPACE and A is PSPACE-hard.

An interactive proof system for A on input x can map x to φ (using $A \le_p^m$ QSAT) and run the interactive proof system for QSAT on input φ. The honest prover is computable in poly time with oracle access to B, and thus with oracle access to A (using $B \le_p^m A$). This still has completeness 1 and soundness $1/3$. Since $\overline{A}$ is PSPACE-complete, it also has such an interactive proof system. By Lemma 15.22, A has a $(1, 1/3)$-checker. ∎

GRAPH ISOMORPHISM also has a poly-time program checker (Exercise 15.15). It's unknown whether NP-complete problems have poly-time program checkers.

15.4 Zero-Knowledge Proofs

Could a prover convince a verifier that a CNF is satisfiable without revealing anything about a satisfying assignment? This sounds contradictory but is actually possible using a *zero-knowledge* interactive proof system. We conclude Part III with this plot twist.

15.4.1 Definition

Zero-knowledge means the verifier gains no knowledge that he couldn't figure out by himself. The honest prover can convince the honest verifier that $A(x) = 1$, but no verifier—even a dishonest one—could trick the honest prover into revealing anything further. A verifier could simulate the honest prover's messages on his own, so interacting with the honest prover can't give a verifier any computational power he didn't already have. Counterintuitively, the honest prover's messages are convincing but unsurprising.

Definition. A *perfect zero-knowledge proof system* for a decision problem A is a poly-time private-coin interactive proof system with a randomized honest prover, such that:

- Completeness c: $A(x) = 1 \Rightarrow$ for the honest prover: $\mathbf{Pr}$[honest verifier accepts] $\ge c$
- Soundness s: $A(x) = 0 \Rightarrow$ for every prover: $\mathbf{Pr}$[honest verifier accepts] $\le s$
- Zero-knowledge: For every poly-time randomized verifier, there exists a poly-time randomized *simulator* program that, for every 1-input, aborts with probability $\le 1/2$ and conditioned on not aborting, outputs a sample of the *view* (randomness and received messages) of this verifier interacting with the honest prover. ◂

Zero-knowledge means every verifier (honest or not) learns nothing on a 1-input: Anything he could compute by interacting with the honest prover, he could compute by himself, by running the simulator to generate his view of the interaction and then doing whatever he would do given that view. For comparison:

- Soundness defends against dishonest provers on 0-inputs.
- Zero-knowledge defends against dishonest verifiers on 1-inputs.

In a *statistical* zero-knowledge proof system, the simulator's output distribution only needs to be close to the verifier's view in statistical distance (§11.1.1). In a *computational* zero-knowledge proof system, the simulator's output distribution only needs to be indistinguishable from the verifier's view by poly-size circuits (§11.1.2, §12.2.1).

Zero-knowledge proof systems are important in cryptography. For example, they're useful for *identification schemes*, in which one party proves their identity (that they are who they claim to be) by demonstrating that they possess certain secret knowledge—like a password—without revealing anything that could let someone impersonate them.

15.4.2 Zero-Knowledge for GRAPH ISOMORPHISM

Theorem 15.24. GRAPH ISOMORPHISM *has a perfect zero-knowledge proof system with completeness* 1 *and soundness* $1/2$.

Proof idea. The prover could convince the verifier that $G_1 \cong G_2$ by exhibiting an isomorphism, but then the verifier would learn this isomorphism, which he couldn't find on his own. Instead, the prover samples a random graph H that's isomorphic to G_1 and G_2, and then the verifier randomly picks either G_1 or G_2 and challenges the prover to exhibit an isomorphism between this graph and H. A simulator can sample H by randomly permuting either G_1 or G_2, and if it happens to permute the same graph that the verifier picks for the challenge, then the simulator already has an isomorphism between this graph and H, and has thus generated the verifier's view unaided. A subtlety is that a dishonest verifier might pick the challenge graph in a way that depends on H, rather than randomly and independently of H. The simulator must pick either G_1 or G_2 to permute before finding out which one the verifier picks for the challenge. If the simulator picks randomly, it gets lucky with probability $1/2$, and aborts otherwise. ■

Proof. On input (G_1, G_2):

Perfect zero-knowledge proof system for GRAPH ISOMORPHISM (15.22)

honest prover sends a uniformly random graph H isomorphic to G_1 and G_2
honest verifier sends a uniformly random $j \in \{1,2\}$
honest prover sends a uniformly random isomorphism q from G_j to H
honest verifier accepts iff q is a permutation and $q(G_j) = H$

Completeness 1: Suppose $G_1 \cong G_2$ and consider the honest verifier's interaction with the honest prover. Regardless of H and j, there exists an isomorphism from G_j to H. The honest verifier confirms that q is such an isomorphism and accepts.

Soundness $1/2$: Suppose $G_1 \ncong G_2$ and consider the honest verifier's interaction with an arbitrary prover. Either $G_1 \ncong H$ or $G_2 \ncong H$, so with probability $\geq 1/2$ over j, we have $G_j \ncong H$ and the honest verifier rejects regardless of q.

Zero-knowledge: Suppose $G_1 \cong G_2$ and consider an arbitrary poly-time verifier's interaction with the honest prover. Let $V(G_1, G_2; r; H) \in \{1,2\}$ be the verifier's message on input (G_1, G_2) with randomness r after receiving message H from the honest prover. The verifier's actual view is (r, H, q) where H is a uniformly random graph isomorphic to G_1 and G_2, and q is a uniformly random isomorphism from G_j to H, where $j = V(G_1, G_2; r; H)$.

Simulator of the verifier's view (15.23)

let $H \leftarrow p(G_i)$ for uniformly random $i \in \{1,2\}$ and permutation $p: [n] \to [n]$
let $j \leftarrow V(G_1, G_2; r; H)$ for uniformly random r
if $i \neq j$: abort
output (r, H, p)

For every H isomorphic to G_1 and G_2, the number of isomorphisms from G_i to H doesn't depend on i or on H (as shown in the proof of Lemma 15.3). Therefore in the simulated view, H is a uniformly random graph isomorphic to G_1 and G_2, and independent of i. Thus $\mathbf{Pr}[\text{abort}] = \mathbf{Pr}[i \neq j] = 1/2$ (since i and j are independent), and p is a uniformly random isomorphism from G_i to H. Conditioned on not aborting, the distribution of r, H is unchanged and p is a uniformly random isomorphism from G_j to H. Thus the actual view is identical to the simulated view conditioned on not aborting. ■

15.4.3 Zero-Knowledge for NP

Every problem in NP (or even in PSPACE) has a computational zero-knowledge proof system. For clarity, we prove an idealized version in a model with physical lockboxes, which could be implemented with commitment schemes (§ 12.3.5). The prover puts a message in an opaque lockbox, locks the box, and sends the box to the verifier. Later, the prover sends the physical key to the verifier, who unlocks the box and reads the message. In the meantime:

- *Hiding*: The verifier learns nothing about the message, since the box is locked and opaque.
- *Binding*: The prover can't change the message, since the verifier has the box. The prover *committed* to the message—he can't pretend he had put something else in the box.

The prover may use multiple lockboxes with separate keys, so sending a particular key only lets the verifier unlock the corresponding box. The verifier's view consists of his own randomness and the messages in whatever boxes the prover lets him unlock.

Theorem 15.25. *Every problem in* NP *has a lockbox zero-knowledge proof system with completeness* 1 *and soundness* 1/2.

Proof idea. Consider GRAPH 3-COLORING. The prover could convince the verifier that the graph has a proper 3-coloring by exhibiting one, but then the verifier would learn this coloring, which he couldn't find on his own. Instead, the prover commits to an entire 3-color assignment but only reveals the colors of the endpoints of one edge, of the verifier's choosing. If the 3-color assignment isn't proper, the verifier has a not-too-small chance of randomly choosing a non-multicolored edge and catching the prover red-handed (or green-handed, or blue-handed). If the 3-color assignment is proper, the verifier unfortunately still learns something—the colors of an edge's endpoints. To fix this, the prover randomly permutes the colors, so the verifier just sees two random distinct colors. ■

Proof. It suffices to prove this for GRAPH 3-COLORING, which is NP-complete (Theorem 2.25). The input is $G = (V, E)$. The set of colors is $[3] = \{1, 2, 3\}$.

Lockbox zero-knowledge proof system for GRAPH 3-COLORING (15.24)

honest prover picks any proper 3-coloring $c\colon V \to [3]$ of G
honest prover picks a uniformly random permutation $p\colon [3] \to [3]$
for each node $v \in V$:
    honest prover sends a locked box labeled v containing the message $p(c(v))$
honest verifier sends a uniformly random edge $\{u, v\} \in E$
honest prover checks whether $\{u, v\} \in E$ and if so:
    honest prover sends the keys for the boxes labeled u and v
    honest verifier accepts iff these unlocked boxes contain distinct colors in $[3]$
else: honest prover halts and sends no keys

Completeness 1: Suppose G has a proper 3-coloring c, and consider the honest verifier's interaction with the honest prover. Assigning each node v the color $p(c(v))$ yields a proper 3-coloring since p is a permutation. For any edge $\{u, v\} \in E$, the honest verifier confirms that $p(c(u)) \neq p(c(v))$ and accepts.

Soundness $1 - 1/|E|$: Suppose G has no proper 3-coloring, and consider the honest verifier's interaction with an arbitrary prover. Whatever messages the prover puts in the boxes, they form a function d with domain V. For at least one edge $\{u, v\} \in E$, either $d(u) = d(v)$ or $d(u) \notin [3]$ or $d(v) \notin [3]$ (otherwise d would be a proper 3-coloring, ignoring any isolated nodes). With probability $\geq 1/|E|$, the honest verifier picks such an edge and subsequently rejects (whether the prover sends the corresponding two keys or not) by the binding property.

Zero-knowledge: Suppose G has a proper 3-coloring c, and consider an arbitrary poly-time verifier's interaction with the honest prover. The verifier's message doesn't depend on p, by the hiding property. If the verifier sends an edge $\{u, v\} \in E$, then the verifier sees $p(c(u))$ and $p(c(v))$ in the boxes labeled u and v. This view is trivial to simulate: Since $c(u) \neq c(v)$ and p is a uniformly random permutation, $\big(p(c(u)), p(c(v))\big)$ is uniformly distributed over $\big\{(1,2), (1,3), (2,1), (2,3), (3,1), (3,2)\big\}$. If the verifier's message isn't an edge of G, then the verifier gets no response from the honest prover.

Amplification: The honest verifier and honest prover repeat this $|E|$ times independently, and the honest verifier accepts iff he would accept in every run. The completeness remains 1. The soundness becomes $(1 - 1/|E|)^{|E|} \leq (e^{-1/|E|})^{|E|} = 1/e \leq 1/2$. Zero-knowledge still holds because a verifier's view (besides his randomness) is uniform over $\big\{(1,2), (1,3), (2,1), (2,3), (3,1), (3,2)\big\}$ in each run that he sends an edge of G. ■

Exercises

15.1 **(a)** Draw $p(G)$ for the permutation p and graph G in Figure 15.7.

(b) What are all the automorphisms of the G in Figure 15.7? How many graphs are isomorphic to G?

15.2 A *partial permutation* is a partial function $p\colon [n] \to [n]$ such that $p(v) \neq p(w)$ for all $v \neq w$ such that $p(v)$ and $p(w)$ are defined. A permutation q is *consistent with* a partial permutation p iff $q(v) = p(v)$ for all v such that $p(v)$ is defined.

CONSISTENT GRAPH ISOMORPHISM	(15.25)
Input: Undirected graphs G_1 and G_2 with nodes $[n]$, and a partial permutation p	
Output: Does there exist an isomorphism from G_1 to G_2 that's consistent with p?	

(GRAPH ISOMORPHISM is the special case where $p(v)$ is undefined for all v.)

(a) Prove CONSISTENT GRAPH ISOMORPHISM $\leq_p^m$ GRAPH ISOMORPHISM.

(b) Prove that $\overline{\text{CONSISTENT GRAPH ISOMORPHISM}}$ has a poly-time private-coin Arthur–Merlin proof system akin to the one for $\overline{\text{GRAPH ISOMORPHISM}}$ (Theorem 15.1). Work with the original graphs G_1 and G_2 rather than relying on Exercise 15.2.a, which augments the graphs.

15.3 Prove AM $\subseteq$ NP/poly.

p

v	1	2	3	4	5
$p(v)$	3	4	1	5	2

G

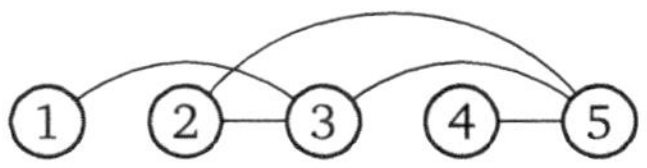

Figure 15.7: Permutation and graph for Exercise 15.1

15.4 Prove that MA and AM are unchanged if we require completeness 1 instead of 2/3. Hint: Strengthen the inclusions $\mathsf{MA} \subseteq \Sigma_2\mathsf{P}$ and $\mathsf{AM} \subseteq \Pi_2\mathsf{P}$ like how the proof of Theorem 7.41 strengthens $\mathsf{BPP} \subseteq \Sigma_2\mathsf{P} \cap \Pi_2\mathsf{P}$.

15.5 **(a)** Prove that if $\mathsf{coNP} \subseteq \mathsf{AM}$ then $\Sigma_2\mathsf{P} = \Pi_2\mathsf{P}$.

(b) Conclude that Graph Isomorphism isn't NP-complete unless the polynomial hierarchy collapses.

15.6 Prove that if $\mathsf{NP} \subseteq \mathsf{P/poly}$ then $\mathsf{MA} = \mathsf{AM}$.

15.7 SBP (small bounded-error probabilistic polynomial time) is the set of all decision problems A for which there exist a poly-time randomized program Π and a function $\varepsilon(N) > 0$ that's computable in poly$N$ time given N (and may be as small as $1/2^{\text{poly}N}$), such that for every input x of size N:

$$A(x) = 1 \Rightarrow \mathbf{Pr}_r\big[\Pi(x;r) \text{ accepts}\big] \geq 2\varepsilon(N)$$
$$A(x) = 0 \Rightarrow \mathbf{Pr}_r\big[\Pi(x;r) \text{ accepts}\big] \leq \varepsilon(N)$$

(a) Prove $\mathsf{MA} \subseteq \mathsf{SBP}$.

(b) Prove $\mathsf{SBP} \subseteq \mathsf{AM}$.

15.8 Suppose A and B are decision problems, and A has a poly-time randomized oracle reduction to B (with error probability 1/3) that makes a single query y to B, and the distribution of y depends only on the size of the input x to A. Prove that if $B \in \mathsf{NP}$ then $A \in \mathsf{AM/poly}$. (In defining AM/poly, we put no constraints on Arthur's output when he's given wrong advice.) Hint: Let the advice be $\mathbf{Pr}_y\big[B(y) = 1\big]$.

15.9 Prove that if A has a poly-time private-coin interactive proof system with completeness > 0 and soundness 0, then $A \in \mathsf{NP}$.

15.10 Step into Merlin's shoes and convince Arthur that $(\overline{x_1} \vee x_2 \vee \overline{x_4}) \wedge (\overline{x_1} \vee \overline{x_3} \vee x_4)$ has exactly 12 satisfying assignments, using the sum-check protocol with the field $\mathbb{Z}_{29}$. If Arthur randomly picks $(a_1, a_2, a_3, a_4) = (4, 18, 11, 2)$, what messages should the honest Merlin send, and why would Arthur accept?

15.11 In this exercise, you'll directly design a poly-space algorithm for the honest prover in the interactive proof system for QSat from § 15.2.4 (without appealing to the generic inclusion $\mathsf{IP} \subseteq \mathsf{PSPACE}$ as in Lemma 15.18).

(a) Show that if Q is any univariate polynomial and Q' is Q with the variable linearized, then $Q'(x) = (1-x) \cdot Q(0) + x \cdot Q(1)$.

(b) Recall the polynomials $P_{i,j}$ from the analysis of the interactive proof system for QSAT. Design a poly-space recursive subroutine eval$(i, j, a_1, \ldots, a_i)$ that returns $P_{i,j}(a_1, \ldots, a_i)$ for field elements $a_1, \ldots, a_i$.

(c) Design a poly-space algorithm for the honest prover, who sends the coefficients of:

$$\begin{aligned} Q_{i,0}(x_i) &= P_{i,0}(a_1, \ldots, a_{i-1}, x_i) \\ Q_{i,j}(x_j) &= P_{i,j}(\ldots, a_{j-1}, x_j, a_{j+1}, \ldots) \quad \text{when } j > 0 \end{aligned}$$

Hint: Use Exercise 15.11.b and a poly-time (hence poly-space) algorithm for recovering the coefficients of any univariate polynomial of degree $\leq m$ from the polynomial's values on any $m+1$ points, in other words, DECODING POLYNOMIAL CODES FROM ERASURES (Theorem 9.13).

15.12 Recall Exercise 5.7: If EXP $\subseteq$ P/poly then EXP $= \Sigma_2$P. Strengthen this to show that if EXP $\subseteq$ P/poly then EXP $=$ MA.

15.13 *Anti-triangles* are size-3 independent sets in graphs.

#ANTI-TRIANGLE	(15.26)
Input: Undirected graph G, nonnegative integer k	
Output: Does G have exactly k anti-triangles?	

(a) Suppose we reduce #ANTI-TRIANGLE to #TRIANGLE by complementing the graph (like reducing INDEPENDENT SET to CLIQUE in §2.4.1) and we apply the doubly efficient interactive proof system for #TRIANGLE (Theorem 15.20). Why doesn't this yield a doubly efficient interactive proof system for #ANTI-TRIANGLE?

(b) Design a doubly efficient interactive proof system for #ANTI-TRIANGLE.

15.14 Prove that if $A \leq_p^m A'$ and $A' \leq_p^m A$ and A' has a poly-time (c,s)-checker, then A has a poly-time (c,s)-checker.

15.15 **(a)** Design a poly-time search-to-decision reduction for GRAPH ISOMORPHISM. (In the search version, the output is an isomorphism.) Hint: Use Exercise 15.2.a.

(b) Prove GRAPH ISOMORPHISM has a poly-time $(1, 1/3)$-checker.

15.16 Use PCP $\subseteq$ MIP (Lemma 15.16) to prove that A has a poly-time $(2/3, 1/3)$-checker iff A and $\overline{A}$ have poly-time two-prover interactive proof systems with completeness 2/3 and soundness 1/3 where the honest provers are computed by poly-time oracle reductions to A.

15.17 Consider the lockbox zero-knowledge proof system for GRAPH 3-COLORING with completeness 1 and soundness $1 - 1/|E|$ (Theorem 15.25). Suppose we change the honest prover so he sends the keys for the boxes labeled u and v even when $\{u, v\} \notin E$. Prove that if this is still zero-knowledge, then NP $=$ RP.

15.18 Prove that the following is a lockbox zero-knowledge proof system with completeness 1 and soundness 1/2 for UNDIRECTED FULL CYCLE on input $G = ([n], E)$. This problem is NP-complete (§2.5.1).

Lockbox zero-knowledge proof system for UNDIRECTED FULL CYCLE (15.27)

honest prover picks any full cycle C of G
honest prover picks a uniformly random permutation $p\colon [n] \to [n]$
for each pair of nodes $\{u, v\}$:
  honest prover sends a locked box labeled $\{u, v\}$ containing the message:
    1 if $\{u, v\}$ is an edge in $p(G)$, and 0 otherwise
honest verifier sends a uniformly random bit b
if $b = 0$:
  honest prover sends p and all $\binom{n}{2}$ keys
  honest verifier accepts iff p is a permutation and the unlocked boxes form $p(G)$
if $b = 1$:
  honest prover sends the keys for the boxes corresponding to edges of $p(C)$
  honest verifier accepts iff these unlocked boxes all contain 1 and form a full cycle

Notes

The quasi-polynomial-time algorithm for GRAPH ISOMORPHISM is due to [38].

Arthur–Merlin proof systems were introduced by [37, 43], which also proved GRAPH NONISOMORPHISM $\in$ AM (Theorem 15.2), MA $\subseteq$ AM (Theorem 15.4), MA $\subseteq \Sigma_2$P (Theorem 15.6), and AM $\subseteq \Pi_2$P (Theorem 15.7). The theorem that private coins can be replaced with public coins in Arthur–Merlin proof systems is due to [209]. Theorems showing AM = NP under certain nonuniform lower bound conjectures are due to [31, 312, 374], and a sort of converse is known [36].

Interactive proof systems were introduced by [208]. The sum-check protocol for #SAT $\in$ IP (Theorem 15.11) is due to [352]. IP = PSPACE (Theorem 15.8) is due to [483], and the proof we presented is due to [488].

Multi-prover interactive proof systems were introduced by [61], which also proved $\mathsf{MIP}_{\mathrm{poly}\,N}$ = MIP. The results MIP = PCP $\subseteq$ NEXP (Lemma 15.14, Lemma 15.15, Lemma 15.16) are due to [168]. MIP = NEXP (Theorem 15.13) is due to [39].

For surveys on delegating computation using interactive proof systems, see [199, 518]. The doubly efficient interactive proof system for #TRIANGLE (Theorem 15.20) is due to [517, 205]. The theorem that doubly efficient interactive proof systems exist for all problems in NC is due to [210]. The theorem that doubly efficient interactive proof systems with $O(1)$ rounds of interaction exist for all problems in TISP[poly N, polylog N] is due to [438].

Program checking (also known as instance checking) was introduced by [70].

Zero-knowledge proof systems were introduced by [208]. Perfect zero-knowledge for GRAPH ISOMORPHISM (Theorem 15.24), statistical zero-knowledge for GRAPH NONISOMORPHISM, and computational zero-knowledge for NP assuming one-way functions exist (Theorem 15.25) are due to [203]. Computational zero-knowledge for IP = PSPACE assuming one-way functions exist is due to [266, 60]. Statistical zero-knowledge has a raft of remarkable properties [403, 528]. For surveys on zero-knowledge proof systems and their applications, see [529, 518, 328].

Exercise 15.4 is due to [179]. Exercise 15.5 is due to [82]. Exercise 15.6 is due to [32]. Exercise 15.7 is due to [80]. Exercise 15.8 is due to [161]. Exercise 15.12 is due to [40, 39]. Exercise 15.18 is due to [67].

Part IV

CONCRETE MODELS

Chapter 16

Decision Trees and Branching Programs

Informally, a *concrete* model of computation is nonuniform (separate algorithms for different input sizes) and fairly simple to define. In contrast, the model from Chapter 1 is uniform (one algorithm for all input sizes) and has a largish instruction set. Chapter 5 introduced important concrete models based on dags (directed acyclic graphs):

- *Circuits* (for nonuniform time) and their tree counterparts *formulas*.
- *Branching programs* (for nonuniform space) and their tree counterparts *decision trees*.

Size complexities for these models are interleaved as follows, ignoring constant factors:

$$\text{circuit} \leq \text{branching program} \leq \text{formula} \leq \text{decision tree}$$

Besides being natural to study in their own right, these concrete models offer a line of attack on the thorny goal of proving time and space complexity lower bounds:

- If a problem has no poly-size circuits, then it has no poly-time algorithm.
- If a problem has no poly-size branching programs, then it has no log-space algorithm.

Proving such concrete lower bounds seems more approachable since the models are "no-frills." When we're unable to prove conjectured lower bounds, we can scale back our ambitions and prove lower bounds under various restrictions on these concrete models (such as the tree counterparts). This clarifies the reach of known lower bound techniques and brings into focus the specific difficulties we must overcome to prove lower bounds for unrestricted models.

"If we don't know how to prove $\mathsf{P} \neq \mathsf{NP}$, what *can* we prove?" Part I contained some modest progress. Now Part IV takes a different tack. The best known size complexity lower bounds for NP problems are linear for circuits, quadratic for branching programs, cubic for formulas, and exponential for decision trees.

Chapter 18 is on circuits and formulas. This chapter is on branching programs and decision trees. First, we investigate depth complexity for branching programs and decision trees—this corresponds to nonuniform time complexity if we only count "read" instructions toward the time. We investigate size complexity at the end of this chapter. Branching programs and decision trees are equivalent for depth but not for size.

16.1 Deterministic Query Complexity

16.1.1 The Model

Definition. A *decision tree* is an out-tree (with edges directed away from the root) where each internal node is labeled by an input variable and has two outgoing edges labeled 0 (to the left child) and 1 (to the right child), and each leaf is labeled by an output bit.

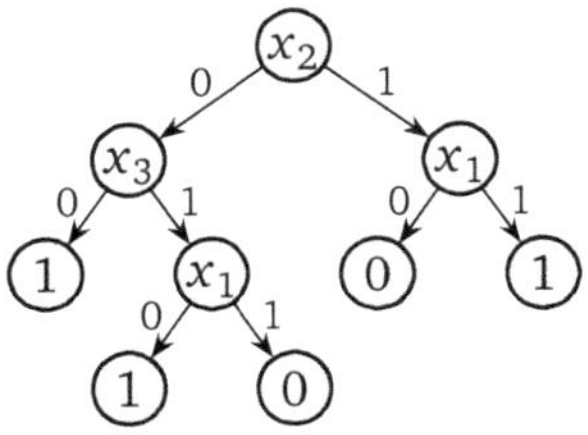


```
if x2 = 0:
    if x3 = 0: output 1
    else:
        if x1 = 0: output 1
        else: output 0
else:
    if x1 = 0: output 0
    else: output 1
```

x_1	x_2	x_3	$f(x)$
0	0	0	1
0	0	1	1
0	1	0	0
0	1	1	0
1	0	0	1
1	0	1	0
1	1	0	1
1	1	1	1

Figure 16.1: Example decision tree

A decision tree is a kind of algorithm to compute a function $f\colon \{0,1\}^N \to \{0,1\}$. On input $a \in \{0,1\}^N$, it traverses a path from the root: At a node labeled x_i, it *queries* (reads) this input bit and follows the edge labeled a_i. It outputs the label of the leaf reached. Requerying a variable on a root-to-leaf path is disallowed since it would be pointless. ◄

Figure 16.1 shows an example. A decision tree is effectively a program of nested "if ... else"s. A decision tree with only one node (the root is a leaf) computes a constant function.

A decision tree's *depth* is the length (number of edges) of a longest root-to-leaf path. This equals the *query efficiency*—the maximum over all $a \in \{0,1\}^N$ of the number of bits queried on input a. The deterministic *query complexity* of $f\colon \{0,1\}^N \to \{0,1\}$, denoted $\mathrm{Det}(f)$, is the depth of a shallowest decision tree that computes f. Every f has $\mathrm{Det}(f) \le N$ since f is computed by a depth-N decision tree that queries all N bits (so all 2^N inputs lead to different leaves). We think of $\mathrm{polylog}\, N$ as "efficient" in this setting.

A total decision problem with word size 1 is a function $F\colon \{0,1\}^+ \to \{0,1\}$, which we view as an infinite family of functions $F_1, F_2, F_3, \dots$ where $F_N\colon \{0,1\}^N \to \{0,1\}$ is F on inputs of size N. In this chapter, we also consider families that are defined for infinitely many N (not necessarily all N). The query complexity of such a family F is the function $\mathrm{Det}(F)$ that maps N to $\mathrm{Det}(F_N)$, for all N such that F_N is defined. For big-Ω lower bounds on $\mathrm{Det}(F)$, we only quantify over N for which F_N is defined.

For illustration, consider a family called INDEX: For $N = 2^k + k$, define $\textsc{Index}_N(x, y) = x_y$ where the binary number $y = y_{k-1} \cdots y_0 \in \{0, 1, \dots, 2^k - 1\}$ is an index into $x = x_0 \cdots x_{2^k-1}$. This is also called the *address* or *multiplexer* function (Mux_k from §5.2.3). To compute $\textsc{Index}_N$, a decision tree can query all k bits of y and then query the bit x_y and output it, so $\mathrm{Det}(\textsc{Index}) \le k + 1 \approx \log N$. Figure 16.2 shows this for $k = 2$.

A uniform program for F yields a decision tree for F_N: The root's label is the first input variable the program reads (for input size N), and its left child's label is the second input variable the program reads if the first read got a 0, and so on. The decision tree's query efficiency (depth) is the program's *read efficiency*—the maximum over all size-N inputs of the number of read instructions executed. So to design a shallow decision tree family, we may design a program that reads few input bits. (Reading the entire input is necessary for many problems, but not all problems.) A query complexity lower bound implies a *read complexity* lower bound and therefore a time complexity lower bound, since each read is a time step. This approach can't yield superlinear time lower bounds, though.

Decision trees model situations where retrieving individual parts of the input is a bottleneck, perhaps because the input is stored elsewhere or is generated by sensors rather than being stored.

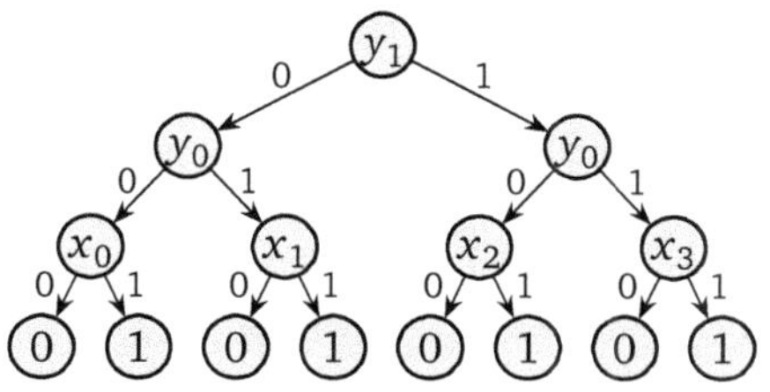

Figure 16.2: Decision tree for INDEX with $k=2$

This represents one challenge of big data processing—determining which parts of the data are helpful to look at.

Decision trees also model how an oracle reduction interacts with its oracle (§1.8). Making a query z to an oracle for a decision problem B corresponds to querying the bit indexed by z in the big bit string representing B's truth table. For each input to the reduction, there exists a decision tree whose input is an oracle's truth table and whose output is the reduction's output: The root's label corresponds to the first z the reduction queries, and its left child's label corresponds to the second z the reduction queries if the first query got a 0, and so on.

16.1.2 Lower Bounds

To prove lower bounds, it helps to characterize the query complexity of $f\colon \{0,1\}^N \to \{0,1\}$ with a "querier versus adversary game": The input to f is not fixed in advance. In each round, the querier picks an input variable (that wasn't already picked), and then the adversary picks a bit to assign that variable. The game ends when f's value is determined. For some parameter d, the querier wins iff the game ends after $\le d$ rounds. (This is like the mistake complexity game in §13.6.3.)

More precisely: A *partial assignment* is a string $a \in \{0,1,*\}^N$ where $*$ means "unassigned," and the *restriction* $f|_a$ is the function that takes any assignment to a's unassigned variables and evaluates f on the "filled out" assignment (§2.3.5). After each round of the game, some partial assignment a records the results of all the queries so far (but not the order of the queries). The game ends when $f|_a$ is a constant function, which means $f(x)$ is the same for all inputs x consistent with a (so there's no need to query more of x).

Example. Suppose $N=4$ and in the first round, the querier picks x_3 and the adversary assigns it 1, and in the second round, the querier picks x_1 and the adversary assigns it 0. Then $a = 0{*}1{*}$ and $f|_a(x_2x_4) = f(0x_21x_4)$. ♦

A decision tree for f is a querier strategy: An internal node specifies the querier's next move, based on everything that happened so far. The depth is the maximum number of rounds until the game ends.

- $\mathrm{Det}(f) \le d$ iff some querier strategy guarantees the game ends after $\le d$ rounds no matter how the adversary plays.
- $\mathrm{Det}(f) > d$ iff some adversary strategy guarantees the game lasts for $> d$ rounds no matter how the querier plays: After round d, $f|_a$ is still nonconstant, which means $f(x)=0$ and $f(x')=1$ for some x and x' consistent with the current a.

To prove a lower bound on query complexity, we design an adversary strategy that prolongs the game. This is less onerous than considering each possible shallow decision tree and arguing that it errs on some input. Intuitively, the adversary should pick bits that keep f's value "up in the air" as long as possible.

If $\mathrm{Det}(f) = N$, we call f *evasive* since the adversary can force the querier to query all N variables, keeping him in suspense till the bitter end. A family F is evasive iff each F_N is evasive.

OR is evasive, where $\text{OR}_N(x) = 1$ iff x has at least one 1: The adversary responds 0 to each query. After $N-1$ queries, the value of OR_N could still go either way since the last remaining variable's value could be 0 or 1. This implies a sublinear time hierarchy: $\mathsf{TIME}[N] \not\subseteq \mathsf{TIME}[o(N)]$ since $\text{OR} \in \mathsf{TIME}[N]$ and $\text{OR} \notin \mathsf{TIME}[o(N)]$.

MAJORITY is evasive, where $\text{MAJORITY}_N(x) = 1$ iff x has more than $N/2$ many 1s: The adversary responds 1 to the first $\lfloor N/2 \rfloor$ queries and 0 to subsequent queries. After $N-1$ queries in total, the remaining unqueried variable could be assigned 0 to get a 0-input, or 1 to get a 1-input, so $\text{MAJORITY}_N|_a$ is nonconstant. (Or, the adversary could alternate $1, 0, 1, 0, \ldots$.)

Consider a family called TRIBES: For $N = n^2$, treat the input x as an $n \times n$ binary matrix and define $\text{TRIBES}_N(x) = 1$ iff x has at least one all-1s row. (Rows are "tribes" of variables.) TRIBES is evasive: The adversary responds 1 to every query but responds 0 to any query that's the last remaining in its row. After $N-1$ queries, the current a has $n-1$ rows with a single 0 each, and one row that's all-1s except for a single unqueried variable. That unqueried variable could be assigned 0 to get a 0-input, or 1 to get a 1-input, so $\text{TRIBES}_N|_a$ is nonconstant.

Now, we generalize the TRIBES lower bound. TRIBES_N is expressed by $\bigvee_{i \in [n]} \bigwedge_{j \in [n]} x_{i,j}$, which is a *read-once* formula, meaning every variable appears exactly once in the formula.

Theorem 16.1. *Every read-once formula expresses an evasive function.*

Proof idea. Short-circuiting an $\wedge$ or $\vee$ gate would render another variable irrelevant, so the adversary avoids doing that. Since the formula is read-once, each query could only cause one short-circuit. ■

Proof. Suppose a read-once formula $\varphi(x_1 \cdots x_N)$ expresses $f \colon \{0,1\}^N \to \{0,1\}$. Assume $\neg$ gates have been pushed to the input variables (preserving the read-once property). For any partial assignment $a \in \{0, 1, *\}^N$, the contracted formula $\varphi|_a$ expresses the restricted function $f|_a$ (§5.2.2).

Adversary strategy for a read-once formula	(16.1)

initialize $\psi \leftarrow \varphi$ and $a \leftarrow ** \cdots *$
repeat $N-1$ times:
  the querier picks some variable x_i
  if x_i feeds into an $\vee$ gate or $\overline{x_i}$ feeds into an $\wedge$ gate in ψ: assign $a_i \leftarrow 0$
  if x_i feeds into an $\wedge$ gate or $\overline{x_i}$ feeds into an $\vee$ gate in ψ: assign $a_i \leftarrow 1$
  delete from ψ the literal we just assigned
  if the $\vee$ or $\wedge$ gate it fed into now has fan-in 1:
    delete the gate from ψ and use its incoming wire as its outgoing wire

This adversary strategy maintains the invariant that $\psi = \varphi|_a$ and every unqueried variable still appears in ψ. When only one variable x_i remains unqueried, $\varphi|_a$ is either x_i or $\overline{x_i}$ (since $\psi = \varphi|_a$ and x_i still appears in ψ by the invariant), so $f|_a$ is nonconstant. ■

Theorem 16.2. $\mathrm{Det}(\text{INDEX}) = k + 1$ *where* $N = 2^k + k$.

Proof. In §16.1.1 we noted the upper bound Det(INDEX) $\le k+1$. For the matching lower bound Det(INDEX) $> k$, the adversary's strategy doesn't even matter. Suppose after k rounds, the querier has queried some $m \le k$ bits of y and $k-m < 2^{k-m}$ bits of x. Among the 2^{k-m} binary numbers in $\{0,1,\ldots,2^k-1\}$ consistent with the y part of the current a, at least one is an unqueried index of x. Assigning y this index, and assigning the corresponding bit of x either 0 or 1, we get two inputs consistent with a but with different values of INDEX_N. Thus $\text{INDEX}_N|_a$ remains nonconstant. This proof just confirms the intuitively obvious necessity of reading the entire index y and the corresponding bit of x. ■

16.1.3 Graph Properties

Represent an undirected graph $G = ([n], E)$ as a bit string g of length $N = \binom{n}{2}$ indexed by unordered pairs $\{u,v\} \subseteq [n]$, where $g_{\{u,v\}} = 1$ iff $\{u,v\} \in E$. A *graph property* is a family of functions $F_N\colon \{0,1\}^N \to \{0,1\}$ for $N = \binom{n}{2}$ such that if g and h represent isomorphic graphs, then $F_N(g) = F_N(h)$. In other words, permuting nodes doesn't affect whether a graph has the property. CONNECTED—defined by $F_N(g) = 1$ iff g represents a connected graph—is a graph property since node names are irrelevant to whether a graph is connected. BIPARTITE is another example of a graph property. A decision tree for a graph property gets a graph as input and makes queries of the form "Is $\{u,v\} \in E$?"

Theorem 16.3. CONNECTED *is evasive.*

Proof. Abbreviate $f = \text{CONNECTED}_N$. The adversary always responds 0 unless it has to respond 1 to avoid dooming the graph to be disconnected. More precisely: Let $a \in \{0,1,*\}^N$ be the partial assignment recording the results of queries so far. Given a query $\{u,v\}$, the adversary assigns $a_{\{u,v\}} \leftarrow 0$ unless that would make $f|_a$ the constant-0 function, in which case the adversary assigns $a_{\{u,v\}} \leftarrow 1$.

We claim that $f|_a$ stays nonconstant until the Nth round. If the adversary assigns $a_{\{u,v\}} \leftarrow 0$, then $f|_a$ doesn't become constant-0, and it can't become constant-1 (since excluding an edge can't make a graph become connected). If the adversary assigns $a_{\{u,v\}} \leftarrow 1$, then $f|_a$ can't become constant-0 (since including an edge can't make a graph become disconnected), but suppose for contradiction it becomes constant-1 even though some $\{s,t\}$ remains unqueried. Since every graph consistent with this a is connected, there already exists a path P between s and t using edges assigned 1 in a. Rewind to the latest round in which an edge $\{q,r\}$ of P was queried, and consider the partial assignment a in this round. The adversary assigned $a_{\{q,r\}} \leftarrow 1$ because if $a_{\{q,r\}} = 0$ then no connected graph would be consistent with a, and if $a_{\{q,r\}} = 1$ then some connected graph g is consistent with a. But replacing $\{q,r\}$ with $\{s,t\}$ in g yields a graph h that's consistent with the a with $a_{\{q,r\}} = 0$ (since $a_{\{s,t\}} = *$) and is still connected: Any walk using $\{q,r\}$ in g can be rerouted using P and $\{s,t\}$ in h. Upon reaching q, the walk instead takes a detour following P from q to either s or t, then $\{s,t\}$, then the rest of P back to r, and then resumes the original walk. The non-$\{q,r\}$ edges of P are in h since they were all queried before $\{q,r\}$. ■

Not all undirected graph properties are evasive (Exercise 16.6). It's slightly simpler to demonstrate a nonevasive *directed graph property*. Represent a directed graph $G = ([n], E)$ as a bit string g of length $N = n(n-1)$ indexed by ordered pairs $(u,v) \in [n]^2$ with $u \ne v$, where $g_{(u,v)} = 1$ iff $(u,v) \in E$. A *celebrity* is a node with all $n-1$ possible incoming edges (everyone knows the celebrity) but no outgoing edges (the celebrity knows nobody). The graph property CELEBRITY asks whether a given directed graph has a celebrity.

Theorem 16.4. Det(CELEBRITY) $= \Theta(n) = \Theta(\sqrt{N})$.

Proof idea. For the upper bound: If $(u, v) \notin E$ then v isn't a celebrity. If $(u, v) \in E$ then u isn't a celebrity. So one query rules out one node. After narrowing it down to a single node with $O(n)$ queries, we check whether that node is really a celebrity with $O(n)$ more queries.

For the lower bound: It takes $\Omega(n)$ queries just to touch every node. ■

Proof. The following decision tree maintains the set S of *contenders*, which are nodes where each possible incoming edge is 1 or $*$, and each possible outgoing edge is 0 or $*$. For every graph consistent with the results of queries so far, any celebrity must be in S.

Decision tree for CELEBRITY (16.2)

```
initialize S ← [n]
repeat n − 1 times:
    pick any distinct nodes u, v ∈ S and query (u, v)
    if it's 0: remove v from S
    if it's 1: remove u from S
let w be the only remaining node in S
for each node u ≠ w:
    if (u, w) hasn't been queried: query (u, w) and reject if it's 0
    if (w, u) hasn't been queried: query (w, u) and reject if it's 1
accept
```

If the input graph has a celebrity, then the first phase finds it and the second phase confirms it and accepts. Conversely, if the decision tree accepts, then the graph has a celebrity w. The first phase makes $n-1$ queries, and the second phase makes $\le 2(n-1)$ queries, so Det(CELEBRITY) $\le 3(n-1) = O(n)$.

To show Det(CELEBRITY) $\ge n/2 = \Omega(n)$, the adversary's strategy doesn't even matter. Each query touches two nodes, so the first $\lceil n/2 \rceil - 1$ queries touch at most $n-1$ nodes. At this point, an untouched node could be a celebrity, or the graph might have no celebrity (if an untouched node's edges all get assigned 0). ■

Exercise 16.10 pinpoints Det(CELEBRITY) $= 3(n-1) - \lfloor \log n \rfloor$ by improving both the upper and lower bounds.

CONNECTED is *monotone*—inserting an edge (flipping an input bit from 0 to 1) can't disconnect a connected graph (can't flip the output from 1 to 0). CELEBRITY is nonmonotone—inserting an edge can make a graph no longer have a celebrity. It has long been conjectured that every nonconstant monotone graph property is evasive. It's known that every nonconstant monotone undirected graph property has query complexity $\Omega(N)$ and is evasive when n is a prime power.

16.1.4 Reductions

In general, an efficient reduction from a problem A to a problem B shows that A's complexity is not much higher than B's, because a hypothetical efficient algorithm for B could be combined with the reduction to get an efficient algorithm for A. We consider a special type of mapping reduction tailored to query complexity. A *projection* is a function $P\colon \{0,1\}^N \to \{0,1\}^M$ such that each bit of $P(x)$ is either a literal (x_i or $\overline{x_i}$) or a constant (0 or 1). For example, $P(x_1x_2x_3) = 0\overline{x_3}1x_2x_30x_2$. A *projection reduction* from $f\colon \{0,1\}^N \to \{0,1\}$ to $g\colon \{0,1\}^M \to \{0,1\}$ is a projection $P\colon \{0,1\}^N \to \{0,1\}^M$ such that $f(x) = g(P(x))$ for all x.

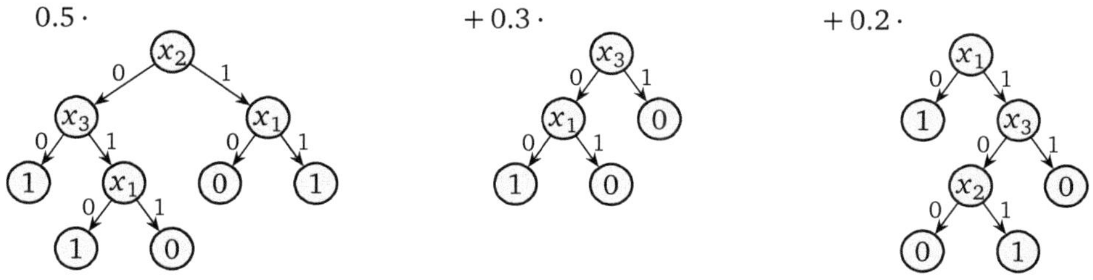

Figure 16.3: Example randomized decision tree

Lemma 16.5. *If P is a projection reduction from f to g, then* $\mathrm{Det}(f) \le \mathrm{Det}(g)$.

Proof. We turn a depth-$\mathrm{Det}(g)$ decision tree for $g(y_1 \cdots y_M)$ into a decision tree for $f(x_1 \cdots x_N)$ without increasing the depth. For any node that queries y_j:

- If $P(x)_j = x_i$, make the node query x_i.
- If $P(x)_j = \overline{x_i}$, make the node query x_i and swap its left and right subtrees.
- If $P(x)_j = 0$, delete the node and its right subtree, and replace it with its left child.
- If $P(x)_j = 1$, delete the node and its left subtree, and replace it with its right child.

On input x, the new decision tree runs the original on input $P(x)$ and outputs $g(P(x)) = f(x)$. ■

We know $\mathrm{Det}(\textsc{Majority}) = N$ from §16.1.2, but a "quick and dirty" way to see the weaker bound $\mathrm{Det}(\textsc{Majority}) = \Omega(N)$ is by a projection reduction from $\textsc{Or}_{\lceil N/2 \rceil}$ to $\textsc{Majority}_N$ that maps x to $P(x) = (x$ followed by $\lfloor N/2 \rfloor$ many 1s). A single 1 in x "tips the scale" in $P(x)$:

- If $\textsc{Or}_{\lceil N/2 \rceil}(x) = 0$ then $\textsc{Majority}_N(P(x)) = 0$ since $P(x)$ has $\le N/2$ many 1s.
- If $\textsc{Or}_{\lceil N/2 \rceil}(x) = 1$ then $\textsc{Majority}_N(P(x)) = 1$ since $P(x)$ has $> N/2$ many 1s.

It follows that $\mathrm{Det}(\textsc{Majority}_N) \ge \mathrm{Det}(\textsc{Or}_{\lceil N/2 \rceil}) = \lceil N/2 \rceil$ by Lemma 16.5.

16.2 Randomized Query Complexity

16.2.1 The Model

A *randomized decision tree* is a distribution over deterministic decision trees. Its depth is the largest depth of any deterministic decision tree that has positive probability.

Example. The depth-3 randomized decision tree in Figure 16.3 gives probability 0.5 to the left tree, 0.3 to the middle tree, and 0.2 to the right tree. To run the randomized decision tree, we sample a constituent deterministic decision tree and run it. On input 110, the left, middle, and right trees output 1, 0, 1 respectively, so the randomized decision tree outputs 1 with probability $0.5 + 0.2 = 0.7$. ♦

We define two-sided, one-sided, and zero-sided error randomized query complexities of $f\colon \{0,1\}^N \to \{0,1\}$ in the spirit of BPP, RP, and ZPP. The notation here may seem slightly abnormal but is compatible with other notation later in this chapter.

- Like BPP: $\mathrm{Rand}_{0,1}(f)$ is the depth of a shallowest randomized decision tree that computes f with two-sided error 1/3, meaning $\mathbf{Pr}\big[\text{output} \ne f(x)\big] \le 1/3$ for each input x. The subscript 0, 1 means it may err on 0-inputs and on 1-inputs.

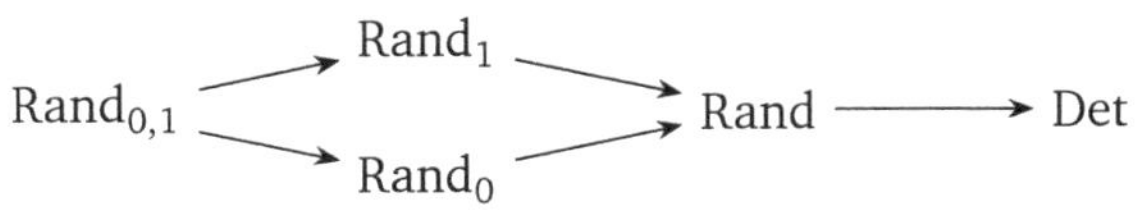

Figure 16.4: Randomized query complexities, where $\longrightarrow$ denotes $\leq$

- Like RP: $\text{Rand}_1(f)$ is the depth of a shallowest randomized decision tree that computes f with one-sided error $1/3$ on the side of 1-inputs, meaning $\mathbf{Pr}[\text{output} = 0] \leq 1/3$ for each 1-input and $\mathbf{Pr}[\text{output} = 1] = 0$ for each 0-input.
- Like coRP: $\text{Rand}_0(f)$ is the depth of a shallowest randomized decision tree that computes f with one-sided error $1/3$ on the side of 0-inputs, meaning $\mathbf{Pr}[\text{output} = 1] \leq 1/3$ for each 0-input and $\mathbf{Pr}[\text{output} = 0] = 0$ for each 1-input.
- Like ZPP: We can define zero-sided-error randomized query complexity in three ways, which are within constant factors of each other. These correspond to the original definition of ZPP in § 7.2.2, the characterization ZPP = RP ∩ coRP (Lemma 7.3), and the characterization of ZPP as "correct always, efficient in expectation" (Theorem 7.15).
  - $\text{Rand}(f)$ is the depth of a shallowest randomized decision tree such that $\mathbf{Pr}\big[\text{output} \in \{f(x), \bot\}\big] = 1$ and $\mathbf{Pr}[\text{output} = \bot] \leq 1/3$ for each input x.
  - $\text{Rand}'(f) = \max\big(\text{Rand}_1(f), \text{Rand}_0(f)\big)$. We have $\text{Rand}'(f) \leq \text{Rand}(f) \leq \text{Rand}_1(f) + \text{Rand}_0(f) \leq 2\text{Rand}'(f)$ by the same argument as Lemma 7.3.
  - $\text{Rand}^*(f)$ is the minimum, over all randomized decision trees with $\mathbf{Pr}\big[\text{output} = f(x)\big] = 1$ for each input x, of $\max_x\big(\mathbf{E}[\text{number of queries on input } x]\big)$. We have $\text{Rand}(f) \leq 3\text{Rand}^*(f)$ and $\text{Rand}^*(f) \leq 1.5\text{Rand}(f)$ by the same argument as Theorem 7.15.

$\text{Rand}_{0,1}(f) \leq \text{Rand}_b(f) \leq \text{Rand}(f) \leq \text{Det}(f)$ for both $b \in \{0,1\}$ (Figure 16.4). These randomized query complexities are amenable to amplification like in §7.3.

16.2.2 Upper Bounds

Lemma 16.6. $\text{Rand}_1(\text{OR}) \leq \lceil 2N/3 \rceil$.

Proof. Pick a uniformly random $i \in [N]$, query $x_i x_{i+1} x_{i+2} \cdots x_{i+\lceil 2N/3 \rceil - 1}$ where indices wrap around (so x_{N+1} means x_1), and accept iff at least one query was a 1. Figure 16.5 shows this for $N = 3$. If $\text{OR}_N(x) = 0$ then $\mathbf{Pr}[\text{accept}] = 0$. If $\text{OR}_N(x) = 1$ then $\mathbf{Pr}[\text{accept}] \geq \lceil 2N/3 \rceil / N \geq 2/3$, since if $x_j = 1$ and $i \in \big\{j, j-1, j-2, \ldots, j - \lceil 2N/3 \rceil + 1\big\}$ (wrapping around) then this accepts. ∎

To do better with two-sided error, we take advantage of erring on the 0-input.

Lemma 16.7. $\text{Rand}_{0,1}(\text{OR}) \leq \lceil N/2 \rceil$.

Proof. With probability $1/3$, accept (with no queries). With the remaining probability $2/3$, pick a uniformly random $i \in [N]$, query $x_i x_{i+1} x_{i+2} \cdots x_{i+\lceil N/2 \rceil - 1}$ (wrapping around), and accept iff at least one query was a 1. Figure 16.6 shows this for $N = 4$. If $\text{OR}_N(x) = 0$ then $\mathbf{Pr}[\text{accept}] = 1/3$. If $\text{OR}_N(x) = 1$ then $\mathbf{Pr}[\text{accept}] \geq (1/3) + (2/3)\lceil N/2 \rceil / N \geq 2/3$. ∎

Next, we illustrate zero-sided error with the Rand* version: A randomized decision tree for

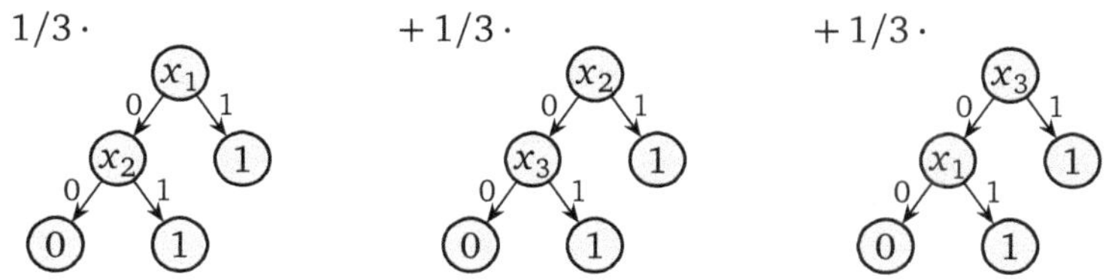

Figure 16.5: One-sided-error randomized decision tree for OR_3

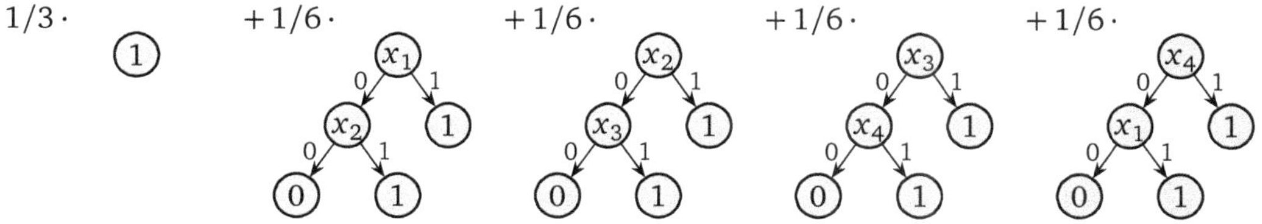

Figure 16.6: Two-sided-error randomized decision tree for OR_4

---

f is a distribution over deterministic decision trees T for f, and its efficiency is:

$$\begin{aligned} & \max_x(\mathbf{E}[\text{number of queries on input } x]) \\ = \; & \max_x\left(\textstyle\sum_T \mathbf{Pr}[T] \cdot (\text{length of } T\text{'s root-to-leaf path on input } x)\right) \end{aligned}$$

MAJORITY_3 evaluates to 1 iff at least two of the three input bits are 1s. We know MAJORITY is evasive (§16.1.2), so $\text{Det}(\text{MAJORITY}_3) = 3$.

Lemma 16.8. $\text{Rand}^*(\text{MAJORITY}_3) \le 8/3$.

Proof. Figure 16.7 shows a deterministic decision tree for MAJORITY_3. If $x_1 = x_2$ then that's the majority bit (no need to query x_3), otherwise x_3 is the tiebreaker. Permute the variables uniformly at random and apply that deterministic decision tree to the permuted variables. In other words, randomly pick two variables to query, and if they have unequal values then query the remaining variable as the tiebreaker. For $x \in \{000, 111\}$, this always makes two queries. For $x \in \{001, 010, 011, 100, 101, 110\}$, this makes two queries with probability 1/3 (if x's two equal bits are queried first) and three queries with probability 2/3, so $\mathbf{E}[\text{number of queries}] = (1/3) \cdot 2 + (2/3) \cdot 3 = 8/3$. ■

16.2.3 Lower Bounds

To prove a randomized worst-case lower bound, it suffices to prove a deterministic average-case lower bound for an input distribution of our choosing:

Lemma 16.9. $\text{Rand}_{0,1}(f) > d$ *if there exists a distribution D over $\{0,1\}^N$ such that for every depth-d deterministic decision tree T,* $\mathbf{Pr}_{x\sim D}\big[T(x) \ne f(x)\big] > 1/3$.

Proof. We prove the contrapositive. Suppose $\text{Rand}_{0,1}(f) \le d$ by some depth-d randomized decision tree, which is a distribution R over depth-d deterministic decision trees. Consider any distribution D over $\{0,1\}^N$. Taking probabilities over $T \sim R$ and $x \sim D$:

$$\min_T\left(\mathbf{Pr}_x\big[T(x) \ne f(x)\big]\right) \;\le\; \mathbf{Pr}_{T,x}\big[T(x) \ne f(x)\big] \;\le\; \max_x\left(\mathbf{Pr}_T\big[T(x) \ne f(x)\big]\right) \;\le\; 1/3$$

Thus for some depth-d deterministic decision tree T, $\mathbf{Pr}_x\big[T(x) \ne f(x)\big] \le 1/3$. ■

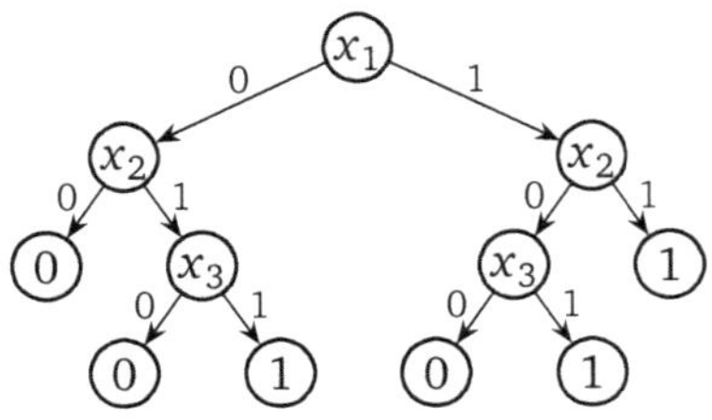

Figure 16.7: Deterministic decision tree for MAJORITY_3

We view this as a "querier versus adversary game" quite different from the one for deterministic lower bounds (§ 16.1.2): The querier randomly picks a depth-d deterministic decision tree T from a distribution of his choice. Simultaneously (with no back-and-forth), the adversary randomly picks an input x from a distribution of his choice. The adversary wins iff $T(x) \neq f(x)$. If the adversary can win with probability $> 1/3$ (no matter how the querier plays), then the querier can't win with probability $\geq 2/3$. To prove a lower bound, we design an input distribution to make things tough for decision trees.

Theorem 16.10. $\text{Rand}_{0,1}(\text{OR}) = \lceil N/2 \rceil$.

Proof idea. If a shallow deterministic decision tree succeeds on the 0-input, then it probably won't notice if we sneak a 1 into a random position, since the position is unlikely to be one of the few queried on the 0-input. Then the decision tree errs on the 1-input since it reaches the same leaf as the 0-input. ■

Proof. The upper bound is Lemma 16.7. We prove the matching lower bound using Lemma 16.9. For some small $\delta > 0$, define a distribution D over $\{0,1\}^N$:

$$D(x) = \begin{cases} 1/3 + \delta & \text{if } x \text{ is all-0s} \\ (2/3 - \delta)/N & \text{if } x \text{ has exactly one } 1 \\ 0 & \text{otherwise} \end{cases}$$

Consider any depth-($\lceil N/2 \rceil - 1$) deterministic decision tree T. If the leftmost root-to-leaf path (where all queries are 0s) accepts, then T errs on the all-0s input, which has probability $> 1/3$. Now, suppose the leftmost path rejects. If x has exactly one 1 but the leftmost path doesn't query the 1, then T follows this path on x and errs. There are $\geq \lfloor N/2 \rfloor + 1$ many such inputs x since the leftmost path queries $\leq \lceil N/2 \rceil - 1$ variables. So this happens with probability $\geq (\lfloor N/2 \rfloor + 1) \cdot (2/3 - \delta)/N$, which is $> 1/3$ if δ is small enough, since $(\lfloor N/2 \rfloor + 1)/N > 1/2$. In both cases, $\mathbf{Pr}_{x \sim D}\big[T(x) \neq \text{OR}_N(x)\big] > 1/3$. ■

This implies $\mathsf{TIME}[N] \not\subseteq \mathsf{BPTIME}[o(N)]$.

There's a similar technique for zero-sided-error lower bounds:

Lemma 16.11. $\text{Rand}^*(f) > d$ *if there exists a distribution D over $\{0,1\}^N$ such that for every deterministic decision tree T that computes f, $\mathbf{E}_{x \sim D}\big[$number of queries T makes to $x\big] > d$.*

Proof. We prove the contrapositive. Suppose $\text{Rand}^*(f) \leq d$ by some randomized decision tree, which is a distribution R over deterministic decision trees that compute f. Consider any distribution D over $\{0,1\}^N$. Taking expectations over $T \sim R$ and $x \sim D$, and letting the random variable Q be the number of queries T makes to x:

$$\min_T\big(\mathbf{E}_x[Q]\big) \leq \mathbf{E}_{T,x}[Q] \leq \max_x\big(\mathbf{E}_T[Q]\big) \leq d$$

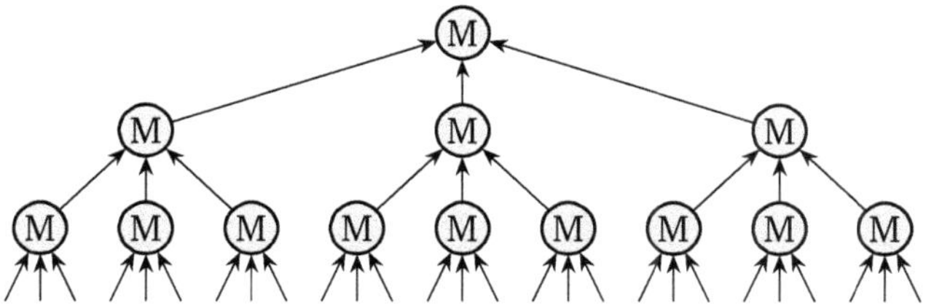

Figure 16.8: MAJ TREE function

Thus for some deterministic decision tree T that computes f, $\mathbf{E}_x[Q] \le d$. ∎

In this variant of the querier versus adversary game, the querier randomly picks a deterministic decision tree T that computes f, and simultaneously, the adversary randomly picks an input x. The number of queries T makes to x is how much money the querier pays the adversary. If the adversary can make the payment $> d$ in expectation, then the querier can't make the payment $\le d$ in expectation.

Theorem 16.12. Rand*(MAJORITY$_3$) $= 8/3$.

Proof. The upper bound is Lemma 16.8. We prove the matching lower bound using Lemma 16.11. Let D be the uniform distribution over $\{001, 010, 100\}$. Consider any deterministic decision tree T that computes MAJORITY$_3$. Note that T always makes at least two queries, since T only terminates after seeing two of the same bit in the input. Say T queries x_i first, and if $x_i = 0$ then T queries x_j second, and if $x_i = 1$ then T queries x_k second. With probability $1/3$, $x_i = 0$ and $x_j = 1$ and T makes three queries. With probability $1/3$, $x_i = 1$ and $x_k = 0$ and T makes three queries. Thus $\mathbf{E}_{x\sim D}\big[\text{number of queries } T \text{ makes to } x\big] \ge \frac{1}{3}\cdot 3 + \frac{1}{3}\cdot 3 + \frac{1}{3}\cdot 2 = 8/3$. ∎

16.2.4 Game Tree Evaluation

Game tree evaluation demonstrates the power of randomized decision trees. As a warmup, consider MAJORITY$_3$ recursively composed with itself: Define MAJ TREE$_N$: $\{0,1\}^N \to \{0,1\}$ by MAJ TREE$_1(x) = x$ and for $N > 1$ a power of 3:

$$\begin{aligned}\text{MAJ TREE}_N(x) \;=\; \text{MAJORITY}_3\big(&\text{MAJ TREE}_{N/3}(\text{first third of } x),\\ &\text{MAJ TREE}_{N/3}(\text{middle third of } x),\\ &\text{MAJ TREE}_{N/3}(\text{last third of } x)\big)\end{aligned}$$

Figure 16.8 depicts this with $N = 3^3$ and letting M stand for MAJORITY$_3$.

Theorem 16.13. Rand*(MAJ TREE) $\le N^{\log_3(8/3)} < N^{0.893}$.

Proof. This returns MAJ TREE$_N(x)$ with probability 1:

Recursive zero-sided-error randomized decision tree for MAJ TREE	(16.3)

eval(x):
  if $N = 1$: query and return x
  let w be either the first, middle, or last third of x, with probability $1/3$ each
  let y and z be the other two thirds of x
  if eval(y) = eval(z): return that bit
  else: return eval(w)

Let the random variable Q_x be the number of queries on input x. For each $d = \log_3(N) \geq 0$ (the depth of MAJ TREE) define:

$$q_d = \max_{x \in \{0,1\}^{3^d}} \big(\mathbf{E}[Q_x]\big)$$

We claim eval maintains the invariant that $q_d \leq (8/3)^d$. This holds for the base case $d = 0$ since $q_0 = 1 = (8/3)^0$. To see that the invariant is maintained, assume it holds for $d-1$, and consider any $x \in \{0,1\}^{3^d}$. At least two of the three bits

$$\text{eval(first third of } x\text{)}, \ \text{eval(middle third of } x\text{)}, \ \text{eval(last third of } x\text{)}$$

are equal. With probability $\geq 1/3$ we have $\text{eval}(y) = \text{eval}(z)$, conditioned on which:

$$\mathbf{E}[Q_x] = \mathbf{E}[Q_y] + \mathbf{E}[Q_z] \leq q_{d-1} + q_{d-1} \leq 2 \cdot (8/3)^{d-1}$$

With probability $\leq 2/3$ we have $\text{eval}(y) \neq \text{eval}(z)$, conditioned on which:

$$\mathbf{E}[Q_x] = \mathbf{E}[Q_y] + \mathbf{E}[Q_z] + \mathbf{E}[Q_w] \leq q_{d-1} + q_{d-1} + q_{d-1} \leq 3 \cdot (8/3)^{d-1}$$

Overall:

$$\mathbf{E}[Q_x] \leq (1/3) \cdot 2 \cdot (8/3)^{d-1} + (2/3) \cdot 3 \cdot (8/3)^{d-1} = (2/3 + 2) \cdot (8/3)^{d-1} = (8/3)^d$$

We conclude $\text{Rand}^*(\text{MAJ TREE}) \leq q_d \leq (8/3)^d = N^{\log_3(8/3)}$. ■

Now, consider a two-player game:

- The players alternate turns: P1, P2, P1, P2, and so on.
- The game always lasts exactly d turns, where d is even.
- In each turn, the player has two possible moves.
- The winner is determined by the whole sequence of moves.

For example, QSAT has this form (§3.1). View such a game as a binary tree: P1 picks a child of the root, then P2 picks a child of that node, and so on, ending at a leaf labeled 1 or 0 indicating whether P1 wins. Put $\vee$ gates at nodes where P1 picks a child, and $\wedge$ gates at nodes where P2 picks a child, and variables at the leaves. In this formula, each input bit indicates whether P1 wins after a particular sequence of moves, and the output indicates whether P1 has a winning strategy.

AND-OR TREE is the problem of evaluating this formula: For $N = 2^d$ where d is even, $\text{AND-OR TREE}_N : \{0,1\}^N \to \{0,1\}$ is a depth-d bounded-fan-in read-once monotone formula whose layers alternate between $\vee$ and $\wedge$: The output is an $\vee$ gate, the next layer is two $\wedge$ gates, then four $\vee$ gates, then eight $\wedge$ gates, and so on, then 2^{d-1} $\wedge$ gates, then $N = 2^d$ input variables. The top of Figure 16.9 shows this for $d = 4$. Equivalently, recursively define AND-OR TREE by $\text{AND-OR TREE}_1(x) = x$ and for $N > 1$ a power of 4:

$$\begin{aligned}\text{AND-OR TREE}_N(x) = \text{OR}_2\big(&\text{AND}_2\big(\text{AND-OR TREE}_{N/4}(\text{first quarter of } x),\\ &\qquad \text{AND-OR TREE}_{N/4}(\text{second quarter of } x)\big),\\ &\text{AND}_2\big(\text{AND-OR TREE}_{N/4}(\text{third quarter of } x),\\ &\qquad \text{AND-OR TREE}_{N/4}(\text{fourth quarter of } x)\big)\big)\end{aligned}$$

We can evaluate game trees faster with randomness than without:

Theorem 16.14. $\text{Rand}^*(\text{AND-OR TREE}) \leq O(N^{\log_2(c)}) < N^{0.754}$ *where* $c = (1+\sqrt{33})/4 < 1.687$.

Proof idea. We exploit short-circuiting: If $\text{OR}_2(x) = 1$, or if $\text{AND}_2(x) = 0$, and we randomly choose one of the two input bits to query, then with probability $\geq 1/2$ we'll know the output without needing to query the other bit. This advantage accumulates in a subtle way throughout the tree. The analysis is simpler to describe after noticing that the tree of $\wedge$ and $\vee$ gates is equivalent to a tree of nand ("negated and") gates. ■

Let $\text{NAND}_2(x_1x_2) = \neg(x_1 \wedge x_2)$. Recursively define NAND TREE by $\text{NAND TREE}_1(x) = x$ and for $N > 1$ a power of 2:

$$\begin{aligned}\text{NAND TREE}_N(x) &= \text{NAND}_2\big(\text{NAND TREE}_{N/2}(\text{left half of } x),\\ &\qquad \text{NAND TREE}_{N/2}(\text{right half of } x)\big)\end{aligned}$$

$\text{AND-OR TREE}_N = \text{NAND TREE}_N$ when N is a power of 4, as Figure 16.9 illustrates: Replace each $\vee$ with an $\wedge$ having $\neg$s on its three wires, and then group each $\neg$ with the $\wedge$ below it.

Proof of Theorem 16.14. This returns $\text{NAND TREE}_N(x)$ with probability 1:

Recursive zero-sided-error randomized decision tree for NAND TREE (16.4)

```
eval(x):
    if N = 1: query and return x
    let y be either the left or the right half of x, with probability 1/2 each
    let z be the other half of x
    if eval(y) = 0: return 1
    else: return ¬eval(z)
```

Let the random variable Q_x be the number of queries on input x. For each $d = \log_2(N) \geq 0$ and $b \in \{0,1\}$ define:

$$q_{d,b} = \max_{b\text{-inputs } x \in \{0,1\}^{2^d}} \big(\text{E}[Q_x]\big)$$

Here are two observations for $d > 0$:

- $q_{d,0} \leq 2q_{d-1,1}$ since for any 0-input $x \in \{0,1\}^{2^d}$, both y and z are 1-inputs and so:

$$\text{E}[Q_x] = \text{E}[Q_y] + \text{E}[Q_z] \leq 2q_{d-1,1}$$

- $q_{d,1} \leq q_{d-1,1}/2 + q_{d-1,0}$ since for any 1-input $x \in \{0,1\}^{2^d}$, either the left or the right half of x is a 0-input, so eval(x) always calls eval on a 0-input, but with probability $\leq 1/2$ it first calls eval on a 1-input.

We claim eval maintains the invariant that $q_{d,1} \leq c^d$. This holds for $d = 0$ since $q_{0,1} = 1 = c^0$ and for $d = 1$ since $q_{1,1} \leq q_{0,1}/2 + q_{0,0} = 1.5 < 1.686 < c^1$. To see that the invariant is maintained, assume it holds for $d-1$ and $d-2$, and combine the above observations:

$$q_{d,1} \leq q_{d-1,1}/2 + 2q_{d-2,1} \leq c^{d-1}/2 + 2c^{d-2} = (1/2c + 2/c^2)c^d = c^d$$

The mysterious $c = (1+\sqrt{33})/4$ comes from solving $1/2c + 2/c^2 = 1$ using the quadratic formula. Finally, $q_{d,0} \leq 2q_{d-1,1} \leq 2c^{d-1} = O(c^d)$ and therefore:

$$\max_{x \in \{0,1\}^{2^d}} \big(\text{E}[Q_x]\big) = \max(q_{d,1}, q_{d,0}) \leq O(c^d)$$

We conclude $\text{Rand}^*(\text{NAND TREE}) \leq O(c^d) = O(N^{\log_2(c)})$. ■

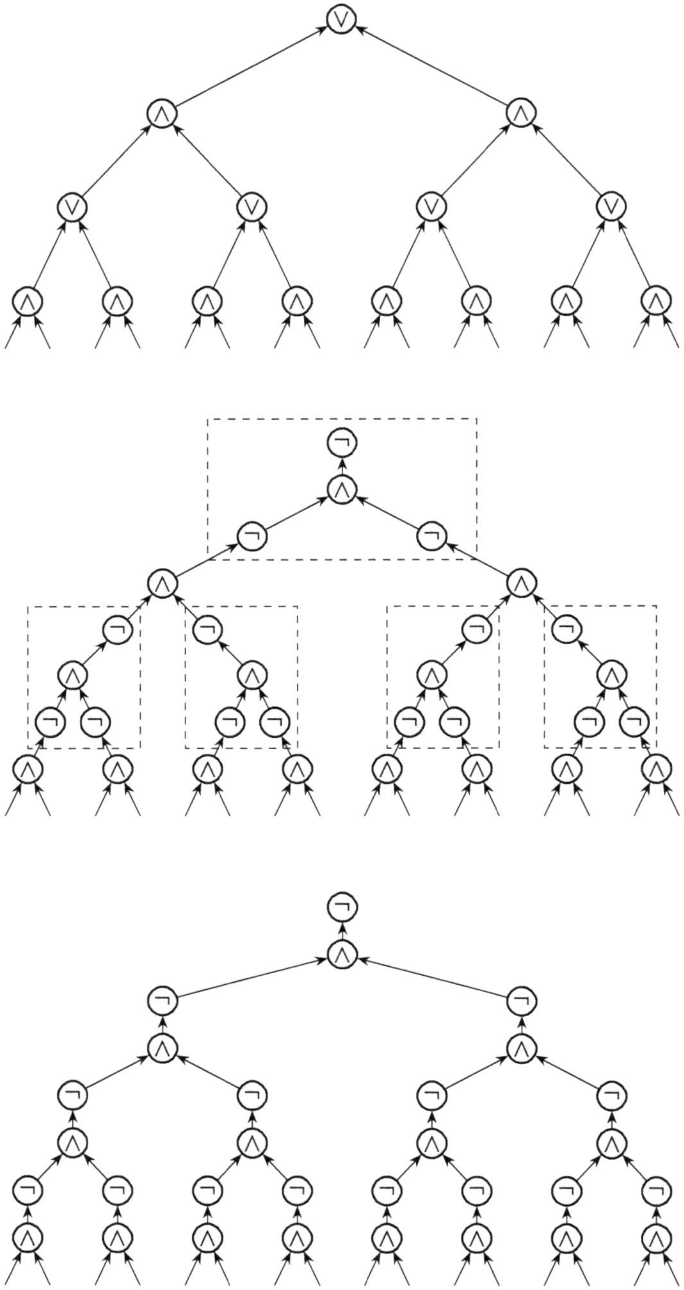

Figure 16.9: AND-OR TREE is equivalent to NAND TREE

Separation means an upper bound and a lower bound for the same problem. For instance, the separation $\mathsf{P} \not\subseteq \mathsf{L}$ would mean some problem has a poly-time algorithm but no log-space algorithm. We saw some simple separations between randomized and deterministic query complexities—functions for which some randomized decision tree is more efficient than every deterministic decision tree. We showed that recursive composition can "amplify" such separations, yielding functions with randomized query complexities significantly lower than their deterministic query complexities. This joins a list of various types of amplification we've encountered:

- Success probability amplification for randomized algorithms (§7.3).
- Hardness amplification for average-case complexity (§10.4).
- Gap amplification for hardness of approximation (§14.2).

Specifically:

- $\text{Rand}^*(\text{MAJ TREE}) \leq N^{\log_3(8/3)} < N^{0.893}$.
- $\text{Det}(\text{MAJ TREE}) = N$ (Exercise 16.12).
- $\text{Rand}^*(\text{AND-OR TREE}) \leq O(N^{\log_2(c)}) < N^{0.754}$.
- $\text{Det}(\text{AND-OR TREE}) = N$ since it's a read-once formula (Theorem 16.1).

Surprisingly, our randomized decision tree for MAJ TREE is not the best possible. It's known that $\text{Rand}^*(\text{MAJ TREE}) < N^{0.887}$ and $\text{Rand}_{0,1}(\text{MAJ TREE}) > N^{0.868}$. It remains open to pin down MAJ TREE's randomized query complexity. Our randomized upper bound for AND-OR TREE, however, is tight even for two-sided error: $\text{Rand}_{0,1}(\text{AND-OR TREE}) \geq \Omega(N^{\log_2(c)})$. No randomized decision tree can evaluate game trees using fewer queries than ours. It was long conjectured that AND-OR TREE exhibits the largest possible separation between randomized and deterministic query complexities: $\text{Rand}_{0,1}(F) \geq \Omega\big(\text{Det}(F)^{\log_2(c)}\big)$ for all F. This is false, as we prove in §16.5 by a technique totally different from recursive composition. Before that, we develop relevant tools with interesting diversions along the way.

16.3 Certificate Complexity

16.3.1 The Model

Definition. A *certificate* for $f\colon \{0,1\}^N \to \{0,1\}$ is a partial assignment $a \in \{0,1,*\}^N$ such that the restriction $f|_a$ is a constant function, in other words, $f(x)$ is the same bit for every $x \in \{0,1\}^N$ consistent with a. If that bit is b, we call a a b-certificate.

A certificate for (f, x) is a certificate for f that x is consistent with, in other words, it reveals enough of x's bits to determine f's value (regardless of the unrevealed bits). A certificate's *size* is its number of non-$*$s (revealed bits). $\text{Cert}(f, x)$ is the size of a smallest certificate for (f, x), in other words, the fewest bits of x that could be revealed to *certify* (be sure of) $f(x)$.

The *certificate complexity* of f is $\text{Cert}(f) = \max_x\big(\text{Cert}(f, x)\big)$. ◄

Example. For the f in Figure 16.10, $*01$ and $1{*}1$ are 0-certificates, and $**0$ and $01*$ are 1-certificates.

$\text{Cert}(f, 010) = 1$ since of all the certificates for $(f, 010)$, the smallest is $**0$ of size 1. To convince a querier that $f(010) = 1$, we could direct them to query just the last input bit.

$\text{Cert}(f, 011) = 2$ since of all the certificates for $(f, 011)$, the smallest is $01*$ of size 2. To convince a querier that $f(011) = 1$, we could direct them to query just the first two input bits.

x	$f(x)$
000	1
001	0
010	1
011	1
100	1
101	0
110	1
111	0

Figure 16.10: Example function for introducing certificate complexity

Cert(f) $= 2$ since every input is consistent with a size-2 certificate for f, and some input is not consistent with any size-1 certificate for f. ♦

A certificate complexity upper bound means for every input, we can certify the output by revealing few input bits. A certificate complexity lower bound means for some input, we can't certify the output by revealing few input bits.

$$\begin{aligned}\text{Cert}(f) \le d &\iff \forall x \left(\exists \text{ certificate } a \text{ for } (f,x)\right): \ a \text{ has size} \le d \\ &\iff \forall x \left(\exists a \text{ of size} \le d \text{ consistent with } x\right) \left(\forall y \text{ consistent with } a\right): \ f(y) = f(x)\end{aligned}$$

$$\begin{aligned}\text{Cert}(f) > d &\iff \exists x \left(\forall \text{ certificate } a \text{ for } (f,x)\right): \ a \text{ has size} > d \\ &\iff \exists x \left(\forall a \text{ of size} \le d \text{ consistent with } x\right) \left(\exists y \text{ consistent with } a\right): \ f(y) \ne f(x)\end{aligned}$$

Every f has Cert(f) $\le N$ since every input is its own size-N certificate. In general, it doesn't matter whether "size-d certificate" means "size exactly d" or "size at most d," since we can enlarge any certificate for (f,x) by assigning more bits.

Lemma 16.15. Cert(f) $\le$ Det(f) *for all* f.

Proof. Let $d =$ Det(f). Consider a depth-d decision tree computing f. For each leaf, the associated partial assignment a (recording the results of queries along the path from the root) is a size-d certificate for f, since all inputs consistent with a lead to that leaf and have the same output. For every x, the decision tree's computation path on x yields a size-d certificate for (f,x). ■

Theorem 16.16. Cert(OR) $= N$.

Proof. Let $f = \text{OR}_N$. To certify $f(00\cdots0) = 0$, revealing all N bits is necessary since changing a $*$ to a 1 would yield a 1-input. Formally, Cert(f) $\ge$ Cert($f, 00\cdots0$) $\ge N$ because the only certificate for $(f, 00\cdots0)$ is $00\cdots0$ itself: Each other a is consistent with a 1-input and hence isn't a 0-certificate. (To certify $f(x) = 1$, revealing a single 1 is sufficient, so Cert(f,x) ≤ 1. It doesn't matter that almost all inputs are easy to certify, when the other input is hard to certify.) ■

Theorem 16.17. Cert(MAJORITY) $= \lfloor N/2 \rfloor + 1$.

Proof. Let $f = \text{MAJORITY}_N$. To certify $f(x) = 1$, revealing $\lfloor N/2 \rfloor + 1$ many 1s is necessary (otherwise changing all $*$s to 0s would yield a 0-input) and sufficient, so Cert(f,x) $= \lfloor N/2 \rfloor + 1$. To certify $f(x) = 0$, revealing $\lceil N/2 \rceil$ many 0s is necessary and sufficient, so Cert(f,x) $= \lceil N/2 \rceil \le \lfloor N/2 \rfloor + 1$. ■

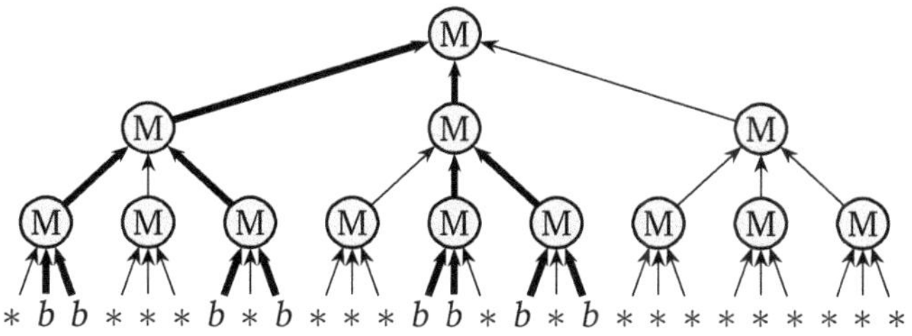

Figure 16.11: Certificate for MAJ TREE

$\text{TRIBES}_N(x) = 1$ iff the $n \times n$ binary matrix x has at least one all-1s row (where $N = n^2$).

Theorem 16.18. $\text{Cert}(\text{TRIBES}) = n = \sqrt{N}$.

Proof. Let $f = \text{TRIBES}_N$. To certify $f(x) = 1$, revealing an all-1s row is necessary (otherwise changing all $*$s to 0s would yield a 0-input) and sufficient, so $\text{Cert}(f, x) = n$ (the number of columns). To certify $f(x) = 0$, revealing a 0 in each row is necessary (otherwise changing all $*$s to 1s would yield a 1-input) and sufficient, so $\text{Cert}(f, x) = n$ (the number of rows). ∎

Theorem 16.19. $\text{Cert}(\text{MAJ TREE}) = N^{\log_3(2)} \approx N^{0.631}$.

Proof. Let $f = \text{MAJ TREE}_N$ where $N = 3^d$. We show $\text{Cert}(f) = 2^d$.

$\text{Cert}(f) \le 2^d$: For any input x, say with $f(x) = b$, we show $\text{Cert}(f, x) \le 2^d$. In the ternary tree of "MAJORITY_3 gates," the root evaluates to b. Pick two children of the root that also evaluate to b. For both of them, pick two children that evaluate to b, and so on. This forms a binary tree with 2^d leaves. Revealing the b at each such leaf (and letting other leaves be $*$s) yields a certificate for (f, x). Figure 16.11 depicts a b-certificate for MAJ TREE_{3^3}.

$\text{Cert}(f) \ge 2^d$: We prove something stronger: *Every* certificate for f has size $\ge 2^d$. For any a of size $< 2^d$, we show a isn't a certificate for f. In the ternary tree of "MAJORITY_3 gates," define a node's *size* (with respect to a) as the number of non-$*$ leaves in its subtree. Since the root has size $< 2^d$, at most one child has size $\ge 2^{d-1}$, so we can pick two children of size $< 2^{d-1}$. For both of them, at most one child has size $\ge 2^{d-2}$, so we can pick two children of size $< 2^{d-2}$, and so on. This forms a binary tree with 2^d leaves, each of which has size $< 2^0$ and is thus a $*$ in a. For either $b \in \{0, 1\}$, changing each such $*$ to b makes the tree evaluate to b, so a isn't a certificate. ∎

16.3.2 One-Sided Certificate Complexity

For each $b \in \{0, 1\}$, define $\text{Cert}_b(f) = \max_{b\text{-inputs } x}\big(\text{Cert}(f, x)\big)$, so $\text{Cert}(f) = \max\big(\text{Cert}_1(f), \text{Cert}_0(f)\big)$. For example:

- $\text{Cert}_1(\text{OR}) = 1$ and $\text{Cert}_0(\text{OR}) = N$ from the proof of Theorem 16.16.
- $\text{Cert}_1(\text{TRIBES}) = \text{Cert}_0(\text{TRIBES}) = n = \sqrt{N}$ from the proof of Theorem 16.18.

A 1-certificate is like an NP witness: A prover can convince a query-efficient verifier that $f(x) = 1$ by showing a small 1-certificate a for (f, x). After querying the relevant variables and confirming that x is consistent with a, the verifier knows $f(x) = 1$ (despite not knowing the rest of x) since a is a 1-certificate for f.

We prove two characterizations of Cert_1.

x	$f(x)$
000	1
001	0
010	1
011	1
100	0
101	0
110	1
111	0

size-2 1-certificates for f: $01*$ $0*0$ $*10$

2-DNF for f: $(\overline{x_1} \wedge x_2) \vee (\overline{x_1} \wedge \overline{x_3}) \vee (x_2 \wedge \overline{x_3})$

Figure 16.12: Example of equivalence between one-sided certificate complexity and DNF width

Lemma 16.20. $\mathrm{Cert}_1(f)$ *equals the smallest* k *for which some* k*-DNF expresses* f.

Proof. Every size-k partial assignment a corresponds to a width-k term $\bigwedge_{i:a_i=1} x_i \wedge \bigwedge_{i:a_i=0} \overline{x_i}$ that accepts exactly the inputs consistent with a.

$\geq$: If $\mathrm{Cert}_1(f) \leq k$ then f is expressed by the k-DNF φ whose terms correspond to all size-k 1-certificates for f: Every 1-input of f is consistent with some size-k 1-certificate for f and is thus accepted by the corresponding term of φ. Every 0-input of f is inconsistent with every 1-certificate for f and is thus rejected by every term of φ.

$\leq$: If some k-DNF φ expresses f, then $\mathrm{Cert}_1(f) \leq k$: Every 1-input is accepted by some term of φ and is thus consistent with the corresponding size-k partial assignment a, which is a 1-certificate for f since every input consistent with a is accepted by that term of φ. ■

Figure 16.12 demonstrates Lemma 16.20. Likewise, $\mathrm{Cert}_0(f)$ equals the smallest k for which some k-DNF expresses $\overline{f}$, or equivalently, some k-CNF expresses f.

A depth-d *verifier decision tree* for f is a set of depth-d deterministic decision trees such that each 1-input is accepted by at least one decision tree in the set, and each 0-input is rejected by all decision trees in the set. (The "witness" says which decision tree to run.)

Lemma 16.21. $\mathrm{Cert}_1(f)$ *equals the depth of a shallowest verifier decision tree for* f.

Proof. $\geq$: Suppose $\mathrm{Cert}_1(f) \leq k$, so some k-DNF φ expresses f. Obtain a depth-k verifier decision tree for f by turning each width-k term of φ into a depth-k deterministic decision tree. Every 1-input is accepted by some term of φ and thus by some decision tree in this set. Every 0-input is rejected by every term of φ and thus by every decision tree in this set.

$\leq$: Suppose f has a depth-k verifier decision tree. We may assume all root-to-leaf paths query exactly k variables. For each accepting leaf in each constituent decision tree, define a width-k term that accepts exactly the inputs that would lead to the leaf (as in Theorem 6.21). The $\vee$ of all these terms is a k-DNF expressing f, so $\mathrm{Cert}_1(f) \leq k$. ■

16.3.3 P Versus NP ∩ coNP

We define query complexity analogues of the time complexity classes P, NP, and coNP. A family F is *total* iff F_N is a total function for all N such that F_N is defined.

- P^{qc} is the class of all total F with $\mathrm{Det}(F) \le \mathrm{polylog}\, N$.
- $\mathsf{NP}^{\mathsf{qc}}$ is the class of all total F with $\mathrm{Cert}_1(F) \le \mathrm{polylog}\, N$.
- $\mathsf{coNP}^{\mathsf{qc}}$ is the class of all total F with $\mathrm{Cert}_0(F) \le \mathrm{polylog}\, N$.

So $\mathsf{NP}^{\mathsf{qc}} \cap \mathsf{coNP}^{\mathsf{qc}}$ is the class of all total F with $\mathrm{Cert}(F) \le \mathrm{polylog}\, N$. For time complexity, it's widely conjectured that $\mathsf{P} \ne \mathsf{NP} \cap \mathsf{coNP}$ (even for total problems). But the following theorem implies $\mathsf{P}^{\mathsf{qc}} = \mathsf{NP}^{\mathsf{qc}} \cap \mathsf{coNP}^{\mathsf{qc}}$ (for total problems).

Theorem 16.22. $\mathrm{Det}(f) \le \mathrm{Cert}_1(f) \cdot \mathrm{Cert}_0(f) \le \mathrm{Cert}(f)^2$ *for all* f.

This is tight since for $f = \textsc{Tribes}_N$ we have $\mathrm{Det}(f) = N = \mathrm{Cert}_1(f) \cdot \mathrm{Cert}_0(f) = \mathrm{Cert}(f)^2$.

Two terms *overlap* when they have at least one variable in common. For example, $\overline{x_1} \wedge x_2$ overlaps $\overline{x_2} \wedge x_3$.

Lemma 16.23. *If DNFs* φ_1 *and* φ_0 *express* f *and* $\overline{f}$ *respectively, then every term of* φ_1 *overlaps every term of* φ_0.

Proof of Lemma 16.23. Suppose for contradiction φ_1 and φ_0 express f and $\overline{f}$ but some terms T_1 and T_0 of φ_1 and φ_0 depend on disjoint sets of variables. We can assign T_1's variables to satisfy T_1 and assign T_0's variables to satisfy T_0, yielding an input x satisfying both φ_1 and φ_0, so $f(x) = 1 = \overline{f}(x)$, which is a contradiction. (It matters that f is total, since if $f(x)$ were undefined then x could satisfy both φ_1 and φ_0.) ∎

Proof of Theorem 16.22. Suppose $\mathrm{Cert}_1(f) = k_1$ so a k_1-DNF φ_1 expresses f, and $\mathrm{Cert}_0(f) = k_0$ so a k_0-DNF φ_0 expresses $\overline{f}$ (Lemma 16.20). We design an algorithm that computes f with $\le k_1 \cdot k_0$ queries, so $\mathrm{Det}(f) \le k_1 \cdot k_0$. Throughout the algorithm, the partial assignment a records the results of queries so far. For each $b \in \{0,1\}$, $\varphi_b|_a$ is the contraction of φ_b with a plugged in: Delete from φ_b each term having at least one literal that evaluates to 0, and delete from all other terms of φ_b any literals that evaluate to 1. (In the algorithm and analysis, φ_1 and φ_0 play asymmetric roles. Swapping their roles would be fine.)

Decision tree for f using DNFs for f and $\overline{f}$	(16.5)
repeat until $f|_a$ is a constant function: pick any term of $\varphi_1|_a$ and query the term's variables output the constant value of $f|_a$	

We argue that this makes $\le k_1 \cdot k_0$ queries. Each iteration makes $\le k_1$ queries since each term of $\varphi_1|_a$ has $\le k_1$ variables. We show there are $\le k_0$ iterations. In each iteration, since $\varphi_1|_a$ expresses $f|_a$ and $\varphi_0|_a$ expresses $\overline{f|_a}$, the term picked from $\varphi_1|_a$ overlaps every term of $\varphi_0|_a$ (Lemma 16.23). So each term of $\varphi_0|_a$ either disappears or shrinks, since at least one of its variables is queried. Since φ_0's terms have width k_0, and the maximum width of $\varphi_0|_a$'s terms decreases in each iteration, one of the following happens within k_0 iterations:

- $\varphi_0|_a$ has a width-0 term and thus always accepts, so $f|_a$ is constant 0.
- $\varphi_0|_a$ has no terms and thus always rejects, so $f|_a$ is constant 1.

The algorithm can't get stuck by picking a width-0 term of $\varphi_1|_a$, or with $\varphi_1|_a$ having no terms to pick from, since then $f|_a$ would be constant and the algorithm would have halted. ∎

Example. Let $f = \overline{\textsc{Tribes}_4}$, so $\mathrm{Cert}_1(f) = \mathrm{Cert}_0(f) = 2$:

$$\varphi_1 = (\overline{x_1} \wedge \overline{x_3}) \vee (\overline{x_1} \wedge \overline{x_4}) \vee (\overline{x_2} \wedge \overline{x_3}) \vee (\overline{x_2} \wedge \overline{x_4}) \qquad \varphi_0 = (x_1 \wedge x_2) \vee (x_3 \wedge x_4)$$

Trivially, f has a depth-4 decision tree since $N = 4$, but let's illustrate the algorithm from Theorem 16.22 anyway. Suppose we pick the term $(\overline{x_1} \wedge \overline{x_3})$ from φ_1, query x_1 and x_3, and get $x_1 = 0$ and $x_3 = 1$, so $a = 0{*}1{*}$:

$$\varphi_1|_a = (\overline{x_4}) \vee (\overline{x_2} \wedge \overline{x_4}) \qquad \varphi_0|_a = (x_4)$$

Suppose we pick the term $(\overline{x_4})$ from $\varphi_1|_a$, query x_4, and get $x_4 = 1$, so $a = 0{*}11$:

$$\varphi_1|_a = \text{no terms} \qquad \varphi_0|_a = ()$$

Now $\varphi_1|_a$ always rejects and $\varphi_0|_a$ always accepts, so $f|_a(x_2) = 0$ for all x_2. ♦

16.4 Sensitivity

We introduce two complexity measures that are useful for relating deterministic and randomized query complexities and are interesting in their own right.

16.4.1 The Model

Definition. For any $x \in \{0,1\}^N$ and index $i \in [N]$, x^i is x with the ith bit flipped. The *sensitivity* of $f\colon \{0,1\}^N \to \{0,1\}$ is $\mathrm{Sens}(f) = \max_x\big(\mathrm{Sens}(f,x)\big)$ where $\mathrm{Sens}(f,x)$ is the number of indices i such that $f(x^i) \neq f(x)$ (f is *sensitive* to the ith bit of x). The one-sided versions are $\mathrm{Sens}_b(f) = \max_{b\text{-inputs } x}\big(\mathrm{Sens}(f,x)\big)$ for each $b \in \{0,1\}$, so $\mathrm{Sens}(f) = \max\big(\mathrm{Sens}_1(f), \mathrm{Sens}_0(f)\big)$. ◄

To show $\mathrm{Sens}_b(f) \geq k$, we exhibit a b-input x and k distinct indices to which f is sensitive.

Example. For the function f in Figure 16.13, we have $\mathrm{Sens}(f,010) = 1$ since $f(110) = f(010)$ (insensitive to 1st bit) and $f(000) = f(010)$ (insensitive to 2nd bit) and $f(011) \neq f(010)$ (sensitive to 3rd bit). We have $\mathrm{Sens}_1(f) = \max(2,2) = 2$ and $\mathrm{Sens}_0(f) = \max(1,1,0,1,0,1) = 1$ and $\mathrm{Sens}(f) = \max(2,1) = 2$. ♦

$\mathrm{Sens}_0(\textsc{Or}) = N$ because on the 0-input, flipping any single bit yields a 1-input. $\mathrm{Sens}_1(\textsc{Or}) = 1$ because on a 1-input with one 1, the 1 is the only bit that can be flipped to get the 0-input, and on a 1-input with multiple 1s, no single bit can be flipped to get the 0-input.

We know certificate complexity is polynomially related to deterministic query complexity (Theorem 16.22). Sensitivity is, too: For some constants c, d we have $\mathrm{Det}(f) \leq c\,\mathrm{Sens}(f)^d$ for all f. This was a notorious conjecture for a long time. We won't fully prove it, but in § 16.4.3 we prove the crucial part that eluded researchers for decades. First, we consider a more complicated variant of sensitivity that's simpler to relate to deterministic query complexity.

Definition. For any $x \in \{0,1\}^N$ and set of indices $I \subseteq [N]$ (a *block*), x^I is x with all bits indexed by I flipped. For example, $01101^{\{2,4,5\}} = 00110$. The *block sensitivity* of $f\colon \{0,1\}^N \to \{0,1\}$ is $\mathrm{BSens}(f) = \max_x\big(\mathrm{BSens}(f,x)\big)$ where $\mathrm{BSens}(f,x)$ is the largest k for which there exist k disjoint blocks $I_1, \ldots, I_k$ such that $f(x^{I_j}) \neq f(x)$ for all $j \in [k]$ (f is *sensitive* to block I_j of x). The one-sided versions are $\mathrm{BSens}_b(f) = \max_{b\text{-inputs } x}\big(\mathrm{BSens}(f,x)\big)$ for each $b \in \{0,1\}$, so $\mathrm{BSens}(f) = \max\big(\mathrm{BSens}_1(f), \mathrm{BSens}_0(f)\big)$. ◄

To show $\mathrm{BSens}_b(f) \geq k$, we exhibit a b-input x and k disjoint blocks to which f is sensitive.

$\mathrm{Sens}(f,x) \leq \mathrm{BSens}(f,x)$ and so $\mathrm{Sens}_b(f) \leq \mathrm{BSens}_b(f)$ and $\mathrm{Sens}(f) \leq \mathrm{BSens}(f)$, because if f is sensitive to indices $i_1, \ldots, i_k$ on input x, then f is sensitive to blocks $I_1 = \{i_1\}, \ldots, I_k = \{i_k\}$ on input x. The freedom to have larger blocks means $\mathrm{BSens}(f)$ could be greater than $\mathrm{Sens}(f)$:

x	$f(x)$	$\text{Sens}(f,x)$
000	0	1
001	1	2
010	0	1
011	1	2
100	0	0
101	0	1
110	0	0
111	0	1

Figure 16.13: Example function for introducing sensitivity

Theorem 16.24. $\text{BSens}(F) \geq N/2$ *and* $\text{Sens}(F) \leq \sqrt{N}$ *for some family* F.

Proof. For even n and $N = n^2$, treat the input x as an $n \times n$ binary matrix, and define $F_N(x) = 1$ iff some row is all-0s except for two 1s in columns j and $j+1$ for some odd j.

BSens$(F_N) \geq n^2/2$ because on the all-0s input, F_N is sensitive to these disjoint blocks, of which there are $n/2$ in each of the n rows:

$$\begin{array}{llll} \{(1,1),(1,2)\}, & \{(1,3),(1,4)\}, & \ldots, & \{(1,n-1),(1,n)\} \\ \{(2,1),(2,2)\}, & \{(2,3),(2,4)\}, & \ldots, & \{(2,n-1),(2,n)\} \\ \vdots & \vdots & & \vdots \\ \{(n,1),(n,2)\}, & \{(n,3),(n,4)\}, & \ldots, & \{(n,n-1),(n,n)\} \end{array}$$

$\text{Sens}_1(F_N) \leq n$ because on a 1-input, say where row i is all-0s except for two 1s in columns j and $j+1$ for some odd j, F_N can't be sensitive to any bits outside of row i (but might be sensitive to the n bits in row i).

$\text{Sens}_0(F_N) \leq n$ because on a 0-input, F_N is sensitive to at most one bit in each of the n rows. For example: If a row is 000100 then F_N is sensitive only to the row's third bit. If a row is 010011 then F_N is sensitive only to the row's second bit. ■

16.4.2 Relationship with Certificate Complexity

Lemma 16.25. $\text{BSens}(f,x) \leq \text{Cert}(f,x)$ *and so* $\text{BSens}_b(f) \leq \text{Cert}_b(f)$ *and* $\text{BSens}(f) \leq \text{Cert}(f)$.

Proof. Suppose f is sensitive to disjoint blocks $I_1, \ldots, I_k$ on input x. We claim that every certificate for (f,x) must assign at least one variable in each of these blocks and therefore have size $\geq k$. If x is consistent with a but a assigns no variables in some I_j, then x^{I_j} is also consistent with a but $f(x^{I_j}) \neq f(x)$, so a isn't a certificate for f. ■

Lemma 16.26. $\text{Cert}_1(f) \leq \text{BSens}_1(f) \cdot \text{Sens}_0(f)$ *for all* f.

Proof. Consider any 1-input x. Let $I_1, \ldots, I_k$ be as many disjoint blocks as possible such that f is sensitive to each I_j on input x, where $k = \text{BSens}(f,x) \leq \text{BSens}_1(f)$. For each j, let H_j be a smallest subset of I_j to which f is still sensitive on input x. Then x^{H_j} is a 0-input, and f is sensitive to each index $i \in H_j$ on input x^{H_j} because $(x^{H_j})^i = x^{H_j \setminus \{i\}}$ is a 1-input since $H_j \setminus \{i\}$ is smaller than H_j. Thus $|H_j| \leq \text{Sens}(f, x^{H_j}) \leq \text{Sens}_0(f)$. Define the partial assignment a by $a_i = x_i$ if $i \in H_1 \cup \cdots \cup H_k$ and $a_i = *$ otherwise. Then a has size $\leq k \cdot \text{Sens}_0(f)$, and x is consistent with a, and we claim a is a certificate for f, which implies $\mathrm{Cert}(f,x) \le k \cdot \mathrm{Sens}_0(f) \le \mathrm{BSens}_1(f) \cdot \mathrm{Sens}_0(f)$. Consider any y consistent with a. Then $I = \{i : y_i \ne x_i\}$ is disjoint from each of $H_1, \ldots, H_k$. By the maximality of k, f can't be sensitive to block I on input x, so $y = x^I$ is a 1-input. ■

The next lemma strengthens $\mathrm{Det}(f) \le \mathrm{Cert}_1(f) \cdot \mathrm{Cert}_0(f)$ (Theorem 16.22) since $\mathrm{BSens}_0(f) \le \mathrm{Cert}_0(f)$ (Lemma 16.25).

Lemma 16.27. $\mathrm{Det}(f) \le \mathrm{Cert}_1(f) \cdot \mathrm{BSens}_0(f)$ *for all* f.

Proof. Suppose $\mathrm{Cert}_1(f) = k_1$ so a k_1-DNF φ expresses f (Lemma 16.20), and $\mathrm{BSens}_0(f) = k_0$. Consider the algorithm to compute f from the proof of Theorem 16.22. We improve the analysis to show it makes $\le k_1 \cdot k_0$ queries, so $\mathrm{Det}(f) \le k_1 \cdot k_0$. Throughout the algorithm, the partial assignment a records the results of queries so far, and $\varphi|_a$ is the contraction of φ with a plugged in.

Decision tree for f (16.6)

repeat until $f|_a$ is a constant function:
    pick any term of $\varphi|_a$ and query the term's variables
output the constant value of $f|_a$

Each iteration makes $\le k_1$ queries since each term of $\varphi|_a$ has $\le k_1$ variables. We show there are $\le k_0$ iterations on every input.

First, consider any 0-input x, and let k be the number of iterations. We claim that $k \le \mathrm{BSens}(f,x) \le k_0$. Let $I_1, \ldots, I_k$ be the disjoint blocks of indices queried on input x in iterations $1, \ldots, k$ respectively. For each $j \in [k]$, there exists $H_j \subseteq I_j$ such that x^{H_j} satisfies the corresponding term of φ and is thus a 1-input. (In that term, any literals with variables indexed by $I_1 \cup \cdots \cup I_{j-1}$ are already satisfied, since the term wasn't removed from $\varphi|_a$.) This means f is sensitive to each of the disjoint blocks $H_1, \ldots, H_k$ on input x, so $k \le \mathrm{BSens}(f,x)$.

On any 1-input x, there are $\le k_0$ iterations as well: Suppose for contradiction the algorithm hasn't halted after k_0 iterations on input x. At this point, some 0-input y is consistent with a, since $f|_a$ is not constant. But on input y, the algorithm would execute the same first k_0 iterations as on input x and thus not halt yet, contradicting the previous paragraph.

The algorithm can't get stuck by picking a width-0 term of $\varphi|_a$, or with $\varphi|_a$ having no terms to pick from, since then $f|_a$ would be constant and the algorithm would have halted. ■

16.4.3 The Sensitivity Theorem

A "club" of query complexity measures are polynomially related to each other: deterministic (Det), randomized ($\mathrm{Rand}_{0,1}$), certificate (Cert), sensitivity (Sens), block sensitivity (BSens), and others beyond the scope of this book. We admitted certificate complexity to the club in Theorem 16.22. We admit block sensitivity now.

Theorem 16.28. $\mathrm{Det}(f) \le \mathrm{BSens}(f)^3$ *for all* f.

Proof. Combining Lemma 16.27 and Lemma 16.26:

$$\begin{aligned}\mathrm{Det}(f) &\le \mathrm{BSens}_1(f) \cdot \mathrm{Sens}_0(f) \cdot \mathrm{BSens}_0(f)\\ &\le \mathrm{BSens}(f) \cdot \mathrm{Sens}(f) \cdot \mathrm{BSens}(f) \le \mathrm{BSens}(f)^3\end{aligned}$$

■

Sensitivity's membership in the club was a notorious, frustrating conjecture for decades. Almost since its inception, this *sensitivity conjecture* was known to follow from a certain other conjecture: Recall that the n-dimensional hypercube is the undirected graph with nodes $\{0,1\}^n$ where two nodes (bit strings) are neighbors iff they differ at only one index. A simple fact is that every set S of more than half the nodes contains a node with at least one neighbor in S (Theorem A.3). The long-conjectured strengthening—whose celebrated confirmation implied sensitivity's belated admission to the club—is that every set S of more than half the nodes contains a node with at least n^c neighbors in S, for some constant $c > 0$.

Theorem 16.29. *Every $S \subseteq \{0,1\}^n$ with $|S| > 2^{n-1}$ contains a node with $\geq \sqrt{n}$ neighbors in S.*

Theorem 16.30. $\mathrm{Det}(f) \leq 2\mathrm{Sens}(f)^6$ *for all f.*

We won't prove that Theorem 16.29 implies Theorem 16.30, which would be a somewhat lengthy detour. The proof of Theorem 16.29 is surprisingly short but comes "out of left field." Let's sit back and enjoy the show without worrying about how the proof was discovered. (Proper intuition involves eigenvectors in linear algebra.)

Proof of Theorem 16.29 (ancillary). We will find a $2^n \times 2^n$ matrix A_n with rows and columns indexed by $\{0,1\}^n$ (in lexicographic order) and a $2^n \times 1$ vector y such that:

(i) $(A_n)_{u,v} \in \{1,-1\}$ if u and v are neighbors, and otherwise $(A_n)_{u,v} = 0$.
(ii) y is nonzero.
(iii) $y_v = 0$ for all $v \notin S$.
(iv) $A_n y = \sqrt{n} y$ (over $\mathbb{R}$).

Let u be a node with the largest value of $|y_u|$. We have $|y_u| > 0$ by *(ii)*, so $u \in S$ by *(iii)*.

$$\begin{aligned}
\sqrt{n}\,|y_u| &= \left|(A_n y)_u\right| && \textit{(iv)}\\
&= \left|\textstyle\sum_v (A_n)_{u,v} y_v\right| \\
&\leq \textstyle\sum_v \left|(A_n)_{u,v}\right| |y_v| && \text{(Lemma A.28)}\\
&= \textstyle\sum_{\text{neighbors } v \in S \text{ of } u} |y_v| && \textit{(i), (iii)}\\
&\leq (\text{number of neighbors } v \in S \text{ of } u)\,|y_u| && (|y_v| \leq |y_u|)
\end{aligned}$$

Dividing both sides by $|y_u| > 0$ shows that $\sqrt{n} \leq$ number of neighbors $v \in S$ of u.

Recursively define A_n by $A_0 = \begin{bmatrix} 0 \end{bmatrix}$ and for $n > 0$,

$$A_n = \begin{bmatrix} A_{n-1} & I_{n-1} \\ I_{n-1} & -A_{n-1} \end{bmatrix}$$

where I_m is the $2^m \times 2^m$ identity matrix. Figure 16.14 shows A_1, A_2, A_3.

The recursive definition maintains *(i)* as an invariant: For entries $(A_n)_{u,v}$ in the upper left or lower right quadrants, u and v agree on their first bit, so *(i)* is maintained. For entries $(A_n)_{u,v}$ in the upper right or lower left quadrants, u and v disagree on their first bit, so they're neighbors iff they agree on all other bits, and thus I_{n-1} yields *(i)*.

The recursive definition also maintains the invariant that $(A_n)^2 = nI_n$, by block-wise matrix multiplication:

$$\begin{aligned}
A_n A_n &= \begin{bmatrix} A_{n-1}A_{n-1} + I_{n-1}I_{n-1} & A_{n-1}I_{n-1} + I_{n-1}(-A_{n-1}) \\ I_{n-1}A_{n-1} + (-A_{n-1})I_{n-1} & I_{n-1}I_{n-1} + (-A_{n-1})(-A_{n-1}) \end{bmatrix} \\
&= \begin{bmatrix} (n-1)I_{n-1} + I_{n-1} & A_{n-1} - A_{n-1} \\ A_{n-1} - A_{n-1} & I_{n-1} + (n-1)I_{n-1} \end{bmatrix} = \begin{bmatrix} nI_{n-1} & 0 \\ 0 & nI_{n-1} \end{bmatrix} = nI_n
\end{aligned}$$

$$A_1 = \left[\begin{array}{c|c} 0 & 1 \\ \hline 1 & 0 \end{array}\right]$$

$$A_2 = \left[\begin{array}{cc|cc} 0 & 1 & 1 & 0 \\ 1 & 0 & 0 & 1 \\ \hline 1 & 0 & 0 & -1 \\ 0 & 1 & -1 & 0 \end{array}\right]$$

$$A_3 = \left[\begin{array}{cccc|cccc} 0 & 1 & 1 & 0 & 1 & 0 & 0 & 0 \\ 1 & 0 & 0 & 1 & 0 & 1 & 0 & 0 \\ 1 & 0 & 0 & -1 & 0 & 0 & 1 & 0 \\ 0 & 1 & -1 & 0 & 0 & 0 & 0 & 1 \\ \hline 1 & 0 & 0 & 0 & 0 & -1 & -1 & 0 \\ 0 & 1 & 0 & 0 & -1 & 0 & 0 & -1 \\ 0 & 0 & 1 & 0 & -1 & 0 & 0 & 1 \\ 0 & 0 & 0 & 1 & 0 & -1 & 1 & 0 \end{array}\right]$$

Figure 16.14: Matrices in the proof of the sensitivity theorem

For $n > 0$ define a $2^n \times 2^{n-1}$ matrix:

$$B_n = \begin{bmatrix} A_{n-1} + \sqrt{n} I_{n-1} \\ I_{n-1} \end{bmatrix}$$

By block-wise matrix multiplication:

$$A_n B_n = \begin{bmatrix} A_{n-1}(A_{n-1} + \sqrt{n} I_{n-1}) + I_{n-1} I_{n-1} \\ I_{n-1}(A_{n-1} + \sqrt{n} I_{n-1}) + (-A_{n-1}) I_{n-1} \end{bmatrix} = \begin{bmatrix} \sqrt{n} A_{n-1} + n I_{n-1} \\ \sqrt{n} I_{n-1} \end{bmatrix} = \sqrt{n} B_n$$

Let B_n^* be the $< 2^{n-1}$ many rows of B_n not indexed by S. There exists a nonzero $2^{n-1} \times 1$ vector x such that $B_n^* x$ is all 0s by Theorem A.29 (since this is a system of $< 2^{n-1}$ linear equations in 2^{n-1} unknowns). Hence for $y = B_n x$:

(ii) y is nonzero since if $x_w \neq 0$ then $y_{1w} = x_w \neq 0$.
(iii) $y_v = 0$ for all $v \notin S$.
(iv) $A_n y = A_n B_n x = \sqrt{n} B_n x = \sqrt{n} y$. ∎

16.5 Deterministic Versus Randomized

16.5.1 Derandomization

We now admit randomized query complexity to the club of measures polynomially related to deterministic query complexity: $\mathsf{P}^{\mathsf{qc}} = \mathsf{ZPP}^{\mathsf{qc}} = \mathsf{RP}^{\mathsf{qc}} = \mathsf{BPP}^{\mathsf{qc}}$. First, we observe $\mathsf{RP}^{\mathsf{qc}} \subseteq \mathsf{NP}^{\mathsf{qc}}$:

Lemma 16.31. $\mathrm{Cert}_1(f) \leq \mathrm{Rand}_1(f)$ *for all* f.

Proof. Ignoring the probabilities in a one-sided-error randomized decision tree for f (in which each constituent deterministic decision tree has positive probability) yields a verifier decision tree of the same depth for f: Each 1-input is accepted by at least one decision tree in the set, and each 0-input is rejected by all decision trees in the set. Thus $\mathrm{Cert}_1(f) \leq \mathrm{Rand}_1(f)$ by Lemma 16.21. ∎

Lemma 16.32. $\mathrm{BSens}(f) \leq 2\mathrm{Rand}_{0,1}(f)$ *for all* f.

Proof. Suppose $\mathrm{BSens}(f) = k$ with f sensitive to some disjoint blocks $I_1, \ldots, I_k$ on some input x. Assume $f(x) = 0$, since the proof is symmetric if $f(x) = 1$. Define the partial function $g\colon \{0,1\}^k \to \{0,1\}$ by $g(y) = 0$ if y is all-0s, and $g(y) = 1$ if y has exactly one 1. That is, g is $\textsc{Or}_k$ except undefined on inputs with multiple 1s. There exists a projection reduction from g to f that maps y to z, where z is x but with the bits indexed by I_j flipped if $y_j = 1$:

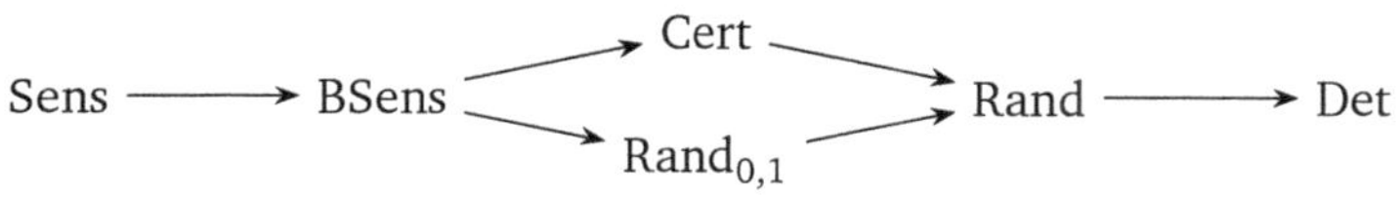

Figure 16.15: Club of polynomially related measures

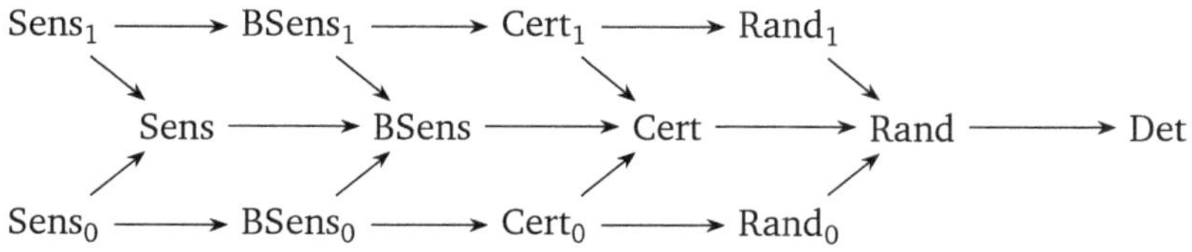

Figure 16.16: How the one-sided measures fit in

- If $i \in I_j$ for some j, then $z_i = x_i \oplus y_j$ (the literal y_j if $x_i = 0$, or $\overline{y_j}$ if $x_i = 1$).
- If $i \notin I_j$ for all j, then $z_i = x_i$ (a constant).

Indeed $g(y) = f(z)$ for all y on which g is defined:

- If $g(y) = 0$ then $z = x$, so $f(z) = 0$.
- If $g(y) = 1$ with $y_j = 1$ then $z = x^{I_j}$, so $f(z) = 1$ since f is sensitive to I_j on input x.

$\mathrm{Rand}_{0,1}(g) \le \mathrm{Rand}_{0,1}(f)$ follows by the same reasoning as in Lemma 16.5: A randomized decision tree for g on input y can simulate a randomized decision tree for f on input z.

We have $\mathrm{Rand}_{0,1}(g) \ge k/2$: Theorem 16.10 says $\mathrm{Rand}_{0,1}(\textsc{Or}_k) \ge k/2$, and the same proof works for g since the input distribution in that proof is only over valid inputs to g (strings with at most one 1). In conclusion, $\mathrm{Rand}_{0,1}(f) \ge \mathrm{Rand}_{0,1}(g) \ge k/2$. ∎

We derandomize one-sided-error randomized decision trees with quadratic overhead:

Theorem 16.33. $\mathrm{Det}(f) \le 2\mathrm{Rand}_1(f)^2$ *for all* f.

Proof. $\mathrm{Det}(f) \le \mathrm{Cert}_1(f) \cdot \mathrm{BSens}_0(f) \le \mathrm{Rand}_1(f) \cdot 2\mathrm{Rand}_1(f)$ by Lemma 16.27, Lemma 16.31, and Lemma 16.32. We used $\mathrm{BSens}_0(f) \le \mathrm{BSens}(f) \le 2\mathrm{Rand}_{0,1}(f) \le 2\mathrm{Rand}_1(f)$. ∎

We derandomize two-sided-error randomized decision trees with cubic overhead:

Theorem 16.34. $\mathrm{Det}(f) \le 8\mathrm{Rand}_{0,1}(f)^3$ *for all* f.

Proof. $\mathrm{Det}(f) \le \mathrm{BSens}(f)^3 \le (2\mathrm{Rand}_{0,1}(f))^3$ by Theorem 16.28 and Lemma 16.32. ∎

In summary: Figure 16.15 shows the club of polynomially related measures (omitting Rand_1 and Rand_0 for clarity), where $\longrightarrow$ means (left side) $\le O$(right side). Figure 16.16 shows how the one-sided measures fit in (omitting $\mathrm{Rand}_{0,1}$ for clarity).

16.5.2 Separation

$\mathrm{Det}(F) \le \mathrm{Cert}(F)^2$ for all families F (Theorem 16.22) and $\mathrm{Det}(F) \ge \mathrm{Cert}(F)^2$ for some family F (namely $\textsc{Tribes}$). That is, the largest possible separation between deterministic and certificate

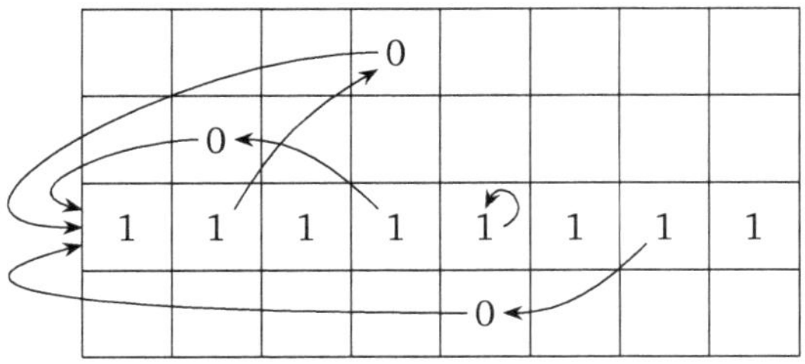

Figure 16.17: Example input for separating deterministic and randomized query complexities

complexities is quadratic. The largest possible separation between deterministic and randomized complexities is at most quadratic for zero-sided and one-sided error (Theorem 16.33) and at most cubic for two-sided error (Theorem 16.34), but can it really be that large? It was long conjectured that the answer is no and that AND-OR TREE exhibits the largest possible separation, which is subquadratic. We refute this by proving an almost-quadratic separation even for zero-sided error. So the largest separation is essentially quadratic for zero-sided and one-sided, and somewhere between quadratic and cubic for two-sided (an annoying open question). We only consider families whose relevant complexity measures are superconstant, so something trivial like $\text{Det}(F) \geq 1$ and $\text{Rand}_{0,1}(F) \leq \sqrt[3]{1}$ wouldn't count as a separation.

Theorem 16.35. $\text{Det}(F) \geq N/\text{polylog}N$ *and* $\text{Rand}(F) \leq \sqrt{N}\,\text{polylog}N$ *for some family* F.

Proof idea. Since Cert $\leq$ Rand, a quadratic separation between Det and Rand is stronger than a quadratic separation between Det and Cert. Let's recall the latter to get our bearings: Defining $f(x) = 1$ iff the $n \times n$ binary matrix x has at least one all-1s row (TRIBES), we have $\text{Det}(f) \geq n^2$ and $\text{Cert}(f) \leq n$. Unfortunately $\text{Rand}(f) \geq \Omega(n^2)$ (Exercise 16.20), so we adapt this f to make it easier for randomized decision trees without making it easier for deterministic decision trees.

First, we redefine f so $f(x) = 1$ iff the $n \times n$ binary matrix x has *exactly* one all-1s row. We still have $\text{Det}(f) \geq n^2$ and $\text{Cert}(f) \leq 2n$: A 1-certificate is an all-1s row and a 0 in each other row. A 0-certificate is either two all-1s rows or a 0 in each row. Unfortunately $\text{Rand}(f) \geq \Omega(n^2)$ still, but this f is a better starting point. To strengthen the Cert upper bound to a Rand upper bound, we further adapt f.

Since evaluating f requires finding a certificate, the key idea is to embed information about a certificate into the input itself, so a randomized querier can probably find it but an adversary can hide it from a deterministic querier. We augment 1-inputs to be "self-certifying" in the sense that the input contains pointers to the all-1s row and to a 0 in each other row. A 1-input is an $n \times 2n$ matrix with a unique all-1s row, and where half of this row's entries also contain pointers to 0s in the other rows. (Only half so an adversary can hide them.) If a querier somehow locates the all-1s row, it can read the whole row to learn where to find 0s in all other rows and be certain that $f(x) = 1$. To help a randomized querier locate the all-1s row, the pointed-to 0s point back to the all-1s row. So in every row that's not all-1s, some 0 entry has a pointer to the all-1s row. Reading any row that has few 0s would help narrow down the set of candidates for the all-1s row. A randomized querier can estimate the fraction of 0s in each remaining candidate row to find a row with few 0s and thereby home in on the all-1s row quickly.

For example, Figure 16.17 illustrates a 1-input with $n = 4$. In this input's all-1s row: The 1st pointer points to the column of a 0 in row 1. The 2nd pointer points to the column of a 0 in row 2. The 3rd pointer doesn't matter since row 3 has no 0s (but we keep this pointer for notational convenience). The 4th pointer points to the column of a 0 in row 4. ■

Proof (ancillary). For every n and for some alphabet Z, we define $f: Z^{2n^2} \to \{0,1\}$ such that $\mathrm{Det}(f) > n^2$ and $\mathrm{Rand}(f) \le O(n \log^2 n)$, assuming each query reads an entire symbol from the input. (Each internal node in a decision tree has $|Z|$ children corresponding to the queried variable's possible values.) At the end of the proof, we turn f into a boolean function exhibiting a similar separation, by simply encoding symbols in Z as bit strings.

With alphabet $Z = (\{0\} \times \{1,2,\ldots,n\}) \cup (\{1\} \times \{1,2,\ldots,2n,\mathrm{null}\})$, the input $x \in Z^{2n^2}$ is an $n \times 2n$ matrix with entries in Z. A 0-*entry* has the form (0, row pointer). A 1-*entry* has the form (1, column pointer or null).

Row i in x is *special* iff it consists of 1-entries with n column pointers $j_1, \ldots, j_n$ interspersed with n null pointers, such that in each row $h \neq i$, column j_h contains a 0-entry with row pointer i. In other words, row i is special iff it has $(1, j_1), \ldots, (1, j_n)$ (from left to right) interspersed with $(1,\mathrm{null}), \ldots, (1,\mathrm{null})$, such that $x_{h,j_h} = (0,i)$ for each $h \neq i$. Intuitively, a special row's entries are 1s pointing to 0s in all other rows, and those 0s point back to the special row.

We can check whether any particular row i is special with $3n-1$ queries: We query the $2n$ entries in row i and reject if they aren't all 1-entries or don't have exactly n column pointers. Then, assuming they're all 1-entries and have n column pointers $j_1, \ldots, j_n$, we query the $n-1$ entries x_{h,j_h} for $h \neq i$ and accept iff they're all $(0,i)$.

Define $f(x) = 1$ iff x has a special row. $\mathrm{Det}(f) > n^2$ by this adversary strategy: In each row, answer the earliest n queries $(1,\mathrm{null}), \ldots, (1,\mathrm{null})$ and the next n queries $(0,1), (0,2), \ldots, (0,n)$. After n^2 queries in total, some row i has had $\le n$ queries (since if each of the n rows had $> n$ queries, there would be $> n^2$ queries in total) and thus:

- Some 0-input is consistent with the results of queries so far: Let each row have a 0-entry if it doesn't already. Then no row is special.
- Some 1-input is consistent with the results of queries so far: Continue the adversary strategy to assign all remaining entries outside of row i. For each row $h \neq i$, let j_h be the column containing $(0,i)$. Let j_i be arbitrary. In row i, assign $(1, j_1), \ldots, (1, j_n)$ to the first n remaining entries and $(1,\mathrm{null})$ to any further remaining entries. Then row i is special.

$\mathrm{Rand}(f) \le O(n \log^2 n)$ by this randomized decision tree:

Zero-sided-error randomized decision tree for f (16.7)

```
initialize I ← [n]
for k ← 1,2,...:
    for each i ∈ I:
        query ⌈2^(k+2) ln n⌉ entries sampled independently and uniformly at random from row i
        if at least one of these is a 0-entry: remove i from I
    if |I| = 0: reject
    pick an arbitrary i ∈ I and query all entries in row i
    if at least one of these is a 0-entry:
        update I ← (I ∖ {i}) ∩ {row pointers of 0-entries in row i}
        if |I| > n/2^k: abort
        if |I| = 0: reject
    else: check whether row i is special and accept if so, and reject if not
```

If it accepts, then of course $f(x) = 1$. We argue that if $f(x) = 1$, then it doesn't reject. Each row removed from I is nonspecial because either it contains a 0-entry, or another row's 0-entries all don't point to it. Thus if row i^* is special then i^* remains in I throughout, so the algorithm never rejects with $|I| = 0$, and if it finds a row i with only 1-entries, then it sees that $i = i^*$ is special and accepts.

We argue that $\mathbf{Pr}[\text{abort}] \leq 1/3$ for every input x. At the start of iteration k, say that row $i \in I$ is *bad* iff it has $> n/2^k$ many 0-entries. In each bad row, a uniformly random entry is a 1-entry with probability $< 1-(n/2^k)/2n = 1-1/2^{k+1} \leq \mathrm{e}^{-1/2^{k+1}}$, so the row remains in I (in the middle of iteration k) with probability $< (\mathrm{e}^{-1/2^{k+1}})^{\lceil 2^{k+2}\ln n\rceil} \leq \mathrm{e}^{-2\ln n} = 1/n^2$. If the algorithm aborts in iteration k, then whichever row i is picked in the middle of the iteration must be bad. By a union bound over the $\leq n$ many bad rows:

$$\begin{aligned}\mathbf{Pr}[\text{abort in iteration } k] &\leq \mathbf{Pr}[\text{some bad row remains in } I \text{ in the middle of iteration } k]\\ &\leq \textstyle\sum_{\text{bad rows } i \text{ in iteration } k} \mathbf{Pr}[i \text{ remains in } I \text{ in the middle of iteration } k]\\ &\leq n \cdot 1/n^2 \;=\; 1/n\end{aligned}$$

The k loop has $\leq \lfloor \log n\rfloor + 1$ iterations because when $k > \log n$, it would halt with either $|I| \geq 1 > n/2^k$ or $|I| = 0$. By a union bound:

$$\mathbf{Pr}[\text{abort}] \;\leq\; \textstyle\sum_{k=1}^{\lfloor \log n\rfloor+1} \mathbf{Pr}[\text{abort in iteration } k] \;\leq\; \big(\lfloor \log n\rfloor + 1\big)/n \;\leq\; 1/3$$

Finally, we argue that the algorithm makes $O(n\log^2 n)$ queries. Iteration k starts with $|I| \leq n/2^{k-1}$ (otherwise iteration $k-1$ would have aborted) and makes $\leq \lceil 2^{k+2}\ln n\rceil$ queries in each row $i \in I$, so the inner loop over $i \in I$ makes $\leq (n/2^{k-1})\cdot\lceil 2^{k+2}\ln n\rceil \leq O(n\log n)$ queries. Then, after picking a remaining $i \in I$, the algorithm queries all $2n$ entries in row i and if they're all 1-entries, it makes $\leq n-1$ further queries. Overall, each of the outer loop's $O(\log n)$ iterations makes $O(n\log n)$ queries.

To conclude, we turn $f\colon Z^{2n^2} \to \{0,1\}$ into $F_N\colon \{0,1\}^N \to \{0,1\}$ where $N = 2n^2\lceil \log|Z|\rceil = \Theta(n^2\log n)$ by representing symbols in Z as strings in $\{0,1\}^{\lceil \log|Z|\rceil}$. (Some symbols get two representations if $|Z|$ isn't a power of 2.)

$\mathrm{Det}(F_N) \geq \mathrm{Det}(f) > n^2 \geq \Omega(N/\log N)$ since we could turn any decision tree for F_N into a same-depth decision tree for f by simulating each query to a bit of F_N's input with a query to the corresponding symbol of f's input.

$\mathrm{Rand}(F_N) \leq \mathrm{Rand}(f)\cdot\lceil \log|Z|\rceil \leq O(n\log^3 n) \leq O(\sqrt{N}\log^{2.5} N)$ since we could turn any randomized decision tree for f into a randomized decision tree for F_N by simulating each query to a symbol of f's input with queries to all $\lceil \log|Z|\rceil$ corresponding bits of F_N's input. ■

16.6 Decision Tree Size

For convenience, we define a decision tree's *size* as its number of leaves. This is within a factor of 2 of its number of nodes (Lemma A.7). The *decision tree size complexity* of $f\colon \{0,1\}^N \to \{0,1\}$, denoted $\mathrm{DTSize}(f)$, is the size of a smallest decision tree that computes f. Every f has $\mathrm{DTSize}(f) \leq 2^N$ since f is computed by a size-2^N decision tree that queries all N bits.

16.6.1 Simple Bounds

Lemma 16.36. $\mathrm{DTSize}(f) \geq \mathrm{Det}(f) + 1$ *for all* f.

Proof. Consider any decision tree for f. The path from the root to some leaf v has $\geq \mathrm{Det}(f)$ internal nodes, each of which has a child that is off the path and that has at least one leaf in its subtree. Thus the decision tree has $\geq \mathrm{Det}(f)$ leaves in addition to v. ■

DTSize(OR) $\le N+1$ since a trivial decision tree for OR_N has $N+1$ leaves (of which N accept and 1 rejects), which is tight since DTSize(OR) $\ge$ Det(OR) $+1 = N+1$. This demonstrates that we can't always turn small decision trees into shallow decision trees. In contrast, we can always turn small formulas into shallow formulas (Theorem 6.22).

Lemma 16.37. *If every certificate for f has size $\ge d$, then* DTSize$(f) \ge 2^d$.

Proof. Consider any decision tree for f. For each leaf, the associated partial assignment (the results of queries along the path from the root) is a certificate for f and so has size $\ge d$. Since every root-to-leaf path has length $\ge d$, there must be $\ge 2^d$ leaves. ■

Here are some consequences of Lemma 16.37:

- It captures the technique we used to prove DTSize(PARITY) $\ge 2^N$ (Theorem 5.21).
- DTSize(INDEX) $\ge 2^{k+1}$ (where $N = 2^k + k$) since the proof of Theorem 16.2 shows that every certificate has size $\ge k+1$. This matches the upper bound DTSize(INDEX) $\le 2^{k+1}$ from the decision tree in §16.1.1.
- DTSize(MAJORITY) $\ge 2^{N/2}$ since every certificate must reveal at least half the input bits.
- DTSize(TRIBES) $\ge 2^n = 2^{\sqrt{N}}$ since every certificate must reveal either an all-1s row or a 0 in each row of the $n \times n$ input matrix.
- DTSize(MAJ TREE) $\ge 2^d$ (where $N = 3^d$) since the proof of Theorem 16.19 shows that every certificate has size $\ge 2^d$.

The next section improves the MAJORITY and TRIBES lower bounds using a more sophisticated technique. For MAJORITY, the trivial upper bound 2^N is almost tight. For TRIBES, the trivial upper bound $2^N = (2^n)^n$ is far from tight:

Theorem 16.38. DTSize(TRIBES) $\le n^0 + n^1 + n^2 + \cdots + n^n = O(n^n)$.

Proof. Consider this decision tree:

Decision tree for TRIBES	(16.8)

for $i \leftarrow 1,\ldots,n$:
    read row i's bits from left to right, stopping as soon as a 0 is seen
    if no 0 was seen in row i: accept
reject	

There are n^n rejecting leaves since each of the n rows has n possible locations for its first 0. There are n^{i-1} accepting leaves corresponding to row i being the first all-1s row, since each of the first $i-1$ rows has n possible locations for its first 0. Thus the decision tree has $n^0 + n^1 + n^2 + \cdots + n^{n-1} + n^n = (n^{n+1} - 1)/(n-1) = O(n^n)$ leaves. ■

16.6.2 Fooling Sets

For any bit b, a *b-fooling set* for $f: \{0,1\}^N \to \{0,1\}$ is a set S of b-inputs such that for all distinct $x, y \in S$, there exists a $\overline{b}$-input z such that $z_i \in \{x_i, y_i\}$ for all i. (This is unrelated to "fooling" in the context of pseudorandomness.)

Lemma 16.39. DTSize(f) *is at least the size of a largest fooling set for f. Specifically, if f has a b-fooling set of size s, then every decision tree for f has at least s leaves that output b.*

Proof. Let S be a b-fooling set of size s for f. We claim that in every decision tree for f, inputs in S must lead to different leaves, so at least s many leaves output b. Suppose for contradiction that in some decision tree for f, some distinct $x, y \in S$ lead to the same leaf, which outputs b. There exists a $\overline{b}$-input z such that $z_i \in \{x_i, y_i\}$ for all i. Thus z also leads to the same leaf as x and y, and the decision tree is "fooled" into incorrectly outputting b on input z. ■

The trivial upper bound DTSize(MAJORITY) $\leq 2^N$ is almost tight:

Theorem 16.40. DTSize(MAJORITY) $\geq 2^{(1-o(1))N}$.

Proof. Assume N is even. (It's similar when N is odd.) The set of all weight-$N/2$ inputs is a 0-fooling set because for any two such inputs $x \neq y$, if we define z by $z_i = x_i \vee y_i \in \{x_i, y_i\}$ for all i, then z is a 1-input since it has weight $> N/2$. This 0-fooling set has size $\binom{N}{N/2} \geq 2^N/(N+1) \geq 2^{(1-o(1))N}$ since $\sum_{k=0}^{N} \binom{N}{k} = 2^N$ and $\binom{N}{N/2}$ is the largest of the $N+1$ many binomial coefficients $\binom{N}{0}$, $\binom{N}{1}, \ldots, \binom{N}{N-1}, \binom{N}{N}$: The latter sequence increases up to $\binom{N}{N/2}$ and decreases thereafter because $\binom{N}{k}/\binom{N}{k-1} = (N-k+1)/k$ is > 1 for $k \leq N/2$ and < 1 for $k > N/2$. ■

The upper bound DTSize(TRIBES) $\leq O(n^n)$ (Theorem 16.38) is almost tight:

Theorem 16.41. DTSize(TRIBES) $\geq n^n$.

Proof. The set of all inputs with exactly one 0 in each row is a 0-fooling set of size n^n: Consider any two such inputs $x \neq y$. For some row i and column j, we have $x_{i,j} = 0$ and $y_{i,j} = 1$. If z is x except $z_{i,j} = y_{i,j}$, then z is a 1-input since row i is all-1s. ■

16.7 Branching Program Size

A *branching program* is a dag with a designated start node, and where each nonsink node is labeled by an input variable and has two outgoing edges labeled 0 and 1, and with two sinks labeled 0 (reject) and 1 (accept). On input $a \in \{0,1\}^N$, it traverses a path from the start node: At a node labeled x_i, it *queries* (reads) this input bit and follows the edge labeled a_i. It outputs the label of the sink reached.

A branching program's *depth* is the length (number of edges) of a longest start-to-sink path. Everything about decision tree depth applies to branching program depth also (Theorem 6.1.*(ii)*).

For convenience, we define a branching program's *size* as its number of nonsink nodes. The *branching program size complexity* of $f\colon \{0,1\}^N \to \{0,1\}$, denoted BPSize($f$), is the size of a smallest branching program that computes f. Every f has BPSize(f) $<$ DTSize(f) $\leq 2^N$ since a decision tree has fewer internal nodes than leaves, and coalescing the leaves into two sinks yields a branching program.

16.7.1 General Branching Programs

BPSize(F) $\geq \Omega(2^N/N)$ for some F (Theorem 5.20), but the nonconstructive proof doesn't explicitly describe any particular such F. The largest known BPSize lower bound for any $F \in$ NP is roughly quadratic. We now develop the technique to prove this. For any $I \subseteq [N]$, say $a \in \{0,1,*\}^N$ is an *I-partial assignment* iff $a_i = *$ for all $i \in I$ and $a_i \neq *$ for all $i \notin I$. For any $f\colon \{0,1\}^N \to \{0,1\}$ and I-partial assignment a, say $f|_a$ is an *I-restriction* of f. Distinct I-partial assignments might yield the same I-restriction of f. Figure 16.18 shows an example.

x_3x_4	$f\|_{00**}(x_3x_4)$
00	1
01	0
10	1
11	1

x_1x_2	x_3x_4	$f(x_1x_2x_3x_4)$
00	00	1
00	01	0
00	10	1
00	11	1
01	00	0
01	01	1
01	10	1
01	11	0
10	00	0
10	01	0
10	10	0
10	11	1
11	00	1
11	01	0
11	10	1
11	11	1

x_3x_4	$f\|_{01**}(x_3x_4)$
00	0
01	1
10	1
11	0

x_3x_4	$f\|_{10**}(x_3x_4)$
00	0
01	0
10	0
11	1

x_3x_4	$f\|_{11**}(x_3x_4)$
00	1
01	0
10	1
11	1

Figure 16.18: This f has four $\{3,4\}$-partial assignments but only three distinct $\{3,4\}$-restrictions

Lemma 16.42. *If f has r distinct I-restrictions, then every branching program for f has at least $(\log r)/(|I|+2\log\log r)$ nodes labeled by variables indexed by I.*

Proof. Consider any branching program B for f, with s nodes labeled by variables indexed by I. For every I-partial assignment a, the contraction $B|_a$ is a size-s branching program computing the restriction $f|_a$ (§5.5.2). Let t be the number of possible size-s branching programs with variables indexed by I. Then $t \le |I|^s((s+1)!)^2 \le (|I|s^2)^s$ since we may assume the start node is first in a topological order and the sinks are last, and the jth nonsink node has $|I|$ options for its variable and $(s+2-j)^2$ options for its two outneighbors.

Since f has r many I-restrictions but B has at most t many I-contractions, we have $t \ge r$ and thus $s \ge (\log r)/(|I|+2\log\log r)$. This is because if $s < (\log r)/(|I|+2\log\log r)$ then:

$$t \;\le\; (|I|s^2)^s \;<\; (\log^2 r)^s \;<\; (2^{2\log\log r})^{(\log r)/2\log\log r} \;=\; 2^{\log r} \;=\; r \qquad \blacksquare$$

For n a power of 2 and $N = 2n\log n$, define ELEMENT DISTINCTNESS$_N(x) = 1$ iff the $n \times 2\log n$ binary matrix x has distinct rows (no two rows are equal). We can solve this problem in quasi-linear time and space by sorting the rows and comparing adjacent pairs of rows, or in log space by comparing all pairs of rows, which yields BPSize(ELEMENT DISTINCTNESS) $\le \operatorname{poly} N$.

Theorem 16.43. BPSize(ELEMENT DISTINCTNESS) $\ge \Omega(n^2) = \Omega((N/\log N)^2)$.

Proof. Let f = ELEMENT DISTINCTNESS$_N$. For each $i \in [n]$, let I_i be the indices of row i's entries. We claim that f has at least $\binom{n^2}{n-1}$ distinct I_i-restrictions. Consider any size-$(n-1)$ subset

$S \subseteq \{0,1\}^{2\log n}$ of the n^2 possible row strings. For an I_i-partial assignment a that assigns S's elements to non-i rows, we have $f|_a(y) = 1$ iff $y \notin S$. Thus the $\binom{n^2}{n-1}$ possibilities of S yield distinct I_i-restrictions.

Now, we claim that $\binom{n^2}{n-1} \geq n^n$: If we partition a size-n^2 set U into n size-n parts, then exactly n^n size-$(n-1)$ subsets $S \subseteq U$ contain at most one element from each part: There are n options for which part has no elements included in S, and for each of the other $n-1$ parts, there are n options for which element to include in S.

By Lemma 16.42 with $r = n^n$ and $\log r = n \log n$, every branching program for f has at least

$$(\log r)/(|I_i| + 2\log\log r) \;=\; (n\log n)/(2\log n + 2\log(n\log n)) \;\geq\; (n\log n)/(6\log n) \;=\; n/6$$

nodes labeled by variables in row i. Since this holds for each of the n rows, every branching program for f has size $\geq n^2/6$. ■

16.7.2 Read-Once Branching Programs

A straightforward branching program for MAJORITY$_N$ reads the input from left to right, remembering how many 1s and how many 0s there have been, and accepts once it has seen $> N/2$ many 1s, and rejects once it has seen $\geq N/2$ many 0s. Figure 16.19 shows this for $N = 5$: Rows correspond to number of 1s so far (which could be $0, \ldots, \lfloor N/2 \rfloor$ before accepting), and columns correspond to number of 0s so far (which could be $0, \ldots, \lceil N/2 \rceil - 1$ before rejecting). This shows BPSize(MAJORITY) $\leq (\lfloor N/2 \rfloor + 1) \cdot \lceil N/2 \rceil \leq N^2$. Surprisingly, BPSize(MAJORITY) $\leq N \operatorname{polylog} N$ by a much more complicated branching program.

The straightforward branching program for MAJORITY$_N$ is *read-once*, which means every start-to-sink path reads each variable at most once. ROBPSize(f) is the size of a smallest read-once branching program that computes f. In this model, input bits are fleeting—unavailable for rereading—but can be stored in work memory at a cost in space. Perhaps input bits come from sensors that can't reproduce their readings on demand. ROBPSize(f) < DTSize(f) since decision trees are read-once.

For MAJORITY, the straightforward read-once upper bound is exactly tight:

Theorem 16.44. ROBPSize(MAJORITY) $= (\lfloor N/2 \rfloor + 1) \cdot \lceil N/2 \rceil = \Theta(N^2)$.

Proof idea. To show that every read-once branching program's nodes must remember how many 1s and how many 0s have been read, we use a variant of the fooling set technique (§16.6.2): We specify paths—rather than inputs—that must lead to different nodes. The read-once property ensures that every start-to-sink path is traversed by some input. (For example, a non-read-once branching program could have a path that reads $x_1 = 0$ then $x_2 = 1$ then $x_1 = 1$, which no input would traverse.) Thus to find a "bad" input—which a too-small read-once branching program errs on—it suffices to find a bad path. ■

Proof. We already observed the upper bound. For the lower bound, let's just consider odd N. (The case of even N is essentially the same.) Consider any read-once branching program B for MAJORITY$_N$. Any path from the start node that reads $\leq \lfloor N/2 \rfloor$ many 1s and $\leq \lfloor N/2 \rfloor$ many 0s is traversed by some 0-input and some 1-input (since B is read-once) and thus doesn't reach a sink. For each pair $(k,\ell) \in \{0,\ldots,\lfloor N/2 \rfloor\}^2$, let $v_{k,\ell}$ be the nonsink node reached by the path $P_{k,\ell}$ where the edge labels are k many 1s followed by ℓ many 0s. We claim the nodes $v_{k,\ell}$ are distinct, so B has at least $\lceil N/2 \rceil^2$ nonsink nodes. Suppose for contradiction $v_{k,\ell} = v_{k',\ell'}$ for some $(k,\ell) \neq (k',\ell')$. Suppose $k \neq k'$, say $k < k'$. (The case $\ell \neq \ell'$ is analogous.) Let Q be the path

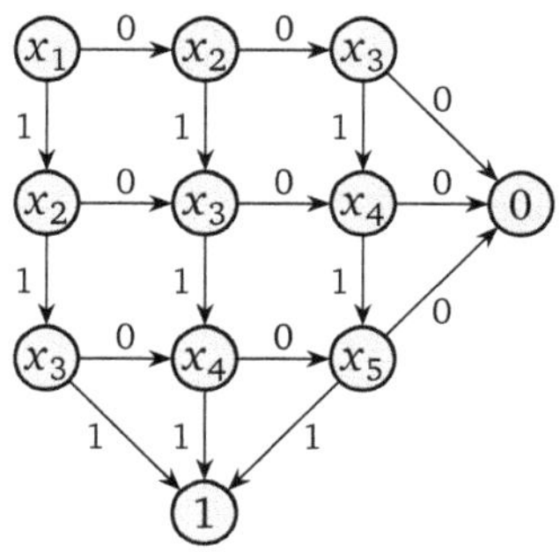

Figure 16.19: Read-once branching program for $\text{M}\textsc{ajority}_5$

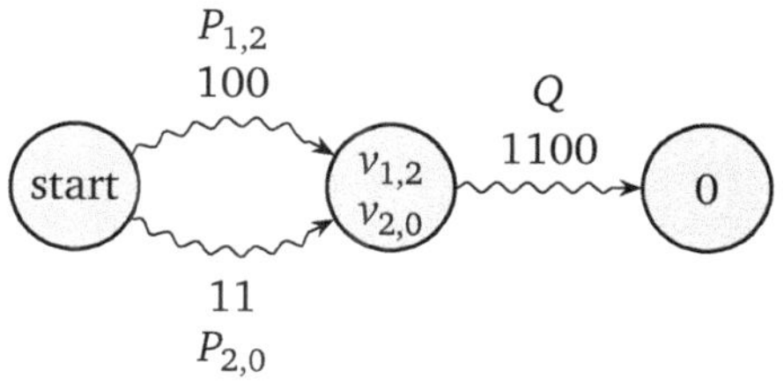

Figure 16.20: Example for Theorem 16.44

from $v_{k,\ell} = v_{k',\ell'}$ where the edge labels are $\lfloor N/2 \rfloor - k$ many 1s followed by $\lceil N/2 \rceil - \ell$ many 0s. The combined path $P_{k,\ell}Q$ reads $\lfloor N/2 \rfloor$ many 1s and doesn't read $\lceil N/2 \rceil$ many 0s until the very last query, so Q must end at the reject node. But since B is read-once, some input traverses the combined path $P_{k',\ell'}Q$ and is rejected despite having $k' + \lfloor N/2 \rfloor - k \geq \lceil N/2 \rceil$ many 1s. Thus B doesn't compute $\text{M}\textsc{ajority}_N$. Figure 16.20 shows an example with $N = 7$. ∎

Exponential ROBPSize lower bounds are known for some explicit families.

16.7.3 Streaming Branching Programs

A *streaming* branching program (§7.8.1) is a read-once branching program that always reads the entire input from left to right: The nodes are partitioned into layers with the start node in layer 1 and the sinks in layer $N+1$, and all nodes in layer $i \leq N$ read the ith input bit and have edges to layer $i+1$. SBPSize(f) is the size of a smallest streaming branching program that computes f. (The read-once branching program for MAJORITY in §16.7.2 isn't quite streaming, because it sometimes skips to a sink without reading the rest of the input.) This is a nonuniform model of streaming algorithms (§8.5.3).

Recall that $\text{I}\textsc{ndex}_N(x,y) = x_y$ where $N = 2^k + k$ and the k-bit binary number y is an index into the 2^k-bit string x. The natural decision tree for INDEX shows ROBPSize(INDEX) $\leq 2^{k+1} - 1 = O(N)$ but crucially reads y before x. Streaming branching programs must read x before y, and INDEX prods this sore spot of the model. All of x must be remembered, since any bit of x might be the correct output:

Theorem 16.45. SBPSize(INDEX) $\geq 2^{2^k} = 2^{(1-o(1))N}$.

Proof. Consider any streaming branching program B of size $< 2^{2^k}$. In particular, layer $2^k + 1$ has $< 2^{2^k}$ nodes. By the pigeonhole principle, some distinct strings $x, x' \in \{0,1\}^{2^k}$ lead B to the same node v in layer $2^k + 1$. For some $y \in \{0,1\}^k$, we have $x_y \neq x'_y$ and thus $\text{I}\textsc{ndex}_N(x,y) \neq \text{I}\textsc{ndex}_N(x',y)$. But $B(x,y) = B(x',y)$ since these inputs traverse the same path after reaching v. (B forgets whether it saw x or x' so far.) Thus B errs on either (x,y) or (x',y). ∎

Another perspective is *one-way communication*: Alice has x. Bob has y. Bob wants to know x_y. Alice can send Bob a message that depends on x. Bob can't send Alice anything. We argued that Alice must send Bob all of x (a 2^k-bit message) since she has no idea which bit Bob wants. Nodes in layer $2^k + 1$ of a streaming branching program correspond to messages Alice could send Bob. This segues into the next chapter, on two-way (back and forth) communication.

Exercises

16.1 Prove GREATER THAN is evasive, where GREATER THAN$(x, y) = 1$ iff $x > y$ where $x = x_{n-1} \cdots x_0$ and $y = y_{n-1} \cdots y_0$ are binary numbers in $\{0, 1, \ldots, 2^n - 1\}$.

16.2 Prove that if $f : \{0,1\}^N \to \{0,1\}$ is nonconstant and *symmetric*, meaning $f(x)$ only depends on x's weight (number of 1s), then f is evasive.

16.3 Prove that if $f : \{0,1\}^N \to \{0,1\}$ has an odd number of 1-inputs, then f is evasive.

16.4 Define $F : \{0,1\}^+ \to \{0,1\}$ by $F(x) = 1$ iff x contains the substring 01.

(a) Prove that if N is odd then F_N is nonevasive. Hint: Query the even-index bits first.

(b) Prove that if N is even then F_N is evasive, and if N is odd then $\text{Det}(F_N) = N - 1$. Hint: Use Exercise 16.3.

16.5 Define $F : \{0,1\}^+ \to \{0,1\}$ by $F(x) = 1$ iff x contains the substring 11.

(a) Prove that if $N \bmod 3 = 1$ then F_N is nonevasive. Hint: Query the second bit first.

(b) Prove that if $N \bmod 3 \neq 1$ then F_N is evasive, and if $N \bmod 3 = 1$ then $\text{Det}(F_N) = N - 1$. Hint: Use Exercise 16.3. To determine (number of 1-inputs of F_N) mod 2, consider three cases for whether $x_N = 0$ or $x_{N-1}x_N = 01$ or $x_{N-1}x_N = 11$.

16.6 Prove that the undirected graph property "Is there a degree-$(n-4)$ node w, each of whose neighbors is only adjacent to w?" is nonevasive for $n \geq 12$ nodes. Hint: First, look for w by querying all possible edges between the first $\lfloor n/2 \rfloor$ nodes and the last $\lceil n/2 \rceil$ nodes.

16.7 Prove that the undirected graph property "Is there a cycle?" is evasive for $n \geq 3$ nodes.

16.8 **(a)** Prove that the directed graph property "Is there an outdegree-0 node?" is evasive.

(b) Prove that the undirected graph property "Is there a degree-0 node?" is evasive. Hint: Design an adversary strategy that maintains the following invariant (for the partial assignment a recording the results of queries so far): The edges $\{u, v\}$ with $a_{\{u,v\}} = 1$ form a tree connecting a subset of nodes S. For every $\{u, v\} \subseteq S$, we have $a_{\{u,v\}} \neq *$. For every $u \notin S$, there exists $v \in S$ with $a_{\{u,v\}} = *$.

16.9 Prove CELEBRITY $\in \mathsf{TIME}[\sqrt{N}]$ when the input is encoded as an adjacency matrix.

16.10 Theorem 16.4 showed $\text{Det}(\text{CELEBRITY}) = \Theta(n)$. Prove $\text{Det}(\text{CELEBRITY}) = 3(n-1) - \lfloor \log n \rfloor$.

(a) Prove the upper bound. Hint: During the querier versus adversary game, define a node v's *query-degree* $\text{qdeg}(v)$ as the number of v's edges (incoming and outgoing) that have been queried so far. Adjust the decision tree from Theorem 16.4 so it queries (u, v) for distinct contenders u, v of lowest query-degrees. Argue that $\text{qdeg}(w) \geq \lfloor \log n \rfloor$ at the start of the second phase.

(b) Prove the lower bound. Hint: Prove that the following adversary strategy's first phase maintains the invariant that after round $i \leq n - 1$, every node in T is a contender and $|T| = n - i$ and $\sum_{t \in T} 2^{\text{qdeg}(t)} \leq n$.

Adversary strategy for CELEBRITY	(16.9)

initialize $T \leftarrow [n]$
repeat $n-1$ times:
    the querier picks some (u,v)
    if $u, v \in T$:
        if $\text{qdeg}(u) \leq \text{qdeg}(v)$: respond 0 and remove v from T
        else: respond 1 and remove u from T
    else: respond arbitrarily and remove from T either:
        u if $u \in T$, or v if $v \in T$, or an arbitrary node otherwise
let w be the only remaining node in T
repeat:
    the querier picks some (u,v)
    respond 0 if $u = w$, or 1 if $v = w$, or arbitrarily otherwise	

16.11 For any functions $f\colon \{0,1\}^N \to \{0,1\}$ and $g\colon \{0,1\}^M \to \{0,1\}$, define their *composition* $f \circ g^N\colon (\{0,1\}^M)^N \to \{0,1\}$ by $(f \circ g^N)(y^1, y^2, \ldots, y^N) = f\big(g(y^1), g(y^2), \ldots, g(y^N)\big)$ where each y^i is a block of M variables. Prove $\text{Det}(f \circ g^N) = \text{Det}(f)\text{Det}(g)$.

16.12 Prove MAJ TREE is evasive.

16.13 **(a)** Design a poly-space algorithm for this function problem.

QUERY COMPLEXITY OF CIRCUIT	(16.10)
Input: Circuit computing some $f\colon \{0,1\}^n \to \{0,1\}$ Output: $\text{Det}(f)$	

(b) Design a poly-time algorithm for this function problem.

QUERY COMPLEXITY OF TRUTH TABLE	(16.11)
Input: Truth table of some $f\colon \{0,1\}^n \to \{0,1\}$ Output: $\text{Det}(f)$	

Hint: For each partial assignment a in increasing order of number of $*$s, compute $\text{Det}(f|_a)$.

16.14 If $f\colon \{0,1\}^N \to \{0,1\}$ is a partial function (possibly undefined on some inputs), then $\text{Det}(f)$ is the depth of a shallowest decision tree that computes f for all inputs on which f is defined. The querier versus adversary game ends when $f|_a$ evaluates to the same bit for all inputs on which $f|_a$ is defined (or when it's undefined on all inputs).

Define PARITY OF SORTED to be PARITY but only defined on inputs in which all 0s precede all 1s. Prove $\text{Det}(\text{PARITY OF SORTED}) = \lceil \log(N+1) \rceil$.

16.15 Query complexity for search problems is defined just like for decision problems. On input x, a decision tree must reach a leaf that is labeled with an acceptable solution for x (or reports that none exists).

Prove that for every unsatisfiable 2-CNF φ with N variables, the following (fixed input size) search problem has deterministic query complexity $O(\log N)$: The input is an assignment $x \in \{0,1\}^N$, and the output is any clause of φ that x doesn't satisfy. Hint: Exercise 2.12.

16.16 (a) Design a technique for lower bounding Rand_1 analogous to Lemma 16.9's technique for lower bounding $\text{Rand}_{0,1}$.

(b) Use it to prove $\text{Rand}_1(\text{OR}) = \lceil 2N/3 \rceil$.

16.17 Prove $\text{Rand}_{0,1,\varepsilon}(\text{OR}) = \left\lceil \frac{1-2\varepsilon}{1-\varepsilon} N \right\rceil$ where $\text{Rand}_{0,1,\varepsilon}$ is like $\text{Rand}_{0,1}$ but with error probability ε instead of $1/3$.

16.18 MAJORITY_5 evaluates to 1 iff at least three of the five input bits are 1s.

(a) Prove $\text{Rand}^*(\text{MAJORITY}_5) = 4.5$.

(b) Define MAJ_5 TREE like MAJ TREE but using MAJORITY_5 instead of MAJORITY_3. Prove $\text{Rand}^*(\text{MAJ}_5\ \text{TREE}) \leq N^{\log_5(4.5)} < N^{0.935}$.

16.19 Recall that $\text{INDEX}_N(x, y) = x_y$ where the binary number $y = y_{k-1} \cdots y_0$ is an index into $x = x_0 \cdots x_{2^k-1}$ (where $N = 2^k + k$). Prove $\text{Rand}_{0,1}(\text{INDEX}) \geq k+1$ using Lemma 16.9.

(a) Prove that $D =$ uniform distribution over $\{0,1\}^{2^k} \times \{0,1\}^k$ *doesn't* work for this.

(b) Prove that the following distribution D works: Sample $y \in \{0,1\}^k$ and $b \in \{0,1\}$ independently and uniformly at random, and for each $i \in \{0,1\}^k$ let $x_i = \oplus(i) \oplus b$ (the parity of i, xored with b).

16.20 Recall that $\text{TRIBES}_N(x) = 1$ iff the $n \times n$ binary matrix x has at least one all-1s row (where $N = n^2$).

(a) Prove $\text{Rand}^*(\text{TRIBES}) = \Omega(N)$ using Lemma 16.11 with the input distribution D_0 that's uniformly random over all matrices with exactly one 0 in each row.

(b) Strengthen this to prove $\text{Rand}_{0,1}(\text{TRIBES}) = \Omega(N)$ using Lemma 16.9 (but with error $1/5$ instead of $1/3$) with the input distribution $D = D_0/2 + D_1/2$ (toss a coin to choose whether to sample from D_0 or D_1) where D_1 is like D_0 but with a uniformly random row being all-1s. Hint: Show that every depth-$N/400$ deterministic decision tree is unlikely to query more than $n/10$ many 0s of $x \sim D_0$.

16.21 For any $f: \{0,1\}^N \to \{0,1\}$ and M, define $g: (\{0,1\}^N)^M \to \{0,1\}$ by $g(x^1, x^2, \ldots, x^M) = f(x^1) \vee f(x^2) \vee \cdots \vee f(x^M)$.

(a) Prove $\text{Rand}_1(g) \leq M \cdot \text{Rand}_1(f)$.

(b) Prove $\text{Rand}_0(g) \leq O(M) \cdot \text{Rand}_0(f)$.

16.22 For N a power of 2, exhibit a projection reduction from PARITY_N to AND-OR TREE_{N^2}.

16.23 Determine the exact certificate complexity for each of these:

(a) INDEX

(b) CONNECTED

(c) CELEBRITY

(d) AND-OR TREE

16.24 A decision tree or DNF for a partial function f must output $f(x)$ for all x such that $f(x)$ is defined. Det(f) is the depth of a shallowest decision tree for f. Cert$_1$(f) is the smallest k for which some k-DNF expresses f. Cert$_0$(f) is the smallest k for which some k-DNF expresses $\overline{f}$.

(a) Theorem 16.22 showed that $\mathsf{P}^{\mathsf{qc}} = \mathsf{NP}^{\mathsf{qc}} \cap \mathsf{coNP}^{\mathsf{qc}}$ for total functions. Prove that this is false for partial functions. Hint: For even N, define the partial function $F_N\colon \{0,1\}^N \to \{0,1\}$ where the input is promised to have exactly one 1, and $F_N(x) = 1$ if the 1 is in the left half, and $F_N(x) = 0$ if the 1 is in the right half.

(b) Suppose a partial function f has a k_1-DNF φ_1 and $\overline{f}$ has a k_0-DNF φ_0 such that no x (for which $f(x)$ may be undefined) satisfies both φ_1 and φ_0. Prove Det(f) $\leq k_1 \cdot k_0$.

16.25 Consider any $f\colon \{0,1\}^N \to \{0,1\}$ and $x \in \{0,1\}^N$ and $J \subseteq [N]$, and define the partial assignment a by $a_i = x_i$ if $i \in J$ and $a_i = *$ if $i \notin J$. Prove that a is a certificate for f iff J intersects every block of x that f is sensitive to.

16.26 Prove that if f is monotone (flipping input bits from 0 to 1 never flips the output from 1 to 0) then Sens(f) = BSens(f) = Cert(f).

16.27 Prove that BSens$_0$(f) $\geq k$ iff there exists a projection reduction from g to f, where the partial function $g\colon \{0,1\}^k \to \{0,1\}$ is defined by $g(y) = 0$ if y is all-0s, and $g(y) = 1$ if y has exactly one 1.

16.28 A DNF is *unambiguous* iff every input satisfies at most one term. UCert$_1$(f) is the smallest k for which some unambiguous k-DNF expresses f. $\mathsf{UP}^{\mathsf{qc}}$ is the class of all total F with UCert$_1$(F) $\leq$ polylog N. This is the query complexity analogue of UP (§8.3.1).

(a) Prove UCert$_1$(f) $\leq$ Det(f) for all f.

(b) Prove that if UCert$_1$(f) $= k$ then the number of 1-inputs of f is a multiple of 2^{N-k}. Conclude that UCert$_1$(OR) $= N$.

(c) Prove Det(f) $\leq$ UCert$_1$(f)^2 for all f, and hence $\mathsf{P}^{\mathsf{qc}} = \mathsf{UP}^{\mathsf{qc}}$.

(d) Prove that the largest possible separation between Det and UCert$_1$ is essentially quadratic: Det(F) $\geq N/$polylog N and UCert$_1$(F) $\leq \sqrt{N}$ polylog N for some family F. Hint: This is like the Det versus Rand separation (Theorem 16.35) but without row pointers from 0s. The input $x \in Z^{2n^2}$ is an $n \times 2n$ matrix with entries in $Z = \{0\} \cup (\{1\} \times \{1, 2, \ldots, 2n, \text{null}\})$. Define $f(x) = 1$ iff some row i is *special*, meaning it has $(1, j_1), \ldots, (1, j_n)$ interspersed with $(1, \text{null}), \ldots, (1, \text{null})$, such that $x_{h, j_h} = 0$ for each $h \neq i$.

16.29 Prove that if $f\colon \{0,1\}^N \to \{0,1\}$ has a 1-fooling set of size s, then every DNF for f has at least s many terms.

16.30 **(a)** Prove that PARITY has randomized decision tree size complexity $\Omega(2^N)$ (with two-sided error probability 1/3).

(b) Deduce that AND-OR TREE has randomized decision tree size complexity $\Omega(2^{\sqrt{N}})$ by a projection reduction from PARITY (Exercise 16.22).

16.31 This exercise concerns "decision trees" where internal nodes can evaluate certain functions of the input, not just query individual input variables.

(a) Let $\text{Det}^{\oplus}(f)$ be the depth of a shallowest decision tree for f where each internal node can evaluate the parity of any subset of input variables. Define $\text{Rand}_1^{\oplus}(f)$ analogously. Prove $\text{Det}^{\oplus}(\textsc{Or}) = N$ and $\text{Rand}_1^{\oplus}(\textsc{Or}) = O(1)$. Hint: Every underdetermined homogeneous system of linear equations over $\mathbb{Z}_2$ has a nontrivial solution (Theorem A.29).

(b) Let $\text{Det}^{\wedge}(f)$ be the depth of a shallowest decision tree for f where each internal node can evaluate the $\wedge$ of any subset of input variables. Let $\text{Det}^{(0)}(f)$ be the "depth" of a "shallowest" ordinary decision tree for f where only edges labeled 0 contribute to the "depth." Prove $\text{Det}^{(0)}(f) \leq \text{Det}^{\wedge}(f) \leq \text{Det}^{(0)}(f) \cdot O(\log N)$ for all $f\colon \{0,1\}^N \to \{0,1\}$.

(c) Let $\text{Det}^{\text{Term}}(f)$ be the depth of a shallowest decision tree for f where each internal node can evaluate any term. Prove $\text{Det}^{\text{Term}}(f) \approx \log(\text{DTSize}(f))$, specifically $\log_2(\text{DTSize}(f))/\log_2(N+1) \leq \text{Det}^{\text{Term}}(f) \leq \log_{3/2}(\text{DTSize}(f))$ for all $f\colon \{0,1\}^N \to \{0,1\}$. Hint: The latter $\leq$ is like balancing formulas (Theorem 6.22).

16.32 Prove that a branching program B is read-once (every start-to-sink path in B reads each variable at most once) iff on every input, B reads each variable at most once.

16.33 For arbitrary $K \leq N$, define $f\colon \{0,1\}^N \to \{0,1\}$ by $f(x) = 1$ iff x has at least K many 1s. Determine $\text{ROBPSize}(f)$.

Notes

For a survey on query complexity, see [97]. For a survey of inclusions and separations between pairs of query complexity measures, see Table 1 in [2].

The conjecture that every nonconstant monotone graph property is evasive is also known as the Aanderaa–Karp–Rosenberg conjecture [448]. Nonevasiveness of Celebrity (Theorem 16.4) is due to [448]. Every nonconstant monotone undirected graph property has deterministic query complexity $\Omega(N)$ [445, 470] and randomized query complexity $\Omega(N^{2/3})$ [229] and is evasive when the number of nodes is a prime power [283].

In contrast to our notation Rand, Rand_0, Rand_1, and $\text{Rand}_{0,1}$, the literature often uses subscripts 0 for zero-sided error and 1 for one-sided error and no subscript for two-sided error. Our notation is more compatible with Cert, Cert_0, Cert_1, though.

Deducing randomized worst-case lower bounds from deterministic average-case lower bounds (Lemma 16.9 and Lemma 16.11) is due to [568] and is often called "Yao's principle."

$\text{Rand}^*(\textsc{Maj Tree}) < N^{0.887}$ is due to [358]. $\text{Rand}_{0,1}(\textsc{Maj Tree}) > N^{0.868}$ is due to [211].

$\text{Rand}^*(\textsc{And-Or Tree}) = \Theta(N^{\log_2(c)})$ where $c = (1+\sqrt{33})/4$ is due to [458]. The qualitatively stronger lower bound $\text{Rand}_{0,1}(\textsc{And-Or Tree}) \geq \Omega(N^{\log_2(c)})$ is due to [460].

$\text{Det}(f) \leq \text{Cert}_1(f) \cdot \text{Cert}_0(f) \leq \text{Cert}(f)^2$ (Theorem 16.22) is due to [233, 69, 515].

$\text{BSens}(F) \geq \Omega(\text{Sens}(F)^2)$ for some F (Theorem 16.24) is due to [454].

$\text{Cert}_1(f) \leq \text{BSens}_1(f) \cdot \text{Sens}_0(f)$ (Lemma 16.26) is due to [392].

$\text{Det}(f) \leq \text{Cert}_1(f) \cdot \text{BSens}_0(f)$ (Lemma 16.27) is due to [51].

The key component of the sensitivity theorem (Theorem 16.29) is due to [255], with simplifications due to Shalev Ben-David and Donald Knuth. The fact that this implies the sensitivity theorem (Theorem 16.30) is due to [397, 218, 369].

$\text{Det}(f) \le 2\text{Rand}_1(f)^2$ (Theorem 16.33) and $\text{Det}(f) \le 8\text{Rand}_{0,1}(f)^3$ (Theorem 16.34) are due to [392]. The essentially quadratic separation between Det and Rand (Theorem 16.35), as well as an essentially quadratic separation between Rand_0 and Rand_1, are due to [24].

An essentially cubic separation between $\text{Rand}_{0,1}$ and Sens is due to [59]. An essentially cubic separation between Cert and Sens is due to [46]. An essentially quadratic separation between Cert and BSens is due to [190].

A historically important application of query complexity of partial functions is in proving "relativization" barriers [45], which imply limitations on diagonalization.

DTSize(MAJ TREE) and DTSize(AND-OR TREE) are $2^{\Omega(N)}$ [279].

Log of randomized decision tree size complexity is polynomially related to log of deterministic decision tree size complexity, up to a polylog N factor [113].

For a text on branching programs, see [556].

BPSize(ELEMENT DISTINCTNESS) $\ge \Omega((N/\log N)^2)$ (Theorem 16.43) follows from [386]. It's known that BPSize(MAJORITY) is N polylog N [494] and $\omega(N)$ [44]. ROBPSize(MAJORITY) $\ge \Omega(N^2)$ (Theorem 16.44) follows from [361].

Exercise 16.6 is due to [64]. Exercise 16.13.b is due to [225]. Exercise 16.15 is due to [348]. Exercise 16.26 is due to [392]. Exercise 16.28.d is due to [215]. Exercise 16.31.b is due to [345]. Exercise 16.31.c is due to [113].

Regarding Exercise 16.13, QUERY COMPLEXITY OF CIRCUIT is PSPACE-hard and QUERY COMPLEXITY OF TRUTH TABLE is NC^1-hard [344].

Chapter 17

Communication Protocols

Suppose the input is distributed across multiple parties, who send each other messages to collaboratively solve a problem on their joint input. They wish to minimize the total amount of communication over the network. Other challenges of distributed computing include synchronization (machines might have unpredictable delays) and fault tolerance (the system shouldn't fail if one machine fails). Also, the usual resources of time and space still matter. But this chapter focuses on the number of bits communicated. We assume local computation costs are cheap enough to disregard, and communication is predictable and reliable. We also assume there are only two parties, Alice and Bob (borrowing terminology from cryptography). Our hands will be full even with these assumptions.

We prove that some distributed problems can be solved with little communication, while others require lots of communication. We'll also see applications of communication complexity to settings that don't explicitly feature communication: Some kinds of computations involve information flowing implicitly from place to place, which we treat as messages between parties.

17.1 Deterministic Communication Complexity

17.1.1 Two-Party Protocols

Consider a function $f: X \times Y \to \{0,1\}$ where X and Y are finite sets. Alice gets input $x \in X$, Bob gets input $y \in Y$, and they should both output $f(x,y)$. A *communication protocol* is an algorithm for this setting. At each step, a protocol specifies whether the computation is finished and if so, the output value, and if not, who talks and what message they send, based on their own input and all the messages so far. See Figure 17.1. The precise definition is in §17.1.2.

Every f has a trivial protocol: Alice sends Bob x using $\lceil \log |X| \rceil$ bits. Then Bob, who now knows both x and y, evaluates $f(x,y)$ and sends Alice this one bit. They both output $f(x,y)$ after communicating $\lceil \log |X| \rceil + 1$ bits in total. If $|Y| < |X|$, they could swap their roles. Often $X = Y = \{0,1\}^N$, in which case a trivial protocol uses $N+1$ bits of communication. Some functions admit more clever protocols that use less communication.

Consider Parity: $X = Y = \{0,1\}^N$ and $f(x,y)$ is the parity (mod 2 sum) of all $2N$ bits in the joint input (x,y). Here's a protocol with two bits of communication: Alice sends Bob x's parity (one bit). Bob sends Alice y's parity (one bit). They both output the xor of these two bits.

Consider Majority: $X = Y = \{0,1\}^N$ and $f(x,y) = 1$ iff $\text{weight}(xy) > N$ (where weight means number of 1s). Here's a protocol with $\lceil \log(N+1) \rceil + 1$ bits of communication: Alice sends Bob $\text{weight}(x) \in \{0,\ldots,N\}$ using $\lceil \log(N+1) \rceil$ bits. Then, Bob sends Alice the bit indicating whether $\text{weight}(x) + \text{weight}(y) > N$. They both output this bit.

A charming example is Clique Versus Independent Set: For some undirected graph G (with no multi-edges or self-loops) known in advance to both parties, X is the set of all cliques in G (subsets of nodes with all possible edges between them), and Y is the set of all independent

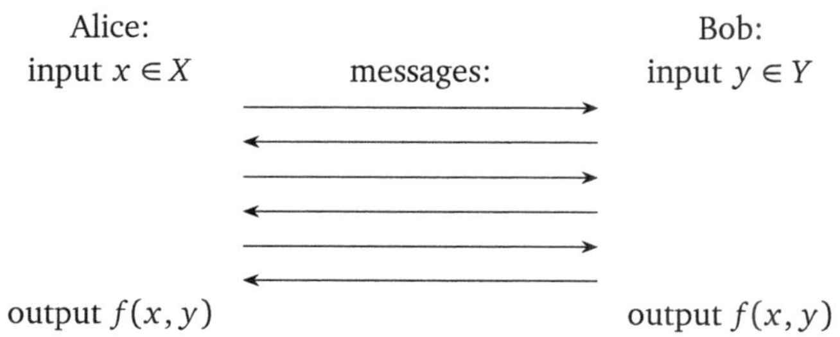

Figure 17.1: Alice and Bob communicate to compute f

sets in G (subsets of nodes with no edges between them). Alice gets a clique x, and Bob gets an independent set y. Note that $|x \cap y| \in \{0,1\}$ because if $x \cap y$ contained distinct nodes u and v, then $\{u,v\}$ would be an edge (since $u,v \in x$ and x is a clique) but not an edge (since $u,v \in y$ and y is an independent set). The goal is to compute $f(x,y) = |x \cap y|$ (determine whether x and y have a node in common).

Theorem 17.1. *For every n-node graph G,* Clique Versus Independent Set *has a protocol with* $O(\log^2 n)$ *bits of communication.*

Proof idea. Suppose x and y have a unique node w in common. Alice and Bob try to find w quickly by ruling out as many other nodes as possible. If Alice tells Bob the identity of some node $u \in x$, this rules out u's non-neighbors since w and u are neighbors. If Bob tells Alice the identity of some node $v \in y$, this rules out v's neighbors since w and v are non-neighbors. It's always possible for either Alice or Bob to eliminate about half the remaining nodes, since w itself is either neighbors with or non-neighbors with at least half the remaining nodes (besides itself). Thus Alice and Bob can narrow it down to a single candidate for w after $O(\log n)$ iterations, each of which communicates $O(\log n)$ bits to identify a node u or v. ■

Proof. Here's the protocol. A node is considered neither a neighbor nor a non-neighbor of itself.

Protocol for Clique Versus Independent Set on a graph G (17.1)

initialize $S \leftarrow$ set of all n nodes
repeat until $|S| = 1$:
  if $x \cap S$ contains a node u with $\leq (|S|-1)/2$ neighbors in S:
    Alice sends Bob such a u, and they remove u's non-neighbors from S
  else:
    Alice tells Bob there's no such node
    if $y \cap S$ contains a node v with $\leq (|S|-1)/2$ non-neighbors in S:
      Bob sends Alice such a v, and they remove v's neighbors from S
    else: Bob rejects and tells Alice to reject
let w be the unique remaining node in S
Alice says whether $w \in x$, and Bob says whether $w \in y$, and they accept iff $w \in x \cap y$

The protocol maintains the invariant that $x \cap y \subseteq S$ because if Alice sends u, then no node of x is removed from S, and if Bob sends v, then no node of y is removed from S. If the loop reaches $|S| = 1$, then the output is correct by the invariant: $x \cap y$ is either $\{w\}$ or $\emptyset$. To conclude that the protocol is correct, we argue that if $|x \cap y| = 1$ then Alice and Bob don't reject inside the loop:

Suppose $x \cap y$ contains a node w, and consider any loop iteration. Then $w \in x \cap S$ and $w \in y \cap S$ by the invariant. Among the $|S|-1$ nodes in S besides w, either at most half are neighbors of w and so Alice sends $u = w$ or another u, or at most half are non-neighbors of w and so Bob sends $v = w$ or another v. In either case, they don't reject.

Now, we analyze the efficiency. In each iteration, $|S|-1$ decreases by at least a factor of 2: Letting S and S' denote the set before and after some iteration, we have $|S'| \le (|S|-1)/2+1$ because S' retains $\le (|S|-1)/2$ many neighbors of u or non-neighbors of v, and the $+1$ is for u or v itself. Thus $|S'|-1 \le (|S|-1)/2$. After at most $\lceil \log n \rceil$ iterations, the loop must reach $|S| = 1$ (or reject). Each iteration communicates $\log n + O(1)$ bits. In total, $O(\log^2 n)$ bits are communicated. ∎

17.1.2 The Model

Protocols are like decision trees except each internal node is labeled by a function of either Alice's input or Bob's input (rather than by an input variable).

Definition. A *protocol* with domain $X \times Y$ is an out-tree (with edges directed away from the root) where each internal node v is labeled by $\big(\text{Alice}, \ g_v : X \to \{0,1\}\big)$ or $\big(\text{Bob}, \ g_v : Y \to \{0,1\}\big)$ and has two outgoing edges labeled 0 (to the left child) and 1 (to the right child), and each leaf is labeled by an output bit.

A protocol is a kind of algorithm to compute a *two-party function* $f : X \times Y \to \{0,1\}$. On input (x,y), it traverses a path from the root: At a node labeled $\big(\text{Alice}, \ g_v : X \to \{0,1\}\big)$, it follows the edge labeled $g_v(x)$ (Alice sends Bob this bit). At a node labeled $\big(\text{Bob}, \ g_v : Y \to \{0,1\}\big)$, it follows the edge labeled $g_v(y)$ (Bob sends Alice this bit). It outputs the label of the leaf reached. ◀

A protocol with only one node (the root is a leaf) computes a constant function.

If a node v in a protocol is *unused* (never reached on any input), then we might as well remove v's subtree and replace v's parent with v's sibling.

A protocol's *depth* is the length (number of edges) of a longest root-to-leaf path. The depth of a protocol without unused nodes equals the *communication efficiency*—the maximum over all $(x,y) \in X \times Y$ of the number of bits communicated on input (x,y). The deterministic *communication complexity* of $f : X \times Y \to \{0,1\}$, denoted $\text{Det}(f)$, is the depth of a shallowest protocol that computes f. (Det also denotes query complexity in Chapter 16, but the context will always disambiguate this overloaded notation.)

If F is an infinite family of two-party functions $F_N : \{0,1\}^N \times \{0,1\}^N \to \{0,1\}$, then $\text{Det}(F)$ is the function that maps N to $\text{Det}(F_N)$, for all N such that F_N is defined. Every such F has $\text{Det}(F) \le N+1$ because Alice can send Bob her entire N-bit input, and then Bob can send Alice the output bit. For big-Ω lower bounds on $\text{Det}(F)$, we only quantify over N for which F_N is defined. We may also consider families where the input sets don't have the form $\{0,1\}^N \times \{0,1\}^N$. For example, Clique Versus Independent Set is a family where each graph G (rather than each integer N) has an associated two-party function.

For any protocol and any input, the *transcript* is the bit string consisting of the edge labels along the root-to-leaf computation path. The transcript's length is the number of bits communicated. The bits themselves don't really matter, because we could swap any node's left and right subtrees. Intuitively, transcripts correspond to leaves. Also, we may assume the last communicated bit is the output.

Each message is one bit, but the parties need not alternate. A party could send multiple bits consecutively, as a single *round*. In practice, fewer rounds may be better. But this chapter focuses mainly on the total number of bits, regardless of who sends them.

A *(combinatorial) rectangle* is a cartesian product $A \times B \subseteq X \times Y$, for some $A \subseteq X$ and $B \subseteq Y$.

Lemma 17.2. *For each node v in a protocol, the set $R_v \subseteq X \times Y$ of all inputs that lead to v is a rectangle.*

Proof. We claim that following any path from the root maintains the invariant that R_v is a rectangle. First, $R_{\text{root}} = X \times Y$. To see that the invariant is maintained, assume $R_v = A \times B$ for some v with children v_0 and v_1. If Alice talks at v, then A is partitioned into A_0 and A_1 where $A_c = \{x \in A : g_v(x) = c\}$, so $R_v = A \times B$ is partitioned into $R_{v_0} = A_0 \times B$ and $R_{v_1} = A_1 \times B$. That is, (x, y) leads to v_c iff (x, y) leads to v and $g_v(x) = c$. If Bob talks at v, then B is partitioned into B_0 and B_1 where $B_c = \{y \in B : g_v(y) = c\}$, so $R_v = A \times B$ is partitioned into $R_{v_0} = A \times B_0$ and $R_{v_1} = A \times B_1$. In both cases, R_{v_0} and R_{v_1} are rectangles. ■

If $R_v = A \times B$ and Alice talks at v, then the protocol can just specify $g_v : A \to \{0,1\}$ rather than $g_v : X \to \{0,1\}$, because if $x \notin A$ then (x, y) doesn't reach v and so $g_v(x)$ is immaterial. If Bob talks at v, then the protocol can just specify $g_v : B \to \{0,1\}$ rather than $g_v : Y \to \{0,1\}$.

A protocol's leaves partition $X \times Y$ into rectangles. (Not every partition into rectangles corresponds to a protocol, though.) With respect to $f : X \times Y \to \{0,1\}$, a rectangle R is *monochromatic* iff $f(x, y)$ is the same for all $(x, y) \in R$. The bit $f(x, y)$ is the "color" of input (x, y), and "monochromatic" means "only one color." In other words, R is monochromatic iff the *restriction* $f|_R : R \to \{0,1\}$ is a constant function, where naturally $f|_R(x, y) = f(x, y)$ for all $(x, y) \in R$. If v is a leaf in a protocol for f, then R_v is monochromatic since v's output label is the color of all inputs that lead to v:

Corollary 17.3. *The leaves of a protocol for $f : X \times Y \to \{0,1\}$ partition $X \times Y$ into monochromatic rectangles.* ■

Every $f : X \times Y \to \{0,1\}$ corresponds to a binary matrix M with rows indexed by X and columns indexed by Y, where $M_{x,y} = f(x, y)$. The restriction of f to a rectangle $A \times B$ corresponds to the submatrix of M with (possibly noncontiguous) rows A and columns B. Sometimes it helps to visualize a rectangle's rows and columns as contiguous even though they needn't be.

Example. Figure 17.2 shows the matrix of some $f : \{0,1\}^2 \times \{0,1\}^2 \to \{0,1\}$ and a depth-2 protocol computing f, so $\text{Det}(f) \leq 2$. The black bits in each node v correspond to R_v. For instance, input $(10, 00)$ leads to the second leaf from the left, with transcript 01. ♦

17.1.3 Lower Bounds

For case studies, we consider these families of functions $F_N : \{0,1\}^N \times \{0,1\}^N \to \{0,1\}$.

- EQUALITY: $\text{EQ}_N(x, y) = 1$ iff $x = y$.
- GREATER THAN: $\text{GT}_N(x, y) = 1$ iff $x > y$ as binary numbers in $\{0, \ldots, 2^N - 1\}$.
- DISJOINTNESS: $\text{DISJ}_N(x, y) = 1$ iff $\{i : x_i = 1\}$ is disjoint from $\{i : y_i = 1\}$.
- INNER PRODUCT: $\text{IP}_N(x, y) = x \odot y = \sum_i x_i y_i \bmod 2$.

Figure 17.3 shows these functions with $N = 2$.

A protocol's *size* is its number of leaves (transcripts), like a decision tree's size (§16.6). Note that size $\leq 2^{\text{depth}}$ and thus depth $\geq \log(\text{size})$, so to prove depth lower bounds, it suffices to prove size lower bounds. We present two techniques, which are analogues of two techniques for decision tree size lower bounds: the "fooling set" method (Lemma 16.39) and the "no small certificate" method (Lemma 16.37).

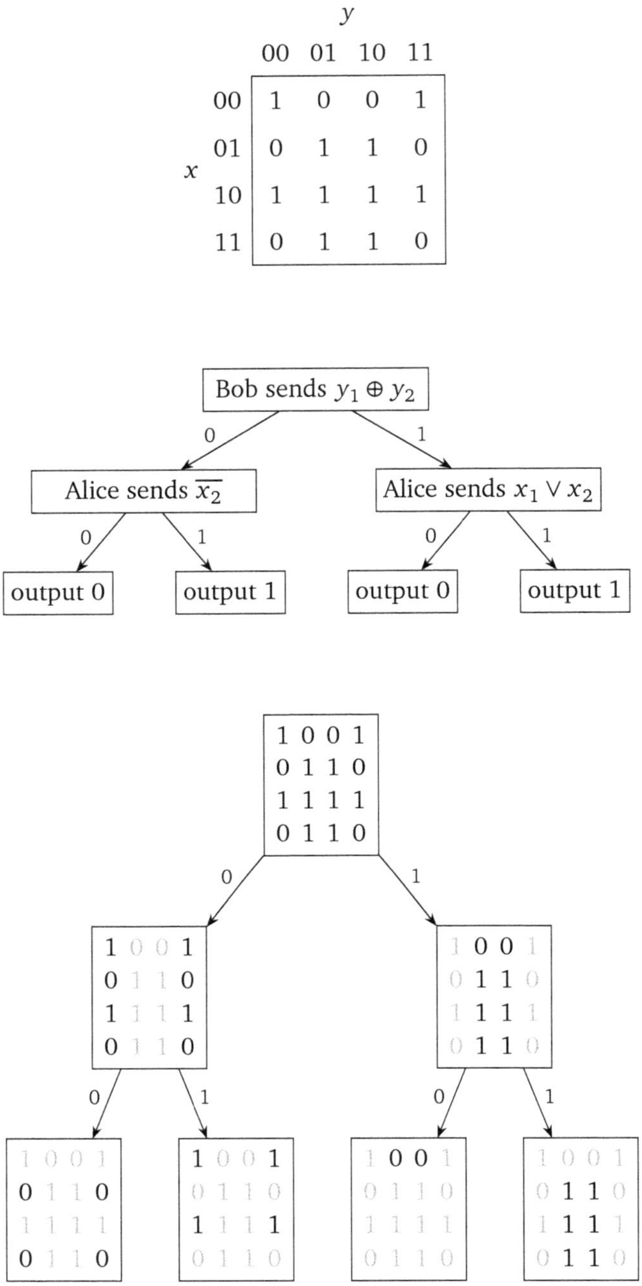

Figure 17.2: Example communication protocol

EQ$_2$

	00	01	10	11
00	1	0	0	0
01	0	1	0	0
10	0	0	1	0
11	0	0	0	1

GT$_2$

	00	01	10	11
00	0	0	0	0
01	1	0	0	0
10	1	1	0	0
11	1	1	1	0

DISJ$_2$

	00	01	10	11
00	1	1	1	1
01	1	0	1	0
10	1	1	0	0
11	1	0	0	0

IP$_2$

	00	01	10	11
00	0	0	0	0
01	0	1	0	1
10	0	0	1	1
11	0	1	1	0

Figure 17.3: "Case study" two-party functions with $N = 2$

For any bit b, a *b-fooling set* for $f : X \times Y \to \{0,1\}$ is a set S of b-inputs such that for all distinct $(x,y),(x',y') \in S$, either (x,y') or (x',y) is a $\overline{b}$-input. Figure 17.4 illustrates a 1-fooling set of size 3.

Lemma 17.4. *If f has a b-fooling set of size $s \geq 2$, then* $\mathrm{Det}(f) > \log s$.

Proof. Let S be a b-fooling set of size s for f. We claim that in every protocol for f, inputs in S must lead to different leaves, so the protocol has at least s leaves that output b and at least one leaf that outputs $\overline{b}$ (since $s \geq 2$) and thus has size $> s$ and depth $> \log s$. Suppose for contradiction that in some protocol for f, some distinct $(x,y),(x',y') \in S$ lead to the same leaf v, which outputs b. Since $(x,y),(x',y') \in R_v$ and R_v is a rectangle (Lemma 17.2), we have $(x,y'),(x',y) \in R_v$ (because if $R_v = A \times B$ then $x,x' \in A$ and $y,y' \in B$). Thus the protocol outputs b on both inputs $(x,y'),(x',y)$, which is incorrect since at least one of them is a $\overline{b}$-input. ■

Theorem 17.5. $\mathrm{Det}(\text{EQUALITY}) = N + 1$.

Proof. $S = \{(x,x) : x \in \{0,1\}^N\}$ (the matrix's diagonal) is a 1-fooling set for EQ$_N$ because for all distinct $(x,x),(x',x')$, either (x,x') or (x',x) (in fact, both) is a 0-input since $x \neq x'$. Therefore $\mathrm{Det}(\text{EQ}_N) > \log|S| = N$ (Lemma 17.4). ■

Theorem 17.6. $\mathrm{Det}(\text{GREATER THAN}) = N + 1$.

Proof. $S = \{(x,x) : x \in \{0,1\}^N\}$ (the matrix's diagonal) is a 0-fooling set for GT$_N$ because for all distinct $(x,x),(x',x')$, either (x,x') or (x',x) is a 1-input since either $x > x'$ or $x' > x$. Therefore $\mathrm{Det}(\text{GT}_N) > \log|S| = N$ (Lemma 17.4). ■

Theorem 17.7. $\mathrm{Det}(\text{DISJOINTNESS}) = N + 1$.

Proof. $S = \{(x,\overline{x}) : x \in \{0,1\}^N\}$ (where $\overline{x}$ is the bitwise negation) is a 1-fooling set for DISJ$_N$ because for all distinct $(x,\overline{x}),(x',\overline{x'})$ with $x_i \neq x'_i$ for some i, either $(x,\overline{x'})$ or $(x',\overline{x})$ is a 0-input since either $x_i = \overline{x'}_i = 1$ or $x'_i = \overline{x}_i = 1$. Therefore $\mathrm{Det}(\text{DISJ}_N) > \log|S| = N$ (Lemma 17.4). ■

INNER PRODUCT has no fooling set of size $> (N+1)^2$ (though we won't prove this), so the "fooling set" method can't yield $\mathrm{Det}(\text{INNER PRODUCT}) \geq \omega(\log N)$. We use the "no large monochromatic rectangle" method, which is an analogue of the "no small certificate" method. The size of a rectangle $A \times B$ is $|A \times B| = |A||B|$.

Lemma 17.8. *If every monochromatic rectangle for $f : X \times Y \to \{0,1\}$ has size $\leq s$, then* $\mathrm{Det}(f) \geq \log(|X||Y|/s)$.

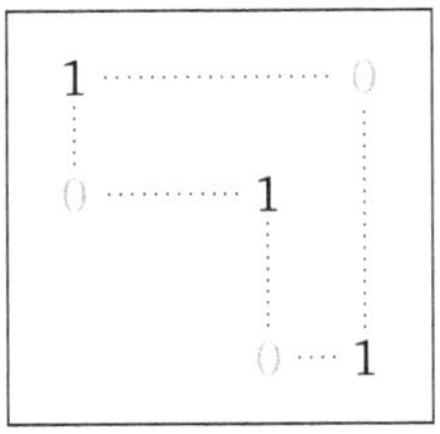

Figure 17.4: 1-fooling set of size 3

Proof. The leaves of a protocol for f partition the set of all $|X||Y|$ inputs into monochromatic rectangles (Corollary 17.3), each of which has size $\le s$, so the number of leaves is $\ge |X||Y|/s$. ■

Theorem 17.9. Det(INNER PRODUCT) $\ge N$.

Proof. This is not difficult to prove using standard linear algebra, but instead we use Corollary 11.32, which says that in the matrix of IP_N, every submatrix of size $\ge 2^N/4\varepsilon^2$ is ε-balanced—the fraction of entries that are 1s is within $\pm\varepsilon$ of $1/2$. Every rectangle of size $> 2^N$ has size exactly $2^N/4\varepsilon^2$ for some $\varepsilon < 1/2$ and is therefore ε-balanced and thus not monochromatic—the fraction of entries that are 1s is > 0 and < 1. Since every monochromatic rectangle has size $\le 2^N$, $\mathrm{Det}(\mathrm{IP}_N) \ge \log\big(2^N 2^N/2^N\big) = N$ (Lemma 17.8). ■

17.1.4 Reductions

We consider a special type of mapping reduction tailored to communication complexity: Alice and Bob can compute the mapping without communicating. This is like how projection reductions are tailored to query complexity (§16.1.4). A *rectangular reduction* from $f\colon X \times Y \to \{0,1\}$ to $f'\colon X' \times Y' \to \{0,1\}$ is a pair of functions $h_{\text{Alice}}\colon X \to X'$ and $h_{\text{Bob}}\colon Y \to Y'$ such that $f(x,y) = f'\big(h_{\text{Alice}}(x), h_{\text{Bob}}(y)\big)$ for all $(x,y) \in X \times Y$.

Lemma 17.10. *If* $(h_{\text{Alice}}, h_{\text{Bob}})$ *is a rectangular reduction from* f *to* f'*, then* $\mathrm{Det}(f) \le \mathrm{Det}(f')$.

Proof. We turn a depth-$\mathrm{Det}(f')$ protocol for f' into a protocol for f without increasing the depth: On input (x,y), Alice evaluates $x' = h_{\text{Alice}}(x)$, and Bob evaluates $y' = h_{\text{Bob}}(y)$, and they run the protocol for f' on input (x',y'), which outputs $f'(x',y') = f(x,y)$. ■

So to deduce a lower bound for f' from a lower bound for f, we can exhibit a rectangular reduction from f to f'. Let's see two examples.

The upper bound Det(MAJORITY) $\le \lceil \log(N+1) \rceil + 1$ (§17.1.1) is essentially tight:

Theorem 17.11. Det(MAJORITY) $> \log(N+1)$.

Proof. Define $f' = \mathrm{MAJ}_N\colon \{0,1\}^N \times \{0,1\}^N \to \{0,1\}$ by $f'(x',y') = 1$ iff $\mathrm{weight}(x'y') > N$. Define $f\colon \{0,\dots,N\} \times \{0,\dots,N\} \to \{0,1\}$ by $f(x,y) = 1$ iff $x > y$. That is, f is effectively GREATER THAN but with $\{0,\dots,N\}$ instead of $\{0,\dots,2^N-1\}$. Since $\big\{(x,x) : x \in \{0,\dots,N\}\big\}$ is a 0-fooling set of size $N+1$ for f, we have $\mathrm{Det}(f) > \log(N+1)$ like in Theorem 17.6. By Lemma 17.10, it suffices to exhibit a rectangular reduction from f to f': Map (x,y) to $(x',y') = (1^x 0^{N-x}, 1^{N-y} 0^y)$. Then $f'(x',y') = f(x,y)$ since $\mathrm{weight}(x'y') = x + N - y$ is $> N$ iff $x > y$. ■

Let CIS_G be the CLIQUE VERSUS INDEPENDENT SET function for a graph G. Theorem 17.1 says $\mathrm{Det}(\mathrm{CIS}_G) \le O(\log^2 n)$ for all n-node graphs G.

Theorem 17.12. $\mathrm{Det}(\mathrm{CIS}_G) > \log n$ *for all n-node graphs G.*

Proof idea. The special case of CIS_G where Alice's and Bob's sets each contain one node amounts to checking whether these two nodes are equal. ■

Proof. Define $f' = \mathrm{CIS}_G$ by $f'(x', y') = |x' \cap y'|$ where x' is a clique and y' is an independent set in $G = (V, E)$. Define $f: V \times V \to \{0,1\}$ by $f(x,y) = 1$ iff $x = y$. That is, f is effectively EQUALITY but with the set of nodes V instead of $\{0,1\}^N$. Since $\{(x,x) : x \in V\}$ is a 1-fooling set of size n for f, we have $\mathrm{Det}(f) > \log n$ like in Theorem 17.5. By Lemma 17.10, it suffices to exhibit a rectangular reduction from f to f': Map (x, y) to $(x', y') = (\{x\}, \{y\})$. (Individual nodes are cliques and independent sets.) Then $f'(x', y') = f(x, y)$ since $|x' \cap y'| = 1$ iff $x = y$. ■

It's known that $\mathrm{Det}(\mathrm{CIS}_G)$ is close to $\Omega(\log^2 n)$ for some n-node graphs G, but even a $\omega(\log n)$ lower bound was an open question for a long time.

17.1.5 Balancing Protocols

Our communication complexity lower bound techniques were based on "depth ≥ log(size)". Maybe, for some functions, we could prove a depth lower bound that's much better than log(size)? No, because protocols can be balanced like formulas can (Theorem 6.22). We can turn any small protocol into an equivalent shallow protocol:

$$\text{depth of new protocol} \leq O\big(\log(\text{size of original protocol})\big)$$

So if we're not picky about constant factors, then to lower bound depth, we might as well lower bound log(size). (This is not true for decision trees.)

Theorem 17.13. *If f has a size-ℓ communication protocol, then* $\mathrm{Det}(f) \leq 2\log_{3/2}(\ell)$.

Proof. Let T be a size-ℓ protocol for f. (T for "tree," ℓ for "leaves.") For any non-root node v:

- Let $R_v = A_v \times B_v$ be the rectangle of inputs that reach v.
- Let T_v be the protocol rooted at v. Thus, T_v agrees with T on inputs in R_v.
- Let T_{-v} be T but with v's subtree deleted and with v's parent deleted and replaced with v's sibling. Thus, T_{-v} agrees with T on inputs not in R_v.

This recursive subroutine returns a depth-$2\log_{3/2}(\ell)$ protocol T' for f:

Algorithm to balance a protocol (17.2)

```
balance(T):
    if T has only one leaf: return T
    if T has ℓ ≥ 2 leaves:
        find a node v whose subtree has ≤ 2ℓ/3 but > ℓ/3 leaves using Lemma 6.23
        let (T_v)' ← balance(T_v) and (T_−v)' ← balance(T_−v)
        return T' in which Alice says whether x ∈ A_v, and Bob says whether y ∈ B_v,
            and if both hold then they run (T_v)', and otherwise they run (T_−v)'
```

This maintains the invariant that T' agrees with T on all inputs, since on inputs in R_v, T' runs $(T_v)'$ which agrees with T_v, and on inputs not in R_v, T' runs $(T_{-v})'$ which agrees with T_{-v}. Since T_v and T_{-v} each have $\leq 2\ell/3$ leaves, the number of levels of recursive calls—not counting base case calls, which correspond to leaves—is $\leq \log_{3/2}(\ell)$. Each level contributes 2 to the depth (Alice and Bob each send one bit). Thus T' has depth $\leq 2\log_{3/2}(\ell)$, so $\mathrm{Det}(f) \leq 2\log_{3/2}(\ell)$. ■

17.2 Randomized Communication Complexity

17.2.1 The Models

We consider two models of randomized communication protocols: *private-coin* and *public-coin*. In the private-coin model, Alice and Bob can't see each other's coin tosses, unless they send each other the outcomes and get "charged" for the communication. In the public-coin model, a single sequence of coin tosses is visible to both Alice and Bob without any communication—perhaps they did the coin tosses together in advance (like agreeing on a private key for cryptography in Chapter 12). Public coins are less realistic than private coins, but it hardly matters because we prove that public coins can be made private with little overhead in communication.

- In a private-coin protocol, Alice and Bob get independent and uniformly random strings $r_{\text{Alice}}, r_{\text{Bob}} \in \{0,1\}^m$. At each Alice node, her message is a function of (x, r_{Alice}). At each Bob node, his message is a function of (y, r_{Bob}).
- In a public-coin protocol, Alice and Bob get the same uniformly random string $r \in \{0,1\}^m$. At each Alice node, her message is a function of (x, r). At each Bob node, his message is a function of (y, r).

The randomness efficiency m may be arbitrarily large. Instead of just the uniform distribution over $\{0,1\}^m$, we could allow arbitrary distributions, but this would have virtually no effect since we can approximate any distribution to any precision using enough uniform coin tosses. For example, to simulate probabilities $1/3$ and $2/3$, we could partition $\{0,1\}^m$, for some large m, into sets of size $\approx (1/3)2^m$ and $\approx (2/3)2^m$.

We define randomized communication complexities of $f : X \times Y \to \{0,1\}$ using the same notation as randomized query complexities (§ 16.2) but with ^{priv} and ^{pub} superscripts.

- Like BPP: $\text{Rand}_{0,1}^{\text{priv}}(f)$ is the depth of a shallowest private-coin protocol that computes f with two-sided error $1/3$, meaning $\mathbf{Pr}\big[\text{output} \neq f(x,y)\big] \leq 1/3$ for each input (x,y). The subscript 0, 1 means it may err on 0-inputs and on 1-inputs.
- Like RP: $\text{Rand}_1^{\text{priv}}(f)$ is the depth of a shallowest private-coin protocol that computes f with one-sided error $1/3$ on the side of 1-inputs, meaning $\mathbf{Pr}[\text{output} = 0] \leq 1/3$ for each 1-input and $\mathbf{Pr}[\text{output} = 1] = 0$ for each 0-input.
- Like coRP: $\text{Rand}_0^{\text{priv}}(f)$ is the depth of a shallowest private-coin protocol that computes f with one-sided error $1/3$ on the side of 0-inputs, meaning $\mathbf{Pr}[\text{output} = 1] \leq 1/3$ for each 0-input and $\mathbf{Pr}[\text{output} = 0] = 0$ for each 1-input.
- Like ZPP: We won't study the zero-sided-error version $\text{Rand}^{\text{priv}}(f)$.

$\text{Rand}_{0,1}^{\text{pub}}(f) \leq \text{Rand}_{0,1}^{\text{priv}}(f)$ (and similarly for one-sided and zero-sided error) since we can treat private coins $r_{\text{Alice}} \in \{0,1\}^m$ and $r_{\text{Bob}} \in \{0,1\}^m$ as public coins $r_{\text{Alice}} r_{\text{Bob}} \in \{0,1\}^{2m}$ where each party can see all the coins but only looks at their own half.

All these randomized communication complexities are amenable to amplification, as usual.

17.2.2 Public Coins

EQUALITY is the poster child of randomized communication complexity. One practical motivation of EQUALITY is checking consistency of replicated databases. Another is verifying that the ISO file of an operating system we're about to install is an exact, uncorrupted copy of the official server's file: x is the server's copy, y is our copy, and we want to know whether $x = y$. This is often done by applying a hash function (such as SHA256) to our copy and comparing with the official copy's hash, which is small enough to be posted on a trusted webpage. A theoretical explanation is that the hash function is effectively randomized (Chapter 8), with the randomness already sampled and hardcoded: If $x = y$ then they definitely hash to the same value, and if $x \neq y$ then they're unlikely to hash to the same value. Let's consider this from first principles.

$\mathrm{Rand}_0^{\mathrm{pub}}(\textsc{Equality}) = O(1)$ is nearly trivial since there's no limit on the length of the public random string r: Alice and Bob treat their inputs $x, y \in \{0,1\}^N$ as indices into $r \in \{0,1\}^{2^N}$, communicate the two bits r_x and r_y, and accept iff $r_x = r_y$. Thus **Pr**[accept] is 1 if $x = y$, and $1/2$ if $x \neq y$ (which can be amplified). Since $\mathrm{Det}(\textsc{Equality}) = N+1$ (Theorem 17.5), this shows that deterministic and randomized communication complexities can be arbitrarily far apart. In contrast, deterministic and randomized query complexities are polynomially related (§16.5.1).

Such an exorbitant amount of randomness is permitted but feels silly. Here's an EQUALITY protocol using only $r \in \{0,1\}^N$: Alice and Bob communicate the two bits $x \odot r$ and $y \odot r$ (where $\odot$ is the dot product mod 2) and accept iff $x \odot r = y \odot r$. Thus **Pr**[accept] is 1 if $x = y$, and $1/2$ if $x \neq y$ by the random subsum principle (Lemma 7.2.*(ii)*). Here are two perspectives:

- We could use any pairwise avoiding hash function $h\colon \{0,1\}^m \times \{0,1\}^N \to \{0,1\}^\ell$ (§8.1): Alice sends Bob $h_r(x)$, and Bob tells Alice to accept iff $h_r(x) = h_r(y)$. Thus **Pr**[accept] is 1 if $x = y$, and $\leq 1/2^\ell$ if $x \neq y$. This is $\ell + 1$ bits of communication. Dot product mod 2 is a pairwise avoiding hash function $h_r(x) = x \odot r$.
- We could use any error correcting code $E\colon \{0,1\}^N \to \{0,1\}^{2^m}$ with constant relative distance (§9.1): The inputs $x, y \in \{0,1\}^N$ are messages (for the code, not for Alice and Bob to send each other), and the randomness $r \in \{0,1\}^m$ is an index into the codewords. Alice and Bob communicate the two bits $E(x)_r$ and $E(y)_r$ and accept iff $E(x)_r = E(y)_r$. Thus **Pr**[accept] is 1 if $x = y$, and $\leq 1 - (\text{relative distance of } E) = 1 - \Omega(1)$ if $x \neq y$ (which can be amplified). The dot product code $E(x)_r = x \odot r$ has relative distance $1/2$. Any code with codeword length $2^m \leq \mathrm{poly}\,N$ yields an EQUALITY protocol with $m = O(\log N)$ random bits.

Theorem 17.14. $\mathrm{Rand}_{0,1}^{\mathrm{pub}}(\textsc{Greater Than}) \leq O(\log N \log\log N)$.

Proof. View $x = x_{N-1} \cdots x_0$ and $y = y_{N-1} \cdots y_0$ as binary numbers. Recall that $\mathrm{GT}_N(x,y) = 1$ iff $x > y$, in other words, $x \neq y$ and $x_i = 1$ and $y_i = 0$ for the most significant index i such that $x_i \neq y_i$. GREATER THAN has a deterministic oracle reduction (not rectangular) to EQUALITY, using binary search to find the most significant index i such that $x_i \neq y_i$. This maintains the invariant that $u \geq i \geq \ell$ (and u, m, ℓ stand for upper, middle, lower):

Oracle reduction from GREATER THAN to EQUALITY (17.3)

```
if x = y: reject
initialize u ← N − 1 and ℓ ← 0
while u > ℓ:
    let m ← ⌈(u + ℓ)/2⌉
    if x_u ··· x_m ≠ y_u ··· y_m: update ℓ ← m
    else: update u ← m − 1
output x_u
```

We replace each of the $k = O(\log N)$ oracle calls with an EQUALITY protocol amplified to have error probability $1/3k$ and depth $O(\log k)$. The overall depth is $O(k \log k)$, and:

$$\mathbf{Pr}[\text{err}] \leq \mathbf{Pr}\big[\exists j : j\text{th oracle call errs}\big] \leq \textstyle\sum_{j=1}^{k} \mathbf{Pr}\big[j\text{th oracle call errs}\big] \leq k/3k = 1/3 \qquad \blacksquare$$

$\text{Rand}_{0,1}^{\text{pub}}(\text{Greater Than}) \leq O(\log N)$ by a more complicated protocol.

17.2.3 Private Coins

We can turn a public-coin protocol into a private-coin one by having Alice toss all the coins and send them to Bob. If the public-coin protocol tosses m coins and communicates d bits, then the private-coin protocol communicates $m + d$ bits. For example, the public-coin Equality protocol based on an asymptotically good error correcting code tosses $O(\log N)$ coins and communicates $O(1)$ bits, so $\text{Rand}_0^{\text{priv}}(\text{Equality}) \leq O(\log N)$.

This motivates derandomization—decreasing the number of coin tosses. Recall from §11.1.3 that $G\colon \{0,1\}^\ell \to \{0,1\}^m$ is an *ε-pseudorandom generator* (*ε-PRG*) for a set H of functions $h\colon \{0,1\}^m \to \{0,1\}$ iff G *ε-fools* every $h \in H$, meaning $\mathbf{Pr}\big[h(G(U_\ell)) = 1\big]$ and $\mathbf{Pr}\big[h(U_m) = 1\big]$ are within $\pm\varepsilon$ of each other (where U_ℓ, U_m are the uniform distributions over $\{0,1\}^\ell$ and $\{0,1\}^m$).

Theorem 17.15. $\text{Rand}_{0,1}^{\text{priv}}(F) \leq O\big(\text{Rand}_{0,1}^{\text{pub}}(F) + \log N\big)$ *for every family F of two-party functions $F_N\colon \{0,1\}^N \times \{0,1\}^N \to \{0,1\}$. The same holds for one-sided error.*

Proof. Consider a $1/3$-error m-public-coin depth-d protocol for $f = F_N$, where $d = \text{Rand}_{0,1}^{\text{pub}}(f)$. For each input $(x,y) \in \{0,1\}^N \times \{0,1\}^N$, define $h_{x,y}\colon \{0,1\}^m \to \{0,1\}$ where $h_{x,y}(r)$ is the protocol's output on input (x,y) and randomness r. Let H be the set of all 2^{2N} of these functions $h_{x,y}$. There exists a $1/7$-PRG G for H with seed length $\ell = O(\log\log|H|) = O(\log N)$ (Theorem 11.4). Consider the private-coin protocol where Alice samples a seed $s \sim U_\ell$ and sends it to Bob, and then they run the public-coin protocol using $r = G(s)$. The new protocol has depth $\ell + d$ and error probability

$$\mathbf{Pr}\big[h_{x,y}(G(U_\ell)) \neq f(x,y)\big] \leq \mathbf{Pr}\big[h_{x,y}(U_m) \neq f(x,y)\big] + 1/7 \leq 1/3 + 1/7 < 1/2$$

since G $1/7$-fools $h_{x,y}$. Amplification yields $\text{Rand}_{0,1}^{\text{priv}}(f) \leq O(d + \log N)$. $\blacksquare$

For example, we can derandomize the "dot product mod 2" public-coin Equality protocol using a $1/7$-bias generator with seed length $O(\log N)$ (§11.2), yielding another explicit protocol for $\text{Rand}_0^{\text{priv}}(\text{Equality}) \leq O(\log N)$.

Theorem 17.15 implies $\text{Rand}_{0,1}^{\text{priv}}(\text{Greater Than}) \leq O\big(\text{Rand}_{0,1}^{\text{pub}}(\text{Greater Than}) + \log N\big) = O(\log N + \log N) = O(\log N)$.

Theorem 17.16. $\text{Det}(F) \leq 2^{O(\text{Rand}_{0,1}^{\text{priv}}(F))}$ *for all F.*

Proof. Consider a $1/3$-error m-private-coin depth-d protocol for $f = F_N$, where $d = \text{Rand}_{0,1}^{\text{priv}}(f)$, viewed as a size-$2^d$ deterministic protocol T with input $\big((x, r_{\text{Alice}}), (y, r_{\text{Bob}})\big)$ where $r_{\text{Alice}}, r_{\text{Bob}} \in \{0,1\}^m$. Let $p_{x,y} = \mathbf{Pr}\big[T\big((x, r_{\text{Alice}}), (y, r_{\text{Bob}})\big) = 1\big]$ over uniformly random $(r_{\text{Alice}}, r_{\text{Bob}})$, so $p_{x,y} \geq 2/3$ if $f(x,y) = 1$, and $p_{x,y} \leq 1/3$ if $f(x,y) = 0$.

- For each leaf v, let $A_v \times B_v$ be the rectangle of all $\big((x, r_{\text{Alice}}), (y, r_{\text{Bob}})\big)$ that lead to v.
- For each x, let $a_{v,x} = \mathbf{Pr}\big[(x, r_{\text{Alice}}) \in A_v\big]$.
- For each y, let $b_{v,y} = \mathbf{Pr}\big[(y, r_{\text{Bob}}) \in B_v\big]$.

	$\text{Rand}_{0,1}^{\text{pub}}$	$\text{Rand}_{0,1}^{\text{priv}}$	Det
EQUALITY	$\Theta(1)$	$\Theta(\log N)$	$\Theta(N)$
GREATER THAN	$\Theta(\log N)$	$\Theta(\log N)$	$\Theta(N)$
DISJOINTNESS	$\Theta(N)$	$\Theta(N)$	$\Theta(N)$
INNER PRODUCT	$\Theta(N)$	$\Theta(N)$	$\Theta(N)$

Figure 17.5: Communication complexities of four running example functions

Thus $p_{x,y} = \sum_{\text{accepting leaf } v} \mathbf{Pr}\big[((x, r_{\text{Alice}}), (y, r_{\text{Bob}})) \in A_v \times B_v\big] = \sum_{\text{accepting leaf } v} a_{v,x} b_{v,y}$. To deterministically compute $f(x,y)$, Alice could send Bob $a_{v,x}$ for every accepting leaf v, and then Bob could evaluate $p_{x,y} = \sum_{\text{accepting leaf } v} a_{v,x} b_{v,y}$ and tell Alice whether it's $\geq 2/3$ or $\leq 1/3$. This takes $O(m2^d)$ bits of communication, since each $a_{v,x}$ is $O(m)$ bits. We improve this to $O(d2^d)$ bits of communication. It suffices for Bob to obtain an approximation $\widetilde{p}_{x,y}$ within $\pm 1/7$ of $p_{x,y}$, and tell Alice to accept iff $\widetilde{p}_{x,y} > 1/2$, because:

- If $f(x,y) = 1$ then $\widetilde{p}_{x,y} \geq p_{x,y} - 1/7 \geq 2/3 - 1/7 > 1/2$.
- If $f(x,y) = 0$ then $\widetilde{p}_{x,y} \leq p_{x,y} + 1/7 \leq 1/3 + 1/7 < 1/2$.

For every accepting leaf v, Alice sends Bob some $\widetilde{a}_{v,x}$ within $\pm 2^{-d}/7$ of $a_{v,x}$ using $O(d)$ bits. Then, Bob evaluates $\widetilde{p}_{x,y} = \sum_{\text{accepting leaf } v} \widetilde{a}_{v,x} b_{v,y}$, which is within $\pm \sum_{\text{accepting leaf } v} (2^{-d}/7) b_{v,y} \leq \sum_{\text{accepting leaf } v} 2^{-d}/7 \leq 1/7$ of $p_{x,y} = \sum_{\text{accepting leaf } v} a_{v,x} b_{v,y}$. Thus $\text{Det}(f) \leq O(d2^d) \leq 2^{O(d)}$. ■

17.2.4 Lower Bounds

Theorem 17.16 says $\text{Rand}_{0,1}^{\text{priv}}(F) \geq \Omega(\log \text{Det}(F))$ for all F. Therefore $\text{Rand}_{0,1}^{\text{priv}}(\text{EQUALITY}) \geq \Omega(\log \text{Det}(\text{EQUALITY})) \geq \Omega(\log N)$ (Theorem 17.5), matching the upper bound from § 17.2.3. In summary, $\text{Rand}_{0,1}^{\text{pub}}(\text{EQUALITY}) = \Theta(1)$ and $\text{Rand}_{0,1}^{\text{priv}}(\text{EQUALITY}) = \Theta(\log N)$, which shows that the $+ \log N$ overhead in making public coins private (Theorem 17.15) is unavoidable in general. Figure 17.5 shows the communication complexities of our four running examples. Proving the randomized lower bounds for GREATER THAN (public-coin), DISJOINTNESS, and INNER PRODUCT involves more sophisticated techniques.

First, observe that randomized worst-case lower bounds follow from deterministic average-case lower bounds, just like with decision trees (Lemma 16.9):

Lemma 17.17. $\text{Rand}_{0,1}^{\text{pub}}(f) > d$ *if there exists a distribution D over $X \times Y$ such that for every depth-d deterministic protocol T,* $\mathbf{Pr}_{(x,y)\sim D}\big[T(x,y) \neq f(x,y)\big] > 1/3$.

Proof. We prove the contrapositive. Suppose $\text{Rand}_{0,1}^{\text{pub}}(f) \leq d$ by some depth-d public-coin protocol, which is a distribution P over depth-d deterministic protocols. Consider any distribution D over $X \times Y$. Taking probabilities over $T \sim P$ and $(x,y) \sim D$:

$$\begin{aligned} \min_T\big(\mathbf{Pr}_{x,y}\big[T(x,y) \neq f(x,y)\big]\big) &\leq \mathbf{Pr}_{T,(x,y)}\big[T(x,y) \neq f(x,y)\big] \\ &\leq \max_{x,y}\big(\mathbf{Pr}_T\big[T(x,y) \neq f(x,y)\big]\big) \leq 1/3 \end{aligned}$$

Thus for some depth-d deterministic protocol T, $\mathbf{Pr}_{x,y}\big[T(x,y) \neq f(x,y)\big] \leq 1/3$. ■

Definition. For a function $f : X \times Y \to \{0,1\}$, let $R \subseteq X \times Y$ denote a rectangle and D denote a distribution over $X \times Y$. The *discrepancy* measures are:

$$\begin{aligned}
\mathrm{Disc}_D(f,R) &= \left|D\big(R \cap f^{-1}(1)\big) - D\big(R \cap f^{-1}(0)\big)\right| \\
\mathrm{Disc}_D(f) &= \max_R\big(\mathrm{Disc}_D(f,R)\big) \\
\mathrm{Disc}(f) &= \min_D\big(\mathrm{Disc}_D(f)\big)
\end{aligned}$$

◄

$\mathrm{Disc}(f) \le \delta$ iff there exists a distribution D such that for every rectangle R,

$$\mathbf{Pr}_{(x,y)\sim D}\big[(x,y) \in R \text{ and } f(x,y) = 1\big] \text{ and } \mathbf{Pr}_{(x,y)\sim D}\big[(x,y) \in R \text{ and } f(x,y) = 0\big]$$

are within $\pm\delta$ of each other. Intuitively, this means if R has not-too-small probability under D, then R must be fairly balanced between 1-inputs and 0-inputs.

Lemma 17.18. $\mathrm{Rand}_{0,1}^{\mathrm{pub}}(f) \ge \log\big(1/\mathrm{Disc}(f)\big) - O(1)$ *for all* f.

Proof. Let $\delta = \mathrm{Disc}(f) = \mathrm{Disc}_D(f)$ for some D. Let $d = \lceil \log(1/3\delta) \rceil - 1 \ge \log(1/\delta) - 3$. To prove $\mathrm{Rand}_{0,1}^{\mathrm{pub}}(f) > d$, it suffices to show that for every depth-d deterministic protocol T, we have $D(E) > 1/3$ where $E = \big\{(x,y) : T(x,y) \ne f(x,y)\big\}$ is the error event (Lemma 17.17). For each leaf v of T, let R_v be the rectangle of inputs that lead to v. Within R_v, E coincides with either $f^{-1}(1)$ (if v outputs 0) or $f^{-1}(0)$ (if v outputs 1).

$$\begin{aligned}
D(\overline{E}) - D(E) &= \textstyle\sum_{\text{leaf } v}\Big(D\big(R_v \cap \overline{E}\big) - D\big(R_v \cap E\big)\Big) \\
&\le \textstyle\sum_{\text{leaf } v}\left|D\big(R_v \cap f^{-1}(1)\big) - D\big(R_v \cap f^{-1}(0)\big)\right| \\
&= \textstyle\sum_{\text{leaf } v} \mathrm{Disc}_D(f,R) \;\le\; \sum_{\text{leaf } v} \delta \;\le\; 2^d\delta \;<\; 1/3
\end{aligned}$$

Since $D(\overline{E}) + D(E) = 1$, this implies $D(E) > 1/3$. ■

Theorem 17.19. $\mathrm{Rand}_{0,1}^{\mathrm{pub}}(\textsc{Inner Product}) = \Theta(N)$.

Proof. Let $f = \mathrm{IP}_N$. It suffices to prove $\mathrm{Disc}(f) \le 1/2^{N/2}$ (Lemma 17.18). Let D be the uniform distribution over $\{0,1\}^N \times \{0,1\}^N$, and consider any rectangle R. Corollary 11.32 says that in every size-$2^N/(2\varepsilon)^2$ submatrix of f's matrix, the fraction of 1s is within $\pm\varepsilon$ of 1/2 and thus within $\pm 2\varepsilon$ of the fraction of 0s. That is, $D\big(R \cap f^{-1}(1)\big)/D(R)$ and $D\big(R \cap f^{-1}(0)\big)/D(R)$ are within $\pm 1/\sqrt{2^N D(R)}$, and thus $D\big(R \cap f^{-1}(1)\big)$ and $D\big(R \cap f^{-1}(0)\big)$ are within $\pm\sqrt{D(R)/2^N} \le 1/2^{N/2}$. ■

$\mathrm{Disc}(\textsc{Greater Than}) \le O(1/\sqrt{N})$ (but we won't prove it), so $\mathrm{Rand}_{0,1}^{\mathrm{pub}}(\textsc{Greater Than}) \ge \Omega(\log N)$, matching the $O(\log N)$ upper bound.

For $\mathrm{Rand}_{0,1}^{\mathrm{pub}}(\textsc{Disjointness})$, the discrepancy method unfortunately can't yield a lower bound better than $\Omega(\log N)$:

Claim 17.20. $\mathrm{Disc}(\textsc{Disjointness}) > 1/3N$.

Proof. Let $f = \textsc{Disj}_N$ and consider any distribution D. We find a rectangle R such that $D\big(R \cap f^{-1}(1)\big)$ and $D\big(R \cap f^{-1}(0)\big)$ aren't within $\pm 1/3N$. If $D\big(f^{-1}(0)\big) \le 1/3$ then it's not within $\pm 1/3N$ of $D\big(f^{-1}(1)\big) \ge 2/3$, so we let $R = \{0,1\}^N \times \{0,1\}^N$. Now, assume $D\big(f^{-1}(0)\big) > 1/3$. For each $i \in [N]$, let R_i be the rectangle of all (x,y) with $x_i = y_i = 1$. Since $R_1 \cup R_2 \cup \cdots \cup R_N = f^{-1}(0)$, for some $R = R_i$ we have $D\big(R \cap f^{-1}(0)\big) = D(R) \ge D\big(f^{-1}(0)\big)/N > 1/3N$ and $D\big(R \cap f^{-1}(1)\big) = 0$, which aren't within $\pm 1/3N$. ■

Instead, we use a method known as *corruption*. This hinges on the following lemma, which we won't prove since it's somewhat difficult.

Lemma 17.21. *For $f = \textsc{Disj}_N$, there exist a constant $c > 0$ and an input distribution D such that $D\big(f^{-1}(1)\big) = 1/2$ and for every rectangle R, we have $D\big(R \cap f^{-1}(0)\big) \geq c \cdot D\big(R \cap f^{-1}(1)\big) - 1/2^{cN}$.*

Theorem 17.22. $\text{Rand}_{0,1}^{\text{pub}}(\textsc{Disjointness}) = \Theta(N)$.

Proof. For $f = \textsc{Disj}_N$, let c and D be from Lemma 17.21, and let $d = cN + \log(c/8)$. By amplification, we may assume the error probability is $c/8$ in the definition of $\text{Rand}_{0,1}^{\text{pub}}$ and in Lemma 17.17. Thus, it suffices to prove that for every depth-d deterministic protocol T:

$$D\big(T^{-1}(1) \cap f^{-1}(0)\big) + D\big(T^{-1}(0) \cap f^{-1}(1)\big) \; > \; c/8$$

For each leaf v of T, let R_v be the rectangle of inputs that lead to v. The accepting leaves v partition $T^{-1}(1)$ into at most 2^d rectangles R_v.

$$\begin{aligned}
D\big(T^{-1}(1) \cap f^{-1}(0)\big) &= \textstyle\sum_{\text{accepting leaf } v} D\big(R_v \cap f^{-1}(0)\big) \\
&\geq \textstyle\sum_{\text{accepting leaf } v} \Big(c \cdot D\big(R_v \cap f^{-1}(1)\big) - 1/2^{cN}\Big) \qquad \text{(Lemma 17.21)} \\
&\geq c \cdot \textstyle\sum_{\text{accepting leaf } v} D\big(R_v \cap f^{-1}(1)\big) - 2^d/2^{cN} \\
&= c \cdot D\big(T^{-1}(1) \cap f^{-1}(1)\big) - c/8
\end{aligned}$$

Since $D\big(f^{-1}(1)\big) = 1/2$, either $D\big(T^{-1}(0) \cap f^{-1}(1)\big) \geq 1/4 > c/8$ or $D\big(T^{-1}(1) \cap f^{-1}(1)\big) > 1/4$, in which case $D\big(T^{-1}(1) \cap f^{-1}(0)\big) > c/4 - c/8 = c/8$. ■

Theorem 17.22 is a cornerstone of communication complexity and a workhorse in many of its application areas.

17.3 Asymmetry

So far, we cared about the total number of bits communicated, regardless of who sends them. Now, we distinguish between Alice's messages and Bob's messages. In the extreme *one-way* setting, only one party talks to the other (§17.3.1). More generally, with two-way communication, we count Alice's bits and Bob's bits separately and prove tradeoffs: If one party is laconic, the other must be verbose (§17.3.2).

As a case study, we focus on the quintessentially asymmetric function $\textsc{Index}_N : \{0,1\}^N \times [N] \to \{0,1\}$ defined by $\textsc{Index}_N(x, y) = x_y$ where Bob gets an index $y \in [N]$ into Alice's string $x = x_1 x_2 \cdots x_N \in \{0,1\}^N$. (In Chapter 16, N was the number of bits in (x, y), but here N is the number of bits in x.) Bob can send y to Alice, who can respond with x_y. But if Bob talks less, then Alice must talk a lot more. Formalizing this illustrates the basics of asymmetric communication complexity.

17.3.1 One-Way Communication

In the *one-way* communication model, Alice sends Bob a message based on her input x, and then Bob outputs a bit based on his input y and the message. Alice doesn't need to know the output. The depth is the number of bits in Alice's message. Formally, a depth-d deterministic one-way protocol with domain $X \times Y$ is a pair of functions $g : X \to \{0,1\}^d$ and $h : Y \times \{0,1\}^d \to \{0,1\}$

where $g(x)$ is Alice's message and $h(y, g(x))$ is Bob's output. $\mathrm{Det}^{\rightarrow}(f)$ is the depth of a shallowest deterministic one-way protocol that computes f. $\mathrm{Rand}_{0,1}^{\mathrm{pub},\rightarrow}(f)$ is the depth of a shallowest public-coin one-way protocol that computes f with two-sided error $1/3$.

Observation 17.23. $\mathrm{Det}^{\rightarrow}(f) = \lceil \log(\text{number of distinct rows in } f\text{'s matrix}) \rceil$ *for all* f.

Proof. $\leq$: Alice can send that many bits to identify her row to Bob, assuming identical rows have been coalesced.

$\geq$: Distinct rows must have distinct messages, because if x and x' have the same message $g(x) = g(x')$ and Bob gets y such that $f(x, y) \neq f(x', y)$, then Bob's output $h(y, g(x)) = h(y, g(x'))$ would be wrong for one of those two inputs. Thus the number of messages is at least the number of distinct rows. ■

$\mathrm{Det}^{\rightarrow}(\textsc{Index}) = N$ since $\textsc{Index}_N$'s matrix has 2^N distinct rows. This is the same reasoning as the streaming branching program size lower bound for $\textsc{Index}$ (Theorem 16.45).

In the one-way setting, randomized worst-case lower bounds follow from deterministic average-case lower bounds, for the same reason as the two-way setting (Lemma 17.17):

Lemma 17.24. $\mathrm{Rand}_{0,1}^{\mathrm{pub},\rightarrow}(f) > d$ *if there exists a distribution* D *over* $X \times Y$ *such that for every depth-*d *deterministic one-way protocol* T, $\mathbf{Pr}_{(x,y)\sim D}\big[T(x, y) \neq f(x, y)\big] > 1/3$. ■

Theorem 17.25. $\mathrm{Rand}_{0,1}^{\mathrm{pub},\rightarrow}(\textsc{Index}) = \Theta(N)$.

Proof. Let $d = \lfloor 0.01N \rfloor$. Let D be the uniform distribution over $\{0,1\}^N \times [N]$. It suffices to prove that for every depth-d deterministic one-way protocol T, $\mathbf{Pr}_{(x,y)\sim D}\big[T(x, y) \neq x_y\big] > 1/3$ (Lemma 17.24). Let $g\colon \{0,1\}^N \to \{0,1\}^d$ be Alice's message function and $h\colon [N] \times \{0,1\}^d \to \{0,1\}$ be Bob's output function, so $T(x, y) = h(y, g(x))$. For each message $m \in \{0,1\}^d$, Bob's "guess" for x is:

$$z^m \;=\; h(1, m)h(2, m)\cdots h(N, m) \;\in\; \{0,1\}^N$$

Let $B^m = \big\{x : \mathrm{dist}(z^m, x) \leq 0.4N\big\}$ be the ball of radius $0.4N$ centered at z^m. By Lemma 9.4, $|B^m| \leq 2^{H(0.4)N} \leq 2^{0.98N}$ where $H(p) = p\log_2(1/p) + (1-p)\log_2(1/(1-p))$. Therefore:

$$\begin{aligned}\mathbf{Pr}_x\big[x \notin B^{g(x)}\big] \;\geq\; \mathbf{Pr}_x\big[x \notin \textstyle\bigcup_m B^m\big] \;&\geq\; 1 - \textstyle\sum_m \mathbf{Pr}_x\big[x \in B^m\big] \\ &\geq\; 1 - 2^d \cdot 2^{0.98N}/2^N \;\geq\; 1 - 2^{-0.01N} \;\geq\; 0.9\end{aligned}$$

If $x \notin B^{g(x)}$ then $\mathbf{Pr}_y\big[T(x, y) \neq x_y\big] = \mathbf{Pr}_y\big[(z^{g(x)})_y \neq x_y\big] = \mathrm{dist}(z^{g(x)}, x)/N > 0.4$. Combining:

$$\begin{aligned}\mathbf{Pr}_{x,y}\big[T(x, y) \neq x_y\big] \;&\geq\; \mathbf{Pr}_{x,y}\big[T(x, y) \neq x_y \text{ and } x \notin B^{g(x)}\big] \\ &=\; \mathbf{Pr}_x\big[x \notin B^{g(x)}\big] \cdot \mathbf{Pr}_{x,y}\big[T(x, y) \neq x_y \,\big|\, x \notin B^{g(x)}\big] \\ &>\; 0.9 \cdot 0.4 \;>\; 1/3\end{aligned}$$

■

This implies that $\textsc{Index}$ has randomized streaming branching program size complexity $2^{\Omega(N)}$.

This also implies $\mathrm{Rand}_{0,1}^{\mathrm{pub},\rightarrow}(\textsc{Disjointness}) = \Theta(N)$ since $\textsc{Index}_N$ has a rectangular reduction to $\textsc{Disj}_N$ that maps (x, y) to (x', y') where x' is the bitwise negation of x, and y' has a 1 at index y and 0s elsewhere. This is a much simpler proof than the qualitatively stronger two-way lower bound for $\textsc{Disjointness}$ (Theorem 17.22).

17.3.2 Tradeoffs

In an (a,b)-*protocol*, Alice sends at most a bits in total, and Bob sends at most b bits in total, for every input. INDEX_N has an $(N,1)$-protocol where Alice sends x and then Bob sends x_y. INDEX_N has a $(1,\lceil\log N\rceil)$-protocol where Bob sends y and then Alice sends x_y. Getting "the best of both worlds" is impossible, but we can essentially interpolate between the two extremes using a little more back-and-forth: INDEX_N has a $(\lceil N/2^{b-1}\rceil, b)$-protocol (for any $1 \le b \le \lceil\log N\rceil$) where Bob sends the least significant $b-1$ bits of y, then Alice sends the bits of x whose indices are consistent with Bob's message, and then Bob sends x_y. Could even more back-and-forth yield a better tradeoff between Alice's and Bob's communication? Not significantly:

Theorem 17.26. INDEX_N *has no* $(\lceil N/2^{b+1}\rceil - b - 2, b)$*-protocol for any* b.

We develop a general technique for proving asymmetric communication complexity lower bounds. Say $f: X \times Y \to \{0,1\}$ is (s,t)-*rich* iff for at least s many $x \in X$, we have $f(x,y) = 1$ for at least t many $y \in Y$. That is, f's matrix has at least s rows that each have at least t 1s. A rectangle R is 1-*monochromatic* iff $f(x,y) = 1$ for all $(x,y) \in R$.

Lemma 17.27. f *has no* (a,b)*-protocol if* f *is* (s,t)*-rich but has no* 1*-monochromatic* $\lceil s/2^{a+b}\rceil \times \lceil t/2^b\rceil$ *rectangle.*

Proof of Lemma 17.27. Assuming f has an (a,b)-protocol and is (s,t)-rich, we design an algorithm to find a 1-monochromatic $\lceil s/2^{a+b}\rceil \times \lceil t/2^b\rceil$ rectangle.

Let $R_v = A_v \times B_v$ be the rectangle of inputs that lead to node v in the protocol. Say v has children v_0 and v_1, and suppose v is (p,q)-rich, which means the restriction $f|_{R_v}$ is (p,q)-rich.

- If Alice talks at v, then either v_0 or v_1 is $(p/2,q)$-rich since among the p or more rows in A_v that each have q or more 1s in $B_v = B_{v_0} = B_{v_1}$, either at least half are in A_{v_0} or at least half are in A_{v_1}.
- If Bob talks at v, then either v_0 or v_1 is $(p/2,q/2)$-rich since among the p or more rows in $A_v = A_{v_0} = A_{v_1}$ that each have q or more 1s in B_v, either at least half have $q/2$ or more 1s in B_{v_0} or at least half have $q/2$ or more 1s in B_{v_1}.

This algorithm maintains the invariant that v is (p,q)-rich:

Algorithm to find a large 1-monochromatic rectangle using an asymmetric protocol (17.4)

```
initialize v ← root and (p,q) ← (s,t)
while v is not a leaf:
    say v has children v0 and v1
    if Alice talks at v:
        update v ← whichever of v0 or v1 is (p/2,q)-rich; update (p,q) ← (p/2,q)
    if Bob talks at v:
        update v ← whichever of v0 or v1 is (p/2,q/2)-rich; update (p,q) ← (p/2,q/2)
```

This reaches a leaf v that's $(s/2^{a+b}, t/2^b)$-rich since Alice sends at most a bits (each of which halves p) and Bob sends at most b bits (each of which halves p and halves q). Thus R_v has $\ge \lceil s/2^{a+b}\rceil > 0$ rows and $\ge \lceil t/2^b\rceil > 0$ columns and is monochromatic (since v is a leaf) and therefore 1-monochromatic (since it contains at least one 1-input). ∎

Proof of Theorem 17.26. Let $a = \lceil N/2^{b+1} \rceil - b - 2$ and $s = 2^{N-1}$ and $t = \lceil N/2 \rceil$. $\textsc{Index}_N$ is (s,t)-rich since at least half of all $x \in \{0,1\}^N$ have weight $\geq N/2$. But no $\lceil s/2^{a+b} \rceil \times \lceil t/2^b \rceil$ rectangle $A \times B$ is 1-monochromatic, because only $2^{N-\lceil t/2^b \rceil} < \lceil s/2^{a+b} \rceil$ many $x \in \{0,1\}^N$ have 1s in the positions indexed by B. Thus $\textsc{Index}_N$ has no (a,b)-protocol (Lemma 17.27). ■

The richness method can also be applied to "lopsided $\textsc{Disjointness}$," in which Alice's string x has a particular weight k and Bob's string y has a particular weight ℓ. The trivial upper bounds are that Alice could use $k \log N$ bits to send Bob the locations of 1s in x, or Bob could use $\ell \log N$ bits to send Alice the locations of 1s in y. Ignoring the $\log N$ factors, these trivial protocols are optimal and there's no tradeoff: In every protocol, either Alice sends $\Omega(k)$ bits or Bob sends $\Omega(\ell)$ bits, assuming $k + \ell \leq N/2$ (Exercise 17.18).

17.4 Applications

This section showcases the breadth of applications of communication complexity. Another application awaits in Chapter 18.

17.4.1 Streaming Algorithms

A streaming algorithm (§ 8.5.3) takes one pass through the input (the data stream) from left to right, using its limited memory space to maintain a summary of the input so far. One-way communication lower bounds imply streaming space lower bounds, because streaming space upper bounds imply one-way communication upper bounds: Split the input stream into two parts, and give Alice the first part and give Bob the rest. Alice runs a streaming algorithm on her part and then sends Bob the algorithm's memory contents (configuration) at that point—a "message" from the past to the future. Bob picks up where Alice left off and continues running the streaming algorithm on his part of the input to obtain the output.

Often, the input is a length-m stream of elements from $[n]$, and the output depends only on each element's *frequency* (number of occurrences in the input). Let's consider these two statistics of a data stream:

- "Highest frequency": The frequency of the most frequent element.
- "Distinct elements": The number of elements with nonzero frequency.

For motivation, if elements are IP addresses of packets going through a network router, then a high frequency might indicate a denial-of-service attack.

A small-space streaming algorithm for "distinct elements" uses randomization and approximation (Theorem 8.19): $O(\log n)$ space suffices for a constant factor approximation (which can be improved to any constant factor > 1) with constant error probability. We prove lower bounds:

- "Highest frequency" needs large space even if we allow randomization and approximation.
- "Distinct elements" needs large space if we allow randomization but not approximation.
- "Distinct elements" needs large space if we allow approximation but not randomization.

We assume randomized algorithms have error probability $1/3$.

Theorem 17.28. *Every randomized streaming algorithm for approximating the highest frequency within factor $< \sqrt{2}$ uses space $\Omega(n)$.*

Proof. We reduce from INDEX. Suppose Π is a space-s randomized streaming algorithm that approximates the highest frequency within factor $< \sqrt{2}$ when the stream's elements are from $[n]$. We turn Π into a depth-s public-coin one-way protocol for INDEX_n, which implies $s \geq \Omega(n)$ (Theorem 17.25). On input $(x, y) \in \{0,1\}^n \times [n]$: Alice runs Π with the stream being the indices $i_1, i_2, \ldots, i_\ell$ of 1s in x (using public coins for Π's randomness), then sends Bob Π's memory contents. Bob continues running Π with the single element y appended to the stream. Bob accepts iff Π's output is $> \sqrt{2}$. This is correct because:

- If $x_y = 1$ then $(i_1, \ldots, i_\ell, y)$ has highest frequency 2 (since $y =$ some i_j), so Π's output is $> 2/\sqrt{2} = \sqrt{2}$ with probability $\geq 2/3$.
- If $x_y = 0$ then $(i_1, \ldots, i_\ell, y)$ has highest frequency 1 (since $y \neq$ all i_j), so Π's output is $< \sqrt{2} \cdot 1 = \sqrt{2}$ with probability $\geq 2/3$. ■

Theorem 17.29. *Every randomized streaming algorithm for exactly computing the number of distinct elements uses space* $\Omega(n)$.

Proof. We reduce from INDEX. Suppose Π is a space-s randomized streaming algorithm that exactly computes the number of distinct elements when the stream's elements are from $[n]$. We turn Π into a depth-$(s + O(\log n))$ public-coin one-way protocol for INDEX_n, which implies $s \geq \Omega(n)$ (Theorem 17.25). On input $(x, y) \in \{0,1\}^n \times [n]$: Alice runs Π with the stream being the indices $i_1, i_2, \ldots, i_\ell$ of 1s in x (using public coins for Π's randomness), then sends Bob Π's memory contents and ℓ. Bob continues running Π with the single element y appended to the stream. Bob accepts iff Π outputs ℓ. This is correct because:

- If $x_y = 1$ then $(i_1, \ldots, i_\ell, y)$ has ℓ distinct elements (since $y =$ some i_j), so Π outputs ℓ with probability $\geq 2/3$.
- If $x_y = 0$ then $(i_1, \ldots, i_\ell, y)$ has $\ell + 1$ distinct elements (since $y \neq$ all i_j), so Π outputs $\ell + 1 \neq \ell$ with probability $\geq 2/3$. ■

Theorem 17.30. *Every deterministic streaming algorithm for approximating the number of distinct elements within factor* 1.1 *uses space* $\Omega(n)$.

Proof. We reduce from EQUALITY. Suppose Π is a space-s deterministic streaming algorithm that approximates the number of distinct elements within factor 1.1 when the stream's elements are from $[20n]$. We turn Π into a depth-s deterministic one-way protocol for EQ_n, which implies $s \geq n = \Omega(20n)$ (Observation 17.23). Let $E\colon \{0,1\}^n \to \{0,1\}^{10n}$ be an error correcting code with relative distance ≥ 0.3 and rate 0.1 (Theorem 9.3). Identify the set of elements $[20n]$ with $[10n] \times \{0,1\}$. On input $(x, y) \in \{0,1\}^n \times \{0,1\}^n$: Alice computes $x' = E(x)$, and Bob computes $y' = E(y)$. Alice runs Π with the stream being $(1, x'_1), (2, x'_2), \ldots, (10n, x'_{10n})$, then sends Bob Π's memory contents. Bob continues running Π with $(1, y'_1), (2, y'_2), \ldots, (10n, y'_{10n})$ appended to the stream. Bob accepts iff Π's output is $\leq 11n$. This is correct because:

- If $x = y$ then $x' = y'$ and $\big((1, x'_1), \ldots, (10n, x'_{10n}), (1, y'_1), \ldots, (10n, y'_{10n})\big)$ has $10n$ distinct elements, so Π's output is $\leq 1.1 \cdot 10n = 11n$.
- If $x \neq y$ then $\text{dist}(x', y') \geq 3n$ and $\big((1, x'_1), \ldots, (10n, x'_{10n}), (1, y'_1), \ldots, (10n, y'_{10n})\big)$ has $\geq 13n$ distinct elements, so Π's output is $\geq 13n/1.1 > 11n$. ■

17.4.2 Data Structures

Definition. A *data structure problem* is a pair (X, Q) where X is a finite set of possibilities of data to be stored, and Q is a set of *query* functions $q: X \to \{0,1\}$ (not to be confused with oracle queries or queries made by decision trees). Technically, a data structure problem is an infinite family of such pairs (X, Q). ◄

For example:

- Set membership: $X = \{0,1\}^N$ and $Q = \{q_1, q_2, \ldots, q_N\}$ where $q_i(x) = x_i$: The data is a subset of $[N]$ represented by its characteristic bit string x, and the query q_i asks whether i is in that subset.
- Range sum mod 2: $X = \{0,1\}^N$ and $Q = \{q_{i,j} : 1 \le i \le j \le N\}$ where $q_{i,j}(x) = x_i \oplus x_{i+1} \oplus \cdots \oplus x_j$.
- Directed graph reachability: X is the set of all directed graphs with nodes $[n]$ and $Q = \{q_{v,w} : v, w \in [n]\}$ where $q_{v,w}(x) = 1$ iff node w is reachable from v in the graph x.

Here are some generalizations:

- We defined decision problems. We could also consider function or search problems.
- We defined *static* problems. A *dynamic* data structure problem also has a set U of *update* functions $u: X \to X$. Given an initial $x \in X$ and a sequence of updates $u^1, u^2, \ldots, u^m \in U$, any query would then be applied to the updated data $u^m(\cdots u^2(u^1(x))\cdots)$.

(For example, "stack" is a dynamic data structure function problem where "push a particular item" is an update and "pop" is a combination of the "peek" query and "remove" update.) We just consider static decision problems.

Definition. A space-s time-t *data structure algorithm* for (X, Q) consists of an *encoding* function $E: X \to \{0,1\}^s$ and depth-t decision trees $T_q: \{0,1\}^s \to \{0,1\}$ for all $q \in Q$, such that $T_q(E(x)) = q(x)$ for all x and q. The data x is preprocessed into the s-bit string $E(x)$, and then any query q can be answered by adaptively reading at most t bits of $E(x)$. Reading a bit is called *probing* (which confusingly corresponds to "querying" from Chapter 16). ◄

The number of probes is a proxy for time. We won't care about the time to compute $E(x)$. Every problem has two extreme algorithms:

- Time-optimal: With $t = 1$ and $s = |Q|$, let $E(x)$ be the answers $q(x)$ for all possible queries $q \in Q$ in some order. Answering a query just requires one probe.
- Space-optimal: With $s = t = \lceil \log |X| \rceil$, let $E: X \to \{0,1\}^s$ be any injection (different values of x get encoded differently). Answering a query may require probing all t bits. Every algorithm must have space $\ge \lceil \log |X| \rceil$ if the query answers collectively determine the data (that is, if there don't exist $x \ne x'$ such that $q(x) = q(x')$ for all q), because then any encoding must be injective.

For set membership, encoding x as itself and answering q_i by probing x_i is simultaneously time-optimal and space-optimal.

For range sum mod 2, we achieve $s = N$ and $t = 2$ (space-optimal and nearly time-optimal) by letting $E(x)_k = x_1 \oplus x_2 \oplus \cdots \oplus x_k$ (for all $k \in [N]$) and answering $q_{i,j}$ by probing $E(x)_j$ and $E(x)_{i-1}$ (which is implicitly 0 if $i = 1$) and returning $E(x)_j \oplus E(x)_{i-1}$. If we want $t = 1$, then $s \ge |Q| = \binom{N}{2} + N$ is necessary because different queries would have to probe different bits: If two different queries $q_{i,j}$ and $q_{i',j'}$ probed the same bit, then they'd be negations of each other. But some index k is in one of $\{i,\ldots,j\}$ or $\{i',\ldots,j'\}$ but not in the other, so flipping x_k would flip the value of one of $q_{i,j}$ or $q_{i',j'}$ but not of the other, so they aren't negations of each other.

More generally, an algorithm may encode x using *cells*, each of which holds a w-bit word and can be probed in one time step. (We considered $w = 1$ above.) The space s is the number of cells, and the time t is the worst-case number of cell probes. That is, $E: X \to (\{0,1\}^w)^s$ and each non-leaf node in a query decision tree $T_q: (\{0,1\}^w)^s \to \{0,1\}$ is labeled with a cell index and has 2^w children corresponding to the possible values of the word in the cell.

Asymmetric communication complexity (§17.3.2) is useful for proving data structure lower bounds. In an (a,b)-protocol, Alice sends at most a bits in total, and Bob sends at most b bits in total, for every input. For every data structure problem (X,Q), define a two-party function $f: X \times Q \to \{0,1\}$ by $f(x,q) = q(x)$. Alice has the data, and Bob has the query. For example, for set membership, $f = \text{INDEX}_N$.

Lemma 17.31. *A data structure problem has no space-s time-t word-size-w algorithm if the associated f has no $(tw,\ t\lceil\log s\rceil + 1)$-protocol.*

Proof. We prove the contrapositive. Suppose (X,Q) has a space-s time-t word-size-w algorithm with encoding function E and decision trees T_q for all $q \in Q$. Here's a $(tw,\ t\lceil\log s\rceil + 1)$-protocol to compute $f(x,q) = q(x) = T_q(E(x))$: Alice and Bob simulate T_q (which Bob knows) on input $E(x)$ (which Alice knows). For each of the t probes, Bob sends the cell's index ($\lceil\log s\rceil$ bits), and then Alice sends the cell's contents (w bits), and Bob descends to the corresponding child in T_q. Upon reaching a leaf of T_q, Bob sends the output (one bit). ■

For example, suppose the data is $x \subseteq [N]$ of size k, and each query corresponds to some $y \subseteq [N]$ of size $\ell > k$ and asks whether x is disjoint from y. The time-optimal algorithm achieves $t = 1$ and $s = \binom{N}{\ell} \le N^\ell$. The space-optimal algorithm achieves $s = t = \left\lceil \log \binom{N}{k} \right\rceil \le k \log N$. Essentially no tradeoff is possible: f is lopsided DISJOINTNESS, which has no $(k/4,\ \ell/4)$-protocol (Exercise 17.18) and thus no $(t,\ t\lceil\log s\rceil + 1)$-protocol where $t = k/4$ and $s = 2^{\ell/k-2}$. So this data structure problem has no space-s time-t word-size-1 algorithm (Lemma 17.31). For every algorithm, either the time is almost as bad as in the space-optimal algorithm, or the space is almost as bad as in the time-optimal algorithm.

Many data structure lower bounds can be proven by reductions from lopsided DISJOINTNESS.

17.4.3 Integrated Circuit Layout

A VLSI (very large scale integrated) chip is a kind of circuit whose wires, gates, and input nodes are laid out on a rectangular grid. In each time step, every wire carries a bit between neighboring positions on the grid. A wire may carry different bits in different steps. The details don't matter here. A chip's *area* is width × height, and its parallel *time* is the number of steps to obtain the output. Communication complexity is useful for proving area-time tradeoffs: Small chips must be slow, and fast chips must be large.

For any $f: \{0,1\}^{2N} \to \{0,1\}$ and any *equipartition* of $[2N]$ into equal-size sets S and $\overline{S}$, let $f_{S,\overline{S}}: \{0,1\}^N \times \{0,1\}^N \to \{0,1\}$ be the two-party version where Alice gets the input bits indexed by S, and Bob gets the input bits indexed by $\overline{S}$.

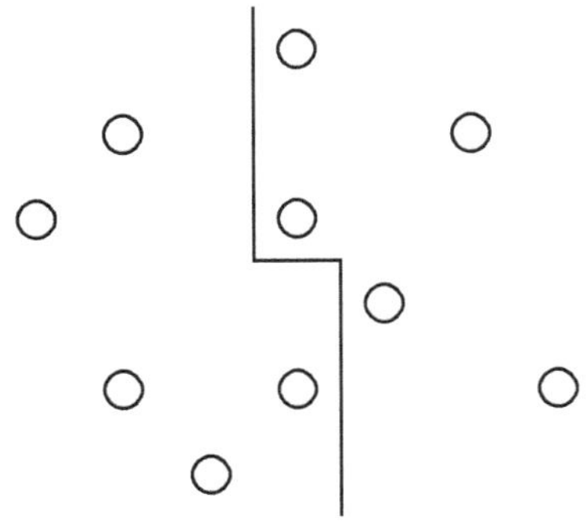

Figure 17.6: VLSI layout example

Theorem 17.32. *If an area-A time-T VLSI chip computes f, then* $\mathrm{Det}(f_{S,\overline{S}}) \le (\sqrt{A}+1)T+1$ *for some equipartition* $(S,\overline{S})$.

Proof. Assume height $\le$ width, so height $\le \sqrt{A}$. First, suppose the input nodes are all in different columns. Some vertical line partitions the $2N$ input nodes into N on the left, indexed by S, and N on the right, indexed by $\overline{S}$. At most $\sqrt{A}$ many wires cross this vertical line. A protocol for $f_{S,\overline{S}}$ can simulate each time step of the chip by having Alice send Bob the values on the left-to-right wires across the line, and Bob send Alice the values on the right-to-left wires across the line. Each of the $\le T$ time steps involves $\le \sqrt{A}$ bits of communication, so the protocol has depth $\le \sqrt{A}T+1$, where the $+1$ is for the output bit. If the input nodes aren't all in different columns, then we add a "shoulder" to the vertical line to get an equipartition of the input nodes, with $\le \sqrt{A}+1$ wires crossing. ■

Example. Figure 17.6 depicts a width-7 height-6 grid and a "vertical line with a shoulder" equipartitioning the $2N = 10$ input nodes. ♦

The contrapositive is that if a communication lower bound holds for every equipartition of f's input variables, then essentially the same lower bound on $\sqrt{A}T$ holds for VLSI chips computing f. For example, it's known that multiplying two N-bit integers requires $\sqrt{A}T \ge \Omega(N)$. Squaring both sides, such results are often called "AT^2 lower bounds."

17.5 Search Problems

With a two-party search problem, each input $(x,y) \in X \times Y$ has an associated set of acceptable solutions, and the goal is to output any acceptable solution (it doesn't matter which one) or report that the set is empty. The leaves of a protocol for a search problem partition $X \times Y$ into monochromatic rectangles, where *monochromatic* means that some solution (the protocol's output) is acceptable for all inputs in the rectangle, or that all such inputs have no acceptable solutions. Our lower bound techniques for decision problems generally don't apply to search problems, so we develop new techniques. This section's results have applications to circuit and formula lower bounds (Chapter 18).

17.5.1 Finding Opposite Bits

Denote the parity of $x \in \{0,1\}^N$ by $\oplus(x) = x_1 \oplus x_2 \oplus \cdots \oplus x_N$. OPPOSITE PARITY is the search problem where Alice gets $x \in \{0,1\}^N$ with $\oplus(x) = 1$, Bob gets $y \in \{0,1\}^N$ with $\oplus(y) = 0$, and they want to output an index $i \in [N]$ such that $x_i \neq y_i$ (which exists since $x \neq y$).

Det(OPPOSITE PARITY) $\geq \log N$ because for every $i \in [N]$, some input's only acceptable solution is i and so every protocol has at least one leaf labeled i, and thus every protocol has size $\geq N$ and depth $\geq \log N$.

Theorem 17.33. Det(OPPOSITE PARITY$_N$) $= 2\log N$ *if N is a power of* 2.

Proof. Let $f =$ OPPOSITE PARITY$_N$ with domain $X \times Y$.

$\leq$: Alice and Bob do binary search: They first tell each other the parities of the left halves of x and y. If these parities are opposite, then Alice and Bob restrict their attention to the left halves. Otherwise, they restrict their attention to the right halves of x and y, which have opposite parities. Alice and Bob repeat this—maintaining the invariant that the current segments of x and y have opposite parities—until the current segments each have one bit, whose index Alice and Bob output. In each of the $\log N$ phases, 2 bits are communicated, so Det(f) $\leq 2\log N$.

$\geq$: Consider any depth-d size-s protocol for f. For each leaf v, let R_v be the rectangle of inputs that lead to v. Let $Z \subseteq X \times Y$ be the set of all inputs (x,y) with $\text{dist}(x,y) = 1$, that is, (x,y) has only one acceptable solution. No two inputs in $Z \cap R_v$ are in the same row or in the same column, because if two such inputs were in the same row (or similarly, in the same column), say $(x,y),(x,y') \in Z \cap R_v$ with $y \neq y'$, then their unique acceptable solutions would be different (since $x_i \neq y_i$ and $x_j \neq y'_j$ for some $j \neq i$), so the protocol would err on one of them. Letting $z_v = |Z \cap R_v|$, this implies R_v has $\geq z_v$ rows and $\geq z_v$ columns and therefore $\geq z_v^2$ inputs. By Corollary A.27:

$$|X \times Y| \;=\; \textstyle\sum_{\text{leaf } v} |R_v| \;\geq\; \sum_{\text{leaf } v} z_v^2 \;\geq\; \left(\sum_{\text{leaf } v} z_v\right)^2 / s \;=\; |Z|^2/s$$

We have $|X| = |Y| = 2^{N-1}$ since half of all strings have parity 1, and $|Z| = N2^{N-1}$ since for each x with parity 1, flipping any one of the N bits yields some y with parity 0. We conclude that

$$s \;\geq\; |Z|^2/|X \times Y| \;=\; (N2^{N-1})^2/(2^{N-1})^2 \;=\; N^2$$

so the protocol has depth $d \geq \log s \geq 2\log N$. ■

17.5.2 Finding a Fork

FORK is the search problem parameterized by integers $k \geq 2$ and $n \geq 1$ where Alice gets $x \in [k]^n$, Bob gets $y \in [k]^n$, and they want to output a *fork*, which is an index $i \in \{0,1,\ldots,n\}$ such that $x_i = y_i$ and $x_{i+1} \neq y_{i+1}$, assuming implicitly that $x_0 = y_0$ and $x_{n+1} \neq y_{n+1}$. A fork always exists: If $x_1 \neq y_1$ then 0 is a fork. If $x_n = y_n$ then n is a fork. Otherwise, at least one $i \in \{1,\ldots,n-1\}$ is a fork.

Theorem 17.34. Det(FORK) $= \Theta\big((\log k)(\log n)\big)$.

This multivariate big-Θ means Det(FORK$_{k,n}$) is within a constant factor of $(\log k)(\log n)$ for all $k \geq 2$ and all $n \geq 1$.

Proof (ancillary). Big-O: This protocol maintains the invariant that $x_\ell = y_\ell$ and $x_u \neq y_u$:

Binary search protocol for FORK	(17.5)

```
initialize ℓ ← 0 and u ← n+1
while u ≥ ℓ+2:
    let m ← ⌊(ℓ+u)/2⌋
    Alice sends x_m, and Bob says whether x_m = y_m
    if x_m = y_m: update ℓ ← m
    if x_m ≠ y_m: update u ← m
output ℓ
```

Each iteration communicates $O(\log k)$ bits. After $O(\log n)$ iterations, the protocol reaches $u = \ell+1$ and correctly outputs ℓ.

Big-Ω: We may assume n has been rounded down to a power of 2. We may also assume k is even and $k \geq 256$ because if $2 \leq k < 256$, then $\text{Det}(\text{FORK}_{k,n}) \geq \Omega(\log n)$ is trivial: For every $i \in \{0, 1, \ldots, n\}$, some input's only fork is i and so every protocol has a leaf labeled i, and thus every protocol has size $\geq n+1$ and depth $\geq \log(n+1)$.

The idea is to prove that every protocol must be "like binary search": After $\Omega(\log k)$ bits of communication, we can focus on either the left half or the right half of the input, and then repeat this $\Omega(\log n)$ times while staying nonmonochromatic. Throughout the analysis, the restricted protocol might only work on a somewhat large set of inputs, rather than all inputs.

For a set $S \subseteq [k]^n$, let FORK_S be $\text{FORK}_{k,n}$ restricted to inputs $(x, y) \in S \times S$. For $\delta > 0$ (a "density" parameter), let $d_{\delta,n}$ be the minimum of $\text{Det}(\text{FORK}_S)$ over all $S \subseteq [k]^n$ with $|S| \geq \delta k^n$.

Lemma 17.35. *$d_{\delta,n} > 0$ if $\delta > 1/k$.*

Lemma 17.36. *$d_{\delta,n} \geq d_{\delta/2,n} + 1$ if $d_{\delta,n} > 0$.*

Lemma 17.37. *$d_{\delta,n} \geq d_{\sqrt{\delta}/2,n/2}$ if $\delta \geq 16/k$.*

Before proving the lemmas, we combine them to prove the lower bound. Starting with $d_{1,n} = \text{Det}(\text{FORK}_{k,n})$, we can afford to apply Lemma 17.36 $\Omega(\log k)$ times while keeping $\delta \geq 16/k$ (using Lemma 17.35 to justify the $d_{\delta,n} > 0$ hypothesis) and then apply Lemma 17.37 once to get $\delta \geq \sqrt{16/k}/2 = 2/\sqrt{k}$ while halving n. (Intuitively, this corresponds to binary search sending $O(\log k)$ bits to halve n in one iteration.) We repeat this reasoning $\log n$ times—accumulating $\Omega(\log k)$ bits of communication each time—until n reaches 1. Specifically, letting $c = \lfloor \log(\sqrt{k}/8) \rfloor$, which is $\Omega(\log k)$ since $k \geq 256$, we have $(2/\sqrt{k})/2^c \geq 16/k$ and thus:

$$d_{2/\sqrt{k},n} \;\geq\; d_{16/k,n} + c \;\geq\; d_{2/\sqrt{k},n/2} + c$$

Repeating this $\log n$ times and letting $\delta = 2/\sqrt{k}$:

$$\text{Det}(\text{FORK}_{k,n}) \;=\; d_{1,n} \;\geq\; d_{\delta,n} \;\geq\; d_{\delta,n/2} + c \;\geq\; d_{\delta,n/4} + 2c \;\geq\; \cdots \;\geq\; d_{\delta,1} + (\log n)c \;\geq\; (\log n)c$$

This concludes the proof that $\text{Det}(\text{FORK}) \geq \Omega\big((\log k)(\log n)\big)$, except for the three lemmas. ■

Proof of Lemma 17.35 (ancillary). We show $\text{Det}(\text{FORK}_S) > 0$, in other words, the rectangle $S \times S$ is not monochromatic, for all $S \subseteq [k]^n$ with $|S| \geq \delta k^n$, assuming $\delta > 1/k$. For every such S, there exist $x, y \in S$ with $x_n \neq y_n$, because if x_n were the same for all $x \in S$, then $|S| \leq k^{n-1} < \delta k^n$. On input $(x, x) \in S \times S$, the only fork is n. On input $(x, y) \in S \times S$, n isn't a fork since $x_n \neq y_n$. Thus $S \times S$ is not monochromatic. ■

Proof of Lemma 17.36 (ancillary). We prove $d_{\delta/2,n} \leq d_{\delta,n} - 1$ assuming $d_{\delta,n} > 0$. Let $S \subseteq [k]^n$ with $|S| \geq \delta k^n$ be such that $\mathrm{Det}(\textsc{Fork}_S) = d_{\delta,n}$. Consider a depth-$d_{\delta,n}$ protocol Π for $\textsc{Fork}_S$. Partition S into S_0 and S_1, where S_b is all elements of S on which b is the first bit communicated (viewing S as rows if Alice talks first, or as columns if Bob talks first). Let S' be the larger of S_0 and S_1, and let b be the corresponding bit. Then $|S'| \geq (\delta/2)k^n$, and $\textsc{Fork}_{S'}$ has a depth-$(d_{\delta,n}-1)$ protocol Π' in which Π's first bit of communication is skipped and assumed to be b. (Π''s root is the b-child of Π's root.) Thus $d_{\delta/2,n} \leq \mathrm{Det}(\textsc{Fork}_{S'}) \leq d_{\delta,n} - 1$. ■

Proof of Lemma 17.37 (ancillary). Let $S \subseteq [k]^n$ with $|S| \geq \delta k^n$ be such that $\mathrm{Det}(\textsc{Fork}_S) = d_{\delta,n}$. Consider a depth-$d_{\delta,n}$ protocol Π for $\textsc{Fork}_S$. Let $u, v \in [k]^{n/2}$ denote the left and right halves of any tuple $uv \in [k]^n$. For each u, let $V_u = \{v : uv \in S\} \subseteq [k]^{n/2}$. Let $U = \{u : |V_u| \geq (\delta/2)k^{n/2}\} \subseteq [k]^{n/2}$.

Either U or some V_u has size $\geq \sqrt{\delta/2}k^{n/2}$ (and intuitively, these two cases correspond to binary search restricting attention to the left or right half, respectively) because if U and all V_u had size $< \sqrt{\delta/2}k^{n/2}$, then:

$$\begin{aligned} |S| \;=\; \textstyle\sum_u |V_u| \;&\leq\; |U| \cdot \max_{u \in U} |V_u| \;+\; |\overline{U}| \cdot \max_{u \notin U} |V_u| \\ &<\; \sqrt{\delta/2}k^{n/2} \cdot \sqrt{\delta/2}k^{n/2} \;+\; k^{n/2} \cdot (\delta/2)k^{n/2} \\ &=\; (\delta/2)k^n + (\delta/2)k^n \;=\; \delta k^n \end{aligned}$$

First, suppose $|V_u| \geq \sqrt{\delta/2}k^{n/2}$ for some u. Then $\textsc{Fork}_{V_u}$ has a depth-$d_{\delta,n}$ protocol Π_u where $\Pi_u(x,y)$ runs $\Pi(ux,uy)$ and subtracts $n/2$ from the output. This works because for all $x, y \in V_u$ (with $x_0 = y_0 = u_{n/2}$ implicitly), we have $ux, uy \in S$ and so $\Pi(ux,uy)$ outputs a fork $i \in \{0,\ldots,n\}$ for (ux,uy), which means $(ux)_i = (uy)_i$ and $(ux)_{i+1} \neq (uy)_{i+1}$, which implies $i \in \{n/2,\ldots,n\}$ and $x_{i-n/2} = y_{i-n/2}$ and $x_{i-n/2+1} \neq y_{i-n/2+1}$, so $i-n/2$ is a fork for (x,y). Hence $d_{\sqrt{\delta}/2,n/2} \leq d_{\sqrt{\delta/2},n/2} \leq \mathrm{Det}(\textsc{Fork}_{V_u}) \leq d_{\delta,n}$.

Now, suppose $|U| \geq \sqrt{\delta/2}k^{n/2}$. We claim that some $U' \subseteq U$ of size $\geq (\sqrt{\delta}/2)k^{n/2}$ and some $v^u, w^u \in V_u$ for each $u \in U'$ have the property that for all $x, y \in U'$, v^x and w^y differ in every coordinate. Assuming the claim is true, $\textsc{Fork}_{U'}$ has a depth-$d_{\delta,n}$ protocol Π' where $\Pi'(x,y)$ runs $\Pi(xv^x, yw^y)$. This works because for all $x, y \in U'$ (with $x_{n/2+1} = v_1^x \neq w_1^y = y_{n/2+1}$ implicitly), we have $xv^x, yw^y \in S$ and so $\Pi(xv^x, yw^y)$ outputs a fork $i \in \{0,\ldots,n\}$ for (xv^x, yw^y), which means $(xv^x)_i = (yw^y)_i$ and $(xv^x)_{i+1} \neq (yw^y)_{i+1}$, which implies $i \in \{0,\ldots,n/2\}$ (since v^x and w^y differ in every coordinate) and $x_i = y_i$ and $x_{i+1} \neq y_{i+1}$, so i is a fork for (x,y). Hence $d_{\sqrt{\delta}/2,n/2} \leq \mathrm{Det}(\textsc{Fork}_{U'}) \leq d_{\delta,n}$.

We prove the claim using the probabilistic method. For each $j \in \{1,\ldots,n/2\}$ independently, let $K_j \subseteq [k]$ be a uniformly random subset of size $k/2$. With respect to an outcome $K = (K_1,\ldots,K_{n/2})$:

- u is *v-good* iff there exists $v^u \in V_u \cap (K_1 \times \cdots \times K_{n/2})$.
- u is *w-good* iff there exists $w^u \in V_u \cap (\overline{K_1} \times \cdots \times \overline{K_{n/2}})$.
- u is *good* iff u is v-good and w-good.

We shortly prove the "subclaim" that $\mathbf{Pr}[u \text{ is } v\text{-good}] \geq 0.9$ for each $u \in U$. By symmetry, this also means $\mathbf{Pr}[u \text{ is } w\text{-good}] \geq 0.9$ and therefore $\mathbf{Pr}[u \text{ is good}] \geq 0.8$ for each $u \in U$. Then for uniformly random $u \in U$:

$$\max_K\big(\mathbf{Pr}_u[u \text{ is good}]\big) \;\geq\; \mathbf{Pr}_{K,u}[u \text{ is good}] \;\geq\; \min_u\big(\mathbf{Pr}_K[u \text{ is good}]\big) \;\geq\; 0.8$$

Thus for some K, at least 0.8 fraction of all $u \in U$ are good. Let U' be the set of all good $u \in U$ with respect to this K, so $|U'| \geq 0.8|U| \geq 0.8\sqrt{\delta/2}k^{n/2} \geq (\sqrt{\delta}/2)k^{n/2}$. For all $x, y \in U'$, v^x and w^y differ in every coordinate j since $v_j^x \in K_j$ and $w_j^y \in \overline{K_j}$.

Finally, to prove the subclaim, consider any $u \in U$. We can sample K by sampling $k/2$ independent, uniformly random tuples $z^1, \ldots, z^{k/2} \in [k]^{n/2}$ and letting K_j consist of $z_j^1, \ldots, z_j^{k/2}$ (which might not be distinct) along with more uniformly random elements of $[k]$, if necessary, to bring the number of distinct elements in K_j up to exactly $k/2$. Of course, if at least one of $z^1, \ldots, z^{k/2}$ is in V_u, then there exists $v^u \in V_u \cap (K_1 \times \cdots \times K_{n/2})$ and so u is v-good.

$$\begin{aligned}
\mathbf{Pr}[u \text{ is not } v\text{-good}] &\leq \mathbf{Pr}\left[z^1, \ldots, z^{k/2} \notin V_u\right] \\
&= \mathbf{Pr}\left[z^1 \notin V_u\right] \cdots \mathbf{Pr}\left[z^{k/2} \notin V_u\right] && \text{(independence)} \\
&\leq (1-\delta/2) \cdots (1-\delta/2) && (|V_u| \geq (\delta/2)k^{n/2} \text{ since } u \in U) \\
&\leq (\mathrm{e}^{-\delta/2})^{k/2} && \text{(Fact 7.6)} \\
&\leq \mathrm{e}^{-4} && \text{(assumption that } \delta \geq 16/k) \\
&\leq 0.1 && \blacksquare
\end{aligned}$$

Exercises

17.1 For a directed cycle on a set of n nodes V, define $f: V \times V \to \{0,1\}$ by $f(u,v) = 1$ iff the path from u to v has length $< n/2$. Use the fooling set method to prove $\mathrm{Det}(f) > \log n$.

17.2 In Theorem 17.5 we showed that the EQUALITY function EQ_N has a 1-fooling set of size 2^N. Prove that a largest 0-fooling set for EQ_N has size 3, assuming $N \geq 2$.

17.3 Prove that if D is a distribution over $f^{-1}(1)$ such that $D(R) \leq \delta$ for every rectangle $R \subseteq f^{-1}(1)$, then $\mathrm{Det}(f) \geq \log(1/\delta)$. Also explain why this method is more general than the 1-fooling set method (Lemma 17.4).

17.4 Prove $\mathrm{Det}(f) \geq \log\big(\log(\text{number of distinct rows in } f\text{'s matrix})\big)$ for all f.

(a) Prove this using an "adversary argument": In any protocol for f, consider a root-to-leaf path that repeatedly steps to whichever child has more distinct rows in its associated rectangle.

(b) Give an alternative proof by relating two-way and one-way communication.

17.5 Prove that if $f^{-1}(1)$ is a union of at most 2^{k_1} rectangles, and $f^{-1}(0)$ is a union of at most 2^{k_0} rectangles, then $\mathrm{Det}(f) \leq O(k_1 \cdot k_0)$. This is the communication complexity analogue of $\mathrm{Det}(f) \leq \mathrm{Cert}_1(f) \cdot \mathrm{Cert}_0(f)$ for query complexity (Theorem 16.22). Hint: For each rectangle of 1-inputs and each rectangle of 0-inputs, they are disjoint and are therefore either row-disjoint or column-disjoint.

17.6 For $f: \{0,1\}^N \to \{0,1\}$ and $g: X \times Y \to \{0,1\}$, define the *composition* $f \circ g^N : X^N \times Y^N \to \{0,1\}$ by $(f \circ g^N)\big((x^1, \ldots, x^N), (y^1, \ldots, y^N)\big) = f\big(g(x^1, y^1), \ldots, g(x^N, y^N)\big)$. Prove that $\mathrm{Det}^{\mathrm{cc}}(f \circ g^N) \leq \mathrm{Det}^{\mathrm{qc}}(f) \cdot \mathrm{Det}^{\mathrm{cc}}(g)$ where $\mathrm{Det}^{\mathrm{cc}}$ is communication complexity and $\mathrm{Det}^{\mathrm{qc}}$ is query complexity.

17.7 Prove $\text{DTSize}(f) \geq 2^{\Omega(\text{Det}(f))}$ for all $f\colon \{0,1\}^N \times \{0,1\}^N \to \{0,1\}$, where Det is communication complexity and DTSize is decision tree size complexity (which ignores the distinction between Alice's and Bob's input bits).

17.8 Every partial two-party function $f: X \times Y \to \{0,1\}$ corresponds to a partial binary matrix M with rows indexed by X and columns indexed by Y, where $M_{x,y} = f(x,y) \in \{0,1,*\}$, where $*$ means "undefined." The communication complexity $\text{Det}(f)$ is the depth of a shallowest protocol that computes f for all inputs on which f is defined. The leaves of a protocol for f partition $X \times Y$ into rectangles that are monochromatic, which means "doesn't contain both a 0-input and a 1-input."

COMMUNICATION COMPLEXITY OF PARTIAL MATRIX	(17.6)
Input: Partial binary matrix corresponding to some f, and integer $d \geq 0$	
Output: Is $\text{Det}(f) \leq d$?	

(a) Prove that this problem is in NP.

(b) Prove that for $d = 2$, this problem is in P. Hint: Reduce to GRAPH 2-COLORING.

(c) Prove that for $d = 3$, this problem is NP-complete by the following reduction from GRAPH 4-COLORING: Map $G = (V,E)$ to the matrix of $f: V \times V \to \{0,1\}$ where $f(u,v)$ is 1 if $u = v$, is 0 if $\{u,v\} \in E$, and is undefined otherwise. Hint: Without loss of generality, a depth-3 protocol has only four accepting leaves.

17.9 For some tree $G = (V,E)$ (a connected undirected graph with no cycles) known in advance to both parties, define $f: V \times V \to \{0,1\}$ by $f(u,v) = 1$ iff $\{u,v\} \in E$. (Are Alice's node and Bob's node adjacent?) Prove $\text{Rand}_0^{\text{pub}}(f) = O(1)$.

17.10 Define $f\colon \{0,1\}^N \times \{0,1\}^N \to \{0,1\}$ by $f(x,y) = 1$ iff $\text{dist}(x,y) \leq 1$. (Do x and y differ in at most one bit position?)

(a) Use the fooling set method to prove $\text{Det}(f) \geq N$ if $N \geq 2$.

(b) Prove $\text{Rand}_0^{\text{pub}}(f) = O(1)$. Hint: Randomly partition the N coordinates into two parts.

(c) Show how to do the partitioning with only $O(\log N)$ public coins using a pairwise avoiding hash function.

17.11 In a private-coin *simultaneous messages* protocol, Alice and Bob each send a multi-bit message (which is a function of their own input and randomness) to a "referee," who announces the output as a function of the two messages. (The referee does not see the input or randomness.) Prove that EQUALITY has such a protocol with $O(\sqrt{N})$-bit messages and one-sided error. Hint: Alice and Bob encode their inputs with an asymptotically good error correcting code. They can't communicate with each other to agree on which codeword coordinate to compare, so they arrange the coordinates into a square, and Alice picks which row and Bob picks which column.

17.12 **(a)** Design a technique for lower bounding $\text{Rand}_1^{\text{pub}}$ analogous to Lemma 17.17's technique for lower bounding $\text{Rand}_{0,1}^{\text{pub}}$.

(b) Prove that if f has a 1-fooling set of size $s \geq 2$, then $\text{Rand}_1^{\text{pub}}(f) > \log(2s/3)$. Conclude that $\text{Rand}_1^{\text{pub}}(\text{EQUALITY}) \geq N$.

17.13 In this exercise, you'll prove that for all $\varepsilon \geq 1/N$, the public-coin communication complexity of DISJOINTNESS with two-sided error probability $1/2-\varepsilon$ is $\Theta(\varepsilon N)$.

(a) Prove the $O(\varepsilon N)$ upper bound.

(b) For calibration, use amplification to deduce a $\Omega(\varepsilon^2 N)$ lower bound from the $\Omega(N)$ lower bound for error probability $1/3$ (Theorem 17.22).

(c) A (d,α,β)*-protocol* for f is a depth-d public-coin protocol that accepts 1-inputs with probability $\geq \alpha$ and accepts 0-inputs with probability $\leq \beta$. Prove that for every integer $k \geq 1$, if f has a (d,α,β)-protocol, then f has a (dk,α^k,β^k)-protocol.

(d) Prove that for every $c > 0$, if f has a $(d,1/2+\varepsilon,1/2-\varepsilon)$-protocol, then f has a $(dk,\alpha,(c/4)\alpha)$-protocol where $k = \lceil \ln(4/c)/2\varepsilon \rceil$ and $\alpha = (1/2+\varepsilon)^k$.

(e) Prove that if f has a $(dk,\alpha,(c/4)\alpha)$-protocol, then for all distributions D_1 and D_0 over $f^{-1}(1)$ and $f^{-1}(0)$, there exists a depth-dk deterministic protocol T such that $D_1(A) \geq \alpha/2$ and $D_0(A) \leq (c/2)D_1(A)$ where $A = T^{-1}(1)$ is the event that T accepts.

(f) For $f = \text{DISJ}_N$, let c and $D = D_1/2 + D_0/2$ be from Lemma 17.21 (the corruption property). Prove that for every depth-dk deterministic protocol T, $D_0(A) \geq cD_1(A) - 2^{dk}/2^{cN-1}$ where $A = T^{-1}(1)$ is the event that T accepts.

(g) Assemble the pieces to deduce the $\Omega(\varepsilon N)$ lower bound.

17.14 **(a)** Show how $\text{Rand}_{0,1}^{\text{priv}}(\text{INDEX}) \geq \Omega(\log N)$ follows from $\text{Det}^{\rightarrow}(\text{INDEX}) \geq N$.

(b) Show how $\text{Rand}_{0,1}^{\text{pub}}(\text{INDEX}) \geq \Omega(\log N)$ follows from $\text{Rand}_{0,1}^{\text{pub}}(\text{INNER PRODUCT}) \geq \Omega(N)$.

17.15 Exhibit an n-node graph G with $\text{Rand}_{0,1}^{\text{pub},\rightarrow}(\text{CIS}_G) = \Theta(n)$.

17.16 **(a)** For any $f: X \times Y \to \{0,1\}$ and $x \in X$, define $f^x: Y \to \{0,1\}$ by $f^x(y) = f(x,y)$. Prove that the VC dimension (§13.4) of the concept class $\{f^x : x \in X\}$ equals the largest N for which there exists a rectangular reduction from INDEX_N to f.

(b) Conclude that $\text{Rand}_{0,1}^{\text{pub},\rightarrow}(f) \geq \Omega\big(\text{VC dimension of } \{f^x : x \in X\}\big)$.

(c) Let $\text{Rand}_{0,1}^{\text{pub},\leftarrow}$ be like $\text{Rand}_{0,1}^{\text{pub},\rightarrow}$ except Bob sends a message to Alice, who produces the output. Prove $\text{Rand}_{0,1}^{\text{pub},\leftarrow}(\text{INDEX}) = \Theta(\log N)$ using the VC dimension method.

17.17 Prove an analogue of Lemma 17.27 for one-sided-error randomized protocols: f has no public-coin (a,b)-protocol with one-sided error ε on the side of 1-inputs if f is (s,t)-rich but has no 1-monochromatic $\lceil (1-\sqrt{\varepsilon})s/2^{a+b} \rceil \times \lceil (1-\sqrt{\varepsilon})t/2^b \rceil$ rectangle. Hint: Obtain an average-case deterministic protocol like in Exercise 17.12.a, then use Lemma 17.27 as a black box.

17.18 Let f be "lopsided DISJOINTNESS" where $\text{weight}(x) = k$ and $\text{weight}(y) = \ell$ for some parameters k,ℓ such that $k+\ell \leq N/2$. Use the richness method (Lemma 17.27) to prove that f has no $(k/4,\ \ell/4)$-protocol. By swapping Alice and Bob if necessary, you may assume $k \geq \ell$. Hint: $\binom{N}{k}/c^k \geq \binom{N/c}{k}$ for all $c \geq 1$.

17.19 Prove that every randomized streaming algorithm for approximating the highest frequency within factor $< \sqrt{2}$ uses space $\Omega(n)$ even if the algorithm may take a constant number of passes over the input (instead of just one pass). Hint: Use the two-way communication lower bound for DISJOINTNESS (Theorem 17.22).

17.20 Prove $\mathrm{Rand}^{\mathrm{pub}}(\text{OPPOSITE PARITY}) \geq 2\log N - O(1)$. This is the depth of a shallowest public-coin protocol such that for every input, **Pr**[output is an acceptable solution] $\geq 2/3$.

17.21 Prove $\mathrm{Det}(\text{FORK}_{2,n}) \geq 2\log(n+1)$ by reducing from $\text{OPPOSITE PARITY}_{n+1}$.

17.22 In $\text{UNDIRECTED FORK}_{k,n}$, Alice and Bob get $(x, y) \in [k]^n \times [k]^n$ and want to output an *undirected fork*, which is an index $i \in \{0, 1, \ldots, n\}$ such that either $x_i = y_i$ and $x_{i+1} \neq y_{i+1}$ or $x_i \neq y_i$ and $x_{i+1} = y_{i+1}$, assuming implicitly that $x_0 = y_0$ and $x_{n+1} \neq y_{n+1}$. Of course, $\mathrm{Det}(\text{UNDIRECTED FORK}) \leq \mathrm{Det}(\text{FORK})$ since forks are undirected forks (though not all undirected forks are forks). Prove $\mathrm{Det}(\text{UNDIRECTED FORK}) \geq \Omega\big((\log k)(\log n)\big)$.

17.23 UNIVERSAL SEARCH is the partial two-party search problem where Alice and Bob get $(x, y) \in \{0,1\}^N \times \{0,1\}^N$ such that $x \neq y$ (so inputs with $x = y$ are invalid) and want to output an index $i \in [N]$ such that $x_i \neq y_i$.

(a) Prove a randomized communication upper bound for UNIVERSAL SEARCH by reducing to EQUALITY.

(b) Prove a deterministic communication lower bound for UNIVERSAL SEARCH by reducing from EQUALITY.

Notes

For texts on communication complexity, see [324, 329, 452, 426]. The seminal paper [569] introduced the subject. A protocol's depth is also called its "cost."

The $O(\log^2 n)$ upper bound for CLIQUE VERSUS INDEPENDENT SET (Theorem 17.1) is due to [566]. The matching lower bound is due to [215] (deterministic) and [212] (randomized).

The fooling set method originated in [569, 341]. Rectangular reductions, and communication analogues of traditional complexity classes and completeness, were introduced by [41].

The conversion of public coins to private coins (Theorem 17.15) is due to [388].

$\mathrm{Rand}^{\mathrm{pub}}_{0,1}(\text{GREATER THAN}) \leq O(\log N)$ is due to [395, 160]. Also, $\mathrm{Disc}(\text{GREATER THAN}) \leq O(1/\sqrt{N})$ is due to [89]. Other proofs of $\mathrm{Rand}^{\mathrm{pub}}_{0,1}(\text{GREATER THAN}) \geq \Omega(\log N)$ are due to [549, 425]. Also, $\mathrm{Rand}^{\mathrm{pub},\rightarrow}_{0,1}(\text{GREATER THAN}) = \Theta(N)$ is due to [373].

$\mathrm{Rand}^{\mathrm{pub}}_{0,1}(\text{INNER PRODUCT}) = \Theta(N)$ (Theorem 17.19) is due to [125].

$\mathrm{Rand}^{\mathrm{pub}}_{0,1}(\text{DISJOINTNESS}) = \Theta(N)$ (Theorem 17.22) is originally due to [284]. The corruption-based proof (Lemma 17.21) is due to [432]. A conceptually different proof is due to [47].

$\mathrm{Rand}^{\mathrm{pub},\rightarrow}_{0,1}(\text{INDEX}) = \Theta(N)$ (Theorem 17.25) is due to [321].

The richness method for asymmetric lower bounds (Lemma 17.27), and the deterministic lower bound for lopsided DISJOINTNESS (Exercise 17.18), are due to [373]. The randomized lower bound for lopsided DISJOINTNESS is due to [409, 141].

The streaming lower bounds in §17.4.1 (and Exercise 17.19) are due to [18].

For a survey on data structure lower bounds, see [372]. The connection between static data structures and asymmetric communication complexity is due to [371] and expanded on in [373].

The connection between communication and area-time tradeoffs for VLSI (Theorem 17.32) is due to [519, 341]. The lower bound for multiplication is due to [4, 90].

The lower bound for FORK (Theorem 17.34) is due to [220].

Exercise 17.5, which implies the analogue of $\mathsf{P} = \mathsf{NP} \cap \mathsf{coNP}$ for total functions in communication complexity, is due to [12, 230]. Exercise 17.8.c is due to [257]. Exercise 17.11 is due to [23]. Exercise 17.13 is due to [216]. Exercise 17.16 is due to [321].

Regarding Exercise 17.8, Communication Complexity of Total Matrix (in which the matrix has no undefined entries) is NP-complete [245, 184]. This was open for a long time.

Regarding Exercise 17.10, the randomized communication complexity of deciding whether $\text{dist}(x, y) \leq k$ is $\Theta(k \log k)$ if $k^2 \leq N/3$ [457].

Regarding Exercise 17.11, the communication complexity of Equality in the private-coin simultaneous messages model is $\Theta(\sqrt{N})$ [389, 42].

Chapter 18

Circuits and Formulas

A *circuit* is a dag where sources are input variables, nonsource nodes are $\wedge$, $\vee$, or $\neg$ gates, edges are wires, and one node is designated as the output. A *formula* is a tree-like circuit, where the output node (root) has fan-out 0, and every non-output node has fan-out 1, and different input nodes (leaves) may represent the same variable. The class of decision problems with poly-size circuit families is P/poly (§5.3.3). The class of decision problems with poly-size formula families is NC^1/poly (§6.5.2).

The best known size lower bounds for NP problems are linear for circuits (cN for some constant $c > 1$) and polynomial for formulas (N^c for some constant $c > 1$). For every constant c, some problem in $\Sigma_2\mathsf{P}$ doesn't have size-N^c circuits (Exercise 5.14). But it's not even known whether $\mathsf{NEXP} \not\subseteq \mathsf{NC}^1$/poly, which would require proving a superpolynomial formula size lower bound. We prove superpolynomial size lower bounds for NP problems for special types of circuits and formulas:

- *Shallow* means the gates are partitioned into few layers, with wires going from lower to higher layers. Each layer of gates can be evaluated in one parallel time step.
- *Monotone* means there are no $\neg$ gates, only $\wedge$ and $\vee$ gates.

As a case study, we consider Parity: $\{0,1\}^+ \to \{0,1\}$ defined by $\text{Parity}_N(x) = x_1 \oplus x_2 \oplus \cdots \oplus x_N$, which is 1 iff x has odd *weight* (number of 1s). We prove that the Parity upper bounds for circuits, formulas, and shallow circuits from Chapter 6 are essentially tight. We also prove:

- A superpolynomial monotone formula size lower bound for the NL-complete problem Directed Reachability, showing that only $\neg$ gates stand between us and a separation of NC^1 and NL.
- A superpolynomial monotone circuit size lower bound for the NP-complete problem Clique, showing that only $\neg$ gates stand between us and a separation of P and NP.

We conclude by elucidating why lower bounds for general circuits are so elusive: The kinds of lower bound techniques we apply to special types of circuits are subject to a barrier that inhibits them from applying to general circuits. Ironically, this barrier says that a "natural" proof of a strong lower bound would yield a similarly strong upper bound as a byproduct.

18.1 Gate Elimination

In this section, circuits always have bounded fan-in. We do two elementary demonstrations of the *gate elimination* technique for proving circuit size lower bounds. The key observation is that if a possibly-negated input variable (x_i or $\neg x_i$) feeds into an $\wedge$ or $\vee$ gate, and if we assign the variable any bit and contract the circuit (§5.2.2), then the gate is eliminated:

- An $\wedge$ gate with an incoming 0 becomes constant 0.
- An $\wedge$ gate with an incoming 1 is bypassed.
- An $\vee$ gate with an incoming 1 becomes constant 1.
- An $\vee$ gate with an incoming 0 is bypassed.

Bypassed means the gate's other incoming wire goes directly to its outgoing wires.

For each integer $k \geq 0$, define k-THRESHOLD: $\{0,1\}^+ \to \{0,1\}$ by k-THRESHOLD$(x) = 1$ iff weight$(x) \geq k$. Abbreviate k-THRESHOLD as F^k. For all $N \geq 2$, F_N^2 has a circuit with only $3N-5$ many $\wedge$ and $\vee$ gates: For each $i \leftarrow 2,\ldots,N$, compute $w_i^1 = F_i^1(x_1 \cdots x_i)$ and $w_i^2 = F_i^2(x_1 \cdots x_i)$ (and finally output w_N^2) as follows: $w_2^1 = x_1 \vee x_2$ and $w_2^2 = x_1 \wedge x_2$ and for $i > 2$, $w_i^1 = w_{i-1}^1 \vee x_i$ and $w_i^2 = w_{i-1}^2 \vee (w_{i-1}^1 \wedge x_i)$. There are two gates for $i = 2$ and three gates for each $i > 2$, but w_N^1 isn't needed. This upper bound of $\approx 3N$ can be improved to $\approx 2N$, but that's more difficult. We complement this with a $\approx 2N$ lower bound:

Theorem 18.1. *Every bounded-fan-in circuit for* 2-THRESHOLD$_N$ *has at least* $2N-3$ *many* $\wedge$ *and* $\vee$ *gates.*

Proof. This is trivial for $N \leq 2$, so assume $N \geq 3$. Consider any circuit C for F_N^2 with as few $\wedge/\vee$ gates as possible. Consider the first $\wedge/\vee$ gate u in some topological order. Two possibly-negated variables x_i and x_j feed into u. Either x_i or x_j, possibly negated, also feeds into another $\wedge/\vee$ gate v, because otherwise the three partial assignments with $x_i x_j \in \{00, 01, 11\}$ would yield only two contractions of C (in which u becomes constant 0 or 1) but three restrictions of F_N^2 (namely F_{N-2}^2, F_{N-2}^1, F_{N-2}^0, which are different since $N \geq 3$). Say x_j, possibly negated, feeds into v. Figure 18.1 depicts this with the optional $\neg$ gates in gray. Assigning $x_j \leftarrow 0$ and contracting C eliminates u and v, yielding a circuit for F_{N-1}^2 with at least two fewer $\wedge/\vee$ gates. Repeating this until two variables remain eliminates $\geq 2(N-2)$ many $\wedge/\vee$ gates. Then, an $\wedge/\vee$ gate remains for F_2^2. Thus C has $\geq 2(N-2)+1$ many $\wedge/\vee$ gates. ■

$\oplus_N =$ PARITY$_N$ has a circuit with only $3N-3$ many $\wedge$ and $\vee$ gates: $(\cdots(((x_1 \oplus x_2) \oplus x_3) \oplus x_4) \cdots) \oplus x_N$ has $N-1$ "xor gates," each of which corresponds to two $\wedge$ gates and one $\vee$ gate (and two $\neg$ gates). This upper bound is exactly tight:

Theorem 18.2. *Every bounded-fan-in circuit for* PARITY$_N$ *has at least* $3N-3$ *many* $\wedge$ *and* $\vee$ *gates.*

Proof. Consider any circuit C for $\oplus_N$ with as few $\wedge/\vee$ gates as possible. Consider the first $\wedge/\vee$ gate u in some topological order. Two possibly-negated variables x_i and x_j feed into u. Then x_j, possibly negated, also feeds into another $\wedge/\vee$ gate v, because otherwise assigning x_i a certain bit and contracting C would make u a constant and thus yield a circuit for either $\oplus_{N-1}$ or $\overline{\oplus_{N-1}}$ that doesn't depend on x_j, contradicting the fact that $\oplus_{N-1}$ depends on all its variables. Neither v nor $\neg v$ is the output, because assigning x_j a certain bit would make v a constant, which can't happen for $\oplus_N$ (if $N \geq 2$). Thus v, possibly negated, feeds into an $\wedge/\vee$ gate w, and $w \neq u$ since u is the first $\wedge/\vee$ gate in the topological order. Figure 18.2 depicts this with the optional $\neg$ gates in gray. Assigning x_j a certain bit and contracting C makes v a constant and eliminates u, v, w, yielding a circuit for either $\oplus_{N-1}$ or $\overline{\oplus_{N-1}}$ with at least three fewer $\wedge/\vee$ gates. Repeating this until one variable remains eliminates $\geq 3(N-1)$ many $\wedge/\vee$ gates. Thus C has $\geq 3(N-1)$ many $\wedge/\vee$ gates. ■

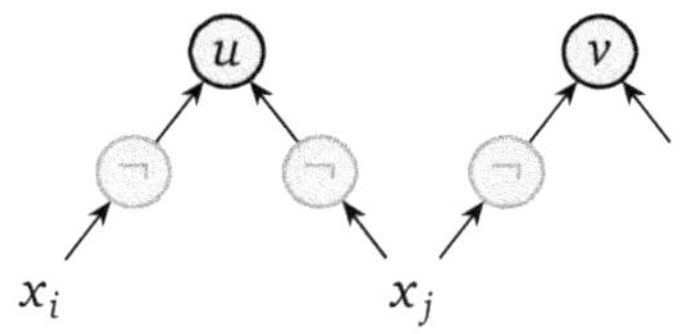

Figure 18.1: Gate elimination for 2-THRESHOLD

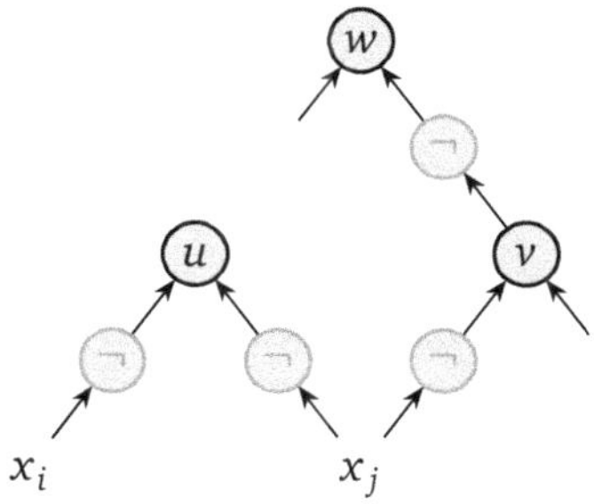

Figure 18.2: Gate elimination for PARITY

The gate elimination method, with more elaborate case analyses, yields linear lower bounds with slightly higher constant factors for other NP problems. But no superlinear circuit size lower bound is known for any NP problem.

18.2 Circuits and Polynomials

Now, we consider shallow unbounded-fan-in circuits.

Theorem 18.3. PARITY *has depth-d circuit size complexity* $2^{\Omega(N^{1/2d})}$.

This doesn't quite match the $2^{O(N^{1/(d-1)})}$ upper bound from Theorem 6.2. We prove the tight $2^{\Omega(N^{1/(d-1)})}$ lower bound in §18.3 by a different technique. Anyway, Theorem 18.3 already implies PARITY $\notin$ AC^0/poly because for constant d, the $2^{N^{\Omega(1)}}$ lower bound is superpolynomial. The hidden constant in the exponent $\Omega(N^{1/2d})$ doesn't depend on d, so we get a lower bound even when d is a function of N, but the lower bound is trivial when $d \geq \frac{1}{2}\log N$ since $N^{1/\log N} = 2$.

The proof of Theorem 18.3 involves multivariate polynomials over finite fields. In this section, "degree" means total degree. The idea is that low-degree polynomials can approximate small shallow circuits but can't approximate PARITY. Since PARITY$_N(x)$ is computed by the degree-1 polynomial $x_1 + x_2 + \cdots + x_N$ over $\mathbb{Z}_2$, we use a different field, $\mathbb{Z}_3$. The polynomial approximating a circuit has the same variables as the circuit, and although any values from $\mathbb{Z}_3$ could be plugged into the polynomial's variables, we only plug in values from $\{0,1\}$.

Proof of Theorem 18.3. We combine two lemmas:

- §18.2.1: For every depth-d size-s circuit $C\colon \{0,1\}^N \to \{0,1\}$ and every $k \geq 1$, some $\mathbb{Z}_3$-polynomial of degree $\leq (2k)^d$ agrees with C on $\geq 1 - s/3^k$ fraction of $\{0,1\}^N$.
- §18.2.2: Every $\mathbb{Z}_3$-polynomial of degree $\leq \sqrt{N}/2$ agrees with PARITY$_N$ on $\leq 4/5$ fraction of $\{0,1\}^N$.

Pick $k = \lfloor (\sqrt{N}/2)^{1/d}/2 \rfloor = \Omega(N^{1/2d})$ so the two degree bounds essentially match: For every depth-d size-s circuit for PARITY$_N$, some $\mathbb{Z}_3$-polynomial of degree $\leq (2k)^d \leq \sqrt{N}/2$ agrees with the circuit on $\geq 1 - s/3^k$ but $\leq 4/5$ fraction of $\{0,1\}^N$. Rearranging $1 - s/3^k \leq 4/5$ yields $s \geq 3^k/5 = 2^{\Omega(N^{1/2d})}$. ∎

This is quantitatively weaker than the lower bound in §18.3 but has a qualitative advantage: It can handle circuits with "mod 3 gates" since they wouldn't increase the polynomial's degree.

18.2.1 Polynomials Approximate Shallow Circuits

Lemma 18.4. *For every depth-d size-s circuit $C: \{0,1\}^N \to \{0,1\}$ and every $k \geq 1$, some $\mathbb{Z}_3$-polynomial of degree $\leq (2k)^d$ agrees with C on $\geq 1-s/3^k$ fraction of $\{0,1\}^N$.*

Proof idea. Like we've seen several times (Lemma 10.3, Lemma 16.9, Lemma 17.17), to design a "deterministic average-case" polynomial, it suffices to design a "randomized worst-case" polynomial simulating C. We handle each gate separately, and then combine the polynomials for individual gates in the same way C combines the gates, with the error probability accumulating over the s gates by a union bound.

Warmup: We design a low-degree randomized polynomial over $\mathbb{Z}_2$ (rather than $\mathbb{Z}_3$) to simulate an $\vee$ gate with incoming wires $y = (y_1, \ldots, y_m)$. The polynomial $1-(1-y_1)(1-y_2)\cdots(1-y_m)$ has high degree m and no error: It agrees with $\vee$ on all $y \in \{0,1\}^m$. The randomized polynomial $b \cdot y = b_1y_1 + \cdots + b_my_m$ (for a uniformly random tuple of coefficients $b \in \mathbb{Z}_2^m$) has low degree 1 and one-sided error: If $\vee(y) = 0$ then $b \cdot y = 0$. If $\vee(y) = 1$ then $\mathbf{Pr}[b \cdot y \neq 1] = 1/2$ by the random subsum principle (Lemma 7.2.*(i)*). To balance the tradeoff between degree and error probability, we combine these approaches. The randomized polynomial

$$Q(y) = \vee(b^1 \cdot y, \ldots, b^k \cdot y) = 1-(1-b^1 \cdot y)\cdots(1-b^k \cdot y)$$

(for independent and uniformly random $b^1 \in \mathbb{Z}_2^m, \ldots, b^k \in \mathbb{Z}_2^m$) has degree k and one-sided error probability $1/2^k$: If $\vee(y) = 0$ then $Q(y) = 0$. If $\vee(y) = 1$ then $\mathbf{Pr}\big[Q(y) \neq 1\big] = 1/2^k$. A similar thing works over $\mathbb{Z}_3$, but we use $(b \cdot y)^2$ instead of $b \cdot y$ because squaring turns 2 into 1; then Q has degree $2k$ and error probability $1/3^k$.

Each layer of gates contributes $\leq 2k$ to the degree of the polynomial for the whole circuit, and these degrees multiply together over the d layers, so we get degree $\leq (2k)^d$. ■

Proof. We design a distribution over N-variate $\mathbb{Z}_3$-polynomials P of degree $\leq (2k)^d$ such that $\mathbf{Pr}_P\big[P(x) \neq C(x)\big] \leq s/3^k$ for every $x \in \{0,1\}^N$. This implies $\mathbf{Pr}_{P,x}\big[P(x) \neq C(x)\big] \leq s/3^k$ for uniformly random x, which implies $\mathbf{Pr}_x\big[P(x) \neq C(x)\big] \leq s/3^k$ for some P.

Consider an $\vee$ gate with incoming wires $y = (y_1, \ldots, y_m)$. We design a distribution over polynomials Q of degree $\leq 2k$ such that $\mathbf{Pr}\big[Q(y) \neq \vee(y)\big] \leq 1/3^k$ for every $y \in \{0,1\}^m$.

- First, consider the degree-1 polynomial $b \cdot y = b_1y_1 + \cdots + b_my_m$ for a uniformly random tuple of coefficients $b \in \mathbb{Z}_3^m$. If $\vee(y) = 0$ then $b \cdot y = 0$. If $\vee(y) = 1$, say $y_j = 1$, then $b \cdot y$ is uniformly distributed over $\mathbb{Z}_3$ because regardless of $b_1y_1 + \cdots + b_{j-1}y_{j-1} + b_{j+1}y_{j+1} + \cdots + b_my_m$, we add to it b_jy_j which is independent and uniform over $\mathbb{Z}_3$.
- Next, consider the degree-2 polynomial $(b \cdot y)^2$ for a uniformly random $b \in \mathbb{Z}_3^m$. If $\vee(y) = 0$ then $(b \cdot y)^2 = 0$. If $\vee(y) = 1$ then $\mathbf{Pr}\big[(b \cdot y)^2 \neq 1\big] = \mathbf{Pr}\big[b \cdot y \notin \{1,2\}\big] = 1/3$ since $1^2 = 2^2 = 1$ and $b \cdot y$ is uniform over $\mathbb{Z}_3$.
- Finally, consider the degree-$2k$ polynomial

  $$Q(y) = \vee\big((b^1 \cdot y)^2, \ldots, (b^k \cdot y)^2\big) = 1-\big(1-(b^1 \cdot y)^2\big)\cdots\big(1-(b^k \cdot y)^2\big)$$

  for independent and uniformly random $b^1 \in \mathbb{Z}_3^m, \ldots, b^k \in \mathbb{Z}_3^m$. If $\vee(y) = 0$ then $Q(y) = 0$. If $\vee(y) = 1$ then $\mathbf{Pr}\big[Q(y) \neq 1\big] = 1/3^k$.

We may assume the circuit C only has $\vee$ and $\neg$ gates, since an $\wedge$ gate $\wedge(y_1, \ldots, y_m)$ is equivalent to $\neg(\vee(\neg y_1, \ldots, \neg y_m))$. To turn C into a random polynomial P, replace the ith $\vee$ gate $\vee_i(y_1, \ldots, y_m)$ with an independently sampled polynomial $Q_i(y_1, \ldots, y_m)$ as above, and replace each $\neg$ gate $\neg y_1$ with the polynomial $1-y_1$. For example, the circuit $C(x) = \vee\big(x_1, \neg(\vee(x_2, \neg x_3))\big)$ becomes the polynomial $P(x) = Q_1\big(x_1, 1-Q_2(x_2, 1-x_3)\big)$ for independent Q_1, Q_2.

For each input $x \in \{0,1\}^N$, we have $P(x) = C(x)$ if there's no error at any $\vee$ gate, in other words, if $Q_i(y) = \vee_i(y)$ for all i, where y is the incoming bits to $\vee_i$ on input x. By a union bound over C's $\vee$ gates, of which there are at most s:

$$\mathbf{Pr}\big[P(x) \neq C(x)\big] \;\leq\; \mathbf{Pr}[\text{some } Q_i \text{ errs}] \;\leq\; \textstyle\sum_i \mathbf{Pr}[Q_i \text{ errs}] \;\leq\; s/3^k$$

P has degree $\leq (2k)^d$ because each of the d layers of $\vee$ gates multiplies the degree by $\leq 2k$: When we plug polynomials into Q_i's variables, the degree becomes at most $2k$ (the degree of Q_i) times the maximum degree of the polynomials we plug in. ■

18.2.2 Polynomials Don't Approximate Parity

Lemma 18.5. *Every $\mathbb{Z}_3$-polynomial of degree $\leq \sqrt{N}/2$ agrees with* PARITY_N *on $\leq 4/5$ fraction of $\{0,1\}^N$.*

Proof. First, we change perspective: "Sum over $\mathbb{Z}_2$" (parity) becomes "product over $\mathbb{Z}_3$" if we change 0 to 1 and change 1 to $-1 = 2$: For all $x \in \{1,-1\}^N$,

$$x_1 x_2 \cdots x_N \;=\; \big((x_1-1) \oplus (x_2-1) \oplus \cdots \oplus (x_N-1)\big) + 1$$

since this is -1 iff x has an odd number of -1s. Let P be a $\mathbb{Z}_3$-polynomial of degree $\leq \sqrt{N}/2$ that agrees with PARITY_N on some $S \subseteq \{0,1\}^N$. Then $Q(x) = P(x_1-1,\ldots,x_N-1)+1$ is a $\mathbb{Z}_3$-polynomial of degree $\leq \sqrt{N}/2$ that agrees with the product function $x_1 \cdots x_N$ on $T = \big\{x : (x_1-1,\ldots,x_N-1) \in S\big\} \subseteq \{1,-1\}^N$, which has the same size as S. We prove $|T| \leq (4/5)2^N$.

Since we only care about inputs in $T \subseteq \{1,-1\}^N$, we may assume $\mathbb{Z}_3$-polynomials are multilinear (each individual degree is ≤ 1) because $x_i^2 = 1$ for both $x_i \in \{1,-1\}$. For all $I \subseteq [N]$ and $x \in T$:

$$\textstyle\prod_{i\in I} x_i \;=\; \big(\prod_{i\in[N]} x_i\big)\big(\prod_{i\in[N]\setminus I} x_i\big) \;=\; Q(x)\big(\prod_{i\in[N]\setminus I} x_i\big)$$

So every monomial of degree $|I| \geq N/2 + \sqrt{N}/4$ agrees with a polynomial of degree $\leq \sqrt{N}/2 + (N-|I|) \leq N/2 + \sqrt{N}/4$ on T. Therefore, every polynomial agrees with a polynomial of degree $\leq N/2 + \sqrt{N}/4$ on T. Every function $f: T \to \mathbb{Z}_3$ is expressed by a polynomial $\sum_{a\in T} f(a) \prod_{i\in[N]}(2 - a_i x_i)$, so f is expressed by a polynomial of degree $\leq N/2 + \sqrt{N}/4$. This implies

$$3^{|T|} \;\leq\; 3^{\binom{N}{0}+\binom{N}{1}+\binom{N}{2}+\cdots+\binom{N}{\lfloor N/2+\sqrt{N}/4\rfloor}}$$

because the left side is the number of such functions (3 options for $f(x)$ for each $x \in T$) and the right side is the number of such polynomials (3 options for the coefficient of $\prod_{i\in I} x_i$ for each $I \subseteq [N]$ of size $\leq N/2 + \sqrt{N}/4$). Therefore:

$$\begin{aligned}|T| &\leq \Big(\tbinom{N}{0} + \tbinom{N}{1} + \cdots + \tbinom{N}{\lceil N/2\rceil - 1}\Big) + \tbinom{N}{\lceil N/2\rceil} + \cdots + \tbinom{N}{\lfloor N/2+\sqrt{N}/4\rfloor} \\ &\leq (2^N/2) + (2^N/\sqrt{N}) + \cdots + (2^N/\sqrt{N}) \qquad \text{(Claim 18.6 below)} \\ &\leq (2^N/2) + (\sqrt{N}/4+1)\cdot(2^N/\sqrt{N}) \;\leq\; (4/5)2^N\end{aligned}$$

■

Claim 18.6. $\binom{n}{k} \leq 2^n/\sqrt{n}$ *for all $n \geq 1$ and k.*

Proof (ancillary). First, assume n is even and $k = n/2$.

$$\binom{n}{n/2}/2^n = \frac{n!}{(n/2)!(n/2)!2^n} = \frac{n\cdot(n-1)\cdot(n-2)\cdots 2\cdot 1}{\big(n\cdot(n-2)\cdot(n-4)\cdots 4\cdot 2\big)\cdot\big(n\cdot(n-2)\cdot(n-4)\cdots 4\cdot 2\big)}$$
$$= \frac{n\cdot(n-1)\cdot(n-2)\cdot(n-3)\cdots 4\cdot 3\cdot 2\cdot 1}{n\cdot\quad n\quad\cdot(n-2)\cdot(n-2)\cdots 4\cdot 4\cdot 2\cdot 2}$$
$$= \frac{n-1}{n}\cdot\frac{n-3}{n-2}\cdots\frac{3}{4}\cdot\frac{1}{2} \leq \frac{n}{n+1}\cdot\frac{n-2}{n-1}\cdots\frac{4}{5}\cdot\frac{2}{3}$$

$$\Big(\binom{n}{n/2}/2^n\Big)^2 \leq \Big(\frac{n-1}{n}\cdot\frac{n-3}{n-2}\cdots\frac{3}{4}\cdot\frac{1}{2}\Big)\cdot\Big(\frac{n}{n+1}\cdot\frac{n-2}{n-1}\cdots\frac{4}{5}\cdot\frac{2}{3}\Big)$$
$$= \frac{n\cdot(n-1)\cdot(n-2)\cdots 4\cdot 3\cdot 2\cdot 1}{(n+1)\cdot n\cdot(n-1)\cdot(n-2)\cdots 4\cdot 3\cdot 2} = \frac{1}{n+1} \leq \frac{1}{n}$$

Thus $\binom{n}{n/2} \leq 2^n/\sqrt{n}$. If n is odd, then $\binom{n}{\lceil n/2\rceil} = \frac{1}{2}\binom{n+1}{(n+1)/2} \leq \frac{1}{2}2^{n+1}/\sqrt{n+1} \leq 2^n/\sqrt{n}$. For all $n \geq k \geq 1$, we have $\binom{n}{k}/\binom{n}{k-1} = (n-k+1)/k$, which is ≥ 1 if $k \leq \lceil n/2\rceil$ and ≤ 1 if $k > \lceil n/2\rceil$. Thus $\binom{n}{0}, \binom{n}{1}, \ldots, \binom{n}{n-1}, \binom{n}{n}$ increases up to $\binom{n}{\lceil n/2\rceil} \leq 2^n/\sqrt{n}$ and decreases thereafter. ■

18.3 Circuits and Random Restrictions

Theorem 18.7. Parity *has depth-d circuit size complexity* $2^{\Omega(N^{1/(d-1)})}$.

This improves Theorem 18.3 and matches the $2^{O(N^{1/(d-1)})}$ upper bound from Theorem 6.2. In particular, Parity has depth-3 circuit size complexity $2^{\Theta(\sqrt{N})}$. It's unknown whether any problem in NP has even higher depth-3 circuit size complexity.

18.3.1 The Random Restriction Method

For a function $f\colon \{0,1\}^N \to \{0,1\}$ and partial assignment $a \in \{0,1,*\}^N$, the restriction $f|_a$ is f but with a's non-stars hardcoded and with a's stars left as unassigned variables. Given an assignment to a's star variables, $f|_a$ combines it with a and evaluates f on the resulting full assignment. If a has M stars, then $f|_a\colon \{0,1\}^M \to \{0,1\}$.

We introduce a general technique for proving lower bounds: Show that if f has an efficient algorithm in some model (circuit, formula, branching program, or decision tree), then a random partial assignment probably simplifies the algorithm a lot but doesn't simplify f much. If the contracted algorithm can't compute the restricted f, then the original algorithm couldn't compute the original f. A lower bound for the simpler model implies a lower bound for the original model.

Before developing this technique for circuit lower bounds, we do a warmup demonstration: Random partial assignments make small decision trees shallow, so we could derive decision tree size lower bounds from depth lower bounds.

Lemma 18.8. *If f has a size-s decision tree, then for a uniformly random partial assignment a:*

$$\mathbf{Pr}\big[f|_a \text{ has a depth-}d\text{ decision tree}\big] \geq 1 - s(2/3)^{d+1}$$

Proof. Let T be a decision tree for f with s leaves. For any partial assignment a, define the contracted decision tree $T|_a$ from T as follows. For each node u that queries x_i:

- If $a_i = 0$, delete u's right subtree and replace u with its left child.
- If $a_i = 1$, delete u's left subtree and replace u with its right child.

For each node v, let T^v be the subtree rooted at v, and let q^v be the partial assignment recording the results of queries along the root-to-v path. Then T^v is deleted if a and q^v assign some variable opposite bits. Let L be the set of all nodes at distance $d+1$ from T's root, of which there are $\leq s$. If T^v is deleted for every $v \in L$, then $T|_a$ has depth $\leq d$.

$$\begin{aligned}
& \mathbf{Pr}\big[f|_a \text{ has no depth-}d\text{ decision tree}\big] \\
\leq\ & \mathbf{Pr}\big[T|_a \text{ has depth} \geq d+1\big] \\
\leq\ & \mathbf{Pr}\big[\text{for some } v \in L,\ T^v \text{ isn't deleted}\big] \\
\leq\ & \textstyle\sum_{v\in L} \mathbf{Pr}\big[T^v \text{ isn't deleted}\big] && \text{(union bound)} \\
\leq\ & \textstyle\sum_{v\in L} \mathbf{Pr}\big[a_i \in \{q_i^v, *\} \text{ for all } i \text{ with } q_i^v \neq *\big] \\
=\ & \textstyle\sum_{v\in L} \prod_{i \text{ with } q_i^v \neq *} \mathbf{Pr}\big[a_i \in \{q_i^v, *\}\big] && (a_1, a_2, \ldots \text{ are fully independent}) \\
=\ & \textstyle\sum_{v\in L} (2/3)^{d+1} && (a_i \text{ is uniform over } \{0,1,*\}) \\
\leq\ & s(2/3)^{d+1} && \blacksquare
\end{aligned}$$

Corollary 18.9. *f has decision tree size complexity $> s$ if $f|_a$ has decision tree depth complexity $> \log_{3/2}(2s)$ for every a with at least $N/4$ stars, assuming N is sufficiently large.*

Proof. We prove the contrapositive. Suppose f has a size-s decision tree. A uniformly random partial assignment a has at least $N/4$ stars with probability $\geq 1 - e^{-N/144} \geq 1 - 1/e > 1/2$ if $N \geq 144$ (Lemma 7.20), and $f|_a$ has a depth-d decision tree with probability $\geq 1 - s(2/3)^{d+1} > 1/2$ for $d = \lfloor \log_{3/2}(2s) \rfloor$ (Lemma 18.8), so by a union bound, a has at least $N/4$ stars and $f|_a$ has a depth-d decision tree with probability > 0. Thus for some a with at least $N/4$ stars, $f|_a$ has a depth-d decision tree. ■

Next, we take off the training wheels and deal with circuits. There are two commonly used types of distributions over partial assignments a:

- For each i independently, $\mathbf{Pr}[a_i = *] = p$ and $\mathbf{Pr}[a_i = 0] = \mathbf{Pr}[a_i = 1] = (1-p)/2$ for some parameter p. (This is the uniform distribution when $p = 1/3$.)
- The uniform distribution over all M-*partial assignments*, which have exactly M stars. This is intuitively similar to the $p = M/N$ distribution above, but is sometimes more convenient because the number of stars isn't random.

18.3.2 Switching Lemma

The titular "switching lemma," which we prove in §18.3.3, says that a random partial assignment "switches" a k-DNF to an ℓ-CNF:

Lemma 18.10. *If $f: \{0,1\}^N \to \{0,1\}$ has a k-DNF, then for a uniformly random M-partial assignment a, where $M \leq N/2$:*

$$\mathbf{Pr}\big[f|_a \text{ has no } \ell\text{-CNF}\big] \leq (16kM/N)^\ell$$

By symmetry, this also holds with the roles of "DNF" and "CNF" swapped. The factor of 16 is unimportant and can be improved. Also, a qualitatively stronger version of the switching lemma has "depth-ℓ decision tree" instead of "ℓ-CNF" (Exercise 18.7.a).

Now, we'll see an application of the switching lemma to shallow circuits. We assume circuits have $\neg$ gates pushed to the input variables, and the layers of $\wedge$ and $\vee$ gates strictly alternate between $\wedge$ and $\vee$, and the size is the number of $\wedge$ and $\vee$ gates.

A *certificate* for f is a partial assignment a such that $f|_a$ is a constant function, in other words, $f(x)$ is the same bit for all $x \in \{0,1\}^N$ consistent with a. A certificate's *size* is its number of assigned bits (non-$*$s). Lemma 16.37 says that if f has no small certificate, then f has large decision tree size complexity. Now, we prove that if f has no small certificate, then f has large depth-d circuit size complexity.

Lemma 18.11. *If $f: \{0,1\}^N \to \{0,1\}$ has a depth-d size-s circuit, then f has a certificate with at least $N/32(32k)^{d-2} - k$ many $*$s, where $k = 2\log s$.*

This implies that PARITY has depth-d circuit size complexity $2^{\Omega(N^{1/(d-1)})}$:

Proof of Theorem 18.7. Every certificate for PARITY_N has no $*$s. If PARITY_N has a depth-d size-s circuit, then by Lemma 18.11 it has a certificate with $\geq N/32(32k)^{d-2} - k$ many $*$s, where $k = 2\log s$. Rearranging $0 \geq N/32(32k)^{d-2} - k$ yields $(32k)^{d-1} \geq N$ and thus $k \geq N^{1/(d-1)}/32$, so $s \geq 2^{N^{1/(d-1)}/64}$. ■

Proof idea for Lemma 18.11. Suppose layer 1 (the gates closest to the literals) has $\wedge$ gates, and layer 2 has $\vee$ gates, and layer 3 has $\wedge$ gates, and so on. Also suppose for now that each gate in layer 1 has "medium" fan-in k. Then each gate in layer 2 computes a k-DNF, as the top of Figure 18.3 shows. A random partial assignment probably switches all these k-DNFs to k-CNFs by the switching lemma with $\ell = k$, as the middle of Figure 18.3 shows. These k-CNFs' $\wedge$ gates are absorbed into layer 3's $\wedge$ gates, which now compute k-CNFs, as the bottom of Figure 18.3 shows. The circuit's depth decreased by 1. We repeat this to decrease the depth by 1 again: Another random partial assignment (to the first partial assignment's $*$s) switches the bottom k-CNFs to k-DNFs whose $\vee$ gates merge with the next layer. After $d-2$ applications of the switching lemma, the whole circuit becomes a k-DNF or k-CNF (depth 2), which has a size-k certificate by definition. A preliminary application of the switching lemma justifies our assumption about the fan-in of layer 1 gates. ■

This idea resembles the flipping and merging of quantifiers in the proof that if $\mathsf{NP} = \mathsf{coNP}$ then PH collapses to NP (Theorem 4.23). There's an analogy between query complexity and time complexity: Decision trees correspond to P, DNFs correspond to NP (Lemma 16.20), and constant-depth circuits correspond to PH. So circuit complexity is a natural extension of query complexity.

If a is a partial assignment and b is a partial assignment to a's $*$ variables, define the combined partial assignment ab by $(ab)_i = a_i$ if $a_i \neq *$, and $(ab)_i = b_i$ if $b_i \neq *$, and $(ab)_i = *$ otherwise. (Despite the notation, this isn't concatenation.)

Example. The gray stars mean b must not assign any variables that a assigned:

$$\begin{aligned} a &= * \; 0 \; * \; * \; 1 \; 0 \; * \\ b &= * \; * \; 1 \; * \; * \; * \; 0 \\ ab &= * \; 0 \; 1 \; * \; 1 \; 0 \; 0 \end{aligned}$$

♦

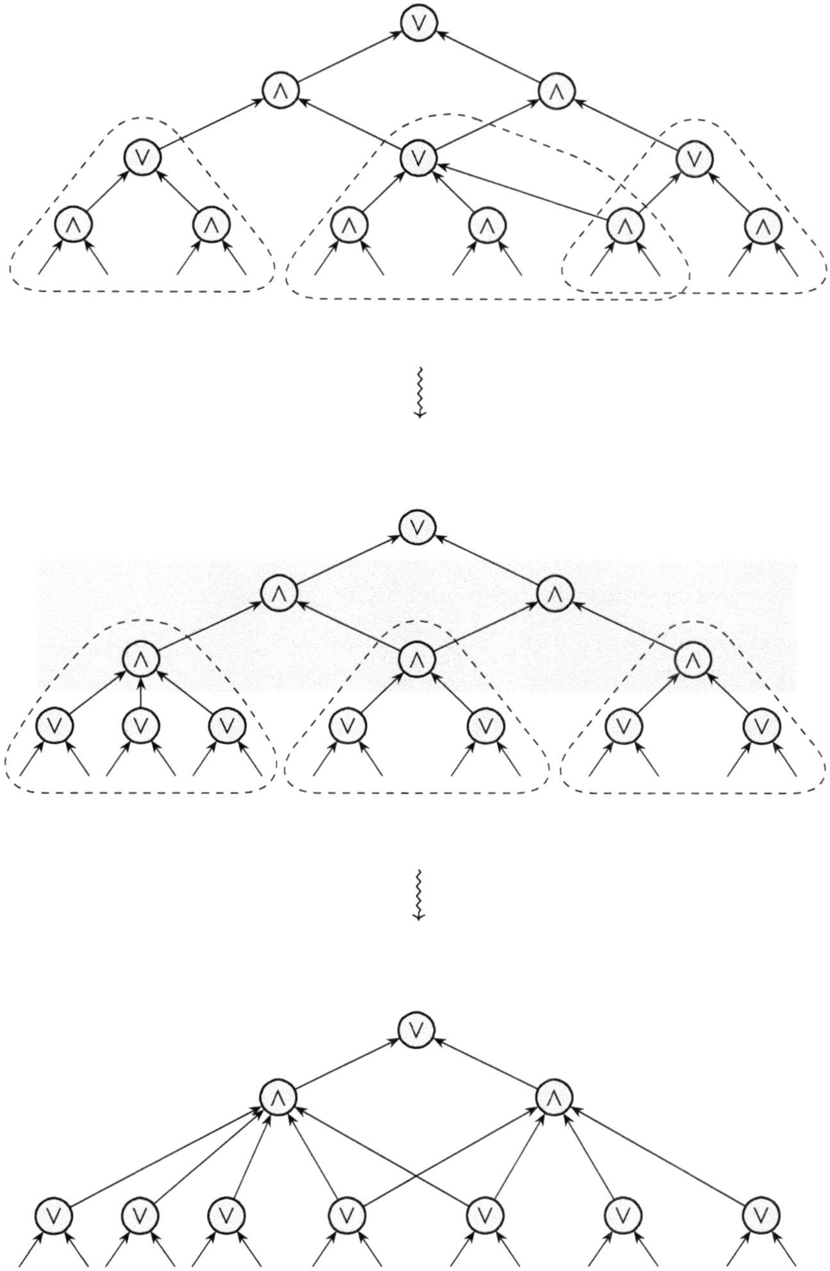

Figure 18.3: Using the switching lemma to collapse a depth-4 circuit to a depth-3 circuit

Proof of Lemma 18.11. Let $k = \ell = 2\log s$. For all $g: \{0,1\}^N \to \{0,1\}$ and a uniformly random M-partial assignment a where $M = N/32k$, the bound in Lemma 18.10 is $(16kM/N)^\ell = (1/2)^\ell = 1/s^2$ and thus:

- If g has a k-DNF, then $\mathbf{Pr}\big[g|_a$ has no k-CNF$\big] \le 1/s^2$.
- If g has a k-CNF, then $\mathbf{Pr}\big[g|_a$ has no k-DNF$\big] \le 1/s^2$.

Suppose $f: \{0,1\}^N \to \{0,1\}$ has a depth-d size-s circuit. The layers of $\wedge$ and $\vee$ gates are numbered $1, \ldots, d$ where the literals feed into layer 1, and each layer i feeds into layer $i+1$, and layer d is the output gate. Assume layer i has $\wedge$ gates if i is odd, and $\vee$ gates if i is even.

- Layer 1: Let $M_1 = N/32$. Let a^1 be a uniformly random M_1-partial assignment to the N variables. For each gate g in layer 1, let B_g be the *bad* event that g, which is a 1-CNF (an $\wedge$ of literals), doesn't switch to a k-DNF under a^1. By the switching lemma, $\mathbf{Pr}[B_g] \le (16M_1/N)^k = (1/2)^k = 1/s^2$.
- Layer $i \leftarrow 2, \ldots, d-1$: Let $M_i = M_{i-1}/32k$. Let a^i be a uniformly random M_i-partial assignment to the M_{i-1} many $*$ variables of $a^1 \cdots a^{i-1}$. Assume i is even. For each gate g in layer i, let B_g be the *bad* event that g doesn't compute a k-CNF under $a^1 \cdots a^i$ but computes a k-DNF under $a^1 \cdots a^{i-1}$. By the switching lemma:

  $$\mathbf{Pr}[B_g] \;\le\; \mathbf{Pr}\big[g \text{ isn't a } k\text{-CNF under } a^1 \cdots a^i \,\big|\, g \text{ is a } k\text{-DNF under } a^1 \cdots a^{i-1}\big] \;\le\; 1/s^2$$

  If i is odd, the same holds with "CNF" and "DNF" interchanged.

By a union bound over all s gates, $\mathbf{Pr}[B_g$ holds for at least one $g] \le \sum_g \mathbf{Pr}[B_g] \le s/s^2 < 1$. Thus for some outcome $a^1 \cdots a^{d-1}$, no bad event holds, in which case:

- Each $\wedge$ gate in layer 1 becomes a k-DNF under a^1. After absorbing these k-DNFs' $\vee$ gates into layer 2's $\vee$ gates, the latter become k-DNFs under a^1.
- Each $\vee$ gate in layer 2 becomes a k-CNF under a^1a^2. After absorbing these k-CNFs' $\wedge$ gates into layer 3's $\wedge$ gates, the latter become k-CNFs under a^1a^2.
- And so on, until the whole circuit becomes a k-CNF (if d is odd) or k-DNF (if d is even) under $a^1 \cdots a^{d-1}$, which has M_{d-1} many $*$s.

The final k-CNF or k-DNF has a size-k certificate a^d (falsifying some clause or satisfying some term). Thus $a^1 \cdots a^d$ is a certificate for f with $M_{d-1} - k = N/32(32k)^{d-2} - k$ many $*$s. ■

18.3.3 Proof of the Switching Lemma

We begin with preliminaries for the proof. A 0-*certificate* for f is a partial assignment a such that $f|_a$ is the constant-0 function, in other words, $f(x) = 0$ for all $x \in \{0,1\}^N$ consistent with a. A 0-certificate's *size* is its number of assigned bits (non-$*$s). A 0-certificate is *minimal* iff no smaller 0-certificate can be obtained by changing an assigned bit to $*$. The next claim essentially follows from Lemma 16.20, but we provide a self-contained proof:

Claim 18.12. *If f has no ℓ-CNF, then f has a minimal* 0*-certificate of size* $> \ell$.

Proof of Claim 18.12. We prove the contrapositive. Suppose every minimal 0-certificate for f has size $\le \ell$. Define a CNF ψ as the conjunction, over all minimal 0-certificates b, of the clause $\bigvee_{i:b_i=0} x_i \vee \bigvee_{i:b_i=1} \overline{x_i}$, which rejects exactly the inputs consistent with b. This ψ expresses f:

- If $\psi(x) = 0$ then some clause of ψ rejects x, so x is consistent with the corresponding minimal 0-certificate, and thus $f(x) = 0$.
- If $f(x) = 0$ then the smallest 0-certificate of f that x is consistent with must be minimal, so the corresponding clause of ψ rejects x, and thus $\psi(x) = 0$.

Each clause of ψ has width $\leq \ell$. To turn ψ into an ℓ-CNF, repeatedly replace any clause C of width $< \ell$ with $(C \vee x_i) \wedge (C \vee \overline{x_i})$ for some variable x_i not in C. ■

Suppose φ is a DNF and a is a partial assignment. To obtain the contracted DNF $\varphi|_a$, delete from φ each term having at least one literal that evaluates to 0 under a (since the term is already unsatisfied), and delete from all other terms of φ any literals that evaluate to 1 under a (leaving only literals whose variables are $*$s in a). A term of φ *survives* in $\varphi|_a$ iff it doesn't evaluate to 0 under a (but may or may not shrink due to deletion of literals). A DNF with no terms always evaluates to 0. A DNF with an empty term always evaluates to 1.

If a is a partial assignment and b is a partial assignment to a's $*$ variables, define the combined partial assignment ab by $(ab)_i = a_i$ if $a_i \neq *$, and $(ab)_i = b_i$ if $b_i \neq *$, and $(ab)_i = *$ otherwise. By analogy with multiplication, we also have "division": $(ab)/b = a$.

Proof idea for Lemma 18.10. We want to show that the set of all *bad* M-partial assignments a (meaning $f|_a$ has no ℓ-CNF) is small compared to the set of all M-partial assignments. A technique for showing a set is small is to "encode" its elements as distinct elements of some other small set. To show the encodings are distinct, we "decode" them to the original elements.

It would suffice to encode bad M-partial assignments as M'-partial assignments for a small enough $M' < M$, because there are far fewer M'-partial assignments than M-partial assignments (since there are far fewer options for placing $*$s, and only somewhat more options for assigning bits to non-$*$s). This suggests encoding a bad a as ab where b is a minimal 0-certificate for $f|_a$ of size $> \ell$ (Claim 18.12). We'd like to decode ab to $a = (ab)/b$, but this would require knowing which variables b assigns. For this, we modify the encoding.

Let φ be a k-DNF for f. Then b's effect on $\varphi|_a$ helps us encode which variables b assigns, without enlarging the encoding much. Since $\varphi|_a$ doesn't always evaluate to 0 (by minimality of b), it has at least one surviving term. Let b^1 be b but only assigning variables in the first term T^1 of φ that survives in $\varphi|_a$. This b^1 assigns at least one such variable since it eliminates T^1 (since b is a 0-certificate). Let c^1 be b^1 but with some bits flipped as needed to satisfy the corresponding literals in T^1 and thus *not* eliminate T^1. Putting ac^1 in the encoding lets the decoder identify T^1 as the first term that survives in $\varphi|_{ac^1}$. This drastically narrows down which variables b^1 assigns—they're among the k variables in T^1. We augment the encoding to say which of those k variables are assigned by b^1 (and c^1). Now the decoder knows c^1. To repeat this (until the encoding assigns enough variables beyond a), the decoder must also know b^1. So we augment the encoding to say how b^1 differs from c^1. ■

Proof of Lemma 18.10. Assume f has a k-DNF φ, whose terms are ordered in some arbitrary way. Let R be the set of all M-partial assignments a such that $f|_a$ has no ℓ-CNF. We'll exhibit an injection from R to some set S of size $\binom{N}{M-\ell}2^{N-(M-\ell)}(4k)^\ell$, which implies $|R| \leq |S|$. There are $\binom{N}{M}2^{N-M}$ many M-partial assignments since there are $\binom{N}{M}$ options for which variables are $*$s and 2^{N-M} options for assigning bits to non-$*$ variables. Therefore,

$$\mathbf{Pr}\big[f|_a \text{ has no } \ell\text{-CNF}\big] \leq \frac{\binom{N}{M-\ell}2^{N-(M-\ell)}(4k)^\ell}{\binom{N}{M}2^{N-M}} = \frac{\binom{N}{M-\ell}(8k)^\ell}{\binom{N}{M}} \leq (16kM/N)^\ell$$

using:

$$\binom{N}{M-\ell}/\binom{N}{M} = \frac{N(N-1)\cdots(N-(M-\ell)+1)}{(M-\ell)(M-\ell-1)\cdots 1} / \frac{N(N-1)\cdots(N-M+1)}{M(M-1)\cdots 1}$$
$$= \frac{M(M-1)\cdots(M-\ell+1)}{(N-M+\ell)(N-M+\ell-1)\cdots(N-M+1)} \le \frac{M^\ell}{(N-M)^\ell} \le \left(\frac{M}{N/2}\right)^\ell$$

Let $S = \big(\text{set of all } (M-\ell)\text{-partial assignments}\big) \times \big([k]\times\{\text{same},\text{flip}\}\times\{\text{continue},\text{done}\}\big)^\ell$. The injection will "encode" $a \in R$ as $(d,e)\in S$. To prove it's an injection, we "decode" $(d,e)\in S$ back to $a\in R$. First, we design an encoder/decoder where $(d,e)\notin S$, with d having $< M-\ell$ many $*$s and e having $>\ell$ many entries. Afterward, we tweak the encoder/decoder so $(d,e)\in S$.

Consider any $a \in R$. Since $f|_a$ has no ℓ-CNF, $f|_a$ has a minimal 0-certificate b of size $>\ell$ (Claim 18.12). View b as a partial assignment to all of φ's variables, with automatic $*$s for variables that a assigns.

This algorithm encodes a. (We elucidate the algorithm with an example after the proof.)

Encoding algorithm for the switching lemma (18.1)

encode(a):
    for $i \leftarrow 1,2,\ldots$ until $b^1b^2\cdots b^i = b$:
        let T^i be the first term of φ that survives in $\varphi|_{ab^1\cdots b^{i-1}}$
        let b^i be b but only assigning variables in $T^i|_{ab^1\cdots b^{i-1}}$ (changing other bits to $*$s)
        let c^i be b^i but with some bits flipped so as not to eliminate T^i
        for each variable that b^i and c^i assign: append to e the tuple with components:
            $j\in[k]$ if this variable is the jth within T^i
            "same" or "flip" for whether or not b^i and c^i agree on this variable's value
            "done" or "continue" for whether or not it's the last such variable
    output (d,e) where $d \leftarrow ac^1c^2\cdots c^h$ and h is the last i

In the encoder's ith iteration, $\varphi|_{ab^1\cdots b^{i-1}}$ has at least one term, since otherwise $b^1\cdots b^{i-1}$ would be a 0-certificate of $f|_a$, contradicting b's minimality. Thus T^i indeed exists. Also, ab makes T^i evaluate to 0 (since b is a 0-certificate of $f|_a$) and $ab^1\cdots b^{i-1}$ doesn't, so b^i assigns at least one more variable in T^i. This ensures progress, so the encoding eventually terminates with $b^1b^2\cdots b^h = b$.

This algorithm decodes (d,e) assuming it's a's encoding.

Decoding algorithm for the switching lemma (18.2)

decode(d,e):
    for $i \leftarrow 1,2,\ldots$ until reaching the end of e:
        let T^i be the first term of φ that survives in $\varphi|_{d^{i-1}}$ (where $d^0 = d$)
        for each subsequent entry of e (picking up where we left off) through the next "done":
            consider the jth variable within T^i, where j is the entry's first component
            let c^i assign this variable the same bit that d does
            let b^i assign this variable the same bit if "same" or the opposite bit if "flip"
        let $d^i \leftarrow (d^{i-1}/c^i)b^i$
    output $a \leftarrow d/(c^1c^2\cdots c^h)$ where h is the last i

The decoder maintains the invariant that $d^i = ab^1\cdots b^ic^{i+1}\cdots c^h$, which holds initially with $d^0 = d = ac^1c^2\cdots c^h$. The decoder finds the same T^i as the encoder because the first term of

φ that survives in $\varphi|_{ab^1\cdots b^{i-1}}$ also survives in $\varphi|_{d^{i-1}} = \varphi|_{ab^1\cdots b^{i-1}c^i\cdots c^h}$ since c^i doesn't eliminate this term, and $c^{i+1}\cdots c^h$ doesn't even touch this term. By the definition of e, the decoder then finds the same c^i and b^i as the encoder, and maintains the invariant with d^i. The decoder has the same number of iterations h as the encoder, halting after exhausting e to find $c^1c^2\cdots c^h$.

Finally, we tweak this so $(d,e) \in S$ by making d have exactly $M-\ell$ many $*$s and e have exactly ℓ entries: If the encoder reaches an iteration where $b^1b^2\cdots b^i$ has exactly ℓ bits, then it stops there. Otherwise, in the first iteration where $b^1b^2\cdots b^i$ would have more than ℓ bits, it limits b^i (and c^i) to assign just enough bits to bring the total to ℓ, and stops there. The same decoder works. ■

Example. Suppose $T^i = (\overline{x_2} \wedge x_3 \wedge x_5 \wedge x_6 \wedge \overline{x_7})$ and $b^i = *1{*}{*}10*$, where the gray stars are variables not in T^i. Then $c^i = *0{*}{*}11*$ and we append (1, flip, continue), (3, same, continue), (4, flip, done) to e, since b^i assigns the 1st, 3rd, and 4th variables within T^i (namely x_2, x_5, and x_6) and c^i assigns the 1st and 4th differently to satisfy the corresponding literals $\overline{x_2}$ and x_6 of T^i. (Possibly, $ab^1\cdots b^{i-1}$ assigned $x_3 = 1$ or $x_7 = 0$, but that's irrelevant here.) ♦

18.4 Formulas and Random Restrictions

We develop a random restriction method for proving formula size lower bounds. In this section, formulas always have negations pushed to the leaves and have bounded fan-in: Leaves are literals, and non-leaves are $\wedge$ or $\vee$ gates with exactly two children. A formula's size is the number of leaves. As a special case, constant functions have formula size complexity 0 in this section (the formula is "empty").

18.4.1 Shrinkage

A formula probably shrinks a lot when we contract it with a random partial assignment:

Lemma 18.13. *If $f\colon \{0,1\}^N \to \{0,1\}$ has formula size complexity s, then for a uniformly random M-partial assignment a:*

$$\mathbf{E}\big[\text{formula size complexity of } f|_a\big] \le (M/N)^{1.5}s + 1$$

Proof idea. We might intuitively expect a formula to shrink by a factor M/N on average, because M/N is the fraction of unassigned variables, corresponding to surviving leaves in the formula. But even more shrinkage sometimes occurs, because assigning a value to a leaf sometimes makes other leaves disappear. For example, in $x_1 \wedge x_2$, although assigning $x_1 = 1$ only eliminates the x_1 leaf, assigning $x_1 = 0$ also eliminates the x_2 leaf (despite x_2 remaining unassigned) due to short-circuiting: Feeding 0 into an $\wedge$ gate or 1 into an $\vee$ gate renders the gate's other subformula irrelevant. On average, short-circuiting happens half the time (the .5 in the 1.5 exponent). But what if short-circuiting eliminates leaves that would be eliminated anyway because they're assigned values? The following lemma addresses this. ■

Say a formula is *minimal* iff no smaller formula computes the same function. Leaves labeled x_i or $\overline{x_i}$ are *i-leaves*. Leaves that are *under* (in the subformula rooted at) the sibling of an i-leaf are *i-sibling-leaves*.

Lemma 18.14. *In a minimal formula, no i-leaf is an i-sibling-leaf.*

Proof of Lemma 18.14. For any formula φ, we argue that if some i-leaf v is under the sibling of another i-leaf w, then φ isn't minimal—we construct a smaller formula ψ that computes the same function.

First, suppose v and w are labeled x_i and w's parent is an $\vee$ gate. Obtain ψ by contracting φ after replacing v with 0. Then ψ agrees with φ on every assignment: If $x_i = 0$ then our modification is faithful, and if $x_i = 1$ then our tampering doesn't matter because the $\vee$ gate evaluates to 1 anyway.

All other cases (whether v is labeled x_i or $\overline{x_i}$, and w is labeled x_i or $\overline{x_i}$, and w's parent is an $\wedge$ or $\vee$ gate) are completely analogous: Some bit $x_i = b$ would make w short-circuit its parent, and we replace v with $\overline{b}$ if v is labeled x_i, or with b if v is labeled $\overline{x_i}$. On any assignment, if $x_i = \overline{b}$ then v gets the right bit, and if $x_i = b$ then it doesn't matter that v gets the wrong bit. ■

Proof of Lemma 18.13. First, suppose $M = N - 1$. Consider a minimal formula φ for f, with $s > 1$ leaves. (If $s \leq 1$, the lemma is trivial because of the $+1$.) Let s_i be the number of i-leaves, so $s = s_1 + \cdots + s_N$. Let t_i be the number of i-sibling-leaves, so $t_i \geq s_i$ because each i-leaf has a sibling (since $s > 1$) and all i-leaves have disjoint sibling subformulas (Lemma 18.14). For each i-leaf, some assignment to x_i makes the parent a constant and thus eliminates not only that leaf but also the leaves under its sibling. So each i-sibling-leaf is eliminated by at least one assignment to x_i. Thus $t_i \leq t_{i,0} + t_{i,1}$ where $t_{i,b}$ is the number of i-sibling-leaves eliminated by assigning $x_i = b$. Let $r_{i,b}$ be the total number of leaves eliminated by assigning $x_i = b$. Then $r_{i,b} \geq s_i + t_{i,b}$ because assigning $x_i = b$ eliminates all s_i many i-leaves and $t_{i,b}$ many i-sibling-leaves, which are distinct (Lemma 18.14). Thus:

$$r_{i,0} + r_{i,1} \;\geq\; (s_i + t_{i,0}) + (s_i + t_{i,1}) \;\geq\; 2s_i + t_i \;\geq\; 3s_i$$

For a random $(N-1)$-partial assignment a, which assigns $x_i = b$ for a random i and b:

$$\mathbf{E}\big[\text{number of leaves eliminated}\big] \;=\; \tfrac{1}{2N}\textstyle\sum_i (r_{i,0} + r_{i,1}) \;\geq\; \tfrac{1}{2N}\sum_i 3s_i \;=\; 1.5s/N$$

$$\begin{aligned}\mathbf{E}\big[\text{formula size complexity of } f|_a\big] &\leq \mathbf{E}\big[\text{size of } \varphi|_a\big]\\ &= s - \mathbf{E}\big[\text{number of leaves eliminated}\big]\\ &\leq s - 1.5s/N \;=\; (1 - 1.5/N)s \;\leq\; (1 - 1/N)^{1.5}s\end{aligned}$$

$(1 - 1.5/N) \leq (1 - 1/N)^{1.5}$ holds by squaring both sides and expanding.

For any $M < N$, to sample a random M-partial assignment a, we can sample a random $(N-1)$-partial assignment, then a random $(N-2)$-partial assignment on the remaining $N-1$ variables, then a random $(N-3)$-partial assignment on the remaining $N-2$ variables, and so on, until M variables remain. Applying the above bound repeatedly:

$$\begin{aligned}\mathbf{E}\big[\text{formula size complexity of } f|_a\big] &\leq \Big(\frac{M}{M+1}\Big)^{1.5}\Big(\frac{M+1}{M+2}\Big)^{1.5}\cdots\Big(\frac{N-2}{N-1}\Big)^{1.5}\Big(\frac{N-1}{N}\Big)^{1.5}s\\ &= \Big(\frac{M}{M+1}\cdot\frac{M+1}{M+2}\cdots\frac{N-2}{N-1}\cdot\frac{N-1}{N}\Big)^{1.5}s\\ &= (M/N)^{1.5}s\end{aligned}$$

This is assuming the intermediate restrictions of f have formula size complexity > 1. The $+1$ in the lemma handles restrictions with complexity ≤ 1 (for which the bound wouldn't otherwise hold). ■

Example. The formula at the top of Figure 18.4 has size $s = 10$. The 2-leaves are highlighted in boxes. There are $s_2 = 4$ many 2-leaves and $t_2 = 6$ many 2-sibling-leaves.

- Assigning $x_2 = 0$ eliminates $r_{2,0} = 7$ leaves—the 2-leaves and the $t_{2,0} = 3$ many 2-sibling-leaves labeled $x_1, \overline{x_5}, x_6$. Feeding $x_2 = 0$ into an $\wedge$ gate and $\overline{x_2} = 1$ into an $\vee$ gate eliminates the subformulas rooted at the siblings. The contracted formula is $(x_3 \vee \overline{x_4}) \wedge \overline{x_7}$.
- Assigning $x_2 = 1$ eliminates $r_{2,1} = 7$ leaves—the 2-leaves and the $t_{2,1} = 3$ many 2-sibling-leaves labeled $x_3, \overline{x_4}, \overline{x_7}$. Feeding $\overline{x_2} = 0$ into an $\wedge$ gate and $x_2 = 1$ into an $\vee$ gate eliminates the subformulas rooted at the siblings. The contracted formula is $x_1 \wedge (\overline{x_5} \wedge x_6)$. ♦

The shrinkage exponent can be improved from 1.5 to essentially 2, but that's much tougher to prove.

18.4.2 Formula Size Lower Bound

Lemma 18.13 implies that PARITY$_N$ has formula size complexity $s \geq \Omega(N^{1.5})$: For some 2-partial assignment a, PARITY$_N|_a$ has formula size complexity $\leq (2/N)^{1.5}s + 1$, which must be ≥ 2 since PARITY$_N|_a$ depends on both its variables. Rearranging yields $s \geq (N/2)^{1.5}$. Using the stronger shrinkage lemma with exponent 2 instead of 1.5 shows that PARITY$_N$ has formula size complexity $\Omega(N^2)$. We prove the latter bound in § 18.5 using a different technique.

Now, we use Lemma 18.13 to prove that some problem in P has formula size complexity $\geq N^{2.5-o(1)}$. Using the stronger shrinkage lemma with exponent 2 instead of 1.5 shows that this problem actually has formula size complexity $\geq N^{3-o(1)}$. (No supercubic formula size lower bound is known for any problem in NP.) This problem is like INDEX (§ 16.1, § 17.3) except the bits of the index are parities of bit strings.

In this section, $\oplus\colon \{0,1\}^n \to \{0,1\}$ is PARITY$_n$. For $n = 2^\ell$, define $f\colon \{0,1\}^n \times (\{0,1\}^n)^\ell \to \{0,1\}$ by $f(x,y) = x\big(\oplus(y^1),\ldots,\oplus(y^\ell)\big)$ where x is the truth table of a function $x\colon \{0,1\}^\ell \to \{0,1\}$, and $y = (y^1,\ldots,y^\ell)$. Alternatively, $f(x,y) = x_{\oplus(y^1)\cdots\oplus(y^\ell)}$ where the binary number $\oplus(y^1)\cdots\oplus(y^\ell)$ is an index into $x = x_0x_1\cdots x_{n-1}$. The total input size is $N = (1+\ell)n$.

Theorem 18.15. *f defined above has formula size complexity $\geq N^{2.5-o(1)}$.*

Proof idea. Ignoring polylog N factors: Hardwire some $x\colon \{0,1\}^\ell \to \{0,1\}$ that has formula size complexity $\geq N$. A random partial assignment to y probably shrinks f's formula size complexity by a factor $\geq N^{1.5}$ if there aren't too many $*$s. But the formula size complexity probably remains $\geq N$ (because of x) if there aren't too few $*$s. So f has formula size complexity $\geq N^{1.5}\cdot N$. ■

Proof. Say f has formula size complexity s. Some $g\colon \{0,1\}^\ell \to \{0,1\}$ has formula size complexity $t \geq \Omega(2^\ell/\ell) = \Omega(n/\log n)$ (Theorem 5.8). Hardwire this g for x to get the function $f_g(y) = f(g,y) = g\big(\oplus(y^1),\ldots,\oplus(y^\ell)\big)$ with formula size complexity $s_g \leq s$. For any partial assignment $a = (a^1,\ldots,a^\ell) \in (\{0,1,*\}^n)^\ell$, say $f_g|_a$ has formula size complexity $s_{g,a}$. If a^i has at least one $*$ for each i, then $s_{g,a} \geq t$ because we can turn any formula for $f_g|_a$ into a formula for g by plugging in arbitrary bits for all but one $*$ in each a^i, and possibly negating the remaining variables. (This is because if we obtain b^i from a^i by assigning bits to all but one $*$, then $\oplus|_{b^i}$ is either the remaining variable or its negation.) For a uniformly random m-partial assignment a where $m = \lceil \ell(1+\ln\ell)\rceil$:

$$\begin{aligned}\mathbf{Pr}[a^i \text{ has no } *\text{s}] &= \binom{(\ell-1)n}{m}\Big/\binom{\ell n}{m} = \frac{((\ell-1)n)((\ell-1)n-1)\cdots((\ell-1)n-m+1)}{(\ell n)(\ell n-1)\cdots(\ell n-m+1)}\\ &\leq \left(\frac{(\ell-1)n}{\ell n}\right)^m = (1-1/\ell)^m \leq e^{-m/\ell} \leq 1/e\ell < 1/2\ell\end{aligned}$$

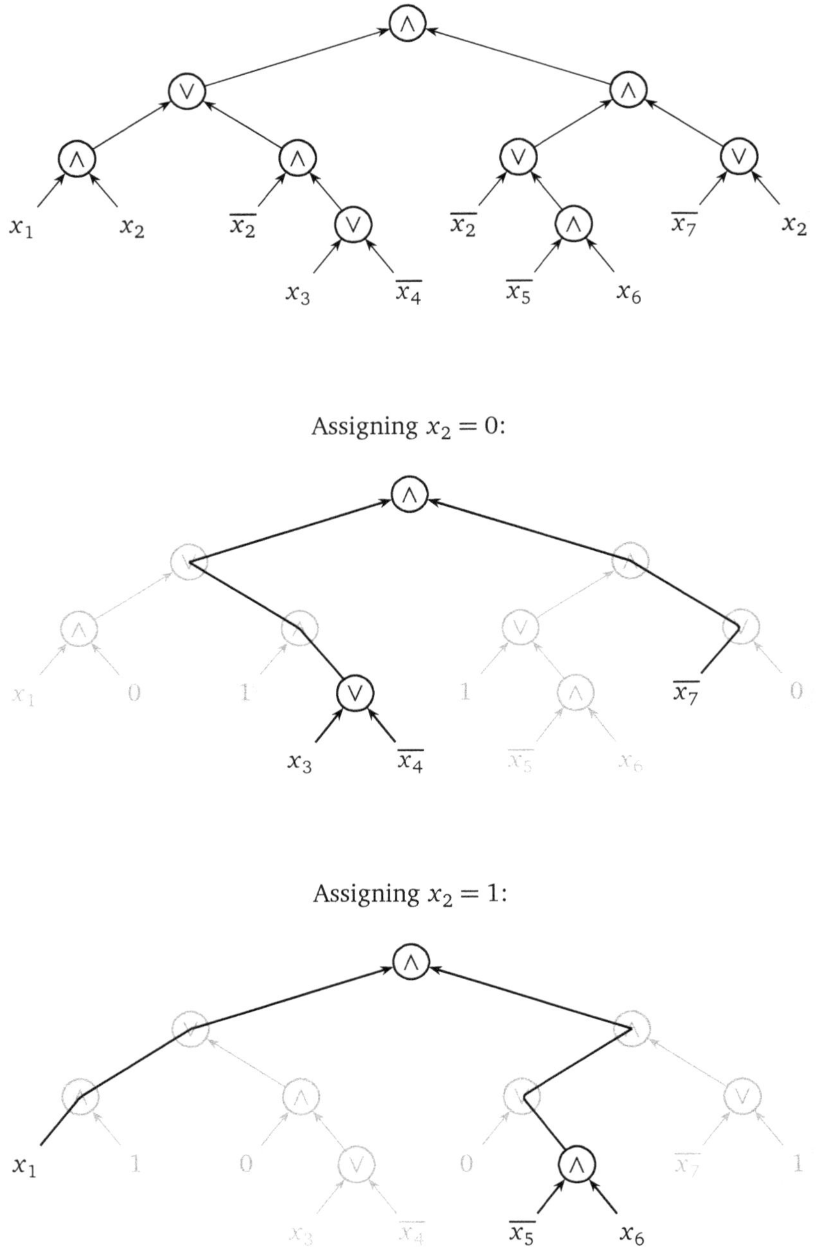

Figure 18.4: Formula shrinkage

By a union bound:

$$\mathbf{Pr}[s_{g,a} < t] \le \mathbf{Pr}[a^i \text{ has no } {*}\text{s for some } i] \le \textstyle\sum_i \mathbf{Pr}[a^i \text{ has no } {*}\text{s}] < \ell/2\ell = 1/2$$

$\mathbf{E}[s_{g,a}] \le rs_g + 1$ where $r = (m/\ell n)^{1.5} = O((\log\log n/n)^{1.5})$ (Lemma 18.13). Therefore $\mathbf{Pr}\big[s_{g,a} > 2rs_g + 2\big] < 1/2$ (Lemma 7.13). By a union bound, $\mathbf{Pr}\big[s_{g,a} < t \text{ or } s_{g,a} > 2rs_g + 2\big] < 1/2 + 1/2 = 1$. So for some a, we have $t \le s_{g,a} \le 2rs_g + 2$, which implies:

$$s \ge s_g \ge (t-2)/2r \ge \Omega(t/r) \ge \Omega\Big(\frac{n/\log n}{(\log\log n/n)^{1.5}}\Big) \ge n^{2.5-o(1)} \ge N^{2.5-o(1)}$$

■

18.5 Formulas and Communication Protocols

We use communication complexity (Chapter 17) to prove formula depth lower bounds, and therefore also formula size lower bounds (§6.5.2) and circuit depth lower bounds (§6.1.1). In this section, formulas always have negations pushed to the leaves and have bounded fan-in. A formula's size is the number of leaves.

18.5.1 Formulas Are Protocols

Let's compare formulas and protocols.

A *formula* with domain $\{0,1\}^N$ is a binary in-tree where each leaf's label is an input variable or its negation, and each non-leaf's label is $\vee$ or $\wedge$. On input z, a formula outputs the value of the root after evaluating all nodes from the leaves to the root.

A *protocol* with domain $X \times Y$ is a binary out-tree where each leaf's label is an output value, and each non-leaf v's label is $\big(\text{Alice}, g_v : X \to \{0,1\}\big)$ or $\big(\text{Bob}, g_v : Y \to \{0,1\}\big)$. On input (x, y), a protocol outputs the label of the leaf reached by the path from the root where at v, Alice sends $g_v(x)$ or Bob sends $g_v(y)$, and $0 =$ "go left" and $1 =$ "go right."

The *shape* of a formula or protocol is the underlying undirected binary tree T.

For any $f : \{0,1\}^N \to \{0,1\}$, let f^* be the two-party search problem where Alice gets $x \in f^{-1}(1)$, Bob gets $y \in f^{-1}(0)$, and they want to output an index $i \in [N]$ such that $x_i \ne y_i$ (which exists since $x \ne y$).

Example. The top of Figure 18.5 shows a formula and a protocol of the same shape, but doesn't specify the protocol's g_v functions. The formula computes $f : \{0,1\}^3 \to \{0,1\}$ shown on the bottom left. The corresponding f^* is on the bottom right. It turns out that with suitable g_v functions, the protocol on the top right computes f^*. Let's demonstrate the idea on input $(x, y) = (001, 101)$: Alice and Bob start at the formula's root, which evaluates to 1 on x and 0 on y. Alice says this $\vee$ gate's right child evaluates to 1 on x, and they step to that node, which also evaluates to 0 on y. Then, Bob says this $\wedge$ gate's left child evaluates to 0 on y, and they step to that node, which also evaluates to 1 on x. Then, Alice says this $\vee$ gate's right child evaluates to 1 on x, and they step to that node, which also evaluates to 0 on y. This leaf is labeled $\overline{z_1}$, so Alice and Bob output the index 1 since $\overline{x_1} = 1$ and $\overline{y_1} = 0$ implies $x_1 \ne y_1$. ♦

The next lemma formalizes this example's idea. Like P-completeness of GEOGRAPHY ON A DAG (Theorem 5.17), computing from input to output is equivalent to playing a two-player game from output to input.

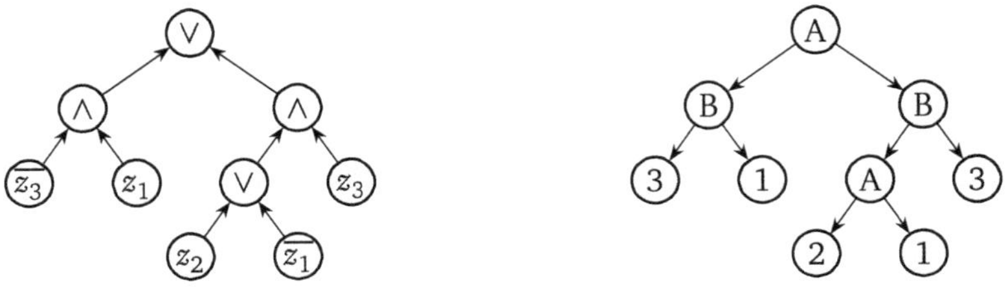

z	$f(z)$
000	0
001	1
010	0
011	1
100	1
101	0
110	1
111	1

$f^*(x,y)$	000	010	101
001	$\{3\}$	$\{2,3\}$	$\{1\}$
011	$\{2,3\}$	$\{3\}$	$\{1,2\}$
100	$\{1\}$	$\{1,2\}$	$\{3\}$
110	$\{1,2\}$	$\{1\}$	$\{2,3\}$
111	$\{1,2,3\}$	$\{1,3\}$	$\{2\}$

Figure 18.5: Formula for f and protocol for f^* of the same shape

Lemma 18.16. *f has a shape-T formula iff f^* has a shape-T protocol. Consequently:*

$$\begin{aligned}\textit{formula size complexity of } f &= \textit{protocol size complexity of } f^* \\ \textit{formula depth complexity of } f &= \textit{protocol depth complexity of } f^*\end{aligned}$$

Proof. $\Rightarrow$: Suppose f has a shape-T formula. We design a shape-T protocol for f^*. On input (x,y), Alice and Bob follow a root-to-leaf path in T, maintaining the invariant that every node on this path in the formula evaluates to 1 on input x and to 0 on input y.

- At an $\vee$ gate: At least one child evaluates to 1 on x. Both children evaluate to 0 on y. Alice sends a bit identifying some child that evaluates to 1 on x.
- At an $\wedge$ gate: At least one child evaluates to 0 on y. Both children evaluate to 1 on x. Bob sends a bit identifying some child that evaluates to 0 on y.

They reach a leaf labeled z_i or $\overline{z_i}$, which evaluates to 1 on x and 0 on y, so they output i since $x_i \neq y_i$.

$\Leftarrow$: Suppose f^* has a shape-T protocol. We design a shape-T formula for f by turning Alice nodes into $\vee$ gates and Bob nodes into $\wedge$ gates, and turning any leaf that outputs i into either z_i or $\overline{z_i}$ (to be specified shortly). For each node v, let $A_v \times B_v \subseteq f^{-1}(1) \times f^{-1}(0)$ be the rectangle of inputs that lead to v in the protocol. We show that in the formula, v evaluates to 1 on all $x \in A_v$ and to 0 on all $y \in B_v$. This implies that the whole formula indeed computes f.

At a leaf v that outputs i, we have $x_i \neq y_i$ for all $(x,y) \in A_v \times B_v$, so either $x_i = 1$ for all $x \in A_v$ and $y_i = 0$ for all $y \in B_v$, in which case the leaf becomes the positive literal z_i, or $x_i = 0$ for all $x \in A_v$ and $y_i = 1$ for all $y \in B_v$, in which case the leaf becomes the negative literal $\overline{z_i}$.

Working our way up the tree, at any non-leaf v with children v_0, v_1 such that v_0 evaluates to 1 on all $x \in A_{v_0}$ and 0 on all $y \in B_{v_0}$, and v_1 evaluates to 1 on all $x \in A_{v_1}$ and 0 on all $y \in B_{v_1}$:

- If Alice talks at v, so v becomes an $\vee$ gate:
  For $x \in A_v = A_{v_0} \cup A_{v_1}$, either v_0 or v_1 evaluates to 1, so v evaluates to 1.
  For $y \in B_v = B_{v_0} = B_{v_1}$, both v_0 and v_1 evaluate to 0, so v evaluates to 0.
- If Bob talks at v, so v becomes an $\wedge$ gate:
  For $y \in B_v = B_{v_0} \cup B_{v_1}$, either v_0 or v_1 evaluates to 0, so v evaluates to 0.
  For $x \in A_v = A_{v_0} = A_{v_1}$, both v_0 and v_1 evaluate to 1, so v evaluates to 1. ■

Theorem 18.17. PARITY *has formula size complexity* $\Theta(N^2)$.

Proof. Upper bound: We observed this in §6.1.2. Lower bound: $\text{PARITY}^*_N = \text{OPPOSITE PARITY}_N$ (§17.5.1) is the search problem where Alice gets $x \in \{0,1\}^N$ with $\oplus(x) = 1$, Bob gets $y \in \{0,1\}^N$ with $\oplus(y) = 0$, and they want to output an index $i \in [N]$ such that $x_i \neq y_i$. It suffices to prove that OPPOSITE PARITY has protocol size complexity $\geq N^2$ (Lemma 18.16). This was shown in the proof that OPPOSITE PARITY has protocol depth complexity $\geq 2\log N$ (Theorem 17.33). ■

18.5.2 Monotone Formulas Are Protocols

A monotone formula's leaves are positive literals. If a monotone formula computes $f\colon \{0,1\}^N \to \{0,1\}$, then f is monotone: Flipping input bits from 0 to 1 never flips the output from 1 to 0. Much stronger lower bounds are known for monotone formulas than for general (nonmonotone) formulas.

For any monotone $f\colon \{0,1\}^N \to \{0,1\}$, let f' be the two-party search problem where Alice gets $x \in f^{-1}(1)$, Bob gets $y \in f^{-1}(0)$, and they want to output an index $i \in [N]$ such that $x_i = 1$ and $y_i = 0$. Such an i exists since otherwise, we could transform x to y by flipping some input bits from 0 to 1, contradicting the monotonicity of f. With f' it's unacceptable to output i such that $x_i = 0$ and $y_i = 1$, though with f^* that's acceptable. This superficially minor difference greatly affects our ability to prove communication lower bounds.

Lemma 18.18. *A monotone f has a shape-T monotone formula iff f' has a shape-T protocol. Consequently:*

$$\begin{aligned} \textit{monotone formula size complexity of } f &= \textit{protocol size complexity of } f' \\ \textit{monotone formula depth complexity of } f &= \textit{protocol depth complexity of } f' \end{aligned}$$

Proof. $\Rightarrow$: Turn a monotone formula for f into a protocol for f' exactly as in the proof of Lemma 18.16. On input (x, y), Alice and Bob reach a leaf labeled z_i, which evaluates to 1 on x and 0 on y, so they output i since $x_i = 1$ and $y_i = 0$.

$\Leftarrow$: Turn a protocol for f' into a monotone formula for f exactly as in the proof of Lemma 18.16. At a leaf v that outputs i, we have $x_i = 1$ for all $x \in A_v$ and $y_i = 0$ for all $y \in B_v$, so the leaf becomes the positive literal z_i. ■

Define $\text{DIRECTED REACHABILITY}_{n^2}\colon \{0,1\}^{n^2} \to \{0,1\}$ as a monotone function: The input is an n-node directed graph z encoded as an $n \times n$ adjacency matrix: $z_{i,j} = 1$ iff there's an edge from node i to node j. The output is 1 iff the graph has a walk from node $s = 1$ to node $t = n$. This is monotone since adding edges to a graph can't destroy an existing walk.

Theorem 18.19. Directed Reachability *has monotone formula size complexity* $2^{\Theta(\log^2 n)}$.

Proof. Upper bound: Directed Reachability $\in$ NL $\subseteq$ AC^1 $\subseteq$ NC^2 via middle-first search (Theorem 6.9), so it has a circuit of depth $O(\log^2 n)$ and thus a formula of the same depth and size $2^{O(\log^2 n)}$. This circuit and formula turn out to be monotone: For all nodes i and j and all $k \in \{0, \dots, \lceil \log n \rceil\}$, the circuit has $v_{i,j,k}$ that evaluates to 1 iff the input graph z has a walk from i to j of length $\leq 2^k$. For $i \neq j$ we have $v_{i,j,0} = z_{i,j}$, and for $i = j$ we have $v_{i,j,0} = 1$. For $k > 0$ we have $v_{i,j,k} = \bigvee_{\text{node } h}(v_{i,h,k-1} \wedge v_{h,j,k-1})$. The output is $v_{1,n,\lceil \log n \rceil}$. Each k contributes $O(\log n)$ many bounded-fan-in layers, so the total depth is $O(\log^2 n)$.

Lower bound: By balancing (Theorem 6.24), it suffices to prove f = Directed Reachability$_{n^2}$ has monotone formula depth complexity $\Omega(\log^2 n)$. By Lemma 18.18, it suffices to prove f' has protocol depth complexity $\Omega(\log^2 n)$.

Fork$_{k,m}$ (§ 17.5.2) is the search problem where Alice gets $x \in [k]^m$, Bob gets $y \in [k]^m$, and they want to output a *fork*, which is an index $i \in \{0, 1, \dots, m\}$ such that $x_i = y_i$ and $x_{i+1} \neq y_{i+1}$, assuming implicitly that $x_0 = y_0$ and $x_{m+1} \neq y_{m+1}$, say $x_0 = y_0 = 1$ and $x_{m+1} = k$ and $y_{m+1} = k - 1$.

We reduce Fork$_{k,m}$ to f' where $n = k(m+2)$ and $k = m \approx \sqrt{n}$. Then Theorem 17.34 does the heavy lifting: Both problems have protocol depth complexity $\Omega\big((\log k)(\log m)\big) = \Omega(\log^2 n)$.

The inputs to f' will be layered graphs with nodes $[k] \times \{0, 1, \dots, m+1\}$: Layer i is the nodes $[k] \times \{i\}$, and each edge goes from some layer i to layer $i+1$. The start and destination nodes are $s = (1, 0)$ and $t = (k, m+1)$.

- Map $x \in [k]^m$ to a graph x' having just the path

  $$(x_0, 0) \to (x_1, 1) \to (x_2, 2) \to \cdots \to (x_m, m) \to (x_{m+1}, m+1)$$

  from $(1, 0) = s$ to $(k, m+1) = t$. Thus $f(x') = 1$ (t is reachable from s).
- Map $y \in [k]^m$ to a graph y' having the path

  $$(y_0, 0) \to (y_1, 1) \to (y_2, 2) \to \cdots \to (y_m, m) \to (y_{m+1}, m+1)$$

  from $(1, 0) = s$ to $(k-1, m+1) \neq t$, and each node not on this path has edges to all nodes in the next layer in y'. The latter edges don't create any new paths from s, so $f(y') = 0$ (t isn't reachable from s).

Another way to describe the layered graphs x' and y' is:

- $(v, i) \to (w, i+1)$ is an edge of x' iff $x_i = v$ and $x_{i+1} = w$.
- $(v, i) \to (w, i+1)$ is a non-edge of y' iff $y_i = v$ and $y_{i+1} \neq w$.

A protocol for Fork$_{k,m}$ on input (x, y) could run a protocol for f' on input (x', y') to find an acceptable solution $(v, i) \to (w, i+1)$ (an edge of x' that's a non-edge of y') and then output i, which is a fork for (x, y) since $x_i = v = y_i$ and $x_{i+1} = w \neq y_{i+1}$. Hence the protocol depth complexity of Fork$_{k,m}$ is no greater than that of f'. ■

Example. Figure 18.6 illustrates the reduction from Fork$_{3,3}$ to Directed Reachability$'_{15^2}$ on input $x = (2, 1, 3)$ and $y = (2, 2, 3)$, with implicit "bookends" $x_0 = y_0 = 1$ and $x_4 = 3$ and $y_4 = 2$. The forks are the indices 1 and 3: The edges of x' coming out of layers 1 and 3 are non-edges of y'. (By the way, in layer 0, only the 1st node is relevant, and in layer $m+1$, only the kth and $(k-1)$st nodes are relevant, so the other nodes in these two layers are grayed out.) ♦

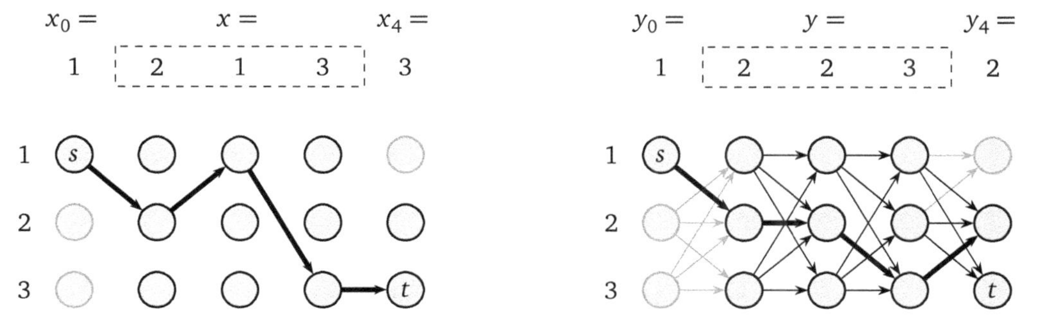

Figure 18.6: Reducing FORK to DIRECTED REACHABILITY′

DIRECTED REACHABILITY $\in$ NL is conjectured to have *non*monotone formula size complexity $2^{\Omega(\log^2 n)}$, which would imply $\mathsf{NC}^1 \neq \mathsf{NL}$. Only $\neg$ gates stand between us and a separation of NC^1 and NL! In fact, UNDIRECTED REACHABILITY $\in$ L has monotone formula size complexity $2^{\Omega(\log^2 n)}$ (Exercise 18.11), so if it weren't for pesky $\neg$ gates, we could even prove $\mathsf{NC}^1 \neq \mathsf{L}$.

Alas, a protocol for DIRECTED REACHABILITY* might find an edge of y' that's a non-edge of x' (instead of the other way around), which wouldn't help to find a fork. This seemingly small distinction between the monotone and nonmonotone settings is actually, as yet, an insurmountable obstacle to proving strong nonmonotone formula lower bounds via communication complexity.

18.6 Monotone Circuits

Now, we'll see that only $\neg$ gates stand between us and a separation of P and NP. We consider bounded-fan-in monotone circuits and let "size" mean "number of gates."

A *k-clique* in an undirected graph G is a size-k subset S of G's nodes such that every pair of nodes in S has an edge between them. Encode $G = ([n], E)$ as a length-$\binom{n}{2}$ bit string x indexed by unordered pairs $\{u, v\} \subseteq [n]$, where $x_{\{u,v\}} = 1$ iff $\{u, v\} \in E$. Think of x as the graph itself, even though technically it's a bit string representing the graph.

Theorem 18.20. *Define* $f_{n,k} \colon \{0,1\}^{\binom{n}{2}} \to \{0,1\}$ *by* $f_{n,k}(x) = 1$ *iff the graph* x *has a* k*-clique. If* $k \leq n^{1/5}$ *then* $f_{n,k}$ *has monotone circuit size complexity* $\geq n^{\sqrt{k}/4}$.

$f_{n,k}$ has a monotone circuit of size $\binom{n}{k}\binom{k}{2} \leq n^k$ that tries all possible k-cliques. Theorem 18.20 says this upper bound is nearly tight. When $k = n^{1/5}$, we get a superpolynomial lower bound of $n^{\Omega(n^{1/10})} = N^{\Omega(N^{1/20})}$ where $N = \binom{n}{2}$ is the input size. If only we could handle $\neg$ gates, we'd conclude that the NP-complete problem CLIQUE (Corollary 2.20) is not in P/poly, and therefore $\mathsf{P} \neq \mathsf{NP}$. Unfortunately, all hell breaks loose if we allow $\neg$ gates, and the known techniques for monotone circuit size lower bounds are to no avail.

Proof. Define distributions D_1 and D_0 over 1-inputs and 0-inputs, respectively, of $f = f_{n,k}$:

- D_1 is the uniform distribution over all graphs x containing a k-clique and no other edges.
- To sample $x \sim D_0$, pick a uniformly random function $h \colon [n] \to [k-1]$ and let $x_{\{u,v\}} = 1$ iff $h(u) \neq h(v)$. This graph has no k-clique, because every set of k nodes contains two nodes $u \neq v$ with $h(u) = h(v)$ (by the pigeonhole principle) and therefore isn't a clique.

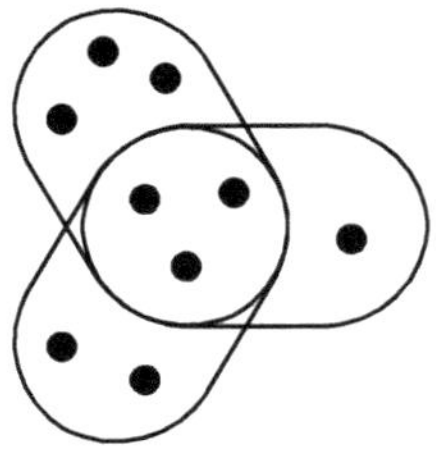

Figure 18.7: Sunflower with three petals

The *clique indicator* for a set of nodes $C \subseteq [n]$ is the term

$$T_C(x) = \bigwedge_{\{u,v\}\subseteq C} x_{\{u,v\}}$$

indicating whether C is a clique in x. If $|C| \le \ell = \sqrt{k}$ then by a union bound:

$$\begin{aligned}\mathbf{Pr}_{x\sim D_0}\big[T_C(x)=0\big] &\le \textstyle\sum_{\{u,v\}\subseteq C} \mathbf{Pr}_{x\sim D_0}\big[x_{\{u,v\}}=0\big] \\ &= \textstyle\sum_{\{u,v\}\subseteq C} \mathbf{Pr}_{h:\,[n]\to[k-1]}\big[h(u)=h(v)\big] \le \binom{\ell}{2}/(k-1) \le 1/2\end{aligned}$$

Supposing f has a size-s monotone circuit where $s = n^{\sqrt{k}/4}$, we'll define f' such that:

- f' is an (m,ℓ)*-clique-DNF*, which has at most m terms, each of which is a clique indicator T_C with $|C| \le \ell$.
- f' approximates f in the sense that $\mathbf{Pr}_{x\sim D_1}\big[f'(x)=1\big] \ge 3/4$ and $\mathbf{Pr}_{x\sim D_0}\big[f'(x)=0\big] \ge 3/4$.

This yields a contradiction: If f' has no terms, then $\mathbf{Pr}_{x\sim D_1}\big[f'(x)=1\big]=0<3/4$. If f' has at least one term T_C, then $\mathbf{Pr}_{x\sim D_0}\big[f'(x)=0\big] \le \mathbf{Pr}_{x\sim D_0}\big[T_C(x)=0\big] \le 1/2 < 3/4$.

The construction of f' involves a new concept: A *sunflower* with *core* set C is a collection of *petal* sets that each contain C but are otherwise pairwise disjoint. The core C may be $\emptyset$. See Figure 18.7.

Lemma 18.21. *For every collection of more than $\ell!(p-1)^\ell$ distinct sets each of size $\le \ell$, some p of them form a sunflower.*

We postpone Lemma 18.21's proof to the end of this section. *Plucking* a sunflower means replacing all its petal sets with the single core set. For every (q,ℓ)-clique-DNF $T_{C_1} \vee \cdots \vee T_{C_q}$ with $q > m = \ell!(p-1)^\ell$ distinct terms, some p of the sets $C_1,\ldots,C_q$ form a sunflower, which we can pluck to get a $(q-p+1,\ell)$-clique-DNF by replacing the corresponding terms with the core's clique indicator. We can repeat this plucking process until there are at most m terms.

The following algorithm shows the construction of f'. Identifying each node g in the circuit with the monotone function of x that it computes, we approximate g with an (m,ℓ)-clique-DNF g'. Recalling that $\ell = k^{1/2}$ and $s = n^{\ell/4}$, we choose $p = 3\log s \le \ell \log n$ and note that $m = \ell!(p-1)^\ell \le (\ell p)^\ell \le (k\log n)^\ell \le s/2$ since $k \le n^{1/5}$.

Algorithm to approximate a monotone circuit with an (m,ℓ)-clique-DNF (18.3)

for each node g in a topological order of the circuit:
  if g is an input node $x_{\{u,v\}}$: let $g' = g = T_{\{u,v\}}$
  otherwise g has inneighbors a and b, say with $a' = \bigvee_{i\in[q]} T_{A_i}$ and $b' = \bigvee_{j\in[r]} T_{B_j}$
  if $g = a \vee b$: to obtain g' from $g^* = a' \vee b' = \left(\bigvee_{i\in[q]} T_{A_i}\right) \vee \left(\bigvee_{j\in[r]} T_{B_j}\right)$:
    repeatedly pluck a p-petal sunflower until there are at most m terms
  if $g = a \wedge b$: to obtain g' from $g^* = a' \wedge b' = \bigvee_{(i,j)\in[q]\times[r]}\left(T_{A_i} \wedge T_{B_j}\right)$:
    replace each $T_{A_i} \wedge T_{B_j}$ with the clique indicator $T_{A_i \cup B_j}$
    delete any $T_{A_i \cup B_j}$ with $|A_i \cup B_j| > \ell$
    repeatedly pluck a p-petal sunflower until there are at most m terms
let $f' = g'$ for the output node g

First, we prove $\mathbf{Pr}_{x\sim D_1}\left[f'(x) = 1\right] \geq 3/4$. If $f'(x) < f(x)$ then $g'(x) < g^*(x)$ for some gate g, because the first g (in the topological order) with $g'(x) < g(x)$ must be a gate (not an input node) with $g'(x) < g^*(x)$ since otherwise $g^*(x) < g(x)$ and thus either $a'(x) < a(x)$ or $b'(x) < b(x)$ (where a and b are the inneighbors of g) since the circuit is monotone. Thus it suffices to prove $\mathbf{Pr}_{x\sim D_1}\left[g'(x) < g^*(x)\right] \leq 1/4s$ for every gate g, since then by a union bound over all s gates:

$$\begin{aligned}\mathbf{Pr}_{x\sim D_1}\left[f'(x)=0\right] &\leq \mathbf{Pr}_{x\sim D_1}\left[g'(x)<g^*(x) \text{ for some gate } g\right]\\ &\leq \textstyle\sum_{\text{gate } g} \mathbf{Pr}_{x\sim D_1}\left[g'(x)<g^*(x)\right] \leq s/4s = 1/4\end{aligned}$$

If $g = a \vee b$, then $\mathbf{Pr}_{x\sim D_1}\left[g'(x) < g^*(x)\right] = 0$ since plucking can't flip the output from 1 to 0. Now, suppose $g = a \wedge b$. Replacing $T_{A_i} \wedge T_{B_j}$ with $T_{A_i\cup B_j}$ can't flip the output from 1 to 0 when x contains a clique on $S \subseteq [n]$ and no other edges, because if $\left(T_{A_i} \wedge T_{B_j}\right)(x) = 1$ then $A_i \cup B_j \subseteq S$ and thus $T_{A_i\cup B_j}(x) = 1$. Plucking can't flip the output from 1 to 0. The only issue is that deleting $T_{A_i\cup B_j}$ may flip the output from 1 to 0. If (i,j) is *bad* in the sense that $|A_i \cup B_j| > \ell$, then:

$$\begin{aligned}\mathbf{Pr}_{x\sim D_1}\left[T_{A_i\cup B_j}(x)=1\right] &= \mathbf{Pr}_{S\subseteq[n]:|S|=k}\left[A_i \cup B_j \subseteq S\right]\\ &\leq \binom{n-\ell}{k-\ell}\Big/\binom{n}{k} = \frac{k(k-1)\cdots(k-\ell+1)}{n(n-1)\cdots(n-\ell+1)} \leq (k/n)^\ell \leq 1/n^{4\ell/5}\end{aligned}$$

By a union bound:

$$\begin{aligned}\mathbf{Pr}_{x\sim D_1}\left[g'(x)<g^*(x)\right] &\leq \mathbf{Pr}_{x\sim D_1}\left[T_{A_i\cup B_j}(x)=1 \text{ for some bad } (i,j)\right]\\ &\leq \textstyle\sum_{\text{bad } (i,j)} \mathbf{Pr}_{x\sim D_1}\left[T_{A_i\cup B_j}(x)=1\right] \leq m^2/n^{4\ell/5} \leq (s/2)^2/s^3 = 1/4s\end{aligned}$$

Now, we prove $\mathbf{Pr}_{x\sim D_0}\left[f'(x) = 0\right] \geq 3/4$. Like above, it suffices to prove $\mathbf{Pr}_{x\sim D_0}\left[g'(x) > g^*(x)\right] \leq 1/4s$ for every gate g. First, suppose $g = a \vee b$. Plucking a sunflower $C_1, \ldots, C_p$ with core C flips the output from 0 to 1 with probability

$$\begin{aligned}&\leq \mathbf{Pr}_{x\sim D_0}\left[T_{C_1}(x)=\cdots=T_{C_p}(x)=0 \text{ and } T_C(x)=1\right]\\ &\leq \mathbf{Pr}_{x\sim D_0}\left[T_{C_1}(x)=\cdots=T_{C_p}(x)=0 \,\middle|\, T_C(x)=1\right]\\ &= \textstyle\prod_{i\in[p]} \mathbf{Pr}_{x\sim D_0}\left[T_{C_i}(x)=0 \,\middle|\, T_C(x)=1\right]\\ &\leq \textstyle\prod_{i\in[p]} \mathbf{Pr}_{x\sim D_0}\left[T_{C_i}(x)=0\right]\\ &\leq (1/2)^p\end{aligned}$$

where the third line is by conditional independence (since the petals are pairwise disjoint outside C), and the fourth line is because conditioning on C being a clique only decreases the probability that C_i isn't a clique, and we showed the fifth line earlier. Since at most m sunflowers are plucked, $\mathbf{Pr}_{x\sim D_0}\big[g'(x) > g^*(x)\big] \le m/2^p \le (s/2)/s^3 \le 1/4s$. Now, suppose $g = a \wedge b$. Replacing $T_{A_i} \wedge T_{B_j}$ with $T_{A_i \cup B_j}$ can't flip the output from 0 to 1. Deleting $T_{A_i \cup B_j}$ can't flip the output from 0 to 1. Since plucking a p-petal sunflower flips the output from 0 to 1 with probability $\le 1/2^p$, and at most m^2 sunflowers are plucked, $\mathbf{Pr}_{x\sim D_0}\big[g'(x) > g^*(x)\big] \le m^2/2^p \le (s/2)^2/s^3 = 1/4s$. ∎

Proof of Lemma 18.21 (ancillary). The following algorithm finds a p-petal sunflower among $q > \ell!(p-1)^\ell$ distinct sets each of size $\le \ell$. Here, p is fixed but ℓ and q can vary.

Algorithm to find a sunflower (18.4)

```
find-sunflower(A_1,...,A_q):
    find as many pairwise disjoint sets among A_1,...,A_q as possible
    assume they're A_1,...,A_t for convenience
    if t ≥ p: return A_1,...,A_p
    find u ∈ A_1 ∪ ··· ∪ A_t that's in as many of A_1,...,A_q as possible
    let B_1,...,B_r denote the sets among A_1,...,A_q containing u
    return find-sunflower(B_1 ∖ {u},...,B_r ∖ {u}) but with u added back to each set
```

If $t \ge p$ then $A_1,\dots,A_p$ form a sunflower with an empty core since they're pairwise disjoint. This covers the base case $\ell = 1$ since distinct singletons are pairwise disjoint. Now, assume $t < p$ and $\ell > 1$. Each of $A_1,\dots,A_q$ contains at least one element of $A_1 \cup \cdots \cup A_t$ (since otherwise such a set would be disjoint from each of $A_1,\dots,A_t$, contradicting the maximality of t). Since $\big|A_1 \cup \cdots \cup A_t\big| \le \ell t \le \ell(p-1)$, this means u is in $\ge 1/\ell(p-1)$ fraction of the sets $A_1,\dots,A_q$. That is, $r \ge q/\ell(p-1) > (\ell-1)!(p-1)^{\ell-1}$. Also, the distinct sets $B_1 \setminus \{u\},\dots,B_r \setminus \{u\}$ each have size $\le \ell - 1$. Thus by the invariant, the recursive call returns a p-petal sunflower among $B_1 \setminus \{u\},\dots,B_r \setminus \{u\}$, which is a sunflower among $A_1,\dots,A_q$ after adding u back in to the core. ∎

Sunflowers also have applications in other areas of complexity theory, including hardness of approximation, cryptography, communication complexity, and data structures.

18.7 Natural Proofs Barrier

We've had decent success in proving lower bounds for special types of circuits. Why is proving lower bounds for general circuits much tougher? We'd like to show P ≠ NP by proving that an NP-complete problem requires superpolynomial-size circuits. Unfortunately, known lower bound techniques fall flat on their faces when we don't rein in the circuits somehow. Why? This book's final plot twist is that computational complexity is self-sabotaging: Every lower bound technique that's *natural* (in a certain sense) effectively dooms itself to fail on general circuits. Imprecisely but evocatively: *The lower bound we'd like to prove inhibits us from proving it.* More accurately: Any potential natural proof of a strong lower bound would also yield a similarly strong upper bound that—while not exactly contradicting the desired lower bound—is qualitatively at odds with it, and is conjectured to be false. As §2.2.3 forewarned, this barrier is evidence that to show P ≠ NP, we would need a drastically new idea (an unnatural proof). And so the book comes full circle, dredging up our consternation at P versus NP.

x							S									
00	0	0	0	0	0	0	0	0	1	1	1	1	1	1	1	1
01	0	0	0	0	1	1	1	1	0	0	0	0	1	1	1	1
10	0	0	1	1	0	0	1	1	0	0	1	1	0	0	1	1
11	0	1	0	1	0	1	0	1	0	1	0	1	0	1	0	1
p	0	0	0	0	0	0	0	0	0	1	1	1	0	1	1	1

Figure 18.8: Natural property example

Summary: To prove that some function f has no small circuit, we would identify some property that f has but that functions with small circuits don't have. And unless our approach is rather unconventional, this property would be *natural*:

- It can be decided somewhat efficiently whether any given function has the property.
- The property holds for random functions (with high probability), not just for a specific f.

Almost all known lower bounds for special types of nonmonotone circuits are via such *natural proofs*. (We consider nonmonotone circuits since there's no simple, standard definition of a "random monotone function.") For general circuits, a natural property would hold for random functions but not for small circuits, so we could distinguish random functions from pseudorandom functions (§12.4) using the algorithm for deciding whether a function has the natural property. This would refute a standard cryptographic assumption analogous to $\mathsf{P} \neq \mathsf{NP}$.

18.7.1 Natural Properties

Identify a function $f\colon \{0,1\}^N \to \{0,1\}$ with its truth table $f \in \{0,1\}^{2^N}$, so $f(x) = f_x$. In this section, a circuit's size is its number of $\wedge$ and $\vee$ gates.

Definition. A function $p\colon \{0,1\}^{2^N} \to \{0,1\}$ is a (t,ε)-*natural property* for a set of functions $S \subseteq \{0,1\}^{2^N}$ iff:

- *Constructiveness*: p is computed by a size-t circuit.
- *Largeness*: $p(f) = 1$ for $> \varepsilon$ fraction of all f.
- *Usefulness*: $p(f) = 0$ for all $f \in S$. ◀

Example. Figure 18.8 shows all 16 functions $f\colon \{0,1\}^2 \to \{0,1\}$ and a $p\colon \{0,1\}^{2^2} \to \{0,1\}$ which is a $(2,\varepsilon)$-natural property for the shaded set of functions S, for all $\varepsilon < 6/16$. For example, $f = 0101$ is the function with $f(00) = 0$, $f(01) = 1$, $f(10) = 0$, $f(11) = 1$, and we have $f \in S$ and $p(f) = 0$.

- *Constructiveness*: p is computed by the size-2 circuit $p(f) = f_{00} \wedge (f_{10} \vee f_{11})$.
- *Largeness*: $p(f) = 1$ for 6 of the 16 many f.
- *Usefulness*: $p(f) = 0$ for all $f \in S$. ♦

We generally consider infinite families of natural properties parameterized by N.

Here's the connection to circuit lower bounds: If p is a natural property for the set S of functions computed by size-s circuits, and if $p(f) = 1$, then by usefulness, f has no size-s circuit. Constructiveness and largeness aren't necessary for deducing a lower bound, but they "naturally" hold for the kinds of properties people have devised:

- Constructiveness means the property is not too bizarre. We can efficiently check whether any given f has the property. Typically $t \le 2^{O(N)} = \text{poly}(2^N)$, so evaluating $p(f)$ takes time polynomial in the length of f's truth table.
- Largeness means lots of functions have the property, not just the particular f we want a lower bound for. Intuitively, largeness ought to hold because if some f has a lower bound, then all the "hardest" functions (random ones) should have a lower bound too. Typically $\varepsilon \ge 1/2^{O(N)} = 1/\text{poly}(2^N)$.

Conceivably, we might prove strong circuit lower bounds via unnatural properties, which are not constructive or not large. But so far, researchers haven't had much success with that. Almost all known circuit lower bound proofs are natural or can be made natural with some adjustment.

Example. The depth-d circuit size lower bound for PARITY via the switching lemma (§18.3) uses this property: $p(f) = 1$ iff f has no certificate with at least $M = N/32(32k)^{d-2} - k$ many $*$s, where $k = 2\log s$. If $s = 2^{N^{1/(d-1)}/128}$ then p is $\left(2^{O(N)}, 1 - o(1)\right)$-natural for depth-$d$ size-s circuits:

- *Constructiveness*: $p(f)$ can be computed in time $2^{O(N)}$ (and so by a size-$2^{O(N)}$ circuit) by trying all 3^N partial assignments, except those with fewer than M many $*$s, and checking whether any of the corresponding restrictions of f are constant by examining all entries in the truth table.
- *Largeness*: $p(f) = 1$ for most functions f: Say a partial assignment a with at least M many $*$s is *good*, so $p(f) = 1$ iff f has no good certificate. For uniformly random f:

$$\begin{aligned}
\mathbf{Pr}\left[p(f) = 0\right] &= \mathbf{Pr}\left[\text{some good } a \text{ is a certificate for } f\right] \\
&\le \textstyle\sum_{\text{good } a} \mathbf{Pr}\left[a \text{ is a certificate for } f\right] \\
&= \textstyle\sum_{\text{good } a} \Big(\prod_{x \text{ consistent with } a} \mathbf{Pr}\left[f(x) = 0\right] + \\
&\qquad\qquad \textstyle\prod_{x \text{ consistent with } a} \mathbf{Pr}\left[f(x) = 1\right]\Big) \\
&\le 3^N\left((1/2)^{2^M} + (1/2)^{2^M}\right) \\
&\le o(1) \qquad\qquad (\text{since } M \ge N^{1/(d-1)}/64)
\end{aligned}$$

- *Usefulness*: $p(f) = 0$ for all f computed by depth-d size-s circuits (Lemma 18.11). ♦

In some cases, such as the "polynomial approximation" method from §18.2, making the proof natural takes extra work.

18.7.2 Natural Proofs Break Pseudorandom Functions

A seeded function $F: \{0,1\}^\ell \times \{0,1\}^n \to \{0,1\}$ is a (t,ε)-pseudorandom function (PRF) iff every size-t oracle circuit C (where each oracle gate has n incoming wires and one outgoing wire) can't distinguish by more than ε whether its oracle is $F_r: \{0,1\}^n \to \{0,1\}$ defined by $F_r(x) = F(r,x)$ for a uniformly random seed $r \in \{0,1\}^\ell$, or is a uniformly random function $g: \{0,1\}^n \to \{0,1\}$. That is, $\mathbf{Pr}\left[C(F_{U_\ell}) = 1\right]$ and $\mathbf{Pr}\left[C(U_{n\to 1}) = 1\right]$ are within $\pm\varepsilon$, where U_ℓ is the uniform distribution over $\{0,1\}^\ell$, and $U_{n\to 1}$ is the uniform distribution over all $g: \{0,1\}^n \to \{0,1\}$. We're using n for pseudorandom functions and N for natural properties.

Theorem 18.22. *If there exists a (t,ε)-pseudorandom function computed by a size-s circuit with $n \ge N$, then there doesn't exist a $(t - 2^N, \varepsilon)$-natural property for size-s circuits.*

Proof. We prove the contrapositive. Suppose $p\colon \{0,1\}^{2^N} \to \{0,1\}$ is a $(t-2^N, \varepsilon)$-natural property for size-s circuits, and $F\colon \{0,1\}^\ell \times \{0,1\}^n \to \{0,1\}$ is computed by a size-s circuit. We show that F isn't a (t,ε)-PRF. Consider this oracle circuit C:

Oracle circuit to break a pseudorandom function using a natural property	(18.5)
given access to oracle $g\colon \{0,1\}^n \to \{0,1\}$: obtain $f\colon \{0,1\}^N \to \{0,1\}$ by querying $f(x) = g(x0^{n-N})$ for each $x \in \{0,1\}^N$ output $p(f)$ by feeding the truth table of f into the circuit for p	

f is the restriction of g under the partial assignment $*^N 0^{n-N}$. If $g = F_r$ for any seed r, then f has a size-s circuit (a contraction of F's size-s circuit), so $C(g) = p(f) = 0$ (usefulness). If g is uniformly random, then f is too, so $C(g) = p(f) = 1$ for $> \varepsilon$ fraction of all g (largeness). Thus $\mathbf{Pr}\big[C(U_{n\to 1}) = 1\big] - \mathbf{Pr}\big[C(F_{U_\ell}) = 1\big] > \varepsilon - 0 = \varepsilon$. Also, C is a size-t oracle circuit since it consists of 2^N oracle gates and p's size-$(t-2^N)$ circuit (constructiveness). Thus F isn't a (t,ε)-PRF. ■

Example. Suppose $t = 2^{n^{1/3}}$ and $s = n^4$ and $\varepsilon = 1/5$ and $n = N^6$, so $t = 2^{N^2}$ and $s = N^{24}$. Under the plausible assumption that there exists a $(2^{n^{1/3}}, 1/5)$-pseudorandom function computed by a size-n^4 circuit, there doesn't exist a $(2^{N^2} - 2^N, 1/5)$-natural property for size-N^{24} circuits. So we shouldn't expect to prove a circuit size lower bound of N^{24} without using a property that either holds for few functions or is so strange that, given a truth table of size $M = 2^N$, the property can't be computed by a circuit of size $2^{N^2} - 2^N \approx M^{\log M}$. ◆

This barrier casts a pall over the circuit lower bound successes described earlier in this chapter. Trying to prove P ≠ NP by adapting known techniques is like trying to reach the moon by building a taller skyscraper—we need a spaceship but have no idea how to build one. The natural proofs barrier helps researchers avoid wasting time on futile proof attempts. We hope the reader is galvanized to circumvent the barrier and further unravel the mysteries of efficient computation.

Exercises

18.1 Define $F\colon \{0,1\}^+ \to \{0,1\}$ by $F(x) = 1$ iff weight(x) is divisible by 3. Prove that every bounded-fan-in circuit for F_N has at least $2N-3$ many $\wedge$ and $\vee$ gates.

18.2 For even N, define $\textsc{Equality}_N\colon \{0,1\}^N \to \{0,1\}$ by $\textsc{Equality}_N(x) = 1$ iff $x_1 \cdots x_{N/2} = x_{N/2+1} \cdots x_N$. Prove that every bounded-fan-in circuit for $\textsc{Equality}_N$ has at least $2N-1$ many $\wedge$ and $\vee$ gates.

18.3 Prove that 2-Threshold has monotone formula size complexity $O(N \log N)$ using a divide-and-conquer approach.

18.4 In the proof of Lemma 18.4, we designed a distribution over $\mathbb{Z}_3$-polynomials Q of degree 2 such that $\mathbf{Pr}\big[Q(y) \neq \vee(y)\big] \le 1/3$ for every $y \in \{0,1\}^m$.

(a) Design a distribution over $\mathbb{Z}_3$-polynomials Q of degree 4 such that $\mathbf{Pr}\big[Q(y) \neq f(y)\big] \le 1/3$ for every $y \in \{0,1\}^m$, where $f = 2\text{-}\textsc{Threshold}_m$.

(b) Design a distribution over $\mathbb{R}$-polynomials Q of degree $O(\log m)$ such that $\mathbf{Pr}\big[Q(y) \neq \vee(y)\big] \le 1/3$ for every $y \in \{0,1\}^m$. Hint: Use $Q(y) = 1 - (1 - b^1 \cdot y) \cdots (1 - b^k \cdot y)$ for independent (but not uniformly distributed) $b^1 \in \{0,1\}^m, \ldots, b^k \in \{0,1\}^m$.

18.5 Prove that Parity has depth-d circuit size complexity $2^{\Omega(N^{1/2d})}$ even when we allow gates that evaluate to 1 iff the number of incoming 1s is divisible by 5.

18.6 (a) Prove that for every constant d, there exists a constant $e > 0$ such that Majority has depth-d circuit size complexity $2^{\Omega(N^e)}$, by reducing from Parity.

(b) Prove that $\binom{n}{n/2} \geq 2^n/\sqrt{2n}$ if n is even and $\binom{n}{\lceil n/2 \rceil} \geq 2^n/\sqrt{2(n+1)}$ if n is odd. (See Claim 18.6.)

(c) Prove that $\text{Majority}_N(x) = x_1$ for $1/2 + \Omega(1/\sqrt{N})$ fraction of inputs x. Therefore, Majority has no average-case lower bound for circuits that succeed on $1/2 + \Omega(1/\sqrt{N})$ fraction of inputs.

18.7 (a) Prove a stronger version of the switching lemma (Lemma 18.10) with "depth-ℓ decision tree" instead of "ℓ-CNF." Hint: Show that for a random partial assignment a, the following decision tree that simulates $\varphi|_a$ is probably shallow:

Decision tree to simulate a contracted DNF	(18.6)

```
for each term T of φ|a (in the same order as the corresponding terms of φ):
    if T hasn't been eliminated so far:
        query all unqueried variables in T
        if T is satisfied: accept
reject
```

(b) Adapt Lemma 18.11 to prove that if $f: \{0,1\}^N \to \{0,1\}$ has a depth-d size-s circuit, then for a uniformly random $N/32(32k)^{d-1}$-partial assignment a where $k = 2\log s$:

$$\mathbf{Pr}\big[f|_a \text{ has no depth-}k\text{ decision tree}\big] \leq 1/s$$

(c) Prove that every depth-d circuit either computes Parity_N on $\leq 1/2 + 1/2^{\Omega(N^{1/d})}$ fraction of inputs or has size $2^{\Omega(N^{1/d})}$. (By the way, using this average-case lower bound in the PRG framework of § 11.4 yields a PRG that fools depth-d circuits.)

18.8 Consider computational problems where the goal is to take uniformly random bits as input, and output a sample from some probability distribution. Assume the distribution is uniform over input-output pairs of Parity: The goal is to output $(x, \oplus(x)) \in \{0,1\}^{n+1}$ where $x \in \{0,1\}^n$ is uniformly random. The obvious approach is to sample x and then compute $\oplus(x)$, but AC^0-type circuits can't do this. Prove that this distribution can be sampled by an AC^0-type (in fact, NC^0-type) circuit using a different approach.

18.9 Prove that Majority has formula size complexity $\Omega(N^2)$. (Exercise 6.11.b showed that Majority has formula size complexity at most poly N.)

18.10 Describe a depth-$O(\log^2 n)$ communication protocol for Directed Reachability′, defined in § 18.5.2.

18.11 Prove that Undirected Reachability has monotone formula size complexity $2^{\Omega(\log^2 n)}$, using the Undirected Fork communication lower bound from Exercise 17.22. Also, illustrate the reduction on input $x = (3, 2, 1)$ and $y = (2, 3, 1)$.

18.12 The connection between formulas and protocols (§ 18.5) is useful for proving formula size lower bounds and circuit depth lower bounds. This exercise develops a similar connection for circuit size lower bounds. Here, circuits have negations pushed to the input variables and have bounded fan-in. A circuit for f is a dag such that:

- Each source is a literal.
- Each non-source is an $\vee$ or $\wedge$ gate with two inneighbors.
- The unique sink outputs 1 on all $x \in X = f^{-1}(1)$ and 0 on all $y \in Y = f^{-1}(0)$.

A *rectangle dag* for f^* is a dag where each node v has an associated rectangle $A_v \times B_v \subseteq X \times Y$ such that:

- Each sink's rectangle is monochromatic with respect to f^*.
- Each non-sink v has two outneighbors v_0 and v_1, and either $A_v \subseteq A_{v_0} \cup A_{v_1}$ and $B_v \subseteq B_{v_0} \cap B_{v_1}$ or $A_v \subseteq A_{v_0} \cap A_{v_1}$ and $B_v \subseteq B_{v_0} \cup B_{v_1}$.
- The unique source's rectangle is $X \times Y$.

The *shape* of a circuit or rectangle dag is the underlying dag G. The *size* is the number of nodes. Let G^* be G with all edge directions reversed. Protocols are tree-shaped rectangle dags, like how formulas are tree-shaped circuits.

Prove that f has a shape-G circuit iff f^* has a shape-G^* rectangle dag. Consequently, the circuit size complexity of f equals the rectangle dag size complexity of f^*.

18.13 Prove that for every constant $0 < c < 1$, no $(2^{4n^c}, 1/2)$-pseudorandom function is computed by a depth-d size-$2^{n^{c/(d-1)}/128}$ circuit.

Notes

Books on circuit complexity include [555, 463, 552, 278].

The theorem that 2-THRESHOLD has a circuit family with $(2 + o(1))N$ many $\wedge$ and $\vee$ gates is due to [151] and references therein.

The gate elimination lower bound for PARITY (Theorem 18.2) is due to [471].

The polynomial approximation method for lower bounding PARITY's depth-d circuit size complexity (Theorem 18.3) is known as the "Razborov–Smolensky theorem" [431, 498]. Surprisingly, the polynomial approximation method also has applications to algorithm design, as surveyed in [562]. This method for constant-depth circuit size lower bounds also applies to circuits with "mod m gates" for prime m. For composite m, strong lower bounds are known for problems in NEXP [561].

The random restriction method for proving the tight lower bound on PARITY's depth-d circuit size complexity (Theorem 18.7) is the culmination of a line of work [180, 13, 571, 236, 433]. In the literature, "restriction" sometimes means "partial assignment," and what we call "restriction" is sometimes called "subfunction." Other applications of the switching lemma to AC^0-type circuits include learning algorithms [338], pseudorandom generators [393, 355], and extractors [548].

Formula shrinkage with exponent 1.5 (Lemma 18.13) is due to [508], and with exponent 2 is due to [237] with an alternative proof due to [512]. The $N^{2.5-o(1)}$ formula size lower bound for a problem in P is due to [25].

The notorious "KRW conjecture" [290] concerns circuit/formula depth complexity and would imply $\mathsf{P} \neq \mathsf{NC}^1$.

The connection between formulas and communication (Lemma 18.16 and Lemma 18.18) is known as the "Karchmer–Wigderson game" [291]. The formula size lower bound for PARITY (Theorem 18.17) is originally due to [308, 307]. The monotone formula size lower bounds for DIRECTED REACHABILITY (Theorem 18.19) and UNDIRECTED REACHABILITY (Exercise 18.11) are due to [291, 220]. The communication complexity framework can also be used to prove monotone formula size lower bounds for detecting cliques in graphs [193] and detecting perfect matchings in graphs [429].

The monotone circuit size lower bound for detecting cliques (Theorem 18.20) is due to [430, 16]. The sunflower lemma (Lemma 18.21) is due to [157], and a celebrated strengthening is due to [22]. Some monotone functions have exponentially smaller nonmonotone circuit size complexity than monotone circuit size complexity [514, 214].

We have monotone analogues of $\mathsf{P} \neq \mathsf{NP}$ (Theorem 18.20) and $\mathsf{NC}^1 \neq \mathsf{L}$ (Theorem 18.19 and Exercise 18.11). Monotone analogues of $\mathsf{L} \neq \mathsf{NL}$ [417] and $\mathsf{NC}^i \neq \mathsf{NC}^{i+1}$ for all i [428] and $\mathsf{NC} \neq \mathsf{P}$ [428] have also been proven.

The natural proofs barrier (§18.7) is due to [434]. Natural proofs also have applications to computational learning theory [108].

Regarding the fact that 2-THRESHOLD has monotone formula size complexity $O(N \log N)$ (Exercise 18.3): k-THRESHOLD has monotone formula size complexity $O(N \log N)$ for every constant $k \geq 2$ [301, 176], and 2-THRESHOLD has nonmonotone formula size complexity $\Omega(N \log N)$ [322, 390].

Exercise 18.4.b is due to [56, 516]. Exercise 18.12 is due to [499].

Epilogue

This is a brief survey of other important topics in computational complexity.

Fine-Grained Complexity

We typically consider "polynomial time" to be "efficient." But the polynomial's degree matters a lot when inputs are large, as often happens in computational biology, finance, social media, transportation, and other domains. When N is one billion, linear time is fine but quadratic time may be far too slow. How can complexity theory provide guidance about when to hope for algorithms with lower-degree running times?

Suppose a problem is solvable in $O(N^2)$ time, and we conjecture it's not solvable in $O(N^c)$ time for any constant $c < 2$. To give evidence for this conjecture, we could prove that it follows from some generic, widely believed conjecture, like $\mathsf{P} \neq \mathsf{NP}$. Unfortunately, the "$\mathsf{P} \neq \mathsf{NP}$ hypothesis" is too coarse-grained to distinguish $O(N^3)$ from $O(N^{2.99})$. A fine-grained analogue known as the *strong exponential-time hypothesis* (SETH) says, informally, that not only does SAT have no poly-time algorithm, but brute force (trying all 2^n assignments to the CNF's n variables) is essentially the fastest possible SAT algorithm when the clauses are wide. Formally, SETH is the conjecture that for every $c < 2$, there exists k such that k-SAT isn't solvable in $O(c^n)$ time. Using *fine-grained reductions*, it's possible to pinpoint some problems' time complexities (up to low-order factors) assuming SETH. Some other fine-grained hypotheses (presumably incomparable to SETH) are also used for this purpose.

Parameterized Complexity

We generally measure a problem's complexity in terms of one parameter—the input size N. This doesn't always paint the full picture. Some problems have another natural parameter k that depends on the input. It's sometimes helpful to describe efficiency in terms of both parameters N and k, because if k is small in practice, then the dependence on k doesn't matter too much.

Consider INDEPENDENT SET where the parameter k is the desired size of an independent set (specified as part of the input). The brute force algorithm that tries all subsets of k nodes runs in time $N^{k+O(1)}$, which is a polynomial when k is a constant. So despite being NP-complete, INDEPENDENT SET is tractable when k is a constant. But this still leaves something to be desired: The exponent of N depends on k, so the time efficiency degrades significantly as k increases. A *fixed-parameter tractable* problem has an algorithm running in time $f(k) \cdot N^{O(1)}$ where $f(k)$ is an arbitrary function (typically exponential) of k alone, and the exponent in $N^{O(1)}$ doesn't depend on k. This makes a big difference: If $N = 1{,}000$ and $k = 5$, for example, then $N^k = 1{,}000{,}000{,}000{,}000{,}000$ is dizzyingly large, while $2^k \cdot N^2 = 32{,}000{,}000$ is manageable. Unfortunately, INDEPENDENT SET is conjectured not to be fixed-parameter tractable.

How about NODE COVER parameterized by the desired size k of a node cover? Standard reductions between INDEPENDENT SET and NODE COVER (§2.4.1) don't preserve k at all, and therefore imply nothing about the relationship between the parameterized complexities of these problems. In fact, Node Cover is fixed-parameter tractable, by the following recursive algorithm. The key observation is that if $\{u, v\}$ is an edge in G, then a size-k node cover would contain either u or v, so either $G - u$ (the graph without u and u's edges) or $G - v$ would have a size-$(k-1)$ node cover.

Fixed-parameter algorithm for Node Cover (E.1)

```
solve(G, k):
    if G has no edges: return true
    if k = 0: return false
    let {u, v} be an arbitrary edge of G
    return solve(G − u, k − 1) ∨ solve(G − v, k − 1)
```

Each non-leaf call spawns at most two recursive calls, with decremented k. So the tree of calls has at most 2^k leaves and $O(2^k)$ nodes, where k is the original parameter. Each call contributes $O(N)$ time, so the overall time efficiency is $O(2^k N)$.

Parameterized complexity theory features a whole new menagerie of algorithmic techniques, complexity classes, reductions, and completeness results.

Proof Complexity

The NP-completeness of Sat yields an effective strategy for solving various problems in practice: Transform inputs into CNFs and apply an industrial-strength Sat solver. But how can a Sat solver convince someone its output is correct? This issue is also relevant to interactive theorem provers (proof assistants) and automated theorem provers.

We can convince someone φ is satisfiable by presenting a satisfying assignment. How can we convince someone φ is unsatisfiable? This is the essence of NP versus coNP. One way is a *resolution refutation*. The idea is that if clauses $(C_1 \vee x_i)$ and $(C_2 \vee \overline{x_i})$ are present, then we may append the clause $(C_1 \vee C_2)$ to the CNF. For example, if $(\overline{x_1} \vee x_3)$ and $(x_2 \vee \overline{x_3} \vee \overline{x_4})$ are present, we may append $(\overline{x_1} \vee x_2 \vee \overline{x_4})$. If the original CNF is satisfiable, then so is the augmented CNF, because any assignment that satisfies $(C_1 \vee x_i) \wedge (C_2 \vee \overline{x_i})$ also satisfies $(C_1 \vee C_2)$ since either $x_i = 0$ and C_1 is satisfied, or $x_i = 1$ and C_2 is satisfied. Contrapositive: If the augmented CNF is unsatisfiable, then so is the original CNF. Thus to convince someone the original CNF is unsatisfiable, it suffices to convince them the augmented CNF is unsatisfiable. We can apply the resolution rule repeatedly, deriving more and more clauses until the CNF is obviously unsatisfiable because it contains an empty clause, derived from clauses (x_i) and $(\overline{x_i})$. A resolution refutation is a dag (directed acyclic graph) where each source is an original clause, each nonsource is a clause derived from its two inneighbors, and the unique sink is the empty clause.

Example. $(x_1 \vee x_2 \vee x_3) \wedge (\overline{x_1} \vee x_2) \wedge (\overline{x_2} \vee x_3) \wedge (x_1 \vee \overline{x_3}) \wedge (\overline{x_1} \vee \overline{x_2} \vee \overline{x_3})$ is unsatisfiable because the cycle of implications $(x_1 \Rightarrow x_2) \wedge (x_2 \Rightarrow x_3) \wedge (x_3 \Rightarrow x_1)$ says the three variables have the same value, but $(x_1 \vee x_2 \vee x_3)$ says they're not all 0, and $(\overline{x_1} \vee \overline{x_2} \vee \overline{x_3})$ says they're not all 1. Figure E.1 shows a resolution refutation for this CNF. ♦

Every unsatisfiable CNF has at least one resolution refutation, and may have many (of varying sizes) since there may be many options for which pair of clauses to combine at each step. An unsatisfiable CNF's *resolution complexity* is the size of a smallest resolution refutation for it. An upper bound for an unsatisfiable CNF shows that it has a small resolution refutation ("easy to

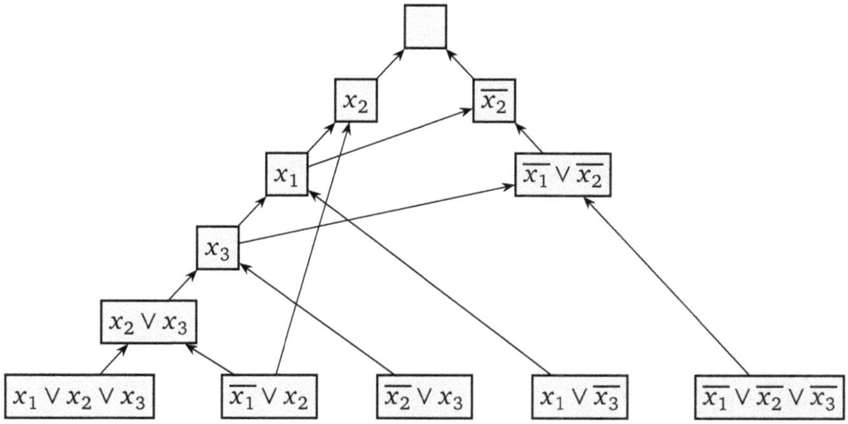

Figure E.1: Example resolution refutation

verify"), while a lower bound shows that all of its resolution refutations are large ("hard to verify").

If a SAT solver uses resolution to ascertain unsatisfiability, then the SAT solver will necessarily be slow on unsatisfiable CNFs with large resolution complexity, since a refutation takes a long time just to write down (much less find).

Other proof systems (with corresponding complexity measures) are more general than resolution. Some are based on algebraic or geometric principles. Proof systems are like concrete models of verifiers and have close connections to all the other concrete models in Part IV.

Expander Graphs

Expander graphs are undirected graphs that have few edges but are "highly connected": Every set of at most half the nodes has a relatively large neighborhood. It's not difficult to show that such graphs exist nonconstructively by the probabilistic method. Explicit constructions of expander graphs—where each node's list of neighbors can be computed very efficiently—are somewhat tough to design and analyze. Expanders are a kind of pseudorandom graph, useful because they are not random but "behave like" they are. They have a spectacular variety of applications in computational complexity, including UNDIRECTED REACHABILITY $\in$ L, the PCP theorem, pseudorandom generators, randomness extractors, randomness-efficient amplification, error correcting codes, sorting networks, and proof complexity.

Harmonic Analysis

We touched on *harmonic analysis* of boolean functions in § 11.2.3 and § 14.4.4. The idea is to represent $f: \{0,1\}^n \to \{0,1\}$ as a linear combination (over $\mathbb{R}$) of parity functions (on subsets of input variables). The linear combination's coefficients make certain information about f more transparent. This tool for analyzing properties of boolean functions is part of complexity theory's "infrastructure," with applications in probabilistically checkable proofs and hardness of approximation, pseudorandomness, average-case complexity, computational learning theory, and lower bounds for many concrete models of computation.

Program Size Complexity

Informally, a string's *program size complexity* is the size of a smallest program that outputs that string (and takes no input). This is a measure of "incompressibility" or "amount of information."

Example. The string 1010101010101010101010101010101010101010 contains little information. It's just 20 copies of "10" and is thus output by a fairly small program (with Reg[0] initialized to 0):

Program to write 1010101010101010101010101010101010101010 (E.2)

```
0. write 1
1. write 0
2. let Reg[0] ← Reg[0] + 1
3. if Reg[0] < 20 then goto line 0
4. halt
```

In contrast, the string 1110100110100111101100001001000100101100 lacks discernible patterns and presumably can't be output by any program much smaller than the trivial one that has the whole string hardcoded (with 40 "write" instructions for the 40 bits). ♦

To formally define a program's *size*, we'd need to account for not only the number of lines of code, but also the number of registers, the sizes of hardcoded constants, and the word size.

Program size complexity has connections to derandomization, average-case complexity, cryptography, and computational learning theory.

Complexity of Counting

Every poly-time verifier (for an NP problem) has an associated function problem: Given an input x, how many witnesses w would make the verifier accept? The complexity class of all such counting problems is called #P ("sharp P"). We studied approximate counting of witnesses in § 8.4, but now we consider exact counting. For example, the problem of counting satisfying assignments to a CNF is in #P, and turns out to be #P-complete, even for monotone 2-CNFs. So a counting problem may be #P-complete even when the associated decision problem (would at least one witness make the verifier accept?) is in P. Another problem where that happens is counting perfect matchings in a bipartite graph. Remarkably, there exists a fully poly-time randomized approximation scheme for counting perfect matchings in a bipartite graph. Another marvelous theorem is that, although counting witnesses seems incomparable to the polynomial hierarchy, it's actually "harder": Every problem in PH has a poly-time reduction to a #P problem.

Arithmetic Complexity

An *arithmetic circuit* is like a logic circuit but with $+$ and $\cdot$ gates (instead of $\wedge, \vee, \neg$ gates) and with sources labeled by variables and constants in some field. Arithmetic circuits express multivariate polynomials. A measure of the complexity of a polynomial is the size of a smallest arithmetic circuit that expresses it. An arithmetic analogue of P versus NP is the so-called VP versus VNP question, which is also open but potentially easier to resolve. Unlike the situation with logic circuits, we know slightly superlinear lower bounds for arithmetic circuits, but we don't know strong lower bounds for constant-depth arithmetic circuits, even for depth 4. This is partly explained by a surprising theorem that strong lower bounds for depth-4 arithmetic circuits would actually imply strong lower bounds for unbounded-depth arithmetic circuits. Another major goal in arithmetic complexity is to derandomize polynomial identity testing (§7.1.2); significant progress has been made for restricted types of arithmetic circuits.

Property Testing

When the input is huge, even linear time might be too slow. A *property tester* is a randomized sublinear-time algorithm for a certain kind of promise problem, which asks whether the input has some property or is "far" from having the property.

For example, suppose the input is the adjacency matrix of an undirected graph, and consider the property of *triangle-freeness,* meaning the graph contains no size-3 clique. (We encountered this property in § 15.3.2.) A property tester should accept with high probability if the input graph is triangle-free and should reject with high probability if the input graph disagrees with every triangle-free graph on at least ε fraction of all $\binom{n}{2}$ possible edges. It's unsurprising but very non-obvious that the following tester works: For a certain k depending only on ε, pick k triples of nodes uniformly at random, and accept iff none of these triples is a triangle in the input graph.

There's a wealth of techniques for upper and lower bounds for testing various properties. Property testers also play an important role in probabilistically checkable proofs, for example the linearity tester we analyzed in § 14.4.4.

Quantum Computing

Quantum mechanics is a branch of physics concerning counterintuitive behavior of subatomic particles. In theory, this behavior can be harnessed by *quantum algorithms* to solve some problems more efficiently than "classical" randomized algorithms.

Here's the basic difference between the randomized and quantum settings: A randomized computation has probabilities, which are nonnegative and sum to 1. A quantum computation has *amplitudes,* which may be negative, and their squares sum to 1. In more detail, suppose $\{0,1\}^m$ is the set of all configurations of the memory. These m bits are called *qubits* in the quantum setting.

- Each step of a randomized computation yields a distribution over configurations—a linear combination $\sum_{C\in\{0,1\}^m} p_C C$ where the coefficient p_C is the probability of configuration C, and where each $p_C \geq 0$ and $\sum_C p_C = 1$. For example, $\frac{1}{4}00 + \frac{1}{3}01 + \frac{1}{6}10 + \frac{1}{4}11$.
- Each step of a quantum computation yields a *superposition* over configurations—a linear combination $\sum_{C\in\{0,1\}^m} a_C C$ where the coefficient a_C is the *amplitude* of configuration C, and where each $a_C \in \mathbb{R}$ and $\sum_C a_C^2 = 1$. For example, $\frac{1}{\sqrt{4}}00 - \frac{1}{\sqrt{3}}01 + \frac{1}{\sqrt{6}}10 - \frac{1}{\sqrt{4}}11$.

Steps of a quantum computation are local operations (quantum gates) guaranteed to maintain $\sum_C a_C^2 = 1$. The qubits aren't really "in" any particular configuration until we *measure* them and observe configuration C with probability a_C^2. We could just measure a single qubit, say the first, and observe 0 with probability $\sum_{C:C_1=0} a_C^2$, and observe 1 with probability $\sum_{C:C_1=1} a_C^2$. The amplitudes of all configurations inconsistent with the measurement outcome get set to 0, and all other amplitudes automatically get rescaled so their squares sum to 1, and the computation may continue from there.

A key feature of the quantum setting—with no analogue in the randomized setting—is *interference*: Positive and negative amplitudes for the same configuration may "cancel out" during a computation step.

Example. Let $m = 1$, and represent $a_0 0 + a_1 1$ as the column vector $\begin{bmatrix} a_0 & a_1 \end{bmatrix}^\top$.

$$\begin{bmatrix} \frac{1}{\sqrt{2}} & \frac{1}{\sqrt{2}} \\ \frac{1}{\sqrt{2}} & -\frac{1}{\sqrt{2}} \end{bmatrix} \begin{bmatrix} \frac{1}{\sqrt{2}} \\ \frac{1}{\sqrt{2}} \end{bmatrix} = \begin{bmatrix} 1 \\ 0 \end{bmatrix}$$

We start with the superposition $a_0 = a_1 = \frac{1}{\sqrt{2}}$, for which a measurement would yield 0 or 1 with equal probabilities. But after the computation step that multiplies by the 2×2 matrix on the left, we have $a_0 = 1$ and $a_1 = 0$, so a measurement would definitely yield 0. The interference $\frac{1}{\sqrt{2}}\frac{1}{\sqrt{2}} - \frac{1}{\sqrt{2}}\frac{1}{\sqrt{2}} = 0$ eliminates the configuration 1 from the superposition. ♦

A poly-time quantum algorithm can factor integers (though presumably no poly-time randomized algorithm can). This will have profound implications for cryptography if practical quantum computers are ever built. Also, quantum computing can quadratically speed up evaluation of the OR function (detecting a 1 without examining each input bit separately).

BQP is the complexity class of decision problems solved by poly-time quantum algorithms. We have BPP $\subseteq$ BQP since we can simulate coin tosses by measuring qubits in the superposition $\frac{1}{\sqrt{2}}0 + \frac{1}{\sqrt{2}}1$. It's known that BQP $\subseteq$ PP, and it's conjectured that NP $\not\subseteq$ BQP (quantum computing isn't especially helpful for solving NP-complete problems). It's known that QIP = PSPACE (the quantum analogue of IP = PSPACE), so quantum interactive proofs are no more powerful than classical ones. Generally, any model with deterministic and randomized variants also has a quantum variant. For example, there's considerable research on quantum query complexity and quantum communication complexity.

Complexity Beyond Computer Science

Many processes in the natural and social sciences are like computations because they effect "global" transformations by sequences of "local" operations. This occurs in quantum physics, statistical physics, molecular biology, evolutionary biology, economics, and sociology, for example. The computational "lens" on the sciences has spawned mutually beneficial collaborations with all these disciplines. Computational complexity theory is an important tool for understanding how the world works.

Notes

Here are texts and surveys on fine-grained complexity [564, 91], parameterized complexity [164], proof complexity [53, 475, 139, 400, 418, 320], expander graphs and their applications [250], harmonic analysis of boolean functions and its applications [402], program size complexity [335], complexity of counting [165], arithmetic complexity [99, 491], property testing [198, 65], and quantum computing [391, 310, 298, 367].

The notion of program size complexity is attributed to Solomonoff [500], Kolmogorov [317], and Chaitin [110].

For a simple proof of the #P-completeness of counting satisfying assignments of a monotone 2-CNF, see [554]. The #P-completeness of counting perfect matchings in a bipartite graph, and of related problems, are due to [532, 533]. The fully poly-time randomized approximation scheme for counting perfect matchings in a bipartite graph is due to [272]. The theorem that PH reduces to #P is known as "Toda's theorem" [520].

The theorem that strong lower bounds for arithmetic circuits would follow from strong lower bounds for depth-4 arithmetic circuits is due to [11].

The poly-time quantum algorithm for factoring integers is due to [489]. The quadratic quantum speedup for evaluating the OR function is due to [224]. $\mathsf{BQP} \subseteq \mathsf{PP}$ is due to [6]. $\mathsf{QIP} = \mathsf{PSPACE}$ is due to [271].

Appendix

Discrete Math Background

We assume the reader is familiar with basic discrete math notation, terminology, and proof techniques. This appendix briefly reviews essential definitions and proofs of useful lemmas.

A.1 Combinatorics

A.1.1 Discrete Structures

A *set* is an unordered collection of distinct *elements*, written between braces. The *size* (number of elements) of a set S is denoted $|S|$. The *empty set* is denoted $\emptyset$. The set $\{1, 2, 3, \ldots, n\}$ is denoted $[n]$. The set of positive integers is $\mathbb{N}_+$. The set of nonnegative integers is $\mathbb{N}$. The set of integers is $\mathbb{Z}$. The set of real numbers is $\mathbb{R}$. The notation $x \in S$ means x is an element of the set S. The notation $S \subseteq T$ means S is a *subset* of T. These operations produce new sets from sets S and T:

$$\begin{aligned} \textit{Union:} \quad S \cup T &= \{x : x \in S \text{ or } x \in T \text{ (or both)}\} \\ \textit{Intersection:} \quad S \cap T &= \{x : x \in S \text{ and } x \in T\} \\ \textit{Difference:} \quad S \setminus T &= \{x : x \in S \text{ and } x \notin T\} \end{aligned}$$

If some "universe" set U is understood from context, and $S \subseteq U$, then the *complement* of S is $\overline{S} = U \setminus S$. We have $\overline{S \cup T} = \overline{S} \cap \overline{T}$ and $\overline{S \cap T} = \overline{S} \cup \overline{T}$. Sets S and T are *disjoint* when $S \cap T = \emptyset$.

A *tuple* is a finite, ordered sequence of elements, written between parentheses. An n-tuple has *length* (number of components) n. An *ordered pair* is a 2-tuple. The ith component of a tuple x is denoted x_i. The *cartesian product* of sets $S_1, S_2, \ldots, S_n$ is the set of all n-tuples whose ith component comes from S_i, for each index $i \in [n]$:

$$S_1 \times S_2 \times \cdots \times S_n = \big\{(x_1, x_2, \ldots, x_n) : x_1 \in S_1 \text{ and } x_2 \in S_2 \text{ and } \cdots \text{ and } x_n \in S_n\big\}$$

S^n denotes the cartesian product of n copies of a set S. In particular, $\{0,1\}^n$ is the set of all length-n bit strings, since strings are just tuples written without parentheses or commas. Also, $\{0,1\}^+$ is the set of all nonempty bit strings. The *characteristic bit string* of a set $S \subseteq [n]$ is $x \in \{0,1\}^n$ such that $x_i = 1$ if $i \in S$, and $x_i = 0$ if $i \notin S$. The *lexicographic order* of $\{0,1\}^n$ is the numerical order if we interpret bit strings as binary (base 2) numbers 0 through $2^n - 1$, so x is earlier than y if $x_i = 0$ and $y_i = 1$ for the first (most significant) index i such that $x_i \neq y_i$. If $x \in (\{0,1\}^m)^n$ is an n-tuple of length-m bit strings, then x_i is the ith string, and $x_{i,j}$ is its jth bit. Alternative notation: x^i is the ith string, and x^i_j is its jth bit.

For a *function* (or *mapping*) $f : S \to T$ from *domain* set $S \neq \emptyset$ to *codomain* set $T \neq \emptyset$, we can plug in any *preimage* $x \in S$ and *evaluate* f to get the *image* $f(x) \in T$. We say f *maps* x to $f(x)$. Each $x \in S$ has exactly one image, but each $y \in T$ can have any number (zero or more) of preimages. The set of all preimages of y is $f^{-1}(y) = \big\{x \in S : f(x) = y\big\}$. An *injection* is a function where each codomain element has at most one preimage. A *surjection* is a function where each codomain element has at least one preimage. A *bijection* is a function where each codomain

P	not / negation $\neg P$
1	0
0	1

P	Q	and / conjunction $P \wedge Q$	or / disjunction $P \vee Q$	xor / exclusive or $P \oplus Q$	if then / implication $P \Rightarrow Q$	iff / if and only if $P \Leftrightarrow Q$
1	1	1	1	0	1	1
1	0	0	1	1	0	0
0	1	0	1	1	1	0
0	0	0	0	0	1	1

Figure A.1: Truth tables for logical connectives

element has exactly one preimage. For any $f: S \to T$ and $g: R \to S$, define the *composed* function $f \circ g: R \to T$ by $(f \circ g)(x) = f(g(x))$. For a *partial function*, $f(x)$ may be undefined for some values of x. When we evaluate a partial function f, there's an implicit *promise* that x is such that $f(x)$ is defined. A *total function* is an ordinary function, which is defined on all x in the domain.

Figure A.1 shows the *truth tables* for standard *logical connectives* that operate on boolean variables P and Q (representing propositions) that take values 1 (true) or 0 (false). Negation has higher precedence than binary connectives, so for example, $\neg P \vee Q$ means $(\neg P) \vee Q$. Also, $\overline{P}$ means $\neg P$. Two logic formulas are *equivalent* (denoted with $\equiv$, which is not a logical connective) when they have the same truth table. Here are some commonly used equivalences:

$$\begin{array}{lll} \overline{P \vee Q} \equiv \overline{P} \wedge \overline{Q} & P \Rightarrow Q \equiv \overline{P} \vee Q & P \Leftrightarrow Q \equiv \overline{P \oplus Q} \\ \overline{P \wedge Q} \equiv \overline{P} \vee \overline{Q} & P \Rightarrow Q \equiv \overline{Q} \Rightarrow \overline{P} & P \Leftrightarrow Q \equiv (P \Rightarrow Q) \wedge (Q \Rightarrow P) \end{array}$$

We extend the logical connectives to *bitwise operators* on bit strings (rather than individual bits) by operating on each coordinate separately. For instance, $\wedge: \{0,1\}^n \times \{0,1\}^n \to \{0,1\}^n$ is bitwise "and".

$\forall$ and $\exists$ are the *universal* and *existential* quantifiers: If $P(x)$ is a *predicate* whose truth value depends on the variable x, then "$\forall x: P(x)$" means "for all x in the domain, $P(x)$ holds," and "$\exists x: P(x)$" means "there exists an x in the domain such that $P(x)$ holds."

Here's a reminder about big-O and friends, for functions on nonnegative integers:

- $f = O(g)$ means $(\exists c > 0)\ (\exists n_0 \in \mathbb{N})\ (\forall n \geq n_0)\ (f(n) \leq c \cdot g(n))$.
- $f = o(g)$ means $(\forall c > 0)\ (\exists n_0 \in \mathbb{N})\ (\forall n \geq n_0)\ (f(n) \leq c \cdot g(n))$.
- $f = \Omega(g)$ means $g = O(f)$.
- $f = \omega(g)$ means $g = o(f)$.
- $f = \Theta(g)$ means $f = O(g)$ and $g = O(f)$ both hold.

A.1.2 Counting

Addition principle: If $S_1, \ldots, S_n$ partition S, then $|S| = \sum_{i=1}^{n} |S_i|$.
Subtraction principle: If $S \subseteq T$ then $|S| = |T| - |T \setminus S|$.
Multiplication principle: If $S = S_1 \times \cdots \times S_n$ then $|S| = \prod_{i=1}^{n} |S_i|$.
Division principle: If $S_1, \ldots, S_n$ partition S and have the same size s, then $n = |S|/s$.

Lemma A.1. $2^0 + 2^1 + 2^2 + \cdots + 2^{n-2} + 2^{n-1} = 2^n - 1$.

Proof. We can evaluate this geometric sum with the "telescoping" trick:

$$2^0 + \cdots + 2^{n-1} = (2-1)(2^0 + \cdots + 2^{n-1}) = (2^1 + \cdots + 2^n) - (2^0 + \cdots + 2^{n-1}) = 2^n - 2^0 = 2^n - 1$$

A more enlightening approach shows that both sides count the same thing in different ways: Let S be the set of all length-n bit strings besides the all-0 string. Then $|S| = 2^n - 1$ since $|\{0,1\}^n| = 2^n$ by the multiplication principle. Partition S according to the first 1's index: $S = S_1 \cup \cdots \cup S_n$ where $S_k = \{x \in \{0,1\}^n : x_1 \cdots x_{k-1} x_k = 0 \cdots 01\}$. Then $|S_k| = |\{0,1\}^{n-k}| = 2^{n-k}$. By the addition principle, $|S| = |S_1| + \cdots + |S_n| = 2^{n-1} + \cdots + 2^0$. ■

A *permutation* is an ordering of $[n]$ (or another size-n set), in other words, an n-tuple where each element of $[n]$ appears exactly once. There are $n! = n \cdot (n-1) \cdot (n-2) \cdots 3 \cdot 2 \cdot 1$ permutations because there are n options for the first component, and then $n-1$ options for the second component (namely, any element of $[n]$ except the one used for the first component), then $n-2$ options for the third component, and so on. This is a more general form of the multiplication principle: The set of all permutations of $[n]$ is not a cartesian product since the options for each component depend on the other components.

A *combination* is a size-k subset of $[n]$ (or another size-n set). There are $\binom{n}{k} = \frac{n!}{k!(n-k)!}$ combinations: If we wanted to count *ordered* size-k subsets (k-tuples of distinct elements) of $[n]$, there would be n options for the first component, then $n-1$ options for the second, and so on, then $n-(k-1)$ options for the kth component, for a total of $n \cdot (n-1) \cdots (n-k+1) = n!/(n-k)!$ such tuples. Partitioning the set of all such tuples so each part contains all $k!$ different orderings of some size-k subset, the division principle says the number of parts—and hence the number of size-k subsets—is $\frac{n!}{k!(n-k)!}$. As corner cases, $\binom{n}{0} = \binom{n}{n} = 1$ since $0! = 1$.

A bit string's *weight* is its number of 1s. There are $\binom{n}{k}$ length-n weight-k bit strings. Partitioning $\{0,1\}^n$ by weight, the addition principle says $2^n = \sum_{k=0}^{n} \binom{n}{k}$. Another way to see this is by plugging $x = 1$ and $y = 1$ into the *binomial formula* $(x+y)^n = \sum_{k=0}^{n} \binom{n}{k} x^k y^{n-k}$, which holds since to completely expand $(x+y)^n$ into a sum of 2^n many terms, we obtain each term by selecting x or y from each of the n factors, and there are $\binom{n}{k}$ ways to choose a term with k factors of x and $n-k$ factors of y. Due to its role in the binomial formula, $\binom{n}{k}$ is called a *binomial coefficient*.

The *pigeonhole principle* says if more than n pigeons fly into n holes, then some hole gets more than one pigeon (since there aren't enough holes to go around). Some variants are: If fewer than n pigeons fly into n holes, then some hole is pigeonless. If exactly n pigeons fly into n holes and every hole gets at most one pigeon, then every hole gets exactly one pigeon. If exactly n pigeons fly into n holes and every hole gets at least one pigeon, then every hole gets exactly one pigeon. We summarize all the variants abstractly using a function f where pigeon x flies into hole $f(x)$:

Fact A.2 (Pigeonhole principle). *For every function $f : S \to T$ where S and T are finite:*

- *If $|S| > |T|$ then f is not an injection.*
- *If $|S| < |T|$ then f is not a surjection.*
- *If $|S| = |T|$ and f is an injection, then f is a bijection.*
- *If $|S| = |T|$ and f is a surjection, then f is a bijection.*

The *distance* $\text{dist}(x,y)$ between $x \in \{0,1\}^n$ and $y \in \{0,1\}^n$ is the number of indices i for which $x_i \neq y_i$. The distance $\text{dist}(S)$ of $S \subseteq \{0,1\}^n$ is the minimum of $\text{dist}(x,y)$ over all distinct $x, y \in S$. (If $|S| \leq 1$, then $\text{dist}(S) = \infty$.)

Theorem A.3. *There exists $S \subseteq \{0,1\}^n$ with $|S| \geq k$ and $\text{dist}(S) > 1$ iff $k \leq 2^{n-1}$.*

Proof. $\Rightarrow$: We prove the contrapositive: For any $S \subseteq \{0,1\}^n$ with $|S| > 2^{n-1}$, we show $\text{dist}(S) = 1$. Define $f : S \to \{0,1\}^{n-1}$ by $f(x) = x_1 \cdots x_{n-1}$. Since $|S| > |\{0,1\}^{n-1}|$, the pigeonhole principle says f is not an injection: There exist distinct $x, y \in S$ with $f(x) = f(y)$. Since $x_1 \cdots x_{n-1} = y_1 \cdots y_{n-1}$, we have $x_n \neq y_n$ and $\text{dist}(S) \leq \text{dist}(x,y) = 1$.

$\Leftarrow$: Let $S \subseteq \{0,1\}^n$ be all even-weight strings. We have $|S| = 2^{n-1}$ because for each of the 2^{n-1} strings $x_1 \cdots x_{n-1}$, there's exactly one bit x_n such that $\text{weight}(x_1 \cdots x_n)$ is even. To show $\text{dist}(S) > 1$, we argue that $\text{dist}(x,y) > 1$ for any distinct strings $x, y \in S$. Going from one even-weight string to another requires flipping multiple bits, because flipping only one bit would make the weight go up or down by 1 and therefore become odd. ■

In § 16.4.3 we prove that for every $S \subseteq \{0,1\}^n$ with $|S| > 2^{n-1}$, some string in S has distance 1 from not just one other string in S, but at least $\sqrt{n}$ other strings in S. Such an improvement to Theorem A.3 was a notorious open question for decades.

A.2 Graphs

A.2.1 General Graphs

A *graph* $G = (V, E)$ consists of a finite set V of *nodes* (also known as *vertices*), which we visualize as circles, and a finite set E of *edges* connecting pairs of nodes. In an *undirected* graph, an edge is an unordered pair $\{u, v\}$ and may be traversed in either direction. In a *directed* graph, an edge is an ordered pair (u, v) and may only be traversed from u to v. Sometimes we allow *multi-edges* (multiple copies of the same edge) and/or *self-loops* (edges that go from a node to itself).

In an undirected graph, the *degree* $\deg(v)$ of a node v is the number of edges with v as an endpoint (but a self-loop contributes 2 to the degree). In a directed graph, the *indegree* $\text{indeg}(v)$ is the number of incoming edges to v, and the *outdegree* $\text{outdeg}(v)$ is the number of outgoing edges from v (so a self-loop contributes 1 to the indegree and 1 to the outdegree). A *source* node has indegree 0. A *sink* node has outdegree 0.

Lemma A.4. *For every undirected graph (with multi-edges and self-loops allowed), the sum of the degrees of all nodes is an even number.*

Proof. Consider any undirected graph $G = (V, E)$. Each non-self-loop edge contributes 1 to the degrees of two nodes, and each self-loop contributes 2 to the degree of one node, so each edge contributes 2 to $\sum_{v \in V} \deg(v)$. Thus $\sum_{v \in V} \deg(v) = 2 \cdot |E|$, which is even. ■

A *walk* in a graph goes from node to node to node (and so on) by traversing edges, and may reuse edges. A *trail* is a walk that doesn't reuse edges. A *path* is a trail that doesn't revisit nodes. A *cycle* is like a path but it returns to the starting node (and therefore need not have a distinguished starting node). Node v is *reachable* from node u when there exists a walk from u to v.

An undirected graph is *connected* when every two nodes are reachable from each other. A directed graph is *strongly connected* when every two nodes are reachable from each other. A disconnected undirected graph is partitioned into multiple *connected components*.

The next lemma demonstrates the "proof by algorithm" technique: To prove that something exists, we can exhibit an algorithm that finds it. Proving that an iterative algorithm is correct typically involves identifying an *invariant*, which is a property that holds at the boundaries between iterations of the loop. A correctness proof shows:

- The invariant holds before the first iteration.
- The invariant is *maintained*: If it holds before an iteration, then it holds after the iteration.
- The loop is guaranteed to terminate.
- If the invariant holds when the loop terminates, then the output is correct.

Since the invariant holds before the first iteration, it also holds after the first iteration, which implies it also holds after the second iteration, and so on. (This proof strategy is *induction*.) Since the invariant holds when the loop terminates, the algorithm outputs what we want.

Lemma A.5. *For every graph and nodes u and v, if there exists a walk from u to v then there exists a path from u to v.*

We prove this for directed graphs, but the same argument works for undirected graphs. Multi-edges and self-loops are allowed but aren't pertinent.

Proof. Consider any directed graph.

Algorithm to turn a walk into a path	(A.1)

let P be a walk $(u \to \cdots \to v)$
while the nodes on P are not all distinct:
    find a repeated node w on $P = (u \to \cdots \to w \underbrace{\to \cdots \to w}_{S} \to \cdots \to v)$
    remove the segment S, so P becomes $(u \to \cdots \to w \to \cdots \to v)$
output P

This algorithm maintains the invariant that P is a walk from u to v. The invariant holds before the first iteration, so it holds after every iteration. The loop terminates because P's length (number of edges) decreases in every iteration (since S contains at least one edge, and no edges are ever added to P) but can't go below 0. When the loop terminates, P is a walk from u to v (by the invariant) and has no repeated nodes (by the loop's termination condition), so P is a path from u to v. ■

A.2.2 Trees

A connected undirected graph with no cycles is a *tree*.

Theorem A.6. *For every connected undirected graph (with multi-edges allowed but self-loops not allowed), the following are equivalent:*

(i) For every two nodes u and v, there is only one path between u and v.
(ii) For every edge e, deleting e would disconnect the graph.
(iii) The graph is a tree.

Proof. Consider any connected undirected graph.

(i) ⇒ (ii): We prove the contrapositive. Suppose deleting some edge $e = \{u, v\}$ (with $u \neq v$ since e is not a self-loop) would not disconnect the graph. This means there exists a walk—and hence a path by Lemma A.5—between u and v that doesn't use e. Also, e itself is a path between u and v. Thus there is more than one path between u and v.

(ii) ⇒ (iii): We prove the contrapositive. Suppose the graph has a cycle. Since there are no self-loops, the cycle has length at least 2. We claim that deleting an edge e on the cycle would

not disconnect the graph. For any two nodes u and v (not necessarily e's endpoints), we show that there exists a walk between u and v that doesn't use e. Since the original graph is connected, there exists a path P between u and v by Lemma A.5. If P doesn't use e then we're done, so assume P uses e. To get from u to v without using e: Follow P from u to an endpoint of e, then follow the cycle to e's other endpoint, then follow the rest of P to v. (Intuitively, we reroute P to avoid e by using the cycle as a detour.)

(iii) $\Rightarrow$ *(i)*: We prove the contrapositive. Suppose there exist two nodes u and v with at least two different paths P_1 and P_2 between them.

First, we claim that some edge is on one of these two paths but not on the other. Suppose for contradiction P_1 and P_2 use the same edges but in different orders. Following P_1 and P_2 from u to v, consider the first step where they use different edges, say P_1 uses edge $\{w, x\}$ and P_2 uses edge $\{w, y\}$. Since P_1 and P_2 use the same edges, P_1 must eventually use the edge $\{w, y\}$, contradicting the fact that P_1 is a path and therefore doesn't revisit w. This proves the claim.

Say e is an edge on P_1 but not on P_2. There is a walk between e's endpoints that doesn't use e itself: Follow P_1 from one endpoint of e to u, then P_2 from u to v, then P_1 from v to e's other endpoint. By Lemma A.5 (using the graph with e deleted), there exists a path between e's endpoints that doesn't use e. Adding e to this path creates a cycle. ∎

A *rooted tree* dangles downward from a designated *root* node. A node's *parent* is its neighbor node on the path from the root, and its *children* are its other neighbor nodes. The root has no parent. Nodes with no children are *leaves*. Non-leaf nodes are *internal* nodes. A rooted tree is *binary* when every internal node has exactly two children. A node's *ancestors* are the nodes reachable by walking toward the root, and its *descendants* are the nodes reachable by walking away from the root. The *subtree* rooted at node v consists of v's descendants (including v itself) and the edges connecting them: It's one of the two connected components formed by deleting the edge between v and its parent, assuming v is not the root.

The next lemma demonstrates the "proof by algorithm" technique with a recursive algorithm. Proving that a recursive algorithm is correct typically involves identifying an *invariant*, which is a relationship between the arguments and return value for any invocation. An invariant has the form: "For all arguments with this property, the return value has that property." A *base case* is an invocation that makes no recursive calls. A correctness proof shows:

- The invariant holds for the base cases.
- The invariant is *maintained*: If it holds for each recursive call made by an invocation, then it also holds for that invocation.
- The recursion is guaranteed to terminate.
- If the invariant holds for the original invocation, then the return value yields a correct output.

Since the invariant holds for the base cases, it also holds for the invocations that only make base case calls. Since it holds for those invocations, it also holds for any invocation in which each recursive call is one of those or a base case. And so on for all invocations. (This is a fancy version of induction.) Since the invariant holds for the original invocation, the algorithm outputs what we want.

Lemma A.7. *Every binary tree has exactly one more leaf than internal nodes.*

Proof. Consider any binary tree. For every node v, let ℓ_v and k_v be the number of leaves and number of internal nodes (respectively) in the subtree rooted at v. The following recursive subroutine maintains the invariant that for every node v in the tree, count-nodes(v) returns (ℓ_v, k_v) and that $\ell_v - k_v = 1$.

Recursive algorithm to prove that a binary tree has one more leaf than internal nodes (A.2)

```
count-nodes(v):
    if v is a leaf: return (ℓ_v, k_v) = (1,0)
    let u and w be v's children
    let (ℓ_u, k_u) = count-nodes(u)
    let (ℓ_w, k_w) = count-nodes(w)
    return (ℓ_v, k_v) = (ℓ_u + ℓ_w, k_u + k_w + 1)
```

The invariant trivially holds for the base cases (when v is a leaf). To verify that count-nodes(v) maintains the invariant, assume the invariant holds for count-nodes(u) and count-nodes(w). The leaves in v's subtree are the leaves in u's and w's subtrees, and there are $\ell_u + \ell_w = \ell_v$ such leaves. The internal nodes in v's subtree are the internal nodes in u's and w's subtrees along with v itself, and there are $k_u + k_w + 1 = k_v$ such nodes (where the $+1$ is for v). Furthermore:

$$\ell_v - k_v \;=\; (\ell_u + \ell_w) - (k_u + k_w + 1) \;=\; (\ell_u - k_u) + (\ell_w - k_w) - 1 \;=\; 1 + 1 - 1 \;=\; 1$$

So the invariant holds for count-nodes(v). The recursion terminates because count-nodes(v) is only called once for each v. The lemma is true since the invariant holds for count-nodes(root). ■

A.2.3 Directed Acyclic Graphs

A directed graph with no cycles is a *directed acyclic graph*, or *dag* for short.

Lemma A.8. *Every dag has at least one source and at least one sink.*

Proof. To prove that a dag G has a sink, we show that if G has no sink then the following algorithm finds a cycle in G and therefore G isn't a dag:

Algorithm to find a cycle in a graph with no sink (A.3)

```
let u_1 be an arbitrary node
for i = 1,2,3,...:
    pick an arbitrary outgoing edge from u_i, and let u_{i+1} be the other endpoint
    if u_{i+1} = u_j for some j ≤ i: halt and output the cycle (u_j → u_{j+1} → ··· → u_i → u_j)
```

This algorithm maintains the invariant that $u_1 \to u_2 \to \cdots \to u_i$ is a path in G, since it terminates as soon as it revisits a node. The invariant holds before the first iteration (since (u_1) is a path of length 0), so it holds after every iteration. The loop terminates since there are only finitely many nodes, so revisiting is inevitable. When the loop terminates during the last iteration, the output is a cycle since $u_j \to u_{j+1} \to \cdots \to u_i$ is a path (by the invariant) and $u_i \to u_j$ is an edge (by the termination condition).

To see that every dag G has at least one source, define the directed graph G' by reversing the direction of each edge of G. Then G' is also a dag, since reversing a cycle in G' would yield a cycle in G. We know G' has a sink, which is a source in G. ■

A *topological order* of a directed graph is a permutation $v_1, v_2, \ldots, v_n$ of the nodes (picking a node to call v_1, picking another node to call v_2, and so on) such that every edge goes from a lower-index node to a higher-index node. Formally, if (v_i, v_j) is an edge then $i < j$. Informally, we arrange the nodes in a line so all edges point to the right.

Theorem A.9. *For every directed graph G (with multi-edges and self-loops allowed), G is a dag iff G has a topological order.*

Proof. Consider any directed graph G with n nodes.

$\Leftarrow$: We prove the contrapositive. Suppose G has a cycle. To show that G has no topological order, we consider any permutation $v_1, \ldots, v_n$ and show that some edge (v_i, v_j) has $j \le i$. Let i be the largest index of any node on the cycle, and let j be the index of the next node on the cycle. Thus v_i has an edge to v_j, but $j \le i$ since v_j is on the cycle.

$\Rightarrow$: Suppose G is a dag. The following algorithm finds a topological order. Throughout the algorithm, H changes, but G always refers to the original dag.

Algorithm to find a topological order of a dag (A.4)

initialize H to be G
for $i = 1, 2, \ldots, n$:
    let v_i be a source of H
    delete v_i (and its outgoing edges) from H

The algorithm maintains the invariant that H is a dag, since deleting nodes and edges from a dag can't create a cycle. Lemma A.8 says H indeed has a source in every iteration (so the algorithm doesn't get stuck). To see that $v_1, v_2, \ldots, v_n$ is a topological order of G, consider any edge (v_i, v_j) of G. We need to show that $i < j$, so suppose for contradiction that $j \le i$. We can't have $j = i$, since a self-loop is a cycle and a dag has none of those. Thus $j < i$, which means when v_j is deleted, v_i still remains in H. Since (v_i, v_j) is an edge, v_j has indegree at least 1 and is thus not a source in H at the moment v_j is deleted, which contradicts how the algorithm works. ■

A.3 Probability

A.3.1 Probability Spaces

A *discrete probability space* consists of a finite (or in some cases, countably infinite) set S called the *sample space*, and a probability $\mathbf{Pr}[s] \ge 0$ for each *outcome* $s \in S$, such that $\sum_{s \in S} \mathbf{Pr}[s] = 1$. The *distribution* is the function $D : S \to \mathbb{R}_{\ge 0}$ where $D(s) = \mathbf{Pr}[s]$. We let $s \sim D$ denote that outcome s is *sampled* from distribution D. The *support* is the set of all outcomes having nonzero probability. In a *uniform* probability space, $\mathbf{Pr}[s] = 1/|S|$ for every $s \in S$.

An *event* $A \subseteq S$ has probability $\mathbf{Pr}[A] = \sum_{s \in A} \mathbf{Pr}[s]$. In particular, $\mathbf{Pr}[\emptyset] = 0$ and $\mathbf{Pr}[S] = 1$. For a uniform probability space, $\mathbf{Pr}[A] = |A|/|S|$ and so computing probabilities is just a matter of counting.

For any function $f : S \to T$ and distribution D over S, applying f to a sample $s \sim D$ yields a sample $f(s) \sim f(D)$ from the distribution $f(D)$ over T defined by $\mathbf{Pr}_{f(D)}[t] = \mathbf{Pr}_{s \sim D}\big[f(s) = t\big] = \sum_{s : f(s) = t} \mathbf{Pr}_D[s] = \mathbf{Pr}_D\big[f^{-1}(t)\big]$. This coalesces the event $f^{-1}(t) \subseteq S$ into an outcome $t \in T$.

A *joint* distribution is a distribution D over a cartesian product sample space $S = S_1 \times S_2$. We obtain the *marginal* distribution D_1 over S_1 by ignoring S_2: To sample $s_1 \sim D_1$, we sample $(s_1, s_2) \sim D$ and just view s_1 as the outcome, so $D_1(s_1) = \sum_{s_2 \in S_2} D(s_1, s_2)$. The marginal distribution D_2 over S_2 is analogous. This generalizes to more than two coordinates.

The probability of event B *conditioned on* (or *given*) event A is $\mathbf{Pr}[B \mid A] = \mathbf{Pr}[B \cap A]/\mathbf{Pr}[A]$, assuming $\mathbf{Pr}[A] \neq 0$. If D is the original distribution, then $(D \mid A)$ denotes the conditioned distribution, where $(D \mid A)(s)$ is $\mathbf{Pr}[s]/\mathbf{Pr}[A]$ if $s \in A$, and 0 if $s \notin A$. With a uniform probability space, $\mathbf{Pr}[B \mid A] = |B \cap A|/|A|$.

Events A and B are *independent* when $\mathbf{Pr}[A \cap B] = \mathbf{Pr}[A] \cdot \mathbf{Pr}[B]$, which is equivalent to $\mathbf{Pr}[B \mid A] = \mathbf{Pr}[B]$ if $\mathbf{Pr}[A] \neq 0$. Functions $f_1 : S \to T_1$ and $f_2 : S \to T_2$ are independent when for all $(t_1, t_2) \in T_1 \times T_2$, the events $f_1^{-1}(t_1)$ and $f_2^{-1}(t_2)$ are independent. Events A and B are *conditionally independent* given event C when $\mathbf{Pr}[A \cap B \mid C] = \mathbf{Pr}[A \mid C] \cdot \mathbf{Pr}[B \mid C]$, in other words, A and B are independent under the distribution $(D \mid C)$.

More than two events $A_1, \ldots, A_n$ are *fully* independent when not only $\mathbf{Pr}[A_1 \cap A_2 \cap \cdots \cap A_n] = \mathbf{Pr}[A_1] \cdot \mathbf{Pr}[A_2] \cdots \mathbf{Pr}[A_n]$ holds, but a similar equation holds for every sub-collection of the n events:

$$\text{for every nonempty } I \subseteq [n]\text{:}\;\; \mathbf{Pr}\left[\textstyle\bigcap_{i \in I} A_i\right] = \textstyle\prod_{i \in I} \mathbf{Pr}[A_i]$$

Functions $f_1 : S \to T_1, \ldots, f_n : S \to T_n$ are fully independent when for all $(t_1, \ldots, t_n) \in T_1 \times \cdots \times T_n$, the events $f_1^{-1}(t_1), \ldots, f_n^{-1}(t_n)$ are fully independent.

For any two distributions D_1 over S_1 and D_2 over S_2, the joint distribution D over $S_1 \times S_2$ defined by $D(s_1, s_2) = D_1(s_1) \cdot D_2(s_2)$ has D_1 and D_2 as its marginals. We describe D as "sample $s_1 \sim D_1$ and $s_2 \sim D_2$ independently," because any event or function depending only on s_1 is independent of any event or function depending only on s_2. This generalizes to more than two coordinates.

If events $A_1, \ldots, A_n$ partition S, then $(B \cap A_1), \ldots, (B \cap A_n)$ partition B, so $\mathbf{Pr}[B] = \sum_{i=1}^{n} \mathbf{Pr}[B \cap A_i]$. Using $\mathbf{Pr}[B \cap A_i] = \mathbf{Pr}[A_i] \cdot \mathbf{Pr}[B \mid A_i]$, the *law of total probability* is:

$$\mathbf{Pr}[B] \;=\; \textstyle\sum_{i=1}^{n} \mathbf{Pr}[A_i] \cdot \mathbf{Pr}[B \mid A_i]$$

(If $\mathbf{Pr}[A_i] = 0$, the ith term would be omitted.) For partitions with two parts, the law is $\mathbf{Pr}[B] = \mathbf{Pr}[A] \cdot \mathbf{Pr}[B \mid A] + \mathbf{Pr}[\overline{A}] \cdot \mathbf{Pr}[B \mid \overline{A}]$ where $\overline{A} = S \setminus A$ is the *complement* event.

For arbitrary events $A_1, \ldots, A_n$ (not partitioning S, and not fully independent), the *chain rule* is:

$$\mathbf{Pr}[A_1 \cap \cdots \cap A_n] \;=\; \mathbf{Pr}[A_1] \cdot \mathbf{Pr}[A_2 \mid A_1] \cdot \mathbf{Pr}[A_3 \mid A_1 \cap A_2] \cdots \mathbf{Pr}[A_n \mid A_1 \cap \cdots \cap A_{n-1}]$$

On the right side, the ith factor's numerator cancels out the $(i+1)$st factor's denominator.

A.3.2 Random Variables

For any discrete probability space with sample space S and distribution D, a *random variable* is a function $X : S \to \mathbb{R}$, which assigns a number to each outcome. Applying X to a sample $s \sim D$ yields a sample $X(s) \sim X(D)$ from the distribution $X(D)$ over numbers. A random variable's *expectation* is

$$\mathbf{E}[X] \;=\; \textstyle\sum_s \mathbf{Pr}[s] \cdot X(s) \;=\; \textstyle\sum_x \mathbf{Pr}[X = x] \cdot x$$

where "$X = x$" is the event $X^{-1}(x)$. The *indicator* random variable of an event A is defined by $X(s) = 1$ if $s \in A$, and $X(s) = 0$ if $s \notin A$. An indicator's expectation is the event's probability: $\mathbf{E}[X] = \mathbf{Pr}[A] \cdot 1 + \mathbf{Pr}[\overline{A}] \cdot 0 = \mathbf{Pr}[A]$.

For any random variable X and constant $c \in \mathbb{R}$, define the random variable cX by $(cX)(s) = c \cdot X(s)$. For any *joint* random variables $X_1, \ldots, X_n$ (on the same probability space), define the random variable $X_1 + \cdots + X_n$ by $(X_1 + \cdots + X_n)(s) = X_1(s) + \cdots + X_n(s)$. The distributive property implies *linearity of expectation*, which is surprisingly useful:

$$\mathbf{E}[cX] = c\,\mathbf{E}[X] \qquad \text{and} \qquad \mathbf{E}[X_1 + \cdots + X_n] = \mathbf{E}[X_1] + \cdots + \mathbf{E}[X_n]$$

We can combine these into a single, general form:

$$\mathbf{E}[c_1X_1 + \cdots + c_nX_n] = c_1\,\mathbf{E}[X_1] + \cdots + c_n\,\mathbf{E}[X_n]$$

The *binomial random variable* with parameters n and p is the number of heads in n tosses of a coin with heads probability p: $S = \{\mathrm{H}, \mathrm{T}\}^n$ and if s has k heads, then $D(s) = p^k(1-p)^{n-k}$ and $X(s) = k$. For $k \in \{0, 1, \ldots, n\}$, we have $\mathbf{Pr}[X = k] = \binom{n}{k}p^k(1-p)^{n-k}$ since $\binom{n}{k}$ many outcomes have k heads, and they all have the same probability. The probabilities indeed sum to 1 by the binomial formula:

$$\textstyle\sum_{k=0}^{n} \mathbf{Pr}[X = k] = \sum_{k=0}^{n} \binom{n}{k}p^k(1-p)^{n-k} = (p + (1-p))^n = 1^n = 1$$

It's tricky to evaluate $\mathbf{E}[X] = \sum_{k=0}^{n} \mathbf{Pr}[X = k] \cdot k$ directly, but it's simpler when we exploit linearity:

Lemma A.10. *If X is the binomial random variable with parameters n and p, then $\mathbf{E}[X] = np$.*

Proof. For $i \in [n]$, let X_i be the indicator random variable for the event that the ith toss is heads, and note that $\mathbf{E}[X_i] = \mathbf{Pr}_{s\sim D}[s_i = \mathrm{H}] = p$. We have $X = X_1 + \cdots + X_n$ since the sum has a 1 for each H in s. By linearity of expectation, $\mathbf{E}[X] = \mathbf{E}[X_1] + \cdots + \mathbf{E}[X_n] = p + \cdots + p = np$. ■

For any random variable X and event A with nonzero probability, the *conditional expectation* $\mathbf{E}[X \mid A]$ is X's expectation under the conditioned distribution $(D \mid A)$:

$$\mathbf{E}[X \mid A] = \textstyle\sum_s \mathbf{Pr}[s \mid A] \cdot X(s) = \sum_x \mathbf{Pr}[X = x \mid A] \cdot x$$

The *law of total expectation* says if events $A_1, \ldots, A_n$ partition S, then:

$$\mathbf{E}[X] = \textstyle\sum_{i=1}^{n} \mathbf{Pr}[A_i] \cdot \mathbf{E}[X \mid A_i]$$

(If $\mathbf{Pr}[A_i] = 0$, the ith term would be omitted.) For partitions with two parts, the law is $\mathbf{E}[X] = \mathbf{Pr}[A] \cdot \mathbf{E}[X \mid A] + \mathbf{Pr}[\overline{A}] \cdot \mathbf{E}[X \mid \overline{A}]$.

The *geometric random variable* with parameter $p > 0$ is the number of tosses of a coin with heads probability p until getting a heads: $S = \{\mathrm{H}, \mathrm{TH}, \mathrm{TTH}, \ldots\}$ and if s has $k-1$ tails and one heads, then $D(s) = (1-p)^{k-1}p$ and $X(s) = k$. (We ignore the outcome with infinitely many tails because it has probability $(1-p)^\infty = 0$ since $p > 0$.) The probabilities indeed sum to 1 by a geometric series, using $q = 1-p$:

$$\begin{aligned}\textstyle\sum_{k=1}^{\infty} \mathbf{Pr}[X = k] &= \textstyle\sum_{k=1}^{\infty}(1-p)^{k-1}p = (1-q)\sum_{k=1}^{\infty} q^{k-1} \\ &= \left(q^0 + q^1 + q^2 + \cdots\right) - \left(q^1 + q^2 + q^3 + \cdots\right) = q^0 = 1\end{aligned}$$

(If $p = 1$, then $0^0 = 1$.) It's tricky to evaluate $\mathbf{E}[X] = \sum_{k=1}^{\infty} \mathbf{Pr}[X = k] \cdot k$ directly, but it's simpler when we exploit the law of total expectation:

Lemma A.11. *If X is the geometric random variable with parameter $p > 0$, then $\mathbf{E}[X] = 1/p$.*

Proof. Partition the sample space into the event $A = \{H\}$ that the first toss is already heads, and the event $\overline{A}$ that more than one toss occurs. We have $\mathbf{E}[X \mid A] = X(H) = 1$. If the first toss is tails, then the number of additional tosses to get a heads is distributed exactly as in the unconditioned probability space: $\mathbf{E}[X \mid \overline{A}] = 1 + \mathbf{E}[X]$. By the law of total expectation:

$$\mathbf{E}[X] = \mathbf{Pr}[A] \cdot \mathbf{E}[X \mid A] + \mathbf{Pr}[\overline{A}] \cdot \mathbf{E}[X \mid \overline{A}] = p \cdot 1 + (1-p) \cdot (1 + \mathbf{E}[X]) = 1 + (1-p) \cdot \mathbf{E}[X]$$

Rearranging yields $\mathbf{E}[X] = 1/p$. ∎

Joint random variables $X_1, \ldots, X_n$ are fully independent when for every tuple of numbers $(x_1, \ldots, x_n)$, the events "$X_1 = x_1$", ..., "$X_n = x_n$" are fully independent. For any joint random variables $X_1, \ldots, X_n$, define the random variable $X_1 \cdots X_n$ by $(X_1 \cdots X_n)(s) = X_1(s) \cdots X_n(s)$.

Lemma A.12. $\mathbf{E}[X_1 \cdots X_n] = \mathbf{E}[X_1] \cdots \mathbf{E}[X_n]$ *if* $X_1, \ldots, X_n$ *are fully independent joint random variables.*

Proof. Using full independence of the events "$X_1 = x_1$", ..., "$X_n = x_n$":

$$\begin{aligned} \mathbf{E}\left[\textstyle\prod_{i=1}^{n} X_i\right] &= \textstyle\sum_{x_1,\ldots,x_n} \mathbf{Pr}\left[X_1 = x_1 \text{ and } \cdots \text{ and } X_n = x_n\right] \cdot \prod_{i=1}^{n} x_i \\ &= \textstyle\sum_{x_1,\ldots,x_n} \prod_{i=1}^{n} \mathbf{Pr}[X_i = x_i] \cdot x_i \\ &= \textstyle\prod_{i=1}^{n} \sum_{x_i} \mathbf{Pr}[X_i = x_i] \cdot x_i \\ &= \textstyle\prod_{i=1}^{n} \mathbf{E}[X_i] \end{aligned}$$

∎

Lemma A.13. *The probability of getting an odd number of heads in n tosses of a coin with heads probability p is* $\frac{1}{2} - \frac{1}{2}(1-2p)^n$.

Proof. If we multiply together some factors of -1, then each factor makes the result flip between 1 and -1, so the result is -1 if there are an odd number of factors, and is 1 otherwise. Defining $X_i(s) = -1$ if $s_i = H$, and $X_i(s) = 1$ if $s_i = T$, we have $(X_1 \cdots X_n)(s) = -1$ if s has an odd number of heads, and $(X_1 \cdots X_n)(s) = 1$ if s has an even number of heads. We have $\mathbf{E}[X_i] = p \cdot (-1) + (1-p) \cdot 1 = 1 - 2p$. Letting A be the event of getting an odd number of heads, $\mathbf{E}[X_1 \cdots X_n] = \mathbf{Pr}[A] \cdot (-1) + (1 - \mathbf{Pr}[A]) \cdot 1 = 1 - 2\mathbf{Pr}[A]$. Since $X_1, \ldots, X_n$ are fully independent, $1 - 2\mathbf{Pr}[A] = \mathbf{E}[X_1 \cdots X_n] = \mathbf{E}[X_1] \cdots \mathbf{E}[X_n] = (1-2p)^n$. Thus $\mathbf{Pr}[A] = \frac{1}{2} - \frac{1}{2}(1-2p)^n$. ∎

A.3.3 The Probabilistic Method

To use the *probabilistic method* to prove that an object with a certain property exists, we show that an object sampled randomly from some distribution has the property with positive probability. This is *nonconstructive* because it doesn't explicitly describe any particular object with the property.

One version of the probabilistic method uses the *union bound*: For any events $A_1, \ldots, A_n$, we have $\mathbf{Pr}[A_1 \cup \cdots \cup A_n] \leq \mathbf{Pr}[A_1] + \cdots + \mathbf{Pr}[A_n]$. If the latter is < 1 then the former is < 1, so some outcome is in none of the events. The next theorem demonstrates this technique.

An $n \times n$ *binary matrix* M is a square 2-dimensional array of 0s and 1s with rows indexed by $[n]$ and columns indexed by $[n]$. For nonempty sets $I \subseteq [n]$ and $J \subseteq [n]$, let $M_{I,J}$ denote the *submatrix* consisting of entries with row indices in I and column indices in J. A submatrix is *monochromatic* when either every entry is 0 or every entry is 1. Thinking of 0 as "white" and 1 as "black," monochromatic means the whole submatrix is a single color. Logs are base 2 by default.

Theorem A.14. *For every $n \geq 2$, there exists an $n \times n$ binary matrix with no monochromatic $k \times k$ submatrix where $k = \lceil 2 \log n \rceil$.*

Proof idea. Call a matrix "bad" if it has a monochromatic $k \times k$ submatrix, and "good" otherwise. We show that with positive probability (in fact, high probability), a uniformly random matrix is good. For each $k \times k$ set of positions, we show that the "bad event" that this submatrix is monochromatic has probability $< 1/$(the number of bad events). The union of all bad events therefore has probability < 1, so a random matrix is bad with probability < 1. Hence a good matrix exists. ■

Proof. Pick a uniformly random $n \times n$ binary matrix M. For each $I \subseteq [n]$ and $J \subseteq [n]$ with $|I| = |J| = k$, let $A_{I,J}$ be the event that $M_{I,J}$ is monochromatic. $\mathbf{Pr}[A_{I,J}] = 2 \cdot 2^{-k^2} = 2^{-k^2+1}$ because we can partition $A_{I,J}$ into two events corresponding to $M_{I,J}$ being only 0s or only 1s, and both of these events have probability $(1/2)^{k^2}$ (since the k^2 many bits of $M_{I,J}$ are independent, and each has probability 1/2 of being the target bit). There are $\binom{n}{k}$ possibilities for I and $\binom{n}{k}$ possibilities for J, so there are $\binom{n}{k}^2$ many $A_{I,J}$ events. By a union bound:

$$\mathbf{Pr}\left[\bigcup_{I,J} A_{I,J}\right] \leq \sum_{I,J} \mathbf{Pr}[A_{I,J}] = \binom{n}{k}^2 \cdot 2^{-k^2+1}$$

We show that the latter bound is < 1, which implies that some outcome M is in none of the $A_{I,J}$ events and hence has no monochromatic $k \times k$ submatrix. To do this, we show that an even bigger (but tidier) bound is < 1. Let's work with $\binom{n}{k} = \frac{n \cdot (n-1) \cdots (n-k+1)}{k \cdot (k-1) \cdots 1}$ first. This increases if we increase the numerator and decrease the denominator. We increase the numerator to n^k by changing each factor to n. We decrease the denominator to 2 by changing the k factor to 2 (using $k \geq 2$ since $n \geq 2$) and all other factors to 1. In summary, $\binom{n}{k} \leq n^k/2$. Since $k \geq 2 \log n$, we have $n \leq 2^{k/2}$. Combining these bounds, $\binom{n}{k} \leq n^k/2 \leq (2^{k/2})^k/2 = 2^{k^2/2-1}$. Putting everything together:

$$\mathbf{Pr}\left[\bigcup_{I,J} A_{I,J}\right] \leq \binom{n}{k}^2 \cdot 2^{-k^2+1} \leq 2^{k^2-2} \cdot 2^{-k^2+1} = 2^{k^2-k^2-1} = 1/2 < 1$$ ■

This proof shows that not only some, but most $n \times n$ binary matrices have no monochromatic $k \times k$ submatrix. Despite their abundance, such matrices are quite difficult to find! The probabilistic proof doesn't describe any particular such matrix. Nobody knows how to explicitly construct such a matrix (for arbitrary n). After herculean effort, researchers have found explicit constructions achieving $k = \log^{O(1)} n$. Achieving $k = o(\log n)$ is impossible.

Another version of the probabilistic method uses expectation. It's intuitive that the average of some numbers can't be greater than all those numbers. The following lemma is more general.

Lemma A.15. *For every random variable X on a discrete probability space, there exists an outcome s such that $X(s) \geq \mathbf{E}[X]$ and $\mathbf{Pr}[s] > 0$. Symmetrically, there also exists an outcome s such that $X(s) \leq \mathbf{E}[X]$ and $\mathbf{Pr}[s] > 0$.*

Proof. Suppose for contradiction that $X(s) < \mathbf{E}[X]$ for every outcome s with $\mathbf{Pr}[s] > 0$. Thus, $\mathbf{Pr}[s] \cdot X(s) < \mathbf{Pr}[s] \cdot \mathbf{E}[X]$ for every s with $\mathbf{Pr}[s] > 0$ (since for all real numbers $a > 0$ and $b < c$, we have $ab < ac$). Outcomes s with $\mathbf{Pr}[s] = 0$ contribute $\mathbf{Pr}[s] \cdot X(s) = 0$ to the expectation, so we can sum over s with $\mathbf{Pr}[s] > 0$:

$$\mathbf{E}[X] = \sum_s \mathbf{Pr}[s] \cdot X(s) < \sum_s \mathbf{Pr}[s] \cdot \mathbf{E}[X] = \mathbf{E}[X] \cdot \sum_s \mathbf{Pr}[s] = \mathbf{E}[X] \cdot 1$$

This gives the contradiction $\mathbf{E}[X] < \mathbf{E}[X]$. ■

This provides a technique to prove that an outcome with a certain property exists: Design a random variable X such that "$X(s) \geq \mathbf{E}[X]$" implies s has the property.

A.4 Algebra

A.4.1 Fields

A *field* is a set of numbers that contains two special numbers 0 and 1 and is equipped with four arithmetic operators $+, -, \cdot, /$ (with division by 0 disallowed) obeying these familiar *axioms* for all numbers a, b, c (not necessarily distinct):

$$\begin{aligned}
\textit{Commutative:}\quad & a+b=b+a \text{ and } a\cdot b=b\cdot a\\
\textit{Associative:}\quad & a+(b+c)=(a+b)+c \text{ and } a\cdot(b\cdot c)=(a\cdot b)\cdot c\\
\textit{Distributive:}\quad & a\cdot(b+c)=(a\cdot b)+(a\cdot c)\\
\textit{Identity:}\quad & a+0=a \text{ and } a\cdot 1=a\\
\textit{Additive inverse:}\quad & a-a=0 \text{ and } b-a=b+(0-a)\\
\textit{Multiplicative inverse:}\quad & a/a=1 \text{ and } b/a=b\cdot(1/a) \text{ assuming } a\neq 0
\end{aligned}$$

Other familiar arithmetic properties follow from these axioms.

The notations $-a$ and a^{-1} are shorthands for the numbers $0-a$ and $1/a$. The inverse axioms imply that the $-$ and $/$ operators are redundant: Subtracting a means adding $-a$, and dividing by a means multiplying by a^{-1}.

The set of real numbers $\mathbb{R}$ is a field. The set of integers $\mathbb{Z}$ isn't a field, because b/a isn't always an integer. For computer science applications, *finite fields* are helpful. Defining these involves modular arithmetic.

If $m > 1$ and a are integers, then "dividing a by m" decomposes $a = q\cdot m + r$ with *quotient* $q \in \mathbb{Z}$ and *remainder* $r \in \mathbb{Z}_m = \{0, 1, 2, \ldots, m-1\}$. The remainder is denoted "a mod m". A standard fact is that for addition, subtraction, and multiplication "mod m", all integers with the same remainder are equivalent to each other, so we might as well use the remainder itself:

$$\begin{aligned}
(a+b) \bmod m &= \big((a \bmod m)+(b \bmod m)\big) \bmod m\\
(a-b) \bmod m &= \big((a \bmod m)-(b \bmod m)\big) \bmod m\\
(a\cdot b) \bmod m &= \big((a \bmod m)\cdot(b \bmod m)\big) \bmod m
\end{aligned}$$

Define arithmetic operators $+, -, \cdot : \mathbb{Z}_m \times \mathbb{Z}_m \to \mathbb{Z}_m$ by:

$$a+b=(a+b) \bmod m \qquad a-b=(a-b) \bmod m \qquad a\cdot b=(a\cdot b) \bmod m$$

On the left sides of these equalities, $+, -, \cdot$ are the new operators being defined, and on the right sides, $+, -, \cdot$ are the ordinary integer operators. The first five field axioms hold for these operators on $\mathbb{Z}_m$. The last axiom says to think of division by a as multiplication by the multiplicative inverse a^{-1}, which is some field element such that $a\cdot a^{-1}=1$. From this perspective, division in $\mathbb{Z}_m$ can actually make sense. Unfortunately, some nonzero elements might have no multiplicative inverse, in which case $\mathbb{Z}_m$ isn't a field. Fortunately, if $p > 1$ is a *prime* number (not divisible by any positive integer besides 1 and p itself), then $\mathbb{Z}_p$ is a field:

Theorem A.16. *For every prime p, every nonzero $a \in \mathbb{Z}_p$ has a unique "mod p" multiplicative inverse.*

We use the "proof by algorithm" technique to find a "mod p" multiplicative inverse of a, and we separately prove that a has only one such inverse. To facilitate the algorithm, we prove something more general. Two positive integers (a, b) are *coprime* (or *relatively prime*) to each other when they have no common divisor besides 1—that is, there's no integer $d > 1$ such that $a = q_1 d$ and $b = q_2 d$ for some integers q_1 and q_2. A "mod b" multiplicative inverse of a is an $x \in \mathbb{Z}_b$ such that $ax \bmod b = 1$. Since a prime p is coprime to every nonzero $a \in \mathbb{Z}_p$, Theorem A.16 is a corollary of the following:

Theorem A.17. *If $0 < a < b$ and (a, b) are coprime, then a has a unique* "mod b" *multiplicative inverse.*

Proof idea. We design a recursive subroutine to find such an inverse. Two lemmas tell us what arguments to pass to the recursive call, and what to do with the call's return value. We say a is "mod b" invertible when a has a "mod b" multiplicative inverse.

	(a, b) are coprime		a is "mod b" invertible	
Lemma A.18	$\Downarrow$		$\Uparrow$	Lemma A.19
	$(b \bmod a, a)$ are coprime	$\Rightarrow$	$(b \bmod a)$ is "mod a" invertible	
		recursion		

■

Lemma A.18. *If $1 < a < b$ and (a, b) are coprime, then $0 < (b \bmod a) < a$ and $(b \bmod a, a)$ are coprime.*

Proof of Lemma A.18. Assuming $1 < a < b$, we show that if either $(b \bmod a) = 0$ or $(b \bmod a, a)$ aren't coprime, then (a, b) aren't coprime. If $(b \bmod a) = 0$ then $a > 1$ itself is a common divisor of a and b. Now, suppose $(b \bmod a, a)$ aren't coprime, so $(b \bmod a) = q_1 d$ and $a = q_2 d$ for some integers $d > 1$ and q_1 and q_2. Since $b = q_3 a + (b \bmod a)$ for some integer q_3, we have $b = q_3 q_2 d + q_1 d = (q_3 q_2 + q_1) d$. Thus d is also a divisor of both a and b, so (a, b) aren't coprime. ■

Lemma A.19. *If $1 < a < b$ and $(b \bmod a)$ is* "mod a" *invertible, then a is* "mod b" *invertible.*

Proof of Lemma A.19. Assume $1 < a < b$ and $(b \bmod a)$ has a "mod a" multiplicative inverse s, which means $(b \bmod a)s \bmod a = 1$, in other words $(b \bmod a)s = q_1 a + 1$ for some integer q_1. Combining this with $b = q_2 a + (b \bmod a)$ for some integer q_2, we get $(b - q_2 a)s = q_1 a + 1$. Rearranging this yields $a(-q_1 - q_2 s) = (-s)b + 1$, which says $at = q_3 b + 1$ where $t = -q_1 - q_2 s$ and $q_3 = -s$. This means $at \bmod b = 1$, so a has a "mod b" multiplicative inverse $(t \bmod b)$ since $a(t \bmod b) \bmod b = at \bmod b = 1$. ■

Proof of Theorem A.17. The following recursive subroutine maintains the invariant that if $0 < a < b$ and (a, b) are coprime, then find-inverse(a, b) returns a "mod b" multiplicative inverse of a.

Algorithm to find a multiplicative inverse of an integer (A.5)

```
find-inverse(a, b):
    if a = 1: return 1
    s ← find-inverse(b mod a, a)
    return (−q1 − q2 s) mod b where:
        q1 is the integer quotient of (b mod a)s divided by a
        q2 is the integer quotient of b divided by a
```

The base cases are when $a = 1$ and the subroutine returns 1, which is correct since $(1 \cdot 1) \bmod b = 1$. To prove that find-inverse(a, b) maintains the invariant when $a > 1$, we assume the invariant holds for find-inverse$(b \bmod a, a)$ and show that it also holds for find-inverse(a, b). Suppose $1 < a < b$ and (a, b) are coprime. Then $0 < (b \bmod a) < a$ and $(b \bmod a, a)$ are coprime by Lemma A.18. Thus s is a "mod a" multiplicative inverse of $(b \bmod a)$ by the invariant. The return value $(-q_1 - q_2 s) \bmod b$ is a "mod b" multiplicative inverse of a by the proof of Lemma A.19. The recursion terminates since the first argument decreases (but stays positive) in each successive call, so it eventually reaches a base case.

Now that we know a has at least one "mod b" multiplicative inverse (since find-inverse(a, b) returns one), we show that a has only one such inverse. Assuming t and u are "mod b" multiplicative inverses of a, we show that $t = u$. Doing all calculations "mod b": We have $a(t-u) = at - au = 1 - 1 = 0$. Multiplying both sides by t, the left side becomes $t(a(t-u)) = (ta)(t-u) = 1 \cdot (t-u) = t - u$, while the right side becomes $t \cdot 0 = 0$. In summary, $(t-u) \bmod b = 0$, which implies $t = u$ since $t, u \in \mathbb{Z}_b$. ∎

A.4.2 Polynomials

A *polynomial* P over a field $\mathbb{F}$ is a sum of *monomials*, each of which is a coefficient times a variable x raised to a natural number power. Every coefficient is an element of $\mathbb{F}$, and the elements of $\mathbb{F}$ may be plugged in for x, and we evaluate P using $\mathbb{F}$'s arithmetic operators. A polynomial P over $\mathbb{F}$ expresses a function $P : \mathbb{F} \to \mathbb{F}$. We slightly abuse notation by letting P denote both the expression and the function.

If several monomials have the same power of x, we can collect them into a single monomial by summing the coefficients. A polynomial P's *degree*, denoted $\deg(P)$, is the highest power of x with a nonzero coefficient in P's *canonical form*, which we obtain by collecting terms so that all monomials have different powers of x:

$$P(x) = c_d \cdot x^d + c_{d-1} \cdot x^{d-1} + \cdots + c_2 \cdot x^2 + c_1 \cdot x + c_0$$

Here, d is the degree, $c_d \neq 0$ is the *leading coefficient*, and c_0 is the *constant term* (the coefficient of x^0, where $0^0 = 1$). A polynomial has degree 0 when its canonical form is just a nonzero constant term. The polynomial whose coefficients are all 0 is the *zero polynomial* and has degree $-\infty$. Polynomials with the same canonical form are considered identical. If $P(x) = \sum_k b_k \cdot x^k$ and $Q(x) = \sum_k c_k \cdot x^k$ are canonical-form polynomials over the same field, then:

- $P + Q$ is the polynomial $\sum_k (b_k + c_k) x^k$.
  $(P + Q)(x) = P(x) + Q(x)$ for all x, and $\deg(P + Q) \leq \max(\deg(P), \deg(Q))$.
- $P \cdot Q$ is the polynomial $\sum_k (b_k c_0 + b_{k-1} c_1 + b_{k-2} c_2 + \cdots + b_0 c_k) \cdot x^k$.
  $(P \cdot Q)(x) = P(x) \cdot Q(x)$ for all x, and $\deg(P \cdot Q) = \deg(P) + \deg(Q)$.

A *root* of a polynomial P is a field element a such that $P(a) = 0$.

Theorem A.20. *Over every field, every nonzero polynomial of degree d has at most d many roots.*

Corollary A.21. *Over every field, if P and Q are distinct polynomials of degree $\leq d$, then $P(a) = Q(a)$ holds for at most d many field elements a.*

Proof of Corollary A.21. The polynomial $P - Q$ is nonzero since $P \neq Q$, and $\deg(P - Q) \leq \max(\deg(P), \deg(Q)) \leq d$. By Theorem A.20, $P - Q$ has at most d many roots. The roots of $P - Q$ are the field elements a such that $P(a) - Q(a) = 0$, in other words, $P(a) = Q(a)$. ∎

Over the field $\mathbb{Z}_p$ (for a prime p), distinct polynomials of degree $< p$ express different functions, because $P(a) = Q(a)$ holds for at most $p-1$ of the p possible values of a, and so $P(a) \neq Q(a)$ for at least one $a \in \mathbb{Z}_p$.

To prepare for the proof of Theorem A.20, recall integer division: For all integers p and $m > 0$, there exist unique integers q (the quotient) and r (the remainder) such that $p = q \cdot m + r$ and $0 \leq r < m$. Something similar holds for polynomial division:

Lemma A.22. *Over every field, for all polynomials P and $M \neq 0$, there exist unique polynomials Q (the quotient) and R (the remainder) such that $P = Q \cdot M + R$ and* $\deg(R) < \deg(M)$.

Proof of Lemma A.22. First, we prove the existence of Q and R. The following recursive subroutine maintains the invariant that for all polynomials P and $M \neq 0$, divide(P, M) returns a pair of polynomials (Q, R) such that $P = Q \cdot M + R$ and $\deg(R) < \deg(M)$.

Algorithm for polynomial division	(A.6)

divide(P, M):
  if $\deg(P) < \deg(M)$: return $(0, P)$
  let bx^d be P's leading monomial (so $b \neq 0$ and $d = \deg(P) \geq 0$)
  let cx^e be M's leading monomial (so $c \neq 0$ and $e = \deg(M) \leq d$)
  $(Q', R) \leftarrow$ divide(P', M) where $P' = P - (b/c)x^{d-e} \cdot M$
  return (Q, R) where $Q = (b/c)x^{d-e} + Q'$

The invariant trivially holds for the base cases when $\deg(P) < \deg(M)$. To see that divide(P, M) maintains the invariant when $\deg(P) \geq \deg(M)$, assume the invariant holds for divide(P', M), that is, $P' = Q' \cdot M + R$ and $\deg(R) < \deg(M)$. Then by definition:

$$P = (b/c)x^{d-e} \cdot M + P' = (b/c)x^{d-e} \cdot M + \big(Q' \cdot M + R\big) = \big((b/c)x^{d-e} + Q'\big) \cdot M + R = Q \cdot M + R$$

The recursion terminates because $\deg(P)$ decreases in each successive call: $\deg(P') < \deg(P)$ because the leading monomial of $(b/c)x^{d-e} \cdot M$ is $(b/c)x^{d-e} \cdot cx^e = bx^d$, which cancels the leading monomial of P in the definition of P'. The invariant directly implies the existence of Q and R.

Now, we prove that Q and R are unique. Suppose for contradiction there exist some other polynomials S and T (either $S \neq Q$ or $T \neq R$) such that $P = S \cdot M + T$ and $\deg(T) < \deg(M)$. Then $0 = P - P = (Q \cdot M + R) - (S \cdot M + T) = (Q - S) \cdot M + (R - T)$. But the latter polynomial is nonzero because: If $S \neq Q$ then $\deg(R - T) < \deg(M) \leq \deg((Q - S) \cdot M)$. If $S = Q$ and $T \neq R$ then $0 \cdot M + (R - T)$ is nonzero. ∎

Lemma A.23. *Over every field, if P is a polynomial and $P(a) = 0$, then $P(x) = Q(x) \cdot (x - a)$ for some polynomial Q.*

Proof of Lemma A.23. Suppose $P(a) = 0$. Divide P by $M(x) = x - a$ using Lemma A.22 to get $P = Q \cdot M + R$. Since $\deg(R) < \deg(M) = 1$, R is a constant. We have $R = 0$ and therefore $P = Q \cdot M$ because $0 = P(a) = Q(a) \cdot M(a) + R = Q(a) \cdot (a - a) + R = 0 + R = R$. ∎

Proof of Theorem A.20. Rewriting the statement as an implication: For every nonzero polynomial P, if $\deg(P) = d$ then P has at most d many roots. We prove the contrapositive. Assume P has at least $d + 1$ many roots: $P(a_1) = P(a_2) = \cdots = P(a_{d+1}) = 0$ for some distinct field elements

$a_1, a_2, \ldots, a_{d+1}$. We claim that $P = Q \cdot (x - a_1) \cdot (x - a_2) \cdots (x - a_{d+1})$ for some polynomial Q (which must be nonzero since P is nonzero), in which case

$$\deg(P) = \deg(Q) + \deg(x - a_1) + \cdots + \deg(x - a_{d+1}) \geq 0 + 1 + \cdots + 1 = d + 1$$

since the degree of a product equals the sum of the degrees. Here's an iterative algorithm to find Q, using Lemma A.23 to peel off the $(x - a_i)$ factors one at a time:

Algorithm to factor a polynomial using its roots (A.7)

```
let Q_{d+1} = P
for i ← d+1, d, d−1, ..., 1:
    let Q_{i−1} be a polynomial such that Q_i = Q_{i−1} · (x − a_i)
output Q = Q_0
```

This maintains the invariant that $P = Q_i \cdot (x - a_{i+1}) \cdots (x - a_{d+1})$ and $a_1, \ldots, a_i$ are roots of Q_i. The invariant holds at the beginning ($i = d + 1$) by assumption. To see that the invariant is maintained, suppose it holds for some $i \geq 1$. In particular, since $Q_i(a_i) = 0$, Lemma A.23 says that indeed $Q_i = Q_{i-1} \cdot (x - a_i)$ for some polynomial Q_{i-1} (so the algorithm doesn't get stuck). Thus:

$$P = Q_i \cdot (x - a_{i+1}) \cdots (x - a_{d+1}) = Q_{i-1} \cdot (x - a_i) \cdot (x - a_{i+1}) \cdots (x - a_{d+1})$$

Furthermore, $a_1, \ldots, a_{i-1}$ are roots of Q_{i-1} because for every $j \leq i - 1$, we have $Q_{i-1}(a_j) = Q_i(a_j)/(a_j - a_i) = 0$ since a_j is a root of Q_i and $a_j \neq a_i$. So the invariant also holds for $i - 1$. The loop certainly terminates. In summary, since the invariant holds for $i = 0$, we have $P = Q \cdot (x - a_1) \cdot (x - a_2) \cdots (x - a_{d+1})$ as claimed. ■

A.4.3 Vectors

A *scalar* is a field element. A *vector* is a tuple of scalars. For all vectors v and w with the same number of components, and every scalar c:

- cv is the vector $(cv_1, cv_2, \ldots)$, using the field's multiplication.
- $v + w$ is the vector $(v_1 + w_1, v_2 + w_2, \ldots)$, using the field's addition.
- $v \cdot w$ is the scalar $v_1 w_1 + v_2 w_2 + \cdots$, using the field's multiplication and addition.

$v \cdot w$ is the *dot product*. Here's the linearity property:

Lemma A.24. *For all vectors u, v, w with the same number of components, and every scalar c:*

(i) $(cv) \cdot w = c(v \cdot w)$
(ii) $u \cdot (v + w) = (u \cdot v) + (u \cdot w)$ *and* $u \cdot (v - w) = (u \cdot v) - (u \cdot w)$

Proof. For *(i)*,

$$(cv) \cdot w = \textstyle\sum_i (cv_i) w_i = c \sum_i v_i w_i = c(v \cdot w)$$

using the distributive axiom to factor out the c. For *(ii)*:

$$u \cdot (v + w) = \textstyle\sum_i u_i (v_i + w_i) = \sum_i (u_i v_i + u_i w_i) = \left(\sum_i u_i v_i\right) + \left(\sum_i u_i w_i\right) = (u \cdot v) + (u \cdot w)$$

Subtraction is similar. ■

Since dot product is commutative, we also have $v\cdot(cw) = c(v\cdot w)$ and $(v+w)\cdot u = (v\cdot u)+(w\cdot u)$ and $(v-w)\cdot u = (v\cdot u)-(w\cdot u)$.

When the field is $\mathbb{Z}_2$, we also denote the dot product $v\cdot w$ by $v \odot w$, by analogy with $\oplus$ (xor), which is addition in $\mathbb{Z}_2$. For the rest of this section, we deal exclusively with the field $\mathbb{R}$.

Lemma A.25. *$v\cdot v \geq 0$ for every vector $v \in \mathbb{R}^n$. Furthermore, $v\cdot v = 0$ iff v is the zero vector.*

Proof. This holds for scalars ($n = 1$) because a real number's square is always nonnegative, and 0 is the only real number whose square is 0. For $n > 1$, we have $v\cdot v = \sum_i v_i^2 \geq \sum_i 0 = 0$, and if $v_i = 0$ for each i then $v\cdot v = \sum_i 0^2 = 0$, and if $v_j \neq 0$ for some j then $v\cdot v \geq v_j^2 > 0$ since $v_i^2 \geq 0$ for each $i \neq j$. ■

This classic inequality makes occasional appearances in computational complexity proofs:

Theorem A.26. *$(v\cdot w)^2 \leq (v\cdot v)(w\cdot w)$ for all vectors $v \in \mathbb{R}^n$ and $w \in \mathbb{R}^n$.*

Proof. If v is the zero vector, then $(v\cdot w)^2 \leq (v\cdot v)(w\cdot w)$ because the left side is 0 (since $v\cdot w = \sum_i v_i w_i = \sum_i 0 w_i = \sum_i 0 = 0$) and the right side is also 0 (since $v\cdot v = 0$).

For the rest of the proof, assume v is nonzero, so $v\cdot v > 0$ by Lemma A.25. Define the vectors $x = (v\cdot w)v$ and $y = (v\cdot v)w$. By Lemma A.24.*(i)*:

$$x\cdot x = (v\cdot w)^2(v\cdot v) \qquad x\cdot y = (v\cdot w)(v\cdot v)(v\cdot w) = (v\cdot w)^2(v\cdot v) \qquad y\cdot y = (v\cdot v)^2(w\cdot w)$$

Applying Lemma A.25 and Lemma A.24.*(ii)*, and noting that $x\cdot y = x\cdot x$:

$$0 \leq (x-y)\cdot(x-y) = (x\cdot x) - 2(x\cdot y) + (y\cdot y) = -(x\cdot x) + (y\cdot y)$$

Rearranging yields $x\cdot x \leq y\cdot y$. Plugging in our expressions for $x\cdot x$ and $y\cdot y$, we have $(v\cdot w)^2(v\cdot v) \leq (v\cdot v)^2(w\cdot w)$. Dividing both sides by $v\cdot v$ (which is positive) produces $(v\cdot w)^2 \leq (v\cdot v)(w\cdot w)$. ■

Corollary A.27. *$\left(\sum_i |v_i|\right)^2 \leq n\sum_i v_i^2$ for every vector $v \in \mathbb{R}^n$.*

Proof. Define a vector $w \in \mathbb{R}^n$ such that $w_i = 1$ if $v_i \geq 0$, and $w_i = -1$ if $v_i < 0$. Note that $|v_i| = v_i w_i$ and $w_i^2 = 1$ for each index i. By Theorem A.26:

$$\left(\sum_i |v_i|\right)^2 = \left(\sum_i v_i w_i\right)^2 = (v\cdot w)^2 \leq (v\cdot v)(w\cdot w) = \left(\sum_i v_i^2\right)\left(\sum_i w_i^2\right) = n\sum_i v_i^2 \qquad ■$$

Lemma A.28. *$\left|\sum_i v_i\right| \leq \sum_i |v_i|$ for every vector $v \in \mathbb{R}^n$.*

Proof. Consider two cases: If $v_1 + \cdots + v_n \geq 0$ then $|v_1 + \cdots + v_n| = v_1 + \cdots + v_n \leq |v_1| + \cdots + |v_n|$ since $v_i \leq |v_i|$ for each index i. If $v_1 + \cdots + v_n < 0$ then $|v_1 + \cdots + v_n| = -(v_1 + \cdots + v_n) = (-v_1) + \cdots + (-v_n) \leq |v_1| + \cdots + |v_n|$ since $v_i \geq -|v_i|$ and thus $-v_i \leq |v_i|$ for each index i. ■

A.4.4 Matrices

A *matrix* is a rectangular 2-dimensional array of scalars. An $m \times n$ matrix has m rows and n columns. Row 1 is the top, row m is the bottom, column 1 is the leftmost, and column n is the rightmost. The entry in row i and column j of a matrix A is $A_{i,j}$. The *transpose* of an $m \times n$ matrix A is the $n \times m$ matrix $A^\top$ such that $A^\top_{j,i} = A_{i,j}$ for each $i \in [m]$ and $j \in [n]$. A $1 \times n$ matrix is a *row vector* v, and we abbreviate $v_{1,j}$ as v_j. An $m \times 1$ matrix is a *column vector* v, and we abbreviate $v_{i,1}$ as v_i. We can treat a scalar as a 1×1 matrix.

If v is a $1 \times n$ row vector and w is an $n \times 1$ column vector, then vw is the dot product $v \cdot w = \sum_{i=1}^{n} v_i w_i$. If A is an $m \times n$ matrix and v is an $n \times 1$ column vector, then Av is the $m \times 1$ column vector whose ith entry is the dot product of A's ith row and v. If A is an $m \times n$ matrix and v is a $1 \times m$ row vector, then vA is the $1 \times n$ row vector whose jth entry is the dot product of v and A's jth column.

This is among the most fundamental results in linear algebra:

Theorem A.29. *Over every field, for every $n \times (n+1)$ matrix A, there exists a nonzero column vector x such that Ax is the zero vector.*

This says every underdetermined homogeneous system of linear equations has a nontrivial solution. Viewing the entries of x as unknowns and the entries of each row of A as coefficients, the system is:

$$\begin{bmatrix} A_{1,1} & A_{1,2} & \cdots & A_{1,n+1} \\ A_{2,1} & A_{2,2} & \cdots & A_{2,n+1} \\ \vdots & \vdots & & \vdots \\ A_{n,1} & A_{n,2} & \cdots & A_{n,n+1} \end{bmatrix} \begin{bmatrix} x_1 \\ x_2 \\ \vdots \\ x_n \\ x_{n+1} \end{bmatrix} = \begin{bmatrix} 0 \\ 0 \\ \vdots \\ 0 \end{bmatrix} \qquad \begin{aligned} A_{1,1}x_1 + A_{1,2}x_2 + \cdots + A_{1,n+1}x_{n+1} &= 0 \\ A_{2,1}x_1 + A_{2,2}x_2 + \cdots + A_{2,n+1}x_{n+1} &= 0 \\ &\vdots \\ A_{n,1}x_1 + A_{n,2}x_2 + \cdots + A_{n,n+1}x_{n+1} &= 0 \end{aligned}$$

Underdetermined means there are more unknowns than equations. *Homogeneous* means the right-hand side is all 0s. The trivial solution would just assign $x_j = 0$ for all j. In a *nontrivial* solution, $x_j \neq 0$ for at least one j, which means the column vector x is nonzero.

To prove Theorem A.29, we argue that a standard algorithm for solving systems of linear equations is guaranteed to find a nonzero solution in the underdetermined homogeneous case.

Proof. Let A_i denote A's ith row. The following recursive subroutine maintains the invariant that for every $n \times (n+1)$ matrix A, solve(A) returns a nonzero column vector x such that Ax is the zero vector.

Algorithm to solve an underdetermined homogeneous system of linear equations (A.8)

solve(A):
  if A's last column is all 0s: return $x = \begin{bmatrix} 0 & \cdots & 0 & 1 \end{bmatrix}^\top$
  if $n = 1$: return $x = \begin{bmatrix} 1 & -A_{1,1}/A_{1,2} \end{bmatrix}^\top$
  since A's last column is not all 0s, suppose $A_{n,n+1} \neq 0$ for simplicity of notation
  $y \leftarrow$ solve(B) where B is the $(n-1) \times n$ matrix such that for each $i \in [n-1]$:
    $B_i = A_i - (A_{i,n+1}/A_{n,n+1})A_n$ but with the last entry (which would be 0) deleted
  return $x = y$ but with $x_{n+1} = -(A_{n,1}y_1 + A_{n,2}y_2 + \cdots + A_{n,n}y_n)/A_{n,n+1}$ appended

For the base cases when A's last column is all 0s, the invariant holds by definition. For the base cases when $n = 1$ and $A_{1,2} \neq 0$, the invariant holds since:

$$Ax = A_{1,1}1 + A_{1,2}(-A_{1,1}/A_{1,2}) = A_{1,1} - A_{1,1} = 0$$

For all other A, to see that solve(A) maintains the invariant, we assume the invariant holds for solve(B) and argue that it also holds for solve(A): Assuming y is nonzero and By is zero, we show that x is nonzero and Ax is zero. Observe that x is nonzero since y is. Now, we argue that $A_i x = 0$ for each $i \in [n]$. When $i = n$:

$$A_n x = A_{n,1}y_1 + A_{n,2}y_2 + \cdots + A_{n,n}y_n + A_{n,n+1}x_{n+1} = 0$$

Now, suppose $i < n$. In the definition of B_i, the deleted last entry would have been:

$$A_{i,n+1} - (A_{i,n+1}/A_{n,n+1})A_{n,n+1} = 0$$

So regardless of x_{n+1}'s value,

$$0 = B_i y = \big(A_i - (A_{i,n+1}/A_{n,n+1})A_n\big)x = A_i x - (A_{i,n+1}/A_{n,n+1})A_n x = A_i x$$

by distributivity and $A_n x = 0$. The recursion terminates because B has fewer rows than A and so the recursion eventually reaches a base case. ∎

If A and B are $m \times n$ matrices, then $A+B$ is the $m \times n$ matrix such that $(A+B)_{i,j} = A_{i,j} + B_{i,j}$, using the field's addition. If A is an $\ell \times m$ matrix and B is an $m \times n$ matrix, then AB is the $\ell \times n$ matrix such that $(AB)_{h,j} = \sum_{i=1}^{m} A_{h,i}B_{i,j}$ is the dot product of A's hth row and B's jth column. Matrix multiplication is associative (meaning $(AB)C = A(BC)$, so we can just write ABC) and distributive (meaning $(A+B)C = AC + BC$) but not commutative (so sometimes $AB \neq BA$), assuming the matrices have compatible sizes. If A is an $n \times n$ matrix and $\ell \in \mathbb{N}$, then A^ℓ is ℓ copies of A multiplied together. In particular, $A^1 = A$ and A^0 is the $n \times n$ *identity matrix*, with 1s on its diagonal (upper left to lower right) and 0s elsewhere. The notation $A^\ell_{i,j}$ is ambiguous since $(A^\ell)_{i,j}$ doesn't generally equal $(A_{i,j})^\ell$.

We conclude with a topic that combines many concepts from this appendix.

Consider any directed graph G with set of nodes $[n]$. If self-loops are allowed but multi-edges aren't, then G's *adjacency matrix* is the $n \times n$ matrix A where $A_{i,j} = 1$ if G has an edge from node i to node j, and $A_{i,j} = 0$ if G has no such edge. If multi-edges (including multi-self-loops) are allowed, then $A_{i,j}$ is the number of (i,j) edges. The sum of row i's entries is node i's outdegree. The sum of column j's entries is node j's indegree. An undirected graph's adjacency matrix is the adjacency matrix of the directed version in which each edge $\{i,j\}$ is replaced with a pair of edges (i,j) and (j,i). We focus on directed graphs since they're more general.

A walk goes from node to node to node (and so on) by traversing edges, and may reuse edges. A walk's length is the number of edge traversals (steps).

Lemma A.30. *If A is a directed graph's adjacency matrix, then $(A^\ell)_{i,j}$ is the number of length-ℓ walks that start at node i and end at node j.*

Proof. This holds by definition when $\ell \leq 1$. Next, consider $\ell = 2$: For any node k, the number of walks that visit nodes i,k,j (in that order) equals $A_{i,k}A_{k,j}$ by the multiplication principle (since there are $A_{i,k}$ many (i,k) edges and $A_{k,j}$ many (k,j) edges). By the addition principle, we can partition the set of all length-2 walks from i to j according to their second node k, to see that the total number of such walks is $\sum_{k=1}^{n} A_{i,k}A_{k,j} = (A^2)_{i,j}$. We repeat this reasoning to handle $\ell = 3,4,\ldots$: Assuming we already know that the entries of $A^{\ell-1}$ count walks of length $\ell - 1$, we count the number of length-ℓ walks from i to j by using the addition principle (partitioning the set of such walks according to their second node k) and multiplication principle to get $\sum_{k=1}^{n} A_{i,k}(A^{\ell-1})_{k,j} = (AA^{\ell-1})_{i,j} = (A^\ell)_{i,j}$. ∎

A *random walk* of length ℓ starts at a designated node i, and in each step, it follows a uniformly random outgoing edge from the current node. The graph's *transition matrix* is the $n \times n$ matrix T where $T_{i,j} = (\text{number of } (i,j) \text{ edges})/\operatorname{outdeg}(i)$ is the probability of being at node j after one step from node i. The sum of the entries in any individual row of T is 1.

Lemma A.31. *If T is a directed graph's transition matrix, then $(T^{\ell})_{i,j}$ is the probability that a length-ℓ random walk starting at node i ends at node j.*

Proof. This holds by definition when $\ell \le 1$. Next, consider $\ell = 2$: For any node k, the probability that the random walk visits nodes i, k, j (in that order) equals

$$\mathbf{Pr}[\text{second node is } k]\,\mathbf{Pr}[\text{last node is } j \,|\, \text{second node is } k] \;=\; T_{i,k}T_{k,j}$$

by the chain rule (since conditioned on the second node being k, the marginal distribution of the second edge is the same as a random walk of length 1 from k). By the law of total probability, we can partition the set of all length-2 walks from i according to their second node k, to get:

$$\mathbf{Pr}[\text{last node is } j] \;=\; \textstyle\sum_{k=1}^{n} \mathbf{Pr}[\text{second node is } k \text{ and last node is } j] \;=\; \sum_{k=1}^{n} T_{i,k}T_{k,j} \;=\; (T^2)_{i,j}$$

We repeat this reasoning to handle $\ell = 3, 4, \ldots$: Assuming we already know that the entries of $T^{\ell-1}$ are the relevant probabilities for walks of length $\ell - 1$, we calculate the probability that a length-ℓ random walk from i ends at j by using the law of total probability (partitioning the set of such walks according to their second node k) and chain rule to get $\sum_{k=1}^{n} T_{i,k}(T^{\ell-1})_{k,j} = (TT^{\ell-1})_{i,j} = (T^{\ell})_{i,j}$. (Again, conditioned on the second node being k, the marginal distribution of the last $\ell - 1$ steps is the same as a random walk of length $\ell - 1$ from k.) ∎

Another perspective: Suppose instead of starting at a designated node i, the random walk starts at a random node sampled from some distribution represented by a $1 \times n$ row vector v where v_i is the probability of starting at node i. Then the row vector vT is the distribution over nodes after one step of the random walk: $(vT)_j$ is the probability that a uniformly random edge out of a random node i distributed according to v goes to node j. Since the distribution after one step is vT, the distribution after another step is $(vT)T = vT^2$, and so on: vT^{ℓ} is the distribution of the ending node of a length-ℓ random walk with starting node distributed according to v.

References

[1] Scott Aaronson. $P \stackrel{?}{=} NP$. In *Open Problems in Mathematics*, pages 1–122. Springer, 2016. doi:10.1007/978-3-319-32162-2_1 [p. 135]

[2] Scott Aaronson, Shalev Ben-David, Robin Kothari, Shravas Rao, and Avishay Tal. Degree vs. approximate degree and quantum implications of Huang's sensitivity theorem. In *Proceedings of the 53rd Symposium on Theory of Computing (STOC)*, pages 1330–1342. ACM, 2021. doi:10.1145/3406325.3451047 [p. 616]

[3] Scott Aaronson and Avi Wigderson. Algebrization: A new barrier in complexity theory. *ACM Transactions on Computation Theory*, 1(1):2:1–2:54, 2009. doi:10.1145/1490270.1490272 [p. 194]

[4] Harold Abelson and Peter Andreae. Information transfer and area-time tradeoffs for VLSI multiplication. *Communications of the ACM*, 23(1):20–23, 1980. doi:10.1145/358808.358814 [p. 645]

[5] Leonard Adleman. Two theorems on random polynomial time. In *Proceedings of the 19th Symposium on Foundations of Computer Science (FOCS)*, pages 75–83. IEEE, 1978. doi:10.1109/SFCS.1978.37 [p. 309]

[6] Leonard Adleman, Jonathan DeMarrais, and Ming-Deh Huang. Quantum computability. *SIAM Journal on Computing*, 26(5):1524–1540, 1997. doi:10.1137/S0097539795293639 [p. 683]

[7] Leonard Adleman and Ming-Deh Huang. Primality testing and abelian varieties over finite fields. In *Lecture Notes in Mathematics*, volume 1512. Springer, 1992. doi:10.1007/BFb0090185 [p. 308]

[8] Leonard Adleman, Carl Pomerance, and Robert Rumely. On distinguishing prime numbers from composite numbers. *Annals of Mathematics*, 117(1):173–206, 1983. doi:10.2307/2006975 [p. 308]

[9] Manindra Agrawal and Somenath Biswas. Primality and identity testing via Chinese remaindering. *Journal of the ACM*, 50(4):429–443, 2003. doi:10.1145/792538.792540 [p. 308]

[10] Manindra Agrawal, Neeraj Kayal, and Nitin Saxena. PRIMES is in P. *Annals of Mathematics*, 160(2):781–793, 2004. doi:10.4007/annals.2004.160.781 [p. 308]

[11] Manindra Agrawal and V. Vinay. Arithmetic circuits: A chasm at depth four. In *Proceedings of the 49th Symposium on Foundations of Computer Science (FOCS)*, pages 67–75. IEEE, 2008. doi:10.1109/FOCS.2008.32 [p. 683]

[12] Alfred Aho, Jeffrey Ullman, and Mihalis Yannakakis. On notions of information transfer in VLSI circuits. In *Proceedings of the 15th Symposium on Theory of Computing (STOC)*, pages 133–139. ACM, 1983. doi:10.1145/800061.808742 [p. 646]

[13] Miklós Ajtai. Σ_1^1-formulae on finite structures. *Annals of Pure and Applied Logic*, 24(1):1–48, 1983. doi:https://doi.org/10.1016/0168-0072(83)90038-6 [p. 675]

[14] Miklós Ajtai, János Komlós, and Endre Szemerédi. Sorting in $c \log n$ parallel steps. *Combinatorica*, 3(1):1–19, 1983. doi:10.1007/BF02579338 [p. 135]

[15] Romas Aleliunas, Richard Karp, Richard Lipton, László Lovász, and Charles Rackoff. Random walks, universal traversal sequences, and the complexity of maze problems. In *Proceedings of the 20th Symposium on Foundations of Computer Science (FOCS)*, pages 218–223. IEEE, 1979. doi:10.1109/SFCS.1979.34 [p. 309]

[16] Noga Alon and Ravi Boppana. The monotone circuit complexity of boolean functions. *Combinatorica*, 7(1):1–22, 1987. doi:10.1007/BF02579196 [p. 676]

[17] Noga Alon, Oded Goldreich, Johan Håstad, and René Peralta. Simple construction of almost k-wise independent random variables. *Random Structures and Algorithms*, 3(3):289–304, 1992. doi:10.1002/rsa.3240030308 [p. 423]

[18] Noga Alon, Yossi Matias, and Mario Szegedy. The space complexity of approximating the frequency moments. *Journal of Computer and System Sciences*, 58(1):137–147, 1999. doi:10.1006/JCSS.1997.1545 [pp. 331, 645]

[19] Noga Alon and Joel Spencer. *The Probabilistic Method*. Discrete Mathematics and Optimization. Wiley, 4th edition, 2016. [p. 308]

[20] Noga Alon and Benny Sudakov. Bipartite subgraphs and the smallest eigenvalue. *Combinatorics, Probability, and Computing*, 9(1):1–12, 2000. doi:10.1017/S0963548399004071 [p. 309]

[21] Omar Alrabiah, Venkatesan Guruswami, Pravesh Kothari, and Peter Manohar. A near-cubic lower bound for 3-query locally decodable codes from semirandom CSP refutation. In *Proceedings of the 55th Symposium on Theory of Computing (STOC)*, pages 1438–1448. ACM, 2023. doi:10.1145/3564246.3585143 [p. 384]

[22] Ryan Alweiss, Shachar Lovett, Kewen Wu, and Jiapeng Zhang. Improved bounds for the sunflower lemma. *Annals of Mathematics*, 194(3):795–815, 2021. doi:10.4007/annals.2021.194.3.5 [p. 676]

[23] Andris Ambainis. Communication complexity in a 3-computer model. *Algorithmica*, 16(3):298–301, 1996. doi:10.1007/BF01955678 [p. 646]

[24] Andris Ambainis, Kaspars Balodis, Aleksandrs Belovs, Troy Lee, Miklos Santha, and Juris Smotrovs. Separations in query complexity based on pointer functions. *Journal of the ACM*, 64(5):32:1–32:24, 2017. doi:10.1145/3106234 [p. 617]

[25] Alexander Andreev. On a method for obtaining more than quadratic effective lower bounds for the complexity of π-schemes. *Moscow University Mathematics Bulletin*, 42(1):24–29, 1987. [p. 675]

[26] Dana Angluin. Queries and concept learning. *Machine Learning*, 2(4):319–342, 1988. doi:10.1007/BF00116828 [p. 505]

[27] Dana Angluin and Michael Kharitonov. When won't membership queries help? *Journal of Computer and System Sciences*, 50(2):336–355, 1995. doi:10.1006/JCSS.1995.1026 [p. 506]

[28] Sanjeev Arora and Boaz Barak. *Computational Complexity: A Modern Approach*. Cambridge University Press, 2009. doi:10.1017/CBO9780511804090 [p. 71]

[29] Sanjeev Arora, Carsten Lund, Rajeev Motwani, Madhu Sudan, and Mario Szegedy. Proof verification and hardness of approximation problems. In *Proceedings of the 33rd Symposium on Foundations of Computer Science (FOCS)*, pages 14–23. IEEE, 1992. doi:10.1109/SFCS.1992.267823 [p. 543]

[30] Sanjeev Arora and Shmuel Safra. Probabilistic checking of proofs: A new characterization of NP. In *Proceedings of the 33rd Symposium on Foundations of Computer Science (FOCS)*, pages 2–13. IEEE, 1992. doi:10.1109/SFCS.1992.267824 [p. 543]

[31] Vikraman Arvind and Johannes Köbler. On pseudorandomness and resource-bounded measure. *Theoretical Computer Science*, 255(1-2):205–221, 2001. doi:10.1016/S0304-3975(99)00164-4 [p. 576]

[32] Vikraman Arvind, Johannes Köbler, Uwe Schöning, and Rainer Schuler. If NP has polynomial-size circuits, then MA = AM. *Theoretical Computer Science*, 137(2):279–282, 1995. doi:10.1016/0304-3975(95)91133-B [p. 576]

[33] Bengt Aspvall, Michael Plass, and Robert Tarjan. A linear-time algorithm for testing the truth of certain quantified boolean formulas. *Information Processing Letters*, 8(3):121–123, 1979. doi:10.1016/0020-0190(79)90002-4 [pp. 135, 161]

[34] Giorgio Ausiello, Alberto Marchetti-Spaccamela, Pierluigi Crescenzi, Giorgio Gambosi, Marco Protasi, and Viggo Kann. *Complexity and Approximation: Combinatorial Optimization Problems and Their Approximability Properties*. Springer, 1999. doi:10.1007/978-3-642-58412-1 [p. 542]

[35] Per Austrin. Balanced max 2-sat might not be the hardest. In *Proceedings of the 39th Symposium on Theory of Computing (STOC)*, pages 189–197. ACM, 2007. doi:10.1145/1250790.1250818 [p. 542]

[36] Barış Aydınlıoğlu, Dan Gutfreund, John Hitchcock, and Akinori Kawachi. Derandomizing Arthur-Merlin games and approximate counting implies exponential-size lower bounds. *Computational Complexity*, 20(2):329–366, 2011. doi:10.1007/s00037-011-0010-8 [p. 576]

[37] László Babai. Trading group theory for randomness. In *Proceedings of the 17th Symposium on Theory of Computing (STOC)*, pages 421–429. ACM, 1985. doi:10.1145/22145.22192 [p. 576]

[38] László Babai. Graph isomorphism in quasipolynomial time. In *Proceedings of the 48th Symposium on Theory of Computing (STOC)*, pages 684–697. ACM, 2016. doi:10.1145/2897518.2897542 [p. 576]

[39] László Babai, Lance Fortnow, and Carsten Lund. Non-deterministic exponential time has two-prover interactive protocols. *Computational Complexity*, 1:3–40, 1991. doi:10.1007/BF01200056 [pp. 383, 576]

[40] László Babai, Lance Fortnow, Noam Nisan, and Avi Wigderson. BPP has subexponential time simulations unless EXPTIME has publishable proofs. *Computational Complexity*, 3:307–318, 1993. doi:10.1007/BF01275486 [pp. 383, 576]

[41] László Babai, Peter Frankl, and Janos Simon. Complexity classes in communication complexity theory. In *Proceedings of the 27th Symposium on Foundations of Computer Science (FOCS)*, pages 337–347. IEEE, 1986. doi:10.1109/SFCS.1986.15 [p. 645]

[42] László Babai and Peter Kimmel. Randomized simultaneous messages: Solution of a problem of Yao in communication complexity. In *Proceedings of the 12th Conference on Computational Complexity (CCC)*, pages 239–246. IEEE, 1997. doi:10.1109/CCC.1997.612319 [p. 646]

[43] László Babai and Shlomo Moran. Arthur–Merlin games: A randomized proof system, and a hierarchy of complexity classes. *Journal of Computer and System Sciences*, 36(2):254–276, 1988. doi:10.1016/0022-0000(88)90028-1 [p. 576]

[44] László Babai, Pavel Pudlák, Vojtech Rödl, and Endre Szemerédi. Lower bounds to the complexity of symmetric boolean functions. *Theoretical Computer Science*, 74(3):313–323, 1990. doi:10.1016/0304-3975(90)90080-2 [p. 617]

[45] Theodore Baker, John Gill, and Robert Solovay. Relativizations of the P =? NP question. *SIAM Journal on Computing*, 4(4):431–442, 1975. doi:10.1137/0204037 [pp. 194, 617]

[46] Kaspars Balodis, Shalev Ben-David, Mika Göös, Siddhartha Jain, and Robin Kothari. Unambiguous DNFs and Alon–Saks–Seymour. In *Proceedings of the 62nd Symposium on Foundations of Computer Science (FOCS)*, pages 116–124. IEEE, 2021. doi:10.1109/FOCS52979.2021.00020 [p. 617]

[47] Ziv Bar-Yossef, T. S. Jayram, Ravi Kumar, and D. Sivakumar. An information statistics approach to data stream and communication complexity. *Journal of Computer and System Sciences*, 68(4):702–732, 2004. doi:10.1016/j.jcss.2003.11.006 [p. 645]

[48] David Mix Barrington. Bounded-width polynomial-size branching programs recognize exactly those languages in NC^1. *Journal of Computer and System Sciences*, 38(1):150–164, 1989. doi:10.1016/0022-0000(89)90037-8 [p. 264]

[49] Leonid Bassalygo. New upper bounds for error-correcting codes. *Problemy Peredachi Informatsii*, 1(4):41–45, 1965. In Russian. [p. 359]

[50] Kenneth Batcher. Sorting networks and their applications. In *Proceedings of the Spring Joint Computer Conference*, pages 307–314. American Federation of Information Processing Societies, 1968. doi:10.1145/1468075.1468121 [p. 135]

[51] Robert Beals, Harry Buhrman, Richard Cleve, Michele Mosca, and Ronald de Wolf. Quantum lower bounds by polynomials. *Journal of the ACM*, 48(4):778–797, 2001. doi:10.1145/502090.502097 [p. 616]

[52] Paul Beame, Stephen Cook, and James Hoover. Log depth circuits for division and related problems. *SIAM Journal on Computing*, 15(4):994–1003, 1986. doi:10.1137/0215070 [p. 264]

[53] Paul Beame and Toniann Pitassi. Propositional proof complexity: Past, present, and future. In *Current Trends in Theoretical Computer Science: Entering the 21st Century*, pages 42–70. World Scientific, 2001. doi:10.1142/9789812810403_0001 [p. 682]

[54] Donald Beaver and Joan Feigenbaum. Hiding instances in multioracle queries. In *Proceedings of the 7th International Symposium on Theoretical Aspects of Computer Science (STACS)*, pages 37–48. Springer, 1990. doi:10.1007/3-540-52282-4_30 [p. 383]

[55] Richard Beigel and David Eppstein. 3-coloring in time $O(1.3289^n)$. *Journal of Algorithms*, 54(2):168–204, 2005. doi:10.1016/j.jalgor.2004.06.008 [p. 135]

[56] Richard Beigel, Nick Reingold, and Daniel Spielman. The perceptron strikes back. In *Proceedings of the 6th Structure in Complexity Theory Conference (STRUCTURES)*, pages 286–291. IEEE, 1991. doi:10.1109/SCT.1991.160270 [p. 676]

[57] Mihir Bellare, Oded Goldreich, and Erez Petrank. Uniform generation of NP-witnesses using an NP-oracle. *Information and Computation*, 163(2):510–526, 2000. doi:10.1006/inco.2000.2885 [p. 331]

[58] Shai Ben-David, Benny Chor, Oded Goldreich, and Michael Luby. On the theory of average case complexity. *Journal of Computer and System Sciences*, 44(2):193–219, 1992. doi:10.1016/0022-0000(92)90019-F [p. 383]

[59] Shalev Ben-David, Pooya Hatami, and Avishay Tal. Low-sensitivity functions from unambiguous certificates. In *Proceedings of the 8th Innovations in Theoretical Computer Science Conference (ITCS)*, pages 28:1–28:23. Schloss Dagstuhl, 2017. doi:10.4230/LIPICS.ITCS.2017.28 [p. 617]

[60] Michael Ben-Or, Oded Goldreich, Shafi Goldwasser, Johan Håstad, Joe Kilian, Silvio Micali, and Phillip Rogaway. Everything provable is provable in zero-knowledge. In *Proceedings of the 8th International Cryptology Conference (CRYPTO)*, pages 37–56. Springer, 1988. doi:10.1007/0-387-34799-2_4 [p. 576]

[61] Michael Ben-Or, Shafi Goldwasser, Joe Kilian, and Avi Wigderson. Multi-prover interactive proofs: How to remove intractability assumptions. In *Proceedings of the 20th Symposium on Theory of Computing (STOC)*, pages 113–131. ACM, 1988. doi:10.1145/62212.62223 [p. 576]

[62] Charles Bennett and John Gill. Relative to a random oracle A, $\mathrm{P}^A \neq \mathrm{NP}^A \neq \text{co-NP}^A$ with probability 1. *SIAM Journal on Computing*, 10(1):96–113, 1981. doi:10.1137/0210008 [p. 309]

[63] Elwyn Berlekamp and Lloyd Welch. Error correction for algebraic block codes. United States Patent 4,633,470, 1986. [p. 358]

[64] Marc Best, Peter van Emde Boas, and Hendrik Lenstra. A sharpened version of the Aanderaa–Rosenberg conjecture. *Mathematisch Centrum Amsterdam*, 30, 1974. [p. 617]

[65] Arnab Bhattacharyya and Yuichi Yoshida. *Property Testing: Problems and Techniques*. Springer, 2022. doi:10.1007/978-981-16-8622-1 [p. 682]

[66] Jarosław Błasiok. Optimal streaming and tracking distinct elements with high probability. *ACM Transactions on Algorithms*, 16(1):3:1–3:28, 2020. doi:10.1145/3309193 [p. 331]

[67] Manuel Blum. How to prove a theorem so no one else can claim it. In *Proceedings of the International Congress of Mathematicians*, pages 1444–1451, 1986. [p. 576]

[68] Manuel Blum, Ashok Chandra, and Mark Wegman. Equivalence of free boolean graphs can be decided probabilistically in polynomial time. *Information Processing Letters*, 10(2):80–82, 1980. doi:10.1016/S0020-0190(80)90078-2 [p. 309]

[69] Manuel Blum and Russell Impagliazzo. Generic oracles and oracle classes. In *Proceedings of the 28th Symposium on Foundations of Computer Science (FOCS)*, pages 118–126. IEEE, 1987. doi:10.1109/SFCS.1987.30 [p. 616]

[70] Manuel Blum and Sampath Kannan. Designing programs that check their work. *Journal of the ACM*, 42(1):269–291, 1995. doi:10.1145/200836.200880 [p. 576]

[71] Manuel Blum, Michael Luby, and Ronitt Rubinfeld. Self-testing/correcting with applications to numerical problems. *Journal of Computer and System Sciences*, 47(3):549–595, 1993. doi:10.1016/0022-0000(93)90044-W [p. 543]

[72] Manuel Blum and Silvio Micali. How to generate cryptographically strong sequences of pseudo-random bits. *SIAM Journal on Computing*, 13(4):850–864, 1984. doi:10.1137/0213053 [p. 456]

[73] Anselm Blumer, Andrzej Ehrenfeucht, David Haussler, and Manfred Warmuth. Occam's razor. *Information Processing Letters*, 24(6):377–380, 1987. doi:10.1016/0020-0190(87)90114-1 [p. 505]

[74] Anselm Blumer, Andrzej Ehrenfeucht, David Haussler, and Manfred Warmuth. Learnability and the Vapnik–Chervonenkis dimension. *Journal of the ACM*, 36(4):929–965, 1989. doi:10.1145/76359.76371 [p. 505]

[75] Andrej Bogdanov, Zeev Dvir, Elad Verbin, and Amir Yehudayoff. Pseudorandomness for width-2 branching programs. *Theory of Computing*, 9(7):283–293, 2013. doi:10.4086/toc.2013.v009a007 [p. 424]

[76] Andrej Bogdanov and Alon Rosen. Pseudorandom functions: Three decades later. In *Tutorials on the Foundations of Cryptography*, pages 79–158. Springer, 2017. doi:10.1007/978-3-319-57048-8_3 [p. 457]

[77] Andrej Bogdanov and Muli Safra. Hardness amplification for errorless heuristics. In *Proceedings of the 48th Symposium on Foundations of Computer Science (FOCS)*, pages 418–426. IEEE, 2007. doi:10.1109/FOCS.2007.25 [p. 384]

[78] Andrej Bogdanov and Luca Trevisan. Average-case complexity. *Foundations and Trends in Theoretical Computer Science*, 2(1):1–106, 2006. doi:10.1561/0400000004 [p. 383]

[79] Andrej Bogdanov and Luca Trevisan. On worst-case to average-case reductions for NP problems. *SIAM Journal on Computing*, 36(4):1119–1159, 2006. doi:10.1137/S0097539705446974 [p. 384]

[80] Elmar Böhler, Christian Glaßer, and Daniel Meister. Error-bounded probabilistic computations between MA and AM. *Journal of Computer and System Sciences*, 72(6):1043–1076, 2006. doi:10.1016/J.JCSS.2006.05.001 [p. 576]

[81] Maria Luisa Bonet and Samuel Buss. Size-depth tradeoffs for boolean formulae. *Information Processing Letters*, 49(3):151–155, 1994. doi:10.1016/0020-0190(94)90093-0 [p. 264]

[82] Ravi Boppana, Johan Håstad, and Stathis Zachos. Does co-NP have short interactive proofs? *Information Processing Letters*, 25(2):127–132, 1987. doi:10.1016/0020-0190(87)90232-8 [p. 576]

[83] Allan Borodin. Computational complexity and the existence of complexity gaps. *Journal of the ACM*, 19(1):158–174, 1972. doi:10.1145/321679.321691 [p. 194]

[84] Allan Borodin. On relating time and space to size and depth. *SIAM Journal on Computing*, 6(4):733–744, 1977. doi:10.1137/0206054 [p. 264]

[85] Allan Borodin, Stephen Cook, Patrick Dymond, Walter Ruzzo, and Martin Tompa. Two applications of inductive counting for complementation problems. *SIAM Journal on Computing*, 18(3):559–578, 1989. doi:10.1137/0218038 [pp. 264, 309]

[86] Allan Borodin, Stephen Cook, and Nicholas Pippenger. Parallel computation for well-endowed rings and space-bounded probabilistic machines. *Information and Control*, 58:113–136, 1983. doi:10.1016/S0019-9958(83)80060-6 [p. 309]

[87] Allan Borodin, Danny Dolev, Faith Fich, and Wolfgang Paul. Bounds for width two branching programs. *SIAM Journal on Computing*, 15(2):549–560, 1986. doi:10.1137/0215040 [p. 264]

[88] Joshua Brakensiek, Neng Huang, and Uri Zwick. Tight approximability of MAX 2-SAT and relatives, under UGC. In *Proceedings of the 35th Symposium on Discrete Algorithms (SODA)*, pages 1328–1344. SIAM, 2024. doi:10.1137/1.9781611977912.53 [p. 542]

[89] Mark Braverman and Omri Weinstein. A discrepancy lower bound for information complexity. *Algorithmica*, 76(3):846–864, 2016. doi:10.1007/s00453-015-0093-8 [p. 645]

[90] Richard Brent and Hsiang-Tsung Kung. The area-time complexity of binary multiplication. *Journal of the ACM*, 28(3):521–534, 1981. doi:10.1145/322261.322269 [p. 645]

[91] Karl Bringmann. Fine-grained complexity theory. In *Proceedings of the 36th International Symposium on Theoretical Aspects of Computer Science (STACS)*, pages 4:1–4:7. Schloss Dagstuhl, 2019. doi:10.4230/LIPICS.STACS.2019.4 [p. 682]

[92] R. Leonard Brooks. On colouring the nodes of a network. *Mathematical Proceedings of the Cambridge Philosophical Society*, 37(2):194–197, 1941. doi:10.1017/S030500410002168X [p. 135]

[93] Nader Bshouty, Richard Cleve, and Wayne Eberly. Size-depth tradeoffs for algebraic formulas. *SIAM Journal on Computing*, 24(4):682–705, 1995. doi:10.1137/S0097539792232586 [p. 264]

[94] Nader Bshouty, Richard Cleve, Ricard Gavaldà, Sampath Kannan, and Christino Tamon. Oracles and queries that are sufficient for exact learning. *Journal of Computer and System Sciences*, 52(3):421–433, 1996. doi:10.1006/jcss.1996.0032 [p. 505]

[95] Harry Buhrman, Richard Cleve, Michal Koucký, Bruno Loff, and Florian Speelman. Computing with a full memory: Catalytic space. In *Proceedings of the 46th Symposium on Theory of Computing (STOC)*, pages 857–866. ACM, 2014. doi:10.1145/2591796.2591874 [pp. 161, 309]

[96] Harry Buhrman and Lance Fortnow. One-sided versus two-sided error in probabilistic computation. In *Proceedings of the 16th International Symposium on Theoretical Aspects of Computer Science (STACS)*, pages 100–109. Springer, 1999. doi:10.1007/3-540-49116-3_9 [p. 309]

[97] Harry Buhrman and Ronald de Wolf. Complexity measures and decision tree complexity: A survey. *Theoretical Computer Science*, 288(1):21–43, 2002. doi:10.1016/S0304-3975(01)00144-X [p. 616]

[98] Andrei Bulatov. A dichotomy theorem for nonuniform CSPs. In *Proceedings of the 58th Symposium on Foundations of Computer Science (FOCS)*, pages 319–330. IEEE, 2017. doi:10.1109/FOCS.2017.37 [p. 136]

[99] Peter Bürgisser, Michael Clausen, and Mohammad Amin Shokrollahi. *Algebraic Complexity Theory*. Grundlehren der mathematischen Wissenschaften. Springer, 1997. doi:10.1007/978-3-662-03338-8 [p. 682]

[100] Samuel Buss. The boolean formula value problem is in ALOGTIME. In *Proceedings of the 19th Symposium on Theory of Computing (STOC)*, pages 123–131. ACM, 1987. doi:10.1145/28395.28409 [p. 264]

[101] Samuel Buss, Stephen Cook, Arvind Gupta, and Vijaya Ramachandran. An optimal parallel algorithm for formula evaluation. *SIAM Journal on Computing*, 21(4):755–780, 1992. doi:10.1137/0221046 [p. 264]

[102] Samuel Buss and Ryan Williams. Limits on alternation trading proofs for time-space lower bounds. *Computational Complexity*, 24(3):533–600, 2015. doi:10.1007/s00037-015-0104-9 [p. 194]

[103] Jin-Yi Cai. $S_2^p \subseteq \mathrm{ZPP}^{\mathrm{NP}}$. *Journal of Computer and System Sciences*, 73(1):25–35, 2007. doi:10.1016/j.jcss.2003.07.015 [p. 309]

[104] Jin-Yi Cai and Richard Lipton. Subquadratic simulations of balanced formulae by branching programs. *SIAM Journal on Computing*, 23(3):563–572, 1994. doi:10.1137/S0097539790181336 [p. 264]

[105] Jin-Yi Cai and D. Sivakumar. Sparse hard sets for P: Resolution of a conjecture of Hartmanis. *Journal of Computer and System Sciences*, 58(2):280–296, 1999. doi:10.1006/jcss.1998.1615 [p. 231]

[106] Jin-Yi Cai and D. Sivakumar. Resolution of Hartmanis' conjecture for NL-hard sparse sets. *Theoretical Computer Science*, 240(2):257–269, 2000. doi:10.1016/S0304-3975(99)00234-0 [p. 231]

[107] Ran Canetti. More on BPP and the polynomial-time hierarchy. *Information Processing Letters*, 57(5):237–241, 1996. doi:10.1016/0020-0190(96)00016-6 [p. 309]

[108] Marco Carmosino, Russell Impagliazzo, Valentine Kabanets, and Antonina Kolokolova. Learning algorithms from natural proofs. In *Proceedings of the 31st Computational Complexity Conference (CCC)*, pages 10:1–10:24. Schloss Dagstuhl, 2016. doi:10.4230/LIPICS.CCC.2016.10 [p. 676]

[109] Larry Carter and Mark Wegman. Universal classes of hash functions. *Journal of Computer and System Sciences*, 18(2):143–154, 1979. doi:10.1016/0022-0000(79)90044-8 [p. 331]

[110] Gregory Chaitin. On the simplicity and speed of programs for computing infinite sets of natural numbers. *Journal of the ACM*, 16(3):407–422, 1969. doi:10.1145/321526.321530 [p. 682]

[111] Sourav Chakraborty, N. V. Vinodchandran, and Kuldeep Meel. Distinct elements in streams: An algorithm for the (text) book. In *Proceedings of the 30th European Symposium on Algorithms (ESA)*, pages 34:1–34:6. Schloss Dagstuhl, 2022. doi:10.4230/LIPICS.ESA.2022.34 [p. 331]

[112] Ashok Chandra, Dexter Kozen, and Larry Stockmeyer. Alternation. *Journal of the ACM*, 28(1):114–133, 1981. doi:10.1145/322234.322243 [p. 161]

[113] Arkadev Chattopadhyay, Yogesh Dahiya, Nikhil Mande, Jaikumar Radhakrishnan, and Swagato Sanyal. Randomized versus deterministic decision tree size. In *Proceedings of the 55th Symposium on Theory of Computing (STOC)*, pages 867–880. ACM, 2023. doi:10.1145/3564246.3585199 [p. 617]

[114] Eshan Chattopadhyay. Recent advances in randomness extraction. *Entropy*, 24(7):880, 2022. doi:10.3390/e24070880 [p. 423]

[115] Eshan Chattopadhyay and Jesse Goodman. Improved extractors for small-space sources. In *Proceedings of the 62nd Symposium on Foundations of Computer Science (FOCS)*, pages 610–621. IEEE, 2021. doi:10.1109/FOCS52979.2021.00066 [p. 424]

[116] Eshan Chattopadhyay and David Zuckerman. Explicit two-source extractors and resilient functions. *Annals of Mathematics*, 189(3):653–705, 2019. doi:10.4007/annals.2019.189.3.1 [p. 424]

[117] Hubie Chen. *Computability and Complexity*. MIT Press, 2023. [p. 71]

[118] Lijie Chen, Ce Jin, Ryan Williams, and Hongxun Wu. Truly low-space element distinctness and subset sum via pseudorandom hash functions. In *Proceedings of the 33rd Symposium on Discrete Algorithms (SODA)*, pages 1661–1678. SIAM, 2022. doi:10.1137/1.9781611977073.67 [p. 308]

[119] Lijie Chen and Roei Tell. Simple and fast derandomization from very hard functions: Eliminating randomness at almost no cost. In *Proceedings of the 53rd Symposium on Theory of Computing (STOC)*, pages 283–291. ACM, 2021. doi:10.1145/3406325.3451059 [p. 424]

[120] Lijie Chen and Roei Tell. New ways of studying the BPP = P conjecture. *SIGACT News*, 54(2):44–69, 2023. doi:10.1145/3604943.3604950 [p. 423]

[121] Kuan Cheng and William Hoza. Hitting sets give two-sided derandomization of small space. *Theory of Computing*, 18(21):1–32, 2022. doi:10.4086/toc.2022.v018a021 [p. 424]

[122] Kuan Cheng and Yichuan Wang. $\mathrm{BPL} \subseteq \mathrm{L\text{-}AC}^1$. In *Proceedings of the 39th Computational Complexity Conference (CCC)*, pages 32:1–32:14. Schloss Dagstuhl, 2024. doi:10.4230/LIPICS.CCC.2024.32 [p. 309]

[123] Herman Chernoff. A measure of asymptotic efficiency for tests of a hypothesis based on the sum of observations. *Annals of Mathematical Statistics*, 23(4):493–507, 1952. doi:10.1214/aoms/1177729330 [p. 309]

[124] Andrew Chiu, George Davida, and Bruce Litow. Division in logspace-uniform NC^1. *RAIRO - Theoretical Informatics and Applications*, 35(3):259–275, 2001. doi:10.1051/ita:2001119 [pp. 71, 264]

[125] Benny Chor and Oded Goldreich. Unbiased bits from sources of weak randomness and probabilistic communication complexity. *SIAM Journal on Computing*, 17(2):230–261, 1988. doi:10.1137/0217015 [pp. 424, 645]

[126] Benny Chor and Oded Goldreich. On the power of two-point based sampling. *Journal of Complexity*, 5(1):96–106, 1989. doi:10.1016/0885-064X(89)90015-0 [p. 331]

[127] Benny Chor, Oded Goldreich, Johan Håstad, Joel Friedman, Steven Rudich, and Roman Smolensky. The bit extraction problem or t-resilient functions. In *Proceedings of the 26th Symposium on Foundations of Computer Science (FOCS)*, pages 396–407. IEEE, 1985. doi:10.1109/SFCS.1985.55 [p. 424]

[128] Moon-Jung Chung and Bala Ravikumar. Strong nondeterministic Turing reduction—A technique for proving intractability. *Journal of Computer and System Sciences*, 39(1):2–20, 1989. doi:10.1016/0022-0000(89)90017-2 [p. 135]

[129] Vasek Chvátal. A greedy heuristic for the set-covering problem. *Mathematics of Operations Research*, 4(3):233–235, 1979. doi:10.1287/MOOR.4.3.233 [p. 542]

[130] Richard Cleve. Towards optimal simulations of formulas by bounded-width programs. *Computational Complexity*, 1:91–105, 1991. doi:10.1007/BF01200059 [p. 264]

[131] Alan Cobham. The intrinsic computational difficulty of functions. *Logic, Methodology, and Philosophy of Science*, pages 24–30, 1965. [p. 72]

[132] Alan Cobham. The recognition problem for the set of perfect squares. In *Proceedings of the 7th Symposium on Switching and Automata Theory (SWAT/FOCS)*, pages 78–87. IEEE, 1966. doi:10.1109/SWAT.1966.30 [p. 231]

[133] Aviad Cohen and Avi Wigderson. Dispersers, deterministic amplification, and weak random sources. In *Proceedings of the 30th Symposium on Foundations of Computer Science (FOCS)*, pages 14–19. IEEE, 1989. doi:10.1109/SFCS.1989.63449 [p. 331]

[134] Beate Commentz-Walter. Size-depth tradeoff in monotone boolean formulae. *Acta Informatica*, 12(3):227–243, 1979. doi:10.1007/BF00264580 [p. 264]

[135] Beate Commentz-Walter and Jürgen Sattler. Size-depth tradeoff in non-monotone boolean formulae. *Acta Informatica*, 14(3):257–269, 1980. doi:10.1007/BF00264256 [p. 264]

[136] Stephen Cook. The complexity of theorem-proving procedures. In *Proceedings of the 3rd Symposium on Theory of Computing (STOC)*, pages 151–158. ACM, 1971. doi:10.1145/800157.805047 [pp. 72, 135]

[137] Stephen Cook. A hierarchy for nondeterministic time complexity. *Journal of Computer and System Sciences*, 7(4):343–353, 1973. doi:10.1016/S0022-0000(73)80028-5 [p. 194]

[138] Stephen Cook and Pierre McKenzie. Problems complete for deterministic logarithmic space. *Journal of Algorithms*, 8(3):385–394, 1987. doi:10.1016/0196-6774(87)90018-6 [p. 264]

[139] Stephen Cook and Phuong Nguyen. *Logical Foundations of Proof Complexity*. Perspectives in Logic. Cambridge University Press, 2010. doi:10.1017/CBO9780511676277 [p. 682]

[140] Stephen Cook and Robert Reckhow. Time bounded random access machines. *Journal of Computer and System Sciences*, 7(4):354–375, 1973. doi:10.1016/S0022-0000(73)80029-7 [p. 71]

[141] Anirban Dasgupta, Ravi Kumar, and D. Sivakumar. Sparse and lopsided set disjointness via information theory. In *Proceedings of the 16th International Workshop on Randomization and Computation (RANDOM)*, pages 517–528. Springer, 2012. doi:10.1007/978-3-642-32512-0_44 [p. 645]

[142] Holger Dell, Valentine Kabanets, Dieter van Melkebeek, and Osamu Watanabe. Is Valiant–Vazirani's isolation probability improvable? *Computational Complexity*, 22(2):345–383, 2013. doi:10.1007/s00037-013-0059-7 [p. 331]

[143] Richard DeMillo and Richard Lipton. A probabilistic remark on algebraic program testing. *Information Processing Letters*, 7(4):193–195, 1978. doi:10.1016/0020-0190(78)90067-4 [p. 308]

[144] Scott Diehl and Dieter van Melkebeek. Time-space lower bounds for the polynomial-time hierarchy on randomized machines. *SIAM Journal on Computing*, 36(3):563–594, 2006. doi:10.1137/050642228 [p. 309]

[145] Irit Dinur. The PCP theorem by gap amplification. *Journal of the ACM*, 54(3):12:1–12:44, 2007. doi:10.1145/1236457.1236459 [p. 543]

[146] Irit Dinur, Subhash Khot, Guy Kindler, Dor Minzer, and Muli Safra. Towards a proof of the 2-to-1 games conjecture? In *Proceedings of the 50th Symposium on Theory of Computing (STOC)*, pages 376–389. ACM, 2018. doi:10.1145/3188745.3188804 [p. 542]

[147] Irit Dinur and Shmuel Safra. On the hardness of approximating minimum vertex cover. *Annals of Mathematics*, 162(1):439–485, 2005. doi:10.4007/annals.2005.162.439 [p. 542]

[148] Irit Dinur and David Steurer. Analytical approach to parallel repetition. In *Proceedings of the 46th Symposium on Theory of Computing (STOC)*, pages 624–633. ACM, 2014. doi:10.1145/2591796.2591884 [p. 542]

[149] Ding-Zhu Du and Ker-I Ko. *Theory of Computational Complexity*. Wiley, 2nd edition, 2014. doi:10.1002/9781118595091 [p. 71]

[150] Devdatt Dubhashi and Alessandro Panconesi. *Concentration of Measure for the Analysis of Randomized Algorithms*. Cambridge University Press, 2009. doi:10.1017/CBO9780511581274 [p. 309]

[151] Paul Dunne. *Techniques for the Analysis of Monotone Boolean Networks*. PhD thesis, University of Warwick, 1984. [p. 675]

[152] Patrick Dymond and Martin Tompa. Speedups of deterministic machines by synchronous parallel machines. *Journal of Computer and System Sciences*, 30(2):149–161, 1985. doi:10.1016/0022-0000(85)90011-X [p. 264]

[153] Jack Edmonds. Paths, trees, and flowers. *Canadian Journal of Mathematics*, 17:449–467, 1965. doi:10.4153/CJM-1965-045-4 [p. 72]

[154] Jack Edmonds. Optimum branchings. *Journal of Research of the National Bureau of Standards*, 71B(4):233–240, 1967. doi:10.6028/jres.071b.032 [p. 72]

[155] Klim Efremenko. 3-query locally decodable codes of subexponential length. *SIAM Journal on Computing*, 41(6):1694–1703, 2012. doi:10.1137/090772721 [p. 384]

[156] Andrzej Ehrenfeucht, David Haussler, Michael Kearns, and Leslie Valiant. A general lower bound on the number of examples needed for learning. *Information and Computation*, 82(3):247–261, 1989. doi:10.1016/0890-5401(89)90002-3 [p. 505]

[157] Paul Erdős and Richard Rado. Intersection theorems for systems of sets. *Journal of the London Mathematical Society*, 35(1):85–90, 1960. doi:10.1112/jlms/s1-35.1.85 [p. 676]

[158] Shimon Even, Alon Itai, and Adi Shamir. On the complexity of timetable and multicommodity flow problems. *SIAM Journal on Computing*, 5(4):691–703, 1976. doi:10.1137/0205048 [p. 135]

[159] Shimon Even and Robert Tarjan. A combinatorial problem which is complete in polynomial space. *Journal of the ACM*, 23(4):710–719, 1976. doi:10.1145/321978.321989 [p. 161]

[160] Uriel Feige, Prabhakar Raghavan, David Peleg, and Eli Upfal. Computing with noisy information. *SIAM Journal on Computing*, 23(5):1001–1018, 1994. doi:10.1137/S0097539791195877 [p. 645]

[161] Joan Feigenbaum and Lance Fortnow. Random-self-reducibility of complete sets. *SIAM Journal on Computing*, 22(5):994–1005, 1993. doi:10.1137/0222061 [pp. 384, 576]

[162] Philippe Flajolet, Éric Fusy, Olivier Gandouet, and Frédéric Meunier. HyperLogLog: The analysis of a near-optimal cardinality estimation algorithm. *Discrete Mathematics and Theoretical Computer Science Proceedings*, AH:137–156, 2007. Conference on Analysis of Algorithms. doi:10.46298/dmtcs.3545 [p. 331]

[163] Philippe Flajolet and G. Nigel Martin. Probabilistic counting algorithms for data base applications. *Journal of Computer and System Sciences*, 31(2):182–209, 1985. doi:10.1016/0022-0000(85)90041-8 [p. 331]

[164] Jörg Flum and Martin Grohe. *Parameterized Complexity Theory*. Springer, 2006. doi:10.1007/3-540-29953-X [p. 682]

[165] Lance Fortnow. Counting complexity. In *Complexity Theory Retrospective II*, pages 81–107. Springer, 1998. [p. 682]

[166] Lance Fortnow. Time-space tradeoffs for satisfiability. *Journal of Computer and System Sciences*, 60(2):337–353, 2000. doi:10.1006/jcss.1999.1671 [p. 194]

[167] Lance Fortnow, Richard Lipton, Dieter van Melkebeek, and Anastasios Viglas. Time-space lower bounds for satisfiability. *Journal of the ACM*, 52(6):835–865, 2005. doi:10.1145/1101821.1101822 [p. 194]

[168] Lance Fortnow, John Rompel, and Michael Sipser. On the power of multi-prover interactive protocols. *Theoretical Computer Science*, 134(2):545–557, 1994. doi:10.1016/0304-3975(94)90251-8 [p. 576]

[169] Steven Fortune. A note on sparse complete sets. *SIAM Journal on Computing*, 8(3):431–433, 1979. doi:10.1137/0208034 [p. 231]

[170] Steven Fortune, John Hopcroft, and James Wyllie. The directed subgraph homeomorphism problem. *Theoretical Computer Science*, 10(2):111–121, 1980. doi:10.1016/0304-3975(80)90009-2 [pp. 136, 542]

[171] Aviezri Fraenkel and David Lichtenstein. Computing a perfect strategy for $n \times n$ chess requires time exponential in n. *Journal of Combinatorial Theory, Series A*, 31(2):199–214, 1981. doi:10.1016/0097-3165(81)90016-9 [p. 161]

[172] Aviezri Fraenkel, Edward Scheinerman, and Daniel Ullman. Undirected edge geography. *Theoretical Computer Science*, 112(2):371–381, 1993. doi:10.1016/0304-3975(93)90026-P [p. 161]

[173] Michael Fredman and Dan Willard. Surpassing the information theoretic bound with fusion trees. *Journal of Computer and System Sciences*, 47(3):424–436, 1993. doi:10.1016/0022-0000(93)90040-4 [p. 71]

[174] Rūsiņš Freivalds. Probabilistic machines can use less running time. In *Proceedings of the 7th International Federation for Information Processing (IFIP) Congress*, pages 839–842. North–Holland, 1977. [p. 308]

[175] Yoav Freund and Robert Schapire. A decision-theoretic generalization of on-line learning and an application to boosting. *Journal of Computer and System Sciences*, 55(1):119–139, 1997. doi:10.1006/jcss.1997.1504 [p. 505]

[176] Joel Friedman. Constructing $O(n \log n)$ size monotone formulae for the k-th threshold function of n boolean variables. *SIAM Journal on Computing*, 15(3):641–654, 1986. doi:10.1137/0215047 [p. 676]

[177] Alan Frieze and Colin McDiarmid. Algorithmic theory of random graphs. *Random Structures and Algorithms*, 10(1-2):5–42, 1997. doi:10.1002/(SICI)1098-2418(199701/03)10:1/2<5::AID-RSA2>3.0.CO;2-Z [p. 383]

[178] Martin Fürer. Faster integer multiplication. *SIAM Journal on Computing*, 39(3):979–1005, 2009. doi:10.1137/070711761 [p. 71]

[179] Martin Fürer, Oded Goldreich, Yishay Mansour, Michael Sipser, and Stathis Zachos. On completeness and soundness in interactive proof systems. *Advances in Computing Research*, 5:429–442, 1989. [p. 576]

[180] Merrick Furst, James Saxe, and Michael Sipser. Parity, circuits, and the polynomial-time hierarchy. *Mathematical Systems Theory*, 17(1):13–27, 1984. doi:10.1007/BF01744431 [p. 675]

[181] Ariel Gabizon, Ran Raz, and Ronen Shaltiel. Deterministic extractors for bit-fixing sources by obtaining an independent seed. *SIAM Journal on Computing*, 36(4):1072–1094, 2006. doi:10.1137/S0097539705447049 [p. 424]

[182] Michael Garey and David Johnson. *Computers and Intractability: A Guide to the Theory of NP-Completeness*. W. H. Freeman, 1979. [p. 135]

[183] Michael Garey, David Johnson, and Larry Stockmeyer. Some simplified NP-complete graph problems. *Theoretical Computer Science*, 1(3):237–267, 1976. doi:10.1016/0304-3975(76)90059-1 [p. 135]

[184] Serge Gaspers, Zixu He, and Simon Mackenzie. NP-hardness and ETH-based inapproximability of communication complexity via relaxed interlacing. Technical Report 2508.05597, arXiv, 2025. [p. 646]

[185] Peter Gemmell, Richard Lipton, Ronitt Rubinfeld, Madhu Sudan, and Avi Wigderson. Self-testing/correcting for polynomials and for approximate functions. In *Proceedings of the 23rd Symposium on Theory of Computing (STOC)*, pages 32–42. ACM, 1991. doi:10.1145/103418.103429 [p. 384]

[186] Peter Gemmell and Madhu Sudan. Highly resilient correctors for polynomials. *Information Processing Letters*, 43(4):169–174, 1992. doi:10.1016/0020-0190(92)90195-2 [p. 384]

[187] Edgar Gilbert. A comparison of signalling alphabets. *Bell System Technical Journal*, 31(3):504–522, 1952. doi:10.1002/j.1538-7305.1952.tb01393.x [p. 358]

[188] John Gilbert, Thomas Lengauer, and Robert Tarjan. The pebbling problem is complete in polynomial space. *SIAM Journal on Computing*, 9(3):513–524, 1980. doi:10.1137/0209038 [p. 161]

[189] John Gill. Computational complexity of probabilistic Turing machines. *SIAM Journal on Computing*, 6(4):675–695, 1977. doi:10.1137/0206049 [p. 309]

[190] Justin Gilmer, Michael Saks, and Srikanth Srinivasan. Composition limits and separating examples for some boolean function complexity measures. *Combinatorica*, 36(3):265–311, 2016. doi:10.1007/S00493-014-3189-X [p. 617]

[191] Michel Goemans and David Williamson. New 3/4-approximation algorithms for the maximum satisfiability problem. *SIAM Journal on Discrete Mathematics*, 7(4):656–666, 1994. doi:10.1137/S0895480192243516 [p. 542]

[192] Michel Goemans and David Williamson. Improved approximation algorithms for maximum cut and satisfiability problems using semidefinite programming. *Journal of the ACM*, 42(6):1115–1145, 1995. doi:10.1145/227683.227684 [pp. 542, 543]

[193] Mikael Goldmann and Johan Håstad. A simple lower bound for monotone clique using a communication game. *Information Processing Letters*, 41(4):221–226, 1992. doi:10.1016/0020-0190(92)90184-W [p. 676]

[194] Oded Goldreich. *The Foundations of Cryptography: Volume 1, Basic Techniques*. Cambridge University Press, 2001. doi:10.1017/CBO9780511546891 [p. 456]

[195] Oded Goldreich. *The Foundations of Cryptography: Volume 2, Basic Applications*. Cambridge University Press, 2004. doi:10.1017/CBO9780511721656 [p. 456]

[196] Oded Goldreich. *Computational Complexity: A Conceptual Perspective*. Cambridge University Press, 2008. doi:10.1017/CBO9780511804106 [p. 71]

[197] Oded Goldreich. In a world of P = BPP. In *Studies in Complexity and Cryptography*, pages 191–232. Springer, 2011. doi:10.1007/978-3-642-22670-0_20 [p. 424]

[198] Oded Goldreich. *Introduction to Property Testing*. Cambridge University Press, 2017. doi:10.1017/9781108135252 [p. 682]

[199] Oded Goldreich. On doubly-efficient interactive proof systems. *Foundations and Trends in Theoretical Computer Science*, 13(3):158–246, 2018. doi:10.1561/0400000084 [p. 576]

[200] Oded Goldreich. Two comments on targeted canonical derandomizers. In *Computational Complexity and Property Testing*, pages 24–35. Springer, 2020. doi:10.1007/978-3-030-43662-9_4 [p. 424]

[201] Oded Goldreich, Shafi Goldwasser, and Silvio Micali. How to construct random functions. *Journal of the ACM*, 33(4):792–807, 1986. doi:10.1145/6490.6503 [p. 457]

[202] Oded Goldreich and Leonid Levin. A hard-core predicate for all one-way functions. In *Proceedings of the 21st Symposium on Theory of Computing (STOC)*, pages 25–32. ACM, 1989. doi:10.1145/73007.73010 [pp. 331, 456]

[203] Oded Goldreich, Silvio Micali, and Avi Wigderson. Proofs that yield nothing but their validity or all languages in NP have zero-knowledge proof systems. *Journal of the ACM*, 38(3):691–729, 1991. doi:10.1145/116825.116852 [p. 576]

[204] Oded Goldreich, Noam Nisan, and Avi Wigderson. On Yao's XOR-Lemma. In *Studies in Complexity and Cryptography*, pages 273–301. Springer, 2011. doi:10.1007/978-3-642-22670-0_23 [p. 384]

[205] Oded Goldreich and Guy Rothblum. Simple doubly-efficient interactive proof systems for locally-characterizable sets. In *Proceedings of the 9th Innovations in Theoretical Computer Science Conference (ITCS)*, pages 18:1–18:19. Schloss Dagstuhl, 2018. doi:10.4230/LIPICS.ITCS.2018.18 [p. 576]

[206] Oded Goldreich, Salil Vadhan, and Avi Wigderson. Simplified derandomization of BPP using a hitting set generator. In *Studies in Complexity and Cryptography*, pages 59–67. Springer, 2011. doi:10.1007/978-3-642-22670-0_8 [p. 424]

[207] Shafi Goldwasser and Silvio Micali. Probabilistic encryption. *Journal of Computer and System Sciences*, 28(2):270–299, 1984. doi:10.1016/0022-0000(84)90070-9 [p. 456]

[208] Shafi Goldwasser, Silvio Micali, and Charles Rackoff. The knowledge complexity of interactive proof systems. *SIAM Journal on Computing*, 18(1):186–208, 1989. doi:10.1137/0218012 [p. 576]

[209] Shafi Goldwasser and Michael Sipser. Private coins versus public coins in interactive proof systems. *Advances in Computing Research*, 5:73–90, 1989. [pp. 331, 576]

[210] Shafi Goldwasser, Yael Tauman Kalai, and Guy Rothblum. Delegating computation: Interactive proofs for muggles. *Journal of the ACM*, 62(4):27:1–27:64, 2015. doi:10.1145/2699436 [p. 576]

[211] Mika Göös and T. S. Jayram. A composition theorem for conical juntas. In *Proceedings of the 31st Computational Complexity Conference (CCC)*, pages 5:1–5:16. Schloss Dagstuhl, 2016. doi:10.4230/LIPICS.CCC.2016.5 [p. 616]

[212] Mika Göös, T. S. Jayram, Toniann Pitassi, and Thomas Watson. Randomized communication vs. partition number. *ACM Transactions on Computation Theory*, 10(1):4:1–4:20, 2018. doi:10.1145/3170711 [p. 645]

[213] Mika Göös, Pritish Kamath, Toniann Pitassi, and Thomas Watson. Query-to-communication lifting for P^{NP}. *Computational Complexity*, 28(1):113–144, 2019. doi:10.1007/S00037-018-0175-5 [p. 506]

[214] Mika Göös, Pritish Kamath, Robert Robere, and Dmitry Sokolov. Adventures in monotone complexity and TFNP. In *Proceedings of the 10th Innovations in Theoretical Computer Science Conference (ITCS)*, pages 38:1–38:19. Schloss Dagstuhl, 2019. doi:10.4230/LIPICS.ITCS.2019.38 [p. 676]

[215] Mika Göös, Toniann Pitassi, and Thomas Watson. Deterministic communication vs. partition number. *SIAM Journal on Computing*, 47(6):2435–2450, 2018. doi:10.1137/16M1059369 [pp. 617, 645]

[216] Mika Göös and Thomas Watson. Communication complexity of set-disjointness for all probabilities. *Theory of Computing*, 12(1):1–23, 2016. doi:10.4086/TOC.2016.V012A009 [p. 646]

[217] Parikshit Gopalan, Raghu Meka, Omer Reingold, Luca Trevisan, and Salil Vadhan. Better pseudorandom generators from milder pseudorandom restrictions. In *Proceedings of the 53rd Symposium on Foundations of Computer Science (FOCS)*, pages 120–129. IEEE, 2012. doi:10.1109/FOCS.2012.77 [p. 384]

[218] Craig Gotsman and Nathan Linial. The equivalence of two problems on the cube. *Journal of Combinatorial Theory, Series A*, 61(1):142–146, 1992. doi:10.1016/0097-3165(92)90060-8 [p. 616]

[219] Raymond Greenlaw, H. James Hoover, and Walter Ruzzo. *Limits to Parallel Computation: P-Completeness Theory*. Oxford University Press, 1995. doi:10.1093/oso/9780195085914.001.0001 [p. 231]

[220] Michelangelo Grigni and Michael Sipser. Monotone separation of logarithmic space from logarithmic depth. *Journal of Computer and System Sciences*, 50(3):433–437, 1995. doi:10.1006/jcss.1995.1033 [pp. 645, 676]

[221] Geoffrey Grimmett and Colin McDiarmid. On colouring random graphs. *Mathematical Proceedings of the Cambridge Philosophical Society*, 77(2):313–324, 1975. doi:10.1017/S0305004100051124 [p. 383]

[222] Mikhail Grinchuk. Sharpening an upper bound on the adder and comparator depths. *Journal of Applied and Industrial Mathematics*, 3(1):61–67, 2009. doi:10.1134/S1990478909010086 [p. 264]

[223] Joshua Grochow. NP-hard sets are not sparse unless P = NP: An exposition of a simple proof of Mahaney's theorem, with applications. Technical Report TR16-162, Electronic Colloquium on Computational Complexity (ECCC), 2016. [p. 231]

[224] Lov Grover. A fast quantum mechanical algorithm for database search. In *Proceedings of the 28th Symposium on Theory of Computing (STOC)*, pages 212–219. ACM, 1996. doi:10.1145/237814.237866 [p. 683]

[225] David Guijarro, Víctor Lavín, and Vijay Raghavan. Exact learning when irrelevant variables abound. *Information Processing Letters*, 70(5):233–239, 1999. doi:10.1016/S0020-0190(99)00063-0 [p. 617]

[226] Venkatesan Guruswami, Sanjeev Khanna, Rajmohan Rajaraman, Bruce Shepherd, and Mihalis Yannakakis. Near-optimal hardness results and approximation algorithms for edge-disjoint paths and related problems. *Journal of Computer and System Sciences*, 67(3):473–496, 2003. doi:10.1016/S0022-0000(03)00066-7 [p. 542]

[227] Venkatesan Guruswami, Christopher Umans, and Salil Vadhan. Unbalanced expanders and randomness extractors from Parvaresh–Vardy codes. *Journal of the ACM*, 56(4):20:1–20:34, 2009. doi:10.1145/1538902.1538904 [p. 424]

[228] Dan Gutfreund, Ronen Shaltiel, and Amnon Ta-Shma. If NP languages are hard on the worst-case, then it is easy to find their hard instances. *Computational Complexity*, 16(4):412–441, 2007. doi:10.1007/s00037-007-0235-8 [p. 384]

[229] Péter Hajnal. An $\Omega(n^{4/3})$ lower bound on the randomized complexity of graph properties. *Combinatorica*, 11(2):131–143, 1991. doi:10.1007/BF01206357 [p. 616]

[230] Bernd Halstenberg and Rüdiger Reischuk. Different modes of communication. *SIAM Journal on Computing*, 22(5):913–934, 1993. doi:10.1137/0222057 [p. 646]

[231] Richard Hamming. Error detecting and error correcting codes. *Bell System Technical Journal*, 29(2):147–160, 1950. doi:10.1002/j.1538-7305.1950.tb00463.x [p. 359]

[232] Steve Hanneke. The optimal sample complexity of PAC learning. *Journal of Machine Learning Research*, 17(38):1–15, 2016. [p. 505]

[233] Juris Hartmanis and Lane Hemachandra. One-way functions and the nonisomorphism of NP-complete sets. *Theoretical Computer Science*, 81(1):155–163, 1991. doi:10.1016/0304-3975(91)90323-T [p. 616]

[234] Juris Hartmanis and Richard Stearns. On the computational complexity of algorithms. *Transactions of the American Mathematical Society*, 117:285–306, 1965. [p. 194]

[235] David Harvey and Joris van der Hoeven. Integer multiplication in time $O(n \log n)$. *Annals of Mathematics*, 193(2):563–617, 2021. doi:https://doi.org/10.4007/annals.2021.193.2.4 [p. 71]

[236] Johan Håstad. Almost optimal lower bounds for small depth circuits. In *Proceedings of the 18th Symposium on Theory of Computing (STOC)*, pages 6–20. ACM, 1986. doi:10.1145/12130.12132 [p. 675]

[237] Johan Håstad. The shrinkage exponent of De Morgan formulas is 2. *SIAM Journal on Computing*, 27(1):48–64, 1998. doi:10.1137/S0097539794261556 [p. 675]

[238] Johan Håstad. Clique is hard to approximate within $n^{1-\varepsilon}$. *Acta Mathematica*, 182(1):105–142, 1999. doi:10.1007/BF02392825 [p. 542]

[239] Johan Håstad. Some optimal inapproximability results. *Journal of the ACM*, 48(4):798–859, 2001. doi:10.1145/502090.502098 [p. 542]

[240] Johan Håstad, Russell Impagliazzo, Leonid Levin, and Michael Luby. A pseudorandom generator from any one-way function. *SIAM Journal on Computing*, 28(4):1364–1396, 1999. doi:10.1137/S0097539793244708 [pp. 424, 456]

[241] Pooya Hatami and William Hoza. Paradigms for unconditional pseudorandom generators. *Foundations and Trends in Theoretical Computer Science*, 16(1-2):1–210, 2024. doi:10.1561/0400000109 [pp. 423, 424]

[242] Alexander Healy, Salil Vadhan, and Emanuele Viola. Using nondeterminism to amplify hardness. *SIAM Journal on Computing*, 35(4):903–931, 2006. doi:10.1137/S0097539705447281 [p. 384]

[243] Shuichi Hirahara. Average-case hardness of NP from exponential worst-case hardness assumptions. In *Proceedings of the 53rd Symposium on Theory of Computing (STOC)*, pages 292–302. ACM, 2021. doi:10.1145/3406325.3451065 [p. 384]

[244] Shuichi Hirahara. NP-hardness of learning programs and partial MCSP. In *Proceedings of the 63rd Symposium on Foundations of Computer Science (FOCS)*, pages 968–979. IEEE, 2022. doi:10.1109/FOCS54457.2022.00095 [p. 457]

[245] Shuichi Hirahara, Rahul Ilango, and Bruno Loff. Communication complexity is NP-hard. Technical Report TR25-094, Electronic Colloquium on Computational Complexity (ECCC), 2025. [p. 646]

[246] Dorit Hochbaum, editor. *Approximation Algorithms for NP-Hard Problems*. PWS Publishing Company, 1997. [p. 542]

[247] Wassily Hoeffding. Probability inequalities for sums of bounded random variables. *Journal of the American Statistical Association*, 58(301):13–30, 1963. doi:10.1080/01621459.1963.10500830 [p. 309]

[248] Thomas Holenstein. Parallel repetition: Simplification and the no-signaling case. *Theory of Computing*, 5(1):141–172, 2009. doi:10.4086/toc.2009.v005a008 [p. 542]

[249] Steven Homer and Alan Selman. *Computability and Complexity Theory*. Texts in Computer Science. Springer, 2nd edition, 2011. doi:10.1007/978-1-4614-0682-2 [p. 71]

[250] Shlomo Hoory, Nathan Linial, and Avi Wigderson. Expander graphs and their applications. *Bulletin of the Americal Mathematical Society*, 43:439–561, 2006. doi:10.1090/S0273-0979-06-01126-8 [p. 682]

[251] Shlomo Hoory, Avner Magen, and Toniann Pitassi. Monotone circuits for the majority function. In *Proceedings of the 10th International Workshop on Randomization and Computation (RANDOM)*, pages 410–425. Springer, 2006. doi:10.1007/11830924_38 [p. 264]

[252] John Hopcroft, Rajeev Motwani, and Jeffrey Ullman. *Introduction to Automata Theory, Languages, and Computation*. Pearson, 3rd edition, 2006. [p. 71]

[253] John Hopcroft, Wolfgang Paul, and Leslie Valiant. On time versus space. *Journal of the ACM*, 24(2):332–337, 1977. doi:10.1145/322003.322015 [p. 161]

[254] William Hoza. Better pseudodistributions and derandomization for space-bounded computation. In *Proceedings of the 25th International Conference on Randomization and Computation (RANDOM)*, pages 28:1–28:23. Schloss Dagstuhl, 2021. doi:10.4230/LIPICS.APPROX/RANDOM.2021.28 [p. 309]

[255] Hao Huang. Induced subgraphs of hypercubes and a proof of the sensitivity conjecture. *Annals of Mathematics*, 190(3):949–955, 2019. doi:10.4007/annals.2019.190.3.6 [p. 616]

[256] W. Cary Huffman and Vera Pless. *Fundamentals of Error-Correcting Codes*. Cambridge University Press, 2003. doi:10.1017/CBO9780511807077 [p. 358]

[257] Rahul Ilango, Bruno Loff, and Igor Oliveira. NP-hardness of circuit minimization for multi-output functions. In *Proceedings of the 35th Computational Complexity Conference (CCC)*, pages 22:1–22:36. Schloss Dagstuhl, 2020. doi:10.4230/LIPICS.CCC.2020.22 [p. 646]

[258] Neil Immerman. Nondeterministic space is closed under complementation. *SIAM Journal on Computing*, 17(5):935–938, 1988. doi:10.1137/0217058 [p. 161]

[259] Russell Impagliazzo. Hard-core distributions for somewhat hard problems. In *Proceedings of the 36th Symposium on Foundations of Computer Science (FOCS)*, pages 538–545. IEEE, 1995. doi:10.1109/SFCS.1995.492584 [p. 384]

[260] Russell Impagliazzo. A personal view of average-case complexity. In *Proceedings of the 10th Structure in Complexity Theory Conference (STRUCTURES)*, pages 134–147. IEEE, 1995. doi:10.1109/SCT.1995.514853 [pp. 383, 457]

[261] Russell Impagliazzo, Valentine Kabanets, and Avi Wigderson. In search of an easy witness: Exponential time vs. probabilistic polynomial time. *Journal of Computer and System Sciences*, 65(4):672–694, 2002. doi:10.1016/S0022-0000(02)00024-7 [p. 309]

[262] Russell Impagliazzo and Leonid Levin. No better ways to generate hard NP instances than picking uniformly at random. In *Proceedings of the 31st Symposium on Foundations of Computer Science (FOCS)*, pages 812–821. IEEE, 1990. doi:10.1109/FSCS.1990.89604 [p. 383]

[263] Russell Impagliazzo and Michael Luby. One-way functions are essential for complexity based cryptography. In *Proceedings of the 30th Symposium on Foundations of Computer Science (FOCS)*, pages 230–235. IEEE, 1989. doi:10.1109/SFCS.1989.63483 [p. 456]

[264] Russell Impagliazzo, Noam Nisan, and Avi Wigderson. Pseudorandomness for network algorithms. In *Proceedings of the 26th Symposium on Theory of Computing (STOC)*, pages 356–364. ACM, 1994. doi:10.1145/195058.195190 [p. 424]

[265] Russell Impagliazzo and Avi Wigderson. P = BPP if E requires exponential circuits: Derandomizing the XOR lemma. In *Proceedings of the 29th Symposium on Theory of Computing (STOC)*, pages 220–229. ACM, 1997. doi:10.1145/258533.258590 [pp. 384, 424]

[266] Russell Impagliazzo and Moti Yung. Direct minimum-knowledge computations. In *Proceedings of the 7th International Cryptology Conference (CRYPTO)*, pages 40–51. Springer, 1987. doi:10.1007/3-540-48184-2_4 [p. 576]

[267] Russell Impagliazzo and David Zuckerman. How to recycle random bits. In *Proceedings of the 30th Symposium on Foundations of Computer Science (FOCS)*, pages 248–253. IEEE, 1989. doi:10.1109/SFCS.1989.63486 [p. 331]

[268] Shigeki Iwata and Takumi Kasai. The Othello game on an $n \times n$ board is PSPACE-complete. *Theoretical Computer Science*, 123(2):329–340, 1994. doi:10.1016/0304-3975(94)90131-7 [p. 161]

[269] Jeffrey Jackson. An efficient membership-query algorithm for learning DNF with respect to the uniform distribution. *Journal of Computer and System Sciences*, 55(3):414–440, 1997. doi:10.1006/JCSS.1997.1533 [p. 506]

[270] Zahra Jafargholi, Hamidreza Jahanjou, Eric Miles, Jaideep Ramachandran, and Emanuele Viola. From RAM to SAT. Technical Report TR12-125, Electronic Colloquium on Computational Complexity (ECCC), 2012. [p. 135]

[271] Rahul Jain, Zhengfeng Ji, Sarvagya Upadhyay, and John Watrous. QIP = PSPACE. *Journal of the ACM*, 58(6):30:1–30:27, 2011. doi:10.1145/2049697.2049704 [p. 683]

[272] Mark Jerrum, Alistair Sinclair, and Eric Vigoda. A polynomial-time approximation algorithm for the permanent of a matrix with nonnegative entries. *Journal of the ACM*, 51(4):671–697, 2004. doi:10.1145/1008731.1008738 [p. 683]

[273] Mark Jerrum, Leslie Valiant, and Vijay Vazirani. Random generation of combinatorial structures from a uniform distribution. *Theoretical Computer Science*, 43:169–188, 1986. doi:10.1016/0304-3975(86)90174-X [p. 331]

[274] David Johnson. Approximation algorithms for combinatorial problems. *Journal of Computer and System Sciences*, 9(3):256–278, 1974. doi:10.1016/S0022-0000(74)80044-9 [p. 542]

[275] David Johnson. The NP-completeness column: An ongoing guide. *Journal of Algorithms*, 3(3):288–300, 1982. doi:10.1016/0196-6774(82)90026-8 [p. 135]

[276] Selmer Johnson. A new upper bound for error-correcting codes. *IRE Transactions on Information Theory*, 8(3):203–207, 1962. doi:10.1109/TIT.1962.1057714 [p. 358]

[277] D. Joshi. A note on upper bounds for minimum distance codes. *Information and Control*, 1(3):289–295, 1958. doi:10.1016/S0019-9958(58)80006-6 [p. 358]

[278] Stasys Jukna. *Boolean Function Complexity: Advances and Frontiers*, volume 27 of *Algorithms and Combinatorics*. Springer, 2012. doi:10.1007/978-3-642-24508-4 [pp. 231, 675]

[279] Stasys Jukna, Alexander Razborov, Petr Savický, and Ingo Wegener. On P versus NP $\cap$ co-NP for decision trees and read-once branching programs. *Computational Complexity*, 8(4):357–370, 1999. doi:10.1007/S000370050005 [p. 617]

[280] Jørn Justesen. Class of constructive asymptotically good algebraic codes. *IEEE Transactions on Information Theory*, 18(5):652–656, 1972. doi:10.1109/TIT.1972.1054893 [p. 359]

[281] Valentine Kabanets and Jin-Yi Cai. Circuit minimization problem. In *Proceedings of the 32nd Symposium on Theory of Computing (STOC)*, pages 73–79. ACM, 2000. doi:10.1145/335305.335314 [p. 457]

[282] Valentine Kabanets and Russell Impagliazzo. Derandomizing polynomial identity tests means proving circuit lower bounds. *Computational Complexity*, 13(1-2):1–46, 2004. doi:10.1007/s00037-004-0182-6 [p. 309]

[283] Jeff Kahn, Michael Saks, and Dean Sturtevant. A topological approach to evasiveness. *Combinatorica*, 4(4):297–306, 1984. doi:10.1007/BF02579140 [p. 616]

[284] Bala Kalyanasundaram and Georg Schnitger. The probabilistic communication complexity of set intersection. *SIAM Journal on Discrete Mathematics*, 5(4):545–557, 1992. doi:10.1137/0405044 [p. 645]

[285] Jesse Kamp, Anup Rao, Salil Vadhan, and David Zuckerman. Deterministic extractors for small-space sources. *Journal of Computer and System Sciences*, 77(1):191–220, 2011. doi:10.1016/j.jcss.2010.06.014 [p. 424]

[286] Jesse Kamp and David Zuckerman. Deterministic extractors for bit-fixing sources and exposure-resilient cryptography. *SIAM Journal on Computing*, 36(5):1231–1247, 2007. doi:10.1137/S0097539705446846 [p. 424]

[287] Ravindran Kannan. Circuit-size lower bounds and non-reducibility to sparse sets. *Information and Control*, 55(1-3):40–56, 1982. doi:10.1016/S0019-9958(82)90382-5 [p. 231]

[288] Ravindran Kannan. Towards separating nondeterminism from determinism. *Mathematical Systems Theory*, 17(1):29–45, 1984. doi:10.1007/BF01744432 [p. 194]

[289] George Karakostas, Jeff Kinne, and Dieter van Melkebeek. On derandomization and average-case complexity of monotone functions. *Theoretical Computer Science*, 434:35–44, 2012. doi:10.1016/j.tcs.2012.02.017 [p. 424]

[290] Mauricio Karchmer, Ran Raz, and Avi Wigderson. Super-logarithmic depth lower bounds via the direct sum in communication complexity. *Computational Complexity*, 5(3-4):191–204, 1995. doi:10.1007/BF01206317 [p. 675]

[291] Mauricio Karchmer and Avi Wigderson. Monotone circuits for connectivity require super-logarithmic depth. *SIAM Journal on Discrete Mathematics*, 3(2):255–265, 1990. doi:10.1137/0403021 [p. 676]

[292] Richard Karp. Reducibility among combinatorial problems. In *Proceedings of a Symposium on the Complexity of Computer Computations*, pages 85–103, 1972. [pp. 72, 135, 194]

[293] Richard Karp and Richard Lipton. Turing machines that take advice. *L'Enseignement Matheématique*, 28:191–209, 1982. doi:10.5169/seals-52237 [p. 231]

[294] Richard Karp and Michael Luby. Monte-Carlo algorithms for enumeration and reliability problems. In *Proceedings of the 24th Symposium on Foundations of Computer Science (FOCS)*, pages 56–64. IEEE, 1983. doi:10.1109/SFCS.1983.35 [p. 331]

[295] Richard Karp, Eli Upfal, and Avi Wigderson. Constructing a perfect matching is in random NC. *Combinatorica*, 6(1):35–48, 1986. doi:10.1007/BF02579407 [p. 308]

[296] Jonathan Katz and Yehuda Lindell. *Introduction to Modern Cryptography*. CRC Press, 3rd edition, 2021. doi:10.1201/9781351133036 [p. 456]

[297] Jonathan Katz and Luca Trevisan. On the efficiency of local decoding procedures for error-correcting codes. In *Proceedings of the 32nd Symposium on Theory of Computing (STOC)*, pages 80–86. ACM, 2000. doi:10.1145/335305.335315 [p. 384]

[298] Phillip Kaye, Raymond Laflamme, and Michele Mosca. *An Introduction to Quantum Computing*. Oxford University Press, 2006. doi:10.1093/oso/9780198570004.001.0001 [p. 682]

[299] Michael Kearns and Umesh Vazirani. *An Introduction to Computational Learning Theory*. MIT Press, 1994. doi:10.7551/mitpress/3897.001.0001 [p. 505]

[300] Iordanis Kerenidis and Ronald de Wolf. Exponential lower bound for 2-query locally decodable codes via a quantum argument. *Journal of Computer and System Sciences*, 69(3):395–420, 2004. doi:10.1016/j.jcss.2004.04.007 [p. 384]

[301] L. S. Khasin. Complexity bounds for the realization of monotonic symmetrical functions by means of formulas in the basis $\vee$, &, $-$. *Soviet Physics – Doklady*, 14:1149–1151, 1970. [p. 676]

[302] Subhash Khot. On the power of unique 2-prover 1-round games. In *Proceedings of the 34th Symposium on Theory of Computing (STOC)*, pages 767–775. ACM, 2002. doi:10.1145/509907.510017 [p. 542]

[303] Subhash Khot, Guy Kindler, Elchanan Mossel, and Ryan O'Donnell. Optimal inapproximability results for MAX-CUT and other 2-variable CSPs? *SIAM Journal on Computing*, 37(1):319–357, 2007. doi:10.1137/S0097539705447372 [p. 543]

[304] Subhash Khot, Dor Minzer, and Muli Safra. On independent sets, 2-to-2 games, and Grassmann graphs. In *Proceedings of the 49th Symposium on Theory of Computing (STOC)*, pages 576–589. ACM, 2017. doi:10.1145/3055399.3055432 [p. 542]

[305] Subhash Khot, Dor Minzer, and Muli Safra. Pseudorandom sets in Grassmann graph have near-perfect expansion. In *Proceedings of the 59th Symposium on Foundations of Computer Science (FOCS)*, pages 592–601. IEEE, 2018. doi:10.1109/FOCS.2018.00062 [p. 542]

[306] Subhash Khot and Oded Regev. Vertex cover might be hard to approximate to within $2-\varepsilon$. *Journal of Computer and System Sciences*, 74(3):335–349, 2008. doi:10.1016/j.jcss.2007.06.019 [p. 542]

[307] Valerii Khrapchenko. Complexity of the realization of a linear function in the class of π-circuits. *Mathematical Notes of the Academy of Sciences of the USSR*, 9(1):21–23, 1971. doi:10.1007/BF01405045 [p. 676]

[308] Valerii Khrapchenko. Method of determining lower bounds for the complexity of π-schemes. *Mathematical Notes of the Academy of Sciences of the USSR*, 10:474–479, 1971. doi:10.1007/BF01747074 [p. 676]

[309] Valerii Khrapchenko. On a relation between the complexity and the depth of formulas. *Methods of Discrete Analysis in Synthesis of Control Systems*, 32:76–94, 1978. [p. 264]

[310] Alexei Kitaev, Alexander Shen, and Mikhail Vyalyi. *Classical and Quantum Computation*. American Mathematical Society, 2002. doi:10.1090/gsm/047 [p. 682]

[311] Jon Kleinberg. *Approximation Algorithms for Disjoint Paths Problems*. PhD thesis, Massachusetts Institute of Technology, 1996. [p. 542]

[312] Adam Klivans and Dieter van Melkebeek. Graph nonisomorphism has subexponential size proofs unless the polynomial-time hierarchy collapses. *SIAM Journal on Computing*, 31(5):1501–1526, 2002. doi:10.1137/S0097539700389652 [p. 576]

[313] Adam Klivans and Rocco Servedio. Boosting and hard-core set construction. *Machine Learning*, 51(3):217–238, 2003. doi:10.1023/A:1022949332276 [p. 384]

[314] Adam Klivans and Rocco Servedio. Learning DNF in time $2^{\widetilde{O}(n^{1/3})}$. *Journal of Computer and System Sciences*, 68(2):303–318, 2004. doi:10.1016/J.JCSS.2003.07.007 [p. 506]

[315] Ker-I Ko. Some observations on the probabilistic algorithms and NP-hard problems. *Information Processing Letters*, 14(1):39–43, 1982. doi:10.1016/0020-0190(82)90139-9 [p. 309]

[316] Konstantinos Koiliaris and Chao Xu. Faster pseudopolynomial time algorithms for subset sum. *ACM Transactions on Algorithms*, 15(3):40:1–40:20, 2019. doi:10.1145/3329863 [p. 135]

[317] Andrey Kolmogorov. Three approaches to the quantitative definition of information. *International Journal of Computer Mathematics*, 2(1-4):157–168, 1968. doi:10.1080/00207166808803030 [p. 682]

[318] Yasuo Komamiya. Application of logical mathematics to information theory. In *Proceedings of the 3rd Japan National Congress on Applied Mathematics*, page 437, 1953. [p. 358]

[319] Dexter Kozen. *Theory of Computation*. Texts in Computer Science. Springer, 2006. doi:10.1007/1-84628-477-5 [p. 71]

[320] Jan Krajíček. *Proof Complexity*. Number 170 in Encyclopedia of Mathematics and Its Applications. Cambridge University Press, 2019. doi:10.1017/bsl.2023.13 [p. 682]

[321] Ilan Kremer, Noam Nisan, and Dana Ron. On randomized one-round communication complexity. *Computational Complexity*, 8(1):21–49, 1999. doi:10.1007/S000370050018 [pp. 645, 646]

[322] Rafail Krichevskii. Complexity of contact circuits realizing a function of logical algebra. *Soviet Physics – Doklady*, 8:770–772, 1964. [p. 676]

[323] Melven Krom. The decision problem for a class of first-order formulas in which all disjunctions are binary. *Zeitschrift für Mathematische Logik und Grundlagen der Mathematik*, 13(1-2):15–20, 1967. doi:10.1002/malq.19670130104 [p. 135]

[324] Eyal Kushilevitz and Noam Nisan. *Communication Complexity*. Cambridge University Press, 1997. doi:10.1017/CBO9780511574948 [p. 645]

[325] Richard Ladner. On the structure of polynomial time reducibility. *Journal of the ACM*, 22(1):155–171, 1975. doi:10.1145/321864.321877 [pp. 136, 194]

[326] Kasper Green Larsen. Bagging is an optimal PAC learner. In *Proceedings of the 36th Conference on Learning Theory (COLT)*, pages 450–468. PMLR, 2023. [p. 505]

[327] Clemens Lautemann. BPP and the polynomial hierarchy. *Information Processing Letters*, 17(4):215–217, 1983. doi:10.1016/0020-0190(83)90044-3 [p. 309]

[328] Ryan Lavin, Xuekai Liu, Hardhik Mohanty, Logan Norman, Giovanni Zaarour, and Bhaskar Krishnamachari. A survey on the applications of zero-knowledge proofs. Technical Report 2408.00243, arXiv, 2024. [p. 576]

[329] Troy Lee and Adi Shraibman. Lower bounds in communication complexity. *Foundations and Trends in Theoretical Computer Science*, 3(4):263–398, 2009. doi:10.1561/0400000040 [p. 645]

[330] Jure Leskovec, Anand Rajaraman, and Jeffrey Ullman. *Mining of Massive Datasets*. Cambridge University Press, 3rd edition, 2020. doi:10.1017/9781108684163 [p. 331]

[331] Leonid Levin. Universal sequential search problems. *Problems of Information Transmission*, 9(3):265–266, 1973. [p. 135]

[332] Leonid Levin. Average case complete problems. *SIAM Journal on Computing*, 15(1):285–286, 1986. doi:10.1137/0215020 [p. 383]

[333] Leonid Levin. One-way functions and pseudorandom generators. *Combinatorica*, 7(4):357–363, 1987. doi:10.1007/BF02579323 [p. 384]

[334] Harry Lewis and Christos Papadimitriou. *Elements of the Theory of Computation*. Prentice Hall, 2nd edition, 1998. [p. 71]

[335] Ming Li and Paul Vitányi. *An Introduction to Kolmogorov Complexity and Its Applications*. Texts in Computer Science. Springer, 4th edition, 2019. doi:10.1007/978-3-030-11298-1 [p. 682]

[336] Xin Li. Two source extractors for asymptotically optimal entropy, and (many) more. In *Proceedings of the 64th Symposium on Foundations of Computer Science (FOCS)*, pages 1271–1281. IEEE, 2023. doi:10.1109/FOCS57990.2023.00075 [p. 424]

[337] David Lichtenstein and Michael Sipser. GO is polynomial-space hard. *Journal of the ACM*, 27(2):393–401, 1980. doi:10.1145/322186.322201 [p. 161]

[338] Nathan Linial, Yishay Mansour, and Noam Nisan. Constant depth circuits, Fourier transform, and learnability. *Journal of the ACM*, 40(3):607–620, 1993. doi:10.1145/174130.174138 [p. 675]

[339] Jacobus van Lint. *Introduction to Coding Theory*. Springer, 3rd edition, 1999. doi:10.1007/978-3-642-58575-3 [p. 358]

[340] Richard Lipton. New directions in testing. In *Distributed Computing And Cryptography*, volume 2 of *DIMACS Series in Discrete Mathematics and Theoretical Computer Science*, pages 191–202. DIMACS/AMS, 1989. doi:10.1090/dimacs/002/13 [p. 383]

[341] Richard Lipton and Robert Sedgewick. Lower bounds for VLSI. In *Proceedings of the 13th Symposium on Theory of Computing (STOC)*, pages 300–307. ACM, 1981. doi:10.1145/800076.802482 [p. 645]

[342] Nick Littlestone. Learning quickly when irrelevant attributes abound: A new linear-threshold algorithm. *Machine Learning*, 2(4):285–318, 1988. doi:10.1007/BF00116827 [p. 505]

[343] Sixue Liu. Chain, generalization of covering code, and deterministic algorithm for k-SAT. In *Proceedings of the 45th International Colloquium on Automata, Languages, and Programming (ICALP)*, pages 88:1–88:13. Schloss Dagstuhl, 2018. doi:10.4230/LIPIcs.ICALP.2018.88 [p. 135]

[344] Bruno Loff and Alexey Milovanov. The hardness of decision tree complexity. In *Proceedings of the 42nd International Symposium on Theoretical Aspects of Computer Science (STACS)*, pages 66:1–66:13. Schloss Dagstuhl, 2025. doi:10.4230/LIPIcs.STACS.2025.66 [p. 617]

[345] Bruno Loff and Sagnik Mukhopadhyay. Lifting theorems for equality. In *Proceedings of the 36th International Symposium on Theoretical Aspects of Computer Science (STACS)*, pages 50:1–50:19. Schloss Dagstuhl, 2019. doi:10.4230/LIPICS.STACS.2019.50 [p. 617]

[346] László Lovász. On the ratio of optimal integral and fractional covers. *Discrete Mathematics*, 13(4):383–390, 1975. doi:10.1016/0012-365X(75)90058-8 [p. 542]

[347] László Lovász. On determinants, matchings, and random algorithms. In *Proceedings of the 2nd International Symposium on Fundamentals of Computation Theory (FCT)*, pages 565–574. Akademie Verlag, 1979. [p. 308]

[348] László Lovász, Moni Naor, Ilan Newman, and Avi Wigderson. Search problems in the decision tree model. *SIAM Journal on Discrete Mathematics*, 8(1):119–132, 1995. doi:10.1137/S0895480192233867 [p. 617]

[349] Chi-Jen Lu, Shi-Chun Tsai, and Hsin-Lung Wu. Improved hardness amplification in NP. *Theoretical Computer Science*, 370(1-3):293–298, 2007. doi:10.1016/j.tcs.2006.10.009 [p. 384]

[350] Michael Luby and Charles Rackoff. How to construct pseudorandom permutations from pseudorandom functions. *SIAM Journal on Computing*, 17(2):373–386, 1988. doi:10.1137/0217022 [p. 457]

[351] Michael Luby and Avi Wigderson. Pairwise independence and derandomization. *Foundations and Trends in Theoretical Computer Science*, 1(4):237–301, 2005. doi:10.1561/0400000009 [pp. 331, 424]

[352] Carsten Lund, Lance Fortnow, Howard Karloff, and Noam Nisan. Algebraic methods for interactive proof systems. *Journal of the ACM*, 39(4):859–868, 1992. doi:10.1145/146585.146605 [p. 576]

[353] Oleg Lupanov. A method of circuit synthesis. *Izvesitya VUZ, Radiofizika*, 1:120–140, 1958. In Russian. [p. 231]

[354] Oleg Lupanov. On the complexity of realization of functions of propositional calculus by formulas. *Problemy Kibernetiki*, 3:61–80, 1960. In Russian. [p. 231]

[355] Xin Lyu. Improved pseudorandom generators for AC^0 circuits. In *Proceedings of the 37th Computational Complexity Conference (CCC)*, pages 34:1–34:25. Schloss Dagstuhl, 2022. doi:10.4230/LIPICS.CCC.2022.34 [p. 675]

[356] Xin Lyu and Weihao Zhu. Time-space tradeoffs for element distinctness and set intersection via pseudorandomness. In *Proceedings of the 34th Symposium on Discrete Algorithms (SODA)*, pages 5243–5281. SIAM, 2023. doi:10.1137/1.9781611977554.CH190 [p. 308]

[357] Florence MacWilliams and Neil Sloane. *The Theory of Error-Correcting Codes*. North–Holland, 1977. [p. 358]

[358] Frédéric Magniez, Ashwin Nayak, Miklos Santha, Jonah Sherman, Gábor Tardos, and David Xiao. Improved bounds for the randomized decision tree complexity of recursive majority. *Random Structures and Algorithms*, 48(3):612–638, 2016. doi:10.1002/RSA.20598 [p. 616]

[359] Sanjeev Mahajan and H. Ramesh. Derandomizing approximation algorithms based on semidefinite programming. *SIAM Journal on Computing*, 28(5):1641–1663, 1999. doi:10.1137/S0097539796309326 [p. 543]

[360] Stephen Mahaney. Sparse complete sets of NP: Solution of a conjecture of Berman and Hartmanis. *Journal of Computer and System Sciences*, 25(2):130–143, 1982. doi:10.1016/0022-0000(82)90002-2 [p. 231]

[361] William Masek. A fast algorithm for the string editing problem and decision graph complexity. Master's thesis, Massachusetts Institute of Technology, 1976. [p. 617]

[362] Noam Mazor and Rafael Pass. Counting unpredictable bits: A simple PRG from one-way functions. In *Proceedings of the 21st Theory of Cryptography Conference (TCC)*, pages 191–218. Springer, 2023. doi:10.1007/978-3-031-48615-9_7 [p. 456]

[363] Raghu Meka, Omer Reingold, and Avishay Tal. Pseudorandom generators for width-3 branching programs. In *Proceedings of the 51st Symposium on Theory of Computing (STOC)*, pages 626–637. ACM, 2019. doi:10.1145/3313276.3316319 [p. 424]

[364] Dieter van Melkebeek. A survey of lower bounds for satisfiability and related problems. *Foundations and Trends in Theoretical Computer Science*, 2(3):197–303, 2006. doi:10.1561/0400000012 [pp. 135, 194]

[365] Dieter van Melkebeek and Konstantin Pervyshev. A generic time hierarchy with one bit of advice. *Computational Complexity*, 16(2):139–179, 2007. doi:10.1007/s00037-007-0227-8 [p. 309]

[366] Dieter van Melkebeek and Gautam Prakriya. Derandomizing isolation in space-bounded settings. *SIAM Journal on Computing*, 48(3):979–1021, 2019. doi:10.1137/17M1130538 [p. 161]

[367] N. David Mermin. *Quantum Computer Science: An Introduction*. Cambridge University Press, 2007. doi:10.1017/CBO9780511813870 [p. 682]

[368] Albert Meyer and Larry Stockmeyer. The equivalence problem for regular expressions with squaring requires exponential space. In *Proceedings of the 13th Symposium on Switching and Automata Theory (SWAT/FOCS)*, pages 125–129. IEEE, 1972. doi:10.1109/SWAT.1972.29 [p. 194]

[369] Gatis Midrijānis. Exact quantum query complexity for total boolean functions. Technical Report quant-ph/0403168, arXiv, 2004. [p. 616]

[370] Gary Miller. Riemann's hypothesis and tests for primality. *Journal of Computer and System Sciences*, 13(3):300–317, 1976. doi:10.1016/S0022-0000(76)80043-8 [p. 308]

[371] Peter Bro Miltersen. Lower bounds for union-split-find related problems on random access machines. In *Proceedings of the 26th Symposium on Theory of Computing (STOC)*, pages 625–634. ACM, 1994. doi:10.1145/195058.195415 [p. 645]

[372] Peter Bro Miltersen. Cell probe complexity – A survey. In *Proceedings of the 19th Conference on Foundations of Software Technology and Theoretical Computer Science (FSTTCS), Advances in Data Structures Workshop*. Springer, 1999. [p. 645]

[373] Peter Bro Miltersen, Noam Nisan, Shmuel Safra, and Avi Wigderson. On data structures and asymmetric communication complexity. *Journal of Computer and System Sciences*, 57(1):37–49, 1998. doi:10.1006/JCSS.1998.1577 [p. 645]

[374] Peter Bro Miltersen and N. V. Vinodchandran. Derandomizing Arthur–Merlin games using hitting sets. *Computational Complexity*, 14(3):256–279, 2005. doi:10.1007/S00037-005-0197-7 [p. 576]

[375] Michael Mitzenmacher and Eli Upfal. *Probability and Computing: Randomized Algorithms and Probabilistic Analysis*. Cambridge University Press, 2nd edition, 2017. [p. 308]

[376] Cristopher Moore and Stephan Mertens. *The Nature of Computation*. Oxford University Press, 2011. doi:10.1093/acprof:oso/9780199233212.001.0001 [p. 71]

[377] Elchanan Mossel, Ryan O'Donnell, and Krzysztof Oleszkiewicz. Noise stability of functions with low influences: Invariance and Optimality. In *Proceedings of the 46th Symposium on Foundations of Computer Science (FOCS)*, pages 21–30. IEEE, 2005. doi:10.1109/SFCS.2005.53 [p. 543]

[378] Rajeev Motwani and Prabhakar Raghavan. *Randomized Algorithms*. Cambridge University Press, 1995. doi:10.1017/CBO9780511814075 [p. 308]

[379] David Muller. Application of boolean algebra to switching circuit design and to error detection. *Transactions of the IRE Professional Group on Electronic Computers*, 3(3):6–12, 1954. doi:10.1109/IREPGELC.1954.6499441 [p. 359]

[380] David Muller. Complexity in electronic switching circuits. *IRE Transactions on Electronic Computers*, EC-5(1):15–19, 1956. doi:10.1109/TEC.1956.5219786 [p. 231]

[381] Ketan Mulmuley, Umesh Vazirani, and Vijay Vazirani. Matching is as easy as matrix inversion. *Combinatorica*, 7(1):105–113, 1987. doi:10.1007/BF02579206 [pp. 161, 308]

[382] Cody Murray and Ryan Williams. On the (non) NP-hardness of computing circuit complexity. *Theory of Computing*, 13(1):1–22, 2017. doi:10.4086/toc.2017.v013a004 [p. 457]

[383] S. Muthukrishnan. Data streams: Algorithms and applications. *Foundations and Trends in Theoretical Computer Science*, 1(2):117–236, 2005. doi:10.1561/0400000002 [p. 331]

[384] Joseph Naor and Moni Naor. Small-bias probability spaces: Efficient constructions and applications. *SIAM Journal on Computing*, 22(4):838–856, 1993. doi:10.1137/0222053 [pp. 423, 424]

[385] Moni Naor. Bit commitment using pseudorandomness. *Journal of Cryptology*, 4(2):151–158, 1991. doi:10.1007/BF00196774 [p. 457]

[386] Eduard Nechiporuk. On a Boolean function. *Soviet Mathematics – Doklady*, 7(4):999–1000, 1966. [p. 617]

[387] V. Nepomnjaščiĭ. Rudimentary predicates and Turing calculations. *Soviet Mathematics – Doklady*, 11:1462–1465, 1970. [p. 194]

[388] Ilan Newman. Private vs. common random bits in communication complexity. *Information Processing Letters*, 39(2):67–71, 1991. doi:10.1016/0020-0190(91)90157-D [p. 645]

[389] Ilan Newman and Mario Szegedy. Public vs. private coin flips in one round communication games. In *Proceedings of the 28th Symposium on Theory of Computing (STOC)*, pages 561–570. ACM, 1996. doi:10.1145/237814.238004 [p. 646]

[390] Ilan Newman and Avi Wigderson. Lower bounds on formula size of boolean functions using hypergraph entropy. *SIAM Journal on Discrete Mathematics*, 8(4):536–542, 1995. doi:10.1137/S0895480190283595 [p. 676]

[391] Michael Nielsen and Isaac Chuang. *Quantum Computation and Quantum Information*. Cambridge University Press, 2011. doi:10.1017/CBO9780511976667 [p. 682]

[392] Noam Nisan. CREW PRAMs and decision trees. *SIAM Journal on Computing*, 20(6):999–1007, 1991. doi:10.1137/0220062 [pp. 616, 617]

[393] Noam Nisan. Pseudorandom bits for constant depth circuits. *Combinatorica*, 11(1):63–70, 1991. doi:10.1007/BF01375474 [p. 675]

[394] Noam Nisan. Pseudorandom generators for space-bounded computation. *Combinatorica*, 12(4):449–461, 1992. doi:10.1007/BF01305237 [p. 423]

[395] Noam Nisan. The communication complexity of threshold gates. *Combinatorics, Paul Erdős is Eighty*, 1:301–315, 1993. [p. 645]

[396] Noam Nisan. RL $\subseteq$ SC. *Computational Complexity*, 4:1–11, 1994. doi:10.1007/BF01205052 [p. 423]

[397] Noam Nisan and Mario Szegedy. On the degree of boolean functions as real polynomials. *Computational Complexity*, 4:301–313, 1994. doi:10.1007/BF01263419 [p. 616]

[398] Noam Nisan and Avi Wigderson. Hardness vs randomness. *Journal of Computer and System Sciences*, 49(2):149–167, 1994. doi:10.1016/S0022-0000(05)80043-1 [p. 424]

[399] Noam Nisan and David Zuckerman. Randomness is linear in space. *Journal of Computer and System Sciences*, 52(1):43–52, 1996. doi:10.1006/jcss.1996.0004 [p. 424]

[400] Jakob Nordström. Pebble games, proof complexity, and time-space trade-offs. *Logical Methods in Computer Science*, 9(3), 2013. doi:10.2168/LMCS-9(3:15)2013 [p. 682]

[401] Ryan O'Donnell. Hardness amplification within NP. *Journal of Computer and System Sciences*, 69(1):68–94, 2004. doi:10.1016/j.jcss.2004.01.001 [p. 384]

[402] Ryan O'Donnell. *Analysis of Boolean Functions*. Cambridge University Press, 2014. doi:10.1017/CBO9781139814782 [pp. 543, 682]

[403] Tatsuaki Okamoto. On relationships between statistical zero-knowledge proofs. *Journal of Computer and System Sciences*, 60(1):47–108, 2000. doi:10.1006/JCSS.1999.1664 [p. 576]

[404] Igor Oliveira and Rahul Santhanam. Pseudo-derandomizing learning and approximation. In *Proceedings of the 22nd International Conference on Randomization and Computation (RANDOM)*, pages 55:1–55:19. Schloss Dagstuhl, 2018. doi:10.4230/LIPIcs.APPROX-RANDOM.2018.55 [p. 72]

[405] Øystein Ore. Über höhere Kongruenzen (On higher congruences). *Norsk Matematisk Forenings Skrifter Ser I*, (7), 1922. In German. [p. 308]

[406] Alain Pajor. *Sous-Espaces l_1^n des Espaces de Banach (l_1^n Subspaces of Banach Spaces)*, volume 16 of *Travaux en Cours*. Hermann, Paris, 1985. In French. [p. 505]

[407] Christos Papadimitriou. *Computational Complexity*. Addison–Wesley, 1994. [p. 71]

[408] Mike Paterson and Leslie Valiant. Circuit size is nonlinear in depth. *Theoretical Computer Science*, 2(3):397–400, 1976. doi:10.1016/0304-3975(76)90090-6 [p. 264]

[409] Mihai Pătraşcu. Unifying the landscape of cell-probe lower bounds. *SIAM Journal on Computing*, 40(3):827–847, 2011. doi:10.1137/09075336X [p. 645]

[410] Junqiang Peng and Mingyu Xiao. A fast algorithm for SAT in terms of formula length. In *Proceedings of the 24th International Conference on Theory and Applications of Satisfiability Testing (SAT)*, pages 436–452. Springer, 2021. doi:10.1007/978-3-030-80223-3_30 [p. 135]

[411] Rene Peralta. On the randomness complexity of algorithms. CS Research Report TR 90-1, University of Wisconsin–Milwaukee, 1990. [p. 423]

[412] Nicholas Pippenger. On simultaneous resource bounds. In *Proceedings of the 20th Symposium on Foundations of Computer Science (FOCS)*, pages 307–311. IEEE, 1979. doi:10.1109/SFCS.1979.29 [p. 231]

[413] David Pisinger. Linear time algorithms for knapsack problems with bounded weights. *Journal of Algorithms*, 33(1):1–14, 1999. doi:10.1006/jagm.1999.1034 [p. 135]

[414] Leonard Pitt and Leslie Valiant. Computational limitations on learning from examples. *Journal of the ACM*, 35(4):965–984, 1988. doi:10.1145/48014.63140 [pp. 505, 506]

[415] Leonard Pitt and Manfred Warmuth. Prediction-preserving reducibility. *Journal of Computer and System Sciences*, 41(3):430–467, 1990. doi:10.1016/0022-0000(90)90028-J [p. 505]

[416] Morris Plotkin. Binary codes with specified minimum distance. *IRE Transactions on Information Theory*, 6(4):445–450, 1960. doi:10.1109/TIT.1960.1057584 [p. 358]

[417] Aaron Potechin. Bounds on monotone switching networks for directed connectivity. *Journal of the ACM*, 64(4):29:1–29:48, 2017. doi:10.1145/3080520 [p. 676]

[418] Pavel Pudlák. *Logical Foundations of Mathematics and Computational Complexity: A Gentle Introduction*. Springer, 2013. doi:10.1007/978-3-319-00119-7 [p. 682]

[419] Pavel Pudlák and Stanislav Žák. Space complexity of computations. Technical report, University of Prague, 1983. [p. 231]

[420] Edward Pyne. Derandomizing logspace with a small shared hard drive. *Computational Complexity*, 34(2):13, 2025. doi:10.1007/S00037-025-00275-6 [p. 309]

[421] Michael Rabin. Mathematical theory of automata. In *Proceedings of a Symposium in Applied Mathematics*, volume 19, pages 153–175. American Mathematical Society, 1966. [p. 72]

[422] Michael Rabin. Probabilistic algorithm for testing primality. *Journal of Number Theory*, 12(1):128–138, 1980. doi:10.1016/0022-314X(80)90084-0 [p. 308]

[423] Md Lutfar Rahman and Thomas Watson. Complexity of unordered CNF games. *ACM Transactions on Computation Theory*, 12(3):18:1–18:18, 2020. doi:10.1145/3397478 [p. 161]

[424] Md Lutfar Rahman and Thomas Watson. 6-uniform maker-breaker game is PSPACE-complete. *Combinatorica*, 43(3):595–612, 2023. doi:10.1007/s00493-023-00026-7 [p. 161]

[425] Sivaramakrishnan Natarajan Ramamoorthy and Makrand Sinha. On the communication complexity of greater-than. In *Proceedings of the 53rd Allerton Conference on Communication, Control, and Computing*, pages 442–444. IEEE, 2015. doi:10.1109/ALLERTON.2015.7447037 [p. 645]

[426] Anup Rao and Amir Yehudayoff. *Communication Complexity and Applications*. Cambridge University Press, 2020. doi:10.1017/9781108671644 [p. 645]

[427] Ran Raz. A parallel repetition theorem. *SIAM Journal on Computing*, 27(3):763–803, 1998. doi:10.1137/S0097539795280895 [p. 542]

[428] Ran Raz and Pierre McKenzie. Separation of the monotone NC hierarchy. *Combinatorica*, 19(3):403–435, 1999. doi:10.1007/S004930050062 [p. 676]

[429] Ran Raz and Avi Wigderson. Monotone circuits for matching require linear depth. *Journal of the ACM*, 39(3):736–744, 1992. doi:10.1145/146637.146684 [p. 676]

[430] Alexander Razborov. Lower bounds for the monotone complexity of some boolean functions. *Soviet Mathematics – Doklady*, 31(2):354–357, 1985. [p. 676]

[431] Alexander Razborov. Lower bounds on the size of bounded depth circuits over a complete basis with logical addition. *Mathematical Notes of the Academy of Sciences of the USSR*, 41(4):333–338, 1987. doi:10.1007/BF01137685 [p. 675]

[432] Alexander Razborov. On the distributional complexity of disjointness. *Theoretical Computer Science*, 106(2):385–390, 1992. doi:10.1016/0304-3975(92)90260-M [p. 645]

[433] Alexander Razborov. Bounded arithmetic and lower bounds in boolean complexity. In *Feasible Mathematics II*, pages 344–386. Birkhäuser Boston, 1995. doi:10.1007/978-1-4612-2566-9_12 [p. 675]

[434] Alexander Razborov and Steven Rudich. Natural proofs. *Journal of Computer and System Sciences*, 55(1):24–35, 1997. doi:10.1006/jcss.1997.1494 [p. 676]

[435] Irving Reed. A class of multiple-error-correcting codes and the decoding scheme. *Transactions of the IRE Professional Group on Information Theory*, 4(4):38–49, 1954. doi:10.1109/TIT.1954.1057465 [p. 359]

[436] Irving Reed and Gustave Solomon. Polynomial codes over certain finite fields. *Journal of the Society for Industrial and Applied Mathematics*, 8(2):300–304, 1960. doi:10.1137/0108018 [p. 358]

[437] Omer Reingold. Undirected connectivity in log-space. *Journal of the ACM*, 55(4):17:1–17:24, 2008. doi:10.1145/1391289.1391291 [p. 309]

[438] Omer Reingold, Guy Rothblum, and Ron Rothblum. Constant-round interactive proofs for delegating computation. *SIAM Journal on Computing*, 50(3):STOC16–255–STOC16–340, 2021. doi:10.1137/16M1096773 [p. 576]

[439] Omer Reingold, Luca Trevisan, and Salil Vadhan. Pseudorandom walks on regular digraphs and the RL vs. L problem. In *Proceedings of the 38th Symposium on Theory of Computing (STOC)*, pages 457–466. ACM, 2006. doi:10.1145/1132516.1132583 [p. 309]

[440] Klaus Reinhardt and Eric Allender. Making nondeterminism unambiguous. *SIAM Journal on Computing*, 29(4):1118–1131, 2000. doi:10.1137/S0097539798339041 [p. 161]

[441] Stefan Reisch. Hex ist PSPACE-vollständig (Hex is PSPACE-complete). *Acta Informatica*, 15:167–191, 1981. In German. doi:10.1007/BF00288964 [p. 161]

[442] Gabriel Renault and Simon Schmidt. On the complexity of the misère version of three games played on graphs. *Theoretical Computer Science*, 595:159–167, 2015. doi:10.1016/j.tcs.2015.06.034 [p. 161]

[443] John Riordan and Claude Shannon. The number of two-terminal series-parallel networks. *Journal of Mathematics and Physics*, 21:83–93, 1942. doi:10.1002/sapm194221183 [p. 231]

[444] Ronald Rivest. Learning decision lists. *Machine Learning*, 2(3):229–246, 1987. doi:10.1007/BF00058680 [p. 505]

[445] Ronald Rivest and Jean Vuillemin. On recognizing graph properties from adjacency matrices. *Theoretical Computer Science*, 3(3):371–384, 1976. doi:10.1016/0304-3975(76)90053-0 [p. 616]

[446] John Robson. The complexity of Go. In *Proceedings of the 9th World Computer Congress, Information Processing (IFIP)*, pages 413–417. North–Holland, 1983. [p. 161]

[447] John Robson. N by N Checkers is Exptime complete. *SIAM Journal on Computing*, 13(2):252–267, 1984. doi:10.1137/0213018 [p. 161]

[448] Arnold Rosenberg. On the time required to recognize properties of graphs: A problem. *SIGACT News*, 5(4):15–16, 1973. doi:10.1145/1008299.1008302 [p. 616]

[449] Benjamin Rossman. Formulas versus circuits for small distance connectivity. *SIAM Journal on Computing*, 47(5):1986–2028, 2018. doi:10.1137/15M1027310 [p. 263]

[450] Ron Roth. *Introduction to Coding Theory*. Cambridge University Press, 2006. doi:10.1017/CBO9780511808968 [p. 358]

[451] Jörg Rothe. *Complexity Theory and Cryptology: An Introduction to Cryptocomplexity*. Texts in Theoretical Computer Science. Springer, 2005. doi:10.1007/3-540-28520-2 [p. 456]

[452] Tim Roughgarden. Communication complexity (for algorithm designers). *Foundations and Trends in Theoretical Computer Science*, 11(3-4):217–404, 2016. doi:10.1561/0400000076 [p. 645]

[453] Eyal Rozenman and Salil Vadhan. Derandomized squaring of graphs. In *Proceedings of the 9th International Workshop on Randomization and Computation (RANDOM)*, pages 436–447. Springer, 2005. doi:10.1007/11538462_37 [p. 309]

[454] David Rubinstein. Sensitivity vs. block sensitivity of boolean functions. *Combinatorica*, 15(2):297–299, 1995. doi:10.1007/BF01200762 [p. 616]

[455] Alexander Russell and Ravi Sundaram. Symmetric alternation captures BPP. *Computational Complexity*, 7(2):152–162, 1998. doi:10.1007/s000370050007 [p. 309]

[456] Gerald Sacks. Multiple error correction by means of parity checks. *IRE Transactions on Information Theory*, 4(4):145–147, 1958. doi:10.1109/IRETIT.1958.6741947 [p. 358]

[457] Mert Sağlam. Near log-convexity of measured heat in (discrete) time and consequences. In *Proceedings of the 59th Symposium on Foundations of Computer Science (FOCS)*, pages 967–978. IEEE, 2018. doi:10.1109/FOCS.2018.00095 [p. 646]

[458] Michael Saks and Avi Wigderson. Probabilistic boolean decision trees and the complexity of evaluating game trees. In *Proceedings of the 27th Symposium on Foundations of Computer Science (FOCS)*, pages 29–38. IEEE, 1986. doi:10.1109/SFCS.1986.44 [p. 616]

[459] Michael Saks and Shiyu Zhou. $\mathrm{BP_H SPACE}(S) \subseteq \mathrm{DSPACE}(S^{3/2})$. *Journal of Computer and System Sciences*, 58(2):376–403, 1999. doi:10.1006/jcss.1998.1616 [p. 309]

[460] Miklos Santha. On the Monte Carlo boolean decision tree complexity of read-once formulae. *Random Structures and Algorithms*, 6(1):75–88, 1995. doi:10.1002/RSA.3240060108 [p. 616]

[461] Norbert Sauer. On the density of families of sets. *Journal of Combinatorial Theory, Series A*, 13(1):145–147, 1972. doi:10.1016/0097-3165(72)90019-2 [p. 505]

[462] John Savage. Computational work and time on finite machines. *Journal of the ACM*, 19(4):660–674, 1972. doi:10.1145/321724.321731 [p. 231]

[463] John Savage. *Models of Computation: Exploring the Power of Computing*. Addison–Wesley, 1998. [pp. 231, 675]

[464] Walter Savitch. Relationships between nondeterministic and deterministic tape complexities. *Journal of Computer and System Sciences*, 4(2):177–192, 1970. doi:10.1016/S0022-0000(70)80006-X [p. 161]

[465] Marcus Schaefer. Deciding the Vapnik–Červonenkis dimension is Σ_3^{p}-complete. *Journal of Computer and System Sciences*, 58(1):177–182, 1999. doi:10.1006/JCSS.1998.1602 [p. 506]

[466] Marcus Schaefer and Christopher Umans. Complexity theory column 37: Completeness in the polynomial-time hierarchy: Part I: A compendium. *ACM SIGACT News*, 33(3), 2002. doi:10.1145/582475.582484 [p. 194]

[467] Marcus Schaefer and Christopher Umans. Complexity theory column 38: Completeness in the polynomial-time hierarchy: Part II. *ACM SIGACT News*, 33(4), 2002. doi:10.1145/601819.601829 [p. 194]

[468] Thomas Schaefer. The complexity of satisfiability problems. In *Proceedings of the 10th Symposium on Theory of Computing (STOC)*, pages 216–226. ACM, 1978. doi:10.1145/800133.804350 [p. 136]

[469] Thomas Schaefer. On the complexity of some two-person perfect-information games. *Journal of Computer and System Sciences*, 16(2):185–225, 1978. doi:10.1016/0022-0000(78)90045-4 [p. 161]

[470] Robert Scheidweiler and Eberhard Triesch. A lower bound for the complexity of monotone graph properties. *SIAM Journal on Discrete Mathematics*, 27(1):257–265, 2013. doi:10.1137/120888703 [p. 616]

[471] Claus-Peter Schnorr. Zwei lineare untere Schranken für die Komplexität Boolescher Funktionen (Two linear lower bounds on the complexity of boolean functions). *Computing*, 13(2):155–171, 1974. In German. doi:10.1007/BF02246615 [p. 675]

[472] Arnold Schönhage and Volker Strassen. Schnelle Multiplikation großer Zahlen (Fast multiplication of large numbers). *Computing*, 7(3-4):281–292, 1971. In German. doi:10.1007/BF02242355 [p. 71]

[473] Uwe Schöning. A probabilistic algorithm for k-SAT based on limited local search and restart. *Algorithmica*, 32(4):615–623, 2002. doi:10.1007/s00453-001-0094-7 [p. 308]

[474] Jack Schwartz. Fast probabilistic algorithms for verification of polynomial identities. *Journal of the ACM*, 27(4):701–717, 1980. doi:10.1145/322217.322225 [p. 308]

[475] Nathan Segerlind. The complexity of propositional proofs. *Bulletin of Symbolic Logic*, 13(4):417–481, 2007. doi:10.2178/bsl/1203350879 [p. 682]

[476] Joel Seiferas, Michael Fischer, and Albert Meyer. Separating nondeterministic time complexity classes. *Journal of the ACM*, 25(1):146–167, 1978. doi:10.1145/322047.322061 [p. 194]

[477] Alan Selman. P-selective sets, tally languages, and the behavior of polynomial time reducibilities on NP. *Mathematical Systems Theory*, 13:55–65, 1979. doi:10.1007/BF01744288 [p. 231]

[478] Igor Sergeev. Complexity and depth of formulas for symmetric boolean functions. *Moscow University Mathematics Bulletin*, 71(3):127–130, 2016. doi:10.3103/S0027132216030098 [p. 264]

[479] Igor Sergeev. On a relation between the depth and complexity of monotone boolean formulas. *Journal of Applied and Industrial Mathematics*, 13(4):746–752, 2020. doi:10.1134/S1990478919040161 [p. 264]

[480] Ronen Shaltiel. An introduction to randomness extractors. In *Proceedings of the 38th International Colloquium on Automata, Languages, and Programming (ICALP)*, pages 21–41. Springer, 2011. doi:10.1007/978-3-642-22012-8_2 [p. 423]

[481] Ronen Shaltiel and Christopher Umans. Simple extractors for all min-entropies and a new pseudo-random generator. *Journal of the ACM*, 52(2):172–216, 2005. doi:10.1145/1059513.1059516 [p. 424]

[482] Yakov Shalunov. Improved bounds on the space complexity of circuit evaluation. Technical Report TR25-078, Electronic Colloquium on Computational Complexity (ECCC), 2025. [p. 231]

[483] Adi Shamir. IP = PSPACE. *Journal of the ACM*, 39(4):869–877, 1992. doi:10.1145/146585.146609 [p. 576]

[484] Claude Shannon. The synthesis of two-terminal switching circuits. *Bell System Technical Journal*, 28(1):59–98, 1949. doi:10.1002/j.1538-7305.1949.tb03624.x [p. 231]

[485] Claude Shannon, Robert Gallager, and Elwyn Berlekamp. Lower bounds to error probability for coding on discrete memoryless channels, Part I. *Information and Control*, 10(1):65–103, 1967. doi:10.1016/S0019-9958(67)90052-6 [p. 359]

[486] Claude Shannon, Robert Gallager, and Elwyn Berlekamp. Lower bounds to error probability for coding on discrete memoryless channels, Part II. *Information and Control*, 10(5):522–552, 1967. doi:10.1016/S0019-9958(67)91200-4 [p. 359]

[487] Saharon Shelah. A combinatorial problem; stability and order for models and theories in infinitary languages. *Pacific Journal of Mathematics*, 41(1):247–261, 1972. doi:10.2140/pjm.1972.41.247 [p. 505]

[488] Alexander Shen. IP = PSPACE: Simplified proof. *Journal of the ACM*, 39(4):878–880, 1992. doi:10.1145/146585.146613 [p. 576]

[489] Peter Shor. Polynomial-time algorithms for prime factorization and discrete logarithms on a quantum computer. *SIAM Journal on Computing*, 26(5):1484–1509, 1997. doi:10.1137/S0097539795293172 [p. 683]

[490] Victor Shoup. New algorithms for finding irreducible polynomials over finite fields. *Mathematics of Computation*, 54(189):435–447, 1990. doi:10.1090/S0025-5718-1990-0993933-0 [p. 358]

[491] Amir Shpilka and Amir Yehudayoff. Arithmetic circuits: A survey of recent results and open questions. *Foundations and Trends in Theoretical Computer Science*, 5(3-4):207–388, 2010. doi:10.1561/0400000039 [p. 682]

[492] Alistair Sinclair and Mark Jerrum. Approximate counting, uniform generation and rapidly mixing Markov chains. *Information and Computation*, 82(1):93–133, 1989. doi:10.1016/0890-5401(89)90067-9 [p. 331]

[493] Richard Singleton. Maximum distance q-nary codes. *IEEE Transactions on Information Theory*, 10(2):116–118, 1964. doi:10.1109/TIT.1964.1053661 [p. 358]

[494] Rakesh Sinha and Jayram Thathachar. Efficient oblivious branching programs for threshold and mod functions. *Journal of Computer and System Sciences*, 55(3):373–384, 1997. doi:10.1006/JCSS.1997.1530 [p. 617]

[495] Michael Sipser. A complexity theoretic approach to randomness. In *Proceedings of the 15th Symposium on Theory of Computing (STOC)*, pages 330–335. ACM, 1983. doi:10.1145/800061.808762 [p. 309]

[496] Michael Sipser. The history and status of the P versus NP question. In *Proceedings of the 24th Symposium on Theory of Computing (STOC)*, pages 603–618. ACM, 1992. doi:10.1145/129712.129771 [p. 135]

[497] Michael Sipser. *Introduction to the Theory of Computation*. Cengage, 3rd edition, 2012. [p. 71]

[498] Roman Smolensky. Algebraic methods in the theory of lower bounds for boolean circuit complexity. In *Proceedings of the 19th Symposium on Theory of Computing (STOC)*, pages 77–82. ACM, 1987. doi:10.1145/28395.28404 [p. 675]

[499] Dmitry Sokolov. Dag-like communication and its applications. In *Proceedings of the 12th International Computer Science Symposium in Russia (CSR)*, pages 294–307. Springer, 2017. doi:10.1007/978-3-319-58747-9_26 [p. 676]

[500] Ray Solomonoff. A formal theory of inductive inference. Part I. *Information and Control*, 7(1):1–22, 1964. doi:10.1016/S0019-9958(64)90223-2 [p. 682]

[501] Robert Solovay and Volker Strassen. A fast Monte-Carlo test for primality. *SIAM Journal on Computing*, 6(1):84–85, 1977. doi:10.1137/0206006 [p. 308]

[502] Emanuel Sperner. Ein Satz über Untermengen einer endlichen Menge (A theorem about subsets of a finite set). *Mathematische Zeitschrift*, 27(1):544–548, 1928. In German. doi:10.1007/BF01171114 [p. 506]

[503] Philip Spira. On time-hardware complexity tradeoffs for boolean functions. In *Proceedings of the 4th Hawaii Symposium on System Sciences*, pages 525–527. Western Periodicals, 1971. [p. 264]

[504] Richard Stearns, Juris Hartmanis, and Philip Lewis. Hierarchies of memory limited computations. In *Proceedings of the 6th Symposium on Switching Circuit Theory and Logical Design (SWCT/FOCS)*, pages 179–190. IEEE, 1965. doi:10.1109/FOCS.1965.11 [p. 194]

[505] Douglas Stinson. Combinatorial techniques for universal hashing. *Journal of Computer and System Sciences*, 48(2):337–346, 1994. doi:10.1016/S0022-0000(05)80007-8 [p. 331]

[506] Larry Stockmeyer. On approximation algorithms for #P. *SIAM Journal on Computing*, 14(4):849–861, 1985. doi:10.1137/0214060 [p. 331]

[507] Larry Stockmeyer and Albert Meyer. Word problems requiring exponential time. In *Proceedings of the 5th Symposium on Theory of Computing (STOC)*, pages 1–9. ACM, 1973. doi:10.1145/800125.804029 [p. 161]

[508] Bella Subbotovskaya. Realizations of linear functions by formulas using ∨, &, —. *Soviet Mathematics – Doklady*, 2:110–112, 1961. [p. 675]

[509] Madhu Sudan, Luca Trevisan, and Salil Vadhan. Pseudorandom generators without the XOR lemma. *Journal of Computer and System Sciences*, 62(2):236–266, 2001. doi:10.1006/jcss.2000.1730 [pp. 384, 424]

[510] Róbert Szelepcsényi. The method of forced enumeration for nondeterministic automata. *Acta Informatica*, 26(3):279–284, 1988. doi:10.1007/BF00299636 [p. 161]

[511] Amnon Ta-Shma. Explicit, almost optimal, epsilon-balanced codes. In *Proceedings of the 49th Symposium on Theory of Computing (STOC)*, pages 238–251. ACM, 2017. doi:10.1145/3055399.3055408 [p. 359]

[512] Avishay Tal. Shrinkage of De Morgan formulae by spectral techniques. In *Proceedings of the 55th Symposium on Foundations of Computer Science (FOCS)*, pages 551–560. IEEE, 2014. doi:10.1109/FOCS.2014.65 [p. 675]

[513] John Talbot and Dominic Welsh. *Complexity and Cryptography: An Introduction*. Cambridge University Press, 2006. doi:10.1017/CBO9780511755286 [p. 456]

[514] Éva Tardos. The gap between monotone and non-monotone circuit complexity is exponential. *Combinatorica*, 8(1):141–142, 1988. doi:10.1007/BF02122563 [p. 676]

[515] Gábor Tardos. Query complexity, or why is it difficult to separate $NP^A \cap coNP^A$ from P^A by random oracles A? *Combinatorica*, 9(4):385–392, 1990. doi:10.1007/BF02125350 [p. 616]

[516] Jun Tarui. Probabilistic polynomials, AC^0 functions, and the polynomial-time hierarchy. *Theoretical Computer Science*, 113(1):167–183, 1993. doi:10.1016/0304-3975(93)90214-E [p. 676]

[517] Justin Thaler. Semi-streaming algorithms for annotated graph streams. In *Proceedings of the 43rd International Colloquium on Automata, Languages, and Programming (ICALP)*, pages 59:1–59:14. Schloss Dagstuhl, 2016. doi:10.4230/LIPICS.ICALP.2016.59 [p. 576]

[518] Justin Thaler. Proofs, arguments, and zero-knowledge. *Foundations and Trends in Privacy and Security*, 4(2-4):117–660, 2022. doi:10.1561/3300000030 [p. 576]

[519] Clark Thompson. Area-time complexity for VLSI. In *Proceedings of the 11th Symposium on Theory of Computing (STOC)*, pages 81–88. ACM, 1979. doi:10.1145/800135.804401 [p. 645]

[520] Seinosuke Toda. PP is as hard as the polynomial-time hierarchy. *SIAM Journal on Computing*, 20(5):865–877, 1991. doi:10.1137/0220053 [p. 683]

[521] Boris Trakhtenbrot. Turing computations with logarithmic delay. *Algebra and Logic*, 3(4):33–48, 1964. [p. 194]

[522] Luca Trevisan. Extractors and pseudorandom generators. *Journal of the ACM*, 48(4):860–879, 2001. doi:10.1145/502090.502099 [p. 424]

[523] Luca Trevisan, Gregory Sorkin, Madhu Sudan, and David Williamson. Gadgets, approximation, and linear programming. *SIAM Journal on Computing*, 29(6):2074–2097, 2000. doi:10.1137/S0097539797328847 [p. 543]

[524] Luca Trevisan and Salil Vadhan. Extracting randomness from samplable distributions. In *Proceedings of the 41st Symposium on Foundations of Computer Science (FOCS)*, pages 32–42. IEEE, 2000. doi:10.1109/SFCS.2000.892063 [p. 424]

[525] Alan Turing. On computable numbers, with an application to the Entscheidungsproblem. *Proceedings of the London Mathematical Society*, s2-42(1):230–265, 1937. doi:10.1112/plms/s2-42.1.230 [p. 71]

[526] Alan Turing. Systems of logic based on ordinals. *Proceedings of the London Mathematical Society*, s2-45(1):161–228, 1939. doi:10.1112/plms/s2-45.1.161 [p. 72]

[527] Christopher Umans. The minimum equivalent DNF problem and shortest implicants. *Journal of Computer and System Sciences*, 63(4):597–611, 2001. doi:10.1006/jcss.2001.1775 [p. 194]

[528] Salil Vadhan. *A Study of Statistical Zero-Knowledge Proofs*. PhD thesis, Massachusetts Institute of Technology, 1999. [p. 576]

[529] Salil Vadhan. The complexity of zero knowledge. In *Proceedings of the 27th Conference on Foundations of Software Technology and Theoretical Computer Science (FSTTCS)*, pages 52–70. Springer, 2007. doi:10.1007/978-3-540-77050-3_5 [p. 576]

[530] Salil Vadhan. Pseudorandomness. *Foundations and Trends in Theoretical Computer Science*, 7(1-3):1–336, 2012. doi:10.1561/0400000010 [p. 423]

[531] Leslie Valiant. Graph-theoretic arguments in low-level complexity. In *Proceedings of the 6th Symposium on Mathematical Foundations of Computer Science (MFCS)*, pages 162–176. Springer, 1977. doi:10.1007/3-540-08353-7_135 [p. 264]

[532] Leslie Valiant. The complexity of computing the permanent. *Theoretical Computer Science*, 8(2):189–201, 1979. doi:10.1016/0304-3975(79)90044-6 [p. 683]

[533] Leslie Valiant. The complexity of enumeration and reliability problems. *SIAM Journal on Computing*, 8(3):410–421, 1979. doi:10.1137/0208032 [p. 683]

[534] Leslie Valiant. Exponential lower bounds for restricted monotone circuits. In *Proceedings of the 15th Symposium on Theory of Computing (STOC)*, pages 110–117. ACM, 1983. doi:10.1145/800061.808739 [p. 264]

[535] Leslie Valiant. Short monotone formulae for the majority function. *Journal of Algorithms*, 5(3):363–366, 1984. doi:10.1016/0196-6774(84)90016-6 [p. 264]

[536] Leslie Valiant. A theory of the learnable. *Communications of the ACM*, 27(11):1134–1142, 1984. doi:10.1145/1968.1972 [p. 505]

[537] Leslie Valiant and Vijay Vazirani. NP is as easy as detecting unique solutions. *Theoretical Computer Science*, 47(3):85–93, 1986. doi:10.1016/0304-3975(86)90135-0 [p. 331]

[538] Vladimir Vapnik and Alexey Chervonenkis. On the uniform convergence of relative frequencies of events to their probabilities. *Theory of Probability and Its Applications*, 16(2):264–280, 1971. doi:10.1137/1116025 [p. 505]

[539] Rom Varshamov. Estimate of the number of signals in error correcting codes. *Doklady Akademii Nauk SSSR*, 117:739–741, 1957. In Russian. [p. 358]

[540] Umesh Vazirani. Efficiency considerations in using semi-random sources. In *Proceedings of the 19th Symposium on Theory of Computing (STOC)*, pages 160–168. ACM, 1987. doi:10.1145/28395.28413 [p. 331]

[541] Vijay Vazirani. *Approximation Algorithms*. Springer, 2001. doi:10.1007/978-3-662-04565-7 [p. 542]

[542] H. Venkateswaran. Properties that characterize LOGCFL. *Journal of Computer and System Sciences*, 43(2):380–404, 1991. doi:10.1016/0022-0000(91)90020-6 [p. 264]

[543] H. Venkateswaran. Circuit definitions of nondeterministic complexity classes. *SIAM Journal on Computing*, 21(4):655–670, 1992. doi:10.1137/0221040 [p. 231]

[544] Karsten Verbeurgt. Learning DNF under the uniform distribution in quasi-polynomial time. In *Proceedings of the 3rd Workshop on Computational Learning Theory (COLT)*, pages 314–326. Morgan Kaufmann, 1990. doi:10.1016/b978-1-55860-146-8.50027-8 [p. 506]

[545] Emanuele Viola. On approximate majority and probabilistic time. *Computational Complexity*, 18(3):337–375, 2009. doi:10.1007/s00037-009-0267-3 [p. 309]

[546] Emanuele Viola. On the power of small-depth computation. *Foundations and Trends in Theoretical Computer Science*, 5(1):1–72, 2009. doi:10.1561/0400000033 [p. 264]

[547] Emanuele Viola. The sum of D small-bias generators fools polynomials of degree D. *Computational Complexity*, 18(2):209–217, 2009. doi:10.1007/s00037-009-0273-5 [p. 423]

[548] Emanuele Viola. Extractors for circuit sources. *SIAM Journal on Computing*, 43(2):655–672, 2014. doi:10.1137/11085983X [pp. 424, 675]

[549] Emanuele Viola. The communication complexity of addition. *Combinatorica*, 35(6):703–747, 2015. doi:10.1007/s00493-014-3078-3 [p. 645]

[550] Emanuele Viola. Sampling lower bounds: Boolean average-case and permutations. *SIAM Journal on Computing*, 49(1):119–137, 2020. doi:10.1137/18M1198405 [p. 424]

[551] Emanuele Viola and Avi Wigderson. Norms, XOR lemmas, and lower bounds for polynomials and protocols. *Theory of Computing*, 4(1):137–168, 2008. doi:10.4086/toc.2008.v004a007 [p. 384]

[552] Heribert Vollmer. *Introduction to Circuit Complexity: A Uniform Approach*. Texts in Theoretical Computer Science. Springer, 1999. doi:10.1007/978-3-662-03927-4 [pp. 231, 675]

[553] Thomas Watson. Query complexity in errorless hardness amplification. *Computational Complexity*, 24(4):823–850, 2015. doi:10.1007/s00037-015-0117-4 [p. 384]

[554] Thomas Watson. The complexity of estimating min-entropy. *Computational Complexity*, 25(1):153–175, 2016. doi:10.1007/S00037-014-0091-2 [p. 682]

[555] Ingo Wegener. *The Complexity of Boolean Functions*. Wiley–Teubner, 1987. [pp. 231, 675]

[556] Ingo Wegener. *Branching Programs and Binary Decision Diagrams: Theory and Applications*. SIAM, 2000. doi:10.1137/1.9780898719789 [p. 617]

[557] Ingo Wegener. *Complexity Theory: Exploring the Limits of Efficient Algorithms*. Springer, 2005. doi:10.1007/3-540-27477-4 [p. 71]

[558] Avi Wigderson. Improving the performance guarantee for approximate graph coloring. *Journal of the ACM*, 30(4):729–735, 1983. doi:10.1145/2157.2158 [p. 543]

[559] Avi Wigderson. *Mathematics and Computation: A Theory Revolutionizing Technology and Science*. Princeton University Press, 2019. doi:10.1515/9780691192543 [p. 71]

[560] Ryan Williams. Time-space tradeoffs for counting NP solutions modulo integers. *Computational Complexity*, 17(2):179–219, 2008. doi:10.1007/s00037-008-0248-y [p. 194]

[561] Ryan Williams. Nonuniform ACC circuit lower bounds. *Journal of the ACM*, 61(1):2:1–2:32, 2014. doi:10.1145/2559903 [p. 675]

[562] Ryan Williams. The polynomial method in circuit complexity applied to algorithm design. In *Proceedings of the 34th Conference on Foundations of Software Technology and Theoretical Computer Science (FSTTCS)*, pages 47–60. Schloss Dagstuhl, 2014. doi:10.4230/LIPICS.FSTTCS.2014.47 [p. 675]

[563] Ryan Williams. Simulating time with square-root space. In *Proceedings of the 57th Symposium on Theory of Computing (STOC)*, pages 13–23. ACM, 2025. doi:10.1145/3717823.3718225 [p. 231]

[564] Virginia Vassilevska Williams. On some fine-grained questions in algorithms and complexity. In *Proceedings of the International Congress of Mathematicians (ICM)*, pages 3447–3487. World Scientific, 2018. doi:10.1142/9789813272880_0188 [p. 682]

[565] David Williamson and David Shmoys. *The Design of Approximation Algorithms*. Cambridge University Press, 2011. doi:10.1017/CBO9780511921735 [p. 542]

[566] Mihalis Yannakakis. Expressing combinatorial optimization problems by linear programs. *Journal of Computer and System Sciences*, 43(3):441–466, 1991. doi:10.1016/0022-0000(91)90024-Y [p. 645]

[567] Mihalis Yannakakis. On the approximation of maximum satisfiability. *Journal of Algorithms*, 17(3):475–502, 1994. doi:10.1006/JAGM.1994.1045 [p. 542]

[568] Andrew Yao. Probabilistic computations: Toward a unified measure of complexity. In *Proceedings of the 18th Symposium on Foundations of Computer Science (FOCS)*, pages 222–227. IEEE, 1977. doi:10.1109/SFCS.1977.24 [p. 616]

[569] Andrew Yao. Some complexity questions related to distributive computing. In *Proceedings of the 11th Symposium on Theory of Computing (STOC)*, pages 209–213. ACM, 1979. doi:10.1145/800135.804414 [p. 645]

[570] Andrew Yao. Theory and applications of trapdoor functions. In *Proceedings of the 23rd Symposium on Foundations of Computer Science (FOCS)*, pages 80–91. IEEE, 1982. doi:10.1109/SFCS.1982.45 [p. 456]

[571] Andrew Yao. Separating the polynomial-time hierarchy by oracles. In *Proceedings of the 26th Symposium on Foundations of Computer Science (FOCS)*, pages 1–10. IEEE, 1985. doi:10.1109/SFCS.1985.49 [p. 675]

[572] Chee-Keng Yap. Some consequences of non-uniform conditions on uniform classes. *Theoretical Computer Science*, 26(3):287–300, 1983. doi:10.1016/0304-3975(83)90020-8 [p. 231]

[573] Sergey Yekhanin. Locally decodable codes. *Foundations and Trends in Theoretical Computer Science*, 6(3):139–255, 2012. doi:10.1561/0400000030 [p. 384]

[574] Stathis Zachos. Probabilistic quantifiers and games. *Journal of Computer and System Sciences*, 36(3):433–451, 1988. doi:10.1016/0022-0000(88)90037-2 [p. 309]

[575] Stathis Zachos and Hans Heller. A decisive characterization of BPP. *Information and Control*, 69(1-3):125–135, 1986. doi:10.1016/S0019-9958(86)80044-4 [p. 309]

[576] Stanislav Žák. A Turing machine time hierarchy. *Theoretical Computer Science*, 26(3):327–333, 1983. doi:10.1016/0304-3975(83)90015-4 [p. 194]

[577] Dmitriy Zhuk. A proof of CSP dichotomy conjecture. In *Proceedings of the 58th Symposium on Foundations of Computer Science (FOCS)*, pages 331–342. IEEE, 2017. doi:10.1109/FOCS.2017.38 [p. 136]

[578] Richard Zippel. Probabilistic algorithms for sparse polynomials. In *Proceedings of an International Symposium on Symbolic and Algebraic Manipulation (EUROSAM)*, pages 216–226. Springer, 1979. doi:10.1007/3-540-09519-5_73 [p. 308]

[579] David Zuckerman. Linear degree extractors and the inapproximability of max clique and chromatic number. *Theory of Computing*, 3(1):103–128, 2007. doi:10.4086/TOC.2007.V003A006 [p. 542]

Index

Symbols

#Anti-Triangle, 575
#P, 680
#Sat, 556
#Triangle, 565
$\leq_f^m$, 184
$\leq_\ell^m$, 61, 127, 143, 243
$\leq_{nc^1}^m$, 244
$\leq_p^m$, 52, 87, 143
$\leq_\ell^o$, 64, 160, 197
$\leq_p^o$, 51, 197, 279
0-input, 21
1-input, 21
(2 out of 3)-Sat, 159
2-QSat, 143, 157
2-Sat, 130, 159
2-Threshold, 648, 673
2-Xor Sat, 158
3-NAE Sat, 540
3-QSat, 143, 157
3-Sat, 93, 516

A

A Select, 228
abort, 275, 322, 497, 570
AC^0/poly, 238, 649
accept, 24
accuracy in PAC learning, 459
AC^i, 237
AC^i/poly, 238
active adversary, 427
active learning, 488
AdaBoost, 485
adaptive, 56, 443
addition principle, 686
additive inverse, 697
adjacency list, 15, 247
adjacency matrix, 15, 247, 704
adjusted multilinear code, 372
Adjusted Σ_3Sat, 505
adversary, 427, 581, 588
advice, 195
agnostic learning, 506
ALG, 508
algorithm, 9, 24
Alice and Bob, 428, 618
All Gates Circuit Sat, 230
Almost Clique, 131
(α, β)-Gap *B*, 515
alphabet, 342, 350
AM, 549
AM/poly, 574
amortized analysis, 47
amplification, 277, 484, 553, 593
ancestor node, 690
And-Or Path, 263
And-Or Tree, 590
answer segment, 57
anti-dictatorship, 389, 462
Any Directed Full Path, 132
A_{pad}, 163
approximate counting of witnesses, 318, 548
approximation algorithm, 507, 634
arithmetic circuit, 305, 680
arithmetic complexity, 680
arithmetic formula, 268
arithmetization, 556
Arthur, 544
Arthur of *V*, 551
Arthur–Merlin proof system, 545
assignment, 89
associative, 697
asymmetric communication complexity, 631, 637
asymptotically good code, 337, 352
augmented polynomial code, 352
automorphism, 548
auxiliary variable, 118
average-case, 42, 360, 403, 435, 587, 650

B

Balanced Directed Reachability, 307
Balanced Partition, 110
Balanced Tripartition, 132
balancing, 250, 263, 616, 625
ball of bit strings, 333, 338, 632
Barely 3-Sat, 132
barrier theorem, 87, 194, 670
Barrington's theorem, 264
base case, 690
base+offset addressing, 31
Berlekamp–Welch algorithm, 358
BFS, *see* breadth-first search
big-*O*, 14, 686

big-Ω, 18, 380, 686
big-Θ, 686
bijection, 257, 435, 685
binary decision diagram, *see* branching program
binary entropy function, 338
binary matrix, 695
binary search, 151, 490, 627, 639
binary tree, 690
binding in a commitment scheme, 441, 572
binomial coefficient, 687
binomial formula, 479, 687
binomial random variable, 287, 694
bipartite graph, 78, 522
bit flip error, 332
BIT OF CONFIGURATION OF Π, 200
bit string field, 346, 391
bit-fixing source, 421
block cipher, *see* pseudorandom permutation
block sensitivity, 598
block size of a pseudorandom function, 443
block size of a streaming branching program, 295
boolean variable, 89, 686
boosting, 485
bootstrapping, *see* self-compilation
bottom, 275, 332
bounded error, 274
bounded fan-in, 201, 234
bounded word size, 40
BP*L, 307, 421
BPL, 290, 294
BPL-complete, 301, 391
BPP, 274, 280, 402, 585
BPP-complete, 300, 391
$\mathsf{BPP}^{\mathsf{qc}}$, 602
BPSize(), 608
BPSPACE[S], 290
BPTIME[T], 274
BQP, 682
branch instruction, 24
branching program, 219, 608
BRANCHING PROGRAM EVALUATION, 225, 245
BRANCHING PROGRAM SAT, 230
branching program size complexity, 221, 608
branching program size hierarchy, 223
breadth-first search, 12, 28
Brooks' theorem, 135
brute force, 9, 11, 73, 84, 489
BSens(), 598
$\mathrm{BSens}_0()$, 598
$\mathrm{BSens}_1()$, 598
bubble sort, 121
bundle of wires, 205

C

call stack, 32
canonical form polynomial, 699
carry look-ahead adder, 238
cartesian product, 621, 685
cascade insertion, 48
catalytic space, 161, 306
CELEBRITY, 583, 612
Cert(), 593
$\mathrm{Cert}_0()$, 595
$\mathrm{Cert}_1()$, 595
certificate, 135, 593, 654
certificate complexity, 593, 599
chain rule, 693
chaining in a hash table, 328
character, 535
characteristic bit string, 391, 493, 685
Chebyshev's inequality, 309
checkpoint configuration, 144, 181
Chernoff–Hoeffding bound, 309
child node, 690
chosen plaintext attack, 451, 455
ciphertext, 428
circuit, 201, 223, 232, 647
CIRCUIT EVALUATION, 209, 214
CIRCUIT GAP MAJORITY, 300, 391
CIRCUIT SAT, 218
CIRCUIT SAT APPROXIMATE SAMPLING, 322, 499
CIRCUIT SAT COUNTING, 319
circuit size complexity, 206, 647
circuit size hierarchy, 207
clause, 90, 393
CLIQUE, 99, 131, 667
clique, 98, 618, 667
CLIQUE VERSUS INDEPENDENT SET, 618
closed under and, 129
closed under complement, 126
closed under or, 129
CNF, 90, 112, 137, 471, 510, 678
code, *see* error correcting code
code of a program, 24
codeword, 332
codomain, 685
coirreducible polynomials, 347
collapse of complexity classes, 178, 197, 282, 301
collision in a hash function, 310
collision probability, 423
color assignment, 76
column vector, 703
combination, 687
combinatorial rectangle, *see* rectangle
commitment scheme, 441, 454, 572

communication complexity, 620, 663
Communication Complexity of Partial Matrix, 643
communication protocol, *see* protocol
commutative, 697
comparator, 120
comparison network, 120, 135
compatibility mode, 39, 165
complement of a boolean function, 91
complement of a decision problem, 126, 154
complement of a graph, 99
complement of a set, 98, 685, 693
complete bipartite graph, 101
completeness of a verifier, 84, 526, 544
complexity, 17
complexity class, 40
component CNF, 117, 121, 187
composition of functions, 257, 546, 613, 686
computability, 71
computational learning theory, 458, 538
computational problem, *see* problem
computational security, 431
computational zero-knowledge, 570
concatenated code, 353
concentration bound, 284, 408, 481
concept, 458
concept class, 459
concrete model of computation, 579
conditional expectation, 511, 694
conditional independence, 292, 670, 693
conditional probability, 693
confidence in PAC learning, 459
configuration, 44, 115, 144, 199, 225, 243
Configuration of Π, 199
conjunction, 90, 686
conjunctive normal form, *see* CNF
coNL, 154
Connected, 583
Connected Equitable 3-Coloring, 132
connected graph, 688
coNP, 126, 176
coNP^{qc}, 597
Consistency for 3-Term DNFs, 472
Consistent Graph Isomorphism, 573
consistent learning, 464, 480, 538
consistent with, 96
constant term, 699
constructible word size, 38, 196
Containment in Sorted List, 67
contraction of a branching program, 221, 609
contraction of a circuit, 204, 378
contraction of a CNF, 97, 115, 130
contraction of a decision tree, 652
contraction of a DNF, 130, 597, 657
contraction of a formula, 660
control flow instructions, 24, 168, 213
Cook reduction, 72
coprime numbers, 697
coRP, 275, 586
correctness, 9, 25
corruption, 332, 631
counter mode encryption scheme, 450
counterexample, 488
counting witnesses, 318, 680
Critical Graph 3-Coloring, 192
cross a cut, 133
crude source of randomness, 409
cryptographic pseudorandom generator, 435
cryptography, 427, 496, 571, 671
cubic consistency check, 541
cut in a graph, 133
cycle, 688
cyclic permutation, 258

D

dag, 68, 201, 219, 691
Dag Decision, 159
data processing instructions, 24, 167, 213
data structure, 12, 45, 636
decision list, 466
decision problem, 10, 21
decision tree, 220, 419, 579
decision tree size complexity, 221, 606, 652
decoding, 332
Decoding Polynomial Codes from Erasures, 344, 382, 575
Decoding Polynomial Codes from Symbol Changes, 345, 382
decryption, 428
defragmentation, 45
degree of a node, 107, 688
degree of a polynomial, 268, 699
Degree-d k-Coloring, 107
delayed diagonalization, 173, 303, 308
delegation, 565
depth of a circuit/formula, 232, 649
depth of a communication protocol, 620
depth of a decision tree/branching program, 232, 580
dequeue, 12
derandomization, 276, 280, 294, 390, 602, 628
descendant node, 690
Det(), 580, 620
$\mathrm{Det}^{\rightarrow}()$, 632
deterministic algorithm, 267
diagonal-constant matrix, 314

diagonalization, 169, 196
dichotomy theorem, 136
dictatorship, 389, 462
dictionary data structure, 45, 310
difference of sets, 685
digital signature, 451
direct product lemma, 384
directed acyclic graph, *see* dag
DIRECTED FULL CYCLE, 102
DIRECTED FULL PATH, 75, 102
DIRECTED FULL TRAIL, 76
directed graph, 688
DIRECTED LONGEST PATH DECISION, 74
DIRECTED MIN PATH HEIGHT, 70
DIRECTED REACHABILITY, 11, 28, 148, 151, 154, 665
DIRECTED REACHABILITY ON A DAG, 159, 229
DIRECTED REACHABILITY SEARCH, 13, 68
DIRECTED SHORTEST PATH, 13, 55, 68
DIRECTED SHORTEST PATH DECISION, 55, 148
DIRECTED SUBSET REACHABILITY, 50
directed switching network, 230
discrepancy, 630
disjoint, 685
DISJOINTNESS, 621, 630, 644
disjunction, 90, 686
disjunctive normal form, *see* DNF
distance between bit strings, 332, 687
distance between nodes, 13, 513
distance of an error correcting code, 333
distinguisher, 404
distribution, 385, 692
distributional problem, 360
distributive, 10, 697
divide and conquer, 144, 181
DIVISION, 71
division principle, 548, 686
DNF, 90, 472, 596
DNF SAT COUNTING, 330
DNF SAT EXACT SAMPLING, 330
domain of a function, 685
domain of a quantifier, 686
DOMINATING SET, 131
dot product, 410, 701
dot product code, 335, 354, 368, 439, 529, 627
doubly efficient interactive proof system, 565
downward self-reducible, 130
DP, 194
DTSize(), 606
dynamic programming, 80, 209, 216, 297

E

E, 41, 402
edge, 688
EDGE DISJOINT PATHS, 134
efficiency, 14, 17, 25
element, 685
ELEMENT DISTINCTNESS, 68, 328, 609
Elias–Bassalygo bound, 359
empty set, 685
encoding for a data structure, 636
encoding of a message, 332
encoding of input/output, 19
encoding to show a set is small, 657
encryption, 428
enqueue, 12
epoch, 144, 181
ε-balanced code, 355, 392
ε-bias generator, 391, 419, 542, 628
EQUALITY, 621, 626, 673
EQUITABLE 2-COLORING, 132
equivalence query, 488, 497
equivalent circuits, 202
equivalent formulas, 686
erasure, 332, 344
error correcting code, 332, 392, 417, 627
Euler's theorem, 135
Eulerian trail, *see* full trail
evaluate a circuit, 201
evaluate a function, 685
EVALUATE TO ZERO EVERYWHERE, 305
evaluation tree, 138, 554
evasive, 582
Eve, 428
event, 692
EXACT INDEPENDENT SET, 175
exact learning, 487
EXACT PATH LENGTH IN A DAG, 133
exclusive or, *see* xor
existential quantifier, 686
EXP, 41, 162
EXP-complete, 127, 143
expander graph, 326, 679
expectation, 284, 693, 696
exponential time, 41
extended breadth-first search, 13, 68, 513
extractor, 409

F

family of circuits, 202
family of concept classes, 463
family of error correcting codes, 334
fan-in, 201, 232
fan-out, 201
feasible solution, 507
feature, 458

fetch-execute cycle, 167, 210
field, 346, 697
FINAL ∀ OF V, 180, 283
FINAL ∃ OF V, 179, 198
FIND WITNESS FOR V, 130, 364
fine-grained complexity, 677
finite field, 268, 313, 348, 649, 697
fixed-parameter tractability, 677
flat distribution, 414
flattening a code, 350, 372
focused reduction, 184
fooling a function, 388
fooling set, 607, 621
forest, 69
FOREST REACHABILITY, 69, 262
FORK, 639, 666
formula, 89, 201, 223, 249, 647
FORMULA EVALUATION, 252
formula size complexity, 206, 659
Fourier analysis, *see* harmonic analysis
FPRAS, *see* fully poly-time randomized approximation scheme
frame pointer, 32
frequency in a data stream, 634
fresh store, 47
full cycle, 102
full derandomization, 390
full path, 75
FULL PATH IN A DAG, 133
full trail, 76
fully independent, 288, 693
fully poly-time randomized approximation scheme, 319, 680
function, 685
function problem, 21

G

gadget, 100
Galois field, *see* finite field
game, 138, 143, 216, 491, 581, 588, 590
game tree evaluation, 140, 589
GAP MAJORITY, 306
gap-amplifying reduction, 519, 523
gap-introducing reduction, 514
gap-preserving reduction, 516
garbage in, garbage out, 21
gate, 201, 268
gate elimination, 647
GENERAL ITERATED ADDITION, 69
generator, 214, 227
generator matrix, 336
GEOGRAPHY, 142, 145
GEOGRAPHY ON A DAG, 216
GEOGRAPHY ON A DAG WITH TARGETS, 230
geometric random variable, 285, 362, 694
Gilbert–Varshamov bound, 358
Goldreich–Levin theorem, 456
graph, 688
GRAPH 2-COLORING, 93, 133, 158, 643
GRAPH 3-COLORING, 106, 134, 473, 539, 572
GRAPH 3-COLORING WITH FORBIDDEN COLORS, 159
GRAPH 4-COLORING, 107, 643
GRAPH ISOMORPHISM, 546, 571
GRAPH k-COLORING, 76
GRAPH NONISOMORPHISM, 546
graph property, 583
GREATER THAN, 68, 612, 621, 627
greedy algorithm, 55, 78, 96, 338, 361, 510, 513
group theory, 258, 548
growth function, 475

H

Hadamard code, *see* dot product code
halfspace, 478, 485
halt instruction, 24
halving algorithm, 489, 497
Hamiltonian path, *see* full path
Hamming bound, 359
Hamming distance, *see* distance between bit strings
Hamming weight, *see* weight
hardcore bit, 436, 442
hardcore set of inputs, 383
hardness amplification, 375
hardness of approximation, 514, 527
harmonic analysis, 394, 535, 679
hash function, 310, 627
hash mixing, 324, 382, 395, 440
$\mathsf{HEUR}_\varepsilon\mathsf{BPP}$, 363
$\mathsf{HEUR}_\varepsilon\mathsf{P}$, 362
$\mathsf{HEUR}_\varepsilon\mathsf{P/poly}$, 363
heuristic, 360
hiding in a commitment scheme, 441, 572
Hierholzer's algorithm, 135
hitting set generator, 424
homogeneous system of equations, 703
honest prover, 564
hybrid argument, 405, 437
hypothesis, 458
hypothesis class, 463

I

identical arithmetic formulas, 268
identically zero, 268
identity in a field, 697

identity matrix, 704
identity permutation, 258, 546
if and only if, *see* iff
iff, 686
image, 435, 685
Immerman–Szelepcsényi theorem, 161
implementation, 24
implication, 686
implication graph, 130
improper learning, 463, 472, 538
in-tree, 201, 245, 663
IN-TREE REACHABILITY, 245
inclusion of complexity classes, 41
indegree, 688
independent distributions, 410, 693
independent events, 693
INDEPENDENT HALF, 131
independent random variables, 287, 695
INDEPENDENT SET, 73, 98, 360, 517, 677
independent set, 73, 360, 618
INDEPENDENT SET GAP COUNTING, 132
INDEPENDENT SET SEARCH, 361
INDEX, 580, 611, 631, 661
indicator polynomial, 344
indicator random variable, 286, 693
indirect branch, 31
indirect diagonalization, 190
indistinguishable distributions, 387, 431
individual degree, 270, 559
induction, 689, 690
injection, 657, 685
INNER PRODUCT, 621, 630
inner product, *see* dot product
input segment, 24
input size, 21
insertion sort, 47
instance, 71
instance checker, *see* program checker
interactive proof system, 552
internal node, 690
INTERPRETATION, 167
INTERPRETATION FOR SPACE, 171
interpreter, 166, 171
intersection, 685
invariant, 16, 140, 688, 690
inverse of a permutation, 257, 546
IP, 553
irreducible polynomial, 346
isolation of witnesses, 316
isomorphic graphs, 545, 583
isomorphism, 546
ITERATED ADDITION, 53, 79, 239, 298
iterative algorithm, 688

J

Johnson bound, 358
joint distribution, 692
joint random variables, 693
junta, 389, 419
Justesen code, 359

K

k-CNF, 90, 653
k-DNF, 90, 653
k-INDEPENDENT SET, 74
k-QSAT, 143
k-SAT, 92
k-wise uniform hash function, 329
Karchmer–Wigderson game, 676
Karp reduction, 72
Karp–Lipton theorem, 231
key, 428
Kolmogorov complexity, *see* program size complexity
KRW conjecture, 675

L

L, 43, 143, 149, 291
L/poly, 196, 295
L^2, 151, 297
label cover, 522
labeled example, 458
Ladner's theorem, 136
Lagrange interpolation, 358
language, 71
law of total expectation, 512, 694
law of total probability, 693
layered branching program, 253, 295
layered graph, 66, 666
leading coefficient, 699
leaf node, 690
learning reduction, 470
LEAST SIGNIFICANT BIT OF MEDIAN, 69
leftover hash lemma, 424
length of a layered branching program, 253
lexicographic order, 685
line number, 24
linear combination, 393, 529, 535
linear error correcting code, 336
linear exponential time, 41
linearity of dot product, 272, 535, 701
linearity of expectation, 287, 511, 694
linearizing a variable, 559
list decoding, 341, 375, 381, 418, 439
literal, 90, 203
little-o, 18, 686
little-ω, 192, 686
load instruction, 24

locally correctable code, 530
locally decodable code, 367, 439, 530
locally testable code, 530, 535
log-bounded word size, 40
log-space mapping reduction, 61
log-space oracle reduction, 64
log-space-uniform, 214, 227
logarithmic space, 43
logic circuit, *see* circuit
logic formula, *see* formula
lopsided DISJOINTNESS, 634, 637, 644
lower bound, 17, 162, 579, 670

M

MA, 550
MAC, *see* message authentication code
machine learning, 458
Mahaney's theorem, 231
maintain an invariant, 689, 690
MAJ TREE, 589
MAJORITY, 229, 263, 608, 610, 674
map, 51, 685
mapping, *see* function
mapping reduction, 52
marginal distribution, 692
Markov's inequality, 309
mask, 36
matrix, 703
MATRIX MULTIPLICATION, 272, 566
MATRIX MULTIPLICATION VERIFICATION, 272, 305, 393
MAX 2-SAT DECISION, 133
MAX 3-NAE SAT, 540
MAX 3-SAT, 523, 527
MAX CUT, 543
MAX CUT DECISION, 133
MAX EDGE DISJOINT PATHS, 512, 521, 539
MAX GRAPH 3-COLORING, 539
MAX INDEPENDENT SET, 517, 519
MAX k-LABEL COVER, 523
MAX k-SAT, 510
MAX SET COVERAGE, 538
MAX SHY SET, 540
MAX UNIQUE k-LABEL COVER, 525
MAX $\mathbb{Z}_2$ LINEAR SYSTEM SAT, 539
MAX $\mathbb{Z}_2$ QUADRATIC SYSTEM SAT, 542
MCSP, *see* MINIMUM CIRCUIT SIZE PROBLEM
membership query, 488, 493
memory access instructions, 24, 168, 213
memory space, *see* space
merge sort, 47, 120
Merlin, 544
MERLIN OF V, 552
Merlin–Arthur proof system, 550
message, 332, 427, 552, 618
message authentication code, 451, 456
meta complexity, 454
method of conditional expectations, 511
middle-first counting, 297
middle-first search, 151, 153, 242, 297
Millennium Prize Problems, 85
MIN AND MAX, 67
MIN COLORING OF 3-COLORABLE GRAPHS, 539
MIN NODE COVER, 508
MIN SET COVER, 509, 538
min-entropy, 409
MINIMUM CIRCUIT SIZE PROBLEM, 453
MIP, 562
MISÈRE GEOGRAPHY, 157
mistake bound model, 488
mistake complexity, 491
mixture of distributions, 414, 422
mod, 697
model of computation, 23
modulo, *see* mod
monochromatic, 412, 621, 633, 638, 695
monomial, 699
monotone circuit, 203, 421, 471, 667
MONOTONE CIRCUIT EVALUATION, 215
monotone CNF, 129, 157
monotone DNF, 129, 493
monotone formula, 252, 665
monotone function, 493, 665
monotone mux, 252
monotone term, 490
MOST SIGNIFICANT BIT OF MEDIAN, 69
multi-edges, 688
multilinear code, 369, 382
multilinear polynomial, 305, 358, 369, 536, 651
multiplexer, 205, 250, 580
MULTIPLICATION, 9, 28, 239, 298, 435
MULTIPLICATION DECISION, 10
multiplication of matrices, 704
multiplication principle, 686
multiplicative approximation, 319
multiplicative inverse of a polynomial, 346
multiplicative inverse of an integer, 697
multivariate polynomial, 270
mux, *see* multiplexer

N

NAE SAT, 133
NAND TREE, 591
natural proof, 670
NC^1, 252

NC^1/poly, 252, 257
NC^2, 299
NC^i, 237
NC^i/poly, 238
needle in a haystack, 81
negation, 667, 686
negligible function, 431
NEXP, 127, 162, 562
Nisan's generator, 423
Nisan–Wigderson generator, 424
NL, 147, 667
NL-complete, 149
NLPCP[$\log N$], 541
no-input, *see* 0-input
node, 688
NODE COVER, 98, 508, 677
node cover, 98
NODE DISJOINT PATHS, 134
NODE KAYLES, 157
nonadaptive, 54, 527
nonconstructive, 207, 389, 415, 695
nondeterministic, 82
nontrivial solution, 703
nonuniform, 195, 579
NOT A SORTING NETWORK, 135
NOT-ALL-EQUAL SATISFIABILITY, *see* NAE SAT
NP, 82, 84, 176, 527
NP search problem, 364
NP-complete, 88, 127, 218, 472, 515
NP-hard, 88, 507
NP-intermediate, 89, 194, 453
NP/poly, 573
$\mathsf{NP}^{\mathrm{qc}}$, 597
NPSPACE, 153
NSPACE[S], 147
NTIME[T], 84, 158, 172
NTISP[T, S], 193

O

objective function, 507
oblivious, 120, 263
Occam's razor, 505
odd-even merge sort, 124, 187
one-sided error, 274, 277
one-time pad, 430
one-way communication, 611, 631, 634
one-way function, 435
one-way permutation, 435
OPPOSITE PARITY, 639
OPT, 508
optimization problem, 13, 507
oracle circuit, 443, 496
oracle program, 568
oracle reduction, 51
out-tree, 220, 246, 579, 620
OUT-TREE REACHABILITY, 246
outcome, 692
outdegree, 688
OUTPUT OF Π WITH RANDOMNESS, 301
OUTPUT OF V WITH WITNESS, 218
output segment, 24
OWF, *see* one-way function
OWP, *see* one-way permutation

P

P, 41
P-complete, 215
P/poly, 195, 280
PAC learning, 459
padding, 162, 207, 302
pairwise avoiding hash function, 311, 423, 627
pairwise independent, 311, 325
pairwise uniform hash function, 311, 395, 439, 541, 548
parallel computation, 232
parallel repetition, 523
parameterized complexity, 677
parameterized line, 370
parameterized parabola, 382
parent node, 690
PARITY, 222, 235, 240, 647, 665
parity, 391, 535
parity code, 335
PARITY OF SORTED, 613
partial assignment, 96, 204, 581, 608, 652
partial function, 21, 686
partially evaluate a circuit, 204
passive adversary, 427
path, 75, 688
path forming game, 141, 145, 216
PCP, *see* probabilistically checkable proof
PCP theorem, 526
PCP[$\log N, k$], 527
PCP[$\mathrm{poly} N, k$], 528
PEBBLE GAME, 160
perceptron, 478
perebor, 135
perfect security, 429
perfect zero-knowledge, 570
permutation, 257, 305, 435, 546, 687
permutation branching program, 259
PH, 177
$\Pi_2\mathsf{P}$, 551
Π_2SAT, 192
pigeonhole principle, 44, 100, 340, 611, 687
$\Pi_\ell\mathsf{P}$, 176

Π_ℓTIME[T], 176
plain witness, 316
planar graph, 77
PLAY QSAT, 158
play-to-decision reduction, 157, 228
Plotkin bound, 358
point function, 461
poly$N$, 41
poly-bounded word size, 41
poly-time-uniform, 214
polylog$N$, 41
polynomial, 267, 556, 649, 699
polynomial code, 342, 351
polynomial hierarchy, 175, 197, 281, 308
POLYNOMIAL IDENTITY TESTING, 271, 557
polynomial space, 43
polynomial time, 41, 677
POLYNOMIAL ZERO TESTING, 271
polynomial-time hierarchy, *see* polynomial hierarchy
power set, 21
PP, 274, 305, 682
P^{qc}, 597
precomputation, 195, 214
predicate, 686
predictor, 404
preimage, 435, 685
PRF, *see* pseudorandom function
PRG, *see* pseudorandom generator
PRIMALITY TESTING, 276, 558
primary-school algorithm, 9, 28
prime field, 268, 557
prime number, 557, 697
private coins, 545, 626
private-key cryptography, 427
probabilistic method, 280, 339, 389, 408, 511, 695
probabilistically checkable proof, 526, 562
probability space, 692
probably approximately correct learning, *see* PAC learning
probe, 636
problem, 9, 21
program, 24
program checker, 567
program counter, 24, 167
program protector, 568
program size complexity, 680
projection reduction, 584
promise problem, 21, 300
proof complexity, 678
proper coloring, 76
proper learning, 463
property testing, 535, 681
protocol, 618, 663
prover, 544
PRP, *see* pseudorandom permutation
PSAMP, 364
pseudorandom function, 442, 455, 496, 672
pseudorandom generator, 388, 416, 432, 628
pseudorandom permutation, 448
PSPACE, 43, 139, 142, 199, 553
PSPACE-complete, 143, 559, 569
public coins, 547, 626
public-key cryptography, 427
pure source of randomness, 409, 429

Q

QSAT, 137, 144, 559
quadratic consistency check, 532
QUANTIFIED SATISFIABILITY, *see* QSAT
quantifier, 137, 175, 301, 686
quantum computing, 42, 681
quasi-linear time, 41, 119, 565
quasi-polynomial time, 70, 546
quasi-quadratic time, 117
querier versus adversary game, 581, 588
query a data structure, 636
query an oracle, 50, 367
query complexity, 580
QUERY COMPLEXITY OF CIRCUIT, 613
QUERY COMPLEXITY OF TRUTH TABLE, 613
query efficiency, 526, 580
query instruction, 57, 568
query segment, 56
queue, 12, 30
quotient of integer division, 697
quotient of polynomial division, 346, 700

R

Rand(), 586
Rand′(), 586
Rand*(), 586
Rand_0(), 586
$\text{Rand}_{0,1}$(), 585
Rand_1(), 586
random restriction, 652, 659
random subsum principle, 271, 314, 335, 391, 529, 536, 650
random variable, 284, 693
random walk, 290, 307, 322, 705
randomized algorithm, 267
randomized approximation scheme, 319, 330
randomized decision tree, 585
randomized halving algorithm, 497
randomized hash function, 311
randomized verifier, 526, 545, 549

randomness efficiency, 390, 527
randomness extractor, *see* extractor
randomness segment, 273, 290
randomness-efficient amplification, 326, 419, 439, 541
$\mathrm{Rand}_0^{\mathrm{priv}}()$, 626
$\mathrm{Rand}_{0,1}^{\mathrm{priv}}()$, 626
$\mathrm{Rand}_1^{\mathrm{priv}}()$, 626
$\mathrm{Rand}_0^{\mathrm{pub}}()$, 626
$\mathrm{Rand}_{0,1}^{\mathrm{pub}}()$, 626
$\mathrm{Rand}_{0,1}^{\mathrm{pub},\rightarrow}()$, 632
$\mathrm{Rand}_1^{\mathrm{pub}}()$, 626
rate of an error correcting code, 334
Razborov–Smolensky theorem, 675
reachable, 11, 688
read instruction, 24, 327, 580
read-advice instruction, 195
read-answer instruction, 58
read-once branching program, 305, 610
READ-ONCE BRANCHING PROGRAM EQUIVALENCE, 305
read-once formula, 582
read-rand instruction, 273, 307
read-witness instruction, 83, 147, 176, 527
received word, 332
rectangle, 621
rectangular reduction, 624
recursive algorithm, 139, 242, 297, 554, 690
reduction, 49, 197, 244, 279, 469, 584, 624
Reed–Muller code, 359
Reed–Solomon code, *see* polynomial code
register, 24
register-only, 37, 43
reject, 24
relation, 71
relative distance of an error correcting code, 334
relatively prime numbers, *see* coprime numbers
relativization, 194, 617
remainder of integer division, 697
remainder of polynomial division, 346, 700
repetition code, 334
resolution refutation, 678
resource, 14, 274
restriction of a function, 96, 204, 581, 608, 621, 652
retrieval, 117, 121
richness, 633
ripple carry adder, 208, 238
RL, 290
ROBPSize(), 610
ROBUST INDEPENDENT SET, 192
robustness, 30, 42, 202, 220, 247
ROCK SCISSORS PAPER COLORING, 128
root node, 690
root of a polynomial, 270, 699
round-robin tournament, 228
row vector, 703
RP, 275, 586
$\mathrm{RP}^{\mathrm{qc}}$, 602
RTIME[T], 275
running time, *see* time

S
$\mathrm{S_2P}$, 306
SAC^i, 262
sample, 692
sample complexity, 474
SAT, 91, 114, 162, 219, 510
SAT SEARCH, 95
SATISFIABILITY, *see* SAT
satisfiable, 91, 218
satisfying assignment, 91, 218, 510
Sauer–Shelah lemma, 505
Savitch's theorem, 161
SBP, 574
SBPSize(), 611
SC, 72
scalar, 701
Schwartz–Zippel lemma, 308
search problem, 13, 21, 638
search-to-decision reduction, 54, 66, 95, 130, 198, 282, 319
seed, 388, 412
seeded extractor, 412
seeded function, 443
selector, 205
self-compilation, 170
self-loop, 292, 688
semi-unbounded fan-in, 262
Sens(), 598
$\mathrm{Sens}_0()$, 598
$\mathrm{Sens}_1()$, 598
sensitivity, 598
separation of complexity classes, 41
separation of complexity measures, 593, 603
set, 685
set cover, 509
set data structure, 310
set system, 406, 509
shape of a formula/protocol, 663
shattered set, 475
shift of a set of bit strings, 281
short circuit, 141, 224, 582, 591, 659
shrinkage of formulas, 659

SHY SET, 131, 540
Σ_2P, 281, 551
Σ_2SAT, 193
Σ_ℓP, 176
Σ_ℓTIME[T], 176
simultaneous messages protocol, 643
single-elimination tournament, 205
Singleton bound, 358
sink node, 200, 688
size of a branching program, 220, 608
size of a circuit, 201, 375, 431
size of a decision tree, 606, 652
size of a formula, 250, 659
size of a protocol, 621
size of a set, 685
SIZE OF F, 184
skew circuit, 230
SMALL EXACT PATH LENGTH IN A DAG, 133
SMALL ITERATED ADDITION, 20, 27
SMALL SUBSET SUM, 80, 128
small-bias generator, *see* ε-bias generator
SMALLER CNF, 175
socks, 546
solve a problem, 9, 25
sorting network, 120, 135, 187, 421
soundness of a verifier, 84, 526, 544
source node, 200, 688
space, 15, 25, 137, 241
space hierarchy, 171, 302
SPACE[S], 42, 171
sparse decision problem, 228
spectral graph theory, 293
Sperner's theorem, 506
split a wire, 204
SQUARING, 262
stable set, *see* independent set
stable sort, 122
stack frame, 32, 140
star, 96
statistical distance, 385
statistical zero-knowledge, 570
STINGY 2-SAT, 131
store instruction, 24
strategy, 138, 553
stream cipher, 432
streaming algorithm, 326, 634
streaming branching program, 295, 394, 611
STREAMING BRANCHING PROGRAM GAP MAJORITY, 301, 391
streaming verifier, 147, 541
strict inclusion, 41
STRONG CONNECTIVITY, 159
strong exponential-time hypothesis, 677
strong seeded extractor, 423
strongly connected graph, 159, 540, 688
submatrix, 695
subroutine, 32, 50
subset, 685
SUBSET SUM, 79, 110
SUBSET SUM GAME, 158
SUBSET SUM TO ZERO, 110
subtraction principle, 686
subtree, 690
SUCCINCT VC DIMENSION, 505
sum-check protocol, 556, 566
sunflower, 668
support, 692
surjection, 685
switching lemma, 653, 674
symbol change error, 342, 345
symmetric function, 612
syntactic sugar, 33
system of linear equations, 345, 528, 703
system of quadratic equations, 531, 542

T

tag of a message authentication code, 451
TAUTOLOGY, 127
teacher, 491
tensor product, 532
term, 90, 393, 465
termination instructions, 24, 168, 213
threshold function, 421, 459
tight program, 33, 167
time, 14, 25
time hierarchy, 168, 172, 229, 302
time-space lower bound, 162, 190
TIME[T], 41, 168
TISP[T, S], 43, 162, 401
Toda's theorem, 683
topological layering, 234
TOPOLOGICAL ORDER, 68
topological order, 68, 209, 217, 691
total degree, 270
total function, 21, 206, 596, 686
total problem, 206, 300, 580, 596
total variation distance, *see* statistical distance
tractable, 42
trail, 76, 688
training data, 458
transcript, 115, 181, 199, 620
transition matrix, 292, 705
transitive property of reductions, 56, 64, 66, 186
transpose, 703
TRAVELING SALESPERSON, 75

tree, 689
triangle, 565, 681
TRIANGLE DETECTION, 68
triangle inequality, 333, 386
TRIBES, 607
TRUE QUANTIFIED BOOLEAN FORMULA, *see* QSAT
truth table, 89, 686
TRUTH TABLE VC DIMENSION, 504
tuple, 685
Turing machine, xiv, 71
Turing reduction, 72
TWO EDGE DISJOINT PATHS, 516
two's complement, 26, 208
two-party function, 620
two-prover one-round game, 523
two-sided error, 274, 278
two-source extractor, 410, 422

U
$\mathrm{UCert}_1()$, 615
UL, 160
ultimate reduction to SAT, 186
UNAMBIGUOUS DIRECTED REACHABILITY, 161
unambiguous DNF, 615
unambiguous encoding, 19
UNAMBIGUOUS SAT, 317, 329
unambiguous verifier, 160, 316
unbounded fan-in, 201, 235, 649
underdetermined system of equations, 703
UNDIRECTED CONNECTIVITY, 71
UNDIRECTED FORK, 645, 674
UNDIRECTED FULL CYCLE, 575
UNDIRECTED FULL PATH, 103
undirected graph, 688
UNDIRECTED REACHABILITY, 158, 290, 307, 674
UNDIRECTED SHORTEST PATH DECISION, 159
uniform distribution, 692
uniform program, 195
union, 685
union bound, 695
unique games conjecture, 525
UNIQUE SAT, 193
univariate polynomial, 267, 699
UNIVARIATE POLYNOMIAL IDENTITY TESTING, 268, 557
UNIVARIATE POLYNOMIAL ZERO TESTING, 268
universal program, *see* interpreter
universal quantifier, 686
UNIVERSAL SEARCH, 645
universe, 685
UNORDERED QSAT, 160
UP, 316, 329
upper bound, 17
$\mathrm{UP}^{\mathrm{qc}}$, 615

V
Valiant–Vazirani theorem, 331
valid input, 21, 300
validation, 484
Vandermonde matrix, 358
variance, 286, 325
VC dimension, 475, 644
vector, 701
verifier, 81, 176, 544
verifier decision tree, 596
VERIFIER INTERPRETATION, 174
VERIFIER INTERPRETATION WITH WITNESS, 173
vertex, *see* node
VERTEX COVER, *see* NODE COVER
vertex cover, *see* node cover
VLSI, 512, 637
VNP, 680
VP, 680

W
walk, 75, 688
Walsh code, *see* dot product code
weak PCP theorem, 528
weight, 335, 687
WHICH IS SATISFIABLE, 135
width of a layered branching program, 253
width of a term/clause, 90
wire in a circuit, 201
wire in a sorting network, 121
witness, 81, 526
witness segment, 83, 147, 176, 527
word, 20
WORD OF F, 184
Word RAM, xiv, 71
word size of a problem, 21
word size of a program, 25, 38
work memory, 16
work segment, 24
worst-case, 17, 360
worst-case to average-case reduction, 367
write instruction, 24
write-query instruction, 57

X
xor, 686
xor lemma, 375

Y
yes-input, *see* 1-input
yogurt, 412

Z

$\mathbb{Z}_2$ LINEAR SYSTEM SAT, 528
$\mathbb{Z}_2$ QUADRATIC SYSTEM SAT, 531
zero polynomial, 268, 699
zero-knowledge proof system, 570
zero-sided error, 275
ZPL, 290
ZPP, 275, 285, 586
$\mathsf{ZPP}^{\mathsf{qc}}$, 602
ZPTIME[T], 275

For EU product safety concerns, contact us at Calle de José Abascal, 56–1°,
28003 Madrid, Spain or eugpsr@cambridge.org.

www.ingramcontent.com/pod-product-compliance
Ingram Content Group UK Ltd.
Pitfield, Milton Keynes, MK11 3LW, UK
UKHW050859281026
477038UK00005B/93
* 9 7 8 1 0 0 9 7 5 2 3 3 6 *